W9-CAR-145

Welcome to the companion Web site for
The Bedford Guide for College Writers
bedfordstmartins.com/bedguide

You need value, and you want practical help with improving your writing. The companion Web site for *The Bedford Guide for College Writers* gives you both, with lots of free and open resources that you can use anywhere, anytime.

- Try interactive activities and exercises for writing, researching, and grammar.
- See models of student writing.
- Get help with drafts.
- Find more information about authors in *The Bedford Guide for College Writers.*
- Watch videos of real-world writers.
- Take tutorials on designing documents, charts, and graphs; evaluating and citing sources; and analyzing visuals.
- Download useful forms.
- Find reliable research links and get help with citing sources.
- Search for solutions to common grammar and spelling problems.

The Bedford Guide
for College Writers

NINTH EDITION

The Bedford Guide *for* College Writers

with Reader, Research Manual, and Handbook

X. J. Kennedy | Dorothy M. Kennedy | Marcia F. Muth

Bedford/St. Martin's

Boston ♦ New York

For Bedford/St. Martin's

Senior Executive Editor: Leasa Burton
Senior Developmental Editor: Martha Bustin
Senior Production Editor: Anne Noonan
Senior Production Supervisor: Dennis Conroy
Senior Marketing Manager: Molly Parke
Associate Editor: Sophia Snyder
Editorial Assistant: Mallory Moore
Production Assistant: David Ayers
Copy Editors: Jacqueline Rebisz and Dan Otis
Indexer: Leoni McVey
Photo Researcher: Susan McDermott Barlow
Permissions Manager: Kalina Ingham Hintz
Senior Art Director: Anna Palchik
Text Design: Lisa Buckley
Cover Design: Donna Dennison
Cover Art/Cover Photo: Bean Lark/Corbis
Composition: Graphic World, Inc.
Printing and Binding: RR Donnelley and Sons

President: Joan E. Feinberg
Editorial Director: Denise B. Wydra
Editor in Chief: Karen S. Henry
Director of Marketing: Karen R. Soeltz
Director of Production: Susan W. Brown
Associate Director, Editorial Production: Elise S. Kaiser
Managing Editor: Elizabeth M. Schaaf

Library of Congress Control Number: 2010929465

5   4   3   2   1   0
f   e   d   c   b   a

For information, write: Bedford/St. Martin's, 75 Arlington Street, Boston, MA 02116 (617-399-4000)

ISBN: 978-0-312-65663-8 (Instructor's Annotated Edition)
ISBN: 978-0-312-60153-9 (hardcover Student Edition)
ISBN: 978-0-312-60159-1 (paperback Student Edition)

Acknowledgments

Acknowledgments and copyrights are continued at the back of the book on pages A-69–A-72, which constitute an extension of the copyright page. It is a violation of the law to reproduce these selections by any means whatsoever without the written permission of the copyright holder.

To the Instructor

The ninth edition of *The Bedford Guide for College Writers* is a thorough revision, coordinated around the goal of helping students become the confident, resourceful, and independent writers they need to be. The qualities that have contributed to the book's enduring success—an emphasis on active learning and a focus on transferable skills—have been strengthened, updated, and implemented in new and more effective ways. At the same time, this revision reflects the new student population and the changing world that people live and write in, through relevant material on online learning, more student writing, and fresh photographs and design. The book incorporates a broader conception of students' educational backgrounds and the work they will do in college. All changes, large and small, throughout every section, help this edition deliver on the promise of its title, making *The Bedford Guide for College Writers* truly a current, practical, and flexible resource.

Several key interrelated ideas have shaped this book from the beginning. First, *students learn best by doing*. *The Bedford Guide* therefore includes an exceptional number of opportunities for practice and self-assessment. Throughout the book, we intersperse class-tested "Learning by Doing" activities and assignments in a helpful rhythm with concise instruction and models of writing. Students have frequent opportunities to apply what they have learned and become comfortable with each step in the process as they go along.

Second, we intend *The Bedford Guide for College Writers* to be an effective, engaging text that gives students *everything they need to write well—all in one flexible book*. Written and developed as four books in one, it offers a process-oriented rhetoric, a provocative thematic reader, an up-to-date research manual, and a comprehensive handbook. *The Bedford Guide* gives students all the tools they need to succeed as writers.

Most important, the focus of the book is *building transferable skills*. Recognizing that the college composition course may be one of a student's last classes with in-depth writing instruction, we have made every effort to ensure that *The Bedford Guide* develops resourceful, confident writers. It offers supportive, step-by-step guidance; "Why Writing Matters" features; a new chapter, "Strategies for Future Writing"; and varied, end-of-chapter "Additional Writing Assignments." These features and others prepare students to apply what they have learned to less guided assignments in other courses and in the workplace. This book is designed to help students meet whatever rhetorical challenges lie ahead, in college and in life.

Built on these cornerstone concepts, the enduring success of *The Bedford Guide* has been gratifying. And especially gratifying has been the way that this book has been able to evolve over time. New ideas on teaching and writing and excellent suggestions from users of the book continue to improve and enrich this work. In addition to the changes mentioned above, the ninth edition has many thought-provoking new readings, more on visual literacy, a new series of "Learning by Doing" activities, and more about APA documentation style. These changes and others throughout the book do even more to involve students in their own development as writers.

Everything You Need

The ninth edition continues to offer four coordinated composition books integrated into one convenient text — all of them now even better resources for students. *The Bedford Guide* is also available in a brief version, containing the rhetoric and reader, and in an e-book version. (For more details on the e-book and other exciting new resources accompanying *The Bedford Guide,* see pp. xii–xix. For more information on what is new in the ninth edition, see p. viii.)

BOOK 1 A Writer's Guide

This uniquely accessible — yet thorough — process-oriented rhetoric helps students become better writers, regardless of their skill level. Addressing all the assignments and topics typically covered in a first-year writing course, it is divided into four parts.

Part One, "A College Writer's Processes," introduces students to the interconnected processes of writing (Chapter 1), reading (Chapter 2), and critical thinking (Chapter 3). In the ninth edition, more examples of student writing appear throughout these chapters, and new coverage of visual literacy enhances Chapter 2, "Reading Processes."

In Part Two, "A Writer's Situations," nine core chapters — each including two sample readings (one by a student) — guide students step-by-step through a full range of common first-year writing assignments. The rhetorical situations in Part Two include recalling an experience (Chapter 4), observing a scene (Chapter 5), interviewing a subject (Chapter 6), comparing and contrasting (Chapter 7), explaining causes and effects (Chapter 8), taking a stand (Chapter 9), proposing a solution (Chapter 10), evaluating and reviewing (Chapter 11), and supporting a position with sources (Chapter 12). New "Why Writing Matters" features, readings, visuals, "Responding to an Image" chapter openers for class discussion and journal writing, and "Additional Writing Assignments" make these chapters even more interesting for students. If followed sequentially, these chapters lead students gradually into the rigorous analytical writing that will comprise most of their college writing. Rearranged and selected chapters readily support a course emphasizing argument, source-based writing, or other rhetorical or thematic approaches.

Part Three, "Other Writing Situations," offers helpful strategies and examples to focus students' efforts in five special rhetorical situations: responding to literature (Chapter 13), responding to visual representations (Chapter 14), writing online (Chapter 15), writing and presenting under pressure (Chapter 16), and writing in the workplace (Chapter 17). With the addition of the new Chapter 15, "Writing Online," and new sections on visual analysis in Chapter 14, Part Three even more closely matches rhetorical situations that students encounter in college today.

Part Four, "A Writer's Strategies," is a convenient resource for approaching different writing processes. The first chapter, the new "Strategies: A Case Study" (Chapter 18), follows a student as she develops her "Recalling an Experience" paper through multiple drafts, showing the revision process in action. It also includes her self-reflective portfolio letter. The next five chapters explain and further illustrate stages of common writing processes: generating ideas (Chapter 19), stating a thesis and planning (Chapter 20), drafting (Chapter 21), developing (Chapter 22), and revising and editing (Chapter 23), now including advice for meeting with and decoding comments from an instructor. Marginal annotations in the earlier parts of the book guide students to these chapters, which collectively serve as a writer's toolbox. Another new chapter, "Strategies for Future Writing" (Chapter 24), concludes this part, helping students adapt and apply what they have learned to other rhetorical situations they will encounter, including assignments in other courses.

BOOK 2 A Writer's Reader

A Writer's Reader is a thematic reader, unique in a book of this kind. The reader offers thirty-three selections—nineteen of them new—arranged around five themes that provide a meaningful context for students, giving them something to write about. The themes are families (Chapter 25), men and women (Chapter 26), popular culture (Chapter 27), electronic technology (Chapter 28), and a new chapter, explorations on living well (Chapter 29). Added in response to reviewer requests, this last theme considers what different people value as components of a life well lived. Apparatus that encourages critical thinking and writing accompanies each reading. A rhetorical table of contents (p. xxxvii) helps students see how the selections are coordinated with *A Writer's Guide* and how selections serve as models of writing situations assigned there. A biographical headnote and a brief prereading tip or question introduce each reading. Each selection is followed by questions on meaning, writing strategies, critical reading, vocabulary, and connections to other selections; journal prompts; and suggested writing assignments, one personal and the other analytical. These questions move students from reading carefully for both thematic and rhetorical elements to applying new strategies and insights in their own writing.

BOOK 3 A Writer's Research Manual

A Writer's Research Manual is a remarkably comprehensive guide to source-based writing, detailing all the essential steps for print, electronic, and field research. It covers planning and managing a research project (Chapter 30), working with sources (Chapter 31), finding sources (Chapter 32), evaluating sources (Chapter 33), integrating sources (Chapter 34), writing the research paper (Chapter 35), and documenting sources using MLA style (Chapter 36) and APA style (Chapter 37). Chapters 36 and 37 include extensive coverage of MLA and APA documentation, with one hundred MLA-style models and sixty-nine APA-style models. Additionally, the ninth edition includes a new example of an MLA research paper and a complete research paper showing APA documentation. In the appendices, a "Quick Research Guide" conveniently—and briefly—reviews how to find, evaluate, integrate, cite, and document sources.

BOOK 4 A Writer's Handbook

A most complete handbook, with superior ESL coverage (in "ESL Guidelines"), this useful reference includes clear explanations of grammar, style, and usage topics. It also includes nearly fifty exercise sets for practice in and out of class. Answers to half of the questions in each set are provided in the back of the book so that students can check their understanding. Frequent cross-references in the handbook refer students to additional practices on *Exercise Central*, the largest bank of free online grammar exercises. These practices, written specifically for *The Bedford Guide*, include ESL exercises to accompany all the ESL guidelines in the book. Beyond the coverage in the handbook, a "Quick Editing Guide" in the appendices gives special attention to the most troublesome grammar and editing problems.

New to the Ninth Edition

The ninth edition focuses on giving students even more opportunities for learning by doing and developing transferable skills. Through innovative activities, assignments, visuals, readings, and examples of students' work, this new edition engages students and prepares them for the writing challenges they will encounter in college and beyond. The changes reflect classroom experiences, advances from the always-developing field of composition, and the insightful suggestions of many helpful reviewers.

Focus on Active Learning and Transferable Writing Skills

A new series of "Learning by Doing" activities provides creative ways for students—working alone, in pairs, or in groups—to practice and apply the topics under discussion to their own papers. Emphasizing such practical skills as developing your thesis, focusing your introduction, and selecting reliable sources, dozens of these interactive practices appear throughout Book One, *A Writer's Guide,* and Book Three, *A Writer's Research Manual,* alternating with and reinforcing the presentation of key concepts. These short, focused assignments can be done in class, online, or as homework. (See "Learning by Doing: Selecting Reliable Sources," p. 232, for an example.)

A new chapter, "Strategies: A Case Study," follows one student's process through several drafts of her "Recalling an Experience" paper and includes questions for writers to ask as they develop and revise their own papers. This chapter also shows the changes that the student makes to her paper in response to peer review comments and feedback from her instructor as well as her reflective portfolio letter.

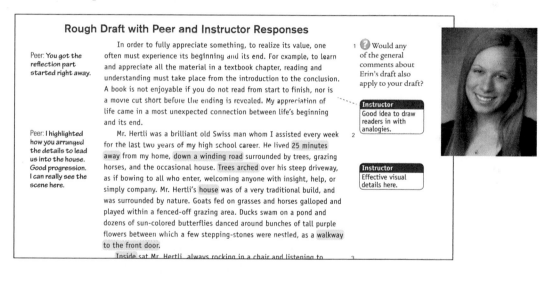

Rough Draft with Peer and Instructor Responses

Peer: You got the reflection part started right away.

In order to fully appreciate something, to realize its value, one often must experience its beginning and its end. For example, to learn and appreciate all the material in a textbook chapter, reading and understanding must take place from the introduction to the conclusion. A book is not enjoyable if you do not read from start to finish, nor is a movie cut short before the ending is revealed. My appreciation of life came in a most unexpected connection between life's beginning and its end.

1   Would any of the general comments about Erin's draft also apply to your draft?

Instructor
Good idea to draw readers in with analogies.

Peer: I highlighted how you arranged the details to lead us into the house. Good progression. I can really see the scene here.

Mr. Hertli was a brilliant old Swiss man whom I assisted every week for the last two years of my high school career. He lived 25 minutes away from my home, down a winding road surrounded by trees, grazing horses, and the occasional house. Trees arched over his steep driveway, as if bowing to all who enter, welcoming anyone with insight, help, or simply company. Mr. Hertli's house was of a very traditional build, and was surrounded by nature. Goats fed on grasses and horses galloped and played within a fenced-off grazing area. Ducks swam on a pond and dozens of sun-colored butterflies danced around bunches of tall purple flowers between which a few stepping-stones were nestled, as a walkway to the front door.

2

Instructor
Effective visual details here.

Inside sat Mr. Hertli, always rocking in a chair and listening to

3

A new chapter, "Strategies for Future Writing," helps students transfer the skills they learn in composition to other writing situations across the curriculum. Handy checklists guide students through assignment and genre analysis.

A new chapter, "Writing Online," gives brief, practical advice on organizing files, communicating with instructors and peers (through messages, profiles, and threaded discussions), and using a course management system.

The new "Why Writing Matters" features connect the assignment chapters with rhetorical situations in college and beyond, inviting students to apply what they learn about a particular type of writing. (See "Why Comparing and Contrasting Matter," p. 117, for an example.)

Unique "Take Action" charts guide students through assessing and addressing challenging aspects of writing. These self-assessment charts are designed to help even students of varying skill levels become stronger and more independent writers. Specifically, the charts help students reflect on their own writing, identify its weaknesses, and then use concrete and relevant strategies for strengthening their papers. "Take Action" charts address such important issues as supporting a stand, integrating sources, and strengthening thesis statements.

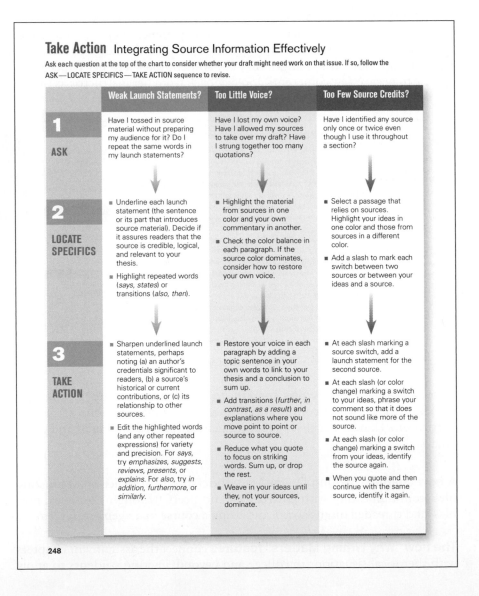

Take Action Integrating Source Information Effectively

Ask each question at the top of the chart to consider whether your draft might need work on that issue. If so, follow the ASK—LOCATE SPECIFICS—TAKE ACTION sequence to revise.

	Weak Launch Statements?	Too Little Voice?	Too Few Source Credits?
1 ASK	Have I tossed in source material without preparing my audience for it? Do I repeat the same words in my launch statements?	Have I lost my own voice? Have I allowed my sources to take over my draft? Have I strung together too many quotations?	Have I identified any source only once or twice even though I use it throughout a section?
2 LOCATE SPECIFICS	▪ Underline each launch statement (the sentence or its part that introduces source material). Decide if it assures readers that the source is credible, logical, and relevant to your thesis. ▪ Highlight repeated words (*says, states*) or transitions (*also, then*).	▪ Highlight the material from sources in one color and your own commentary in another. ▪ Check the color balance in each paragraph. If the source color dominates, consider how to restore your own voice.	▪ Select a passage that relies on sources. Highlight your ideas in one color and those from sources in a different color. ▪ Add a slash to mark each switch between two sources or between your ideas and a source.
3 TAKE ACTION	▪ Sharpen underlined launch statements, perhaps noting (a) an author's credentials significant to readers, (b) a source's historical or current contributions, or (c) its relationship to other sources. ▪ Edit the highlighted words (and any other repeated expressions) for variety and precision. For *says,* try *emphasizes, suggests, reviews, presents,* or *explains.* For *also,* try *in addition, furthermore,* or *similarly.*	▪ Restore your voice in each paragraph by adding a topic sentence in your own words to link to your thesis and a conclusion to sum up. ▪ Add transitions (*further, in contrast, as a result*) and explanations where you move point to point or source to source. ▪ Reduce what you quote to focus on striking words. Sum up, or drop the rest. ▪ Weave in your ideas until they, not your sources, dominate.	▪ At each slash marking a source switch, add a launch statement for the second source. ▪ At each slash (or color change) marking a switch to your ideas, phrase your comment so that it does not sound like more of the source. ▪ At each slash (or color change) marking a switch from your ideas, identify the source again. ▪ When you quote and then continue with the same source, identify it again.

248

Updated guidelines and expanded coverage of APA, now in a separate chapter, include a full model research paper documented in APA style, recognizing the diversity of students' careers and majors. The ninth edition of *The Bedford Guide* also contains updated MLA and APA documentation guidelines.

More Visuals and an Open, Accessible Design

A new design makes the book both easier to use and more engaging, with powerful visuals that draw readers into the book. The new art program, with accompanying prompts and visual assignments, invites students to look more closely and to think and write more deeply about the world they see.

This image shows German artist Johan Lorbeer during one of his "still-life performances" outside of the Chemnitz city hall.

Responding to an Image
A scene like this one might look and feel quite different to different observers, depending on their vantage points, emotions, backgrounds, and experiences. In this image, what prominent element attracts your attention? Who are the various observers? Which details might be important for them? Which details might matter more to one observer than another? Although

77

Revised Chapter 14, "Responding to Visual Representations," contains two new student essays, an advertisement analysis paper and a photo essay, as well as a guided assignment for analyzing a visual representation.

New visual and multimodal options in the expanded end-of-chapter "Additional Writing Assignments" include more choices of assignments and more opportunities for collaborative projects. Located at the ends of each of the assignment chapters in Part Two, "A Writer's Situations," these flexible alternatives often link the particular type of writing being explored to other disciplines, genres, and real-world scenarios. (See "Additional Writing Assignments," pp. 180–82, for an example.)

Explanatory graphics and diagrams help to clarify concepts for visual learners — and all students.

A new "Quick Format Guide" at the back of the book is easy for students to consult when formatting academic essays, designing documents, and incorporating charts and diagrams into their papers.

More Varied Readings and Examples of Student Writing

Readings in the ninth edition reflect a wider range of experience and a recognition that students coming to the composition class vary in age, work background, familiarity with technology, life situations, and other factors.

With twenty-six new readings by both students and professionals (seven in Part Two, "A Writer's Situations"; nineteen in *A Writer's Reader*) and more in-text examples throughout the book, topics better connect to the realities of students' lives. New selections by students appear in Chapter 2, "Reading Processes"; Chapter 3, "Critical Thinking Processes"; and Chapter 14, "Responding to Visual Representations." In Chapter 16, "Writing and Presenting under Pressure," a new section on oral presentations also contains students' work.

A new reader chapter, "Explorations on Living Well" (Chapter 29), takes up an enduring question: What does it means to live a fulfilling life?

You Get More Digital Choices for *The Bedford Guide for College Writers,* Ninth Edition

The Bedford Guide for College Writers, Ninth Edition, does not stop with a book. Online, you will find both free and affordable premium resources to help students get even more out of the book and your course. You will also find convenient instructor resources, such as downloadable sample syllabi, additional classroom activities, and even a nationwide community of teachers. For ideas and assistance on using these resources in your course, please see the WPA Correlation Guide on pages xliii–xlix. This guide shows how *The Bedford Guide* and its accompanying materials support Writing Program Administrators (WPA) course outcomes. To learn more about or order any of the products below, contact your Bedford/St. Martin's sales representative,

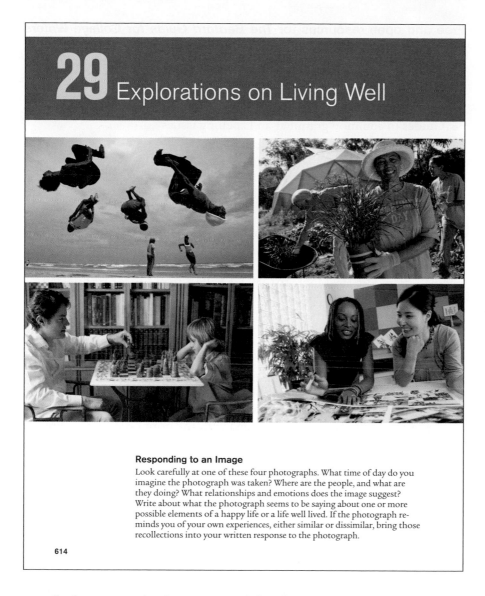

29 Explorations on Living Well

Responding to an Image

Look carefully at one of these four photographs. What time of day do you imagine the photograph was taken? Where are the people, and what are they doing? What relationships and emotions does the image suggest? Write about what the photograph seems to be saying about one or more possible elements of a happy life or a life well lived. If the photograph reminds you of your own experiences, either similar or dissimilar, bring those recollections into your written response to the photograph.

614

e-mail sales support (<sales_support@bfwpub.com>), or visit the Web site at <bedfordstmartins.com/bedguide/catalog>.

Companion Web Site for *The Bedford Guide for College Writers* <bedfordstmartins.com/bedguide>

Use this site to send students to free and open resources, choose flexible premium resources to supplement your print text, or upgrade to an expanding collection of helpful digital content.

Free and open resources for *The Bedford Guide for College Writers* provide students with easy-to-access reference materials, visual tutorials, and support for working with sources. The companion Web site includes:

- Additional writing assignments and "Learning by Doing" activities
- Expanded "Take Action" charts to help with drafts
- Guides to common grammar and spelling issues
- Five free videos of real writers from *VideoCentral*
- More models of student writing
- *TopLinks* and *AuthorLinks* with reliable online sources

VideoCentral is a growing collection of videos for the writing class that captures real-world, academic, and student writers talking about how and why they write. Writer and teacher Peter Berkow interviewed hundreds of people — from Michael Moore to Cynthia Selfe — to produce fifty brief videos about topics such as revising and getting feedback. *VideoCentral* can be packaged for free with *The Bedford Guide for College Writers*. An activation code is required.

Re:Writing Plus gathers all of Bedford/St. Martin's premium digital content for composition into one online collection. It includes hundreds of model documents, the first-ever peer review game, and *VideoCentral*. *Re:Writing Plus* can be purchased separately or packaged with the print book at a significant discount. An activation code is required.

E-book Options

E-books offer all the content of the print texts at roughly half the price. If you are interested in an e-book, you have two options. Bedford/St. Martin's e-books are online texts that let students search, highlight, and bookmark, making it easier to study and access key content. For teachers, these e-books make it easy to give students just the book they want to deliver: customize and rearrange chapters, add and share notes, and link to quizzes, activities, and other resources. You can package a Bedford/St. Martin's e-book free with the print text.

If your students are interested in an e-book that they can download to their computers, Bedford/St. Martin's has partnered with CourseSmart to make many of its books available as CourseSmart e-books, which offer page-by-page fidelity, highlighting, and note taking. You choose whether to download the e-book to access it from one machine or purchase the online version to access it from wherever you are.

CompClass for The Bedford Guide for College Writers, Ninth Edition <yourcompclass.com>

An easy-to-use online course space designed for composition students and instructors, *CompClass for The Bedford Guide for College Writers,* Ninth Edition, comes preloaded with *The Bedford Guide for College Writers,* Ninth Edition *e-Book,* as well as other Bedford/St. Martin's premium digital content, including *VideoCentral.* Powerful assignment and assessment tools make it easier to customize content and to keep track of your students' progress. *CompClass for The Bedford Guide for College Writers,* Ninth Edition, can be purchased separately at <yourcompclass.com> or packaged with the print book at a significant discount. An activation code is required.

More Options for Students

Add more value to your text by choosing one of the following resources, free when packaged with *The Bedford Guide for College Writers.* To learn more about package options or any of the products below, contact your Bedford/ St. Martin's sales representative or visit the Web site at <bedfordstmartins .com/bedguide/catalog>.

i·series available on CD-ROM and online. This popular series presents multimedia tutorials in a flexible format—because there are things you cannot do in a book.

- *ix: visual exercises* helps students put into practice key rhetorical and visual concepts.
- *i·claim: visualizing argument* offers a new way to see argument—with six tutorials, an illustrated glossary, and over seventy multimedia arguments.
- *i·cite: visualizing sources* brings research to life through an animated introduction, four tutorials, and hands-on source practice.

Both *ix* and *i·cite* are part of *Re:Writing Plus,* our premium collection of e-learning resources for English, <bedfordstmartins.com/rewritingplus>.

Portfolio Keeping, **Second Edition,** by Nedra Reynolds and Rich Rice, provides all the information students need to use the portfolio method successfully in a writing course. *Portfolio Teaching,* a companion guide for instructors, provides the practical information instructors and writing program administrators need to use the portfolio method successfully in a writing course.

Oral Presentations in the Composition Course: A Brief Guide, by Matthew Duncan and Gustav W. Friedrich, offers students the advice they need to plan, prepare, and present their work effectively. With sections on analyzing audiences, choosing effective language, using visual aids, collaborating on group presentations, and dealing with the fear of public speaking, this booklet helps students develop strong oral presentations.

Instructor Resources <bedfordstmartins.com/bedguide/catalog>

Bedford/St. Martin's wants to make it easy for you to find the support you need — and to get it quickly.

Instructor's Annotated Edition of The Bedford Guide for College Writers puts information right where busy instructors need it: on the pages of the book itself. The marginal annotations offer teaching tips, analysis tips with readings, last-minute in-class activities, vocabulary glosses, additional assignments, and cross-references to other ancillaries.

Practical Suggestions for Teaching with The Bedford Guide for College Writers, by Dana Waters of Dodge City Community College, Shirley Morahan, and Sylvia A. Holladay, helps instructors plan and teach their composition course. This text is available in print or in a PDF that can be downloaded from the Bedford/St. Martin's online catalog or the companion Web site. The instructor's manual includes practical advice on designing an effective course and teaching writing online. It also contains sample syllabi, chapter-by-chapter support, and suggestions for using the electronic media package.

Teaching Composition: Background Readings, Third Edition, edited by T. R. Johnson of Tulane University, addresses the concerns of both first-year and veteran writing instructors. This collection includes thirty professional readings on composition and rhetoric written by leaders in the field. The selections are accompanied by helpful introductions, activities, and practical insights for inside and outside the classroom. The new edition offers up-to-date advice on avoiding plagiarism, classroom blogging, and more.

TeachingCentral offers the entire list of Bedford/St. Martin's print and on-line professional resources in one place. You will find landmark reference works, sourcebooks on pedagogical issues, award-winning collections, and practical advice for the classroom — all free for instructors.

Bits collects creative ideas for teaching a range of composition topics in an easily searchable blog format. A community of teachers — leading scholars, authors, and editors — discuss revision, research, grammar and style, technology, peer review, and much more. Take, use, adapt, and pass the ideas around. Then, come back to the site to comment or share your own suggestion.

Content cartridges for the most common course management systems — Blackboard, WebCT, Angel, and Desire2Learn — allow you to easily download Bedford/St. Martin's digital materials for your course.

Testing Tool Kit: A Writing and Grammar Test Bank. This CD-ROM allows instructors to create secure, customized tests and quizzes. The prebuilt diagnostic tests are also included.

Ordering Information

To order any of the ancillaries, please contact your Bedford/St. Martin's sales representative, e-mail sales support at <sales_support@bfwpub.com>, or visit our Web site at <bedfordstmartins.com>. Note that activation codes are required for *VideoCentral, Re:Writing Plus,* and *CompClass.* Codes can be purchased separately or packaged with the print book at a significant discount.

To order *VideoCentral* packaged with the print book, use these ISBNs:
- with *Reader, Research Manual,* and *Handbook* (hardcover): 978-0-312-58508-2
- with *Reader, Research Manual,* and *Handbook* (paperback): 978-0-312-58509-9
- with *Reader* (paperback only): 978-0-312-58500-6

To order *Re:Writing Plus* packaged with the print book, use these ISBNs:
- with *Reader, Research Manual,* and *Handbook* (hardcover): 978-0-312-58441-2
- with *Reader, Research Manual,* and *Handbook* (paperback): 978-0-312-58422-1
- with *Reader* (paperback only): 978-0-312-58425-2

To order the online, interactive e-book packaged with the print book, use these ISBNs:
- with *Reader, Research Manual,* and *Handbook* (hardcover): 978-0-312-58669-0
- with *Reader, Research Manual,* and *Handbook* (paperback): 978-0-312-58672-0
- with *Reader* (paperback only): 978-0-312-58666-9

To order the online or downloadable CourseSmart e-book, use this ISBN:
- with *Reader, Research Manual,* and *Handbook:* 978-0-312-65680-5

(continued)

Ordering Information (*continued*)

To order the Bedford/St. Martin's e-book,
go to <bedfordstmartins.com/ebooks>.
To order the CourseSmart e-book, go to <CourseSmart.com>.

To order *CompClass for The Bedford Guide for College Writers,* Ninth
Edition, packaged with the print book, use these ISBNs:
- with *Reader, Research Manual,* and *Handbook* (hardcover):
  978-0-312-58668-3
- with *Reader, Research Manual,* and *Handbook* (paperback):
  978-0-312-58671-3
- with *Reader* (paperback only): 978-0-312-58667-6

To order *ix visual exercises* packaged with the print book, use these
ISBNs:
- with *Reader, Research Manual,* and *Handbook* (hardcover):
  978-0-312-58440-5
- with *Reader, Research Manual,* and *Handbook* (paperback):
  978-0-312-58489-4
- with *Reader* (paperback only): 978-0-312-58424-5

To order *i-claim: visualizing argument* packaged with the print book,
use these ISBNs:
- with *Reader, Research Manual,* and *Handbook* (hardcover):
  978-0-312-58439-9
- with *Reader, Research Manual,* and *Handbook* (paperback):
  978-0-312-58488-7
- with *Reader* (paperback only): 978-0-312-58437-5

To order *i-cite: visualizing sources* packaged with the print book, use
these ISBNs:
- with *Reader, Research Manual,* and *Handbook* (hardcover):
  978-0-312-58438-2
- with *Reader, Research Manual,* and *Handbook* (paperback):
  978-0-312-58442-9
- with *Reader* (paperback only): 978-0-312-58423-8

To order *Portfolio Keeping* packaged with the print book, use these
ISBNs:
- with *Reader, Research Manual,* and *Handbook* (hardcover):
  978-0-312-59530-2

Ordering Information (*continued*)

- with *Reader, Research Manual,* and *Handbook* (paperback): 978-0-312-59576-0
- with *Reader* (paperback only): 978-0-312-59579-1

To order *Oral Presentations in the Composition Course* packaged with the book, use these ISBNs:

- with *Reader, Research Manual,* and *Handbook* (hardcover): 978-0-312-59529-6
- with *Reader, Research Manual,* and *Handbook* (paperback): 978-0-312-59575-3
- with *Reader* (paperback only): 978-0-312-59578-4

Thanks and Appreciation

Many individuals contributed significantly to the ninth edition of *The Bedford Guide for College Writers,* and we extend our sincerest thanks to all of them.

Editorial Advisory Board

As we began to prepare the ninth edition, we assembled an editorial advisory board to respond to the many significant changes we planned and to share ideas about how to make the book more useful to both students and teachers. These dedicated instructors responded thoroughly and insightfully to new features of the text, answered innumerable questions, and suggested many ideas, activities, and assignments. They also submitted student papers and in ways large and small helped to shape the new and revised sections of the ninth edition. We are extremely grateful to each one of them:

- Kathleen Beauchene, Community College of Rhode Island
- Jan Bone, Roosevelt University and Harper College
- John Dethloff, Lone Star College
- Thomas Eaton, Southeast Missouri State University
- Sonia Feder-Lewis, Saint Mary's University of Minnesota
- Karen Keaton Jackson, North Carolina Central University
- Beth Koruna, Bohecker College–Columbus
- Denise Longsworth, Bohecker College–Columbus
- Leigh Martin, Community College of Rhode Island
- Annie Nguyen, Community College of Baltimore County

- Terry Novak, Johnson and Wales University
- Arthur L. Schuhart, Northern Virginia Community College–Annandale
- Candice Simmons, Johnson and Wales University
- Dana Waters, Dodge City Community College

Other Colleagues

We also extend our gratitude to instructors across the country who took time and care to review this edition, to participate in a focus group, to send us their students' work, and to share excellent suggestions gleaned from their experience. For this we thank

- Mary Ellen Ackerman, Dennis-Yarmouth Regional High School
- Mary Baken, Webster University
- Crystal Brothe, University of Northern Colorado
- Karen Davis Brown, Winnetonka High School
- Sarah Canfield-Fuller, Shenandoah University
- Terri Carine, RETS College
- Sandra L. Cavender, Middle Tennessee State University
- Laurie Lopez Coleman, San Antonio College
- Connie Corbett-Whittier, Friends University
- Dale Dittmer, Chippewa Valley Technical College
- Rosary Fazende-Jones, Phillips Community College of the University of Arkansas
- Patrick Finn, Chandler-Gilbert Community College
- Lisa J. Friedrich-Harris, Baker College
- LaDonna Friesen, Central Bible College
- Caroline Gebhard, Tuskegee University
- Barbara Gleason, City College of New York
- M. Suzanne Harper, Penn State Worthington Scranton
- Stephen B. Heller, Adlai E. Stevenson High School
- Virginia Scott Hendrickson, Missouri State University
- Marlene Hess, Ferris State University
- Susanna Hoeness-Krupsaw, University of Southern Indiana
- Eileen Medeiros, Johnson & Wales University
- Mike Michaud, Rhode Island College
- Heather Michael, McLennan Community College
- Anthony C. Miller Sr., Buffalo State College
- Julie A. Myatt, Middle Tennessee State University

- Kimme Nuckles, Baker College
- Roy Kenneth Pace II, Valdosta State University
- Zachary Perkinson, East Carolina University
- Marianne G. Pindar, Lackawanna College–Hazelton Center
- Amy Rosenbluth, Lakeland Community College
- Samantha Ruckman, Arizona State University
- Joyce Russo, Lakeland Community College
- Sara E. Selby, Waycross College
- Suzanne Skipper, Lake Howell High School
- Lori Weber, Lakeland Community College
- Bridgette Weir, Nashville State Community College

We also want to acknowledge the tremendous and enduring help provided by reviewers of previous editions. Their expert ideas and suggestions live on in the pages of this edition.

Alice B. Adams, Rosemary R. Adams, Ted Allder, Patricia Allen, Steve Amidon, David Auchter, Renee Bangerter, Stuart Barbier, Marci Bartolotta, Barry Batorsky, Shannon Beasley, Randolph A. Beckham, Pamela J. Behrens, Carmine J. Bell, Kay Berg, Tanya Boler, Jeannie Boniccki, Debbie Boyd, Barbara Brown, Ty Buckman, Rita Buscher-Weeks, Joan Campbell, Tom Casey, Steve Cirrone, Susan Romayne Clark, Ted Contreras, Nancy Cook, Jane Corbly, Monica Cox, Carolyn Craft, Sheilah Craft, Mary Cullen, P. R. Dansby, Fred D'Astoli, Ed Davis, Patricia Ann Delamar, Helen Duclos, Irene Duprey-Gutierrez, Corinna Evett, Carol Luers Eyman, Leora Freedman, Julie Freeman, Sandy Fuhr, Jan Fulwiler, Pamela Garvey, Mary Ann Gauthier, Michael Gavin, Olga Geissler, Robert Gmerlin, Aaron Goldweber, Daniel Gonzales, Sherry F. Gott, Daniel V. Gribbin, Robert Grindy, Joyce Hall, Jefferson Hancock, Alyssa Harad, Johnnie Hargrove, Judy Hatcher, Elaine Hays, Diana Hicks, Marita Hinton, Tom Hodges, Jane Holwerda, Patricia Hunt, Elizabeth Jarok, Barbara Jensen, Greg Jewell, Jean L. Johnson, Ted Johnston, Andrew Jones, Anne D. Jordan, M. L. Kayser, Cynthia Kellogg, Dimitri Keriotis, Kate Kiefer, Yoon Sik Kim, Kaye Kolkmann, Fred A. Koslowski III, Brandy Kreisler, Sandra Lakey, Norman Lanquist, Colleen Lloyd, Stephen Ma, Susan Peck MacDonald, Jennifer Madej, Janice Mandile, Phil Martin, Gerald McCarthy, Miles S. McCrimmon, Jackie McGrath, Jenna Merritt, Elizabeth Metzger, Eric Meyer, Libby Miles, Sandra Moore, Cleatta Morris, Robert Morse, Sheryl A. Mylan, Clement Ndulute, Jerry Nelson, Peggy J. Oliver, Laura Osborne, Brit Osgood-Treston, Mike Palmquist, Geraldine C. Pelegano, Laurel S. Peterson, Mary F. Pflugshaupt, John F. Pleimann, Kenneth E. Poitras, Michael Punches, Patrice Quarg, Jeanie Page Randall, Betty Ray, Joan Reteshka, Mark Reynolds, Kira Roark, Peggy Roche, Dawn Rodrigues, Ann Westmoreland Runsick, Karin Russell, Wendy Schmidt, Nancy J. Schneider, Janis Schulte, Susan Schurman, Patricia C. Schwindt,

Herbert Shapiro, Andrea Shaw, Elizabeth Smart, Ognjen Smiljanic, Allison Smith, Patrick Smith, David Sorrells, Ann Spencer-Livingstone, Lori Spillane, Scott R. Stankey, Leroy Sterling, Dean Stover, Ellen Straw, Monnette Sturgill, Ronald Sudol, Darlene Summers, David Tammer, William G. Thomas, Daphne Thompson, Janice M. Vierk, Dave Waddell, Christopher Walker, Laurie Walker, Carol Westcamp, Patricia South White, Susan Whitlow, Jim Wilcox, Carmiele Wilkerson, Mary Zacharias, and Valerie P. Zimbaro.

Contributors

The ninth edition could not have been completed without the help of numerous individuals. Special thanks go to Dana Waters (Dodge City Community College) for once again revising *Practical Suggestions*. Jan Bone, of Roosevelt University and Harper College, and Thomas Eaton, of Southeast Missouri State University, contributed a new chapter, "Teaching Writing Online," to *Practical Suggestions*. Text from two faculty members — Kathleen Beauchene at Community College of Rhode Island and Pamela Laird at University of Colorado Denver — appears in and enhances Chapter 15, "Writing Online," and Chapter 24, "Strategies for Future Writing," respectively. Jeff Ousborne wrote excellent apparatus for the new reading selections. Art researcher Susan McDermott Barlow helped us take the book in an even more visually rich direction, finding eye-catching and thought-provoking photographs and other images. She also cleared permissions for the art. Katrina M. Washington efficiently cleared text permissions under the able guidance of Kalina Hintz. Candace Rardon was our special student consultant on many matters concerning student writing and brought her great energy and valuable perspective to the project. Erika Hayden contributed online activities to *The Bedford Guide*'s companion Web site and compiled links on authors featured in the reader.

For the appealingly clear and functional new design that graces the ninth edition, we thank the very talented and patient graphic designer Lisa Buckley. Anna Palchik, senior art director, also played a crucial role in the design, from the first imagining to the late fine-tuning stages.

Student Writers

We offer sincere thanks to all the students who have challenged us over the years to find better ways to help them learn. In particular, we would like to thank those who granted us permission to use their essays in the ninth edition. Focused as this textbook is on student writing, we consider it essential to provide effective model essays by students. The writings of Linn Bourgeau, Betsy Buffo, Jonathan Burns, Anne Cahill, Tim Chabot, Yun Yung Choi, David Ian Cohn, Michael Coil, Heather Colbenson, Sarah Goers, Kelly Grecian, Stephanie Hawkins, Cindy Keeler, Heidi Kessler, Melissa Lamberth, Daniel Matthews, Angela Mendy, Susanna Olsen, Dennis O'Neil, Ross Rocketto,

Lindsey Schendel, Robert G. Schreiner, Lillian Tsu, Donna Waite, and Carrie Williamson were included in earlier editions as well as this one. New to the ninth edition are the writings of Richard Anson, Cristina Berrios, Josh Birnbaum, Andrew Bustin, Heather Church, Olof Eriksson, Marjorie Lee Garretson, Jennifer Miller, Shari O'Malley, Candace Rardon, Lorena A. Ryan-Hines, Michelle Sausen, Erin Schmitt, Rachel Steinhaus, Stephanie Switzer, Lacey Taylor, Joshua Tefft, Leah Threats, Joel Torres, Arthur Wasilewski, and Christopher Williams.

Editorial

At Bedford/St. Martin's three individuals merit special recognition. President Joan E. Feinberg and editorial director Denise B. Wydra (also a former editor of *The Bedford Guide*) continue to contribute invaluable suggestions for improving the book for both students and instructors. We also greatly value the guidance of editor in chief Karen S. Henry, who has helped sustain the direction of the book throughout many editions and who has provided perceptive advice at crucial points in the development of the current edition.

The editorial effort behind this edition was truly a team endeavor. Marcia F. Muth assumed a major authorial role in the seventh edition, answering needs expressed by users with many exciting new features. She has continued in that role through the ninth edition, bringing innovation to every part of the book and making it an even stronger resource for all students, regardless of their skill level. Senior editor Martha Bustin brought fresh eyes and great insight to this edition, encouraging lively innovation while patiently coordinating text, design, and images. Associate editor Sophia Snyder skillfully and thoughtfully developed *A Writer's Reader,* the companion Web site, and e-book. She was a key team member, tackling many crucial and time-sensitive jobs, large and small. Editorial assistant Mallory Moore joined the team when the book was in its final stages and lent her calm and efficient help to ongoing work on the front and end matter and the print and electronic ancillaries. Rebecca Merrill guided the production of the electronic resources, bringing creativity and energy to the development of the e-book and other parts of the book's ancillary package.

Other members of the Bedford/St. Martin's staff contributed greatly to the ninth edition. Many thanks and heartfelt appreciation go to Anne Noonan, who, with an exacting eye, great patience, and good humor, shepherded the book through production, with the assistance of David Ayers and Kerri Cardone. We especially appreciate her care in overseeing the design updates and the production of the book's growing art program. Sue Brown, Elise Kaiser, and Elizabeth Schaaf were immensely helpful in overseeing production. Donna Dennison oversaw the lovely redesign of the book's cover. Molly Parke skillfully coordinated the marketing of the book and offered much good advice based on feedback from the field. Karen Melton Soeltz and Jane Helms also offered valuable marketing advice. The book's promotion was ably handled by Shelby Disario. Pelle Cass created a colorful and appealing brochure. Pelle also kindly and generously granted permission for the inclusion of several photographs from his series *Selected People*.

Marcia Muth is especially grateful to the School of Education and Human Development at the University of Colorado Denver for sponsoring her writing workshops. She also thanks CU Online for its many creative suggestions about online instruction, especially those in *The CU Online Handbook: Teach Differently: Create and Collaborate*. Special appreciation also goes to Mary Finley, University Library at California State University Northridge, and Rodney Muth, University of Colorado Denver, for expert advice. Finally, we once again thank our friends and families for their unwavering patience, understanding, and encouragement.

Contents

BOOK 1 A WRITER'S GUIDE

BOOK 2

A WRITER'S READER

BOOK 4

A WRITER'S HANDBOOK

Introduction: Grammar, or The Way Words Work   779

APPENDICES AND OTHER RESOURCES

RHETORICAL CONTENTS

*(Essays listed in order of appearance; * indicates student essays)*

SELECTED VISUAL CONTENTS

Visual Essays, Series, and Collages

Workplace Documents

FEATURES OF *THE BEDFORD GUIDE*, NINTH EDITION, AND ANCILLARIES

Correlated to the Writing Program Administrators (WPA) Outcomes Statement

WPA Goals and Learning Outcomes	Support in *The Bedford Guide*, Ninth Edition
Rhetorical Knowledge: Student Outcomes	
Focus on a purpose	<ul><li>Purpose and Audience (pp. 11–16)</li><li>Chs. 4–14, including thesis development and revision</li><li>Ch. 20: Strategies for Stating a Thesis and Planning (pp. 400–01)</li><li>Ch. 23: Strategies for Revising and Editing with revision for purpose, thesis, and audience (pp. 460–62)</li><li>Companion Web site: Visualizing Purpose tutorial</li><li>*VideoCentral**: videos on rhetorical purpose</li></ul>*For instructors* The following ancillaries contain helpful tips, strategies, and resources for teaching purpose, as well as for the other topics considered throughout this chart.<ul><li>*Instructor's Annotated Edition of The Bedford Guide for College Writers*, Ninth Edition</li><li>*Practical Suggestions for Teaching with The Bedford Guide for College Writers*, Ninth Edition</li></ul>
Respond to the needs of different audiences	<ul><li>Writing for Your Audience and Targeting a College Audience (pp. 12–16)</li><li>Using Evidence to Appeal to Your Audience (pp. 43–45)</li><li>Chs. 4–12, with situational consideration of audience and Peer Response questions</li><li>Attention to specific audiences such as Messages to Your Instructor (pp. 316–17), Online Threaded Discussions (pp. 319–21), workplace (p. 353), and research (p. 649)</li><li>Ch. 24: Strategies for Future Writing (pp. 479–83)</li><li>Shaping Your Topic for Your Purpose and Audience (pp. 400–01)</li><li>Revising for Audience (pp. 461–62), Working with a Peer Editor (pp. 463–65), and Meeting with Your Instructor (p. 464)</li><li>Companion Web site: Visualizing audience tutorial</li></ul>
Respond appropriately to different kinds of rhetorical situations	<ul><li>Part Two: A Writer's Situations (pp. 56–252) with detailed advice on responding to varied rhetorical situations from recalling an experience to supporting a position with sources</li><li>Chs. 4–12 with opening "Why Writing Matters" feature illustrating college, workplace, and community situations (e.g., pp. 59 and 221–22)</li><li>Part Three: Other Writing Situations (pp. 254–369): responding to literature and visuals; writing online, under pressure, and at work</li><li>Ch. 24: Strategies for Future Writing (pp. 478–90)</li><li>Companion Web site: Learning by Doing activities for Part Two; Visualizing context tutorial</li></ul>

* This resource is available packaged with the print book. See the preface for details.

WPA Goals and Learning Outcomes	Support in *The Bedford Guide*, Ninth Edition
Rhetorical Knowledge: Student Outcomes	
Use conventions of format and structure appropriate to the rhetorical situation	▪ Examples of effective structure in Part Two (see sample annotations, pp. 157–60) ▪ Ch. 15 on file management and templates (pp. 325–28) ▪ Chs. 36 and 37 with sample MLA and APA papers ▪ Quick Format Guide ▪ Quick Research Guide ▪ Companion Web site: exercises on effective structure; models of student papers and professional essays
Adopt appropriate voice, tone, and level of formality	▪ Ch. 40: Word Choice (pp. 849–53) ▪ Purpose and audience coverage (pp. 11–16 and throughout) ▪ Facing the Challenge: Finding Your Voice (pp. 229–30) and Join the Academic Exchange (pp. 234 and 236–39)
Understand how genres shape reading and writing	▪ Part Two: A Writer's Situations (pp. 56–253) with professional and student essays, guided writing advice, and opening and closing images for analysis for a variety of rhetorical situations ▪ Why Writing Matters sections opening each Part Two chapter with applications in college, at work, in the community (e.g., p. 156). ▪ Part Three: Other Writing Situations (pp. 254–369) with responding to literature and visuals and writing online, under pressure, and at work ▪ Ch. 24: Strategies for Future Writing, including genre analysis ▪ *A Writer's Reader* with 33 readings in five thematic groups ▪ *A Writer's Research Manual* (pp. 643–776) and Quick Research Guide (pp. A-18–A-35) ▪ Companion Web site: Writing activities for Part Two of the book; model documents
Write in several genres	▪ Rhetorical strategies for varied situations in Part Two, including student and professional examples, Why Writing Matters, Facing the Challenge, and Discovery, Revision, and Editing checklists (e.g., pp. 136–54) ▪ Part Three: Other Writing Situations (pp. 254–369) with responding to literature and visuals and writing online, under pressure, and at work ▪ Ch. 24: Strategies for Future Writing, including disciplinary assumptions, genre analysis, and a Genre Checklist (pp. 481–85) ▪ *A Writer's Research Manual* (pp. 643–776) and Quick Research Guide (pp. A-18–A-35) ▪ Companion Web site: Additional activities prompting students to write in multiple genres

* This resource is available packaged with the print book. See the preface for details.

WPA Goals and Learning Outcomes	Support in *The Bedford Guide*, Ninth Edition
Critical Thinking, Reading, and Writing: Student Outcomes	
Use writing and reading for inquiry, learning, thinking, and communicating	■ Part One: writing, reading, and critical-thinking processes ■ Parts Two, Three, and Four emphasizing the connection between reading and writing ■ *A Writer's Reader* with 33 readings grouped thematically ■ Critical reading apparatus in Part Two: A Writer's Situations (e.g., pp. 60, 63) and in *A Writer's Reader* (e.g., pp. 602, 608–09) ■ Companion Web site: Writing activities linked to Part Two of the book emphasizing connection between reading and critical thinking; Reading Critically video *For instructors:* ■ *Practical Suggestions for Teaching with The Bedford Guide for College Writers,* Ch. 3, Teaching Critical Thinking and Writing ■ *Teaching Composition: Background Readings:* Ch. 1, Teaching Writing: Key Concepts, Philosophies, Frameworks, and Experiences
Understand a writing assignment as a series of tasks, including finding, evaluating, analyzing, and synthesizing appropriate primary and secondary sources	■ Chs. 4–14 breaking writing assignments into guided tasks ■ Ch. 18: Strategies: A Case Study showing one student's stages writing an essay ■ Ch. 12: Supporting a Position with Sources ■ Ch. 30: Planning and Managing Your Research Project ■ Ch. 31: Working with Sources, including capturing information and developing an annotated bibliography ■ Chs. 32–34 on finding, evaluating, integrating, and synthesizing sources (pp. 676–716) ■ Quick Research Guide ■ Companion Web site: Additional Learning by Doing activity on finding and evaluating credible sources ■ *i·cite: visualizing sources**: Tutorials and practice on citing all kinds of sources ■ *VideoCentral**: Videos on integrating sources
Integrate students' own ideas with those of others	■ *A Writer's Reader* with journal prompts, writing suggestions, and paired essays ■ Ch. 12: Supporting a Position with Sources (pp. 220–53) ■ Chs. 32–34 on finding, evaluating, integrating and synthesizing sources (pp. 676–716) ■ Quick Research Guide ■ Companion Web site: Research and documentation advice and models, activities on supporting a position with sources ■ *i·cite: visualizing sources**: Tutorials and practice on incorporating sources
Understand the relationships among language, knowledge, and power	■ Ch. 40: Appropriateness (pp. 849–53) and Bias (pp. 857–60) ■ Purpose and Audience (pp. 11–16) and audience analysis throughout ■ Selections in *A Writer's Reader* on language and literacy by Tan, Rodriguez, and others ■ Companion Web site: Why Writing Matters video *For instructors:* ■ *Teaching Composition: Background Readings:* Ch. 4, Issues in Writing Pedagogy: Institutional Politics and the Other

WPA Goals and Learning Outcomes	Support in *The Bedford Guide*, Ninth Edition
Processes: Student Outcomes	
Be aware that it usually takes multiple drafts to create and complete a successful text	■ Ch. 1: Writing Processes (pp. 6–16) with process overview ■ Chs. 4–14 with situation-specific process guidance ■ Part Four writing processes in detail, including Ch. 18: Strategies: A Case Study (pp. 370–84) showing one student's stages ■ Companion Web site: Models of revising and editing; exercises on revising for emphasis ■ *Portfolio Keeping,* Second Edition,* discussing portfolio keeping as a reflection of writing processes *For instructors:* *Teaching Composition: Background Readings:* Ch. 2, Thinking about the Writing Process
Develop flexible strategies for generating ideas, revising, editing, and proofreading	■ Ch. 1: A Writer's Processes with an overview of generating ideas, planning, drafting, developing, revising, editing, and proofreading (pp. 6–16) ■ Parts Two and Three with situation-specific process strategies ■ Part Four: A Writer's Strategies with detailed coverage of writing processes (pp. 370–490) ■ Companion Web site: Models of revising and editing; exercises on revising for emphasis; Getting Started video *For instructors:* *Teaching Composition: Background Readings:* Revising a Draft (pp. 195–246); Ch. 3, Responding to and Evaluating Student Writing
Understand writing as an open process that permits writers to use later invention and rethinking to revise their work	■ Ch. 20: Strategies for Revising and Editing ■ Revision coverage with examples in every Part Two chapter ■ Recurring presentation of a flexible and recursive process of writing (pp. 7–11) ■ Companion Web site: Revising video; an example of revising and editing; exercises on revising for emphasis ■ *Portfolio Keeping,* Second Edition,* discussing portfolio keeping as a reflection of writing processes *For instructors:* ■ *Teaching Composition: Background Readings:* Ch. 2, Thinking about the Writing Process
Understand the collaborative and social aspects of writing processes	■ Learning by Doing features including collaborative activities (e.g., pp. 110, 149, 171) and Peer Response guidelines ■ Part Two: Additional Writing Assignments with collaborative options (e.g., pp. 133–34) ■ Ch. 30 advice, Planning Collaborative Research (pp. 654–55) ■ *Re:Writing Plus**: *Peer Factor* with games and best practices for peer review ■ *Portfolio Keeping,* Second Edition*, Ch. 4, Keeping Company and Working with Others, addressing community and peer response ■ *Oral Presentations in the Composition Course: A Brief Guide**: Ch. 9, Presenting as a Group *For instructors:* ■ *Practical Suggestions for Teaching with The Bedford Guide for College Writers,* Ch. 2, Creating a Writing Community

* This resource is available packaged with the print book. See the preface for details.

WPA Goals and Learning Outcomes	Support in *The Bedford Guide*, Ninth Edition
Processes: Student Outcomes	
Learn to critique their own and others' works	• Ch. 23: Strategies for Revising and Editing with peer-editing advice (pp. 463–65) • Peer Response sections for each chapter in Part Two • Ch. 15: Writing Online with online assessment (pp. 329–32) • Self-assessment Take Action charts (e.g., p. 177) • Ch. 24: Strategies for Future Writing with Connecting Expectations and Assessments (pp. 480–81) • Companion Web site: Peer response worksheets • *Re:Writing Plus**: *Peer Factor* with games and best practices for peer review • *Portfolio Keeping,* Second Edition*, Ch. 4, Keeping Company and Working with Others, addressing community and peer response • *Oral Presentations in the Composition Course: A Brief Guide**: Ch. 10, Evaluating Presentations *For instructors:* • *Practical Suggestions for Teaching with The Bedford Guide for College Writers,* Ch. 2, Creating a Writing Community
Learn to balance the advantages of relying on others with the responsibility of doing their part	• Face-to-face and online individual, paired, small-group, and whole-class Learning by Doing activities throughout • Ch. 30 advice, Planning Collaborative Research (pp. 646–57) • Ethical explorations in Ch. 3: Critical Thinking Processes, Ch. 12, Supporting a Position with Sources, Ch. 15: Writing Online, and Ch. 34: Integrating Sources, and the Quick Research Guide • *Portfolio Keeping,* Second Edition*, Ch. 4, Keeping Company and Working with Others, addressing community and peer response *For instructors:* • *Practical Suggestions for Teaching with The Bedford Guide for College Writers,* Ch. 2, Creating a Writing Community
Use a variety of technologies to address a range of audiences	• Ch. 14: Responding to Visual Representations • Ch. 15: Writing Online • Ch. 16, including oral presentations with visuals • *A Writer's Research Manual* with online strategies throughout (pp. 643–775) • Quick Research Guide, including Searching for Recommended Sources (pp. A-22–A-24) • Quick Format Guide, including a section on integrating and crediting visuals (pp. A-8–A-12) • Companion Web site: tutorials on presentation slides, preparing charts and graphs, and designing documents • *ix visual exercises**: Interactive assignments and guided analysis offer practice with multimedia texts *For instructors:* • *Practical Suggestions for Teaching with The Bedford Guide for College Writers,* Part One, Writing Online • *Teaching Composition: Background Readings:* Teaching Writing with Computers (pp. 305–37); Teaching Visual Literacy (pp. 337–76)

WPA Goals and Learning Outcomes	Support in *The Bedford Guide*, Ninth Edition
Knowledge of Conventions	
Learn common formats for different kinds of texts	■ Advice on various types of assignments in Part Two and Part Three ■ Quick Format Guide with MLA and APA paper and table formats ■ Examples of varied formats for online course (pp. 315–21) and business (pp. 354–65) communication, portfolio letters (pp. 344–46 and 382–84), résumés and application letters (pp. 355–61), presentation visuals (pp. 366–68), and questionnaires (pp. 693–95) ■ Companion Web site: Tutorials on designing documents, preparing effective charts and graphs ■ *ix visual exercises**: Interactive assignments and guided analysis for practice with multimedia texts *For instructors:* *Teaching Composition: Background Readings:* Teaching Visual Literacy (pp. 337–76)
Develop knowledge of genre conventions ranging from structure and paragraphing to tone and mechanics	■ Part Two: A Writer's Situations and Part Three, Other Writing Situations ■ Ch. 24: Strategies for the Future, including Genre Checklist and Learning by Doing genre analysis (pp. 481–88) ■ Part Four: A Writer's Strategies, including chapters on planning, drafting, and developing ■ Chs. 40: Word Choice, 41: Punctuation, and 42: Mechanics ■ Companion Web site: Genre-based activities in Writing Activities for Part Two; Why Proofreading Matters video
Practice appropriate means of documenting their work	■ Ch. 12: Supporting a Position with Sources (pp. 220–53) ■ Chs. 31–34 on working with, finding, evaluating, integrating, and synthesizing sources, including annotated bibliographies (pp. 674–75) ■ Source Navigators (pp. 660–67) ■ Ch. 36 (MLA) and Ch. 37 (APA) with sample entries and full papers ■ Quick Research Guide (pp. A-36–A-56) ■ Companion Web site: *The Bedford Bibliographer* for help in collecting sources and creating bibliography; exercises on MLA and APA style ■ *i-cite: visualizing sources**: Tutorials and practice on citing all kinds of sources
Control such surface features as syntax, grammar, punctuation, and spelling	■ *A Writer's Handbook* (pp. 777–873) with exercises ■ Quick Editing Guide (pp. A-36–A-56) ■ Part Two revising and editing advice, including cross-references to relevant topics in the Quick Editing Guide ■ Ch. 20: Strategies for Revising and Editing ■ Companion Web site: Take Action charts; exercises focusing on all aspects of grammar, from sentence structure to spelling ■ *Re:Writing Plus**: *Make-a-Paragraph Kit*'s animated tutorials on grammar issues *For instructors:* ■ *Practical Suggestions for Teaching with The Bedford Guide for College Writers,* Ch. 4, Providing Support for Underprepared Students

* This resource is available packaged with the print book. See the preface for details.

WPA Goals and Learning Outcomes	Support in *The Bedford Guide*, Ninth Edition
Composing in Electronic Environments	
Use electronic environments for drafting, reviewing, revising, editing, and sharing texts	■ Ch. 15: Writing Online, including course management systems ■ Additional Writing Assignments in Parts Two and Three with online options ■ Ch. 20: Strategies for Revising and Editing ■ *Portfolio Keeping*, Second Edition*, discussion of electronic presentation of portfolios ■ *CompClass for The Bedford Guide for College Writers** ■ Companion Web site: Additional Writing Online activity; Learning by Doing: Becoming Familiar with Your Course Management System *For instructors:* ■ *Practical Suggestions for Teaching with The Bedford Guide for College Writers:* Chs. 5 and 6, Teaching Writing Online and Assessing Student Writing ■ *Teaching Composition: Background Readings:* Teaching Writing with Computers (pp. 305–37)
Locate, evaluate, organize, and use research material collected from electronic sources	■ Reading Online and Multimodal Texts, pp. 33–34 ■ Chs. 31–34 on working with, finding, evaluating, and integrating sources, including annotated bibliographies (pp. 674–75) ■ Quick Research Guide ■ Companion Web site: *The Bedford Bibliographer* for help in collecting sources and creating bibliography; research checklists ■ *i-cite: visualizing sources**: Tutorials and practice on citing electronic sources *For instructors:* ■ *Practical Suggestions for Teaching with The Bedford Guide for College Writers:* Chs. 5 and 6, Teaching Writing Online, and Assessing Student Writing ■ *Teaching Composition: Background Readings:* Teaching Writing with Computers (pp. 305–37)
Understand and exploit the differences in the rhetorical strategies and in the affordances available for both print and electronic composing processes and texts	■ Ch. 15: Writing Online ■ Part Four: A Writer's Strategies ■ Reading Online and Multimodal Texts, pp. 33–34 ■ *A Writer's Reader*, Ch. 28: E-Technology, including six provocative essays ■ Companion Web site: tutorials on Web design, preparing charts and graphs, and designing documents with a word processor *For instructors:* ■ *Practical Suggestions for Teaching with The Bedford Guide for College Writers*, Part One, Using Technology in Your Composition Course and Teaching Writing Online ■ *Teaching Composition: Background Readings:* Teaching Writing with Computers (pp. 305–37)

How to Use *The Bedford Guide for College Writers*

Just as you may be unsure of what to expect from your writing course, you may be unsure of what to expect from your writing textbook. You may even be wondering how any textbook can improve your writing. In fact, a book alone can't make you a better writer, but practice can, and *The Bedford Guide for College Writers* is designed to make your writing practice effective and productive. This text offers help — easy to find and easy to use — for writing essays most commonly assigned in college.

Underlying *The Bedford Guide* is the idea that writing is a necessary and useful skill beyond the writing course. The skills you will learn throughout this book are transferable to other areas of your life — future courses, jobs, and community activities — making *The Bedford Guide* both a time-saver and a money-saver. The following sections describe how you can get the most out of this text.

Finding Information in *The Bedford Guide*

In *The Bedford Guide,* it is easy to find what you need when you need it. Each of the tools described here directs you to useful information — fast.

Brief List of Contents. Open the book to the inside front cover. At a glance you can see a list of the topics in *The Bedford Guide.* If you are looking for a specific chapter, this brief list of contents is the quickest way to find it.

Detailed List of Contents. Beginning on p. xxv, the longer, more detailed list of contents breaks down the topics covered within each chapter of the book. Use this list to find a specific part of a chapter. For example, if you have

I

Contents

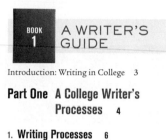

BOOK 1   A WRITER'S GUIDE

been asked to read Olof Eriksson's paper, "The Problems with Masculinity," a quick scan of the detailed contents will show you that it begins on page 24.

Rhetorical List of Contents. This list, beginning on page xxxvii, includes all the readings in *The Bedford Guide,* organized by writing strategy or situation, such as "Explaining Causes and Effects," or "Evaluating and Reviewing." Use this list to locate examples of the kind of writing you are doing and to see how other writers have approached their material.

Selected List of Visuals. On page xli is a list of many of the photographs or other visual images in *The Bedford Guide,* arranged by type, genre, or purpose. This list can help you locate photographs, such as an "Advertisement" or "Visual Essays," to analyze or compare in your writing. In our increasingly visual age, knowing how to read and analyze visuals and then to write about them is a particularly valuable skill.

Locator Guide. If you find yourself stuck at any stage of the writing process, open the book to the inside back cover and its facing page. There you will find the page numbers of useful checklists, self-assessment flowcharts, activities, ESL boxes, and other resources. If you are having trouble writing an opening to your paper, for example, this Locator Guide makes it easy for you to turn to the right place at the right time.

LOCATOR GUIDE
Active Learning and Transferable Skills

Learning by Doing
A Selected List of Activities

From *A Writer's Guide*
Considering Purpose   12
Considering Audience   13
Considering a College Audience   16
Annotating a Passage   22
Responding in a Journal   23

Exploring Your CMS   323
Preparing a Template   325
Organizing Your Files   326
Planning a Job Application   360
Writing a Reflective Letter   384
Discovering a Thesis   404
Outlining   421
Opening and Concluding   432
437

Analogy, argument from, 179
Analysis, 26, 37, 37 (fig.)
   in critical reading, 26, 26 (fig.)
   of genre models, 483–85
   of literature, 270–71
   of process, 450–52
   of readers' points of view, 172
   of subject, 448–50
Analytical reading, 25–29, 26 (fig.)
and
   pronoun-antecedent agreement
      and, 815
   subject-verb agreement and, 805
Annotated bibliography, 490, 674–75

Index. *The Bedford Guide*'s index is an in-depth list of the book's contents in alphabetical order. Turn to page I-1 when you want to find the information available in the book for a particular topic. This example shows you all the places to look for help with analyzing material, a common assignment in college.

Guide to the Handbook. On page 778 you will find a guide that shows you at a glance the entire contents of *A Writer's Handbook.* Turn to this guide when you need help editing your essays. It gives page numbers for each handbook topic, such as "sentence fragments." If English is not your native language, turn to the Locator Guide on the inside back cover for a list of "ESL Guidelines" included in the handbook.

Marginal Cross-References. You can find additional information quickly by using the references in the margins — notes on the sides of each page that tell you where to turn in the book or on the book's companion Web site. For online resources, visit **<bedfordstmartins.com/bedguide>** for more help or for other activities related to what you are reading.

Color-Coded Pages. Several sections of *The Bedford Guide* are color-coded to make them easy to find.

- "MLA Style" (pp. 724 52). If you need help using MLA guidelines to document the sources you have used in your paper, turn to the green-edged pages.

- "APA Style" (pp. 754–75). If you need help using APA guidelines to document the sources you have used in your paper, turn to the turquoise-edged pages.

- "Quick Format Guide" (pp. A-1–A-17). If you need help formatting your paper, turn to this section at the back of the book, which is designated with yellow-edged pages.

- "Quick Research Guide" (pp. A-18–A-35). If you need fast help with research processes, sources, or the basics of MLA or APA style, turn to this section at the back of the book, which is designated with orange-edged pages.

- "Quick Editing Guide" (pp. A-36–A-56). If you need help as you edit your writing, turn to this section at the back of the book, which is designated with purple-edged pages.

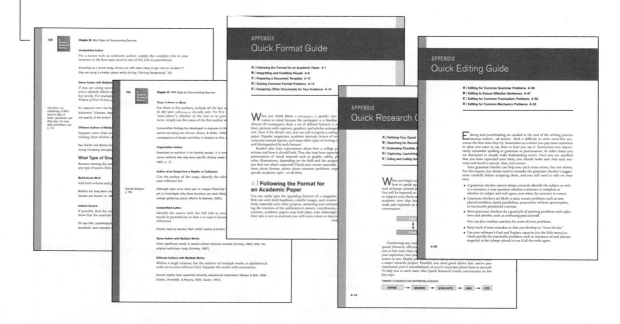

Color-Coded Tabs. Your instructor may use correction symbols, such as "agr" for subject-verb agreement, to indicate areas in your draft that need editing. Tabs at the top of each page in *A Writer's Handbook* link these common correction symbols with explanations, examples, and exercises related to the particular editing problem. The example below shows a page from the handbook.

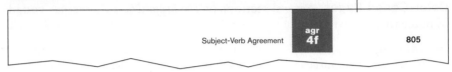

| | Subject-Verb Agreement | **agr 4f** | 805 |

Answers to Exercises. As you complete the exercises in the handbook, you will want to know if you are learning what is expected. Turn to pages A-64–A-68 in the back of the book to find the correct answers to the lettered exercises.

Becoming a Better Writer by Using *The Bedford Guide*

The Bedford Guide includes readings, checklists, activities, and other features that will help you to improve your writing and to do well in college and on the job.

Model Readings. *The Bedford Guide* is filled with examples of both professional and student essays, located on the beige pages in *A Writer's Guide* and in *A Writer's Reader.* All these essays are accompanied by informative notes about the author, prereading questions, definitions of difficult words, questions for thinking more deeply about the reading, and suggestions for writing.

Reading Annotations. Student essays include questions in the margins to spark your imagination and your ideas as you read. Professional essays in *A Writer's Guide* include annotations to point out notable features, such as the thesis and supporting points.

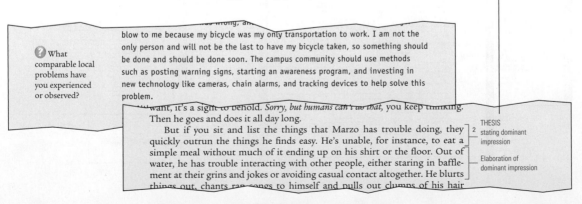

? What comparable local problems have you experienced or observed?

blow to me because my bicycle was my only transportation to work. I am not the only person and will not be the last to have my bicycle taken, so something should be done and should be done soon. The campus community should use methods such as posting warning signs, starting an awareness program, and investing in new technology like cameras, chain alarms, and tracking devices to help solve this problem.

...want, it's a sight to behold. *Sorry, but humans can't do that,* you keep thinking. Then he goes and does it all day long.

But if you sit and list the things that Marzo has trouble doing, they quickly outrun the things he finds easy. He's unable, for instance, to eat a simple meal without much of it ending up on his shirt or the floor. Out of water, he has trouble interacting with other people, either staring in bafflement at their grins and jokes or avoiding casual contact altogether. He blurts things out, chants rap songs to himself and pulls out clumps of his hair

2 THESIS stating dominant impression

Elaboration of dominant impression

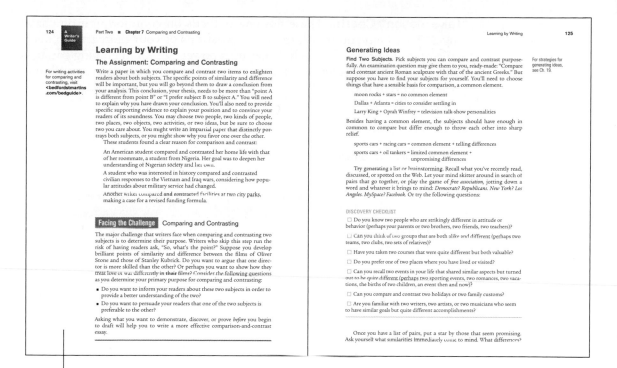

Clear Assignments. In Chapters 4 to 14, the "Learning by Writing" section presents the assignment for the chapter and guides you through the process of writing that type of essay. The "Facing the Challenge" section in each of these chapters helps you through the most complicated step in the assignment.

"Learning by Doing." These activities are designed to let you practice and apply what you are learning to your own writing. They encourage you to make key concepts your own so that you will be able to take what you have learned and apply it in other writing situations and contexts in college and in the workplace.

Learning by Doing   Selecting Reliable Sources

When you choose your own sources, you need to evaluate them to be certain that they are reliable choices that your audience will respect. When your sources are identified in your assignment, you still need to know their strengths, weaknesses, and limitations so that you introduce and use them effectively. Bring your articles, essays, and other sources to a small-group evaluation session. Using the guideline in C3 in the Quick Research Guide (pp. A-24–A-26), discuss your common sources or a key source selected by each writer in the group. Look for aspects that you might mention in a paper to bolster a source's credibility with readers (for example, the author's professional affiliation). Look as well for limitations that might restrict what a source can support.

"Take Action" Charts. These flowcharts focus on common writing challenges. They help you to ask the right questions of your draft and to take active steps to revise effectively. They are a powerful tool in helping you become an independent writer, able to assess what you have written and improve it on your own.

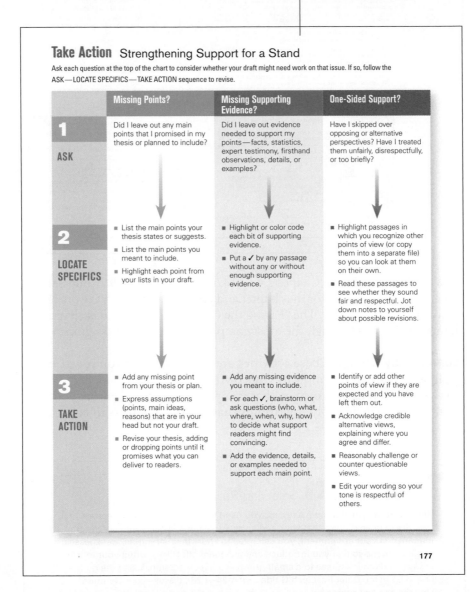

Take Action Strengthening Support for a Stand

Ask each question at the top of the chart to consider whether your draft might need work on that issue. If so, follow the ASK — LOCATE SPECIFICS — TAKE ACTION sequence to revise.

	Missing Points?	Missing Supporting Evidence?	One-Sided Support?
1 **ASK**	Did I leave out any main points that I promised in my thesis or planned to include?	Did I leave out evidence needed to support my points — facts, statistics, expert testimony, firsthand observations, details, or examples?	Have I skipped over opposing or alternative perspectives? Have I treated them unfairly, disrespectfully, or too briefly?
2 **LOCATE SPECIFICS**	■ List the main points your thesis states or suggests. ■ List the main points you meant to include. ■ Highlight each point from your lists in your draft.	■ Highlight or color code each bit of supporting evidence. ■ Put a ✔ by any passage without any or without enough supporting evidence.	■ Highlight passages in which you recognize other points of view (or copy them into a separate file) so you can look at them on their own. ■ Read these passages to see whether they sound fair and respectful. Jot down notes to yourself about possible revisions.
3 **TAKE ACTION**	■ Add any missing point from your thesis or plan. ■ Express assumptions (points, main ideas, reasons) that are in your head but not your draft. ■ Revise your thesis, adding or dropping points until it promises what you can deliver to readers.	■ Add any missing evidence you meant to include. ■ For each ✔, brainstorm or ask questions (who, what, where, when, why, how) to decide what support readers might find convincing. ■ Add the evidence, details, or examples needed to support each main point.	■ Identify or add other points of view if they are expected and you have left them out. ■ Acknowledge credible alternative views, explaining where you agree and differ. ■ Reasonably challenge or counter questionable views. ■ Edit your wording so your tone is respectful of others.

177

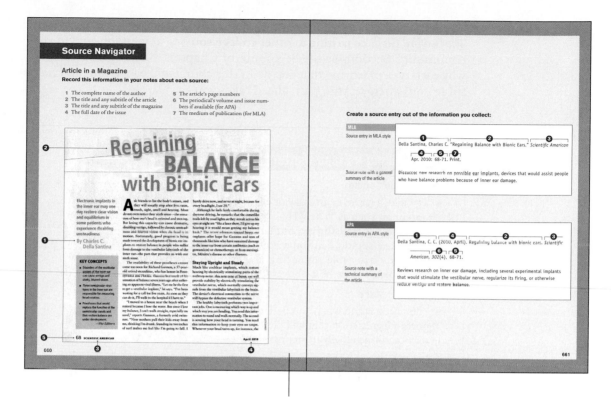

Resources for Crediting Sources. Source Navigators, on pages 660–67, show you where to look in several major types of sources so that you can quickly find the details needed to credit these sources correctly.

Helpful Checklists. Easy-to-use checklists help you to consider your purpose and audience, discover something to write about, get feedback from a peer, revise your draft, and edit for grammatical correctness, using references to the "Quick Editing Guide" (pages A-36–A-56).

AUDIENCE CHECKLIST

☐ Who are your readers? What is their relationship to you?

☐ What do they know about this topic? What do you want them to learn?

☐ How much detail will they want to read about this topic?

☐ What objections are they likely to raise as they read? How can you anticipate and overcome their objections?

☐ What's likely to convince them? What's likely to offend them?

☐ What tone and style would most effectively influence them?

Why Writing Matters. You will apply the writing skills that you learn using *The Bedford Guide* to writing in other college courses, at your job, and in your community. Sections at the beginning of Chapters 4 through 12 consider why each type of writing that you do in this course will be relevant and helpful to you, wherever your path ahead takes you.

Why Taking a Stand Matters

In a College Course

- You take a stand in an essay or exam when you respond, pro or con, to a statement such as "The Web, like movable type for printing, is an invention that has transformed human communication."
- You take a stand when you write research papers that support your position on juvenile sentencing, state support for higher education, or tax breaks for new home buyers.

In the Workplace

- You take a stand when you persuade others that your case report supports a legal action that will benefit your clients or that your customer-service initiative will attract new business.

In Your Community

- You take a stand when you write a letter to the editor appealing to voters to support a local bond issue.

When have you taken a stand in your writing? In what circumstances are you likely to do so again?

A Writer's Guide Contents

Introduction: Writing in College

As a college writer you probably wrestle with the question, What should I write? You may feel you have nothing to say or nothing worth saying. Sometimes your difficulty lies in understanding the requirements of your writing situation, sometimes in finding a topic, and sometimes in uncovering information about it. Perhaps you, like many other college writers, have convinced yourself that professional writers have some special way of discovering ideas for writing. But they have no magic. In reality, what they have is experience and confidence, the products of lots of practice writing.

In *The Bedford Guide for College Writers,* we want you to become a better writer by actually writing. To help you do so, we'll give you a lot of practice as well as useful advice about writing to help you build your skills and confidence. Because writing and learning to write are many-faceted tasks, each part of *A Writer's Guide* is devoted to a different aspect of writing. Together, these four parts contribute to a seamless whole, much like the writing process itself.

Part One, "A College Writer's Processes." This part introduces writing, reading, and thinking critically—essential processes for meeting college expectations.

Part Two, "A Writer's Situations." The nine chapters in Part Two form the core of *The Bedford Guide*. Each presents a writing situation and then guides you as you write a paper in response. You'll develop skills in recalling, observing, interviewing, comparing and contrasting, explaining causes and effects, taking a stand, proposing a solution, evaluating and reviewing, and supporting a position with sources.

Part Three, "Other Writing Situations." This part leads you through five special situations that most students encounter at some point—writing about literature, writing about visuals, and writing online, under pressure, and in the workplace.

Part Four, "A Writer's Strategies." Part Four opens with one student's writing strategies, showing how a paper evolves from idea to final form. The rest of the part is packed with tips and activities that you can use to generate ideas, plan, draft, develop, revise, edit, and carry forward to the future what you have learned as a writer.

PART ONE

A COLLEGE WRITER'S PROCESSES

1 Writing Processes

You are already a writer with long experience. In school you have taken notes, written book reports and term papers, answered exam questions, perhaps kept a journal. In the community or on the job you've composed letters and e-mails. You've sent messages to friends, made lists, maybe even written songs or poetry. All this experience is about to pay off as you tackle college writing, learning by doing.

In this book our purpose is to help you to write better, deeper, clearer, and more satisfying papers than you have ever written before and to learn to do so by actually writing. Throughout the book we'll give you a lot of practice—in writing processes, patterns, and strategies—to build confidence. And we'll pose various writing situations and say, "Go to it!"

Writing, Reading, and Critical Thinking

In college you will expand what you already know about writing. You may be asked not only to recall an experience but also to reflect upon its significance. Or you may be asked to go beyond summarizing positions about an issue to present your own position or propose a solution. Above all, you will be reading and thinking critically—not just stacking up facts but analyzing what you discover, deciding what it means, and weighing its value. You will need to read—and write—actively, engaging with the ideas of others. At the same time, you will need to think critically, analyzing and judging those ideas. You will use criteria—models, conventions, principles, standards—to assess or evaluate what you are doing.

For more on reading critically, see Ch. 2. For more on thinking critically, see Ch. 3.

WRITER'S CHECKLIST

☐ Have you achieved your purpose?

☐ Have you considered your audience?

☐ Have you clearly stated your point as a thesis or unmistakably implied it?

☐ Have you supported your point with enough reliable evidence to persuade your audience?

6

☐ Have you arranged your ideas logically so that each follows from, supports, or adds to the one before it?

☐ Have you made the connections among ideas clear to a reader?

☐ Have you established an appropriate tone?

In large measure, learning to write well is learning what questions to ask as you write. Throughout *A Writer's Guide,* we include questions, suggestions, and activities to help you accomplish your writing tasks and reflect on your own processes as you write, read, and think critically.

For information and journal questions about the Part One photograph, see p. A-72.

A Process of Writing

Writing can seem at times an overwhelming drudgery, worse than scrubbing floors; at other moments, it's a sport full of thrills—like whizzing downhill on skis, not knowing what you'll meet around a bend. Surprising and unpredictable as the process may seem, nearly all writers do similar things:

- They generate ideas.
- They plan, draft, and develop their papers.
- They revise and edit.

These three activities form the basis of most effective writing processes, and they lie at the heart of each chapter in Part Two, "A Writer's Situations."

For full chapters on stages of the writing process, see Chs. 18–24.

For more help with every stage of the writing process, visit <bedfordstmartins.com/bedguide>.

Getting Started

Two considerations—what you want to accomplish as a writer and how you want to appeal to your audience—will shape the direction of your writing. Clarifying your purpose and considering your audience are likely to increase your confidence as a writer. Even so, your writing process may take you in unexpected directions. Because writing activities aren't lockstep stages, you won't necessarily proceed in a straight line. You can skip around, work on several parts at a time, test a fresh approach, or circle back over what's already done. While gathering material, you may feel an urge to play with a sentence until it clicks. Or while writing a draft, you may backtrack to look for more material.

Generating Ideas

The first activity in writing—finding a topic and something to say about it—is often the most challenging and least predictable. Each chapter in Part Two includes a section called "Generating Ideas," which is filled with examples, questions, checklists, and visuals designed to trigger ideas and associations that will help you begin the chapter's writing assignment.

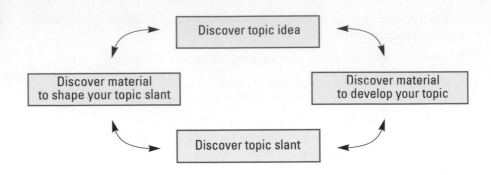

Discovering What to Write About. You may get an idea while talking with friends, riding your bike, or staring out the window. Sometimes a topic lies near home, in a conversation or an everyday event. Often, your reading will raise questions that call for investigation. Even if a particular writing assignment doesn't appeal to you, your challenge is to find a slant that does. Find it, and words will flow—words to engage readers and accomplish your purpose.

Discovering Material. To shape and support your ideas, you'll need facts and figures, reports and opinions, examples and illustrations. How do you find supporting material that makes your slant on a topic clear and convincing to your audience? Luckily you have numerous sources at your fingertips. You can recall your experience and knowledge, observe things around you, converse with others who are knowledgeable, read enlightening materials that draw you to new approaches, and think critically about all these sources.

For an online class discussion of writing processes, see pp. 319–21.

Learning by Doing Reflecting on Ideas

Think over past writing experiences at school or work. How do you get your ideas? Where do they come from? Where do you turn for related material? List or write a few sentences about your most reliable sources of inspiration and information. Discuss your experiences with others in class or online, noting any new approaches you would like to try.

Planning, Drafting, and Developing

Next you will plan your paper, write a draft, and develop your ideas further. Each chapter in Part Two has a section titled "Planning, Drafting, and Developing" to help you through these stages for the assignment in that chapter.

Planning. Having discovered a burning idea to write about (or at least a smoldering one) and some supporting material (but maybe not enough yet), you will sort out what matters most. If you see one main point, or thesis, test various ways of stating it, given your purpose and audience:

MAYBE	Parking in the morning before class is annoying.
OR	Campus parking is a big problem.

Next arrange your ideas and material in a sensible order that will clarify your point. For example, you might group and label your ideas, make an outline, or analyze the main point, breaking it down into parts:

> Parking on campus is a problem for students because of the long lines, inefficient entrances, and poorly marked spaces.

But if no clear thesis emerges quickly, don't worry. You may find one while you draft — that is, while you write an early version of your paper.

Drafting. When your ideas begin to emerge, you want to welcome them — lure them forth, not tear them apart — or they might go back into hiding. Don't be afraid to take risks at this stage: you'll probably be surprised and

For practice choosing a main point, visit **<bedfordstmartins .com/bedguide>**.

Processes for Planning, Drafting, and Developing

pleased at what happens, even though your first version will be rough. Writing takes time; a paper usually needs several drafts and may need a clearer introduction, stronger conclusion, more convincing evidence, or even a fresh start when your subject is unfamiliar or complicated.

Developing. Weave in explanations, definitions, examples, details, and varied evidence to make your ideas clear and persuasive. For example, you may define an at-risk student, illustrate the problems of single parents, or supply statistics about hit-and-run accidents. If you need specific support for your point, use strategies for developing ideas — or return to those for generating ideas. Work in your insights if they fit.

For advice on using a few sources, see the Quick Research Guide, pp. A-18–A-35.

Learning by Doing 🎥 Reflecting on Drafts

Reflect on your past writing experiences. How do you usually plan, draft, and develop your writing? How well do your methods work? How do you adjust them to the situation or type of writing you're doing? Which part of actually producing a draft do you most dread, enjoy, or wish to change? Why? Write down your reflections, and then discuss your experiences with others in class or online.

Revising and Editing

You might want to relax once you have a draft, but for most writers, revising begins the work in earnest. Each chapter in Part Two has a "Revising and Editing" section with checklists and suggestions for working with a peer.

Revising. Revising means both reseeing and rewriting, making major changes so that your paper accomplishes what you want it to. In fact, you may revise what you know and what you think while you're writing or when you reread. You then might reconsider your purpose and audience, rework your thesis, decide what to put in or leave out, rearrange for clarity,

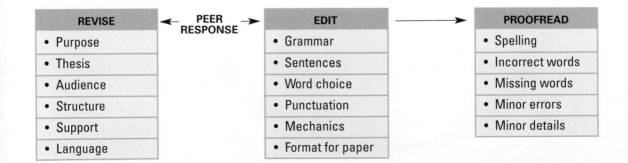

REVISE	← PEER → RESPONSE	EDIT	→	PROOFREAD
• Purpose		• Grammar		• Spelling
• Thesis		• Sentences		• Incorrect words
• Audience		• Word choice		• Missing words
• Structure		• Punctuation		• Minor errors
• Support		• Mechanics		• Minor details
• Language		• Format for paper		

move sentences or paragraphs around, and express or connect ideas better. Perhaps you'll add costs to a paper on parking problems or switch attention to fathers instead of mothers as you consider teen parenthood.

If you put aside your draft for a few hours or a day, you can reread it with fresh eyes and a clear mind. Other students can also help you—sometimes more than a textbook or an instructor can—by responding to your drafts as engaged readers.

Editing. Editing means refining details, improving wording, and correcting flaws that may stand in the way of your readers' understanding and enjoyment. Don't edit too early, though, because you may waste time on parts that you later revise out. In editing, you usually make these repairs:

- Drop unnecessary words; choose lively and precise words.
- Replace incorrect or inappropriate wording.
- Rearrange words in a clearer, more emphatic order.
- Combine short, choppy sentences, or break up long, confusing ones.
- Refine transitions for continuity of thought.
- Check grammar, usage, punctuation, and mechanics.

For editing advice, see the Quick Editing Guide, pp. A-36–A-56. For format advice, see the Quick Format Guide, pp. A-1–A-17.

Proofreading. Finally you'll proofread, taking a last look, checking correctness, and catching doubtful spellings or word-processing errors.

Learning by Doing 🖼 Reflecting on Finishing

Think over your past high-pressure writing experiences such as major papers at school, reports at work, or personal projects such as launching a blog or Web site. What steps do you take to rethink and refine your writing before submitting or posting it? What prompts you to make major changes? How do you try to satisfy the concerns or quirks of your main reader or a broader audience? Work with others in class or online to collect and share your best ideas about how to wrap up writing projects.

Purpose and Audience

At any moment in the writing process, two questions are worth asking:

Why am I writing?   **Who is my audience?**

Writing for a Reason

For more on planning with your purpose in mind, see pp. 400–01. For more on revising for purpose, see pp. 460–61.

Like most college writing assignments, every assignment in this book asks you to write for a definite reason. For example, in Chapter 4 you'll be asked to recall a memorable experience in order to explain its importance for you; in Chapter 9, you'll take a stand on a controversy in order to convey your position and persuade readers to respect it. Be careful not to confuse the sources and strategies you are asked to apply in these assignments with your ultimate purpose for writing. "To compare and contrast two things" is not a very interesting purpose; "to compare and contrast two Web sites *in order to explain which is more reliable*" implies a real reason for writing. In most college writing, your ultimate purpose will be to explain something to your readers or to convince them of something.

To sharpen your concentration on your purpose, ask yourself from the start: What do I want to do? And, in revising, Did I do what I meant to do? These practical questions will help you slice out irrelevant information and remove other barriers to getting your paper where you want it to go.

Learning by Doing 🖉 Considering Purpose

Imagine that you are in the following writing situations. For each, write a sentence or two summing up your purpose as a writer.

1. The instructor in your psychology course has assigned a paragraph about the meanings of three essential terms in your readings.
2. You're very upset about a change in financial-aid procedures and plan to write a letter asking the registrar to remedy the problem.
3. You're starting a blog about your first year at college so your extended family can envision the environment and share your experiences.
4. Your supervisor wants you to write an article about the benefits of a new company service for the customer newsletter.
5. Your MySpace or Facebook profile seemed appropriate last year, but you want to revise it now that you're attending college and have a job with future prospects.

Writing for Your Audience

For more on planning for your readers, see pp. 400–01. For more on revising for them, see pp. 461–62.

Your audience, or your readers, may or may not be defined in your assignment. Consider the following examples:

ASSIGNMENT 1   Discuss the advantages and disadvantages of home-schooling.

ASSIGNMENT 2   In a letter to parents of school-aged children, discuss the advantages and disadvantages of homeschooling.

If your assignment defines an audience, as the second example does, you will need to think about how to approach those readers and what to assume about their relationship to your topic. For example, what points would you include in a discussion aimed at parents? How would you organize your ideas? Would you discuss advantages or disadvantages first? On the other hand, how might your approach differ if the assignment read this way?

ASSIGNMENT 3   In a newsletter article for teachers, discuss the advantages and disadvantages of homeschooling.

Audiences may be identified by characteristics, such as occupation (teachers) or role (parents), that suggest values to which a writer might appeal. As the chart on page 14 suggests, you can analyze the preferences, biases, and concerns of your audience in order to engage and influence readers more successfully. When you consider what readers know, believe, and value, you can aim your writing toward them with a better chance of hitting your mark.

AUDIENCE CHECKLIST

☐ Who are your readers? What is their relationship to you?

☐ What do they know about this topic? What do you want them to learn?

☐ How much detail will they want to read about this topic?

☐ What objections are they likely to raise as they read? How can you anticipate and overcome their objections?

☐ What's likely to convince them? What's likely to offend them?

☐ What tone and style would most effectively influence them?

Learning by Doing 🎯 Considering Audience

Read the following renewal notices directed to subscribers of two magazines, *Zapped!* and *The Atlantic*. Examine the style, tone, language, sequence of topics, or other features of each letter. Write two short paragraphs—one about each letter—explaining what you can conclude about the letter's target audience and its appeal to that audience.

Audience Characteristics and Expectations

	General Audience	College Instructor	Work Supervisor	Campus Friend
Reader's Relationship to You	Imagined but not known personally	Known briefly in a class context	Known for some time in a job context	Known in campus and social contexts
Reason for Reading Your Writing	Curious attitude and interest in your topic assumed	Professional responsibility for your knowledge and skills	Managerial interest in and reliance on your job performance	Personal interest based on shared circumstances
Knowledge About Your Topic	Level of awareness assumed and gaps addressed with logical presentation	Well informed about college topics but wants to see what you know	Informed about the business and expects reliable information from you	Friendly but may or may not be informed beyond social interests
Forms and Formats Expected	Essay, article, letter, report, or other format	Essay, report, research paper, or other academic format	Memo, report, Web page, e-mail, or letter using company format	Chats, notes, blog entries, or other informal messages
Language and Style Expected	Formal, using clear words and sentences	Formal, following academic conventions	Appropriate for advancing you and the company	Informal, using abbreviations, phrases, and slang
Attitude and Tone Expected	Interested and thoughtful about the topic	Serious and thoughtful about the topic and course	Respectful, showing reliability and work ethic	Friendly and interested in shared experiences
Amount of Detail Expected	Sufficient detail to inform or persuade the reader envisioned	Enough sound or research-based evidence to support your thesis	General or technical information as needed	Much detail or little, depending on the topic

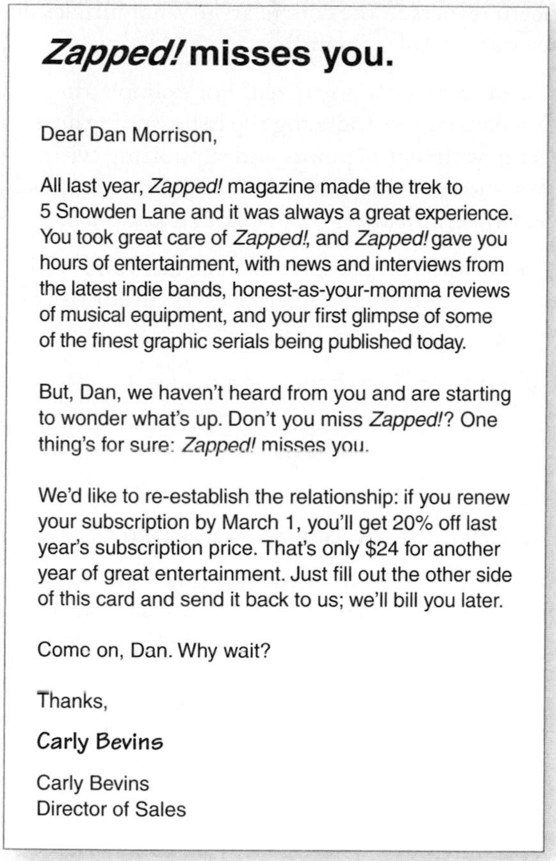

Zapped! misses you.

Dear Dan Morrison,

All last year, *Zapped!* magazine made the trek to 5 Snowden Lane and it was always a great experience. You took great care of *Zapped!*, and *Zapped!* gave you hours of entertainment, with news and interviews from the latest indie bands, honest-as-your-momma reviews of musical equipment, and your first glimpse of some of the finest graphic serials being published today.

But, Dan, we haven't heard from you and are starting to wonder what's up. Don't you miss *Zapped!*? One thing's for sure: *Zapped!* misses you.

We'd like to re-establish the relationship: if you renew your subscription by March 1, you'll get 20% off last year's subscription price. That's only $24 for another year of great entertainment. Just fill out the other side of this card and send it back to us; we'll bill you later.

Come on, Dan. Why wait?

Thanks,

Carly Bevins

Carly Bevins
Director of Sales

Figure 1.1 Letter from *Zapped!*

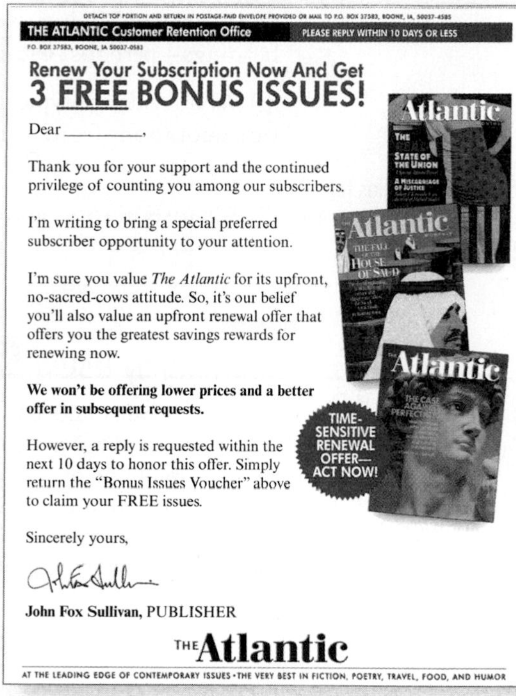

DETACH TOP PORTION AND RETURN IN POSTAGE-PAID ENVELOPE PROVIDED OR MAIL TO P.O. BOX 37583, BOONE, IA, 50037-4585

THE ATLANTIC Customer Retention Office PLEASE REPLY WITHIN 10 DAYS OR LESS

P.O. BOX 37583, BOONE, IA 50037-0583

Renew Your Subscription Now And Get
3 FREE BONUS ISSUES!

Dear ________,

Thank you for your support and the continued privilege of counting you among our subscribers.

I'm writing to bring a special preferred subscriber opportunity to your attention.

I'm sure you value *The Atlantic* for its upfront, no-sacred-cows attitude. So, it's our belief you'll also value an upfront renewal offer that offers you the greatest savings rewards for renewing now.

We won't be offering lower prices and a better offer in subsequent requests.

However, a reply is requested within the next 10 days to honor this offer. Simply return the "Bonus Issues Voucher" above to claim your FREE issues.

Sincerely yours,

John Fox Sullivan, PUBLISHER

THE **Atlantic**

AT THE LEADING EDGE OF CONTEMPORARY ISSUES • THE VERY BEST IN FICTION, POETRY, TRAVEL, FOOD, AND HUMOR

Figure 1.2 Letter from *The Atlantic*

Targeting a College Audience

Many of your college assignments, like Assignment 1 on page 12, may assume that you are addressing general college readers, represented by your instructor and possibly your classmates. Such readers typically expect clear, logical writing with supporting evidence to explain or persuade. Of course, the format, approach, or evidence may differ by field. For example, biologists might expect the findings from your experiment while literature specialists might look for relevant quotations from the novel you're analyzing.

COLLEGE AUDIENCE CHECKLIST

☐ How has your instructor advised you to write for readers? What criteria related to audience will be used for grading your papers?

☐ What do the assigned readings in your course assume about an audience? Has your instructor recommended models or sample readings?

☐ What topics and issues concern readers in the course area? What puzzles do they want to solve? How do they want to solve them?

☐ How is writing in the course area commonly organized? For example, do writers tend to follow a persuasive pattern — introducing the issue, stating an assertion or a claim, backing the claim with logical points and supporting evidence, acknowledging other views, and concluding? Or do they use conventional headings — perhaps *Abstract, Introduction, Methodology, Findings,* and *Discussion*?

☐ What evidence typically supports ideas or interpretations — facts and statistics, quotations from texts, summaries of research, references to authorities or prior studies, experimental findings, observations, or interviews?

☐ What style, tone, and level of formality do writers in the field use?

For more strategies for future college writing, see Ch. 24.

Learning by Doing 🖊 Considering a College Audience

Use the checklist above to examine reading or writing assignments for one of your courses. What are some prominent features of writing in the area, and which of these might be expected in student papers? How would your college paper differ from writing on the same topic for another audience (such as a letter to the editor, a newspaper article, a consumer brochure, an explanation for young students, or a Web page)?

Additional Writing Activities

1. Select a typical passage from a textbook or a reading assigned in a course. Rewrite the passage for a specific nonacademic audience (such as readers of a particular magazine or newspaper, visitors to a certain Web site, or amateurs interested in the topic).

2. Find a nonacademic article, pamphlet, or Web page. Try your hand at rewriting a passage from it to present the material as a college textbook or reading in the field might. Then write an informal paragraph explaining why this task was easy, challenging, or impossible.

3. Write a few paragraphs or an online posting about your personal goals as a writer during this class. What do you already do well as a writer? What do you need or want to improve? What do you hope to accomplish during the course? How might you benefit, in college or elsewhere, from improving your writing?

Reading Processes 2

What's so special about college reading? Don't you pick up the book, start on the first page, and keep going, just as you have ever since you met *The Cat in the Hat*? Reading from beginning to end works especially well when you are eager to find out what happens next, as in a thriller, or what to do next, as in a cookbook. On the other hand, much of what you read in college — textbooks, scholarly articles, research reports, or the papers of your peers — is complicated. Dense, challenging material like this often requires closer, slower reading and deeper thinking — in short, a process for reading critically.

A Process of Critical Reading

Reading critically means approaching whatever you read in an active, questioning manner. This essential college-level skill changes reading from a spectator sport to a contact sport. You no longer sit in the stands, watching graceful skaters glide by. Instead, you charge right into a rough-and-tumble hockey game, gripping your stick and watching out for your teeth.

Critical reading, like critical thinking, is not an isolated activity. It is a continuum of strategies that thoughtful people use every day to grapple with new information, to integrate it with existing knowledge, and to apply it to problems in daily life and academic courses. Many readers do similar things:

For more on critical thinking, see Ch. 3.

- They get ready to do their reading.
- They respond as they read.
- They read on literal and analytical levels.

Building your critical reading skills can bring many benefits, especially if you aren't a regular reader. You'll open the door to information you've never encountered and ideas unlikely to come up with friends. For this course alone, you will be prepared to evaluate strengths and weaknesses of essays by professionals, students, and classmates. If you research a topic, you will be ready to figure out what your sources say, what they assume and imply, whether they are sound, and how you might use them to help make your point. In addition, you can apply your expanded skills in other courses, your job, and your community.

Many instructors help you develop your skills, especially once you realize that they want to improve your critical reading, not complicate your life. Some try to prepare you by previewing a reading so you learn its background or structure. Others supply reading questions so you know what to look for or give motivational credit for reading responses. Still others may share their own reading processes with you, revealing what they read first (maybe an essay's opening and conclusion) or how they might decide to skip a section (such as the methods in a research report whose conclusions they want first).

In the end, however, making the transition to college reading requires your time and energy — and both will be well spent. Once you build your skills as a critical reader, you'll save time by reading more effectively, and you'll save energy by improving both your reading and your writing.

Learning by Doing 🖌 Describing Your Reading Strategies

Briefly describe your reading strategies in different situations. For example, how do you read a magazine, newspaper, or popular novel? What are your goals when you do this kind of reading? What's different about reading the material assigned in college? What techniques do you use for reading assignments? Working with others in class or online, collect your best ideas about how to cope effectively, especially in classes with lots of reading.

Scene from *Hansel and Gretel*, a Grimm's fairy tale, on a German postage stamp (1961).

Getting Started

College reading is active reading. Your instructors expect you to do far more than recognize the words on the page. They want you to read their assignments critically and then to think and write critically about what you have read. Many offer pointers about readings: they want to help you follow the trail of bread crumbs through the forest as you read.

▪ If you know the old tale of Hansel and Gretel, you will remember those resourceful children who dropped crumbs as they walked so that they could retrace their steps through the deep, dark woods. If so, you are interacting with this book, bringing to it your memories

and experience, and you won't stop to puzzle over woods and crumbs.
You'll just keep reading.

- If you have never met those two children, you may have to stop and
  puzzle out how they might connect to the reading process.

Many readers—even college professors—feel lost when they begin complex
texts about something new. However, experienced critical readers hike
through the intellectual woods with confidence because they know how to
use many reading strategies. You can learn and practice such strategies, too,
following the trail of bread crumbs left by other writers and dropping them
for your readers as well.

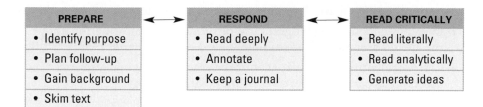

PREPARE	RESPOND	READ CRITICALLY
• Identify purpose	• Read deeply	• Read literally
• Plan follow-up	• Annotate	• Read analytically
• Gain background	• Keep a journal	• Generate ideas
• Skim text		

Preparing to Read

Before you read, think ahead about how to approach the reading process—
how to make the most of the time you spend reading.

Thinking about Your Purpose. Naturally enough, your overall goal for
doing most college reading is to be successful in your courses. When you
begin to read, ask questions like these about your immediate purpose:

- What are you reading?
- Why are you reading? What do you want to do with the reading?
- What does your instructor expect you to learn from the reading?
- Do you need to memorize details, find main points, or connect ideas?
- How does this reading build on, add to, contrast with, or otherwise re-
  late to other reading assignments in the course?

Planning Your Follow-Up. When you are required to read or to select a
reading, ask yourself what your instructor expects to follow it:

- Do you need to be ready to discuss the reading during class?
- Will you need to mention it or analyze it during an examination?

- Will you need to write about it or its topic?
- Do you need to find its main points? Sum it up? Compare it? Question it? Spot its strengths and weaknesses? Draw useful details from it?

Gaining Some Background. Knowing a reading's background, context, approach, or frame of reference can help you predict where the reading is likely to go and understand how it relates to other readings. Begin with the resources readily available to you:

- Do the syllabus, reading schedule, and class notes reveal your instructor's purpose in assigning the reading? What can you learn from any reading questions, tips about what to watch for, or connections with other readings?
- Does your text have short introductions to readings, your book a jacket or preface, or your article an introduction or abstract that sums it up?
- Does any enlightening biographical or professional information about the author accompany the reading?
- Can you identify or speculate about the reading's original audience based on its content, style, tone, or publication history?

Skimming the Text. Before you actively read a text, begin by skimming it—quickly reading only enough to introduce yourself to it. If the reading has a table of contents or subheadings, read those first to figure out what material it covers and how it is organized. Read the first paragraph and then the first (or first and last) sentence of each paragraph that follows. If the material has any visuals, read the captions.

Learning by Doing 🎯 Preparing to Read

Working with a selection from the reader in this book, try out a few strategies for preparing to read. Then sum up your experience—which strategies worked, which didn't, and whether you feel prepared to read the selection critically. Discuss your accounts with others in class or online.

Responding to Reading

You may be accustomed to reading simply for facts or main ideas. However, critical reading is far more active than fact hunting. It requires responding, questioning, and challenging as you read.

Reading Deeply. College assignments often require more concentration from you as a reader than other readings do. Use the following questions to explore the complexities below the surface:

- Are difficult or technical terms defined in specific ways? How might you highlight, list, or record such terms so that you master them?
- How might you record or recall the details in the reading? How could you track or diagram interrelated ideas to grasp their connections?
- How do word choice, tone, and style alert you to the complex purpose of a reading that is layered or indirect rather than straightforward?
- How might you trace the progression of ideas in the reading? How do headings, previews of what's coming up, summaries of what's gone before, and transitions signal the organization?
- Does the reading include figurative or descriptive language, references to other works, or recurring themes? How do these enrich the reading?
- Can you answer any reading questions in your textbook, assignment, study guide, or syllabus? Can you restate headings in question form to create your own questions and then supply the answers? For example, change "Major Types of X" to "What are the major types of X?"

For more on figurative language, see p. 268.

Annotating the Text. Writing notes on the page (or on a photocopy if the material is not your own) is a useful way to trace the author's points, question them, and add your own comments as they pop up. The following passage ends the introduction of "The New Science of Siblings," written by Jeffrey Kluger (with reporting by Jessica Carsen, Wendy Cole, and Sonja Steptoe) and featured as the cover story in the July 10, 2006, *Time* (pp. 47–48). Notice how one writer annotated this passage:

For more on evaluating what you read, see section C in the Quick Research Guide, pp. A-24–A-26.

For a Critical Reading Checklist, see pp. 28–29.

Key point — both obvious and surprising

Our spouses arrive comparatively late in our lives; our parents eventually leave us. Our siblings may be the only people we'll ever know who truly qualify as partners for life. "Siblings," says family sociologist Katherine Conger of the University of California, Davis, "are with us for the whole journey."

Good quote — from UC Davis authority

Scary — I never thought of my sister this way!

Sums up past studies but new to me

Within the scientific community, siblings have not been wholly ignored, but research has been limited mostly to discussions of birth order. Older sibs were said to be strivers; younger ones rebels; middle kids the lost souls. The stereotypes were broad, if not entirely untrue, and there the discussion mostly ended.

Not exactly! My sister's definitely a striver, but I'm no rebel

But all that's changing. At research centers in the United States, Canada, Europe, and elsewhere, investigators are launching a wealth of new studies into the sibling dynamic, looking at ways brothers and sisters steer one another into—or away from—risky behavior; how they form a protective buffer against family upheaval; how they educate one another about the opposite sex; how all siblings compete for family recognition and come to terms—or blows—over such impossibly charged issues as parental favoritism.

Wow — global research!

Have to go for the drama — competition and favorites!!

Cousins-example — pulled together when parents split

When you annotate a reading, don't passively highlight big chunks of text. Instead, use a pen or pencil (or add a comment to a file) to respond actively. Next, read slowly and carefully so that you can follow what the reading says and how it supports its point. Record your own reactions, not what you think you are supposed to say:

- Jot down things you already know or have experienced to build your own connection to the reading.
- Circle key words, star or check ideas when you agree or disagree, add arrows to mark connections, or underline key points, ideas, or definitions to learn the reading's vocabulary.
- Add question marks or questions about meaning or implications.
- Separate main points from supporting evidence and detail. Then you can question a conclusion, or challenge the evidence that supports it. (Main points often open a section or paragraph, followed by supporting detail, but sometimes this pattern is reversed.)
- React to quotable sentences or key passages. If they are hard to understand, restate them in your own words, or sum them up.
- Consider how the reading appeals to your head, heart, or conscience.

Learning by Doing 🎥 Annotating a Passage

For a sample annotated passage, see p. 21.

Annotate the following passage on a recent trend.

Every woman's dream is to find the perfect spouse and settle down for life, right? Although this may be the dream of some, it doesn't reflect reality, according to a recent analysis of census data. Based on this analysis, the *New York Times* reported that, for the first time in history, most U.S. women are single ("51% of Women Are Now Living without Spouse," 16 Jan. 2007; reported by Sam Roberts). Specifically, in 2005, 51 percent of women reported being unmarried, up from 49 percent in 2000 and 35 percent in 1950.

The *Times* and other media sources have pointed to several factors behind the shift, including the fact that women are waiting longer to get married. "We don't need men anymore," said twenty-nine-year-old New York City resident Jessica Cohen, in an interview with CBS News ("More Women Saying, 'I Don't,'" 16 Jan. 2007; reported by Kelly Wallace). As Cohen explained, "I mean, we want men, we want someone to share everything with, but I don't think we need to rush."

Other women are choosing to live with partners instead of marrying. Many divorced women are staying single or delaying remarriage. As divorced Baltimore attorney Catherine Flynn told MSNBC, "I get to make the choices myself about where I live, how I live, how I decorate my house" ("Watch Out, Men! More Women Opt to Live Alone," 16 Jan. 2007; reported by Dawn Fratangelo). And in another trend behind the shift, women are living longer as widows.

Social commentators who have studied marriage trends say that women today simply have more choices than were available in past generations. Many are financially independent and are even willing to raise children on their own. Freed from the need to find someone to support them as soon as possible, these women can take more time to find a partner with whom they are emotionally, intellectually, and spiritually compatible. But even then, they might not marry such a man, as the *Times* story shows.

Keeping a Reading Journal. A reading journal is an excellent place to record not just what you read but how you respond to it. It helps you read actively and build a reservoir of ideas for follow-up writing. Use a special notebook, a computer file, or easy-to-sort cards for a research project to address questions like these:

For advice on keeping a writer's journal, see Ch. 19.

- What is the subject of the reading? What is the writer's stand?
- What does the writer take for granted? What assumptions does he or she begin with? Where are these stated or suggested?
- What are the writer's main points? What evidence supports them?
- Do you agree with what the writer has said? Do his or her ideas clash with your ideas or question something you take for granted?
- Has the writer told you more than you wanted to know or failed to tell you something you wish you knew?
- What conclusions can you draw from the reading?
- Has the reading opened your eyes to new ways of viewing the subject?

Learning by Doing 🎥 Responding in a Reading Journal

Return to the passage that you annotated on pages 22–23. Write a brief journal entry about this passage. Concentrate on two points: what the passage says and how you respond.

Learning from Another Writer: Reading Summary and Response

For another reading response with a summary, critique, and application, see pp. 29–30.

Olof Eriksson's instructor asked students to write a one-page reading response, including a summary and a personal response, before writing each assigned essay. Your instructor may also ask you to keep a reading journal or to submit or post online your responses to readings. Your assignment might require brief features such as these:

- Summary: a short statement in your own words of the reading's main points (without your opinion, evaluation, or judgment).
- Paraphrase: a restatement of a passage using your own words and sentences.
- Quotation: a noteworthy expression or statement in the author's exact words, presented in quotation marks and correctly cited.

For more on citing sources, see E1–E2 in the Quick Research Guide, pp. A-30–A-35.

- Personal response: a statement and explanation of your reaction to the reading.
- Critique: your evaluation of the strengths or weaknesses of the reading.
- Application: a connection between the reading and your experience.
- Question: a point of curiosity or uncertainty that you wish the writer had covered.

Olof Eriksson   Student Summary and Response

The Problems with Masculinity

Robert Jensen writes in his essay "The High Cost of Manliness" about masculinity   1
and how our culture creates expectations of certain traits from the males in our
society. He strongly opposes this view of masculinity and would prefer that sociological constructs like masculinity and femininity were abolished. As examples of
expected traits, he mentions strength and competition. Males are supposed to take
what they want and avoid showing weaknesses. Then Jensen points out negative
consequences of enforcing masculinity, things like rape and men having trouble
showing vulnerability. He counters the argument of differences in biology between
males and females by pointing out that we do not know how much comes from
biology and how much comes from culture, but that both certainly matter and we
should do what we can. He is also concerned about giving positive attributes to
masculinity, as that effectively tells us they only belong with males. He ends by
observing that we are facing challenges now that cannot be met with the current
view of masculinity.

I agree with what Jensen says, and I find it a problem today that the definition [2] of masculinity is so closely connected to competition and aggression. Even so, I find that my own definition of masculinity is very close to the general one. I would say it is to be strong and determined, always winning. I'm sure most people have a similar idea of what it is, even as most people would disagree logically. That is why we need to make an effort to change our culture, just as Jensen argues. If we can either abolish masculinity and femininity or simply change them into a lot more neutral and closely related terms, then we will be a lot closer to real equality between the genders. This change will not only help remove most of the negative impacts Jensen brought up but also help pave a better way for future generations, reducing their problems.

Works Cited

Jensen, Robert. "The High Cost of Manliness." *The Bedford Guide for College Writers.* 9th ed. Ed. X. J. Kennedy, Dorothy M. Kennedy, and Marcia F. Muth. Boston: Bedford, 2011. 532–35. Print.

Questions to Start You Thinking

Meaning

1. According to Eriksson, what is the topic of Jensen's essay, and what is Jensen's position on this topic? Where does Eriksson present this information?

2. What is Eriksson's personal response to the essay? Where does he present his views?

Writing Strategies

3. How does Eriksson consider his audience as he organizes and develops his summary and response?

4. What kinds of material from the essay does Eriksson use to develop his summary?

Reading on Literal and Analytical Levels

Educational expert Benjamin S. Bloom identified six levels of cognitive activity: knowledge, comprehension, application, analysis, synthesis, and evaluation.[1] Each level acts as a foundation for the next. Each also demands higher thinking skills than the previous one. Experienced readers, however, jump among these levels, gathering information and insight as they occur. (See the reading skills figure on the next page.)

[1]Benjamin S. Bloom et al., *Taxonomy of Educational Objectives, Handbook 1: Cognitive Domain* (New York: McKay, 1956).

The first three levels are literal skills, the building blocks of thought. The last three levels — analysis, synthesis, and evaluation — are the analytical skills that your instructors especially want you to develop. To read critically, you must engage with a reading on both literal and analytical levels. Suppose you read in your history book a passage about Franklin Delano Roosevelt (FDR), the only American president elected to four consecutive terms of office.

Knowing. Once you read the passage, even if you have little background in American history, you can decode and recall the information it presents about FDR and his four terms in office.

Comprehending. To understand the passage, you need to know that a term for a U.S. president is four years and that *consecutive* means "continuous." Thus, FDR was elected to serve for sixteen years.

Applying. To connect this knowledge to what you already know, you think of other presidents — George Washington, who served two terms; Grover Cleveland, who served two terms but not consecutively; Jimmy Carter, who served one term; and the second George Bush, who served two terms. Then you realize that being elected to four terms is quite unusual. In fact, the Twenty-second Amendment to the Constitution, ratified in 1951, now limits a president to two terms.

Analyzing. You can scrutinize FDR's four terms from various angles, selecting a principle for analysis that suits your purpose. Then you can use this principle to break the information into its components or parts. For example, you might analyze FDR's tenure in relation to that of other presidents. Why has FDR been the only president elected to serve four terms? What circumstances contributed to three reelections?

Literal and Analytical Reading Skills
The information in this figure is adapted from Benjamin S. Bloom et al., *Taxonomy of Educational Objectives, Handbook 1: Cognitive Domain* (New York: McKay, 1956).

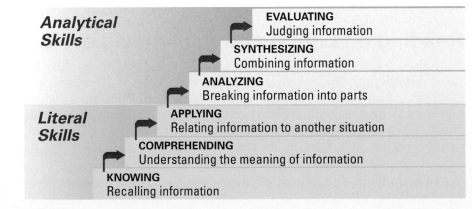

Synthesizing. To answer your questions, you may have to read more or review past readings. Then you begin synthesizing—recombining information, pulling together facts and opinions, identifying evidence accepted by all or most sources, examining any controversial evidence, and drawing conclusions that reliable evidence seems to support. For example, it would be logical to conclude that the special circumstances of the Great Depression and World War II contributed to FDR's four terms, not that Americans reelected him out of pity because he had polio.

Evaluating. Finally, you evaluate the significance of your new knowledge to your understanding of Depression-era politics and to your assessment of your history book's approach. For instance, you might ask yourself, Why has the book's author chosen to make this point? How does it affect the rest of the discussion? And you may also have formed your own opinion that FDR's four-term presidency is understandable in light of the events of the 1930s and 1940s, that the author has mentioned this fact to highlight the era's unique political atmosphere, and that, in your opinion, it is evidence neither for nor against FDR's excellence as a president.

Learning by Doing 📷 Reading Analytically

Think back to something you have read recently that helped you make a decision, perhaps a newspaper or magazine article, an electronic posting, or a college brochure. How did you analyze what you read, breaking the information into parts? How did you synthesize it, combining it with what you already knew? How did you evaluate it, judging its significance for your decision?

For additional critical reading activities, visit **<bedfordstmartins .com/bedguide>**.

Generating Ideas from Reading

Like flints that strike each other and cause sparks, readers and writers provoke one another. For example, when your class discusses an essay, you may be surprised by the range of insights your classmates report. Of course, they may be equally surprised by what you see. Above all, reading is a dynamic process. It may change your ideas instead of support them. Here are suggestions for unlocking the potential of a good text.

For more on generating ideas, see Ch. 19.

Looking for Meaty Pieces. Spur your thinking about current topics by browsing through essay collections or magazines in the library or online. Try *Atlantic, Harper's, New Republic, Commentary,* or special-interest magazines such as *Architectural Digest* or *Scientific American.* Check the editorials and op-ed columns in your local newspaper, the *New York Times,* or the *Wall Street Journal.* Also search the Internet on challenging subjects (such as film classics or homeless children). Look for articles that are meaty, not superficial, and that are written to inform and convince, not to entertain or amuse.

Logging Your Reading. For several days keep a log of the articles that you find. Record the author, title, and source for each promising piece so that you can easily find it again. Briefly note the subject and point of view as well, so you identify a range of possibilities.

Recalling Something You Have Already Read. What have you read lately that started you thinking? Return to a recent reading—a chapter in a humanities textbook, an article assigned in sociology, a research study for biology.

Paraphrasing and Summarizing Complex Ideas. Do you sometimes feel overwhelmed by a challenging reading? If so, read slowly and carefully. Then consider two common methods of recording and integrating ideas from sources into papers.

For more on paraphrase and summary, see Ch. 12 and D4–D5 in the Quick Research Guide, pp. A-28–A-29.

- Paraphrase: restate an author's complicated ideas fully but in your own language, using different wording and different sentence patterns.
- Summarize: reduce an author's main point to essentials, using your own clear, concise, and accurate language.

Accurately recording what a reading says can help you grasp its ideas, especially on literal levels. Once you understand what it says, you can agree, disagree, or question.

Reading Critically. Instead of just soaking up what a thought-provoking reading says, engage in a dialogue or conversation with the writer. Criticize. Wonder. Argue back. Demand convincing evidence. Use the following checklist to get started.

CRITICAL READING CHECKLIST

☐ What problems and issues does the author raise?

☐ What is the author's purpose? Is it to explain or inform? To persuade? To amuse? In addition to this overall purpose, is the author trying to accomplish some other agenda?

☐ How does the author appeal to you as a reader? Where do you agree and disagree? Where do you want to say "Yeah, right!" or "I don't think so!"?

☐ How does this piece relate to your own experiences or thoughts? Have you encountered anything similar? Does the topic or approach intrigue you?

☐ Are there any important words or ideas that you don't understand? If so, do you need to reread or turn to a dictionary or reference book?

☐ What is the author's point of view? What does the author assume or take for granted? Where does the author reveal these assumptions? Do they make the selection seem weak or biased?

☐ Which statements are facts, verifiable by observation, firsthand testimony, or research? Which are opinions? Does one or the other dominate?

☐ Is the writer's evidence accurate, relevant, and sufficient? Do you find it persuasive?

For more on facts and opinions, see pp. 40–41.

For more on evaluating evidence, see C1–C3 in the Quick Research Guide, pp. A-24–A-26.

Analyzing Writing Strategies. Reading widely and deeply can reveal what others say and how they shape and state it. For some readings in this book, notes in the margin identify key features such as the introduction, thesis statement or main idea, major points, and supporting evidence. Ask questions such as these to help you identify writing strategies:

WRITING STRATEGIES CHECKLIST

☐ How does the author introduce the reading and try to engage the audience?

☐ Where does the author state or imply the main idea or thesis?

☐ How is the text organized? What main points develop the thesis?

☐ How does the author supply support—facts, data, statistics, expert opinions, experiences, observations, explanations, examples, other information?

☐ How does the author connect or emphasize ideas for readers?

☐ How does the author conclude the reading?

☐ What is the author's tone? How do the words and examples reveal the author's attitude, biases, or assumptions?

Learning from Another Writer: Reading Summary, Critique, and Application

This student journal entry responds to an essay from the July 14, 2003, issue of *Time* reprinted in the last edition of this book. The entry includes a summary, a critique, and an application.

Stephanie Switzer
Student Journal Entry

A Response to "Free the Children"

For another reading response, see pp. 24–25.

<u>Summary</u>: In "Free the Children," Nancy Gibbs explains why she believes children need the summer as a time away from the stresses of the world and as a time for freedom. Gibbs thinks that children should have summers that don't count and don't matter. Their time should be spent investigating the outdoors and having adventures, not preparing for the upcoming school year. According to Gibbs, "The experts have long charted the growing stress and disappearing downtime of modern children; now they say the trend extends across class and region" (471). A child's summer shouldn't be clogged and booked up like the rest of the year but should be relaxing and full of grace. What Gibbs isn't saying, though, is that we should let our children run amok and continually get themselves into dangerous situations. With Amber Alerts being ever present, it is important for parents to stay on their guard but also to give their child some much-needed freedom from school. Gibbs says that "apart from the challenge of trusting our kids, there is the challenge of trusting ourselves, steering by the stars of instinct and memory rather than parent peer pressure or all those guidebooks on how to raise a Successful Child" (472).

<u>Critique</u>: It seemed to me that you could tell that this article was written by a parent who had concerns for her child. I could not agree more with the opinions of Nancy Gibbs in this essay. I think that Gibbs did a good job of balancing a summer of freedom with a summer that does not altogether leave behind discipline and parents. She gave a personal example about her own daughter neglecting to call home. Gibbs realized that she was just curious but still disciplined her. Also, I think that Gibbs did a good job of getting readers to think back to their own childhood as they were reading, with examples of red rover and other things from their youth.

<u>Application</u>: This article has helped me to realize what I need to do when I am a parent. I know now that I can't reign over my children's whole summer with work for them. I need to be able to let them do their own thing and worry about the future when the time is right. This article also reminded me of my own childhood when I would go to camp every year and just have fun. I would run around with my friends without a care in the world. Now I wish I could have that time back and be that reckless youth again without the strains of work and school on me anymore.

Works Cited

Gibbs, Nancy. "Free the Children." *The Bedford Guide for College Writers*. 8th ed. Ed. X. J. Kennedy, Dorothy M. Kennedy, and Marcia F. Muth. Boston: Bedford, 2008. 470–72. Print.

Questions to Start You Thinking

Meaning

1. According to Switzer, what is the topic of Gibbs's essay, and what is Gibbs's position on this topic? Where does Switzer present this information?

2. What are Switzer's main points in her critique?

3. How does Switzer apply this reading to her own life?

Writing Strategies

4. Following her instructor's directions, how has Switzer identified the three parts of her reading response? If she had not used this method, how else might she have alerted a reader to each shift in focus?

5. How does Switzer develop her summary? What kinds of material does she draw from the essay?

Learning by Doing 🎬 Reading Critically

Using the advice in this chapter, critically read the following essay from the *Chicago Tribune Online*. First, add your own notes and comments in the margin, responding on both literal and analytical levels. Second, add notes about the writers' writing strategies. (Sample annotations are supplied to help you get started.) Finally, write out a brief summary of the reading and your own well-reasoned conclusions about it.

For a sample annotated passage, see p. 21.

Jeffery M. Leving and Glenn Sacks
Women Don't Want Men? Ha!

The recent census data finding that for the first time the majority of American women are unmarried is being greeted in a largely celebratory tone. One newspaper explains, "Who needs a man? Not most women." MSNBC warns, "Watch out, men! More women opt to live alone." CBS says, "More women saying 'I don't.'" One newspaper cartoon depicts a happily divorced woman remembering her ex-husband bellowing, "Where's my dinner?! Iron my shirts!! Lose weight!!!" Several others depict women pondering the single life as their fat, lazy husbands drink beer and watch TV sports. One female blogger summed up the female blogosphere's reaction—"Hurray for all single women! You go girls!" 1

The message is clear—men don't measure up and are no longer needed nor often even wanted. Since women have careers now, we are told, men's tra- 2

Writers sum up sources, but not all women would agree

ditional contribution—financial support—has become largely irrelevant, and men do not now nor did they ever contribute much more than that.

In reality, men give a lot to their families—as much as women do. The cur- 3
rent trend away from marriage and toward divorce and/or remaining single has more to do with overcritical women and their excessive expectations than it does with unsuitable men.

The most common charge leveled at men is that they don't hold up their 4
end in the home. Men do work, many critics say, but women work too, and also do most of the childcare and housework—the "second shift."

Research contradicts this. Census data show that only 40 percent of mar- 5
ried women with children under eighteen work full-time, and more than a quarter do not hold a job outside the home. According to the Bureau of Labor Statistics' 2004 Time Use Survey, men spend 1½ times as many hours working as women do, and full-time employed men still work significantly more hours than full-time employed women. When work outside the home and inside the home are properly considered, it is clear that men do at least as much as women. A 2002 University of Michigan Institute for Social Research survey found that women do eleven more hours of housework a week than men, but men work at their jobs fourteen hours a week more than women. According to the Bureau of Labor Statistics, men's total time at leisure, sleeping, doing personal-care activities, or socializing is a statistically meaningless 1 percent higher than women's. The Families and Work Institute in New York City found that fathers, despite their greater market labor load, provide three-fourths as much childcare as mothers do. And these studies do not account for the fact, strongly supported by federal Department of Labor data, that men's jobs tend to be more dangerous and physically straining than women's.

To what, then, do we attribute women's discontent with marriage and re- 6
lationships and the fact that they initiate the vast majority of divorces? A new *Woman's Day* magazine poll found that 56 percent of married women would not or might not marry their husbands if they could choose again.

Nobody would dispute that, in selecting a mate, women are more discern- 7
ing than men. This is an evolutionary necessity—a woman must carefully evaluate who is likely to remain loyal to her and protect and provide for her and her children. If a man and a woman go on a blind date and don't hit it off, the man will shrug and say "It went OK." The woman will give five reasons why he's not right for her.

A woman's discerning, critical nature doesn't disappear on her wedding 8
day. Most marital problems and marriage counseling sessions revolve around why the wife is unhappy with her husband, even though they could just as easily be about why the husband is unhappy with the wife. In this common predivorce scenario there are only two possibilities—either she's a great wife and he's a lousy husband, or she's far more critical of him than he is of her. Usually it's the latter.

Despite last week's media homilies, it's doubtful that many men or 9
women are truly happy alone. Much of women's cheerful "I don't need a

man/I love my cats" reaction has a hollow ring to it and sounds a lot more like whistling in the dark than a celebration.

Yes, there are some men who make poor mates but not nearly enough to account for the divorce epidemic and the decline of marriage. While it's easy to blame men, many of the wounds women bear from failed relationships and loneliness are self-inflicted.

Reading Online and Multimodal Texts

Traditionally, a literate person was someone who could read and write. That definition remains current, but the texts that people now read and write are not necessarily printed material. The opportunities to read and write have vastly increased with the development of online technologies and multimodal texts that combine visual, audio, and written materials. Such texts do not necessarily have a fixed form because they may include sound and motion that cannot be confined to a printed page. Further, they may be randomly or routinely updated. In addition, readers can access them flexibly, through pages and links rather than in a strict sequence and scan them quickly (see below). More innovations, unimaginable now, might well emerge even before you graduate from college.

For more on responding to images, see Ch. 14.

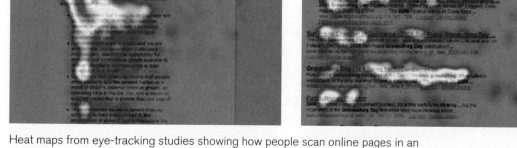

Heat maps from eye-tracking studies showing how people scan online pages in an F-shaped pattern.

What might these changes mean for you as a reader and writer? Your critical reading skills are likely to be increasingly useful because the essential challenge of deep, thoughtful reading applies to graphic novels, blogs, photo essays, and YouTube videos just as it applies to printed books, articles, and essays. In fact, some might argue that texts using multiple components and appealing to multiple senses require even more thorough scrutiny to grasp what they are saying and how they are saying it. Here are some suggestions about how you might apply your critical skills in these new contexts:

- Concentrate on your purpose to stay focused when you read online or multimodal texts, especially if those texts tug you further and further away from your original search or material.

- Create an online file, reading journal, research journal, or writer's blog so that you have a handy location for responding to new materials.

- Bookmark meaty online readings, sites, or multimodal texts so that you can easily return to them to examine their details. Look not only at what you see or hear but also at what the material suggests and how it appeals to you.

- View the features and effects of visual or multimodal texts as carefully as you read printed texts. Observe composition, symmetry, sequence, shape, color, brightness, and other visual components.

- Listen for the presence and impact of audio characteristics such as sound effects (accuracy, clarity, volume, timing, emotional impact), speech (pitch, tone, dialect, accent, pace), and music (instrumentation, vocals, melody, rhythm, harmony, musical roots, cuts, remix decisions).

- Examine visual or multimodal materials critically—analyzing components, synthesizing varied information, and evaluating effects.

- Evaluate research material that presents evidence to support your points or to challenge other views so that you rely on trustworthy sources.

- Be careful to secure any necessary permission to add someone else's visual or other material to your own text and to credit your source appropriately.

- Generate even more ideas by rereading this chapter and thinking about how you could apply the skills presented here in new situations.

Learning by Doing 🎥 Reading a Web Site

Working with a small group on a laptop in class, at the computer lab, or online, examine a Web site about a topic that you might want to investigate for a college research project. Critically "read" and discuss the site's written text, images, organization, and other features that might persuade you that it would or would not be a reliable source.

Additional Writing Activities

1. Select an essay from the reader in this book. Annotate the essay, marking both its key ideas and your own reactions to it. Then write two paragraphs, one summarizing the reading and the other explaining your personal response to it.

2. Follow up on Activity 1, working with others who have responded to the same essay. Share your summaries, noting the strengths of each. Then develop a collaborative summary that briefly and fairly presents the main points of the reading. (You can merge your existing summaries or make a fresh start.) When you finish the group summary, decide which methods of summarizing work best.

3. Follow up on Activity 1 by adding a critique, application, or question for the author to your response.

4. Select a passage from the textbook or readings for another course you are taking or have taken. Annotate the passage, and make some notes using the Critical Reading Checklist and the Writing Strategies Checklist (pp. 28–29) as guides. Pay special attention to the reading's purpose and its assumptions about its audience. Write a paragraph or two about your critical examination of the passage.

5. **Visual Activity.** Select a Web page, a blog entry, a YouTube video, a photo from an online gallery, or another brief online text. "Read" this text critically, adapting and using reading processes and skills from this chapter. Write a short summary and response, including a link or a printout of the page or section to which you have responded.

3 Critical Thinking Processes

Critic, from the Greek word *kritikos*, means "one who can judge and discern"—in short, someone who thinks critically. College will have given you your money's worth if it leaves you better able to judge and discern—to determine what is more and less important, to make distinctions and recognize differences, to generalize from specifics, to draw conclusions from evidence, to grasp complex concepts, to choose wisely. The effective thinking that you will need in college, on the job, and in your daily life is active and purposeful, not passive and ambling. It is critical thinking.

A Process of Critical Thinking

You use critical thinking every day to solve problems and make decisions. Suppose you don't have enough money both to pay your tuition and to buy the car you need. First, you might pin down the causes of your financial problem. Next, you might examine your options to find the best solution, as shown in the graphic on page 36.

Learning by Doing [ICON] Thinking Critically to Solve a Campus Problem

With classmates, identify a common problem for students at your college— juggling a busy schedule, parking on campus, making a class change, joining a social group, or some other issue. Working together, use critical thinking to explore the problem and identify possible solutions.

Getting Started

For more on critical reading, see Ch. 2.

Using critical thinking, you can explore many problems step by step and reach reasonable solutions. Critical thinking, like critical reading, draws on a cluster of intellectual strategies and skills.

These three activities — analysis, synthesis, and evaluation — are the core of critical thinking. They are not new to you, but applying them rigorously in college-level reading and writing may be. When you approach college reading and writing tasks, instructors will expect you (and you should expect yourself) to think, read, write, and think some more.

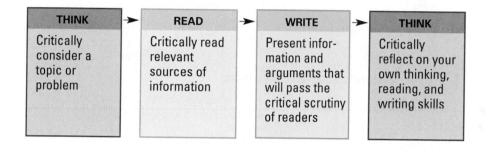

Critical Thinking Skill	Definition	Applications for Readers	Applications for Writers
Analysis	Breaking down information into its parts and elements	Analyzing the information in articles, reports, and books to grasp the facts and concepts they contain	Analyzing events, ideas, processes, and structures to understand them and explain them to readers
Synthesis	Putting together elements and parts to form new wholes	Synthesizing information from several sources, examining implications, and drawing conclusions supported by reliable evidence	Synthesizing source materials with your own thoughts in order to convey the unique combination to others
Evaluation	Judging according to standards or criteria	Evaluating a reading by determining standards for judging, applying them to the reading, and arriving at a conclusion about its significance, value, or credibility	Evaluating something in writing by convincing readers that your standards are reasonable and that the subject either does or does not meet those standards

> ## **?** *Problem*
> *You can't afford both your college tuition and the car you need.*

Solution

1 IDENTIFY CAUSES

Causes in your control:
Expensive vacation?
Credit-card debt?

Causes out of your control:
Medical emergency?
Job loss?
Tuition increase?
Financial aid policy change?

2 ANALYZE, SYNTHESIZE, AND EVALUATE OPTIONS

Do without a car	*(how?)*	• Get rides with family or friends? • Take public transportation?
Decrease your tuition	*(how?)*	• Take fewer courses?
Get more money	*(how?)*	• Get a loan from the bank? • Get a loan from the college? • Get a loan from a family member? • Get another job?

3 REACH A LOGICAL CONCLUSION

Apply for a short-term loan through the college for tuition.

Critical Thinking Processes in Action

Learning by Doing 🔖 Thinking Critically to Explore an Issue

You have worked hard on a group presentation that will be a major part of your grade—and each member of the group will get the same grade. Two days before the project is due, you discover that one group member has plagiarized heavily from sources well known to your instructor. Working together with classmates, use critical thinking to explore your problem and determine what you might do.

Applying Critical Thinking to Academic Problems

As you grapple with academic problems and papers, you'll be expected to use your critical thinking skills—analyzing, synthesizing, and evaluating—as you read and write. You may simply dive in, using each skill as needed.

However, the very wording of an assignment or examination question may alert you to a skill that your instructor expects you to use, as the first sample assignment in each set illustrates in the chart below.

Using Critical Thinking for College Assignments

Critical Thinking Skill	Sample College Writing Assignments
Analysis: breaking into parts and elements based on a principle	■ Describe the immediate causes of the 1929 stock market crash. (Analyze by using the principle of immediate causes to identify and explain the reasons for the 1929 crash.) ■ Trace the stages through which a bill becomes federal law. ■ Explain and illustrate the three dominant styles of parenting. ■ Define *romanticism,* identifying and illustrating its major characteristics.
Synthesis: combining parts and elements to form new wholes	■ Discuss the following statement: High-minded opposition to slavery was only one cause, and not a very important one, of the animosity between North and South that in 1861 escalated into civil war. (Synthesize by combining the causes or elements of the North-South animosity, going beyond the opposition to slavery, to form a new whole: your conclusion that accounts for the escalation into civil war.) ■ Imagine that you are a trial lawyer in 1921, charged with defending Nicola Sacco and Bartolomeo Vanzetti, two anarchists accused of murder. Argue for their acquittal on whatever grounds you can justify.
Evaluation: judging according to standards or criteria	■ Present and evaluate the most widely accepted theories that account for the disappearance of the dinosaurs. (Evaluate, based on standards such as scientific merit, the credibility of each theory.) ■ Defend or challenge the idea that houses and public buildings should be constructed to last no longer than twenty years. ■ Contrast the models of the solar system advanced by Copernicus and by Kepler, showing how the latter improved on the former.

Learning by Doing Thinking Critically to Respond to an Academic Problem

Working with a classmate or small group, select a sample assignment (not already explained) from the table above or from one of your classes. Explain how you would approach the assignment to demonstrate your critical thinking. Share your strategies for tackling college assignments.

Supporting Critical Thinking with Evidence

As you write a college paper, you try to figure out your purpose, position, and strategies for getting readers to follow your logic and accept your points. Your challenge, of course, is not just to think clearly but to demonstrate your thinking to others, to persuade them to pay attention to what you say. And sound evidence is what critical readers want to see.

For advice on using a few sources, see the Quick Research Guide, pp. A-18–A-35.

Sound evidence supports your main idea or thesis, convincing readers by substantiating your points. It also bolsters your credibility as a writer, demonstrating the merit of your position. When you write, you need to marshal enough appropriate evidence to clarify, explain, and support your ideas. Then you need to weave claims, evidence, and your own interpretations together into a clearly reasoned explanation or argument.

Types of Evidence

For more on using evidence in a paper that takes a stand, see pp. 168–72.

What is evidence? It is anything that demonstrates the soundness of a claim. Facts, statistics, firsthand observations, and expert testimony are four reliable forms of evidence. Other evidence might include examples, illustrations, details, and opinions. Depending on the purpose of your assignment, some kinds of evidence weigh more heavily than others. For example, readers might appreciate your memories of livestock care on the farm in an essay recalling your childhood summers. However, they would probably discount your memories in an argumentative paper about ethical agricultural methods unless you could show that your memories are representative or that you are an expert on the subject. Personal experience may strengthen an argument but generally is not sufficient as its sole support. If you are in doubt about the type of evidence an assignment requires, ask your instructor whether you should use sources or rely on personal experience and examples.

Facts. Facts are statements that can be verified objectively, by observation or by reading a reliable account. They are usually stated dispassionately: "If you pump the air out of a five-gallon varnish can, it will collapse." Of course, we accept many of our facts based on the testimony of others. For example, we believe that the Great Wall of China exists although we may never have seen it with our own eyes.

Sometimes people say facts are true statements, but truth and sound evidence may be confused. Consider the truth of these statements:

The tree in my yard is an oak.	*True* because it can be verified
A kilometer is 1,000 meters.	*True* using the metric system
The speed limit on the highway is 65 miles per hour.	*True* according to law

Fewer fatal highway accidents have occurred since the new exit ramp was built.	*True* according to research studies
My favorite food is pizza.	*True* as an opinion
More violent criminals should receive the death penalty.	*True* as a belief
Murder is wrong.	*True* as a value judgment

Some would claim that each statement is true, but when you think critically, you should avoid treating opinions, beliefs, judgments, or personal experience as true in the same sense that verifiable facts and events are true.

Statistics. Statistics are facts expressed in numbers. What portion of American children are poor? According to statistics from the U.S. Census Bureau, 13.2 million children (or 18.2 percent of all children) lived in poverty in 2008 compared with 11.7 million (or 16.3 percent) in 2001. Clear as such figures seem, they may raise complex questions. For example, how significant is the increase in the poverty rate over seven years? Has the percentage fluctuated or steadily increased? What percentage of children were poor over longer terms such as fifteen years or twenty?

Most writers, without trying to be dishonest, interpret statistics to help their causes. The statement "Fifty percent of the populace have incomes above the poverty level" might substantiate the fine job done by the government of a developing nation. Putting the statement another way—"Fifty percent of the populace have incomes below the poverty level"—might use the same statistic to show the inadequacy of the government's efforts.

Even though a writer is free to interpret a statistic, statistics should not be used to mislead. On the wrapper of a peanut candy bar, we read that a one-ounce serving contains only 150 calories. The claim is true, but the bar weighs 1.6 ounces. Gobble it all—more likely than eating 62 percent of it—and you'll ingest 240 calories, a heftier snack than the innocent statistic on the wrapper suggests. Because abuses make some readers automatically distrustful, use figures fairly when you write, and make sure they are accurate. If you doubt a statistic, compare it with figures reported by several other sources. Distrust a statistical report that differs from every other report unless it is backed by further evidence.

Few people save some of a candy bar to eat later.

Should you want to contact a campus expert, turn to Ch. 6 for advice about interviews.

Expert Testimony. By "experts," we mean people with knowledge gained from study and experience in a particular field. The test of an expert is whether his or her expertise stands up to the scrutiny of others who are knowledgeable in that field. The views of Michael Jordan on how to play offense in basketball carry authority. So do the views of economist and former Federal Reserve chairman Alan Greenspan on what causes inflation. However, Jordan's take on the economy or Greenspan's thoughts on basketball might not be authoritative. Also consider whether the expert has any bias or special interest that would affect reliability. Statistics on cases of lung cancer attributed to smoking might be better taken from government sources than from the tobacco industry.

Firsthand Observation. Firsthand observation is persuasive. It can add concrete reality to abstract or complex points. You might support the claim "The Meadowfield waste recycling plant fails to meet state guidelines" by recalling your own observations: "When I visited the plant last January, I was struck by the number of open waste canisters and by the lack of protective gear for the workers who handle these toxic materials daily."

For more on observation, see Ch. 5.

As readers, most of us tend to trust the writer who declares, "I was there. This is what I saw." Sometimes that trust is misplaced, however, so always be wary of a writer's claim to have seen something that no other evidence supports. Ask yourself, Is this writer biased? Might the writer have (intentionally or unintentionally) misinterpreted what he or she saw? Of course, your readers will scrutinize your firsthand observations, too; take care to reassure them that your observations are unbiased and accurate.

Learning by Doing 🔲 Looking for Evidence

For more on selecting evidence to persuade readers, see pp. 171–72.

Using the issue you explored for the activity on page 36, what would you need to support your identification, explanation, or solution of the problem? Working with classmates, identify the kinds of evidence that would be most useful. Where or how might you find such evidence?

Testing Evidence

For advice on evaluating sources of evidence, see C in the Quick Research Guide, pp. A-18–A-35.

As both a reader and a writer, always critically test and question evidence to see whether it is strong enough to carry the weight of the writer's claims.

EVIDENCE CHECKLIST

☐ Is it accurate?
- Do the facts and figures seem accurate based on what you have found in published sources, reports by others, or reference works?
- Are figures or quoted facts copied correctly?

☐ Is it reliable?
- Is the source trustworthy and well regarded?
- Does the source acknowledge any commercial, political, advocacy, or other bias that might affect the quality of its information?
- Does the writer supplying the evidence have appropriate credentials or experience? Is the writer respected as an expert in the field?
- Do other sources agree with the information?

☐ Is it up-to-date?
- Are facts and statistics—such as population figures—current?
- Is the information from the latest sources?

☐ Is it to the point?
- Does the evidence back the exact claim made?
- Is the evidence all pertinent? Does any of it drift from the point to interesting but irrelevant evidence?

☐ Is it representative?
- Are examples typical of all the things included in the writer's position?
- Are examples balanced? Do they present the topic or issue fairly?
- Are contrary examples acknowledged?

☐ Is it appropriately complex?
- Is the evidence sufficient to account for the claim made?
- Does it avoid treating complex things superficially?
- Does it avoid needlessly complicating simple things?

For information on mistakes in thinking, see pp. 50–51 and pp. 178–79.

☐ Is it sufficient and strong enough to back the claim and persuade readers?
- Are the amount and quality of the evidence appropriate for the claim and for the readers?
- Is the evidence aligned with the existing knowledge of readers?
- Does the evidence answer the questions readers are likely to ask?
- Is the evidence vivid and significant?

Using Evidence to Appeal to Your Audience

One way to select evidence and to judge whether it is appropriate and sufficient is to consider the types of appeals—logical, emotional, and ethical. Most effective arguments work on all three levels, using all three types of appeals with evidence that supports all three.

For more on appeals, see pp. 173–74.

Logical Appeal (Logos)

When writers use a logical appeal (*logos,* or "word" in Greek), they appeal to the reader's mind or intellect. This appeal relies on evidence that is factual, objective, clear, and relevant. Critical readers expect to find logical evidence that supports major claims and statements.

Example: If a writer were arguing for term limits for legislators, she wouldn't want to base her argument on the evidence that some long-term legislators were or weren't reelected (irrelevant) or that the current system is unfair to young people who want to get into politics (illogical). Instead, she might argue that the absence of term limits encourages corruption, using evidence of legislators who repaid lobbyists for campaign contributions with key votes.

Emotional Appeal (Pathos)

When writers use an emotional appeal (*pathos,* or "suffering" in Greek), they appeal to the reader's heart. They choose language, facts, quotations, examples, and images that evoke emotional responses. Of course, convincing writing does touch readers' hearts as well as their minds. Without this heartfelt tug, a strict logical appeal may seem cold and dehumanized.

> Example: If a writer opposed hunting seals for their fur, he might combine statistics about the number of seals killed each year and the overall population decrease with a vivid description of baby seals being slaughtered.

Some writers use emotional words and sentimental examples to manipulate readers—to arouse their sympathy, pity, or anger in order to convert them without much logical evidence—but dishonest emotional appeals may alienate readers.

> Example: Instead of basing an argument against a political candidate on pitiful images of scrawny children living in roach-infested squalor, a good writer would report the candidate's voting record on issues that affect children.

Ethical Appeal (Ethos)

When writers use an ethical appeal (*ethos,* or "character" in Greek), they call on the reader's sense of fairness and trust. They select and present evidence in a way that will make the audience trust them, respect their judgment, and believe what they have to say. The best logical argument in the world falls flat when readers don't take the writer seriously. How can you use an ethical appeal to establish your credibility as a writer? First you need to establish your credentials in the field through experience, reading, or interviews that helped you learn about the subject.

> Example: If you are writing about water quality, tell your readers about the odor, taste, and color of your local water. Identify medical or environmental experts you have contacted or whose publications you have read.

Demonstrate your knowledge through the information you present, the experts and sources you cite, and the depth of understanding you convey. Establish a rapport with readers by indicating values and attitudes that you share with them and by responding seriously to opposing arguments. Finally, use language that is precise, clear, and appropriate in tone.

Learning by Doing 🎬 Identifying Types of Appeals

Bring to class or post links for the editorial or opinion page from a newspaper, newsmagazine, or blog with a strong point of view. Read some of the pieces, and identify the types of appeals used by each author to support his or her point. With classmates, evaluate the effectiveness of these appeals.

Learning from Another Writer: Rhetorical Analysis

Richard Anson was asked to find an outside selection about a class reading topic, read the selection critically, and then write a brief rhetorical analysis. The purpose of the rhetorical analysis was to identify the reading's audience and the logical, emotional, and ethical appeals to that audience used by the writer. Anson's selection, an essay from 1998, provided a historical perspective on the power of popular culture to distract young adults from significant current events.

Richard Anson   **Student Rhetorical Analysis**

Young Americans and Media News

In a world where young adults have been more interested in *American Idol* than in who is running for president, it is critical to take a step back and look at the factors involved prior to the presidential election of 2008. Stephen Earl Bennett has done just that in "Young Americans' Indifference to Media Coverage of Public Affairs," an essay that appeared in *PS: Political Science & Politics*, a journal that focuses on contemporary politics and the teaching thereof. Being featured in this journal, as well as being a Fellow of the Center for the Study of Democratic Citizenship at the University of Cincinnati, easily establishes Bennett's trustworthy character or ethos.

Given where the article was published, it is safe to say that he is trying to reach an audience of professors in the field of political science and possibly policy makers as well. With this assumption, however, Bennett makes an error. His essay focuses solely on facts and numbers and not at all on the audience's emotions. A reader would be hard-pressed to find any appeals to emotion (pathos) in his essay at all and could liken it to an instruction manual on American youth's indifference to current events. Professors may be more likely to respond to the logical appeal (logos) of facts and numbers than some other readers, but they are still human, and very few humans enjoy reading instruction manuals for fun. For example, Bennett starts off with "Although young Americans are normally less engaged in politics than their elders (Converse with Niemi 1971), today's youth are more withdrawn from public affairs than earlier birth cohorts were when they were young (Bennett 1997)" (Bennett 1). In this first sentence alone, Bennett is citing from two other sources, one of which happens to be his own. There is nothing wrong with jumping right in, but this is a little over the top and very dry for an introduction.

The idea that more people vote for *American Idol* than their own president in the leading democratic nation in the world is just pathetic. There's no other way to describe it. On this point, Bennett agrees with other readings discussed in class. He also agrees that current affairs and news need to be more widely taught in schools across the nation and that something needs to be done to attract American youth to the news. The Bennett article was published in 1998, and maybe the interest of young voters in the 2008 presidential election shows that Americans have started listening.

3

Works Cited

Bennett, Stephen Earl. "Young Americans' Indifference to Media Coverage of Public Affairs." *PS: Political Science & Politics* 31.3 (1998): 535–41. *General OneFile.* Web. 15 Oct. 2009.

Questions to Start You Thinking

Meaning

1. According to Anson, what position about the political engagement of young people does Bennett take?

2. What is Anson's position about Bennett's article?

Writing Strategies

3. Why do you think that Anson begins his essay with information about the article and its author instead of a summary of Bennett's main points?

4. Why do you think that Anson decided to arrange his discussion of the three appeals — ethos, pathos, and logos — in that order?

Presenting Your Critical Thinking

For more on taking a stand, see Ch. 9; on proposals, see Ch. 10; on evaluation, see Ch. 11; and on supporting a position, see Ch. 12.

Why do you have to worry about critical thinking? Isn't it enough just to tell everybody else what you think? That tactic probably works fine when you casually debate with your friends. After all, they already know you, your opinions, and your typical ways of thinking. They may even find your occasional rant entertaining. Whether they agree or disagree, they probably tolerate your ideas because they are your friends.

When you write a paper in college, however, you face a different type of audience, one that expects you to explain what you assume, what you advocate, and why you hold that position. That audience wants to learn the specifics—reasons you find compelling, evidence that supports your view, and connections that relate each point to your position. Because approaches and answers to complex problems may differ, your college audience expects reasoning, not emotional pleading or bullying or preaching.

How you reason and how you present your reasoning are important parts of gaining the confidence of college readers. College papers typically develop their points based on logic, not personal opinions or beliefs. Most are organized logically, often as a series of reasons, each making a claim, a statement, or an assertion that is backed up with persuasive supporting evidence. Your assignment or your instructor may recommend ways such as the following for showing your critical thinking.

Reasoning Deductively or Inductively. When you state a *generalization,* you present your broad, general point, viewpoint, or conclusion.

For more about the statement-support pattern, see A3 in the Quick Research Guide, pp. A-18–A-35.

> The admissions requirements at Gerard College are unfair.

On the other hand, when you supply a *particular,* you present an instance, a detail, an example, an item, a case, or other specific evidence to demonstrate that a general statement is reasonable.

> A Gerard College application form shows the information collected by the admissions office. Under current policies, standardized test scores are weighted more heavily than better predictors of performance, such as high school grades. Qualified students who do not test well often face a frustrating admissions process, as Irma Lang's situation illustrates.

Your particulars consist of details that back up your broader point; your generalizations connect the particulars so that you can move beyond isolated, individual cases.

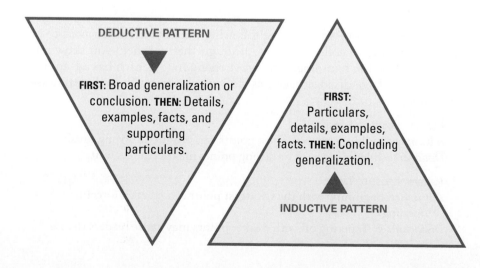

DEDUCTIVE PATTERN

FIRST: Broad generalization or conclusion. **THEN:** Details, examples, facts, and supporting particulars.

FIRST: Particulars, details, examples, facts. **THEN:** Concluding generalization.

INDUCTIVE PATTERN

For more about thesis statements, see Ch. 20.

Most college papers are organized *deductively*. They begin with a general statement (often a thesis) and then present particular cases to support or apply it. Readers like this pattern because it reduces mystery; they learn right away what the writer wants to show. Writers like this pattern because it helps them state up front what they want to accomplish (even if they have to figure some of that out as they write and state it more directly as they revise). Papers organized deductively sacrifice suspense but gain directness and clarity.

On the other hand, some papers are organized *inductively*. They begin with the particulars—a persuasive number of instances, examples, or details—and lead up to the larger generalization that they support. Because readers have to wait for the generalization, this pattern allows them time to adjust to an unexpected conclusion that they might initially reject. For this reason, writers favor this pattern when they anticipate resistance from their audience and want to move gradually toward the broader point.

For more on inductive and deductive reasoning, see pp. 445–47.

Building Sequences and Scaffolds. You may use several strategies for presenting your reasoning, depending on what you want to show and how you think you can show it most persuasively. You may develop a line of reasoning, a series of points and evidence, running one after another in a sequence or building on one another to support a persuasive scaffold (see p. 49).

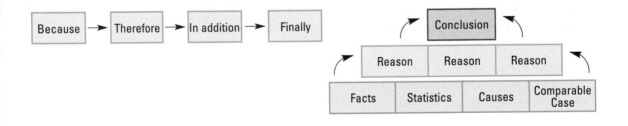

For more strategies for developing, see Ch. 22.

Developing Logical Patterns. The following patterns are often used to organize reasoning in college papers. Although they can help you show relationships, they don't automatically prove them. In fact, each has advantages but may also have disadvantages, as the sample strengths and weaknesses illustrate.

> *Pattern:* Least to Most
> *Advantage:* Building up to the best points can produce a strong finish.
> *Disadvantage:* Holding back on strong points makes readers wait.
>
> *Pattern:* Most to Least
> *Advantage:* Beginning with the strongest point can create a forceful opening.
> *Disadvantage:* Tapering off with weaker points may cause readers to lose interest.

LEAST TO MOST PATTERN

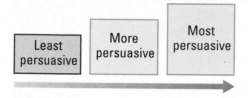

MOST TO LEAST PATTERN

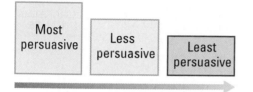

Pattern: Comparison and Contrast

Advantage: Readers can easily relate comparable points about things of like kind.

Disadvantage: Some similarities or differences don't guarantee or prove others.

For more on comparison and contrast, see Ch. 7.

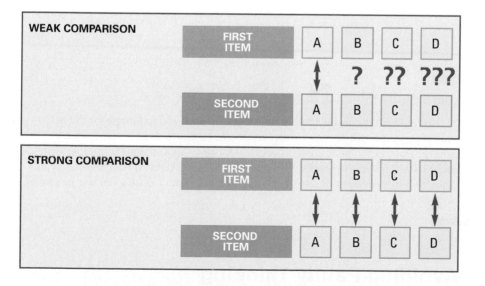

Pattern: Cause and Effect

Advantage: Tracing causes or effects can tightly relate and perhaps predict events.

Disadvantage: Weak links can call into question all relationships in a series of events.

For more on cause and effect, see Ch. 8.

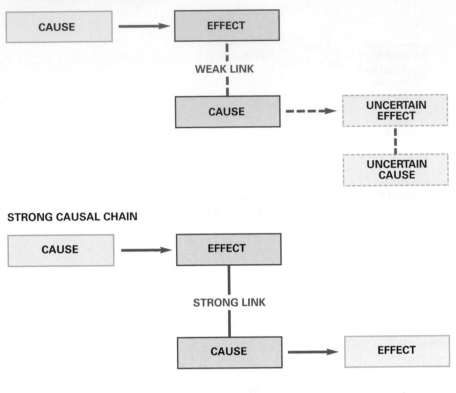

WEAK CAUSAL CONNECTIONS

STRONG CAUSAL CHAIN

Learning by Doing 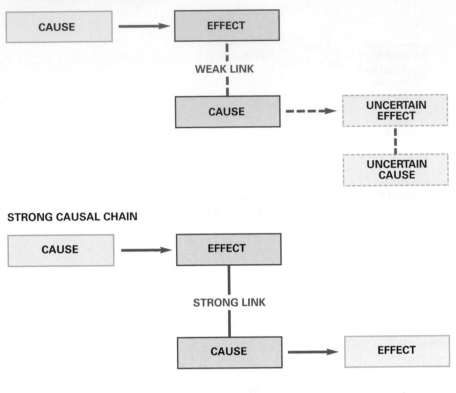 Testing Logical Patterns

Continuing with the issue and the possible evidence you explored for the activities on pages 36 and 42, work with classmates to figure out several different patterns you could use to present your evidence to an audience of people who could help to solve the problem or address the issue. What would be the advantages or disadvantages of each pattern, given your issue, audience, and possible evidence?

Avoiding Faulty Thinking

For specific logical fallacies, see pp. 178–79.

Common mistakes in thinking can distort evidence or lead to wrong conclusions. How can you avoid such mistakes as you write or spot them as you read? A good strategy is to look carefully at the ways in which you (or the author of a reading) describe events, relate ideas, identify reasons, supply evidence, and draw conclusions.

	Sound Reasoning	Weak Reasoning
Comparisons	Comparison that uses substantial likeness to project other similarities:	Inaccurate comparison that relies on slight or superficial likenesses to project other similarities:
	Like the third graders in the innovative reading programs just described, the children in this town also could become better readers.	Like kittens eagerly stalking mice in the fields, young readers should gobble up the tasty tales that were the favorites of their grandparents.
Causes and Effects	Causal analysis that relies on well-substantiated and specific connections relating events and outcomes:	Faulty reasoning that oversimplifies causes, confuses them with coincidences, or assumes a first event must cause a second:
	City water reserves have suffered from below-average rainfall, above-average heat, and steadily increasing consumer demand.	One cause—and one alone—accounts for the ten-year drought that has dried up local water supplies.
Reasons	Logical reasons that are supported by relevant evidence and presented with fair and thoughtful consideration:	Faulty reasons that rely on bias, emotion, or unrelated personal traits or that accuse, flatter, threaten, or inspire fear:
	As the recent audit indicates, all campus groups that spend student activity fees should prepare budgets, keep clear financial records, and substantiate expenses	All campus groups, especially the arrogant social groups, must stop ripping off the average student's fees and threatening to run college costs sky high.
Evidence	Evidence that is accurate, reliable, current, relevant, fair, and sufficient to persuade readers:	Weak evidence that is insufficient, dated, unreliable, slanted, or emotional:
	Both the statistics from international agencies and the accounts of Sudanese refugees summarized earlier suggest that, while a fair immigration policy needs to account for many complexities, it should not lose sight of compassion.	As five-year-old Lannie's frantic flight across the Canadian border in 1988 proves, refugees from all the war-torn regions around the world should be welcomed here because this is America, land of the free.
Conclusions	Solid conclusions that are based on factual evidence and recognize multiple options or complications:	Hasty conclusions that rely on insufficient evidence, assumptions, or simplistic two-option choices:
	As the recent campus wellness study has demonstrated, college students need education about healthy food and activity choices.	The campus health facility should refuse to treat students who don't eat healthy foods and exercise daily.

Use the following questions to help you refine your reasoning as you plan, draft, or revise a college paper:

LOGICAL REASONING CHECKLIST

☐ Have you reviewed your assignment or syllabus, looking for advice or requirements about the kind of reasoning or evidence expected?

☐ Have you developed your reasoning on a solid foundation? Are your initial assumptions sound? Do you need to identify, explain, or justify them?

☐ Is your thesis or position stated clearly? Are its terms explained or defined?

☐ Have you presented your reasons for thinking that your thesis is sound? Have you arranged them in a sequence that will make sense to your audience? Have you used transitions to introduce and connect them so that readers can't miss them?

☐ Have you used evidence that your audience will respect to support each reason you present? Have you favored objective, research-based evidence (facts, statistics, and expert testimony that others can substantiate) rather than personal experiences or beliefs that others cannot or may not share?

☐ Have you explained your evidence so that your audience can see how it supports your points and applies to your thesis? Have you used transitions to specify relationships for readers?

☐ Have you enhanced your own credibility by acknowledging, rather than ignoring, other points of view? Have you integrated or countered these views?

☐ Have you adjusted your tone and style so that you come across as reasonable and fair-minded? Have you avoided arrogant claims about proving (rather than showing) points?

☐ If you have used any sources, have you credited them as expected by academic readers?

Learning by Doing 📷 Analyzing Reasoning

Analyze the following newspaper column and letter, looking for clear reasoning as well as flaws in logic. For each, identify its position, its sequence of reasons or points, its supporting evidence, and its methods of appealing to readers. The column by Al Knight appeared in the *Denver Post* on November 22, 2006.

Al Knight

Perhaps We Should Move to Save Dogs from Their Owners

The election earlier this month settled a lot of the state's big issues, like who will sit in the governor's office, but there are plenty of little problems that were left for another day. One of them is whether Colorado should join a handful of other states and prohibit pickup owners from plying the state's major highways with one or several dogs loose in the truck bed.   1

Colorado is a big state with lots of open road. Anyone who has traveled 2
those roads will have seen a truck owner speeding down the highway with his
pet or pets running from side to side in the open bed, seemingly inches from
certain disaster. There is, alas, more than the prospect of disaster. According
to one estimate, 100,000 dogs are killed each year by either falling out of or
being intentionally tossed out of careening pickup trucks.

Some states—including Virginia, Florida, New Hampshire, California, 3
Rhode Island, Massachusetts, and Oregon—have passed legislation regulating the practice. Some localities and counties also have local ordinances on
the subject. In all of these locations, proponents advanced arguments dealing
with public as well as animal safety. A frolicking dog in the back of a pickup
is an obvious distraction and hazard, not only for the truck owner and the
dog but for anybody else on or near that road or highway.

As to animal safety, as far back as 1988, the Society for the Prevention of 4
Cruelty to Animals did a study in Massachusetts that was based on interviews with 141 veterinarians. The organization found that those vets had
treated 592 dogs that year for injuries received when tossed from the bed of a
pickup. The Humane Society, in an article titled "Why Dogs and Pickup
Trucks Don't Mix," stated the obvious quite nicely: "If your truck hits a
bump, or if you step on the brakes suddenly or swerve to avoid an obstacle,
your dog can easily be thrown from the truck bed and onto the road.
Chances are, this will injure or kill your dog. But even if it doesn't, being
struck by another vehicle probably will. Also, other drivers may cause an accident by swerving to avoid hitting your dog."

The question remains whether the plainly unwise practice of transporting 5
loose dogs in pickup beds should be regulated. Would such a law, for example, interfere with the rights of farmers, ranchers, hunters, and others who

might have a reason to transport dogs in this fashion? Well, the handful of states that have addressed that concern have carved out narrow exceptions to cover those situations. Oregon, for example, has an exception for ranching and farming which is limited to noninterstate highways and population centers with less than 5,000 people. In Tennessee, where a bill was considered and later defeated, the measure had a narrow exception for licensed hunters. In Texas, where there has been a petition drive urging the legislature to act, a proposed law has exceptions for hunters and ranchers. These exceptions haven't satisfied everyone. During the Tennessee debate, one lawmaker complained that the proposed statute would "absolutely destroy the way people live with these animals."

Hysteria aside, there are good arguments to be made in favor of a state   6
statute requiring the use of carriers or restraints:

- The current system doesn't work. While many dogs can survive a ride in the back of a pickup, many will not.
- Public education doesn't seem to be a good option. The typical pickup/ dog owner surely knows the risks but has chosen to ignore them. More education is unlikely to change that fact.
- Enforcement of a statute would be a breeze. The dog is typically in plain sight. A safety officer need not listen to the kind of stories offered when someone is stopped for speeding or a seat-belt violation. It would be hard for a driver to claim the officer was mistaken and that "the dog wasn't really in the bed of the pickup in the first place."

If one of the new legislators in Colorado wants to take on the task of   7
passing such a law, next year would be a good time to start.

Letter from an Irate Dog Owner

Dear Editor:

Even a city slicker should be able to see why dogs belong in pickup trucks. All dogs love riding out in the air. They need room to jump around. And you'd better just zip your lip if you see me driving down I-25 with my dog.

Who would want Colorado to turn into one of those wimpy states that amends its constitution whenever some bleeding heart starts feeling sorrowful about wolves or dolphins? Maybe we should bring fur coats back here instead of trying to force hard-working citizens to take their dogs out of their trucks. This whole issue stinks!

Dog owners have the right to do whatever they want with their animals. This is the kind of law that only busybodies would support. If you're thinking of supporting this issue, you'd better think again. Besides, if my dog had any complaints, he'd have to take them up with me!

An Irate Dog Owner

Additional Writing Activities

1. List your main reasons (and some supporting details) for and against doing something: going somewhere, joining something, buying something, or the like. Then outline one presentation directed to someone who would agree with you and another directed to someone who would disagree. Do your two plans differ? If so, how and why?

2. Working with a group, survey several opinion pieces. Refer to Presenting Your Critical Thinking (pp. 46–50) to help you identify the patterns the writers use to present their views. Then speculate about why they chose to organize as they did.

3. Select an editorial, opinion column, or brief blog entry that takes a clear stand on an issue. Analyze its stand, main points, evidence, and appeals to readers. Write a paragraph explaining how it makes its case. Then write a second paragraph stating and justifying your judgment about how well it succeeds.

4. If you disagree with the opinion piece that you analyzed in Activity 3, write a paragraph or two explaining and supporting your own point of view.

5. Divide a page into three columns, or create a table in a file. Label each column with a type of appeal: logical, emotional, ethical. Pick a limited, local issue about which you have a definite view, and identify a specific audience that you might be able to persuade to agree with or at least consider your position. Start filling in the columns with persuasive evidence that supports your view. Discuss your table with one or two classmates to decide what evidence would most effectively appeal to your specific audience.

6. **Visual Activity.** Select a Web page, a powerful photo, a cartoon, a graphical display of information, or another text that uses an image to help make its point about an issue. Adapt the critical thinking skills in this chapter to analyze this visual text, examining its evidence and its appeals to viewers. Write a paragraph or two explaining how it makes its case, including a link to the item or a printout.

PART TWO

A WRITER'S SITUATIONS

4 Recalling an Experience

Responding to an Image

Look carefully at one of the photographs in the grid. In your view, when was this photograph taken? Who might the person or people be? Where are they, and why are they there? What are they doing? What relationships and emotions does the picture suggest with its focal point and arrangement? Write about an experience the image helps you recall or about a possible explanation of events in this picture. Use vivid detail to convey what happened to you or what might have happened to the people in the picture.

Writing from recall is writing from memory, a writer's richest—and handiest—resource. Recall is clearly necessary when you write of a personal experience, a favorite place, a memorable person. Recall also helps you probe your memories of specific events. For example, in a literacy narrative you might examine the significance of your experiences learning to read or write. On the other hand, in a reflection you might begin with an incident that you recall and then explore the ideas that evolve from it.

Even when an instructor hands you a subject that seems to have nothing to do with you, your memory is the first place to look. Suppose you have to write a psychology paper about how advertisers prey on consumers' fears. Begin with what you remember. What ads have sent chills down your back? What ads have suggested that their products could save you from a painful social blunder, a lonely night, or a deadly accident? All by itself, memory may not give you enough to write about, but you will rarely go wrong if you start by jotting down something remembered.

For information and journal questions about the Part Two photograph, see p. A-72.

Why Recalling an Experience Matters

In a College Course

- You recall your experiences of visiting or living in another region or country to introduce and add authority to your sociology paper on cultural differences.
- You recall and record both routine and unusual events as the foundation for the reflective journal you keep during your internship or clinical experience.

In the Workplace

- You recall past successes, failures, or customer comments to provide compelling reasons for adopting your proposals for changing a product or service.

In Your Community

- You recall your own experiences taking standardized tests to add impact to your appeal to the local school board to change the testing program at your child's school.

When have you recalled experiences in your writing? What did these recollections add to your writing? In what situations might you rely on recollection again in future writing?

A Writer's Guide

Learning from Other Writers

Here are two samples of good writing from recall—one by a professional writer, one by a college student. To help you begin to analyze the first reading, look at the notes in the margin. They identify features such as the main idea, or thesis, and the first of the main events that support it in a paper written from recall.

As You Read These Recollections

For more examples of writing from recall, visit **<bedfordstmartins .com/bedguide>**.

As you read these essays, ask yourself the following questions:

1. Is the perspective of the essay primarily that of a child or an adult? Why do you think so?

2. What does the author realize after reflecting on the events recalled? Does the realization come soon after the experience or later, when the writer examines the events from a more mature perspective?

3. How does the realization change the individual?

Russell Baker

The Art of Eating Spaghetti

In this essay from his autobiography *Growing Up* (1982), columnist Russell Baker recalls being sixteen in urban Baltimore and wondering what to do with his life.

Introduction

The only thing that truly interested me was writing, and I knew that sixteen-year-olds did not come out of high school and become writers. I thought of writing as something to be done only by the rich. It was so obviously not real work, not a job at which you could earn a living. Still, I had begun to think of myself as a writer. It was the only thing for which I seemed to have the smallest talent, and, silly though it sounded when I told people I'd like to be a writer, it gave me a way of thinking about myself which satisfied my need to have an identity.   1

THESIS stating main idea

The notion of becoming a writer had flickered off and on in my head since the Belleville days, but it wasn't until my third year in high school that the possibility took hold. Until then I'd been bored by everything associated with English courses. I found English grammar dull and baffling. I hated the assignments to turn out "compositions," and went at them like heavy labor, turning out leaden, lackluster paragraphs that were agonies for teachers to read and for me to write. The classics thrust on me to read seemed as deadening as chloroform.   2

Major event 1

When our class was assigned to Mr. Fleagle for third-year English I anticipated another grim year in that dreariest of subjects. Mr. Fleagle was notorious among City students for dullness and inability to inspire. He was said to be stuffy, dull, and hopelessly out of date. To me he looked to be sixty or sev-   3

Lady Macbeth, played by Maria Guleghina, Royal Opera House, London.

enty and prim to a fault. He wore primly severe eyeglasses, his wavy hair was primly cut and primly combed. He wore prim vested suits with neckties blocked primly against the collar buttons of his primly starched white shirts. He had a primly pointed jaw, a primly straight nose, and a prim manner of speaking that was so correct, so gentlemanly, that he seemed a comic antique.

I anticipated a listless,° unfruitful year with Mr. Fleagle and for a long   4
time was not disappointed. We read *Macbeth*. Mr. Fleagle loved *Macbeth* and wanted us to love it too, but he lacked the gift of infecting others with his own passion. He tried to convey the murderous ferocity of Lady Macbeth one day by reading aloud the passage that concludes

> ... I have given suck, and know
> How tender 'tis to love the babe that milks me.
> I would, while it was smiling in my face,
> Have plucked my nipple from his boneless gums. ...

Support for major event 1

The idea of prim Mr. Fleagle plucking his nipple from boneless gums was too much for the class. We burst into gasps of irrepressible snickering. Mr. Fleagle stopped.

"There is nothing funny, boys, about giving suck to a babe. It is the—the   5
very essence of motherhood, don't you see."

He constantly sprinkled his sentences with "don't you see." It wasn't   6
a question but an exclamation of mild surprise at our ignorance. "Your

listless: Lacking energy or enthusiasm.

pronoun needs an antecedent, don't you see," he would say, very primly. "The purpose of the Porter's scene, boys, is to provide comic relief from the horror, don't you see."

Late in the year we tackled the informal essay. "The essay, don't you see, is the . . ." My mind went numb. Of all forms of writing, none seemed so boring as the essay. Naturally we would have to write informal essays. Mr. Fleagle distributed a homework sheet offering us a choice of topics. None was quite so simpleminded as "What I Did on My Summer Vacation," but most seemed to be almost as dull. I took the list home and dawdled until the night before the essay was due. Sprawled on the sofa, I finally faced up to the grim task, took the list out of my notebook, and scanned it. The topic on which my eye stopped was "The Art of Eating Spaghetti." 7

This title produced an extraordinary sequence of mental images. Surging up out of the depths of memory came a vivid recollection of a night in Belleville when all of us were seated around the supper table—Uncle Allen, my mother, Uncle Charlie, Doris, Uncle Hal—and Aunt Pat served spaghetti for supper. Spaghetti was an exotic treat in those days. Neither Doris nor I had ever eaten spaghetti, and none of the adults had enough experience to be good at it. All the good humor of Uncle Allen's house reawoke in my mind as I recalled the laughing arguments we had that night about the socially respectable method for moving spaghetti from plate to mouth. 8

Suddenly I wanted to write about that, about the warmth and good feeling of it, but I wanted to put it down simply for my own joy, not for Mr. Fleagle. It was a moment I wanted to recapture and hold for myself. I wanted to relive the pleasure of an evening at New Street. To write it as I wanted, however, would violate all the rules of formal composition I'd learned in school, and Mr. Fleagle would surely give it a failing grade. Never mind. I would write something else for Mr. Fleagle after I had written this thing for myself. 9

When I finished it the night was half gone and there was no time left to compose a proper, respectable essay for Mr. Fleagle. There was no choice next morning but to turn in my private reminiscence° of Belleville. Two days passed before Mr. Fleagle returned the graded papers, and he returned everyone's but mine. I was bracing myself for a command to report to Mr. Fleagle immediately after school for discipline when I saw him lift my paper from his desk and rap for the class's attention. 10

"Now, boys," he said, "I want to read you an essay. This is titled 'The Art of Eating Spaghetti.'" 11

And he started to read. My words! He was reading *my words* out loud to the entire class. What's more, the entire class was listening. Listening attentively. Then somebody laughed, then the entire class was laughing, and not in contempt and ridicule, but with openhearted enjoyment. Even Mr. Fleagle stopped two or three times to repress a small prim smile. 12

I did my best to avoid showing pleasure, but what I was feeling was pure ecstasy at this startling demonstration that my words had the power to make 13

reminiscence: Memory.

people laugh. In the eleventh grade, at the eleventh hour as it were, I had discovered a calling. It was the happiest moment of my entire school career. When Mr. Fleagle finished he put the final seal on my happiness by saying, "Now that, boys, is an essay, don't you see. It's—don't you see—it's of the very essence of the essay, don't you see. Congratulations, Mr. Baker."

For the first time, light shone on a possibility. It wasn't a very heartening possibility, to be sure. Writing couldn't lead to a job after high school, and it was hardly honest work, but Mr. Fleagle had opened a door for me. After that I ranked Mr. Fleagle among the finest teachers in the school.

14

Conclusion restating thesis

Questions to Start You Thinking

Meaning

1. In your own words, state what Baker believes he learned in the eleventh grade about the art of writing. What incidents or statements help identify this lesson for readers? What lesson, if any, did you learn from the essay?

2. Why do you think Baker included this event in his autobiography?

3. Have you ever changed your mind about something you had to do, as Baker did about writing? Or about a person, as he did about Mr. Fleagle?

Writing Strategies

4. What is the effect, in paragraph 3, of Baker's repetitions of the words *prim* and *primly*? What other devices does he use to characterize Mr. Fleagle vividly? Why do you think Baker uses so much space to portray his teacher?

5. What does the quotation from *Macbeth* add to Baker's account? Had the quotation been omitted, what would have been lost?

6. How does Baker organize the essay? Why does he use this order?

Robert G. Schreiner   Student Essay

What Is a Hunter?

In this college essay, Robert G. Schreiner uses vivid details to bring to life a significant childhood event.

What is a hunter? This is a simple question with a relatively straightforward answer. A hunter is, according to *Webster's New Collegiate Dictionary*, a person who hunts game (game being various types of animals hunted or pursued for various reasons). However, a second question is just as simple but without such a straightforward answer: What characteristics make up a hunter? As a child, I had always considered the most important aspect of the hunter's person to be his ability to use

1

a rifle, bow, or whatever weapon was appropriate to the type of hunting being done. Having many relatives in rural areas of Virginia and Kansas, I had been exposed to rifles a great deal. I had done extensive target shooting and considered myself to be quite proficient in the use of firearms. I had never been hunting, but I had always thought that since I could fire a rifle accurately I would make a good hunter.

One Christmas holiday, while we were visiting our grandparents in Kansas, my grandfather asked me if I wanted to go jackrabbit hunting with him. I eagerly accepted, anxious to show off my prowess° with a rifle. A younger cousin of mine also wanted to come, so we all went out into the garage, loaded two .22 caliber rifles and a 20-gauge shotgun, hopped into the pickup truck, and drove out of town. It had snowed the night before, and to either side of the narrow road swept six-foot-deep powdery drifts. The wind twirled the fine crystalline snow into whirling vortexes° that bounced along the icy road and sprayed snow into the open windows of the pickup. As we drove, my grandfather gave us some pointers about both spotting and shooting jackrabbits. He told us that when it snows, jackrabbits like to dig out a hollow in the top of a snowdrift, usually near a fencepost, and lie there soaking up the sunshine. He told us that even though jackrabbits are a grayish brown, this coloration is excellent camouflage in the snow, for the curled-up rabbits resemble rocks. He then pointed out a few rabbits in such positions as we drove along, showing us how to distinguish them from exposed rocks and dirt. He then explained that the only way to be sure that we killed the rabbit was to shoot for the head and, in particular, the eye, for this was on a direct line with the rabbit's brain. Since we were using solid point bullets, which deform into a ball upon impact, a hit anywhere but the head would most likely only wound the rabbit.

My grandfather then slowed down the pickup and told us to look out for the rabbits hidden in the snowdrifts. We eventually spotted one about thirty feet from the road in a snow-filled gully. My cousin wished to shoot the first one, so he hopped out of the truck, balanced the .22 on the hood, and fired. A spray of snow erupted about a foot to the left of the rabbit's hollow. My cousin fired again, and again, and again, the shots pockmarking the slope of the drift. He fired once more and the rabbit bounced out of its hollow, its head rocking from side to side. He was hit. My cousin eagerly gamboled into the snow to claim his quarry.° He brought it back holding it by the hind legs, proudly displaying it as would a warrior the severed head of his enemy. The bullet had entered the rabbit's right shoulder and exited through the neck. In both places a thin trickle of crimson marred the gray sheen of the rabbit's pelt. It quivered slightly and its rib cage pulsed with its labored breathing. My cousin was about to toss it into the back of the pickup when my grandfather pointed out that it would be cruel to allow the rabbit to bleed slowly to death and instructed my cousin to bang its head against the side of the pickup to kill it. My cousin then proceeded to bang the rabbit's head against the

2

3

How does the writer convey his grandfather's definition of hunting?

prowess: Superior skill.   **vortex:** Rotation around an axis, as in a whirlwind.
quarry: Prey.

yellow metal. Thump, thump, thump, thump; after a minute or so my cousin loudly proclaimed that it was dead and hopped back into the truck.

The whole episode sickened me to some degree, and at the time I did not know why. We continued to hunt throughout the afternoon, and feigning boredom, I allowed my cousin and grandfather to shoot all of the rabbits. Often, the shots didn't kill the rabbits outright so they had to be killed against the pickup. The thump, thump, thump of the rabbits' skulls against the metal began to irritate me, and I was strangely glad when we turned around and headed back toward home. We were a few miles from the city limits when my grandfather slowed the truck to a stop, then backed up a few yards. My grandfather said he spotted two huge "jacks" sitting in the sun in a field just off the road. He pointed them out and handed me the .22, saying that if I didn't shoot something the whole afternoon would have been a wasted trip for me. I hesitated and then reluctantly accepted the rifle. I stepped out onto the road, my feet crunching on the ice. The two rabbits were about seventy feet away, both sitting upright in the sun. I cocked and leveled the rifle, my elbow held almost horizontal in the military fashion I had learned to employ. I brought the sights to bear on the right eye of the first rabbit, compensated° for distance, and fired. There was a harsh snap like the crack of a whip and a small jolt to my shoulder. The first rabbit was gone, presumably knocked over the side of the snowdrift. The second rabbit hadn't moved a muscle; it just sat there staring with that black eye. I cocked the rifle once more and sighted a second time, the bead of the rifle just barely above the glassy black orb that regarded me so passively. I squeezed the trigger. Again the crack, again the jolt, and again the rabbit disappeared over the top of the drift. I handed the rifle to my cousin and began making my way toward the rabbits. I sank into powdery snow up to my waist as I clambered to the top of the drift and looked over.

4 ❓ Why do you think that the writer reacts as he does?

On the other side of the drift was a sight that I doubt I will ever forget. There was a shallow, snow-covered ditch on the leeward side of the drift and it was into this ditch that the rabbits had fallen, at least what was left of the rabbits. The entire ditch, in an area about ten feet wide, was spattered with splashes of crimson blood, pink gobbets of brain, and splintered fragments of bone. The twisted corpses of the rabbits lay in the bottom of the ditch in small pools of streaming blood. Of both the rabbits, only the bodies remained, the heads being completely gone. Stumps of vertebrae protruded obscenely from the mangled bodies, and one rabbit's hind legs twitched spasmodically. I realized that my cousin must have made a mistake and loaded the rifle with hollowpoint explosive bullets instead of solid ones.

5

I shouted back to the pickup, explaining the situation, and asked if I should bring them back anyway. My grandfather shouted back, "No, don't worry about it, just leave them there. I'm gonna toss these jacks by the side of the road anyway; jackrabbits aren't any good for eatin'."

6

compensate: Counterbalance.

❓ Why do you think the writer returns in silence?

Looking at the dead, twitching bodies I thought only of the incredible waste of   7
life that the afternoon had been, and I realized that there was much more to being
a hunter than knowing how to use a rifle. I turned and walked back to the pickup,
riding the rest of the way home in silence.

Questions to Start You Thinking

Meaning

1. Where in the essay do you first begin to suspect the writer's feelings about hunting? What in the essay or in your experience led you to this perception?

2. How would you characterize the writer's grandfather? How would you characterize his cousin?

3. How did the writer's understanding of himself change as a result of this hunting experience?

Writing Strategies

4. How might the essay be strengthened or weakened if the opening paragraph were cut out? Without this paragraph, how would your understanding of the author and his change be different?

5. Would Schreiner's essay be more or less effective if he explained in the last paragraph what he means by "much more to being a hunter"?

6. What are some of Schreiner's memorable images?

7. Using highlighters or marginal notes, identify the essay's introduction, thesis, major events, support for each event, and conclusion. How effective is the organization of this essay?

Learning by Writing

The Assignment: Recalling a Personal Experience

For writing activities for recalling an experience, visit
<bedfordstmartins .com/bedguide>.

Write about one specific experience that changed how you acted, thought, or felt. Use your experience as a springboard for reflection. Your purpose is not merely to tell an interesting story but to show your readers — your instructor and your classmates — the importance of that experience for you.

We suggest you pick an event that is not too personal, too subjective, or too big to convey effectively to others. Something that happened to you or that you observed, an encounter with a person who greatly influenced you, a decision that you made, or a challenge or an obstacle that you faced will be easier to recall (and to make vivid for your readers) than an interior experience like a religious conversion or falling in love.

These students recalled experiences heavy and light:

One writer recalled guitar lessons with a teacher who at first seemed harsh but who turned out to be a true friend.

Another student recalled a childhood trip when everything went wrong and she discovered the complexities of change.

Another recalled competing with a classmate who taught him a deeper understanding of success.

Facing the Challenge   Writing from Recall

The major challenge writers confront when writing from recall is to focus their essays on a main idea. When writing about a familiar—and often powerful—experience, it is tempting to include every detail that comes to mind and equally easy to overlook familiar details that would make the story's relevance clearer to the reader.

When you are certain of your purpose in writing about a particular event—what you want to show readers about your experience—you can transform a laundry list of details into a narrative that connects events clearly around a main idea. You can select details that work together to convey the significance of your experience. To help you decide what to show your readers, respond to each of the following questions in a few sentences:

- What was important to you about the experience?
- What did you learn from it?
- How did it change you?
- How would you reply to a reader who asked "So what?"

Once you have decided on your main point about the experience, you should select the details that best illustrate that point and show readers why the experience was important to you.

Generating Ideas

You may find that the minute you are asked to write about a significant experience, the very incident will flash to mind. Most writers, though, will need a little time for their memories to surface. Often, when you are busy doing something else—observing the scene around you, talking with someone, reading about someone else's experience—the activity can trigger a recollection. When a promising one emerges, write it down. Perhaps, like Russell Baker, you found success when you ignored what you thought you were supposed to do in favor of what you really wanted to do. Perhaps, like Robert Schreiner, you learned from a painful experience.

For more on each strategy for generating ideas in this section or for additional strategies, see Ch. 19.

Try Brainstorming. When you brainstorm, you just jot down as many ideas as you can. You can start with a suggestive idea — *disobedience, painful lesson, childhood, peer pressure* — and list whatever occurs through free association. You can also use the questions in the following checklist:

DISCOVERY CHECKLIST

☐ Did you ever break an important rule or rebel against authority? What did you learn from your actions?

☐ Did you ever succumb to peer pressure? What were the results of going along with the crowd? What did you learn?

☐ Did you ever regard a person in a certain way and then have to change your opinion of him or her? What produced this change?

☐ Did you ever have to choose between two equally attractive alternatives? How might your life have been different if you had chosen differently?

☐ Have you ever been appalled by witnessing an act of prejudice or insensitivity? What did you do? Do you wish you had done something different?

Try Freewriting. Devote ten minutes to freewriting — simply writing without stopping. If you get stuck, write "I have nothing to say" over and over, until ideas come. They will come. After you finish, you can circle or draw lines between related items, considering what main idea connects events.

Try Doodling or Sketching. As you recall an experience such as breaking your arm during a soccer tournament, try sketching whatever helps you

recollect the event and its significance. Turn doodles into words by adding comments on main events, notable details, and their impact on you.

Try Mapping Your Recollections. Identify a specific time period such as your birthday last year, the week when you decided to enroll in college, or a time when you changed in some way. On a blank page, on movable sticky notes, or in a computer file, record all the details you can recall about that time — people, statements, events, locations, and related physical descriptions.

Try a Reporter's Questions. Once you recall an experience you want to write about, ask "the five **W**'s and an **H**" that journalists find useful.

- **W**ho was involved?
- **W**hat happened?
- **W**here did it take place?
- **W**hen did it happen?
- **W**hy did it happen?
- **H**ow did the events unfold?

    Any question might lead to further questions — and to further discovery.

- **Who** was involved? ⟶ What did the others look like?
    - What did they say or do?
    - Would their words supply any lively quotations?
- **What** happened? ⟶ What did you think as the event unfolded?
    - When did you see the importance of the experience?

Consider Sources of Support. Because your memory drops details as well as retains them, you may want to check your recollections of an experience. Did you keep a journal at the time? Do your memories match those of a friend or family member who was there? Was the experience a turning point (big game, graduation, new home, birth of a child) that you or your family would have documented with photos? Was it sufficiently public (such as a demonstration or community catastrophe) or universal (such as a campus event) to have been recorded in a newspaper? If so, these resources can refresh your memory so that you rediscover forgotten details or angles.

Learning by Doing 🎨 Creating Your Writing Space

If you are online, in a computer lab, or on your laptop, begin your first writing assignment right now by creating your electronic writing space. Open, label, and save a file for generating ideas. (Systematically label your writing files for submission as directed or with your name, course, assignment, and writing stage, draft number, or date so that their sequence is clear: Marcus Recall Ideas 9-14-10 or Chung W110 Recall 1. Store the first file to a course folder or a subfolder for each assignment.) If you are in a face-to-face class, label a new page in your notebook so that your ideas are easy to find. Now use your new file or your notebook to brainstorm, freewrite, or try another strategy for generating ideas.

Planning, Drafting, and Developing

For more strategies for planning, drafting, and developing papers, see Chs. 20, 21, and 22.

Now, how will you tell your story? If the experience is still fresh in your mind, you may be able simply to write a draft, following the order of events and shaping your story as you go along. If you want to plan before you write, here are some suggestions.

For more on stating a thesis, see pp. 401–10.

For exercises on choosing effective thesis statements, visit **<bedfordstmartins .com/bedguide>**.

Start with a Main Idea, or Thesis. As you think about the experience, jot down a few words that identify it and express its importance to you. Next, begin to shape these words into a sentence that states the significance of the experience — the main idea that you want to convey to a reader. If you aren't certain yet about what that idea is or how to put it into words, just begin writing. You can work again on your thesis as you revise.

TOPIC IDEA + SLANT	reunion in Georgia + really liked meeting family
WORKING THESIS	When I went to Georgia for a family reunion, I enjoyed meeting many relatives.

Learning by Doing Stating the Importance of Your Experience

Work up to stating your thesis by completing these two sentences: The most important thing about my experience is _____. I want to share this so that my readers _____. Exchange your sentences with a classmate or a small group, either in person or online. Ask each other questions about what you want to convey to help each writer sharpen ideas about the experience and express them in a working thesis.

For examples of time markers and other transitions, see pp. 433–37.

Establish a Chronology. Retelling an experience is called *narration*, and the simplest way to organize is chronologically — relating the essential events in the order in which they occurred. On the other hand, sometimes you can start an account of an experience in the middle and then, through *flashback*, fill in whatever background a reader needs to know.

Richard Rodriguez, for instance, begins *Hunger of Memory* (Boston: David R. Godine, 1982), a memoir of his bilingual childhood, with an arresting sentence:

> I remember, to start with, that day in Sacramento, in a California now nearly thirty years past — when I first entered a classroom, able to understand about fifty stray English words.

The opening hooks our attention. In the rest of his essay, Rodriguez fills us in on his family history, on the gulf he came to perceive between the public language (English) and the language of his home (Spanish).

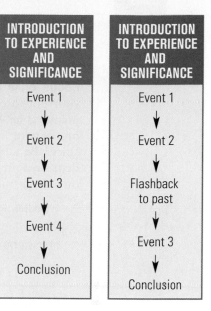

Learning by Doing 🖉 Selecting and Arranging Events

Open a new file, or start a new page in your notebook or outline organizer. List the main events in the order in which they occurred during the experience you plan to write about. Next, sum up the main idea you want to convey to readers. Then decide whether each event in your list supports that main idea. Drop unrelated events, or refine your main idea to reflect the importance of the events more accurately. Exchange files or pages with a classmate, and test each other's sequence of events against the main idea. Note clear connections and engaging events. Add question marks and comments if you notice shifts, gaps, irrelevant events, or missing connections. Use these comments to improve your selection of events and the clarity of your main idea.

Show Your Audience What Happened. How can you make your recollections come alive for your readers? Look again at Russell Baker's account of Mr. Fleagle teaching *Macbeth* and at the way Robert G. Schreiner depicts his cousin putting the wounded rabbits out of their misery. These two writers have not merely told us what happened; they have *shown* us, by creating scenes that we can see in our mind's eye.

As you tell your story, zoom in on at least two or three specific scenes. Show your readers exactly what happened, where it occurred, what was said, who said it. Use details and words that appeal to all five senses — sight, sound, touch, taste, smell. Carefully position any images you include to clarify visual details for readers. (Be sure that your instructor approves such additions.)

Revising and Editing

After you have written an early draft, put it aside for a day or two — or a few hours if your deadline is looming. Then read it over carefully. Try to see it through the eyes of one of your readers, noting both the pleasing parts and

For more on providing details, see pp. 441–43.

For exercises on supporting a thesis, visit **<bedfordstmartins .com/bedguide>**.

For more on adding visuals, see the Quick Format Guide, pp. A-1–A-17.

For more revising and editing strategies, see Ch. 23.

the confusing spots. Revise to ensure that you've expressed your thoughts and feelings clearly and strongly in a way that will reach your readers.

Focus on a Main Idea, or Thesis. As you read over the essay, return to your purpose: What was so important about this experience? Why is it so memorable? Will readers be able to see why this experience was a crucial one in your life? Will they understand how your life has been different ever since? Be sure that you specify a genuine difference, reflecting the incident's real impact on you. In other words, revise to keep your essay focused on a single main idea or thesis.

WORKING THESIS	When I went to Georgia for a family reunion, I enjoyed meeting many relatives.
REVISED THESIS	Meeting my Georgia relatives showed me how powerfully two values — generosity and resilience — unite my family.

Peer Response   Recalling an Experience

For general questions for a peer editor, see p. 465.

Have a classmate or friend read your draft and suggest how you might present the main idea about your experience more clearly and vividly. Ask your peer editor questions such as these about writing from recall:

- What do you think the writer's main idea or thesis is? Where is it stated or clearly implied? Why was this experience significant?

- What emotions do the people in the essay feel? How did *you* feel while reading the essay?

- Where does the essay come alive? Underline images, descriptions, and dialogue that seem especially vivid.

- If this paper were yours, what is the one thing you would be sure to work on before handing it in?

Add Concrete Detail. Ask whether you have made events come alive for your audience by recalling them in sufficient concrete detail. Be specific enough that your readers can see, smell, taste, hear, and feel what you experienced. Make sure that all your details support your main idea or thesis. Notice again Robert Schreiner's focus in his second paragraph on the world outside his own skin: his close recall of the snow, of his grandfather's pointers about the habits of jackrabbits and the way to shoot them.

Learning by Doing 🎤 Appealing to the Senses

Working online or in person with a classmate, exchange short passages from your drafts. As you read each other's paragraphs, highlight the sensory details—the sights, sounds, tastes, touches, and smells that bring a description to life. As you notice each detail, jot down the sense to which it appeals in the margin, or add a comment to the file. Return each passage to the writer, review the notes about yours, and decide whether you need to strengthen your description with more— or more varied—details.

Follow a Clear Sequence. Reconsider the order of events in terms of your audience, looking for changes that might make your essay easier to follow. For example, if a classmate seems puzzled about the sequence of your draft, you might make a rough outline or list of the main events to check the clarity of your arrangement. Or you might add more transitions to connect events and clarify where your account is going.

For more on outlining, see pp. 413–21.

For more on transitions, see pp. 433–37.

Revise and rewrite until you've related your experience and its impact as well as you can. Here are some useful questions about revising your paper:

REVISION CHECKLIST

☐ Where have you shown why this experience was important and how it changed your life?

☐ How have you engaged readers so that they will want to keep reading? Will they find your paper dramatic, instructive, or revealing? Will they see and feel what you experienced?

☐ Why do you begin your narration as you do? Is there another place in the draft that would make a better beginning?

☐ If the events are not in chronological order, how have you made the organization easy for readers to follow?

☐ In what ways does the ending provide a sense of finality?

☐ Do you stick to a point? Is everything relevant to your main idea or thesis?

☐ If you portray any people, how have you made their importance clear? Which details make them seem real, not just shadowy figures?

☐ Does any dialogue sound like real speech? Read it aloud. Try it on a friend.

After you have revised your recall essay, edit and proofread it. Carefully check the grammar, word choice, punctuation, and mechanics—and then correct any problems you find. On page 74 are some questions to get you started.

For more editing and proofreading strategies, see pp. 473–76.

EDITING CHECKLIST

For more help, find the relevant checklist sections in the Quick Editing Guide on p. A-36. Turn also to the Quick Format Guide beginning on p. A-1.

☐ Is your sentence structure correct? Have you avoided writing fragments, comma splices, or fused sentences?   A1, A2

☐ Have you used correct verb tenses and forms throughout? When you present a sequence of past events, is it clear what happened first and what happened next?   A3

☐ When you use transitions and other introductory elements to connect events, have you placed any needed commas after them?   C1

☐ In your dialogue, have you placed commas and periods before (inside) the closing quotation mark?   C3

☐ Have you spelled everything correctly, especially the names of people and places? Have you capitalized names correctly?   D1, D2

Also check the format of your paper, using the Quick Format Guide. Be sure that you follow the style expected by your instructor for features such as the heading, title, running head with page numbers, margins, and paragraph indentation.

When you have made all the changes you need to make, save your file, print out a clean copy of your paper or attach the file — and submit it.

Additional Writing Assignments

1. Choose a person outside your immediate family who had a marked effect on your life, either good or bad. Jot down ten details that might help a reader understand what that person was like. Consider the person's physical appearance, way of talking, and habits as well as any memorable incidents. When your list is finished, look back at "The Art of Eating Spaghetti" to identify the kinds of detail Baker uses in his portrait of Mr. Fleagle, noting any you might add to your list. Then write a paper in which you portray that person, including details to help your audience experience his or her impact on you.

2. Recall a place you were once fond of — your grandmother's kitchen, a tree house, a library, a locker room, a vacation retreat. What made it different from other places? Why was it important to you? What do you feel when you remember it? Write a paper that uses specific, concrete details to explain to your audience why this place was memorable. If you have a photograph of the place, look at it to jog your memory, and consider including it in your paper.

3. Write a paper or the text for a podcast in which you recall some familiar ceremony, ritual, or observation. Such a tradition can pertain to a holiday, a rite of passage (confirmation, bar or bat mitzvah, college orientation, graduation), a sporting event, a family custom. How did the tradition originate? Who takes part? How has it changed through the years? What does it add to the lives of those who observe it? Share with your audience the importance of the tradition to you, using whatever information you recall.

4. Recall how you learned to read, write, or see how literacy could shape or change your life. What early experiences with reading or writing do you recall? How did these experiences affect you? Which were positive or negative? Were they turning points for you? Write an essay about the major events in your literacy story—your personal account of your experiences learning to read or write—so that your audience understands the impact of those events on you.

5. Respond to one of the four preceding assignments by writing a reflective journal entry, a letter, or an entry for a personal blog to share your recollections with a specific audience—such as yourself, students or a teacher at your old school, a younger relative, your own children (real or future), or a person involved in your experience.

6. **Visual Assignment.** Examine the images of different environments on this page and the next page. What do you recall about an experience in a similar urban, natural, or social environment? What events took place there? What role, if any, did the environment play in shaping the experience? How did you react to those events? What was their importance to you? How did the experience change you, your ideas, or your decisions? Write a reflective essay that briefly recalls your experience and then reflects on its importance or consequences for you. Add your own photo to your text, if you wish.

This image shows German artist Johan Lorbeer during one of his "still-life performances" outside of the Chemnitz city hall.

Responding to an Image

A scene like this one might look and feel quite different to different observers, depending on their vantage points, emotions, backgrounds, and experiences. In this image, what prominent element attracts your attention? Who are the various observers? Which details might be important for them? Which details might matter more to one observer than another? Although visual details are obviously central, feel free to describe sound, smell, and touch, as well as any emotions that might come into play.

Most writers begin to write by recalling what they know. Then they look around and add what they observe. Some writing consists almost entirely of observation—a reporter's eyewitness account of a fire, an anthropologist's field notes, a clinical report by a nurse detailing a patient's condition, a scientist's account of a laboratory experiment, a traveler's blog or photo essay. In fact, observation plays a large role in any writing that describes a person, place, or thing. In other instances, observation provides support, details to make a point clear or convincing. For example, a case study might report information from interviews and analyze artifacts— whether ancient bowls, new playgound equipment, or decades of airport records. However, to make its abstractions and statistics more vivid, it also might integrate compelling observation.

If you need more to write about, open your eyes—and your other senses. Take in not only what you can see but also what you can hear, smell, touch, and taste. Then when you write, report your observations in concrete detail. Of course, you can't record everything your senses bring you. You must be selective based on what's important and relevant for your purpose and your audience. To make a football game come alive for readers of your college newspaper, you might mention the overcast cold weather and the spicy smell of bratwurst. But if your purpose is primarily to explain which team won and why, you might stress the muddy playing field, the most spectacular plays, and the players who scored.

Why Observing a Scene Matters

In a College Course

- You observe and report compelling information from field trips in sociology, criminal justice, or anthropology as well as impressions of a play, a concert, an exhibit, or a historical site for a humanities or fine arts class.
- You observe clinical practices in health or education, habitats for plants and animals, the changing night sky, or lab experiments to report accurate information and to improve your own future practice.

In the Workplace

- You observe and analyze to lend credibility to your case study as a nurse, teacher, or social worker or to your site report as an engineer or architect.

In Your Community

- You observe, photograph, and report on hazards (a dangerous intersection, a poorly lighted park, a run-down building), needs (a soccer arena, a performing arts center), or disasters (an accident, a crime scene, a flood) to motivate action by authorities or fellow citizens.

🄠 When have you reported or included observations in your writing? How did these observations contribute to your writing? In what situations might you use observation again in future writing?

Learning from Other Writers

Here are two essays by writers who observe their surroundings and reflect on their observations. As you begin to analyze the first reading, look at the notes in the margin. They identify features such as the main impression created in the observation and stated in the thesis, the first of the locations observed, and the supporting details that describe the location.

As You Read These Observations

As you read these essays, ask yourself the following questions:

For more examples of writing from observation, visit <bedfordstmartins.com/bedguide>.

1. Specifically, what does the writer observe? Places? People? Behavior? Nature? Things?

2. What senses does the writer rely on? What sensory images does each writer develop? Find some striking passages in which the writer reports his or her observations. What makes these passages memorable to you?

3. Why does the writer use observation? What conclusion does the writer draw from reflecting on the observations?

Eric Liu

The Chinatown Idea

Eric Liu is an educator, lecturer, and author of *Guiding Lights* (2005) about mentorship. In this selection from *The Accidental Asian* (1998), he describes a childhood visit to Chinatown in New York City.

Another family outing, one of our occasional excursions to the city. It was a Saturday. I was twelve. I remember only vaguely what we did during the day—Fifth Avenue, perhaps, the museums, Central Park, Carnegie Hall. But I recall with precision going to Chinatown as night fell.   1   Introduction

We parked on a side street, a dim, winding way cluttered with Chinese placards° and congested with slumbering Buicks and Chevys. The license   2   Vantage point 1

placards: Posters, signs.

plates — NEW YORK, EMPIRE STATE — seemed incongruous here, foreign. We walked a few blocks to East Broadway. Soon we were wading through thick crowds on the sidewalk, passing through belts of aroma: sweat and breath, old perfume, spareribs. It was late autumn and chilly enough to numb my cheeks, but the bustle all around gave the place an electric warmth. Though it was evening, the scene was lit like a stage, thanks to the aluminum lamps hanging from every produce stand. Peddlers lined the street, selling steamed buns and chicken feet and imitation Gucci bags. Some shoppers moved along slowly. Others stopped at each stall, inspecting the greens, negotiating the price of fish, talking loudly. I strained to make sense of the chopped-off twangs of Cantonese coming from every direction, but there were more tones than I knew: my ear was inadequate; nothing was intelligible.

— Supporting detail

This was the first time I had been in Chinatown after dark. Mom held   3
Andrea's hand as we walked and asked me to stay close. People bumped us, brushed past, as if we were invisible. I felt on guard, alert. I craned my neck as we walked past a kiosk° carrying a Chinese edition of *Playboy*. I glanced sidelong at the teenage ruffians on the corner. They affected an air of menace with their smokes and leather jackets, but their feathery almost-mustaches and overpermed hair made them look a bit ridiculous. Nevertheless, I kept my distance. I kept an eye on the sidewalk, too, so that I wouldn't soil my shoes in the streams of putrid° water that trickled down from the alleyways and into the parapet° of trash bags piled up on the curb.

I remember going into two stores that night. One was the Far Eastern   4
Bookstore. It was on the second floor of an old building. As we entered, the sounds of the street fell away. The room was spare and fluorescent. It looked like an earnest community library, crowded with rows of chest-high shelves. In the narrow aisles between shelves, patrons sat cross-legged on the floor, reading intently. If they spoke at all it was in a murmur. Mom and Dad each found an absorbing book. They read standing up. My sister and I, meanwhile, wandered restlessly through the stacks, scanning the spines for stray English words or Chinese phrases we might recognize. I ended up in children's books and leafed through an illustrated story about the three tigers. I couldn't read it. Before long, I was tugging on Dad's coat to take us somewhere else.

The other shop, a market called Golden Gate, I liked much more. It was   5
noisy. The shoppers swarmed about in a frenzy. On the ground level was an emporium° of Chinese nonperishables: dried mushrooms, spiced beef, seaweed, shredded pork. Open crates of hoisin sauce° and sesame chili paste. Sweets, like milky White Rabbit chews, coconut candies, rolls of sour "haw flakes." Bags of Chinese peanuts, watermelon seeds. Down a narrow flight of stairs was a storehouse of rice cookers, ivory chopsticks, crockery, woks that hung from the wall. My mother carefully picked out a set of rice bowls and serving platters. I followed her to the long checkout line, carrying a basket full of groceries we wouldn't find in Poughkeepsie. I watched with wonder as the cashier tallied up totals with an abacus.

kiosk: Booth.   **putrid:** Rotten; decaying.   **parapet:** Wall, as on a castle.   **emporium:** Marketplace.   **hoisin sauce:** A sweet brown sauce that is a popular Chinese condiment.

We had come to this store, and to Chinatown itself, to replenish our supply of things Chinese: food and wares, and something else as well. We had ventured here from the colorless outer suburbs to touch the source, to dip into a pool of undiluted Chineseness. It was easier for my parents, of course, since they could decode the signs and communicate. But even I, whose bond to his ancestral culture had frayed down to the inner cord of *appetite* — even I could feel somehow fortified by a trip to Chinatown.

Yet we knew that we couldn't stay long — and that we didn't really want to. We were Chinese, but we were still outsiders. When any peddler addressed us in Cantonese, that became obvious enough. They seemed so familiar and so different, these Chinatown Chinese. Like a reflection distorted just so. Their faces were another brand of Chinese, rougher-hewn. I was fascinated by them. I liked being connected to them. But was it because of what we shared — or what we did not? I began that night to distinguish between my world and theirs.

It was that night, too, as we were making our way down East Broadway, that out of the blur of Chinese faces emerged one that we knew. It was Po-Po's° face. We saw her just an instant before she saw us. There was surprise in her eyes, then hurt, when she peered up from her parka. Everyone hugged and smiled, but this was embarrassing. Mom began to explain: we'd been uptown, had come to Chinatown on a whim, hadn't wanted to barge in on her unannounced. Po-Po nodded. We made some small talk. But the realization that her daily routine was our tourist's jaunt,° that there was more than just a hundred miles between us, consumed the backs of our minds like a flame

6   THESIS   stating main impression

7

Conclusion drawn from observation

8

Po-Po: The narrator's grandmother.   **jaunt:** Trip, outing.

to paper. We lingered for a minute, standing still as the human current flowed past, and then we went our separate ways.

Afterward, during the endless drive home, we didn't talk about bumping 9 into Po-Po. We didn't talk about much of anything. I looked intently through the window as we drove out of Chinatown and sped up the FDR Drive, then over the bridge. Manhattan turned into the Bronx, the Bronx into Yonkers, and the seams of the parkway clicked along in soothing intervals as we cruised northward to Dutchess County. I slipped into a deep, open-mouthed slumber, not awakening until we were back in Merrywood, our development, our own safe enclave. I remember the comforting sensation of being home: the sky was clear and starry, the lawn a moon-bathed carpet. We pulled into our smooth blacktop driveway. Silence. It was late, perhaps later than I'd ever stayed up. Still, before I went to bed, I made myself take a shower.

Questions to Start You Thinking

Meaning

1. Why do Liu and his family go to Chinatown?
2. How do Liu and his family feel when they encounter Po-Po? What observations and descriptions lead you to that conclusion?
3. What is the significance of the last sentence? How does it capture the essence of Liu's Chinatown experience?

Writing Strategies

4. In which paragraphs or sections does the writer's use of sensory details capture the look, feel, or smell of Chinatown? In general, how successfully has Liu included various types of observations and details?
5. How does Liu organize his observations? Is this organization effective? Why or why not?
6. Which of the observations and events in this essay most clearly reveal that Liu considers himself to be a "tourist"?

Michael Coil   **Student Essay**

Communications

For his first-year composition class, Michael Coil took a fresh look at a familiar location.

What kinds of places does this building bring to mind?

Walking into the county government building, a visitor would not imagine what 1 goes on in the basement twenty-four hours a day, seven days a week. The building is so quiet, and nobody is in sight. I make my way down the stairs and into the basement. A long hallway and an inconspicuous,° unmarked brown wooden door lead me

inconspicuous: Not noticeable.

to the communications center, where the radio traffic for all of Dodge City and Ford County is handled. Nothing along the way even hints at the amount of emotion that is felt in this small space.

Inside the center a kitchen is connected to a workspace with a large glass window that looks in on the main room. An office for the supervisor sits closed and locked, and a bathroom hides around the corner. The smell of constantly brewing coffee is thick, as though permanently tattooed on the air. I step through the kitchen and past the long window into the Dispatch Room. As a police officer for the city, I have been in the Dispatch Room many times, but I have never sat and thought of everything that goes on there. I begin to see things through new eyes.

The first thing to attract my attention is the number of computers at the workstations. I see three individual stations, each with a tall leather chair and a computer keyboard. At each station is a line of computer screens of various shapes and sizes, all brightly lit and streaming with information. A large green digital clock on the wall keeps the time, and a stack of printers taller than I am decorates the wall beside me. I notice a quiet hum from the many hard drives and printer fans. It is cold outside, but still the heat of the machines makes it necessary to run the air conditioner.

A television hangs from the ceiling in the corner. I can tell it's muted because it makes no sound though lines streaming with information slide off the screen. The reporters on the screen appear to be talking about Iraq. The anchorman looks angry, but nobody in the room pays him any attention. The only real noise is from the three 911 dispatchers talking happily. The mood is light, and conversation seems to come very easily.

A phone rings, and one of the dispatchers answers. She enters something on her screen and then hangs up. She tells me that the hospital was calling to ask them to page one of the on-call doctors. The dispatchers resume their conversation. They are casual and friendly, and their conversation ranges from what they ate today to the personalities of their dogs at home. I find it easy to talk with them, and I can tell that spending so much time side by side in this room brings the three dispatchers together like close friends.

After a few minutes the phone rings again. The situation is different this time. The first phone that rang was a normal ring without unusual volume or tone, but this one makes my blood churn. It is loud, obnoxious,° and ugly. It's like combining the screech of a vulture and the wail of a dying animal. The air becomes thick and tense. The conversation stops in mid-sentence, and I can feel all of the dispatchers tense up in anticipation of what they are about to hear. The three of them pick up the phone, and one begins to talk. Another begins to type on the computer screen, and the third gets on the radio and dispatches the call to the police. From where I am sitting at the rear of the workspace, I can hear the woman on the phone screaming. I can't quite decipher° what she is saying, but by the dispatcher's rising tone, I can tell it is

2

③ When have you had a similar change in perception?

3

4

5

6

② How can a ring be "obnoxious"?

obnoxious: Offensive, intolerable.   **decipher:** Interpret.

not good. Repeatedly the caller is told to calm down and tell what's going on. With each command the dispatcher's voice gets more edgy. Hearts are racing now, and the room fills with dread. "Somebody is breaking into my house," the voice on the line finally pushes out. I read the screen and see that she lives not far from where we are sitting. It only takes a minute or two for the first unit to arrive, but sitting and listening to that poor woman's plea for help makes that short time feel like an eternity. The officers inform the dispatcher that they are in front of the house, and they don't see anybody. The person must have left just moments before they got there. The dispatcher speaking with the woman leans back slowly in her chair, causing it to groan softly. She rubs her hands on her face as though she were sweating and suddenly goes back into her casual mode. She politely tells the woman to answer the door because the police are standing out front, then pauses a moment and says goodbye.

> *How have you responded to the sounds that the writer has described?*

Several minutes pass before I can collect myself and begin to process everything I just saw and heard. I feel as though I had been sitting in the house with that distraught woman watching helplessly. I feel suddenly tired, stressed, and still my nerves are shaking from the adrenaline. The dispatchers, however, return to their conversation without missing a beat. The tension filters silently away, and the mood becomes friendly again. Only a unique and brave person could willingly face challenges like that one on a day-to-day basis.   7

As I walk out of the communications room, I see multiple cartoons cut out of the newspaper and taped to the doorway. I think to myself, What a difficult task it must be to come back down after eight hours on the emotional rollercoaster. It would be so easy for the dispatchers to become bitter, angry people, but they are quite the opposite. They are inviting and friendly, and though they will always deny it, they are modern-day heroes waiting to come to our rescue. Day and night they sit, behind the brown unmarked wooden door, at the end of the long marble hallway, always ready to help.   8

Questions to Start You Thinking

Meaning

1. Is the Dispatch Room as "quiet" as Coil originally suspects as he enters the building? Which paragraph best supports your answer?
2. In paragraph 8, Coil uses the term "modern-day heroes" to describe the dispatchers. What details in his account support that description?
3. What does Coil learn about himself from his visit to the Dispatch Room?

Writing Strategies

4. How does comparing and contrasting the dispatchers' behavior before a call and during a call help Coil create a vivid impression of the room?
5. Which sense does Coil use most effectively? Point to a few examples that support your choice.

6. Paragraph 6 includes the only dialogue in the essay. What is its effect?

7. Using highlighters or marginal notes, identify the essay's introduction, thesis, major vantage points for observation, details supporting each part of the observation, and conclusion. How effective is this organization?

Learning by Writing

The Assignment: Observing a Scene

Observe a place near your campus, home, or job and the people who frequent this place. Then write a paper in which you describe the place, the people, and their actions so as to convey the spirit of the place and offer some insight into the impact of the place on the people.

For writing activities for observing a scene, visit **<bcdfordstmartins .com/bedguide>**.

This assignment is meant to start you observing closely enough that you go beyond the obvious. Go somewhere nearby, and station yourself where you can mingle with the people there. Open your senses — all of them, so that you see, smell, taste, hear, and feel. Jot down what you immediately notice, especially the atmosphere and its effect on the people there. Take notes describing the location, people, actions, and events you see. Then use your observations to convey the spirit of the scene. What is your main impression of the place? Of the people there? Of the relationship between the people and the place? Remember, your purpose is not only to describe the scene but also to express thoughts and feelings connected with what you observe.

Three student writers wrote about these observations:

One student, who works nights in the emergency room, observed the scene and the community that abruptly forms when an accident victim arrives: medical staff, patient, friends, and relatives.

Another observed a bar mitzvah celebration that reunited a family for the first time in many years.

Another observed the activity in the bleachers in a baseball stadium before, during, and after a game.

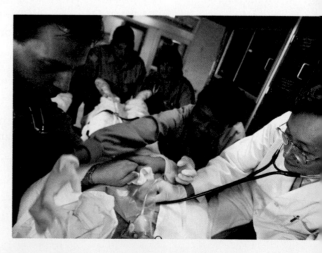

When you select the scene you wish to observe, find out from the person in charge whether you'll need to request permission to observe there, as you might at a school, business, or other restricted or privately owned site.

Facing the Challenge   Observing a Scene

The major challenge writers face when writing from observation is to select compelling details that fully convey an engaging main impression of a scene. As we experience the world, we are bombarded by sensory details, but our task as writers is to choose those that bring a subject alive for readers. For example, describing an oak as "a big tree with green leaves" is too vague to help readers envision the tree or grasp what is unique about it. Consider:

- What colors, shapes, and sizes do you see?
- What tones, pitches, and rhythms do you hear?
- What textures, grains, and physical features do you feel?
- What fragrances and odors do you smell?
- What sweet, spicy, or other flavors do you taste?

After recording the details that define the scene, ask two more questions:

- What overall main impression do these details establish?
- Which specific details will best show the spirit of this scene to a reader?

Your answers will help you decide which details to include in your paper.

Generating Ideas

For more on each strategy for generating ideas in this section or for additional strategies, see Ch. 19.

Although setting down observations might seem cut-and-dried, to many writers it is true discovery. Here are some ways to generate such observations.

Brainstorm. First, you need to find a scene to observe. What places interest you? Which are memorable? Start brainstorming—listing rapidly any ideas that come to mind. Here are a few questions to help you start your list:

DISCOVERY CHECKLIST

☐ Where do people gather for some event or performance (a stadium, a church, a theater, an auditorium)?

☐ Where do people get together for some activity (a gym, a classroom)?

☐ Where do crowds form while people are getting things or services (a shopping mall, a dining hall or student union, a dentist's waiting room)?

☐ Where do people pause on their way to yet another destination (a light-rail station, a bus or subway station, an airport, a restaurant on the toll road)?

☐ Where do people go for recreation or relaxation (an arcade, a ballpark)?

☐ Where do people gather (a fire, a party, a wedding, a graduation, an audition)?

Get Out and Look. If nothing on your list strikes you as compelling, plunge into the world to see what you see. Visit a city street or country hillside, a campus building or practice field, a contest, a lively scene — a mall, an airport, a fast-food restaurant, a student hangout — or a scene with only a few people sunbathing, walking dogs, or tossing Frisbees. Stand off in a corner for a while, and then mix and move to gain different views of the scene.

Record Your Observations. Michael Coil's essay "Communications" began with some notes Coil made about his county communications center and the phone traffic it receives. He was able to mine those notes for details to bring his subject to life.

Your notes on a subject — or tentative subject — can be taken in any order or methodically. To draw up an "observation sheet," fold a sheet of paper in half lengthwise. Label the left column "Objective," and impartially list what you see, like a zoologist looking at a new species of moth. Label the right column "Subjective," and list your thoughts and feelings about what you observe. If possible, keep your subject before you as you write.

The quality of your paper will depend in large part on the truthfulness and accuracy of your observations. Your objective notes will trigger more subjective ones.

Elvis impersonators gather to audition in a Las Vegas contest.

Objective	Subjective
The ticket holders form a line on the weathered sidewalk outside the old brick hall, standing two or three deep all the way down the block.	This place has seen concerts of all kinds — you can feel the history as you wait, as if the hall protects the crowds and the music.
Groups of friends talk, a few couples hug, and some guys burst out in staccato laughter as they joke.	The crowd seems relaxed and friendly, all waiting to hear their favorite group.
Everyone shuffles forward when the doors finally open, looking around at the crowd and slowly edging toward the entrance.	The excitement and energy grow with the wait, but it's just the concert ritual — the prelude to a perfect night.

Include a Range of Images. Have you captured not just sights but sounds, touches, odors? Have you observed from several vantage points or on several occasions to deepen your impressions? Have you added sketches or doodles to your notes, perhaps drawing the features or mapping the shape of the place? Can you begin writing as you continue to observe your subject? Have you noticed how other writers use *images,* evoking sensory experience, to record what they sense? In the memoir *Northern Farm* (New York: Rinehart, 1948), naturalist Henry Beston describes a remarkable sound: "the voice of ice," the midwinter sound of a whole frozen pond settling and expanding in its bed.

> Sometimes there was a sort of hollow oboe sound, and sometimes a groan with a delicate undertone of thunder. . . . Just as I turned to go, there came from below one curious and sinister crack which ran off into a sound like the whine of a giant whip of steel lashed through the moonlit air.

Learning by Doing 🔲 Enriching Sensory Detail

Review the detail in your observation notes. Because observers often note first what they see, mark references to other senses by underlining sounds, circling smells, and boxing textures or touches or by adding different color highlights to your file. (Mark taste, too, if appropriate.) Compare your coverage with that of a classmate or small group, either in class or online. Add more varied details from memory, or list what you want to observe when you return to the scene to do more listening, sniffing, tasting, or touching. (You can also use this activity to analyze sensory details in paragraphs from the two essays opening this chapter.)

Planning, Drafting, and Developing

For more strategies for planning, drafting, and developing, see Chs. 20, 21, and 22.

After recording your observations, look over your notes or your observation sheet, circling whatever looks useful. Maybe you can rewrite your notes into a draft, throwing out details that don't matter, leaving those that do. Maybe you'll need a plan to help you organize all the observations, laying them out graphically or in a simple scratch outline.

Start with a Main Impression or Thesis. What main insight or impression do you want to get across? Answering this question will help you decide which details to include and which to omit. It will also help you avoid a dry recitation of observed facts.

PLACE OBSERVED	Smalley Green after lunch
MAIN IMPRESSION	relaxing activity is good after a morning of classes
WORKING THESIS	After their morning classes, students have fun relaxing on Smalley Green with their dogs and Frisbees.

For more on stating a thesis, see pp. 401–10.

For exercises on choosing effective thesis statements, visit **<bedfordstmartins .com/bedguide>**.

Organize to Show Your Audience Your Point. How do you map out a series of observations? Your choice will depend on your purpose in writing and the main impression that you want to create. Whatever your choice, be sure to add transitions—words or phrases that guide the reader from one vantage point, location, or idea to the next. Consider options such as the ones at the top of the next page.

As you create your "picture," you bring a place to life using the details that capture its spirit. If your instructor approves, consider whether adding a photograph, sketch, diagram, or other illustration—with a caption—would enhance your written observation.

For more organization strategies, see pp. 410–13.

For transitions that mark place or direction, see p. 435.

Learning by Doing 🎥 Experimenting with Organization

Take a second look at the sequence in which you have arranged the details in your observation. Select a different yet promising sequence, and then test it by outlining your draft (or reorganizing another file) in that order. Ask classmates for their reactions as you consider which sequence will most effectively convey your main impression.

Revising and Editing

Your revising, editing, and proofreading will all be easier if you have taken accurate notes on your observations. But what if, when you look over your draft, you find that you don't have enough detail? If you have any doubts, go back to the scene, and take more notes to flesh out your draft.

For more revising and editing strategies, see Ch. 23.

Focus on a Main Impression or Thesis. As you begin to revise, ask a friend to read your observation, or read it yourself as if you had never visited the place you observed. While reading, you might notice gaps that would puzzle a reader or decide that the spirit of the place seems understated. Consider whether the main impression you want to convey would be clearer if you sharpened its description in your thesis.

SPATIAL MOVEMENT	top	left	near	center
	↓	↓	↓	↓
	bottom	right	far	edge

PROMINENT FEATURES	least: Sunday suit, light blue blouse, dramatic flowered hat
	↓
	most: Grandma's sharp eyes, spotting the best in others

SPECIFIC DETAILS TO GENERAL IMPRESSION	souvenir sellers calling, small waves slapping tour boats, and pungent fish frying on Fisherman's Wharf
	↓
	In all this commotion, a visitor sees the wharf's vitality.

COMMON AND ORDINARY TO UNUSUAL FEATURES	mounds of bright leaves, crisp fall air, children bouncing
	↓
	the sheer joy of every moment at the playground across from the pediatric cancer center

Sequential Organization of Details

WORKING THESIS	After their morning classes, students have fun relaxing on Smalley Green with their dogs and Frisbees.
REVISED THESIS	When students, dogs, and Frisbees accumulate on Smalley Green after lunch, they show how much campus learning takes place outside of class.

For exercises on supporting a thesis, visit <bedfordstmartins .com/bedguide>.

Add Relevant and Powerful Details. Next, check your selection of details. Does each detail contribute to your main impression? Should any details be dropped or added? Should any be rearranged so that your organization, moving from point to point, is clearer? Could any observations be described more vividly or powerfully? Could more precise or more concrete wording strengthen the way you present the details? Could any vague words such as *very, really, great,* or *beautiful* be replaced with more specific words? (As you spot too much repetition of certain words, use your soft-

ware's Find function in the Edit menu to locate all of them so you can reword for variety.)

Learning by Doing 🎥 Strengthening Your Main Impression

Complete these two sentences: The main impression that I want to show my audience is _____. The main insight that I want to share is _____.
Exchange sentences with a classmate or small group, and then each read aloud
your draft while the others listen in terms of the impression and insight you want
to convey. After each reading, discuss revision options with the writer—cuts, additions, changes—to strengthen that impression.

Peer Response 👥 Observing a Scene

Let a classmate or friend respond to your draft, suggesting how to use detail to
convey your main impression more powerfully. Ask your peer editor to answer
questions such as these about writing from observation:

- What is the main insight or impression you carry away from this writing?
- Which sense does the writer use particularly well? Are any senses neglected
  that could be used?
- Can you see and feel what the writer experienced? Would more details make
  this writing more compelling? Put check marks wherever you want more detail.
- How well has the writer used evidence from the senses to build a main impression? Which sensory impressions contribute most strongly to the overall picture? Which seem superfluous?
- If this paper were yours, what is the one thing you would be sure to work on
  before handing it in?

For general questions
for a peer editor, see
p. 465.

To see where your draft could need work, consider these questions:

REVISION CHECKLIST

☐ Have you accomplished your purpose—to convey to readers your overall
impression of your subject and to share some telling insight about it?

☐ What can you assume your readers know? What do they need to be told?

☐ Have you gathered enough observations to describe your subject? Have
you observed with *all* your senses when possible—even smell and taste?

☐ Have you been selective, including details that effectively support your overall impression?

☐ Which observations might need to be checked for accuracy? Which might need to be checked for richness or fullness?

☐ Is your organizational pattern the most effective for your subject? Is it easy for readers to follow? Would another pattern work better?

For more editing and proofreading strategies, see pp. 473–76.

After you have revised your essay, edit and proofread it. Carefully check the grammar, word choice, punctuation, and mechanics — and then correct any problems. If you have added details while revising, consider whether they have been sufficiently blended with the ideas already there. Here are some questions to get you started:

EDITING CHECKLIST

For more help, find the relevant checklist sections in the Quick Editing Guide on pp. A-36–A-56. Turn also to the Quick Format Guide beginning on p. A-1.

☐ Is your sentence structure correct? Have you avoided writing fragments, comma splices, and fused sentences?   **A1, A2**

☐ Have you used an adjective whenever describing a noun or pronoun? Have you used an adverb whenever describing a verb, adjective, or adverb? Have you used the correct form when comparing two or more things?   **A7**

☐ Is it clear what each modifier in a sentence modifies? Have you created any dangling or misplaced modifiers?   **B1**

☐ Have you used parallel structure wherever needed, especially in lists or comparisons?   **B2**

Additional Writing Assignments

1. To develop your powers of observation, go for a walk, recording your observations in two or three detailed paragraphs. Let your walk take you through either an unfamiliar scene or a familiar scene worth a closer look than you normally give it (such as a supermarket, a city street, an open field). Avoid a subject so familiar that you would struggle to see it from a fresh perspective (such as a dormitory corridor or a parking lot). Sum up your impression of the place, including any opinion you form through your close observations.

2. Try this short, spontaneous writing exercise. Begin the assignment immediately after class, and turn it in the same afternoon.

> Go to a nearby public place—a café, library, copy center, art gallery—and select a person who catches your eye, who somehow intrigues you. Try to choose someone who looks as if she or he will stay put for a while. Settle yourself where you can observe your subject unobtrusively. Take notes, if you can do so without being observed.
>
> Now, carefully and tactfully (we don't want any fistfights or lawsuits) notice everything you can about this person. Start with physical characteristics, but focus on other things too. How does the person talk? Move? What does the person's body language tell you?
>
> Write a paragraph describing the person. Pretend that the person is going to hold up a bank ten minutes from now, and the police will expect you to supply a full and accurate description.

3. The perspective of a tourist, an outsider alert to details, often reveals the distinctive character of places and people. Think of some place you have visited as an outsider in the past year, and jot down any notable details you recall. Or spend a few minutes as a tourist right now. Go to a busy spot on or off campus, and record your observations of anything you find amusing, surprising, puzzling, or intriguing. Then write an essay on the unique character of the place.

4. Select an observation site that relates to your current or possible career plans. For example, you might choose a medical facility (for nursing or medical school), a school or playground (for education), or an office complex or work site (for business). Observe carefully at this location, noting details that contribute to your main impression of the place and your insight about the site or about the work that goes on there. Write an essay using rich detail to convey these points to an audience that might be interested in the same career path.

5. Observe the details of a specific place on campus as if you were seeing it for the first time. Write about the main impression and insight about it that you wish to convey in an essay for a campus audience, a letter to a prospective student (who will want to know the relevance of the place), or an entry on your travel blog for foreign tourists (who will want to know why they should add this stop to their travel itinerary). If you wish, include your own photograph of the scene or a standard campus shot; add a caption that expresses its essence.

6. **Visual Assignment.** Use one of the photographs on pages 94 and 95 to explore the importance of the observer's point of view. After a preliminary examination of the details of the scene, select your vantage point as an observer, and identify the audience you plan to address (for example, readers who would or would not share your perspective). Observe the image carefully, and write an essay using its details to support your main impression of the scene from your perspective and to develop your specific insight about the scene, directed to your audience.

Responding to an Image

Suppose that you had an opportunity to interview Supreme Court Justice Sonia Sotomayor, President Barack Obama, basketball player and Olympian Yao Ming, or actor and philanthropist Angelina Jolie. What two or three questions would you most like to ask the interviewee? Based on the person's public image and his or her personality as revealed in these photos, what kind of response would you expect to receive? How do you think the photographer has tried to bring the person to life or suggest something about the person?

Don't know what to write about? Go talk with someone. Meet for half an hour with an anthropology professor, and you probably will have plenty of material for a paper. Just as likely, you can get a paper's worth of information from a ten-minute exchange with a mechanic who relines brakes. Both the mechanic and the professor are experts. But even people who aren't usually considered experts may tell you things you didn't know and provide you with material.

As this chapter suggests, you can direct a conversation by asking questions to elicit what you want to find out. You do so in an *interview* — a special kind of conversation with a purpose — usually to help you understand the other person or to find out what that person knows. You may use what you learn to profile the character or personality of the individual interviewed. However, interviews also provide expert information about a topic, intriguing firsthand accounts of an event or an era, or systematic research samples of selected or representative people.

Why Interviewing a Subject Matters

In a College Course

- You interview people for your American Studies course, talking in person, by telephone or Web call, or through e-mail. You seek firsthand knowledge about a moment in history that engages you from a veteran, a civil rights activist, a disaster survivor, or a person who experienced a local or regional event.
- You interview a person who mentors college students or sponsors internships for field experience to gain career advice (perhaps from an early childhood educator, public safety officer, health-care provider, alternative energy developer, artist, catering manager).

In the Workplace

- You interview an "informed source" for a news site, a financial planner for a profile in your company newsletter, your customers or clients for feedback on company products and services, or involved parties who can clarify an insurance or legal claim.

In Your Community

- You contact experts to learn about composting food waste through the new city program or about installing a ramp to make your home accessible for your child who uses a wheelchair.

A
Writer's
Guide

❓ Who would you like to interview as an intriguing personality? Who would you like to interview to learn answers or get advice about some of your questions? In what situations might you conduct interviews in the future?

Learning from Other Writers

Here are two essays whose writers talked to someone and reported the conversations, using direct quotations and telling details to reveal engaging personalities. To help you begin to analyze the first reading, look at the notes in the margin. They identify features such as the main idea, or thesis, and the quotations providing support.

For more examples of writing based on interviews, visit **<bedfordstmartins .com/bedguide>**.

As You Read These Interview Essays

As you read these essays, ask yourself the following questions:

1. Was the conversation reported from an informal discussion or planned as an interview? Does the writer report the conversation directly or indirectly?

2. What does the interview show about the character and personality of the individual speaking? What does it show about the author who is listening?

3. Why do you think the writer draws on conversation?

Paul Solotaroff

The Surfing Savant

Paul Solotaroff is the author of *The Body Shop* (2010) about his experiences with muscle-building and steroids. For this article, published in the April 2010 *Rolling Stone*, he interviewed Clay Marzo, a young man who does not fit neatly into the role of "celebrity athlete."

Opening description bringing subject to life

P
ut him in the water and Clay Marzo is magic, a kid with so much grace and daring that you laugh in disbelief to watch him surf. Every day he's out there in the South Pacific, shredding huge swells° till he's faint with hunger and near the verge of dehydration. He doesn't really ride waves as much as *fly* them, soaring above the sea foam upside down and spinning the

1

swells: Sets of long, stable ocean waves.

nose of his board in whiplash twists. Just two years out of high school, Marzo is remaking a sport held hostage by rules and hack judges, turning it into a cross between aquatic parkour° and X Games° stunt work. Call it what you want, it's a sight to behold. *Sorry, but humans can't do that,* you keep thinking. Then he goes and does it all day long.

2   But if you sit and list the things that Marzo has trouble doing, they quickly outrun the things he finds easy. He's unable, for instance, to eat a simple meal without much of it ending up on his shirt or the floor. Out of water, he has trouble interacting with other people, either staring in bafflement at their grins and jokes or avoiding casual contact altogether. He blurts things out, chants rap songs to himself and pulls out clumps of his hair when anxious. When he speaks, which isn't often, he seems younger than his 20 years, mumbling like a bashful eighth-grader. For years, the rap on Marzo was that, for all his gifts, he's a pothead who chokes in competitions. And then there were the nastier names he's had to deal with, slurs that burned in deep: *retard, moron, slacker, zombie.* In middle school, Marzo was treated so badly that his mother, Jill, had to pull him out and teach him at home, where he wouldn't be punched for staring at wanna-be thugs. His agonizing shyness has fractured his family and sparked ugly set-tos with his father, Gino, an old-school hard-hat striver who accused him of flaking off and screwing up his shot at stardom. That charge hurts Clay more than the others combined: When your own father misconceives you so badly, how can you hope that strangers will understand?

THESIS stating dominant impression

Elaboration of dominant impression

Background and challenges

3   Now, pushing back from lunch at a Maui fish stand, bits of ahi po'boy° dotting his face and lap, Marzo wears the grin of a birthday boy who gets to eat as much cake as he wants. To see him like this, hands clasped across belly, is to encounter a kid whose first and last directive° is pure, physical joy. But the facts are more complex and less happy. Marzo has Asperger's syndrome, a form

Clay Marzo, surfer.

parkour: An activity in which participants travel as quickly and efficiently as possible through spaces and around obstacles.   **X Games:** A twice-yearly sporting event focused on extreme action sports.   **ahi po'boy:** Tuna fish sandwich.   **directive:** Guiding principle.

of high-functioning autism that causes no end of social confusion and anguish, and that commonly burdens those afflicted with a single, smothering obsession: bird songs or train routes or the history of naval warfare. "Though Asperger's teens are typically bright and verbal, they can't connect with kids their age or with people they don't know well," says Dr. Michael Linden, an autism specialist who diagnosed Marzo at the age of 18, after a dozen years of botched assessments. "Feelings are a foreign language to them, and they're unable to pick up social cues. A lot of them retreat from relationships and get stuck in a special activity or interest that they devote themselves to intensely."

Like a lot of Aspies, as some with the diagnosis have taken to calling themselves, Marzo is a baffling mix of powers and deficits. He has no interest in the written word (and has read few of the dozens of stories about him in sports magazines, which regularly anoint° him one of surfing's saviors) but is brilliant, even clairvoyant,° in the water. Looking at the horizon, Marzo can read waves that others can't and intuit where they'll break before they crest. Traveling raises such dread in him that he's sick with nausea days before boarding a plane, but he gets up each morning and surfs lethal points on Maui's western shore. The kinds of waves he lives on don't crash near sandy beaches; instead, he climbs down lava cliffs to reach breaks rife with boulders and a seafloor of spear-tipped coral reefs that can turn a surfer's chest to chum.° His body is a travelogue° of scars and welts, but it bores him to talk about the dangers he courts—the boards he routinely snaps taking hellish falls; the waves that hold him down till his lungs scream, half a minute or more during really heavy sets. Only once, he says, has he been afraid of the surf. "There were tiger sharks behind me," he says, wiping a quarter-size splotch of mayo off his cheek. "They were pretty big, so I bailed quick." . . .

I think back on our first—and last—sit-down chat, in which he all but fled the room, screaming. It began well enough, with Marzo talking about his childhood and name-checking his heroes, like Bruce Irons° and Kalani Robb.° "Those guys invented the moves," he says. "We were just trying to take them farther." Then, out of the blue, he announces that surfing is the thing that "saved" him. "It's the best drug ever," he says, "and I'm lucky to have it."

I gently ask what it saved him from. He stares out the window and starts to yank his forelock. "I just . . . see things different, from the back of my brain," he says. "Other people see 'em from the front, I guess. It's not good or bad, just how I am. Sort of makes it harder, though, you know?"

"How so?"

His free hand paws the side of his trunks, damp in the air-chilled room. "Well, I need people's help to get stuff done. Telling me where to go and what to say, and sometimes I don't like that, or I'm tired and don't want . . ."

anoint: Choose based on a position of authority.   **clairvoyant:** Able to see or feel things that cannot be perceived with the normal range of senses.   **chum:** Ground-up meat or fish, thrown in the water as bait when fishing.   **travelogue:** A journal or description of a person's travels.   **Bruce Irons** (1979–): Professional surfer from Hawaii.   **Kalani Robb** (1977–): Actor and surfer from Hawaii.

Quotation from expert

Dominant impression restated

Details supporting the dominant impression

Quotations showing subject's personality

4

5

6

7

8

The sentence just hangs there, whirring in space. I hold off, giving him   9
room to work through the tangle of half-formed thoughts. Instead, he tugs
his hair so hard that a clump comes off in his fingers. Panicked, I ask about
the feeling he gets when he does something splendid on a wave. "I can't describe it," he says, slouching so low that he burrows into his chest. "Just pleasure, I guess. Where you want it over and over, and do anything to get it. . . .
Are we almost done?"

"Just one more," I say, looking at a poster-size photo on the wall. In it,   10
Marzo is stock-still on his board, raising his arms in benediction° as a
20-foot wave hulks above him. In the undepicted instant after the photo was
taken, he paddled coolly around the edge of the wave before it smashed him
to bits on the rocks. "What do you think when you see that picture?" I ask.

He mashes his lower lip, but releases the hair he's wrapped around a   11
clenched index finger. "I was stoked," he says. "That wave was *bombing*, and
there was another, even bigger, right behind it."

> Body language included as well as spoken language

What he doesn't add is that he had just returned from a nightmare trip   12
and felt blessed to be home again. Marzo is a creature of waves, but of *these*
waves, the rocky, shark-toothed waters of Maui that he knows by heart. Look
at him now, out beyond the reef, doing tricks to raise his flagging spirits. In
surf no bigger than a picket fence, he's positioned himself above the swell,
skimming like a coin from crest to crest. Just as each dies, he spies a new section to carve his name upon, hurling his board up the short-sleeve face to
ride the foam again. He's forgotten the guys watching from their pickup
trucks, and the small crowd up here with our mouths agape, and the father
he can't please, and the brother who cut him dead—all of that's gone now,
carried away by the hunchbacked westerly waves. He'll surf until lunchtime,
then come back after a nap, and if not for the tiger sharks that hunt these
waters once the sun goes down, he might never get out of the bliss machine,
which makes no claims, only grants them.

> Physical description supporting the dominant impression

> Restatement of thesis

Questions to Start You Thinking

Meaning

1. How is Marzo "a baffling mix of powers and deficits" (paragraph 4)?

2. How does Marzo's Asperger's syndrome affect his attitude toward his
own celebrity?

3. Why does Marzo call surfing "the best drug ever" (paragraph 5)?

Writing Strategies

4. Solotaroff quotes Dr. Michael Linden, an autism specialist, in paragraph 3. How does the quotation contribute to the essay?

benediction: The act of blessing.

5. How does Solotaroff seem to feel about his dominant impression of Marzo? What observations and details does he include to affect your impression of him?

6. How does Solotaroff combine physical description and direct quotation of Marzo in the second half of the essay? Would the essay be as effective if he focused more on one or the other? Why or why not?

Lorena A. Ryan-Hines   Student Essay

Looking Backwards, Moving Forward

Lorena Ryan-Hines, a student in a nursing program, wrote this essay after interviewing an experienced professional in her field.

Someone once said, "You cannot truly know where you are going unless you know   1
where you have come from." I don't think I understood this statement until I got the opportunity to sit down with Joan Gilmore, assistant director of nursing at Smithville Health Care Center. With the blur of everyday activities going on during the change of third shift to first shift at the nursing home, I had never recognized what value Joan could bring to the younger nurses. Once we started to talk, I began to realize that, although I am a nurse, I don't know much about how nursing has evolved over the years. During our conversation, I discovered how much history, wisdom, and advice Joan has to share.

⬤ Can you
identify with
Ryan-Hines's work
environment and
relationship with
Joan? In what ways?

Joan tries to stay as active as she can working on the floor so she does not use   2
an office. We decided just to sit down in one of the multi-purpose conference rooms. Joan looks very good for a woman of her age. In fact, no one would ever suspect by looking at her that she is a young sixty-four years old. She is approximately 5'2" tall and dressed in white scrub pants with a flowered scrub top. Although her hair is dyed, the color is a nice natural tone for her. She is not flashy or outspoken, but she knows what she is doing. However, if she has a question, she does not have a problem asking someone else.

When we first sat down, we started talking about how she grew up. She was the   3
third child of seven children. Her father worked in a factory and also farmed over one hundred acres. Her mom stayed home to take care of the children. As I watched her talk about her upbringing, a glaze seemed to roll across her face. I could see a slight twinkle in her eyes. She almost appeared to be back in that time and space of childhood. She went on to explain to me that she decided to go to nursing school because it was one of the few jobs, forty-five years ago, that could be productive for a woman.

She decided to enter the three-year program at St. Elizabeth Hospital's School   4
for Nursing in Dayton, Ohio. Students were not allowed to be married and had to live

in the nursing school's brick dormitory. Whenever they were in class and on the floors of the hospital, they were required to wear their uniforms, light blue dresses with white pin stripes. The student nursing cap, the "dignity cap" as Joan called it, was all white. When students graduated, they earned their black stripe which distinguished them as registered nurses. Joan said that she did not think we should continue to wear the all-white uniforms or nursing caps. However, she conveyed a sense of sadness when she said, "I think we have gone too far to the left these days because everyone dresses and looks the same. I think as a nurse you have worked hard and earned the right to stand out somehow."

Why do you think that the "dignity cap" was so important for Joan?

I asked Joan about the pros and cons of being a registered nurse and whether she ever regretted her decision. Her philosophy is that being a nurse is a calling. Although nursing pay is generally considered a decent living wage, sometimes dealing with management, long hours, and the grief of tough cases is hard. Through experience and commitment, a nurse learns to take each day as it comes and grow with it. Even though life-and-death situations can be very stressful and the fast-paced nursing world can be draining, nurses can never forget that patients are people. For Joan, when patients are demanding and short fused, they are not really angry at the nurses but at the situation they are in. She believes that a nurse is always able to help her patients in some way, be it physical or emotional.

5

The advice Joan gave me about becoming a new registered nurse may be some of the best advice of my life. Each registered nurse specialty has its demands. She recommended working for a while in a medical surgery area. This area is a great place to gain knowledge and experience about multiple acute illnesses and disease processes. From there, nurses can move forward and find the specialty areas that best suit them. This fit is important because nurses need to be knowledgeable and confident, leaders who are not afraid to ask questions when they do not know the answers. To gain the respect of others, nurses also must be willing to help and to let others help them because no one can be a nurse all alone. Joan recommended being courteous, saying "please" and "thank you" when asking someone to do something as well as encouraging others with different talents. Lastly, she urged me always to do my best and be proud of my accomplishments.

6

Afterwards, I thanked her for the advice and her time. She got up smiling and simply walked out of the room and back to the job she has loved for so many years. I found myself sitting back down for a few minutes to reflect on everything she had just told me. Nursing from yesterday to today has changed not only with the technological advances but even the simplest things. Uniforms are nothing like they were forty years ago. The rules back then could never be enforced today. Some things will never change though, like the simple respect a nurse gives another human being. The profound advice Joan gave me is something I will carry with me for the rest of my personal and professional career.

7 Have you ever received valuable advice from someone like Joan? How has that advice affected you and your decisions?

Works Cited

Gilmore, Joan. Personal interview. 4 June 2009.

Questions to Start You Thinking

Meaning

1. What is the main point of Ryan-Hines's essay?

2. What kind of person is Joan Gilmore? How does Ryan-Hines feel about her?

3. How is Gilmore's history the history of nursing during the last decades? Is an interview an effective method of relating the history of a profession? Why or why not?

Writing Strategies

4. Why does Ryan-Hines begin her essay with a quotation and an impression of the nursing home? How does this opening serve as a frame for her conversation with Joan?

5. What details does Ryan-Hines use to describe Joan? What senses does she draw on? Does she provide enough detail for you to form a clear image of Joan?

6. How much of the interview does Ryan-Hines quote directly? Why does she choose to quote directly rather than paraphrase in these places? Would her essay be stronger if she used more of Joan's own words?

7. Using highlighters or marginal notes, identify the essay's introduction, thesis, major emphases, supporting details for each emphasis, and conclusion. How effective is the organization of this essay?

Learning by Writing

The Assignment: Interviewing

For writing activities for interview-based writing, visit <bedfordstmartins .com/bedguide>.

Write a paper about someone who interests you and base the paper primarily on a conversation with that person. Select any acquaintance, relative, or person you have heard about whose traits, interests, activities, background, or outlook on life might intrigue your readers. Your purpose is to show this person's character and personality—to bring your subject to life for your readers—through his or her conversation.

These students found notable people to interview:

One student wrote about a high school science teacher who had quit teaching for a higher-paying job in the computer industry, only to return three years later to the classroom.

One writer recorded the thoughts and feelings of a discouraged farmer she had known since childhood.

To interview someone for information about something, see Additional Writing Assignments on pp. 112–15.

Another learned about adjustment to life in a new country by talking to his neighbor from Somalia.

Facing the Challenge   Writing from an Interview

The major challenge writers face when writing from an interview is to find a clear focus for the paper. They must first sift through the huge amount of information generated in an interview and then decide what dominant impression of the subject to present in an essay. Distilling the material you have gathered into a focused, overall impression may seem overwhelming. As a writer, however, you have the responsibility to select and organize your material for your readers, not simply transcribe your notes.

To identify possible angles, jot down answers to these questions:

- What did you find most interesting about the interview?
- What topics did your subject talk about the most?
- What did he or she become most excited or animated about?
- What topics generated the most interesting quotations?

Your answers should help you to determine a dominant impression—the aspect of your interviewee's character or personality that you want to emphasize for your readers. Once you have this focus, you can pick the details and direct quotations from the interview that best illustrate the points you want to make. Use direct quotations strategically and sparingly to reveal the character traits that you wish to emphasize. Select colorful quotations that allow readers to "hear" your subject's distinctive voice. Make sure that all quotations—long or short—are accurate. To capture the dynamic of conversation, include your own observations as well as actual quotations.

Generating Ideas

If an image of the perfect subject has flashed into your mind, consider yourself lucky, and set up an appointment with that person at once. If you have drawn a blank, you'll need to cast about for a likely interview subject.

For more on each strategy for generating ideas in this section or for additional strategies, see Ch. 19.

Brainstorm for Possible Subjects. Try brainstorming for a few minutes to see what pops into your mind. Your subject need not be spectacular or unusual; ordinary lives can make fascinating reading.

DISCOVERY CHECKLIST

☐ Are you acquainted with anyone whose life has been unusually eventful, stressful, or successful?

☐ Are you curious about why someone you know made a certain decision or how that person got to his or her current point in life?

☐ Is there an expert or a leader whom you admire or are puzzled by?

☐ Do you know someone whose job or hobby interests you?

☐ What older person could tell you about life thirty or even fifty years ago?

☐ Who has passionate convictions about society, politics, sex, or childrearing?

☐ Whose background and life history would you like to know more about?

☐ Whose lifestyle, values, or attitudes are utterly different from your own and from those of most people you know?

Former President Richard Nixon, right, is interviewed by David Frost, May 5, 1977. Their exchanges later inspired an award-winning play and the movie *Frost/Nixon*.

Tap Local Interview Resources. Investigate campus resources such as the directory, student guide, Web page, departmental faculty lists, student activity officers and sponsors, recent yearbook photographs, stories from the newspaper archives, or facilities such as the theater, media, or sports centers. Look for students, staff, or faculty with intriguing backgrounds or experiences. Campuses and libraries often maintain lists or databases of local authorities, researchers, and authors available for press contacts or expert advice. Identify several prospects in case your first choice isn't available.

Set Up an Interview. Find out whether your prospect will grant an interview, talk at length—an hour, say—and agree to appear in your paper. If you sense reluctance, your wisest course is to find another subject.

Don't be timid about asking for an interview. After all, your request is flattering, acknowledging that person as someone with valuable things to say. Try to schedule the interview on your subject's own ground—his or her home or workplace. The details you observe in those surroundings can make your essay more vivid.

Prepare Questions. The interview will go better if you are an informed interviewer with prepared questions. Find out a bit about your subject's life history, experience, affiliations, and interests, and then work on your questions. Ask about the person's background, everyday tasks, favorite activities, and hopes to encourage your subject to open up. Asking for a little imagining may elicit a revealing response. (If your house were on fire, what would you try to save? If you had your life to live over, what would you do differently?)

You can't find out everything about someone, but you can focus on whatever aspects best reveal his or her personality. Good questions will help you lead the conversation where you want it to go, get it back on track when it strays, and avoid awkward silences. For example, to interview someone with an unusual job or hobby, you might ask questions like these:

- How long have you been a park ranger?
- How did you get involved in this work?
- How have you learned about the physical features and ecological balance in your park?
- What happens in a typical day? What do you like most or least?
- How has this job changed your life or your concerns?
- What are your plans and hopes for the future?

One good question can get some people talking for hours, and four or five may be enough for any interview, but it's better to prepare too many than too few. You can easily skip any that seem irrelevant during the interview. Simply listening and responding may encourage genuine communication.

Peer Response Preparing Questions for an Interview

Ask a classmate to read the questions you plan to use in your interview and then to respond to the following:

- Are the questions appropriate for the person who will be interviewed?
- Will the questions help gather the information you are seeking?
- Are any of the questions unclear? How could you rephrase them?
- Do any of the questions seem redundant? Irrelevant?
- What additional questions might you ask?

Be Flexible and Observant. Sometimes a question won't interest your subject as much as you hoped. Or the person may seem reluctant to answer, especially if you're unwittingly trespassing into private territory, such as someone's love life. Don't badger. If you wait silently for a bit, you might be rewarded. If not, just go on to the next question. Anytime the conversation drifts, you can always steer it back: "But to get back to what you were saying about . . ."

Sometimes the most rewarding question simply grows out of what the subject says or an item you note in the environment. Observing your subject's clothing, expressions, mannerisms, and equipment may also suggest unexpected facets of personality. For example, Ryan-Hines describes Joan Gilmore's appearance as she introduces her character.

For more on using observation, see Ch. 5.

Decide How to Record the Interview. Many interviewers use only paper and pen or pencil to take notes unobtrusively. Even though they can't write down everything the person says, they want to look the subject in the eye and keep the conversation lively. As you take notes, be sure to record or sketch details on the scene—names and dates, numbers, addresses, surroundings, physical appearance. Also jot down memorable words just as the speaker says them. Put quotation marks around them so that when you transcribe your notes later, you will know that they are quoted directly.

A telephone or an e-mail interview sounds easy but lacks the lively interplay you can achieve face-to-face. You'll miss observing the subject's possessions, which so often reveal personality, or seeing your subject's smiles, frowns, or other body language. Meet in person if possible.

Many professionals advise against using a recorder because it may inhibit the subject and make the interviewer lazy about concentrating on the subject's responses. Too often, the objections go, it tempts the interviewer simply to quote the rambling conversation from the recording without shaping it into good writing. If you do bring a recorder to your interview, be sure that the person you're talking with has no objections. Arm yourself with a pad of paper and a pen or pencil just in case the recorder malfunctions. Perhaps the best practice is to record the interview but at the same time take notes. Write down the main points, and use your recording as a backup when you need to check quotations for accuracy or include more words from the interview.

As soon as the interview ends, rush to the nearest desk, and write down everything you remember but couldn't record. The questions you prepared for the interview will guide your memory, as will notes you took while talking.

Learning by Doing 🎙 Transcribing Your Interview Notes

After your interview, follow the lead of reporters and other interviewers who routinely store digital conversations. If you recorded the interview, try to type out the exact conversation. If you took notes, type as much of the interview as possible from them. If you have both, combine them in one file, but use bold for your notes so you don't confuse them with direct quotations from the recording. Save this record of your original research—the complete, unedited transcript and your notes—with a descriptive name. If you use voice recognition software such as Dragon Naturally Speaking, you may save typing time by reading aloud your notes and by restating each of your subject's comments on the tape if the software does not recognize the second voice. Begin your draft in a new file so that you do not change or lose any of your interview record. Check your record for accuracy when you summarize; copy and paste from it when you quote, adding quotation marks to show exact words from the interview.

Planning, Drafting, and Developing

After your interview, you may have a good notion of what to include in your first draft, what to emphasize, what to quote directly, what to summarize. But if your notes seem a confused jumble, what should you do?

For more strategies for planning, drafting, and developing, see Chs. 20, 21, and 22.

Evaluate Your Material. Remember your purpose: to reveal your subject's character and personality through conversation. Start by listing details you're likely to include. As you sift your material, you may find these questions useful:

> What part of the conversation gave you the most insight into your subject's character and circumstances?
>
> Which direct quotations reveal the most about your subject? Which are the most amusing, pithy, witty, surprising, or outrageous?
>
> Which objects in the subject's environment provide you with valuable clues about his or her interests?
>
> What, if anything, did your subject's body language reveal? Did it suggest discomfort, pride, self-confidence, shyness, pomposity?
>
> What did tone or gestures tell you about the person's state of mind?
>
> How can you summarize your subject's character or personality?
>
> Does one theme run through your material? If so, what is it?

Photographs, sketches, or your own doodles also may help you clarify the dominant impression and main emphases for your paper.

Focus Your Thesis on a Dominant Impression. Most successful portraits focus on a single dominant impression of the interview subject.

For more on stating a thesis, see pp. 401–10.

DOMINANT IMPRESSION	Del talked a lot about the freedom of the press.
WORKING THESIS	Del Sampat is a true believer in the freedom of the press.

For exercises on choosing effective thesis statements, visit **< bedfordstmartins .com/bedguide>**.

If you have lots of material and if, as often happens, your conversation rambled, you may want to develop the dominant impression by emphasizing just a few things about your subject—personality traits, views on particular topics, or shaping influences. To find such a focus, try grouping your details in three layers of notes, following the pattern in the graphic below:

1. Dominant Impression   ☐
2. Main Emphases   ☐   ☐
     points about traits, views, influences
3. Supporting Details   ☐   ☐   ☐   ☐   ☐
     quotations, reported words, description

Learning by Doing 🎙 Stating a Dominant Impression

How would you characterize in one sentence the person you interviewed? What single main impression do you want to convey? Specify your ideas by completing this sentence: My dominant impression of _____ is _____.
Share your sentence with a classmate or small group, either in person or online. Respond to each other's sentences to help each writer achieve a sentence that is both thoughtful and clear.

For more on selecting and presenting quotations, see D3 (p. A-27) and D6 (p. A-29) in the Quick Research Guide. For more on using visuals, see pp. 366–68.

Bring Your Subject to Life for Your Audience. At the beginning of your paper, can you immediately frame the person you interviewed? A quotation, a bit of physical description, a portrait of your subject at home or at work can bring the person instantly to life in your reader's mind. If your instructor approves adding an image, consider where to place it so that it supplements your text but does not overshadow your essay.

When you quote directly, be as accurate as possible, and don't put into quotation marks anything your subject didn't say. Sometimes you may want to quote a whole sentence or more, sometimes just a phrase. Keep evaluating your quotations until they all convey the essence of your subject.

Double-Check Important Information. You may find that you can't read your hasty handwriting or that some crucial bit of information escaped when you were taking notes. In such a case, telephone or e-mail the person you interviewed to ask specific questions without taking much time. You may also want to read back to your subject any direct quotations you intend to use so that he or she can confirm their accuracy.

Revising and Editing

For more revising and editing strategies, see Ch. 23.

As you read over your first draft, keep in mind that your purpose was to make the person you interviewed come alive for your reader.

Peer Response 👥 Interviewing a Subject

For general questions for a peer editor, see p. 465. For peer response worksheets, visit **<bedfordstmartins .com/bedguide>**.

Have a classmate or friend read your draft and suggest how to make the portrait more vivid, complete, and clear. Ask your peer editor to answer questions such as these about writing from an interview:

- Does the essay opening make you want to know the person portrayed? If so, how has the writer interested you? If not, what gets in your way?
- What seems to make the person interviewed interesting to the writer?
- What is the writer's dominant impression of the person interviewed?

- Does the writer include any details that contradict or are unrelated to the dominant impression or insight?
- Do the quoted words or reported speech "sound" real to you? Do any quotations seem at odds with the dominant impression of the person?
- Would you drop any conversation the writer used? If so, mark it.
- Do you have questions about the subject that aren't answered?
- If this paper were yours, what is the one thing you would be sure to work on before handing it in?

Focus on Your Main Idea or Thesis. Once you have finished a draft, you may still feel swamped by too much information. Will readers find your essay overloaded? Will they understand the dominant impression you want to convey about the person you have interviewed? To be certain that they will, first polish and refine your thesis.

WORKING THESIS   Del Sampat is a true believer in the freedom of the press.

REVISED THESIS   Del Sampat, news editor for the *Campus Times,* sees every story he writes as an opportunity to exercise and defend the freedom of the press.

Learning by Doing 🔘 Screening Your Details

Using your revised thesis as a guide, look again at the quotations and other details in your draft. Keep only those that support your thesis and enhance the dominant impression. Drop the others, even if they are vivid or catchy. Then select a passage from your draft—perhaps one that still seems slightly off track—and ask for an opinion from a classmate as you decide whether all the details in the passage strengthen the dominant impression expressed in your thesis.

For exercises on supporting a thesis, visit **<bedfordstmartins.com/bedguide>**.

REVISION CHECKLIST

☐ Are the details focused on a dominant impression you want to emphasize? Are all of them relevant? How do you convey the impression to readers?

☐ How do the parts of the conversation you've reported reveal the subject's unique personality, character, mood, or concerns?

☐ Should your paper have a stronger beginning? Is your ending satisfactory?

☐ Should some quotations be summarized or indirectly quoted? Should some explanation be enlivened by adding specific quotations?

□ When the direct quotations are read out loud, do they sound as if they're from the mouth of the person you're portraying?

□ Where might you need to add revealing details about the person's surroundings, personal appearance, or mannerisms?

□ Have you included your own pertinent observations and insights?

□ Does any of your material strike you now as irrelevant or dull?

For more editing and proofreading strategies, see pp. 473–76.

For more help, find the relevant checklist sections in the Quick Editing Guide on p. A-36. Turn also to the Quick Format Guide beginning on p. A-1.

After you have revised your essay, edit and proofread it. Carefully check the grammar, word choice, punctuation, and mechanics — and then correct any problems you find.

EDITING CHECKLIST

□ Is it clear what each pronoun refers to so that the *he*'s, *she*'s, and *they*'s are not confusing? Does each pronoun agree with (match) its antecedent?   A6

□ Have you used the correct case (*he* or *him*) for all your pronouns?   A5

□ Is your sentence structure correct? Have you avoided writing fragments, comma splices, or fused sentences?   A1, A2

□ Have you used quotation marks, ellipses (to show the omission of words), and other punctuation correctly in all your quotations?   C3

Additional Writing Assignments

1. Interview someone from whom you can learn, possibly someone whose profession interests you or whose advice can help you solve a problem or make a decision. Your purpose will be to communicate what you have learned, not to characterize the person you interview.

2. Write a paper based on an interview with at least two members of your extended family about some incident that is part of your family lore. Direct your paper to younger relatives. If accounts of the event don't always agree, combine them into one vivid account, noting that some details may be more trustworthy than others. Give credit to your sources.

3. Briefly talk with fifteen or twenty students on your campus to find out what careers they are preparing for. What are their reasons for their choices? Are they feeling uncertain about a career, pursuing the one they have always wanted, or changing careers for better employment options? Are most looking for a career that pays well or one that offers personal satisfaction? Write a short essay summing up what you find out. Provide some quotations to flesh out your survey. From the information you have gathered, characterize your classmates. Are they materialists? Idealists? Practical people? (Ask your instructor if any campus permission is needed before you begin these interviews.)

4. With your whole class or a small group, collaborate to interview someone on campus or from the local community with special knowledge or expertise about a matter that concerns the group. Plan the interview by working together to resolve these questions:

> What do you want to find out? What lines of questioning will you pursue? What topic will each student ask about? How much time will each group member have to ask a series of questions? Who will record the interview (if your subject agrees)? Who will take notes (as your record or your backup)?

Preview each other's questions to avoid duplication. Ask open-ended, rather than yes/no, questions to encourage discussion. Your group's product can be many individual papers or one collaborative effort (such as a paper, an online threaded discussion, or a blog), as your instructor directs.

5. With the approval of your instructor, plan an individual or collaborative interview project with a possible public outcome — an article for the campus newspaper or alumni magazine, a page for the course Web site, a podcast for the campus radio station, a multimodal presentation for future students (combining written text with audio clips or photographs), or some other option that you or your group have the expertise to prepare. Once this project is planned and approved, analyze the purpose and audience of the proposed outlet; select someone on campus to interview whose knowledge or experience might assist or intrigue its audience. Develop your questions, conduct your interview, and present it. Stay focused on sharing the subject's expertise with your audience.

6. **Visual Assignment.** Select one of the photographs on pages 114–15 to explore the experience of an interview from the standpoint not of what is spoken but of what is communicated through expression, body language, clothing, environment, and other nonverbal cues that can be captured in an image. Use your careful analysis of the photograph to support your thesis about the interview relationship it portrays.

7 Comparing and Contrasting

Responding to an Image

The large photograph of the young couple was taken at Woodstock in August 1969 and then featured on the cover for the album and the poster for the movie that recorded the event. The smaller insert, taken before the event's fortieth anniversary, shows the same couple, Nick and Bobbi Ercoline, now married for decades. Examine the two photographs carefully, noting similarities and differences. What does each image convey about its era? What does each convey about the couple, whether age twenty or sixty?

What qualities made the original image iconic? What similar or different qualities are captured in the more recent image?

Which city—Dallas or Atlanta—has more advantages and more drawbacks for a young single person thinking of settling down to a career? Which of two advertisements for the same toy appeals more effectively to parents who want to get durability as well as educational value for their money? As singers and songwriters, how are Beyoncé Knowles and Taylor Swift similar and dissimilar? Such questions invite answers that set two subjects side by side.

When you compare, you point out similarities; when you contrast, you discuss differences. When you write about two complicated subjects, usually you will need to do both. Considering Mozart and Bach, you might find that each has traits the other has—or lacks. Instead of concluding that one is great and the other inferior, you might conclude that they're two distinct composers, each with an individual style. On the other hand, if your main purpose is to judge between two subjects (as when you'd recommend moving either to Dallas or to Atlanta), you would look especially for positive and negative features, weigh the attractions and faults of each city, and then stick your neck out and make your choice.

Why Comparing and Contrasting Matter

In a College Course

- You compare and contrast to "evaluate" the relative merits of Norman Rockwell and N. C. Wyeth in an art history course or the relative accuracy of two Civil War Web sites for a history course.
- You compare and contrast to "describe" a little-known subject, such as medieval funeral customs, by setting it next to a similar yet familiar subject, such as modern funeral traditions.

In the Workplace

- You compare and contrast your company's products or services with those of competitors, just as your experience, education, and personal attributes were compared and contrasted with those of others before you were hired.

In Your Community

- You compare and contrast your options in choosing a financial aid package, cell phone contract, childcare provider, bike helmet, or new mayor.

❓ What are some instances when you compare or contrast products, services, opportunities, options, solutions, or other things? When might you use comparison, contrast, or both in your writing? What would you expect them to contribute?

Learning from Other Writers

In this chapter you will be asked to write a paper setting two subjects side by side, comparing and contrasting them. Let's see how two other writers have used these familiar habits of thought in writing. To help you begin to analyze the first reading, look at the notes in the margin. They identify features such as the thesis, or main idea, the sequence of the broad subjects considered, and the specific points of comparison and contrast.

For more examples of writing based on comparing and contrasting, visit <**bedfordstmartins .com/bedguide**>.

As You Read These Comparisons and Contrasts

As you read these essays, ask yourself the following questions:

1. What two (or more) items are compared and contrasted? Does the writer use comparison only? Contrast only? A combination of the two? Why?

2. What is the purpose of the comparison and contrast? What idea does the information support or refute?

3. How does the writer organize the essay? Why?

Suzanne Britt

Neat People vs. Sloppy People

Suzanne Britt takes a lighthearted look at neat and sloppy people in this selection from her essay collection *Show and Tell* (1983).

Introduction

THESIS
Setting up subjects

Subject A

Point 1

Point 2

I've finally figured out the difference between neat people and sloppy people. The distinction is, as always, moral. Neat people are lazier and meaner than sloppy people.

Sloppy people, you see, are not really sloppy. Their sloppiness is merely the unfortunate consequence of their extreme moral rectitude.° Sloppy people carry in their mind's eye a heavenly vision, a precise plan, that is so stupendous, so perfect, it can't be achieved in this world or the next.

Sloppy people live in Never-Never Land. Someday is their métier.° Someday they are planning to alphabetize all their books and set up home catalogs. Someday they will go through their wardrobes and mark certain items for tentative mending and certain items for passing on to relatives of similar shape and size. Someday sloppy people will make family scrapbooks into which they will put newspaper clippings, postcards, locks of hair, and the dried corsage from their senior prom. Someday they will file everything on the surface of their desks, including the cash receipts from coffee purchases

1

2

3

---

rectitude: Correctness, decency.   **métier:** Trade, specialty.

at the snack shop. Someday they will sit down and read all the back issues of *The New Yorker*.

For all these noble reasons and more, sloppy people never get neat. They aim too high and wide. They save everything, planning someday to file, order, and straighten out the world. But while these ambitious plans take clearer and clearer shape in their heads, the books spill from the shelves onto the floor, the clothes pile up in the hamper and closet, the family mementos accumulate in every drawer, the surface of the desk is buried under mounds of paper, and the unread magazines threaten to reach the ceiling.   4

The messy desk of Albert Einstein, 1955.

Sloppy people can't bear to part with anything. They give loving attention to every detail. When sloppy people say they're going to tackle the surface of a desk, they really mean it. Not a paper will go unturned; not a rubber band will go unboxed. Four hours or two weeks into the excavation, the desk looks exactly the same, primarily because the sloppy person is meticulously creating new piles of papers with new headings and scrupulously stopping to read all the old book catalogs before he throws them away. A neat person would just bulldoze the desk.   5

Exaggeration to make a point and add humor

Neat people are bums and clods at heart. They have cavalier° attitudes toward possessions, including family heirlooms. Everything is just another dust-catcher to them. If anything collects dust, it's got to go and that's that. Neat people will toy with the idea of throwing the children out of the house just to cut down on the clutter.   6

Neat people don't care about process. They like results. What they want to do is get the whole thing over with so they can sit down and watch the rasslin' on TV. Neat people operate on two unvarying principles: Never handle any item twice, and throw everything away.   7

The only thing messy in a neat person's house is the trash can. The minute something comes to a neat person's hand, he will look at it, try to decide if it has immediate use and, finding none, throw it in the trash.   8

Neat people are especially vicious with mail. They never go through their mail unless they are standing directly over a trash can. If the trash can is beside the mailbox, even better. All ads, catalogs, pleas for charitable contributions, church bulletins, and money-saving coupons go straight into the trash can without being opened. All letters from home, postcards from Europe, bills, and paychecks are opened, immediately responded to, then dropped in the trash can. Neat people keep their receipts only for tax purposes. That's it. No sentimental salvaging of birthday cards or the last letter a dying relative ever wrote. Into the trash it goes.   9

cavalier: Dismissive.

Neat people place neatness above everything, even economics. They are   10
incredibly wasteful. Neat people throw away several toys every time they walk
through the den. I knew a neat person once who threw away a perfectly good
dish drainer because it had mold on it. The drainer was too much trouble to
wash. And neat people sell their furniture when they move. They will sell a
Another exaggeration for effect La-Z-Boy recliner while you are reclining in it.

Neat people are no good to borrow from. Neat people buy everything in   11
expensive little single portions. They get their flour and sugar in two-pound
bags. They wouldn't consider clipping a coupon, saving a leftover, reusing
plastic nondairy whipped cream containers, or rinsing off tin foil and drap-
ing it over the unmoldy dish drainer. You can never borrow a neat person's
newspaper to see what's playing at the movies. Neat people have the paper all
wadded up and in the trash by 7:05 A.M.

Neat people cut a clean swath° through the organic as well as the inor-   12
ganic world. People, animals, and things are all one to them. They are so in-
Concluding exaggeration for effect sensitive. After they've finished with the pantry, the medicine cabinet, and
the attic, they will throw out the red geranium (too many leaves), sell the dog
(too many fleas), and send the children off to boarding school (too many
scuff marks on the hardwood floors).

Questions to Start You Thinking

Meaning

1. Does Britt favor one group over the other? Which details or statements
   support your response?

2. Based on the details presented here, to which group do you belong?
   What specific details describe you most accurately?

3. What is Britt's purpose in contrasting neat people and sloppy people?
   Is her goal to explain or to convince? Or is it something else?

Writing Strategies

4. In the introductory paragraph, Britt jumps right into the essay. Is that
   technique effective? How else might she have begun her essay?

5. Which method of organization does Britt use to arrange her essay?
   How effectively does she switch between her two subjects of "sloppy"
   and "neat"?

6. From reading this essay, are readers to assume that "sloppy" and "neat"
   people have nothing in common? Why?

swath: Path.

Tim Chabot

Take Me Out to the Ball Game, but Which One?

Student Tim Chabot compares and contrasts baseball and basketball, asking which deserves the title of America's national pastime.

For much of the twentieth century, baseball has been considered the national [1] pastime of the United States. Hank Aaron, home runs, and hot dogs seem as American as Thanksgiving. Many American presidents, from Eisenhower to Obama, have participated in the tradition of a celebrity throwing out the first ball on opening day of a new baseball season. But beginning in the 1990s, baseball stars were being eclipsed by the stars of another game invented in America—basketball. Some argue that Michael Jordan and Shaquille O'Neal, basketball greats and household names, are more famous than any current pitcher or home run king. This shift has raised a question in the minds of many: Should baseball continue to be considered our national pastime, or should basketball take its place?

❓ Why do you think the writer raises this question here?

Both sports are very popular with American sports fans. In addition, both games [2] attract fans of all races—white, African American, Asian American, Hispanic—and all classes, rich and poor, educated and uneducated. Baseball has become a national treasure through its appeal to a wide, wide audience. At a Saturday afternoon game, men, women, grandparents, and kids of all ages wait to catch a fly ball. The appeal of basketball is growing, the sport having become popular in urban and rural areas, on high school and college campuses. Both sports are played in quite a variety of locations. Baseball games occur on neighborhood sandlots as well as official diamonds. Basketball requires little space and equipment, so pickup basketball games occur in almost every neighborhood park and virtually anywhere that a hoop can be rigged up.

Although both sports are popular with American fans, attending a baseball game [3] is quite different from attending a basketball game. Baseball is a family-oriented spectator sport. Because of the widely diverse baseball fans with varied attention spans, attending a baseball game is like going to an open-air carnival, and the game itself is only one of the many spectacles. If fans are bored with the game, they can listen to the vendors hawking ice cream, watch a fight brewing in the bleacher seats, stand in line to buy peanuts or hot dogs, participate in "the wave," or just bask in the sun. Only diehard fans keep a constant eye on the game itself, because there are frequent breaks in the play.

❓ Do you agree with the analogy between baseball and an "open-air carnival"?

In contrast, the central spectacle of any basketball arena is definitely the game [4] itself. Few distractions to entertain a casual fan occur, except for cheerleaders for college teams. Basketball arenas are always indoors, and the games are usually at night, creating an atmosphere that is urban and adult. The constant motion of the sport rivets° attention to the game itself. Attending a basketball game can be

rivets: Commands or fixes attention to.

❓ What other differences in attending the games come to mind?

compared to an exciting night on the town, while watching a baseball game is like relaxing with the family in the backyard.

The pace of the two games is also quite different. The leisurely pace of a base-ball game contributes to its popularity because it offers relaxation to harried Americans. Each batter may spend several minutes at the plate, hit a few foul balls, and reach a full count of three balls and two strikes before getting on base, hitting a routine pop fly, or striking out. While batters slow things down by stepping out of the box to practice their swing, pitchers stall the play by "holding the runners on" to prevent stolen bases. The substitution of relief pitchers suspends the game and gives spectators an opportunity to purchase junk food or memorabilia. In games in which star pitchers duel, the audience may see only a few men on base in nine innings and a very low score. Also, the tradition of the seventh-inning stretch underscores baseball's appeal to a person who wants to take it easy and relax. 5

On the other hand, the quick pace of basketball has contributed to its popularity in our fast-paced society. Players run down the court at sometimes exhausting speed for a "fast break," successful baskets can occur merely seconds apart, each team may score as many as one hundred points a game, and the ball changes sides hundreds of times, as opposed to every half-inning in baseball. Games can be won or lost in the few seconds before the final buzzer. Basketball players are always in motion, much like American society. The pounding excitement of basketball appeals to people who play hard as well as work hard. 6

These two sports require different athletic abilities from the players. Although baseball games are slow-paced, the sport places a premium on athletic precision and therefore showcases strategy and skill rather than brute physical strength. The choice of a pitch, the decision to bunt or to steal a base, and the order of batters are all careful strategic moves that could affect the outcome of the whole game. Baseball has been called the "thinking person's game" because of its emphasis on statistics and probabilities. Although mental strategy and dexterity° are emphasized, physical strength is important, too. A strong arm obviously increases the power of a player's throw or of his swing, and speed is essential in running bases. But intimidating physical ability is not necessarily a required element to become a major league player, and even out-of-shape players can become stars if their bats are hot. The importance of skill over brawn has contributed to baseball's popularity not merely as a spectator sport but also as a sport in which millions of Americans participate, from Little League to neighborhood leagues for adults. 7

❓ Do you agree that baseball requires "skill" and basketball "brawn"?

Unlike baseball, basketball emphasizes physical power, stamina, and size since jumping high, running fast, and just being tall with long legs and big hands usually contribute to a player's success. Skill and dexterity are certainly necessary in executing a slam dunk or dribbling past a double team, but these skills are usually 8

dexterity: Skill in using the hands or body.

combined with physical strength. In order to be a successful rebounder, a player needs to be extremely aggressive and occasionally commit fouls. Many more injuries occur on basketball courts than on baseball fields. Perhaps the physical power and intimidation required in basketball have led to the media's focus on individual players' star qualities. Magic, Bird, Jordan, Shaq, and LeBron James are icons° who have taken the place of baseball stars of previous generations like Joe DiMaggio, Ted Williams, and Babe Ruth. Furthermore, in the international arena of the Olympics, basketball came to be seen as a symbol of American strength and power, as the 1992 Dream Team demolished all of its opponents.

If the rest of the world now equates basketball with America, should we consider   9
it to be our true national pastime? The increasing popularity of basketball seems to reflect the change in American society in the past few decades, a change to a more fast-paced and aggressive culture. But basketball doesn't yet appeal to as diverse an audience as does baseball, and thus it doesn't seem to deserve to be called a national phenomenon—yet. Until kids, women, and grandparents are as prevalent at a Lakers game as are young males, baseball will retain its title as the national pastime. But the exciting speed of basketball may soon have more appeal than the leisurely pace of baseball.

Why do you agree or disagree with this conclusion?

Questions to Start You Thinking

Meaning

1. In what specific ways does Chabot claim that baseball and basketball are similar? In what ways are these two sports different? Do the similarities outweigh the differences, or vice versa?

2. Can you think of other ways these two sports are similar and different?

3. Would you nominate another sport, say soccer or ice hockey, for the national pastime? If so, why?

Writing Strategies

4. Is Chabot's support for his comparison and contrast sufficient and balanced? Explain.

5. What transitional devices does Chabot use to indicate when he is comparing and when he is contrasting?

6. What is Chabot's thesis? Why does Chabot state it where he does?

7. Using highlighters or marginal notes, identify the essay's introduction, thesis, contrasting subjects, points of comparison and contrast, and conclusion. How effective is the organization of this essay?

icons: Images or symbols.

Learning by Writing

The Assignment: Comparing and Contrasting

For writing activities for comparing and contrasting, visit **<bedfordstmartins .com/bedguide>**.

Write a paper in which you compare and contrast two items to enlighten readers about both subjects. The specific points of similarity and difference will be important, but you will go beyond them to draw a conclusion from your analysis. This conclusion, your thesis, needs to be more than "point A is different from point B" or "I prefer subject B to subject A." You will need to explain why you have drawn your conclusion. You'll also need to provide specific supporting evidence to explain your position and to convince your readers of its soundness. You may choose two people, two kinds of people, two places, two objects, two activities, or two ideas, but be sure to choose two you care about. You might write an impartial paper that distinctly portrays both subjects, or you might show why you favor one over the other.

These students found a clear reason for comparison and contrast:

An American student compared and contrasted her home life with that of her roommate, a student from Nigeria. Her goal was to deepen her understanding of Nigerian society and her own.

A student who was interested in history compared and contrasted civilian responses to the Vietnam and Iraq wars, considering how popular attitudes about military service had changed.

Another writer compared and contrasted facilities at two city parks, making a case for a revised funding formula.

Facing the Challenge   Comparing and Contrasting

The major challenge that writers face when comparing and contrasting two subjects is to determine their purpose. Writers who skip this step run the risk of having readers ask, "So, what's the point?" Suppose you develop brilliant points of similarity and difference between the films of Oliver Stone and those of Stanley Kubrick. Do you want to argue that one director is more skilled than the other? Or perhaps you want to show how they treat love or war differently in their films? Consider the following questions as you determine your primary purpose for comparing and contrasting:

■ Do you want to inform your readers about these two subjects in order to provide a better understanding of the two?

■ Do you want to persuade your readers that one of the two subjects is preferable to the other?

Asking what you want to demonstrate, discover, or prove *before* you begin to draft will help you to write a more effective comparison-and-contrast essay.

Generating Ideas

Find Two Subjects. Pick subjects you can compare and contrast purposefully. An examination question may give them to you, ready-made: "Compare and contrast ancient Roman sculpture with that of the ancient Greeks." But suppose you have to find your subjects for yourself. You'll need to choose things that have a sensible basis for comparison, a common element.

For strategies for generating ideas, see Ch. 19.

> moon rocks + stars = no common element
>
> Dallas + Atlanta = cities to consider settling in
>
> Larry King + Oprah Winfrey = television talk-show personalities

Besides having a common element, the subjects should have enough in common to compare but differ enough to throw each other into sharp relief.

> sports cars + racing cars = common element + telling differences
>
> sports cars + oil tankers = limited common element + unpromising differences

Try generating a list or brainstorming. Recall what you've recently read, discussed, or spotted on the Web. Let your mind skitter around in search of pairs that go together, or play the game of *free association*, jotting down a word and whatever it brings to mind: *Democrats? Republicans. New York? Los Angeles. MySpace? Facebook.* Or try the following questions:

DISCOVERY CHECKLIST

☐ Do you know two people who are strikingly different in attitude or behavior (perhaps your parents or two brothers, two friends, two teachers)?

☐ Can you think of two groups that are both alike and different (perhaps two teams, two clubs, two sets of relatives)?

☐ Have you taken two courses that were quite different but both valuable?

☐ Do you prefer one of two places where you have lived or visited?

☐ Can you recall two events in your life that shared similar aspects but turned out to be quite different (perhaps two sporting events, two romances, two vacations, the births of two children, an event then and now)?

☐ Can you compare and contrast two holidays or two family customs?

☐ Are you familiar with two writers, two artists, or two musicians who seem to have similar goals but quite different accomplishments?

Once you have a list of pairs, put a star by those that seem promising. Ask yourself what similarities immediately come to mind. What differences?

Can you jot down several of each? Are these striking, significant similarities and differences? If not, move on until you discover a workable pair.

Limit the Scope of Your Paper. If you propose to compare and contrast Japanese literature and American literature in 750 words, your task is probably impossible. But to cut down the size of this subject, you might compare and contrast, say, a haiku of Bashō about a snake with a short poem about a snake by Emily Dickinson. This topic you could cover adequately in 750 words.

Explore Each Member of Your Pair to Build Support. As you examine your two subjects, your goal is twofold. You want to analyze each using a similar approach so that you have a reasonable basis for comparison and contrast. You also want to find the details and examples that you'll need to support your points. Consider these sources of support:

For more on interviewing, see Ch. 6.

For advice on finding a few useful sources, turn to B1–B2 in the Quick Research Guide, pp. A-23–A-24. For more on using sources for support, see Ch. 12.

■ Two events, processes, procedures	Ask a reporter's questions—5 *W*'s (who, what, where, when, why) and an *H* (how).
■ Two events from the past	Using the same questions, interview someone present at each event, or read news or other accounts.
■ Two perceptions (public and private)	Interview someone behind the scenes; read or listen to contrasting views.
■ Two approaches or viewpoints	Browse online for Web sites or pages that supply different examples.
■ Two policies or options	Look for articles reporting studies or government statistics.

Learning by Doing 🖉 Making a Comparison-and-Contrast Table

After deciding what to compare, write down what you know about subject A and then subject B. Next, divide a page or use your computer menu to create a table with three columns (up and down) and at least half a dozen rows (across). Use the first row to label the columns:

Categories	Subject A	Subject B

Now read over your notes on subject A. When you spot related details, identify a logical category for them, and enter that category name in the left column of the second row. Then add the related details for subject A in the middle column. Repeat this process, labeling more rows as categories and filling in corresponding details for subject A. (Draw more lines, or use the table menu to add new rows as needed.)

   Next, review your notes on subject B. If some details fall into categories already listed in your table, add those details in the subject B column for each category. If new categories emerge, add them in new rows along with the subject B details. After you finish with your notes, round out the table—adding details to fill in empty cells, combining or adding categories. Select the most promising categories from your table as common features for logical comparison and contrast in your essay.

Planning, Drafting, and Developing

As you start planning your paper, be prepared to cover both subjects in a similar fashion. Return to your table or make a scratch outline so that you can refine your points of comparison or contrast, consolidate supporting details, and spot gaps in your information. Remind yourself of your goal in comparing and contrasting the two subjects. What is it you want to show, argue, or find out?

For more on planning, drafting, and developing, see Chs. 20, 21, and 22.

State Your Purpose in a Thesis. You need a reason to place two subjects side by side—a reason that you and your audience will find compelling and worthwhile. Ask yourself if you prefer one subject in the pair over the other. What reasons can you give for your preference? It's also all right not to have a preference; you can try instead to understand both subjects more clearly, making a point about each or both. Comparing and contrasting need not be a meaningless exercise. Try instead to think clearly and pointedly in order to explain an idea about which you care.

For more on stating a thesis, see pp. 401–10.

TWO SUBJECTS	two teaching styles in required biology courses
REASON	to show why one style is better
WORKING THESIS	Although students learn a lot in both of the required introductory biology courses, one class teaches information and the other teaches how to be a good learner.

For exercises on choosing and supporting effective thesis statements, visit **<bedfordstmartins .com/bedguide>**.

Learning by Doing 📷 Pinpointing Your Purpose

Following the model above on teaching styles, specify your two subjects, identify your reason for comparing, and state your working thesis, making it as pointed as you can. To learn how others react to your purpose, exchange statements with a classmate or small group in person or online. Discuss possibilities for increasing clarity and purposefulness.

Select a Pattern to Help Your Audience Follow Your Evidence. Besides understanding your purpose and thesis, readers also need to follow your supporting evidence—the clusters of details that reveal the nature of each subject you consider. They're likely to expect you to follow one of two ways to organize a comparison-and-contrast essay.

OPPOSING PATTERN, SUBJECT BY SUBJECT	ALTERNATING PATTERN, POINT BY POINT
Subject A	Point 1
Point 1	Subject A
Point 2	Subject B
Point 3	
	Point 2
Subject B	Subject A
Point 1	Subject B
Point 2	
Point 3	Point 3
	Subject A
	Subject B

Although both patterns present the same information, each has its own advantages and disadvantages.

Use the Opposing Pattern of Organization. When you use the opposing pattern of subject by subject, you state all your observations about subject A and then do the same for subject B. In the following paragraph from *Whole Brain Thinking* (New York: William Morrow, 1984), Jacquelyn Wonder and Priscilla Donovan use the opposing pattern of organization to explain the differences in the brains of females and males.

Subject A: Female brain

Point 1: Development
Point 2: Consequences
Shift to subject B:
Male brain

Point 1: Development
Point 2: Consequences

> At birth there are basic differences between male and female brains. The female cortex is more fully developed. The sound of the human voice elicits more left-brain activity in infant girls than in infant boys, accounting in part for the earlier development in females of language. Baby girls have larger connectors between the brain's hemispheres and thus integrate information more skillfully. This flexibility bestows greater verbal and intuitive skills. Male infants lack this ready communication between the brain's lobes; therefore, messages are routed and rerouted to the right brain, producing larger right hemispheres. The size advantage accounts for males having greater spatial and physical abilities and explains why they may become more highly lateralized and skilled in specific areas.

For a single paragraph or a short essay, the opposing pattern can effectively unify all the details about each subject, like neat versus sloppy people in Suzanne Britt's essay. For a long essay or a complicated subject, it has a drawback: readers might find it difficult to remember all the separate information about subject A while reading about subject B.

Use the Alternating Pattern of Organization. There's a better way to organize most longer papers: the *alternating pattern* of *point by point*. Using this method, you take up one point at a time, applying it first to one subject and then the other. Tim Chabot uses this pattern to lead the reader along clearly and carefully, looking at each subject before moving on to the next point. His outline might have looked like this:

THESIS: The exciting speed of basketball may soon have more appeal than the leisurely pace of baseball.

I.   Similarities of fans
    A.   Appeal to diverse groups
       1.   Baseball
       2.   Basketball
    B.   Varied locations
       1.   Baseball
       2.   Basketball

II.   Difference in atmosphere at game
    A.   Baseball as a diverse family-oriented spectator sport
       1.   Many distractions
       2.   Frequent breaks in play
    B.   Basketball as game-focused sport
       1.   Few distractions
       2.   Constant game activity

III.   Difference in pace of game
    A.   Leisurely pace of baseball
       1.   Slow batters
       2.   Stalling pitchers
       3.   Substitution of relief pitchers
       4.   Low score
       5.   Seventh-inning stretch
    B.   Quick pace of basketball
       1.   Fast players
       2.   High scores
       3.   Frequent changes of sides
       4.   Constant motion

IV.   Different athletic abilities of players
    A.   Baseball as a mental game
       1.   Emphasis on athletic precision
          a.   Strategy
          b.   Skill
          c.   Decision making
       2.   Physical strength less important

Fans with a portable generator watch the All-Star Game at San Diego's Jack Murphy Stadium.

LeBron James, Shaquille O'Neal, and Kobe Bryant in action.

    B. Basketball as a physical game
      1. Emphasis on physical power
        a. Jumping high
        b. Running fast
        c. Being tall and big
        d. Being aggressive
      2. Importance of skill and dexterity

For more on outlines, see pp. 413–21. For Tim Chabot's full paper, see pp. 121–23.

Add Transitions. Once your essay is organized, you can bring cohesion to it through effective transitional words and phrases — *on the other hand, in contrast, also, both, yet, although, finally, unlike.* Your choice of wording will depend on the content, but keep it varied and smooth. Jarring, choppy transitions distract attention instead of contributing to a unified essay, each part working to support a meaningful thesis.

For more on transitions, see pp. 433–37.

Learning by Doing 📷 Building Cohesion with Transitions

Working on paper or in a file, add color highlights to mark each transitional expression already in your draft. Then check any passages without much highlighting to decide whether your audience will need more cues to see how your ideas connect. Next, check each spot where you switch from one subject or point to another to be sure that readers can easily make the shift. Finally, smooth out the wording of your transitions so that they are clear and helpful, not repetitious or mechanical. Test your changes on a reader by exchanging drafts with a classmate.

Revising and Editing

Focus on Your Thesis. Reconsider your purpose when you review your draft. If your purpose is to illuminate two subjects impartially, ask whether you have given readers a balanced view. Obviously it would be unfair to set forth all the advantages of Oklahoma City and all the disadvantages of Honolulu and then conclude that Oklahoma City is superior on every count.

For more on revising and editing strategies, see Ch. 23.

Of course, if you love Oklahoma City and can't stand Honolulu, or vice versa, go ahead: don't be balanced; take a stand. Even so, you will want to include the same points about each city and to admit, in all honesty, that Oklahoma City has its faults. One useful way to check for balance or thoroughness is to outline your draft and give the outline a critical look.

Peer Response 👥 Comparing and Contrasting

You may want a classmate or friend to respond to your draft, suggesting how to present your two subjects more clearly. Ask your peer editor to answer questions like these about comparison and contrast:

For general questions for a peer editor, see p. 465.

- How does the introduction motivate you to read the entire essay?
- What is the point of the comparison and contrast of the two subjects? Is the thesis stated in the essay, or is it implied?
- Is the essay organized by the opposing pattern or by the alternating pattern? Is the pattern appropriate, or would the other one work better?
- Are the same categories discussed for each item? If not, should they be?
- Are there enough details for you to understand the comparison and contrast? Put a check where more details or examples would be useful.
- If this paper were yours, what is the one thing you would be sure to work on before handing it in?

If classmates have made suggestions, perhaps about clearer wording to sharpen distinctions, use their ideas as you rework your thesis.

WORKING THESIS   Although students learn a lot in both of the required introductory biology courses, one class teaches information and the other teaches how to be a good learner.

REVISED THESIS   Although students learn the basics of biology in both of the required introductory courses, one class teaches how to memorize information and the other teaches an invaluable lesson: how to be an active learner.

Vary Your Wording. Make sure, as you go over your draft, that you have escaped a monotonous drone: A does this, B does that; A has these advantages, B has those. Comparison and contrast needn't result in a paper as symmetrical as a pair of sneakers. Revising and editing give you a chance to add lively details, transitions, dashes of color, and especially variety:

The menu is another major difference between the Cozy Cafe and the Wilton

Inn. For lunch, the Cozy Cafe offers sandwiches, hamburgers, and chili. ~~For~~ *L*unch, *at*

the Wilton Inn ~~offers~~ *features* dishes such as fajitas, shrimp salads, and onion soup topped

with Swiss cheese. ~~For dinner, the Cozy Cafe continues to serve the lunch menu and~~

~~adds~~ *adding* home-style comfort foods such as meatloaf, stew, macaroni and cheese, and

barbecued ribs. ~~By dinner,~~ *after five o'clock* the Wilton's specialties for the day are posted—perhaps

marinated buffalo steak or orange-pecan salmon.

REVISION CHECKLIST

☐ Does your introduction present your topic and main point clearly? Is it interesting enough to make a reader want to read the whole essay?

☐ Is your reason for doing all the comparing and contrasting unmistakably clear? What do you want to demonstrate, argue for, or find out? Do you need to reexamine your goal?

☐ Have you used the same categories for each item so that you treat them fairly? In discussing each feature, do you always look at the same thing?

☐ Have you selected points of comparison and supporting details that will intrigue, enlighten, and persuade your audience?

☐ What have you concluded about the two? Do you prefer one to the other? If so, is this preference (and your rationale for it) clear?

☐ Does your draft look thin at any point for lack of evidence? If so, how might you develop your ideas?

☐ Have you used the best possible arrangement, given your subject and your point?

☐ Are there any spots where you need to revise a boringly mechanical, monotonous style ("On one hand, . . . now on the other hand")?

For more editing and proofreading strategies, see pp. 473–76.

After you have revised your comparison-and-contrast essay, edit and proofread it. Carefully check the grammar, word choice, punctuation, and mechanics — and then correct any problems you may find.

For more help, find the relevant checklist sections in the Quick Editing Guide on p. A-36. Turn also to the Quick Format Guide beginning on p. A-1.

EDITING CHECKLIST

☐ Have you used the correct comparative forms (for two things) and superlative forms (for three or more) for adjectives and adverbs?	A7
☐ Is your sentence structure correct? Have you avoided writing fragments, comma splices, or fused sentences?	A1, A2
☐ Have you used parallel structure in your comparisons and contrasts? Are your sentences as balanced as your ideas?	B2
☐ Have you used commas correctly after introductory phrases and other transitions?	C1

Additional Writing Assignments

1. Listen to two different recordings of the same piece of music as performed by two different groups, orchestras, or singers. What elements of the music does each stress? What contrasting attitudes toward the music do you detect? In an essay, compare and contrast these versions.

2. Write an essay in which you compare and contrast the subjects in any of the following pairs for the purpose of throwing light on both. In a short paper, you can trace only a few similarities and differences, but don't hesitate to observe, visit the library, or interview a friendly expert.

For more on using sources to support a position, see Ch. 12 and the Quick Research Guide beginning on p. A-18.

> Women and men as single parents
> Living at home and living away from home
> The coverage of a world event on television and in a newspaper
> The experience of watching a film on a DVD and in a theater
> The styles of two athletes playing in the same position (two pitchers, two quarterbacks, two goalies)
> English and another language
> Your college and a rival college
> Two differing views of a current controversy
> Northern and southern California (or two other regions)
> Two similar works of architecture (two churches, two skyscrapers, two city halls, two museums, two campus buildings)
> Two articles, essays, or Web sites about the same topic
> Two short stories, two poems, or two literary works about the same theme

3. In a serious or nonserious way, introduce yourself to your class by comparing and contrasting yourself with someone else. You might choose either a real person or a character in a film, a TV series, a novel, or a comic strip, but you and this other person should have much in common. Choose a few points of comparison (an attitude, a habit, or a way of life), and deal with each in an essay or, if your instructor approves, a mixed-media format.

4. With a classmate or small group, choose a topic, problem, or campus issue about which your views differ to some extent. Agree on several main points of contrast that you want each writer to consider. Then have each person write a paragraph summing up his or her position or point of view on the matter, concentrating on those main points. After your passages are written, collaboratively develop an introduction that outlines the issue, identifies the main points, and previews the contrasting views. Arrange the paragraphs effectively, add transitions, and write a collaborative conclusion. Revise and edit as needed to produce an orderly, coherent collaborative essay.

5. Compare and contrast yourself with a classmate in a collaborative essay. Decide together what your focus will be: Your backgrounds? Your paths to

college? Your career goals? Your lives outside the classroom? Your study habits? Your taste in music or clothes? Your politics? Have each writer use this focus to work on a detailed analysis of himself or herself. Then compare your analyses, clarify the purpose and thesis of your comparison, and decide how to shape the essay. If your instructor approves, you might prepare a mixed-media presentation or post your essay through the course management system to introduce yourselves to the class.

6. **Visual Assignment.** The following images are selected from *What the World Eats,* a book that shows families around the world with their food for a week. Compare and contrast two of the images here in an essay, following the advice in this chapter. Be sure that you identify the purpose of your comparison, organize your subjects and points effectively, and support your points with details that you observe in the images.

The Aboubakar family of Darfur province, Sudan, in a refugee camp in Chad with a week's worth of food (cost: $1.22 USD).

The Mendoza family and a servant in their courtyard in Guatemala, with a week's worth of food (cost: $75.70 USD).

The Revis family at home in Raleigh, North Carolina, with a week's worth of food (cost: $341.98 USD).

8 Explaining Causes and Effects

Responding to an Image

This image suggests both causes and effects. What causes can you identify? What effects? Also consider artistic choice — the selection of the scene and the vantage point from which it was photographed. What mood does the photograph create? How does it affect you personally?

When a house burns down, an insurance company assigns a claims adjuster to look into the disaster and ask, Why? He or she investigates to find the answer — the *cause* of the fire, whether lightning, a cooking mishap, or a match that someone deliberately struck — and presents it in a written report. The adjuster also details the *effects* of the fire — what was destroyed or damaged, what repairs will be needed, how much they will cost.

Often in college you are asked to investigate and think like the insurance adjuster, tracing causes or identifying effects. To do so, you have to gather information to marshal evidence. Effects, by the way, are usually easier to identify than causes. Results of a fire are apparent to an onlooker the next day, although its cause may be obscure. For this reason, seeking causes and effects may be an uncertain pursuit, and you are unlikely to set forth definitive explanations with absolute certainty. Despite these uncertainties, causes and effects intrigue investigative journalists, stock market analysts, historians, and geographers, as well as families who look for one generation's impact on another.

Why Explaining Causes and Effects Matters

In a College Course

- You explore causes or effects to add depth to your papers whether you are investigating teen parenthood in sociology, romanticism in American fiction, or head traumas in speech pathology.
- You identify causes (such as those for the decline of the U.S. auto industry) or effects (such as those of widespread unemployment in Detroit) in essay exams.

In the Workplace

- You consider causes and effects when you recommend changing from one advertising campaign to another to improve sales or from an old procedure to a new one to improve quality, efficiency, or safety.

In Your Community

- You use causal analysis to help you advocate for more rigorous standards for the fuel efficiency of new vehicles or for stronger school board support for preschool programs.

❓ When have you explained causes, effects, or both in your writing? What situations are likely to require this kind of analysis?

Learning from Other Writers

The following essays explore causes and effects, each examining a different environment. To help you begin to analyze the first reading, look at the notes in the margin. They identify features such as the thesis, or main idea, and the first of the causes or effects that develop it in a paper analyzing cause and effect.

As You Read These Cause-and-Effect Essays

For more examples of writing that explains causes and effects, visit **<bedfordstmartins .com/bedguide>**.

As you read these essays, ask yourself the following questions:

1. Does the writer explain causes? Or effects? Or both? Why?
2. Does the writer perceive and explain a chain or series of causal relationships? If so, how are the various causes and effects connected?
3. What evidence does the writer supply? Is the evidence sufficient to clarify the causal relationships and to provide credibility to the essay?

Jeffrey Pfeffer

Lay Off the Layoffs

Jeffrey Pfeffer, a professor at Stanford University's Graduate School of Business, examines the common business practice of laying off workers in an economic downturn. In this essay, originally published in *Newsweek* in February 2010, he considers the effects of layoffs — for both workers and businesses.

Introduction to situation —

On Sept. 12, 2001, there were no commercial flights in the United States. It was uncertain when airlines would be permitted to start flying again — or how many customers would be on them. Airlines faced not only the tragedy of 9/11 but the fact that [the] economy was entering a recession.° So almost immediately, all the U.S. airlines, save one, did what so many U.S. corporations are particularly skilled at doing: they began announcing tens of thousands of layoffs. Today the one airline that didn't cut staff, Southwest, still has never had an involuntary layoff in its almost 40-year history. It's now the largest domestic U.S. airline and has a market capitalization° bigger than all its domestic competitors combined. As its former head of human resources once told me: "If people are your most important assets,° why would you get rid of them?" . . .

1

recession: A long period of widespread economic decline.   **market capitalization:** The estimated value of a company or stock.   **assets:** Resources.

It's difficult to study the causal effect of layoffs—you can't do double-blind,° placebo-controlled° studies as you can for drugs by randomly assigning some companies to shed workers and others not, with people unaware of what "treatment" they are receiving. Companies that downsize are undoubtedly different in many ways (the quality of their management, for one) from those that don't. But you can attempt to control for differences in industry, size, financial condition, and past performance, and then look at a large number of studies to see if they reach the same conclusion.

Question raised about effects

2

That research paints a fairly consistent picture: layoffs don't work. And for good reason. In *Responsible Restructuring*, University of Colorado professor Wayne Cascio lists the direct and indirect costs of layoffs: severance pay; paying out accrued vacation and sick pay; outplacement costs; higher unemployment insurance taxes; the cost of rehiring employees when business improves; low morale and risk-averse survivors; potential lawsuits, sabotage, or even workplace violence from aggrieved employees or former employees; loss of institutional memory and knowledge; diminished trust in management; and reduced productivity. . . .

THESIS

3

Effects specified

Some managers compare layoffs to amputation: that sometimes you have to cut off a body part to save the whole. As metaphors go, this one is particularly misplaced. Layoffs are more like bloodletting, weakening the entire organism. That's because of the vicious cycle that typically unfolds. A company cuts people. Customer service, innovation, and productivity fall in the face of a smaller and demoralized workforce. The company loses more ground, does more layoffs, and the cycle continues. That's part of the story of now-defunct Circuit City, the electronics retailer that decided it needed to get rid of its 3,400 highest-paid (and almost certainly most effective) sales associates to cut its costs. Fewer people with fewer skills in the Circuit City stores permitted competitors such as Best Buy to gain ground, and once the death spiral started, it was hard to stop. Circuit City filed for bankruptcy in 2008 and closed its doors last March.

4

Causal chain traced

Beyond the companies where layoffs take place, widespread downsizing can have a big impact on the economy—a phenomenon that John Maynard Keynes° taught us about decades ago, but one that's almost certainly going on now. The people who lose jobs also lose incomes, so they spend less. Even workers who don't lose their jobs but are simply fearful of layoffs are likely to cut back on spending too. With less aggregate° demand in the economy, sales fall. With smaller sales, companies lay off more people, and the cycle continues. That's why places where it is harder to shed workers—such as (can

5

double-blind: A testing procedure in which neither participants nor experimenters know what treatment participants are receiving, used to eliminate accidental bias.   **placebo-controlled:** A testing procedure in which one group of participants receives an accepted or experimental treatment and another group receives an inactive or false treatment (the *placebo*).   **John Maynard Keynes** (1883–1946): British economist who introduced new ideas about economics during the 1930s.   **aggregate:** Overall.

I dare say it?) France—have held up comparatively better during the global economic meltdown. Workers there are confident that they'll remain employed, so they needn't pull back on spending so dramatically.

The airline industry provides a case study of the downside of retrench-   6 ment.° After the layoffs following 9/11, airline service deteriorated and flying became a truly unpleasant experience. That carried predictable consequences: the number of "premium" passenger trips, defined as full-fare coach, first-, or business-class fares (where airlines make their biggest margins), declined by 47 percent between 2000 and 2007. According to an industry survey published in 2008, in the preceding 12 months airlines had lost $9.6 billion in revenue as people voluntarily flew less because they found the experience so noxious.° In a fixed-cost industry like airlines, that was the difference between an industrywide loss and profitability. . . .

As bad as the effects of layoffs are on companies and the economy, per-   7 haps the biggest damage is done to the people themselves. . . . When people lose their jobs, they get angry and depressed—not a big surprise. Angry and depressed people who believe they have been treated unfairly can lose psychological control and exact vengeance on those they deem responsible. We have all seen too-frequent cable-news coverage of the fired employee who returns to the workplace with a gun and wounds or kills people. It's not just the occasional anecdote. Research shows that people who had no history of violent behavior were six times more likely to exhibit violent behavior after a layoff than similar people who remained employed.

And some research has looked directly at the health consequences of los-   8 ing one's job or being unemployed on mortality. A study in New Zealand found that for people 25 to 64 years old, being unemployed increased the likelihood of committing suicide by 2.5 times. When two meat-processing plants closed in New Zealand, epidemiologists° followed what happened to their employees over an eight-year period. The odds of self-harm and the rate of admission to hospitals for mental-health problems increased significantly compared with people who remained employed. A recent National Bureau of Economic Research working paper reported that in the United States, job displacement led to a 12 to 20 percent increase in death rates during the following 20 years, implying a loss of life expectancy of 1.5 years for an employee who loses his job at the age of 40. Even in societies with strong social-welfare provisions, job loss is traumatic. A study of plant closures in Sweden reported a 44 percent increase in the mortality risk among men during the first four years following the loss of work.

Anyone who's suffered a layoff or watched a loved one lose a job can un-   9 derstand why downsizees exhibit increased rates of alcoholism, smoking, drug abuse, and depression. In economic terms, we should think of these as

---

retrench ment: Cutting back.   **noxious:** Unpleasant and harmful.   **epidemiologists:** People who study health and illness in large populations.

"externalities",° just like air and water pollution, since many of the costs of these behaviors and ailments are borne by the larger society.

Despite all the research suggesting downsizing hurts companies, manag-   10
ers everywhere continue to do it. That raises an obvious question: why? Part of the answer lies in the immense pressure corporate leaders feel—from the media, from analysts, from peers—to follow the crowd no matter what. When SAS Institute, the $2 billion software company, considered going pub-lic about a decade ago, its potential underwriter° told the company to do things that would make it look more like other software companies: pay sales people on commission, offer stock options, and cut back on the lavish bene-fits that landed SAS at No. 1 on *Fortune*'s annual Best Places to Work list. (SAS stayed private.) It's an example of how managerial behavior can be con-tagious, spreading like the flu across companies. One study of downsizing over a 15 year period found a strong "adoption effect"—companies copied the behavior of other firms to which they had social ties.

The facts seem clear. Layoffs are mostly bad for companies, harmful for   11
the economy, and devastating for employees. This is not news, or should not be. There is substantial research literature in fields from epidemiology to or-ganizational behavior documenting these effects. The damage from overzeal-ous downsizing will linger even as the economy recovers—and as it does, per-haps managers will learn from their mistakes.

Conclusion
restating thesis

Questions to Start You Thinking

Meaning

1. Why is the comparison of layoffs to amputations misguided, according to Pfeffer (paragraph 4)?

2. How does widespread downsizing affect the wider economy?

3. Pfeffer discusses how layoffs can make workers angry and depressed. What are the wider effects of this anger and depression?

Writing Strategies

4. Pfeffer begins the essay with the story of Southwest Airlines after 9/11. Is this an effective beginning? Why or why not? In what other ways might he have begun his essay?

5. Pfeffer uses a mixture of anecdotal evidence and scientific studies to dis-cuss the causes and effects of layoffs. How effective is this mix? Does he depend too strongly on one or the other? Why or why not?

6. Does Pfeffer's essay deal predominantly with causes or effects? Where and to what degree does he examine each of these? How would his essay change if he changed his focus?

---

externalities: Hidden or indirect costs of economic activities.   **underwriter:** Financial backer.

Yun Yung Choi   **Student Essay**

Invisible Women

Yun Yung Choi examines the adoption of a new state religion in her native Korea and the effects of that adoption on Korean women.

❓ How would you have answered this question?

For me, growing up in a small suburb on the outskirts of Seoul, the adults' preference for boys seemed quite natural. All the important people that I knew—doctors, lawyers, policemen, and soldiers—were men. On the other hand, most of the women that I knew were either housekeepers or housewives whose duty seemed to be to obey and please the men of the family. When my teachers at school asked me what I wanted to be when I grew up, I would answer, "I want to be the wife of the president." Because all women must become wives and mothers, I thought, becoming the wife of the president would be the highest achievement for a woman. I knew that the birth of a boy was a greatly desired and celebrated event, whereas the birth of a girl was a disappointing one, accompanied by the frequent words of consolation for the sad parents: "A daughter is her mother's chief help in keeping house."

These attitudes toward women, widely considered the continuation of an unbroken chain of tradition, are, in fact, only a few hundred years old, a relatively short period considering Korea's long history. During the first half of the Yi dynasty, which lasted from 1392 to 1910, and during the Koryo period, which preceded the Yi dynasty, women were treated almost as equals with many privileges that were denied them during the latter half of the Yi dynasty. This turnabout in women's place in Korean society was brought about by one of the greatest influences that shaped the government, literature, and thoughts of the Korean people—Confucianism.°

Throughout the Koryo period, which lasted from 918 to 1392, and throughout the first half of the Yi dynasty, according to Laurel Kendall in her book *View from the Inner Room*, women were important and contributing members of the society and not marginal and dependent as they later became. Women were, to a large extent, in command of their own lives. They were permitted to own property and receive inheritances from their fathers. Wedding ceremonies were held in the bride's house, where the couple lived, and the wife retained her surname. Women were also allowed freedom of movement—that is, they were able to go outside the house without any feelings of shame or embarrassment.

With the introduction of Confucianism, however, the rights and privileges that women enjoyed were confiscated. The government of the Yi dynasty made great efforts to incorporate into society the Confucian ideologies, including the principle of *agnation*. This principle, according to Kendall, made men the important members of society and relegated° women to a dependent position. The government succeeded in Confucianizing the country and encouraging the acceptance of Confucian

1

2

3

4

Confucianism: Ethical system based on the teachings of Chinese philosopher Confucius (551–479 B.C.).

proverbs such as the following: "Men are honored, but women are abased." "A daughter is a 'robber woman' who carries household wealth away when she marries."

The unfortunate effects of this Confucianization in the lives of women were numerous. The most noticeable was the virtual confinement of women. They were forced to remain unseen in the *anbang*, the inner room of the house. This room was the women's domain, or, rather, the women's prison. Outside, a woman was carried through the streets in a closed sedan chair. Walking outside, she had to wear a veil that covered her face and could travel abroad only after nightfall. Thus, it is no wonder that Westerners traveling through Korea in the late nineteenth century expressed surprise at the apparent absence of women in the country.

Women received no formal education. Their only schooling came from government textbooks. By giving instruction on the virtuous° conduct of women, these books attempted to fit women into the Confucian stereotype—meek, quiet, and obedient. Thus, this Confucian society acclaimed particular women not for their talent or achievement but for the degree of perfection with which they were able to mimic the stereotype.

A woman even lost her identity in such a society. Once married, she became a stranger to her natal° family, becoming a member of her husband's family. Her name was omitted from the family *chokpo*, or genealogy book, and was entered in the *chokpo* of her in-laws as a mere "wife" next to her husband's name.

Even a desirable marriage, the ultimate hope for a woman, failed to provide financial and emotional security for her. Failure to produce a son was legal grounds for sending the wife back to her natal home, thereby subjecting the woman to the greatest humiliation and to a life of continued shame. And because the Confucian ideology stressed a wife's devotion to her husband as the greatest of womanly virtues, widows were forced to avoid social disgrace by remaining faithfully unmarried, no matter how young they were. As women lost their rights to own or inherit property, these widows, with no means to support themselves, suffered great hardships. Thus, as Sandra Martielle says in *Virtues in Conflict*, what the government considered "the ugly custom of remarriage" was slowly eliminated at the expense of women's happiness.

This male-dominated system of Confucianism is one of the surviving traditions from the Yi dynasty. Although the Constitution of the Republic of Korea proclaimed on July 17, 1948, guarantees individual freedom and sexual equality, these ideals failed to have any immediate effect on the Korean mentality that stubbornly adheres to its belief in the superiority of men. Women still regard marriage as their prime objective in life, and little girls still wish to become the doctor's wife, the lawyer's wife, and even the president's wife. But as the system of Confucianism is slowly being forced out of existence by new legal and social standards, perhaps a day will come, after all, when a little girl will stand up in class and answer, "I want to be the president."

relegated: Reduced to a less important position.   **virtuous:** Moral, honorable.   **natal:** Relating to one's birth.

(?) How do you respond to this historical background?

6

7

8

9

(?) Why do you think the writer ends with this quotation?

Questions to Start You Thinking

Meaning

1. What effect does Choi observe? What cause does she attribute it to?

2. What specific changes in Korean culture does Choi attribute to the introduction of Confucianism?

3. What evidence do you find of the writer's critically rethinking an earlier belief and then revising it? What do you think may have influenced her to change her belief?

Writing Strategies

4. What does Choi gain by beginning and ending with her personal experience?

5. Where does Choi use the strategy of comparing and contrasting?

6. How does Choi consider readers for whom her culture might be foreign?

7. Using highlighters or marginal notes, identify the essay's introduction, thesis, major causes or effects, supporting explanations and details for each of these, and conclusion. How effective is the organization?

Learning by Writing

The Assignment: Explaining Causes and Effects

For writing activities for cause and effect, visit **<bedfordstmartins .com/bedguide>**.

Pick a disturbing fact or situation that you have observed, and seek out its causes and effects to help you and your readers understand the issue better. You may limit your essay to the causes *or* the effects, or you may include both but emphasize one more than the other. Yun Yung Choi uses the last approach when she identifies the cause of the status of Korean women (Confucianism) but spends most of her essay detailing effects of this cause.

The situation you choose may have affected you and people you know well, such as student loan policies, the difficulty of working while going to school, or a challenge facing your family. It might have affected people in your city or region—a small voter turnout in an election, decaying bridge supports, or pet owners not using pooper-scoopers. It may affect society at large—identity theft, immigration laws, or the high cost of health care. It might be gender or racial stereotypes on television, binge drinking at parties, spouse abuse, teenage suicide, global warming, student debt, or the use of dragnets for ocean fishing. Don't think you must choose an earthshaking topic to write a good paper. On the contrary, you will do a better job if you are personally familiar with the situation you choose.

These students selected topics of personal concern for causal analysis:

One student cited her observations of the hardships faced by Indians in rural Mexico as one cause of rebellions there.

Another analyzed the negative attitudes of men toward women at her workplace and the resulting tension, inefficiency, and low production.

A third contended that buildings in Miami are not constructed to withstand hurricanes due, for one reason, to an inadequate inspection system.

Facing the Challenge   Causes and Effects

The major challenge writers face when exploring causal relationships is how to limit the subject. When you explore a given phenomenon—whether local unemployment or the success of your favorite band—devoting equal space to all possible causes and effects will either overwhelm your readers or put them to sleep. Instead, you need to decide what you want to show your readers—and then emphasize the causal relationships that help achieve this purpose.

Rely on your purpose to help you decide which part of the relationship—cause or effect—to stress and how to limit your ideas to strengthen your overall point. If you are writing about your family's transportation problems, for example, you may be tempted to discuss all the possible *causes* and then analyze all the *effects* it has had on you. Your readers, however, won't want to know about every single complication. Both you and your readers will have a much easier time if you make some decisions about your focus:

- Do you want to concentrate on *causes* or *effects*?
- Which of your explanations are most and least compelling?
- How can you emphasize the points that are most important to you?
- Which relatively insignificant or irrelevant ideas can you omit?

Generating Ideas

Find a Topic. What familiar situation would be informative or instructive to explore? This assignment leaves you the option of writing from what you know, what you can find out, or a combination of the two. Begin by letting your thoughts wander over the results of a particular situation. Has the situation always been this way? Or has it changed in the last few years? Have things gotten better or worse?

When your thoughts begin to percolate, jot down likely topics. Then choose the idea that you care most about and that promises to be neither too large nor too small. A paper confined to the causes of a family's move from New Jersey to Montana might be a single sentence: "My father's company transferred him." But the subsequent effects of the move on the family might become an interesting essay. On the other hand, you might need hundreds of pages to study all the effects of gangs in urban high schools. Instead, you might select just one unusual effect, such as gang members staking out territory in the parking lot of a local school.

For more strategies for generating ideas, see Ch. 19.

DISCOVERY CHECKLIST

☐ Has a difficult situation resulted from a change in your life (a lost job or a new one; a fluctuation in income; personal or family upheaval following death, divorce, accident, illness, or good fortune; a new school)?

☐ Has the environment changed (due to a drought, a flood or a storm, a fire, a new industry, the collapse of an old industry)?

☐ Has a disturbing situation been caused by an invention (the computer, the laptop, the DVD player, the television, the ATM, the cell phone)?

☐ Do certain employment trends cause you concern (for women in management, for young people in rural areas, for males in nursing)?

☐ Is a situation on campus or in your neighborhood, city, or state causing problems for you (traffic, housing costs, population, health care)?

Learning by Doing 🖐️ Visualizing the Situation

Working by yourself or with a group, try mapping to investigate likely causes and effects in the situation you have selected. Use a blank page with movable sticky notes, note cards, a computer file where you can position chunks or boxes of text, or software for clustering ideas. Identify causes and effects, and then arrange them to show their relationships or their relative importance.

List Causes and Effects. After noting causes and effects, consider which are immediate (evident and close at hand), which are remote (underlying, more basic, or earlier), and how you might arrange them in a logical sequence or causal chain.

Causes and effects during a mishap in Connemara, Ireland, in 2004.

FOCUS ON CAUSAL CHAIN

Remote Causes		Immediate Causes		Situation		Immediate Effects		Remote Effects
Foreign competition	→	Sales, profits drop	→	Clothing factory closing	→	Jobs vanish	→	Town flounders

Once you have figured out the basic causal relationships, focus on complexities or implications. Probe more deeply for contributing, related, or even hidden factors. When you begin to draft your paper, these ideas will be a rich resource, allowing you to concentrate on the causes or effects you find most important and skip any that are minor.

For more on thinking critically, see Ch. 3.

FOCUS ON IMMEDIATE EFFECTS

Factory workers lose jobs	→	Households curtail spending
Grocery and other stores suffer	→	Businesses fold
Workers lose health coverage	→	Health needs ignored
Retirees fear benefits lost	→	Confidence erodes

FOCUS ON REMOTE EFFECTS

Town economy undermined

Food pantry, social services overwhelmed

Hospital limits services and doctors leave

Unemployed and young people leave

Learning by Doing 📷 Making a Cause-and-Effect Table

Use the Table menu in your word processor or draw on paper a four-column table to help you assess the importance of causes and effects. Divide up your causes and effects, making entries under each heading. Refine your table as you relate, order, or limit your points.

Major Cause	Minor Cause	Major Effect	Minor Effect

For advice on finding a few pertinent sources, turn to the Quick Research Guide, beginning on p. A-18.

Consider Sources of Support. After identifying causes and effects, note your evidence next to each item. You can then see at a glance exactly where you need more material. Star or underline any causes and effects that stand out as major ones. A way to rate the items on your list is to ask, How significant is this cause? Would the situation not exist without it? (This major cause deserves a big star.) Or would the situation have arisen without it, for some other reason? (This minor cause might still matter but be less important.) Has this effect had a resounding impact? Is it necessary to explain the results adequately?

As you set priorities—identifying major causes or effects and noting missing information—you may wish to talk with others, use a search engine, or browse the library Web site for sources of supporting ideas, concrete details, and reliable statistics. For example, you might look for illustrations of the problem, accounts of comparable situations, or charts showing current data and projections.

Planning, Drafting, and Developing

For Choi's complete essay, see pp. 142–44. For more about informal outlines, see pp. 414–17.

Start with a Scratch Outline and Thesis. Yun Yung Choi's "Invisible Women" follows a clear plan based on a brief scratch outline that simply lists the effects of the change:

Intro — Personal anecdote
- Tie with Korean history
- Then add working thesis: The turnabout for women resulted from the influence of Confucianism in all aspects of society.

Comparison and contrast of status of women before and after Confucianism
Effects of Confucianism on women
1. Confinement
2. Little education
3. Loss of identity in marriage
4. No property rights
Conclusion: Impact still evident in Korea today but some hints of change

For exercises on choosing effective thesis statements, visit <bedfordstmartins.com/bedguide>.

For more about stating your main point in a thesis, see pp. 401–10.

The paper makes its point: it identifies Confucianism as the reason for the status of Korean women and details four specific effects of Confucianism on women in Korean society. And it shows that cause and effect are closely related: Confucianism is the cause of the change in the status of Korean women, and Confucianism has had specific effects on Korean women.

Organize to Show Causes and Effects to Your Audience. The main part of your paper — showing how the situation came about (the causes) or what followed as a result (the effects) or both — more than likely will follow one of these patterns:

I. The situation	I. The situation	I. The situation
II. Its causes	II. Its effects	II. Its causes
		III. Its effects

You can begin planning your paper by grouping the causes and effects and then classifying them as major or minor. If, for example, you are writing about the reasons more college students accumulate credit-card debt now than they did a generation ago, you might list the following:

1. available credit for students
2. high credit limits with high interest
3. reduced or uncertain income
4. excessive buying

On reflection you might decide that available credit, credit limits, and interest rates are determined by the credit card industry, government regulation, and current economic conditions. These factors certainly affect students, but you are more interested in causes and effects that individual students might be able to influence in order to minimize their debt. You turn to your own situation to consider whether your growing debt is due to too little income or too many expenses. You could then organize the causes from least to most important, giving the major one more space and the final place in your essay. When your plan seems logical to you, discuss it or share your draft with a classmate, a friend, or your instructor. Ask whether your organization will make sense to someone else.

Introduce the Situation. When you draft the first part of your paper, describe the situation you want to explain in no more than two or three paragraphs. Make clear to your readers your task — explaining causes, explaining effects, or explaining both. Instead of doing this in a flat, mechanical fashion ("Now I am going to explain the causes"), announce your task casually, naturally, as if you were talking to someone: "At first, I didn't realize that keeping six pet cheetahs in our backyard would bother the neighbors." Or, tantalize your readers as one writer did in a paper about her father's sudden move to a Trappist monastery: "The real reason for Father's decision didn't become clear to me for a long while."

Learning by Doing 🔘 Focusing Your Introduction

Read aloud the draft of your introduction for a classmate or small group, or post it for online discussion. Ask your readers first to identify where you state the main point of your essay — why you are explaining causes or effects. Then ask them to share their helpful observations about the clarity of that statement or about any spots where your introduction bogs down in detail or skips over essentials.

For more on using sources for support, see Ch. 12 or the Quick Research Guide beginning on p. A-18.

For exercises on supporting a thesis, visit <bedfordstmartins .com/bedguide>.

For more revising and editing strategies, see Ch. 23.

Work in Your Evidence. Some writers want to rough out a cause-and-effect draft, positioning all the major points first and then circling back to pull in supporting explanations and details. Others want to plunge deeply into each section—stating the main point, elaborating, and working in the evidence all at once. Tables, charts, and graphs can often consolidate information that substantiates or illustrates causes or effects. If such additions would strengthen your essay, place your graphics near the related text discussion, supporting but not duplicating it.

Revising and Editing

Because explaining causes and effects takes hard thought, set aside plenty of time for rewriting. As Yun Yung Choi approached her paper's final version, she wanted to rework her thesis with greater precision and more detail.

WORKING THESIS	The turnabout for women resulted from the influence of Confucianism in all aspects of society.
REVISED THESIS	This turnabout in women's place in Korean society was brought about by one of the greatest influences that shaped the government, literature, and thoughts of the Korean people—Confucianism.

She also faced a problem pointed out by classmates: how to make a smooth transition from recalling her own experience to probing causes.

(emphasize that everyone thinks that) ⟶ *widely*

, a relatively short time, considering Korea's long history

These attitudes toward women, ~~which I once~~ believed to be the continuation of an unbroken chain of tradition, are, in fact, only a few hundred years old. During the *[tell when]* first half of the Yi dynasty, which lasted from 1392 to 1910, and during [the Koryo period,] women were treated almost as equals, with many privileges that were denied them during the latter half of the Yi dynasty. This upheaval in women's place in Korean society was brought about by one of the greatest influences that shaped the government, literature, and thoughts of the Korean people: Confucianism. Because of Confucianism, my birth was not greeted with joy and celebration but rather with these words of consolation: "A daughter is her mother's chief help in keeping house."

(belongs in opening paragraph)

Peer Response 👥 Explaining Causes and Effects

Have a classmate or friend read your draft, considering how you've analyzed causes or effects. Ask your peer editor to answer questions such as the following:

For an explanation of causes:

- Does the writer explain, rather than merely list, causes?
- Do the causes seem logical and possible?
- Are there other causes that the writer might consider? If so, list them.

For an explanation of effects:

- Do all the effects seem to be results of the situation the writer describes?
- Are there other effects that the writer might consider? If so, list them.

For all cause-and-effect papers:

- What is the writer's thesis? Does the explanation of causes or effects help the writer accomplish the purpose of the essay?
- Is the order of supporting ideas clear? Can you suggest a better organization?
- Are you convinced by the writer's logic? Do you see any logical fallacies?
- Are any causes or effects hard to accept?
- Do the writer's evidence and detail convince you? Put stars where more or better evidence is needed.
- If this paper were yours, what is the one thing you would be sure to work on before handing it in?

For general questions for a peer editor, see p. 465. For peer response worksheets, visit <**bedfordstmartins .com/bedguide**>.

REVISION CHECKLIST

☐ Have you shown your readers your purpose in presenting causes or effects?

☐ Is your explanation thoughtful, searching, and reasonable?

☐ Where might you need to reorganize or add transitions so your paper is easy for readers to follow?

If you are tracing causes,

☐ Have you made it clear that you are explaining causes?

☐ Do you need to add any significant causes?

☐ At what points might you need to add more evidence to convince readers that the causal relationships are valid, not just guesses?

☐ Do you need to drop any remote causes you can't begin to prove? Or any assertions made without proof?

☐ Have you oversimplified by assuming that only one small cause accounts for a large phenomenon or that one thing caused another just because the one preceded the other?

For more on evidence, see pp. 49–50. For more on mistakes in thinking called logical fallacies, see pp. 178–79.

If you are determining effects,

☐ Have you made it clear that you are explaining effects?

☐ What possible effects have you left out? Are any of them worth adding?

☐ At what points might you need to supply more evidence that these effects have occurred?

☐ Could any effect have resulted not from the cause you describe but from some other cause?

For more editing and proofreading strategies, see pp. 473–76.

For more help, find the relevant checklist sections in the Quick Editing Guide on p. A-36. Turn also to the Quick Format Guide beginning on p. A-1.

After you have revised your cause-and-effect essay, edit and proofread it. Carefully check the grammar, word choice, punctuation, and mechanics — and then correct any problems you find.

EDITING CHECKLIST

☐ Have you used correct verb tenses and forms throughout? When you describe events in the past, is it clear what happened first and what happened next?   **A3**

☐ Have you avoided creating fragments when adding causes or effects? (Check revisions carefully, especially those beginning "*Because . . .*" or "*Causing . . . .*") Have you avoided comma splices or fused sentences when trying to integrate ideas smoothly?   **A1, A2**

☐ Do your transitions and other introductory elements have commas after them, if these are needed?   **C1**

Additional Writing Assignments

1. Pick a change that has taken place during your lifetime — a noticeable, lasting transformation produced by an event or a series of events. Write an essay exploring its causes, effects, or both to help you and your audience understand that change better. The change might have affected only you, such as a move, a decision, or an alteration in a strong personal opinion or belief. It might have also affected others in your community (a new zoning law), in a region (the growth of a new industry), or in society at large (general access to the Internet). Or it might be a new invention, medical breakthrough, or deep-down shift in the structure or attitudes of society.

2. Reflect on your background and experience to identify a major event, person, circumstance, habit, routine, or other factor that significantly shaped you as a person. In your journal, write informally about the nature of this cause and its effects on you. Use this entry to develop a cause-and-effect essay about yourself that will enlighten a reader about how you came to be the person that you are now or are now becoming.

3. Read a newspaper or magazine article that probes the causes of some contemporary problem: the shortage of certain types of jobs, for instance, or tuition increases in your state. Can you suggest causes that the article writer ignored? Write an essay in which you argue that the author has or has not done a good job of explaining the causes of this problem.

4. Write a formal letter or memo addressed to someone who could make a change that you advocate. Support this change by explaining causes, effects, or both. You might, for example, address a college official to support a specific change in a campus event or policy, the principal to advocate for a change at your child's school, your supervisor at work to encourage a change in procedures, or a county official to promote a change in services or regulations.

5. **Visual Assignment.** Write an essay explaining the causes, effects, or both captured or implied in the images below and on page 154. Follow the advice in this chapter, making sure that you establish the purpose of your explanation, effectively identify and organize the causes or effects, and support your points with details that you observe in the images.

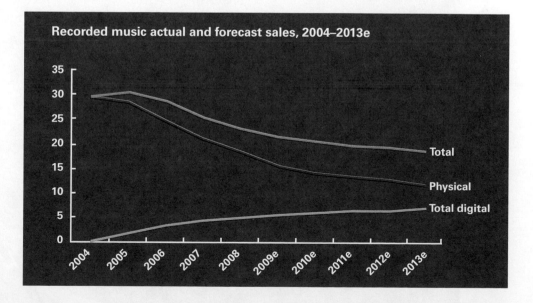

Responding to an Image

The banner in this image identifies a group and its position. What is the stance being taken? What issues and concerns might have led to this position? Based on the image, what event do you think it portrays? What might the photographer have wanted to convey?

Both in and outside of class, you'll hear controversial issues discussed—
health care, immigration policy, standardized testing, disaster preparedness, global outsourcing of jobs, copyright issues. Even in academic
fields, experts don't always agree, and issues may remain controversies for
years. Taking a stand in response to such issues will help you understand
the controversy and clarify what you believe. Such writing is common in
editorials, letters to the editor, or columns on the op-ed page in print and
online news outlets. It is also the foundation of persuasive brochures, partisan blogs, and Web pages that take a stand.

Writing of this kind has a twofold purpose—to state, and to win your
readers' respect for, an opinion. What you say might or might not change a
reader's opinion. But if you fulfill your purpose, a reader at least will see
good reasons for your views. In taking a stand, you do these things:

- You state your opinion or stand.
- You give reasons with evidence to support your position.
- You enlist your readers' trust.
- You consider and respect what your readers probably think and feel.

Why Taking a Stand Matters

In a College Course

- You take a stand in an essay or exam when you respond, pro or con, to a
  statement such as "The Web, like movable type for printing, is an invention that has transformed human communication."
- You take a stand when you write research papers that support your
  position on juvenile sentencing, state support for higher education, or
  tax breaks for new home buyers.

In the Workplace

- You take a stand when you persuade others that your case report supports a legal action that will benefit your clients or that your customer-
  service initiative will attract new business.

In Your Community

- You take a stand when you write a letter to the editor appealing to voters
  to support a local bond issue.

  ❓ When have you taken a stand in your writing? In what circumstances
  are you likely to do so again?

Learning from Other Writers

In the following two essays, the writers take a stand on issues of importance to them. To help you begin to analyze the first reading, look at the
notes in the margin. They identify features such as the thesis, or main idea,
and the first of the points that support it in a paper that takes a stand.

As You Read These Essays That Take a Stand

As you read these essays, ask yourself the following questions:

1. What stand does the writer take? Is it a popular opinion, or does it
   break from commonly accepted beliefs?

2. How does the writer appeal to readers?

3. How does the writer support his or her position? Is the evidence sufficient to gain your respect? Why or why not?

For more such
writings, visit
**<bedfordstmartins
.com/bedguide>**.

Suzan Shown Harjo

Last Rites for Indian Dead

As a result of persuasive efforts such as Suzan Shown Harjo's essay, the Native American Graves Protection and Repatriation Act was passed in 1990.

What if museums, universities, and government agencies could put
your dead relatives on display or keep them in boxes to be cut up and
otherwise studied? What if you believed that the spirits of the dead could not
rest until their human remains were placed in a sacred area?

    1   Introduction appeals
to readers

     The ordinary American would say there ought to be a law—and there is,
for ordinary Americans. The problem for American Indians is that there are
too many laws of the kind that make us the archaeological property of the
United States and too few of the kind that protect us from such insults.

    2   THESIS
taking a stand

Point 1

     Some of my own Cheyenne relatives' skulls are in the Smithsonian Insti-
tution today, along with those of at least 4,500 other Indian people who were
violated in the 1800s by the U.S. Army for an "Indian Crania Study." It wasn't
enough that these unarmed Cheyenne people were mowed down by the cav-
alry at the infamous Sand Creek massacre; many were decapitated and their
heads shipped to Washington as freight. (The Army Medical Museum's collection is now in the Smithsonian.) Some had been exhumed° only hours
after being buried. Imagine their grieving families' reaction on finding their
loved ones disinterred° and headless.

    3   Supporting evidence

exhumed: Dug up out of the earth.   **disinterred:** Taken out of a place of burial.

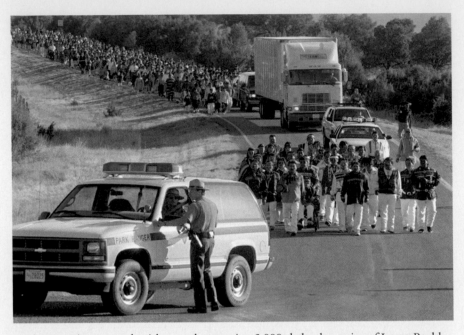

Native Americans march with a truck returning 2,000 skeletal remains of Jemez Pueblo Indian ancestors for reburial in New Mexico. The remains had been in the collections of Harvard University.

Supporting evidence

Some targets of the army's study were killed in noncombat situations and 4 beheaded immediately. The officer's account of the decapitation of the Apache chief Mangas Coloradas in 1863 shows the pseudoscientific nature of the exercise. "I weighed the brain and measured the skull," the good doctor wrote, "and found that while the skull was smaller, the brain was larger than that of Daniel Webster."

These journal accounts exist in excruciating detail, yet missing are any 5 records of overall comparisons, conclusions, or final reports of the army study. Since it is unlike the army not to leave a paper trail, one must wonder about the motive for its collection.

The total Indian body count in the Smithsonian collection is more than 6 19,000, and it is not the largest in the country. It is not inconceivable that the 1.5 million of us living today are outnumbered by our dead stored in museums, educational institutions, federal agencies, state historical societies, and private collections. The Indian people are further dehumanized by being exhibited alongside the mastodons and dinosaurs and other extinct creatures.

Where we have buried our dead in peace, more often than not the sites 7 have been desecrated. For more than two hundred years, relic-hunting has been a popular pursuit. Lately, the market in Indian artifacts has brought this abhorrent activity to a fever pitch in some areas. And when scavengers come upon Indian burial sites, everything found becomes fair game, including sacred burial offerings, teeth, and skeletal remains.

One unusually well-publicized example of Indian grave desecration occurred two years ago in a western Kentucky field known as Slack Farm, the site of an Indian village five centuries ago. Ten men — one with a business card stating "Have Shovel, Will Travel" — paid the landowner $10,000 to lease digging rights between planting seasons. They dug extensively on the forty-acre farm, rummaging through an estimated 650 graves, collecting burial goods, tools, and ceremonial items. Skeletons were strewn about like litter.   8

What motivates people to do something like this? Financial gain is the first answer. Indian relic-collecting has become a multimillion-dollar industry. The price tag on a bead necklace can easily top $1,000; rare pieces fetch tens of thousands.   9   *Question used as transition*

And it is not just collectors of the macabre° who pay for skeletal remains. Scientists say that these deceased Indians are needed for research that someday could benefit the health and welfare of living Indians. But just how many dead Indians must they examine? Nineteen thousand?   10

There is doubt as to whether permanent curation of our dead really benefits Indians. Dr. Emery A. Johnson, former assistant Surgeon General, recently observed, "I am not aware of any current medical diagnostic or treatment procedure that has been derived from research on such skeletal remains. Nor am I aware of any during the thirty-four years that I have been involved in American Indian . . . health care."   11

Indian remains are still being collected for racial biological studies. While the intentions may be honorable, the ethics of using human remains this way without the full consent of relatives must be questioned.   12

Some relief for Indian people has come on the state level. Almost half of the states, including California, have passed laws protecting Indian burial sites and restricting the sale of Indian bones, burial offerings, and other sacred items. Representative Charles E. Bennett (D-Fla.) and Senator John McCain (R-Ariz.) have introduced bills that are a good start in invoking the federal government's protection. However, no legislation has attacked the problem head-on by imposing stiff penalties at the marketplace, or by changing laws that make dead Indians the nation's property.   13

Some universities — notably Stanford, Nebraska, Minnesota, and Seattle — have returned, or agreed to return, Indian human remains; it is fitting that institutions of higher education should lead the way.   14

Congress is now deciding what to do with the government's extensive collection of Indian human remains and associated funerary objects. The secretary of the Smithsonian, Robert McC. Adams, has been valiantly° attempting to apply modern ethics to yesterday's excesses. This week, he announced that the Smithsonian would conduct an inventory and return all Indian skeletal remains that could be identified with specific tribes or living kin.   15

macabre: Gruesome, ghastly.   **valiantly:** Bravely.

But there remains a reluctance generally among collectors of Indian re- 16
mains to take action of a scope that would have a quantitative impact and
a healing quality. If they will not act on their own—and it is highly unlikely
that they will—then Congress must act.

Transition to
concluding proposal

The country must recognize that the bodies of dead American Indian 17
people are not artifacts to be bought and sold as collector's items. It is not
appropriate to store tens of thousands of our ancestors for possible future
research. They are our family. They deserve to be returned to their sacred
burial grounds and given a chance to rest.

Conclusion
proposes action

The plunder of our people's graves has gone on too long. Let us rebury 18
our dead and remove this shameful past from America's future.

Questions to Start You Thinking

Meaning

1. What is the issue Harjo identifies? How extensive does she show it to be?

2. What is Harjo's position on this issue? Where does she first state it?

3. What evidence does Harjo present to refute the claim that housing
   skeletal remains of Native Americans in museums is necessary for
   medical research and may benefit living Indians?

Writing Strategies

4. What assumptions do you think Harjo makes about her audience?

5. What types of evidence does Harjo use to support her argument? How
   convincing is the evidence to you?

6. How does Harjo use her status as a Native American to enhance her
   position? Would her argument be as credible if it were written by someone of another background?

7. How does she appeal to the emotions of the readers in the essay? In what
   ways do these strategies strengthen or detract from her logical reasons?

8. Why does Harjo discuss what legislatures and universities are doing in
   response to the situation?

Marjorie Lee Garretson   Student Essay

More Pros Than Cons in a Meat-Free Life

Marjorie Lee Garretson's opinion piece originally appeared in *The Daily Mississippian*, the
student newspaper of the University of Mississippi, in April of 2010.

What would you say if I told you there was a way to improve your overall health, 1
decrease environmental waste and save animals from inhumane treatment at the
same time? You would probably ask how this is possible. The answer is quite simple:

go vegetarian. Vegetarians are often labeled as different or odd, but if you take a closer look at their actions, vegetarians reap multiple benefits meat eaters often overlook or choose to ignore for convenience.

The health benefits vegetarians acquire lead us to wonder why more people are not jumping on the meat-free bandwagon. On average, vegetarians have a lower body mass index,° significantly decreased cancer rates and longer life expectancies. In addition, Alzheimer's disease° and osteoporosis° were linked to diets containing dairy, eggs and meat.

The environment also encounters benefits from vegetarians. It takes less energy and waste to produce vegetables and grains than the energy required to produce meat. To produce one pound of meat it is estimated to require 16 pounds of grain and up to 5,000 gallons of water, which comes from adding the water used to grow the grain crop as well as the animal's personal water consumption. Also, according to the Environmental Protection Agency, the runoff of fecal matter from meat factories is the single most detrimental° pollutant to our water supply. In fact, it is said to be the most significant pollutant in comparison to sources of all other industries combined.

The inhumane treatment of animals is common at most animal factories. The living conditions chickens, cows, pigs and other livestock are forced into are far removed from their natural habitats. The goal of animal agriculture nowadays seems to be minimizing costs without attention to the sacrifices being made to do so. Animals are crammed into small cages where they often cannot even turn around. Exercise is denied to the animals to increase energy toward the production of meat. Female cows are pumped with hormones to allow their bodies to produce triple the amount of milk they are naturally capable of. Chickens are stuffed tightly into wire cages, and conditions are manipulated to increase egg production cycles. When chickens no longer lay eggs and cows cannot produce milk, they are transported to slaughterhouses where their lives are taken from them—often piece by piece.

Animal factory farms do a great job convincing Americans that their industry is vital to our health because of the protein, calcium and other nutrients available in chicken, beef and milk. We are bombarded with "Got Milk?" ads featuring various celebrities with white milk mustaches. We are told the egg is a healthy breakfast choice and lean protein is the basis of many good weight loss diets. What all of the ads and campaigns for animal products leave out are all the hormones injected into the animals to maximize production. Also, the tight living conditions allow for feces to contaminate the animals, their environment and the potential meat they are growing. It is ironic how irate° Americans react to puppy mills and the inhumane treatment of household pets, but for our meat and dairy products we look the other way. We pretend it is fine to confine cows, pigs and chickens to tiny spaces and give

2 Do you find Garretson's discussion of the health benefits of vegetarianism convincing? Why or why not?

3 Is it possible to decrease damage to the environment from factory farms without becoming a vegetarian? What other options might there be?

5

Do you agree that Americans are hypocritical about the different treatment of household pets and farm animals? Why or why not?

---

body mass index: A measurement of body fat, based on height and weight.   **Alzheimer's disease:** An incurable brain disorder causing memory loss and dementia.   **osteoporosis:** A disease which causes an increased risk of bone fractures.   **detrimental:** Harmful.   **irate:** Angry.

them hormones and treat them inhumanely in their life and often in the way they are killed. We then cook and consume them at our dinner tables with our families and friends.

Therefore, I encourage you to consider a meat-free lifestyle not only for the sake of the animals and the environment, but most importantly your personal health. All of your daily nutrients can be found in plant-based sources, and oftentimes when you make the switch to being a vegetarian, your food choices expand because you are willing to use vegetables and grains in innovative ways at the dinner table. Going vegetarian is a life-changing decision and one you can be proud of because you know it is for your own health as well as the greater good. 6

Questions to Start You Thinking

Meaning

1. What points does Garretson make to support her position that vegetarianism has multiple benefits?

2. What, according to Garretson, are the environmental consequences of meat-eating?

3. In the author's view, why is it especially troubling that we are willing to "look the other way" (paragraph 5) on the inhumane treatment of farm animals?

Writing Strategies

4. What kind of support does Garretson use to back up her claims about the benefits of vegetarianism? Do you find her argument effective? Why or why not?

5. To what extent does Garretson account for other points of view? How does the inclusion (or absence) of opposing views affect your opinion on the issue?

6. This article was written as an editorial for a student newspaper. How might Garretson change the article if she were submitting it as an essay or research paper?

7. Using highlighters or marginal notes, identify the essay's introduction, thesis, major points or reasons, supporting evidence for each point, and conclusion. How effective is the organization of this essay?

Learning by Writing

The Assignment: Taking a Stand

For writing activities for taking a stand, visit <bedfordstmartins .com/bedguide>.

Find a controversy that rouses your interest. It might be a current issue, a long-standing one, or a matter of personal concern: military benefits for national guard troops sent to war zones, the contribution of sports to a school's educational mission, or the need for menu changes at the cafeteria to accommodate ethnic, religious, and personal preferences. Your purpose isn't to solve a social or moral problem but to make clear exactly where you stand on an issue and to persuade your readers to respect your position, perhaps even to accept it. As you reflect on your topic, you may change your position, but don't shift positions in the middle of your essay.

Assume that your readers are people who may or may not be familiar with the controversy, so provide some background or an overview to help them understand the situation. Furthermore, your readers may not have taken sides yet or may hold a position different from yours. You'll need to consider their views and choose strategies that will enlist their support.

Each of these students took a clear stand:

> A writer who pays her own college costs disputed the opinion that working during the school year provides a student with valuable knowledge. Citing her painful experience, she maintained that devoting full time to studies is far better than juggling school and work.

> Another writer challenged his history textbook's portrayal of Joan of Arc as "an ignorant farm girl subject to religious hysteria."

> A member of the wrestling team argued that the number of weight categories in wrestling should be increased because athletes who overtrain to qualify for the existing categories often damage their health.

Facing the Challenge   Taking a Stand

The major challenge writers face when taking a stand is to gather enough relevant evidence to support their position. Without such evidence, you'll convince only those who agreed with you in the first place. You also won't persuade readers by ranting emotionally about an issue or insulting as ignorant those who hold different opinions. Moreover, few readers respect an evasive writer who avoids taking a stand.

What does work is respect—yours for the views of readers who will, in turn, respect your opinion, even if they don't agree with it. You convey—and gain—respect when you anticipate readers' objections or counterarguments, demonstrate knowledge of these alternate views, and present evidence that addresses others' concerns as it strengthens your argument.

Joan of Arc (1412–1431), heroine, martyr, saint, and cultural icon who boldly led French forces against the English.

A
Writer's
Guide

　　To anticipate and find evidence that acknowledges other views, list groups that might have strong opinions on your topic. Then try putting yourself in the shoes of a member of each group by writing a paragraph on the issue from that point of view.

- What would that person's opinion be?
- On what grounds might he or she object to your argument?
- How can you best address these concerns and overcome objections?

Your paragraph will suggest additional evidence to support your claims.

Generating Ideas

For this assignment, you will need to select an issue, take a stand, develop a clear position, and assemble evidence that supports your view.

For more strategies for generating ideas, see Ch. 19.

Find an Issue. The topic for this paper should be an issue or controversy that interests both you and your audience. Try brainstorming a list of possible topics. To get started, look at the headlines of a newspaper or newsmagazine, review the letters to the editor, check the political cartoons on the opinion page, or watch for stories or photos on civic demonstrations or protests. You might also consult the index to *CQ Researcher* in the library, watch a news broadcast, use a search engine to browse news or opinion Web sites, talk with friends, or consider topics raised in class. If you keep a journal, look over your entries to see what has perplexed or angered you. If you need to understand the issue better or aren't sure you want to take a stand on it, investigate by freewriting, reading, or turning to other sources.

　　Once you have a list of possible topics, drop those that seem too broad or complex or that you don't know much about. Weed out anything that might not hold your interest or that of your readers. From your new, shorter list, pick the issue or controversy for which you can make the strongest argument.

Start with a Question and a Thesis. At this stage, many writers find it useful to pose the issue as a question—a question that will be answered through the position they take. Skip vague questions that most readers wouldn't debate, or convert them to questions that allow different stands.

| VAGUE QUESTION | Is stereotyping bad? |
| CLEARLY DEBATABLE | Should we fight gender stereotypes in advertising? |

You can help focus your position by stating it in a sentence—a thesis, or statement of your stand. Your statement can answer your question:

For more on stating a thesis, see pp. 401–09.

| WORKING THESIS | We should expect advertisers to fight rather than reinforce gender stereotypes. |
| OR | Most people who object to gender stereotypes in advertising need to get a sense of humor. |

Your thesis should invite continued debate by taking a strong position that could be argued rather than stating a fact.

FACT	Hispanics constitute 16 percent of the community but only 3 percent of our school population.
WORKING THESIS	Our school should increase its outreach to the Hispanic community, which is underrepresented on campus.

Learning by Doing Asking Your Question

Using your list of possible topics, start writing down questions you might want to answer. Work individually or with a classmate to review both of your lists. Weed out questions that are vague or that would be difficult to debate. For questions with potential, write out some working thesis statements until you settle on a statement you want to support.

Use Formal Reasoning to Refine Your Position. When you take a position about a debatable matter, you are likely to use reasoning as well as specific evidence to support your position. A *syllogism* is a series of statements, or premises, used in traditional formal logic to lead deductively to a logical conclusion.

MAJOR STATEMENT	All students must pay tuition.
MINOR STATEMENT	You are a student.
CONCLUSION	Therefore, you must pay tuition.

For a syllogism to be logical, ensuring that its conclusion always applies, its major and minor statements must be true, its definitions of terms must remain stable, and its classification of specific persons or items must be accurate. In real-life arguments, such tidiness may be hard to achieve.

For example, maybe we all agree with the major statement just above. All students must pay tuition. However, some students owe tuition, but it is paid for them through a loan or scholarship. Others are admitted under special programs, such as a free-tuition benefit for families of college employees or a back-to-college program for retirees. Further, the word *student* is general; it might apply to students at public high schools who pay no tuition. Next, everyone might agree that you are a student, but maybe you haven't completed registration or the computer has mysteriously dropped you from the class list. Such complications can threaten the success of your conclusion, especially if your audience doesn't accept it. In fact, many civic and social arguments revolve around questions such as these: What— exactly—is the category or group affected? Is its definition or consequence stable—or does it vary? Who falls in or out of the category?

Use Informal Toulmin Reasoning to Refine Your Position. A contemporary approach to logic is presented by the philosopher Stephen Toulmin (1922– 2009) in *The Uses of Argument*. He describes an informal way of arguing that acknowledges the power of assumptions in our day-to-day reasoning. This approach starts with a concise statement—the essence of an argument— that makes a claim and supplies a reason to support it.

$$\overline{\text{CLAIM}} \qquad \qquad \overline{\text{REASON}}$$
Students should boycott the snack bar <u>because</u> the food costs too much.

You develop a claim by supporting your reasons with evidence—your *data* or grounds. For example, your evidence might include facts about the cost of lunches on campus, especially in contrast to local fast-food options, and statistics about the limited resources of most students enrolled at your campus.

However, most practical arguments rely on a *warrant*, your thinking about the connection or relationship between your claim and your supporting data. Because you accept this connection and assume that it applies, you generally assume that others also take it for granted. For instance, nearly all students probably would accept your assumption that a campus snack bar should serve the needs of its customers. Many might also agree that students should take action rather than allow a campus facility to take advantage of them by charging high prices. Even so, you could state your warrant directly if you thought that your readers would not see the same connection that you do. You also could back up your warrant, if necessary, in various ways:

- using facts, perhaps based on quality and cost comparisons with food service operations on other campuses
- using logic, perhaps based on research findings about the relationship between cost and nutrition for institutional food as well as the importance of good nutrition for brain function and learning
- making emotional appeals, perhaps based on happy memories of the snack bar or irritation with its options
- making ethical appeals, perhaps based on the college mission statement or other expressions of the school's commitment to students

As you develop your reasoning, you might adjust your claim or your data to suit your audience, your issue, or your refined thinking. For instance, you might *qualify* your argument (perhaps limiting your objections to most, but not all, of the lunch prices). You might also add a *rebuttal* by identifying an *exception* to it (perhaps excluding the fortunate, but few, students without financial worries due to good jobs or family support). Or you might simply reconsider your claim, concluding that the campus snack bar is, after all, convenient for students and that the manager might be willing to offer more inexpensive options without a student boycott.

———————— REVISED CLAIM ———————— ┐ ┌— REASON —
The snack bar should offer less expensive options because most

students can't afford a balanced meal at current prices.

Toulmin reasoning is especially effective for making claims like these:

- Fact — *Loss of polar ice can accelerate ocean warming.*
- Cause — *The software company went bankrupt because of its excessive borrowing and poor management.*
- Value — *Cell phone plan A is a better deal than cell phone plan B.*
- Policy — *Admissions policies at Triborough University should be less restrictive.*

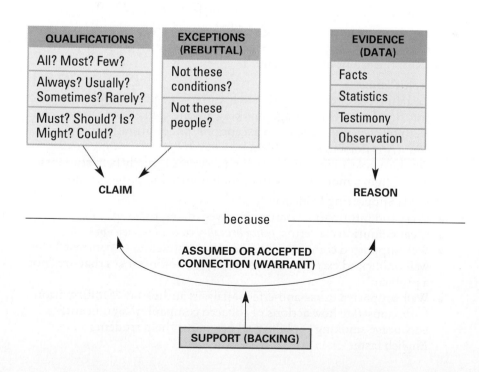

DISCOVERY CHECKLIST

☐ What issue or controversy concerns you? What current debate engages you?

☐ What position do you want to take? How can you state your stand? What evidence might you need to support it?

☐ How might you refine your working thesis? How could you make statements more accurate, definitions clearer, or categories more exact?

☐ What assumptions are you making? What clarification of or support for these assumptions might your audience need?

☐ How might you qualify your thesis? What exceptions should you note? What other views might you want to recognize?

Select Evidence to Support Your Position. When you state your claim, you state your overall position. You also may state supporting claims as topic sentences that establish your supporting points, introduce supporting evidence, and help your reader follow your reasoning. To decide how to support a claim, try to reduce it to its core question. Then figure out what reliable and persuasive evidence might answer the question. As you begin to look for supporting evidence, consider the issue in terms of the three general types of claims — claims that require substantiation, provide evaluation, and endorse policy.

1. Claims of Substantiation: What Happened?

   These claims require examining and interpreting information in order to resolve disputes about facts, circumstances, causes or effects, definitions, or the extent of a problem.

   Sample Claims:
   a. Certain types of cigarette ads, such as the once-popular Joe Camel ads, significantly encourage smoking among teenagers.
   b. Despite a few well-publicized exceptions, police brutality in this country is not a major problem.
   c. On the whole, bilingual education programs actually help students learn English more quickly than total immersion programs do.

   Possible Supporting Evidence:
   - Facts and information: parties involved, dates, times, places
   - Clear definitions of terms: *police brutality* or *total immersion*
   - Well-supported comparison and contrast: statistics to contrast "a few well-publicized exceptions" with a majority of instances that are "not a problem"
   - Well-supported cause-and-effect analysis: authoritative information to demonstrate how actions of tobacco companies "significantly encourage smoking" or bilingual programs "help students learn English faster"

2. Claims of Evaluation: What Is Right?

These claims consider right or wrong, appropriateness or inappropriateness, and worth or lack of worth involved in an issue.

Sample Claims:
a. Research using fetal tissue is unethical in a civilized society.
b. English-only legislation promotes cultural intolerance in our society.
c. Keeping children in foster care for years, instead of releasing them for adoption, is wrong.

Possible Supporting Evidence:
- Explanations or definitions of appropriate criteria for judging: deciding what's "unethical in a civilized society"
- Corresponding details and reasons showing how the topic does or does not meet the criteria: details or applications of English-only legislation that meet the criteria for "cultural intolerance" or reasons with supporting details that show why years of foster care meet the criteria for being "wrong"

3. Claims of Policy: What Should Be Done?

These claims challenge or defend approaches for achieving generally accepted goals.

Sample Claims:
a. The federal government should support the distribution of clean needles to reduce the rate of HIV infection among intravenous drug users.
b. Denying illegal immigrant children enrollment in public schools will reduce the problem of illegal immigration.
c. All teenagers accused of murder should be tried as adults.

Possible Supporting Evidence:
- Explanation and definition of the policy goal: assuming that most in your audience agree that it is desirable to reduce "the rate of HIV infection" or "the problem of illegal immigration" or to try murderers in the same way regardless of age
- Corresponding details and reasons showing how your policy recommendation would meet the goal: results of "clean needle" trials or examples of crime statistics and cases involving teen murderers
- Explanations or definitions of the policy's limits or applications, if needed: why some teens should not be tried as adults because of their situations

Consider Your Audience as You Develop Your Claim. The nature of your audience might influence the type of claim you choose to make. For example, suppose that the nurse or social worker at the high school you attended or that your children now attend proposed distributing free condoms to students. The following table illustrates how the responses of different audiences to this proposal might vary with the claim. As you develop your claims, try to put yourself in the place of your audience. For example, if you are a former student, what claim would most effectively persuade you? If you are the parent of a teenager, what claim would best address both your general views and your specific concerns about your own child?

Audience	Type of Claim	Possible Effect on Audience
Conservative parents who believe that free condoms would promote immoral sexual behavior	*Evaluation:* In order to save lives and prevent unwanted pregnancies, distributing free condoms in high school is our moral duty.	Counterproductive if the parents feel that they are being accused of immorality for not agreeing with the proposal
Conservative parents who believe that free condoms would promote immoral sexual behavior	*Substantiation:* Distributing free condoms in high school can effectively reduce pregnancy rates and the spread of STDs, especially AIDS, without substantially increasing the rate of sexual activity among teenagers.	Possibly persuasive, based on effectiveness, if parents feel that their desire to protect their children from harm, no matter what, is recognized and the evidence deflates their main fear (promoting sexual activity)
School administrators who want to do what's right but don't want hordes of angry parents pounding down the school doors	*Policy:* Distributing free condoms in high school to prevent unwanted pregnancies and the spread of STDs, including AIDS, is best accomplished as part of a voluntary sex education program that strongly emphasizes abstinence as the primary preventative.	Possibly persuasive if administrators see that the proposal addresses health and pregnancy issues without setting off parental outrage (by proposing a voluntary program that would promote abstinence, thus addressing a primary concern of parents)

For more about forms of evidence, see pp. 40–43.

For more about using sources, see Ch. 12 and the Quick Research Guide beginning on p. A-18.

Assemble Supporting Evidence. Your claim stated, you'll need evidence to support it. What is evidence? It is anything that demonstrates the soundness of your position and the points you make in your argument—facts, statistics, observations, expert testimony, illustrations, examples, and case studies.

The three most important sources of evidence are these:

1. *Facts, including statistics.* Facts are statements that can be verified by objective means; statistics are facts expressed in numbers. Facts usually form the basis of a successful argument.

2. *Expert testimony.* Experts are people with knowledge of a particular field gained from study and experience.

3. *Firsthand observation.* Your own observations can be persuasive if you can assure your readers that your account is accurate.

For more on logical fallacies, see pp. 178–79.

Of course, evidence must be used carefully to avoid defending logical fallacies—common mistakes in thinking—and making statements that lead to wrong conclusions. Examples are easy to misuse (claiming proof by example or using too few examples). Because two professors you know are dissatisfied with state-mandated testing programs, you can't claim that all or even most professors are. Even if you surveyed more professors at your school, you could speak only generally of "many professors." To claim more, you might need to conduct scientific surveys, access reliable statistics in the library or on the Internet, or solicit the views of a respected expert in the area.

Learning by Doing 🎦 Supporting a Claim

In a small group, have each person write out, in one complete sentence, the core claim or position he or she plans to support. Drop all these "position statements" into a hat, with no names attached. Then draw and read each aloud in turn, inviting the group to suggest useful supporting evidence and possible sources for it. Ask someone in the group to act as a recorder, listing suggestions on a separate page for each claim. Finally, match up writers with claims, and share reactions. (If you are working online, follow your instructor's directions, possibly sending your statement privately to your instructor for anonymous posting for a threaded discussion.) If this activity causes you to alter your stand, be thankful: it will be easier to revise now than later.

Record Evidence. For this assignment, you will need to record your evidence in written form. Take notes in a notebook, on index cards, or in a computer file. Be sure to note exactly where each piece of information comes from. Keep the form of your notes flexible so that you can easily rearrange them as you plan your draft.

Test and Select Evidence to Persuade Your Audience. Now that you've collected some evidence, you need to sift through it to decide which pieces of information to use. Evidence is useful and trustworthy when it is accurate, reliable, up-to-date, to the point, representative, appropriately complex, and sufficient and strong enough to back the claim and persuade your readers. You may find that your evidence supports a stand different from the one you intended to take. Might you find some facts, testimony, and observations that would support your original position after all? Or should you rethink your position? If so, revise your working thesis. Does your evidence cluster around several points or reasons? If so, use your evidence to help plan the sequence of your essay.

In addition, consider whether information presented visually would strengthen your case or make your evidence easier for readers to grasp.

For more on testing evidence, see pp. A-8–A-12.

For more on the use of visuals and their placement, see section B in the Quick Format Guide, pp. A-8–A-12.

- Graphs can effectively show facts or figures.
- Tables can convey terms or comparisons.
- Photographs or other illustrations can substantiate situations.

Test each visual as you would test other evidence for accuracy, reliability, and relevance. Mention each visual in your text, and place the visual close to that reference. Cite the source of any visual you use and of any data you consolidate in your own graph or table.

Most effective arguments take opposing viewpoints into consideration whenever possible. Use these questions to help you assess your evidence from this standpoint.

ANALYZE YOUR READERS' POINTS OF VIEW

- What are their attitudes? Interests? Priorities?
- What do they already know about the issue?
- What do they expect you to say?
- Do you have enough appropriate evidence that they'll find convincing?

FOCUS ON THOSE WITH DIFFERENT OR OPPOSING OPINIONS

- What are their opinions or claims?
- What is their evidence?
- Who supports their positions?
- Do you have enough appropriate evidence to show why their claims are weak, only partially true, misguided, or just plain wrong?

ACKNOWLEDGE AND REBUT THE COUNTERARGUMENTS

- What are the strengths of other positions? What might you want to concede or grant to be accurate or relevant?
- What are the limitations of other positions? What might you want to question or challenge?
- What facts, statistics, testimony, observations, or other evidence would support questioning, qualifying, challenging, or countering other views?

Planning, Drafting, and Developing

Reassess Your Position and Your Thesis. Now that you have looked into the issue, what is your current position? If necessary, revise the thesis that you formulated earlier. Then summarize your reasons for holding this view, and list your supporting evidence.

For exercises on choosing and supporting effective thesis statements, visit <**bedfordstmartins .com/bedguide**>.

WORKING THESIS	We should expect advertisers to fight rather than reinforce gender stereotypes.
REFINED THESIS	Consumers should spend their shopping dollars thoughtfully in order to hold advertisers accountable for reinforcing rather than resisting gender stereotypes.

Learning by Doing 🎬 Refining Your Plans

Follow the steps outlined in the previous section: update your thesis to match your current view, summarize the reasons behind that position, and list your supporting evidence. Ask a classmate for a second opinion on these plans, and continue reworking them if your exchange generates significant questions or ideas.

Organize Your Material to Persuade Your Audience. Arrange your notes into the order you think you'll follow, perhaps making an outline. One useful pattern is the classical form of argument:

1. Introduce the subject to gain the readers' interest.
2. State your main point or thesis.
3. If useful, supply the historical background or an overview of the situation.
4. Present your points or reasons, and provide evidence to support them.
5. Refute the opposition.
6. Reaffirm your main point.

For more on outlines, see pp. 413–21.

Especially when you expect readers to be hostile to your position, you may want to take the opposite approach: refute the opposition first, then replace those views by building a logical chain of evidence that leads to your main point, and finally state your position. If you state your position too early, you might alienate resistant readers or make them defensive. Of course, you can always try both approaches to see which one works better. Note also that some papers will be mostly based on refutation (countering opposing views) and some mostly on confirmation (directly supporting your position). Others might even alternate refutation and confirmation rather than separate them.

Define Your Terms. To prevent misunderstanding, make clear any unfamiliar or questionable terms used in your thesis. If your position is "Humanists are dangerous," give a short definition of what you mean by *humanists* and by *dangerous* early in the paper.

Attend to Logical, Emotional, and Ethical Appeals. The logical appeal engages readers' intellect; the emotional appeal touches their hearts; the ethical appeal draws on their sense of fairness and reasonableness. A persuasive argument usually operates on all three levels. For example, you might use all three appeals to support a thesis about the need to curb accidental gunshot deaths, as the following table illustrates.

For more on appeals, see pp. 42–44.

Type of Appeal	Ways of Making the Appeal	Possible Supporting Evidence
Logical (logos)	■ Rely on clear reasoning and sound evidence to influence a reader's thinking. ■ Demonstrate what you claim, and don't claim what you can't demonstrate. ■ Test and select your evidence.	■ Supply current and reliable statistics about gun ownership and accidental shootings. ■ Prepare a bar graph that shows the number of incidents each year in Lion Valley during the past ten years, using data from the county records. ■ Describe the immediate and long-term consequences of a typical shooting accident.
Emotional (pathos)	■ Choose examples and language that will influence a reader's feelings. ■ Include effective images, but don't overdo them. ■ Complement logical appeals, but don't replace them.	■ Describe the wrenching scenario of a father whose college-age son unexpectedly returns home at 3 A.M. The father mistakes his son for an intruder and shoots him, throwing the family into turmoil. ■ Use quotations and descriptions from newspaper accounts to show reactions of family members and neighbors.
Ethical (ethos)	■ Use a tone and approach that appeal to your reader's sense of fairness and reasonableness. ■ Spell out your values and beliefs, and acknowledge values and beliefs of others with different opinions. ■ Establish your credentials, if any, and the credentials of experts you cite. ■ Instill confidence in your readers so that they see you as a caring, trustworthy person with reliable views.	■ Establish your reasonable approach by acknowledging the views of hunters and others who store guns at home and follow recommended safety procedures. ■ Supply the credentials or affiliation of experts ("Ray Fontaine, public safety director for the town of Lion Valley"). ■ Note ways in which experts have established their authority ("During my interview with Ms. Dutton, she related recent incidents involving gun accidents in the home, testifying to her extensive knowledge of this issue in our community.")

Learning by Doing 🎦 Making Columns of Appeals

Use columns to help you write about your logical, emotional, and ethical appeals. Go to the Format menu in your word processor, select Columns, and click on the preset three-column pattern. (Or draw three columns on paper.) Under "Logical Appeals," write the claims and support that rely on reasoning and sound evidence. Under "Emotional Appeals," note the claims and support that may affect readers' emotions. Under "Ethical Appeals," add your claims and support based on values, both your values and those of opposing points of view as you understand them. As you reread each column, consider how to relate your claims and support across columns, how to organize your ideas persuasively, and how best to merge or separate your logical, emotional, and ethical appeals. Add color coding if you want to identify related ideas.

Logical Appeals	Emotional Appeals	Ethical Appeals

Credit Your Sources. As you write, make your sources of evidence clear. One simple way to do so is to incorporate your source into the text: "According to an article in the October 18, 2010, issue of *Time*" or "As to my history professor, Dr. Harry Cleghorn . . ."

For pointers on integrating and documenting sources, see Ch. 12 and D6 (p. A-29) and E1–E2 (pp. A-30–A-35) in the Quick Research Guide.

Revising and Editing

When you're writing a paper taking a stand, you may fall in love with the evidence you've gone to such trouble to collect. Taking out information is hard to do, but if it is irrelevant, redundant, or weak, the evidence won't help your case. Play the crusty critic as you reread your paper. Consider outlining what it actually includes so that you can check for missing or unnecessary points or evidence. Pay special attention to the suggestions of friends or classmates who read your draft for you. Apply their advice by ruthlessly cutting unneeded material, as in the following passage:

For more revising and editing strategies, see Ch. 23.

> The school boundary system requires children who are homeless or whose families move frequently to change schools repeatedly. ~~They often lack clean clothes, winter coats, and required school supplies.~~ As a result, these children struggle to establish strong relationships with teachers, to find caring advocates at school, and even to make friends to join for recess or lunch.

Peer Response 👥 Taking a Stand

Enlist several other students to read your draft critically and tell you whether they accept your arguments. For a paper in which you take a stand, ask your peer editors to answer questions such as these:

For general questions for a peer editor, see p. 465.

- Can you state the writer's claim?
- Do you have any problems following or accepting the reasons for the writer's position? Would you make any changes in the reasoning?
- How persuasive is the writer's evidence? What questions do you have about it? Can you suggest good evidence the writer has overlooked?

- Has the writer provided enough transitions to guide you through the argument?

- Has the writer made a strong case? Are you persuaded to his or her point of view? If not, is there any point or objection that the writer could address to make the argument more compelling?

- If this paper were yours, what is the one thing you would be sure to work on before handing it in?

For online Take Action help, visit **<bedfordstmartins .com/bedguide>**.

Use the Take Action chart (p. 177) to help you figure out how to improve your draft. Skim across the top to identify questions you might ask about strengthening support for your stand. When you answer a question with "Yes" or "Maybe," move straight down the column to Locate Specifics under that question. Use the activities there to pinpoint gaps, problems, or weaknesses. Then move straight down the column to Take Action. Use the advice that suits your problem as you revise.

REVISION CHECKLIST

☐ Is your main point, or thesis, clear? Do you stick to it rather than drifting into contradictions?

☐ Where might you need better reasons or more evidence?

☐ Have you tried to keep in mind your readers and what would appeal to them? Where have you answered their likely objections?

☐ Have you defined all necessary terms and explained your points clearly?

☐ Is your tone suitable for your readers? Are you likely at any places to alienate them, or, at the other extreme, to sound weak or apologetic?

☐ Might your points seem stronger if arranged in a different sequence?

☐ Have you unfairly omitted any evidence that would hurt your case?

☐ In rereading your paper, do you have any excellent, fresh thoughts? If so, where might you make room for them?

For more editing and proofreading strategies, see pp. 473–76.

After you have revised your argument, edit and proofread it. Carefully check the grammar, word choice, punctuation, and mechanics — and then correct any problems you find. Wherever you have given facts and figures as evidence, check for errors in names and numbers.

Take Action Strengthening Support for a Stand

Ask each question at the top of the chart to consider whether your draft might need work on that issue. If so, follow the ASK—LOCATE SPECIFICS—TAKE ACTION sequence to revise.

	Missing Points?	Missing Supporting Evidence?	One-Sided Support?
1 ASK	Did I leave out any main points that I promised in my thesis or planned to include?	Did I leave out evidence needed to support my points—facts, statistics, expert testimony, firsthand observations, details, or examples?	Have I skipped over opposing or alternative perspectives? Have I treated them unfairly, disrespectfully, or too briefly?
2 LOCATE SPECIFICS	■ List the main points your thesis states or suggests. ■ List the main points you meant to include. ■ Highlight each point from your lists in your draft.	■ Highlight or color code each bit of supporting evidence. ■ Put a ✓ by any passage without any or without enough supporting evidence.	■ Highlight passages in which you recognize other points of view (or copy them into a separate file) so you can look at them on their own. ■ Read these passages to see whether they sound fair and respectful. Jot down notes to yourself about possible revisions.
3 TAKE ACTION	■ Add any missing point from your thesis or plan. ■ Express assumptions (points, main ideas, reasons) that are in your head but not your draft. ■ Revise your thesis, adding or dropping points until it promises what you can deliver to readers.	■ Add any missing evidence you meant to include. ■ For each ✓, brainstorm or ask questions (who, what, where, when, why, how) to decide what support readers might find convincing. ■ Add the evidence, details, or examples needed to support each main point.	■ Identify or add other points of view if they are expected and you have left them out. ■ Acknowledge credible alternative views, explaining where you agree and differ. ■ Reasonably challenge or counter questionable views. ■ Edit your wording so your tone is respectful of others.

For more help, find the relevant checklist sections in the Quick Editing Guide on p. A-36. Turn also to the Quick Format Guide beginning on p. A-1.

EDITING CHECKLIST

☐ Is it clear what each pronoun refers to? Does each pronoun agree with (match) its antecedent? Do pronouns used as subjects agree with their verbs? Carefully check sentences that make broad claims about *everyone, no one, some, a few,* or some other group identified by an indefinite pronoun.   A6

☐ Have you used an adjective whenever describing a noun or pronoun? Have you used an adverb whenever describing a verb, adjective, or adverb? Have you used the correct form when comparing two or more things?   A7

☐ Have you set off your transitions, other introductory elements, and interrupters with commas, if these are needed?   C1

☐ Have you spelled and capitalized everything correctly, especially names of people and organizations?   D1, D2

☐ Have you correctly punctuated quotations from sources and experts?   C3

Recognizing Logical Fallacies

For more on faulty thinking, see p. A-37.

Logical fallacies are common mistakes in thinking that may lead to wrong conclusions or distort evidence. Here are a few familiar logical fallacies.

Term	Explanation	Example
Non Sequitur	Stating a claim that doesn't follow from your first premise or statement; Latin for "It does not follow"	Jenn should marry Mateo. In college he got all A's.
Oversimplification	Offering easy solutions for complicated problems	If we want to end substance abuse, let's send every drug user to prison for life. (Even aspirin users?)
Post Hoc Ergo Propter Hoc	Assuming a cause-and-effect relationship where none exists even though one event preceded another; Latin for "after this, therefore because of this"	After Jenny's black cat crossed my path, everything went wrong, and I failed my midterm.
Allness	Stating or implying that something is true of an entire class of things, often using *all, everyone, no one, always,* or *never*	Students enjoy studying. (All students? All subjects? All the time?)

(continued on next page)

Term	Explanation	Example
Proof by Example or Too Few Examples	Presenting an example as proof rather than as illustration or clarification; overgeneralizing (the basis of much prejudice)	Armenians are great chefs. My neighbor is Armenian, and can he cook!
Begging the Question	Proving a statement already taken for granted, often by repeating it in different words or by defining a word in terms of itself	Rapists are dangerous because they are menaces. Happiness is the state of being happy.
Circular Reasoning	Supporting a statement with itself; a form of begging the question	He is a liar because he simply isn't telling the truth.
Either/Or Reasoning	Oversimplifying by assuming that an issue has only two sides, a statement must be true or false, a question demands a yes or no answer, or a problem has only two possible solutions (and one that's acceptable)	What are we going to do about global warming? Either we stop using all of the energy-consuming vehicles and products that cause it, or we just learn to live with it.
Argument from Dubious Authority	Using an unidentified authority to shore up a weak argument or an authority whose expertise lies outside the issue, such as a television personality selling insurance	According to some of the most knowing scientists in America, smoking two packs a day is as harmless as eating oatmeal cookies.
Argument *ad Hominem*	Attacking an individual's opinion by attacking his or her character, thus deflecting attention from the merit of a proposal; Latin for "against the man"	Diaz may argue that we need to save the whales, but he's the type who gets emotional over nothing.
Argument from Ignorance	Maintaining that a claim has to be accepted because it hasn't been disproved or that it has to be rejected because it has not been proved	Despite years of effort, no one has proved that ghosts don't exist; therefore, we should expect to see them at any time. No one has ever shown that life exists on any other planet; clearly the notion of other living things in the universe is absurd.
Argument by Analogy	Treating an extended comparison between familiar and unfamiliar items, based on similarities and ignoring differences, as evidence rather than as a useful way of explaining	People were born free as the birds; it's cruel to expect them to work.
Bandwagon Argument	Suggesting that everyone is joining the group and readers who don't may miss out on happiness, success, or a reward	Purchasing the new Swallowtail admits you to the nation's most elite group of drivers.

Additional Writing Assignments

1. Write a letter to the editor of your newspaper or a newsmagazine in which you agree or disagree with the publication's editorial stand on a current question. Make clear your reasons for holding your view.

2. Write one claim each of substantiation, of evaluation, and of policy for or against a specific policy or proposal. Indicate an audience each claim might address effectively. Then list reasons and types of evidence you might need to support one of these claims. Finally, for the same claim, indicate what opposing viewpoints you would need to consider and how you could best do so.

3. Write a short paper, blog entry, or class posting expressing your view on one of these topics or another that comes to mind. Make clear your reasons for thinking as you do.

For more on supporting a position with sources, see Ch. 12.

Bilingual education	Raising the minimum wage
Nonsmokers' rights	Protecting the polar bears
Dealing with date rape	Controlling terrorism
Salaries of professional athletes	Prayer in public schools

4. Find a letter to the editor, opinion piece, or blog that takes a stand that you disagree with. Write a response to that piece, countering its points, presenting your points, and supporting them with evidence. Decide which audience to address: The writer? Readers likely to support the other selection? Readers with interest in the issue but without loyalty to the original publication? Some other group?

5. Working with a classmate or a small group online, develop a threaded discussion or collaborative blog designed to inform your audience about multiple points of view on an issue. Aim to present the most compelling reasons and evidence to support each view. Counter other views as appropriate with reasons and evidence, but avoid emotional outbursts attacking them. Before you begin posting, decide which view each person will present. Considering your purpose and audience, also decide whether the thread or blog should cover certain points or be organized in a particular way. If you wish to refine your contribution before you post it, write it in a location or file where you can save and return to it. Take some time to revise and edit before you send or paste it into the thread or blog.

6. **Visual Assignment.** Select one of the images on the next page. Analyze its argument, noting its persuasive visual elements. Write an essay that first explains its argument, including its topic and its visual appeals to viewers, and then agrees, disagrees, or qualifies that argument.

A young hospitalized cancer victim watches a fundraising walkathon (2009).

A family in Connecticut reads after dinner.

A cell phone tower in Mono Lake, California, from photographer Robert Voit's series, "New Trees."

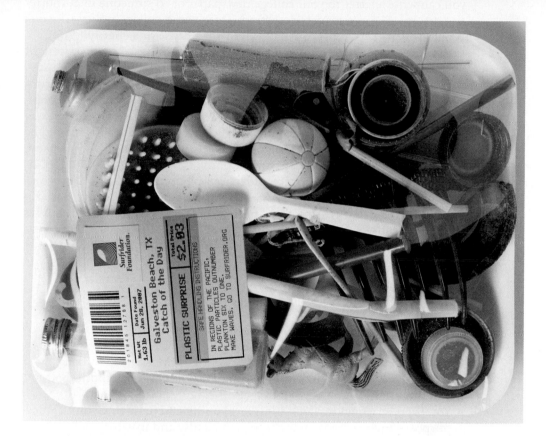

Within the image:

Surfrider Foundation.

Net Wt 1.63 lb   Date Found Jun 28, 2007

Galveston Beach, TX
Catch of the Day

PLASTIC SURPRISE   Total Price $2.03

SAFE HANDLING INSTRUCTIONS:
IN REGIONS OF THE PACIFIC,
PLASTIC PARTICLES OUTNUMBER
PLANKTON SIX TO ONE.
MAKE WAVES. GO TO SURFRIDER.ORG

201845 127881

Responding to an Image

This image from the public service campaign of the Surfrider Foundation, an environmental organization, shows real trash collected from a beach in Galveston. Not only did this image run in various magazines, but the real packages of trash were offered to shoppers at farmer's markets around the country. Examine this image carefully, including its details. What is the problem that the image identifies? Why is the problem presented as it is? How might the presentation help viewers understand the problem? In what ways do the details suggest aspects, dimensions, or variations of the problem? What solutions does the image suggest or imply? Are the solutions realistic and workable? What is your reaction to the presentation of a problem and potential solutions in this way?

Sometimes when you learn of a problem such as the destruction caused by a natural disaster, homelessness, or famine, you say to yourself, "Something should be done about that." You can do something constructive yourself—through the powerful and persuasive activity of writing.

Your purpose in such writing, as political leaders and advertisers well know, is to rouse your audience to action. Even in your daily life at college, you can write a letter to your college newspaper or to someone in authority and try to stir your readers to action. Does some college policy irk you? Would you urge students to attend a rally for a cause or a charity?

The uses of such writing go far beyond these immediate applications. In Chapter 9, you took a stand and backed it up with evidence. Now go a step further, writing a *proposal*—a recommendation for taking action. If, for instance, you have made the claim "Our national parks are in sorry condition," you might urge readers to act—to write to their representatives in Congress or to visit a national park and pick up trash. This paper would be a call to immediate action on the part of your readers. On the other hand, you might suggest that the Department of the Interior be given a budget increase to hire more park rangers, purchase additional park land to accommodate more visitors, and buy more cleanup equipment. You might also suggest that the department could raise funds through sales of park DVDs as well as admissions fees from visitors attracted by the DVDs. This second paper would attempt to forge a consensus about what needs to be done.

Why Proposing a Solution Matters

In a College Course

- You identify a problem and propose a solution, tackling issues such as sealed adoption records, rising costs of prescriptions, overcrowded prisons, and hungry children whose families cannot afford both food and housing.
- You propose a field research study, explaining and justifying your purposes and methods, in order to gain faculty and institutional approval for your capstone project.

In the Workplace

- You propose developing services for a new market to avoid layoffs during an economic downturn.

In Your Community

- You propose starting a tutoring program at the library for the many adults in your region with limited literacy skills.

❓ What solutions have you proposed? What others might you propose? What situations have encouraged you to write proposals?

Learning from Other Writers

The writers of the following two essays propose sensible solutions for pressing problems. To help you begin to analyze the first reading, look at the notes in the margin. They identify features such as the introduction of the problem, the thesis, or main idea, and the introduction of the proposed solution.

As You Read These Proposals

As you read these essays, ask yourself the following questions:

1. What problem does the writer identify? Does the writer rouse you to want to do something about the problem?

2. What solution does the writer propose? What evidence supports the solution? Does the writer convince you to agree with this solution?

3. How is the writer qualified to write on this subject?

For more examples of writing that proposes a solution, visit **<bedfordstmartins .com/bedguide>**.

Wilbert Rideau

Why Prisons Don't Work

Wilbert Rideau, editor of the *Angolite,* the Louisiana State Penitentiary newsmagazine, offers a voice seldom heard in the debate over crime control—that of the criminal.

I was among thirty-one murderers sent to the Louisiana State Penitentiary in 1962 to be executed or imprisoned for life. We weren't much different from those we found here, or those who had preceded us. We were unskilled, impulsive, and uneducated misfits, mostly black, who had done dumb, impulsive things—failures, rejects from the larger society. Now a generation has come of age and gone since I've been here, and everything is much the same as I found it. The faces of the prisoners are different, but behind them are the same impulsive, uneducated, unskilled minds that made dumb, impulsive choices that got them into more trouble than they ever thought existed. The vast majority of us are consigned to suffer and die here so politicians can sell the illusion that permanently exiling people to prison will make society safe. 1

Introduction of the problem

THESIS stating the problem

Getting tough has always been a "silver bullet," a quick fix for the crime and violence that society fears. Each year in Louisiana—where excess is a way of life—lawmakers have tried to outdo each other in legislating harsher mandatory penalties and in reducing avenues of release. The only thing to do with criminals, they say, is get tougher. They have. In the process, the purpose of prison began to change. The state boasts one of the highest lockup rates in the country, imposes the most severe penalties in the nation, and vies to execute more criminals per capita than anywhere else. This state is so 2

A
Writer's
Guide

tough that last year, when prison authorities here wanted to punish an in-
mate in solitary confinement for an infraction,° the most they could inflict
on him was to deprive him of his underwear. It was all he had left.

If getting tough resulted in public safety, Louisiana citizens would be the   3
safest in the nation. They're not. Louisiana has the highest murder rate
among states. Prison, like the police and the courts, has a minimal impact on
crime because it is a response after the fact, a mop-up operation. It doesn't
work. The idea of punishing the few to deter the many is counterfeit because
potential criminals either think they're not going to get caught or they're so
emotionally desperate or psychologically distressed that they don't care
about the consequences of their actions. The threatened punishment, regardless of its severity, is never a factor in the equation. But society, like the incor-
rigible° criminal it abhors, is unable to learn from its mistakes.

Prison has a role in public safety, but it is not a cure-all. Its value is lim-   4
ited, and its use should also be limited to what it does best: isolating young
criminals long enough to give them a chance to grow up and get a grip on
their impulses. It is a traumatic experience, certainly, but it should be only a
temporary one, not a way of life. Prisoners kept too long tend to embrace the
criminal culture, its distorted values and beliefs; they have little choice—
prison is their life. There are some prisoners who cannot be returned to
society—serial killers, serial rapists, professional hit men, and the like—but
the monsters who need to die in prison are rare exceptions in the criminal
landscape.

Crime is a young man's game. Most of the nation's random violence is   5
committed by young urban terrorists. But because of long, mandatory sentences, most prisoners here are much older, having spent fifteen, twenty,
thirty, or more years behind bars, long past necessity. Rather than pay for
new prisons, society would be well served by releasing some of its older prisoners who pose no threat and using the money to catch young street thugs.
Warden John Whitley agrees that many older prisoners here could be freed
tomorrow with little or no danger to society. Release, however, is governed by
law or by politicians, not by penal professionals. Even murderers, those most
feared by society, pose little risk. Historically, for example, the domestic staff
at Louisiana's Governor's mansion has been made up of murderers, hand-
picked to work among the chief-of-state and his family. Penologists° have
long known that murder is almost always a once-in-a-lifetime act. The most
dangerous criminal is the one who has not yet killed but has a history of escalating offenses. He's the one to watch.

Rehabilitation can work. Everyone changes in time. The trick is to influ-   6
ence the direction that change takes. The problem with prisons is that they
don't do more to rehabilitate those confined in them. The convict who enters
prison illiterate will probably leave the same way. Most convicts want to be
better than they are, but education is not a priority. This prison houses

Introduction of the
proposed solution

Transitions (underlined)
for coherence

---

infraction: Violation.   **incorrigible:** Incapable of reform.   **Penologists:** Those who study
prison management and criminal justice.

4,600 men and offers academic training to 240, vocational training to a like number. Perhaps it doesn't matter. About 90 percent of the men here may never leave this prison alive.

The only effective way to curb crime is for society to work to prevent the criminal act in the first place, to come between the perpetrator° and crime. Our youngsters must be taught to respect the humanity of others and to handle disputes without violence. It is essential to educate and equip them with the skills to pursue their life ambitions in a meaningful way. As a community, we must address the adverse life circumstances that spawn criminality. These things are not quick, and they're not easy, but they're effective. Politicians think that's too hard a sell. They want to be on record for doing something now, something they can point to at reelection time. So the drumbeat goes on for more police, more prisons, more of the same failed policies.

7

Conclusion summing up solution

Ever see a dog chase its tail?

8

Questions to Start You Thinking

Meaning

1. Does Rideau convince you that the belief that "permanently exiling people to prison will make society safe" is an "illusion" (paragraph 1)?

2. According to Rideau, why don't prisons work?

3. What does he propose as solutions to the problem of escalating crime? What other solutions can you think of?

Writing Strategies

4. What justifications, if any, for the prison system has Rideau left out of his essay? Do these omissions help or hurt his essay? Why or why not?

5. What evidence does the author provide to support his assertion that Louisiana's "getting tough" policy has not worked? Does he provide sufficient evidence to convince you? Does he persuade you that action is necessary?

6. What would make Rideau's argument for his proposals more persuasive?

7. Other than himself, what authorities does Rideau cite? Why do you think he does this?

8. Does the fact that the author is a convicted criminal strengthen or weaken his argument? Why do you think he mentions this in his first sentence?

9. How do you interpret the last line, "Ever see a dog chase its tail?" Is this line an effective way for Rideau to end his essay? Explain.

perpetrator: One who is responsible for an action or a crime.

Lacey Taylor   **Student Essay**

It's Not Just a Bike

Lacey Taylor drew on personal experience in her essay to identify a problem on her campus and to propose solutions for it.

Imagine one day waking up to find that your car had been stolen. To many   1
students, a bicycle is just like a car. They depend on their bicycles for all their
transportation needs, getting to and from classes and work. Too many bicycles
are being stolen on campus, and this situation has become a major problem for
students who depend on them. In the past year, one friend has had two new
bicycles stolen. Just three months ago, I went home for the weekend, and when
I got back, my bicycle was gone. I could not believe that anyone would do such a
horrible thing, but I was wrong, and someone did do it. This theft was a major
blow to me because my bicycle was my only transportation to work. I am not the
only person and will not be the last to have my bicycle taken, so something should
be done and should be done soon. The campus community should use methods
such as posting warning signs, starting an awareness program, and investing in
new technology like cameras, chain alarms, and tracking devices to help solve this
problem.

Although many solutions are available to help alleviate this problem, some may   2
be as simple as posting signs. Signs are a cheap and easy way to alleviate bike theft.
The signs should read that bicycle theft is a crime, punishable by law, and they
should explain the consequences that go along with stealing bicycles. The signs
would need to be posted at all the bicycle racks just like the signs posted at every
parking spot warning about being a tow-away zone. These signs would not completely solve the problem, but they would discourage some potential bicycle
thieves.

The school also needs to begin a bicycle-theft awareness program. The program   3
should inform students about bicycle theft, warning that it happens all the time and
that it could happen to them. The program also would need to tell students about
certain steps that they could take to avoid becoming victims of bike theft. For example, it could provide information about different methods of bicycle security such
as keeping the serial number in case the bike is stolen and engraving a name on the
bike so that it can be easily identified. The program also should tell students what
to do if a bicycle is actually stolen such as calling the police and filing a report.
This awareness program would prevent many students from ending up with stolen
bicycles.

A more advanced method for solving this problem would be to install security   4
cameras all around campus. The cameras would keep track of all the activity going
on at the bicycle racks and let the person watching the camera know if someone is

What comparable local problems have you experienced or observed?

What simple informative and preventive methods have been used in your community or on your campus to solve problems?

stealing a bicycle. If no one sees the illegal act take place, then the camera tape could be pulled, watched, and used as evidence against the bike thief. For this solution to succeed, the cameras should be placed a certain way, all facing the bike racks and close enough for a viewer to tell what is going on at the racks. The cameras also need to be in plain sight for everyone to see so that anyone considering stealing a bicycle would think twice before acting. After all, no one wants to be caught doing something illegal on camera. Finally, these cameras should be linked to a TV in the lobby of each dorm. Keeping an eye on the TV, watching for any strange activity, should be part of the job of the resident assistant on duty. The resident assistant then could report a bicycle being stolen to the campus police. These cameras would not only ward off some potential criminals but also help to catch the ones who were not scared off.

5

A creative solution would be to invest in chain alarms. These chains contain small wires; if the chains are cut, an alarm in the lock goes off just like a car alarm. This alarm would alert people nearby that someone was stealing a bicycle. The sound also might scare the thief into dropping the bike and running off. These chains could be rented out to students by the transportation department. If the rental cost around ten dollars a semester, the chains would pay for themselves over a short period of time and eventually make a profit for the transportation department. If someone never returned the chain at the end of the semester, the student should be fined, and a hold should be placed on his or her account just as the library does with book fines that must be paid before graduation. These chains would help to catch the bike thieves and also, just like the signs and cameras, help to scare off potential thieves.

6

Finally tracking devices could be placed on all campus bicycles. This would be the most effective solution to the bicycle theft problem because these tracking devices would come into play if all the other solutions failed to do the job. These devices should be small and placed in a hard-to-find spot on the bicycle. If a bike is stolen, then the bike could be traced on a campus police computer and its location identified. Then the police could go through the proper procedure to catch the thief. These tracking devices could be rented out just like the bicycle chains. Even though this method would not stop bicycles from being stolen, it would make it easy to find the bikes and catch the thieves.

Would students on your campus welcome technological solutions to problems like bike theft, or would they worry about privacy, costs, or other issues?

7

Bicycle theft is a major problem that deserves attention. Too many bicycles are being stolen, and bikes are too important to everyday campus life to let this problem go unnoticed. The campus should use simple methods such as posting warning signs or sponsoring an awareness program and also invest in new technology like cameras, chain alarms, and tracking devices to help solve this problem. Bicycle riders should be aware that theft is a problem that could happen to them at any time, but bicycle thieves should not be able to take whatever they like with no action being taken against them. Bicycles, like cars, provide essential transportation, and no one wants to have that necessity stolen.

Questions to Start You Thinking

Meaning

1. What problem does Taylor identify? Does she convince you that this is an important problem? Why, or why not?

2. What solutions does she propose? Why does she arrange them as she does? Which is her strongest solution? Her least convincing? Can you think of other ideas that she might have included?

3. How effectively would Taylor's proposal persuade various members of a campus audience? Which people would she easily persuade? Which might need more convincing? Can you think of other arguments that would appeal to specific readers?

Writing Strategies

4. Is Taylor's argument easy to follow? Why or why not? What kinds of transitions does she use to lead readers through her points? How effective do you find them?

5. Is Taylor's evidence specific and sufficient? Explain.

6. What qualifies Taylor to write about this topic? How do these qualifications contribute to her ability to persuade?

7. Using highlighters or marginal notes, identify the essay's introduction, explanation of the problem, thesis, proposal to solve the problem, and conclusion. How effective is the organization of this essay?

Learning by Writing

The Assignment: Proposing a Solution

For writing activities for proposing a solution, visit **<bedfordstmartins .com/bedguide>**.

In this essay you'll first carefully analyze and explain a specific social, economic, political, civic, or environmental problem—a problem you care about and strongly wish to see resolved. The problem may be large or small, but it shouldn't be trivial. It may affect the whole country or mainly people in your city, campus, or classroom. Show your readers that this problem really exists and that it matters to you and to them. After setting forth the problem, you also may want to explain why it exists. Write for an audience who, once aware of the problem, may be expected to help do something about it.

The second thing you are to accomplish in the essay is to propose one or more ways to solve the problem or at least alleviate it. In making a proposal, you urge action by using words like *should, ought,* and *must*: "This city ought to have a Bureau of Missing Persons"; "Small private aircraft should be banned from flying close to a major commercial airport." Lay out the reasons why your proposal deserves to be implemented; supply evidence that your solution is reasonable and can work. Remember that your purpose is to convince readers that something should be done about the problem.

These students cogently argued for action in their papers:

> Based on research studies and statistics, one student argued that using standardized test scores from the SAT or the ACT as criteria for college admissions is a problem because it favors aggressive students from affluent families. His proposal was to abolish this use of the scores.

> Another argued that speeders racing past an elementary school might be slowed by a combination of more warning signs, surveillance equipment, police patrols, and fines.

> A third argued that cities should consider constructing public buildings with "living walls" in order to reduce energy consumption, improve air quality, and allow for urban agriculture.

A "living wall" or "green wall" is a wall that is completely or partially covered with plants, as shown here at the Musée du Quai Branly in Paris.

Facing the Challenge   Proposing a Solution

The major challenge writers face when writing a proposal is to develop a detailed and convincing solution. Finding solutions is much harder than finding problems. Convincing readers that you have found a reasonable, workable solution is harder still. For example, suppose you propose the combination of a rigorous exercise program and a low-fat diet as a solution for obesity. While these solutions seem reasonable and workable to you, readers who have lost weight and then gained it back might point out that their main problem is not losing weight but maintaining weight loss over time. To account for their concerns and enhance your credibility, you might revise your solution to focus on realistic long-term goals and strategies for sticking to an exercise program. For instance, you might recommend that friends walk together two or three times a week or that employees lobby for a fitness center at work.

To develop a realistic solution that fully addresses a problem and satisfies the concerns of readers, consider questions such as these:

- How might the problem affect different groups of people?
- What range of concerns are your readers likely to have?
- What realistic solution addresses the concerns of readers about *all* aspects of the problem?

Generating Ideas

Identify a Problem. Brainstorm by writing down all the possible topics that come to mind. Observe events around you to identify irritating campus or community problems you would like to solve. Watch for ideas as you read the newspaper or listen to the news. Browse through issue-oriented Web sites. Look for sites sponsored by large nonprofit foundations that accept grant proposals and fund innovative solutions to societal issues. Although a controversy or current issue might start you thinking, be sure to stick to problems that you want to solve as you consider options. Star the ideas that seem to have the most potential.

DISCOVERY CHECKLIST

☐ Can you recall any problem that needs a solution? What problems do you meet every day or occasionally? What problems concern people near you?

☐ What conditions in need of improvement have you observed on television, on the Web, or in your daily activities? What action is called for?

☐ What problems have been discussed recently on campus or in class?

☐ What problems are discussed in blogs, chat rooms, newspapers, or newsmagazines such as *Time, Newsweek,* or *U.S. News & World Report*?

Consider Your Audience. Readers need to believe that your problem is real and your solution is feasible. If you are addressing classmates, maybe they haven't thought about the problem before. Look for ways to make it personal for them, to show that it affects them and deserves their attention.

- Who are your readers? How would you describe them?
- Why should your readers care about this problem? Does it affect their health, welfare, conscience, or pocketbook?

- Have they ever expressed any interest in the problem? If so, what has triggered their interest?
- Do they belong to any organization or segment of society that makes them especially susceptible to — or uninterested in — this problem?
- What attitudes about the problem do you share with your readers? Which of their assumptions or values that differ from yours will affect how they view your proposal?

Learning by Doing 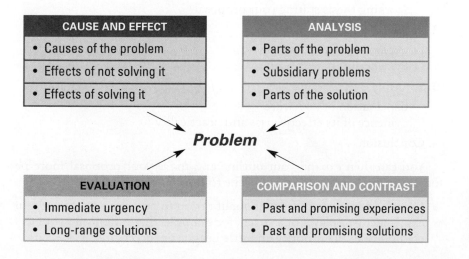 Describing Your Audience

Write a paragraph or so describing the audience you intend to address. Who are they? Which of their circumstances, interests, traits, social circles, attitudes, and values best prepare them to grasp the problem? Which make them most (or least) receptive to your solution? If certain aspects of the problem or the solution especially appeal (or do not appeal) to them, consider how to present your ideas most persuasively. (Save these notes for the next Learning by Doing activity on p. 195.) If you want a second opinion on your audience, share your analysis with a classmate.

Think about Solutions. Once you've chosen a problem, brainstorm — alone or with classmates — for possible solutions, or use your imagination. Some problems, such as reducing international tensions, present no easy solutions. Still, give some strategic thought to any problem that seriously concerns you, even if it has thwarted teams of experts. Sometimes a solution will reveal itself to a novice thinker, and even a small contribution to a partial solution is worth offering.

CAUSE AND EFFECT	ANALYSIS
• Causes of the problem	• Parts of the problem
• Effects of not solving it	• Subsidiary problems
• Effects of solving it	• Parts of the solution

Problem

EVALUATION	COMPARISON AND CONTRAST
• Immediate urgency	• Past and promising experiences
• Long-range solutions	• Past and promising solutions

For more on causes and effects, see Ch. 8 and pp. 457–58. For more on analysis, see pp. 448–50.

For more on comparison and contrast, see Ch. 7. For more on evaluation, see Ch. 11.

For more on evidence, see Ch. 3. For more on using evidence to support an argument, scc pp. 168–72.

For advice on finding a few sources, see sections A and B in the Quick Research Guide, pp. A-18–A-35.

For more on stating a thesis, see pp. 401–10.

For exercises on choosing and supporting effective thesis statements, visit <**bedfordstmartins .com/bedguide**>.

For more on outlines, see pp. 413–21.

Consider Sources of Support. To show that the problem really exists, you'll need evidence and examples. If you feel that further library research will help you justify the problem, now is the time to do it. In addition, previous efforts to solve the problem may help you develop your solution. Consider whether local history archives, newspaper stories, accounts of public meetings, interviews, or Web sites sponsored by interested groups might identify concerns of readers or practical limits of solutions.

Planning, Drafting, and Developing

Start with Your Proposal and Your Thesis. A basic approach is to state your proposal in a sentence that can act as your thesis.

PROPOSAL	Let people get divorced without having to go to court.
WORKING THESIS	The legislature should pass a law allowing couples to divorce without the problem of going to court.

From such a statement, the rest of the argument may start to unfold, often falling naturally into a simple two-part shape:

1. *A claim that a problem exists.* This part explains the problem and supplies evidence of its significance — for example, the costs, adversarial process, and stress of divorce court for a couple and their family.

2. *A claim that something ought to be done about it.* This part proposes a solution to the problem — for example, legislative action to authorize other options such as mediation.

These two parts can grow naturally into an informal outline.

1. Introduction

    Overview of the situation
    Working thesis stating your proposal

2. Problem

    Explanation of its nature
    Evidence of its significance

3. Solution

    Explanation of its nature
    Evidence of its effectiveness and practicality

4. Conclusion

You can then expand your outline and make your proposal more persuasive by including some or all of the following elements:

■ Knowledge or experience that qualifies you to propose a solution (your experience as a player or a coach, for example, that establishes your credibility as an authority on Little League or soccer clubs.)

- Values, beliefs, or assumptions that have caused you to feel strongly about the need for action

- An estimate of the resources — money, people, skills, material — and the time required to implement the solution (perhaps including what is available now and what needs to be obtained)

- Step-by-step actions needed to achieve your solution

- Controls or quality checks to monitor implementation

- Possible obstacles or difficulties that may need to be overcome

- Reasons your solution is better than others proposed or tried already

A sign from part of a popular and successful anti-littering campaign.

- Any other evidence that shows that your suggestion is practical, reasonable in cost, and likely to be effective

Imagine Possible Objections of Your Audience. You can increase the likelihood that readers will accept your proposal in two ways. First, start your proposal by showing that a problem exists. Then, when you turn to your claim that something should be done, begin with a simple and inviting suggestion. For example, a claim that national parks need better care might begin by suggesting that readers head for such a park and personally size up the situation. Besides drawing readers into the problem and the solution, you may think of objections they might raise — reservations about the high cost, complexity, or workability of your plan, for instance. Persuade your readers by anticipating and laying to rest objections that might occur to them.

Learning by Doing 🎯 Making Problem–Solution Columns

A persuasive proposal should show that you understand a problem well enough to suggest solutions while addressing specific audience needs. Considering these ideas in columns can help you see them differently than you do as you write. Open a new file, go to the Format menu, choose Columns, select the three-column format, and label the columns. Use your audience description (p. 193), notes, plan, and working draft to copy and paste ideas into the appropriate columns. Add points as needed so that you can move logically from problem to solution to answering readers' objections point by point. If you can't see how to make solid connections, ask your classmates for advice.

Problems	Solutions	Reader Objections

For pointers on integrating and documenting sources, see Ch. 12 and D6 and E1–E2 (pp. A-29–A-35) in the Quick Research Guide.

Cite Sources Carefully. When you collect ideas and evidence from outside sources, you need to document your evidence—that is, tell where you found everything. Check with your instructor on the documentation method he or she wants you to use. You may also want to identify sources as you introduce them to assure a reader that they are authoritative.

> According to *Newsweek* correspondent Josie Fair, . . .

> In his biography *FDR: The New Deal Years*, Davis reports . . .

> While working as a Senate page in the summer of 2010, I observed . . .

For more about integrating visuals, see section B (pp. A-8–A-12) in the Quick Format Guide.

You can introduce a table, graph, drawing, map, photograph, or other visual evidence in much the same way.

> As the 2000 census figures in Table 1 indicate, . . .

> The photograph showing the run-down condition of the dog park (see Fig. 2) . . .

Revising and Editing

For more revising and editing strategies, see Ch. 23.

As you revise, concentrate on a clear explanation of the problem and solid supporting evidence for the solution. Make your essay coherent and its parts clear to help achieve your purpose of convincing your readers.

Clarify Your Thesis. Your readers are likely to rely on your thesis to identify the problem and possibly to preview your solution. Look again at your thesis from a reader's point of view.

WORKING THESIS	The legislature should pass a law allowing couples to divorce without the problem of going to court.
REVISED THESIS	Because divorce court can be expensive, adversarial, and stressful, passing a law that allows couples to divorce without a trip to court would encourage simpler, more harmonious ways to end a marriage.

Reorganize for Unity and Coherence. When Heather Colbenson revised her first draft, she wanted to clarify the presentation of her problem.

Why would high schools in farming communities drop

agriculture classes and the FFA program? ~~s~~Small schools are
The main reason that

is that
cutting ag programs ~~because~~ the state has not provided

significant funding for the schools to operate. The small

schools have to make cuts, and some small schools are

deciding that the agriculture classes are not as important

as other courses. Some small schools are consolidating to

receive more aid. Many of these schools have been able to

save their ag programs.

Move main reason last for emphasis

Why did I put a solution here? Move to end!

One reason is that m
Many colleges are demanding that students have two years of foreign language.

In small schools, like my own, the students could take either foreign language or ag

classes. Therefore, students choose language classes to fill the college requirement.

When the students leave the ag classes to take foreign language, the number of stu-

dents declines, which makes it easier for school administrators to cut ag classes.

Rewrite this! Not really college requirements but college-prep courses vs. others when budget is tight

Her revised paper was more forcefully organized and more coherent, making it easier for readers to follow. The bridges between ideas were now on paper, not just in her mind.

For strategies for achieving coherence, see pp. 433–37.

Learning by Doing 🔟 Revising for Clear Organization

Check the actual organization of your draft against your plans and the two-part structure commonly used in proposals (see p. 194). Outlining what you've actually done, not what you intended, may help you see your organization as readers will. Does your draft open with a sufficient overview for your audience? Do you state your actual proposal clearly? Does your draft progress from problem to solution without mixing ideas together? Have you included other elements appropriate for your audience? Reorganize and revise as needed.

Be Reasonable. Exaggerated claims for your solution will not persuade your readers. Neither will oversimplifying the problem so that the solution seems more likely to apply. Don't be afraid to express your own reasonable doubts about the completeness of your solution. If necessary, rethink both the problem and the solution.

Peer Response Proposing a Solution

Ask several classmates or friends to review your proposal and solution, answering questions such as these:

For general questions for a peer editor, see p. 465. For peer response worksheets, visit **<bedfordstmartins .com/bedguide>**.

- What is your overall reaction to this proposal? Does it make you want to go out and do something about the problem?
- Are you convinced that the problem is of concern to you? If not, why not?
- Are you persuaded that the writer's solution is workable?
- Has the writer paid enough attention to readers and their concerns?
- Restate what you understand to be the proposal's major points:
    Problem
    Explanation of problem and why it matters
    Proposed solution
    Explanation of proposal and its practicality
    Reasons and procedure to implement proposal
    Proposal's advantages, disadvantages, and responses to other solutions
    Final recommendation
- If this paper were yours, what is the one thing you would be sure to work on before handing it in?

REVISION CHECKLIST

- ☐ Does your introduction invite the reader into the discussion?
- ☐ Is your problem clear? How have you made it relevant to readers?
- ☐ Have you clearly outlined the steps necessary to solve the problem?
- ☐ Where have you demonstrated the benefits of your solution?
- ☐ Have you considered other solutions before rejecting them for your own?
- ☐ Have you anticipated the doubts readers may have about your solution?
- ☐ Do you come across as a well-meaning, reasonable writer willing to admit that you don't know everything? If you sound preachy, have you overused *should* and *must*?

☐ Have you avoided promising that your solution will do more than it can possibly do? Have you made believable predictions for its success?

After you have revised your proposal, edit and proofread it. Carefully check the grammar, word choice, punctuation, and mechanics—and then correct any problems you find. If you have used sources, be sure that you have cited them correctly in your text and added a list of works cited.

Make sure your sentence structure helps you make your points clearly and directly. Don't let yourself slip into the passive voice, a grammatical construction that represents things as happening without any obvious agent: "The problem should be remedied by spending money on prevention." Instead, every sentence should specify who should act: "The dean of students should remedy the problem by spending money on prevention."

For more editing and proofreading strategies, see pp. 473–76. For more on documenting sources, see E1–E2 in the Quick Research Guide, pp. A-30–A-35.

EDITING CHECKLIST

☐ Is it clear what each pronoun refers to? Is any *this* or *that* ambiguous? Does each pronoun agree with (match) its antecedent?   A6

☐ Is your sentence structure correct? Have you avoided writing fragments, comma splices, or fused sentences?   A1, A2

☐ Do your transitions and other introductory elements have commas after them, if these are needed?   C1

☐ Have you spelled and capitalized everything correctly, especially names of people and organizations?   D1, D2

For more help, find the relevant checklist sections in the Quick Editing Guide on p. A-36. Turn also to the Quick Format Guide beginning on p. A-1.

Additional Writing Assignments

1. If you followed the assignment in Chapter 9 and took a stand, now write a few paragraphs extending that paper to propose a solution that argues for action. To gather ideas, brainstorm with classmates first.

2. Choose from the following list a practice that you find inefficient, unethical, unfair, or morally wrong as a solution to a problem. In a few paragraphs, give reasons for your objections. Then narrow the issue as needed to propose a better solution in a persuasive essay directed to an audience that is mostly unaware of the problem.

Censorship	Genetic engineering
Goods made with child labor	Outsourcing jobs
Laboratory experiments on animals	Dumping wastes in the ocean

3. Brainstorm with your classmates to develop a list of campus problems that irritate students or complicate their lives. Write an essay that tackles one of these problems by explaining it and proposing a practical, workable solution to it. (If you can't identify a workable solution, select a different problem.) Address an audience on your campus or in your college system that could implement a solution. Present your ideas to them tactfully. After all, they may also be the ones responsible for creating or at least not solving the problem earlier. (If appropriate, also investigate any campus history that might be involved to help you overcome possible resistance from your audience based on tradition.)

4. Write a memo to your supervisor at work in which you propose an innovation (related to procedures, schedules, policies, or similar matters) that could benefit your department or company.

5. As part of a problem–solution blog, thread, or discussion area for your class, post a concise passage identifying and explaining a problem. (Your instructor may limit the problems to campus, community, student, educational, technology, or topical issues relevant for your class.) Then post a second passage identifying and explaining a solution to the problem you identified. Respond to each other's problem–solution statements with questions, comments, connections, or suggestions to develop a focused exchange about the class proposals.

6. **Visual Assignment.** Select one of the following images. Write an essay that analyzes the problem that it identifies, noting how the elements of the image try to draw the viewer into the problem. Include any solution suggested or implied by the image or your own solution to the problem.

11 Evaluating and Reviewing

Responding to an Image

In what respects does this photograph of a giant-pumpkin weigh-in capture the essence of such competitions? What overall impression does the image convey? What details contribute to this impression? How and where does the photograph direct the viewer's eye? In what ways does this image suggest, represent, or comment on a particular set of criteria and process of evaluation?

Evaluating means judging. You do it when you decide what candidate to vote for, pick which camera to buy, or recommend a new restaurant to your friends. All of us pass judgments—often snap judgments—as we move through a day's routine. A friend asks, "How was that movie you saw last night?" and you reply, "Terrific—don't miss it" or maybe "Pretty good, but it had too much blood and gore for me."

But to *write* an evaluation calls for you to think more critically. As a writer you first decide on *criteria,* or standards for judging, and then come up with evidence to back up your judgment. Your evaluation zeroes in on a definite subject that you inspect carefully in order to reach a considered opinion. The subject might be a film, a book, or a performance that you review. Or it might be a sports team, a product, or a body of research that you evaluate. The possibilities are endless.

Why Evaluating and Reviewing Matter

In a College Course

- You evaluate theories and methods in the fields you study, including long-standing controversies such as the dispute about teaching methods raging in education for the deaf.
- You evaluate instructors, courses, and sometimes campus facilities and services to participate in the process of monitoring and improving your college.

In the Workplace

- You evaluate people, projects, goals, and results, just as your potential was evaluated as a job applicant and your performance is evaluated as an employee.

In Your Community

- You evaluate video games for yourself or your children and review films, music, shows, and restaurants as you decide how to spend your money and time.

❓ What have you evaluated within the last few weeks? How have evaluations and reviews been useful for you? How have you incorporated evaluations and reviews into your writing?

Learning from Other Writers

Here are evaluations by a professional writer and by a student. To help you begin to analyze the first reading, look at the notes in the margin. They identify features such as the thesis, or main idea, the criteria for evaluation, and the evidence supporting the writer's judgment, all typical of essays that evaluate.

As You Read These Evaluations

As you read these essays, ask yourself the following questions:

For more examples of evaluative writing, visit **<bedfordstmartins .com/bedguide>**.

1. Do you consider the writer qualified to evaluate the subject he or she chose? What biases and prejudices might the writer bring to the evaluation?

2. What criteria for evaluation does the writer establish? Are these reasonable standards for evaluating the subject?

3. What is the writer's assessment of the subject? Does the writer provide sufficient evidence to convince you of his or her evaluation?

Seth Stevenson

Soft Sell: Why quiet, understated TV ads are so effective.

Seth Stevenson regularly evaluates advertisements for Slate.com. In this particular Ad Report Card, published in February 2010, Stevenson discusses ads that try to make their points without shouting.

The Spot: A man sits at the counter of a coffee shop, tapping on his laptop. Text bubbles pop on-screen as he trades instant messages with an unseen interlocutor.° "Remember how we used to say 'WHEN' we retire, like it was a sure thing?" types the person at the other end of the chat. "I know," types the man. "Then it became a lot of 'WILL WE' retire." When the imploring° response comes — "How do we get from 'WILL WE' back to 'WHEN WE'?" — the man is at a loss, staring aimlessly out the window. An announcer utters the first spoken words of the spot as the scene fades: "John Hancock. The future is yours." 1

THESIS presenting judgment of trend

In the never-ending battle for your attention, advertisers have experimented with all sorts of A/V° tweaks. Generally, the goal has been amplification: boosting the volume of the announcer's voice or flashing the product price in big, bright numbers. But I've noticed a recent mini-trend of ads that muffle senses instead of attacking them. The most striking example is a commercial for the 2

---

interlocutor: A person who asks questions.   **imploring:** Urgently begging.   **A/V:** Audio-visual.

We never made it to the restaurant.
What better way to celebrate your next anniversary?
A diamond is forever.

DeBeers diamond ad from the mid-1990s "A Diamond Is Forever" campaign.

asthma medication Symbicort. As our spokeswoman prances around singing Symbicort's praises, she is almost completely obscured by shadows. We strain to make out her features even in the tight close-ups on her face. We're left wondering whether this woman is a wanted criminal or has some sort of jarring scar the director wished to hide.

— Introduction to first criterion: clarity

This silhouette technique has been used before—most notably in ads for DeBeers diamonds (shadow people slip on sparkling necklaces) and for the iPod (shadow people bop around to music). In each of those campaigns, though, (1) the people are pure silhouettes, not half-lit noir° freaks and (2) the aim is to showcase the shiny product by fading the humans into the background. In the Symbicort spot, the product—I'm not even sure what form it takes; a pill? an inhalant?—is never seen. The only clear, well-lit image in the ad is of icky bronchial° tissue. I keep waiting for the woman to emerge into sunlight at the close of the ad, symbolizing the newfound happiness Symbicort has brought her. But it never happens. And I'm left wondering: Why would asthma sufferers aspire to an underilluminated lifestyle?

3

— Supporting evidence

Two dueling financial services firms also employ the sense-muting gambit.° In Prudential's "Retirement Red Zone" ads, people silhouetted in solid black and white discuss their retirement preparedness. The idea here seems to be that obscuring our vision will heighten our sense of hearing, forcing us to concentrate on the spot's spoken words. John Hancock's "Cursor" campaign similarly lets us eavesdrop on intimate money conversations. But this time the missing ingredient is aural.° The John Hancock dialoguers text each other over smartphones and laptops, so we hear only the background noise of an airport gate, a coffee shop, or a city park—punctuated by clicking keystrokes and the chimes that signal a new text message has arrived.

4

— Introduction to second criterion: ability to get viewers' attention

These ads have been airing for almost two years now. They continue to be the quietest moments you'll find anywhere on television (save for the

5

noir: Relating to a type of crime literature or movie that features a shadowy, dangerous world and tough characters.   **bronchial:** Associated with the tubes that let air travel in and out of the lungs and within the lungs.   **gambit:** A risky move calculated to gain an advantage, as in chess.   **aural:** Relating to the sense of hearing.

occasional *CBS Sunday Morning* segment consisting solely of static wheat-field footage). "The reality is that very few people only watch TV today—they watch while they're reading a magazine, looking at email, or answering a text," says Jim Bacharach, vice president of brand communications for John Hancock. "What we have found, and confirmed in our tracking studies, is that the quiet of our ads makes people lift their heads and look up."

Supporting evidence ——

The ads mainly run during live sports events, in part because viewers tend not to DVR° live sports and in part because sports programming is the most focused way to reach John Hancock's target market (adults over 35 with investable assets exceeding $250,000). "You'd think sports might skew° heavily male," says Bacharach, "but the programs we're buying—like golf, college football, and the MLB playoffs—are actually closer to a 55-45 percentage split."   6

I asked Bacharach if it's more effective when the ads run during raucous college football games, where their silence offers a stark contrast, instead of during already quiet golf broadcasts. He said he felt that didn't matter much, but that the best placement for these ads is in the middle of a pod° of other commercials, where they stand out from the crowd. "Unfortunately," he acknowledged, "we can't guarantee they'll be placed in the middle of a pod when we buy the airtime."   7

I imagine the best placement of all would be immediately following a ShamWow or Slap Chop ad—where their soothing white noise and gentle chimes might come as welcome antidotes to the bleats of pitchman Vince.°   8

Conclusion underscoring thesis, with a final grade ——

Grade: A-. By zigging where others zag, the John Hancock ads cut through the TV clutter. We pay close attention to their text, following the characters' conversations. And those final moments—in which the cursor blinks with implacable° expectation—artfully symbolize the uncertainty that can accompany big financial decisions. Take a lesson, Symbicort. Form can mesh with function in a manner that clarifies the message instead of dumbfounding the viewer.   9

Questions to Start You Thinking

Meaning

1. What is Stevenson's view of the Symbicort ads?
2. Why do the John Hancock "cursor" ads run mainly during live sports events?
3. What does Stevenson mean when he says that the John Hancock ads are "zigging where others zag" (paragraph 9)?

DVR: Capture on digital video recorder.   **skew:** Tilt statistically towards being.   **pod:** Cluster or group.   **pitchman Vince:** Vince Offer (1964–) appears in commercials for ShamWow, a clean-up towel, and Slap Chop, a food preparation tool.   **implacable:** Not capable of being changed.

Writing Strategies

4. What is Stevenson's overall judgment of the John Hancock ads? What criteria does he use to make this judgment?

5. In your view, how well does he support his judgment? Point to some specific examples in making your case.

6. Stevenson quotes the executive in charge of John Hancock's "brand communications" in paragraphs 5, 6, and 7. How do these quotations contribute to the overall point that Stevenson is making?

7. How would you describe Stevenson's tone, the quality of his writing that reveals his attitude toward his topic and his readers? What specific words, phrases, or sentences contribute to his tone? Does the tone seems appropriate for his purpose and audience?

Dennis O'Neil   **Student Essay**

Katrina Documentary Gives Voice to Survivors

Dennis O'Neil wrote this review of Spike Lee's documentary on Hurricane Katrina for the *Louisville Cardinal*, the newspaper of the University of Louisville.

Spike Lee's film *When the Levees° Broke: A Requiem° in Four Acts* cuts straight to   1
the heart of the Hurricane Katrina tragedy and gives voice to the New Orleans
survivors in an unprecedented° way. The epic,° 256-minute documentary provides a
multitude° of different perspectives on the disaster and demonstrates the tragic
effect that the disaster has had on New Orleans and its citizens.

"It is very important, not just here in the United States but all over the world,   2
that people hear the stories from these individuals, these witnesses, who saw the
horror of what happened in New Orleans," Lee said in a recent interview with HBO.
The film is Lee's third collaboration with HBO (after the Oscar-nominated *4 Little
Girls* as well as *Jim Brown: All American*), which wanted Lee to craft the "documentary
of record" about the tragedy. Three months after Katrina hit, Lee and a small crew
made the first of eight trips to New Orleans to shoot raw footage of the disaster and
gather subjects for interviews. Ultimately,° close to one hundred subjects appear in
the film, all from various walks of life, including academics, military personnel, politicians, celebrities, activists, and residents of New Orleans who were the most
affected by the tragedy.

The film is divided into four one-hour acts with acts 1 and 2 encompassing° the   3
period of time between the earliest threats of Katrina to the point where survivors

---

Levees: Walls or embankments that hold back water to prevent flooding.   **Requiem:** A
solemn chant, song, or other work of art that honors the dead.   **unprecedented:** New;
never achieved before.   **epic:** Large in scope.   **a multitude:** Many.   **Ultimately:** Finally;
in the end.   **encompassing:** Covering; consisting of.

were finally beginning to be evacuated five days after the storm hit. Many of the interview subjects offer strong evidence that the flood of New Orleans was not caused entirely by Katrina but because the city's levee system was not structurally adequate, as it was not strong enough to withstand even a category-three° storm.

❓ What images
or voices from the
Katrina disaster
persist in your
memory?

The film offers harrowing° and graphic° images of the disaster while it was in progress, as well as of the aftermath in which the survivors fled their flooded homes for various sanctuaries° around the city. Lee shows the roof on the New Orleans Superdome slowly turning to rust as the storm progresses and how federal aid, which was so quick to assist the tsunami victims in Asia,° didn't arrive until long after the worst had already occurred.   4

"It was absolutely horrific° conditions," said survivor Fred Johnson to Lee. "It was like being in the middle of a war and all you could do was stand there and feel helpless."   5

Many of the personal tragedies experienced by the survivors are addressed in the film, such as that of Herbert Freeman Jr., a resident of the Lower Ninth Ward neighborhood of New Orleans, whose mother passed away during the disaster. Freeman was forced to leave her dead body sitting in the Superdome with a note attached to her because she couldn't be airlifted out and Freeman couldn't take her with him. She sat there for days before someone noticed her.   6

Acts 3 and 4 of the film heavily depict° the aftermath of the tragedy, as the survivors were shepherded° to various areas of the country to restart their lives. Many of them recount° the various hardships of being separated from family members, looking for new homes, fighting with insurance companies, and experiencing the heartache of losing the only home many of them have ever known.   7

❓ What does
"home" mean to
you? What do you
value in it?

"Thanksgiving was a heart-wrenching situation," said Pastor James Pullings to Lee. "It broke my heart to hear people saying, 'I want to go home, but I have no home to go to.'"   8

Many of the film's most poignant° moments involve survivors returning to New Orleans and being confronted by the devastation that has occurred there. In one scene, the elderly Wilhelmina Blanchard returns to her home and breaks into uncontrollable sobs as she sees the horrific state that it is now in. "I had heard of the devastation," she says through tears, "but I didn't know it was this bad."   9

"You walk through your old neighborhood," says actor Wendell Pierce, "and you see a house with the number two on the door, and you realize, 'Man, two people died in that house.' And it's just so deafeningly quiet."   10

But Lee's ultimate victory with the film is that he doesn't allow the silence to drown out the heart of New Orleans that still beats underneath it. The film's most   11

category-three: A storm characterized by 111- to 130-mph winds and 9- to 12-foot storm surges. Hurricane Katrina made landfall as a category-four storm, with wind speeds up to 140 mph. **harrowing:** Upsetting. **graphic:** Vivid, often in a disturbing way. **sanctuaries:** Places of safety. **tsunami victims in Asia:** A reference to the post-earthquake tidal wave that killed more than 200,000 people in 2004. **horrific:** Horrifying; terrible. **depict:** Show or portray. **shepherded:** Led. **recount:** Recall; describe. **poignant:** Touching or moving.

moving moment occurs when Terence Blanchard, who composed the film's mournful, elegiac° score, walks the ghostly silent streets of New Orleans and plays on his trumpet a soulful jazz lullaby, as if humming a crippled giant to sleep.

"One of the things that I hope this documentary does is remind America that New Orleans is not over with," added Lee. "It's not done."

12

What does "It's not done" suggest to you? How does the 2010 Gulf oil spill affect your response?

Questions to Start You Thinking

Meaning

1. Why did Spike Lee make the documentary described in the essay?

2. What content (visual, testimonial, and so on) did Lee include to make his point about the effects of Hurricane Katrina on its survivors and on New Orleans?

3. What is the "ultimate victory" of the film, according to O'Neil?

Writing Strategies

4. What criteria does O'Neil use to judge Lee's documentary? To what extent has the film met these criteria, according to O'Neil?

5. Does O'Neil provide enough evidence to support his judgment? Why or why not?

6. O'Neil makes extensive use of quotations. Do you find the quotations effective or overdone?

7. Using highlighters or marginal notes, identify the essay's introduction, thesis, criteria for evaluation, supporting evidence, and conclusion. How effective is the organization of the essay?

Learning by Writing

The Assignment: Writing an Evaluation

Pick a subject to evaluate — one you have personal experience with and feel competent to evaluate. This subject might be a movie, a TV program, a piece of music, an artwork, a new product, a government agency, a campus facility or policy, an essay or a reading, or anything else you can think of. Then in a thoughtful essay, analyze your subject and evaluate it. You will need to determine specific criteria for evaluation and make them clear to your readers. In writing your evaluation, you will have a twofold purpose: (1) to set forth your assessment of the quality of your subject and (2) to convince your readers that your judgment is reasonable.

For writing activities for evaluating, visit **<bedfordstmartins .com/bedguide>**.

elegiac: Sorrowful.

These three students wrote lively evaluations:

Composer and pianist George Gershwin (1898–1937), known for *Rhapsody in Blue, An American in Paris,* and many songs for musical shows and movies.

A music major evaluated works by American composer Aaron Copland, finding him trivial and imitative, "without a tenth of the talent or inventiveness that George Gershwin or Duke Ellington had in his little finger."

A student planning a career in business management evaluated a computer firm in which he had worked one summer. His criteria were efficiency, productivity, appeal to new customers, and employee satisfaction.

A student from Brazil, who had seen firsthand the effects of industrial development in the Amazon rain forest, evaluated the efforts of the U.S. government to protect forests and wetlands, comparing them with the efforts of environmentalists in her own country.

Facing the Challenge   Evaluating and Reviewing

The major challenge writers face when writing evaluations is to make clear to their readers the criteria they have used to arrive at their opinion. While you may not be an expert in any field, you should never underestimate your powers of discrimination. When reviewing a movie, for example, you may begin by simply summarizing the story of the film and saying whether you like it or not. However, for readers who wonder whether to see the movie, you need to go further. For example, you might find its special effects, exotic sets, and unpredictable plot effective but wish that the characters had seemed more believable. Based on these criteria, your thesis might maintain that the movie is not realistic but is entertaining and well worth seeing.

Once you've chosen a topic, clarify your standards for evaluating it:

- What features or standards will you use as criteria for evaluating?
- How could you briefly explain each of the criteria for a reader?
- What judgment or evaluation about your topic do the criteria support?

After identifying your criteria, you can examine each in turn. Explaining your criteria will ensure that you move beyond a summary to an opinion or judgment that you can justify to your readers.

Generating Ideas

Find Something to Evaluate. Try *brainstorming* or *mapping* to identify as many possible topics as you can. Select the ones with the most potential. Test your mastery of each option by concisely describing or summarizing it. Spend enough time investigating these possibilities that you can comfortably choose one subject for your essay.

For more strategies for generating ideas, see Ch. 19.

Consider Sources of Support. You'll want to spend time finding material to help you develop a judgment. You may recall a program on television or hunt for an article to read. You might observe a performance or a sports team. An interview or conversation could reveal what others think. Perhaps you'll want to review several examples of your subject: watching several films, listening to several CDs, examining several works of art, or testing several products. You might also browse the Web for information about your subject or attend a campus concert or play.

Establish Your Criteria. Jot down criteria, standards to apply to your subject based on the features of the subject worth considering. How well, for example, does a popular entertainer score on musicianship, rapport with the audience, selection of material, originality? In evaluating Portland as a home for a young careerist, you might ask: Does it offer ample decent-paying entry-level positions in growth firms? Any criterion for evaluation has to fit your subject, audience, and purpose. After all, ample entry-level jobs might not matter to an audience of retirees.

For more on comparing and contrasting, see Ch. 7.

Try Comparing and Contrasting. Often you can readily size up the worth of a thing by setting it next to another of its kind. (When you *compare,* you point to similarities; when you *contrast,* you note differences.) To be comparable, of course, your two subjects need to have plenty in common. The quality of a Harley-Davidson motorcycle might be judged by contrasting it with a Honda but not with a school bus.

For example, if you are writing a paper for a film-history course, you might compare and contrast the classic German horror movie *The Cabinet of Dr. Caligari* with the classic Hollywood movie *Frankenstein,* concluding that *Caligari* is more artistic.

Impressionistic set for *The Cabinet of Dr. Caligari* (1920), in which a man investigates the murder of his friend in a mountain village.

In planning the paper, you might make a table in which you list the characteristics of each film, point by point:

	CALIGARI	FRANKENSTEIN
SETS	Dreamlike and impressionistic	Realistic, but with heavy Gothic atmosphere
	Sets deliberately angular and distorted	Gothic sets
LIGHTING	Deep shadows that throw figures into relief	Torches highlighting monster's face in night scene

By jotting down each point and each bit of evidence side by side, you can outline your comparison and contrast with great efficiency. Once you have listed them, decide on a possible order for the points.

For more on defining, see pp. 443–45.

Try Defining Your Subject. Another technique for evaluating is to define your subject, indicating its nature so clearly that your readers can easily distinguish it from others of its kind. Defining helps readers understand your subject — its structure, habitat, functions. In evaluating a classic television show such as *Roseanne,* you might want to include an *extended* definition of sitcoms over the years, their techniques, views of women, effects on the audience. Unlike a *short definition,* as in a dictionary, an extended definition is intended not simply to explain but to judge: What is the nature of my subject? What qualities make it unique, unlike others of its sort?

Develop a Judgment That You Can Explain to Your Audience. In the end, you will have to come to a decision: Is your subject good, worthwhile, significant, exemplary, preferable — or not? Most writers come to a judgment gradually as they explore their subjects and develop criteria.

DISCOVERY CHECKLIST

☐ What criteria do you plan to use in making your evaluation? Are they clear and reasonably easy to apply?

☐ What evidence can back up your judgments?

☐ Would comparing or contrasting help in evaluating your subject? If so, with what might you compare or contrast your subject?

☐ What qualities define your subject, setting it apart from the rest of its class?

Learning by Doing 🖾 Developing Criteria

With a small group of classmates, meeting in person or online, discuss the subjects each of you plan to evaluate to help each other arrive at sound judgments. Make a detailed report about what you're evaluating. If possible, pass around a product, show a photograph of artwork, play a song on a CD, or read aloud a short literary work or an idea expressed in a reading. Ask your classmates to explain the reasons for their own evaluations. Maybe they'll suggest criteria or evidence that hadn't occurred to you.

Planning, Drafting, and Developing

Start with a Thesis. Reflect a moment: What is your purpose? What is your main point? Try writing a paragraph that sums up the purpose of your evaluation or stating a thesis that summarizes your main point.

For more on stating a thesis, see pp. 401–10.

TOPIC + JUDGMENT	campus revival of *South Pacific* — liked the performers featured in it plus the problems the revival raised
WORKING THESIS	Chosen to showcase the achievements of graduating seniors, the campus revival of *South Pacific* also brings up societal problems.

For exercises on choosing and supporting effective thesis statements, visit **<bedfordstmartins .com/bedguide>**.

Learning by Doing 🖾 Stating Your Overall Judgment

Build your criteria into your working thesis statement by filling in this sentence:

This subject is _____ because it _____.
                 your judgment   your criteria

With a classmate or small group, compare sentences and share ideas about improving your statement of your judgment and criteria. Use this advice to rework and sharpen your working thesis.

Consider Your Criteria. Many writers find that a list of specific criteria gives them confidence and provokes ideas. Consider filling in a chart with three columns — criteria, evidence, judgment — to help focus your thinking.

Develop an Organization. You may want to begin with a direct statement of your judgment: Based on durability, cost, and comfort, the Classic 7 is an ideal campus backpack. On the other hand, you may want to reserve judgment by opening with a question about your subject: How good a film is *The Hurt Locker*? Each approach suggests a different organization:

Thesis or main point   →   Supporting evidence   →   Return to thesis

Opening question   →   Supporting evidence   →   Overall judgment

In either case, you'll supply plenty of evidence — details, examples, possibly comparisons or contrasts — to make your case compelling. You'll also cluster your evidence around your points or criteria for judgment so that readers know how and why you reach your judgment. You might try both patterns of organization to see which works better for your subject and purpose.

Most writers find that an outline — even a rough list — helps them keep track of points to make. If you intend to compare and contrast your subject with something else, one way to arrange the points is *subject by subject:* discuss subject A, and then discuss subject B. For a longer comparison, a better way to organize is *point by point,* applying each point first to one subject and then to the other. If appropriate and approved by your instructor, you also might plan to include a sketch, photograph, or other illustration of your subject or develop a comparative table summarizing the features of similar items you have compared.

Learning by Doing 🎬 Supporting Your Judgments

Consider how well you have linked specific support to your judgments to make your draft interesting and persuasive. Scroll through the file for your draft, and highlight each judgment or opinion in one color. (Look under Format to find Font choices, including color, or use your highlighting options.) Then go back to the beginning, and this time highlight all the facts and evidence in a different color. (If you work on a printed copy, use two highlighters to do the same.)

Now observe the flow of color in your draft. Are your judgments followed by or related to the evidence that supports them? Do you need to add more support at any points? Should you move sentences around to link your support more closely to your judgments? Once you have connected judgments and evidence, reread what you are saying to confirm how well they match. Do you need to modify any judgments or revise any support?

Revising and Editing

For more revising and editing strategies, see Ch. 23.

Focus on Your Thesis. Make your thesis as precise and clear as possible.

WORKING THESIS   Chosen to showcase the graduating seniors, the campus revival of *South Pacific* also brings up societal problems.

REVISED THESIS   The senior showcase, the musical *South Pacific,* spotlights outstanding performers and raises timely societal issues such as prejudice.

Be Fair. Make your judgments reasonable, not extreme. A reviewer can find fault with a film and still conclude that it is worth seeing. There's nothing wrong, of course, with a fervent judgment ("This play is the trashiest excuse for a drama I have ever suffered through"), but consider your readers and their likely reactions. Read some reviews in your local newspaper or online, or watch some movie critics on television to see how they balance their judgments. Because readers will have more confidence in your opinions if you seem fair and reasonable, revise your tone where needed. For example, one writer revised his opening after he realized that he was criticizing the audience rather than evaluating the performance.

The most recent performance by a favorite campus group—Rock Mountain—
disappointing concert   *Although t*
was an ~~incredibly revolting~~ experience. ~~T~~he ~~outlandish~~ crowd ignored the DJ who
people
introduced the group͵ and a few ~~nameless members of one social group spent~~
ed
~~their time~~ toss~~ing~~ around trash cans in front of the stage͵ *, the opening number still*
announced the group's powerful musical presence.

Peer Response 👥 Evaluating and Reviewing

Enlist the advice of a classmate or friend as you determine your criteria for evaluation and your judgment. Ask your peer editor to answer questions like these about your evaluation:

- What is your overall reaction to this essay? Does the writer persuade you to agree with his or her evaluation?
- When you finish the essay, can you tell exactly what the writer thinks of the subject? Where does the writer express this opinion?
- How do you know what criteria the writer is using for evaluation?
- Does the writer give you sufficient evidence for his or her judgment? Put stars wherever more or better evidence is needed.
- What audience does the writer seem to have in mind?
- Would you recommend any changes in the essay's organization?
- If this paper were yours, what is the one thing you would be sure to work on before handing it in?

For general questions for a peer editor, see p. 465. For peer response worksheets, visit **<bedfordstmartins .com/bedguide>**.

REVISION CHECKLIST

☐ Is the judgment you pass on your subject unmistakably clear?

☐ Have you given your readers evidence to support each point you make?

☐ Have you been fair? If you are championing something, have you deliberately skipped over any of its disadvantages or faults? If you are condemning your subject, have you omitted any of its admirable traits?

☐ Have you anticipated and answered readers' possible objections?

☐ If you compare two things, do you look at the same points in both?

For more on comparison and contrast, see Ch. 7.

For more editing and proofreading strategies, see pp. 473–76.

After you have revised your evaluation, edit and proofread it. Carefully check grammar, word choice, punctuation, and mechanics—and then correct any problems you find. Make sentences in which you describe the subject of your evaluation as precise and useful as possible. If you have used comparisons or contrasts, make sure these are clear: don't lose your readers in a fog of vague pronouns or confusing references.

EDITING CHECKLIST

For more help, find the relevant checklist sections in the Quick Editing Guide on p. A-36. Turn also to the Quick Format Guide beginning on A-1.

☐ Is the reference of each pronoun clear? Does each pronoun agree with (match) its antecedent? **A6**

☐ Is it clear what each modifier in a sentence modifies? Have you created any dangling or misplaced modifiers, especially in descriptions of your subject? **B1**

☐ Have you used parallel structure wherever needed, especially in lists or comparisons? **B2**

Additional Writing Assignments

1. Write an evaluation of a college course you have taken or are now taking. Analyze its strengths and weaknesses. Does the instructor present the material clearly, understandably, and engagingly? Can you confer with the instructor if you need to? Are the assignments pointed and purposeful? Is the textbook helpful, readable, and easy to use? Does this course give you your money's worth?

2. Evaluate an unfamiliar magazine, an essay in this textbook, a proposal under consideration at work, a source you have read for a college class, or a recommended academic Web site about an area that interests you. Be sure to specify your criteria for evaluation and identify the evidence that supports your judgments.

3. Evaluate a product that you might want to purchase. Establish the criteria that matter to you—and to the other prospective purchasers who right turned to you for a recommendation. Consider, for example, the product's features, construction, utility, beauty, color, cost, or other criteria that matter to purchasers. Make a clear recommendation to your audience: buy or not.

4. Read these two poems on a similar theme, and decide which seems to you the better poem. In a brief essay, set forth your evaluation. Some criteria to apply might be the poet's choice of concrete, specific words that appeal to the senses and his awareness of his audience.

For more on responding to literature, see Ch. 13.

> **Putting in the Seed**
> ROBERT FROST (1874–1963)
>
> You come to fetch me from my work tonight
> When supper's on the table, and we'll see
> If I can leave off burying the white
> Soft petals fallen from the apple tree
> (Soft petals, yes, but not so barren quite,
> Mingled with these, smooth bean and wrinkled pea),
> And go along with you ere you lose sight
> Of what you came for and become like me,
> Slave to a springtime passion for the earth.
> How Love burns through the Putting in the Seed
> On through the watching for that early birth
> When, just as the soil tarnishes with weed,
> The sturdy seedling with arched body comes
> Shouldering its way and shedding the earth crumbs.

> **Between Our Folding Lips**
> T. E. BROWN (1830–1897)
>
> Between our folding lips
> God slips
> An embryon life, and goes;
> And this becomes your rose.
> We love, God makes: in our sweet mirth
> God spies occasion for a birth.
> *Then is it His, or is it ours?*
> I know not—He is fond of flowers.

5. Visit a restaurant, a museum, or a tourist attraction, and write an evaluation of it for others who might consider a visit. Present your evaluation as an essay, an article for a travel or lifestyle magazine, or a travel blog that informs prospective travelers about local sites and evaluates what they offer. Be sure to specify your criteria and include plenty of detail to create the local color your audience will expect.

6. **Visual Assignment.** Select one pair of the following images, and examine their features carefully. Write an essay that evaluates the items portrayed in the images or the images themselves. Specify for your audience your criteria for judging. Observe carefully to identify enough visual detail to support your judgments.

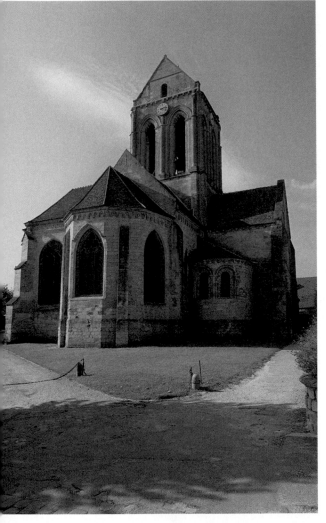

Church at Auvers-sur-Oise, France (2002)

"Church at Auvers-sur-Oise" painted by Vincent van Gogh (1853–1890)

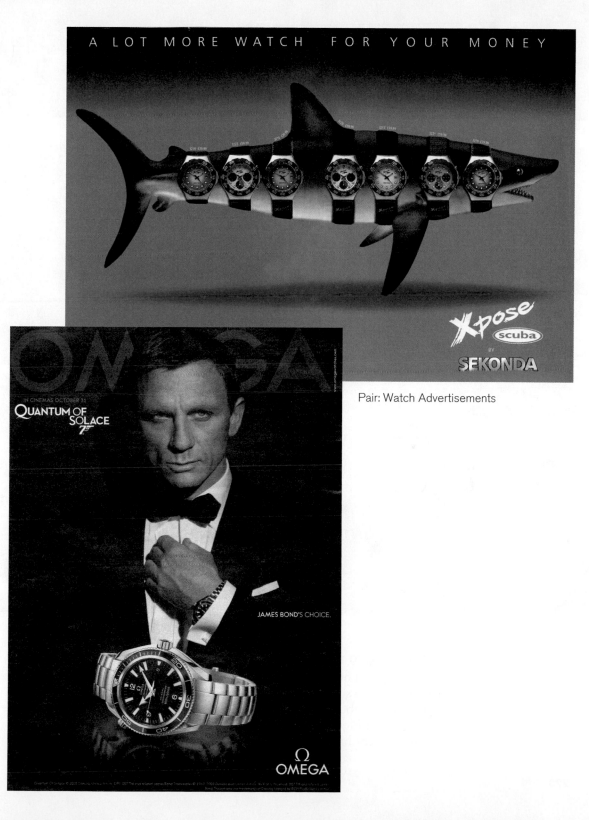

Pair: Watch Advertisements

12 Supporting a Position with Sources

Responding to an Image

These images show activities that might help a student gather evidence from sources to support a position in a college paper. What does each image suggest about possible sources? What do the images suggest about the process of inquiry? Which activities look most intriguing? What other activities might have appeared in images on this page?

Suppose you surveyed a random group of graduating students about the typical college writing assignment. The odds are good that this assignment might boil down to reading a few texts and writing a paper about them. Simple as this description sounds, it does suggest what you probably expect from a college education: an opportunity to absorb and think seriously about provocative ideas. It also suggests the values that lie behind many college expectations — a deep respect for the process of inquiry (the academic method of asking and investigating intriguing questions) and for the products of disciplined inquiry (the analyses, interpretations, and studies in each academic field).

When you first tackle such assignments, you may wonder "How do I figure out what my instructor really wants?" or "How could I possibly do that?" In response, you may turn to peripheral questions such as "How long does my paper have to be?" or "How many sources do I have to use?" instead of facing the central question: "How can I learn the skills I need to use a few sources to develop and support a position in a college paper?"

Unlike a debate or a Super Bowl game, a paper that takes a position generally doesn't have two distinct sides or a single winner. Instead, the writer typically makes a point by joining the ongoing exchange of ideas about an intriguing or challenging topic in the field. Each paper builds on the exchanges of the past — the articles, essays, reports, books, and other texts that convey the perspectives, research findings, and conclusions of others. Although reading such sources may seem daunting, it is a reassuring expectation. After all, you are not expected to know everything yourself but simply to work conscientiously at learning what others know. Your paper, in turn, advances or redirects the exchange in order to convey your well-grounded point of view or to defend your well-reasoned interpretation.

Why Supporting with Sources Matters

In a College Course

- You support a position with sources when you write a sociology paper about families, based on several articles, or a history paper about an event, synthesizing a first-person account, contemporary newspaper account, and scholarly article.
- You support a position with sources when you write an essay presenting your analysis after reading a short story, play, or poem along with several critical essays about it.

In the Workplace

- You support a position with sources when you write a report for your agency, pulling together multiple accounts and records to support your recommendation.

In Your Community

- You support a position with sources when you write a well-substantiated letter to the editor or justify the needs of a local nonprofit group.

❓ What are some instances, besides assigned research papers, when you have used sources to support a position in your writing? What source-based writing might you do at work or in your community?

Learning from Other Writers

For more such writings, visit
<bedfordstmartins .com/bedguide>.

The selections here illustrate how two different writers draw on evidence from sources to substantiate their points. The notes in the margin of the first reading will help you begin to analyze features such as the thesis, or main idea, and the variety of methods used to introduce and integrate information from sources.

As You Read These Essays That Support a Position with Sources

As you read these essays, ask yourself the following questions:

1. What thesis, or main idea, expresses the position supported by the essay? How does the writer try to help readers appreciate the importance of this position?

2. In what ways does the writer use information from sources to develop and support a thesis? Do you find this information relevant and persuasive?

3. How does the writer vary the way each source is introduced and the way information is drawn from it?

Jake Halpern

The Popular Crowd

Works by author and radio producer Jake Halpern include *Braving Home* (2003), a study of people who live in extreme places, and *Dormia* (2009), a fantasy novel. The following selection comes from *Fame Junkies* (2007), Halpern's analysis of celebrity worship. Its references to sources have been adapted to illustrate the use of MLA style.

Americans now appear to be lonelier than ever. In his book *The Loss of Happiness in Market Democracies,* the Yale political scientist Robert Lane notes that the number of people who described themselves as lonely more than quadrupled in the past few decades (85). We have increasingly become a nation of loners—traveling salesmen, Web designers, phone-bank operators, and online day traders who live and work in isolation. According to the U. S. Census Bureau, we also marry later in life. In 1956 the median age for marriage was 22.5 for men and 20.1 for women; by 2004 it was 27.4 for men and 25.8 for women (Russell). This helps to explain something else the Census Bureau has noted: Americans are increasingly living alone. The share of American households including seven or more people dropped from 35.9 percent in 1790, 5.8 percent in 1950, and 1.2 percent in 2004. Meanwhile, the number of households consisting of just one person rose from 3.7 percent in 1790 to 9.3 percent in 1950 and 26.4 percent in 2004. Nowadays, one out of four American households consists of a single person. In recent years this trend has been especially discernible° among young people (Cushman 599; US Census Bureau). Since 1970 the number of youths (ages fifteen to twenty-five) living alone has almost tripled, and the number of young adults (ages twenty-five to thirty-four) living alone has more than quadrupled (Russell).

The combination of loneliness and our innate° desire to belong may be fueling our interest in celebrities and our tendency to form para-social relationships° with them. Only a few research psychologists have seriously explored this possibility, among them Lynn McCutcheon and Dianne Ashe. McCutcheon and Ashe compared results from 150 subjects who had taken three personality tests—one measuring shyness, one measuring loneliness, and one measuring celebrity obsession, on something called the Celebrity Attitudes Scale, or CAS. The CAS asks subjects to rate the veracity° of statements such as "I am obsessed by details of my favorite celebrity's life" and "If I were lucky enough to meet my favorite celebrity, and he/she asked me to do something illegal as a favor, I would probably do it." McCutcheon and Ashe found a correlation among scores on loneliness, shyness, and the CAS (Ashe and McCutcheon 129). Their results led McCutcheon to observe in a subsequent paper, "Perhaps one of the ways [we] cope with shyness and loneliness is to cultivate a 'safe,' non-threatening relationship with a celebrity" (McCutcheon et al. 503).

Another investigation, led by Jacki Fitzpatrick, of Texas Tech University, looked at the correlation° between para-social relationships and actual romantic relationships. Fitzpatrick asked forty-five college students to complete a questionnaire containing several psychological measures, including one that gauged para-social relationships (the Para-social Interaction Scale) and another that gauged romantic relationships (the Multiple Determinants

1

Background information including facts and statistics

2

THESIS presenting position

Supporting evidence, including description of psychological study

Examples quoted from survey

Point 1

Direct quotation

Et al. ("and others") used for source with four or more authors

3

Paraphrase

---

discernible: Distinguishable, noticeable.   **innate:** Inborn from birth.   **para-social relationships:** One-sided friendships, based on the illusion of interaction and mutual knowledge. **veracity:** Truthfulness.   **correlation:** Agreement, parallelism.

Point 2 — of Relationship Commitment Inventory). She and her colleague, Andrea McCourt, discovered that subjects who were less invested in their romantic relationships were more involved in para-social relationships. They concluded, "It makes sense that individuals may use para-social relationships as one way to fulfill desires or address needs (e.g., for attention, companionship) that are unmet in their romances" (Fitzpatrick and McCourt).

Author's position based on study — The Rochester survey,* too, provides evidence that lonely teenagers are especially susceptible to forming para-social relationships with celebrities. Boys who described themselves as lonely were almost twice as likely as others to endorse the statement "My favorite celebrity just helps me feel good and forget about all of my troubles." Girls who described themselves as lonely were almost three times as likely as others to endorse that statement.   4

Paraphrase — Analysis — Conclusion synthesizing sources — Another survey question asked teens whom they would most like to meet for dinner: Jesus Christ, Albert Einstein, Shaquille O'Neal, Jennifer Lopez, 50 Cent, Paris Hilton, or the President. Among boys who said they were not lonely, the clear winner was Jesus Christ; but among those who described themselves as lonely, Jesus finished last and 50 Cent was the clear winner. Similarly, girls who felt appreciated by their parents, friends, and teachers tended to choose dinner with Jesus, whereas those who felt underappreciated were likely to choose Paris Hilton. One possible interpretation of these results is that lonely and underappreciated teens particularly want to befriend the ultimate popular guy or girl. Regardless of who exactly this figure is at a given time, it's clear that many of us—lonely people in particular—yearn to belong to the popular crowd.   5

Works Cited

Each source cited in Halpern's essay listed alphabetically by author, with full publication information

First line of entry placed at left margin; with subsequent lines indented ½"

Ashe, D. D., and Lynn McCutcheon. "Shyness, Loneliness, and Attitude Toward Celebrities." *Current Research in Social Psychology* 6.9 (2001): 124-33. Print.

Cushman, Philip. "Why the Self Is Empty: Toward a Historically Situated Psychology." *American Psychologist* 45.5 (1990): 599-612. Print.

Fitzpatrick, Jacki, and Andrea McCourt. "The Role of Personal Characteristics and Romantic Characteristics in Para-social Relationships: A Pilot Study." *Journal of Mundane Behavior* 2.1 (2001): n. pag. Web. [Author's date of access not known.]

Lane, Robert E. *The Loss of Happiness in Market Democracies*. New Haven: Yale UP, 2000. Print.

McCutcheon, Lynn, Mara Aruguete, Vann B. Scott, Jr., and Kristen L. VonWaldner. "Preference for Solitude and Attitude Toward One's Favorite Celebrity." *North American Journal of Psychology* 6.3 (2004): 499-505. Print.

Russell, Cheryl. *newstrategist.com*. New Strategist Publications, n.d. Web. [Author's date of access not known.]

*The Rochester, NY, survey of 653 fifth to eighth grade students, conducted by Jake Halpern and Carol M. Liebler, is discussed in full in *Fame Junkies* (New York: Houghton Mifflin 2007). [Editor's note]

United States Census Bureau. Fertility and Family Branch. *HH-4: Households by Size: 1960 to Present.* 15 Sept. 2004. *U.S. Census Bureau.* Web. [Author's date of access not known.]

Questions to Start You Thinking

Meaning

1. What position does Halpern take in this essay?

2. In paragraph 1, Halpern refers to America as "a nation of loners." What does he mean by this statement, and how does he see the problem changing in recent decades?

3. How does Halpern suggest that following and watching a celebrity could help people cope with shyness?

4. How has Halpern arranged the main points of his essay? How do these points develop his thesis in paragraph 2 and lead up to paragraph 5?

Writing Strategies

5. What types of evidence does Halpern use to support his position? How convincing is this evidence to you?

6. Halpern alternates between stating some source information in his own words and quoting some directly. What are the advantages and disadvantages of these two approaches?

7. How would you describe Halpern's tone, the quality of his writing that reveals his attitude toward his topic and his readers? What specific words, phrases, or sentences contribute to his tone? Does the tone seem appropriate for his purpose and audience?

8. Compare this selection, excerpted from a book, with an article written for a newspaper (see, for example, "Katrina Documentary Gives Voice to Survivors," p. 207). What differences in formatting, style, and presentation do you notice between the two selections?

Melissa Lamberth   **Student Essay**

Overworked!

Melissa Lamberth wrote this essay for a composition course at Riverside Community College. She used MLA style to cite and list sources.

For more on this citation style, see E1–E2 in the Quick Research Guide, pp. A-18–A-35.

In the song "Nine to Five," Dolly Parton speaks for the overworked employee whose life is drained away by the clock. The amount of time Americans are working is on the increase, and Americans are growing weary.° Shorter workdays or more   1

weary: Tired.

opportunities to take time off need to be available in order to provide a safer, happier, and more energetic workplace.

In her book *The Overworked American*, Schor writes, "The rise of work time was unexpected. For nearly a hundred years, hours had been declining. When this decline abruptly° ended in the late 1940s, it marked the beginning of a new era in work time" (1). Schor explains how this surprising increase has grown during recent years: "Each year, the change is small, amounting to about nine hours, or slightly more than one additional day of work. In any given year, such a small increment° has probably been imperceptible,° but the accumulated increase over two decades is substantial" (2). If Americans are gaining a little over a day of work each year, that is over ten days in a decade! This does not leave much time for family responsibilities or, much less, for leisure time.

Overworked employees may present a problem not only in the household but also in the workplace and even on the road. In his essay "Four Weeks Vacation," Robinson writes, "The health implications° of sleep-deprived° motorists weaving their way to the office or operating machinery on the job are self-evident" (481). An employee may work a few hours of overtime, drive home in traffic for an hour, and then cook or eat dinner with the family. On top of that, there are errands to run and bills to pay. How much time does that leave the individual to rest? This schedule easily could lead to a "sleep-deprived motorist" or an injured machine operator.

The toll that overworked employees take on the family is also evident. In recent years, it has become more and more common for both parents to go to work to support the family. Time is a very important factor in keeping relationships in the household healthy. If both parents are spending a majority of their time working, it may be very difficult to find time to raise the kids and keep a marriage intact. In an article titled "Just What the Worker Needs—Longer Days, No Overtime," Eisenbrey writes, "Women are working many more weeks per year and hours per week, on average, than they did 30 or even 10 years ago. Middle-class married couples with children and a head of household between the ages of 25 and 54 now work an average of 98 weeks a year, compared with 78 weeks in 1969. These changes clearly support Eisenbrey's conclusion. Overtime for either spouse—but especially the mother— can have serious effects on a family."

All these added stresses, caused by overworking, are carried straight back to the workplace the next morning. Negative attitudes set in. Employees start to hate work. As a result, morale goes down in the workplace. It is a vicious° cycle that Americans are stuck in. How can this cycle be stopped? Overtime, for one thing, should not be required but only allowed as an option. If employees have too much extra work to do, employers should consider giving the work to someone else. This could mean hiring another employee or dividing the extra work among employees who are not as busy.

Do you feel overworked? Why or why not?

What do you think of these ideas? Are they practical?

---

abruptly: Suddenly.   **increment:** Unit (of growth, in this case).   **imperceptible:** Not noticeable.   **implications:** Consequences.   **sleep-deprived:** Lacking restorative slumber. **vicious:** Harmful; nasty.

Employees also need to have more opportunities to take time off. If the employee can't take desired time off due to a heavy workload, which is common in the workplace, employers need to consider hiring temporary employees or going through a temp agency to find employees who will work during the regular employee's time off. This work relief will make for a happier, less stressed employee. In an SFGate.com article titled "You Deserve a Month Off," columnist Mark Morford wrote, "We need more time off. A lot more time. Longer vacations. Extended breaks. Chunks of contiguous° time which you can roll around on the tongue of your id° and feel all swoony° and blissed.° When's the last time you saw an unhappy Aussie°? Exactly." Morford is implying that employees need more time off in order to be happier. He went on to say, "It prevents burnouts and ameliorates° loathings° and lightens the spirit and lets the psyche° breathe. . . ." 6

Some employers may claim that hiring temporary employees so that an employee can have time off would not be cost-effective. However, good employees are valuable. With that value in mind, hiring someone for a couple of weeks would be worthwhile so that the regular employee could come back to work rested, refreshed, and more productive than ever! 7

Employers may believe that family- and life-related programs that teach employees how to manage stress and time are the answers to stress in the workplace. That notion may lead some employees to question "Where are we going to get the time for such programs?!?" They have their kids' soccer and softball games, meetings with teachers, dinner to cook, and laundry to do. Employees simply have no time to be involved in those programs. 8

As a response to this overload, an organization named Take Back Your Time announced in 2005 the sixty-fifth anniversary of the forty-hour workweek (Burger). In its honor, this group declared October 24th Take Back Your Time Day. In a press release, John de Graaf, Take Back Your Time's national coordinator, stated, "It's 65 years later, productivity is quadruple what it was then, and still most Americans are working more than 40 hours a week. If 40 hours was enough to support a family then, it should take even less work time now. We need to start by getting the workweek back down to 40 hours." The organization is fighting for protected 40-hour workweeks and for higher wages so that Americans don't have to work more than 40 hours to support a family above the poverty line. They are also fighting for salaried workers who work long hours to be given comp time° for time required of them by their employers that goes over the 40-hour workweek and for time-and-a-half overtime premiums° to be protected and strengthened. 9

🔘 If you had more time, what would you do with it?

These goals are positive stepping-stones that will lead to a more positive workplace. There should be no need for more than 40 hours of work each week when 10

contiguous: Uninterrupted.   **id:** The part of the personality concerned with instincts and basic needs.   **swoony:** Given to fainting (in this case, out of happiness).   **blissed:** Happy.
Aussie: Australian.   **ameliorates:** Makes better.   **loathings:** Hatreds.   **psyche:** Mind.
comp time: Compensatory time—time off given for extra time worked.   **premiums:** Extra payments.

Americans didn't need to work this much 65 years ago. Technology has radically increased productivity. Employers need to embrace this and "let their people go!" Let them take an extra week off! Let them opt out of overtime! Let them get off work a few hours early! In the long run, employees won't be let go, in the literal° sense, because they will be more productive and punctual.° And that is well worth it.

Works Cited

Burger, Gretchen. "Take Back Your Time." *Take Back Your Time*. CRESP at Cornell U, 11 Oct. 2005. Web. 15 Oct. 2005.

Eisenbrey, Ross. "Just What the Worker Needs—Longer Days, No Overtime." *Los Angeles Times*. Los Angeles Times, 14 Feb. 2003. Web. 16 Oct. 2005.

Morford, Mark. "You Deserve a Month Off." *SFGate*. Hearst Communications, 19 Apr. 2002. Web. 12 Oct. 2005.

Robinson, Joe. "Four Weeks Vacation." *The Bedford Guide for College Writers*. 7th ed. Ed. X. J. Kennedy, Dorothy M. Kennedy, Sylvia A. Holladay, and Marcia F. Muth. Boston: Bedford, 2005. 479–84. Print.

Schor, Juliet B. *The Overworked American: The Unexpected Decline of Leisure*. New York: Basic, 1992. Print.

Questions to Start You Thinking

Meaning

1. What position does Lamberth support in this essay?
2. According to Lamberth, what difficulties and risks do overworked people face inside and outside of work?
3. What responsibilities do employers have to improve the lives of overworked employees, according to the author?

Writing Strategies

4. What types of evidence does Lamberth use to support her position? How convincing is this evidence to you?
5. Has Lamberth considered alternative views? How does the inclusion (or lack) of these views contribute to or detract from the essay?
6. Exclamation points are used in several places. Do you find this to be an effective or ineffective stylistic choice?
7. Using highlighters or marginal notes, identify the essay's introduction, thesis, major points, supporting evidence for each point, and conclusion. How effective is the organization of this essay?

literal: Referring to the exact meaning of a word or expression.   **punctual:** On time.

Learning by Writing

The Assignment: Supporting a Position with Sources

Identify a cluster of readings about a topic that interests you. For example, choose some related readings from one of the thematic groups in *A Writer's Reader,* from different thematic groups there, or from a group of related readings assigned in your class. If your topic is assigned and you don't begin with any particular interest in it, develop your intellectual curiosity. Look for an angle, an implication, or a vantage point that will engage you. Try to relate the topic in some way to your own experience. Read (or reread) the selections, considering how each supports, challenges, or deepens your understanding of the topic.

Based on the information in your cluster of readings, develop an enlightening position about the topic that you'd like to share with an audience of college readers. Support this position—your working thesis—using quotations, paraphrases, summaries, and syntheses of the information in the readings as evidence. Present your information from sources clearly, and credit your sources appropriately.

Three students investigated topics of great variety:

One student examined local language usage that combined words from English and Spanish, drawing on essays about language diversity to analyze the patterns and implications of such usage.

Another writer used a cluster of readings about technology to evaluate the privacy issues on a popular Web site for student profiles.

A third, using personal experience with a blended family and several essays on families, challenged misconceptions about today's families.

For writing activities on supporting a position with sources, visit <bedfordstmartins.com/bedguide>.

See the contents of *A Writer's Reader* on p. 494.

Facing the Challenge   Finding Your Voice

The major challenge that writers face when using sources to support a position is finding their own voices. You create your voice as a college writer through your choice of language and angle of vision. You probably want to present yourself as a thoughtful writer with credible insights, a reasonable person a reader will want to hear from.

Finding your own voice may be especially difficult in a source-based paper. After all, you need to read carefully and then capture information to strengthen your discussion by quoting, paraphrasing, or summarizing. You need to introduce it, feed it into your draft, and, of course, credit it. By this time, you'll probably feel that your sources have taken over your paper. You may feel that there's no room left for your own voice and, even if there were, it's too quiet to jostle past the powerful words of your sources. That, however, is your challenge.

As you develop your voice as a college writer and use it to guide your readers' understanding, you'll restrict sources to their proper role as supporting evidence. Don't let them get pushy or dominate your writing. Use these questions to help you strengthen your voice:

For more on evidence, see pp. 39–42 and pp. 168–72.

■ Can you write a list or passage explaining what you'd like readers to hear from your voice? Where could you add more of this in your draft?

■ Have you used your own voice, not quotations or paraphrases from sources, to introduce your topic, state your thesis, and draw conclusions?

■ Have you generally relied on your own voice to open and conclude paragraphs and to reinforce your main ideas in every passage?

■ Have you alternated between your voice and the voices of sources? Can you strengthen your voice if it gets trampled by a herd of sources?

■ Have you used your voice to identify and introduce source material before you present it? Have you used your voice to explain or interpret source material after you include it?

■ Have you used your voice to tell readers why your sources are relevant, how they support your points, and what their limits might be?

■ Have you carefully created your voice as a college writer, balancing passion and personality with rock-solid reasoning?

Whenever you are uncertain about the answers to these questions, make an electronic copy of your file or print it out. Highlight all of the wording in your own voice in a bright, visible color. Check for the presence and prominence of this highlighting, and then revise the white patches (the material drawn from sources) as needed to strengthen your voice.

Generating Ideas

For more strategies for generating ideas, see Ch. 19.

Pin Down Your Working Topic and Your Cluster of Readings. Try to specify what you're going to work on. This task is relatively easy if your instructor has assigned the topic and the required set of readings. If not, figure out what limits your instructor has set and which decisions are yours. Carefully follow any directions about the number or types of sources that you are expected to use. Instead of hunting only for sources that share your initial views about the topic, look for a variety of reliable and relevant sources so that you can broaden, even challenge, your perspective.

For advice about finding and evaluating academic sources, turn to sections B and C in the Quick Research Guide, pp. A-18–A-35.

Consider Your Audience. You are writing for an academic community that is intrigued by your topic (unless your instructor specifies some other group). In addition, your instructor probably holds several expectations. One is a broad goal, making sure that you are prepared to succeed when you write future assignments, including full research papers. For this reason, you'll be expected to quote, paraphrase, and summarize information from sources. Each time you use such material, you'll also need to introduce — or launch — it and credit its source, thus demonstrating essential skills for source-based writing.

In addition, your instructor will want to see your own position emerge from the swamp of information that you are reading. You may feel that your ideas are like a prehistoric creature, dripping as it struggles out of the bog. If so, encourage your creature to wade toward dry land. Jot down your own ideas whenever they pop into mind. Highlight them in color on the page or on the screen. Store them in your writing notebook or a special file so that you can find them, watch them accumulate, and give them well-deserved prominence in your paper.

One Student Thinking through a Topic

General Subject: Men and Women (Ch. 26)

Assigned topic: State and support a position about differences in the behavior of men and women.

What do I know about?

What do I care about?

RECALL PERSONAL EXPERIENCES: Friends at school? Competition for jobs? Pressure on parents to be good role models?

CONSIDER READINGS: Barry? Ehrenreich? Brady? Perrin? Staples? Jensen?

- Stereotypes of women — emotional and caring
- Stereotypes of men — tough and aggressive
- What aboout me? I'm a woman in training to be a police officer — and I'm a mother. I'm emotional, caring, aggressive, and tough.

I bet that men and women are more alike than different. What do the readings say? What evidence do they present?

- **RETURN TO THE READINGS.**
- **TEST AND REFINE YOUR WORKING THESIS.**
- **LOOK FOR EVIDENCE.**

Take an Academic Approach. Your experience and imagination remain your own deep well, an endless reservoir from which you can draw ideas whenever you need them. For an academic paper, this deep well may help you identify an intriguing topic, raise a compelling question about it, or pursue an unusual slant. For example, you might recall talking with your

For more on generating ideas, see Ch. 19.

For more on reading critically, see Ch. 2.

cousin about the high cost of her prescriptions and decide to investigate the controversy about importing low-cost medications from other countries.

Besides drawing on your personal reserves, you'll also be expected to investigate your topic using authoritative sources. These sources—articles, essays, reports, books, Web pages, and other reliable materials—are your second deep well. When one well runs dry for the moment, start pumping the other. As you read critically to tap your second reservoir, you join the academic exchange. This exchange is the flow of knowledge from one credible source to the next as writers and researchers raise questions, seek answers, evaluate information, and advance knowledge. As you inquire about your topic, you'll move from what you already know to deeper knowledge. You'll gain a more complex appreciation of varied perspectives on the topic. Welcome sources that shed light on your inquiry rather than simply agree with a view you already hold.

Learning by Doing 🎯 Selecting Reliable Sources

When you choose your own sources, you need to evaluate them to be certain that they are reliable choices that your audience will respect. When your sources are identified in your assignment, you still need to know their strengths, weaknesses, and limitations so that you introduce and use them effectively. Bring your articles, essays, and other sources to a small-group evaluation session. Using the guideline in C3 in the Quick Research Guide (pp. A-24–A-26), discuss your common sources or a key source selected by each writer in the group. Look for aspects that you might mention in a paper to bolster a source's credibility with readers (for example, the author's professional affiliation). Look as well for limitations that might restrict what a source can support.

Skim Your Sources. When you work with a cluster of readings, you'll need to read them carefully and probably repeatedly. Start out, however, by skimming—quickly reading only enough to find out what direction a selection takes. First, leaf through the reading, glancing at any headings or figure labels. Return to the first paragraph, read it in full, but then read only the first sentence of each subsequent paragraph. At the end, read the final paragraph in full. Then stop to consider what you've already learned. Do the same with your other selections, classifying or comparing them as you begin to think about what they might contribute to your paper.

DISCOVERY CHECKLIST

☐ What topic is assigned or under consideration? What ideas about it emerge as you brainstorm, freewrite, or use another strategy to generate ideas?

□ What cluster of readings will you begin with? What do you already know about them? What have you learned about them simply by skimming?

□ What purpose would you like to achieve in your paper? Who is your primary audience? What will your instructor expect you to accomplish?

□ What clues about how to proceed can you draw from the two sample essays in this chapter or from other readings that your instructor has identified as useful models?

Planning, Drafting, and Developing

Start with a Working Thesis. Sometimes you start reading for a source-based paper with a clear position in mind; other times, you begin simply with your initial response to your sources. Either way, try to state your main idea as a working thesis even if you expect to rewrite it—or even replace it—later on. Once your thesis takes shape in words, you can assess the richness and relevance of your reading based on a clear main idea.

For more on stating a thesis, see pp. 401–10.

For exercises on choosing effective thesis statements, visit **<bedfordstmartins .com/bedguide>**.

| FIRST RESPONSE TO SOURCES | Joe Robinson, author of "Four Weeks Vacation," and others say that workers need more vacation time, but I can't see my boss agreeing to this. |
| WORKING THESIS | Although most workers would like longer vacations, many employers do not believe that they would benefit, too. |

Once your thesis takes shape in words, you can analyze its parts and use them to guide your search for reliable information. Of course you'll look for material to support your view, but often material that questions it proves more valuable, prompting you to rethink your thesis, refine it, or counter more effectively whatever challenges it. For example, the working thesis above breaks into two parts: workers and employers. Each might benefit from, or suffer from, longer vacations. Instead of looking for a source to prove your thesis, you're now ready to look for the light each source can shed on either view (benefit or suffer) held by either party (worker or employer) identified in your thesis.

Learning by Doing Connecting Evidence and Thesis

State your working thesis, no matter how shaky it seems. Examine it to consider what parties or components it mentions, what views they might hold, or whatever else seem relevant. List the parties, views, or other aspects that your evidence from sources might address, whether it supports, qualifies, or challenges your thesis. Keep your working thesis and your evidence list handy as you read.

Read Each Source Thoughtfully. Before you begin copying quotations from a source, read it through, slowly and carefully, in order to understand what it says. During this reading, don't scribble notes or vigorously highlight. Simply read. After you have figured out what the source says, you are ready to decide how you might use its information to support your ideas. Read again, this time sifting and selecting what's relevant to your thesis.

- How does the source use its own sources to support its position?
- Does it review major sources chronologically (by date), thematically (by topic), or by some other method?
- Does it use sources to supply background for its own position? Does it compare its position or research findings with those of other studies?
- What audience does the source address? What was its author's purpose?
- How might you want to use the source?

Join the Academic Exchange. A well-researched article that follows academic conventions will identify its sources for several reasons. First, it gives honest credit to the work on which it relies — work done by other researchers and writers. They deserve this credit because their useful information contributes to the article's credibility and substantiates its points. In addition, the article informs you about its sources so that you, or any other reader, could find them yourself.

The visual on pages 236–37 illustrates how this exchange of ideas and information works and how you, from the moment you begin to use sources in your college writing, join this exchange. The middle of the visual shows the opening of a sample article about a global health problem: obesity. Because this article appears online, it credits its sources by providing a link to each one. A comparable printed article might identify its sources by supplying brief in-text citations (in parentheses in MLA style and APA style), footnotes, numbers keyed to its references, or source identifications in the text itself. To the left of and below the source article are several of its sources. (They, in turn, also supply information about their sources.) The column to the right of the source article illustrates ways that you might capture information from the source.

For more on plagiarism, see D1 in the Quick Research Guide, pp. A-26–A-27.

For an avoiding-plagiarism tutorial, visit **<bedfordstmartins .com/rewriting>**.

Capture Information and Record Source Details. Consider how you might eventually want to capture each significant passage or point from a source in your paper — by quoting the exact words of the source, by paraphrasing its ideas in your own words, or by summarizing its essential point. Keeping accurate notes and records as you work with your sources will help you avoid accidental plagiarism (using someone else's words or ideas without giving the credit due). Accurate notes also help to reduce errors or missing information when you add the source material to your draft.

As you capture information, plan ahead so that you can acknowledge each source following academic conventions. Record the details necessary to identify the source in your discussion and to list it with other sources at the end of your paper. The next sections illustrate how to capture and credit your sources, using examples for a paper that relates land use and threats to wildlife. Compare the examples with the original passage from the source.

For more on citing and listing sources, see E1 and E2 in the Quick Research Guide, pp. A-30–A-35.

Identify Significant Quotations. When an author expresses an idea so memorably that you want to reproduce those words exactly, quote them word for word. Direct quotations can add life, color, and authority; too many can drown your voice and overshadow your point.

ORIGINAL

The tortoise is a creature that has survived virtually unchanged since it first appeared in the geologic record more than 150 million years ago. The species became threatened, however, when ranchers began driving their herds onto Mojave Desert lands for spring grazing, at the very time that the tortoise awakens from hibernation and emerges from its burrows to graze on the greening desert shrubs and grasses. As livestock trampled the burrows and monopolized the scarce desert vegetation, tortoise populations plummeted. (page 152)

The Mojave Desert

Babbitt, Bruce. *Cities in the Wilderness: A New Vision of Land Use in America*. Washington: Island Press-Shearwater, 2005. Print.

TOO MUCH QUOTATION

When "tortoise populations plummeted," a species "that has survived virtually unchanged since it first appeared in the geologic record more than 150 million years ago" (Babbitt 152) had losses that helped to justify setting workable boundaries for the future expansion of Las Vegas.

MEMORABLE QUOTATION

When "tortoise populations plummeted" (Babbitt 152), an unlikely species that has endured for millions of years helped to establish workable boundaries for the future expansion of Las Vegas.

Writers often begin by highlighting or copying too many quotations as they struggle to master the ideas in the source. The better you understand the reading and your own thesis, the more effectively you'll choose quotations. After all, a quotation in itself is not necessarily effective evidence; too many quotations suggest that your writing is padded or lacks originality.

THE ACADEMIC EXCHANGE Suppose that you used the center article to support a position. The various ways you might use this source are shown on the right-hand page. In turn, your source drew on other writings, some of which are shown to the left of and below the center article.

Sources Cited in Your Source

Source: U.S. Department of Agriculture

<www.usda.gov>

AREI Chapter 3.5: Global Resources and Productivity

Keith Wiebe

Abstract—*Global food production has grown faster than population in recent decades, due largely to improved seeds and increased use of fertilizer and irrigation. Soil degradation which has slowed yield growth in some areas, depends on farmers' incentives to adopt conservation practices, but does not threaten food security at the global level.*

Introduction

Increased resource use and improvements in technology and efficiency have increased global food production more rapidly than population in recent decades, but 800 million people remain food insecure (fig. 3.5.1). . . .

Source: World Bank

<web.worldbank.org>

Poverty Analysis: Overview

Trends in poverty over time: Living Standards have improved...

Living standards have risen dramatically over the last decades. The proportion of the developing world's population living in extreme economic poverty -- defined as living on less than $1 per day ($1.08 in 1993 dollars, adjusted to account for differences in purchasing power across countries) -- has fallen from 28 percent in 1990 to 21 percent in 2001.

Substantial improvements in social indicators have accompanied growth in average incomes. Infant mortality rates in low- and middle-income countries have fallen from 86 per 1,000 live births in 1980 to 60 in 2002. Life expectancy in these countries has risen from 60 to 65 between 1980 and 2002. For more health, nutrition and population statistics, see the HNPStats database. . . .

Your Source <www.slate.com>

Please Do Not Feed the Humans
THE GLOBAL EXPLOSION OF FAT.
By William Saletan
Posted Saturday, Sept. 2, 2006, at 8:22 AM ET

In 1894, Congress established Labor Day to honor those who "from rude nature have delved and carved all the grandeur we behold." In the century since, the grandeur of human achievement has multiplied. Over the past four decades, global population has doubled, but food output, driven by increases in productivity, has outpaced it. Poverty, infant mortality, and hunger are receding. For the first time in our planet's history, a species no longer lives at the mercy of scarcity. We have learned to feed ourselves.

We've learned so well, in fact, that we're getting fat. Not just the United States or Europe, but the whole world. Egyptian, Mexican, and South African women are now as fat as Americans. Far more Filipino adults are now overweight than underweight. In China, one in five adults is too heavy, and the rate of overweight in children is 28 times higher than it was two decades ago. In Thailand, Kuwait, and Tunisia, obesity, diabetes, and heart disease are soaring.

Hunger is far from conquered. But since 1990, the global rate of malnutrition has declined an average of 1.7 percent a year. Based on data from the World Health Organization and the U.N. Food and Agriculture Organization, for every two people who are malnourished, three are now overweight or obese. Among women, even in most African countries, overweight has surpassed underweight. The balance of peril is shifting.

Indirect Source: U.S. Department of Labor

<www.dol.gov/opa/aboutdol/laborday.htm>

The History of Labor Day

Labor Day: How it Came About; What it Means

"Labor Day differs in every essential way from the other holidays of the year in any country," said Samuel Gompers, founder and longtime president of the American Federation of Labor. "All other holidays are in a more or less degree connected with conflicts and battles of man's prowess over man, of strife and discord for greed and power, of glories achieved by one nation over another. Labor Day...is devoted to no man, living or dead, to no sect, race, or nation."

Labor Day, the first Monday in September, is a creation of the labor movement and is dedicated to the social and economic achievements of American workers. It constitutes a yearly national tribute to the contributions workers have made to the strength, prosperity, and well-being of our country.

Founder of Labor Day

More than 100 years after the first Labor Day observance, there is still some doubt as to who first proposed the holiday for workers.

Some records show that Peter J. McGuire, general secretary of the Brotherhood of Carpenters and Joiners and a cofounder of the American Federation of Labor, was first in suggesting a day to honor those "who from rude nature have delved and carved all the grandeur we behold."

Information Captured from Your Source

Sample Working Thesis
A clear thesis statement establishes a framework for selecting source material as useful evidence and for explaining its relevance to readers.

WORKING THESIS   In order to counter national and worldwide trends toward obesity, agricultural communities like Grand Junction need to apply their expertise as food producers to the promotion of healthy food products.

Quotation from an Indirect Source
A quotation from an indirect source captures the exact words of an author quoted within the source.

An 1894 action by Congress created a holiday to recognize workers who "delved and carved" to produce what Americans enjoy (qtd. in Saletan).

If possible, go to the original source to be sure that the quotation is accurate and that you are using it appropriately. (See the bottom left-hand page.)

Credit, though disputed, has gone to labor leader Peter McGuire for promoting the recognition of those who "delved and carved all the grandeur we behold" (US Dept. of Labor).

Quotation from a Source
A quotation captures the author's exact words directly from the source.

As Saletan observes, "We have learned to feed ourselves," but the success of agricultural enterprise and technology does not guarantee that well-fed people are healthy.

Paraphrase of a Source
A paraphrase captures an author's specific ideas fully and accurately, restating them in your own words and sentences.

Though the number of hungry people drops nearly 2 percent annually, more people, including African women, are now overfed by a ratio of 3 to 2 and thus have traded the health risks of malnutrition for those of obesity (Saletan).

Summary of a Source
A summary reduces an author's main point to essentials, using your own words and sentences.

Given that a worldwide shift in food security has led to an obesity epidemic (Saletan), consumers need lighter, healthier food options, a goal that the Grand Junction agricultural community can actively support.

MLA Works Cited Entry

AUTHOR'S NAME   TITLE OF ARTICLE   TITLE OF MAGAZINE

Saletan, William. "Please Do Not Feed the Humans: The Global Explosion of Fat." *Slate*.
    Washingtonpost.Newsweek Interactive, 2 Sept. 2006. Web. 28 Sept. 2006.

SPONSOR/PUBLISHER   PUBLICATION DATE   MEDIUM   ACCESS DATE

A Writer's Guide

HOW TO QUOTE

For more on quotations, see D3 in the Quick Research Guide, pp. A-18–A-35.

- Select a quotation that is both notable and pertinent to your thesis.
- Record it accurately, writing out exactly what it says. Include its punctuation and capitalization. Avoid abbreviations that might later be ambiguous.
- Mark both its beginning and ending with quotation marks.
- Note the page or other location (such as an electronic paragraph) where the quotation appears. If the quotation begins on one page but ends on another, mark where the switch occurs so that the credit in your draft will be accurate no matter how much of the quotation you eventually use.
- Double-check the accuracy of each quotation as you record it.

For more on punctuating quotations and using ellipsis marks, see C3 in the Quick Editing Guide, pp. A-36–A-56.

Use an ellipsis mark — three spaced dots (. . .) within a sentence or four dots (. . . .), a period and three spaced dots, concluding a sentence — to show where you leave out any original wording. You may omit wording that doesn't relate to your point, but don't distort the original meaning. For example, if a reviewer calls a movie "a perfect example of poor directing and inept acting," don't quote this comment as "perfect . . . directing and . . . acting."

Paraphrase Specific Information. Paraphrasing involves restating an author's ideas in your own language. A paraphrase is generally about the same length as the original. It conveys the ideas and emphasis of the original in your words and sentences, thus bringing your own voice to the fore. A fresh and creative paraphrase expresses your style without awkwardly jumping between it and your source's style. Be sure to name the source so that your reader knows exactly where you move from one to the other.

Here, again, is the original passage by Bruce Babbitt, followed by a sloppy paraphrase. The paraphrase suffers from a common fault, slipping in too many words from the original. (The borrowed words are underlined in the paraphrase.) Those words need to be expressed in the writer's own language or identified as direct quotations with quotation marks.

ORIGINAL

> The tortoise is a creature that has survived virtually unchanged since it first appeared in the geologic record more than 150 million years ago. The species became threatened, however, when ranchers began driving their herds onto Mojave Desert lands for spring grazing, at the very time that the tortoise awakens from hibernation and emerges from its burrows to graze on the greening desert shrubs and grasses. As livestock trampled the burrows and monopolized the scarce desert vegetation, tortoise populations plummeted. (page 152)

> Babbitt, Bruce. *Cities in the Wilderness: A New Vision of Land Use in America.* Washington: Island Press-Shearwater, 2005. Print.

SLOPPY
PARAPHRASE

Babbitt says that the <u>tortoise is a creature</u> in the Mojave
that is <u>virtually unchanged</u> over <u>150 million years</u>. Over
the millennia, the tortoise would <u>awaken from hibernation</u>
just in time <u>for spring grazing</u> on the new growth of the
region's <u>shrubs and grasses</u>. In recent years <u>the species
became threatened</u>. When cattle started to compete for
the same food, the <u>livestock trampled</u> the tortoise <u>burrows
and monopolized the desert vegetation</u> while the <u>tortoise
populations plummeted</u> (152).

To avoid picking up language from the original as you paraphrase, state
each sentence afresh instead of just changing a few words in the original. If
possible, take a short break, and then check each sentence against the original. Highlight any identical words or sentence patterns, and rework your
paraphrase again. Proper nouns or exact terms for the topic (such as *tortoise*)
do not need to be rephrased.

The next example avoids parroting the original by making different
word choices while reversing or varying sentence patterns.

PARAPHRASE

As Babbitt explains, a tenacious survivor in the Mojave
is the 150-million-year-old desert tortoise. Over the
millennia, the hibernating tortoise would rouse itself each
spring just in time to enjoy the new growth of the limited
regional plants. In recent years, as cattle became rivals
for this desert territory, the larger animals destroyed
tortoise homes, ate tortoise food, and thus eliminated
many of the tortoises themselves (152).

A common option is to blend paraphrase with brief quotation, carefully
using quotation marks to identify any exact words drawn from the source.

BLENDED

Babbitt describes a tenacious survivor in the Mojave, the
150-million-year-old desert tortoise. Over the millennia,
the hibernating tortoise would rouse itself each spring
just in time to munch on the new growth of the sparse
regional plants. As cattle became rivals for the desert food
supply and destroyed the tortoise homes, the "tortoise
populations plummeted" (152).

Even in a brief paraphrase, be careful to avoid slipping in the author's
words or closely shadowing the original sentence structure. If a source says,
"President Obama called an emergency meeting of his cabinet to discuss the
crisis," and you write, "The president called his cabinet to hold an emergency meeting to discuss the crisis," your words are too close to those of the
source. One option is to quote the original, though it doesn't seem worth

quoting word for word. Or, better, you could write, "Summoning his cabinet to an emergency session, Obama laid out the challenge before them."

HOW TO PARAPHRASE

For more on paraphrases, see D4 in the Quick Research Guide, pp. A-18–A-35.

- Select a passage with detailed information relevant to your thesis.
- Reword the passage: represent it accurately but use your own language.
- Change both its words and its sentence patterns. Replace its words with different expressions. Begin and end sentences differently, simplify long sentences, and reorder information.
- Note the page or other location (such as an electronic paragraph) where the original appears in your source. If the passage runs from one page onto the next, record where the page changes so that your credit will be accurate no matter how much of the paraphrase you use.
- After a break, recheck your paraphrase against the original to be certain that it does not repeat the same words or merely replace a few with synonyms. Revise as needed, placing fresh words in fresh arrangements.

For advice on writing a synopsis of a literary work, see pp. 278–79.

Summarize an Overall Point. Summarizing is a useful way of incorporating the general point of a whole paragraph, section, or work. You briefly state the main sense of the original in your own words and also identify the source. Like a paraphrase, a summary uses your own language. However, a summary is generally much shorter than the original; it expresses only the most important ideas — the essence — of the original. This example summarizes the section of Babbitt's book containing the passage quoted on pages 235 and 238–39.

SUMMARY

> According to Bruce Babbitt, former Secretary of the Interior and governor of Arizona, the isolated federal land in the West traditionally has been open to cattle and sheep ranching. These animals have damaged the arid land by grazing too aggressively, and the ranchers have battled wildlife grazers and predators alike to reduce competition with their stock. Protecting species such as the gray wolf and the desert tortoise has meant limiting grazing, an action supported by the public in order to conserve the character and beauty of the public land.

HOW TO SUMMARIZE

For more on summaries, see D5 in the Quick Research Guide, pp. A-18–A-35.

- Select a passage, an article, a chapter, or an entire book whose main idea bears on your thesis.
- Read the selection carefully until you have mastered its overall point.
- Write a sentence or a series of sentences that states its essence in your own words.

Methods of Capturing Information from Sources

	Quotation	Paraphrase	Summary
Format for Wording	Use exact words from the source, and identify any additions, deletions, or other changes	Use your words and sentence structures, translating the content of the original passage	Use your words and sentence structures, reducing the original passage to its core
Common Use	Capture lively and authoritative wording	Capture specific information while conserving its detail	Capture the overall essence of an entire source or a passage in brief form
Advantages	Catch a reader's attention Emphasize the authority of the source	Treat specifics fully without shifting from your voice to the source's	Make a broad but clear point without shifting from your voice to the source's
Common Problems	Quoting too much Quoting inaccurately	Slipping in the original wording Following the original sentence patterns too closely	Losing impact by bogging down in too much detail Drifting into vague generalities
Markers	Add quotation marks to show the source's exact words Use ellipses and brackets to mark any changes Identify source in launch statement or text citation and in list of sources	Identify source in launch statement or text citation and in final list of sources	Identify source in launch statement or text citation and in final list of sources

- Revise your summary until it is as concise, clear, and accurate as possible. Replace any vague generalizations with precise words.
- Name your source as you begin your summary, or identify it in parentheses.

For more on plagiarism, see D1 in the Quick Research Guide, pp. A-18–A-35.

Credit Your Sources Fairly. As you quote, paraphrase, or summarize, be certain to note which source you are using and exactly where the material appears in the original. Carefully citing and listing your sources will give credit where it's due as it enhances your credibility as a careful writer.

Although academic fields prefer specific formats for their papers, MLA style is widely used in composition, English, and other humanities courses. In MLA style, you credit your source twice. First, identify the author's last name (and the page number in the original) in the text as you quote, paraphrase, summarize, or refer to the source. Often you will simply mention the author's name (or a short version of the title if the author is not identified) as you introduce the information from the source. If not, note the name and page number of the original in parentheses after you present the

For a tutorial on avoiding plagiarism, visit <bedfordstmartins.com/rewriting>.

For sample source citations and lists, see the readings on pp. 222–28 and the MLA and APA examples in E in the Quick Research Guide, pp. A-18–A-35.

material: (Walton 88). Next, fully identify the source in an alphabetical list at the end of your paper.

Right now, the methods for capturing information and crediting sources may seem complicated. However, the more you use them, the easier they become. Experienced writers also know some time-tested secrets. For example, how can you save time, improve accuracy, and avoid last-minute stress about sources? The answer is easy. Include in your draft, even your very first one, both the source identification and the location. Add them at the very moment when you first add the material, even if you are just dropping it in so you don't forget it. Later on, you won't have to hunt for the details.

Let Your Draft Evolve. No matter how many quotations, paraphrases, and summaries you assemble, chunks of evidence captured from sources do not—on their own—constitute a solid paper. You need to interpret and explain that evidence for your readers, helping them to see exactly why, how, and to what extent it supports your position.

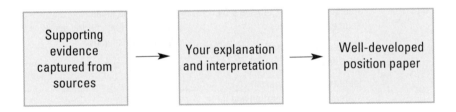

To develop a solid draft, many writers rely on one of two methods, beginning either with the evidence or with the position they wish to support.

METHOD 1 Start with your evidence, using one of these strategies to arrange quotations, paraphrases, and summaries in a logical and compelling order.

- Cut and paste the chunks of evidence, moving them around in a file until they fall into a logical order.
- Print each chunk on a separate page, and arrange the pages on a flat surface like a table, floor, or bed until you reach a workable sequence.
- Label each chunk with a key word, and use the key words to work out an informal outline.

Once your evidence is organized logically, add commentary to connect the chunks for your readers: introduce, conclude, and link the pieces of evidence with your own explanations and interpretations. (Ignore any leftovers from sources unless they cover key points that you still need to integrate.) Let your draft expand as you alternate evidence and interpretation.

METHOD 2 Start with your position or your conclusion, focusing on how you want your paper to present it. You can state your case boldly and directly, explaining your thesis and supporting points in your own words. If

For exercises on supporting a thesis, visit <bedfordstmartins .com/bedguide>.

you feel too uncertain to take that step, you can write out directions, telling yourself what to do in each part of the draft (in preparation for actually doing it). Either way, use this working structure to identify where to embed the evidence from your sources. Let your draft grow as you pull in your sources and expand your comments.

DEVELOPMENT CHECKLIST

☐ Have you quoted only notable passages that add support and authority?

☐ Have you checked your quotations for accuracy and marked where each begins and ends with quotation marks?

☐ Have you paraphrased accurately, reflecting both the main points and the supporting details in the original?

☐ Does each paraphrase use your own words without repeating or echoing the words or the sentence structure of the original?

☐ Have you briefly stated supporting ideas that you wish to summarize, sticking to the overall point without bogging down in details or examples?

☐ Has each summary remained respectful of the ideas and opinions of others, even if you disagree with them?

☐ Have you identified the source of every quotation, paraphrase, summary, or source reference by noting in parentheses the last name of the writer and the page number (if available) where the passage appears in the source?

☐ Have you ordered your evidence logically and effectively?

☐ Have you interpreted and explained your evidence from sources with your own comments in your own voice?

For sample quotations, paraphrases, and summaries, see D3, D4, and D5 in the Quick Research Guide, pp. A-27–A-29.

Revising and Editing

As you read over the draft of your paper, remember what you wanted to accomplish: to develop an enlightening position about your topic and to share this position with a college audience, using sources to support your ideas.

For more on revising and editing strategies, see Ch. 23.

Strengthen Your Thesis. As you begin revising, you may decide that your working thesis is ambiguous, poorly worded, hard to support, or simply off the mark. Revise it so that it clearly alerts readers to your main idea.

WORKING THESIS — Although most workers would like longer vacations, many employers do not believe that they would benefit, too.

REVISED THESIS — Despite assumptions to the contrary, employers who increase vacation time for workers also are likely to increase creativity, productivity, and the bottom line.

For more about launching sources, see D6 in the Quick Research Guide, pp. A-18–A-35.

Launch Each Source. Whenever you quote, paraphrase, summarize, or refer to a source, launch it with a suitable introduction. An effective launch sets the scene for your source material, prepares your reader to accept it, and marks the transition from your words and ideas to those of the source. As you revise your draft, confirm that you effectively launch all of your source material.

As you create a launch statement, often you will first identify the source — by the author's last name or by a short version of the title when the author isn't named — in your introductory sentence. If not, identify the source in parentheses, typically to conclude the sentence. Then try to suggest why you've selected this source and mentioned it at this point, perhaps noting its contribution to your discussion, its credibility, its vantage point, or its relationship to other sources. Vary your launch statements to avoid tedium and to add emphasis. Boost your credibility as a writer by establishing the credibility of your sources.

Here are some typical patterns for launch statements:

As Yung demonstrates, . . .

Although Zeffir maintains . . . , Matson suggests . . .

Many schools educated the young but also unified the community (Hill 22). . . .

In *Forward March*, Smith's study of the children of military personnel, . . .

Another common recommendation is . . . ("Safety Manual").

Making good use of her experience as a travel consultant, Lee explains . . .

These examples follow MLA style. For more about how to capture, launch, and cite sources in your text using either MLA or APA style, see D6 and E1 in the Quick Research Guide, pp. A-18–A-35.

When you quote or paraphrase information from a specific page (or other location, such as a paragraph numbered on a Web page), also include that exact location.

The classic definition of . . . (Bagette 18) is updated to . . . (Zoe par. 4).

Benton distinguishes four typical steps in this process (248–51).

Learning by Doing 📷 Launching Your Sources

Make a duplicate file of your draft or print a copy. Add highlights in one color to mark where you identify each source and in another color to mark material from the source:

The problem of unintended consequences is well illustrated by many environmental changes over recent decades. For instance, if using the Mojave Desert for cattle grazing seemed efficient to ranchers, it also turned out to be destructive for long-time desert residents such as tortoises (Babbitt 152).

Now examine your draft. How do the colors alternate? Do you find color globs where you simply list sources without explaining their contributions? Or do you find material without source identification (typically the author's name) or without a specified location in the original (typically a page number)? Fill in whatever gaps you discover.

———

Synthesize Several Sources. Often you will compare, contrast, or relate two or three sources to deepen your discussion or to illustrate a range of views. When you synthesize, you pull together several sources in the same passage to build a new interpretation or reach a new conclusion. You go beyond the separate contributions of the individual sources to relate the sources to each other and to connect them to your thesis. A synthesis should be easy to follow and use your own wording.

HOW TO SYNTHESIZE

- Summarize (see pp. 240–41) each of the sources you want to synthesize. Boil down each summary to its essence.
- Write a few sentences that state in your own words how the sources are related. For example, are they similar, different, or related? Do they share assumptions and conclusions, or do they represent alternatives, opposites, or opponents? Do they speak to chronology, influence, logical progression, or diversity of opinion?
- Write a few more sentences stating what the source relationships mean for your thesis and the position you develop in your paper.
- Refine your synthesis statements until they are clear and illuminating for your audience. Embed them as you move from one source summary to the next and as you reach new interpretations or conclusions that go beyond the separate sources.

Use Your Own Voice to Interpret and Connect. By the time your draft is finished, you may feel that you have found relevant evidence in your sources but that they now dominate your draft. As you reread, you may discover passages that simply string together ideas from sources.

DRAFT

Easterbrook <u>says</u> in "In Search of the Cause of Autism: How about Television?" that television may injure children who are susceptible to autism. The Centers for Disease Control and Prevention <u>says</u> that autism trails only mental retardation among disabilities that affect children's development. The Kaiser Family Foundation study <u>says</u> that parents use television and other electronic entertainment "to help them

Whole passage repeats "says"

Repeats sentence pattern opening with author

Jumps from one source to the next without transitions

manage their household and keep their kids entertained" (Rideout, Hamel, and Kaiser Family Foundation 4).

When your sources overshadow your thesis, your explanations, and your writing style, revise to restore balance. Try strategies such as these to regain control of your draft:

- Add your explanation and interpretation of the source information so that your ideas are clear.
- Add transitions, and state the connections that you assume are obvious.
- Arrange information in a logical sequence, not in the order in which you read it or recorded notes about it.
- Clarify definitions, justify a topic's importance, and recognize alternative views to help your audience appreciate your position.
- Reword to vary your sentence openings, and avoid repetitive wording.

Thoughtful revision can help readers grasp what you want to say, why you have included each source, and how you think that it supports your thesis.

REVISION

Connects two sources

Adds transitions

Two recent studies take very different looks at the development of children in our society. First, a research study sponsored by the Kaiser Family Foundation examines how parents use television and other electronic options "to help them manage their household and keep their kids entertained" (Rideout, Hamel, and Kaiser Family Foundation 4). Next, based on statistics about how often major developmental disabilities occur in children, the Centers for Disease Control and Prevention reports that autism currently trails only mental retardation among disabilities that affect children's development. Journalist and book author Gregg

Identifies author's experience to add credibility

Easterbrook pulls together these two views, using the title of his article to raise his unusual question: "In Search of the Cause of Autism: How about Television?" He urges

Defines issue and justifies concern

study of his speculation that television may injure children who are vulnerable to autism and joins an ongoing debate about what causes autism, a challenging disability that interferes with children's ability to communicate and interact with other people.

List Your Sources as College Readers Expect. When you use sources in a college paper, you'll be expected to identify them twice: briefly when you draw information from them and fully when you list them at the end of your paper, following a conventional system. The list of sources for the draft and revision in the previous section would include these entries.

Centers for Disease Control and Prevention. "Frequently Asked Questions—
   Prevalence." *Autism Information Center*. CDC, 30 Jan. 2006. Web. 12 Sept. 2006.
Easterbrook, Gregg. "In Search of the Cause of Autism: How about Television?" *Slate*.
   Washingtonpost.Newsweek Interactive, 5 Sept. 2006. Web. 12 Sept. 2006.
Rideout, Victoria, Elizabeth Hamel, and Kaiser Family Foundation. *The Media Family:
   Electronic Media in the Lives of Infants, Toddlers, Preschoolers and Their Parents*.
   Menlo Park: Henry J. Kaiser Family Foundation, 2006. *Kaiser Family Foundation*.
   Web. 12 Sept. 2006.

Learning by Doing 🎯 Checking Your Presentation of Sources

Use your software to help you improve the presentation of source materials in your draft. For example, search for all the quotation marks in your paper. As you find each one, make sure that it is one of a pair surrounding every quotation in your paper. At the same time, be sure that the source and location are identified for each quotation. Try color highlighting in your final list of sources to help you spot and refine details, especially any common personal errors. For instance, if you tend to forget periods after names of authors or to mix up semicolons and colons, highlight those marks in color so that you slow down and focus on them. Then correct or add marks as needed. After you finish correcting your entries, restore the passage to the usual black color.

Use the Take Action chart (p. 248) to help you figure out how to improve your draft. Skim across the top to identify questions you might ask about integrating sources in your draft. When you answer a question with "Yes" or "Maybe," move straight down the column to Locate Specifics under that question. Use the activities there to pinpoint gaps, problems, or weaknesses. Then move straight down the column to Take Action. Use the advice that suits your problem as you revise.

To get online help from the Take Action, visit **<bedfordstmartins .com/bedguide>**.

Peer Response 👥 Supporting a Position with Sources

Have several classmates read your draft critically, considering how effectively you have used your sources to support a position. Ask your peer editors to answer questions such as these:

Take Action Integrating Source Information Effectively

Ask each question at the top of the chart to consider whether your draft might need work on that issue. If so, follow the ASK—LOCATE SPECIFICS—TAKE ACTION sequence to revise.

	Weak Launch Statements?	**Too Little Voice?**	**Too Few Source Credits?**
1 **ASK**	Have I tossed in source material without preparing my audience for it? Do I repeat the same words in my launch statements?	Have I lost my own voice? Have I allowed my sources to take over my draft? Have I strung together too many quotations?	Have I identified any source only once or twice even though I use it throughout a section?
2 **LOCATE SPECIFICS**	■ Underline each launch statement (the sentence or its part that introduces source material). Decide if it assures readers that the source is credible, logical, and relevant to your thesis. ■ Highlight repeated words (*says*, *states*) or transitions (*also*, *then*).	■ Highlight the material from sources in one color and your own commentary in another. ■ Check the color balance in each paragraph. If the source color dominates, consider how to restore your own voice.	■ Select a passage that relies on sources. Highlight your ideas in one color and those from sources in a different color. ■ Add a slash to mark each switch between two sources or between your ideas and a source.
3 **TAKE ACTION**	■ Sharpen underlined launch statements, perhaps noting (a) an author's credentials significant to readers, (b) a source's historical or current contributions, or (c) its relationship to other sources. ■ Edit the highlighted words (and any other repeated expressions) for variety and precision. For *says*, try *emphasizes*, *suggests*, *reviews*, *presents*, or *explains*. For *also*, try *in addition*, *furthermore*, or *similarly*.	■ Restore your voice in each paragraph by adding a topic sentence in your own words to link to your thesis and a conclusion to sum up. ■ Add transitions (*further*, *in contrast*, *as a result*) and explanations where you move point to point or source to source. ■ Reduce what you quote to focus on striking words. Sum up, or drop the rest. ■ Weave in your ideas until they, not your sources, dominate.	■ At each slash marking a source switch, add a launch statement for the second source. ■ At each slash (or color change) marking a switch to your ideas, phrase your comment so that it does not sound like more of the source. ■ At each slash (or color change) marking a switch from your ideas, identify the source again. ■ When you quote and then continue with the same source, identify it again.

- Can you state the writer's position on the topic?
- Do you have any trouble seeing how the writer's points and the supporting evidence from sources connect? How might the writer make the connections clearer?
- How effectively does the writer capture the information from sources? Would you recommend that any of the quotations, paraphrases, or summaries be presented differently?
- Are any of the source citations unclear? Can you tell where source information came from and where quotations and paraphrases appear in a source?
- Is the writer's voice clear? Do the sources drown out the writer's voice in any spots?
- If this paper were yours, what is the one thing you would be sure to work on before handing it in?

For general questions for a peer editor, see p. 491. For peer response worksheets, visit **<bedfordstmartins .com/bedguide>**.

REVISION CHECKLIST

☐ Is your thesis, or main idea, clear? Is it distinguished from the points made by your sources?

☐ Do you speak in your own voice, interpreting and explaining your sources instead of allowing them to dominate your draft?

☐ Have you moved smoothly back and forth between your explanations and your source material?

☐ Have you credited every source in the text and in a list at the end of your paper? Have you carefully included each detail expected in the format for crediting sources?

☐ Have you been careful to quote, paraphrase, summarize, and credit sources accurately and ethically? Have you hunted up missing details, double-checked quotations, and rechecked the accuracy of anything prepared hastily?

After you have revised your paper, edit and proofread it. Carefully check the grammar, word choice, punctuation, and mechanics — and then correct any problems you find. Be certain to check the punctuation with your quotations, making sure that each quotation mark is correctly placed and that you have used other punctuation, such as commas, correctly.

EDITING CHECKLIST

☐ Do all the verbs agree with their subjects, especially when you switch from your words to those of a source?

A4

For more help, find the relevant checklist sections in the Quick Editing Guide on p. A-36. Turn also to the Quick Format Guide beginning on p. A-1.

☐ Do all the pronouns agree with their antecedents, especially when   A6
you use your words with a quotation from a source?

☐ Have you used commas correctly, especially where you integrate   C1
material from sources?

☐ Have you punctuated all your quotations correctly?   C3

Additional Writing Assignments

1. Read several sources about the same topic. Instead of using those sources as evidence to support your own position about the topic, analyze how well they function as sources. State your thesis about them, and analyze their strengths and weaknesses, using clear criteria. (See, for example, the criteria for evaluating sources in C3 in the Quick Research Guide, pp. A-24–A-26.)

2. Locate several different accounts of a notable event in newspapers, magazines, published letters or journals, books, blogs, or other sources, depending on the time when the event occurred. State and support a thesis that explains and accounts for the differences among the accounts. Use the accounts as evidence to support your position.

3. Browse in your library's new book and periodical areas (on site or online) or in specialty search engines to identify a current topic of interest to you. (Adding the current or previous year's date to a search is one way to locate what has recently been published or acquired.) Gather and evaluate a small cluster of resources on your topic, and use those readings to write an essay supporting your position about the new development.

4. Following the directions of your instructor, use several types of sources to support your position in an essay. One option might be to select the paired readings for one theme or two related readings of your own choosing from *A Writer's Reader* and also to interview someone (see Ch. 6) with the academic background or personal experience to act as another valuable source of information on your topic. A second option might be to view and evaluate (see Ch. 11) a film, television program, radio show, blog, Web site, art exhibit, performance, or other event and then to supplement your review by reading several periodical articles or Web commentaries that review the same event, evaluate a different or related production, or discuss criteria for similar types of items or events.

5. Create a concise Web site that addresses a question of interest to you. Select and read a few reliable sources about that question, and then create several

screens or short pages to explain what you have learned. For example, you might want to define or explain aspects of the question, justify the conclusion you have reached, or evaluate alternative answers as well as your own. Identify all of your sources, and supply links when appropriate.

6. **Visual Assignment.** Examine the following images, and analyze one or more of them. Use the image or images to support your position in an essay, perhaps a conclusion about the image or images themselves or about what they portray. Be sure to point out relevant detail to persuade your audience of your view. Cite the images correctly, too, using the style your instructor specifies.

PART THREE

OTHER WRITING SITUATIONS

13 Responding to Literature

As countless readers know, reading fiction gives pleasure and delight. Whether you are reading Stephen King or Stephen Crane, you can be swept up into an imaginative world where you journey to distant lands and meet exotic people. You may also meet characters like yourself and encounter familiar as well as new ways of viewing life. By sharing the experiences of literary characters, you gain insight into your own problems and tolerance of others.

Using Strategies for Literary Analysis

More often than not, a writing assignment in a literature or humanities course will require you first to read closely a literary work (short story, novel, play, or poem) and then to divide it into its elements, explain its meaning, and support your interpretation with evidence from the work. You might also be asked to evaluate a selection or to compare and contrast several pieces that you read. Such analysis is not an end in itself; its purpose is to illuminate the meaning of the work, to help you and others understand it better.

Although there are other ways of writing about literature, this chapter focuses on *literary analysis,* which requires you to analyze, interpret, and evaluate what you read. Because literary analysis has its own vocabulary — as do fields as diverse as scuba diving, gourmet cooking, and engineering — a handy glossary presents terms used to discuss the elements of fiction, poetry, and drama (see pp. 268–69). The chapter also concludes with two writing activities — synopsis (summarizing of the events in a narrative) and paraphrase (expressing the content of a work in your own words) — that can help you prepare to write a literary analysis or to integrate essentials about the literary work into your analysis.

For a sample literary analysis, see pp. 266–67. For a sample synopsis, see pp. 278–79; for a sample paraphrase, see p. 282.

When you start preparing to write a literary analysis, your first step is to read the work closely and mark key points in the text to comprehend its meaning. Your next step is to reread the work, *at least* twice more, each time checking your interpretations and identifying possible evidence to back up your claims as you analyze and evaluate. Use this checklist to structure several close readings, each for a different reason.

READING CHECKLIST

Reading to Comprehend

☐ What is the literal meaning? Write a few sentences explaining the overall situation—what happens to whom, where, when, why, and how.

☐ What are the facts of the situation—the events of the plot, the aspects of the setting, and the major attributes, words, and actions of the characters?

☐ What does all the vocabulary mean, especially in titles and in poems? Look up both unfamiliar words and words whose familiar meanings don't seem to fit the context.

Reading to Analyze

☐ What are the main parts or elements of the work? Read, read aloud, mark, or make notes on theme, character, language, style, symbol, or form.

☐ What does the literary work mean? What does it imply?

☐ What does it suggest about the human condition? How does it expand your understanding? What insights can you apply to your own life?

Reading to Evaluate

☐ How do you assess the work's soundness and plausibility?

☐ Are the words and tone appropriate for the purpose and audience?

☐ Does the author achieve his or her purpose? Is it a worthwhile purpose?

For more on literal and critical reading, see Ch. 2.

For information and journal questions about the Part Three photograph, see p. A-72.

Learning from Other Writers

In a composition course, Jonathan Burns was given an assignment to write a literary analysis of "The Lottery," a provocative short story by Shirley Jackson. Read this story yourself to understand its meaning. Then read on to see what Jonathan Burns made of it.

Shirley Jackson

The Lottery

The morning of June 27th was clear and sunny, with the fresh warmth of a full-summer day; the flowers were blossoming profusely and the grass was richly green. The people of the village began to gather in the square, between the post office and the bank, around ten o'clock; in some towns there were so many people that the lottery took two days and had to be started on   1

June 26th, but in this village, where there were only about three hundred people, the whole lottery took less than two hours, so it could begin at ten o'clock in the morning and still be through in time to allow the villagers to get home for noon dinner.

The children assembled first, of course. School was recently over for the summer, and the feeling of liberty sat uneasily on most of them; they tended to gather together quietly for a while before they broke into boisterous play, and their talk was still of the classroom and the teacher, of books and reprimands. Bobby Martin had already stuffed his pockets full of stones, and the other boys soon followed his example, selecting the smoothest and roundest stones; Bobby and Harry Jones and Dickie Delacroix—the villagers pronounced his name "Dellacroy"—eventually made a great pile of stones in one corner of the square and guarded it against the raids of the other boys. The girls stood aside, talking among themselves, looking over their shoulders at the boys, and the very small children rolled in the dust or clung to the hands of their older brothers or sisters.

Soon the men began to gather, surveying their own children, speaking of planting and rain, tractors and taxes. They stood together, away from the pile of stones in the corner, and their jokes were quiet and they smiled rather than laughed. The women, wearing faded house dresses and sweaters, came shortly after their menfolk. They greeted one another and exchanged bits of gossip as they went to join their husbands. Soon the women, standing by their husbands, began to call to their children, and the children came reluctantly, having to be called four or five times. Bobby Martin ducked under his mother's grasping hand and ran, laughing, back to the pile of stones. His father spoke up sharply, and Bobby came quickly and took his place between his father and his oldest brother.

The lottery was conducted—as were the square dances, the teenage club, the Halloween program—by Mr. Summers, who had time and energy to devote to civic activities. He was a round-faced, jovial man and he ran the coal business, and people were sorry for him, because he had no children and his wife was a scold. When he arrived in the square, carrying the black wooden box, there was a murmur of conversation among the villagers, and he waved and called, "Little late today, folks." The postmaster, Mr. Graves, followed him, carrying a three-legged stool, and the stool was put in the center of the square and Mr. Summers set the black box down on it. The villagers kept their distance, leaving a space between themselves and the stool, and when Mr. Summers said, "Some of you fellows want to give me a hand?" there was a hesitation before two men, Mr. Martin and his oldest son, Baxter, came forward to hold the box steady on the stool while Mr. Summers stirred up the papers inside it.

The original paraphernalia for the lottery had been lost long ago, and the black box now resting on the stool had been put into use even before Old Man Warner, the oldest man in town, was born. Mr. Summers spoke frequently to the villagers about making a new box, but no one liked to upset even as much tradition as was represented by the black box. There was a story that the present box had been made with some pieces of the box that had preceded it, the one that had been constructed when the first people settled down to make a village here. Every year, after the lottery, Mr. Summers began talking again about a new box, but every year the subject was allowed to fade off without anything's being done. The black box grew shabbier each year; by now it was no longer completely black but splintered badly along one side to show the original wood color, and in some places faded or stained.

Mr. Martin and his oldest son, Baxter, held the black box securely on the   6
stool until Mr. Summers had stirred the papers thoroughly with his hand. Because so much of the ritual had been forgotten or discarded, Mr. Summers had been successful in having slips of paper substituted for the chips of wood that had been used for generations. Chips of wood, Mr. Summers had argued, had been all very well when the village was tiny, but now that the population was more than three hundred and likely to keep on growing, it was necessary to use something that would fit more easily into the black box. The night before the lottery, Mr. Summers and Mr. Graves made up the slips of paper and put them in the box, and it was then taken to the safe of Mr. Summers's coal company and locked up until Mr. Summers was ready to take it to the square the next morning. The rest of the year, the box was put away, sometimes one place, sometimes another; it had spent one year in Mr. Graves's barn and another year underfoot in the post office, and some-times it was set on a shelf in the Martin grocery and left there.

There was a great deal of fussing to be done before Mr. Summers declared   7
the lottery open. There were the lists to make up — of heads of families, heads of households in each family, members of each household in each family. There was the proper swearing-in of Mr. Summers by the postmaster, as the official of the lottery; at one time, some people remembered, there had been a recital of some sort, performed by the official of the lottery, a perfunctory, tuneless chant that had been rattled off duly each year; some people believed that the official of the lottery used to stand just so when he said or sang it, others believed that he was supposed to walk among the people, but years and years ago this part of the ritual had been allowed to lapse. There had been, also, a ritual salute, which the official of the lottery had had to use in addressing each person who came up to draw from the box, but this also had changed with time, until now it was felt necessary only for the official to speak to each person approaching. Mr. Summers was very good at all this; in his clean white shirt and blue jeans, with one hand resting carelessly on the black box, he seemed very proper and important as he talked interminably to Mr. Graves and the Martins.

Just as Mr. Summers finally left off talking and turned to the assembled   8
villagers, Mrs. Hutchinson came hurriedly along the path to the square, her sweater thrown over her shoulders, and slid into place in the back of the crowd. "Clean forgot what day it was," she said to Mrs. Delacroix, who stood next to her, and they both laughed softly. "Thought my old man was

out back stacking wood," Mrs. Hutchinson went on, "and then I looked out the window and the kids was gone, and then I remembered it was the twenty-seventh and came a-running." She dried her hands on her apron, and Mrs. Delacroix said, "You're in time, though. They're still talking away up there."

Mrs. Hutchinson craned her neck to see through the crowd and found her husband and children standing near the front. She tapped Mrs. Delacroix on the arm as a farewell and began to make her way through the crowd. The people separated good-humoredly to let her through; two or three people said, in voices just loud enough to be heard across the crowd, "Here comes your Missus, Hutchinson," and "Bill, she made it after all." Mrs. Hutchinson reached her husband, and Mr. Summers, who had been waiting, said cheerfully, "Thought we were going to have to get on without you, Tessie." Mrs. Hutchinson said, grinning, "Wouldn't have me leave m'dishes in the sink, now, would you, Joe?" and soft laughter ran through the crowd as the people stirred back into position after Mrs. Hutchinson's arrival. 9

"Well, now," Mr. Summers said soberly, "guess we better get started, get this over with, so's we can go back to work. Anybody ain't here?" 10

"Dunbar," several people said. "Dunbar, Dunbar." 11

Mr. Summers consulted his list. "Clyde Dunbar," he said. "That's right. He's broke his leg, hasn't he? Who's drawing for him?" 12

"Me, I guess," a woman said, and Mr. Summers turned to look at her. "Wife draws for her husband," Mr. Summers said. "Don't you have a grown boy to do it for you, Janey?" Although Mr. Summers and everyone else in the village knew the answer perfectly well, it was the business of the official of the lottery to ask such questions formally. Mr. Summers waited with an expression of polite interest while Mrs. Dunbar answered. 13

"Horace's not but sixteen yet," Mrs. Dunbar said regretfully. "Guess I gotta fill in for the old man this year." 14

"Right," Mr. Summers said. He made a note on the list he was holding. Then he asked, "Watson boy drawing this year?" 15

A tall boy in the crowd raised his hand. "Here," he said. "I'm drawing for m'mother and me." He blinked his eyes nervously and ducked his head as several voices in the crowd said things like "Good fellow, Jack," and "Glad to see your mother's got a man to do it." 16

"Well," Mr. Summers said, "guess that's everyone. Old Man Warner make it?" 17

"Here," a voice said, and Mr. Summers nodded. 18

A sudden hush fell on the crowd as Mr. Summers cleared his throat and looked at the list. "All ready?" he called. "Now, I'll read the names — heads of families first — and the men come up and take a paper out of the box. Keep the paper folded in your hand without looking at it until everyone has had a turn. Everything clear?" 19

The people had done it so many times that they only half listened to the directions; most of them were quiet, wetting their lips, not looking around. 20

Then Mr. Summers raised one hand high and said, "Adams." A man disengaged himself from the crowd and came forward. "Hi, Steve," Mr. Summers said, and Mr. Adams said, "Hi, Joe." They grinned at one another humorlessly and nervously. Then Mr. Adams reached into the black box and took out a folded paper. He held it firmly by one corner as he turned and went hastily back to his place in the crowd, where he stood a little apart from his family, not looking down at his hand.

"Allen," Mr. Summers said. "Anderson. . . . Bentham."   21

"Seems like there's no time at all between lotteries anymore," Mrs. Delacroix said to Mrs. Graves in the back row. "Seems like we got through with the last one only last week."   22

"Time sure goes fast," Mrs. Graves said.   23

"Clark. . . . Delacroix."   24

"There goes my old man," Mrs. Delacroix said. She held her breath while her husband went forward.   25

"Dunbar," Mr. Summers said, and Mrs. Dunbar went steadily to the box while one of the women said, "Go on, Janey," and another said, "There she goes."   26

"We're next," Mrs. Graves said. She watched while Mr. Graves came around from the side of the box, greeted Mr. Summers gravely, and selected a slip of paper from the box. By now, all through the crowd there were men holding the small folded papers in their large hands, turning them over and over nervously. Mrs. Dunbar and her two sons stood together, Mrs. Dunbar holding the slip of paper.   27

"Harburt. . . . Hutchinson."   28

"Get up there, Bill," Mrs. Hutchinson said, and the people near her laughed.   29

"Jones."   30

"They do say," Mr. Adams said to Old Man Warner, who stood next to him, "that over in the north village they're talking of giving up the lottery."   31

Old Man Warner snorted. "Pack of crazy fools," he said. "Listening to the young folks, nothing's good enough for *them*. Next thing you know, they'll be wanting to go back to living in caves, nobody work anymore, live *that* way for a while. Used to be a saying about 'Lottery in June, corn be heavy soon.' First thing you know, we'd all be eating stewed chickweed and acorns. There's *always* been a lottery," he added petulantly. "Bad enough to see young Joe Summers up there joking with everybody."   32

"Some places have already quit lotteries," Mrs. Adams said.   33

"Nothing but trouble in *that*," Old Man Warner said stoutly. "Pack of young fools."   34

"Martin." And Bobby Martin watched his father go forward. "Overdyke. . . . Percy."   35

"I wish they'd hurry," Mrs. Dunbar said to her older son. "I wish they'd hurry."   36

"They're almost through," her son said.   37

"You get ready to run tell Dad," Mrs. Dunbar said.   38

Mr. Summers called his own name and then stepped forward precisely and selected a slip from the box. Then he called, "Warner."   39

"Seventy-seventh year I been in the lottery," Old Man Warner said as he   40
went through the crowd. "Seventy-seventh time."

"Watson." The tall boy came awkwardly through the crowd. Someone said,   41
"Don't be nervous, Jack," and Mr. Summers said, "Take your time, son."

"Zanini."   42

After that, there was a long pause, a breathless pause, until Mr. Summers,   43
holding his slip of paper in the air, said, "All right, fellows." For a minute, no
one moved, and then all the slips of paper were opened. Suddenly, all the
women began to speak at once, saying, "Who is it?" "Who's got it?" "Is it the
Dunbars?" "Is it the Watsons?" Then the voices began to say, "It's Hutchinson. It's Bill." "Bill Hutchinson's got it."

"Go tell your father," Mrs. Dunbar said to her older son.   44

People began to look around to see the Hutchinsons. Bill Hutchinson   45
was standing quiet, staring down at the paper in his hand. Suddenly, Tessie
Hutchinson shouted to Mr. Summers, "You didn't give him time enough to
take any paper he wanted. I saw you. It wasn't fair!"

"Be a good sport, Tessie," Mrs. Delacroix called, and Mrs. Graves said, "All   46
of us took the same chance."

"Shut up, Tessie," Bill Hutchinson said.   47

"Well, everyone," Mr. Summers said, "that was done pretty fast, and now   48
we've got to be hurrying a little more to get done in time." He consulted his
next list. "Bill," he said, "you draw for the Hutchinson family. You got any
other households in the Hutchinsons?"

"There's Don and Eva," Mrs. Hutchinson yelled. "Make *them* take their   49
chance!"

"Daughters draw with their husbands' families, Tessie," Mr. Summers   50
said gently. "You know that as well as anyone else."

"It wasn't *fair*," Tessie said.   51

"I guess not, Joe," Bill Hutchinson said regretfully. "My daughter draws   52
with her husband's family, that's only fair. And I've got no other family except the kids."

"Then, as far as drawing for families is concerned, it's you," Mr. Summers   53
said in explanation, "and as far as drawing for households is concerned,
that's you, too. Right?"

"Right," Bill Hutchinson said.   54

"How many kids, Bill?" Mr. Summers asked formally.   55

"Three," Bill Hutchinson said. "There's Bill, Jr., and Nancy, and little   56
Dave. And Tessie and me."

"All right, then," Mr. Summers said. "Harry, you got their tickets back?"   57

Mr. Graves nodded and held up the slips of paper. "Put them in the box,   58
then," Mr. Summers directed. "Take Bill's and put it in."

"I think we ought to start over," Mrs. Hutchinson said, as quietly as she   59
could. "I tell you it wasn't *fair*. You didn't give him time enough to choose.
*Every*body saw that."

Mr. Graves had selected the five slips and put them in the box, and he 60 dropped all the papers but those onto the ground, where the breeze caught them and lifted them off.

"Listen, everybody," Mrs. Hutchinson was saying to the people around her. 61

"Ready, Bill?" Mr. Summers asked, and Bill Hutchinson, with one quick 62 glance around at his wife and children, nodded.

"Remember," Mr. Summers said, "take the slips and keep them folded 63 until each person has taken one. Harry, you help little Dave." Mr. Graves took the hand of the little boy, who came willingly with him up to the box. "Take a paper out of the box, Davy," Mr. Summers said. Davy put his hand into the box and laughed. "Take just *one* paper," Mr. Summers said. "Harry, you hold it for him." Mr. Graves took the child's hand and removed the folded paper from the tight fist and held it while little Dave stood next to him and looked up at him wonderingly.

"Nancy next," Mr. Summers said. Nancy was twelve, and her school 64 friends breathed heavily as she went forward, switching her skirt, and took a slip daintily from the box. "Bill, Jr.," Mr. Summers said, and Billy, his face red and his feet overlarge, nearly knocked the box over as he got a paper out. "Tessie," Mr. Summers said. She hesitated for a minute, looking around defiantly, and then set her lips and went up to the box. She snatched a paper out and held it behind her.

"Bill," Mr. Summers said, and Bill Hutchinson reached into the box and 65 felt around, bringing his hand out at last with the slip of paper in it.

The crowd was quiet. A girl whispered, "I hope it's not Nancy," and the 66 sound of the whisper reached the edges of the crowd.

"It's not the way it used to be," Old Man Warner said clearly. "People ain't 67 the way they used to be."

"All right," Mr. Summers said. "Open the papers. Harry, you open little 68 Dave's."

Mr. Graves opened the slip of paper and there was a general sigh through 69 the crowd as he held it up and everyone could see that it was blank. Nancy and Bill, Jr., opened theirs at the same time, and both beamed and laughed, turning around to the crowd and holding their slips of paper above their heads.

"Tessie," Mr. Summers said. There was a pause, and then Mr. Summers 70 looked at Bill Hutchinson, and Bill unfolded his paper and showed it. It was blank.

"It's Tessie," Mr. Summers said, and his voice was hushed. "Show us her 71 paper, Bill."

Bill Hutchinson went over to his wife and forced the slip of paper out of 72 her hand. It had a black spot on it, the black spot Mr. Summers had made the night before with the heavy pencil in the coal-company office. Bill Hutchinson held it up, and there was a stir in the crowd.

"All right, folks," Mr. Summers said. "Let's finish quickly." 73

Although the villagers had forgotten the ritual and lost the original black 74 box, they still remembered to use stones. The pile of stones the boys had made earlier was ready; there were stones on the ground with the blowing scraps of paper that had come out of the box. Mrs. Delacroix selected a stone so large she had to pick it up with both hands and turned to Mrs. Dunbar. "Come on," she said. "Hurry up."

Mrs. Dunbar had small stones in both hands, and she said, gasping for breath, "I can't run at all. You'll have to go ahead and I'll catch up with you." 75

The children had stones already, and someone gave little Davy Hutchinson a few pebbles. 76

Tessie Hutchinson was in the center of a cleared space by now, and she held her hands out desperately as the villagers moved in on her. "It isn't fair," she said. A stone hit her on the side of the head. 77

Old Man Warner was saying, "Come on, come on, everyone." Steve Adams was in the front of the crowd of villagers, with Mrs. Graves beside him. 78

"It isn't fair, it isn't right," Mrs. Hutchinson screamed, and then they were upon her. 79

Questions to Start You Thinking

Meaning

1. Where does this story take place? When?

2. How does this lottery differ from what we usually think of as a lottery? Why would people conduct a lottery such as this?

3. What does this story mean to you?

Writing Strategies

4. Can you see and hear the people in the story? Do they seem to be real or based on fantasy? Who is the most memorable character to you?

5. Are the events believable? Does the ending shock you? Is it believable?

6. Is this story realistic, or is Jackson using these events to represent something else?

Preparing to Write a Literary Analysis

As Jonathan Burns read "The Lottery" for the first time, he was carried along to the startling ending. Then he reread so that he would understand the story well enough to identify and analyze important elements such as setting, character, or tone. He began turning his understanding into text by writing a synopsis to clarify the literal events in the story. Summing up those events immediately suggested writing about the undertone of violence in the story, but he decided that the undertone was so subtle that it would be hard to write about it.

Then he considered writing about the characters in the story, especially Mr. Summers, Tessie Hutchinson, or the memorable Old Man Warner. Burns experimented with that notion by paraphrasing Old Man Warner's comments from one paragraph. But he decided not to focus on the characters because he couldn't think of more than the vague statement that they were memorable. He considered other elements—language, symbols, ambiguity, foreshadowing—and dismissed each in turn. All of a sudden, he hit on the surprise ending. How did Jackson manipulate all the details to generate such a shock?

For Burns's synopsis, see pp. 278–79; for his paraphrase, see p. 282.

To focus his thinking, he brainstormed for possible essay titles about the ending: Death Comes as a Surprise, The Unsuspected Finish, and finally his straightforward choice "The Hidden Truth." After reviewing his notes, Burns realized that Jackson uses characterization, symbolism, and ambiguous description to build up to the ending. He listed details from the story under those three headings to plan his paper informally:

For more on seeking motives of characters, see pp. 395–96.

For more on stating a thesis, organizing ideas, and outlining, see Ch. 20.

Title: The Hidden Truth
Working Thesis: In "The Lottery" Jackson effectively crafts a shock ending.
1. Characterization that contributes to the shock ending
   –The children of the village
   –The adults of the village
   –Conversations among the villagers
2. Symbols that contribute to the shock ending
   –The stones
   –The black box
3. Ambiguous description that contributes to the shock ending
   –The word "lottery"
   –Comments: "clean forgot," "wish they'd hurry," "It isn't fair."
   –Actions: relief, suspense

Then he drafted the following introduction:

For more on introductions, see pp. 428–30.

Unsuspecting, the reader follows Shirley Jackson's softly flowing tale of a rural community's timeless ritual, the lottery. Awareness of what is at stake—the savage murder of one random member—comes slowly. No sooner does the realization set in than the story is over. It is a shock ending.

What creates the shock that the reader experiences reading "The Lottery"? Shirley Jackson carefully produces this effect, using elements such as language, symbolism, and characterization to lure the reader into not anticipating what is to come.

With his synopsis, his paraphrase, his plan, his copy of the story, and this starting point, Burns revised the introduction and wrote his essay.

Jonathan Burns   **Student Literary Analysis**

The Hidden Truth: An Analysis of Shirley Jackson's "The Lottery"

It is as if the first stone thrown strikes the reader as well as Mrs. Hutchinson. 1
And even though there were signs of the stoning to come, somehow the reader is
taken by surprise at Tessie's violent death. What factors contribute to the shock
ending to "The Lottery"? On closer examination of the story, the reader finds that
through all the events leading up to the ending, Shirley Jackson has used
unsuspicious characterizations, unobtrusive symbolism, and ambiguous descriptions
to achieve so sudden an impact.

By all appearances, the village is a normal place with normal people. Children 2
arrive at the scene first, with school just over for the summer, talking of teachers
and books, not of the fact that someone will die today (258). And as the adults
show up, their actions are just as stereotypical: the men talk of farming and taxes,
while the women gossip (258). The scene conveys no trace of hostility, no sense of
dread in anyone: death seems very far away here.

The conversations between the villagers are no more ominous. As the husbands 3
draw slips of paper for their families, the villagers make apparently everyday
comments about the seemingly ordinary event of the lottery. Mr. Summers is
regarded as a competent and respected figure, despite the fact that his wife is
"a scold" (258). Old Man Warner criticizes other towns that have given up their
lottery tradition, and brags about how many lotteries he's seen (261–62). The
characters' comments show the crowd to be more a close-knit community than a
murderous mob.

The symbols of "The Lottery" seem equally ordinary. The stones collected by the 4
boys (258) are unnoticed by the adults and thus seem a trivial detail. The reader
thinks of the "great pile" (258) as children's entertainment, like a stack of imaginary
coins, rather than an arsenal. Ironically, no stones are ever thrown during the
children's play, and no violence is seen in the pile of stones.

Similarly, Jackson describes the box and its history in great detail, but nothing 5
seems unusual about it. It is just another everyday object, stored away in the post
office or on a shelf in the grocery (259). Every other day of the year, the box is in
plain view but goes virtually unnoticed. The only indication that the box has lethal
consequences is that it is painted black (258), yet this is an ambiguous detail, as
a black box can also signify mystery or magic, mystical forces that are sometimes
thought to exist in any lottery.

In her ambiguous descriptions, Jackson refers regularly to the village's lottery and 6
emphasizes it as a central ritual for the people. The word *lottery* itself is ironic, as it
typically implies a winning of some kind, like a raffle or sweepstakes. It is paralleled
to square dances and to the teenage club, all under the direction of Mr. Summers
(258), activities people look forward to. There is no implied difference between the

The numbers in parentheses are page-number citations following MLA style. For more on citing and listing sources, see D6 and E (pp. A-29–A-35) in the Quick Research Guide.

occurrences of this day and the festivities of Halloween: according to Jackson, they are all merely "civic activities" (258). Equally ambiguous are the people's emotions: some of the villagers are casual, such as Mrs. Hutchinson, who arrives late because she "'clean forgot'" what day it is (259), and some are anxious, such as Mrs. Dunbar, who repeats to her son, "'I wish they'd hurry,'" without any sign of the cause of her anxiety (261). With these descriptive details, the reader finds no threat or malice in the villagers, only vague expectation and congeniality.

Even when it becomes clear that the lottery is something no one wants to win, 7 Jackson presents only a vague sense of sadness and mild protest. The crowd is relieved that the youngest of the Hutchinsons, Davy, doesn't draw the fatal slip of paper (263). One girl whispers that she hopes it isn't Nancy (263), and when the Hutchinson children discover they aren't the winners, they beam with joy and proudly display their blank slips (263). Suspense and excitement grow only when the victim is close to being identified. And when Tessie is revealed as the winner of the lottery (263), she merely holds her hands out "desperately" and repeats, "'It isn't fair'" (264).

With a blend of character, symbolism, and description, Jackson paints an overall 8 portrait of a gentle-seeming rural community, apparently no different from any other. The tragic end is sudden only because there is no recognition of violence beforehand, despite the fact that Jackson has provided the reader with plenty of clues in the ample details about the lottery and the people. It is a haunting discovery that the story ends in death, even though such is the truth in the everyday life of all people.

Questions to Start You Thinking

Meaning

1. What is Burns's thesis?
2. What major points does he use to support the interpretation stated in his thesis? What specific elements of the story does he include as evidence?

Writing Strategies

3. How does this essay differ from a synopsis, a summary of the events of the plot? (For a synopsis of "The Lottery," see pp. 278–79.)
4. Does Burns focus on the technique of the short story or on its theme?
5. Is his introduction effective? Compare and contrast it with his first draft (p. 265). What did he change? Which version do you prefer?
6. Why does he explain characterization first, symbolism second, and description last? How effective is this organization? Would discussing these elements in a different order have made much difference?
7. Is his conclusion effective?
8. How does he tie his ideas together as he moves from paragraph to paragraph? How does he keep the focus on ideas and technique instead of plot?

A Glossary of Terms for Literary Analysis

Characters. Characters are imagined people. The author shows you what they are like through their actions, speech, thoughts, attitudes, and background. Sometimes a writer also includes physical characteristics or names or relationships with other people. For example, in "The Lottery," the description of Mr. Summers introduces the lottery official as someone with civic interests who wants to avoid slip-ups (paragraphs 4, 9, and 10).

Figures of Speech. Figures of speech are lively or fresh expressions that vary the expected sequence or sense of words. Some common types of figurative language are the *simile*, a comparison using *like* or *as*; the *metaphor*, an implied comparison; and *personification*, the attribution of human qualities to inanimate or nonhuman creatures or things. In "The Lottery," three boys *guard* their pile of stones "against the *raids*" of others (paragraph 2).

Imagery. Images are words or groups of words that refer to any sense experience: seeing, hearing, smelling, tasting, touching, or feeling. The images in "The Lottery" help readers envision the "richly green" grass (paragraph 1), the smooth and round stones the children gather (paragraph 2), the "hush" that comes over the crowd (paragraph 19), and Mrs. Dunbar "gasping for breath" (paragraph 75).

Irony. Irony results from readers' sense of discrepancy. A simple kind of irony, *sarcasm*, occurs when you say one thing but mean the opposite: "I just love scrubbing the floor." In literature, an *ironic situation* sets up a contrast or incongruity. In "The Lottery," cruel and horrifying actions take place on a sunny June day in an ordinary village. *Ironic dialogue* occurs when a character says one thing, but the audience or reader is aware of another meaning. When Old Man Warner reacts to giving up the lottery as "wanting to go back to living in caves" (paragraph 32), he implies that such a change would return the villages to a more primitive life. His comment is ironic because the reader is aware that this lottery is a primitive ritual. A story has an *ironic point of view* when readers sense a difference between the author and the narrator or the character who perceives the story; Jackson, for instance, clearly does not condone the actions of the villagers.

Plot. Plot is the arrangement of the events of the story—what happens to whom, where, when, and why. If the events follow each other logically and are in keeping with the characters, the plot is *plausible*, or believable. Although the ending of "The Lottery" at first may shock readers, the author uses *foreshadowing*, hints or clues such as the villagers' nervousness about the lottery, to help readers understand future events or twists in the plot.

Most plots place the *protagonist*, or main character, in a *conflict* with the *antagonist*, some other person or group. In "The Lottery," a reader might see Tessie as the protagonist and the villagers as the antagonist. *Conflict* consists of two forces trying to conquer each other or resist being conquered—not merely vaguely defined turmoil. *External conflicts* occur outside an individual—between two people, a person and a group (Tessie versus the villagers), two groups (lottery supporters and opponents), or even a character and the environment. *Internal conflicts* between two opposing forces or desires occur within an individual (such as fear versus hope as the lottery slips are drawn). The *central conflict* is the primary conflict for the protagonist that propels the action of the story. Events of the plot *complicate* the conflict (Tessie arrives late, Bill draws the slip) and lead to the *climax*, the moment when the outcome is inevitable (Tessie draws the black dot). This outcome is the *resolution*, or conclusion (the villagers stone Tessie). Some stories let events unfold without any apparent plot—action and change occur inside the characters.

Point of View. The point of view, the angle from which a story is told, might be the author's or a character's. The *narrator* is the one who tells the story and perceives the events, perhaps with limited knowledge or a part to play. Two common points of view are those of a *first-person narrator* (*I*), the *speaker* who tells the story and a *third-person narrator* (*he, she*) who tells the story from an all-knowing perspective, from the perspective of a single character, or from numerous, shifting perspectives. The point of view may be *omniscient* (the speaker knows all and has access to every character's thoughts and feelings); *limited omniscient* (the speaker knows the thoughts and feelings of one or more characters, but not all); or *objective* (the speaker observes the characters but cannot share their thoughts or feelings). In "The Lottery," a third-person objective narrator seemingly looks on and reports what occurs without knowing what the characters think.

Setting. Setting refers to the time and place of events and may include the season, the weather, and the people in the background. The setting often helps establish a literary work's *mood* or *atmosphere*, the emotional climate that a reader senses. For example, the first sentence of "The Lottery" establishes its setting (paragraph 1).

Symbols. Symbols are tangible objects, visible actions, or characters that hint at meanings beyond themselves. In "The Lottery," the black box suggests outdated tradition, resistance to change, evil, cruelty, and more.

Theme. A theme is a work's main idea or insight—the author's observation about life, society, or human nature. Sometimes you can sum up a theme in a sentence ("Human beings cannot live without illusion"); other times, a theme may be implied, hard to discern, or one of several in a work.

To state a theme, go beyond a work's topic or subject by asking yourself, What does the author say about this subject? Details from the story should support your statement of theme, and your theme should account for the details. "The Lottery" treats subjects such as the unexpected, scapegoating, outmoded rituals, and violence; one of its themes might be stated as "People are selfish, always looking out for number one."

Learning by Writing: Literary Analysis

The Assignment: Analyzing a Literary Work

For this assignment, you are to be a literary critic—analyzing, interpreting, and evaluating a literary selection for your classmates. Your purpose is to deepen their understanding because you will have devoted time and effort to digging out the work's meaning. Even if they too have studied the work carefully, you will try to convince them that your interpretation is valid.

Choose a literary work that intrigues you or expresses a worthwhile meaning. Your selection might be a short story, a poem, a play, or a novel. Be sure to follow directions if your instructor wants to approve your choice, assign the literary work, or limit your options to several works read by your class. After careful analysis of the work, write an essay as the expert critic, explaining the meaning you discern, supporting your interpretation with evidence from the work, and evaluating the effectiveness of literary elements used by the author and the significance of the theme.

You cannot include everything about the work in your paper, so you should focus on one element (such as character, setting, or theme) or the interrelationship of two or three elements (such as characterization and symbolism). Although a summary, or *synopsis*, of the plot is a good beginning point, retelling the story is not a satisfactory literary analysis.

These college writers successfully responded to such an assignment:

One showed how the rhythm, rhymes, and images of Adrienne Rich's poem "Aunt Jennifer's Tigers" mesh to convey the poem's theme of tension between a woman's artistic urge and societal constraints.

Another who was a musician read James Baldwin's "Sonny's Blues" and established Sonny's credibility as a musician—based on attitudes, actions, struggles, relationship with his instrument and with other musicians.

A psychology major concluded that the relationship between Hamlet and Claudius in Shakespeare's *Hamlet* represents in many ways the tension, jealousy, and misunderstanding between stepsons and stepfathers.

Facing the Challenge   Analyzing Literature

The major challenge that writers face when analyzing a literary work is to state and support a thesis that takes a stand. If you simply explain the literal meaning of the work—retelling the story or summing up the topic of an essay or a poem—your readers will be disappointed. Instead, they expect a clear thesis that presents your specific interpretation. They want to see how you analyze the work and which features of the work you use to support your position about it. For instance, your thesis might identify a theme—an insight, main idea, or observation about life—developed in the work. Then your essay would show how selected features of the work express, develop, or illustrate this theme. On the other hand, your thesis might present your analysis of how a story, poem, or play works. Then your essay might discuss how several elements—such as the mood established by the setting, the figurative language used to describe events, and the arc of the plot—work together to develop its meaning. Whatever the case that you argue, your thesis needs to be clearly focused and your supporting evidence needs to come from the words and expressions of the work itself.

Generating Ideas

Read several literary works from the course options to find two or three you like. Next, reread the works that interest you, and select the one that strikes you as especially significant—realistic or universal, moving or disturbing, believable or shocking—with a meaning that you wish to share with your classmates.

Analyzing a literary work is the first step in interpreting meaning and evaluating literary quality. As you read the work, identify its elements and analyze them. Then focus on *one* significant element or a cluster of related elements. As you write, restrict your discussion to that focus.

For more on analysis, see pp. 448–50.

We provide three checklists to guide you in analyzing different types of literature. Each of these is an aid to understanding, *not* an organizational outline for writing about literature. The first checklist focuses on short stories and novels, but some of its questions can help you analyze setting, character, theme, or your reactions as a reader for almost any kind of literary work.

DISCOVERY CHECKLIST
Analyzing a Short Story or a Novel

For a glossary of literary terms, see pp. 268–69.

☐ What is your reaction to the story? Jot it down.

☐ Who is the *narrator*—not the author, but the one who tells the story?

☐ What is the *point of view*?

☐ What is the *setting* (time and place)? What is the *atmosphere* or *mood*?

☐ How does the *plot* unfold? Write a synopsis, or summary, of the events in time order, including relationships among those events (see pp. 278–79).

☐ What are the *characters* like? Describe their personalities, traits, and motivations based on their actions, speech, habits, and so on. What strategies does the author use to develop the characters? Who is the *protagonist*? The *antagonist*? Do any characters change? Are the changes believable?

☐ How would you describe the story's *style*, or use of language? Is it informal, conversational, or formal? Does the story use dialect or foreign words?

☐ What are the *external conflicts* and the *internal conflicts*? What is the *central conflict*? Express the conflicts using the word *versus,* such as "dreams versus reality" or "the individual versus society."

☐ What is the *climax* of the story? Is there any *resolution*?

☐ Are there important *symbols*? What might they mean?

☐ What does the *title* of the story mean?

☐ What are the *themes* of the story? Are they universal (applicable to all people everywhere at all times)? Write down your interpretation of the main theme. How is this theme related to your own life?

☐ What other literary works or life experiences does the story remind you of?

When looking at a poem, consider the elements specific to poetry and those shared with other genres, as the following checklist suggests.

DISCOVERY CHECKLIST
Analyzing a Poem

☐ What is your reaction to the poem? Jot it down.

☐ Who is the *speaker*—not the author, but the one who narrates?

☐ Is there a *setting*? How does it relate to the meaning of the poem? What *mood* or emotional *atmosphere* does it suggest?

☐ Can you put the poem into your own words—paraphrase it?

☐ What is striking about the poem's language? Is it informal or formal? Does it use irony or figurative language: *imagery, metaphor, personification*? Identify repetition or words that are unusual, used in an unusual way, or *archaic* (no longer commonly used). Consider *connotations,* the suggestions conjured by the words: *house* versus *home,* though both refer to the same place.

☐ Is the poem *lyric* (expressing emotion) or *narrative* (telling a story)?

☐ How is the poem structured or divided? Does it use *couplets* (two consecutive rhyming lines), *quatrains* (units of four lines), or other units? How do the beginning and end relate to each other and to the poem as a whole?

☐ Does the poem use *rhyme* (words that sound alike)? If so, how does the rhyme contribute to the meaning?

☐ Does the poem have *rhythm* (regular meter or beat, patterns of accented and unaccented syllables)? How does the rhythm contribute to the meaning?

☐ What does the *title* of the poem mean?

☐ What is the major *theme* of the poem? How does this underlying idea unify the poem? How is it related to your own life?

☐ What other literary works or life experiences does the poem remind you of?

A play is written to be seen and heard, not read. You may analyze what kind it is and how it would appear onstage, as this checklist suggests.

DISCOVERY CHECKLIST
Analyzing a Play

☐ What is your reaction to the play? Jot it down.

☐ Is the play a serious *tragedy* (which arouses pity and fear in the audience and usually ends unhappily with the death or downfall of the *tragic hero*)? Or is it a *comedy* (which aims to amuse and usually ends happily)?

☐ What is the *setting* of the play? What is its *mood*?

☐ In brief, what happens? Summarize each act of the play.

☐ What are the characters like? Who is the *protagonist*? Who is the *antagonist*? Are there *foil characters* who contrast with the main character and reveal his or her traits? Which characters are in conflict? Which change?

☐ Which speeches seem especially significant?

☐ What is the plot? Identify the *exposition* or background information needed to understand the story. Determine the main *external* and *internal* conflicts. What is the *central conflict*? What events *complicate* the central conflict? How are these elements of the plot spread throughout the play?

☐ What is the *climax* of the play? Is there a *resolution* to the action?

☐ What does the *title* mean?

☐ Can you identify any *dramatic irony,* words or actions of a character that carry meaning unperceived by the character but evident to the audience?

☐ What is the major *theme*? Is it universal? How is it related to your life?

☐ What other literary works or life experiences does the play remind you of?

Learning by Doing 🎬 Developing Your Literary Analysis

Once you have chosen and read the work you want to write about, also select an appropriate checklist from the preceding section. Then concentrate on a few questions that seem interesting and potentially fruitful to you. Answer them, jotting notes in a file, on the work itself, or on a separate card or page for each question. If you find a good idea, highlight or underline relevant evidence in the work. If not, try a few more questions until an idea starts to take shape.

Planning, Drafting, and Developing

For more on planning, drafting, and developing, see Chs. 20, 21, and 22.

When you write your analysis, your purpose is to explain the work's deeper meaning. Don't try to impress readers with your brilliance. Instead, regard them as friends in whose company you are discussing something familiar to all, though they may not have studied the work as carefully as you have. This assumption will help you decide how much evidence from the work to include and will reduce summarizing.

Identify Your Support. After you have determined the major element or cluster of elements that you intend to focus on, go through the work again to find all the passages that relate to your main point. Mark them as you find them, or put them on note cards or in a computer file, along with the page references. If you use any quotations, quote exactly.

For more on stating a thesis, see pp. 401–10.

Develop Your Main Idea or Thesis. Begin by trying to express your point in a thesis statement that identifies the literary work and the author. Suppose you start with a working thesis on the theme of "The Lottery":

WORKING THESIS   In "The Lottery," Shirley Jackson reveals the theme.

But this statement is too vague, so you rewrite it to be more precise:

IMPROVED   In "The Lottery" by Shirley Jackson, the theme is tradition.

This thesis is better but still doesn't state the theme clearly or precisely. You try other ways of expressing what Jackson implies about tradition:

IMPROVED   In "The Lottery" by Shirley Jackson, one of the major themes is that outmoded traditions can be harmful.

Adding *one of* shows that this is not the story's only theme, but the rest is vague. What does *outmoded* mean? How are traditions harmful?

MORE PRECISE   In "The Lottery" by Shirley Jackson, one of the major themes is that traditions that have lost their meaning can still move people to act abnormally without thinking.

This thesis is better but may change as you write the analysis. For instance, you might go beyond interpretation of Jackson's ideas by adding *tragic* to convey your evaluation of her observation of the human condition:

EVALUATION ADDED	In "The Lottery," Shirley Jackson reveals the tragic theme that traditions that have lost their meaning can still move people to abnormal and thoughtless action.

Or you might say this, alerting readers to your main points:

PREVIEW ADDED	In "The Lottery," Jackson effectively uses symbolism and irony to reveal the theme that traditions that have lost their meaning can still move people to abnormal action.

Focus on analyzing ideas, not retelling events. Maintain that focus by analyzing your thesis: divide it into parts, and then develop each part in turn. The thesis just presented could be divided into (1) use of symbolism to reveal theme and (2) use of irony to reveal theme. Similarly, you might divide a thesis about character change into the character's original traits, the events that cause change, and the character's new traits.

Learning by Doing 📷 Developing Your Thesis

Follow the pattern for developing a thesis statement in the last section. Start with your working thesis and then improve it, make it more precise, and consider adding an evaluation or preview. Present your thesis drafts to a classmate or small group, perhaps asking them questions like these: What wording needs to be clearer? What idea could I narrow down? What point sounds intriguing? What might a reader want me to emphasize further? Continue to refine your thesis as you work on your essay.

Introduce Your Essay. Tie your beginning to your main idea, or thesis. If you are uncertain how to begin, try one of these openings:

For more on introductions, see pp. 428–30.

- Focus on a character's universality (pointing out that most people might feel as Tessie in "The Lottery" did if their names were drawn).
- Focus on a theme's universality (discussing briefly how traditions seem to be losing their meaning in modern society).
- Quote a striking line from the work ("and then they were upon her" or "'Lottery in June, corn be heavy soon'").
- Make a statement about the work's point, your reaction when you read it, a parallel personal experience, or the writer's technique.

■ Ask a "Have you ever?" question to draw readers into your interpretation.

Peer Response   Responding to Literature

For general questions for a peer editor, see p. 465. For peer response worksheets, visit <bedfordstmartins .com/bedguide>.

Ask one of your classmates to read your draft, considering how effectively you have analyzed the literary work and presented your analysis. Ask your peer editor to answer specific questions such as these:

- What is your first reaction to the literary analysis?
- In what ways does the analysis add to your understanding of the literary work? In what ways does it add to your insights into life?
- Does the introduction make you want to read the rest of the analysis? What changes would you suggest to strengthen the opening?
- Is the main idea clear? Is there sufficient relevant evidence from the work to support that point? Put stars wherever additional evidence is needed. Put a check mark by any irrelevant information.
- Does the writer go beyond plot summary to analyze elements, interpret meaning, and evaluate literary merit? If not, how might the writer revise?
- Is the analysis organized by ideas instead of events? What changes in organization would you suggest?
- Do the transitions guide you smoothly from one point to the next? Do the transitions focus on ideas, not on time or position in the story? Note any places where the writer might add transitions.
- If this paper were yours, what is the one thing you would be sure to work on before handing it in?

For more on citing and listing literary works, see MLA style in E (pp. A-30–A-35) in the Quick Research Guide.

Support Your Interpretation. As you develop your analysis, include supporting evidence—descriptions of setting and character, summaries of events, quotations of dialogue, and other specifics. Cite page numbers (for prose) or line numbers (for poetry) where the details can be found in the work. Integrate evidence from the story with your comments and ideas.

For a list of transitions showing logical connections, see p. 435.

Keep the focus on ideas, not events, by using transition markers that refer to character traits and personality change, not to time. Say "Although Mr. Summers was . . ." instead of "At the beginning of the story Mr. Summers was . . . ." Write "Tessie became . . ." instead of "After that Tessie was . . ." State "The villagers in 'The Lottery' changed . . . ," not "On the next page . . . ."

For more on conclusions, see pp. 430–32.

Conclude Your Essay. When you reach the end, don't just stop writing. Close as you might open—personal experience, comment on technique, quotation — to provide a sense of finality. Refer to or reaffirm your thesis. Often an effective conclusion ties in directly with the introduction.

Revising and Editing

As you read over your draft, keep in mind your thesis and the evidence that supports it.

For more revising and editing strategies, see Ch. 25.

REVISION CHECKLIST

☐ Have you clearly identified the literary work and the author near the beginning of the analysis?

☐ Is your main idea or thesis clear? Does everything else relate to it?

☐ Have you focused on one element or a cluster of related elements in your analysis? Have you organized around these ideas rather than events?

☐ Do your transitions focus on ideas, not on plot or time sequence? Do they guide readers easily from one section or sentence to the next?

☐ Are your interpretations supported by evidence from the literary work? Do you need to add examples of dialogue, action, or description? Have you selected details relevant to the points of analysis, not interesting sidelights?

☐ Have you woven the details from the work smoothly into your text? Have you cited their correct page or line numbers? Have you quoted and cited carefully instead of lifting language without proper attribution?

☐ Do you understand all the words and literary terms you use?

☐ Have you tried to share your insights into the meaning of the work with your readers, or have you slipped into trying to impress them?

After you have revised your literary analysis, check the grammar, word choice, punctuation, and mechanics — and then correct any problems you find. Make sure that you smoothly introduce all of your quotations and references to the work and weave them into your own discussion.

For more editing and proofreading strategies, see pp. 473–76.

EDITING CHECKLIST

☐ Have you used the present tense for events in the literary work and for comments about the author's presentation? **A3**

☐ Have you used quotation marks correctly whenever you give the exact words of the literary work? **C3**

☐ Have you used correct manuscript format for your paper?

For more help, find the relevant checklist sections in the Quick Editing Guide on p. A-36. Turn also to the Quick Format Guide beginning on p. A-1.

Learning from Another Writer: Synopsis

In your literature courses you may write synopses of works to help you prepare to write about them or to sum up concise information about them for your essay. A synopsis can help you get the chronology straight, pick out the significant events and details, and relate the parts of a work to each other and to the work's themes.

A *synopsis* is a summary of the plot of a narrative—a short story, a novel, a play, or a narrative poem. It describes the literal meaning, condensing the story to the major events and most significant details. Do not include your interpretation, but summarize the work in your own words, taking care not to lift language or sentence structure from the work itself.

In preparation for writing his literary analysis of "The Lottery" (pp. 257–64)—to make sure he had the sequence of events clear—Jonathan Burns wrote the following synopsis of the story.

For more on summarizing and paraphrasing, see Ch. 12 and D (pp. A-26–A-30) in the Quick Research Guide.

Jonathan Burns   **Student Synopsis**

A Synopsis of "The Lottery"

Around ten o'clock on a sunny June 27, the villagers gathered in the square for a   1
lottery, expecting to be home in time for lunch. The children came first, gathering
stones and talking as they enjoyed the summer vacation. Then came the men, followed by the women. When parents called, the children joined their families.

Mr. Summers, who always conducted the town lottery, arrived with the black   2
wooden box and placed it on the three-legged stool that Mr. Graves had brought out.
The villagers remained at a distance from these men, but Mr. Martin and his son
reluctantly helped hold the shabby black box as Mr. Summers mixed the papers in it.
Although the townspeople had never replaced the box, they had substituted paper
slips for the original wooden chips. To prepare for the drawing, they listed the
members of every household and swore in Mr. Summers. Although they had dropped
much of the original ritual, the official still greeted each person individually.

Tessie Hutchinson rushed into the square, telling her friend Mrs. Delacroix she   3
had almost forgotten the day. Then she joined her husband and children. When
Mr. Summers asked if everyone was present, he was told that Clyde Dunbar was absent
because of a broken leg but that his wife would draw for the family. Summers noted
that the Watson boy was drawing for his mother and checked to see if Old Man Warner
was present.

The crowd got quiet. Mr. Summers reminded everybody of the procedure and   4
began to call the family names in alphabetical order. People in the group joked and
talked nervously until Mr. Summers finished calling the roll. After a pause, the heads
of households opened their slips. Everybody wondered who had the special slip of

paper, who had won the lottery. They discovered it was Bill Hutchinson. When Tessie complained that the drawing hadn't been done fairly, the others told her to "Be a good sport" (262).

Mr. Graves put five slips into the box, one for each member of the Hutchinson family, although Tessie kept charging unfairness. The children drew first, then Tessie, then Bill. The children opened their slips and held up blank pieces of paper. Bill opened his, also blank. Tessie wouldn't open hers; Bill had to do it for her, revealing its black spot.   5

Mr. Summers urged everyone to complete the process right away. They picked up stones, even young Davy Hutchinson, and started throwing them at Tessie, as she kept screaming, "It isn't fair, it isn't right" (264). Then the villagers stoned her.   6

Questions to Start You Thinking

Meaning

1. In what ways does this synopsis help you understand the story better?
2. Why isn't a synopsis as interesting as a short story?
3. Can you tell from this synopsis whether Burns understands Jackson's story beyond the literal level? How can you tell?

Writing Strategies

4. Does Burns retell the story accurately and clearly? Does he get the events in correct time order? How does he show the relationships of the events to each other and to the whole?
5. Does Burns select the details necessary to indicate what happened in "The Lottery"? Why do you think he omits certain details?
6. Are there any details, comments, or events that you would add to his synopsis? Why or why not?
7. How does this synopsis differ from Burns's literary analysis (pp. 266–67)?

Learning by Writing: Synopsis

The Assignment: Writing a Synopsis of a Story by Kate Chopin

Whenever you need to understand a story or recall a lot of stories, writing a synopsis can help you review a story's specifics. Keep your synopsis of the plot true to the original, noting accurate details in time order. Condensing a story to a few hundred words forces you to focus on what's most important, often leading to a statement of theme.

Kate Chopin was a nineteenth-century American writer whose female characters search for identity and freedom from oppression. Write a synopsis of two to three hundred words of Chopin's "The Story of an Hour."

DISCOVERY CHECKLIST

☐ What are the major events and details of the story?

☐ In what time order do events take place?

☐ How are the story's parts related (without adding interpretations)?

☐ Which of the author's words might you want to quote?

Kate Chopin
The Story of an Hour

Knowing that Mrs. Mallard was afflicted with a heart trouble, great care 1
was taken to break to her as gently as possible the news of her husband's
death.

It was her sister Josephine who told her, in broken sentences, veiled hints 2
that revealed in half concealing. Her husband's friend Richards was there,
too, near her. It was he who had been in the newspaper office when intelligence of the railroad disaster was received, with Brently Mallard's name leading the list of "killed." He had only taken the time to assure himself of its
truth by a second telegram, and had hastened to forestall any less careful, less
tender friend in bearing the sad message.

She did not hear the story as many women have heard the same, with a 3
paralyzed inability to accept its significance. She wept at once, with sudden,
wild abandonment, in her sister's arms. When the storm of grief had spent itself she went away to her room alone. She would have no one follow her.

There stood, facing the open window, a comfortable, roomy armchair. 4
Into this she sank, pressed down by a physical exhaustion that haunted her
body and seemed to reach into her soul.

She could see in the open square before her house the tops of trees that 5
were all aquiver with the new spring life. The delicious breath of rain was in
the air. In the street below a peddler was crying his wares. The notes of a distant song which someone was singing reached her faintly, and countless
sparrows were twittering in the eaves.

There were patches of blue sky showing here and there through the clouds 6
that had met and piled one above the other in the west facing her window.

She sat with her head thrown back upon the cushion of the chair, quite 7
motionless, except when a sob came up into her throat and shook her, as a
child who has cried itself to sleep continues to sob in its dreams.

She was young, with a fair, calm face, whose lines bespoke repression and 8
even a certain strength. But now there was a dull stare in her eyes, whose gaze
was fixed away off yonder on one of those patches of blue sky. It was not a
glance of reflection, but rather indicated a suspension of intelligent thought.

There was something coming to her and she was waiting for it, fearfully. 9
What was it? She did not know; it was too subtle and elusive to name. But
she felt it, creeping out of the sky, reaching toward her through the sounds,
the scents, the color that filled the air.

Now her bosom rose and fell tumultuously. She was beginning to recog- 10
nize this thing that was approaching to possess her, and she was striving to
beat it back with her will—as powerless as her two white slender hands
would have been.

When she abandoned herself a little whispered word escaped her slightly 11
parted lips. She said it over and over under her breath: "Free, free, free!" The
vacant stare and the look of terror that had followed it went from her eyes.
They stayed keen and bright. Her pulses beat fast, and the coursing blood
warmed and relaxed every inch of her body.

She did not stop to ask if it were not a monstrous joy that held her. 12
A clear and exalted perception enabled her to dismiss the suggestion as
trivial.

She knew that she would weep again when she saw the kind, tender 13
hands folded in death; the face that had never looked save with love upon
her, fixed and gray and dead. But she saw beyond that bitter moment a long
procession of years to come that would belong to her absolutely. And she
opened and spread her arms out to them in welcome.

There would be no one to live for during those coming years; she would 14
live for herself. There would be no powerful will bending her in that blind
persistence with which men and women believe they have a right to impose a
private will upon a fellow creature. A kind intention or a cruel intention
made the act seem no less a crime as she looked upon it in that brief moment
of illumination.

And yet she had loved him—sometimes. Often she had not. What did it 15
matter! What could love, the unsolved mystery, count for in face of this possession of self-assertion which she suddenly recognized as the strongest impulse of her being.

"Free! Body and soul free!" she kept whispering. 16

Josephine was kneeling before the closed door with her lips to the 17
keyhole, imploring for admission. "Louise, open the door! I beg; open the
door—you will make yourself ill. What are you doing, Louise? For heaven's
sake open the door."

"Go away. I am not making myself ill." No; she was drinking in a very 18
elixir of life through that open window.

Her fancy was running riot along those days ahead of her. Spring days, 19
and summer days, and all sorts of days that would be her own. She breathed
a quick prayer that life might be long. It was only yesterday she had thought
with a shudder that life might be long.

She arose at length and opened the door to her sister's importunities. 20
There was a feverish triumph in her eyes, and she carried herself unwittingly
like a goddess of Victory. She clasped her sister's waist, and together they descended the stairs. Richards stood waiting for them at the bottom.

Someone was opening the front door with a latchkey. It was Brently Mal- 21
lard who entered, a little travel-stained, composedly carrying his gripsack and
umbrella. He had been far from the scene of the accident, and did not even
know there had been one. He stood amazed at Josephine's piercing cry; at
Richards's quick motion to screen him from the view of his wife.

But Richards was too late. 22

When the doctors came they said she had died of heart disease — of joy 23
that kills.

Learning from Another Writer: Paraphrase

Like a synopsis, a *paraphrase* conveys the meaning of the original piece of literature and the relationships of its parts in your own words. A paraphrase,
however, converts the original poetry to your own prose or the original
prose to your own words in a passage about as long as the original.

As Jonathan Burns read through "The Lottery" preparing to write his
analysis, he paid close attention to several of the characters that he planned
to mention. To sharpen his understanding of Old Man Warner, he wrote a
paraphrase of that character's comments in paragraph 32.

Jonathan Burns   Student Paraphrase

A Paraphrase from "The Lottery"

Old Man Warner criticized people who were willing to give up the lottery as stupid
idiots or uppity young people who were not satisfied with anything. He claimed that
such people would be content to quit work and move to caves. Then he repeated an
old folk expression about a good corn crop following the June lottery and claimed
that without it the villagers would end up living on weeds and nuts. Finally, he maintained that the lottery had been a tradition forever. He even criticized Mr. Summers
as a youngster, faulting him for not being serious enough about the lottery (261).

Questions to Start You Thinking

Meaning

1. In what ways do you think this paraphrase helped Jonathan Burns
   understand Old Man Warner better?

2. Why isn't a paraphrase as interesting as the original passage in a short
   story?

Writing Strategies

3. To what extent does Burns paraphrase clearly and accurately? Would
   you add or drop any details or comments from his paraphrase?

4. How does this paraphrase differ from Burns's synopsis (pp. 278–79)?

Learning by Writing: Paraphrase

The Assignment: Writing a Paraphrase of a Poem

When you study poetry, you can benefit from paraphrasing—expressing the content of a poem in your own words without adding opinions or interpretations. A paraphrase forces you to divide the poem into logical sections, to figure out what the poet says in each section, and to discern how the parts relate. It also prepares you to state its theme—its main idea or insight—in a sentence or two.

See p. 217 and the Additional Writing Assignments section below for poems you might paraphrase.

DISCOVERY CHECKLIST

☐ What are the poem's major sections? What does the poet say in each one?

☐ How are the sections of the poem related?

☐ Are any words unfamiliar or used in a special sense, different from the usual meanings? What do those words mean in the context of the poem?

☐ Does the poet use images to create sensory pictures or figurative language (see p. 268) to create comparisons? How do these contribute to the meaning?

Additional Writing Assignments

1. Analyze the themes of "The Story of an Hour" or another literary work written in an earlier era and assigned by your instructor. Which themes are relevant now? How do they relate to twenty-first-century readers and their issues?

2. Write an essay comparing and contrasting a literary element in two or three short stories or poems.

3. Read the poem below by Robert Frost (1874–1963). Write an essay using a paraphrase of the poem as a springboard for your thoughts on a fork in the road of your life—a decision that made a difference for you.

For more on writing a comparison and contrast essay, see Ch. 7.

For another poem by Robert Frost, see p. 217.

The Road Not Taken
Two roads diverged in a yellow wood,
And sorry I could not travel both
And be one traveler, long I stood
And looked down one as far as I could
To where it bent in the undergrowth;

Then took the other, as just as fair,
And having perhaps the better claim,
Because it was grassy and wanted wear;
Though as for that the passing there
Had worn them really about the same,

And both that morning equally lay
In leaves no step had trodden black.
Oh, I kept the first for another day!
Yet knowing how way leads on to way,
I doubted if I should ever come back.

I shall be telling this with a sigh
Somewhere ages and ages hence:
Two roads diverged in a wood, and I—
I took the one less traveled by,
And that has made all the difference.

For more on writing a comparison and contrast essay, see Ch. 7.

4. Read the poem below by Edwin Arlington Robinson (1869–1935). Have you known and envied someone like Richard Cory, a person everyone thought had it all? What happened to him or her? What did you discover about your impression of the person? Analyze the poem and draw on experience as you write a personal response essay to compare and contrast the person you knew with Richard Cory.

Richard Cory

Whenever Richard Cory went down town,
We people on the pavement looked at him:
He was a gentleman from sole to crown,
Clean favored, and imperially slim.

And he was always quietly arrayed,
And he was always human when he talked;
But still he fluttered pulses when he said,
"Good-morning," and he glittered when he walked.

And he was rich—yes, richer than a king—
And admirably schooled in every grace:
In fine, we thought that he was everything
To make us wish that we were in his place.

So on we worked, and waited for the light,
And went without the meat, and cursed the bread;
And Richard Cory, one calm summer night,
Went home and put a bullet through his head.

For more about analyzing visuals, see Ch. 14. For more on analysis in general, see pp. 448–50.

5. Write a critical analysis of a song, a movie, or a television show. Play or view it several times to pull out specific evidence to support your interpretation. If your instructor approves, present your analysis in a podcast, a multimedia format, or a series of Web pages.

Responding to Visual Representations 14

I mages are a constant and persistent presence in our lives. The sign atop a taxi invites us to try the new ride at a local tourist attraction. A celebrity sporting a milk mustache smiles from the side of a city bus, accompanied by the familiar question, "Got milk?" The lettering on a pickup truck urges us to call for a free landscaping estimate. On television, video, and the Web, advertising images surround us, trying to shape our opinions about everything from personal hygiene products to snack foods to political candidates.

Advertisements are not the only visual representations that affect us. Cartoons, photographs, drawings, paintings, logos, graphics, and other two-dimensional media all work to evoke responses. The critical skills you develop for analyzing these still images also apply to other types of visual representations, including television commercials, films, and stage productions. Whether visual images provoke a smile or a frown, one thing is certain: visuals help to structure our views of reality.

Using Strategies for Visual Analysis

Just as you annotate or respond to a written text, be sure to take notes or use your journal to record your observations and interpretations of images. Include a copy of the image, if available, when you solicit peer review or submit your essay. Begin your visual analysis by conducting a *close reading* of the image. Like a literal and critical reading of a written text, a close reading of an image involves careful, in-depth examination of the advertisement, photograph, cartoon, artwork, or other visual representation. Your close reading should focus on the following three levels of questions:

For a sample visual analysis and visual-analysis activity, visit **<bedfordstmartins .com/bedguide>**.

- **What is the big picture?** What is the source of the image? What is its purpose? What audience does it address? What prominent element in the image stands out? What focal point draws the eye?

- **What characteristics of the image can you observe?** What story does the image tell? What people or animals appear in the image? What are the major elements of the image? How are they arranged?

- **How can you interpret what the image suggests?** What feeling or mood does it create? What is its cultural meaning? What are the roles of any signs, symbols, or language that it includes? What is its theme?

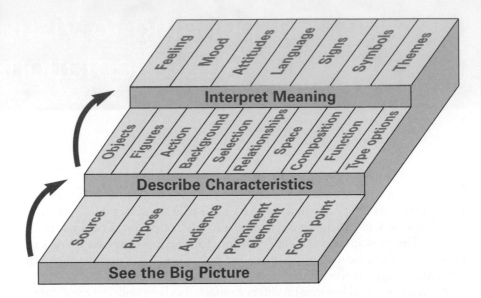

As you apply these three levels of visual analysis, you may discover that your classmates respond differently to some images than you do, just as they might respond differently to a written text. Your personal cultural background and your experiences may influence how you interpret the meaning of an image. As a result, your thesis interpreting the meaning of an image or analyzing its effectiveness will be your own — shaped by your responses and supported by your observations.

For more on literal and critical reading of texts, see Ch. 2. For checklists for analyzing images, see pp. 289, 295, and 300.

Level One: Seeing the Big Picture

Begin your close reading of an image by discovering what you can about its origins and overall composition. If you include the image in a paper, you will need to cite the source and its "author" or artist, just as you would if you were including text from a reading, an article, or a literary work.

For more on crediting sources of visuals, see the Quick Format Guide, p. A-1.

Source, Purpose, and Audience

Identifying the background of an image is sometimes complicated. For example, an image may appear in its original context or in a different situation, used seriously, humorously, or allusively.

- What is the context for the image? If it is an advertisement, when and where did it run? If it is a photograph, painting, or other work of art, who is the artist? Where and how has it been published, circulated, or exhibited?
- What is the purpose of the image?
- What audience does it aim to attract? How does it appeal to viewers?

Prominent Element

Next, examine the overall composition of the image. Look carefully at the whole image and ask yourself, "Is there one prominent element—object, person, background, writing—in the image that immediately attracts my attention?" Examine that element in detail to figure out how and why it draws you into the image.

Figure 14.1 Public Service Announcement with One Prominent Element. *Source:* Act Against Violence.org/Ad Council

Answering that question is easy for a visual that showcases a single object or person, as in Figure 14.1. There, the child is the obvious prominent element. Her dark eyes, framed by her dark hair, draw the viewer to her alert, intent expression. That expression suggests her capacity to learn from all she observes. The text above and below her image reinforces this message as it cautions adults to be careful what they teach children through their own conduct.

Identifying the prominent element can be more complicated for a visual with several characters. For example, which form draws your eye in Figure 14.2? Many people would first notice the dark-haired Caucasian girl. Her prominence can be explained in part by her position at the left side, framed by the white porch railing. People who read from left to right and top to bottom—including most Americans and Europeans—typically read photographs in the same way. For this reason, artists and photographers often position key elements—those they want viewers to see right away—somewhere in the upper left quadrant, drawing the viewer's eye into the image at the upper left corner. (See Figure 14.3.)

Focal Point

There is another reason the reader's eye might be drawn first to the girl on the left: all the other children are turned slightly toward her, straining to see the pages of the magazine she holds. She is positioned to provide a focal point both for the viewer and for the action within the photograph.

Now, look at the child on the right side of the picture. You may have noticed her first. Or, once you did notice her, you may have been surprised that she didn't attract your attention right away. After all, she provides some contrast within the image because she sits apart from the other girls, seems to be a bit younger, and does not appear to be included in their little group. What's more, she's not wearing any clothes. Still, most people won't notice her first. Because of the left-to-right and top-to-bottom reading pattern, most of us view photographs in a Z pattern, as depicted in Figure 14.4. Even though most viewers would notice the child on the far right last, they would still pause to look at her. Thus, the bottom right corner of an image is a second very important position that a skilled photographer can use to hold the viewers' attention. When you look at the "big picture" in this way, you can

Figure 14.2 (top) Photograph of Four Children, Kodak Picture of the Day, October 22, 2000

Figure 14.3 (above left) Photograph Divided into Quarters

Figure 14.4 (above right) Z Pattern Often Used to Read Images

Figure 14.5 (right) Close-Up Detail of Photograph

see the overall composition of the image, identify its prominent element, and determine its focal point.

VISUAL ANALYSIS CHECKLIST
Seeing the Big Picture

☐ What is the source of the image? What is its purpose and audience?

☐ What prominent element in the image immediately attracts your attention? How and why does it draw you into the image?

☐ What is the focal point of the image? How does the image direct your attention to this point? What path does your eye follow as you observe the image?

Learning by Doing 📷 Seeing the Big Picture

Working with a classmate or a small group, select another image in this book such as one that opens a chapter in Part Two: A Writer's Situations or A Writer's Reader. Consider the image's purpose and audience (in its original context or in this book), but concentrate on its prominent element, which draws the viewer's eye, and its focal point, which suggests the center of its action or moment. Share analyses in a class discussion, or explain yours to another group in a brief oral report or an online posting.

Level Two: Observing the Characteristics of an Image

As you read a written text literally, you become aware of what it presents, what it means, and how it applies in other situations. Similarly, your close reading of an image includes observing its *denotative* or literal characteristics. At this stage, you focus on exactly what the image depicts — observing it objectively — rather than probing what it means or signifies.

Cast of Characters

Objects. Examine the condition, colors, sizes, functions, and positions of the objects included in the image. In Figure 14.2, for example, only one object is depicted in the image: a large magazine. Everything else in the image is either a figure or part of the background.

Figures. Look closely at any figures (people, animals) in the image. Consider facial expressions, poses, hairstyles and colors, ages, sexes, ethnicity, possible education or occupation, apparent relationships, and so on.

Figure 14.2 shows four girls, three about eight or nine years old and the fourth a few years younger. Three are Caucasian, and one is African American. The dark-haired Caucasian girl is wearing a colorful bathing suit as is the African American girl. Between them sits a light-haired Caucasian girl, wearing shorts and a flowered T-shirt. They pore over the magazine held by the dark-haired Caucasian girl, engrossed as well as a little puzzled, judging from their facial expressions. The girls seem to be looking at a picture; the magazine is turned sideways with the spine at the bottom.

The fourth child, the youngest, sits slightly apart from the others. Her light hair appears damp — possibly from swimming, we might conclude, because two of the others wear swimsuits. We can see her tanned skin and the small bruises on her legs, probably acquired during play.

Story of the Image

Action. The action shown in an image suggests its "plot" or story, the events surrounding the moment captured in the image. Figure 14.2 captures the four children seated on the steps on a summer day. Because no adults are present and the children look puzzled, maybe they are looking at something they don't understand in the magazine, possibly something adults might frown on. On the other hand, they are not being secretive, so this impression may not be accurate.

Background. The background in an image shows where and when the action takes place. In Figure 14.2, the children are seated on the wooden steps of a blue house. The steps seem part of a back, not a front, porch, relatively small with nowhere to sit except on the steps themselves. The top step is painted blue and the railing white to match the metal door and window frames. In a few places the paint is chipped or worn away. But these small signs of disrepair suggest a lived-in, comfortable house, not that the occupants are poor. The windows next to the steps and on the door reflect leafy summer trees.

Design and Arrangement

Selection of Elements. When you look at the design of an image, reflect on both the elements within the image and their organization.

- What are the major colors and shapes? How are they arranged?
- Does the image look balanced? Are light and dark areas symmetrical?
- Does the image appear organized or chaotic?
- Is one area darker (heavier) or brighter (lighter) than other areas?
- What does the design make you think of — does it evoke a particular emotion, historical period, or memory?

In Figure 14.2, the most prominent shape is the white porch railing that frames the children and draws the viewer's eye toward the action. The image appears balanced, in that the white door provides the backdrop for the youngest child, while the blue siding and white porch railing frame the other girls. Therefore, the image is split down the center, both by the separation of the figures and by the shapes that make up the background. The brightly colored summer clothing worn by the girls on the left side also accentuates the youngest child's monochromatic nakedness.

Relationship of Elements. Visual elements may be related to one another or to written text that appears with them. In Figure 14.2, for instance, the three older girls gather around the magazine, and the youngest child is clearly not part of their group. She is separated physically by a bit of space and by the vertical line formed by the doorframe, which splits the background in two. Moreover, her body is turned slightly away from them and is not clothed. However, her gaze is on the magazine that the others are scrutinizing, an element that connects all four children.

Use of Space. An image may be surrounded by a lot of "white space"— empty space without text or graphics—or it may be "busy," filled with visual and written elements. Effective white space provides relief from a busy layout or directs the reader's eye to key elements. The image in Figure 14.2 uses shapes and colors to guide the viewer's eye, not empty space.

In contrast, look at the image in Figure 14.6. It specifically uses white space to call attention to the Volkswagen's small size. When this advertisement was produced back in 1959, many American cars were large and heavy. The VW, a German import, provided consumers with an alternative type of vehicle, and the advertising emphasized this contrast.

Artistic Choices

Whatever the form of an image, the person who composes it considers its artistic effect, function, and connection to related text.

Composition Decisions. Aesthetic or artistic choices may vary with the designer's preferences and the characteristics of the medium. For example, a photographer might use a close-up, medium, or wide-angle shot—and also determine the angle of the shot, the lighting, and the use of color.

The picture of the four children in Figure 14.2 (p. 288) is a medium shot taken at the children's eye level. Notice in Figure 14.5 how the meaning of the picture changes when we view the girls' faces as a close-up. We have no way of telling where the picture was taken or what the girls are doing; moreover, moving in closer completely cuts out the youngest child. The girls' attentiveness is still apparent, but we can't quite tell what its object is.

In contrast, in the Volkswagen ad (Figure 14.6), the white space creates the effect of a long shot taken from below with a telephoto lens. We see the car as it might appear through the wrong end of a pair of binoculars. This vantage point shrinks the car so that the small vehicle looks even smaller.

Figure 14.6 Volkswagen Advertisement, about 1959

Function Decisions. When an image illustrates a point, the illustration needs to serve the overall purpose of the document. In other words, form should follow function. For example, the 1959 Oldsmobile ad, Figure 14.7, shows people having a good time; in fact, one scene is set near the shore. These illustrations suggest that those who purchase the cars will enjoy life, a notion that undoubtedly suits the advertiser's goals.

Figure 14.7 Oldsmobile Advertisement, 1959

Writers have many illustrations available—photographs, drawings, charts, graphs, tables. Certain types of visuals are especially suited to certain functions. For example, a pie chart effectively conveys parts of a whole, while a photograph captures the drama and intensity of the moment—a child's rescue, a family's grief, an earthquake's toll. When you look at visuals in publications, consider how they function and why the writer might have chosen them.

For sample tables and figures, see B (pp. A-8–A-12) in the Quick Format Guide. For sample photographs, turn to the images opening Chs. 4 to 12 and 25 to 29.

Typeface Options. Many images, especially advertisements, combine image and text, using the typeface to set a mood and convey an impression. For example, **Times New Roman** is a common typeface, easy to read and somewhat conservative, whereas **Comic Sans MS** is considered informal—almost playful—and looks handwritten. Any printed element in an image may be trendy or conservative, large or small, in relation to the image as a whole. Further, it may inform, evoke emotion, or decorate the page.

Look back at Figure 14.6, the 1959 Volkswagen ad. The words "Think small" are printed in a sans serif typeface, one "without serifs," the small tails at the ends of the letters. This type is spare and unadorned, just like the VW itself. The ad also includes significant text across the bottom of the page. While this text is difficult to read in the reproduction in this book, it humorously points out the benefits of driving a small imported vehicle instead of one of the large, roomy cars common at the time.

In contrast to the VW ad campaign, the 1959 Oldsmobile marketing strategy promoted a big vehicle, as Figure 14.7 illustrates. Here the cars are shown in medium to close-up view to call attention to their length. Happy human figures in and beside the cars emphasize their size, and the cars are painted in bright colors, unlike the VW's serviceable black. The type in the ad also promotes the Oldsmobile's size. The primary text in the center of the page is large enough to be read in the reproduction here. It introduces the brand name by opening with the Oldsmobile '59 logo and praises the cars' size, space, power, and other features. Near the bottom of each car image, however, is some "fine print" that is difficult to read in the reproduction—brief notes about other features of the car, such as fuel efficiency.

Other images besides advertisements use type to set a mood or convey feelings and ideas. Figure 14.8 is a design student's response to an assignment that called for using letters to create an image. The simple typeface and stairlike arrangement help viewers "experience" the word *stairway*. Figure 14.9 illustrates how certain typefaces have become associated with countries—even to the point of becoming clichés. In fact, designers of travel posters and brochures often draw on predictable choices like these to suggest a feeling or mood—for example, boldness, tradition, adventure, history.

Just as type can establish a mood or tone, the absence of any written language in an image can also affect us. Recall Figure 14.2 (p. 288), the photograph of the children looking at a magazine. Because we can't see the magazine's title, we are left to wonder—perhaps with amusement—about what has so engrossed them. If the title—*Sports Illustrated*, *Wired*, *People*—were revealed to us, the photograph might seem less intriguing. By leaving us to speculate, the photographer may keep us looking longer and harder at the image.

s
st
sta
stair
stairw
stairwa
stairway

Figure 14.8 Stairway.
Source: Design for Communication: Conceptual Graphic Design Basics

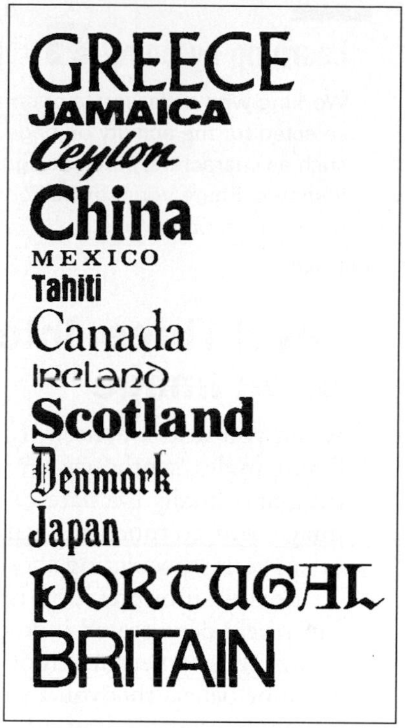

GREECE
JAMAICA
Ceylon
China
MEXICO
Tahiti
Canada
Ireland
Scotland
Denmark
Japan
PORTUGAL
BRITAIN

Figure 14.9 Type as Cultural Cliché.
Source: Publication Design

VISUAL ANALYSIS CHECKLIST
Observing the Characteristics of an Image

☐ What objects are included in the image?

☐ What figures (people or animals) appear in the image?

☐ What action takes place in the image? What is its "plot" or story?

☐ What is in the background? In what place does the action take place?

☐ What elements, colors, and shapes contribute to the design? How are they arranged or balanced? What feeling, memory, or association does the design evoke?

☐ How are the pictorial elements related to one another? How are they related to any written material? What do these relationships tell you as a viewer?

☐ How does the image use space? Does it include a lot of white space, or does it seem cluttered and busy?

☐ What composition decisions has the designer or artist made? What type of shot, shot angle, lighting, or color is used?

☐ What is the function of the image? How does form support function?

☐ What typefaces are used? What impressions do they convey?

Learning by Doing 📷 Observing Characteristics

Working with a classmate or small group, continue analyzing the image you selected for the activity on page 289. Examine one of its major characteristics—such as characters, story, design, or artistic choices—to determine exactly what it shows. Share your conclusions with your class or another group in a brief oral report or an online posting.

Level Three: Interpreting the Meaning of an Image

When you read a written text analytically, you examine its parts from different angles, synthesize the material by combining it with related information, and finally evaluate or judge its significance. When you interpret an image, you do much the same, actively examining what the image *connotes* or suggests, speculating about what it means.

Because interpretation is more personal than observation, this process can reveal deep-seated individual and cultural values. In fact, interpreting an image is sometimes emotional or difficult because it may require you to examine beliefs that you are unaware of holding. You may even become impatient, perhaps feeling that too much is being read into the image.

Like learning to read critically, however, learning to interpret images is a valuable skill. When you see an image that attracts you, chances are good that you like it because it upholds strong cultural beliefs. Through close reading of images, you can examine how image makers are able to perpetuate such cultural values and speculate about why—perhaps analyzing an artist's political motives or an advertiser's economic motives.

General Feeling or Mood

To begin interpreting an image, consider what feeling or mood it creates and how it does so. If you are a woman, you probably recall huddling, around age eight or nine, with a couple of "best friends," as the girls do in Figure 14.2. As a result, the interaction in this photograph may seem very familiar and may evoke fond memories. If you are a man, this photograph may call up somewhat different memories. Although eight-year-old boys also cluster in small groups, their motivations may differ from those behind little girls' huddles. Moreover, anyone who was ignored or excluded at a young age may feel a rush of sympathy for the youngest child; her separation from the older children may dredge up age-old hurt feelings.

For many viewers, the image may also suggest a mood associated with summer: sitting on the back porch after a trip to the swimming pool, spending a carefree day with friends. This "summer" mood is a particular cultural association related to the summers of childhood. By the time we reach college, summer no longer has the same feeling. Work, summer school, separations, and family responsibilities—maybe even for children like those in the picture—obliterate the freedoms of childhood vacations. However, another image might capture or represent a different version of this feeling or mood. As Figure 14.10 illustrates, an adult version of the "summer mood" might use similar colors and bright light to evoke a similar feeling. In this image, the cluster of childhood friends has been replaced by a solitary, reflective person, tapping the beauty of a summer scene through the creative experience of painting.

Figure 14.10 Photograph Conveying a Mood. *Source:* Jonathan Nourok, PhotoEdit

Sociological, Political, Economic, or Cultural Attitudes

On the surface, the Volkswagen ad in Figure 14.6 (p. 292) is simply an attempt to sell a car. But its message might be interpreted to mean "scale down"—lead a less consumer-oriented lifestyle. If Volkswagen had distributed this ad in the 1970s, it would have been unremarkable—faced with the first energy crisis that adversely affected American gasoline prices, many advertisers used ecological consciousness to sell cars. In 1959, however, energy conservation was not really a concern. Contrasted with other automobile ads of its time, the Volkswagen ad seems somewhat eccentric, making the novel suggestion that larger cars are excessively extravagant.

Whereas the Volkswagen ad suggests that "small" refers both to size and affordability, the Oldsmobile ad in Figure 14.7 (p. 293) depicts a large vehicle and implies a large price tag. By emphasizing the Vista-Panoramic view and increased luggage space and by portraying the car near a seashore, the ad leads viewers to think about going on vacation. It thus implies luxury and exclusivity—not everyone can afford this car or the activities it suggests.

Sometimes what is missing from an image is as important as what is included. For instance, Figure 14.11 (p. 298) deliberately contrasts presence and absence, projecting a possible future scene—without the bear—to bring home its message about the need to protect and preserve our national parks and their residents. What's missing also may be more subtle, especially for viewers who wear the blinders of their own times, circumstances, or expectations. For example, viewers of today might readily notice the absence of people of color in the 1959 Oldsmobile ad. An interesting study might investigate what types of magazines originally carried this ad, whether their

Here today...

Figure 14.11 Photograph Using a Missing Element to Convey a Message. *Source:* Public Service Announcement, Americans for National Parks

readers recognized what was missing, and whether (and, if so, how) Oldsmobiles were also advertised in publications aimed at Asian, African, or Spanish-speaking Americans.

Language

Just as you examine figures, colors, and shapes in an image, so you need to examine its words, phrases, and sentences to interpret what it suggests. Does its language provide information, generate an emotional response,

Figure 14.12 Public-Service Advertisement Showing Wordplay. *Source:* Design for Communication: Conceptual Graphic Design Basics

or do both? Do its words repeat a sound or concept, signal a comparison (such as a "new, improved" product), carry sexual overtones, issue a challenge, or offer a definition or philosophy of life? The words in the center of the Oldsmobile ad in Figure 14.7 (p. 293) associate the car with a leisurely, affluent lifestyle. On the other hand, VW's "Think small" ad in Figure 14.6 turns compactness into a goal, a desirable quality in a car and, by extension, in life.

Frequently advertisements employ wordplay—lighthearted or serious—to get their messages across. Consider the public-service advertisement in Figure 14.12, created by a graphic-design student. This ad features a play on the word *tolerance,* which is scrambled on the chalkboard so that the letters in the center read *learn.* The chalkboard, a typical classroom feature, suggests that tolerance is a basic lesson to be learned. Also, the definition of tolerance at the bottom of the ad is much like other definitions students might look up in a dictionary. (It reads, "The capacity for, or practice of, recognizing or respecting the behavior, beliefs, opinions, practices, or rights of others, whether agreeing with them or not.")

Wordplay can also challenge viewers' preconceptions about an image. The billboard in Figure 14.13 shows a romantic—indeed, seductive—scene. The sophisticated couple gaze deeply into each other's eyes as the man kisses

Figure 14.13 Billboard Showing Wordplay. *Source:* Photograph by Bill Aron, PhotoEdit

the woman's hand. However, the verbal exchange undermines that intimate scene and viewers' expectations about what happens next. Instead of a similar compliment in response to "Your scent is intoxicating," the billboard makes plain its antismoking position with the reply: "Yours is carcinogenic." In just seven words, the billboard counters the suave, romantic image of smoking with the reality of smelly, cancer-causing tobacco smoke.

Signs and Symbols

Signs and symbols, such as product logos, are images or words that communicate key messages. In the Oldsmobile ad in Figure 14.7 (p. 293), the product logo doubles as the phrase that introduces the description of the 1959 model. Sometimes a product logo alone may be enough, as in the Hershey chocolate company's holiday ads that include little more than a single Hershey's Kiss.

Themes

The theme of an image is not the same as its plot. When you identify the plot, you identify the story that is told by the image. When you identify the theme, on the other hand, you explain what the image is about. An ad for a diamond ring may tell the story of a man surprising his wife with a ring on their twenty-fifth wedding anniversary, but the advertisement's theme could be sex, romance, commitment, or some other concept. Similarly, the theme of a soft-drink ad might be competition, community, compassion, or individualism. A painting of the ocean might be about cheerfulness, fear, or loneliness.

Through a close reading, you can unearth clues and details to support your interpretation of the theme and convince others of its merit. For example, when you first glance at the image in Figure 14.14, it appears to illustrate a recipe for a tasty margarita. However, the list of ingredients suggests a tale of too many drinks and a drunk-driving accident after running a red light. Instead of promoting an alcoholic beverage or promising relaxing fun, this public-service announcement challenges the assumption that risky behavior won't carry consequences. Its text counters its suggestive image and reminds viewers of its theme — that well-being comes not from alcohol-fueled confidence but from responsible choices.

Figure 14.14 Poster Conveying a Theme.
Source: U.S. Department of Transportation/Ad Council

VISUAL ANALYSIS CHECKLIST
Interpreting the Meaning of an Image

☐ What general feeling do you get from looking at the image? What mood does it create? How does it create this mood?

☐ What sociological, political, economic, or cultural attitudes are reflected?

☐ What language is included in the image? How does the language function?

☐ What signs and symbols can you identify? What role do these play?

☐ What theme or themes can you identify in the image?

Learning by Doing Interpreting Meaning

Working with a classmate or small group, continue analyzing the image you selected for the activity on page 289. Examine one of its major characteristics — such as feeling or mood, attitude, language, signs or symbols, or theme — to interpret what the image might mean. Share your conclusions with your class or another group in a brief oral report or an online posting.

Learning from Another Writer: Visual Analysis

Because visual images surround us in print, on television, in theaters, and on the Web, you may be asked in many courses to respond to them and to analyze them, concentrating on persuasive, cultural, historical, sociological, or other qualities. Rachel Steinhaus analyzed a television commercial to investigate how advertisements persuade us to buy.

Rachel Steinhaus   **Student Analysis of an Advertisement**

"Life, Liberty, and the Pursuit"

The television commercial for the 2008 Cadillac CTS, featuring the star Kate   1
Walsh, epitomizes a car advertisement that focuses not on the vehicle itself, but on
the ideas that the company wants to associate with its product. Rather than focusing on the power and features of the car, the commercial emphasizes the ideas of
sex, social status, freedom, and Americanism, wrapping the car in a shroud of social
contradictions and ideals. Viewers are enticed to see the car as more than a means of
transportation. This other image of the car as a sexual object is what resonates most
clearly with viewers as it illustrates how the ad manipulates their emotions and
ideas in order to sell the product.

This commercial begins with the word *Cadillac* scrawled across a view of a city   2
with the lights creating long stretches across the screen, as though the viewer is in
a car traveling quickly down the street. This effect, the illusion of fast motion, is
maintained throughout the commercial. Kate Walsh, star of the television shows
Private Practice and *Grey's Anatomy*, then lists a number of the car's optional features, from a pop-up navigation system to sunroofs and 40G hard drives, saying
that those opportunities are not what are important "in today's luxury game" (Cadillac). The ad continues to show different aspects of the car as Kate Walsh reveals
what she presumably believes is the most important quality in a car: "When you
turn your car on, does it return the favor?" (Cadillac). A few more images show the
sleek car driving through the city and a tunnel, and then the name of the car, the
phrase "Life, Liberty, and the Pursuit," and the Cadillac logo appear on the screen
sequentially.

The most prominent aspect of this ad is its focus on the automobile as a sex   3
symbol, which is most blatantly expressed by the line in the commercial, "When you
turn it on, does it return the favor?" (Cadillac). This colloquial phrase clearly sends
the message that cars that are not sexy are inferior to the 2008 CTS. The phrase also
personifies the vehicle itself, giving it the capability to turn someone on, which is
generally a human action. This use of personification fits with the idea presented in
"The New Citroen," where Barthes describes the automobile as "humanized art" (89).
The car may be a product with a particular function, but it is designed to look appealing while also having human qualities that allow people to be more emotionally
attached to their car than the average product.

Kate Walsh reinforces the sexual ideas connected to the car in this commercial.   4
Her attire, a dress and heels, is clearly chosen to provide sex appeal. The camera
shots, angled to show her looking over the steering wheel as she delivers the end of
the line and to show her foot as she hits the accelerator in her strappy heels, objec-
tify her as a source of sex appeal (Garfield). Her celebrity status also influences the
viewer's idea of what it would mean to own the car. Although the car's available
features are casually listed, making Cadillac appear modest about its technology

and luxury embellishments, Kate Walsh places the focus on the prospective owner's status. Simply attaching the name of a celebrity to a car is enough to raise interest for some viewers as they imagine themselves owning something that a rich and successful star also enjoys. The combination of Walsh's stardom and her sex appeal becomes the main focus of this advertisement.

In addition to these strong sexual and status connotations, the commercial   5
emphasizes the idea that this car is a solid American product. The tagline at the end of the commercial, "Life, Liberty, and the Pursuit" (Cadillac) is a reference to the well-known line of the Declaration of Independence, automatically connecting the Cadillac CTS to patriotism. Even without finishing the phrase, this added plug connects supporting one's country to buying an American-made Cadillac 2008 CTS. The ad assumes that the typical American viewer will automatically insert the words "of happiness" to complete the phrase and also connect buying a CTS with furthering their own "pursuit of happiness." The context of the phrase within the Declaration of Independence is also important because it describes our inalienable rights, therefore connecting the thought that buying this car is the right of an American.

The open-ended phrase, however, also lends itself to interpretation as a literal   6
statement, alluding to the idea that the Cadillac CTS will give one the freedom to pursue whatever one wishes. In a physical sense, the driver can use the CTS horsepower to pursue other, "lesser" cars. On the other hand, the emotional message is that the driver can pursue different dreams and lifestyles because of the reputation and self-image that the CTS affords. This second interpretation relates well to the celebrity power that Kate Walsh brings to the ad.

The freedom to follow one's dreams goes hand in hand with the freedom of the   7
road that this advertisement conveys. As Walsh goes speeding down a tunnel, nothing inhibits her progress. However, Böhm and the other authors of "Impossibilities of Automobility" see things in a much more realistic light. Both the congestion created by the infrastructure required to support automobiles and our reliance on cars make driving far from pleasurable, according to the article. Driving is often marked by frustration and danger, rather than absolute freedom. Cadillac's commercial, however, ignores these facts, instead showing off speed by the blurred lights as the car flies by and giving Kate Walsh the freedom to go wherever she wishes.

Cadillac's commercial promotes the 2008 CTS without much focus on the car's   8
actual features. Instead, the ad uses appeals to sex, celebrity, freedom, and Americanism. Cadillac is proud to attach its name to a car that could mean so much to the life of the viewer, and the Cadillac logo appears in the commercial no less than six times. Even this constant repetition of the brand name takes away from the car itself, as its name, CTS, is mentioned only once. Despite a lack of focus on the actual vehicle, the advertiser assumes that our culture responds well to the appeals to sex, status, freedom, and patriotism that the automobile industry chooses to show in ads like this one.

Works Cited

Barthes, Roland. "The New Citroen." *Mythologies*. Trans. Annette Lavers. 1957. New York: Hill-Farrar, 2001. 88–90. Print.

Böhm, Steffen, Campbell Jones, Chris Land, and Matthew Paterson. "Impossibilities of Automobility." *Against Automobility*. Ed. Böhm, Jones, Land, and Paterson. Oxford: Wiley-Blackwell, 2006. 1–16. Print.

Cadillac. Advertisement. Web. 8 Mar. 2009. http://www.youtube.com/watch?v=jkEw1rsBUak>.

Garfield, Bob. "Taking Cadillac from Stodgy to Sexy: Kate Walsh." *Advertising Age* 1 Oct. 2007. Web. 8 Mar. 2009.

Questions to Start You Thinking

Meaning

1. How does Steinhaus say that the Cadillac ad sells cars?
2. What selling points does Kate Walsh add to the commercial? What does the wording from the Declaration of Independence add?

Writing Strategies

3. Where does Steinhaus introduce her thesis and her major supporting points?
4. How does Steinhaus ensure that readers know enough about the advertisement to follow her discussion?
5. How does Steinhaus help her audience follow her paper?
6. What different kinds of support does Steinhaus draw from her sources?

Learning by Writing

The Assignment: Analyzing a Visual Representation

Find a print or online advertisement that uses an image to promote a product, service, or nonprofit group. Study the ad carefully, using the three Visual Analysis checklists (pp. 289, 295, and 300) to help you observe the characteristics of the image and interpret its meaning. Write an essay analyzing how the ad uses its visual elements to persuade viewers to accept its message. Include a copy of the ad with your essay or supply a link to it. If your instructor approves, you may select a brochure, flyer, graphic, photo essay, work of art, campus sculpture, campus landmark, or other visual option for analysis.

Facing the Challenge   Analyzing an Image

The major challenge that writers face when analyzing an image is to state a clear thesis about how the image creates its impact and then to support that thesis with relevant detail. Although you may analyze the many details that an image includes, you will need to select and group those that support your thesis in order to develop a successful essay. If you try to pack in too many details, you are likely to distract your audience and bury your main point. On the other hand, if you include too few, your case may seem weak. In addition, you need to select and describe your details carefully so that they persuasively, yet fairly, confirm your points about the image.

Generating Ideas

Browse through print or online publications to gather several possibilities—ads that make clear appeals to viewers. Look for ads that catch your eye and promise rich detail for analysis.

As you consider how an ad tries to attract a viewer's attention, try several approaches. For example, think about its purpose and the audience likely to view the ad where it is published or circulated. Consider the same appeals you might identify in written or spoken texts: its logical appeal to the mind, its emotional appeal to the heart, and its ethical appeal, perhaps to trust in the product or sponsor. Look also for the specific visual components discussed in this chapter—the elements that guide a viewer's attention, develop the ad's persuasive potential, and convey its meaning.

DISCOVERY CHECKLIST

☐ What is the overall meaning and impact of the ad?

☐ How do the ad's visual elements contribute to its persuasiveness?

☐ Which elements appeal most strongly to viewers?

☐ What main points about the ad seem most important? Which details support each point most clearly and fairly?

Planning, Drafting, and Developing

Begin working on a thesis that states how the advertisement tries to attract and influence viewers. For example, you might clarify a consistent persuasive appeal used in major components of the ad, or you might show how several components work together to persuade particular viewers.

WORKING THESIS   The dog food ad has photos of puppies to interest animal lovers.

IMPROVED   The Precious Pooch dog food advertisement uses photos of cuddly puppies to appeal to dog owners.

MORE PRECISE   The Precious Pooch dog food advertisement shows carefully designed photos of cuddly puppies to soften the hearts and wallets of devoted dog owners.

Point out the Details. Identify details—and explain their significance—so that you guide your audience to and through your supporting evidence. Help your readers see exactly which visual elements create an impression, solidify an appeal, or connect with a viewer as you maintain that they do. Avoid general description for its own sake, but supply enough relevant description to make your points clear.

Organize Support for Your Thesis. As you state your thesis more precisely, analyze the position it expresses by breaking it down into main points. Note each main point, and then list the relevant supporting detail from the ad that can clarify and develop each point.

Open and Conclude Effectively. Begin by introducing to your audience both the ad and your thesis about it. Describe the ad briefly but clearly so that your readers start off with an overall understanding of its structure and primary features. State your thesis equally clearly so that your readers know how you view the ad's persuasive strategy. Use your conclusion to pull together your main points and confirm your thesis.

Revising and Editing

Exchange drafts with your peers to learn what is—or isn't—clear to someone else who is not immersed in your ad. Then revise as needed.

REVISION CHECKLIST

☐ Have you briefly described the ad as you open your essay?

☐ Have you stated a clear thesis about how the ad tries to persuade its audience?

☐ Have you identified specific visual features and details that support your view?

☐ Do you need to add more detail about the figures, action, or design of the ad?

☐ Do you need to elaborate on the feeling, attitude, theme, or other meaning conveyed?

☐ Have you moved smoothly between each main point about the effectiveness of the ad and the supporting detail from the ad that demonstrates the point?

After you have revised your visual analysis, check the grammar, word choice, punctuation, and mechanics—then correct any problems you find.

For more help, find the relevant checklist sections in the Quick Editing Guide on p. A-36. Turn also to the Quick Format Guide beginning on p. A-1.

EDITING CHECKLIST

☐ Have you used adjectives and adverbs correctly to present the ad?   A7

☐ Have you placed modifiers correctly so that your descriptions are clear?   B1

☐ Have you used correct manuscript format for your paper?

Learning from Another Writer: Visual Essay

Besides responding to visual representations designed by others, you might have opportunities to create your own series of images and text. Visual essays can record an event or situation, or they can support an observation, interpretation, or position, usually through a combination of image and text or a multimedia text incorporating sound or video. In his prize-winning documentary visual essay, Josh Birnbaum gathered twelve images—five presented here—to capture the spirit of the national wheelchair basketball tournament.

Josh Birnbaum   **Student Photo Essay**

Uphill Battle

Illinois wheelchair basketball players practice for a tournament game as head coach Mike Frogley watches at Oklahoma State University in Stillwater, Okla., on Friday, March 14, 2008.

To ward off boredom on the bus, from left, Aaron Pike, Lars Spenger, Brian Bell, and Matt Buchi play Family Feud on a laptop during the trip to their national tournament on Wednesday, March 12, 2008.

Steve Serio fixes his hair while sitting atop a counter in his hotel room after a wheelchair basketball tournament in Whitewater, Wisc., on March 18, 2006.

Lars Spenger attempts to shoot over Wisconsin-Whitewater defenders during the national championship game on Saturday, March 15, 2008.

From left, Joey Gugliotta, Matt Buchi, Tom Smurr, and Lars Spenger celebrate after Illinois defeated Wisconsin-Whitewater, 63-58, to win the national championship in Stillwater, Okla., on Saturday, March 15, 2008.

Questions to Start You Thinking

Meaning

1. What story does the selection of images tell?

2. Why do you think that the photographer arranged the images out of chronological order? If the first image had been left out, would your understanding of the selection have changed?

Writing Strategies

3. How would you describe the nature of Birnbaum's written text? Why do you think that he uses this approach?

4. What is the effect of Birnbaum's title for his essay?

Additional Writing Assignments

1. **Visual Activity.** Select an image such as an advertisement; a visual from a magazine or image database; or a CD, DVD, or videocassette cover. Make notes on its "literal" characteristics (see pp. 289–95). Then, bring your image and notes to class. In small groups of three to five students, share your images and discuss your literal readings.

2. **Visual Activity.** In a small group, pick one or two of the images that the group members analyzed for activity 1. Ask each group member, in turn, to suggest possible interpretations of the images. (For guidance, see pp. 296–99.) What different interpretations do group members suggest? How do you account for their differences? Share your findings with the rest of the class.

3. **Visual Assignment.** Find a Web page that evokes a strong emotional response. Study the page closely, observing its characteristics and interpreting its meaning. Write an essay in which you explain the techniques by which the page evokes your emotional response. If appropriate, you also may want to define a standard for its type of Web page and evaluate the site in terms of that standard. Include a link to the page with your essay.

4. **Visual Assignment.** Volkswagen continues to produce thought-provoking advertisements like the one shown in Figure 14.6 on page 292. Search online for some of the company's recent ads, or check those out at <www.volksfolks.org/gallery/commercials/>. View one or two of these advertisements, considering such features as their stories or "plots"; the

For criteria for visual analysis, review this chapter. For more on comparison and contrast (Ch. 7), evaluation (Ch. 11), or other relevant situations, turn to Part 2.

choice of figures, settings, and images; the angles from which subjects are filmed; and any text messages included. Based on your analysis of the ads, decide what message you think that the company wants to communicate about its cars. In an essay, describe this message, the audience that Volkswagen seems to be aiming for, and the artistic choices in the ads to appeal to this audience.

5. **Visual Assignment.** Compile a design notebook. Over several weeks, collect ten or twelve images that appeal to you. Your teacher may assign a genre or theme, or you may wish to choose examples of a particular genre such as snack food advertisements, portraits, photographs of campus landmarks, or landscape paintings by different artists. On the other hand, your collection might revolve around a theme, such as friendship, competition, community, or romance. As you collect these images, "read" each one closely, and write short responses explaining your reactions. At the end of the collection period, choose two or three images. Write an essay in which you compare or contrast them, perhaps analyzing how they illustrate the same genre, convey a theme, or appeal to different audiences.

6. **Visual Assignment.** Prepare your own visual essay on a topic that engages or concerns you. Decide on the purpose and audience for your essay. Take, select, and arrange photographs that will help to achieve this purpose. (Use the guidelines in this chapter to help you evaluate your own photos.) Add concise complementary text to the photos. Ask your classmates to review your essay to help you reach the clearest and most effective final form.

7. **Visual Assignment.** Visit a music store, and find a CD cover whose design interests you. Make notes about design choices such as its prominent element and focal point, the use of color and imagery, and the use of typography. Based on the design, try to predict what kind of music is on the CD. If the store has CD-listening stations, try to listen to a track or two. Did the music match your expectations based on the CD design? If you were the CD designer, would you have made any different artistic choices? Write a brief essay discussing your observations, and attach a copy of the CD cover, if possible. (You might be able to print it out from the Web.) As an alternative assignment, listen to some music that's new to you, and design a CD cover for it, applying the elements described in this chapter. Describe in a brief paper the visual elements you would include on your CD cover. If you wish, sketch your design for the cover, using colored pencils or markers or pasting in images or type.

8. **Visual Assignment.** Using the advice in this chapter, analyze an episode in a television series, a film, a multimodal blog, a YouTube or other video, a television or video commercial, a campus theater or dance production, or a similar production. Analyze the visual elements of your selection, and also evaluate it in terms of criteria that you explain to your audience.

Perhaps you are an experienced online writer—constantly texting your friends, chatting with your family, updating your social-network page, blogging, and commenting on YouTube videos. On the other hand, perhaps you need help from your co-workers or from younger or more experienced classmates to figure out how to master new online tasks. Whatever your background, you—like most college students—are already an electronic writer and increasingly likely to be an online writer.

Many college classes are now offered in three formats, all likely to expect online writing:

- face-to-face classes, meeting at a set time and place but possibly with online communication and paper submissions
- online classes with synchronous (scheduled at the same time) or asynchronous (unscheduled, but available when convenient) virtual meetings, discussions, activities, and paper exchanges and submissions
- hybrid (or blended) classes with both in-person and online meetings, discussions, activities, and paper exchanges and submissions

In addition, any of these three class formats may rely on the campus course management system (CMS), a Web-accessible environment where class participants can access information, communicate with each other, and post papers or other assignments. This chapter will help you understand likely online activities and responsibilities in your current course, whatever its format.

Getting Started with Campus and Course Basics

Many schools provide an orientation booklet or program for new or returning students as well as directions or tutorials for accessing and using online campus resources.

CAMPUS FACILITIES CHECKLIST

☐ Where and when do your face-to-face classes meet? If you come to campus only for a few hybrid course meetings, do you have a map and know where to park or find a transit stop?

☐ How do you access the campus e-mail system, your instructor's Web page, your textbook's Web site, the online library, any virtual labs, and other campus resources?

☐ Where is the campus writing center? What services does it provide, and how do you access them? How does it provide assistance: chats or messages, online responses to drafts, telephone calls, face-to-face meetings, or other formats? What should you bring to a consultation?

☐ How do you reach the campus technology center both online and by phone if you have trouble connecting? Is help available 24/7 or only during daytime hours on weekdays?

College instructors generally supply a syllabus, course policies, assignments, assessment criteria, and other information for each course. Especially for online work, remember these two essential survival skills: read first, and then ask questions.

COURSE EXPECTATIONS CHECKLIST

☐ What types of writing are you expected to do? Where can you access the writing assignments and the course schedule or calendar?

☐ What are the deadlines for your essay drafts? What are the deadlines for submitting in-class work or posting online activities? Have you set up a calendar for the term, listing what's due when for all your classes?

☐ What are the directions for posting or submitting assignments as e-mail attachments?

☐ Have you checked for changes in the schedule or syllabus? If face-to-face sessions are canceled due to a campus issue, how do you contact your instructor and classmates online?

☐ How extensively are you expected to participate online? Will participation be measured by time online, frequency or number of comments, length of postings, quality of exchanges, or objective quiz answers? What online activity will the CMS track, and what will your instructor assess?

☐ Have you browsed through your course resources — required, recommended, posted, or linked?

☐ How and when can you reach your instructor online, by phone, or in person? What response time or availability might you expect?

Whatever the format of your course, you are expected to begin with or to gain technical skills sufficient to meet course requirements involving technology. Find out how to tap campus resources for immediate crises, self-help tutorials, and technology consultation.

TECHNOLOGY CHECKLIST

☐ What programs or software will you need for your course? For example, will you need to use Microsoft Office or to read pdf files? Have you installed what's needed?

☐ What computer skills will your course require? Do you know how to cut and paste sections of text to move them, how to add comments to someone else's paper, how to read comments added to your draft, how to attach files to e-mail messages, or how to answer questions like these using your software's Help feature?

☐ How are you expected to exchange papers with peer editors or to transmit papers to your instructor? What file format (such as .doc, .docx, or .rtf) should you use? How do you use Save and Save As to "translate" your files to that format?

☐ How do you access and use your campus CMS (such as eCollege, Black-board, or a local system)? Where can you find a tutorial that explains how to navigate the system?

☐ How do you access the online locations where you will post responses or interact with others — content areas, discussion boards or a forum, blogs, social networks, comment or note options, or other spaces?

☐ Will you need to use other technology — for example, text messaging or Twitter — during your course? If so, where can you get help with it on campus?

Learning by Doing 🔲 Identifying Online Writing Expectations

Review your course syllabus and assignments. List each type of online writing that you will need to do. Write down any problems or questions you can antici-pate. Then map out a plan to begin solving or answering those issues.

Class Courtesy

All of your classes — face-to-face, online, or hybrid — have expectations for conduct and procedures. Some rules, such as keeping food and beverages out of a campus computer lab or laptop-cart classroom, obviously protect the equipment for everyone's benefit. Although explicit rules may vary by campus or instructor, conduct yourself in ways that demonstrate your attentiveness, courtesy, and consideration for others. During a face-to-face class, avoid texting or taking mobile phone calls. When technology problems inevitably arise, ask about solutions instead of blaming the online environment for snags. Online, consider both your tone and level of formality. Use the relative anonymity of online participation to advance your own intellectual growth, not to make negative comments at the expense of others. Think twice before you post each message so you don't regret a hasty attack, a bad joke, a personal revelation, or an emotional rant. If you are uncertain about what is appropriate, ask your instructor for guidelines, and observe the conventions of professional communication. Try to present yourself as — and actually to be — a thoughtful learner who treats others respectfully as colleagues in a learning community.

Online Ethics

Respect class or campus guidelines for online text exchanges with other students. Treat each other courteously and respectfully, address others in an appropriate classroom manner, and follow directions designed to protect each other's privacy and hard work.

In addition, find out whether your papers might be routinely or randomly submitted to a plagiarism-detection site. Be certain that you understand your campus rules about plagiarism and your instructor's directions about online group exchanges so that you do not confuse individual and collaborative work. Further, use sources carefully as you do online research:

- Distinguish your writing and your ideas from those of sources so that you avoid blurring or confusing the two.
- Keep track of sources so that you can credit their words and ideas accurately, following the style expected by your instructor.

For more about using sources, see the Quick Research Guide beginning on p. A-18.

- Respect intellectual property rights by asking permission and crediting your source if you integrate someone else's images or other media in your paper.

Learn the rules for your campus and class, whether it is face-to-face, hybrid, or online.

Learning by Doing 🎯 Making Personal Rules

Using brainstorming or mapping, develop the list of rules only you know that you need—rules that will bring out your best as an online student or online writer. For example, do you need a personal "rule" about checking for your USB drive, card, or portable hard drive after every computer session on campus so you don't lose your work? List your rules in an e-mail message to yourself. Then sum up the most important points in a tweet-length statement. (You can use your software's word count tool to limit this summary to the 140 characters allowed for a "tweet," the short message sent through Twitter.) If you wish, also embed your "rules" in your cell phone notepad for quick reference along with your online course PIN number, if needed. Return to standard English—using correct grammar, punctuation, capitalization, and complete words instead of abbreviations or shorthand—for material submitted to your instructor.

Common Online Writing Situations

The specific expectations for your college writing may be the same whether you hand in your printed paper during class, send the file to your instructor, or post your work in a CMS. However, some assignments might specify required, encouraged, or accepted online features such as links for references or multimedia components. For other online writing, consider the online conventions—the accepted practices your readers are likely to expect—and the class directions.

Messages to Your Instructor

Learning online requires a lot of communication. Because you aren't meeting—and communicating—face-to-face, you need to engage actively in other types of exchanges. First, welcome available communication by reading posted assignments and directions that advise you about how to meet expectations successfully. Next, initiate communication, asking specific questions online about what to do and how to do it.

When you e-mail your instructor with a question, practice respectful professional communication. Think about your audience—a hard-working teacher who probably posts many class materials and responds to many questions from students in different courses. You can guess that a busy instructor appreciates a direct question from a motivated student who wants help. Ask specific questions well before deadlines, and give your instructor plenty of time to reply. Consider your tone so that you sound polite, interested, and clear about what you need to know.

VAGUE	I don't know how to start this assignment.
SPECIFIC	I've listed my ideas in a scratch outline, but I'm not sure what you mean by . . .

If your class is using a CMS, send your message through that system (unless your instructor asks you to use his or her campus e-mail address). Right away your instructor will know which class you're in and, in a small composition class, recognize you by your first name. If you e-mail outside the CMS, send the message from your campus account, and use the subject line to identify the course name or number and your problem: Deadline for Comp 101 Reading or Question about Math 110 Study Guide.

If you are unsure how to address your instructor, begin with "Hello, Professor Welton" or "Hi, Ms. Welton," following the instructor's preference if known. Avoid too much informality, such as greeting your instructor with "Yo, Prof" or "Hiya, Chief," asking "Whatzup with the paper?" or closing with "Later." Conclude with your name (including your last name and a section number if the class is large). Proofread and spell-check your message before you send it so that your writing does not look hasty or careless.

Consider setting your message to return an automatic "read" confirmation — indicating that the recipient has opened the message — so that you do not need to e-mail again to check that the original message arrived. Avoid e-mailing from a personal account that might be mistaken for spam and blocked from the campus system. Remember that your instructor's relationship with you is professional, not social, so do not send social-networking invitations or forward messages about politics, religion, humorous stories, or other personal topics.

Learning by Doing 🗂 Finding a College Voice

Working with a small group in person or online, list at least a dozen popular greetings, closings, and other expressions currently part of your (or your friends') informal voice in text messaging, social networking, or other informal electronic communication. Translate each expression into a clear, polite version without abbreviations, shortcuts, or unconventional grammar — in short, a version appropriate for a message to an instructor in your "college" voice.

Learning from Other Writers: Messages to Your Instructor

Here are two requests sent to the students' instructor in an online composition class, one asking about how to cite an assigned reading and the other about the instructor's comments on a draft.

STUDENT QUESTION ABOUT AN ASSIGNMENT

From: Heather Church

Subject: Reading Response

Hi, Ms. Beauchene,

I want to make sure I am doing this assignment correctly. Is the source an online newspaper article? Also, I can't find out how to cite part of a sentence included in my response. If I quote "binge drinking," for example, do I have to say the page number next to it? I thought that I would cite this as if it is an article with no author. Is that correct?

Thank you.

Heather

STUDENT QUESTION ABOUT COMMENTS ON A DRAFT

From: Arthur Wasilewski

Subject: Comments on Last Paper

Hello, Professor Beauchene,

I would like to ask you a question about your corrections. You changed the last sentence of the last paragraph. I was wondering if you could explain the change. Is it something structural or grammatical? Or was it changed for the sake of style or flow?

Arthur

Questions to Start You Thinking

Meaning

1. Why is Heather Church contacting the instructor? What does she want to know?

2. Why is Arthur Wasilewski contacting the instructor? What does he want to know?

Writing Strategies

3. What impression on their instructor do you think that the students wanted to make? What features of their messages indicate this?

Learning by Doing 🔲 Contacting Your Instructor

Write an e-mail to your instructor requesting information. For example, you might have a question about requirements, assessment criteria for your first essay, procedures for activities such as timed quizzes, or policies such as penalties for late work. Clearly and briefly specify what you want to know. As you ask your question, also try to show your instructor that you are a thoughtful, hardworking learner. Exchange drafts with classmates to learn what they would suggest to make your question clearer or your tone more appropriate.

Online Profile

Because you may never meet your online classmates in person, you may be asked to post a brief online profile introducing yourself to the class. You also might be asked to interview a classmate so that each of you can post an introduction of the other. Such assignments are intended to increase online camaraderie. However, if you feel shy or wish to retain anonymity, cover suggested topics such as academic interests or writing experiences, but stick to general background with limited personal detail. If you prefer not to post a photograph of yourself, consider an image or icon of a pet, possession, or fa-vorite place. If the class already has much in common—for example, all in the same discipline or program—you might include your career plans. Avoid overly personal revelations, gushing enthusiasm, and clipped brevity.

The following profiles, illustrating a personal post and an interview, combine some personal background with academic and career interests.

From: LaTanya Nash

Subject: My Profile as a Future Nurse

After almost a month in the hospital when I was six, I knew that I wanted to be a nurse. That's when I found out how important nurses are to patients and how much they can add to a patient's recovery. I've had after-school and summer jobs in an assisted living center for seniors and a center for children with disabilities. Now that I'm starting college, I'm ready to work on my nursing degree. I'm glad to have this writing class because I've learned from my jobs how important it is for nurses to write clearly.

Learning by Doing 🖝 Posting a Personal Profile

Write a brief personal profile introducing yourself to your instructor and class-mates. Provide enough information about your college interests, background, or goals to give your audience a clear impression about you as a member of the class online learning community. (Avoid any confessional or overly personal reve-lations.) Consider adding a photo or an image representing you or your interests.

From: Lainie Costas

Subject: Interview of Tomas

After interviewing Tomas online, I want to introduce a classmate who has just started college this semester. He has been working since high school—doing everything from washing dishes to making pizzas. Now he's planning on getting a business degree to help him start his own restaurant. He already knows what employees need to do, but he wants to learn about things like business plans, finances, and advertising. Like me, he's a little worried about starting with a writing class, but I know from his messages that he has plenty of interesting things to say.

Learning by Doing 🖝 Introducing a Classmate

E-mail, chat, schedule an online telephone call using a Webcam, or talk in person with a classmate to learn about each other's background, interests, and expectations of the course. (If your instructor assigns the pairs or topics, follow those directions.) Using what you learn, write and post a professional message that introduces your classmate.

⬛

Online Threaded Discussions or Responses

When you add your response to a threaded discussion on a topic or a class reading blog, follow your instructor's directions and read the responses from classmates to clarify how to meet the assignment. Because everyone participating already understands the writing situation, you don't need to write a full introduction to the topic as you would in an essay. Instead, simply dive in as requested — for example, adding your thoughtful comments on a reading, identifying and explaining a key quotation from it, or reflecting on your own reading or writing processes. If you comment on a previous post, do so politely; clarify how your ideas differ without any personal criticism. Follow any length guidelines, and be sure to proofread and spell-check your post.

Learning from Other Writers: Threaded Discussion

The following string of messages begins with the instructor's explanation of the assignment — responding to an assigned reading in one of two specific ways — followed by a few selected responses of students. Notice how each writer responds personally but sticks to the focus by extending the "thread." Directions for other discussions might emphasize different ways of extending the thread — for example, responding specifically to a preceding comment, summarizing several comments and then adding to them, synthesizing and then advancing ideas, raising a different but relevant line of consideration, comparing or contrasting possible responses, tracing possible causes and effects, or other paths that apply your critical thinking skills.

STUDENT ONLINE THREADED DISCUSSION

Instructor Kathleen Beauchene and Students Cristina Berrios, Joshua Tefft, Leah Threats, Arthur Wasilewski, and Joel Torres

Discussion of Writing Processes

Message no. 2706

Author: Kathleen Beauchene (ENGL1010_600_Beauchene)

Date: Saturday, October 10, 2009 2:37pm

In the attached file, you will read about one author's writing process. In your post, you may either comment on a point he makes or share your own writing process, what works or doesn't work for you.

Message no. 2707

Author: Cristina Berrios

Date: Saturday, October 10, 2009 4:02pm

I find that the author's writing process is similar in many ways to how most write, but I do not always have the time to write and rewrite and organize and write and so on. . . . Of course I can see if you are a professional writer rewriting and making sure that your work can be produced to sell, but in my eyes I only need to make sure that my story is interesting, consecutive and progressive, and grammatically correct to the best of my ability. . . . Luckily I work in an office where I can interact closely with colleagues who are willing to listen to my "draft" (some of them are college students as well) and give me feedback.

Message no. 2708

Author: Joshua Tefft

Date: Saturday, October 10, 2009 4:43pm

My writing process, like most people's, is similar to what the author does, given I have a lot of time anyway. I really have trouble with not erasing initial drafts, that is, incomplete drafts. I always find myself too critical of my work before it is anywhere near the final stages. But I've begun to learn to receive outside criticism before I put my own on it; this usually gives me a more open-minded perspective on my writing. But I've realized it's a long process to get the results one wants.

Message no. 2709

Author: Leah Threats

Date: Saturday, October 10, 2009 11:49pm

My writing process includes a lot of thought process before I go anywhere near writing a first draft. Then I begin to write and reread it a few times while in the first paragraph, change wording, cut and paste all over the paper. Then I will move on to the middle of the paper, make sure my introduction has enough to it, and the mid section is full of "beef." Then in the ending, I try to make sure I don't leave the writer thinking, What else? . . . I do take the time to make sure I am not shortchanging my reader. As a person who LOVES to read, I want to be able to draw the reader into whatever it is I am writing to them.

Message no. 2711

Author: Arthur Wasilewski

Date: Sunday, October 11, 2009 1:41pm

I approach the writing process with a shoot-from-the hip mentality. Whatever comes to my head first is usually the right idea. I'll think about the idea throughout the whole day or week, and transcribe it to paper after I've gone through a few mental iterations of my original idea.

Message no. 2713

Author: Joel Torres

Date: Sunday, October 11, 2009 8:21pm

After reading this attachment I realize there are some things I sort of start to do in my own writing process, but stop halfway or do not go through thoroughly. I have used the outline idea from time to time. I should go into more depth and organize the ideas in my papers better in the future though. The whole concept of sleeping between drafts does not sit well with me. I find that when I sit down and write a paper, it is best when I dedicate a couple of hours and get into the "zone" and let the ideas flow through me. If the paper is a research paper, I usually do best when I type it directly onto a word processor. When the assignment is an essay or something along the lines of a written argument or a literary work, I like to handwrite and then go back and type it after. Distractions for me are a huge issue; TV, other Web sites, and just lack of focus definitely hurt my writing and are obstacles I must overcome every time a written assignment is due.

Questions to Start You Thinking

Meaning

1. What did the instructor ask the class to do in the discussion?

2. Highlight or jot down a few key words to sum up the approach of each student in the threaded discussion.

Writing Strategies

3. In what ways do the students show that they are focused on the "thread" that connects their contributions to the discussion?

Learning by Doing 🎯 Joining a Threaded Discussion

Read the preceding sample online discussion of writing processes. Write your own addition to the string, explaining your own process—what works or doesn't work.

Course Management Systems (CMS) and Other Online Tools

Your class, whatever its format, may rely on your own online experience, the features of your campus CMS, or other online options for communication and interaction. In a face-to-face class, you may go online primarily to submit papers, send messages to classmates, or search for library or Web resources. In a hybrid or an online class, your instructor will explain what and how you are expected to contribute: for example, posting a brief profile to introduce yourself to the class, writing three reflective blog entries about your writing processes, adding at least two postings to each threaded discussion about an assigned reading, drafting (for peer response) and then revising four assigned essays, and so forth.

In addition, your instructor may provide cautions about sharing personal or confessional information, especially because your CMS or campus may retain indefinite access to class materials. Your instructor also may offer advice (or assessment criteria) about productive topics to pursue or effective ways to develop your postings or papers. Whatever the friendliness or informality of your class, its online exchanges, comments, and papers will concentrate on exploring and learning about an academic subject.

Course Management Systems

Here's a common — maybe the most common — question asked by online students: What am I supposed to do? And here's a common — maybe the most common — question asked by online instructors: Have you read the course syllabus and schedule? The CMS is the first place to look when you don't know what's due when, how to write the next assignment, or what reading everybody else is doing. To help you navigate, your campus may provide an introductory tutorial for students and a helpline for problems.

If your campus provides and supports a CMS, this efficient and accessible Web-based resource can consolidate all essential class information and coordinate several kinds of interactions. A CMS can accompany an established face-to-face course, substitute for face-to-face meetings in case of campus closure, orchestrate the interactions of an online course, or support the variety of a hybrid. Although your campus CMS has its own design and features, each instructor begins with the shell and then adds the material needed for a specific course. As each instructor selects and arranges the components, the course takes on its own look.

As a student, you typically have individual access to your scores and grades, small-group access to any specific topic or project, and general access to the course information and materials. These materials are crucial. The syllabus lays out the structure of the course. The assignments explain exactly what to do and when. The policies may review campus and class rules about important matters ranging from attendance to zero-tolerance codes of conduct. The class schedule sets deadlines for submitting assignments or taking quizzes, deadlines often enforced by the CMS shutting down access to a drop box or activity. The campus CMS calendar supplies institutional deadlines and policies on incomplete work. Read these materials carefully so you are not surprised about what's expected.

Common Interactive CMS Options

CMS Options	Typical Functions	Components Your Class Might Use
Course Materials	Handy essential information, available online for reference anytime during the course	Course syllabus and calendar, required and background readings, online reserve readings coordinated with the library, optional sources and links, reading or writing assignments, directions for activities, class and lecture notes, study guides, assessment criteria, online tutorials, podcasts, videos, and Webliographies
Course Communication	Convenient and varied systems for course messages and discussions, limited to class members	Convenient e-mail (to the whole class, a small group, or an individual), notices about changes or cancellations, text messaging, social networking, chats, threaded discussions, paper exchanges, a comment system, and a whiteboard for graphics or drawings
Class Profiles	Individual introductions posted for all the class to read, establishing each person's online personality and presence	Descriptions of the individual's background, interests, or expectations of the class, possibly with an option for a photo or other personal representation; possibly CMS reports on whole-class patterns to allow for timely improvements
Threaded Discussions	Series of related exchanges focused on a specific course topic, question, or issue (open to all classmates or only to a group)	Questions and comments exploring and thinking critically about a topic along with any subthreads that evolve during discussion
Text Exchanges and Responses	Drafts and final papers posted for response from other students or for assessment by the instructor	Overall responses to the strengths, weaknesses, and effectiveness of the paper as well as detailed comments noted in the file; possibly options for general or individual feedback requests

Learning by Doing 📷 Exploring Your CMS

Figure out how to accomplish all of the following activities that your CMS offers.
If these tasks are challenging for you, ask for help. If these are easy for you, iden-
tify and explain to your classmates another useful activity that is not listed here.
Report your discoveries, problems, or questions in a message to your class.

> contact the CMS or student help desk or go through the CMS tutorial
> access the CMS class calendar
> write and post your own comment or your response to someone else's
>   comment
> spell-check a message or discussion response
> change the settings for viewing discussions (such as by date, topic, or sender)

send an e-mail from within the CMS to the entire class and to a small group

submit an assignment to a peer for response and then to your instructor

add a journal note or blog entry

search the course material for a key term

find the directions or tutorial for taking online quizzes

view your own grades

Other Online Tools

Some online activities can be organized within either a CMS or a specialized tool or application. Others might be available only separately. If you have trouble accessing or using a specialized tool, don't procrastinate and fall behind; instead, ask for help right away. In addition, pay attention to your instructor's explanations of the activities expected; these explanations often reveal the purposes and goals — what you are expected to do and why.

File Management

Electronic submission of papers is convenient, saving trees as well as time. Writing online has immediacy — potentially a 24/7 audience, instantly ready to read and respond to your writing. On the other hand, online college writing also requires longer-term planning, especially to organize and manage electronic files in classes that encourage revising drafts or developing a portfolio.

For sample pages, see the Quick Format Guide (pp. A-1–A-17). For sample source citations in MLA and APA style, see the Quick Research Guide, pp. A-18–A-35.

Using File Templates. No matter how you submit a college essay or research paper, instructors generally expect you to use MLA, APA, or some other academic style commonly used in the field. These styles specify page layout, font style and size, paragraph indentations, formats for citations, and many other details that determine both the look and the approach of the paper.

Instead of treating each paper as a separate item, set up a template for any style you are required to use in a specific class or field of study. Check your software menu for Tools, File, or Format or go to Help for directions on making a template, a basic paper format with built-in design features. Refine the details, using the samples and checklists in this book as well as your instructor's directions and comments about the format of your drafts. Then, when you begin a new draft, call up your template, and start writing. The template will automatically format the features you have customized. If you need several templates, keep them clearly labeled in a template folder.

Common Interactive Online Options

Online Options	Typical Functions	Applications Your Class Might Use
Class Blogs	Individual or collaborative Web logs or journals for a sequence of public (whole class) or private (small group or instructor) comments on a topic or theme	Regular comments to encourage writing, reflecting, exploring, analyzing, and sharing ideas that also could evolve into more fully developed written pieces
Class Wiki	An encyclopedia of collaborative entries explaining terms relevant to a course topic or issue	An existing or evolving set of essential key terms, activities, concepts, issues, or events
Class Ning	Private social network for class members (as a whole or in special-interest groups) to share information and exchange ideas	List of relevant campus or community events, participant profiles, and a forum or blog to comment on key topics
Text Exchanges	Texts submitted for response from others through messages with attached files (to use software to mark changes and add comments) or a real-time document-sharing Web site (to use the site's comment system)	Overall comments on strengths, weaknesses, and effectiveness as well as suggestions noted in the file (perhaps color coded by respondent); one-on-one exchanges, such as questions and answers, about a draft
Audio Applications	Recorded spoken comments, including responses to drafts, in-person group discussions, presentation or podcast practices, podcasts, course lectures, or interviews	Verbal comments to strengthen personal connections, recorded by the instructor or peers for one student or a group; class interviews of content or research experts (authors, librarians, faculty)
Visual Applications	Organized and archived photos, videos, Web shots, or other images	Visual materials to prompt, inform, illustrate texts, or add to presentation software
Course Resources	Public social-network page, department Web page, program resources, library Web site, open-source materials, online writing lab (OWL), other Web pages	Opportunities for building a supportive online academic group and accessing recommended course resources

Learning by Doing 🔲 Preparing a Template

Set up a template for your papers for your composition class or your portfolio. Follow your instructor's directions about the academic style to follow and any special features to add. Turn to the campus computer lab or writing center if you need help preparing the template or figuring out what it should include.

Naming and Organizing Files. Check your syllabus or assignments to find out whether you need to follow a certain system or pattern for naming your files. Such systems help an instructor to see at a glance who wrote which assignment for which class: Lopez Recall 101Sec2. If you are expected to save or submit your drafts or build a portfolio, you will want to add a draft number, draft code (noting a first draft or a later revision), or a date: Lopez Recall 3, Lopez Recall Dft, Lopez Recall Rev, or Lopez Recall 9-14-10. Remember that your downloaded essay will be separated from your e-mail message; be certain that the file label alone will be clear.

Even if you are not required to submit your drafts, it's a good idea to save each major stage as you develop the paper instead of always reworking the same file. If you set up a folder for your course, perhaps with subfolders for each assignment, your writing records will be organized in a central location. Then you can easily go back to an earlier draft and restore something you cut or show your development to your instructor if asked to do so. You also have a handy backup if you lose a draft or forget to save it to your flash drive (or forget the flash drive itself).

Learning by Doing 🔲 Organizing Your Files

Outline the main principles behind your system for managing files. If your system is random or disorganized, figure out a system that makes sense to you and keeps your writing for several courses well organized. Compare your system with those of a few classmates, and help each other to improve your plans. Then move your existing files into your new or refined system. Maintain your system by storing files where they belong and sticking to the pattern for naming and dating your files.

Inserting Comments. When you need to exchange files with other students for peer responses, use your software menu (Tools, Options, or Inserts), try its Help feature, or find a tutorial to learn how to use the class comment system — track-and-comment word-processing tools, CMS posts, or a document-sharing site with comment options. If the directions seem complicated, print the Help page, and refer to it as you learn the system.

A comment system typically allows you to use color to show cross-outs and additions or to add initials or color to identify comments in "balloons" in the margin. Less formal options include adding comments or a note at the end of a paragraph, highlighted in yellow. Be sure to send your peer response file on time with helpful suggestions.

COMMENT CHECKLIST

☐ For your class, how should you post or send a draft for peer or instructor review?

☐ How do you access Help or a tutorial about adding comments if you need advice?

☐ What do you do to turn the Comment function on and off?

☐ How do you add comments in the text and in balloons or boxes in the margins using the color that identifies you as a reader?

☐ What do you need to do to read, print, save, or delete comments?

☐ How do you access the file-exchange site your class uses?

☐ How do you record and identify your comments on other writers' papers?

☐ How do you retrieve your own draft with the comments of others?

Polishing Electronically. As you revise and edit a draft, use all your resources, online and off. Call up the assignment or syllabus. Review what is required and how it will be assessed. Reread any comments from your peers or instructor. Use the Find or Search menu to hunt for repeated errors or too many repetitions of a favorite word or transition. Use the spelling and grammar checkers in your software or CMS, even for short messages, so that you always present careful work. If your concentration slips, go offline: print out your draft and read it aloud.

Submitting Papers Online. It's usually easy to walk into a face-to-face class and hand in a printed paper. Online, you might hit snags—problems writing a transmittal message if your CMS or e-mail system is down, problems with a drop box or forum that closes early due to an error or power outage, problems attaching a file (or remembering to attach one), problems opening someone else's file. Try to avoid sending an assignment two minutes before the deadline because a time crunch may increase problems.

Many instructors will see "the computer ate my homework" as a problem you should have solved, not an acceptable excuse for late work. If you have trouble transmitting a file, send a short separate message to your instructor to explain how you are solving the problem, or ask your instructor to confirm the file's safe arrival. (Instructors are likely to prefer that you keep explanations and apologies to a minimum, concentrate on solutions, and use an automatic "read" reply to confirm that your message has been received.) If your computer has a problem, you are responsible for going to the lab or using another computer to submit your work on time. If your campus system is temporarily down, you are responsible for submitting your work as soon as access is restored.

No matter what software you use, "translate" your file to whatever format is required—possibly Word (.doc or .docx) but often Rich Text Format • (.rtf), a general format most word-processing software can read. Check your File menu for two different commands: Save (to save the file to the location where you routinely store your class files) and Save As (to save the file in a different format, to a different location, or with a different name). If you consistently add the date at the end of the file name, you will simplify finding and sending the most current version. If you use the same name or the same date for duplicate files in different formats, you also will know that they correspond. Once the correct file is properly formatted, attach it to your message. If your file is returned with comments from your instructor or classmates, give it a new name and date so that it does not replace your original copy.

Backing Up Your Files. No matter how tired or rushed you are, always save and back up your work, preferably using several methods. Use a backup card, portable drive, flash drive, smart stick, file storage site, or whatever is available and efficient for you. Make sure you label or identify your equipment with your name so that you could pull your drive out of the lost-and-found basket at the library or someone could arrange to return it to you. If you are working on a campus computer, carry your drive with you on a neck strap or clipped to your backpack so that your current work is always with you. If you are working on a major project with a tight deadline, attach major drafts to an e-mail to yourself. If you back up your files at home or in your room, do so every day. Then, if a file is damaged or lost, your hard drive fails during finals week, or you leave your drive at the library, you can still finish your writing assignments on time.

FILE CHECKLIST

☐ What academic style and paper format is expected in your class? Have you prepared a template or file format in this style?

☐ Have you saved the files that show your paper's development during several drafts? Have you named or dated them so that the sequence is clear?

☐ Have you named a file you are submitting as directed? Have you used Save As to convert it to the required file format?

☐ Have you developed a file storage system so that you have a folder for each course and a subfolder for all related files for a specific paper?

☐ Do you carry a flash drive or other storage device with you so that you can work on your papers in the computer lab or library whenever you have time?

☐ Do you consistently back up your files every time you write using a flash drive, portable drive, or other device?

Online Assessment

When you hear the word *assessment*, you may automatically think *grade*. However, the grade is simply the spare, conventional marker that sums up your success doing specific academic work during a specific period of time. The first step toward getting a good grade in a composition class — or any class with written projects — is understanding what is expected of your writing. Grades typically sum up whether and to what extent your writing or other activities exhibited certain characteristics.

The outcomes or standards for assessing the qualities and effectiveness of a specific essay for a composition class are probably the same whether a course is face-to-face, hybrid, or online. In fact, your instructor may post or discuss criteria early in the class, perhaps in a rubric — a chart listing characteristics and explaining the quality of achievement expected for each in order to reach particular levels of accomplishment (such as A, B, C, D or advanced, proficient, beginning).

Self-assessment Activities. Learning to assess your own writing can be challenging. You may know how long or hard you worked, but that effort isn't the same as being able to identify and develop expected characteristics. For this reason, some classes look at sample student essays to discuss how well an essay demonstrates desired features. In addition, this book includes many samples of student writing as well as checklists and other self-assessment materials such as the Take Action boxes. You may also be asked to write your own assessment of your success writing a specific paper, collaborating on a group project, or organizing a portfolio.

Online Assessment Procedures. Because online activities can significantly expand the options for class participation, be sure to find out which activities are required and which recommended. Your CMS or other class sites or applications may track and report detailed data on participation such as the following:

- time spent online and active
- time and activity (even keystrokes) within CMS units and tools
- completion of tasks by the deadline or within the allotted time
- number of attempts to complete tasks
- quantity and quality of contributions to threaded discussions (sorted alphabetically to group each individual's contributions)
- number of correct multiple-choice or other objective answers

Also consider nonstatistical measures of your performance and your engagement that might improve your grade. Find out how your instructor will weight or use such information. For example, suppose your instructor asks you to post a question about a challenging reading and also to try to answer two questions from other students. You might receive credit simply for making a conscientious effort to do both, whether your answers were correct or not, because the purpose of the assignment is to generate discussion. On the other hand, if you are asked to post your final, revised version of an essay, posting it would be only the first step, followed by your instructor's assessment based on the criteria for the assignment.

Once you know the many ways that your online participation can be measured, you are prepared to read assignment prompts more critically. For example, suppose you are asked to write a short answer to a question, perhaps with thirty minutes allowed and about 250 words (one double-spaced page) expected. How is your instructor likely to assess your 174 words written in nine minutes? How will your response compare with someone else's 249 words and twenty-nine minutes of attention? Will your instructor think that you felt pressured and rushed, ignored the implications of the directions, didn't care enough to use the time allowed, or simply said what you had to say?

Assessment of Collaborative Work. Sometimes your success is affected or influenced by the work of others. For example, enlightening comments by others may spark your creativity during a discussion. Thoughtful peer responses to an essay can help you reconsider your approach or clarify your most powerful ideas. In return, you can set high standards for your interactions with others, too.

At other times, your class activities are collaborative, and you are expected to work successfully as a group. In such cases, the group should begin by setting fair expectations for everyone: who will do what, who will play which role. When each contributor accepts responsibility under the agreed division of labor, a group often can accomplish far more than an individual. At its best, collaboration also allows group members to learn from others' strengths and experience. For instance, if you are a returning student, you probably will bring maturity and life experience to a group. If you are a traditional college student, you probably will bring confidence about school assignments and online expertise. Taken together, these strengths and perspectives about learning are likely to encourage stronger work from everyone.

To avoid potential conflicts, write out the group plans, individual responsibilities, and deadlines for everyone. Share these agreements with all the group members and your instructor. Keep track of drafts and contributions, especially so that you can document your own contributions if necessary. If you are to provide a self-assessment of the project or a letter to your instructor introducing the project, good records will help you to identify the plans of the group and describe fairly the accomplishments of individual contributors.

Additional Writing Assignments

1. Conduct some research using your college's online catalog. Look up several courses that you will be required or might want to take during the next few terms. What formats — face-to-face, online, or hybrid — are available for these courses? In what ways would the courses differ by format or in other ways, based on the catalog or a linked description? How might each format appeal to your strengths, learning preferences, and educational circumstances? Write a short report that summarizes what you learn and then uses that information to explain which choices might best suit you.

2. Write a comparison-and-contrast essay based on your experiences with face-to-face, online, or hybrid courses. Consider starting with a table with columns to help you systematically compare features of the class formats, the learning requirements or priorities they encourage, any changes in your priorities or activities as a student, or other possible points of comparison.

3. Begin a reflective electronic journal. Add entries daily or several times each week to record ideas, observations, thoughts, and reactions that might enrich your writing. Use your file as a resource as you write assigned essays. Post selections, if you wish, for class or small-group discussion.

4. Keep a blog about your writing experience. (If this will be your first blog, begin by looking for tips or tutorials on your CMS or the site where your class will establish their blogs.) Post regular entries as you work on a specific essay or writing project, commenting on the successes, challenges, and surprises that the college writer meets.

5. Establish a collaborative blog with others in your online class on a key course topic or about possible sources or ideas for the group members' writing or research projects. Decide on a daily or weekly schedule for blogging.

6. Start a threaded discussion about resources for your course topic, current assignment, research project, or other class project. Ask contributors to identify a resource, explain how to locate or access it, evaluate its strengths, and describe any limitations.

7. Set up a small-group or class Wiki, encouraging everyone to identify terms, concepts, strategies, activities, or events of significance to the course, a common academic program, or a shared writing interest. Write and edit collaboratively to arrive at clear, accurate, and useful explanations of these items to help everyone master the course (or program) material.

8. Set up a class Help Board on your CMS, a place where a student could post an immediate problem that has arisen while working on the course reading or writing. (Ask participants to respond to at least two or three other ques-

tions for each one that they post. Ask your instructor to supplement the advice as needed.)

9. Working with a small group, use a document-sharing system to draft an essay or other project, giving all group members and your instructor access to the group process. Without any face-to-face time, work collaboratively through simultaneous or sequential drafting, using chat or other electronic messaging to discuss your work. When your draft is complete, have all participants (including your instructor, if possible) share reflections about both the process and the outcome.

10. Using an available communication system (for example, for a Web-based telephone call, conference call, or video call; for a real-time online meeting; or for an audio chat), set up a conversation with a classmate or a small group. Set a specific time for the meeting, and circulate any necessary materials ahead of time. The purpose of the conversation might be discussing a reading, responding to each other's current draft, reviewing course material before an exam, or a similar group activity. After the conversation, write an evaluation of the experience, including recommendations for the next time you use the technology.

Writing and Presenting Under Pressure 16

M ost college writing is done for assessment—that is, most of the papers you hand in are eventually evaluated and graded. But some college writing tasks exist *only* as methods of assessment, designed to allow you to demonstrate what you have mastered. You often need to do such writing on the spot—a quiz to finish in twenty minutes, a final exam to complete in a few hours, an impromptu essay to dash off in one class period. How do you discover and shape your ideas in a limited time?

In this chapter we provide tips for three types of in-class writing that are commonly used for assessment—the essay exam, the short-answer exam, and the timed writing assignment. We also discuss the writing portfolio, a collection of writing samples that demonstrates your strengths, and the oral presentation, which may include software slides.

Essay Examinations

In many courses an essay exam is the most important kind of in-class writing. Instructors believe that such writing shows that you have examined material critically and can clearly communicate your thoughts about it.

Preparing for the Exam

Some instructors favor the open-book exam, in which you bring your books and perhaps your notes to class for reference. For this exam, ability to memorize and recall is less important than ability to reason and to select what matters. On the other hand—if the exam will be closed book—it's a good idea to fix in your memory vital names, dates, and definitions. Either way, prepare by imagining likely questions and then planning answers. If your instructor has supplied sample questions, pattern new ones after them. To study with a textbook, look for the main ideas in relevant chapters. Ask yourself: How do these ideas relate? How might they be combined? What conclusions can I draw?

Learning from Another Writer: Essay Exam

To look at techniques for answering *any* exam question, let's take one example. A final exam in developmental psychology posed this question:

> What evidence indicates innate factors in perceptual organization? You might find it useful to recall any research that shows how infants perceive depth and forms.

David Ian Cohn sat back in his chair for a few minutes and thought over the reading he'd done for the course. What perception research had used babies for subjects? He jotted down an informal outline, took a deep breath, and wrote a straightforward answer.

David Ian Cohn   **Student Essay Answer**

Response to Psychology Question

Research on infants is probably the best way to demonstrate that some factors in perceptual organization are innate. As the cliff box experiment shows, an infant will avoid what looks like a drop-off, even though its mother calls it and even though it can feel glass covering the drop-off area. The same infant will crawl to the other end of the box, which appears (and is) safe. Apparently, infants do not have to be taught what a cliff looks like.

Psychologists have also observed that infants are aware of size constancy. They recognize a difference in size between a 10 cm box at a distance of one meter and a 20 cm box at a distance of two meters. If this phenomenon is not innate, it is at least learned early, for the subjects of the experiment were infants of sixteen to eighteen months.

When shown various patterns, infants tend to respond more noticeably to patterns that resemble the human face than to those that appear random. This seemingly innate recognition helps the infant distinguish people (such as its mother) from less important inanimate objects.

Infants also seem to have an innate ability to match sight with sound. When simultaneously shown two television screens, each depicting a different subject, while being played a tape that sometimes matched one screen and sometimes the other, infants looked at whichever screen matched what they heard — not always, but at least twice as often.

Questions to Start You Thinking

Meaning

1. What is the main idea of Cohn's answer?
2. If you were the psychology instructor, how could you immediately see that Cohn had thoroughly dealt with the question and only with the question?

Writing Strategies

3. In what places is Cohn's answer concrete and specific, not vague and general?

4. Suppose Cohn had tacked on a concluding sentence: "Thus I have conclusively proved that there are innate factors in perceptual organization, by citing much evidence showing that infants definitely can perceive depth and forms." Would that sentence strengthen his answer? Why, or why not?

Generating Ideas

When the clock is ticking away, generating ideas right on the exam sheet saves time. First read over all the questions carefully. If you don't understand what a question calls for, ask your instructor right away. If you are offered a choice, just cross out questions you are *not* going to answer so you don't waste time on them by mistake. Annotate questions, underline important points, and scribble short definitions. Write reminders that you will notice while you work: TWO PARTS! or GET IN EXAMPLE OF ABORIGINES.

Outline a Concrete Answer. Few people can dash off an excellent essay exam answer without taking time to plan. Instructors prefer answers that are concrete and specific rather than those that wander in the clouds of generality. David Cohn's informal outline helped him cite evidence all the way through — particular experiments with infants.

> Thesis: Research on infants is probably the best way to demonstrate that some factors in perceptual organization are innate.
>
> Cliff box — kid fears drop despite glass, mother; knows shallow side safe
>
> Size constancy — learned early if not intrinsic
>
> Shapes — infants respond more/better to face shape than nonformed
>
> Match sound w/ sight — 2 TVs, look twice as much at right one

Focus on the Question. Instructors prefer answers that are organized and coherent rather than rambling. Often a question will contain directive words that help you define your task: *evaluate, compare, discuss, explain, describe, summarize, trace the development of.* You can put yourself on the right track if you incorporate a form of such a word in your first sentence.

QUESTION	Define socialism, and give examples of its main varieties.
ANSWER	Socialism is defined as . . .
ANSWER	Socialism is an economic and political concept, difficult to define because it takes many forms. It . . .

Planning for Typical Exam Questions

For examples of many methods of development, see Ch. 22.

Most exam questions fall into types. If you can recognize them, you will know how to organize and begin to write.

The cause and effect question mentions *causes, effects,* or both.

> What were the immediate causes of the Dust Bowl in the 1930s?
>
> Describe the main economic effects of a low prime interest rate.

The compare or contrast question asks you to point out similarities (*compare*), differences (*contrast*), or both. Directions to *show similarities* or *identify likenesses* ask for comparisons, while those to *distinguish, differentiate,* or *show differences* ask for contrasts, perhaps to evaluate in what respects one thing is better than the other. You explain not one subject but two, paralleling your points and giving both equal space.

> Compare and contrast *iconic memory* and *eidetic imagery,* defining the terms and indicating the ways in which they differ and are related or alike.

After supplying a one-sentence definition of each term, a student proceeded first to contrast and then to compare, for full credit.

> Iconic memory is a picturelike impression that lasts for only a fraction of a second in short-term memory. Eidetic imagery is the ability to take a mental photograph, exact in detail, as though its subject were still present. But iconic memory soon disappears. Unlike an eidetic image, it does not last long enough to enter long-term memory. IM is common; EI is unusual: very few people have it. Iconic memory and eidetic imagery are similar, however: both record visual images, and every sighted person of normal intelligence has both abilities to some degree.

The definition question requests explanation in many forms, short and extended.

> Explain three common approaches to parenting—*permissive, authoritarian-restrictive,* and *authoritative.* [You should supply a trio of definitions.]
>
> Define the Stanislavsky method of acting, citing outstanding actors who followed it. [You should explain a single method and give examples.]

The demonstration question asks you to back up a statement.

> Demonstrate the truth of Freud's contention that laughter may contain elements of aggression. [You need to explain Freud's claim and supply evidence to support it, maybe crowd scenes, a joke, or examples from reading.]

The discussion question may look like an invitation to ramble, but it isn't.

> Discuss three events that precipitated Lyndon B. Johnson's withdrawal from the 1968 presidential race.

Try rewording the question to help you focus your discussion.

> Why did President Johnson decide not to seek another term? Analyze and briefly explain three causes.

A discussion question may announce itself with *describe, explain,* or *explore.*

> Describe the national experience following passage of the Eighteenth Amendment. What did most Americans learn from it?

Provided you know that this amendment banned the sale, manufacture, and transportation of alcoholic drinks and that it was finally repealed, you can discuss its effects — or perhaps the reasons for its repeal.

The divide or classify question asks you to slice a subject into sections, sort things into kinds, or break the idea, place, person, or process into parts.

> Identify the ways in which each resident of the United States uses, on average, 1,595 gallons of water a day. How and to what degree might a person reduce this amount?

First, divide up water uses — drinking, cooking, bathing, washing cars, and so on. Then give tips for conservation and tell how effective each is.

> What different genres of film did Robert Altman direct? Name at least one outstanding example of each kind.

Sort films into categories — possibly comedy, war, drama, mystery, western — and give examples.

The evaluation question asks you to think critically and present an argument that bases a judgment on criteria.

> Evaluate this idea, giving reasons for your judgements: cities should stop building highways to the suburbs and instead build public lightrail systems.

Other argument questions might begin "Defend the idea of . . ." or "Show weaknesses in the concept of . . ." or otherwise call on you to take a stand.

The process analysis question often begins with *trace.*

> Trace the stages through which a bill becomes a state law.

> Trace the development of the medieval Italian city-state.

Both questions ask you to tell how something occurs or occurred, dividing the process into steps and detailing each step. The next question calls for the other type of process analysis, the "how-to" variety:

> An employee, consistently late for work by fifteen to thirty minutes daily, has been on the job only five months but shows promise of learning skills that your firm needs badly. How would you deal with this situation?

The response question might supply a statement, a comment, or a quotation, asking you to test the writer's opinion against what you know. Carefully read the statement, and jot down contrary or supporting evidence.

> Was the following passage written by Gertrude Stein, Kate Chopin, or Tillie Olsen? On what evidence do you base your answer?
>
> > She waited for the material pictures which she thought would gather and blaze before her imagination. She waited in vain. She saw no pictures of solitude, of hope, of longing, or of despair. But the very passions themselves were aroused within her soul, swaying it, lashing it, as the waves daily beat upon her splendid body. She trembled, she was choking, and the tears blinded her.

If you were familiar with the stories of Kate Chopin, who specializes in physical and emotional descriptions of impassioned women, you would point to language (*swaying, lashing*) that marks the passage as hers.

Learning by Doing 🎥 Asking Questions

Working by yourself or with a study group, review your study guide, class notes, textbook, or other material for an exam. Make your own list of likely questions, or review your instructor's list of sample questions. Then consider each question, and identify its type, using the preceding list or adding other categories as needed. Then underline, circle, or highlight the key words that tell you what your answer needs to do.

Drafting: The Only Version

When you have two or more essay questions to answer, block out your time roughly based on the points or minutes your instructor allots to each. Give extra minutes to a complicated question with several parts. Then pace yourself as you write. For example, wrap up question 2 at 10:30 and move on.

As you draft, give yourself room for second thoughts by writing on only one side of the page in your exam booklet and skipping every other line. Should you wish to add material later, you can do so with ease.

Begin with the Easy Questions. Many students find that it boosts their morale to start with the question they feel best able to answer. Unless your instructor specifies otherwise, why not skip around? Clearly number or label each answer as your instructor does. Then begin in such a way that the instructor will immediately recognize which question you're answering.

QUESTION
Compare and contrast the depression of the 1930s with the recession of 2008 on.

ANSWER
Compared to the paralyzing depression that began in 1929, the recession that began in 2008 seems like . . .

State Your Thesis at the Start. Try making your opening sentence a thesis statement that immediately makes clear the main point. Then the rest of your answer can back up that statement. Get started by turning the question into a statement and using it to begin an answer.

QUESTION
What reasons for leasing cars and office equipment, instead of purchasing them, can be cited for a two-person partnership?

ANSWER
I can cite at least four reasons for a two-person partnership to lease cars and office equipment. First, under present tax laws, the entire cost of a regular payment under a leasing agreement may be deducted. . . .

Stick to the Question. Throwing into your answer everything you have learned in the course defeats the purpose of the exam — to use your knowledge, not to parade it. Answer by selecting and shaping *what matters*. On the other hand, if a question has two parts, answer both.

Name three styles of contemporary architecture and evaluate one of them.

Stay Specific. Pressed for time, some exam takers think, "I haven't got time to get specific here. I'll just sum this up in general." That's a mistake. Every time you throw in a broad statement ("The Industrial Revolution was beneficial for the peasant"), take time to add specific examples ("In Dusseldorf, as Taine tells us, deaths from starvation among displaced Prussian farmworkers dropped from a peak of almost 10 percent a year").

Revising: Rereading and Proofing

If you have paced yourself, you'll have a few minutes left to look over your work. Check that your ideas are clear and hang together. Add sentences wherever new ones are needed. If you recall a key point, add a paragraph on a blank left-hand page. Just draw an arrow to show where it goes. Naturally, errors occur more often when you write under pressure than when you have time to proofread carefully. Make careful corrections by adding words with carets (∧) or neatly striking them out.

When your paper or blue book is returned, consider these questions as you look it over so that you improve your essay-exam skills:

ESSAY EXAM CHECKLIST

☐ Did you answer the whole question, not just part of it?

☐ Did you stick to the point, not throw in unrequested information?

☐ Did you make your general statements clear by citing evidence or examples?

☐ Did you proofread for omissions and lack of clarity?

☐ On what questions do you feel you did a good job, whatever your grade?

☐ If you had to write this exam over again, how would you now go about it?

Short-Answer Examinations

The *short-answer exam* may call on you to identify names or phrases from your reading, in a sentence or a few words.

Identify the following: Clemenceau, Treaty of Versailles, Maginot line.

Georges Clemenceau — This French premier, nicknamed The Tiger, headed a popular coalition cabinet during World War I and at the Paris Peace Conference demanded stronger penalties against Germany.

For more about defining, see pp. 443–45.

Writing a short identification is much like writing a short definition. Mention the general class to which a thing belongs to make clear its nature.

Treaty of Versailles — pact between Germany and the Allies that . . .
Maginot line — fortifications that . . .

Timed Writings

Many composition instructors give you experience in writing on demand by assigning impromptu in-class essays. Their purpose is to test your writing skills, not your recall. Although your time is limited, the setting is controlled, and you can't choose your subject, your usual methods of writing can still serve you well.

Budget Your Time. For an in-class essay with forty-five minutes to write, try to spend ten minutes preparing, thirty minutes writing, and five minutes rereading and making last-minute changes. Plan quickly to avoid rushing to get ideas on paper in an essay—the part you will be graded on.

Consider Types of Topics. Often you can expect the same types of questions for in-class writings as for essay exams. Do what the key words say.

For common types of exam questions, see pp. 336–38.

> What were the *causes* of World War I?
>
> *Compare and contrast* the theories of capitalism and socialism.
>
> *Define* civil rights.

Add your personal twist to a general subject, but note the key words.

> *Analyze* a problem in education that is *difficult to solve.*
>
> *Discuss ways to cope* with stress.

Standardized tests often ask you to respond to a short passage, testing not only your writing ability but also your reading comprehension.

> Thomas Jefferson stated, "If a nation expects to be ignorant and free, in a state of civilization, it expects what never was and never will be." *How* is his comment *relevant* to education today?

Choose Your Topic Wisely. For on-the-spot writing, the trick is to make the topic your own. If you have a choice, pick the one you know most about, not the one you think will impress your readers. They'll be most impressed by logical argument and solid evidence. If you have to write on a broad subject, bring it down to something you have observed or experienced. Have you witnessed traffic jams, power outages, or condos ruining beaches? Then write about increased population, using these examples.

Think before You Write. Despite your limited time, read the instructions or questions carefully, restrict your topic to something you know about, focus on a main idea, and jot down main points for development. If a good hook to open or conclude occurs to you, use it, too.

Don't Try to Be Perfect. No one expects in-class essays to read as smoothly as reports written over several weeks. You can't polish every sentence or remember the exact word for every spot. And never waste time recopying. Devote your time to the more important parts of writing.

Save Time to Proofread. The last few minutes when you read over your work and correct glaring errors may be the best-spent minutes of all. Cross out errors and make neat corrections using asterisks (*), arrows, and carets (^). Especially check for the following:

- letters omitted (*-ed* or *-s*), added (develop*e*), or inverted (rec*ie*ve)
- wrong punctuation (a comma instead of a period)

- omitted apostrophes (*dont* instead of *don't*)
- omitted words ("She going" instead of "She *is* going")
- wrong (*except* instead of *accept*) or misspelled words (*mispelled*)

Learning by Doing 🖐 Thinking Fast

To practice planning quickly for timed writing or tests, brainstorm as a class to explore approaches to sample topics provided in this chapter. Select one class member (or three, in turn) to record ideas on the board. Devote exactly ten minutes of discussion per topic to these key parts of a successful response:

- possible thesis sentences
- possible patterns of organization
- possible kinds and sources of evidence

Expect a wide range of ideas. Spend the last part of class evaluating them.

Portfolio Assessment

Portfolio courses typically emphasize revision and reflection—the ability to identify and discuss your choices, strengths, or learning processes. In such a course, you'll need to save all your drafts and notes, keep track of your choices and changes, and eventually select and submit your best writing in a portfolio. The portfolio is a printed or electronic collection of pieces of writing that represent the writer's best work. Compiled over time and across projects, it showcases a writer's talent, hard work, and ability to make thoughtful choices about content and presentation. For a single course, the portfolio is usually due as the term ends and includes pieces written and revised for that course. Most portfolios also include an introduction (usually a self-assessment or rationale) addressed to readers, who might be teachers, supervisors, evaluators, parents, or classmates.

Understanding Portfolio Assessment

The portfolio method of evaluation and teaching shapes the whole course from beginning to end. For example, your course will probably emphasize responses to your writing—from your classmates and instructor—but not necessarily grades on separate papers. The portfolio method shifts attention to the writing process itself—to discovery, planning, drafting, peer response, revision, editing—allowing time for your skills to develop before the writing "counts" and the portfolio is graded. Because this method is flexible, you need to read your syllabus and assignments carefully and listen well to determine the kind of portfolio you'll be expected to keep, such as these typical types.

A Writing Folder. Students submit all drafts, notes, outlines, scribbles, doodles, and messy pages — in short, all writing done for the course, whether finished or unfinished. Students may also be asked to revise two or three of their most promising pieces for a "presentation portfolio." The folder is usually not accompanied by a reflective cover letter.

A Learning (or Open) Portfolio. Students submit a variety of materials that have contributed to their learning. They may even determine the contents, organization, and presentation of the portfolio which might include photos, other images, or nonprint objects that demonstrate learning.

A Closed Portfolio. Students must turn in assignments that are specified by the instructor, or their options for what to include may be limited.

A Midterm Portfolio. The portfolio is given a trial run at midterm, or the midterm grade is determined by one or two papers that are submitted for evaluation, perhaps accompanied by a brief self-assessment.

A Final or Presentation Portfolio. The portfolio is evaluated at the end of the course after being revised, edited, and polished for presentation.

A Modified or Combination Portfolio. The student has some, but not unlimited, choice in what to include. For example, the instructor may ask for three entries that show certain features or parts of the course.

Find out what kind of portfolio your instructor has in mind. Here's one likely scenario. You are required to submit a modified or combination portfolio — one that contains, for example, three revised papers (out of the five or six drafts required). You decide, late in the term, which three to revise and edit. You also may be asked to reflect on what those choices say about you as a writer, to show your learning in the course, or to explain your decisions while writing a paper. Here are some typical questions your instructor, syllabus, or assignment sheets may answer:

- How many papers should you include in the portfolio?
- Do all these papers need to be revised? If so, what level of revision is expected? What criteria will be used to assess them?
- How much of the course grade is determined by the portfolio? Are portfolio entries graded separately, or does the portfolio receive one grade?
- May you include papers written for other courses or entries other than texts — such as photos, videos, maps, Web pages, or other visuals?
- Should you open with an introduction or a cover letter? What is expected of it: Description? Explanation? Exploration? Reflection? Self-assessment?
- Does each entry need a separate cover sheet? Should descriptions of your processes or choices appear before or after each entry?

Tips for Keeping a Portfolio

Keep Everything, and Stay Organized. Don't throw anything away! Keep all your notes, lists, drafts, outlines, clusters, responses from readers, photocopied articles, and references for works cited. If you have your own computer, *back up everything*. If you use the computer lab, save your work to a drive or card. Use a system to organize your files, and invest in a good folder with pockets. Label their contents as you store the drafts, notes, outlines, and peer review forms for each assignment.

Manage Your Time. The portfolio isn't due until the end of the course (or at midterm), but planning ahead will save you time and frustration. For example, as your instructor returns each assignment with comments, make changes in response while the ideas are fresh. If you don't understand or know how to approach your instructor's comments, ask right away. Make notes about what you want to do. Then, even if you want to let a paper simmer, you will have both a plan and some fresh insight when you work on it again.

For more help with self-assessment, see the For Peer Response questions, the Revision Checklists, and the Take Action sections throughout *The Bedford Guide*. Also, see "Take Action" activities at **<bedfordstmartins .com/bedguide>**.

Practice Self-Assessment. For complex activities, it's important to step back and evaluate your own performance. Maybe you have great ideas but find it hard to organize them. Maybe you write powerful thesis statements but run out of ideas to support them. Don't wait until the portfolio cover letter is due to begin assessing your strengths, weaknesses, or preferences.

Practice self-assessment from the first day of class. After reviewing the syllabus, write a paragraph or two about how you expect to do in this course. What might you do well? Why? What may be hard? Why? For each paper you share with peers or hand in, write a journal entry about what the paper does well and what it still needs. Keep track of your process to plan, research, or draft each paper—where you get stuck and where things click.

Choose the Entries Carefully. If you can select what to include, consider the course emphasis. Of course, you want to select pieces your evaluator will think are "the best," but also consider which show the most promise or potential. Which drafts show creativity, insight, or an unusual approach? Which show variety—different purposes, audiences, or voices? Which show depth—your ability to do thorough research or stay with a topic for several weeks? Also consider the order of the entries—which piece might work best first or last, and how each placement affects the whole.

For a reflective portfolio letter, see p. 383.

Write a Strong Reflective Introduction or Cover Letter. Your introduction—usually a self-assessment in the form of a cover letter, a statement, or a description for each of your entries—could be the most important text you write all semester. Besides introducing readers to your collection and portraying you as a writer, it explains your choices in putting the portfolio together and demonstrates that you can evaluate your work and your writing process.

For many portfolio-based courses, the reflective introduction or cover letter is the "final exam," testing what you've learned about good writing, readers' needs, and the details of a careful self-presentation.

DISCOVERY CHECKLIST

☐ Who will read this reflection?

☐ What qualities of writing will your reader value?

☐ Will the reader suggest changes or evaluate your work?

☐ What will the outcome of the reading be? How much can you influence it?

☐ What do you want to emphasize about your writing? What are you proud of? What have you learned? What did you have trouble with?

☐ How can you present your writing ability in the best light?

If your reader or evaluator is your instructor, look back over responses on your returned papers, and review the course syllabus and assignment sheets. What patterns do you see in your instructor's concerns or directions? What could you tell a friend about this reader's expectations — or pet peeves? Use what you've learned about his or her values as a reader to compose a convincing, well-developed introduction or cover letter.

If your readers or evaluators are unknown, ask your instructor for as much information as possible so you can decide which logical, ethical, or emotional appeals might be most effective. Although you won't know your readers personally, it's safe to assume that they will be trained in portfolio assessment and will share many of your instructor's ideas about good writing. If your college writing program has guidelines, consult them, too.

For more on appeals, see pp. 42–44.

How long should your introduction or cover letter be? Check with your instructor, but regardless of length, develop your ideas or support your claims as in any effective writing. If you are asked to write a letter, follow the format for a business letter: include the date, a salutation, and a closing.

In the reflective introduction, you might try some of the following (but don't try to use all of them):

- Discuss your best entry, and explain why it is your best.
- Detail your revisions — the improvements you want readers to notice.
- Review everything included, touching on the strengths of each.
- Outline your writing and revising process for one or more entries.
- State what the portfolio illustrates about you as a writer, student, researcher, or critical thinker.
- Acknowledge your weaknesses, but show how you've worked to overcome them.

- Acknowledge the influence of your readers on your entries.
- Reflect on what you've learned about writing and reading.
- Lay the groundwork for a positive evaluation of your work.

Polishing the Final Portfolio. From the first page to the last, your portfolio should be ready for public presentation, a product you can take pride in or show to others. Think about creative ways to give your portfolio a final distinctive feature, such as adding a colorful cover, illustrations, a table of contents, or a running head. Although a cheerful cover will not make up for weak writing or careless editing, readers will value your extra effort.

Oral Presentations

In many courses students make oral presentations to classmates and the instructor. Individual presentations might summarize final essays, research reports, or capstone projects. Group or team projects might include pro-and-con debates on controversies, roundtable presentations of viewpoints, organized analyses, problem–solution proposals, or field reports. Such presentations require both thoughtful written materials and confident oral delivery, perhaps using visuals prepared with PowerPoint or other presentation software.

Because presentations draw on multiple skills, you may feel anxious or uncertain about how to prepare. After all, you need to write under pressure, preparing your speaking script or notes as well as the text for any presentation slides. In addition, you need to speak under pressure, making your presentation and possibly fielding questions or adding impromptu responses. You may be assessed on the quality of both your prepared content and your actual presentation. Despite these pressures, each presentation provides valuable experience, preparing you for future class presentations as well as job interviews, workplace reports, professional talks, and community appearances.

Start Early. Get organized, avoid procrastinating, and draw on your writing experience and strategies when a presentation is approaching. Review your assignment and any assessment criteria to be certain you understand what is expected. If you are reporting on a paper or project, finish it well ahead of the deadline. If your presentation requires separate reading or research, get it done early. If you are working with a group, establish a timetable and regular face-to-face meetings or online checkpoints so that everyone is well prepared. This advance work is necessary so that you have time left to plan the presentation as a separate activity instead of just walking into it and looking disorganized or ill-prepared.

Develop Your Oral Presentation. When you begin work on the presentation itself, consider your audience and purpose, the time allotted, and the formality expected. Think hard about an engaging start—something surprising, intriguing, or notable to help your audience focus on your talk. Map out the main points appropriate for your audience and situation, and preview them. Because listeners cannot look back as they might in a printed text, your words need to tell them what's major, what's minor, and what's coming up. Be selective because listeners can absorb only limited detail.

Instead of writing out a speech as you would an essay, record your main points on cards or on a page using easy-to-read type. Then practice — speaking out loud, timing yourself, revising your notes, testing your talk on a friend, or maybe even recording yourself so you can listen or watch for rough spots. If you feel nervous speaking, practice taking a deep breath or counting to five before you begin. Also practice looking around the room to make eye contact with your audience. Connecting with them will turn anonymous faces into sympathetic people.

Align Your Visuals. Once your talk is taking shape, work on any presentation materials such as slides or images for projection or distribution. Listeners appreciate concise visuals that support — but do not repeat — your words. If possible, test the equipment and project a few in the room where you will speak. Sit there, as your audience will, to check how large the type needs to be for easy reading. Try to align your slides with your main points so that they appear steadily and appropriately. Aim for a simple, professional look without exotic designs or dramatic colors. All of this preparation will pay off by improving your presentation and reducing whatever fears you may hold about public speaking.

PRESENTATION CHECKLIST

☐ Have you developed your presentation as effectively as possible?

☐ Do you begin and end with an engaging flair?

☐ Have you stated your points clearly and arranged them so that they are easy to follow?

☐ Are your words, tone, and level of formality well chosen for the situation?

☐ Have you practiced enough to look relaxed and avoid getting lost during your talk?

☐ Have you taken a deep breath and looked around at your audience before starting to speak? Have you continued to make eye contact during your presentation?

☐ Have you projected your voice and spoken slowly so that everyone could hear you?

☐ Does your appearance — posture, dress, hand motions — increase your credibility?

For sample readings written for oral presentation, turn to the radio broadcasts in *A Writer's Reader*: Frank Deford, "NFL: Dodging the Concussion Discussion?" (pp. 573–75); Sarah Adams, "Be Cool to the Pizza Dude" (pp. 615–16); and Harold Taw, "Finding Prosperity by Feeding Monkeys" (pp. 628–29).

☐ Do you stick to the expected time, format, procedure, or other guidelines?

☐ Are your visuals clear, spacious, and easy to read?

☐ Do the design, text, and presentation of your visuals complement your talk?

Learning from Other Writers: Visuals for Oral Presentations

Each of the following images was prepared as part of a series of slides to accompany an oral presentation. The first series, on urban design, was designed by a student for a face-to-face presentation in his geography class. The second, on parental involvement in education, was prepared by a returning student for an online education course.

Andrew Dillon Bustin   Face-to-Face Class Presentation
Traditional Urban Design

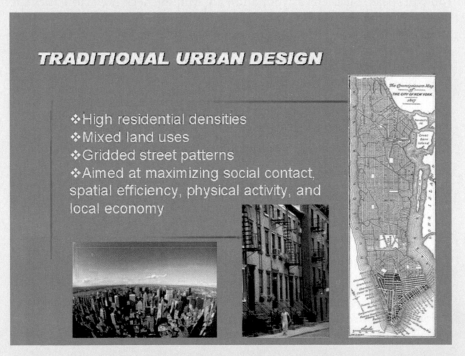

As the student presenter reported on urbanization to his face-to-face geography class, he showed slides with images of the ten most populous cities in the world as well as summaries of key points from sources on this topic. Traditional Urban Design, the example included here, illustrates the combination of text and images.

Questions to Start You Thinking

Meaning

1. What information does the slide present?

2. How do the images relate to the words?

Writing Strategies

3. In what ways does the slide try to appeal to an audience of other students?

4. If the presenter were your classmate, what helpful comments would you make about his slide?

Michelle Sausen   Future Conference Presentation

Parental Involvement

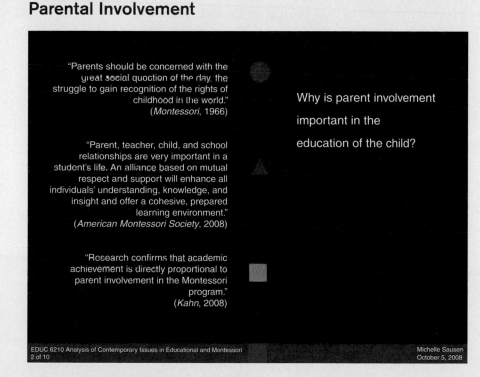

The second slide was prepared for an online course about the Montessori educational philosophy and concentrates on family involvement in the education of children. The student prepared two texts for her last class before graduation: a research report about parental involvement and a slide show on the same topic, designed for future presentation at a professional conference. The slide included here illustrates the presentation of quotations and the use of graphics. The sources quoted on the slide were fully identified in the final slide with this list of references in APA style.

References

American Montessori Society. (n.d.). *Parents and the American Montessori Society*. Retrieved from http://www.amshq.org/parentsPublic.htm

Kahn, D. (1996). *Ten steps to Montessori implementation in public schools*. Retrieved from http://www.montessori-namta.org/NMATA/administrators/implsteps.html

Lillard, A. S. (2007). *Montessori: The science behind the genius*. New York, NY: Oxford University Press.

Montessori, M. (1966). *The secret of childhood*. New York, NY: Ballantine Books.

Questions to Start You Thinking

Meaning

1. What information does the text on the slide present?

Writing Strategies

2. How do the layout and the graphics contribute to the overall effect of the slide?

3. If the presenter were your classmate, what helpful comments would you make about her slide?

Additional Writing Assignments

1. Review the available information about an upcoming examination in one of your classes as well as any advice about such exams in this chapter. Write a set of directions for yourself, explaining the process for preparing for your exam. (Then follow your directions.)

2. Prepare for an examination by writing sample questions that address the major issues in the course. Then outline your possible answers to these questions.

3. Begin to organize your writing portfolio for submission. First, write a paragraph summing up the type of portfolio assigned and listing the components you need to supply. Then outline your current ideas about how to introduce your portfolio and how to organize your portfolio products.

4. Imagine a professional portfolio that would effectively present you and your talents to a prospective employer or an advanced academic program. Write up your plan for this portfolio, including what it would contain, how

you would introduce it, and how you would design it to try to persuade readers to hire or admit you.

5. Prepare an oral presentation on a topic suggested or approved by your instructor. Consider reporting on a reading, expanding the topic of a recent essay, exploring a campus issue that concerns you, identifying the effects on students of physical features of your campus, proposing a change for your campus or workplace, or interpreting a distinctive feature of your community.

6. **Visual Assignment.** Prepare presentation slides or other visuals to project or distribute as part of an oral presentation such as the preceding assignment.

17 Writing in the Workplace

M ost of the world's workplace communication takes place in writing. Although a conversation or voice mail may be forgotten or ignored, a written message provides a permanent record of a business exchange, often calling for action. This chapter first outlines some general guidelines for workplace writing and then shows you some types likely to prove useful in your career — e-mail, résumés, letters, memoranda, brochures, and presentation slides.

Guidelines for Writing in the Workplace

Good workplace writing succeeds in achieving a clear purpose. When you write to a business, your writing represents you; when you write as part of your job, your writing represents your company as well.

EFFECTIVE
WORKPLACE
WRITING

Respectful tone · Clear purpose · Concise, clear, well-organized presentation · Reader's point of view

Know Your Purpose

Your purpose, or reason for writing, helps you select and arrange information; it gives you a standard against which to measure your final draft. Most likely, you will want to create a certain response in your readers.

DISCOVERY CHECKLIST

☐ Do you want to inform — announce something, update others, explain some specialized knowledge, or reply to a request?

☐ Do you want to motivate some action — get a question answered, a wrong corrected, a decision made, or a personnel director to hire you?

☐ When your readers are finished reading what you've written, what do you want them to think? What do you want them to do?

Keep Your Audience in Mind

Consider everything in your workplace writing from your audience's point of view. After all, your purpose is not to express your ideas but to have readers act on them, even if the action is simply to notice your grasp of the situation. If you don't know the person to whom you are writing, make educated guesses based on what you know about the position or company.

Especially when your purpose is to motivate, focus on how "you, the reader" will benefit instead of what "I, the writer" would like.

"I" ATTITUDE	Please send me the form so that I can process your order.
"YOU" ATTITUDE	To make sure that you receive your shipment promptly, please send me the order form.

DISCOVERY CHECKLIST

☐ What do your readers already know about the subject? Are they experts in the field? Have they been kept up to date on the situation?

☐ What do your readers need to know? What information do they expect you to provide? What do they need before they can take action?

☐ What can you assume about your readers' priorities and expectations? Will they expect a clear, efficient overview or detailed background?

☐ What is most likely to motivate readers to take the action you want?

Use an Appropriate Tone

Tone is the quality of writing that reveals your attitude toward your topic and your readers. If you show readers that you respect them, their intelligence, and their feelings, they are far more likely to view you and your message favorably. Most workplace writing today ranges from the informal to the slightly formal. Gone are extremely formal phrases such as *enclosed herewith, be advised that,* or *pursuant to the stated request.* At the other extreme, slang, overfriendliness, or a casual text-messaging style might cast doubts on your seriousness or credibility. Strive for a relaxed and conversational style, using simple sentences, familiar words, and the active voice.

Observe business etiquette in courteous and considerate writing. If you are writing to complain, remember that your reader may not have caused the problem—and courtesy is more likely than sarcasm or insults to motivate help. When delivering bad news, remember that your reader may interpret a bureaucratic response as cold and unsympathetic. And if you have made a mistake, acknowledge it.

☐ Have you avoided slang terms and extremely casual language?

☐ Have you avoided unnecessarily formal or sophisticated words?

☐ Are your sentences of a manageable length?

☐ Have you used the active voice ("I am sending it") rather than the passive voice ("It is being sent")?

☐ Does anything you've written sound blaming or accusatory?

☐ Do you hear a friendly, considerate, competent person behind your words?

☐ Have you asked someone else to read your writing to check for tone?

Present Information Carefully

For sample business documents, see the figures later in this chapter. For more on adding visuals, see the Quick Format Guide beginning on p. A-1.

In business, time is money: time wasted reading irrelevant, poorly written material is money wasted. Organize so that readers can skim or move through your writing quickly and easily. Make the topic absolutely clear from the beginning, usually the first paragraph of a letter or the subject line of a memo or e-mail message. Use a conventional format that your readers will expect (see Figures 17.4 and 17.6 later in this chapter). Break information into easily processed chunks; order these chunks logically and consistently. Finally, use topic sentences and headings (when appropriate) to label each chunk of information and to give your readers an overview of your document.

For more revising and editing strategies, see Ch. 23.

☐ Have you kept your letter, memo, or résumé to a page or two?

☐ Have you cut all unnecessary or wordy explanations?

☐ Have you scrutinized every word to ensure that it can't be misinterpreted? Have you supplied all the background information readers need?

☐ Have you emphasized the most important part of your message? Will readers know what you want them to do?

☐ Have you followed a consistent, logical order and a conventional format?

☐ If appropriate, have you included labels and headings?

E-mail

Because *e-mail* is so easy, speedy, and convenient, it dominates business communication. Communication advances—such as texting and tweeting—may simplify quick exchanges and arrangements. On the other hand, traditional letters and memos may still be preferred for formal, official correspondence. However, e-mail messages easily meet traditional needs because they can be (1) transmitted within organizations (like memos) or between them and other parties (like letters), (2) printed or stored electronically (like permanent file copies), (3) written with standard components and length (like traditional memos or letters in order to serve their functions), or (4) used to cover transmittals (with formal reports, memos, or other documents attached).

E-mail's universality and conversational quality also necessitate professional caution. Although regular correspondents may write informally and overlook each other's quirks, your e-mail messages are part of your company's official record and have no guarantee of privacy. Without warning, your confidential exchange can be intercepted, reviewed by others, forwarded to other computers, distributed electronically, or printed.

Format for E-mail

E-mail headings are predetermined by your system and typically follow memo format: *To:*, *cc:*, *Subject:*, and an automatic *From:* line with your name as sender. Write messages that readers find helpful, efficient, and courteous.

- Use a clear subject line to simplify replying and archiving.
- Move promptly to your purpose: state what you need and when.
- Be concise, adding headings and space between sections if needed.
- Follow company practice as you include or delete a trail of replies.
- Observe company etiquette in copying messages to others.
- Avoid personal statements, humor, or informality that might undermine your professional credibility.

Résumés and Application Letters

The most important business correspondence you write may be the résumé and letter you use to apply for a job. In any economic climate—but especially in a weak one with reduced job prospects—your materials need to be carefully developed and crafted. They need to reflect as many applicable skills and experiences as possible, including your summer, campus, part-time, or full-time employment as you attend college. First, prepare for job prospects by developing opportunities systematically, well before graduation:

- turn to campus career services as well as local library or community resources to investigate job opportunities and useful career strategies
- consider internships or volunteer posts relevant to your goals
- attend preprofessional or career-oriented workshops or gatherings
- network with workplace and professional contacts to learn about your future options and prospects

Remain flexible, too. Instead of looking only for positions with the single job title you want, consider what other roles or fields might give you experience or build your skills on your way to that job. For example, if you are in a public health program and want to join a major city health department, by all means gain expertise that will help you to pursue that job despite the city's recent budget cutbacks. But you also might want to consider rural or statewide positions, hospital outreach programs, corporations with employee health programs, or the growing field of senior care. Be prepared to take advantage of serendipity — the surprise that offers a new or unexpected option.

Finally, as opportunities arise, apply your college writing experience to the workplace in order to draft and revise effectively. Direct, persuasive, correct prose can help you stand out from the crowd.

Résumés

In a résumé, you present yourself as someone who has the qualifications to excel at a job and to be an asset to the organization. Job seekers often have copies of a single résumé on hand, but you may want to customize your résumé for each application if you can easily print attractive copies.

A résumé is highly formatted but allows many decisions about style, organization, and appearance. Unless you have a great deal of relevant work experience, try to keep your résumé to one page. Although many formats are acceptable, this section describes a typical résumé that consists of a heading and labeled sections that detail your experience and qualifications. Within each section, use brief, pointed phrases and clauses rather than complete sentences. Use action verbs (*supervised, ordered, maintained*) and active voice whenever possible. Highlight labels with underlining, boldface, or larger type. Arrange information on the page so that it is pleasing to the eye; use the best paper and clearest printer you can. (See Figure 17.1.)

For electronic applications, you may need to prepare your résumé in several different forms: a text file that you can attach to an e-mail message, an electronically readable version that a company can scan into its database, or a Web version that you can post on your site or a job site (see Figure 17.2). For all these versions, format carefully so that recipients can easily read what you supply. Turn to your campus career center for résumé samples and advice about using alternate formats to your advantage.

Heading. The heading is generally centered (or otherwise pleasingly aligned) on the page with separate lines for your name; street address, city, state, and zip code; phone number; and e-mail address.

Employment Objective. This optional section allows personnel officers to see at a glance your priorities and goals. Try to sound confident and eager but not pompous or presumptuous.

Figure 17.1
Conventional
Résumé

Centers heading with
contact information

Anne Cahill
402 Pigeon Hill Road
Windsor, CT 06095
(860) 555-5763
acahill783@yahoo.com

Labels sections

Objective	Position as Registered Nurse in pediatric hospital setting
Education	**University of Connecticut**, Storrs, CT. Bachelor of Science, Major in nursing, May 2010. GPA: 3.5; licensed as Registered Nurse by the State of Connecticut in June 2010
	Manchester Community Technical College, Manchester, CT. Associate degree in occupational therapy, May 2004. GPA: 3.3.
Work Experience	
9/05–present	**Certified Occupational Therapy Assistant**, Johnson Memorial Hospital, Stafford Springs, CT • Assist children with delayed motor development and cerebral palsy to develop skills for the activities of daily life
9/03–9/05	**Nursing Assistant**, Woodlake Healthcare Center, Tolland, CT • Helped geriatric residents with activities of daily living • Assisted nursing staff in treating acute care patients
9/01–9/03	**Cashier**, Stop and Shop Supermarket, Vernon, CT • Trained newly hired cashiers
Clinical Internships	**St. Francis Hospital**, Hartford, CT • Student Nurse, Maternity and Postpartum, spring 2010
	Hartford Hospital, Hartford, CT • Student Nurse, Pediatrics, fall 2009
	Visiting Nurse and Community Health, Mansfield, CT • Student Nurse, Community, spring 2009
	Manchester General Hospital, Manchester, CT • Student Nurse, Medical-Surgical, fall 2008
Computer Skills	• Proficient with Microsoft Office, Database, and Windows applications and electronic records • Experienced with Internet research
Activities	• Student Union Board of Governors, University of Connecticut, class representative • Intramural soccer
References	Available upon request

Specifies background
and experience

Places current
information first

Adds relevant skills
for health-care record
keeping

Anne Cahill

Objective: **Position as a Registered Nurse in pediatric hospital setting**

- Education
- Experience
- Other Activities
- References
- Contact Me

Profile

New nursing graduate combines proficiency in the latest nursing techniques with significant clinical experience

- Experienced in providing professional, compassionate health-care services to children, others
- Able to work proficiently and productively in hospital settings
- Accustomed to working in a team with a broad range of health professionals and administrators
- Proficient with Microsoft Office, Database, and Windows applications, with electronic records, and with Internet research

Education. This section is almost always included, often first. Specify each postsecondary school you've attended, your major, your date of graduation (or expected graduation), and your grade point average (if it reflects well on you). You can also add any awards, honors, or relevant course work.

Experience. In this key section, list each job with the most recent one first. You can include both full-time and part-time jobs. For each, give the name of the organization, your position, your responsibilities, and the dates you held the job. Describe your involvement in any unusual projects or responsibility for any important developments. Highlight details that show relevant work experience and leadership ability. Minimize information unconnected to the job for which you're applying.

Skills. List any special skills (data processing, technical drawing, multiple languages) that aren't obvious from your education and work experience.

Activities. You can specify either professional interests and activities (*Member of Birmingham Bricklayers Association*) or personal pursuits (*skiing, hiking, needlepoint*) showing that you are dedicated and well-rounded.

References. If a job advertisement requests references, provide them. Always contact your references in advance to make sure they are willing to give you a good recommendation. For each person, list the name, his or her organization and position, and the organization's address and phone number. If references have not been requested, you can simply note "Available on request."

As you prepare your résumé, and possibly your own professional Web site, also consider your electronic trail and workplace etiquette. A prospective employer may well assume that anything you write at work is company correspondence, without personal rights to privacy, and that anywhere you travel online at work will represent or be subsidized by the company. That same employer is unlikely to be amused by your confessional Facebook or MySpace page or your party photos. Even though you might consider social-networking materials personal, they may seem very public to an employer who checks your background and your credibility. Be certain that your electronic presence corresponds with the reliable-future-employee presence you wish to project.

Application Letters

When writing a letter applying for a job, follow all the guidelines for other business letters. Remember that your immediate objective is to obtain an interview. As you compete against other candidates, your letter and résumé are all the employer has to judge you on. If you're responding to an advertisement, read it critically.

For general guidelines for business letters, see pp. 361–63.

- What qualifications are listed? Ideally, you should have them all, but if you lack one, try to find something in your background that compensates, some similar experience in a different form.
- What else can you tell about the organization or position from the ad? How does the organization represent itself? If you're unfamiliar with the company, check its Web site.
- How does the ad describe the ideal candidate? As a team player? A dynamic individual? If you feel that you are the person this organization is looking for, you'll want to portray yourself this way in your letter.

In your letter, you want to spark your readers' interest, convince them that you're qualified, and motivate them to interview you. Whenever possible, address your letter to the person responsible for screening applicants and setting up interviews; you may need to call the organization to find out this person's name. In the first paragraph, identify the job, indicate how you heard about it, and summarize your qualifications. In the second paragraph, expand on your qualifications, highlighting key information on your résumé. Supplement it with details if necessary to show your readers that you're a better candidate than the others. In the third paragraph, restate your interest in the job, ask for an interview, and let your prospective employer know how to reach you. (For a sample application letter, see Figure 17.3.) If you get an interview, follow up with a thank-you note. The note may reemphasize your qualifications and strong interest in the position.

A
Writer's
Guide

Figure 17.3
Application Letter

Follows standard
letter format

Addresses specific person

Identifies job sought and
describes interest

Explains qualifications

Confirms interest and
supplies contact
information

Encloses résumé and
proof of certification

402 Pigeon Hill Road
Windsor, CT 06095
July 8, 2010

Sheryl Sullivan
Director of Nursing
Center for Children's Health and Development
St. Francis Hospital and Medical Center
114 Woodland Street
Hartford, CT 06105

Dear Ms. Sullivan:

I am writing to apply for the full-time position as a pediatric nurse at the Center for Children's Health and Development at St. Francis Hospital, which was advertised on the Eastern Connecticut Health Network Web site. I feel that my varied clinical experiences and my desire to work with children ideally suit me for the job. In addition, I am highly motivated to grow and succeed in the field of health care.

For the past five years, I have worked as a certified occupational therapy assistant. In this capacity, I help children with delayed motor function acquire the skills necessary to achieve as high a level of independence as possible. While working as a COTA, I attended nursing school with the ultimate goal of becoming a pediatric nurse. My varied clinical experiences as a student nurse and my previous experience as a nurse's aide in a geriatric center have exposed me to many types of care. I feel that these experiences have helped me to become a well-rounded caregiver.

I believe that I would be a strong addition to the medical team at the Children's Center. My clinical experiences have prepared me to deal with a wide range of situations. In addition, I am dedicated to maintaining and enhancing the well-being of children. I am enclosing proof of my recent certification as a Registered Nurse in the state of Connecticut. Please write to me at the address above, e-mail me at acahill783@yahoo.com, or call me at (860) 555-5763. Thank you for your consideration. I look forward to hearing from you.

Sincerely,

Anne Cahill

Anne Cahill

Enclosures

Learning by Doing   Planning a Job Application

Look for a job advertisement for a position or in a field that might interest you, using the newspaper, a professional publication, or an organization's Web site. First, analyze the ad to identify what type of applicant it seeks, checking qualifications, experience, ambitions, or other expectations. Then list the kind of information an applicant might supply in response. If possible, discuss your analysis with a classmate to see whether your interpretations match.

Business Letters

To correspond with outside parties, either individuals or groups, organizations use business letters to request and provide information, motivate action, respond to requests, and sell goods and services. Because letters become part of a permanent record, they can be checked later to determine exactly who said what and when. Keep a copy and an electronic backup of every letter you write.

A good business letter is brief—limited to one page if possible. It supplies what the reader needs, no more. A letter of inquiry might simply request a booklet, sample, or promotional piece. A special request might add why you are writing, what you need, and when you need it. On the other hand, a letter of complaint focuses on your problem—what product is involved, when and where you purchased it, why you are unhappy, and how you'd like the problem solved. Include specifics such as product numbers and dates, and maintain a courteous tone. Because they are so brief, business letters are often judged on details—format, appearance, openings, closings.

Format for Business Letters

The format of business letters (see Figure 17.4 on p. 362) is well established by convention. Remember that the physical appearance of a letter is very important.

- Use 8½-by-11-inch bond paper, with matching envelopes. Write on only one side of the page.

- Single-space and use an extra line of space to separate paragraphs and the different elements of the letter. In very short letters, it's acceptable to leave additional space before the inside address.

- Leave margins of at least one inch on both sides; try to make the top and bottom margins fairly even, although you may have a larger bottom margin if your letter is very short.

- Pay attention to grammar, punctuation, and mechanics. Your readers will.

Return Address. This is your address or the address of the company for which you are writing. Abbreviate only the state using its two-letter postal abbreviation. Omit a return address on preprinted letterhead stationery that already provides this information.

Date. Supply this on the line right after the return address. Spell out the month; follow it by the day, a comma, and the year.

Figure 17.4 Letter Using Modified Block Style

Uses standard format for return address, date, and inside address

Uses name of position for salutation

Introduces situation and explains purpose

Requests action

States expectation of resolution

Ends with conventional closing, signature, typed name, and e-mail address (if unknown to addressee)

                                         1453 Illinois Avenue ⎤ — Return address
                                         Miami, FL 33133 ⎦
                                         January 26, 2010 —— Date

Customer Service Department ⎤
Fidelity Products, Inc.   Inside
1192 Plymouth Avenue   address
Little Rock, AR 72210 ⎦

Dear Customer Service Representative: — Salutation

On January 12 I purchased a Fidelity media cabinet (Model XAR) from my local Tech-Mart. I have been unable to assemble the cabinet because the instructions are unclear. These instructions are incomplete (step 6 is missing) and are accompanied by diagrams so small and dark that it is impossible to distinguish the numbers for the different pieces.

Please send me usable instructions. If I do not receive clear instructions within the next three weeks, I will have to return my media cabinet to the Tech-Mart where I purchased it and request a full refund. — Body

I have used your equipment for more than ten years and have been very satisfied, so I was particularly disappointed to find that the media cabinet did not come with clear directions for assembly. I look forward to a prompt resolution of this problem.

                         Sincerely, — Closing

                         James Winter

                         James Winter — Name
                         jwin12@campus.net

Inside Address. This is the address of the person to whom you are writing. Begin with the person's full name and title (*Mr., Ms., Dr., Professor*); when addressing a woman without a professional title, use *Ms.* unless you know that she prefers *Miss* or *Mrs.* The second line should identify the position the person holds (if any), and the third line should name the organization (if you are writing to one). If you don't know who will read your letter, you may start with the name of the position, department, or organization. Avoid abbreviations in the address except for the state.

Salutation. Skip a line, and then type *Dear* followed by the person's title, last name, and a colon. If you don't know the name of the person who will read your letter, you can use the position that person holds (*Dear Editor*) or the name of the organization (*Dear Angell's Bakery*) in place of a name.

Body. Present your message. Leave one line of space between paragraphs; begin each paragraph even with the left margin (no indentations). Paragraphs should generally be no longer than seven or eight typed lines.

Closing. Leave one line of space after the last paragraph, and then use a conventional closing followed by a comma: *Sincerely, Sincerely yours, Respectfully yours, Yours truly*.

Typed Name with Position. Leave four lines of space after the closing, and type your name in full, even if you will sign only your first name. Do not include a title before your name. If you are writing on behalf of an organization, you can include your position on the next line. You may add your e-mail address or telephone number here unless already supplied.

Signature. Print the letter, and sign your name in the space above the typed name. Unless you have a personal relationship with the recipient, use both your first and last names. Do not include a title before your name.

Abbreviations at End. Leave at least two lines of extra space between your typed name and any abbreviations used to communicate more information about the letter. Put each abbreviation on a separate line. If you send a copy to someone other than the recipient, use *cc:* followed by the name of the person or organization receiving a copy. If the letter is accompanied by another document in the same envelope, use *Enc.* or *Enclosure*. If the letter has been typed by someone other than the person who wrote and signed it, the writer's initials are given in capital letters, followed by a slash and the initials of the typist in lowercase letters: *VW/dbw*.

Modified and Full Block Style. To align a letter using *modified block style* (see Figure 17.4), imagine a line running down the center of the page from top to bottom. Place the return address, date, closing, signature, and typed name so the left side of each aligns with this center line. Use *full block style* on letterhead stationery with the organization's name and address. Omit typing the return address, and align all elements at the left margin.

Envelope Formats. The U.S. Postal Service recommends a format with all capital letters, standard abbreviations, and no punctuation; this style is easier for the Postal Service to scan and process. However, conventional envelope format (see Figure 17.5) may be preferred and is always safe to use.

Memoranda

A *memorandum* (*memo* for short) is a form of communication used within a company to request or exchange information, make announcements, and confirm conversations. Memos are frequently used to convey information to

Figure 17.5 Envelope Formats

U.S. Postal Service format

JAMES WINTER
1453 ILLINOIS AVE
MIAMI FL 33133-3955

> CUSTOMER SERVICE DEPT
> FIDELITY PRODUCTS INC
> 1192 PLYMOUTH AVE
> LITTLE ROCK AK 72210-4687

Conventional format

Maria Solis
Customer Service Department
Fidelity Products, Inc.
1192 Plymouth Avenue
Little Rock, AK 72210-4687

> Mr. James Winter
> 1453 Illinois Avenue
> Miami, FL 33133-3955

large groups—an entire team, department, or organization. Generally, the topic is quite narrow and apparent to the reader at a glance. Memos tend to be written in the first person (*I* or *we*) and can range from very informal (if written to a peer) to extremely formal (if written to a high-ranking superior on an important matter). Most are short, but the format can be used to convey proposals and reports; long memos freely use headings, subheadings, lists, and other features that are easy to skim. (See Figure 17.6.)

Format for Memoranda

Although every organization has its own format for memos, the heading generally consists of a series of lines with clear labels (followed by colons).

Date:	(date on which memo is sent)
To:	(person or persons to whom it is primarily addressed)
cc:	(names of anyone else who receives a copy)
From:	(name of the writer)
Subject: *or* Re:	(concise, accurate statement of the memo's topic)

The subject line often determines whether a memo is read. (The old-fashioned abbreviation *Re:* for *regarding* is still used, but we recommend the more common *Subject*.) Accurately sum up the topic in a few words ("Agenda for 12/10 meeting," "Sales estimates for new product line").

Figure 17.6
Memorandum

ininterr
SYSTEMS
INTERLINK SYSTEMS, INC.

To: All Employees
From: Erica Xiang *EX*
Subject: Changes in employee benefits
Date: October 26, 2010

Each fall the Human Resources group looks closely at the company's health insurance benefits to make certain that we are providing an excellent level of coverage in a way that makes economic sense. To that end, we have made some changes to our plan, effective January 1, 2011. Let me outline the three major changes.

1. We are pleased to be able to offer employees the opportunity, through a **Flexible Spending Account**, to pay for dependent care and unreimbursed health expenses on a pre-tax basis, a feature that can result in considerable savings. I have attached a summary and will provide more information on this benefit at our staff meeting tomorrow, October 27, at 10:30 A.M. I will be available immediately after the meeting to answer any specific questions.

2. Those of you who have taken advantage of our **vision care benefit** in the past know that it offers significant help in paying for eye exams, eyeglasses, and contact lenses. The current plan will change slightly on January 1. Employees and covered dependents will be eligible to receive up to $50 each year toward the cost of a routine eye exam and up to $100 every two years toward the cost of eyeglasses or contact lenses. If you see a provider within our health insurance network, you will pay only $10 per office visit.

3. We at Interlink Systems feel strongly that our health insurance benefits are excellent, but as you know, the cost of such plans continues to rise every year. In the interest of maintaining excellent coverage for our employees, we will raise our **employee contribution**. Starting January 1, we are asking employees with single coverage to contribute $12.50 more per pay period toward the cost of medical insurance, and employees who cover dependents to contribute $40 more per pay period. Even with this increase, the amount the company asks its employees to contribute towards the premiums (about 8%) is significantly less than the nationwide average of 30%.

Please contact me if you have questions or concerns about the changes that I have outlined in this memo. You can reach me at x462 or at exiang@interlink.net.

Enclosure

Uses standard format to identify readers, writer, topic, and date

Explains purpose, noting reader's priorities

Previews clear organization in blocks

Uses friendly tone to note new benefit for employees

Offers assistance

Introduces benefit change with positive background

Presents increased cost carefully, noting coverage quality and high employer contribution

Offers more help and supplies contact information

Notes enclosure

Brochures and Presentation Visuals

When you design a workplace brochure, presentation slide, or other visual document, you write the text and also direct a reader's attention using tools such as type options, lists, white space, headings, repetition, and color.

Format for Brochures

For more on understanding visuals, see Ch. 14.

Although workplace brochures do not follow a specific format, artists and designers aim to attract readers' attention by making important elements prominent. Consider Figure 17.7, for example, which shows two of six panels of a student-designed brochure. The image of the mannequin on the brochure's cover immediately draws the eye, but the pattern of light guides readers to the central question: "Is your life out of control?" Other words

Figure 17.7
Sample Brochure.
Source: Art Institute of Boston

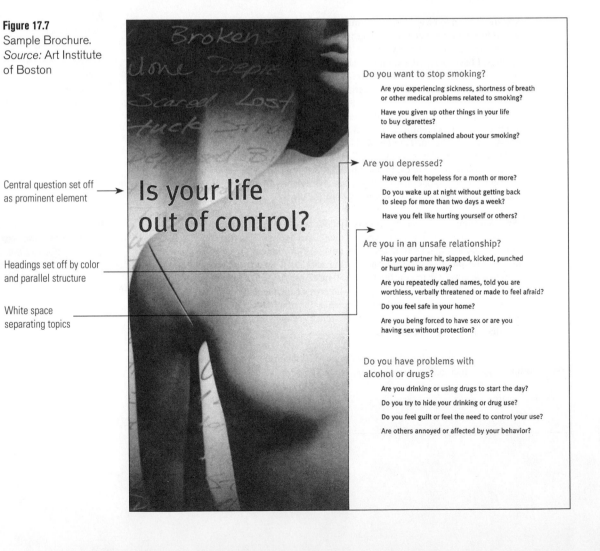

Central question set off as prominent element

Headings set off by color and parallel structure

White space separating topics

Is your life out of control?

Do you want to stop smoking?

Are you experiencing sickness, shortness of breath or other medical problems related to smoking?

Have you given up other things in your life to buy cigarettes?

Have others complained about your smoking?

Are you depressed?

Have you felt hopeless for a month or more?

Do you wake up at night without getting back to sleep for more than two days a week?

Have you felt like hurting yourself or others?

Are you in an unsafe relationship?

Has your partner hit, slapped, kicked, punched or hurt you in any way?

Are you repeatedly called names, told you are worthless, verbally threatened or made to feel afraid?

Do you feel safe in your home?

Are you being forced to have sex or are you having sex without protection?

Do you have problems with alcohol or drugs?

Are you drinking or using drugs to start the day?

Do you try to hide your drinking or drug use?

Do you feel guilt or feel the need to control your use?

Are others annoyed or affected by your behavior?

on the left panel (such as "broken," "stuck," "lost," and "depressed") serve as a suggestive backdrop, but there is no mistaking the main message.

Providing a prominent element helps your readers focus on what you or your organization thinks is most important. As you begin work on any visual document, ask, "What is the main message I want to get across?" Once you have decided on that message, think of ways to give it prominence. For example, if you are designing a brochure, flyer, poster, or postcard, you might want to surround one large headline by significant space, as in the left panel of the brochure. Note also in the right panel how the headings—all questions, parallel in form—appear in color, separated by white space so that readers clearly see the breaks between topics. The inside panels of the brochure respond to the questions posed in the headings, pointing readers toward helpful resources.

For more on parallel structure, see B2 (p. A-48) in the Quick Editing Guide.

Format for Presentation Visuals

Effective use of space is important in visuals—such as PowerPoint or other presentation slides. Providing ample space and limiting the text on each slide helps readers absorb your major points. For example, the slide in Figure 17.8 for a presentation to recruit service learning participants contains too much text, making it hard to read and potentially distracting. In contrast, Figure 17.9 contains less text and more open space, making each

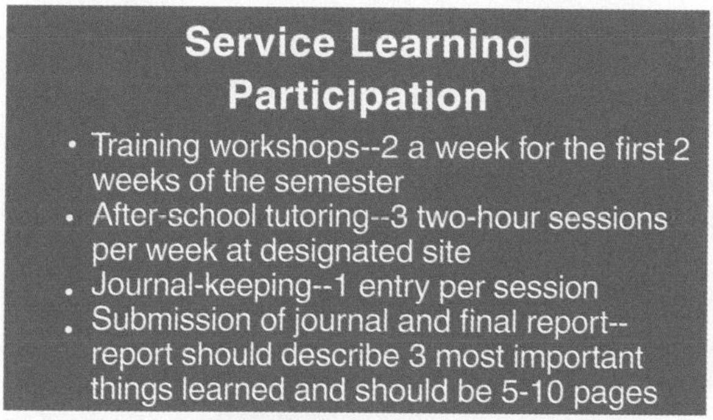

Service Learning Participation

- Training workshops--2 a week for the first 2 weeks of the semester
- After-school tutoring--3 two-hour sessions per week at designated site
- Journal-keeping--1 entry per session
- Submission of journal and final report-- report should describe 3 most important things learned and should be 5-10 pages

Figure 17.8 Presentation Slide with Too Much Text and Too Little Space

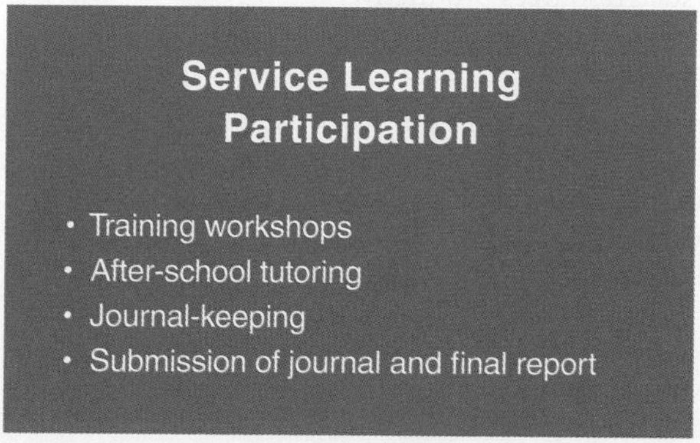

Service Learning Participation

- Training workshops
- After-school tutoring
- Journal-keeping
- Submission of journal and final report

Figure 17.9 Presentation Slide with Brief Text and Effective Use of Space point easier to read. Its bullets highlight the main points, which are meant only to summarize major issues and themes, not to detail the talk. The type sizes for the slides were large enough to be viewed: 44 points for the heading and 32 points for the body.

Finally, the "white space" without text in these slides is actually blue. Some public-speaking experts believe that black type on a white background can be too stark for a slide; instead, they recommend a dark blue background with yellow or white type. However, others believe that black on white is fine and may in fact be what the audience is accustomed to. Presentation software makes it easy for you to experiment with these options or to use your employer's templates.

Additional Writing Assignments

1. Use the job advertisement you located for the activity on pages 360–61, or find one that interests you either for immediate or possible future employment. Write your letter of application for this position, following the advice and format explained in this chapter.

2. Prepare a current résumé, designed as your standard print version or tailored to a specific job advertisement. Follow the advice and format explained in this chapter.

3. Working individually or collaboratively with a small group, conduct a brief research project to investigate the job-hunting or career advice available on campus or in your local community. Identify what you want to learn about these resources or what users might need to know (such as how to access or use them). Prepare a brief report to present your findings to fellow students also interested in using such resources productively.

For more about conducting an interview, see Ch. 6.

4. Interview a personnel manager or another person who hires people in your field of interest. Prepare for the interview by developing a brief set of questions about issues of interest to you — for example, what kinds of jobs are typically available, how the selection process works, what background or other characteristics are typically required or desired, how students might more effectively prepare for employment, what tips the person would give job-seekers, or similar employment- or career-related matters. After the interview, write an essay reporting what you have learned to other interested students. Also write a brief letter (following the business-letter format) thanking the person you interviewed.

5. Prepare your own example of a workplace document introduced in this chapter. After you have drafted, revised, and edited the document, print a second copy. In its margins add notes (like those supplied for many samples in this chapter) to point out features of the format and the content of your document. Revise your document and rework the notes if you wish to make additional changes.

PART FOUR

A WRITER'S STRATEGIES

18 Strategies: A Case Study

For Erin's assignment, see Chapter 4: "Recalling a Personal Experience." For more on writing processes, see Chs. 19–23.

Use the questions in the margin to help you develop your own essay alongside Erin.

When Erin Schmitt enrolled in Rhetoric and Composition I, her first major college assignment was to write an essay reflecting on a personal experience. To get started, she needed to pick a specific experience that she could effectively convey to her readers. Then she needed to reflect on the significance of that experience to convey why it mattered to her. In this chapter, you can follow her writing processes as she generates ideas, develops her first draft, gathers responses from readers, revises and edits her draft, and writes a reflective letter to accompany the essay in her writing portfolio.

Erin Schmitt

Generating Ideas

Erin thought back over her experiences before entering college. She had studied hard to get into college, knowing how important her high school record was for both admissions and financial aid. Although lots of students shared the stress of worrying about grades or money or both, she didn't think that she could narrow those issues to a notable experience. She also knew her local community well, but she thought that her ideas about its issues might work better for the problem-solution assignment coming up later in the term. Then she thought about her last day at her job assisting an elderly man and the compelling recognition she had had just before she came to campus. She started mapping these recollections in the diagram on page 373.

What significant experience do you recall that might engage your readers?

When Erin finished her diagram, she felt confident that she had remembered a significant event and that she could make a compelling point about it. To fill out her ideas, she also answered the six reporter's questions.

How might you generate ideas about your recollections?

Who: Mr. Hertli; me

What: Increased appreciation of life

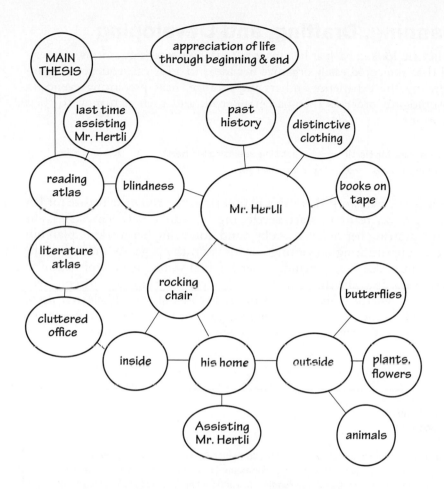

When: While reading an atlas the last time I assisted Mr. Hertli

Where: Mr. Hertli's literature-crammed office/study

Why: Mr. Hertli's blindness

How: Asked to read atlas → confusion → saw child in old, blind Mr. Hertli → appreciation of life

Erin was confident that she had discovered something meaningful to write about. Her reflection about life's connections generated an important recognition. She wanted to share it with readers and thought that she could focus on it as a main idea or thesis to shape her essay. She also had worked for Mr. Hertli for a long time and could remember plenty of vivid details that would bring her experience to life for readers. She could see how her whole paper could fall into place. Now all she needed to do was to figure out how to get it to do that.

 What do you think is the importance of your experience?

For more information and journal questions about the Part Four photograph, see p. A-72.

Planning, Drafting, and Developing

When Erin looked back at her answers to the reporter's questions, she realized that she could easily organize her ideas in a logical sequence: first introducing the experience and its importance, next presenting events in chronological order as they had happened, and then returning to their importance.

What organization would suit your needs?

Assisting Mr. Hertli → Last time assisting Mr. Hertl → Reading atlas → Young and old → Appreciation of life

Once she had worked out this plan, Erin had a rough structure for her essay and was ready to start developing her ideas. Between classes, she started drafting her first version by hand, following her working plan but simply concentrating on getting her ideas on the page. As she wrote, she crossed out false starts, including her original second paragraph. She also inserted words as she thought of them and crossed some out. After all, she didn't care whether this draft was messy because she would clean it up as she keyed it on the computer. The first page of Erin's hand draft appears below, followed by her full word-processor draft for peer review.

How are you starting your draft? What process works for you?

> Erin Schmitt
> 1st Draft
>
> In order to fully appreciate something, to realize its value, one often must experience its beginning and its end. For example, to learn and appreciate all the material in a textbook chapter, reading and understanding must take place from the introduction to the conclusion. A book is not enjoyable if you do not read from start to finish, nor is a movie cut short before the ending is revealed. My appreciation of life came in a most unexpected connection between life's beginning and it's end.

Erin typed her draft, including the changes she had noted in her handwritten draft—omitting paragraph 2, inserting sentence changes, dropping and adding wording, and so forth. Even though this version was still a rough draft, Erin wanted it to be ready for other readers. She and her classmates were going to exchange papers during a workshop for peer response.

Erin expected her classmates to ask about anything that wasn't clear and to respond to the peer response questions for the assignment. Erin also wanted their advice about her own questions:

For Peer Response questions for Erin's assignment, see p. 72.

- Is the scene I'm recalling clear? Does it come alive when you read it?
- Do I reflect enough about what I recall? Should I add more about my insight?

What do you want to ask your readers?

In addition, Erin's instructor required a conference about the draft to discuss revisions that might improve the final version. Erin expected her suggestions to concentrate on the criteria for the assignment: a clear experience with reflection about its significance for the writer. Both sets of comments—handwritten notes and highlighting from a fellow student and electronic "balloons" from her instructor—are shown next to Erin's rough draft.

Rough Draft with Peer and Instructor Responses

In order to fully appreciate something, to realize its value, one often must experience its beginning and its end. For example, to learn and appreciate all the material in a textbook chapter, reading and understanding must take place from the introduction to the conclusion. A book is not enjoyable if you do not read from start to finish, nor is a movie cut short before the ending is revealed. My appreciation of life came in a most unexpected connection between life's beginning and its end.

Peer: *You got the reflection part started right away.*

1 Would any of the general comments about Erin's draft also apply to your draft?

Instructor
Good idea to draw readers in with analogies.

Mr. Hertli was a brilliant old Swiss man whom I assisted every week for the last two years of my high school career. He lived 25 minutes away from my home, down a winding road surrounded by trees, grazing horses, and the occasional house. Trees arched over his steep driveway, as if bowing to all who enter, welcoming anyone with insight, help, or simply company. Mr. Hertli's house was of a very traditional build, and was surrounded by nature. Goats fed on grasses and horses galloped and played within a fenced-off grazing area. Ducks swam on a pond and dozens of sun-colored butterflies danced around bunches of tall purple flowers between which a few stepping-stones were nestled, as a walkway to the front door.

Peer: *I highlighted how you arranged the details to lead us into the house. Good progression. I can really see the scene here.*

2

Instructor
Effective visual details here.

Inside sat Mr. Hertli, always rocking in a chair and listening to books-on-tape in one of the various languages familiar to him. He was very tall, thin, and elderly, and wore dress slacks and a suit jacket no matter what the occasion. His leather shoes were obviously very old, and showed scuffs and wear which told stories of Switzerland, war, research, and accomplishment. Mr. Hertli also wore very dark sunglasses morning and evening to protect the mere one or two percent of his eyesight that had not yet been stolen from him by macular degeneration.

Peer: *I like how you led up to him. You even got his history in with the shoes!*

3

Instructor
Try Edit/Find to catch repetition.

Peer: *The details here end on a big point.*

Peer: *I could see him in ¶3. Now I feel like I know him, too.*

Mr. Hertli was an accomplished man. He had been through   4
immigration, served the United States in war, earned various degrees,
had written a book on evolution and creationism, and was fighting for
his life against a terminal lung disease. He was extremely intelligent,
and it was my job to read him scientific journals and books, record
information and data for his next work-in-progress, manage his
correspondence, fill out paperwork, dispense his medications, and do
nearly all the things a blind person can not do alone.

One particular day, I was assisting Mr. Hertli in his office. Crimson   5
carpeting lined the floor of the tiny literature-crammed room. Journals
and books lay sprawled on every surface, and there was barely room for
a computer on a desk and two chairs somewhere in all the mess. A cord
around Mr. Hertli's head fed oxygen through his nose, while the other
end trailed out the door, down the steps, and into the living room where
an oxygen-dispensing machine always sat, always humming. We sorted
through music, storing old German and Swiss instrumental classics on a
new device for the blind which stored numerous songs, audio books, and
other audio literature for playback. As we waited for the media to
download into the device, Mr. Hertli inquired about recent political
events concerning the country of Georgia. He desired to know the
geographic location of Georgia. "Read the atlas," he said, and although
I had grown to understand and love his thick European accent, I sat
staring at him in bafflement at his words, which he, fortunately, could
not see. I reached under a desk and pushed past books about Darwin,
God, evolution, and history, and found a large, blue-covered atlas, aged
by years of learning, discovery, and research. Brushing the dust off, I
opened the book to the index, and searched for "Georgia." I turned to
the page to which the index directed me, and unsuccessfully tried to
describe Georgia's relation to Turkey, Russia, and Azerbajan. "Show me,"
he said. Show him! How could I, for he could not see, after all, and now
I had to find a way to make him see?!

Instructor
Does everything here support your main idea?

Peer: *The quotes are good, but the whole ¶ seems long — maybe split it? Or drop some detail?*

I placed the wide atlas across his wobbly knees, in his lap, facing   6
him. Taking his hand, I slowly directed Mr. Hertli's finger around the
perimeter of each country, saying. "This is Turkey. To the east, here is
Georgia." He pointed and repeated the countries back to me, and I
asserted that, yes, that was Azerbajan or Russia.

Peer: *Spelled right?*

It was as though I were teaching a small child, who could not read,   7
and who did not know the least about geography. And how strange it
was to be feeling such a way. After all, I was helping a well-educated,
cultured man, in this most elementary, basic way. In this aged man,
nearing the end of his life, I saw the character of a young boy,
beginning to learn a concept new to him.

Peer: *When I read your draft online, my software said this was a fragment. Is it? Are fragments OK in here?*

Peer: *I get what you're saying, but maybe explain it more? This flat statement seems too abrupt.*

This would be the last time I helped Mr. Hertli, as I would be beginning college just a few days later. Mr. Hertli was now completely blind. Like a mother afraid to send her child to school for the first time, I was afraid to cease my assistance of this somewhat helpless man. For when I had seen this connection—the young, new child in the old, I came to realize just how valuable life itself is.

8

Instructor
More reflection here?

Erin also received some overall comments from her readers with suggestions for revision.

❓ What have your readers noted or suggested for your draft?

PEER: I really think you did a good job creating the experience. You're a very descriptive writer, and I liked being able to imagine the experience—the road, the animals, the flowers by the house. I also liked how you used contrasting paragraphs—long paragraph 5 to explain the situation and then short paragraph 6 for the outcome. (But I still think 5 might be too wordy.) You got the reflection part started at the beginning, too, so I knew you were thinking about it. I just wasn't that sure about how you ended with it. My own son traces things with his hands, so I could see what you meant about Mr. Hertli, but I expected you to explain it more. Maybe you could add here to make the conclusion stronger when you revise.

INSTRUCTOR: Erin, you've selected and developed a provocative experience that changed your thinking. However, readers need more explanation and interpretation to share the intensity of your experience. If you explained its significance more fully, your conclusion would be more compelling. I'm wondering if you're trying to find that significance by synthesizing—the reading and thinking skill we discussed in class last week. You seem to be pulling together your actual experience with Mr. Hertli and your insight about the young child who grew up to be this man in order to develop a new idea that goes beyond them. Besides strengthening your concluding reflections as you revise, look also at your fine selection of details. They enrich your description, but try to make sure that all of them are forceful and relevant.

❓ What has your instructor suggested about your draft?

Learning by Doing 🎯 Responding as a Peer

If Erin were in your class, what questions would you want to ask her? What advice for her revision would you supply in your peer response?

Revising and Editing

After Erin met with her peers and her instructor, collecting all the comments about her draft, she began reworking it. To help her focus on the purpose of the essay, she reread the assignment, especially the part where it asked for reflection. She decided that reflecting more would also strengthen her main idea, or thesis—and her instructor had already pointed out the importance of a strong thesis in college writing.

Erin concentrated first on revising her conclusion because all her readers had suggested strengthening it. Then she went back to the beginning of her draft to make other changes, both responding to comments and editing for details. Erin's changes are marked in the following version of her draft. The comments in the margins point out some of her revision and editing decisions.

Revised and Edited Draft

 What is your revision plan for your draft?

What changes do you want to mark in your draft?

Oops! What about a title? Just Mr. Hertli?

In order to fully appreciate something, to realize its value, one often must experience its beginning and its end. For example, to learn and appreciate all the material in a textbook chapter, reading and understanding must take place from the introduction to the conclusion. A book is not enjoyable ~~if you do not~~ from start to finish, nor is a movie cut short before the ending is revealed. My appreciation of life came in a most unexpected connection between life's beginning and its end.

Focus looks OK here.

Mr. Hertli was a brilliant ~~old~~ Swiss man whom I assisted every week for the last two years of my high school career. He lived 25 minutes away from my home, down a winding road, surrounded by trees, grazing horses, *goats, and sheep,* and the occasional house. Trees arched over his steep driveway, as if bowing to all who enter, welcoming anyone with insight, help, or simply company. Mr. Hertli's house was of ~~a very~~ traditional build/ and was surrounded by nature. Goats fed on grasses and horses galloped and played within a fenced-off grazing area. Ducks swam on a pond and dozens of sun-colored butterflies danced around bunches of tall purple flowers between which a few *worn* stepping-stones were nestled/ as a walkway to the front door.

Need to write out numbers that are a word or two

Too much repetition — plus wordy

Inside sat Mr. Hertli, always rocking in a chair and listening to "books-on-tape" in one of the various languages familiar to him. He was ~~very~~ tall, thin, and elderly/ and wore dress slacks and a ~~suit~~ jacket no matter what the occasion. His leather shoes were obviously very old, and *they* showed scuffs and wear which told stories of Switzerland, war, research, and accomplishment. Mr. Hertli also wore ~~very~~ dark

1

2

3

sunglasses morning and evening to protect the mere one or two percent of his ~~eye~~
sight that had not yet been stolen from him by macular degeneration.

Mr. Hertli was an accomplished man. He had been through immigration, served   4
the United States in war, earned various degrees, ~~had~~ written a book on evolution
and creationism, and was *now* fighting for his life against a terminal lung disease. He
was extremely intelligent, and it was my job to read him scientific journals and
books, record information and data for his next work-in-progress, manage his
correspondence, fill out paperwork, dispense his medications, and do nearly all the
things a blind person *can not* do alone.

One particular day, I was assisting Mr. Hertli in his office. Crimson carpeting   5
lined the floor of the tiny literature-crammed room. Journals and books lay sprawled
on every surface~~, and there was~~ *with* barely room for a computer on a desk and two chairs
somewhere in all the mess. *One end of a* ~~A~~ cord around Mr. Hertli's head fed oxygen through
his nose, while the other end trailed out the door, down the steps, and into the
living room where an oxygen-dispensing machine ~~always~~ *constantly* sat, ~~always~~ *constantly* humming. We
sorted through music, storing old German and Swiss instrumental classics on a new
device for the blind which ~~stored numerous songs, audio books, and other audio~~
~~literature~~ *saved audio files* for playback. As we waited for the media to download ~~into the device~~, Mr.
Hertli inquired about recent political events concerning the country of Georgia. He
desired to know the geographic location of Georgia. "Read the atlas," he said, and
although I had grown to understand and love his thick European accent, I sat,
staring ~~at him~~ in bafflement at his words. ~~which he, fortunately, could not see.~~ I
reached under a desk and pushed past books about Darwin, God, evolution, and
history~~, and found~~ *to find* a large, blue-covered atlas, aged by years of learning, *and* discovery~~,~~
~~and research~~. Brushing the dust off, I opened the book to the index, and searched
for "Georgia." I turned to the page to which the index directed me, and
unsuccessfully tried to describe Georgia's relation to Turkey, Russia, and Azerbaijan.
"Show me!" he said. Show him? How could I, for he could not see, after all, and now I
~~had~~ *was* to find a way to make him see!

I placed the wide atlas across his wobbly knees, in his lap, facing him. Taking   6
his hand, I slowly directed Mr. Hertli's *fragile* finger around the perimeter of each country,
saying. "This is Turkey. To the east, here is Georgia." He pointed and repeated the
countries ~~back~~ to me, and I asserted that, yes, that was *indeed* Azerbaijan or Russia *, Armenia,*.

Make this one word

My goal — set the
scene but drop
extra words!

Too much detail
here?

Check commas —
end of the textbook

Luckily my reader
asked about the
spelling.

¶ 5 set up
situation — this ¶
tells what happened

Combine with ¶ 6 — event with meaning?

~~It~~ *This moment* ~~was~~ *felt* as though I were teaching a small child who could not read,   7

and who did not know the least about geography. And how strange it was to be

feeling such a way. After all, I was helping a well-educated, cultured man, in ~~a~~ this

most elementary, basic way! In this aged man, nearing the end of his life, I saw the

character of a *small* young boy, beginning to learn a concept new to him.

My big goal here is adding more reflection.

This would be the last time I helped Mr. Hertli, as I would ~~be beginning~~ *begin* college   8

just a few days later. Mr. Hertli was now completely *, one hundred percent* blind. Like a mother afraid to

send her child to ~~school for the first time~~ *kindergarten*, I was afraid to cease my ~~assistance of this~~ *now care*

for this seemingly ~~somewhat~~ helpless man. For when I had seen this connection, the young*, new* child *new, still learning*

within an man and how unified ~~in the~~ old, I came to realize just how valuable life itself is. *Mr. Hertli showed me how our*

younger selves provide deep roots for us as we get older and how our older selves still preserve our

youth. Young and old, we are all somehow connected, one and the same, no one being of greater worth

than the other. No matter our age, we will always have this link, through generations, and I have grown

to appreciate this of life.

I want to show how old and young connect.

(?) How might you strengthen your essay as you revise and edit?

After Erin finished revising and editing, she spell-checked her final version and proofread it one more time. Then she submitted her final draft.

Final Draft for Submission

Erin Schmitt
ENG 101.004
Essay #1

Mr. Hertli

In order to fully appreciate something, to realize its value, one often must   1 experience its beginning and its end. For example, to learn and appreciate all the material in a textbook chapter, reading and understanding must take place from the introductory paragraph to the conclusion. A book is not enjoyable without reading from start to finish, nor is a movie cut short before the ending is revealed. My appreciation of life came in a most unexpected connection between life's beginning and its end.

Mr. Hertli was a brilliant Swiss man whom I assisted every week for the last two   2 years of my high school career. He lived twenty-five minutes away from my home, down a winding road, surrounded by trees, grazing horses, goats, and sheep, and the occasional house. Trees arched over his steep driveway, as if bowing to all who enter, welcoming anyone with insight, help, or simply company. Mr. Hertli's house was of traditional build and was surrounded by nature. Goats fed on grasses and horses galloped and played within a fenced-off grazing area. Ducks swam on a pond and dozens of sun-colored butterflies danced around bunches of tall purple flowers between which a few worn stepping-stones were nestled as a walkway to the front door.

Inside sat Mr. Hertli, always rocking in a chair and listening to "books-on-tape" in one of the various languages familiar to him. He was tall, thin, and elderly and wore dress slacks and a jacket no matter what the occasion. His leather shoes were obviously very old, and they showed scuffs and wear which told stories of Switzerland, war, research, and accomplishment. Mr. Hertli also wore dark sunglasses morning and evening to protect the mere one or two percent of his sight that had not yet been stolen from him by macular degeneration.   3

Mr. Hertli was an accomplished man. He had been through immigration, served the United States in war, earned various degrees, written a book on evolution and creationism, and was now fighting for his life against a terminal lung disease. He was extremely intelligent, and it was my job to read him scientific journals and books, record information and data for his next work-in-progress, manage his correspondence, fill out paperwork, dispense his medications, and do nearly all the things a blind person cannot do alone.   4

One particular day, I was assisting Mr. Hertli in his office. Crimson carpeting lined the floor of the tiny literature-crammed room. Journals and books lay sprawled on every surface with barely room for a computer on a desk and two chairs somewhere in all the mess. One end of a cord around Mr. Hertli's head fed oxygen through his nose, while the other end trailed out the door, down the steps, and into the living room where an oxygen-dispensing machine constantly sat, constantly humming. We sorted through music, storing old German and Swiss instrumental classics on a new device for the blind which saved audio files for   5

Mr. Peter Hertli

playback. As we waited for the media to download, Mr. Hertli inquired about recent political events concerning the country of Georgia. He desired to know the geographic location of Georgia. "Read the atlas," he said, and although I had grown to understand and love his thick European accent, I sat, staring in bafflement at his words. I reached under a desk and pushed past books about Darwin, God, evolution, and history to find a large, blue-covered atlas, aged by years of learning and discovery. Brushing the dust off, I opened the book to the index and searched for "Georgia." I turned to the page to which the index directed me and unsuccessfully tried to describe Georgia's relation to Turkey, Russia, and Azerbaijan. "Show me!" he said. Show him? How could I, for he could not see, after all, and now I was to find a way to make him see?

I placed the wide atlas across his wobbly knees, in his lap, facing him. Taking   6
his fragile hand, I slowly directed Mr. Hertli's finger around the perimeter of each country, saying. "This is Turkey. To the east, here is Georgia." He pointed and repeated the countries to me, and I asserted that, yes, that was indeed Azerbaijan, Armenia, or Russia. This moment felt as though I were teaching a small child, one who could not read and who did not know the least about geography. And how strange it was to be feeling such a way. After all, I was helping a well-educated, cultured man, in this most elementary, basic way! In this aged man, nearing the end of his life, I saw the character of a small young boy, beginning to learn a concept new to him.

This would be the last time I helped Mr. Hertli, as I would begin college just a   7
few days later. Mr. Hertli was now completely, one hundred percent blind. Like a mother afraid to send her child to kindergarten, I was now afraid to cease my care for this seemingly helpless man. For when I had seen this connection, the new, young child still learning within an old man, I came to realize just how valuable and how unified life itself is. Mr. Hertli showed me how our younger selves provide deep roots for us as we get older and how our older selves still preserve our youth. Young and old, we are all somehow connected, one and the same, no one being of greater worth than the other. No matter our age, we will always have this link, through generations, and I have grown to appreciate this of life.

Reflecting as a Writer

Erin's essay assignment asked her to reflect on her experience as she wrote about its significance for her. In addition, her instructor required a reflective letter, following the time-honored advice of writer and teacher Peter Elbow. Erin needed to consider her goals, strengths, remaining challenges, and responses to readers during her writing process. The letter was to accompany the essay and become a part of her writer's portfolio due at the end of the term.

Reflective Portfolio Letter

Campus Box A-456

September 22, 2010

For sample business
letter formats, see
pp. 361–64.

Dr. Susanna Hoeness-Krupsaw
English Department
State University
1234 University Road
Campustown, OH 23456

Dear Dr. Hoeness-Krupsaw:

The main goal of my essay was to describe accurately and vividly the significant
experience of reading to a blind, elderly man during my last two years of high
school. When writing the essay I was attempting to give the reader insight to the
details and scenery I experienced while visiting this man. By accurately describing
the scene of most significance in great detail, I hoped to convey and emphasize that
significance to the reader.

? What do you
want to say in a
reflective letter?

The strengths I had in writing this essay were in detailing and flow. I believe my
descriptions accurately put images in the mind of the reader. I began my writing
process by planning with a diagram. After creating this diagram, the essay easily
formed in my mind and on paper. However, if I could revise the essay further, I
would focus more on word choice and strength. I would also revise and strengthen
my reflections as well as my concluding paragraph. When writing, I had some
difficulty in putting into words exactly what my experience made me think and feel.

The feedback I received regarding my essay was mostly positive. However, almost all
feedback suggested adding more reflection at the end of my final draft. I believe
this strengthened my essay overall. I would like to get a response from the reader
asserting that my essay vividly conveyed images and that the importance of this
event is easily understood.

I may be contacted regarding this essay at eschmitt@campus.edu or 555-5555.

Sincerely,

Erin E. Schmitt

Enc.

Learning by Doing Writing a Reflective Letter

Select one of the following options, and write a reflective letter to your instructor.

1. Reflect on your responses to Erin's writing strategies and processes. For example, you might consider how her processes do and do not relate to your own or what you have learned from her that you might like to apply to your own writing.
2. Reflect on your own first essay, as Erin did. Consider your goals, strengths, remaining challenges, and responses to readers.

For most writers, the hardest part of writing comes first—confronting a blank page. Fortunately, you can prepare for that moment, both for finding ideas and for getting ready to write. All of the tested techniques that follow have worked for some writers—both professionals and students—and some may work for you.

Finding Ideas

When you begin to write, you need to start the ideas flowing. Sometimes ideas appear effortlessly on the paper or screen, perhaps triggered by the resources around you—something you read, see, hear, discuss, or think about. (See the top half of the graphic below.) But at other times you need idea generators, strategies you can use whenever your ideas dry up or you

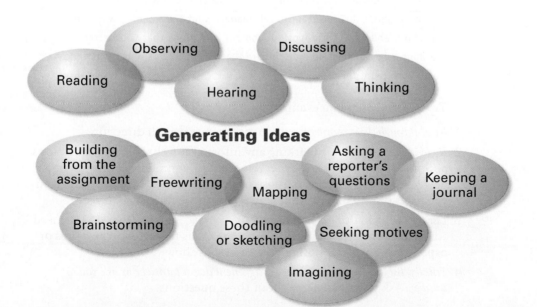

need more examples or evidence. If one strategy doesn't work for a particular writing task, try another. (See the lower half of the graphic.)

Building from Your Assignment

Learning to write is learning what questions to ask yourself. Your assignment may trigger this process by raising some questions and answering others. For example, Ben Tran jotted notes in his book as his instructor and classmates discussed his first assignment—recalling a personal experience.

For more detail about this assignment, turn to pp. 66–67 in Ch. 4.

The assignment clarified what audience to address and what purpose to try to accomplish. Ben's classmates asked about length, format, and due date, but Ben saw three big questions: Which experience should I pick? How did it change me? Why was it so important for me? As class ended, Ben didn't know what he'd write about, but he had figured out the questions to tackle first.

What event? What consequences?

What readers? class + prof.

Write about one specific experience that changed how you acted, thought, or felt. Use your experience as a springboard for reflection. Your purpose is not merely to tell an interesting story but to show your readers—your instructor and your classmates—the importance of that experience for you.

What purpose? 2 parts!

Tell the story but do more—reflect & show importance

Sometimes an assignment assumes that you already understand something critical—how to address a particular audience or what to include in some type of writing. When Amalia Blackhawk read her argument assignment, she jotted down questions to ask her instructor.

Anything OK? Or only newspaper type of issue?

Editor of what?

What's my purpose? Persuading readers to respect my view or to agree?

Select a campus or local issue that matters to you, and write a letter to the editor about it. Be certain to tell readers what the issue is, why it is important, and how you propose to address it. Assume that your letter will appear in a special opinion feature that allows letters longer than the usual word-count limits.

My classmates? The publication's readers?

How long is the usual letter? How long should mine be? Anything else letters like this should do?

Try these steps as you examine an assignment:

1. *Read through the assignment once* to discover its overall direction.

2. *Read it again,* this time marking any information that answers questions about your situation as a writer. Does the assignment identify or suggest your audience, your purpose in writing, the type of paper expected, the parts typical of that kind of writing, or the format required?

3. *List the questions that the assignment raises for you.* Exactly what do you need to decide—the type of topic to pick, the focus to develop, the issues or aspects to consider, or other guidelines to follow?

4. *Finally, list any questions that the assignment doesn't answer or ask you to answer.* Ask your instructor about these questions.

Learning by Doing 🔲 Building from Your Assignment

Select an assignment from this book, another textbook, or another class, and make notes about it. What questions does it answer for you? Which questions or decisions does it direct to you? What other questions might you want to ask your instructor? Then exchange assignments with a classmate; make notes about that assignment, too. With your partner, compare responses to both.

Brainstorming

A *brainstorm* is a sudden insight or inspiration. As a writing strategy, brainstorming uses free association to stimulate a chain of ideas, often to personalize a topic and break it down into specifics. Start with a word or phrase, and spend a set period of time simply listing ideas as rapidly as possible. Write down whatever comes to mind with no editing or going back.

Brainstorming can be a group activity to gain from varied perspectives. At work, it is commonly used to fill a specific need—finding a name for a product or an advertising slogan. In college, you can try group brainstorming with a few others or your entire class. Sit facing one another. Designate one person to record on paper, screen, or chalkboard whatever the others suggest or the best idea in the air at a busy moment. After several minutes of calling out ideas, look over the recorder's list for useful results. Online a group might toss out ideas during a chat or post them for all to consider.

On your own, you might brainstorm to define a topic, generate an example while writing, or come up with a title for a finished paper. Angie Ortiz brainstormed after her instructor assigned a paper ("Demonstrate from your own experience how electronic technology is changing our lives"). First, she wrote *electronic technology* at the top of the page and set her alarm for fifteen minutes. Then she began to scribble words and phrases.

> Electronic technology
> iPod, cell phone, laptop, BlackBerry. Plus TV, cable, DVDs. Too much?!
> Always on call — at home, in car, at school. Always something playing.
> Spend so much time in electronic world — phone calls, texting, tunes. Cuts into time
>   really hanging with friends — face-to-face time.
> Less aware of my surroundings outside of the electronic world?

When her alarm went off, Ortiz took a break. After returning to her list, she crossed out ideas that did not interest her and circled her final promising question. From her rough list, a focus began to emerge: the capacity of the electronic world to expand information but reduce awareness.

When you want to brainstorm, try this advice:

1. *Launch your thoughts with a key word or phrase.* If you need a topic, begin with a general word or phrase (for example, *computer*); if you need an example for a paragraph in progress, use a specific word or phrase (for example, *financial errors computers make*).

2. *Set a time limit.* Ten minutes (or so) is enough for strenuous thinking.

3. *Rapidly list brief items.* Stick to words, phrases, or short sentences that you can quickly scan later.

4. *Don't stop.* Don't worry about spelling, repetition, absurdity, or relevance. Don't judge, and don't arrange: just produce. Record whatever comes into your head, as fast as you can. If your mind goes blank, keep moving, even if you only repeat what you've just written.

When you finish, circle or check anything intriguing. Scratch out whatever looks useless or dull. Then try some conscious organizing: Are any thoughts related? Can you group them? If so, does the group suggest a topic?

Learning by Doing 💾 Brainstorming

From the following list, choose a subject that interests you, that you know something about, and that you'd like to learn more about—in other words, that you might like to write on. Then brainstorm for ten minutes.

travel	fear	exercise
dieting	dreams	automobiles
family	technology	sports
advertisements	animals	education

Now look over your list, and circle any potential paper topic. How well did this exercise work for you? Can you think of variations to make it more useful?

Freewriting

To tap your unconscious by *freewriting,* simply write sentences without stopping for about fifteen minutes. The sentences don't have to be grammatical, coherent, or stylish; just keep them flowing to unlock an idea's potential.

For Ortiz's
brainstorming,
see p. 387.

Generally, freewriting is most productive if it has an aim—for example, finding a topic, a purpose, or a question you want to answer. Angie Ortiz wrote her topic at the top of a page—and then explored her rough ideas.

Electronic devices — do they isolate us? I chat all day online and by phone, but that's quick communication, not in-depth conversation. I don't really spend much time hanging with friends and getting to know what's going on with them. I love listening to my iPod on campus, but maybe I'm not as aware of my surroundings as I could be. I miss seeing things, like the new art gallery that I walk by every day. I didn't even notice the new sculpture park in front! Then, at night, I do assignments on my computer, browse the Web, and watch some cable. I'm in my own little electronic world most of the time. I love technology, but what else am I missing?

The result, as you can see, wasn't polished prose. Still, in a short time she produced a paragraph to serve as a springboard for her essay.

If you want to try freewriting, here's what you do:

1. *Write a sentence or two at the top of your page or file* — the idea you plan to develop by freewriting.

2. *Write without stopping for at least ten minutes.* Express whatever comes to mind, even "My mind is blank," until a new thought floats up.

3. *Don't censor yourself.* Don't cross out false starts or grammar errors. Don't worry about connecting ideas or finding perfect words.

4. *Feel free to explore.* Your initial sentences are a rough guide, not a straitjacket. If you are straying from them, the new direction may be valuable.

5. *Prepare yourself* — if you want to. While you wait for your ideas to start racing, you may want to think about some of these questions:

   What interests you about the topic? What do you care most about? What do you know about it that the next person doesn't?

   What have you read about the topic? Observed or heard about it?

   How might you feel about this topic if you were someone else (a parent, an instructor, a person from another country)?

6. *Repeat the process, looping back to expand a good idea if you wish.* Poke at the most interesting parts to see if they will further unfold:

   What does that mean? If that's true, what then? So what?

   What other examples or evidence does this statement call to mind?

   What objections might a reader raise? How might you answer them?

Learning by Doing 🖋 Freewriting

Select an idea from your current thinking or a brainstorming list. Write it at the top of a page or file, and freewrite for fifteen minutes. Share your freewriting with your classmates. If you wish, loop back to repeat this process.

Doodling or Sketching

If you fill the margins of your notebooks with doodles, harness this artistic energy to generate ideas for writing. Elena Lopez began to sketch her collision with a teammate during a soccer tournament (Figure 19.1). She added stick figures, notes, symbols, and color as she outlined a series of events.

Try this advice as you develop ideas by doodling or sketching:

1. *Give your ideas room to grow.* Open a new file using a drawing program, doodle in pencil on a blank page, or sketch on a series of pages.

2. *Concentrate on your topic, but welcome new ideas.* Begin with a key visual in the center or at the top of a page. Add sketches or doodles as they occur to you to embellish, expand, define, or redirect your topic.

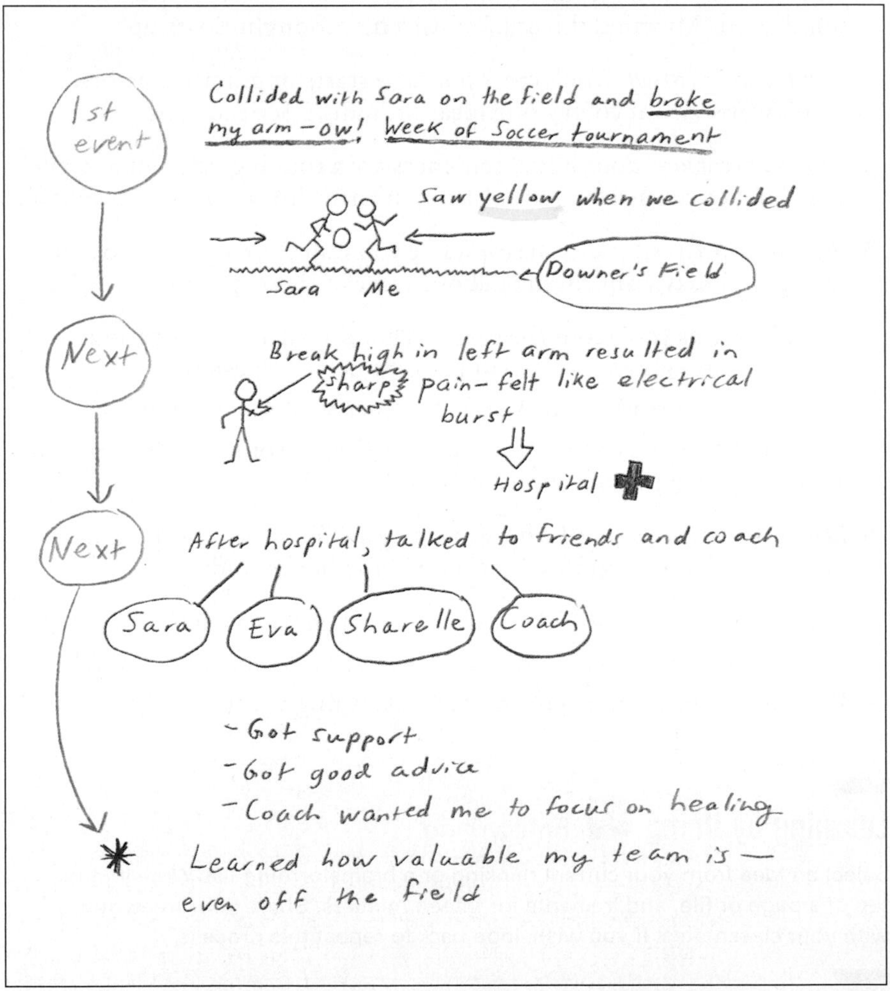

Figure 19.1 Doodling or sketching to generate ideas

3. *Add icons, symbols, colors, figures, labels, notes, or questions.* Freely mix visuals and text, recording ideas without stopping to refine them.

4. *Follow up on your discoveries.* After a break, add notes to make connections, identify sequences, or convert visuals into descriptive sentences.

Learning by Doing 📷 Doodling or Sketching

Start with a doodle or sketch that illustrates your topic. Add related events, ideas, or details to develop your topic visually. Share your material with classmates; use their observations to help you refine your direction as a writer.

Mapping

Mapping taps your visual and spatial creativity as you generate ideas. When you use mapping, you position ideas on the page, in a file, or with cloud software to show their relationships or relative importance — radiating outward from a key term in the center, dropping down from a key word at the top, sprouting upward from a root idea, branching out from a trunk, flowing across the page or screen in a chronological or causal sequence, or following a circular, spiral, sequential, or other familiar form.

Andrew Choi used mapping to gather ideas for his proposal for revitalizing the campus radio station (Figure 19.2). He noted ideas on colored sticky notes — blue for problems, yellow for solutions, and pink for implementation details. Then he moved the sticky notes around on a blank page, arranging them as he connected ideas.

Here are some suggestions for mapping:

1. *Allow space for your map to develop.* Open a new file, try posterboard for arranging sticky notes or cards, or use a large page for notes.

2. *Begin with a topic or key idea.* Using your imagination, memory, class notes, or reading, place a key word at the center or top of a page.

3. *Add related ideas, examples, issues, or questions.* Quickly and spontaneously place these points above, below, or beside your key word.

4. *Refine the connections.* As your map evolves, use lines, arrows, or loops to connect ideas; box or circle them to focus attention; add colors to relate points or to distinguish source materials from your own ideas.

After a break, continue mapping to probe one part more deeply, refine the structure, add detail, or build an alternate map from a different viewpoint. Also try mapping to develop graphics that present ideas in visual form.

See pp. 412–13 on clustering.

Figure 19.2 Mapping to generate ideas

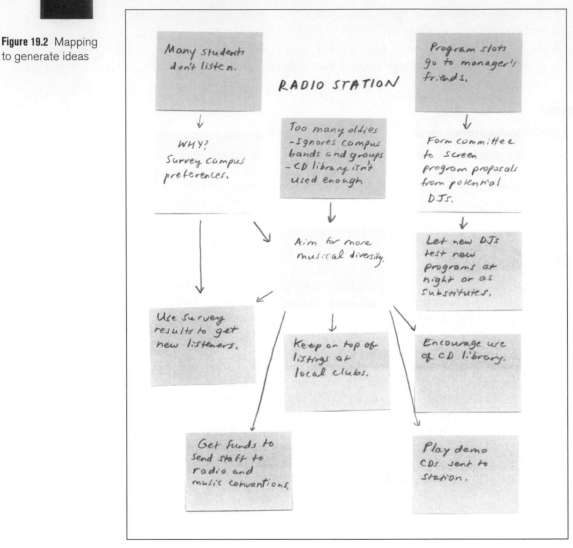

Learning by Doing 📷 Mapping

Start with a key word or idea that you know about. Map related ideas, using visual elements to show how they connect. Share your map with classmates, and then use their questions or comments to refine your mapping.

Imagining

Your imagination is a valuable resource for exploring possibilities—analyzing an option, evaluating an alternative, or solving a problem—to discover surprising ideas, original examples, and unexpected relationships.

Suppose that you asked, "What if the average North American life span were more than a century?" No doubt many more people would be old. How would that shift affect doctors and nurses, hospitals, and other medical facilities? How might city planners respond to the needs of so many more old people? What would the change mean for shopping centers? For television programming? For leisure activities? For Social Security? For taxes?

Use some of the following strategies to unleash your imagination:

1. *Speculate about changes, alternatives, and options.* What common assumption—something most take for granted—might you question or deny? What deplorable condition would you remedy? What changes in policy, practice, or attitude might avoid future problems? What different paths in life each with challenges and promises—might you take?

2. *Shift perspective.* Experiment by taking a point of view other than your usual one. How would someone on the opposite side of an issue respond? How would a plant, an animal, or a Martian? Try shifting the debate (to whether people over sixty-five, not teenagers, should be allowed to drink) or the time frame (from present to past or future).

3. *Envision what might be.* Join the others who have imagined a utopia (an ideal state) or an anti-utopia by envisioning alternatives—a better way of treating illness, electing a president, or ordering a chaotic jumble.

4. *Synthesize.* Synthesizing (generating new ideas by combining previously separate ideas) is the opposite of analyzing (breaking ideas down into component parts). Synthesize to make fresh connections, fusing materials—perhaps old or familiar—into something new.

For more about analysis and synthesis, see pp. 35–37.

Learning by Doing   Imagining

Begin with a problem that cries out for a solution, a condition that requires a remedy, or a situation that calls for change. Ask "What if?" or start with "Suppose that" to trigger your imagination. Share ideas with your classmates.

Asking a Reporter's Questions

Journalists, assembling facts to write a news story, ask themselves six simple questions—the five *W*'s and an *H*:

Who?	Where?	Why?
What?	When?	How?

In the *lead,* or opening paragraph, of a good news story, the writer tries to condense the whole story into a sentence or two, answering all six questions.

> A giant homemade fire balloon [*what*] startled residents of Costa Mesa [*where*] last night [*when*] as Ambrose Barker, 79, [*who*] zigzagged across the sky at nearly 300 miles per hour [*how*] in an attempt to set a new altitude record [*why*].

Later in the news story, the reporter will add details, using the six basic questions to generate more about what happened and why.

For your college writing, use these questions to generate details. They can help you explore the significance of a childhood experience, analyze what happened at a moment in history, or investigate a campus problem. Don't worry if some go nowhere or lead to repetitious answers. Later you'll weed out irrelevant points and keep those that look promising.

For a topic that is not based on your personal experience, you may need to do reading or interviewing to answer some of the questions. Take, for example, the topic of the assassination of President John F. Kennedy, and notice how each question can lead to further questions.

- *Who* was John F. Kennedy? What kind of person was he? What kind of president? Who was with him when he was killed? Who was nearby?
- *What* happened to Kennedy? What events led up to the assassination? What happened during it? What did the media do? What did everyone across the country do? What did someone who remembers this event do?
- *Where* was Kennedy assassinated—city, street, vehicle, seat? Where was he going? Where did the shots likely come from? Where did they hit him? Where did he die?
- *When* was he assassinated—day, month, year, time? When did Kennedy decide to go to this city? When—precisely—were the shots fired? When did he die? When was a suspect arrested?
- *Why* was Kennedy assassinated? What are some of the theories? What solid evidence is available? Why has this event caused controversy?
- *How* was Kennedy assassinated? How many shots were fired? Specifically what caused his death? How can we get at the truth of this event?

Learning by Doing 🖎 Asking a Reporter's Questions

Choose one of the following topics, or use one of your own:

    A memorable event in history or in your life
    A concert or other performance that you have attended
    An accomplishment on campus or an occurrence in your city
    An important speech or a proposal for change
    A questionable stand someone has taken

Answer the six reporter's questions about the topic. Then write a sentence or two synthesizing the answers to the six questions. Incorporate that sentence into an introductory paragraph for an essay that you might write later.

Seeking Motives

In a large part of your college writing, you will try to explain the motives behind human behavior. In a history paper, you might consider how George Washington's conduct shaped the presidency. In a literature essay, you might analyze the motives of Hester Prynne in *The Scarlet Letter*. Because people, including characters in fiction, are so complex, this task is challenging.

For more on writing about literature, see Ch. 13.

If you want to understand any human act, according to philosopher-critic Kenneth Burke, you can break it down into five basic components, a *pentad,* and ask questions about each one. Burke's pentad overlaps the reporter's questions but differs in that it can show how the components of a human act affect one another, taking you deeper into motives.

Suppose that you are preparing to write a political-science paper on President Lyndon Baines Johnson (LBJ), sworn in as president right after President Kennedy's assassination in 1963. A year later, he was elected to the post by a landslide. By 1968, however, Johnson had decided not to run for a second term. You decide to use Burke's pentad to investigate why.

1. *The act*: What was done?

   Announcing the decision to leave office without standing for reelection.

2. *The actor*: Who did it?

   President Johnson.

3. *The agency*: What means did the person use to make it happen?

   A televised address to the nation.

4. *The scene*: Where, when, and under what circumstances did it happen?

   Washington, D.C., March 31, 1968. Protesters against the Vietnam War were gaining influence. The press was increasingly critical of the war. Senator Eugene McCarthy, an antiwar candidate for president, had made a strong showing against LBJ in the New Hampshire primary election.

5. *The purpose or motive for acting*: What could have made the person do it?

   LBJ's motives might have included avoiding a probable defeat, escaping further personal attacks, sparing his family, making it easier for his successor to pull out of the war, and easing bitter dissent among Americans.

To carry Burke's method further, you can pair the five components and begin fruitful lines of inquiry by asking questions about the pairs:

actor to act	act to scene	scene to agency
actor to scene	act to agency	scene to purpose
actor to purpose	act to purpose	agency to purpose

PAIR	actor to agency
QUESTION	What did LBJ [actor] have to do with his televised address [agency]?
ANSWER	Commanding the attention of a vast audience, LBJ must have felt he was in control—even though his ability to control the situation in Vietnam was slipping.

Not all the paired questions will prove fruitful; some may not even apply. But one or two might reveal valuable connections and start you writing.

Learning by Doing 🎬 Seeking Motives

Choose an action that puzzles you—perhaps something you, a family member, or a friend has done; a decision of a historical or current political figure; something in a movie, television program, or literary selection. Then apply Burke's pentad to seek motives for the action. If you wish, also pair up components. When you believe you understand the individual's motivation, write a paragraph explaining the action, and share it with your classmates.

Keeping a Journal

For ideas about keeping a reading journal, see p. 22.

Journal writing richly rewards anyone who engages in it regularly. You can write anywhere or anytime: all you need is a notebook or computer and a few minutes to record an entry. To keep a valuable journal, you need only the honesty and willingness to set down what you think and feel.

Your journal will become a mine studded with priceless nuggets—thoughts, observations, reactions, and revelations that are yours for the taking. As you write, you can rifle your well-stocked journal freely for writing topics, insights, examples, and other material. A journal can be what you want it to be, and the best journal is the one that's useful to *you*.

Reflective Journals. When you write in your journal, put less emphasis on recording what happened, as you would in a diary, than on *reflecting* about what you do or see, hear or read, learn or believe. An entry can be a list or an outline, a paragraph or an essay, a poem or a letter you don't intend to send, even a page of doodling. Describe a person or a place, set down a conversation, or record insights into actions. Consider your pet peeves, fears, dreams, treasures, convictions or moral dilemmas, or the fate of the world — if you were in charge. Use your experience as a writer to nourish and inspire your writing, recording what worked, what didn't, and how you reacted to each.

Responsive Journals. Sometimes you *respond* to something in particular — to your reading for an assignment, to classroom discussions, to a movie, to a conversation or an observation. Faced with a long paper to write, you might assign *yourself* a focused response journal. Then when the time comes to draft your paper, you will have plenty of material to use.

For more on responding to reading, see Ch. 2.

For responsive journal prompts, see the end of each selection in *A Writer's Reader.*

Warm-Up Journals. To prepare for an assignment, you can group ideas, scribble outlines, sketch beginnings, capture stray thoughts, record relevant material. Of course, what starts as a quick comment on an essay (or a responsive journal entry) may turn into the draft of a paper.

E-Journals. Once you create a file and make entries by date or subject, you can record ideas, feelings, images, memories, quotations, and any other writing you wish. You will find it easy to copy and paste inspiring e-mail, quotations from Web pages, or digitized images and sounds. Always identify the source of copied material so that you won't later confuse it with your original writing.

Blogs. Like traditional journals, "Web logs" typically aim for frank, honest, and immediate entries. Unlike journals, they often explore a specific topic and may be available publicly on the Web or privately by invitation. Especially in an online class, you might blog about your writing or research processes.

Learning by Doing 🎦 Keeping a Journal

Keep a journal for at least a week. Each day record your thoughts, feelings, observations, and reactions. Reflect on what happens, and respond to what you read. Try at least one of the responsive prompts following a selection in *A Writer's Reader.* At the end of the week, bring your journal to class, and read aloud to your classmates the entry you like best.

Getting Ready

Once you have generated a suitable topic and some ideas related to that topic, you are ready to get down to the job of actually writing.

Setting Up Circumstances

If you can write only with your shoes off or with a can of soda nearby, set yourself up that way. Some writers need to hear blaring rap music; others need quiet. Create an environment that puts you in the mood for writing.

Devote One Special Place to Writing. Your place should have good lighting and space to spread out. It may be a desk in your room, the dining room table, or a quiet library cubicle — someplace where no one will bother you, where your mind and body will settle in, and preferably where you can leave projects and keep handy your computer and materials.

Establish a Ritual. Some writers find that a ritual relaxes them and helps them get started. You might open a soda, straighten your desk, turn music on (or off), and create a new file on the computer.

Relocate. If you're stuck, try moving from library to home or from kitchen to bedroom. Try an unfamiliar place — a restaurant, an airport.

Reduce Distractions. Most of us can't prevent interruptions, but we can reduce them. If you expect your boyfriend to call, call him before you start writing. If you have small children, write when they are asleep or at school. Turn off your phone, and concentrate hard. Let others know you are serious about writing; allow yourself to give it full attention.

Write at the Time Best for You. Some people think best early in the morning, while others favor the small hours when the world is still and their stern self-critic might be asleep, too. Writing at dawn or in the wee hours also reduces distractions from other people.

Write on a Schedule. Writing at a predictable time of day worked marvels for English novelist Anthony Trollope, who would start at 5:30 A.M., write 2,500 words before 8:30 A.M., and then go to his job at the post office. (He wrote more than sixty books.) Even if you can't set aside the same time every day, it may help to decide, "Today from four to five, I'll write."

Preparing Your Mind

Sometimes ideas, images, or powerful urges to write will arrive like sudden miracles. When they come, even if you are taking a shower or getting ready to go to a movie, yield to impulse and write. Encourage such moments by opening your mind to inspiration.

Talk about Your Writing. Discuss ideas in person, by phone, or online with a classmate or friend, encouraging questions, comments, and suggestions. Or talk to yourself, using a voice-activated recorder, while you sit through traffic jams, walk your dog, or ride your bike.

Lay Out Your Plans. Tell a nearby listener—student next door, spouse, parent, friend—why you want to write this paper, what you'll put in it, how you'll lay it out. If you hear "That sounds good," you'll be encouraged. If you see a yawn, you'll have ideas in motion.

Keep a Notebook or Journal Handy. Always keep some paper in your pocket or backpack or on the night table to write down good ideas that pop into your mind. Imagination may strike in the grocery checkout line, in the doctor's waiting room, or during a lull on the job.

Read. The step from reading to writing is a short one. Even when you're reading for fun, you're involved with words. You might hit on something for your paper. Or read purposefully: Set out to read and take notes.

DISCOVERY CHECKLIST

☐ Is your environment organized for writing? What changes might help you reduce distractions and procrastination?

☐ Have you scheduled enough time to get ready to write? How might you adjust your schedule or your expectations to encourage productivity?

☐ Is your assignment clear? What additional questions might you want to ask about what you are expected to do?

☐ Have you generated enough ideas that interest you? What might help you expand, focus, or deepen your ideas?

20 Strategies for Stating a Thesis and Planning

Starting to write often seems a chaotic activity, but the strategies in this chapter can help create order. For most papers, you will want to consider your purpose and audience and then focus on a central point by discovering, stating, and improving a thesis. To help you arrange your material, the chapter also includes advice on grouping ideas and outlining.

Shaping Your Topic for Your Purpose and Your Audience

For critical questions about audience and more about purpose, see p. 401. For more about both, see pp. 11–15.

As you work on your college papers, you may feel as if you're juggling — selecting weighty points and lively details, tossing them into the air, catching each one as it falls, keeping them all moving in sequence. Busy as you are simply juggling, however, your performance almost always draws a crowd — your instructor, your classmates, or other readers. They'll expect you to attend to their concerns as you try to achieve your purpose — probably informing, explaining, or persuading.

Think carefully about your audience and purpose to plan effectively. If you want to show your classmates and instructor the importance of an event, start by deciding how much detail they need. If most of them have gotten speeding tickets, for instance, they'll need less information about that event than city commuters might. However, to achieve your purpose, you'll need to go beyond what happened to why the event mattered to you. No matter how many tickets your readers have gotten, they won't know the importance of that experience for you unless you share that information. They may incorrectly assume that you were worrying about being late to

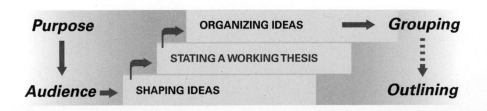

class or paying higher insurance rates when, in fact, you had suddenly realized your narrow escape from an accident like your cousin's and that recognition motivated you to change your driving habits.

Similarly, if you want to persuade county officials to change the way absentee ballots are distributed to college students, you'll need to support your idea with reasons and evidence — drawing on the state election laws and legal precedents familiar to these readers as well as the experiences of student voters. You may need to show not only how your proposal would solve existing problems but also why it would do so better than other proposals.

Plan for your purpose and audience using questions such as these:

- *What is your general purpose?* What would you like to accomplish in your paper? How would you like your readers to react? Do you want them to smile, think, or agree? To understand, learn, accept, respect, care, change, or reply? How might your writing accomplish your aims?

- *Who are your readers?* If they are not clearly identified by your assignment or situation, what do you assume about them? What do they know or want to know? What opinions do they hold? What do they find informative or persuasive? How might you appeal to them?

- *How might you narrow and focus your ideas about the topic,* given what you know or assume about your purpose and audience? Which slant would best accomplish your purpose? What points would appeal most strongly to your readers? What details would engage or persuade them?

- *What qualities of good writing have been discussed in your class,* explained in your syllabus, or identified in assigned readings? What criteria have emerged from exchanges of drafts with classmates or comments from your instructor? How might you shape your writing to demonstrate desirable qualities to readers?

Learning by Doing 🎯 Considering Purpose and Audience

Think back to a recent writing task—a college essay, a job application, a report or memo at work, a letter to a campus office, or some other piece. Write a brief description of your situation as a writer at that time. What was your purpose? Who—exactly—were your readers? How did you account for both as you planned? How might you have made your writing more effective?

Stating and Using a Thesis

Most pieces of effective writing are unified around one main point. That is, all the subpoints and supporting details are relevant to that point. Generally, after you have read an essay, you can sum up the writer's main point in a sentence, even if the author has not stated it explicitly. We call this summary statement a *thesis*.

Explicit Thesis. Often a thesis will be explicit, plainly stated, in the selection itself. In "The Myth of the Latin Woman: I Just Met a Girl Named María" from *The Latin Deli* (Athens: University of Georgia Press, 1993), Judith Ortiz Cofer states her thesis at the end of the first paragraph: "You can leave the Island, master the English language, and travel as far as you can, but if you are a Latina, especially one like me who so obviously belongs to Rita Moreno's gene pool, the Island travels with you." This clear statement, strategically placed, helps readers see her point.

Implicit Thesis. Sometimes a thesis is implicit, indirectly suggested rather than directly stated. In "The Niceness Solution," a selection from Bruce Bawer's *Beyond Queer* (New York: Free Press, 1996), Paul Varnell describes an ordinance "banning rude behavior, including rude speech," passed in Raritan, New Jersey. After discussing a 1580 code of conduct, he identifies four objections to such attempts to limit free speech. He concludes with this sentence: "Sensibly, Raritan Police Chief Joseph Sferro said he would not enforce the new ordinance." Although Varnell does not state his main point in one concise sentence, readers know that he opposes the Raritan law and any other attempts to legislate "niceness."

The purpose of most academic and workplace writing is to inform, to explain, or to convince. To achieve any of these purposes, you must make your main point crystal clear. A thesis sentence helps you clarify your idea and stay on track as you write. It also helps your readers see your point and follow your discussion. Sometimes you may want to imply your thesis, but if you state it explicitly, you ensure that readers cannot miss it.

Learning by Doing 🗂 Identifying Theses

Working in a small group, select five essays from Part Two of this book to read carefully (or your instructor may choose the essays for your group). Then, individually, write out the thesis for each essay. Some thesis sentences are stated outright (explicit), but others are indirect (implicit). Compare and contrast the thesis statements that you identified with those your classmates found, and discuss the similarities and differences. How can you account for the differences? Try to agree on a thesis statement for each essay.

Look for specific advice under headings that mention a thesis in Chs. 4–12. Watch for the red labels that identify thesis examples.

How to Discover a Working Thesis

It's rare for a writer to develop a perfect thesis statement early in the writing process and then to write an effective essay that fits it exactly. What you should aim for is a *working thesis*—a statement that can guide you but that you will ultimately refine. Ideas for a working thesis are probably all around you.

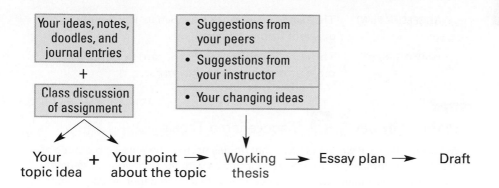

Your topic identifies the area you want to explore. To convert a topic to a thesis, you need to add your own slant, attitude, or point. A useful thesis contains not only the key words that identify your *topic* but also the *point* you want to make or the *attitude* you intend to express.

Topic   +   Slant or Attitude or Point   =   Working Thesis

Suppose you want to identify and write about a specific societal change.

TOPIC IDEA   Old-fashioned formal courtesy

Now you experiment, testing ideas to make the topic your own.

TRIAL   Old-fashioned formal courtesy is a thing of the past.

Although your trial sentence emphasizes change, it's still circular, repeating rather than advancing a workable point. It doesn't say anything new about old-fashioned formal courtesy; it simply defines *old-fashioned*. You still need to state your own slant—maybe why things have changed.

TOPIC IDEA + SLANT   old-fashioned formal courtesy + its decline as gender roles have changed

WORKING THESIS   As the roles of men and women have changed in our society, old-fashioned formal courtesy has declined.

With this working thesis, you could focus on how changing societal attitudes toward gender roles have caused changes in courtesy. Later, when you revise, you may refine your thesis further—perhaps restricting it to courtesy toward the elderly, toward women, or, despite stereotypes, toward men. The chart on page 405 suggests ways to develop a working thesis.

For advice about revising a thesis, see pp. 460–61.

Once you have a working thesis, be sure its point accomplishes the purpose of your assignment. Suppose your assignment asks you to compare and contrast two local newspapers' coverage of a Senate election. Ask yourself what the point of that comparison and contrast is. Simply noting a difference won't be enough to satisfy most readers.

NO SPECIFIC POINT	The *Herald*'s coverage of the Senate elections was different from the *Courier*'s.
WORKING THESIS	The *Herald*'s coverage of the Senate elections was more thorough than the *Courier*'s.

Learning by Doing 🎯 Discovering a Thesis

Write a sentence, a working thesis, that unifies each of the following groups of details. Then compare and contrast your theses with those of your classmates. What other information would you need to write a good paper on each topic? How might the thesis statement change as you write the paper?

1. Cigarettes are expensive.
   Cigarettes can cause fires.
   Cigarettes cause unpleasant odors.
   Cigarettes can cause health problems for smokers.
   Secondhand smoke from cigarettes can cause health problems.

2. Clinger College has a highly qualified faculty.
   Clinger College has an excellent curriculum in my field.
   Clinger College has a beautiful campus.
   Clinger College is expensive.
   Clinger College has offered me a scholarship.

3. Crisis centers report that date rape is increasing.
   Most date rape is not reported to the police.
   Often the victim of date rape is not believed.
   Sometimes the victim of date rape is blamed or blames herself.
   The effects of date rape stay with a woman for years.

How to State a Thesis

Once you have a notion of a topic and main point, use these pointers to state or improve a thesis to guide your planning and drafting.

■ *State the thesis sentence exactly.* Replace vague or general wording with concise, detailed, and down-to-earth language.

TOO GENERAL	There are a lot of troubles with chemical wastes.

Are you going to deal with all chemical wastes, throughout all of history, all over the world? Will you list all the troubles they can cause?

MORE SPECIFIC	Careless dumping of leftover paint is to blame for a recent outbreak of skin rashes in Atlanta.

If you are writing an argument, you need to take a stand on an issue that is debatable and thus would allow others to take different positions. State yours exactly.

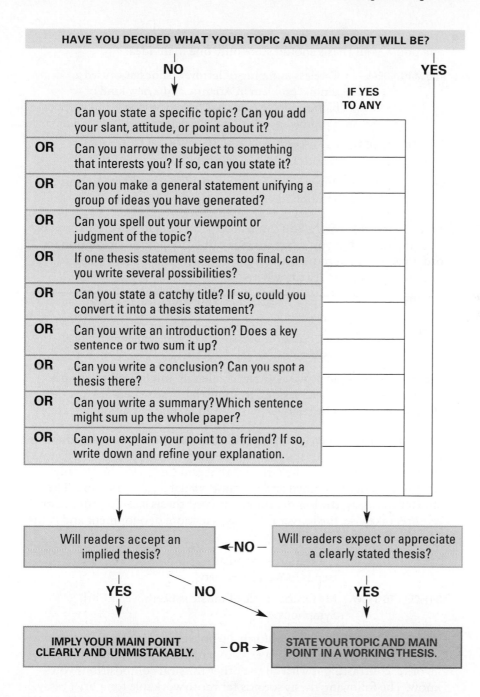

HAVE YOU DECIDED WHAT YOUR TOPIC AND MAIN POINT WILL BE?

NO   YES

IF YES TO ANY

Can you state a specific topic? Can you add your slant, attitude, or point about it?

OR Can you narrow the subject to something that interests you? If so, can you state it?

OR Can you make a general statement unifying a group of ideas you have generated?

OR Can you spell out your viewpoint or judgment of the topic?

OR If one thesis statement seems too final, can you write several possibilities?

OR Can you state a catchy title? If so, could you convert it into a thesis statement?

OR Can you write an introduction? Does a key sentence or two sum it up?

OR Can you write a conclusion? Can you spot a thesis there?

OR Can you write a summary? Which sentence might sum up the whole paper?

OR Can you explain your point to a friend? If so, write down and refine your explanation.

Will readers accept an implied thesis?   ◄ NO ─   Will readers expect or appreciate a clearly stated thesis?

YES   NO   YES

IMPLY YOUR MAIN POINT CLEARLY AND UNMISTAKABLY.   ─ OR ➤   **STATE YOUR TOPIC AND MAIN POINT IN A WORKING THESIS.**

SPECIFIC STAND   The recent health consequences of carelessly dumped leftover paint require Atlanta officials both to regulate and to educate.

■ *State just one central idea in the thesis sentence.* If your paper is to focus on one point, your thesis should state only one main idea.

TOO MANY IDEAS	Careless dumping of leftover paint has caused a serious problem in Atlanta, and a new kind of biodegradable paint has been developed, and it offers a promising solution to one chemical waste dilemma.
ONE CENTRAL IDEA	Careless dumping of leftover paint has caused a serious problem in Atlanta.
OR	A new kind of biodegradable paint offers a promising solution to one chemical waste dilemma.

■ *State your thesis positively.* You can usually find evidence to support a positive statement, but you'd have to rule out every possible exception in order to prove a negative one. Negative statements also may sound half-hearted and seem to lead nowhere.

NEGATIVE	Medical researchers do not know what causes breast cancer.
POSITIVE	The causes of breast cancer still challenge medical researchers.

Presenting the topic positively as a "challenge" might lead to a paper about an exciting quest. Besides, to show that researchers are working on the problem would be relatively easy, given an hour of online research.

■ *Limit your thesis to a statement that you can demonstrate.* A workable thesis is limited so that you can support it with sufficient convincing evidence. It should stake out just the territory that you can cover thoroughly within the length assigned and the time available, and no more. The shorter the essay, the less development your thesis should promise or require. Likewise, the longer the essay, the more development and complexity your thesis should suggest.

DIFFICULT TO SHOW	For centuries, popular music has announced vital trends in Western society.
DIFFICULT TO SHOW	My favorite piece of music is Beethoven's Fifth Symphony.

The first thesis above could inform a whole encyclopedia of music; the second would require that you explain why that symphony is your favorite, contrasting it with all the other musical compositions you know. The following thesis sounds far more workable for a brief essay.

POSSIBLE TO SHOW	In the past two years, a rise in the number of preteenagers has resulted in a comeback for heavy metal on the local concert scene.

Unlike a vague statement or a broad, unrestricted claim, a limited thesis narrows and refines a topic, restricting your essay to a reasonable scope.

TOO VAGUE   Native American blankets are very beautiful.

TOO BROAD   Native Americans have adapted to many cultural shifts.

POSSIBLE TO SHOW   For some members of the Apache tribe, working in high-rise construction has allowed both economic stability and cultural integrity.

If the suggestions in this chapter have helped you draft a working thesis—even an awkward or feeble one—you'll find plenty of advice about improving it in the next few pages and more later about revising it. But what if you're freezing up because your thesis simply won't take shape? First, relax. Your thesis will emerge later on—as your thinking matures and you figure out your paper's true direction, as peer readers spot the idea in your paper you're too close to see, as you talk with your instructor and suddenly grasp how to take your paper where you want it to go. In the meantime, plan and write so that you create a rich environment that will encourage your thesis to emerge.

For more on revising a thesis, see pp. 460–61.

Learning by Doing 🖉 Examining Thesis Statements

Discuss each of the following thesis sentences with your classmates. Answer these questions for each:

For exercises on choosing effective thesis statements, visit **<bedfordstmartins .com/bedguide>**.

Is the thesis stated exactly?
Does the thesis state just one idea?
Is the thesis stated positively?
Is the thesis sufficiently limited for a short essay?
How might the thesis be improved?

1. Teenagers should not get married.
2. Cutting classes is like a disease.
3. Students have developed a variety of techniques to conceal inadequate study from their instructors.
4. Older people often imitate teenagers.
5. Violence on television can be harmful to children.
6. I don't know how to change the oil in my car.

How to Improve a Thesis

Simply knowing what a solid working thesis *should* do may not help you improve your thesis. Whether yours is a first effort or a refined version, turn to the Take Action chart (p. 408) to help you figure out how to improve

To get online help from the Take Action sections, visit **<bedfordstmartins .com/bedguide>**.

Take Action Building a Stronger Thesis

Ask each question at the top of the chart to consider whether your draft might need work on that issue. If so, follow the ASK—LOCATE SPECIFICS—TAKE ACTION sequence to revise.

	Unclear Topic?	Unclear Slant?	Broad Thesis?
1 **ASK**	Could I define or state my topic more clearly? ↓	Could I define or state my slant more clearly? ↓	Could I limit my thesis to develop it more successfully? ↓
2 **LOCATE SPECIFICS**	■ Write out your current working thesis. ■ Circle the words in it that identify your topic. WORKING THESIS (Adaptability) is essential for World Action volunteers. [What, exactly, does the topic *adaptability* mean?] ↓	■ Write out your current working thesis. ■ Underline the words that state your slant, attitude, or point about your topic. WORKING THESIS Volunteering is an invaluable experience. [Why or in what ways is volunteering invaluable?] ↓	■ Write out your current working thesis. ■ Decide whether it establishes a task that you could accomplish given the available time and the expected length. WORKING THESIS Rock and roll has evolved dramatically since the 1950s. [Tracing this history in a few pages would be impossible.] ↓
3 **TAKE ACTION**	■ Rework the circled topic. State it more clearly, and specify what it means to you. ■ Define or identify the topic in terms of your purpose and the likely interests of your audience. REVISED THESIS An ability to adjust to, even thrive under, challenging circumstances is essential for World Action volunteers.	■ Rework your underlined slant. Jot down ideas to sharpen it and express an engaging approach to your topic. ■ Refine it to accomplish your purpose and appeal to your audience. REVISED THESIS Volunteering builds practical skills while connecting volunteers more fully to their communities.	■ Restrict your thesis to a slice of the pie, not the whole pie. ■ Focus on one part or element, not several. Break it apart, and pick only a chunk. ■ Reduce many ideas to one point, or convert a negative statement to a positive one. REVISED THESIS The music of the alternative-rock band Wilco continues to evolve as members experiment with vocal moods and instrumentation.

your thesis. Skim across the top to identify questions you might ask about your working thesis. When you answer a question with "Yes" or "Maybe," move straight down the column to Locate Specifics under that question. Use the activities there to pinpoint gaps, problems, or weaknesses. Then move straight down the column to Take Action. Use the advice that suits your problem as you revise.

How to Use a Thesis to Organize

Often a good, clear thesis will suggest an organization for your ideas.

For more on using a thesis to develop an outline, see pp. 413–17.

WORKING THESIS	Despite the disadvantages of living in a downtown business district, I wouldn't live anywhere else.
FIRST ¶S	Disadvantages of living in the business district
NEXT ¶S	Advantages of living there
LAST ¶	Affirmation of your preference for downtown life

A clear thesis helps to organize you, keeping you on track as you write. Just putting your working thesis into words can stake out your territory. Your thesis can then direct you as you select details and connect sections of the essay. Its purpose is to guide you on a quest, not to limit your ideas.

In addition, your thesis can prepare your readers for the pattern of development or sequence of ideas that you plan to present. As a writer, you look for key words (such as *compare, propose,* or *evaluate*) when you size up an assignment. Such words alert you to what's expected. When you write or revise your thesis, you can use such terms or their equivalents (such as *benefit* or *consequence* instead of *effect*) to preview for readers the likely direction of your paper. Then they, too, will know what to expect.

For more on key terms in college assignments, see p. 38 and pp. 336–38.

WORKING THESIS	Expanding the campus program for energy conservation would bring welcome financial and environmental benefits.
FIRST ¶S	Explanation of the campus energy situation
NEXT ¶S	Justification of the need for the proposed expansion
NEXT ¶S	Financial benefits for the college and students
NEXT ¶S	Environmental benefits for the region and beyond
LAST ¶	Concluding assertion of the value of the expansion

As you write, however, you don't have to cling to a thesis for dear life. If further investigation changes your thinking, you can change your thesis.

WORKING THESIS	Because wolves are a menace to people and farm animals, they ought to be exterminated.
REVISED THESIS	The wolf, a relatively peaceful animal useful in nature's scheme of things, ought to be protected.

You can restate a thesis any time: as you write, revise, or revise again.

Learning by Doing Using a Thesis to Preview

Each of the following thesis statements is from a student paper in a different field. With your classmates, consider how each one previews the essay to come and how you would expect the essay to be organized into sections.

1. Although the intent of inclusion is to provide the best care for all children by treating both special- and general-education students equally, some people in the field believe that the full inclusion of disabled children in mainstream classrooms may not be in the best interest of either type of student. (From "Is Inclusion the Answer?" by Sarah E. Goers)

2. With ancient Asian roots and contemporary European influences, the Japanese language has continued to change and to reflect cultural change as well. (From "Japanese: Linguistic Diversity" by Stephanie Hawkins)

3. *Manifest destiny* was an expression by leaders and politicians in the 1840s to clarify continental extension and expansion and in a sense revitalize the mission and national destiny for Americans. (From ethnic studies examination answer by Angela Mendy)

4. By comparing the *Aeneid* with *Troilus and Criseyde*, one can easily see the effects of the code of courtly love on literature. (From "The Effect of the Code of Courtly Love: A Comparison of Virgil's *Aeneid* and Chaucer's *Troilus and Criseyde*" by Cindy Keeler)

5. The effects of pollutants on the endangered Least Tern entering the Upper Newport Bay should be quantified so that necessary action can be taken to further protect and encourage the species. (From "Contaminant Residues in Least Tern [*Sterna antillarum*] Eggs Nesting in Upper Newport Bay" by Susanna Olsen)

Organizing Your Ideas

When you organize an essay, you select an order for the parts that makes sense and shows your readers how the ideas are connected. Often your organization will not only help a reader follow your points but also reinforce your emphases by moving from beginning to end or from least to most significant, as the table on page 411 illustrates.

Grouping Your Ideas

While exploring a topic, you will usually find a few ideas that seem to belong together—two facts on New York traffic jams, four actions of New York drivers, three problems with New York streets. But similar ideas seldom appear together in your notes because you did not discover them all at the same time. For this reason, you need to sort your ideas into groups and arrange them in sequences. Here are six ways to work:

Organization	Movement	Typical Use	Example
Spatial	Left to right, right to left, bottom to top, top to bottom, front to back, outside to inside	■ Describing a place, a scene, or an environment ■ Describing a person's physical appearance	Describe an ocean vista, moving from the tidepools on the rocky shore to the plastic buoys floating offshore to the sparkling water meeting the sunset sky.
Chronological	What happens first, second, and next, continuing until the end	■ Narrating an event ■ Explaining steps in a procedure ■ Explaining the development of an idea, a school of thought, or a trend	Narrate the events that led up to an accident: leaving home late, stopping for an errand, rushing along the highway, racing up to the intersection.
Logical	General to specific, specific to general, least important to most important, cause to effect, problem to solution	■ Explaining an idea ■ Persuading readers to accept a stand, a proposal, or an evaluation	Analyze the effects of last year's storms by selecting four major consequences, placing the most important one last for emphasis.

1. *Rainbow connections.* List all the main points you're going to express. Don't recopy the rest of your material. Use highlighters or colored pencils to mark points that go together with the same color. When you write, follow the color code, and deal with related ideas at the same time.

2. *Emphasizing ideas.* Make a copy of your file of ideas or notes. Next use your software tools to highlight, categorize, and shape your thinking by grouping or distinguishing your ideas. Mark similar or related ideas in the same way; call out major points. Then move related materials into groups.

   Highlighting

   Boxing

   Showing color

   Using **bold**, *italics*, underlining

   • Adding bullets

   1. Numbering

   Changing fonts

   Varying print sizes

3. *Linking.* Make a list of major points, and then draw lines (in color if you wish) to link related ideas. Figure 20.1 illustrates a linked list for an essay on Manhattan driving. The writer has connected related points, numbered their sequence, and supplied each group with a heading. Each heading will probably inspire a topic sentence to introduce a major division of the essay. Because one point, chauffeured luxury cars, failed to relate to any other, the writer has a choice: drop it or develop ideas about it.

Figure 20.1 The Linking Method for Grouping Ideas

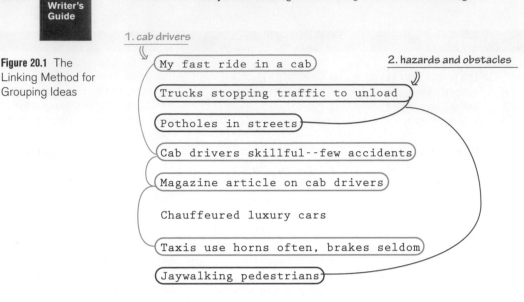

4. *Solitaire.* Collect notes and ideas on roomy (5-by-8-inch) file cards, especially to write about literature or research. To organize, spread out the cards; arrange and rearrange them, as in a game of solitaire. When each idea seems to lead to the next, gather the cards into a deck in this order. As you write, deal yourself a card at a time, and turn its contents into sentences.

5. *Slide show.* Use presentation software to write your notes and ideas on "slides." When you're done, you can view your slides one by one or as a collection. Sort your slides into the most promising order.

For more about mapping, see pp. 391–92.

6. *Clustering.* Like mapping, clustering is a visual method for generating as well as grouping ideas. In the middle of a page, write your topic in a word or a phrase. Then think of the major divisions into which you might break your topic. For an essay on Manhattan drivers, your major divisions might be *types* of drivers: (1) taxi drivers, (2) bus drivers, (3) truck drivers, (4) New York drivers of private cars, and (5) out-of-town drivers of private cars. Arrange these divisions around your topic, and circle them too. Draw lines out from the major topic to the subdivisions. You now have a rough plan for an essay. (See Figure 20.2.)

Around each division, make another cluster of details you might include — examples, illustrations, facts, statistics, bits of evidence, opinions. Circle each specific item, and connect it to the appropriate type of driver. Then expand the details into a paragraph for each type of driver. This technique lets you know where you have enough specific information to make your paper clear and interesting — and where you don't. If one subtopic has no small circles around it (such as "bus drivers" in Figure 20.2), you should either add specifics to expand it or drop it.

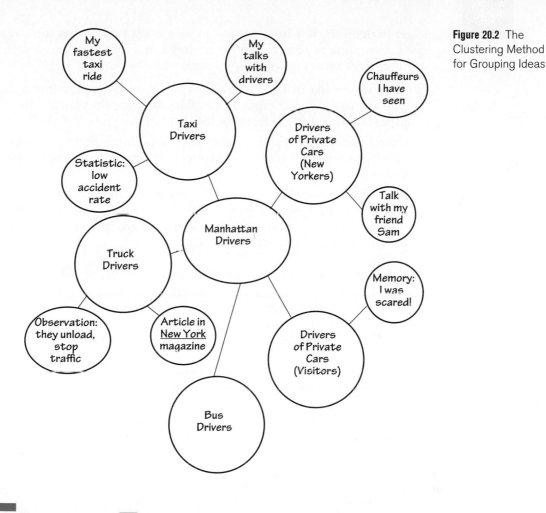

Figure 20.2 The Clustering Method for Grouping Ideas

Learning by Doing 📷 Clustering

Generate clusters for three of the following topics. With your classmates, discuss which one of the three would probably help you write the best paper.

teachers	fast food	civil rights
Internet sites	leisure activities	substance abuse
my favorite restaurants	musicians	technology

Outlining

A familiar way to organize is to outline. A written outline, whether brief or detailed, acts as a map that you make before a journey. It shows where to leave from, where to stop along the way, and where to arrive. If you forget where you are going or what you want to say, you can consult your outline

A
Writer's
Guide

to get back on track. When you turn in your essay, your instructor may request an outline as both a map for readers and a skeletal summary. Here are three ways writers arrive at useful outlines.

For more on thesis statements, see pp. 401–10.

For more on using outlining for revision, see pp. 462–63.

- Some writers like to begin with a working thesis. If it's clear, it may suggest how to develop or expand an outline, allowing the plan for the paper to grow naturally from the idea behind it.
- Others prefer to start with a loose informal outline — perhaps just a list of points to make. If readers find your papers mechanical, such an outline may free up your writing.
- Still others, especially for research papers or complicated arguments, like to lay out a complex job very carefully in a detailed formal outline. If readers find your writing disorganized and hard to follow, this more detailed plan might be especially useful.

Thesis-Guided Outlines. Your working thesis may identify ideas that you can use to organize your paper. (Of course, if it doesn't, you may want to revise your thesis and then return to your outline or vice versa.) For example, suppose that you are assigned an anthropology paper on the people of Melanesia. You decide to focus on the following point:

> Working Thesis: Although the Melanesian pattern of family life may look strange to Westerners, it fosters a degree of independence that rivals our own.

If you lay out your ideas in the same order that they follow in the two parts of this thesis statement, your simple outline would suggest an essay that naturally falls into two parts — features that seem strange and admirable results.

1. Features that appear strange to Westerners
   - A woman supported by her brother, not her husband
   - Trial marriages common
   - Divorce from her children possible for any mother
2. Admirable results of system
   - Wives not dependent on husbands for support
   - Divorce between mates uncommon
   - Greater freedom for parents and children

When you create a thesis-guided outline, look for the key element of your working thesis. This key element can suggest both a useful question to consider and an organization, as the table on page 415 illustrates.

Informal Outlines. For in-class writing, brief essays, and familiar topics, a short or informal outline, also called a *scratch outline,* may serve your needs. Jot down a list of points in the order you plan to make them. Use this outline, for your eyes only, to help you get organized, stick to the point, and remember ideas under pressure. The following example out-

Sample Thesis Statement	Type of Key Element	Examples of Key Element	Question You Might Ask	Organization of Outline
A varied personal exercise program has four main *advantages*.	Plural word	Words such as *benefits*, *advantages*, *teenagers*, or *reasons*	What are the types, kinds, or examples of this word?	List outline headings based on the categories or cases you identify.
Wylie's *interpretation* of Van Gogh's last paintings unifies aesthetic and psychological considerations.	Key word identifying an approach or vantage point	Words such as *claim*, *argument*, *position*, *interpretation*, or *point of view*	What are the parts, aspects, or elements of this approach?	List outline headings based on the components that you identify.
Preparing a pasta dinner for surprise guests can be an easy process.	Key word identifying an activity	Words such as *preparing*, *harming*, or *improving*	How is this activity accomplished, or how does it happen?	Supply a heading for each step, stage, or element that the activity involves.
Although the new wetland preserve will protect only some wildlife, it will bring several long-term benefits to the region.	One part of the sentence subordinate to another	Sentence part beginning with a qualification such as *despite*, *because*, *since*, or *although*	What does the qualification include, and what does the main statement include?	Use a major heading for the qualification and another for the main statement.
When other parents meet Sandie Burns on the soccer field sidelines, they may be surprised to see her wheelchair, but they soon discover that she is a *typical* soccer mom.	General evaluation that assigns a quality or value to someone or something	Evaluative words such as *typical*, *unusual*, *valuable*, *notable*, or other specific qualities	What examples, illustrations, or clusters of details will show this quality?	Add a heading for each extended example or each group of examples or details you want to use.
In spite of these tough economic times, the student senate *should* strongly recommend extended hours for the computer lab.	Claim or argument advocating a certain decision, action, or solution	Words such as *should*, *could*, *might*, *ought to*, *need to*, or *must*	Which reasons and evidence will justify this opinion? Which will counter the opinions of others who disagree with it?	Provide a heading for each major justification or defensive point; add headings for countering reasons.

lines a short paper explaining how outdoor enthusiasts can avoid illnesses carried by unsafe drinking water. It simply lists each of the methods for treating potentially unsafe water that the writer plans to explain.

> Working Thesis: Campers and hikers need to ensure the safety of the water that they drink from rivers or streams.
>
> Introduction: Treatments for potentially unsafe drinking water
>
> 1. Small commercial filter
>   –Remove bacteria and protozoa including salmonella and E. coli
>   –Use brands convenient for campers and hikers
> 2. Chemicals
>   –Use bleach, chlorine, or iodine
>   –Follow general rule: 12 drops per gallon of water
> 3. Boiling
>   –Boil for 5 minutes (Red Cross) to 15 minutes (National Safety Council)
>   –Store in a clean, covered container
>
> Conclusion: Using one of three methods of treating water, campers and hikers can enjoy safe water from natural sources.

This simple outline could easily fall into a five-paragraph essay or grow to eight paragraphs—introduction, conclusion, and three pairs of paragraphs in between. You probably won't know until you write the paper exactly how many paragraphs you'll need.

An informal outline can be even briefer than the preceding one. To answer an exam question or prepare a very short paper, your outline might be no more than an *outer plan*—three or four phrases jotted in a list:

> Isolation of region
> Tradition of family businesses
> Growth of electronic commuting

The process of making an informal outline can help you figure out how to develop your ideas. Say you plan a "how-to" essay analyzing the process of buying a used car, beginning with this thesis:

> Working Thesis: Despite traps that await the unwary, preparing yourself before you shop can help you find a good used car.

The key word here is *preparing*. Considering *how* the buyer should prepare before shopping for a used car, you're likely to outline several ideas:

> –Read car blogs, car magazines, and Consumer Reports.
> –Check craigslist, dealer sites, and classified ads.

    —Make phone calls to several dealers.
    —Talk to friends who have bought used cars.
    —Know what to look and listen for when you test-drive.
    —Have a mechanic check out any car before you buy it.

After some horror stories about people who got taken by car sharks, you can discuss, point by point, your advice. You can always change the sequence, add or drop an idea, or revise your thesis as you go along.

Learning by Doing 🎨 Moving from Outline to Thesis

Write a possible thesis statement based on each of the following informal outlines. Be certain that your thesis expresses a possible slant, attitude, or point (even if you aren't sure that the position is entirely defensible). Share and compare thesis statements with your classmates. What similarities and differences do you find? How do you account for these?

1. Cell Phones
   Get the financial and service plans of various cell-phone companies.
   Read the cell-phone contracts as well as the promotional offers.
   Look for the time period, flexibility, and cancellation provisions.
   Check the calling times, total minutes, and other extra charges.
   Find out about the availability and costs for extended calling locations (international, national, and regional calls).

2. Popular Mystery Novels
   Both Tony Hillerman and Margaret Coel write mysteries with Native American characters and settings.
   Hillerman's novels feature members of the Navajo Tribal Police.
   Coel's novels feature a female attorney who is an Arapaho and a Jesuit priest at the reservation mission who grew up in Boston.
   Hillerman's stories take place mostly on the extensive Navajo Reservation in Arizona, New Mexico, and Utah.
   Coel's are set mostly on the large Wind River Reservation in Wyoming.
   Hillerman and Coel try to convey tribal culture accurately although their mysteries involve different tribes.
   Both also explore similarities, differences, and conflicts between Native American cultures and the dominant culture.

3. Downtown Playspace
   Downtown Playspace has financial and volunteer support but needs more.
   Statistics show the need for a regional expansion of options for children.
   Downtown Playspace will serve visitors at the Children's Museum and local children in Headstart, preschool, and elementary schools.
   It will combine an outdoor playground with indoor technology space.
   Land and a building are available, but both require renovation.

Formal Outlines. A *formal outline* is an elaborate guide, built with time and care, for a long, complex paper. Because major reports, research papers, and senior theses require so much work, some professors and departments ask a writer to submit a formal outline at an early stage and to include one in the final draft. A formal outline shows how ideas relate one to another—which ones are equal and important (*coordinate*) and which are less important (*subordinate*). It clearly and logically spells out where you are going. If you outline again after writing a draft, you can use the revised outline to check your logic then as well, perhaps revealing where to revise.

When you make a full formal outline, follow these steps:

- Place your thesis statement at the beginning.
- List the major points that support and develop your thesis, labeling them with roman numerals (I, II, III).
- Break down the major points into divisions with capital letters (A, B, C), subdivide those using arabic numerals (1, 2, 3), and subdivide those using small letters (a, b, c). Continue until your outline is fully developed. If a very complex project requires further subdivision, use arabic numerals and small letters in parentheses.
- Indent each level of division in turn: the deeper the indentation, the more specific the ideas. Align like-numbered or -lettered headings under one another.
- Cast all headings in parallel grammatical form: phrases or sentences, but not both in the same outline.

For more on parallelism, see B2 (pp. A-48–A-49) in the Quick Editing Guide.

For more on analysis and division, see pp. 448–55.

CAUTION: Because an outline divides or analyzes ideas, some readers and instructors disapprove of categories with only one subpoint, reasoning that you can't divide anything into one part. Let's say that your outline on earthquakes lists a 1 without a 2:

    D. Probable results of an earthquake include structural damage.
       1. House foundations crack.

Logically, if you are going to discuss the *probable results* of an earthquake, you need to include more than one result:

    D. Probable results of an earthquake include structural damage.
       1. House foundations crack.
       2. Road surfaces are damaged.
       3. Water mains break.

Not only have you now come up with more points, but you have also emphasized the one placed last.

A *formal topic outline* for a long paper might include several levels of ideas, as this outline for Linn Bourgeau's research paper illustrates. Such an outline can help you work out both a persuasive sequence for the parts of a paper and a logical order for any information from sources.

Crucial Choices: Who Will Save the Wetlands If Everyone Is at the Mall?

Working Thesis: Federal regulations need to foster state laws and educational requirements that will help protect the few wetlands that are left, restore as many as possible of those that have been destroyed, and take measures to improve the damage from overdevelopment.

    I. Nature's ecosystem
       A. Loss of wetlands nationally
       B. Loss of wetlands in Illinois
          1. More flooding and poorer water quality
          2. Lost ability to prevent floods, clean water, and store water
       C. Need to protect humankind
   II. Dramatic floods
       A. Cost in dollars and lives
          1. Thirteen deaths between 1988 and 1998
          2. Cost about $39 million a year
       B. Great Midwestern Flood of 1993
          1. Lost wetlands in Illinois and other states
          2. Devastation in some states
       C. Flood prevention
          1. Plants and soil
          2. Floodplain overflow
  III. Wetland laws
       A. Inadequately informed legislators
          1. Watersheds
          2. Interconnections in natural water systems
       B. Water purification
          1. Wetlands and water
          2. Pavement and lawns
   IV. Need to save wetlands
       A. New federal definition including all varieties
       B. Re-education about interconnectedness
          1. Ecology at every grade level
          2. Education for politicians, developers, and legislators
       C. No isolated issue or wetlands
       D. Choices in schools, legislature, and people's daily lives

Learning by Doing 🔘 Responding to an Outline

Discuss the formal topic outline above with a small group or the entire class, considering the following questions:

- Would this outline be useful in organizing an essay?
- How is the organization logical? Is it easy to follow? What are other possible arrangements for the ideas?
- Is this outline sufficiently detailed for a paper? Can you spot any gaps?
- What possible pitfalls would the writer using this outline need to avoid?

A topic outline may help you work out a clear sequence of ideas but may not elaborate or connect them. Although you may not be sure how everything will fit together until you write a draft, you may find that a *formal sentence outline* clarifies what you want to say. It also moves you a step closer to drafting topic sentences and paragraphs even though you would still need to add detailed information. Notice how this sentence outline for Linn Bourgeau's research paper expands her ideas.

Crucial Choices: Who Will Save the Wetlands If Everyone Is at the Mall?

Working Thesis: Federal regulations need to foster state laws and educational requirements that will help protect the few wetlands that are left, restore as many as possible of those that have been destroyed, and take measures to improve the damage from overdevelopment.

    I. Each person, as part of nature's ecosystem, chooses how to interact with nature, including wetlands.

      A. The nation has lost over half its wetlands since Columbus arrived.

      B. Illinois has lost even more by legislating and draining away its wetlands.

         1. Destroying wetlands creates more flooding and poorer water quality.

         2. The wetlands could prevent floods, clean the water supply, and store water.

      C. The wetlands need to be protected because they protect and serve humankind.

   II. Floods are dramatic and visible consequences of not protecting wetlands.

      A. The cost of flooding can be tallied in dollars spent and in lives lost.

         1. Thirteen people died in floods between 1988 and 1998.

         2. Flooding typically costs about $39 million a year.

    B. The Great Midwestern Flood of 1993 could have been avoided.

        1. Illinois and other states had lost their wetlands.

        2. Those states also suffered the most devastation.

    C. Preventing floods is a valuable role of wetlands.

        1. Plants and soil manage excess water.

        2. The Mississippi River floodplain was reduced from 60 days of water overflow to 12.

 III. The laws misinterpret or ignore the basic understanding of wetlands.

    A. Legislators need to know that an "isolated wetland" does not exist.

        1. Water travels within an area called a watershed.

        2. The law needs to consider interconnections in natural water systems.

    B. Wetlands naturally purify water.

        1. Water filters and flows in wetlands.

        2. Pavement and lawns carry water over, not through, the soil.

    C. New federal laws should require implementation of what we know.

 IV. Who will save the wetlands if everyone is at the mall?

    A. The federal definition of wetlands should include all the varieties.

    B. The vital concept of interconnectedness means reeducating everyone from legislators to fourth graders.

        1. Ecology must be incorporated into the curriculum at every grade level.

        2. Educating politicians, developers, and legislators is more difficult.

    C. The value of wetlands is not an isolated issue any more than wetlands are isolated from one another.

    D. The choices people make in their schools, legislative systems, and daily lives will determine the future of water quality and flooding.

Learning by Doing 🎯 Outlining

1. Using one of your groups of ideas from the activities in Chapter 19, construct a formal topic outline that might serve as a guide for an essay.
2. Now turn that topic outline into a formal sentence outline.
3. Discuss both outlines with your classmates and your instructor, bringing up any difficulties you encountered. If you get any better notions for organizing your ideas, change the outline.

For exercises on organizing support effectively, visit **<bedfordstmartins .com/bedguide>**.

21 Strategies for Drafting

Learning to write well involves learning what key questions to ask yourself: How can I begin this draft? What should I do if I get stuck? How can I flesh out the bones of my paper? How can I end effectively? How can I keep my readers with me? In this chapter we offer advice to get you going and keep you going, drafting the first paragraph to the last.

Making a Start Enjoyable

A playful start may get you hard at work before you know it.

- **Time Yourself.** Set your watch, alarm, or egg timer, and vow to draft a page before the buzzer sounds. Don't stop for anything. If you're writing nonsense, just push on. You can cross out later.

- **Slow to a Crawl.** If speed quotas don't work, time yourself to write with exaggerated laziness, maybe a sentence every fifteen minutes.

- **Scribble on a Scrap.** If you dread the blank paper or screen, try starting on scrap paper, the back of a list, or a small notebook page.

- **Begin Writing the Part You Find Most Appetizing.** Start in the middle or at the end, wherever the thoughts come easily to mind. As novelist Bill Downey observes, "Writers are allowed to have their dessert first."

- **State Your Purpose.** Set forth what you want to achieve: To tell a story? To explain something? To win a reader over to your way of thinking?

- **Slip into a Reader's Shoes.** Put yourself in your reader's place. Start writing what you'd like to find out from the paper.

- **Nutshell It.** Summarize the paper you want to write. Condense your ideas into one small, tight paragraph. Later you can expand each sentence until the meaning is clear and all points are adequately supported.

- **Shrink Your Immediate Job.** Break the writing task into smaller parts, and do only the first one. Turn out, say, just the first two paragraphs.

- **Seek a Provocative Title.**   Write down a dozen possible titles for your paper. If one sounds strikingly good, don't let it go to waste!
- **Record Yourself.**   Talk a first draft into a recorder or your voice mail. Play it back. Then write. Even if it is hard to transcribe your spoken words, this technique may set your mind in motion.
- **Speak Up.**   On your feet, before an imaginary cheering crowd, spontaneously utter a first paragraph. Then — quick! — record it or write it out.
- **Take Short Breaks.**   Even if you don't feel tired, take a break every half hour or so. Get up, walk around the room, stretch, or get a drink of water. Two or three minutes should be enough to refresh your mind.

Restarting

When you have to write a long or demanding essay that you can't finish in one sitting, you may return to it only to find yourself stalled. You tromp your starter and nothing happens. Your engine seems reluctant to turn over. Try the following suggestions for getting back on the road.

- **Leave Hints for How to Continue.**   If you're ready to quit, jot down what might come next or the first sentence of the next section. When you return, you will face not a blank wall but rich and suggestive graffiti.
- **Pause in Midstream.**   Try breaking off in midsentence or midparagraph. Just leave a sentence trailing off into space, even if you know its closing words. When you return, you can start writing again immediately.
- **Repeat.**   If the next sentence refuses to appear, simply recopy the last one until that shy creature emerges on the page.
- **Reread.**   When you return to work, spend a few minutes rereading what you have already written or what you have planned.
- **Switch Instruments.**   Do you compose on the computer? Try longhand. Or drop your pen to type. Try writing on note cards or colored paper.
- **Change Activities.**   When words won't come, turn to something quite different. Run, walk your dog, cook a meal, or nap. Or reward yourself — after you reach a certain point — with a call to a friend or a TV show. All the while, your unconscious mind will be working on your writing task.

Paragraphing

An essay is written not in large, indigestible lumps but in *paragraphs* — small units, each more or less self-contained, each contributing some new idea in support of the essay's thesis. Writers dwell on one idea at a time, stating it, developing it, illustrating it with examples or a few facts — *showing* readers, with detailed evidence, exactly what they mean.

For more on developing ideas within paragraphs, see Ch. 22.

Paragraphs can be as short as one sentence or as long as a page. Sometimes the length is governed by the writing's audience, purpose, or medium. Journalists expect newspaper readers to gobble up facts like popcorn, quickly skimming short one- or two-sentence paragraphs. College writers, in contrast, should assume their readers expect to read through well-developed paragraphs.

When readers see a paragraph indentation, they interpret it as a pause, a chance for a deep breath. After that signpost, they expect you to concentrate on a new aspect of your thesis for the rest of that paragraph. This chapter gives you advice on guiding readers through your writing — using opening paragraphs to draw them in, topic sentences to focus and control body paragraphs, and concluding paragraphs to wrap up the discussion.

Using Topic Sentences

A *topic sentence* spells out the main idea of a paragraph in the body of an essay. It guides you as you write, and it hooks your readers as they discover what to expect and how to interpret the paragraph. As the topic sentence establishes the focus of the paragraph, it also relates the paragraph to the topic and thesis of the essay as a whole. (In fact, much of the advice on topic sentences for paragraphs also extends to thesis statements for essays.) To convert an idea to a topic sentence, add your own slant, attitude, or point.

For more on thesis statements, see pp. 401–10.

Main Idea   +   Slant or Attitude or Point   =   Topic Sentence

How can you write a good topic sentence? Make it interesting, accurate, and limited. The more pointed and lively your topic sentence, the more it will interest your readers. Even a dull and vague start can be enlivened once you zero in on a specific point.

MAIN IDEA + SLANT   television + everything that's wrong with it

DULL START   There are many things wrong with television.

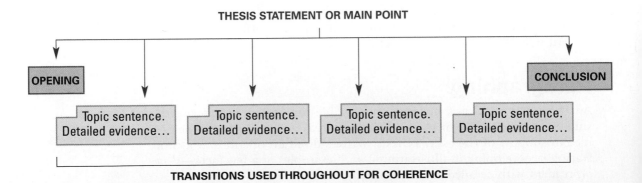

THESIS STATEMENT OR MAIN POINT

OPENING

Topic sentence. Detailed evidence...

Topic sentence. Detailed evidence...

Topic sentence. Detailed evidence...

Topic sentence. Detailed evidence...

CONCLUSION

TRANSITIONS USED THROUGHOUT FOR COHERENCE

POINTED TOPIC SENTENCE	Of all the disappointing television programming, what I dislike most is melodramatic news.
¶ PLAN	Illustrate the point with two or three melodramatic news stories.

A topic sentence also should be an accurate guide to the rest of the paragraph so that readers expect just what the paragraph delivers.

INACCURATE GUIDE	All types of household emergencies can catch people off guard. [The paragraph covers steps for emergency preparedness — not the variety of emergencies.]
ACCURATE TOPIC SENTENCE	Although an emergency may not be a common event, emergency preparedness should be routine at home.
¶ PLAN	Explain how a household can prepare for an emergency with a medical kit, a well-stocked pantry, and a communication plan.

Finally, a topic sentence should be limited so you don't mislead or frustrate readers about what the paragraph covers.

MISLEADING	Seven factors have contributed to the increasing obesity of the average American. [The paragraph discusses only one — portion size.]
LIMITED TOPIC SENTENCE	Portion size is a major factor that contributes to the increasing obesity of average Americans.
¶ PLAN	Define healthy portion sizes, contrasting them with the large portions common in restaurants and packaged foods.

Open with a Topic Sentence. Usually the topic sentence appears first in the paragraph, followed by sentences that clarify, illustrate, and support what it says. It is typically a statement but can sometimes be a question, alerting the reader to the topic without giving away the punchline. This example from "The Virtues of the Quiet Hero," Senator John McCain's essay about "honor, faith, and service," was presented on October 17, 2005, in the "This I Believe" series on National Public Radio's *All Things Considered*. Here, as in all the following examples, we have put the topic sentence in *italics*.

> *Years later, I saw an example of honor in the most surprising of places.* As a scared American prisoner of war in Vietnam, I was tied in torture ropes by my tormentors and left alone in an empty room to suffer through the night. Later in the evening, a guard I had never spoken to entered the room and silently loosened the ropes to relieve my suffering. Just before morning, that same guard came back and retightened the ropes before his less humanitarian comrades returned. He never said a word to me. Some months later on a Christmas morning, as I stood alone in the prison courtyard, that same guard walked up to me and stood next

to me for a few moments. Then with his sandal, the guard drew a cross in the dirt. We stood wordlessly there for a minute or two, venerating the cross, until the guard rubbed it out and walked away.

This paragraph moves from the general to the specific. The topic sentence clearly states at the outset what the paragraph is about. The second sentence introduces the situation McCain recalls. Then the next half-dozen sentences supply two concrete, yet concise, illustrations of his central point.

Place a Topic Sentence near the Beginning. Sometimes the first sentence of a paragraph acts as a transition, linking what is to come with what has gone before. Then the *second* sentence might be the topic sentence. This pattern is illustrated in the following paragraph from "You Wanna Take This Online?" by Jeff Chu (*Time* 8 Aug. 2005). The paragraph before this one recounts thirteen-year-old Taylor Hern's discovery of her name on an online "List of Hos" and ends with her question: "'Who would actually make time in their schedule to do something like that?'"

> Turns out, many of her peers would. *Technology has transformed the lives of teens, including the ways they pick on one another.* If parents and teachers think it's hard to control mean girls and bullying boys in school, they haven't reckoned with cyberspace. Cyberbullying can mean anything from posting pejorative items like the List of Hos to spreading rumors by e-mail to harassing by instant message. It was experienced in the preceding two months by 18 percent of 3,700 middle schoolers surveyed by researchers at Clemson University. Their study is scheduled to be presented at this month's American Psychological Association meeting. The phenomenon peaks at about age thirteen; 21 percent of eighth graders surveyed reported being cyberbullied recently. And incidents of online bullying are like roaches: for every one that's reported, many more go unrecorded. "Our statistics are conservative," says Clemson psychologist Robin Kowalski. "Part of the problem is kids not recognizing that what's happening is a form of bullying."

End with a Topic Sentence. Occasionally a writer, trying to persuade the reader to agree, piles detail on detail. Then, with a dramatic flourish, the writer *concludes* with the topic sentence, as student Heidi Kessler does.

> A fourteen-year-old writes to an advice columnist in my hometown newspaper that she has "done it" lots of times and sex is "no big deal." At the neighborhood clinic where my aunt works, a hardened sixteen-year-old requests her third abortion. A girl-child I know has two children of her own, but no husband. A college student in my dorm now finds herself sterile from a "social disease" picked up during casual sexual encounters. Multiply these examples by thousands. *It seems clear to me that women, who fought so hard for sexual freedom equal to that of men, have emerged from the battle not as joyous free spirits but as the sexual revolution's walking wounded.*

This paragraph moves from the particular to the general—from four examples about individuals to one large statement about American women. By the time you finish the paragraph, you might be ready to accept its conclusion.

Imply a Topic Sentence. It is also possible to find a perfectly unified, well-organized paragraph that has no topic sentence at all, like the following from "New York" (*Esquire* July 1960) by Gay Talese:

> Each afternoon in New York a rather seedy saxophone player, his cheeks blown out like a spinnaker, stands on the sidewalk playing "Danny Boy" in such a sad, sensitive way that he soon has half the neighborhood peeking out of windows tossing nickels, dimes, and quarters at his feet. Some of the coins roll under parked cars, but most of them are caught in his outstretched hand. The saxophone player is a street musician named Joe Gabler; for the past thirty years he has serenaded every block in New York and has sometimes been tossed as much as $100 a day in coins. He is also hit with buckets of water, empty beer cans and eggs, and chased by wild dogs. He is believed to be the last of New York's ancient street musicians.

No one sentence neatly sums up the writer's idea. Like most effective paragraphs that do not state a topic sentence, this one contains something just as good—a *topic idea*. The author doesn't allow his paragraph to wander aimlessly. He knows exactly what he wants to achieve—a description of how Joe Gabler, a famous New York street musician, plies his trade. Because Talese keeps this purpose firmly in mind, the main point—that Gabler meets both reward and abuse—is clear to the reader as well.

Learning by Doing 🔊 Shaping Topic Sentences

Discuss each of the following topic sentences with a small group, answering these questions:

> Will it catch readers' attention? Is it accurate? Is it limited?
> How might you develop the idea in the rest of the paragraph?
> Can you improve it?

1. Television commercials stereotype people.
2. Living away from home for the first time is hard.
3. It's good for a child to have a pet.
4. A flea market is a good place to buy jewelry.
5. Pollution should be controlled.
6. Everybody should recycle wastes.

Writing an Opening

Even writers with something to say may find it hard to begin. Often they are so intent on writing a brilliant opening that they freeze, unable to write at all. They forget even the essentials—set up the topic, stick to what's relevant, and establish a thesis. If you feel like a deer paralyzed by headlights when you face your first page, try these ways of tackling the opening:

- Start with your thesis statement, with or without a full opening paragraph. Fill in the rest later.
- Write your thesis statement—the one you planned or one you'd now like to develop—in the middle of a page. Go back to the top, and concisely add the background a reader needs to see where you're going.
- Write a long beginning for your first draft; then cut it down to the most dramatic, exciting, or interesting essentials.
- Simply set down words—any words—on paper, without trying to write an arresting opening. Rewrite later.
- Write the first paragraph last, after you know exactly where your essay goes.
- Move your conclusion to the beginning, and write a new ending.
- Write a summary for yourself and your readers.

Your opening paragraph should intrigue readers—engaging their minds and hearts, exciting their curiosity, drawing them into the world set forth in your writing.

DISCOVERY CHECKLIST

- ☐ What vital background might readers need?
- ☐ What general situation might help you narrow down to your point?
- ☐ What facts or statistics might make your issue compelling?
- ☐ What powerful anecdote or incident might introduce your point?
- ☐ What striking example or comparison would engage a reader?
- ☐ What question will your thesis—and your essay—answer?
- ☐ What lively quotation would set the scene for your essay?
- ☐ What assertion or claim might be the necessary prelude for your essay?
- ☐ What points should you preview to prepare a reader for what will come?
- ☐ What would compel someone to keep on reading?

Begin with a Story. Often a simple anecdote can capture your readers' interest and thus serve as a good beginning. Here is how Nicholas Kulish opens his essay "Guy Walks into a Bar" (*New York Times* 5 Feb. 2006):

> Recently my friend Brandon and I walked along Atlantic Avenue in Brooklyn looking for a place to watch a football game and to quench our thirst for a cold brew. I pushed open the door and we were headed for a pair of empty stools when we both stopped cold. The bar was packed with under-age patrons.

Most of us, after an anecdote, want to read on. What will the writer say next? What has the anecdote to do with the essay as a whole? Here, Kulish sets the stage for his objections to parents bringing babies and toddlers to bars.

Comment on a Topic or Position. Sometimes a writer expands on a topic, bringing in vital details, as David Morris does to open his article "Rootlessness" (*Utne Reader* May/June 1990):

> Americans are a rootless people. Each year one in six of us changes residences; one in four changes jobs. We see nothing troubling in these statistics. For most of us, they merely reflect the restless energy that made America great. A nation of immigrants, unsurprisingly, celebrates those willing to pick up stakes and move on: the frontiersman, the cowboy, the entrepreneur, the corporate raider.

After stating his point baldly, Morris supplies statistics to support his contention and briefly explains the phenomenon. This same strategy can be used to present a controversial opinion, then back it up with examples.

Ask a Question. An essay can begin with a question and answer, as James H. Austin begins "Four Kinds of Chance," in *Chase, Chance, and Creativity: The Lucky Art of Novelty* (New York: Columbia UP, 1978):

> What is chance? Dictionaries define it as something fortuitous that happens unpredictably without discernible human intention. Chance is unintentional and capricious, but we needn't conclude that chance is immune from human intervention. Indeed, chance plays several distinct roles when humans react creatively with one another and with their environment.

Beginning to answer the question in the first paragraph leads readers to expect the rest of the essay to continue the answer.

End with the Thesis Statement. Opening paragraphs often end by stating the essay's main point. After capturing readers' attention with an anecdote, gripping details, or examples, you lead readers in exactly the direction your essay goes. In response to the question "Should Washington stem the tide of

For more on thesis statements, see pp. 401–10.

both legal and illegal immigration?" ("Symposium." *Insight on the News* 11 Mar. 2002), Daniel T. Griswold uses this strategy to begin his answer:

> Immigration always has been controversial in the United States. More than two centuries ago, Benjamin Franklin worried that too many German immigrants would swamp America's predominantly British culture. In the mid-1800s, Irish immigrants were scorned as lazy drunks, not to mention Roman Catholics. At the turn of the century a wave of "new immigrants" — Poles, Italians, Russian Jews — were believed to be too different ever to assimilate into American life. *Today the same fears are raised about immigrants from Latin America and Asia, but current critics of immigration are as wrong as their counterparts were in previous eras.*

Writing a Conclusion

The final paragraphs of an essay linger longest in readers' minds, as does E. B. White's conclusion to "Once More to the Lake" from *One Man's Meat* (Gardiner, ME: Tilbury House, 1941). In the essay, White describes his return with his young son to a vacation spot he had loved as a child. As the essay ends in an unforgettable image, he recalls how old he really is and realizes the inevitable passing of generations.

> When the others went swimming my son said he was going in, too. He pulled his dripping trunks from the line where they had hung all through the shower and wrung them out. Languidly, and with no thought of going in, I watched him, his hard little body, skinny and bare, saw him wince slightly as he pulled up around his vitals the small, soggy, icy garment. As he buckled the swollen belt, suddenly my groin felt the chill of death.

White's classic ending opens with a sentence that points back to the previous paragraph as it also looks ahead. Then White leads us quickly to his final, chilling insight. And then he stops.

It's easy to say what *not* to do at the end of an essay: don't leave your readers half expecting you to go on. Don't restate all you've just said. Don't introduce a brand-new topic that leads away from your point. And don't signal that the end is near with an obvious phrase like "As I have said." For some answers to "How *do* you write an ending, then?" try this checklist.

DISCOVERY CHECKLIST

☐ What restatement of your thesis would give readers satisfying closure?

☐ What provocative implications of your thesis might answer "What now?" or "What's the significance of what I've said?"

☐ What snappy quotation or statement would wrap up your point?

☐ What closing facts or statistics might confirm the merit of your point?

☐ What final anecdote, incident, or example might round out your ideas?

☐ What question has your essay answered?

☐ What assertion or claim might you want to restate?

☐ What summary might help a reader pull together what you've said?

☐ What would make a reader sorry to finish such a satisfying essay?

End with a Quotation. An apt quotation can neatly round out an essay, as literary critic Malcolm Cowley shows in *The View from Eighty* (New York: Viking, 1980), his discussion of the pitfalls and compensations of old age.

> "Eighty years old!" the great Catholic poet Paul Claudel wrote in his journal. "No eyes left, no ears, no teeth, no legs, no wind! And when all is said and done, how astonishingly well one does without them!"

State or Restate Your Thesis. In a sharp criticism of American schools, humorist Russell Baker in "School vs. Education" ends by stating his main point, that schools do not educate.

> Afterward, the former student's destiny fulfilled, his life rich with Oriental carpets, rare porcelain, and full bank accounts, he may one day find himself with the leisure and the inclination to open a book with a curious mind, and start to become educated.

End with a Brief Emphatic Sentence. For an essay that traces causes or effects, evaluates, or argues, a pointed concluding thought can reinforce your main idea. If you text message or tweet, sending messages with no more than 140 characters through Twitter, occasionally apply those skills in a paragraph. Stick to academic language, but craft a concise, pointed sentence, maybe with a twist. In "Don't Mess with Mother" (*Newsweek* 19 Sept. 2005), Anna Quindlen ends her essay about the environmental challenges posed by post-Katrina New Orleans this way:

> New Orleans will be rebuilt, but rebuilt how? In the heedless, grasping fashion in which so much of this country has been built over the past fifty years, which has led to a continuous loop of floods, fires and filth in the air and water? Or could the new New Orleans be the first city of a new era, in which the demands of development and commerce are carefully balanced against the good of the land and, in the long run, the good of its people? We have been crummy stewards of the Earth, with a sense of knee-jerk entitlement that tells us there is always more where this came from.
> There isn't.

Stop When the Story Is Over. Even a quiet ending can be effective, as long as it signals clearly that the essay is finished. Journalist Martin Gansberg simply stops when the story is over in his true account of the fatal stabbing of a young woman, Kitty Genovese, in full view of residents of a Queens, New York, apartment house. The residents, unwilling to become involved, did nothing to interfere. Here is the last paragraph of "Thirty-eight Who Saw Murder Didn't Call Police" (*New York Times* 17 Mar. 1964):

> It was 4:25 A.M. when the ambulance arrived to take the body of Miss Genovese. It drove off. "Then," a solemn police detective said, "the people came out."

For more exercises on openings and conclusions, visit **<bedfordstmartins .com/bedguide>**.

Learning by Doing 🖋 Opening and Concluding

Openings and conclusions frame an essay, contributing to the unity of the whole. The opening sets up the topic and main idea; the conclusion reaffirms the thesis and rounds off the ideas. Discuss the following with your classmates.

1. Here are two possible opening paragraphs from a student essay on the importance of teaching children how to swim.

   A. Humans inhabit a world made up of over 70 percent water. In addition to these great bodies of water, we have built millions of swimming pools for sports and leisure activities. At one time or another most people will be faced with either the danger of drowning or the challenge of aquatic recreation. For these reasons, it is essential that we learn to swim. Being a competitive swimmer and a swimming instructor, I fully realize the importance of knowing how to swim.

   B. Four-year-old Carl, curious like most children, last spring ventured out onto his pool patio. He fell into the pool and, not knowing how to swim, helplessly sank to the bottom. Minutes later his uncle found the child and brought him to the surface. Because Carl had no pulse, his uncle administered CPR until the paramedics arrived. Eventually the child was revived. During his stay in the hospital, his mother signed him up for beginning swimming classes. Carl was a lucky one. Unlike thousands of other children and adults, he got a second chance.

   1. Which introduction is more effective? Why?
   2. What would the body of this essay consist of? What kinds of evidence would be included?
   3. Write a suitable conclusion for this essay.

2. If you were to read each of the following introductions from professional essays, would you want to read the entire essay? Why?

   A. During my ninth hour underground, as I scrambled up a slanting tunnel through the powdered gypsum, Rick Bridges turned to me and said, "You know, this whole area was just discovered Tuesday." (David Roberts, "Caving Comes into Its Golden Age: A New Mexico Marvel," *Smithsonian* Nov. 1988: 52)

B. From the batting average on the back of a George Brett baseball card to the interest rate fluctuations that determine whether the economy grows or stagnates, Americans are fascinated by statistics. (Stephen E. Nordlinger, "By the Numbers," *St. Petersburg Times* 6 Nov. 1988: 11)

C. "What does it look like under there?"

It was always this question back then, always the same pattern of hello and what's your name, what happened to your eye and what's under there. (Natalie Kusz, "Waiting for a Glass Eye," *Road Song* [New York: Farrar, 1990], rpt. in *Harper's* Nov. 1990)

3. How effective are these introductions and conclusions from student essays? Could they be improved? If so, how? If they are satisfactory, explain why. What would be a catchy yet informative title for each essay?

A. Recently a friend down from New York astonished me with stories of several people infected—some with AIDS—by stepping on needles washed up on the New Jersey beaches. This is just one incident of pollution, a devastating problem in our society today. Pollution is increasing in our world because of greed, apathy, and Congress's inability to control this problem. . . .

Wouldn't it be nice to have a pollution-free world without medical wastes floating in the water and washing up on our beaches? Without cars and power plants spewing greenhouse gases? With every corporation abiding by the laws set by Congress? In the future we can have a pollution-free world, but it is going to take the cooperation of everyone, including Congress, to ensure our survival on this Planet Earth.

B. The divorce rate rose 700 percent in the lasrt century and continues to rise. More than one out of every two couples who are married end up divorcing. Over one million children a year are affected by divorce in the family. From these statistics it is clear that one of the greatest problems concerning the family today is divorce and the adverse effects it has on our society. . . .

Divorce causes problems that change people for life. The number of divorces will continue to exceed the 700 percent figure unless married couples learn to communicate, to accept their mates unconditionally, and to sacrificially give of themselves.

4. Choose one of the topics that you generated in Chapter 19, and write at least three different introductions with conclusions. Ask your classmates which is the most effective.

Adding Cues and Connections

Effective writing proceeds in some sensible order, each sentence following naturally from the one before it. Yet even well-organized prose can be hard to read unless it is *coherent* and smoothly integrates its elements. Readers need cues and connections—devices to tie together words in a sentence, sentences in a paragraph, paragraphs in an essay.

Add Transitional Words and Sentences. You use transitions every day as cues or signals to help others follow your train of thought. For example, you might say to a friend, "Well, *on the one hand,* a second job would help me save money for tuition. *On the other hand,* I'd have less time to study." But some writers rush through, omitting links between thoughts or mistakenly assuming that connections they see will automatically be clear to readers. Often just a word, phrase, or sentence of transition inserted in the right place transforms a disconnected passage into a coherent one.

Many words and phrases specify connections between or within sentences and paragraphs. In the chart on page 435, *transitional markers* are grouped by purpose or the kind of relation or connection they establish.

Occasionally a whole sentence serves as a transition. For example, the opening of one paragraph may hark back to the last one while revealing a new or narrower direction. The following excerpt came from "Preservation Basics: Why Preserve Film," a page on the Web site of the National Film Preservation Foundation (NFPF) at <http://www.filmpreservation.org/>. The first paragraph introduces the organization's mission; the next two each open with transitional sentences that introduce major challenges to that mission. We have italicized the transitional sentences.

> Since Thomas Edison's invention of the kinetoscope in 1893, Americans have traveled the world using motion pictures to tell stories, document traditions, and capture current events. Their work stands as the collective memory of the first century witnessed by the moving image. By saving and sharing these motion pictures, we can illuminate our common heritage with a power and immediacy unique to film.
>
> *Preservationists are working against the clock.* Made on perishable plastic, film decays within years if not properly stored.
>
> *Already the losses are high.* The Library of Congress has documented that fewer than 20 percent of U.S. feature films from the 1920s survive in complete form in American archives; of the American features produced before 1950, only half still exist. For shorts, documentaries, and independently produced works, we have no way of knowing how much has been lost.

The first paragraph establishes the value of "saving and sharing" the American film legacy. The next two paragraphs use key words related to preservation and its absence (*perishable, decays, losses, lost*) to clarify that what follows builds on what has gone before. Each also opens with a short, dramatic transition to one of the major problems: time and existing loss.

Supply Transition Paragraphs. Transitions may be even longer than sentences. In a long and complicated essay, moving clearly from one idea to the next will sometimes require a short paragraph of transition.

Common Transitions

TO MARK TIME	then, soon, first, second, next, recently, the following day, in a little while, meanwhile, after, later, in the past, finally
TO MARK PLACE OR DIRECTION	in the distance, close by, near, far away, above, below, to the right, on the other side, opposite, to the west, next door
TO SUMMARIZE OR RESTATE	in other words, to put it another way, in brief, in simpler terms, on the whole, in fact, in a word, to sum up, in short, in conclusion, to conclude, therefore
TO RELATE CAUSE AND EFFECT OR RESULT	therefore, accordingly, hence, thus, for, so, consequently, as a result, because of, due to, eventually, inevitably
TO ADD OR AMPLIFY OR LIST	and, also, too, besides, as well, moreover, in addition, furthermore, in effect, second, in the second place, again, next
TO COMPARE	similarly, likewise, in like manner, in the same way
TO CONCEDE	whereas, on the other hand, with that in mind, still, and yet, even so, in spite of, despite, at least, of course, no doubt, even though
TO CONTRAST	on the other hand, but, or, however, unlike, nevertheless, on the contrary, conversely, in contrast, instead, counter to
TO INDICATE PURPOSE	to this end, for this purpose, with this aim
TO EXPRESS CONDITION	although, though
TO GIVE EXAMPLES OR SPECIFY	for example, for instance, in this case, in particular, to illustrate
TO QUALIFY	for the most part, by and large, with few exceptions, mainly, in most cases, generally, some, sometimes, typically, frequently, rarely
TO EMPHASIZE	it is true, truly, indeed, of course, to be sure, obviously, without doubt, evidently, clearly, understandably

So far, the physical and psychological effects of driving nonstop for hundreds of miles seem clear. The next consideration is why drivers do this. What causes people to become addicted to their steering wheels?

Use a transition paragraph only when you sense that your readers might get lost if you don't patiently lead them by the hand. If your essay is short, one question or statement beginning a new paragraph will be enough.

A transition paragraph also can aid your movement between one branch of argument and your main trunk or between a digression and your main direction. In this excerpt from *The Film Preservation Guide: The Basics for Archives, Libraries, and Museums* (San Francisco: NFPF, 2004; <http://www.filmpreservation.org/userfiles/image/PDFs/fpg_3.pdf>), the writer introduces the importance of inspecting a film and then devotes the next paragraph to a digression—referring readers to an inspection sheet in the appendix.

> Inspection is the single most important way to date a film, identify its technical characteristics, and detect damage and decay. Much can be learned by examining your film carefully, from start to finish.
>
> A standardized inspection work sheet (see appendix B) lists things to check and helps organize notes. This type of written report is the foundation for future preservation actions. Collecting the information during inspection will help you make informed decisions and enable you to document any changes in film condition over time.
>
> Signs of decay and damage may vary across the length of the film. . . .

The second paragraph acts as a transition, guiding readers to specialized information in the appendix and then drawing them back to the overall purpose of inspection: assessing the extent of damage to a film.

Select Repetition. Another way to clarify the relationship between two sentences, paragraphs, or ideas is to repeat a key word or phrase. Such purposeful repetition almost guarantees that readers will understand how all the parts of a passage fit together. Note the word *anger* in the following paragraph (italics ours) from *Of Woman Born* (New York: Norton, 1976), poet Adrienne Rich's exploration of her relationship with her mother.

> And I know there must be deep reservoirs of *anger* in her; every mother has known overwhelming, unacceptable *anger* at her children. When I think of the conditions under which my mother became a mother, the impossible expectations, my father's distaste for pregnant women, his hatred of all that he could not control, my *anger* at her dissolves into grief and *anger* for her, and then dissolves back again into *anger* at her: the ancient, unpurged *anger* of the child.

Strengthen Pronouns. Because they always refer back to nouns or other pronouns, pronouns serve as transitions by making readers refer back as well. Note how certain pronouns (in italics) hold together the following paragraph from "Misunderstood Michelle" by columnist Ellen Goodman in *At Large* (New York: Summit Books, 1981):

> I have two friends who moved in together many years ago. *He* looked upon this step as a trial marriage. *She* looked upon it as, well, moving in together. *He* was sure that in a matter of time, after *they* had built up trust and confidence, *she* would agree that marriage was the next logical step. *She,* on the other hand, was thrilled that here at last was a man *who* would never push *her* back to the altar.

The paragraph contains other transitions, too: time markers like *many years ago, in a matter of time,* and *after; on the other hand,* which indicates a contrast; and repetition of words related to marriage like *trial marriage, marriage,* and *the altar.* All serve the main purpose of transitions — keeping readers on track.

Learning by Doing Identifying Transitions

Go over one of the papers you have already written for this course, and circle all the transitional devices you can detect. Then exchange papers with a classmate. Can you find additional transitions in the other's paper? Or would you recommend transitions where there aren't any?

For more exercises on transitions, visit **<bedfordstmartins .com/bedguide>**.

22 Strategies for Developing

For examples of development strategies, visit <**bedfordstmartins .com/bedguide**>.

How can you spice up your general ideas with the stuff of real life? How can you tug your readers deeper and deeper into your essays until they say, "I see just what you mean"? Well-developed essays have such power because they back up general points with evidence that comes alive for readers. This chapter covers nine indispensable methods of development—giving examples, providing details, defining, reasoning inductively and deductively, analyzing a subject, analyzing a process, dividing and classifying, comparing and contrasting, and showing causes and effects. A strong essay almost always requires a combination of strategies.

Whenever you develop or revise a piece of writing, you face a challenge: How do you figure out what to do? Sometimes you may suspect that you've wandered into the buffet line at the Writer's Grill. You watch others load their plates, but still you hesitate. What will taste best? How much will fit on your plate? What will create a relaxing experience? For you as a writer, the answers to such questions are individual, depending on your situation, the clarity of your main idea or thesis, and the state of your draft.

DISCOVERY CHECKLIST

Purpose

☐ Does your assignment recommend or require specific methods of development?

☐ Which methods might be most useful to explain, inform, or persuade?

☐ What type of development might best achieve your specific purpose?

Audience

☐ Which strategies would best clarify your topic for readers?

☐ Which would best demonstrate your thesis to your readers?

☐ What kinds of evidence will your specific readers prefer? Which strategies might develop this evidence most effectively?

Thesis

☐ What development does your thesis promise or imply that you will supply?

☐ What sequence of development strategies would best support your thesis?

Essay Development

☐ Has a reader or peer editor pointed out any ideas in your draft that need fuller, more effective, or more logical development?

☐ Where might your readers have trouble following or understanding without more or better development?

Paragraph Development

☐ Should any paragraphs with one or two sentences be developed more fully?

☐ Should any long paragraphs with generalizations, repetition, and wordy phrasing be developed differently so that they are richer and deeper?

Giving Examples

An example — the word comes from the Latin *exemplum,* "one thing chosen from among many" — is a typical instance that illustrates a whole type or kind. Giving examples to support a generalization is probably the most often used means of development. This example, from *In Search of Excellence* (New York: Harper and Row, 1982) by Thomas J. Peters and Robert H. Waterman Jr., explains the success of America's top corporations:

> Although he's not a company, our favorite illustration of closeness to the customer is car salesman Joe Girard. He sold more new cars and trucks, each year, for eleven years running, than any other human being. In fact, in a typical year, Joe sold more than twice as many units as whoever was in second place. In explaining his secret of success, Joe said: "I sent out over thirteen thousand cards every month."
>
> Why start with Joe? Because his magic is the magic of IBM and many of the rest of the excellent companies. It is simply service, overpowering service, especially after-sales service. Joe noted, "There's one thing that I do that a lot of salesmen don't, and that's believe the sale really begins *after* the sale — not before.... The customer ain't out the door, and my son has made up a thank-you note." Joe would intercede personally, a year later, with the service manager on behalf of his customer. Meanwhile he would keep the communications flowing.

Notice how Peters and Waterman focus on the specific, Joe Girard. They don't write *corporation employees* or even *car salespeople.* Instead, they zero in on one particular man to make the point come alive.

Joe Girard	Level 4: Specific Example
car salespeople	Level 3: Even More Specific Group
corporation employees	Level 2: More Specific Group
America's top corporations	Level 1: General Group or Category

This ladder of abstraction moves from the general—America's top corporations—to a specific person—Joe Girard. The specific example of Joe Girard makes closeness to the customer *concrete* to readers: he is someone readers can relate to. To check the level of specificity in a paragraph or an outline, draw a ladder of abstraction for it. Do the same to restrict a broad subject to a topic for a short essay. If you haven't climbed to the fourth or fifth level, you are probably too general and need to add specifics.

An example doesn't have to be a specific individual. Sometimes you can create a picture of something unfamiliar or give an abstraction a personality. In this paragraph from *Prisoners of Silence: Breaking the Bonds of Adult Illiteracy in the United States* (New York: Continuum, 1980), Jonathan Kozol makes real the plight of illiterate people in our healthcare system:

> Illiterates live, in more than literal ways, an uninsured existence. They cannot understand the written details on a health insurance form. They cannot read waivers that they sign preceding surgical procedures. Several women I have known in Boston have entered a slum hospital with the intention of obtaining a tubal ligation and have emerged a few days later after having been subjected to a hysterectomy. Unaware of their rights, incognizant of jargon, intimidated by the unfamiliar air of fear and atmosphere of ether that so many of us find oppressive in the confines even of the most attractive and expensive medical facilities, they have signed their names to documents they could not read and which nobody, in the hectic situation that prevails so often in those overcrowded hospitals that serve the urban poor, had ever bothered to explain.

An example isn't a trivial doodad you add to a paragraph for decoration; it is what holds your readers' attention and makes an idea concrete and tangible. To give plenty of examples is one of the writer's chief tasks, and you can generate more at any point in the writing process. Begin with your experience, even with an unfamiliar topic, or try conversing with others, reading, digging in the library, or browsing on the Web.

For ways to generate ideas, see Ch. 19.

DISCOVERY CHECKLIST

☐ Are your examples relevant to your main idea or thesis?

☐ Are your examples the best ones you can think of? Will readers find them strong and appropriate?

☐ Are your examples truly specific? Or do they just repeat generalities?

☐ From each paragraph, can you draw a ladder of abstraction to at least the fourth level?

Learning by Doing 🔲 Giving Examples

To help you get in the habit of thinking specifically, fill in a ladder of abstraction for five of the following general subjects. Then share your ladders with classmates, and compare and contrast your specifics with theirs.

Examples:

iceberg
lettuce
vegetable
food

Prius
Toyota
hybrid cars
automobiles
land vehicles
transportation

colleges	fast foods	jewelry
college courses	music	books
clothes	movies	buildings
diseases	machines	television

Providing Details

A *detail* is any specific, concrete piece of information—a fact, a bit of the historical record, your own observation. Details make scenes and images more realistic and vivid for readers. They also back up generalizations, convincing readers that the writer can make broad assertions with authority.

Mary Harris "Mother" Jones told the story of her life as a labor organizer in *The Autobiography of Mother Jones* (1925; Chicago: Kerr, 1980). She lends conviction to her generalization about a nineteenth-century coal miner's lot with ample evidence from her own experience and observations.

> Mining at its best is wretched work, and the life and surroundings of the miner are hard and ugly. His work is down in the black depths of the earth. He works alone in a drift. There can be little friendly companionship as there is in the factory; as there is among men who build bridges and houses, working together in groups. The work is dirty. Coal dust grinds itself into the skin, never to be removed. The miner must stoop as he works in the drift. He becomes bent like a gnome.
>
> His work is utterly fatiguing. Muscles and bones ache. His lungs breathe coal dust and the strange, damp air of places that are never filled with sunlight. His house is a poor makeshift and there is little to encourage him to make it attractive. The company owns the ground it stands on, and the miner feels the precariousness of his hold. Around

his house is mud and slush. Great mounds of culm [the refuse left after coal is screened], black and sullen, surround him. His children are perpetually grimy from playing on the culm mounds. The wife struggles with dirt, with inadequate water supply, with small wages, with overcrowded shacks.

Although Mother Jones, not a learned writer, relies on short, simple sentences, her writing is clear and powerful because of the specific details she uses. Her opening states two generalizations: (1) "Mining . . . is wretched work," and (2) the miner's "life and surroundings" are "hard and ugly." She supports these with a barrage of factual evidence and detail, including well-chosen verbs: "Coal dust *grinds* itself into the skin." The result is a moving, convincingly detailed portrait of the miner and his family.

In *Lipstick Jihad: A Memoir of Growing Up Iranian in America and American in Iran* (New York: Public Affairs, 2005), Azadeh Moaveni uses details to evoke the "drama and magic" of a childhood visit to Iran.

> To my five-year-old suburban American sensibilities, exposed to nothing more mystical than the Smurfs, Iran was suffused with drama and magic. After Friday lunch at my grandfather's, once the last plates of sliced cantaloupe were cleared away, everyone retired to the bedrooms to nap. Inevitably there was a willing aunt or cousin on hand to scratch my back as I fell asleep. Unused to the siesta ritual, I woke up after half an hour to find the bed I was sharing with my cousin swathed in a tower of creamy gauze that stretched high up to the ceiling. "Wake up," I nudged him, "we're surrounded!" "It's for the mosquitoes, khareh, ass, go back to sleep." To me it was like a fairy tale, and I peered through the netting to the living room, to the table heaped with plump dates and the dense, aromatic baklava we would nibble on later with tea. The day before I had helped my grandmother, Razi joon, make ash-e gooshvareh, "earring stew"; we made hoops out of the fresh pasta, and dropped them into the vat of simmering herbs and lamb. Here even the ordinary had charm, even the names of stews.

For more on transitions, see pp. 433–37.

To guide readers through her details, Moaveni uses transitions—chronological (*After Friday lunch, after half an hour, The day before*), spatial (*through the netting to the living room*), and thematic (*To me it was like a fairy tale*).

Quite different from Moaveni's personal, descriptive details are Guy Garcia's objective facts in "Influencing America" (*Time* 13 Aug. 2005). Garcia heaps up statistical details to substantiate his claim that Hispanics are "helping to define" mainstream America even though they face "prejudice and enormous social and economic hurdles."

> Nearly a quarter of all Latinos live in poverty; the high school drop out rate for Latino youths between the ages of sixteen and nineteen is 21 percent—more than triple that of non-Hispanic whites. Neo-nativists like Pat Buchanan and Samuel Huntington still argue that the "tsunami" of non–English speakers from Latin America will

destroy everything that America stands for. Never mind that most Hispanics are religious, family-centric, enterprising, and patriotic. In the *Time* poll, 72 percent said they considered moral issues such as abortion and issues of faith important or very important. This year the government announced that undocumented workers were pouring billions into Social Security and Medicare for benefits that they would never be allowed to claim. Of the 27,000 troops serving in the U.S. armed forces who are not U.S. citizens, a large percentage are from Mexico and the rest of Latin America.

Providing details is a simple yet effective way to develop ideas. All it takes is close attention and precise wording to communicate details to readers. What would they see, hear, smell, or feel on the scene? Would a bit of reading or research turn up just the right fact or statistic? Effective details must have a specific purpose: to make your images more evocative or your point more convincing as they support—in some way—your main idea.

For more on observing a scene, see Ch. 5.

DISCOVERY CHECKLIST

☐ Do all your details support your point of view, main idea, or thesis?

☐ Do you have details of sights? Sounds? Tastes? Touch? Smells?

☐ Have you added enough details to make your writing clear and interesting?

☐ Have you arranged your details in an order that is easy to follow?

Learning by Doing 🎧 Providing Details

With classmates or alone, brainstorm specific details on one of the following topics. Include details that appeal to all five senses. Group related details, and write a paragraph or two using them. Begin by stating a main idea that conveys an engaging impression of your topic (not "My grandmother's house was in Topeka, Kansas" but "My grandmother's house was my childhood haven").

the things in my room	a memorable event	my job
my grandmother's home	an unusual person	a classroom
a haunted house	my favorite pet	the cafeteria
a favorite possession	a hospital room	an incident

For more on brainstorming, see pp. 387–88.

For more exercises on supporting details, visit **<bedfordstmartins .com/bedguide>**.

Defining

Define, from the Latin, means "to set bounds to." You define a thing, a word, or a concept by describing it so that it is distinguished from all similar things. If people don't agree on the meaning of a word or an idea, they can't share knowledge about it. Scientists in particular take special care to define their terms precisely. In his article "A Chemist's Definition of pH" from *The Condensed Chemical Dictionary* (New York: Reinhold, 1981), Gessner G. Hawley begins with a brief definition:

> pH is a value taken to represent the acidity or alkalinity of an aqueous solution; it is defined as the logarithm of the reciprocal of the hydrogen-ion concentration of a solution:

$$pH = \ln \frac{1}{[H^+]}$$

If you use a word in a special sense or invent a word, you have to explain it or your readers will be lost. In "The Futile Pursuit of Happiness" (*New York Times,* 7 Sept. 2003), Jon Gertner reports on "affective forecasting," an intriguing area of study by economists and psychologists such as Professors Daniel Gilbert of Harvard and Tim Wilson of the University of Virginia. They are exploring what people expect will bring them happiness and how their expectations pan out. Not surprisingly, their new area of study has generated new terms, as this paragraph explains.

> Gilbert and his collaborator Tim Wilson call the gap between what we predict and what we ultimately experience the *impact bias*—*impact* meaning the errors we make in estimating both the intensity and duration of our emotions and *bias* our tendency to err. The phrase characterizes how we experience the dimming excitement over not just a BMW but also over any object or event that we presume will make us happy. Would a 20 percent raise or winning the lottery result in a contented life? You may predict it will, but almost surely it won't turn out that way. And a new plasma television? You may have high hopes, but the impact bias suggests that it will almost certainly be less cool, and in a shorter time, than you imagine. Worse, Gilbert has noted that these mistakes of expectation can lead directly to mistakes in choosing what we think will give us pleasure. He calls this *miswanting*.

You might define an unfamiliar word to save your readers a trip to the dictionary or a familiar but often misunderstood concept—such as *guerrilla, liberal,* or *minimum wage*—to clarify the meaning you intend. The more complex or ambiguous an idea, a thing, a movement, a phenomenon, or an organization, the longer the definition you will need to clarify the term for your readers.

DISCOVERY CHECKLIST

☐ Have you used definitions to help your readers understand the subject matter, not to show off your knowledge?

☐ Have you tailored your definition to the needs of your audience?

☐ Is your definition specific, clear, and accurate?

☐ Would your definition benefit from an example or from details?

Learning by Doing 🖎 Developing an Extended Definition

Write an extended definition (a paragraph or so) of a word listed below. Begin with a one-sentence definition of the word. Then, instead of turning to a dictionary or textbook, expand and clarify your ideas using strategies in this chapter—examples, details, induction or deduction, analysis, division, classification, comparison, contrast. You may also use *negation* (explaining what something is by stating what it is not). Share your definition with classmates.

education	abuse	exercise	literacy
privacy	jazz	dieting	success
taboo	hip-hop	gossip	fear
prejudice	flu	security	gender

Reasoning Inductively and Deductively

As you develop a typical paragraph, you are likely to rely on both generalizations and particulars. A *generalization* is a broad statement that establishes your point, viewpoint, or conclusion. A *particular* is an instance, a detail, or an example—some specific that supplies evidence that a general statement is reasonable. Your particulars support your generalizations; by presenting compelling instances, details, and examples, you back up your broader point. At the same time, your generalizations pull together your particulars, identifying patterns or connections that relate individual cases.

To link particulars and generalizations, you can use an inductive or deductive process. An *inductive process* begins with the particulars—a convincing number of instances, examples, tests, or experiments. Taken together, these particulars substantiate a larger generalization. In this way a number of long-term studies of weight loss can eventually lead to a consensus about the benefits of walking, eating vegetables, or some other variable. Less formal inductive reasoning is common as people *infer* or conclude that particulars do or do not support a generalization. For example, if your sister ate strawberries three times and got a rash each time, she might infer that she is allergic to strawberries. Induction breaks down when the particulars are too weak or too few to support a generalization: for example, not enough weight-loss studies have comparable results or not enough clear instances occur when strawberries—and nothing else—trigger a reaction.

A *deductive process* begins with a generalization and applies it to another case. When your sister says no to a piece of strawberry pie, she does so because,

For more on reasoning, see Chs. 3 and 9.

For more on the statement-support pattern, see A2 (pp. A-21–A-22) in the Quick Research Guide.

For more on induction and deduction, see Ch. 3.

based on her assumptions, she *deduces* that it, too, will trigger a rash. Deduction breaks down when the initial generalization is flawed or when a particular case doesn't fit the generalization. For instance, suppose that each time your sister ate strawberries she drizzled them with lemon juice, the real culprit. Or suppose that the various weight-loss studies defined low-fat food so differently that no one could determine how their findings might be related.

Once you have reached your conclusions—either by using particulars to support generalizations or by applying reliable generalizations to other particulars—you need to decide how to present your reasoning to readers. Do you want them to follow your process, perhaps examining many cases before reaching a conclusion about them? Or do you want them to learn your conclusion first and then review the evidence? Because academic audiences tend to expect conclusions first, many writers begin essays with thesis statements and paragraphs with topic sentences. On the other hand, if your readers are likely to reject an unexpected thesis initially, you may need to show them the evidence first and then lead them gently to your point.

In "The Good Heart" (*Newsweek,* 3 Oct. 2005), Anne Underwood opens with a paragraph organized inductively: she describes a particular situation that has helped substantiate the broad, even surprising, generalization with which she concludes the paragraph.

> You can call it the Northridge Effect, after the powerful earthquake that struck near Los Angeles at 4:30 on a January morning in 1994. Within an hour, and for the rest of the day, medics responding to people crushed or trapped inside buildings faced a second wave of deaths from heart attacks among people who had survived the tremor unscathed. In the months that followed, researchers at two universities examined coroners' records from Los Angeles County and found an astonishing jump in cardiovascular deaths, from 15.6 on an average day to 51 on the day of the quake itself. Most of these people turned out to have a history of coronary disease or risk factors such as high blood pressure. But those who died were not involved in rescue efforts or trying to dig themselves out of the rubble. Why did they die? In the understated language of the *New England Journal of Medicine,* "emotional stress may precipitate cardiac events in people who are predisposed to such events." To put it simply, they were scared to death.

Underwood goes on to review the impact on heart attack patients of various factors such as anxiety, depression, and childhood trauma. Then, in the following passage, she first states and supports a generalization about the effects of common stresses in adult life, citing the results of an inductive study. In the second paragraph, she deductively applies the generalization to a particular case.

> And if stress in childhood can lead to heart disease, what about current stressors—longer work hours, threats of layoffs, collapsing

pension funds? A study last year in the *Lancet* examined more than 11,000 heart-attack sufferers from 52 countries and found that in the year before their heart attacks, patients had been under significantly more strains — from work, family, financial troubles, depression, and other causes — than some 13,000 healthy control subjects. "Each of these factors individually was associated with increased risk," says Dr. Salim Yusuf, professor of medicine at Canada's McMaster University and senior investigator on the study. "Together, they accounted for 30 percent of overall heart-attack risk." But people respond differently to high-pressure work situations. The key to whether it produces a coronary seems to be whether you have a sense of control over life, or live at the mercy of circumstances and superiors.

That was the experience of John O'Connell, a Rockford, Illinois, laboratory manager who suffered his first heart attack in 1996, at the age of 56. In the two years before, his mother and two of his children had suffered serious illnesses, and his job had been changed in a reorganization. "My life seemed completely out of control," he says. "I had no idea where I would end up." He ended up on a gurney with a clot blocking his left anterior descending artery — the classic "widowmaker." Two months later he had triple bypass surgery. A second heart attack when he was 58 left his cardiologist shaking his head. There's nothing more we can do for you, doctors told him.

DISCOVERY CHECKLIST

☐ Do your generalizations follow logically from your particulars? Can you substantiate what and how much you claim?

☐ Are your particulars typical, numerous, and relevant enough to support your generalizations? Are your particulars substantial enough to warrant the conclusion you have drawn?

☐ Are both your generalizations and your particulars presented clearly? Have you identified your assumptions for your readers?

☐ How do you expect your reasoning patterns to affect your readers? What are your reasons for opening with generalizations or reserving them until the end of a paragraph or passage?

☐ Is your reasoning in an explanatory paper clear and logical? Is your reasoning in an argumentative paper rigorous enough to withstand the scrutiny of readers? Have you avoided generalizing too broadly or illogically connecting generalizations and particulars?

Learning by Doing 🎨 Reasoning Inductively and Deductively

Skim a recent magazine for an article that explores a health, environmental, or economic issue. Read the article, looking for paragraphs organized inductively and deductively. Why do you think the writer chose one pattern or the other in the various sections of the article? How well do those patterns work from a reader's point of view? Sum up your conclusions.

Analyzing a Subject

When you *analyze* a subject, you divide it into its parts and then examine one part at a time. If you have taken any chemistry, you probably analyzed water: you separated it into hydrogen and oxygen, its two elements. You've heard many a commentator or blogger analyze the news, telling us what made up an event—who participated, where it occurred, what happened. Analyzing a news event may produce results less certain and clear-cut than analyzing a chemical compound, but the principle is similar—to take something apart for the purpose of understanding it better.

For more on division and classification, see pp. 452–55. For more on process analysis, see pp. 450–52. For more on cause and effect, see pp. 457–58.

Analysis helps readers grasp something complex: they can more readily take it in as a series of bites than one gulp. For this reason, college textbooks do a lot of analyzing: an economics book divides a labor union into its component parts, an anatomy text divides the hand into its bones, muscles, and ligaments. In your papers, you might analyze and explain to readers anything from a contemporary subculture (What social groups make up the homeless population of Los Angeles?) to an ecosystem (What animals, plants, and minerals coexist in a rain forest?). Analysis is so useful that you can apply it in many situations: breaking down the components of a subject to classify them, separating the stages in a process to see how it works, or identifying the possible results of an event to project consequences.

In *Cultural Anthropology: A Perspective on the Human Condition* (St. Paul: West, 1987), Emily A. Schultz and Robert H. Lavenda briefly but effectively demonstrate by analysis how a metaphor like "the Lord is my shepherd" makes a difficult concept ("the Lord") easy to understand.

> The first part of a metaphor, the metaphorical subject, indicates the domain of experience that needs to be clarified (e.g., "the Lord"). The second part of a metaphor, the metaphorical predicate, suggests a domain of experience which is familiar (e.g., sheep-herding) and which may help us understand what "the Lord" is all about.

In much the same way, Lillian Tsu, a government major at Cornell University, uses analysis in her essay "A Woman in the White House" to identify major difficulties faced by female politicians in the United States.

Although traditionally paternalistic societies like the Philippines and Pakistan and socially conservative states like Great Britain have elected female leaders, particular characteristics of the United States' own electoral system have complicated efforts to elect a female president. Despite social modernization and the progress of the women's movement, the voters of the United States have lagged far behind those of other nations in their willingness to trust in the leadership of a female executive. While the women's movement succeeded in changing Americans' attitudes as to what roles are socially acceptable for women, female candidates have faced a more difficult task in U.S. elections than their male counterparts have. Three factors have been responsible for this situation—political socialization, lack of experience, and open discrimination.

Next, Tsu treats these three factors in turn, beginning each section with a transition that emphasizes the difficulties faced: "One obstacle," "A second obstacle," "A third obstacle." The opening list and the transitions direct readers through a complicated essay, moving from the explanation of the three factors to the final section on implications.

When you plan an analysis, you might label slices in a pielike circle or arrange subdivisions in a list running from smallest to largest or from least to most important. Make sure that your analysis has a purpose—that it will demonstrate something about your subject or tell your readers something they didn't know before. For example, to show the ethnic composition of New York City, you might divide the city geographically into neighborhoods—Harlem, Spanish Harlem, Yorkville, Chinatown, Little Italy. To explain New York's social classes, however, you might start with homeless people and work up to the wealthy elite. The way you slice your subject into pieces will depend in part on the point you want to make about it—and the point you end up making will depend in part on how you've sliced it up. As you develop your ideas, you may also find that you have a stronger point to make—that New York City's social hierarchy is oppressive and unstable, for example.

How can you help your readers follow your analysis? Some writers begin by identifying the subdivisions into which they are going to slice their subject ("The federal government has three branches"). If you name or label each part you mention, define the terms you use, and clarify with examples, you will also help distinguish each part from the others. Finally, using transitions, leading readers from one part to the next, helps make your essay readable.

For more on transitions, see pp. 433–37.

DISCOVERY CHECKLIST

☐ Exactly what will you try to achieve in your analysis?

☐ How does your analysis support your main idea or thesis?

☐ How will you break your subject into parts?

☐ How can you make each part clear to your readers?

☐ What definitions, details, and examples would help clarify each part?

☐ What transitions would clarify your movement from part to part?

Learning by Doing 🔲 Analyzing a Subject

Analyze one of the following subjects by making a list of its basic parts or elements. Then use your list as the basis for a paragraph or short essay explaining each part. Be sure to identify the purpose or point of your analysis. Compare your analysis with those of others in your class who chose the same subject.

a college	a choir, orchestra, or other musical group
a news source	a computer or other technological device
a reality TV show	a basketball, baseball, hockey, or other team
effective teaching	a family, tribe, clan, or neighborhood
a healthy lifestyle	leadership, heroism, or service

Analyzing a Process

Analyzing a process means telling step-by-step how something is, was, or could be done. You can analyze an action or a phenomenon—how a skyscraper is built, how a revolution begins, how sunspots form. You can also explain large, long-ago events that you couldn't possibly have witnessed or complex technical processes that you couldn't personally duplicate. For instance, in "The Case for Cloning" (*Time* 9 Feb. 1998), Madeleine Nash describes the process of cloning cells. Her *informative* process analysis sets forth how something happens.

> Cloning individual human cells . . . is another matter. Biologists are already talking about harnessing for medical purposes the technique that produced the sheep called Dolly. They might, for example, obtain healthy cells from a patient with leukemia or a burn victim and then transfer the nucleus of each cell into an unfertilized egg from which the nucleus has been removed. Coddled in culture dishes, these embryonic clones—each genetically identical to the patient from which the nuclei came—would begin to divide. The cells would not have to grow into a fetus, however. The addition of powerful growth factors could ensure that the clones develop only into specialized cells and tissue. For the leukemia patient, for example, the cloned cells could provide an infusion of fresh bone marrow, and for the burn victim, grafts of brand-new skin. Unlike cells from an unrelated donor, these

cloned cells would incur no danger of rejection; patients would be spared the need to take powerful drugs to suppress the immune system.

In contrast, the *directive*, or "how-to," process analysis tells readers how to do something (how to box, invest for retirement, clean a painting) or how to make something (how to draw a map, blaze a trail, fix chili). Especially on Web sites, directions may consist of simple step-by-step lists with quick advice for browsers. In essays and articles, however, the basics may be supplemented with advice, encouragement, or relevant experience. In "How to Catch More Trout" (*Outdoor Life* May 2006), Joe Brooks identifies the critical stages in the process in his first paragraph:

> Every move you make in trout fishing counts for or against you. The way you approach a pool, how you retrieve, how you strike, how you play the fish, how you land him—all are important factors. If you plan your tactics according to the demands of each situation, you'll catch a lot more trout over a season.

Then Brooks introduces the first stage:

> The first thing you should do is stand by the pool and study it awhile before you fish. Locate the trout that are rising consistently. Choose one (the lowest in the pool, preferably), and work on him. If you rush right in and start casting, you'll probably put down several fish that you haven't seen. And you can scare still more fish by false-casting all over the place. A dozen fish you might have caught with a more careful approach may see the line and go down before you even drop the fly on the surface.

He continues with stages and advice until he reaches the last step:

> The safest way to land a fish is to beach it. If no low bank is handy, you can fight a fish until he is tired and then pull his head against a bank or an up-jutting rock and pick him up. Hold him gently. The tighter your grip, the more likely he is to spurt from your fingers, break your leader tippet, and escape. Even if you intend to put him back, you want to feel that he is really yours—a trout you have cast and caught and released because you planned it that way.

Brooks skillfully addresses his audience—readers of *Outdoor Life,* people who probably already know how to fish and hunt. As his title indicates, Brooks isn't explaining how to catch trout but how to catch *more* trout. For this reason, he skips topics for beginners (such as how to cast) and instead urges readers to try more sophisticated tactics to increase their catch.

Process analysis can also turn to humor, as in this paragraph from "How to Heal a Broken Heart (in One Day)" by student Lindsey Schendel.

> To begin your first day of mourning, you will wake up at 11 a.m., thus banishing any feelings of fatigue. Forget eating a healthy breakfast; toast two waffles, and

plaster them with chocolate syrup instead of maple. Then make sure you have a room of serenity so you may cry in peace. It is important that you go through the necessary phases of denial and depression. Call up a friend or family member while you are still in your serious, somber mood. Explain to that person the hardships you are facing and how you don't know if you can go on. Immediately afterwards, turn on any empowering music, get up, and dance.

For more on transitions, see pp. 433–37.

Like more serious process directions, this paragraph includes steps or stages (sleeping late, eating breakfast, crying and calling, getting up and dancing). They are arranged in chronological order with transitions marking the movement from one to the other (*To begin, then, while, immediately afterwards*).

Process analyses are wonderful ways to show readers the inside workings of events or systems, but they can be difficult to follow. Divide the process into logical steps or stages, and put the steps in chronological order. Add details or examples wherever your description might be ambiguous; use transitions to mark the end of one step and the beginning of the next.

DISCOVERY CHECKLIST

☐ Do you thoroughly understand the process you are analyzing?

☐ Do you have a good reason to analyze a process at this point in your writing? How does your analysis support your main idea or thesis?

☐ Have you broken the process into logical and useful steps? Have you adjusted your explanation of the steps for your audience?

☐ Is the order in which you present these steps the best one possible?

☐ Have you used transitions to guide readers from one step to the next?

Learning by Doing Analyzing a Process

Analyze one of the following processes or procedures in a paragraph or short essay. Then share your process analysis with classmates. Can they follow your analysis easily? Do they spot anything you left out?

registering for college classes   hunting for a job
studying for a test   buying a used car
having the flu (or another illness)   moving

Dividing and Classifying

For more on analyzing a subject, see pp. 448–50.

To divide is to break something down, identifying or analyzing its components. It's far easier to take in a subject, especially a complex one, a piece at a time. The thing divided may be as concrete as a medical center (which you might divide into specialty units) or as abstract as a knowledge of art (which you might divide into sculpture, painting, drawing, and other forms). To classify is to make sense of a potentially bewildering array of things—works of literature, this year's movies—by sorting them into categories (*types* or *classes*) that you can deal with one at a time. Literature is customarily arranged by genre—novels, stories, poems, plays. Movies might be sorted by audience (children, teenagers, mature adults). Dividing and classifying are like two sides of the same coin. In theory, any broad subject can be *divided* into components, which can then be *classified* into categories. In practice, it's often difficult to tell where division stops and classification begins.

In his college textbook *Wildlife Management* (San Francisco: Freeman, 1978), Robert H. Giles Jr. uses division to simplify an especially large, abstract subject: the management of forest wildlife in America. To explain which environmentalists assume which duties, Giles divides forest wildlife management into six levels or areas of concern, arranged roughly from large to small, all neatly presented in fewer than two hundred words.

> There are six scales of forest wildlife management: (1) national,
> (2) regional, (3) state or industrial, (4) county or parish, (5) intra-state
> region, management unit, or watershed, and (6) forest. Each is different.
> At the national and regional levels, management includes decisions on
> timber harvest quotas, grazing policy in forested lands, official stance
> on forest taxation bills, cutting policy relative to threatened and
> endangered species, management coordination of migratory species,
> and research fund allocation. At the state or industrial level, decision
> types include land acquisition, sale, or trade; season setting; and permit
> systems and fees. At the county level, plans are made, seasons set, and
> special fees levied. At the intra-state level, decisions include what
> seasons to recommend, what stances to take on bills not affecting local
> conditions, the sequence in which to attempt land acquisition, and the
> placement of facilities. At the forest level, decisions may include some
> of those of the larger management unit but typically are those of
> maintenance schedules, planting stock, cutting rotations, personnel
> employment and supervision, road closures, equipment use, practices
> to be attempted or used, and boundaries to be marked.

In a textbook lesson on how babies develop from *Human Development* (New York: Freeman, 1984), Kurt W. Fischer and Arlyne Lazerson describe a research project that classified babies into three types by temperament.

> The researchers also found that certain of these temperamental
> qualities tended to occur together. These clusters of characteristics
> generally fell into three types—the easy baby, the difficult baby, and the
> baby who was slow to warm up. The *easy infant* has regular patterns of
> eating and sleeping, readily approaches new objects and people, adapts
> easily to changes in the environment, generally reacts with low or
> moderate intensity, and typically is in a cheerful mood. The *difficult
> infant* usually shows irregular patterns of eating and sleeping, withdraws

from new objects or people, adapts slowly to changes, reacts with great intensity, and is frequently cranky. The *slow-to-warm-up infant* typically has a low activity level, tends to withdraw when presented with an unfamiliar object, reacts with a low level of intensity, and adapts slowly to changes in the environment. Fortunately for parents, most healthy infants — 40 percent or more — have an easy temperament. Only about 10 percent have a difficult temperament, and about 15 percent are slow to warm up. The remaining 35 percent do not easily fit one of the three types but show some other pattern.

When you divide and classify, your point is to make order out of a complex or overwhelming jumble.

- Make sure the components and categories you identify are sensible, given your purpose, and follow the same principle of classification or analysis for all categories. For example, to discuss campus relations, it makes sense to divide the school population into *instructors, students,* and *support staff;* it would make less sense to divide it into *people from the South, people from other states,* and *people from overseas.*

- Try to group apples with apples, not with oranges, so that all the components or categories are roughly equivalent. For example, if you're classifying television shows and you've come up with *reality shows, dramas, talk shows, children's shows, news,* and *cartoons,* then you've got a problem: the last category is probably part of *children's shows.*

- Check that your final system is simple and easy for your readers to understand. Most people can handle only about seven things at once. If you've got more than five or six components or categories, perhaps you need to combine or eliminate some.

DISCOVERY CHECKLIST

☐ How does your division or classification support your main idea or thesis?

☐ Do you use the most logical principle to divide or classify for your purpose?

☐ Do you stick to one principle throughout?

☐ Have you identified components or categories that are comparable?

☐ Have you arranged your components or categories in the best order?

☐ Have you given specific examples for each component or category?

☐ Have you made a complex subject more accessible to your readers?

For more on brainstorming, see pp. 387–88.

Learning by Doing 🎥 Dividing and Classifying

Choose one or two of the following subjects. Brainstorm on each to come up with as many components as you can. With classmates, create one large list by combining items from all who chose each subject. Working together, take the largest list and try to classify the items on it into logical categories. Add or change components or categories if you've overlooked something.

students   customers   sports   families
teachers   Web sites   vacations   drivers

Comparing and Contrasting

Often you can develop ideas by setting a pair of subjects side by side, comparing and contrasting them. When you compare, you point out similarities; when you contrast, you discuss differences. You can use two basic methods of organization for comparison and contrast—the opposing pattern and the alternating pattern—as illustrated for a comparison and contrast of two brothers.

For sample essays and advice on writing a comparison and contrast essay, see Ch. 7.

OPPOSING PATTERN,
SUBJECT BY SUBJECT

Subject A: Jim
  Point 1: Appearance
  Point 2: Personality
  Point 3: Interests
Subject B: Jack
  Point 1: Appearance
  Point 2: Personality
  Point 3: Interests

ALTERNATING PATTERN,
POINT BY POINT

Point 1: Appearance
  Subject A: Jim
  Subject B: Jack
Point 2: Personality
  Subject A: Jim
  Subject B: Jack
Point 3: Interests
  Subject A: Jim
  Subject B: Jack

You need a reason to compare and contrast—a final evaluation, perhaps a decision about which thing is better or another purpose. For example, compare Jack and Jim to do more than point out lanky or curly hair. Use their differences to highlight their powerful bond as brothers or their similarities to support a generalization about a family strength.

The following selection uses both patterns to open Chapter One of *Rousseau's Dog* by David Edmonds and John Eidinow (New York: HarperCollins, 2006). The book tells the story of the bitterness that grew between David Hume and Jean-Jacques Rousseau, two eighteenth-century philosophers with very different views and styles.

On the evening of January 10, 1766, the weather in the English Channel was foul—stormy, wet, and cold. That night, after being held in harbor by unfavorable winds, a packet boat beat its way, rolling and plunging, from Calais to Dover. Among the passengers were two men who had met for the first time some three weeks earlier in Paris, a British diplomat and a Swiss refugee. The refugee was accompanied by his beloved dog, Sultan, small and brown with a curly tail. The

Alternating pattern

diplomat stayed below, tormented by seasickness. The refugee remained on deck all night; the frozen sailors marveled at his hardiness.

Significance

If the ship had foundered, she would have carried to the bottom of the Channel two of the most influential thinkers of the eighteenth century.

Opposing pattern

The diplomat was David Hume. His contributions to philosophy on induction, causation, necessity, personal identity, morality, and theism are of such enduring importance that his name belongs in the league of the most elite philosophers, the league that would also include Plato,

Subject A

Aristotle, Descartes, Kant, and Wittgenstein. A contemporary and friend of Adam Smith's, he paved the way to modern economics; he also modernized historiography.

Subject B

The refugee was Jean-Jacques Rousseau. His intellectual range and achievements were equally staggering. He made epochal contributions to political theory, literature, and education. His autobiography, *The Confessions,* was a stunningly original work, one that has spawned countless successors but still sets the standard for a narrative of self-revelation and artistic development. *Émile,* his educational tract, transformed the debate about the upbringing of children and was instrumental in altering our perceptions of childhood. *On the Social Contract,* his most significant political publication, has been cited as an inspiration for generations of revolutionaries. More fundamentally, Rousseau altered the way we view ourselves, our emotions, and our relationship to society and to the natural world.

As the first chapter continues comparing and contrasting, the difference between the temperaments of the two men—and the potential for deep conflict—grows increasingly clear to readers.

DISCOVERY CHECKLIST

☐ Is your reason for comparing and contrasting unmistakably clear? Does it support or develop your main idea or thesis?

☐ Have you chosen to write about the *major* similarities and differences?

☐ Have you compared or contrasted like things? Have you discussed the same categories or features for each item?

☐ Have you selected points of comparison and supporting details that will intrigue, enlighten, and persuade your audience?

☐ Have you used the best possible arrangement, given your subject and the point you're trying to make?

☐ If you are making a judgment, have you treated both subjects fairly?

☐ Have you avoided moving mechanically from "On the one hand" to "On the other hand"?

Learning by Doing 🎥 Comparing and Contrasting

Write a paragraph or two in which you compare and contrast the subjects in one of the following pairs. Exchange drafts with classmates for response, using questions from the Discovery Checklist.

> baseball and football (or two other sports)
> living in an apartment (or dorm) and living in a house
> two cities, communities, or neighborhoods you are familiar with
> two musicians, artists, or performers
> communicating by two methods
> watching a sports event on television and in person

Identifying Causes and Effects

From the time we are children, we ask why. Why can't I go out and play? Why is the sky blue? Why did my goldfish die? Seeking causes and effects continues into adulthood, so it's a common method of development. To explain causal relationships successfully, think about the subject critically, gather evidence, draw judicious conclusions, and clarify relationships.

In the following paragraph from "What Pop Lyrics Say to Us Today" (*New York Times* 24 Feb. 1985), Robert Palmer speculates on the causes that led young people to turn to rock music for inspiration as well as the effects of their expectations on the musicians of the time.

For sample essays and advice on writing a cause and effect essay, see Ch. 8.

> By the late '60s, the peace and civil rights movements were beginning to splinter. The assassinations of the Kennedys and Martin Luther King had robbed a generation of its heroes, the Vietnam War was escalating despite the protests, and at home, violence was on the rise. Young people turned to rock, expecting it to ask the right questions and come up with answers, hoping that the music's most visionary artists could somehow make sense of things. But rock's most influential artists—Bob Dylan, the Beatles, the Rolling Stones—were finding that serving as the conscience of a generation exacted a heavy toll. Mr. Dylan, for one, felt the pressures becoming unbearable, and wrote about his predicament in songs like "All Along the Watchtower."

Instead of focusing on causes *or* effects, often writers trace a *chain* of cause-and-effect relationships, as Charles C. Mann and Mark L. Plummer do in "The Butterfly Problem" (*Atlantic Monthly* Jan. 1992).

> More generally, the web of species around us helps generate soil, regulate freshwater supplies, dispose of waste, and maintain the quality of the atmosphere. Pillaging nature to the point where it cannot perform these functions is dangerously foolish. Simple self-protection is thus a second motive for preserving biodiversity. When DDT was sprayed in Borneo, the biologists Paul and Anne Ehrlich relate in their book

Extinction (1981), it killed all the houseflies. The gecko lizards that preyed on the flies ate their pesticide-filled corpses and died. House cats consumed the dying lizards; they died too. Rats descended on the villages, bringing bubonic plague. Incredibly, the housefly in this case was part of an intricate system that controlled human disease. To make up for its absence, the government was forced to parachute cats into the area.

DISCOVERY CHECKLIST

☐ Do you clearly tie your use of cause and effect to your main idea or thesis?

☐ Have you identified actual causes? Have you supplied persuasive evidence to support them?

☐ Have you identified actual effects, or are they conjecture? If conjecture, are they logical possibilities? What persuasive evidence supports them?

For more on faulty thinking and logical fallacies, see pp. 50–52 and pp. 178–79.

☐ Have you judiciously drawn conclusions about causes and effects? Have you avoided faulty thinking and logical fallacies?

☐ Have you presented your points clearly and logically so that your readers can follow them easily?

☐ Have you considered other causes or effects, immediate or long-term, that readers might find relevant?

Learning by Doing 🎙 Identifying Causes and Effects

1. Identify some of the *causes* of *five* of the following. Then discuss possible causes with your classmates.

failing an exam	stage fright	stress
an automobile accident	losing/winning a game	going to college
poor/good health	getting/losing a job	getting a scholarship

2. Identify some of the *effects* of *five* of the following. Then discuss possible effects with your classmates.

an insult	dieting	winning the lottery
a compliment	speeding	traveling to another country
learning to read	divorce	drinking while driving

3. Identify some of the *causes and effects* of *one* of the following, doing a little research as needed. How might you use the chain of causes and effects in an essay? Discuss your findings with your classmates.

the online shopping boom	recycling
the attacks of September 11, 2001	a gay marriage court case
the discovery of atomic energy	the uses of solar energy
a major U.S. Supreme Court decision	global climate change
	racial tension

Strategies for Revising and Editing 23

Good writing is rewriting. In this chapter we provide strategies for revising and editing—ways to rethink muddy ideas and emphasize important ones, to rephrase obscure passages and restructure garbled sentences. Our advice applies not only to rewriting whole essays but also to rewriting sentences and paragraphs. In addition, we give you tips for editing and proofreading grammar, spelling, punctuation, and mechanics.

Re-viewing and Revising

Revision means "seeing again"—discovering again, conceiving again, shaping again. It may occur at any and all stages of the writing process, and most writers do a lot of it. *Macro revising* is making large, global, or fundamental changes that affect the overall direction or impact of writing—its

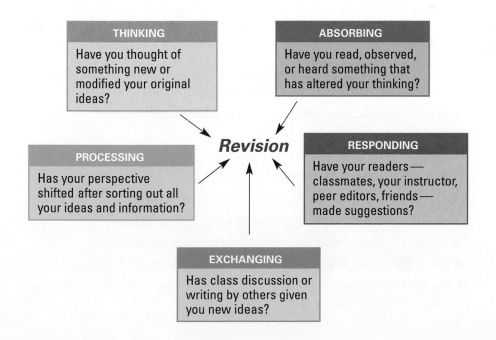

THINKING
Have you thought of something new or modified your original ideas?

ABSORBING
Have you read, observed, or heard something that has altered your thinking?

Revision

PROCESSING
Has your perspective shifted after sorting out all your ideas and information?

RESPONDING
Have your readers—classmates, your instructor, peer editors, friends—made suggestions?

EXCHANGING
Has class discussion or writing by others given you new ideas?

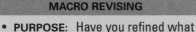

purpose, organization, or audience. Its companion is *micro revising,* paying attention to sentences, words, punctuation, and grammar—including ways to create emphasis and eliminate wordiness.

MACRO REVISING	MICRO REVISING
• **PURPOSE:** Have you refined what you want to accomplish?	• **EMPHASIS:** Can you position your ideas more effectively?
• **THESIS:** Could you state your main point more accurately?	• **CONCISENESS:** Can you spot extra words that you might cut?
• **AUDIENCE:** Should you address your readers differently?	• **CLARITY:** Can you make any sentences and words clearer?
• **STRUCTURE:** Should you reorganize any part of your writing?	
• **SUPPORT:** Do you need to add, drop, or rework your support?	

Revising for Purpose and Thesis

When you revise for purpose, you make sure that your writing accomplishes what you want it to do. If your goal is to create an interesting profile of a person, have you done so? If you want to persuade your readers to take a certain course of action, have you succeeded? Of course, if your project has evolved or your assignment is now clearer to you, the purpose of your final essay may differ from your purpose when you began. To revise for purpose, try to step back and see your writing as other readers will. Concentrate on what's actually in your paper, not what you assume is there.

At this point you'll probably want to revise your working thesis statement (if you've developed one) or create a thesis sentence (if you haven't). First scrutinize your working thesis. Reconsider how it is worded:

For more on stating and improving a working thesis, see pp. 401–07.

- Is it stated exactly in concise yet detailed language?
- Is it focused on only one main idea?
- Is it stated positively rather than negatively?
- Is it limited to a demonstrable statement?

Then consider how accurately your thesis now represents your main idea:

- Does each part of your essay directly relate to your thesis?
- Does each part of your essay develop and support your thesis?
- Does your essay deliver everything your thesis promises?

If you find unrelated or contradictory passages, you have several options: revise the thesis, revise the essay, or revise both.

If you find that your ideas have deepened, your topic has become more complex, or your essay has developed along new lines, you may want to refine or expand your thesis statement accordingly.

WORKING THESIS	The *Herald*'s coverage of the Senate elections was more thorough than the *Courier*'s.
REVISED THESIS	The *Herald*'s coverage of the Senate elections was less timely but more thorough and more impartial than the *Courier*'s.
WORKING THESIS	As the roles of men and women have changed in our society, old-fashioned formal courtesy has declined.
REVISED THESIS	As the roles of men and women have changed in our society, old-fashioned formal courtesy has declined not only toward women but also toward men.

REVISION CHECKLIST

☐ Do you know exactly what you want your essay to accomplish? Can you put it in one sentence: "In this paper I want to . . ."?

☐ Is your thesis stated outright in the essay? If not, have you provided clues so that your readers will know precisely what it is?

☐ Does every part of the essay work to achieve the same goal?

☐ Have you tried to do too much? Does your coverage seem too thin? If so, how might you reduce the scope of your thesis and essay?

☐ Does your essay say all that needs to be said? Is everything—ideas, connections, supporting evidence—on paper, not just in your head?

☐ In writing the essay, have you changed your mind, rethought your assumptions, made a discovery? Does anything now need to be recast?

☐ Do you have enough evidence? Is every point developed fully enough to be clear? To be convincing?

Revising for Audience

An essay is successful only if it succeeds with its particular audience, and what works with one audience can fall flat with another. Your organization, selection of details, word choice, and tone all affect your readers. Visualize one of them poring over the essay, reacting to what you have written. What expressions do you see on that reader's face? Where does he or she have trouble understanding? Where have you hit the mark?

To see one student's revising and editing process, visit **<bedfordstmartins .com/bedguide>**.

REVISION CHECKLIST

☐ Who will read this essay?

☐ Does the essay tell your readers what they want to know, not what they probably know already?

☐ Are there any places where readers might fall asleep? If so, can you shorten, delete, or liven up such passages?

☐ Does the opening of the essay mislead your readers by promising something that the essay never delivers?

☐ Do you unfold each idea in enough detail to make it both clear and interesting? Would readers appreciate more detailed evidence?

☐ Have you anticipated questions your audience might ask?

☐ Where might readers raise serious objections? How might you anticipate their objections and answer them?

☐ Have you used any specialized or technical language that your readers might not understand? If so, have you worked in brief definitions?

☐ What is your attitude toward your audience? Are you chummy, angry, superior, apologetic, preachy? Should you revise to improve your attitude?

☐ Will your readers think you have told them something worth knowing?

Revising for Structure and Support

When you revise for structure and support, you make sure that the order of your ideas, your selection of supporting material, and its arrangement are as effective as possible. You may have all the ingredients of a successful essay—but they may be a confusing mess.

In a well-structured essay, each paragraph, sentence, and phrase serves a clear function. Are your opening and closing paragraphs relevant, concise, and interesting? Is everything in each paragraph on the same topic? Are all ideas adequately developed? Are the paragraphs arranged in the best possible order? Finally, review each place where you lead readers from one idea to the next to be certain that the transition is clear and painless.

An outline can help you discover what you've succeeded in getting on paper. Find the topic sentence of each paragraph in your draft (or create one, if necessary), and list them in order. Label the sentences *I., II., A., B.,* and so on to show the logical relationships of ideas. Do the same with the supporting details under each topic sentence, labeling them also with letters and numbers and indenting appropriately. Now look at the outline. Does it make sense on its own, without the essay to explain it? Would a different order or arrangement be more effective? Do any sections look thin and need more evidence? Are the connections between parts in your head but not on

For more on paragraphs, topic sentences, and transitions, see Ch. 21.

For more on using outlining for planning, see pp. 413–21.

paper? Maybe too many ideas are jammed into too few paragraphs. Maybe you don't include as many specific details and examples as you need — or maybe you need stronger ones. Strengthen the outline and then rewrite to follow it.

REVISION CHECKLIST

☐ Does your introduction set up the whole essay? Does it both grab readers' attention and hint at what is to follow?

☐ Does the essay fulfill all that you promise in your opening?

☐ Would any later passage make a better beginning?

☐ Is your thesis clear early in the essay? If explicit, is it positioned prominently?

☐ Do the paragraph breaks seem logical?

☐ Is the main idea of each paragraph clear? Is it stated in a topic sentence?

☐ Is the main idea of each paragraph fully developed? Where might you need more details or better evidence to be convincing?

☐ Within each paragraph, is each detail or piece of evidence relevant to the topic sentence? If you find a stray bit, should you omit it or move it?

☐ Are all the ideas directly relevant to the main point of the essay?

☐ Would any paragraphs make more sense in a different order?

☐ Does everything follow clearly? Does one point smoothly lead to the next? Would transitions help make the connections clearer?

☐ Does the conclusion follow logically or seem tacked on?

Learning by Doing 🎦 Tackling Macro Revision

Even if you don't know exactly what needs to be changed in a draft, this activity will help you get started making productive changes. Select a draft that would benefit from revision. Then, based on your sense of its greatest need, choose one of the revision checklists to guide a first revision. Let the draft sit for a while. Then work with one of the remaining checklists.

Working with a Peer Editor

Of course, there's no substitute for having someone else go over your writing. Whether you have been asked to write for an audience of classmates or for a different group (the town council or readers of *Newsweek*), having a classmate read your essay is a worthwhile revision strategy. To gain all you can as a writer from a peer review, you need to play an active part:

- Ask your reader questions. (See page 465 for ideas.) Or bring a "Dear Editor" letter or memo, written ahead, to your meeting.
- Be open to new ideas — for focus, organization, or details.
- Use what's helpful, but trust yourself as the writer.

Be a helpful peer editor: offer honest, intelligent feedback, not judgment.

- Look at the big picture: purpose, focus, thesis, clarity, coherence, organization, support.
- When you spot strengths or weaknesses, be specific: note examples.
- Answer the writer's questions, and also use the questions supplied throughout this book to concentrate on essentials, not details.

See specific checklists in the "Revising and Editing" sections in Chs. 4 to 12.

Meeting with Your Instructor

Prepare for your conference on a draft as you prepare for a peer review. Reread your paper; then write out your questions, concerns, or current revision plans. Whether you are meeting face-to-face, online, or by Web phone, arrive on time. Even if you feel shy or anxious, remember that you are working with an experienced reader who wants to help you improve your writing.

- If you already have received comments from your instructor, ask about anything you can't read, don't understand, or can't figure out how to do.
- If you are uncertain about comments from your peers, get your instructor's opinion or clarification.
- If you have a revision plan, ask for suggestions or priorities.
- If more questions arise after your conference, especially about comments on a draft returned there, follow up with a call, e-mail message, question after class, or second conference (as your instructor prefers).

Decoding Your Instructor's Comments

Whether comments are electronic or handwritten, many instructors write two kinds:

- Summary comments — sentences at the end or at the top of your first page — that typically compliment strengths, identify recurring issues, acknowledge changes between drafts, make broad suggestions, and may end with a grade
- Specific comments — brief notes or questions added to your file or in the margins of your printed paper — that typically pinpoint issues in the text.

Brief specific comments may seem like cryptic code or shorthand. They rely on key words, usually to note common, recurring problems that probably

Questions for a Peer Editor

First Questions for a Peer Editor

What is your first reaction to this paper?

What is this writer trying to tell you?

What are this paper's greatest strengths?

Does it have any major weaknesses?

What one change would most improve the paper?

Questions on Meaning

Do you understand everything? Is the draft missing any information that you need to know?

Does this paper tell you anything you didn't know before?

Is the writer trying to cover too much territory? Too little?

Does any point need to be more fully explained or illustrated?

When you come to the end, has the paper delivered what it promised?

Could this paper use a down-to-the-ground revision?

Questions on Organization

Has the writer begun in a way that grabs your interest and quickly draws you into the paper's main idea? Or can you find a better beginning at some later point?

Does the paper have one main idea, or does it juggle more than one?

Would the main idea stand out better if anything were removed or added?

Might the ideas in the paper be more effectively arranged? Do any ideas belong together that now seem too far apart?

Can you follow the ideas easily? Are transitions needed? If so, where?

Does the writer keep to one point of view—one angle of seeing?

Does the ending seem deliberate, as if the writer meant to conclude, not just run out of gas? How might the writer strengthen the conclusion?

Questions on Writing Strategies

Do you feel that this paper addresses you personally?

Do you dislike or object to any statement the writer makes or any wording the writer uses? Is the problem word choice, tone, or inadequate support to convince you? Should the writer keep or change this part?

Does the draft contain anything that distracts you or seems unnecessary?

Do you get bored at any point? How might the writer keep you reading?

Is the language of this paper too lofty and abstract? If so, where does the writer need to come down to earth and get specific?

Do you understand all the words used? Do any specialized words need clearer definitions?

For online peer response worksheets, visit <**bedfordstmartins.com/bedguide**>.

are discussed in class and are related to course criteria. In addition, they may act as reminders, identifying issues that your instructor expects you to look up in your book and solve. A simple analysis — tallying up all the repeated comments in one paper or several — can quickly help you set priorities for revision and editing. Some groups of related comments follow, but turn to your instructor if you need specific translation.

COMMENTS ON PURPOSE	Thesis? Vague Broad Clarify What's your point? So? So what?
POSSIBLE TRANSLATION	You need to state your thesis more clearly and directly so that a reader knows what matters. Concentrate on rewording so that your main idea is plain.
COMMENTS ON ORGANIZATION	Hard to follow Logic? Sequence? Add transitions? Jumpy
POSSIBLE TRANSLATION	You need to reorganize more logically so that your paper is easy for a reader to follow without jumping from point to point. Add transitions or other cues and connections to guide a reader.
COMMENTS ON SENTENCES AND WORDS	Unclear Clarify Awk Repetition Too informal
POSSIBLE TRANSLATION	You need to make your sentence or your wording easier to read and clearer. Rework awkward passages, reduce repetition, and stick to academic language.
COMMENTS ON EVIDENCE	Specify Focus Narrow down Develop more Seems thin
POSSIBLE TRANSLATION	You need to provide more concrete evidence or explain the relevance or nature of your evidence more clearly. Check that each main point is supported by plenty of pertinent and compelling evidence.
COMMENTS ON SOURCES	Likely opponents? Source? Add quotation marks? Too many quotes Add summary Add synthesis Launch source?
POSSIBLE TRANSLATION	You need to add sources that represent views other than your own. You include wording or ideas that sound like a source, not like you, so your quotation marks or a citation might be missing. Instead of tossing in quotations, use your critical thinking skills to sum up ideas, relate them to each other, and introduce them more effectively.
COMMENTS ON SOURCES CREDITS	Cite? MLA? APA?

POSSIBLE TRANSLATION   *Add missing source citations in your text. You need to use the expected academic format to present your citations.*

COMMENTS ON FINAL   MLA? APA? Comma? Period? Cap? Space?
LIST OF SOURCES

POSSIBLE TRANSLATION   *Your entries do not follow the expected format. Check the model entries in this book. Look for the presence, absence, or placement of the specific type of detail noted.*

Revising for Emphasis, Conciseness, and Clarity

After you've revised for the large issues in your draft—purpose, thesis, audience, structure, and support—you're ready to turn your attention to micro revising. Now is the time to look at your language, to emphasize what matters most, and to communicate it concisely and clearly.

Stressing What Counts

An ineffective writer treats all ideas as equals. You can't emphasize merely by monotonous underlining, *italicizing*, putting things in "quotation marks," or throwing them into CAPITALS. Instead, an effective writer decides what matters most and shines a bright light on it using the most emphatic positions in an essay, a paragraph, or a sentence—the beginning and the end.

Stating It First. In an essay, you might start with what matters most. For an economics paper on import quotas (such as the number of foreign cars allowed into a country), student Donna Waite summed up her conclusion.

Although an import quota has many effects, both for the nation imposing the quota and for the nation whose industries must suffer from it, I believe that the most important effect is generally felt at home. A native industry gains a chance to thrive in a marketplace of lessened competition.

A paper that takes a stand or makes a proposal might open with the writer's position.

Our state's antiquated system of justices of the peace is inefficient.

The United States should orbit a human observer around Mars.

In a single sentence, as in an essay, you can stress things at the start. Consider the following unemphatic sentence:

> When Congress debates the Hall-Hayes Act removing existing protections for endangered species, as now seems likely to occur on May 12, it will be a considerable misfortune if this bill should pass, since the extinction of many rare birds and animals would certainly result.

The debate and its probable timing consume the start of the sentence. Here's a better use of this emphatic position:

> The extinction of many rare birds and animals would certainly follow passage of the Hall-Hayes Act.

Now the writer stresses what he most fears — the dire consequences of the act. (A later sentence might add the date and his opinion about passage.)

Stating It Last. To place an idea last can throw weight on it. Emphatic order, proceeding from least important to most, is dramatic: it builds up and up. In a paper on import quotas, however, a dramatic buildup might look contrived. Still, in an essay on how city parks lure visitors to the city, the thesis sentence — summing up the point of the essay — might stand at the very end: "For the urban core, improved parks could bring about a new era of prosperity." Giving evidence first and leading up to the thesis at the end is particularly effective in editorials and informal persuasive essays.

A sentence that uses climactic order, suspending its point until the end, is a *periodic* sentence as novelist Julian Green illustrates.

> Amid chaos of illusions into which we are cast headlong, there is one thing that stands out as true, and that is — love.

Cutting and Whittling

Like pea pickers who throw out dirt and pebbles, good writers remove needless words that clog their prose. One of the chief joys of revising is to watch 200 paunchy words shrink to a svelte 150. To see how saving words helps, let's look at some strategies for reducing wordiness.

For more on transitions, see pp. 433–37.

Cut the Fanfare. Why bother to announce that you're going to say something? Cut the fanfare. We aren't, by the way, attacking the usefulness of transitions that lead readers along.

WORDY	As far as getting ready for winter is concerned, I put antifreeze in my car.
REVISED	To get ready for winter, I put antifreeze in my car.

| WORDY | The point should be made that . . .
Let me make it perfectly clear that . . .
In this paper I intend to . . .
In conclusion I would like to say that . . . |

Use Strong Verbs. Forms of the verb *be* (*am, is, are, was, were*) followed by a noun or an adjective can make a statement wordy, as can *There is* or *There are.* Such weak verbs can almost always be replaced by active verbs.

WORDY	The Akron game was a disappointment to the fans.
REVISED	The Akron game disappointed the fans.
WORDY	There are many people who dislike flying.
REVISED	Many people dislike flying.

Use Relative Pronouns with Caution. When a clause begins with a relative pronoun (*who, which, that*), you often can whittle it to a phrase.

| WORDY | Venus, which is the second planet of the solar system, is called the evening star. |
| REVISED | Venus, the second planet of the solar system, is called the evening star. |

Cut Out Dead Wood. The more you revise, the more shortcuts you'll discover. Phrases such as *on the subject of, in regard to, in terms of,* and *as far as . . . is concerned* often simply fill space. Try reading the sentences below without the words in *italics*.

Howell spoke for the sophomores, and Janet *also spoke* for the seniors.

He is *something of* a clown but *sort of the* lovable *type*.

As a major in *the field of* economics, I plan to concentrate on *the area of* international banking.

The decision as to whether *or not* to go is up to you.

Cut Descriptors. Adjectives and adverbs are often dispensable.

| WORDY | Johnson's extremely significant research led to highly important major discoveries. |
| REVISED | Johnson's research led to major discoveries. |

Be Short, Not Long. While a long word may convey a shade of meaning that a shorter synonym doesn't, in general favor short words over long ones. Instead of *the remainder,* write *the rest;* instead of *activate, start* or *begin;* instead of *adequate* or *sufficient, enough.* Look for the right word—one that wraps an idea in a smaller package.

| WORDY | Andy has a left fist that has a lot of power in it. |
| REVISED | Andy has a potent left. |

By the way, it pays to read. From reading, you absorb words like *potent* and set them to work for you.

Keeping It Clear

Recall what you want to achieve — clear, direct communication with your readers using specific, unambiguous words arranged in logical order.

| WORDY | He is more or less a pretty outstanding person in regard to good looks. |
| REVISED | He is strikingly handsome. |

Read your draft as a brand-new reader would. Return, after a break, to passages that have been a struggle; heal any battle scars by focusing on clarity.

| UNCLEAR | Thus, after a lot of thought, it should be approved by the board even though the federal funding for all the cow-tagging may not be approved yet because it has wide support from local cattle ranchers. |
| CLEAR | In anticipation of federal funding, the Livestock Board should approve the cow-tagging proposal widely supported by local cattle ranchers. |

MICRO REVISION CHECKLIST

☐ Have you positioned what counts at the beginning or the end?

☐ Are you direct, straightforward, and clear?

☐ Do you announce an idea before you utter it? If so, consider chopping out the announcement.

☐ Can you substitute an active verb where you use a form of *be* (*is, was, were*)?

☐ Can you recast any sentence that begins *There is* or *There are*?

☐ Can you reduce to a phrase any clause beginning with *which, who,* or *that*?

☐ Have you added deadwood or too many adjectives and adverbs?

☐ Do you see any long words where short words would do?

☐ Have you kept your writing clear, direct, and forceful?

Learning by Doing 🔘 Tackling Micro Revision

Think over the revisions you've already made and the advice you've received from peers or other readers. Is your paper more likely to seem bland (because it lacks emphasis), wordy (because it needs a good trimming), or foggy (because it needs to be more direct and logical)? Focus on one issue, and concentrate on adding emphasis, cutting extra words, or expressing ideas clearly.

For his composition class, Daniel Matthews was assigned a paper using a few sources. He was to write about an "urban legend," a widely accepted and emotionally appealing—but untrue—tale about events. The following selection from his paper, "The Truth about 'Taps,'" introduces his topic and briefly explains both the legend and the true story about it. The first draft illustrates macro revisions (highlighted in the margin) and micro revisions (marked in the text). Following the draft is the clear and concise final version.

FIRST DRAFT

Anyone who has ever ————————————— Avoid "you" in case
As ~~you know, whenever you have~~ attended the funeral services for a fallen   readers have not shared
^   this experience.
                                              has
veteran of the United States of America, ~~you have~~ stood fast as a lone bugler filled
                                          ^

the air with the mournful ~~and sullenly appropriate~~ last tribute to a defender of the

nation   *T*
~~United States of America.~~ As ~~most of us know,~~ the name of the bugle call is "Taps,"
^   ^
    legend   *has*   *ed*
and the ~~story~~ behind its origin ~~is one that is~~ gaining a popularity ~~of its own~~ as it   Rework paragraph to
        ^   ^   ^   summarize legend when
has   first mentioned.
~~is more and more frequently being~~ circulated in this time of war and terror. Although
^

~~it is clear that~~ this tale ~~of the origin~~ of a beautiful ode to a fallen warrior is ⌐ INSERT:
                                                                                          | According to this story,
                                              As such, i | Union Captain Robert
heartfelt ~~and full of purposeful intent~~, it is an "urban legend." ~~It~~ fails to provide   Ellicombe discovered
                                              ^   that a Confederate
due justice to the memories of the men responsible for the true origin of "Taps."   casualty was, in fact,
                                                                                            his son, a music
              true   ⊙   student in the South.
General Daniel Butterfield is the originator of the bugle call "Taps," ~~formerly~~   The father found "Taps"
              ^   ^   in his son's pocket, and
~~known as "Lights Out."~~ Butterfield served ~~as a general~~ in the Union army during the   the tune was first
                                                                                            played at a military
Civil War and was awarded the Medal of Honor for actions during that time. One of   burial as his son was
                                                                                          ⌐ laid to rest (Coulter).
his most endearing claims to fame is the bugle call "Taps," which he composed at

Harrison's Landing in 1862 (Warner 167). ~~The bugle call~~ "Taps" originates from another call named "Lights Out"~~; this call was~~ used by the Army to signal the end of the day. Butterfield, wanting a new and original call unique to his command, summoned bugler Oliver Willcox Norton to his tent one night. ~~and~~ ᴿrather than compose an altogether new tune, he instead modified the notes to the call "Lights Out" (US Military District of Washington). ~~Then~~ *Shortly thereafter* this call could be heard ~~being used~~ up and down the Union lines as the other commanders ~~who had~~ heard the call ~~liked~~ it and adapted it for their own use. ~~This call, the modified version of "Lights Out" is~~ ~~also in a way~~ *and itself* a derivative of the British bugle call ~~"Tattoo" which is very~~ *"Tattoo," a* similar in both sound and purpose ~~to "Lights Out,"~~ (Villanueva). ~~notes this as well in his paper "24 Notes That Tap Deep Emotion."~~

Group all the discussion of the versions in one place.

Divide long sentence to keep it clear.

Strengthen paragraph conclusion by sticking to its focus.

REVISED DRAFT

Anyone who has ever attended the funeral services for a fallen veteran of the United States of America has stood fast as a lone bugler filled the air with a mournful last tribute to a defender of the nation. The name of the bugle call is "Taps," and the legend behind its origin has gained popularity as it has circulated in this time of war and terror. According to this story, Union Captain Robert Ellicombe discovered that a Confederate casualty was, in fact, his son, a music student in the South. The father found "Taps" in his son's pocket, and the tune was first played at a military burial as his son was laid to rest (Coulter). Although this tale of a beautiful ode to a fallen warrior is heartfelt, it is an "urban legend." As such, it fails to provide due justice to the memories of the men responsible for the true origin of "Taps."

General Daniel Butterfield is the true originator of the bugle call "Taps." Butterfield served in the Union army during the Civil War and was awarded the Medal of Honor for actions during that time. One of his most endearing claims to fame is the bugle call "Taps," which he composed at Harrison's Landing in 1862 (Warner 167). "Taps" originates from another call named "Lights Out," used by the army to signal the end of the day and itself a derivative of "Tattoo," a British bugle call similar in both sound and purpose (Villanueva). Butterfield, wanting a new and original call unique to his command, summoned bugler Oliver Willcox Norton to his tent one night. Rather than compose an altogether new tune, he instead modified the notes to the call "Lights Out" (US Military District of Washington). Shortly thereafter this call could be heard up and down the Union lines as other commanders heard the call and adapted it for their own use.

Editing and Proofreading

Editing means correcting and refining grammar, punctuation, and mechanics. Proofreading means taking a final look to check correctness and to catch spelling or word-processing errors. Don't edit and proofread too

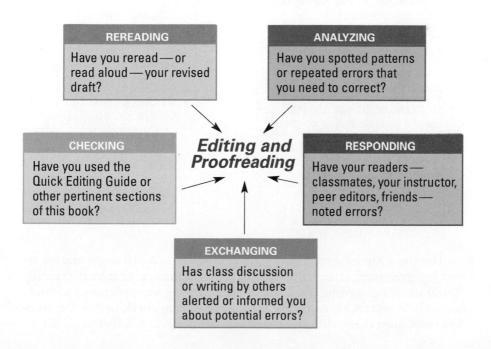

REREADING
Have you reread—or read aloud—your revised draft?

ANALYZING
Have you spotted patterns or repeated errors that you need to correct?

Editing and Proofreading

CHECKING
Have you used the Quick Editing Guide or other pertinent sections of this book?

RESPONDING
Have your readers—classmates, your instructor, peer editors, friends—noted errors?

EXCHANGING
Has class discussion or writing by others alerted or informed you about potential errors?

soon. In your early drafting, don't fret over the spelling of an unfamiliar word; it may be revised out in a later version. After you have revised, you are ready to refine and correct. In college, good editing and proofreading can make the difference between a C and an A. On the job, it may help you get promoted. Readers, teachers, and bosses like careful writers who take time to edit and proofread.

Editing

As you edit, whenever you doubt whether a word or construction is correct, consult a good reference handbook. Learn the grammar conventions you don't understand so you can spot and eliminate problems in your own writing. Practice until you easily recognize major errors such as fragments and comma splices. Ask for assistance from a peer editor or a tutor in the writing center if your campus has one.

EDITING
• **GRAMMAR:** Are your sentences and their parts correct?
• **SENTENCES:** Are your sentences clear and effective?
• **WORD CHOICE:** Are your words correct and well selected?
• **PUNCTUATION:** Do you need to add, correct, or drop any marks?
• **MECHANICS:** Do you need to correct capitals, italics, or other matters?
• **FORMAT:** Do you need to adjust margins, spacing, or headings?

→

PROOFREADING
• **SPELLING:** Have you spell-checked and reread your work attentively?
• **INCORRECT WORDS:** Have you mistakenly picked any wrong words?
• **MISSING WORDS:** Have you left out any words?
• **MINOR ERRORS:** Can you see any small mistakes?
• **MINOR DETAILS:** Do you need to correct any details?

Use the "Quick Editing Guide" (beginning on p. A-00) to get started reviewing grammar, style, punctuation, and mechanics problems typically found in college writing. Look also for definitions, examples, and a checklist to help you tackle each one. Here is an editing checklist for the problems explained there, along with the section letter and number:

EDITING CHECKLIST
Common and Serious Problems in College Writing

The following cross-references refer to the Quick Editing Guide section at the back of this book.

Grammar Problems   *Section Number*

☐ Have you avoided writing sentence fragments?   A1

☐ Have you avoided writing comma splices or fused sentences?   A2

☐ Have you used the correct form for all verbs in the past tense?   A3

☐ Do all verbs agree with their subjects?   A4

☐ Have you used the correct case for all pronouns?   A5

☐ Do all pronouns agree with their antecedents?   A6

☐ Have you used adjectives and adverbs correctly?   A7

Sentence Problems

☐ Does each modifier clearly modify the appropriate sentence element? B1

☐ Have you used parallel structure where necessary?   B2

Punctuation Problems

☐ Have you used commas correctly?   C1

☐ Have you used apostrophes correctly?   C2

☐ Have you punctuated quotations correctly?   C3

Mechanics Problems

☐ Have you used capital letters correctly?   D1

☐ Have you spelled all words correctly?   D2

For help documenting any sources in your paper, turn to sections D6 and E1–E2 (pp. A-18–A-35) in the Quick Research Guide.

Proofreading

All writers make mistakes as they put ideas on paper. Because the mind works faster than the pencil (or the word processor), when you are distracted by someone talking or your cell phone ringing, you may omit a word or put in the wrong punctuation. A moment's break in concentration can lead to errors. Making such mistakes isn't bad—you simply need to take the time to find and correct them. Proofreading does take patience but is a skill you can develop. For instance, when you simply glance at the spelling of *environment,* you may miss the second *n.* When you read normally, you usually see only the shells of words—the first and last letters. You fix your eyes on the print only three or four times per line or less. When you proofread, try to create a situation that will help you concentrate on detail.

- Let a paper sit several days, overnight, or at least a few hours before proofreading so that you allow time to gain perspective.
- Budget enough time to proofread thoroughly. For a long essay or complex research paper with a list of sources, schedule several sessions.
- Ask someone else to read your paper and tell you if it is free of errors. But take pride in your own work. *Don't* let someone else do it for you.
- Use a dictionary or a spell-checker, but remember that a spell-checker recognizes only correct spelling, not correct choices.
- Keep a list of your habitual errors, especially those your instructor has already pointed out. Double-check for these errors (such as leaving off *-s* or *-ed* endings or putting in unnecessary commas).

To proofread effectively, try to look at the letters in each word and the punctuation marks between words. Slow down and concentrate.

PROOFREADING CHECKLIST

☐ Have you read your draft very slowly, looking at every word and letter? Have you tried to see what is actually written, not what you think is there?

☐ Have you read your paper aloud? Have you used speaking to slow yourself down so you can see and hear mistakes?

☐ Have you read the essay backward so that you look at each word instead of getting caught up in the flow of ideas?

☐ Have you read your essay several times, focusing each time on a specific area of difficulty? (For example, read once for spelling, once for punctuation, and once for a problem that recurs in your writing.)

For editing exercises, visit Exercise Central at **<bedfordstmartins .com/bedguide>**.

Learning by Doing Editing and Proofreading

1. Read the following passage carefully. Assume that the organization of the paragraph is satisfactory, but find and correct fifteen errors in sentence structure, grammar, spelling, punctuation, and capitalization. After you have corrected the passage, discuss with your classmates the changes you have made and your reasons for making those changes.

> Robert Frost, one of the most poplar American poets. He was born in San Francisco in 1874, and died in Boston in 1963. His family moved to new England when his father died in 1885. There he completed highschool and attended colledge but never graduate. Poverty and problems filled his life. He worked in a woll mill, on a newspaper, and at varous odd jobs. Because

of ill health he settled on a farm and began to teach school to support his wife and children. Throughout his life he dedicated himself to writing poetry, by 1915 he was in demand for public readings and speaking engagements. He was awarded the Pulitzer Prize for poetry four times—in 1924, 1931, 1937, and 1943. The popularity of his poetry rests in his use of common themes and images. everyone can relate to his universal poems, such as "Birches" and "Stopping by Woods on a Snowy Evening." Students read his poetry in school from seventh grade through graduate school, so almost everyone recognize lines from his best-loved poems. America is proud of it's son, the homespun poet Robert Frost.

2. Select a passage, from this textbook or elsewhere, that is about one hundred words long. Type up the passage, intentionally adding ten errors in grammar, spelling, punctuation, or capitalization. Swap passages with a classmate; proofread, then check each other's work against the originals. Share your proofreading strategies.

24 Strategies for Future Writing

Your college writing course is designed to help you read, write, think, and rewrite. When that course ends, you move on to other courses and other writing assignments. In those future situations, whether or not the assignments and criteria are presented and crafted like those in a composition course, you still will need to read, write, think, and rewrite. The assumption—and the hope—is that your experience in your writing class will equip you to write successfully in your future courses and eventually in your workplace, career, or community. To do so, you will want to transfer your learning and apply it in new situations.

Transferring Knowledge

How to apply what you have learned may seem puzzling, even mysterious. For example, in your next class, would you struggle to start answering a pop quiz question on two creatures, two events, or two theories? Or would you recall what you already have learned about organizing comparison or contrast? In your nursing or teaching clinical program, would you solve on-site problems right away? Or would you struggle every day to interview patients or maintain classroom order?

You've probably had experience of both types: frustration when a new situation challenges your experience and exhilaration when old skills and past practice make something new seem easy. Maybe your background, experience, or confidence makes the difference—or maybe the content area, skill, or kind of knowledge to be transferred does. Either way, how to transfer learning from one situation to another—and how to do so more effectively—often seems a puzzle. To help you solve that puzzle when you need to write different types of papers in different situations, this chapter covers three key questions you might ask:

- What do they want?
- What is it?
- How do I write it?

Learning by Doing 🔟 Transferring Learning

Concentrate for a few minutes on how you have transferred learning in the past. When have you simply tackled a new task and figured out how to succeed? How have you successfully handled new academic situations—different teaching styles, schools of thought, types of assignments, or levels of expectation? Jot down a few notes about your strategies for success. If possible, share them with classmates.

What Do They Want?

When you face a challenging or high-stakes writing assignment, your first question is likely to be What do they want? Your instructor or your supervisor at work may—or may not—provide explicit directions about your task. Either way, your first step is to gather as much information as possible about the assignment.

ASSIGNMENT CHECKLIST

☐ Do you have a written assignment distributed in class, posted online, provided in your syllabus, or included in your job description?

☐ Have you taken notes on verbal advice or directions or read advice posted online by your instructor?

☐ Does your assignment specify or imply a purpose and an audience?

☐ Does your assignment identify a particular approach, activity, method, or product?

☐ Does it require a standard format, perhaps based on a style guide, a sample lab report, headings in a journal article, an evaluation form, past annual reports at work, or some other model?

☐ Does your assignment use key words that you recognize from your writing class or other situations? For instance, does it ask you to compare and contrast, propose a solution, or summarize, drawing on skills you have used in recent essays or exams?

☐ What criteria will be used to assess the success of your writing task?

Analyzing Expectations

When a difficult or unfamiliar writing assignment comes from the instructor in a class where you want or need to succeed or from the boss you have to satisfy, shift your attention from yourself to your audience.

Whether you face your assignment feeling confident, puzzled, or anxious, focus on what is expected. Apply your experience decoding past assignments to analyzing current ones. Do the same with your experience identifying a writing purpose and audience. Try writing notes on or about your assignment to help you tease out all the available clues about how to succeed.

Starting point = problem
+ solution

Need to check grant format

Propose solution — I've done that!

Purpose + Audience

Good — list of required sections

Once you have defined both a problem and a solution that you wish to propose, write your paper as a grant proposal designed to persuade a funding agency to support your proposal. Be sure to include a statement of the problem, a needs assessment, and a specific proposal.

Connecting Expectations and Assessments

Sometimes expectations are expressed through assessment criteria. What are the standards for performance or outcomes in your course or workplace? How will your paper or project be judged? If you will be graded or assigned points based on the presence, absence, or quality of specific features or components, these are also part of "what they want."

You can be awarded a maximum of 25 points for each of these four features: (1) a clear and compelling introduction to your proposal, (2) a well-researched review of relevant literature, (3) a clear explanation of the theoretical framework for examining the problem, and (4) a clear description and justification of the methods proposed for your study.

Try turning your requirements or assessment criteria into a checklist or self-assessment questions for yourself. For example, you might convert the criteria in the previous example to these four questions:

1. Do I have a clear and compelling introduction to my proposal?

2. Have I included a well-researched review of relevant literature?

3. Do I clearly explain my theoretical framework for examining the problem?

4. Do I clearly describe and justify the methods for my study?

If you worry about forgetting or skipping over the assessment details, try breaking out each expectation as a separate question:

1. Do I have an introduction? Is it clear? Is it compelling?

Learning by Doing 🎥 Decoding an Assignment

In a group or individually, select an assignment from another class. First identify its stated expectations. Write a brief statement about what you think the assignment asks you to do and how you might draw on your existing knowledge to do this. If grading criteria are available, turn them into questions that you could ask yourself while working on the assignment. If possible, exchange ideas with your group or a classmate to refine your analyses.

What Is It?

Once you have figured out "what they want," your next challenge is to determine "what it is." As you read and write in a particular field, you may recognize common strategies or approaches. For example, historians frequently use cause-and-effect analysis, natural scientists rely on classification, nurses value accurate description, and specialists in many fields, as varied as film and geology, use comparison and contrast to examine examples, techniques, or theories. In addition, many assignments—such as lab reports, proposals, or reviews—require a genre, or type, of writing defined by specific characteristics and assumptions. Identifying assumptions and genre features will help you to tackle each kind of writing more successfully.

Uncovering Assumptions

In advanced classes, expectations of the field or discipline are likely to underlie those of your individual instructor. Here, your ingenuity is engaged not in the creation of an analytical approach or a method of investigation but in its application to your particular text, project, or research study. For example, your literature essay will probably rely on a close reading of a novel, poem, or play and take an accepted approach to analyzing characters, images, or other components of that work. It probably will not have headings such as Method, Results, or Discussion. However, those divisions are likely essentials for your psychology report on your field study. Such expectations about approach, method, organization, or format reflect the assumptions shared by scholars and researchers in a particular field—their deep agreements, for instance, that a literary study typically relies on textual analysis or that a psychology study typically adheres to and reports certain research procedures.

When a field or approach is new to you, you won't know if your instructor and others in the field already share established ideas about how a paper should develop. How can you find out what is assumed? First, use your experience as a college writer to check your assignment for clues—such as references, maybe without explanation, to a certain type of paper.

Using <u>textual evidence</u>, write an (essay) to <u>analyze</u> the novel's attention to
         ↓   ↓   ↓

Maybe quotations?   *OK*   *Break into elements?*
Repeated images?   *Thesis?*   *Identify components?*
Characters? Setting? Narrator?   *Evidence?*

<u>problems of social justice</u>.
      ↓

Relevance for society?
Cultural commentary?

Prepare a (review of the literature) on your topic, covering <u>advances</u>
             ↓   ↓

What's that? What's in it?   *New studies?*
Find sources??   *New findings?*
Summarize? Or synthesize too?   *New theories?*

during the <u>last decade</u>.
      ↓

Last ten years?
Background OK?

Also consider the readings assigned in the course or field. For example, many journal articles in psychology, sociology, or education open with an abstract, summing up the reading. Should you add an abstract to your paper? Those same articles may have section headings with identical or similar wording. Should your paper use the same headings? Ask your instructor which features of assigned readings are expected in your paper.

By definition, assumptions and conventions (generally accepted ideas about ways to proceed) are taken for granted within an area or field. That's why your instructor may assume that once you enroll in a course you already share a certain set of assumptions, even though you may assume those views are what you need to learn. That's also why two researchers—for instance, an art historian and an eye specialist—could both study a painting but hold different ideas about what's of interest and how to investigate it. One might study techniques for representing light or applying paint while the other might ask how the artist's eyesight affects the definition or brightness of the work. Likewise, the engineers at your job probably view products differently than the marketing team does.

Whenever you enter a class, field, or situation that may operate on assumptions new to you, you need to be curious and observant so that you notice what is shared:

- Preferred kinds of studies, analyses, or topics
- Typical research procedures, stages of analysis, or patterns of organization
- Favored methods of argument or explanation
- Expected kinds and quantities of evidence
- Common use of technical vocabulary, authorial voice, transitions to show shifts, description or explanation, or other features

Then ask what sections, approaches, or features need to be included in your writing. Consider the unstated expectations or criteria that your writing situation—or the situation posed in your assignment—may imply.

Analyzing Genre Models

If you want to find models of a particular written genre, your best resources may be examples such as these:

- assigned, posted, or textbook-supplied readings or examples
- sample essays, projects, or other student examples discussed in class
- published, professional models such as recommended journal articles, research studies, creative works, or Web sites

As you examine these models, reflect on your experience reading and writing past assignments, and bring your relevant skills to your new task. The more experience you gain with a specific genre—whether a review of the literature or a lab report or a literary analysis—the easier and more familiar that form will be. Soon you, too, will absorb its assumptions and conventions.

To identify features of a particular genre, examine several samples of the same genre. Then use the following questions to help you notice which features are shared by all (and seem mandatory) and which appear in some (and seem variable or optional).

For some sets of examples that you might analyze with this checklist, see the poems on p. 217, 283–84; the short stories on p. 266 and 280; the letters on pp. 360, 362, and 383; or the newspaper opinion column on p. 52.

GENRE CHECKLIST
Parts of the Text

☐ How does the text begin—with a title, an abstract (or summary), an opening paragraph about the topic, a description, an address and date, a greeting, or another feature?

☐ What are its sections? Do they appear in a predictable sequence? Are they labeled with headings, act and scene numbers, or other markers? Are they shifts indicated by wording?

□ Does it supply preliminaries (such as a title page, table of contents, or list of figures)?

□ Does it include closing materials (such as a list of sources or an appendix)?

Development

□ How are paragraphs typically developed? Do they begin with topic sentences or work up to the main point? Do they tend to contain one example or several? Are they all about the same length or varied?

□ How are sentences typically developed? Are they similar or varied in terms of length, structure, and opening wording? Do they often begin with transitions? Do they use active (*X did it*) or passive voice (*it was done by X*)? Do they use first person (*I, we*) or third person (*he, she, it, they*)?

□ What tone, style, and level of formality does the text use? Does it expect readers to know certain words or expressions? How does it define terms or technical expressions?

□ What types of assertions, claims, evidence, turns of the argument, or sources does it use?

□ Are sources cited following a specific academic style such as MLA, APA, or another style?

□ Do other features appear to be conventional or typical?

Presentation

□ What does the text look like on a page? Is it mostly running academic text with one-inch margins, a 12-point type font, and a running header? Or does it have uneven lines (as in a letter, poem, or play) or variable placement of text (as in a brochure)?

□ Does the text include diagrams or figures, tables with numerical results, graphs, photographs of places or events, sketches of creatures or objects studied, or other visuals? How are these labeled and credited (if necessary)?

□ How is the final list of sources indented and spaced on the page?

After you analyze the features of several models, compare your observations with the requirements in your assignment. When you find a match, you'll have both directions and an example or pattern. When in doubt, always follow your specific assignment; ask your instructor to clarify any confusing alternatives.

Learning by Doing 🎥 Analyzing a Genre Model

Working individually or in a group, select one or more genre models for analysis. Use the Genre Checklist to help you analyze each sample and identify its characteristic features. If you are working in a group, share your analyses. If you wish, write directions for yourself or for someone else, explaining how to write a particular genre, or type, of paper.

How Do I Write It?

You don't need to start from scratch when you face something new. Beginning with what you know is a valuable way to prepare for what you don't know. When you face a difficult, unfamiliar, or downright mysterious assignment, apply or adapt your past writing processes and experience to that challenge.

- Underline or annotate your assignment to specify the required components.
- Add notes to yourself, especially to identify what you know how to do and what you don't.
- Sort your models to find examples of unfamiliar features or sections.
- Return to the processes used in your writing class so that you generate ideas and plan instead of simply jumping into drafting.
- Turn to the campus writing center, your class study group, or your friends to identify a peer reader; explain your assignment to that person, and then ask for responses to your draft.
- Get a second opinion from another reader if useful.
- Meet with your instructor, or submit your draft for a preliminary reading (if possible). Use your instructor's advice, especially about the big issues, to help you look critically at your own work.
- Revise first to conform to the unfamiliar assignment. Use your analysis of the assignment and criteria to generate your own questions for self-assessment.
- Revise again to improve format, organization, clarity, or other matters.
- Edit to improve conventions and genre features as well as to correct errors.

Learning by Doing 🎥 Reflecting on New Assignments

Reflect on your writing experience. When you face a new assignment, how do you usually get started? What are your most reliable strategies? What adjustments in your processes or strategies have you made or are you making as a college writer? When you face a challenging assignment in a general education course or in a discipline of interest to you, how would you apply what you already know and do as a writer?

Learning from Another Writer: A Multigenre History Assignment

When Shari O'Malley enrolled in the class, "United States Society and Thought since 1860," she analyzed the following multigenre term paper assignment that Professor Laird included in the course packet.

Professor Laird | Term Paper Assignment

Historical Analysis and Argument

Explains approach to history

The ways people have lived and their beliefs and goals and expectations have been the most important ingredients of history. Everything else happens within the contexts of how and why people conduct their lives the way they do. In turn, people's ideas are profoundly related to the conditions of their lives.

Two choices — issue and person

For this paper, therefore, first select an ideological position, a set of behaviors, or a social institution that existed in the United States sometime between 1860 and 1980. Second, select or invent a relatively ordinary person involved with what you have chosen. Possibilities might be a teacher, a successful or failed businessman, an immigrant, a former slave, a local mayor, a suffragette, or a person about to travel west. Then you will need to explore the lives and beliefs of that person as one who supported or rejected the position, activity, or institution you selected.

Show person's point of view

1st part reports research

Your paper will have two parts. One will detail the results of your research, explaining whose position you are taking and the historical situation in which that position was significant in political, business, or domestic matters. It will set the context for the second part, which will make a persuasive argument for the position you have selected based on the person you have selected. The form that your second part takes is up to you. You may simply write an essay, or you may attempt to persuade your audience through a letter, a sermon, diary entries, a dialogue, or a briefing paper for a novelist or screenwriter. Remember that the purpose of this paper is to <u>analyze</u> and to <u>argue</u> from a historical perspective different from your own, showing your understanding of the historical circumstances. Focus on persuasion, not narration or description.

2nd part shows person — can choose genre

Purpose — analyze & argue

Length: 10 to 12 pages in addition to an annotated bibliography at the end that lists the works consulted and explains, in one or two sentences, why each one did or did not help your work. You should consult both primary and secondary sources, including books and articles, to help you understand the nature of your character's life and beliefs.

Also need annotated bib — 3rd part

This assignment offers students an opportunity to gain an enriched understanding of a moment in history. It requires three different sections—a report on research, a presentation of an individual, and an annotated bibliography. It requires various types of writing (as varied as an essay, an annotated bibliography, and a sermon), various critical activities (such as analysis, argument, and persuasion), and various kinds of sources (primary and secondary). Following are selections from Shari O'Malley's paper, illustrating some of the different types of writing that the assignment required. She presented her persuasive argument through half a dozen letters revealing her character's historical perspective. To cite her sources in footnotes and then list them in her bibliography, she also used *Chicago* style, an academic style commonly used in history and other fields and explained in the *Chicago Manual of Style* (16th ed.; Chicago: University of Chicago Press, 2010).

Shari O'Malley   Selections from Student Argument

Recognition

November 5, 1916

Dearest Mother,

I hope all is well in London. I wish for father's safe return daily. Although he is not is actively fighting, his position as radio operator does place him in close proximity to the enemy. The girls working here at the factory anxiously wait for letters from their fathers and husbands, expecting good news but fearing the worst.

During this time of war in our country, I do not regret my decision to live and work here at the factory during father's absence. After all, Britain said, "Do Your Bit, Replace a Man for the Front."[1] Cousin Ralph and I are doing our best to manage the factory for father. Can you believe that I can not have an official title as a manager because Ralph is afraid of what the men may think? I understand that the morale of our troops is our first priority, but I would like some recognition for my hard work.[2] . . .

1. Phil Goodman, "Patriotic Femininity": Women's Morals and Men's Morale During the Second World War," *Gender & History* 10, no. 2 (1998): 278-79.

2. Ibid., 289.

February 14, 1917

Dear Mother,

You mentioned in your last letter that you enjoyed the visit last week from the men working for the war effort. Mother, you are exasperating! Those men work for the state and were checking to make sure you were behaving, to see if you deserve the money you get while father is in the military.[3] This outrageous behavior in the name of the war effort is extremely intrusive to the women at home! Men have no right to come into our private homes and judge our behavior! The war has certainly opened my eyes to many injustices about this country.

Mother, I have some exciting news for you. I met an American soldier stationed nearby, and I must tell you I am quite smitten. His name is Don Jackson, and he is from New Orleans, Louisiana. He is extremely polite and gentlemanly in nature. Don't worry; we are socializing exclusively in public places. . . .

_____

March 18, 1917

Mother,

I was surprised and confused upon receiving your letter. You stated that I should, "Leave political matters to the men." Do you not know that there are currently women fighting for the right to vote in this country and, according to Don Jackson, in America also? Why is it surprising that women are finally standing up for themselves? You say that "You should be trying to find a husband instead of involving yourself in public matters." I know how important marriage is to you, and all of England for that matter, but marriage is not my main objective in life.[4] And how am I supposed to find a husband when all of our men are at the front and yet it is unacceptable to date American military men?[5] . . .

3. Ibid., 289.

4. Susan Kingsley Kent, *Gender and Power in Britain, 1640-1990* (New York: Routledge, 1999), 295-300.

November 24, 1918
Mother,

   I just wanted to let you know that I am safely in America. I think you know
from my previous letters why I have left England. When father returned and basically
told me to give my job back to the men, I was extremely upset and disappointed.
Father practically laughed in my face when I suggested I could work in his position
one day.

   Before Don and I married and left for America, I learned that England had
granted women over thirty years old the vote.[6] . . .

January 4, 1919
My Dear Don,

   I must confess, I think about our short honeymoon constantly. I was so
disappointed you had to go overseas so soon after our marriage, but I know you
will be home before long. . . . Even though I have to wait a few years until I can
apply for citizenship, I am determined to participate in the women's suffrage
movement.[7] . . .

   5. Sonya O. Rose, "Sex, Citizenship, and the Nation in World War II Britain," *American Historical Review* 103, no. 4 (1998): 1147-76.

   6. Kent, *Gender and Power*, 269.

   7. Jenel Virden, *Good-bye, Piccadilly* (Urbana: University of Illinois Press, 1996), 140-41.

SELECTIONS FROM STUDENT'S ANNOTATED BIBLIOGRAPHY

Annotated Bibliography

Goodman, Phil. "Patriotic Femininity": Women's Morals and Men's Morale During the Second World War," *Gender & History* 10, no. 2 (1998): 278-93.

Goodman discusses women's role in the workplace while replacing men serving in WWI and WWII. He also points out the attitudes of the British toward women getting involved with American soldiers serving in Britain.

Kent, Susan Kingsley. *Gender and Power in Britain, 1640-1990*. New York: Routledge, 1999.

Kent gives a thorough history, including the laws that affected the lives of women in Britain and the power of males governing over women's lives. Kent discusses the many ways in which women challenged "separate sphere" ideology and its effects in British society. This information was the determining factor for my main character who was inspired to fight for the vote in America.

Rose, Sonya O. "Sex, Citizenship, and the Nation in World War II Britain." *American Historical Review* 103, no. 4 (1998): 1147-76.

Rose discusses British reaction to African American soldiers from America serving in Britain during WWI and WWII and the fear of British women's sexual involvement with them. Rose identifies women's role as reproducers of Britain's race rather than as political participants, subjects both relevant to my character's situation.

Virden, Jenel. *Good-bye, Piccadilly*. Urbana: University of Illinois Press, 1996.

Virden discusses the conditions of British war brides in America. My main character wishes to gain the right to vote in America, even though she knows she will have a waiting period before obtaining U.S. citizenship.

Questions to Start You Thinking

Meaning

1. What thesis or main idea does O'Malley try to convey in her paper?
2. What is the function of the fictional letter writer in this paper?

Writing Strategies

3. For both sections of O'Malley's term paper briefly illustrated here, mark or list notable features that you think are typical of its genre, or type, of writing.
4. Aside from including the required sections in her paper, what writing techniques does O'Malley use to try to keep a reader's interest?

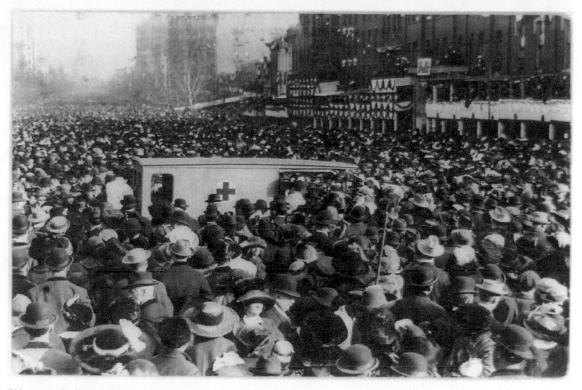

"Women's Suffrage Procession in Washington, DC, March 3, 1913" illustrates the historical issue that concerned the letter writer in the preceding sample history paper. Women across the United States gained the right to vote through the 19th amendment to the Constitution, ratified in 1920.

A
WRITER'S
READER

A Writer's Reader Contents

Introduction: Reading to Write

A Writer's Reader is a collection of thirty-three carefully selected professional essays. We hope, first of all, that you will read these pieces simply for the sake of reading—enjoying and responding to their ideas. Good writers read widely, and in doing so, they increase their knowledge of the craft of writing. Second, we hope that you will actively study these essays as solid examples of the situations and strategies explored in *A Writer's Guide*. The authors represented in this reader have faced the same problems and choices you do when you write. You can learn from studying their decisions, structures, and techniques. Finally, we hope that you will find the content of the essays intriguing—and along with the questions posed after each one, a source of ideas to write about.

Each chapter in *A Writer's Reader* concentrates on a familiar broad theme—families, men and women, popular culture, electronic technology, and the challenge of living well. In some essays the writers focus on the inner world and write personal experience and opinion papers. In others the authors turn their attention to the outer world and write informational and persuasive essays. Within each chapter, the last two selections are a pair of essays on the same subject, illustrating how different writers use different strategies to address similar issues.

Each chapter in the reader begins with an image, a visual activity, and a Web search activity, all intended to stimulate your thinking and writing. Each reading selection is preceded by biographical information about the author, placing him or her—and the piece itself—into a cultural and informational context. Next a reading note, As You Read, suggests a way to consider the selection. Following each reading are five Questions to Start You Thinking that consistently cover the same ground: meaning, writing strategies, critical thinking, vocabulary, and connections with one or more of the other selections in *A Writer's Reader*. Each paired essay is also followed by a question that asks you about a link between the essays. After these questions come a couple of journal prompts designed to get your writing juices flowing. Finally, two possible assignments make specific suggestions for writing. The first assignment is directed toward your inner world, asking you to draw generally on your personal experience and your understanding of the essay. The second is outer directed, asking you to look outside yourself and write an evaluative or argumentative paper, one that may require further reading or research.

For more on journal writing, see pp. 396–97.

Responding to an Image

Carefully examine this family photograph, making thorough notes about the clothing, positions, facial expressions, posture, race, gender, and other attributes of the people. Also, make notes about the surroundings. What might these attributes and surroundings indicate about the occasion? What kind of family does this photograph portray? Does this family portrait remind you of any others you've seen?

Web Search

Search the Library of Congress online archive called American Memory <http://memory.loc.gov> by entering a subject related to your family's history, such as a state or city where your ancestors or family have lived, an industry a relative has worked in, or a historical event or natural disaster that affected your family in some way. Locate and study a specific photograph or document on this subject. Imagine that your family has a direct connection to the photo or document you have found. Write an imaginary narrative about one or more members of your family based on your finding.

For reading activities linked to this chapter, visit **<bedfordstmartins .com/bedguide>**.

Christy De'on Miller
Give Me Five More Minutes

Christy De'on Miller was born in 1955 and grew up in Texas and New Mexico. After serving in the military and working secretarial jobs, she earned a BA in English from Texas Tech University in 2003. Four months after she graduated, her son, Lance Corporal Aaron C. Austin, was killed in Iraq during his second tour of duty as a marine. The following selection, published on Salon.com in 2006, is Miller's moving account of learning the news that her son was killed. A longer version of the essay first appeared in *Operation Homecoming: Iraq, Afghanistan, and the Home Front, in the Words of U.S. Troops and Their Families* (2006), a compilation of writings that soldiers and their loved ones submitted to a project funded by the National Endowment for the Arts.

For more about Christy De'on Miller, visit **<bedfordstmartins .com/bedguide>**.

AS YOU READ: Identify the objects Miller uses to help her recall her son.

On April 26, 2004, I woke up around 4:00 in the morning and turned on the television in my bedroom. At least 12 marines had been injured, and by 6:00 A.M., reporters were saying that one had died. I typed Aaron a letter, as I'd been doing daily for several weeks, trying to sound positive. Outside of mentioning that we had one marine down, I avoided the hard news of the day. 1

It was around 4:00 or 5:00 P.M. when the two marines drove up to my house. The noncommissioned officer began to approach me. It seemed to take an eternity for him to cross my lawn—I think I must have walked some, gone to meet him halfway. 2

He began, "Ma'am, are you Christy Miller? Can we go inside? We need to talk to you." His wasn't an easy job. 3

"No, we've got to do this outside." Mine, still the harder. 4

The other marine, the officer, said, "Ma'am, your son was killed in action today in Al Anbar Province." 5

I said, "My son was killed in the firefight that's on the television right now. He was killed in Fallujah. There's been one marine killed today." 6

There, in that moment, the tiniest and longest length of time, there must've been a mechanical failure, an embodiment of someone's (it couldn't have been mine) heart and brain colliding. 7

"Mine," I finished. Yes, the marine was mine.   8

My son, Lance Corporal Aaron C. Austin, United States Marine Corps   9
machine gunner, team leader Echo Company, Second Battalion, First Marine
Regiment, First Marine Division, was killed in action on April 26, 2004, in
Fallujah, Iraq. He was born on July 1, 1982, at 8:53 P.M. central daylight savings time in Amherst, Texas. Circumcised and sent home on the Fourth of
July, he was my breast-fed, blanket-sucking baby boy, a little Linus° look-
alike. He threw his blanket away when he was ten. God, how I wish for that
blanket now. It surely would carry some scent.

Aaron's company commander, Captain Zembiec, wrote me right after it   10
happened. He wrote,

> Your son was killed in action today. He was conducting a security
> patrol with his company this morning, in enemy territory. His company
> had halted in two buildings, strongpointing° them and looking for
> insurgents. A large number of enemy personnel attacked Aaron and his
> platoon at around 1100. Despite intense enemy machine gun and rocket
> propelled grenade fire, your son fought like a lion. He remained in his
> fighting position until all his wounded comrades could be evacuated
> from the rooftop they were defending. . . . We held a memorial service
> this afternoon in honor of your son. With the exception of the marines
> on security, every man in the company attended the service. Aaron was
> respected and admired by every marine in his company. His death
> brought tears to my eyes, tears that fell in front of my marines. I am
> unashamed of that fact.

From the men who first told me the news, who had stood outside my   11
home, compassionate marines in dress blues, to those who entered my living
room and placed before me the one remaining box of my son's life, and then,
on bent knee, took out a smaller box from within the larger, and handed over
to me Aaron's watch, the one removed from his body at the time of death — it
is to these men that I owe so much.

I began to wear Aaron's watch, which was still on Baghdad time. His   12
watch became my watch. His alarm would go off at 3:28:24. Then again at
3:33:20. Aaron always said, "Give me five more minutes, Mom." This early
alarm, its hidden meaning, meant only for him, for duty on a rooftop possibly, is
5:30 P.M. (the evening before) my time.

When the battery goes dead on a digital watch — it's gone. Blank. Not   13
even a zero. Aaron's watch stopped somewhere between late afternoon on the
twenty-eighth of November and noon on the thirtieth. Since then, I've experienced the first Mother's Day without my son, his twenty-second birthday,
and the homecoming of his unit. More of the "firsts" will soon be behind me.
I don't know if the seconds, thirds, and fourths get any better.

Linus: Character who carries a security blanket in the *Peanuts* comic strip.   **strongpoint-
ing:** In military terms, setting up a location as a heavily protected defensive area.

At times I believe I can learn to live a life without my son. After all, I must. 14
There are other mothers who have lost their boys—car accidents, war, illness—
who can shop for dinner at the local grocer's without the macaroni-and-cheese
boxes suddenly causing them grief. But the memory of him is planted in
everything around me. Inside of me. So much of him has been lost, is fading,
breaking down. His blanket, his watch, his uniform.

The military uses commercial washers to clean personal items before they 15
are handed over to the families. Understandable, but it leaves a synthetic
laundry smell. Aaron's scent is gone. These are the realizations, the moments
I've most dreaded. And they come out of nowhere.

I went through several rounds of "looking for him." Articles, pictures, his 16
voice, things like that. He used to chew on the caps of pens, his dog tags,
everything, so I saved a few things I found like that. You're not ever preparing
for this day, so everything had pretty much been washed, given away, or
thrown out when Aaron deployed.° I did find his voice on a couple of tapes,
including when he was in the third grade, and he was studying for a spelling
test, spelling dinosaur words over and over. Then his voice for a few minutes
back in '98, I think, and then, after his first trip to Iraq when a news station
interviewed him. Each and every new little discovery is uplifting for a while, it
lends hope, and then you remember why you're doing it.

Then one day, I was in a closet, and I looked down and saw a pair of 17
Aaron's house shoes, lizard-striped ones. The shoes brought a smile and tears
and when I grabbed them up, and noticed a kind of grimy stain in the bottom, I sniffed, over and over. I cried, of course, but I was still so happy. It was
the smell of his feet. No one ever expects that kind of smell to be a gift, but to
me, that day, it was. Still, every once in a while, I go and get them out of his
room. Now they sit by his bed, close to our two pairs of boots: jungle boots I
wore in Panama and his pair, from Iraq.

The days have become different. Sorrow is a tile in the mosaic° and 18
flashes of grief still come. But I believe that time does heal. I think it teaches.
The moments pass. I can't say how. It's not of my doing. Sometimes I question. Why has God taken the only child that remained? Left me with no hope
for a grandchild? I'm certain there can be no more. No more children.

And yet I have no particular animosity° for my son's killer. He's a name- 19
less and faceless combatant to me. Should I ever have the opportunity to
meet him, I hope that I'd forgive him. To me, the buck° stops with the
Father. His power stings at times. But He's listened to me; perhaps He's even
cried with me. And yes, I do know what I'm talking about here. It's a belief,
man. Aaron's words. You either believe in God or you don't. Yes, I'd forgive. I
do forgive. There is absolutely nothing I'd do to keep myself from spending
eternity with God and Aaron.

deployed: Traveled with other military personnel to the site of battle.   **mosaic:** A pattern
created through the arrangement of small tiles.   **animosity:** Ill-will, hostility.   **the buck:**
A reference to the saying "The buck stops here," meaning that responsibility for a problem or
situation ultimately rests at this point.

The words *forever* and *eternity* mean something to me now. Before, I 20
wouldn't concentrate on their true definition, on their essence. I thought
they were for later. Now, I have an aching need to know that forever and eternity started long before my time — way before Aaron, before the marines
came to my home that day.

Questions to Start You Thinking

1. **Considering Meaning:**   Where in the essay does Miller refer to its
   title? What is her point in doing so? What other meaning might the
   essay's title have for Miller?

2. **Identifying Writing Strategies:**   Miller uses recall to open her essay
   with a powerful anecdote (paragraphs 1–8). Why do you think she chose
   this strategy? How do you respond to this opening, and how effective
   do you find it?

3. **Reading Critically:**   How would you describe Miller's tone in her
   essay? How does she avoid bitterness in writing about the circumstances of her son's death?

4. **Expanding Vocabulary:**   In paragraphs 2, 19, and 20, Miller uses the
   word *eternity*. What does she mean by *eternity*? What subtle differences
   can you detect in her three uses of the word?

5. **Making Connections:**   Both Miller and Danzy Senna in "The Color
   of Love" (pp. 513–17) end their essays discussing death and spirituality.
   What realizations does each have? In what ways are their insights
   comparable?

Journal Prompts

1. Miller seems intent on recapturing her son's scent. Why do you think
   smells have the power to call up vivid memories? Write about a time or
   two when a smell brought back memories for you.

2. Respond to the saying "Children should not die before their parents
   do." Why do you think it is considered more difficult for a parent to
   lose a child than for a child to lose a parent?

Suggestions for Writing

1. Recall a time when you lost someone for whom you cared a great
   deal — perhaps due to death, a breakup, a move, a family change, or
   some other circumstance. Write an essay in which you describe how
   you responded to this loss. Like Miller, you might use examples and
   description to bring your recollections to life. As you draft, consider
   how your tone could help you convey your feelings through the words
   you choose.

2. The war in which Miller's son died has sparked considerable controversy, especially because ending it proved more difficult than originally anticipated. Write an essay exploring your responses to the war in Iraq or to another war that has affected you, your family, friends, or others you know. To prepare for this essay, you may want to do some brief research to help you recall the events of significance to you.

Anjula Razdan

What's Love Got to Do with It?

Anjula Razdan was a senior editor of the *Utne Reader,* where she wrote on topics ranging from international politics to pop culture. The daughter of Indian immigrants whose marrlage was arranged, Razdan grew up in Illinois and currently works as a freelance writer and editor in Washington, D.C. In this selection, which appeared in the *Utne Reader* in 2003, Razdan asks her readers to consider whether arranging marriages might more effectively create lasting relationships than choosing mates based on romantic attraction. To explore this question, she draws on her own experiences and observations as well as the testimony of experts.

AS YOU READ: Look for Razdan's account of both the benefits and the drawbacks of arranged marriages.

For more about Anjula Razdan, visit **<bedfordstmartins.com/bedguide>**.

One of the greatest pleasures of my teen years was sitting down with a 1 bag of cinnamon Red Hots and a new LaVyrle Spencer romance, immersing myself in another tale of star-crossed lovers drawn together by the heart's mysterious alchemy.° My mother didn't get it. "Why are you reading that?" she would ask, her voice tinged with both amusement and horror. Everything in her background told her that romance was a waste of time.

Born and raised in Illinois by parents who emigrated from India thirty- 2 five years ago, I am the product of an arranged marriage, and yet I grew up under the spell of Western romantic love—first comes love, *then* comes marriage—which both puzzled and dismayed my parents. Their relationship was set up over tea and samosas° by their grandfathers, and they were already engaged when they went on their first date, a chaperoned trip to the movies. My mom and dad still barely knew each other on their wedding day—and they certainly hadn't fallen in love. Yet both were confident that their shared values, beliefs, and family background would form a strong bond that, over time, would develop into love.

"But, what could they possibly know of *real love?*" I would ask myself 3 petulantly° after each standoff with my parents over whether or not I could date in high school (I couldn't) and whether I would allow them to arrange

alchemy: A medieval predecessor of chemistry that aimed to turn base metals into gold.   **samosas:** Small, fried Indian pastries filled with seasoned vegetables or meat. **petulantly:** Irritably.

my marriage (I wouldn't). The very idea of an arranged marriage offended my ideas of both love and liberty—to me, the act of choosing whom to love represented the very essence of freedom. To take away that choice seemed like an attack not just on my autonomy as a person, but on democracy itself.

And, yet, even in the supposedly liberated West, the notion of choosing your mate is a relatively recent one. Until the nineteenth century, writes historian E. J. Graff in *What Is Marriage For? The Strange Social History of Our Most Intimate Institution* (Boston: Beacon Press, 1999), arranged marriages were quite common in Europe as a way of forging alliances, ensuring inheritances, and stitching together the social, political, and religious needs of a community. Love had nothing to do with it.

Fast forward a couple hundred years to twenty-first-century America, and you see a modern, progressive society where people are free to choose their mates, for the most part, based on love instead of social or economic gain. But for many people, a quiet voice from within wonders: Are we really better off? Who hasn't at some point in their life—at the end of an ill-fated relationship or midway through dinner with the third "date-from-hell" this month—longed for a matchmaker to find the right partner? No hassles. No effort. No personal ads or blind dates.

The point of the Western romantic ideal is to live "happily ever after," yet nearly half of all marriages in this country end in divorce, and the number of never-married adults grows each year. Boundless choice notwithstanding, what does it mean when the marital success rate is the statistical equivalent of a coin toss?

"People don't really know how to choose a long-term partner," offers Dr. Alvin Cooper, the director of the San Jose Marital Services and Sexuality Centre and a staff psychologist at Stanford University. "The major reasons that people find and get involved with somebody else are proximity and physical attraction. And both of these factors are terrible predictors of long-term happiness in a relationship."

At the moment we pick a mate, Cooper says, we are often blinded by passion and therefore virtually incapable of making a sound decision.

Psychology Today editor Robert Epstein agrees. "[It's] like getting drunk and marrying someone in Las Vegas," he quips. A former director of the Cambridge Center for Behavioral Studies, Epstein holds a decidedly unromantic view of courtship and love. Indeed, he argues it is our myths of "love at first sight" and "a knight in a shining Porsche" that get so many of us into trouble. When the heat of passion wears off—and it always does, he says—you can be left with virtually nothing "except lawyer's bills."

Epstein points out that many arranged marriages result in an enduring love because they promote compatibility and rational deliberation ahead of passionate impulse. Epstein himself is undertaking a bold step to prove his theory that love can be learned. He wrote an editorial in *Psychology Today* last year seeking women to participate in the experiment with him. He proposed to choose one of the "applicants," and together they would attempt to fall in love—consciously and deliberately. After receiving more than 1,000 responses, none of which seemed right, Epstein yielded just a little to impulse, asking Gabriela, an intriguing Venezuelan woman he met on a plane, to join him in the project. After an understandable bout of cold feet, she eventually agreed.

In a "love contract" the two signed on Valentine's Day this year to seal the 11 deal, Epstein stipulates that he and Gabriela must undergo intensive counseling to learn how to communicate effectively and participate in a variety of exercises designed to foster mutual love. To help oversee and guide the project, Epstein has even formed an advisory board made up of high-profile relationship experts, most notably Dr. John Gray, who wrote the best-selling *Men Are from Mars, Women Are from Venus*. If the experiment pans out, the two will have learned to love each other within a year's time.

It may strike some as anathema° to be so premeditated about the process 12 of falling in love, but to hear Epstein tell it, most unions fail exactly because they aren't intentional enough; they're based on a roll of the dice and a determination to stake everything on love. What this means, Epstein says, is that most people lack basic relationship skills, and, as a result, most relationships lack emotional and psychological intimacy.

A divorced father of four, Epstein himself married for passion—"just like 13 I was told to do by the fairy tales and by the movies"—but eventually came to regret it. "I had the experience that so many people have now," he says, "which is basically looking at your partner and going, 'Who are you?'" Although Epstein acknowledges the non-Western tradition of arranged marriage is a complex, somewhat flawed institution, he thinks we can "distill key elements of [it] to help us learn how to create a new, more stable institution in the West."

Judging from the phenomenon of reality-TV shows like *Married by America* and *Meet My Folks* and the recent increase in the number of professional 14 matchmakers, the idea of arranging marriages (even if in nontraditional ways) seems to be taking hold in this country—perhaps nowhere more powerfully than in cyberspace. Online dating services attracted some twenty million people last year (roughly one-fifth of all singles—and growing), who used sites like Match.com and Yahoo Personals to hook up with potentially compatible partners. Web sites' search engines play the role of patriarchal grandfathers, searching for good matches based on any number of criteria that you select.

Cooper, the Stanford psychologist and author of *Sex and the Internet: A Guidebook for Clinicians* (Brunner-Routledge, 2002)—and an expert in the field 15 of online sexuality—says that because online interaction tends to downplay proximity, physical attraction, and face-to-face interaction, people are more likely to take risks and disclose significant things about themselves. The result is that they attain a higher level of psychological and emotional intimacy

anathema: An abomination; blasphemy.

than if they dated right away or hopped in the sack. Indeed, online dating represents a return to what University of Chicago Humanities Professor Amy Kass calls the "distanced nearness" of old-style courtship, an intimate and protected (cyber)space that encourages self-revelation while maintaining personal boundaries.

And whether looking for a fellow scientist, someone else who's HIV-positive, or a B-movie film buff, an online dater has a much higher likelihood of finding "the one" due to the computer's capacity to sort through thousands of potential mates. "That's what computers are all about—efficiency and sorting," says Cooper, who believes that online dating has the potential to lower the nation's 50 percent divorce rate. There is no magic or "chemistry" involved in love, Cooper insists. "It's specific, operationalizable factors." 16

Love's mystery solved by "operationalizable factors"! Why does that sound a little less than inspiring? Sure, for many people the Internet can efficiently facilitate love and help to nudge fate along. But, for the diehard romantic who trusts in surprise, coincidence, and fate, the cyber-solution to love lacks heart. "To the romantic," observes English writer Blake Morrison in *The Guardian*, "every marriage is an arranged marriage—arranged by fate, that is, which gives us no choice." 17

More than a century ago, Emily Dickinson mocked those who would dissect birds to find the mechanics of song: 18

> *Split the Lark—and you'll find the Music—*
> *Bulb after Bulb, in Silver rolled—*
> *Scantily dealt to the Summer Morning*
> *Saved for your Ear when Lutes be old.*
>
> *Loose the Flood—you shall find it patent—*
> *Gush after Gush, reserved for you—*
> *Scarlet Experiment! Skeptic Thomas!*
> *Now, do you doubt that your Bird was true?*

In other words, writes Deborah Blum in her book, *Sex on the Brain* (Penguin, 1997), "kill the bird and [you] silence the melody." For some, nurturing the ideal of romantic love may be more important than the goal of love itself. Making a more conscious choice in mating may help partners handle the complex personal ties and obligations of marriage; but romantic love, infused as it is with myth and projection and doomed passion, is a way to live *outside* of life's obligations, outside of time itself—if only for a brief, bright moment. Choosing love by rational means might not be worth it for those souls who'd rather roll the dice and risk the possibility of ending up with nothing but tragic nobility and the bittersweet tang of regret. 19

In the end, who really wants to examine love too closely? I'd rather curl up with a LaVyrle Spencer novel or dream up the French movie version of my life than live in a world where the mechanics of love—and its giddy, mysterious buzz—are laid bare. After all, to actually unravel love's mystery is, perhaps, to miss the point of it all. 20

Questions to Start You Thinking

1. **Considering Meaning:** According to the experts whom Razdan quotes, why is cyberspace an ideal venue for facilitating relationships?

2. **Identifying Writing Strategies:** How does Razdan use cause and effect to explain the high divorce rate in the United States?

3. **Reading Critically:** What type of evidence does Razdan use to explore whether arranged marriages are more successful than relationships based on romantic attraction? Do you find the evidence relevant, credible, and sufficient? Why, or why not? What other type of evidence might she have used?

4. **Expanding Vocabulary:** In commenting on her parents' arranged marriage, Razdan asks in paragraph 3, "But, what could they possibly know of *real love*?" How do you define *real love*? Do you think that Razdan would agree with your definition?

5. **Making Connections:** Citing an expert on online sexuality, Razdan writes in paragraph 15 that people who have relationships on the Internet are "more likely to take risks and disclose significant things about themselves." As a result, "they attain a higher level of psychological and emotional intimacy than if they dated right away." Would Sherry Turkle ("How Computers Change the Way We Think," pp. 602–7) agree? How might she respond?

Journal Prompts

1. Write a brief personal ad for a mate, using the writing style associated with personals. Keep in mind that the words you choose and the way you organize your ad reveal something about your personality.

2. One of the experts whom Razdan quotes mentions the myth of "love at first sight" (paragraph 9). Write about a time when you fell in love at first sight or present your opinion on whether such a thing exists.

Suggestions for Writing

1. Write an essay that uses your personal experiences and observations to develop a specific idea presented in Razdan's essay. For example, you might recall your own "date-from-hell" (paragraph 5), a friend's experience with an online dating service, or a matchmaker friend's success rate. Based on your experiences and observations, you might write about current dating practices or about "relationship skills" needed for a successful marriage.

2. Drawing examples from this reading and your own observations, write an essay arguing for or against arranged marriages. You might also do some research to find additional support for your argument.

For more about Judith Warner, visit <bedfordstmartins.com/bedguide>.

Judith Warner

Helicopter Parenting Turns Deadly

Judith Warner was born in New York City on July 4, 1965. She received a bachelor's degree from Brown University and a master's degree from Columbia. Since writing the best-selling biography *Hillary Clinton: The Inside Story* (1993), Warner has continued to tackle what she calls "the politics of everyday life" with a historical and feminist perspective. Her popular nonfiction titles include *You Have the Power: How to Take Back Our Country and Restore Democracy in America* (with Howard Dean, 2004) and *Perfect Madness: Motherhood in the Age of Anxiety* (2005). A former *Newsweek* correspondent in Paris, she has regularly contributed to publications including the *New York Times* (most recently with the online column Domestic Disturbances from which this essay comes), *Boston Globe, Elle, Ms., The New Republic,* and the *Washington Post.* In this essay, Warner discusses the causes and ramifications of a new style of parenting.

AS YOU READ: Identify the changes in parent-child relationships that, for Warner, suggest a troublesome trend underlying tragedies like the death of Megan Meier.

Megan Meier, a 13-year-old from Dardenne Prairie, Missouri, killed herself last year after an online relationship she believed she was having with a cute 16-year-old boy named Josh went very sour. What she didn't know—what her parents would learn six weeks after her death—was that "Josh" was the fictitious° creation of Lori Drew, a then-47-year-old neighbor and the mother of one of Megan's friends.

Or former friends. Megan had, essentially, dropped the other girl when she'd changed schools and tried to put an unhappy chapter of her junior high school life—fraught with weight problems and depression—behind her.

Drew's daughter, one assumes, would have eventually gotten over it. But Drew didn't. Instead, she got revenge.

She created a fake MySpace° profile (she later told police she'd done so to "find out what Megan was saying online" about her daughter, according to a sheriff's report). Working with her daughter, she led Megan to become infatuated° with "Josh." And then she delivered the blow. "I don't like the way you treat your friends," Drew wrote. According to Megan's father, "Josh"'s last e-mail to his daughter read, "You are a bad person and everybody hates you . . . The world would be a better place without you."

The Meier case got massive play in the national media this past week, coming as it did on the heels of a major new survey showing that up to one in three children in the United States have been harassed or bullied online.

But for me the tragedy highlighted another troubling issue that threatens our homes just as steadily as poisonous online communications. That is the disturbing degree to which today's parents—and mothers in particular—frequently lose themselves when they get caught up in trying to smooth out, or steamroll over, the social challenges faced by their children.

fictitious: Made-up, invented.   **MySpace:** Online social networking site.   **infatuated:** Having an extreme, unreasonable attraction or attachment.

You only hear about the most freakish cases, like that of Lori Drew or of 7
Wanda Webb Holloway, the Texas mother who in 1991 tried to pay someone
to murder the mother of her daughter's chief cheerleading rival. ("The motive here was love, a mother's love for a daughter," said a police investigator
at the time.) Yet everyday examples abound of parents whose boundary issues are not so extreme, but still qualify as borderline wacko.

"People now feel like having a good relationship with your child means 8
you're involved in every aspect of your child's life," says Rosalind Wiseman,
author of "Queen Bees & Wannabes" and "Queen Bee Moms & Kingpin
Dads," who travels the country speaking with and counseling parents,
teachers and teens. "Nothing is off-limits" now between parents and their
kids, she says. "There's no privacy and there's no critical thinking."

Wiseman has heard stories of parents who hope to pave their child's way 9
to popularity by luring the in-crowd to parties with promised "loot-bag"
giveaways like iPods and North Face fleeces.° She recently heard of a father
who, happening on an instant-messaging war between his child and a bunch
of children on a sleepover, went over to the other house, called the other father outside, and began a fistfight that ended only after someone called the
police. And of a mother who, unwilling to join her fifth-grade daughter in accepting the apology of another fifth-grader who'd bullied her in the playground, hounded the school incessantly,° pushing for the other child to be
expelled.

Parents, she says, routinely blow a gasket when they get it in their heads 10
that they need to seek revenge on their child's behalf. "It's, 'I've been wronged.
My kid has been wronged, so I've been wronged; therefore I have to do whatever's necessary, including being disgustingly immoral.'"

"Where are the brakes," Wiseman asked, "on parental behavior?" 11

Otherwise put: where does adult behavior end and childish behavior 12
begin?

"Morally speaking, they shouldn't have done that," a 22-year-old writing 13
on Yahoo! Answers this week observed about the Drew case. "But I don't
think they should be held responsible b/c kids are mean to each other every
day. It would not be any different than an actual 13 yr old boy being mean to
another girl."

That, of course, is the whole point. 14

Parents of teenagers are not supposed to act like teenagers. They're not 15
supposed to dress like teenagers or talk like teenagers or spend their days
text-messaging teenagers—as one mom Wiseman encountered did, exchanging expressions of shock and dismay, after her 14-year-old daughter broke up
with a popular and athletic boy. ("I was totally basking in the social status I
was getting from the boy," the very honest mother told Wiseman.)

Or, at least, parents weren't supposed to act like this in the past. 16

"There used to be this kind of parent-child gradient,° where the parent 17
was expected to—and did—function at a different level than the child," says
clinical psychologist Madeline Levine, author of the 2006 book *The Price of*

fleeces: Jackets.   **incessantly:** Without stopping.   **gradient:** Slope.

Privilege, who lectures frequently on child and adolescent issues. Now, she says, "that whole notion of parents being in an entirely different space than their children is disappearing."

In part, Levine blames parenting experts for this turn of events.   18

She blames the self-esteem movement, decades of parenting advice that   19 prized "communication" over limit-setting and safety. She blames the narcissistic needs of parents who want their children to like them at all costs. And in part, when thinking over the fused mother-daughter dyads° she so often encounters in therapy, she indicts this generation of mothers' loneliness, dissatisfaction in work and marriage, stress, sense of failure, and emotional isolation. In the end, she asks, when you're feeling alone and blue, "Who are you sure is going to hang around with you? It's your children."

It's very easy to put up walls to separate the likes of Lori Drew and Wanda   20 Webb Holloway from the rest of us. Most of us, after all, are not sick or profoundly vindictive,° entirely lacking in self-awareness or devoid° of all empathy.°

Still, we have all caught ourselves spending a little too much time worry-   21 ing about (or gloating over) our children's popularity. We spend a lot of time feeling our children's pain and put a lot of thought into shaping their world to offer them the greatest possible degree of happiness. But our kids really need something much bigger from us than that. They desperately need us to grow up.

Questions to Start You Thinking

1. **Considering Meaning:**   According to Warner, parents are overly concerned with their children's pain and popularity. What problems do these tendencies create? What might cause this behavior in parents?

2. **Identifying Writing Strategies:**   Warner emphasizes the extensive coverage that Megan Meier's death received in the media; she uses the sensational account of Meier's suicide to open the essay. What is the significance of this story for Warner—and what did the initial news coverage ignore?

3. **Reading Critically:**   What sources does Warner use? How persuasive are they, and how effectively does she use them?

4. **Expanding Vocabulary:**   In paragraph 19, Warner refers to the "narcissistic needs of parents who want their children to like them at all costs." What does *narcissistic* mean? Why is the term significant for Warner's overall argument?

5. **Making Connections:**   How do the problems Warner highlights among today's "helicopter parents" relate to William F. Buckley Jr.'s argument in "Why Don't We Complain?" (pp. 618–22)? Do you think Buckley would sympathize with her argument? Why or why not?

dyad: Couple; pair.   **vindictive:** Revenge-seeking, unforgiving.   **devoid:** Empty, without.
empathy: The ability to understand another's feelings or motives.

Journal Prompts

1. Warner describes a phenomenon known as "helicopter parenting," in which parents tend to hover over their children. Write a description—humorous or serious—of a "helicopter parent," including his or her behavior, personal characteristics, and motivations.

2. One of Warner's sources, clinical psychologist Madeline Levine, criticizes the "self-esteem movement," which favored "'communication' over limit-setting and safety" between parents and children (paragraph 19). Do you agree that "self-esteem" and excessive "communication" have become problems? Why, or why not?

Suggestions for Writing

1. In a personal essay, discuss your observations or experiences with parents or guardians. How did they balance the need for limits against the need to be "liked"? How would you evaluate them and their attitudes in light of Warner's article?

2. Warner asks, "Where does adult behavior end and childish behavior begin?" (paragraph 12). Levine argues that parents used to occupy "an entirely different space than their children" (paragraph 17). Yet neither writer specifies what these differences mean, except to point out extreme examples of bad behavior by some parents. Write an essay that defines such distinctions or analyzes how societal or cultural changes affect the roles of parents and children.

Alfie Kohn

When a Parent's "I Love You" Means "Do as I Say"

Alfie Kohn was born in 1957 in Miami Beach, Florida. He earned a BA from Brown University after creating his own interdisciplinary course of study and an MA in social sciences from the University of Chicago. An outspoken critic of competition, discipline, and schooling in America, he writes and speaks extensively on human behavior, incentives, education, and parenting. His eleven books on the subject include *Punished by Rewards: The Trouble with Gold Stars, Incentive Plans, A's, Praise, and Other Bribes* (1993) and *No Contest: The Case against Competition* (1986). Other titles that explore national priorities and education initiatives include *The Case against Standardized Testing: Raising the Scores, Ruining the Schools* (2000) and *The Homework Myth: Why Our Kids Get Too Much of a Bad Thing* (2006). In this essay, Kohn examines the negative effects of "conditional parenting," citing new research into the psychology of motivation.

For more about Alfie Kohn, visit **<bedfordstmartins .com/bedguide>**.

AS YOU READ: Identify what Kohn sees as the dominant type of discipline for children today. How does he view these attitudes and methods?

M ore than 50 years ago, the psychologist Carl Rogers suggested that   1
simply loving our children wasn't enough. We have to love them *un-conditionally,* he said—for who they are, not for what they do.

As a father, I know this is a tall order, but it becomes even more challeng-   2
ing now that so much of the advice we are given amounts to exactly the opposite. In effect, we're given tips in *conditional* parenting, which comes in two
flavors: turn up the affection when they're good, withhold affection when
they're not.

Thus, the talk show host Phil McGraw tells us in his book *Family First*   3
(Free Press, 2004) that what children need or enjoy should be offered contingently,° turned into rewards to be doled out or withheld so they "behave according to your wishes." And "one of the most powerful currencies° for a
child," he adds, "is the parents' acceptance and approval."

Likewise, Jo Frost of *Supernanny,* in her book of the same name (Hyper-   4
ion, 2005), says, "The best rewards are attention, praise and love," and these
should be held back "when the child behaves badly until she says she is
sorry," at which point the love is turned back on.

Conditional parenting isn't limited to old-school authoritarians. Some   5
people who wouldn't dream of spanking choose instead to discipline their
young children by forcibly isolating them, a tactic we prefer to call "time
out." Conversely, "positive reinforcement" teaches children that they are
loved, and lovable, only when they do whatever we decide is a "good job."

This raises the intriguing° possibility that the problem with praise isn't   6
that it is done the wrong way—or handed out too easily, as social conservatives insist. Rather, it might be just another method of control, analogous to
punishment. The primary message of all types of conditional parenting is
that children must earn a parent's love. A steady diet of that, Rogers warned,
and children might eventually need a therapist to provide the unconditional
acceptance they didn't get when it counted.

But was Rogers right? Before we toss out mainstream discipline, it would   7
be nice to have some evidence. And now we do.

In 2004, two Israeli researchers, Avi Assor and Guy Roth, joined Edward L.   8
Deci, a leading American expert on the psychology of motivation, in asking
more than 100 college students whether the love they had received from their
parents had seemed to depend on whether they had succeeded in school, practiced hard for sports, been considerate toward others or suppressed° emotions like anger and fear.

It turned out that children who received conditional approval were in-   9
deed somewhat more likely to act as the parent wanted. But compliance°
came at a steep price. First, these children tended to resent and dislike their
parents. Second, they were apt to say that the way they acted was often due
more to a "strong internal pressure" than to "a real sense of choice." More-

---

contingently: Based on conditions.   **currencies:** Things used as a medium of exchange;
money.   **intriguing:** Arousing curiosity or interest.   **suppressed:** Kept in, stopped, withheld.   **compliance:** Cooperation, obedience.

over, their happiness after succeeding at something was usually short-lived, and they often felt guilty or ashamed.

In a companion study, Dr. Assor and his colleagues interviewed mothers 10 of grown children. With this generation, too, conditional parenting proved damaging. Those mothers who, as children, sensed that they were loved only when they lived up to their parents' expectations now felt less worthy as adults. Yet despite the negative effects, these mothers were more likely to use conditional affection with their own children.

This July, the same researchers, now joined by two of Dr. Deci's colleagues 11 at the University of Rochester, published two replications and extensions of the 2004 study. This time the subjects were ninth graders, and this time giving more approval when children did what parents wanted was carefully distinguished from giving less when they did not.

The studies found that both positive and negative conditional parenting 12 were harmful, but in slightly different ways. The positive kind sometimes succeeded in getting children to work harder on academic tasks, but at the cost of unhealthy feelings of "internal compulsion." Negative conditional parenting didn't even work in the short run; it just increased the teenagers' negative feelings about their parents.

What these and other studies tell us, if we're able to hear the news, is that 13 praising children for doing something right isn't a meaningful alternative to pulling back or punishing when they do something wrong. Both are examples of conditional parenting, and both are counterproductive.

The child psychologist Bruno Bettelheim, who readily acknowledged that 14 the version of negative conditional parenting known as time-out can cause "deep feelings of anxiety," nevertheless endorsed it for that very reason. "When our words are not enough," he said, "the threat of the withdrawal of our love and affection is the only sound method to impress on him that he had better conform to our request."

But the data suggest that love withdrawal isn't particularly effective at 15 getting compliance, much less at promoting moral development. Even if we did succeed in making children obey us, though — say, by using positive reinforcement — is obedience worth the possible long-term psychological harm? Should parental love be used as a tool for controlling children?

Deeper issues also underlie a different sort of criticism. Albert Bandura, 16 the father of the branch of psychology known as social learning theory, declared that unconditional love "would make children directionless and quite unlovable" — an assertion entirely unsupported by empirical° studies. The idea that children accepted for who they are would lack direction or appeal is most informative for what it tells us about the dark view of human nature held by those who issue such warnings.

In practice, according to an impressive collection of data by Dr. Deci 17 and others, unconditional acceptance by parents as well as teachers should be accompanied by "autonomy° support": explaining reasons for requests,

empirical: Based on scientific observation.   **autonomy:** Independence.

maximizing opportunities for the child to participate in making decisions, being encouraging without manipulating, and actively imagining how things look from the child's point of view.

The last of these features is important with respect to unconditional parenting itself. Most of us would protest that of course we love our children without any strings attached. But what counts is how things look from the perspective of the children—whether they feel just as loved when they mess up or fall short. 18

Rogers didn't say so, but I'll bet he would have been glad to see less demand for skillful therapists if that meant more people were growing into adulthood having already felt unconditionally accepted. 19

Questions to Start You Thinking

1. **Considering Meaning:** How do parents practice "conditional parenting" (paragraph 2) without full awareness or intention? What problems might conditional parenting cause?

2. **Identifying Writing Strategies:** How does Kohn support his assertion that "so much of the advice we are given amounts to exactly the opposite" (paragraph 2) of the belief that parents should love their children unconditionally?

3. **Reading Critically:** Kohn proposes a model of parenting based on "unconditional acceptance" and "autonomy support" (paragraph 17). How does this approach allow for disciplining children when they behave in inappropriate, immoral, or harmful ways? What does this model suggest about his view of children?

4. **Expanding Vocabulary:** Kohn observes that "Conditional parenting isn't limited to old-school authoritarians" (paragraph 5). What is an *old-school authoritarian*? What connotations does the phrase have? Why does Kohn use it?

5. **Making Connections:** In "Helicopter Parenting Turns Deadly" (pp. 506–8), Judith Warner targets the "self-esteem movement," which encouraged parents to value "'communication' over limit-setting and safety" (p. 508, paragraph 19). How do you think she might respond to Kohn's argument? Which writer seems more persuasive? Why?

Journal Prompts

1. In paragraph 16, Kohn cites the psychologist Albert Bandura, who claims that giving children unconditional love "'would make children directionless and quite unlovable.'" To Kohn, this claim implies a "dark view of human nature." What does this claim suggest to you? What is your view of human nature in this context: "dark" or "light"? What kind of parenting might come from these contrasting views?

2. Kohn suggests that parenting is difficult, especially given the conflicting advice that parents receive. What advice would you give? In your view, how would an ideal parent behave?

Suggestions for Writing

1. In a personal essay, examine the expectation that parents must love their children "unconditionally." Do you think unconditional love is possible, or even desirable, between parents and children?

2. Describe the style of your parents or other parents you know well in the context of Kohn's article. Were they "old-school authoritarians"? Did they practice "conditional parenting" of any kind? How did their children respond to their approach? Then, compare and contrast their style with the recommendations of current guides to parenting in books, magazines, newspapers, or online sources.

Danzy Senna

The Color of Love

Danzy Senna, born in 1970 in Boston, earned her BA at Stanford University and her MFA from the University of California, Irvine. Senna's essays and short stories have been widely anthologized, and her journalistic writing has appeared in such publications as the *Nation,* the *Utne Reader,* and *Newsweek.* Her best-selling novel *Caucasia* (1988) won several awards, and in 2002 she received a prestigious Whiting Award, given each year to ten writers of exceptional ability and promise. Her most recent books are the psychological thriller *Symptomatic* (2004) and the memoir *Where Did You Sleep Last Night?: A Personal History* (2009). In "The Color of Love," Senna, the daughter of a white mother and a black father, explores the complexities — racial and otherwise — of her relationship with her grandmother. The essay originally appeared in *O: The Oprah Magazine* in 2000.

For more about Danzy Senna, visit **<bedfordstmartins .com/bedguide>**.

AS YOU READ: Consider how her grandmother displays both love for Senna and prejudice toward her. How does Senna respond?

We had this much in common: We were both women, and we were both writers. But we were as different as two people can be and still exist in the same family. She was ancient — as white and dusty as chalk — and spent her days seated in a velvet armchair, passing judgments on the world below. She still believed in noble bloodlines; my blood had been mixed at conception. I believed there was no such thing as nobility or class or lineage, only systems designed to keep some people up in the big house and others outside, in the cold.

She was my grandmother. She was Irish but from that country's Protestant elite, which meant she seemed more British than anything. She was an actress, a writer of plays and novels, and still unmarried in her thirties when she came to America to visit. One night while in Boston, she went to a dinner party, where she was seated next to a young lawyer with blood as blue as the ocean. Her pearl earring fell in his oyster soup—or so the story goes—and they fell in love. My grandmother married that lawyer and left her native Ireland for New England.

How she came to have black grandchildren is a story of opposites. It was 1968 in Boston when her daughter—my mother—a small, blonde Wasp° poet, married my father, a tall and handsome black intellectual, in an act that was as rebellious as it was hopeful. The products of that unlikely union—my older sister, my younger brother, and I—grew up in urban chaos, in a home filled with artists and political activists. The old lady across the river in Cambridge seemed to me an endangered species. Her walls were covered with portraits of my ancestors, the pale and dead men who had conquered Africa and built Boston long before my time. When I visited, their eyes followed me from room to room with what I imagined to be an expression of scorn. Among the portraits sat my grandmother, a bird who had flown in to remind us all that there had indeed been a time when lineage and caste° meant something. To me, young and dark and full of energy, she was the missing link between the living and the dead.

But her blood flowed through me, whether I liked it or not. I grew up to be a writer, just like her. And as I struggled to tell my own stories—about race and class and post–civil rights America—I wondered who my grandmother had been before, in Dublin, when she was friend and confidante to literary giants such as William Butler Yeats and Samuel Beckett. Once, while snooping in her bedroom, I discovered her novels, the ones that had been published in Ireland when she was my age. I stared at her photograph on the jacket and wondered about the young woman who wore a mischievous smile. Had she ever worried about becoming so powerful that no man would want her? Did she now feel that she had sacrificed her career and wild Irishwoman dreams to become a wife and mother and proper Bostonian?

I longed to know her—to love her. But the differences between us were real and alive, and they threatened to squelch our fragile connection. She was an alcoholic. In the evening, after a few glasses of gin, she could turn vicious. Though she held antiquated racist views, my grandmother would still have preferred to see my mother married and was saddened when my parents split in the seventies. She believed that a woman without a man was pitiable. The first question she always asked me when she saw me: "Do you have a man?" The second question: "What is he?" That was her way of finding out his race and background. She looked visibly pleased if he was a Wasp, neutral if he was Jewish, and disappointed if he was black.

My mother ignored her hurtful comments but felt them just the same. She spent her visits to my grandmother's house slamming dishes in the

3

4

5

6

Wasp: An acronym (for White Anglo-Saxon Protestant) referring to a member of the prevailing American social class.   **caste:** Class or social group.

kitchen, hissing her anger just out of hearing range, then raving, on the drive home, about what awful thing her mother had said this time. Like my mother, I knew the rule: I was not to disrespect elders. She was old and gray and would soon be gone. But I had inherited my grandmother's short temper. When I got angry, even as a child, I felt as if blood were rushing around in my head, red waves battering the shore. Words spilled from my mouth— cutting, vicious words that I regretted.

One autumn day in Cambridge, at my grandmother's place, I lost my temper. I was home from college for the holidays, staying in her guest room. I woke from a nap to the sound of her enraged voice shouting at what I could only imagine was the television. 7

"Idiot! You damn fool!" she bellowed. "You stupid, stupid woman!" It has to be *Jeopardy!,* I thought. She must be yelling at those tiny contestants on the screen. She knows the answers to those questions better than they do. But when the shouting went on for a beat too long, I went to the top of the stairs and looked down into the living room. She was speaking to a real person: her cleaning lady, a Greek woman named Mary, who was on her hands and knees, nervously gathering the shards of a broken vase. My grandmother stood over her, hands on hips, cursing. 8

"You fool," my grandmother repeated. "How in bloody hell could you have done something so stupid?" 9

"Grandma." I didn't shout her name but said it loudly enough that she, though hard of hearing, glanced up. 10

"Oh, darling!" she piped, suddenly cheerful. "Would you like a cup of tea? You must be dreadfully tired." 11

Mary was on her feet again. She smiled nervously at me, then rushed into the kitchen with the pieces of the broken vase. 12

I told myself to be a good girl, to be polite. But something snapped. I marched down the stairs, and even she noticed something on my face that made her sit in her velvet chair. 13

"Don't you ever talk to her that way," I shouted. "Where do you think you are? Slavery was abolished long ago." 14

I stood over her, tall and long-limbed, daring her to speak. My grandmother shook her head. "It's about race, isn't it?" 15

"Race?" I said, baffled. "Mary's white. This is about respect—treating other human beings with respect." 16

She wasn't hearing me. All she saw was color. "The tragedy about you," she said soberly, "is that you are mixed." I felt those waves in my head: "Your tragedy is that you're old and ignorant," I spat. "You don't know the first thing about me." 17

She cried into her hands. She seemed diminished, a little old woman. She looked up only to say, "You are a cruel girl." 18

I left her apartment trembling yet feeling exhilarated by what I had done. But my elation soon turned to shame. I had taken on an old lady. And for what? Her intolerance was, at her age, deeply entrenched. My rebuttals couldn't change her. 19

Yet that fight marked the beginning of our relationship. I've since decided 20 that when you cease to express anger toward those who have hurt you, you are essentially giving up on them. They are dead to you. But when you express anger, it is a sign that they still matter, that they are worth the fight.

After that argument, my grandmother and I began a conversation. She 21 seemed to see me clearly for the first time, or perhaps she, a "cruel girl" herself, had simply met her match. And I no longer felt she was a relic. She was a living, breathing human being who deserved to be spoken to as an equal.

I began visiting her more. I would drive to Cambridge and sit with 22 her, eating mixed nuts and sipping ginger ale, regaling° her with tales of my latest love drama or writing project. In her presence, I was proudly black and young and political, and she was who she was: subtly racist, terribly elitist, and awfully funny. She still said things that angered me: She bemoaned my mother's marriage to my father, she said that I should marry not for love but for money, and she told me that I needn't identify as black, since I didn't look it. I snapped back at her. But she, with senility creeping in, didn't seem to hear me; each time I came, she said the same things.

Last summer I went into hiding to work on my second novel at a writers' 23 retreat in New Hampshire. The place was a kind of paradise for creative souls, a hideaway where every writer had his or her own cabin in the woods with no phone or television—no distractions to speak of. But I was miserable. I could not write. Even the flies outside my window seemed to whisper, "Go out and play. Forget the novel. Leave it till tomorrow."

I woke one morning at four, the light outside my window still blue. I felt 24 panic and sadness, though I didn't know why. I got up, dressed, and went outside for a walk through the forest. But the panic persisted, and I began to cry. I assumed that my writer's block had seized me suddenly.

That night I ate dinner in the main house and received a call on the pay 25 phone from my mother. She told me my grandmother had fallen and broken her leg. But that wasn't all; she had subsequently suffered a heart attack. Her other organs were failing. I had to hurry if I wanted to say good-bye.

I drove to Boston that night, not believing that we could be losing her. 26 She would make it. I was certain. Sure, she was ninety-two, frail, unable to walk steadily. But she was lucid,° and her tongue was as sharp as ever. Somehow I had imagined her as indestructible, made immortal by power and cruelty and wit.

The woman I found in the hospital bed was barely recognizable. My 27 grandmother had always been fussy about her appearance. She never showed her face without makeup. Even in the day, when it was just she and the cleaning lady, she dressed as if she were ready for a cocktail party. At night she usually had cocktail parties; doddering° old men hovered around her, sipping Scotch and bantering about theater and politics.

My grandmother's face had swollen to twice its normal size, and tubes 28 came out of her nose. She had struggled so hard to pull them out that the

regaling: Entertaining.   **lucid:** Mentally sound.   **doddering:** Feeble.

nurses had tied her wrists to the bed rails. Her hair was gray and thin. Her body was withered and bruised, barely covered by the green hospital gown.

Her hazel eyes were all that was still recognizable, but the expression in them was different from any I had ever seen on her—terror. She was terrified to die. She tried to rise when she saw me, and her eyes pleaded with me to help her, to save her, to get her out of this mess. I stood over her, and I felt only one thing: overwhelming love. Not a trace of anger. That dark gray rage I'd felt toward her was gone as I stroked her forehead and told her she would be okay, even knowing she would not.   29

For two days, my mother, her sisters, and I stood beside my grandmother, singing Irish ballads and reading passages to her from the works of her favorite novelist, James Joyce. For the first time, she could not talk. At one point, she gestured wildly for pen and paper. I brought her the pen and the paper and held them up for her, but she was too weak for even that. What came out was only a faint, incomprehensible line.   30

In death we are each reduced to our essence: the spirit we are when we are born. The trappings we hold on to our whole lives—our race, our money, our sex, our age, our politics—become irrelevant. My grandmother became a child in that hospital bed, a spirit about to embark on an unknown journey, terrified and alone, no matter how many of us were crowded around her. In the final hours, even her skin seemed to lose its wrinkles and take on a waxy glow. Then, finally, the machines around us went silent as she left us behind to squabble in the purgatory° of the flesh.   31

Questions to Start You Thinking

1. **Considering Meaning:** What are the similarities and differences between Senna and her grandmother? How do the differences result in conflict?

2. **Identifying Writing Strategies:** Identify some ways Senna makes her grandmother come alive for readers. Where is her description vivid enough for you to see her as Senna does? Which details are particularly effective? Why?

3. **Reading Critically:** How would you describe the tone of the essay? Support your opinion with specific passages.

4. **Expanding Vocabulary:** In describing her grandmother, Senna explains, "I had imagined her as indestructible, made immortal by power and cruelty and wit" (paragraph 26). In your own words, define *immortal.* How can "power and cruelty and wit" make someone immortal?

5. **Making Connections:** Senna has mixed emotions about confronting her grandmother, telling herself "to be a good girl, to be polite," but

---

purgatory: A place of suffering and remorse (originally, from Roman Catholic beliefs, the place where the souls of the dead suffer for a limited time in order to be cleansed of their sins).

"something snapped" (paragraph 13). In "Why Don't We Complain?" (pp. 618–22), William F. Buckley Jr. also writes about our general "tendency to passive compliance" (paragraph 8) and our reluctance to speak up. What do both writers suggest about the necessity or value of conflict?

Journal Prompts

1. Recall a time when you or someone you know was verbally abused. How did you respond?
2. At the end of her life, Senna's grandmother "gestured wildly for pen and paper" (paragraph 30), but she was unable to write. If she had been able to write a sentence or two, what might she have written to Senna?

Suggestions for Writing

1. Senna notes that "when you cease to express anger toward those who have hurt you, you are essentially giving up on them" (paragraph 20). Write an essay about a time when expressing anger had a positive effect on a relationship. Be sure to recall the events leading up to the confrontation as well as the resolution to the problem.
2. Senna suggests that her grandmother's prejudice is a result of age and ignorance. What other factors might contribute to an individual's prejudices? Write an essay presenting your views about how prejudice develops and what can be done to prevent it.

For more about Amy Tan, visit **<bedfordstmartins .com/bedguide>**.

Amy Tan

Mother Tongue

Amy Tan was born in 1952 in Oakland, California, a few years after her parents immigrated to the United States from China. After receiving a BA in English and linguistics and an MA in linguistics from San Jose State University, Tan worked as a specialist in language development before becoming a freelance business writer in 1981. Tan's first short story (1985) became the basis for her first novel, *The Joy Luck Club* (1990), which was a phenomenal best-seller and was made into a movie. Tan's second novel, *The Kitchen God's Wife* (1991), was equally popular. Throughout her work run themes of family relationships, loyalty, and ways of reconciling past and present. Most recently she published *The Opposite of Fate* (2003), a book of autobiographical essays, and *Saving Fish from Drowning* (2005), a novel. She has also written children's books. "Mother Tongue" first appeared in *Threepenny Review* in 1990. In this essay, Tan explores the effect of her mother's "broken" English — the language Tan grew up with — on her life and writing.

AS YOU READ: Identify the difficulties Tan says exist for a child growing up in a family that speaks nonstandard English.

I am not a scholar of English or literature. I cannot give you much more than personal opinions on the English language and its variations in this country or others.

I am a writer. And by that definition, I am someone who has always loved language. I am fascinated by language in daily life. I spend a great deal of my time thinking about the power of language—the way it can evoke an emotion, a visual image, a complex idea, or a simple truth. Language is the tool of my trade. And I use them all—all the Englishes I grew up with.

Recently, I was made keenly aware of the different Englishes I do use. I was giving a talk to a large group of people, the same talk I had already given to half a dozen other groups. The nature of the talk was about my writing, my life, and my book, *The Joy Luck Club*. The talk was going along well enough, until I remembered one major difference that made the whole talk sound wrong. My mother was in the room. And it was perhaps the first time she had heard me give a lengthy speech, using the kind of English I have never used with her. I was saying things like, "The intersection of memory upon imagination" and "There is an aspect of my fiction that relates to thus-and-thus"—a speech filled with carefully wrought° grammatical phrases, burdened, it suddenly seemed to me, with nominalized° forms, past perfect tenses, conditional phrases, all the forms of Standard English that I had learned in school and through books, the forms of English I did not use at home with my mother.

Just last week, I was walking down the street with my mother, and I again found myself conscious of the English I was using, and the English I do use with her. We were talking about the price of new and used furniture and I heard myself saying this: "Not waste money that way." My husband was with us as well, and he didn't notice any switch in my English. And then I realized why. It's because over the twenty years we've been together I've often used that same kind of English with him, and sometimes he even uses it with me. It has become our language of intimacy, a different sort of English that relates to family talk, the language I grew up with.

So you'll have some idea of what this family talk I heard sounds like, I'll quote what my mother said during a recent conversation which I videotaped and then transcribed.° During this conversation, my mother was talking about a political gangster in Shanghai who had the same last name as her family's, Du, and how the gangster in his early years wanted to be adopted by her family, which was rich by comparison. Later, the gangster became more powerful, far richer than my mother's family, and one day showed up at my mother's wedding to pay his respects. Here's what she said in part:

"Du Yusong having business like fruit stand. Like off the street kind. He is like Du Zong—but not Tsung-ming Island people. The local people call putong, the river east side, he belong to that side local people. That man want to ask Du Zong father take him in like become own family. Du Zong father wasn't look down on him, but didn't take seriously, until that man

---

wrought: Crafted.   **nominalized:** Made into a noun from a verb.   **transcribed:** Made a written copy of what was said.

big like become a mafia. Now important person, very hard to inviting him. Chinese way, came only to show respect, don't stay for dinner. Respect for making big celebration, he shows up. Mean gives lots of respect. Chinese custom. Chinese social life that way. If too important won't have to stay too long. He come to my wedding. I didn't see, I heard it. I gone to boy's side, they have YMCA dinner. Chinese age I was nineteen."

You should know that my mother's expressive command of English be-   7
lies° how much she actually understands. She reads the *Forbes* report, listens to *Wall Street Week,* converses daily with her stockbroker, reads all of Shirley MacLaine's books with ease—all kinds of things I can't begin to understand. Yet some of my friends tell me they understand fifty percent of what my mother says. Some say they understand eighty to ninety percent. Some say they understand none of it, as if she were speaking pure Chinese. But to me, my mother's English is perfectly clear, perfectly natural. It's my mother tongue. Her language, as I hear it, is vivid, direct, full of observation and imagery. That was the language that helped shape the way I saw things, expressed things, made sense of the world.

Lately, I've been giving more thought to the kind of English my mother   8
speaks. Like others, I have described it to people as "broken" or "fractured" English. But I wince when I say that. It has always bothered me that I can think of no way to describe it other than "broken," as if it were damaged and needed to be fixed, as if it lacked a certain wholeness and soundness. I've heard other terms used, "limited English," for example. But they seem just as bad, as if everything is limited, including people's perceptions of the limited English speaker.

I know this for a fact, because when I was growing up, my mother's "lim-   9
ited" English limited *my* perception of her. I was ashamed of her English. I believed that her English reflected the quality of what she had to say. That is, because she expressed them imperfectly her thoughts were imperfect. And I had plenty of empirical evidence to support me: the fact that people in department stores, at banks, and at restaurants did not take her seriously, did not give her good service, pretended not to understand her, or even acted as if they did not hear her.

My mother has long realized the limitations of her English as well. When   10
I was fifteen, she used to have me call people on the phone to pretend I was she. In this guise, I was forced to ask for information or even to complain and yell at people who had been rude to her. One time it was a call to her stockbroker in New York. She had cashed out her small portfolio and it just so happened we were going to go to New York the next week, our very first trip outside California. I had to get on the phone and say in an adolescent voice that was not very convincing, "This is Mrs. Tan."

And my mother was standing in the back whispering loudly, "Why he   11
don't send me check, already two weeks late. So mad he lie to me, losing me money."

belies: Shows to be false.

And then I said in perfect English, "Yes, I'm getting rather concerned. You 12
had agreed to send the check two weeks ago, but it hasn't arrived."

Then she began to talk more loudly. "What he want, I come to New York 13
tell him front of his boss, you cheating me?" And I was trying to calm her
down, make her be quiet, while telling the stockbroker, "I can't tolerate any
more excuses. If I don't receive the check immediately, I am going to have to
speak to your manager when I'm in New York next week." And sure enough,
the following week there we were in front of this astonished stockbroker, and
I was sitting there red-faced and quiet, and my mother, the real Mrs. Tan, was
shouting at his boss in her impeccable broken English.

We used a similar routine just five days ago, for a situation that was far 14
less humorous. My mother had gone to the hospital for an appointment, to
find out about a benign brain tumor a CAT scan had revealed a month ago.
She said she had spoken very good English, her best English, no mistakes.
Still, she said, the hospital did not apologize when they said they had lost the
CAT scan and she had come for nothing. She said they did not seem to have
any sympathy when she told them she was anxious to know the exact diagnosis, since her husband and son had both died of brain tumors. She said they
would not give her any more information until the next time and she would
have to make another appointment for that. So she said she would not leave
until the doctor called her daughter. She wouldn't budge. And when the
doctor finally called her daughter, me, who spoke in perfect English — lo and
behold — we had assurances the CAT scan would be found, promises that a
conference call on Monday would be held, and apologies for any suffering
my mother had gone through for a most regrettable mistake.

I think my mother's English almost had an effect on limiting my possibil- 15
ities in life as well. Sociologists and linguists probably will tell you that a person's developing language skills are more influenced by peers. But I think
that the language spoken in the family, especially in immigrant families
which are more insular,° plays a large role in shaping the language of the
child. And I believe that it affected my results on achievement tests, IQ tests,
and the SAT. While my English skills were never judged as poor, compared to
math, English could not be considered my strong suit. In grade school I did
moderately well, getting perhaps B's, sometimes B-pluses, in English and
scoring perhaps in the sixtieth or seventieth percentile on achievement tests.
But those scores were not good enough to override the opinion that my true
abilities lay in math and science, because in those areas I achieved A's and
scored in the ninetieth percentile or higher.

This was understandable. Math is precise; there is only one correct an- 16
swer. Whereas, for me at least, the answers on English tests were always a
judgment call, a matter of opinion and personal experience. Those tests were
constructed around items like fill-in-the-blank sentence completion, such as,
"Even though Tom was _____ , Mary thought he was _____ ." And the correct answer always seemed to be the most bland combinations of thoughts,
for example, "Even though Tom was shy, Mary thought he was charming,"

---

insular: Detached or isolated; keeping to oneself.

with the grammatical structure "even though" limiting the correct answer to some sort of semantic° opposites, so you wouldn't get answers like, "Even though Tom was foolish, Mary thought he was ridiculous." Well, according to my mother, there were very few limitations as to what Tom could have been and what Mary might have thought of him. So I never did well on tests like that.

The same was true with word analogies, pairs of words in which you were   17
supposed to find some sort of logical, semantic relationship — for example, "*Sunset* is to *nightfall* as _____ is to _____ ." And here you would be presented with a list of four possible pairs, one of which showed the same kind of relationship: *red* is to *stoplight, bus* is to *arrival, chills* is to *fever, yawn* is to *boring.* Well, I could never think that way. I knew what the tests were asking, but I could not block out of my mind the images already created by the first pair, "*sunset* is to *nightfall*" — and I would see a burst of colors against a darkening sky, the moon rising, the lowering of a curtain of stars. And all the other pairs of words — *red, bus, stoplight, boring* — just threw up a mass of confusing images, making it impossible for me to sort out something as logical as saying: "A sunset precedes nightfall" is the same as "a chill precedes a fever." The only way I would have gotten that answer right would have been to imagine an associative situation, for example, my being disobedient and staying out past sunset, catching a chill at night, which turns into feverish pneumonia as punishment, which indeed did happen to me.

I have been thinking about all this lately, about my mother's English,   18
about achievement tests. Because lately I've been asked, as a writer, why there are not more Asian Americans enrolled in creative writing programs. Why do so many Chinese students go into engineering? Well, these are broad sociological questions I can't begin to answer. But I have noticed in surveys — in fact, just last week — that Asian students, as a whole, always do significantly better on math achievement tests than in English. And this makes me think that there are other Asian American students whose English spoken in the home might also be described as "broken" or "limited." And perhaps they also have teachers who are steering them away from writing and into math and science, which is what happened to me.

Fortunately, I happen to be rebellious in nature and enjoy the challenge   19
of disproving assumptions made about me. I became an English major my first year in college, after being enrolled as pre-med. I started writing nonfiction as a freelancer the week after I was told by my former boss that writing was my worst skill and I should hone my talents toward account management.

But it wasn't until 1985 that I finally began to write fiction. And at first I   20
wrote using what I thought to be wittily crafted sentences, sentences that would finally prove I had mastery over the English language. Here's an example from the first draft of a story that later made its way into *The Joy Luck*

---

semantic: Relating to the meaning of language.

Club, but without this line: "That was my mental quandary in its nascent°
state." A terrible line, which I can barely pronounce.

Fortunately, for reasons I won't get into today, I later decided I should en-   21
vision a reader for the stories I would write. And the reader I decided upon
was my mother, because these were stories about mothers. So with this
reader in mind — and in fact she did read my early drafts — I began to write
stories using all the Englishes I grew up with: the English I spoke to my
mother, which for lack of a better term might be described as "simple"; the
English she used with me, which for lack of a better term might be described
as "broken"; my translation of her Chinese, which could certainly be described as "watered down"; and what I imagined to be her translation of her
Chinese if she could speak in perfect English, her internal language, and for
that I sought to preserve the essence, but neither an English nor a Chinese
structure. I wanted to capture what language ability tests can never reveal:
her intent, her passion, her imagery, the rhythms of her speech, and the nature of her thoughts.

Apart from what any critic had to say about my writing, I knew I had suc   22
ceeded where it counted when my mother finished reading my book and gave
me her verdict: "So easy to read."

Questions to Start You Thinking

1. **Considering Meaning:**   What are the Englishes that Tan grew up
   with? What other Englishes has she used in her life? What does each
   English have that gives it an advantage over the other Englishes in certain situations?

2. **Identifying Writing Strategies:**   What examples does Tan use to analyze the various Englishes she uses? How has Tan been able to synthesize her Englishes successfully into her present style of writing fiction?

3. **Reading Critically:**   Although Tan explains that she writes using "all
   the Englishes" she has known throughout her life (paragraph 21), she
   doesn't do that in this essay. What are the differences between the
   English Tan uses in this essay and the kinds she says she uses in her fiction? How does the language she uses here fit the purpose of her essay?

4. **Expanding Vocabulary:**   In paragraph 9, Tan writes that she had
   "plenty of empirical evidence" that her mother's "limited" English meant
   that her mother's thoughts were "imperfect" as well. Define *empirical.*
   What does Tan's use of this word tell us about her present attitude toward the way she judged her mother when she was growing up?

5. **Making Connections:**   Tan worried that her mother's English could
   limit Tan's own "possibilities in life" (paragraph 15), but eventually she
   accepted and appreciated her mother's language — and its positive influence on her writing. In "The Color of Love" (pp. 513–17), Danzy Senna

nascent: Beginning; only partly formed.

engages with her difficult grandmother to deepen their connection — and perhaps to deepen Senna's sense of herself as a writer. What brought about these changes? How did new attitudes evolve? What were the benefits?

Link to the Paired Essay

Tan and Richard Rodriguez ("Public and Private Language," pp. 524–29) recount learning English as they grew up in homes where English was a second language. In what way did they face similar experiences and obstacles? How did learning English affect their self-images and influence their relationships with their families?

Journal Prompts

1. Describe one of the Englishes you use to communicate. When do you use it, and when do you avoid using it?

2. In what ways are you a "translator," if not of language, then of current events and fashions, for your parents or other members of your family?

Suggestions for Writing

1. In a personal essay explain an important event in your family's history, using your family's various Englishes or other languages.

2. Take note of and, if possible, transcribe a conversation you have had with a parent or other family member, with a teacher, and with a close friend. Write an essay comparing and contrasting the "languages" of the three conversations. How do the languages differ? How do you account for these differences? What might happen if someone used "teacher language" to talk to a friend or "friend language" in a class discussion or paper?

For more about Richard Rodriguez, visit **<bedfordstmartins .com/bedguide>**.

Richard Rodriguez

Public and Private Language

Richard Rodriguez, the son of Spanish-speaking Mexican American parents, was born in 1944 and grew up in San Francisco, where he currently lives. He earned a BA at Stanford University and received graduate degrees in English from Columbia University and the University of California at Berkeley. A full-time writer and lecturer, Rodriguez has served as a contributing editor for *Harper's Magazine, U.S. News & World Report,* and the Sunday Opinion section of the *Los Angeles Times.* His work has appeared in many publications, and he regularly contributes to PBS's *News Hour.* His books, which often draw on autobiography to explore race and ethnicity in American society, include *Hunger of Memory* (1982), from which the following selection is drawn; *Days of Obligation: An Argument with My Mexican Father* (1992); and *Brown: The Last Discovery of America*

(2002). In "Public and Private Language," he recounts the origin of his complex views of bilingual education.

AS YOU READ: Discover the ways in which learning English changed Rodriguez's life and his relationship with his family.

Supporters of bilingual education today imply that students like me   1
miss a great deal by not being taught in their family's language. What they seem not to recognize is that, as a socially disadvantaged child, I considered Spanish to be a private language. What I needed to learn in school was that I had the right — and the obligation — to speak the public language of *los gringos*.° The odd truth is that my first-grade classmates could have become bilingual, in the conventional sense of that word, more easily than I. Had they been taught (as upper-middle-class children are often taught early) a second language like Spanish or French, they could have regarded it simply as that: another public language. In my case such bilingualism could not have been so quickly achieved. What I did not believe was that I could speak a single public language.

Without question, it would have pleased me to hear my teachers address   2
me in Spanish when I entered the classroom. I would have felt much less afraid. I would have trusted them and responded with ease. But I would have delayed — for how long postponed? — having to learn the language of public society. I would have evaded — and for how long could I have afforded to delay? — learning the great lesson of school, that I had a public identity.

Fortunately, my teachers were unsentimental about their responsibility.   3
What they understood was that I needed to speak a public language. So their voices would search me out, asking me questions. Each time I'd hear them, I'd look up in surprise to see a nun's face frowning at me. I'd mumble, not really meaning to answer. The nun would persist, "Richard, stand up. Don't look at the floor. Speak up. Speak to the entire class, not just to me!" but I couldn't believe that the English language was mine to use. (In part, I did not want to believe it.) I continued to mumble. I resisted the teacher's demands. (Did I somehow suspect that once I learned public language my pleasing family life would be changed?) Silent, waiting for the bell to sound, I remained dazed, diffident,° afraid.

Because I wrongly imagined that English was intrinsically° a public lan-   4
guage and Spanish an intrinsically private one, I easily noticed the difference between classroom language and the language of home. At school, words were directed to a general audience of listeners. ("Boys and girls. . . .") Words were meaningfully ordered. And the point was not self-expression alone but to make oneself understood by many others. The teacher quizzed: "Boys and girls, why do we use that word in this sentence? Could we think of a better word to use there? Would the sentence change its meaning if the words were

los gringos: Spanish for "foreigners," often used as a derogatory term for English-speaking Americans.   **diffident:** Shy.   **intrinsically:** Essentially; inherently.

differently arranged? And wasn't there a better way of saying much the same thing?" (I couldn't say. I wouldn't try to say.)

Three months. Five. Half a year passed. Unsmiling, ever watchful, my teach-   5
ers noted my silence. They began to connect my behavior with the difficult progress my older sister and brother were making. Until one Saturday morning three nuns arrived at the house to talk to our parents. Stiffly, they sat on the blue living room sofa. From the doorway of another room, spying the visitors, I noted the incongruity° — the clash of two worlds, the faces and voices of school intruding upon the familiar setting of home. I overheard one voice gently wondering, "Do your children speak only Spanish at home, Mrs. Rodriguez?" While another voice added, "That Richard especially seems so timid and shy."

That Rich-heard!   6

With great tact the visitors continued, "Is it possible for you and your   7
husband to encourage your children to practice their English when they are home?" Of course, my parents complied. What would they not do for their children's well-being? And how could they have questioned the Church's authority which those women represented? In an instant, they agreed to give up the language (the sounds) that had revealed and accentuated our family's closeness. The moment after the visitors left, the change was observed. "*Ahora,*° speak to us *en inglés,*"° my father and mother united to tell us.

At first, it seemed a kind of game. After dinner each night, the family   8
gathered to practice "our" English. (It was still then *inglés,* a language foreign to us, so we felt drawn as strangers to it.) Laughing, we would try to define words we could not pronounce. We played with strange English sounds, often overanglicizing our pronunciations. And we filled the smiling gaps of our sentences with familiar Spanish sounds. But that was cheating, somebody shouted. Everyone laughed. In school, meanwhile, like my brother and sister, I was required to attend a daily tutoring session. I needed a full year of special attention. I also needed my teachers to keep my attention from straying in class by calling out, *Rich-heard*—their English voices slowly prying loose my ties to my other name, its three notes, *Ri-car-do.* Most of all I needed to hear my mother and father speak to me in a moment of seriousness in broken—suddenly heartbreaking—English. The scene was inevitable: one Saturday morning I entered the kitchen where my parents were talking in Spanish. I did not realize that they were talking in Spanish however until, at the moment they saw me, I heard their voices change to speak English. Those *gringo* sounds they uttered startled me. Pushed me away. In that moment of trivial misunderstanding and profound insight, I felt my throat twisted by unsounded grief. I turned quickly and left the room. But I had no place to escape to with Spanish. (The spell was broken.) My brother and sisters were speaking English in another part of the house.

Again and again in the days following, increasingly angry, I was obliged to   9
hear my mother and father: "Speak to us *en inglés.*" (*Speak.*) Only then did I

---

incongruity: Lack of harmony or appropriateness.   ***Ahora:*** Spanish for "now."
en inglés: Spanish for "in English."

determine to learn classroom English. Weeks after, it happened: one day in school I had my hand raised to volunteer an answer. I spoke out in a loud voice. And I did not think it remarkable when the entire class understood. That day, I moved very far from the disadvantaged child I had been only days earlier. The belief, that calming assurance that I belonged in public, had at last taken hold.

Shortly after, I stopped hearing the high and loud sounds of *los gringos.* A   10
more and more confident speaker of English, I didn't trouble to listen to *how* strangers sounded, speaking to me. And there simply were too many English-speaking people in my day for me to hear American accents anymore. Conversations quickened. Listening to persons whose voices sounded eccentrically pitched, I usually noted their sounds for an initial few seconds before I concentrated on *what* they were saying. Conversations became content-full. Transparent. Hearing someone's *tone* of voice—angry or questioning or sarcastic or happy or sad—I didn't distinguish it from the words it expressed. Sound and word were thus tightly wedded. At the end of a day, I was often bemused, always relieved, to realize how "silent," though crowded with words, my day in public had been. (This public silence measured and quickened the change in my life.)

At last, seven years old, I came to believe what had been technically true   11
since my birth: I was an American citizen.

But the special feeling of closeness at home was diminished by then.   12
Gone was the desperate, urgent, intense feeling of being at home; rare was the experience of feeling myself individualized by family intimates. We remained a loving family, but one greatly changed. No longer so close; no longer bound tight by the pleasing and troubling knowledge of our public separateness. Neither my older brother nor sister rushed home after school anymore. Nor did I. When I arrived home there would often be neighborhood kids in the house. Or the house would be empty of sounds.

Following the dramatic Americanization of their children, even my parents   13
grew more publicly confident. Especially my mother. She learned the names of all the people on our block. And she decided we needed to have a telephone installed in the house. My father continued to use the word *gringo.* But it was no longer charged with the old bitterness or distrust. (Stripped of any emotional content, the word simply became a name for those Americans not of Hispanic descent.) Hearing him, sometimes, I wasn't sure if he was pronouncing the Spanish word *gringo* or saying gringo in English.

Matching the silence I started hearing in public was a new quiet at home.   14
The family's quiet was partly due to the fact that, as we children learned more and more English, we shared fewer and fewer words with our parents. Sentences needed to be spoken slowly when a child addressed his mother or father. (Often the parent wouldn't understand.) The child would need to repeat himself. (Still the parent misunderstood.) The young voice, frustrated, would end up saying, "Never mind"—the subject was closed. Dinners would be noisy with the clinking of knives and forks against dishes. My mother would smile softly between her remarks; my father at the other end of the

table would chew and chew at his food, while he stared over the heads of his children.

My *mother!* My *father!* After English became my primary language, I no 15 longer knew what words to use in addressing my parents. The old Spanish words (those tender accents of sound) I had used earlier—*mamá* and *papá*—I couldn't use anymore. They would have been all-too-painful reminders of how much had changed in my life. On the other hand, the words I heard neighborhood kids call *their* parents seemed equally unsatisfactory. *Mother* and *Father; Ma, Papa, Pa, Dad, Pop* (how I hated the all-American sound of that last word especially)—all these terms I felt were unsuitable, not really terms of address for *my* parents. As a result, I never used them at home. Whenever I'd speak to my parents, I would try to get their attention with eye contact alone. In public conversations, I'd refer to "my parents" or "my mother and father."

My mother and father, for their part, responded differently, as their chil- 16 dren spoke to them less and less. My mother grew restless, seemed troubled and anxious at the scarcity of words exchanged in the house. It was she who would question me about my day when I came home from school. She smiled at the small talk. She pried at the edges of my sentences to get me to say something more. (What?) She'd join conversations she overheard, but her intrusions often stopped her children's talking. By contrast, my father seemed reconciled to the new quiet. Though his English improved some-what, he retired into silence. At dinner he spoke very little. One night his children and even his wife helplessly giggled at his garbled English pronunci-ation of the Catholic Grace before Meals. Thereafter he made his wife recite the prayer at the start of each meal, even on formal occasions, when there were guests in the house. Hers became the public voice of the family. On offi-cial business, it was she, not my father, one would usually hear on the phone or in stores, talking to strangers. His children grew so accustomed to his si-lence that, years later, they would speak routinely of his shyness. (My mother would often try to explain: both his parents died when he was eight. He was raised by an uncle who treated him like little more than a menial servant. He was never encouraged to speak. He grew up alone. A man of few words.) But my father was not shy, I realized, when I'd watch him speaking Spanish with relatives. Using Spanish, he was quickly effusive.° Especially when talking with other men, his voice would spark, flicker, flare alive with sounds. In Spanish, he expressed ideas and feelings he rarely revealed in English. With firm Spanish sounds, he conveyed confidence and authority English would never allow him.

The silence at home, however, was finally more than a literal silence. 17 Fewer words passed between parent and child, but more profound was the si-lence that resulted from my inattention to sounds. At about the time I no longer bothered to listen with care to the sounds of English in public, I grew careless about listening to the sounds family members made when they

effusive: Talkative; unreserved.

spoke. Most of the time I heard someone speaking at home and didn't distinguish his sounds from the words people uttered in public. I didn't even pay much attention to my parents' accented and ungrammatical speech. At least not at home. Only when I was with them in public would I grow alert to their accents. Though, even then, their sounds caused me less and less concern. For I was increasingly confident of my own public identity.

Today I hear bilingual educators say that children lose a degree of "indi- 18
viduality" by becoming assimilated into public society. (Bilingual schooling was popularized in the seventies, that decade when middle-class ethnics began to resist the process of assimilation—the American melting pot.) But the bilingualists simplistically scorn the value and necessity of assimilation. They do not seem to realize that there are *two* ways a person is individualized. So they do not realize that while one suffers a diminished sense of *private* individuality by becoming assimilated into public society, such assimilation makes possible the achievement of *public* individuality.

Questions to Start You Thinking

1. **Considering Meaning:**   What created the new "silence" in the Rodriguez household? Explain why.

2. **Identifying Writing Strategies:**   How does Rodriguez use comparison and contrast to convey his experience learning English?

3. **Reading Critically:**   How does Rodriguez use dialogue to make the experience he recalls more vivid for his readers? Is this strategy effective in helping him achieve his purpose? Why, or why not?

4. **Expanding Vocabulary:**   Rodriguez uses the terms *private* and *public*. What do these words mean when used as adjectives to describe "language" and "identity"?

5. **Making Connections:**   Rodriguez disagrees with people who claim that assimilation erodes individuality and advocates the "value and necessity of assimilation" (paragraph 18). What does "assimilation" mean, exactly? Is it a necessary process? Does the Latino embrace of "Latino Style" (described by Ruth La Ferla in "Latino Style Is Cool. Oh, All Right: It's Hot," pp. 568–72) represent a resistance to assimilation?

Link to the Paired Essay

Both Rodriguez and Amy Tan ("Mother Tongue," pp. 518–23) grew up in homes in which English was spoken as a second language. Compare and contrast how each writer's mastery of English affected his or her parents.

Journal Prompts

1. Recall a time when your public identity was at odds with your private self.

2. Has an accomplishment that you are proud of ever had a negative effect on another aspect of your life or on other people around you?

Suggestions for Writing

1. If you speak a second language, write an essay recalling your experience learning it. What were some of your struggles? Can you relate to Rodriguez's experience? How do you use that language today? If you do not know a second language, write an essay in which you analyze the possible benefits of learning one. What language would you like to learn? Why?

2. According to Rodriguez, "Supporters of bilingual education today imply that students like me miss a great deal by not being taught in their family's language" (paragraph 1). Rodriguez counters this assumption by showing how his immersion in English allowed him to develop a public identity that ultimately led to his success. At the same time, however, his English-only immersion hurt his family life. Write an essay in which you take a stand on the complex topic of bilingual education, using further reading and research to support your position about how it does or does not benefit students.

Responding to an Image

Examine these photographs, comparing the settings, roles, and body language of the man and woman. What emotions are apparent? If you were to add dialogue to these pictures, what might the man and woman be saying or thinking? Based on your analysis, what general point do the photographs make about gender roles and stereotypes in today's society?

For reading
activities linked to
this chapter, visit
<bedfordstmartins
.com/bedguide>.

Web Search

Use a search engine to find one Web source or publication marketed for women and one marketed for men. Read a few pages of each, and compare and contrast the content. How are they similar? How are they different? Do you think they stereotype women and men? How, and for what reasons?

For more about
Robert Jensen, visit
<bedfordstmartins
.com/bedguide>.

Robert Jensen
The High Cost of Manliness

Robert Jensen was born in 1958 and grew up in Fargo, North Dakota. After earning a BA in social studies and secondary education from Moorhead State University and graduate degrees in journalism from American University and the University of Minnesota, Jensen started his career as a newspaper journalist. He is now a professor of journalism at the University of Texas at Austin, where he teaches courses on media law, ethics, and politics and also regularly contributes to a variety of publications. His recent books include *Citizens of the Empire: The Struggle to Claim Our Humanity* (2004), *The Heart of Whiteness: Confronting Race, Racism, and White Privilege* (2005), and *All My Bones Shake: Seeking a Progressive Path to the Prophetic Voice* (2009). An outspoken critic of current U.S. foreign policy, Jensen gained widespread attention over his series of controversial opinion pieces in the *Houston Chronicle* soon after the September 11 terrorist attacks. In the following essay, which first appeared on *Alternet.org* in September 2006, Jensen calls for abandoning the prevailing definition of masculinity, arguing that it is "toxic" to both men and women.

AS YOU READ: Identify what Jensen sees as the dominant conception of masculinity in contemporary culture. What does he think of this conception?

I t's hard to be a man; hard to live up to the demands that come with the 1
dominant conception of masculinity, of the tough guy.

So, guys, I have an idea—maybe it's time we stop trying. Maybe this mas- 2
culinity thing is a bad deal, not just for women but for us.

We need to get rid of the whole idea of masculinity. It's time to abandon 3
the claim that there are certain psychological or social traits that inherently
come with being biologically male. If we can get past that, we have a chance
to create a better world for men and women.

The dominant conception of masculinity in U.S. culture is easily summa- 4
rized: men are assumed to be naturally competitive and aggressive, and being a
real man is therefore marked by the struggle for control, conquest, and domination. A man looks at the world, sees what he wants, and takes it. Men who don't
measure up are wimps, sissies, fags, girls. The worst insult one man can hurl at
another—whether it's boys on the playground or CEOs in the boardroom—is
the accusation that a man is like a woman. Although the culture acknowledges
that men can in some situations have traits traditionally associated with women
(caring, compassion, tenderness), in the end it is men's strength-expressed-as-

toughness that defines us and must trump any femalelike softness. Those aspects of masculinity must prevail for a man to be a "real man."

That's not to suggest, of course, that every man adopts that view of masculinity. But it is endorsed in key institutions and activities—most notably in business, the military, and athletics—and is reinforced through the mass media. It is particularly expressed in the way men—straight and gay alike—talk about sexuality and act sexually. And our culture's male heroes reflect those characteristics: they most often are men who take charge rather than seek consensus, seize power rather than look for ways to share it, and are willing to be violent to achieve their goals.

That view of masculinity is dangerous for women. It leads men to seek to control "their" women and define their own pleasure in that control, which leads to epidemic levels of rape and battery. But this view of masculinity is toxic for men as well.

If masculinity is defined as conquest, it means that men will always struggle with each other for dominance. In a system premised on hierarchy° and power, there can be only one king of the hill. Every other man must in some way be subordinated to the king, and the king has to always be nervous about who is coming up that hill to get him. A friend who once worked on Wall Street—one of the preeminent° sites of masculine competition—described coming to work as like walking into a knife fight when all the good spots along the wall were taken. Masculinity like this is life lived as endless competition and threat.

No one man created this system, and perhaps none of us, if given a choice, would choose it. But we live our lives in that system, and it deforms men, narrowing our emotional range and depth. It keeps us from the rich connections with others—not just with women and children, but other men—that make life meaningful but require vulnerability.

This doesn't mean that the negative consequences of this toxic masculinity are equally dangerous for men and women. As feminists have long pointed out, there's a big difference between women dealing with the possibility of being raped, beaten, and killed by the men in their lives and men not being able to cry. But we can see that the short-term material gains that men get are not adequate compensation for what we men give up in the long haul—which is to surrender part of our humanity to the project of dominance.

Of course there are obvious physical differences between men and women—average body size, hormones, reproductive organs. There may be other differences rooted in our biology that we don't yet understand. Yet it's also true that men and women are more similar than we are different, and that given the pernicious° effects of centuries of patriarchy° and its relentless devaluing of things female, we should be skeptical of the perceived differences.

hierarchy: A grouping based on relative rank.   **preeminent:** Most important.   **pernicious:** Destructive.   **patriarchy:** Social organization in which the father is supreme; male control of most of the power in a society.

What we know is simple: in any human population, there is wide individ-   11
ual variation. While there's no doubt that a large part of our behavior is
rooted in our DNA, there's also no doubt that our genetic endowment is
highly influenced by culture. Beyond that, it's difficult to say much with any
certainty. It's true that only women can bear children and breast-feed. That
fact likely has some bearing on aspects of men's and women's personalities.
But we don't know much about what the effect is, and given the limits of our
tools to understand human behavior, it's possible we may never know much.

At the moment, the culture seems obsessed with gender differences, in the   12
context of a recurring intellectual fad (called "evolutionary psychology" this
time around, and "sociobiology" in a previous incarnation) that wants to explain all complex behaviors as simple evolutionary adaptations—if a pattern of
human behavior exists, it must be because it's adaptive in some ways. In the
long run, that's true by definition. But in the short term it's hardly a convincing argument to say, "Look at how men and women behave so differently; it
must be because men and women are fundamentally different" when a political system has been creating differences between men and women.

From there, the argument that we need to scrap masculinity is fairly   13
simple. To illustrate it, remember back to right after 9/11. A number of commentators argued that criticisms of masculinity should be rethought. Cannot we now see—recognizing that male firefighters raced into burning
buildings, risking and sometimes sacrificing their lives to save others—that
masculinity can encompass a kind of strength that is rooted in caring and
sacrifice? Of course men often exhibit such strength, just as do women. So,
the obvious question arises: What makes these distinctly masculine characteristics? Are they not simply human characteristics?

We identify masculine tendencies toward competition, domination, and   14
violence because we see patterns of differential behavior; men are more prone
to such behavior in our culture. We can go on to observe and analyze the
ways in which men are socialized to behave in those ways, toward the goal of
changing those destructive behaviors. That analysis is different than saying
that admirable human qualities present in both men and women are somehow primarily the domain of one gender. To assign them to a gender is misguided and demeaning to the gender that is then assumed not to possess
them to the same degree. Once we start saying "strength and courage are
masculine traits," it leads to the conclusion that woman are not as strong or
courageous.

Of course, if we are going to jettison° masculinity, we have to scrap femi-   15
ninity along with it. We have to stop trying to define what men and women
are going to be in the world based on extrapolations° from physical sex differences. That doesn't mean we ignore those differences when they matter,
but we have to stop assuming they matter everywhere.

I don't think the planet can long survive if the current conception of mas-   16
culinity endures. We face political and ecological challenges that can't be met

jettison: Throw out.   **extrapolations:** Predictions.

with this old model of what it means to be a man. At the more intimate level, the stakes are just as high. For those of us who are biologically male, we have a simple choice: we men can settle for being men, or we can strive to be human beings.

Questions to Start You Thinking

1. **Considering Meaning:**   What does Jensen see as the negative consequences of the commonly held idea of masculinity?

2. **Identifying Writing Strategies:**   Where in the essay does Jensen use comparison and contrast in writing about men and women? What is his point in doing so?

3. **Reading Critically:**   In paragraph 5, Jensen admits that not all men conceive of masculinity in terms of competition and aggression. Do you think he goes on to provide enough evidence to support his claim that this view of masculinity is dominant in U.S. culture? Why, or why not?

4. **Expanding Vocabulary:**   In paragraph 12, Jensen refers to the current obsession with gender differences in the United States as a "recurring intellectual fad." What does he mean by this phrase? What does it add to his argument?

5. **Making Connections:**   According to Jensen, "toxic masculinity" (paragraph 9) results from a "political system" that creates "differences between men and women" (paragraph 12). Do you think Brent Staples ("Black Men and Public Space," pp. 536–38) would agree? How are views of black men shaped — or even created — by society? How does the category of race complicate Jensen's analysis?

Journal Prompts

1. Do you agree, as Jensen puts it, that the "worst insult one man can hurl at another . . . is the accusation that a man is like a woman" (paragraph 4)? What do you think about insults that liken a woman to a man?

2. In the essay's final paragraph, Jensen writes that he doesn't think "the planet can long survive if the current conception of masculinity endures." How do you respond to this statement?

Suggestions for Writing

1. Jensen writes in paragraph 13 about the idea of strength. In an essay, discuss how you define *human strength,* considering the physical, the intellectual, and the emotional.

2. Jensen acknowledges that gender differences are in some part determined by biological factors. However, he is more concerned about the influence of social conditioning. Write an essay analyzing how a

particular social force does or does not contribute to stereotypes of
masculinity and femininity. For example, you might consider the influence of some aspect of popular culture, education, sports, or children's
toys. Use examples from your experience as well as other evidence to
support your point.

For more about
Brent Staples, visit
**<bedfordstmartins
.com/bedguide>**.

Brent Staples

Black Men and Public Space

Brent Staples was born in 1951 in Chester, Pennsylvania, and earned a PhD in psychology from the University of Chicago. He wrote for the *Chicago Sun-Times* and *Down
Beat* magazine before joining the *New York Times* in 1985, where he moved from metropolitan news to the *New York Times Book Review*. Since 1990, Staples has been a
member of the *Times* editorial board, writing regular columns on politics and culture. His
work also has appeared in such magazines as *New York Woman, Ms.,* and *Harper's,* and
he is the author of the memoir *Parallel Time: Growing Up in Black and White* (1994). In
the following essay, published in a slightly different version in *Ms.* magazine in September 1986, Staples considers how his presence affects other pedestrians at night.

AS YOU READ: Identify why other pedestrians respond to Staples with anxiety.

My first victim was a woman — white, well dressed, probably in her late   1
twenties. I came upon her late one evening on a deserted street in
Hyde Park, a relatively affluent neighborhood in an otherwise mean, impov-
erished section of Chicago. As I swung onto the avenue behind her, there
seemed to be a discreet, uninflammatory distance between us. Not so. She
cast back a worried glance. To her, the youngish black man — a broad six feet
two inches with a beard and billowing hair, both hands shoved into the pockets of a bulky military jacket — seemed menacingly close. After a few more
quick glimpses, she picked up her pace and was soon running in earnest.
Within seconds, she disappeared into a cross street.

   That was more than a decade ago. I was twenty-one years old, a graduate   2
student newly arrived at the University of Chicago. It was in the echo of that
terrified woman's footfalls that I first began to know the unwieldy inheri-
tance I'd come into — the ability to alter public space in ugly ways. It was clear
that she thought herself the quarry of a mugger, a rapist, or worse. Suffering
a bout of insomnia, however, I was stalking sleep, not defenseless wayfarers.
As a softy who is scarcely able to take a knife to a raw chicken — let alone hold
one to a person's throat — I was surprised, embarrassed, and dismayed all at
once. Her flight made me feel like an accomplice in tyranny. It also made it
clear that I was indistinguishable from the muggers who occasionally seeped
into the area from the surrounding ghetto. The first encounter, and those
that followed, signified that a vast, unnerving gulf lay between nighttime pedestrians — particularly women — and me. And I soon gathered that being
perceived as dangerous is a hazard in itself. I only needed to turn a corner

into a dicey situation, or crowd some frightened, armed person in a foyer somewhere, or make an errant move after being pulled over by a policeman. Where fear and weapons meet—and they often do in urban America—there is always the possibility of death.

In that first year, my first away from my hometown, I was to become thoroughly familiar with the language of fear. At dark, shadowy intersections, I could cross in front of a car stopped at a traffic light and elicit the *thunk, thunk, thunk, thunk* of the driver—black, white, male, or female—hammering down the door locks. On less traveled streets after dark, I grew accustomed to but never comfortable with people crossing to the other side of the street rather than pass me. Then there were the standard unpleasantries with policemen, doormen, bouncers, cabdrivers, and others whose business it is to screen out troublesome individuals *before* there is any nastiness.

I moved to New York nearly two years ago and I have remained an avid night walker. In central Manhattan, the near-constant crowd cover minimizes tense one-on-one street encounters. Elsewhere—in SoHo, for example, where sidewalks are narrow and tightly spaced buildings shut out the sky—things can get very taut indeed.

After dark, on the warrenlike° streets of Brooklyn where I live, I often see women who fear the worst from me. They seem to have set their faces on neutral, and with their purse straps strung across their chests bandolier-style, they forge ahead as though bracing themselves against being tackled. I understand, of course, that the danger they perceive is not a hallucination. Women are particularly vulnerable to street violence, and young black males are drastically overrepresented among the perpetrators of that violence. Yet these truths are no solace against the kind of alienation that comes of being ever the suspect, a fearsome entity with whom pedestrians avoid making eye contact.

It is not altogether clear to me how I reached the ripe old age of twenty-two without being conscious of the lethality nighttime pedestrians attributed to me. Perhaps it was because in Chester, Pennsylvania, the small, angry industrial town where I came of age in the 1960s, I was scarcely noticeable against a backdrop of gang warfare, street knifings, and murders. I grew up one of the good boys, had perhaps a half-dozen fistfights. In retrospect, my shyness of combat has clear sources.

As a boy, I saw countless tough guys locked away; I have since buried several, too. They were babies, really—a teenage cousin, a brother of twenty-two, a childhood friend in his mid-twenties—all gone down in episodes of bravado played out in the streets. I came to doubt the virtues of intimidation early on. I chose, perhaps unconsciously, to remain a shadow—timid, but a survivor.

The fearsomeness mistakenly attributed to me in public places often has a perilous flavor. The most frightening of these confusions occurred in the late 1970s and early 1980s, when I worked as a journalist in Chicago. One day, rushing into the office of a magazine I was writing for with a deadline

warrenlike: Like a maze.

story in hand, I was mistaken for a burglar. The office manager called security and, with an ad hoc° posse, pursued me through the labyrinthine halls, nearly to my editor's door. I had no way of proving who I was. I could only move briskly toward the company of someone who knew me.

Another time I was on assignment for a local paper and killing time before an interview. I entered a jewelry store on the city's affluent Near North Side. The proprietor excused herself and returned with an enormous red Doberman pinscher straining at the end of a leash. She stood, the dog extended toward me, silent to my questions, her eyes bulging nearly out of her head. I took a cursory look around, nodded, and bade her good night. 9

Relatively speaking, however, I never fared as badly as another black male journalist. He went to nearby Waukegan, Illinois, a couple of summers ago to work on a story about a murderer who was born there. Mistaking the reporter for the killer, police officers hauled him from his car at gunpoint and but for his press credentials would probably have tried to book him. Such episodes are not uncommon. Black men trade tales like this all the time. 10

Over the years, I learned to smother the rage I felt at so often being taken for a criminal. Not to do so would surely have led to madness. I now take precautions to make myself less threatening. I move about with care, particularly late in the evening. I give a wide berth° to nervous people on subway platforms during the wee hours, particularly when I have exchanged business clothes for jeans. If I happen to be entering a building behind some people who appear skittish, I may walk by, letting them clear the lobby before I return, so as not to seem to be following them. I have been calm and extremely congenial on those rare occasions when I've been pulled over by the police. 11

And on late-evening constitutionals I employ what has proved to be an excellent tension-reducing measure: I whistle melodies from Beethoven and Vivaldi and the more popular classical composers. Even steely New Yorkers hunching toward nighttime destinations seem to relax, and occasionally they even join in the tune. Virtually everybody seems to sense that a mugger wouldn't be warbling bright, sunny selections from Vivaldi's *Four Seasons*. It is my equivalent of the cowbell that hikers wear when they know they are in bear country. 12

Questions to Start You Thinking

1. **Considering Meaning:** What misconceptions do people have about Staples because he is a young black man? What does he feel causes such misconceptions?

2. **Identifying Writing Strategies:** At the end of the essay, how does Staples use comparison to explain his behavior?

3. **Reading Critically:** What kinds of appeals—emotional, logical, ethical—does Staples use? Are his appeals appropriate for the purpose of his essay? Why, or why not? (For an explanation of kinds of appeals, see pp. 43–45.)

ad hoc: Spur of the moment.   **berth:** Space.

4. **Expanding Vocabulary:**   Define *affluent, uninflammatory* (paragraph 1), *unwieldy, quarry, errant* (paragraph 2), *bandolier, solace* (paragraph 5), *lethality* (paragraph 6), and *bravado* (paragraph 7). Why do you think Staples uses such formal language in this essay?

5. **Making Connections:**   In "The Color of Love" (pp. 513–17), Danzy Senna writes about being the daughter of a black father and a white mother and, in particular, about her relationship with her prejudiced white grandmother. How might Senna and Staples respond to one another's experiences?

Journal Prompts

1. Are stereotypes ever useful? Why, or why not?

2. Have you or someone you know ever been wrongfully stereotyped or prejudged? How did you react?

Suggestions for Writing

1. Staples describes his feelings about being the object of racial fear. Have you or someone you know ever been the object of that fear or other misconceptions based on prejudice or stereotyping? Write a short personal essay discussing the causes and effects of the experience. What preconceptions were involved? How did you or your acquaintance respond?

2. What do you think causes the stereotype of African American men that Staples is addressing? Write an essay that analyzes this stereotype, drawing on several outside sources to support your analysis.

Dave Barry
From Now On, Let Women Kill Their Own Spiders

Dave Barry was born in 1947 in Armonk, New York. According to his own biographical statement, he has been "steadily growing older ever since without ever actually reaching maturity." He attended Haverford College and started his career in journalism at the *Daily Local News* in West Chester, Pennsylvania. As a syndicated writer for the *Miami Herald* from 1983 to 2005, Barry's humorous columns appeared in hundreds of newspapers, and he won the Pulitzer Prize for Commentary in 1988. Barry is the author of numerous books, which include *Dave Barry's Complete Guide to Guys* (1995) and, more recently, *Dave Barry's History of the Millennium (So Far)* (2007) and *I'll Mature When I'm Dead* (2010). The article "From Now On, Let Women Kill Their Own Spiders" first appeared in the *Miami Herald*. In this piece, Barry pokes fun at miscommunication between men and women. Identifying with both, he laughs at how the sexes inevitably bewilder and infuriate each other.

For more about Dave Barry, visit **<bedfordstmartins.com/bedguide>**.

AS YOU READ: Try to discover what Barry is really criticizing.

From time to time I receive letters from a certain group of individuals
that I will describe, for want of a better term, as "women." I have such a
letter here, from a Susie Walker of North Augusta, S.C., who asks the following question: "Why do men open a drawer and say, 'Where is the spatula?' instead of, you know, looking for it?"

This question expresses a commonly held (by women) negative stereotype
about guys of the male gender, which is that they cannot find things around the
house, especially things in the kitchen. Many women believe that if you want to
hide something from a man, all you have to do is put it in plain sight in the refrigerator, and he will never, ever find it, as evidenced by the fact that a man can
open a refrigerator containing 463 pounds of assorted meats, poultry, cold cuts,
condiments, vegetables, frozen dinners, snack foods, desserts, etc., and ask, with
no irony whatsoever, "Do we have anything to eat?"

Now I could respond to this stereotype in a snide° manner by making
generalizations about women. I could ask, for example, how come your average woman prepares for virtually every upcoming event in her life, including
dental appointments, by buying new shoes, even if she already owns as many
pairs as the entire Riverdance troupe. I could point out that, if there were no
women, there would be no such thing as Leonardo DiCaprio. I could ask why
a woman would walk up to a perfectly innocent man who is minding his own
business watching basketball and demand to know if a certain pair of pants
makes her butt look too big, and then, no matter what he answers, get mad
at him. I could ask why, according to the best scientific estimates, 93 percent
of the nation's severely limited bathroom-storage space is taken up by
decades-old, mostly empty tubes labeled "moisturizer." I could point out
that, to judge from the covers of countless women's magazines, the two topics most interesting to women are (1) Why men are all disgusting pigs, and
(2) How to attract men.

Yes, I could raise these issues in response to the question asked by Susie
Walker of North Augusta, S.C., regarding the man who was asking where the
spatula was. I could even ask WHY this particular man might be looking for
the spatula. Could it be that he needs a spatula to kill a spider, because, while
he was innocently watching basketball and minding his own business, a
member of another major gender — a gender that refuses to personally kill
spiders but wants them all dead — DEMANDED that he kill the spider, which
nine times out of ten turns out to be a male spider that was minding its own
business? Do you realize how many men arrive in hospital emergency rooms
every year, sometimes still gripping their spatulas, suffering from painful
spider-inflicted injuries? I don't have the exact statistics right here, but I bet
they are chilling.

As I say, I could raise these issues and resort to the kind of negativity in-
dulged in by Susie Walker of North Augusta, S.C. But I choose not to. I
choose, instead, to address her question seriously, in hopes that, by improving the communication between the genders, all human beings — both men

snide: Sarcastic, especially in a nasty manner.

and women, together—will come to a better understanding of how dense° women can be sometimes.

I say this because there is an excellent reason why a man would open the spatula drawer and, without looking for the spatula, ask where the spatula is: the man does not have TIME to look for the spatula. Why? Because he is busy thinking. Men are almost always thinking. When you look at a man who appears to be merely scratching himself, rest assured that inside his head, his brain is humming like a high-powered computer, processing millions of pieces of information and producing important insights such as, "This feels good!"   6

We should be grateful that men think so much, because over the years they have thought up countless inventions that have made life better for all people, everywhere. The shot clock in basketball is one example. Another one is underwear-eating bacteria. I found out about this thanks to the many alert readers who sent me an article from *New Scientist* magazine stating that Russian scientists—and you KNOW these are guy scientists—are trying to solve the problem of waste disposal aboard spacecraft, by "designing a cocktail of bacteria to digest astronauts' cotton and paper underpants." Is that great, or what? I am picturing a utopian future wherein, when a man's briefs get dirty, they will simply dissolve from his body, thereby freeing him from the chore of dealing with his soiled underwear via the labor-intensive, time-consuming method he now uses, namely, dropping them on the floor.   7

I'm not saying that guys have solved all the world's problems. I'm just saying that there ARE solutions out there, and if, instead of harping endlessly about spatulas, we allow guys to use their mental talents to look for these solutions, in time, they will find them. Unless they are in the refrigerator.   8

Questions to Start You Thinking

1. **Considering Meaning:**   What is Barry satirizing in his essay?

2. **Identifying Writing Strategies:**   Barry's essay is filled with rhetorical questions. Locate some of these, and consider how he answers them. What evidence does he provide to support his answers? How does this evidence affect his tone? How does it affect meaning?

3. **Reading Critically:**   What generalizations about women does Barry make in paragraph 3? How do these serve to support his main point?

4. **Expanding Vocabulary:**   Define *utopian* (paragraph 7). According to Barry, how would underwear-eating bacteria contribute to a utopian future?

5. **Making Connections:**   Both Barry and Judy Brady ("I Want a Wife," pp. 542–44) use satire, humorously attacking human mistakes and shortcomings in their essays. Compare and contrast their use of satire.

dense: Slow-witted.

Journal Prompts

1. Put your imagination to work to suggest other inventions—besides underwear-eating bacteria—that would benefit man- (or woman-) kind. Follow Barry's model and have fun.

2. Discuss a conversation you've heard that involved man or woman bashing. What was the tone of the conversation? How serious were the participants? What are the effects of such remarks?

Suggestions for Writing

1. Using Barry's essay as a model, write an essay satirizing an issue you find unfair, irritating, or just amusing.

2. Stereotypes can be useful in literature and film, but in real life they may be damaging. Write an essay in which you examine real-life stereotypes, recalling behavior you have observed and experienced.

For more about
Judy Brady, visit
**<bedfordstmartins
.com/bedguide>**.

Judy Brady

I Want a Wife

Judy Brady was born in 1937 in San Francisco, where she now makes her home. A graduate of the University of Iowa, Brady has contributed to various publications and has traveled to Cuba to study class relationships and education. She edited the book *1 in 3: Women with Cancer Confront an Epidemic* (1991), drawing on her own struggle with the disease, and she continues to write and speak about cancer and its possible environmental causes. In the following piece, reprinted frequently since it appeared in *Ms.* magazine in December 1971, Brady considers the role of the American housewife. While she has said that she is "not a 'writer,'" this essay shows Brady to be a satirist adept at taking a stand and provoking attention.

AS YOU READ: Ask yourself why Brady says she wants a wife rather than a husband.

belong to that classification of people known as wives. I am A Wife. And, not altogether incidentally, I am a mother.

Not too long ago a male friend of mine appeared on the scene fresh from a recent divorce. He had one child, who is, of course, with his ex-wife. He is looking for another wife. As I thought about him while I was ironing one evening, it suddenly occurred to me that I, too, would like to have a wife. Why do I want a wife?

I would like to go back to school so that I can become economically independent, support myself, and, if need be, support those dependent upon me. I want a wife who will work and send me to school. And while I am going to school I want a wife to take care of my children. I want a wife to keep track of the children's doctor and dentist appointments. And to keep track of mine, too. I want a wife to make sure my children eat properly and are kept clean. I want a wife who will wash the children's clothes and keep them mended. I want a wife who is a good nurturant° attendant to my children, who arranges for their schooling, makes sure that they have an adequate social life with their peers, takes them to the park, the zoo, etc. I want a wife who takes care of the children when they are sick, a wife who arranges to be around when the children need special care, because, of course, I cannot miss classes at school. My wife must arrange to lose time at work and not lose the job. It may mean a small cut in my wife's income from time to time, but I guess I can tolerate that. Needless to say, my wife will arrange and pay for the care of the children while my wife is working.

I want a wife who will take care of *my* physical needs. I want a wife who will keep my house clean. A wife who will pick up after my children, a wife who will pick up after me. I want a wife who will keep my clothes clean, ironed, mended, replaced when need be, and who will see to it that my personal things are kept in their proper place so that I can find what I need the minute I need it. I want a wife who cooks the meals, a wife who is a *good* cook. I want a wife who will plan the menus, do the necessary grocery shopping, prepare the meals, serve them pleasantly, and then do the cleaning up while I do my studying. I want a wife who will care for me when I am sick and sympathize with my pain and loss of time from school. I want a wife to go along when our family takes a vacation so that someone can continue to care for me and my children when I need a rest and change of scene.

I want a wife who will not bother me with rambling complaints about a wife's duties. But I want a wife who will listen to me when I feel the need to explain a rather difficult point I have come across in my course of studies.

I want a wife who will take care of the details of my social life. When my wife and I are invited out by my friends, I want a wife who will take care of the babysitting arrangements. When I meet people at school that I like and want to entertain, I want a wife who will have the house clean, will prepare a special meal, serve it to me and my friends, and not interrupt when I talk about things that interest me and my friends. I want a wife who will have arranged that the children are fed and ready for bed before my guests arrive so that the children do not bother us. I want a wife who takes care of the needs of my guests so that they feel comfortable, who makes sure that they have an ashtray, that they are passed the hors d'oeuvres, that they are offered a second helping of the food, that their wine glasses are replenished when necessary, that their coffee is served to them as they like it. And I want a wife who knows that sometimes I need a night out by myself.

I want a wife who is sensitive to my sexual needs, a wife who makes love passionately and eagerly when I feel like it, a wife who makes sure that I am satisfied. And, of course, I want a wife who will not demand sexual attention when I am not in the mood for it. I want a wife who assumes the complete responsibility for birth control, because I do not want more children. I want a wife who will remain sexually faithful to me so that I do not have to clutter up

nurturant: Kind, loving, nourishing.

my intellectual life with jealousies. And I want a wife who understands that *my* sexual needs may entail more than strict adherence to monogamy. I must, after all, be able to relate to people as fully as possible.

If, by chance, I find another person more suitable as a wife than the wife I already have, I want the liberty to replace my present wife with another one. Naturally, I will expect a fresh, new life; my wife will take the children and be solely responsible for them so that I am left free. 8

When I am through with school and have a job, I want my wife to quit working and remain at home so that my wife can more fully and completely take care of a wife's duties. 9

My God, who *wouldn't* want a wife? 10

Questions to Start You Thinking

1. **Considering Meaning:**   How does Brady define the traditional role of the wife? Does she think that a wife should perform all of the duties she outlines? How can you tell?

2. **Identifying Writing Strategies:**   How does Brady use observation to support her stand? What other approaches does she use?

3. **Reading Critically:**   What is the tone of this essay? How does Brady establish it? Considering that she was writing for a predominantly female—and feminist—audience, do you think Brady's tone is appropriate?

4. **Expanding Vocabulary:**   Why does Brady use such simple language in this essay? What is the effect of her use of such phrases as *of course* (paragraph 2), *Needless to say* (paragraph 3), and *Naturally* (paragraph 8)?

5. **Making Connections:**   How do you think Brady would respond to Cheryl Mendelson's "domestic routine" (paragraph 1) in "My Secret Life" (pp. 545–47)? Compare and contrast Brady's version of a house-wife with Mendelson's.

Journal Prompts

1. Exert your wishful thinking—describe your ideal mate.

2. Begin with a stereotype of a husband, wife, boyfriend, girlfriend, father, or mother, and write a satirical description of that stereotype.

Suggestions for Writing

1. In a short personal essay, explain what you want or expect in a wife, husband, or life partner. Do your hopes and expectations differ from social and cultural norms? If so, in what way(s)? How has your parents' relationship shaped your attitudes and ideals?

2. How has the role of a wife changed since this essay was written? Write an essay comparing and contrasting the twenty-first century wife with the kind of wife Judy Brady claims she wants.

Cheryl Mendelson
My Secret Life

Cheryl Mendelson was born in Jefferson, Pennsylvania, in 1946. She holds a PhD in philosophy from the University of Rochester and a JD from Harvard Law School. Having practiced law in New York City during the 1980s, she went on to become a professor of philosophy, most recently at Barnard. She has published essays on ethical theory in addition to novels and nonfiction. Her works include comprehensive guides to home life and expert motherhood, *Home Comforts: The Art and Science of Keeping House* (1999) as well as *Laundry: The Home Comforts Book of Caring for Clothes and Linens* (2005). Her Morningside Heights trilogy of novels examines the family in a larger social context. In this selection from *Home Comforts,* she discusses the pleasures of domesticity.

For more about Cheryl Mendelson, visit **<bedfordstmartins .com/bedguide>**.

AS YOU READ: Consider your own perceptions and assumptions about housework. How do they compare with Mendelson's characterization of domestic chores?

I am a working woman with a secret life: I keep house. An off-and-on lawyer and professor in public, in private I launder and clean, cook from the hip, and devote serious time and energy to a domestic routine not so different from the one that defined my grandmothers as "housewives." When I want a good read, I reach for my collection of old housekeeping manuals. The part of me that enjoys housekeeping and the comforts it provides is central to my character.   1

Until now, I have almost entirely concealed this passion for domesticity.° No one meeting me for the first time would suspect that I squander° my time knitting or my mental reserves remembering household facts such as the date when the carpets and mattresses were last rotated. Without thinking much about it, I knew I would not want this information about me to get around. After all, I belong to the first generation of women who worked more than they stayed home. We knew that no judge would credit the legal briefs of a housewife, no university would give tenure° to one, no corporation would promote one, and no one who mattered would talk to one at a party.   2

... But most men and many women do not want to identify themselves with homes that they create through their housekeeping and through which they offer of themselves to others.   3

---

domesticity: Home life and household activities.   **squander:** Waste.   **tenure:** Status granted to teachers or professors, often after a probationary period, that protects them from dismissal except for gross incompetence or misconduct.

Their attitudes may have been learned originally at home, but they are 4 constantly reinforced by the media. Advertisements and television programs offer degraded images of household work and workers. Discussions of the subject in magazines and newspapers follow a standard formula. The author confesses either to hating housework or to incompetence at it, jokes about the childish and mischievous aspects of poor housekeeping, then produces a list of "timesaving hints." It is scarcely surprising, then, that so many people imagine housekeeping to be boring, frustrating, repetitive, unintelligent drudgery. I cannot agree. (In fact, having kept house, practiced law, taught, and done many other sorts of work, low- and high-paid, I can assure you that it is actually lawyers who are most familiar with the experience of unintelligent drudgery.) And I am convinced that such attitudes toward housekeeping are needlessly self-defeating. You can be male and domestic. You can have a career and be domestic. You can enjoy keeping house. No one is too superior or intelligent to care for hearth° and home.

Domesticity does not take time or effort but helps save both. It is just an 5 orientation that gives you a sixth sense about the place you live in, and helps you keep it running with the same kind of unconscious and effortless actions that keep you from falling when you walk down stairs. This sixth sense lets you do things fast and cut the right corners, and helps you foresee and forestall the minor domestic disasters—spills, shortages, and conflicts—that can make life miserable when they accumulate. When it is absent, you are like an infant negotiating a flight of stairs for the first time. It feels hard and complicated. You have to focus your whole mind on it, and it wears you out.

Modern housekeeping, despite its bad press, is among the most thoroughly pleasant, significant, and least alienated forms of work that many of us will encounter even if we are blessed with work outside the home that we like. Once, it was so physically onerous° and arduous° that it not infrequently contributed to a woman's total physical breakdown. Today, laundry, cleaning, and other household chores are by and large physically light or moderate work that doctors often recommend to people for their health, as evidence shows that housework is good for weight control and healthy hearts.

Seen from the outside, housework can look like a Sisyphean task that 7 gives you no sense of reward or completion. Yet housekeeping actually offers more opportunities for savoring achievement than almost any other work I can think of. Each of its regular routines brings satisfaction when it is completed. These routines echo the rhythm of life, and the housekeeping rhythm is the rhythm of the body. You get satisfaction not only from the sense of order, cleanliness, freshness, peace and plenty restored, but from the knowl-

---

hearth: The floor of or in front of a fireplace, usually associated with domestic life and comfort.   **onerous:** Heavy, troublesome.   **arduous:** Difficult, requiring great energy and effort.

edge that you yourself and those you care about are going to enjoy these benefits.

Questions to Start You Thinking

1. **Considering Meaning:** How does our society and our popular culture view housework and those who do it, according to Mendelson? What is the effect of these cultural attitudes?

2. **Identifying Writing Strategies:** Who is Mendelson's intended audience for this essay? How can you tell?

3. **Reading Critically:** Mendelson argues that negative attitudes toward housework "are constantly reinforced by the media" (paragraph 4). How does she support this argument? Do you find her approach persuasive? Why or why not?

4. **Expanding Vocabulary:** According to Mendelson, housekeeping is "among the most thoroughly pleasant, significant, and least alienated forms of work that many of us will encounter" (paragraph 6). What does *alienated* mean in this context? How does it help make her point?

5. **Making Connections:** How does Mendelson's characterization of domesticity differ from that of Judy Brady in "I Want a Wife" (pp. 542–44)?

Journal Prompts

1. Do you have a "secret life" of any kind: a passion, a hobby, an aspect of your personality that you keep hidden?

2. What domestic chores do you do for yourself or others? How do you view this work? How has Mendelson's essay affected your attitude?

Suggestions for Writing

1. "My Secret Life" defends housekeeping as satisfying work. What work or activity gives you personal satisfaction? Write a personal essay describing this activity and its relationship to your life and identity.

2. In paragraph 4, Mendelson claims that the media reinforces negative attitudes toward housework. Identify and analyze some pop culture or media examples that illustrate prevailing attitudes toward domestic work and those who do it. Do they support Mendelson's argument or refute it? Explain your answer in an essay.

Linda Babcock and Sara Laschever
Low Goals and Safe Targets

Linda Babcock grew up in Altadena, California, earning a bachelor's degree from the University of California at Irvine and eventually both her master's and PhD in economics from the University of Wisconsin at Madison. Her work on negotiation and dispute resolution has appeared in prominent economics journals as well as the *New York Times*.
Sara Laschever grew up in New Jersey and Connecticut, earning a bachelor's degree in English literature from Princeton University and a master's degree in creative writing from Boston University. In addition to her extensive work as writer and editor, she explored barriers to women's careers in science as research associate and principal interviewer for *Project Access*. This selection is excerpted from Babcock and Laschever's book *Women Don't Ask: Negotiation and the Gender Divide* (2003), which discusses structural and social forces that affect women's negotiation skills in the workplace.

AS YOU READ: What practical advice do Babcock and Laschever provide about negotiating?

For more about Linda Babcock and Sara Laschever, visit **<bedfordstmartins.com/bedguide>**.

Goals, Goals, Goals

Delia and John, both medical researchers with Ph.D.s, were hired by the same medical school at the same time, right out of graduate school. They were both offered the same starting salaries and the same basic budgets to set up their labs. Delia negotiated and successfully raised both her salary and her budget a modest amount. John also negotiated for a higher salary and bigger budget, but he asked for more than Delia asked for—and got more. In addition, John asked for a salary for a full-time research assistant. Having both the bigger budget and the regular assistant boosted John's research productivity substantially. As a result, he was promoted more rapidly than Delia, and the gap between their salaries widened even further.

Why do men outperform women in negotiations? Targets—the goals men and women take into negotiations—have been shown to make a critical difference (Riley, Babcock, & McGinn, 2003; Stevens, Bavetta, & Gist, 1993). John went into his negotiation aiming to get more than Delia aimed to get, he asked for more, and he got more. Extensive research on the relationship between goal-setting and performance—for example, among dieters and recovering addicts—has found that setting concrete, challenging goals consistently improves results (Locke & Latham, 1990). Research confirms that this is true for negotiating as well: People who go into negotiations with more ambitious targets tend to get more of what they want than people who go in with more moderate goals. In the Ivy League MBA study mentioned above, Linda and her colleagues observed that a 30 percent increase in a person's goal going into a negotiation produced, at a minimum, a 10 percent increase in the negotiated amount he or she was able to obtain (Riley et al., 2003). This means that if one person goes into a salary negotiation with a target of $50,000, for example, and another goes in with a target of $65,000 (which is 30 percent higher), the person hoping to get $50,000 might get $50,000, but the other person, who aimed higher, would have a good chance of coming away with $55,000 (10 percent more).

Higher targets have been shown to improve negotiation outcomes for two reasons: They influence the "first offer" a person makes in a negotiation and they influence how quickly or slowly a person concedes from his or her opening position. A first offer is like an opening move in a chess game—it signals a player's intentions, gives an idea of what kind of player he or she is, and sets the stage for everything that follows. First offers play a critical role in producing good negotiated outcomes because they influence the other negotiators' expectations for what you will accept and provide a starting point for the interaction. They also tend to lead to higher final agreements. The impact of higher targets on first offers was demonstrated by another study Linda conducted with Hannah Riley and Kathleen McGinn in which they found a direct one-to-one correlation between targets and first offers—meaning that each dollar increase in a person's goal translated into an increase in his or her first offer of about a dollar. So the higher the goal, the higher the first offer, and the higher the first offer, the higher the likely negotiated settlement (Riley et al., 2003).

Setting high goals is also important because a lack of ambitious goals contributes to another negotiation misstep particularly common among women: conceding too much and conceding too quickly. Someone with relatively modest goals often makes concessions faster than someone with higher goals, who will frequently hold out longer to get more (Galinsky, Mussweiler, & Medvec, 2002; White & Neale, 1994). People who go into a negotiation thinking only about their "bottom line"—the minimum they will accept—may concede as soon as they receive an offer equal or close to that bottom line (Galinsky et al., 2002).

Carol, 38, a doctor, described negotiating with her husband when they bought the house in which they live. "There were two houses that I liked," she explained:

> I liked the house that we bought, and I liked another house. I had narrowed it down to the two, and in retrospect over time it's become clear to me that we probably would have been better off in that other house just because of some of the things it offered that ours doesn't have . . . but my husband really didn't like the other house and he really wanted the one that we got, and so we went with it. But you know, I kind of wonder if I should have fought harder for that other house. . . . I did not persist at all. . . . I was happy that he liked one of the five that I had picked.

Carol's goal and bottom line going into this negotiation had been the same: merely for her husband to agree to buy one of the houses she liked. If she had set a higher goal—for him to recognize and consider the comparative virtues of each choice or to understand her reasons for preferring one of the houses over the others—she might not have conceded so quickly. She might also have come away with a superior outcome and been spared, years later, the regret of realizing that they might have made a better choice.

In contrast, people who go into a negotiation focusing on the top amount   7
they'd like to earn or the best possible outcome tend to hold out longer
(Galinsky et al., 2002). Kirk, a television producer, moved from Chicago to a
smaller city in the Pacific Northwest when his wife changed jobs. Because of
his talent and experience, he quickly found himself at one of the major network affiliates talking to the station manager about a job. Kirk had won several prizes for his work in Chicago, but he knew that this was a smaller television market and he might not be able to earn as much as he'd been making
before. But he also knew that the station was engaged in a fierce battle for
market share with its competitors and that the station manager really wanted
to hire him. So he asked for $85,000, thinking he'd probably get $60,000 or at
most $70,000. When the station manager seemed to balk, instead of conced-
ing, Kirk said, "That's what the market is telling me I can get right now." The
station manager leaned back in his chair, scratched his head, and finally said,
"Okay, I'll give it to you. I think you're worth it." If Kirk had asked for less, obviously he would have gotten less, and if he'd backed down when the station
manager resisted his original figure, he would have gotten less too. He later
learned that he was making $25,000 more than any other producer at the sta-
tion. Although Kirk's credentials undoubtedly accounted for some of this difference, both the high target he took into his negotiation with the station
manager and his resistance to conceding surely made a big difference as well.

Why the Differences?

We know that women typically set less aggressive goals than men, make more   8
modest first offers (Barron, 2003), and concede more rapidly. One of Linda's
studies with Hannah Riley and Kathleen McGinn found male negotiators
setting goals that were about 15 percent more aggressive than those of female negotiators in comparable circumstances (Riley et al., 2003). Looking
simply at the salary realm (although setting high targets produces better results in almost any type of negotiation), the consistency with which women's
lower goals limit how much women are paid has persuaded some researchers
that the gender gap in wages could be all but eliminated if men and women
were to set comparable goals (Stevens et al., 1993).

But why does this happen? We've already discussed some of the causes: 9
Women frequently feel unsure about what they deserve, worry that asking for
too much may threaten a relationship, or fear that the people around them
will react badly if they ask for too much. In addition, women tend to be less optimistic than men about what they can get from a negotiation. They also feel
less comfortable than men with risk taking and often lack confidence in their
negotiating ability—making them ask only for things that will be easy to get.

The sources for
Babcock and
Laschever's study
are presented in
APA style.

References

Barron, L. A. (2003). Ask and you shall receive? Gender differences in negotiator's beliefs about requests for a higher salary. *Human Relations, 56(6)*,
635–662.

Galinsky, A., Mussweiler, T., & Medvec, V. H. (2002). Disconnecting outcomes and evaluations: The role of negotiator reference points. *Journal of Personality and Social Psychology, 83(5),* 1131–1140.

Locke, E. A., & Latham, G. (1990). *A theory of goal setting and task performance.* Englewood Cliffs, NJ: Prentice Hall.

Riley, H. C., Babcock, L., & McGinn, K. (2003). Gender as a situational phenomenon in negotiation. Unpublished manuscript, Carnegie Mellon University, Pittsburgh, PA.

Stevens, C. K., Bavetta, A. G., & Gist, M. E. (1993). Gender differences in the acquisition of salary negotiation skills: The role of goals, self-efficacy, and perceived control. *Journal of Applied Psychology, 78(5),* 723–735.

White, S. B., & Neale, M. A. (1994). The role of negotiator aspirations and settlement expectancies in bargaining outcomes. *Organizational Behavioral and Human Decision Processes, 57,* 303–317.

Questions to Start You Thinking

1. **Considering Meaning:**   What is the relationship between targets and the outcome of negotiations?

2. **Identifying Writing Strategies:**   How does the opening paragraph establish the overall structure and purpose of this reading?

3. **Reading Critically:**   To what extent do the causal relationships presented by the authors seem logical, well substantiated, and fair?

4. **Expanding Vocabulary:**   According to Babcock and Laschever, some researchers believe that "the gender gap in wages could be all but eliminated if men and women were to set comparable goals" (paragraph 8) with regard to salary negotiations. What is the *gender gap*?

5. **Making Connections:**   How might Robert Jensen ("The High Cost of Manliness," pp. 532–35) respond to the research and arguments in "Low Goals and Safe Targets"? How would he perceive men's more effective negotiating skills?

Link to the Paired Essay

How are men and women characterized in Babcock and Laschever's essay and Michael Gurian's "Disappearing Act: Where Have the Men Gone? No Place Good" (pp. 552–56)? What accounts for the differences? In your opinion, which essay seems more relevant or compelling? Why?

Journal Prompts

1. Recount an experience that you have had negotiating with someone, such as a parent, teacher, friend, or boss. What was the outcome? How do you assess your skill as a negotiator?

2. Babcock and Laschever maintain that setting goals improves outcomes (paragraph 2). Do you tend to set specific goals in your life? In what ways does your experience support or challenge the authors' claim?

Suggestions for Writing

1. Over the past two decades, many popular books have provided advice on how to negotiate well. Write your own brief guide to negotiating, based on your own perceptions and experiences.

2. Near the end of the reading, Babcock and Laschever propose several possible reasons for gender disparity in negotiation strategies, including differences in risk taking (paragraph 9). What factors — biological, cultural, economic, historical — do you see as affecting the way men and women negotiate differently? Write an essay using further reading and research to support your position.

For more about Michael Gurian, visit <**bedfordstmartins .com/bedguide**>.

Michael Gurian

Disappearing Act: Where Have the Men Gone? No Place Good

Michael Gurian has worked as a family therapist, corporate consultant, and educator at Gonzaga University, Eastern Washington University, and Ankara University. He is a cofounder of the Gurian Institute, which focuses on using neurobiology research in schools, corporations, and public policy. Much of his research and writing is in the area of neurobiological gender difference. His twenty-five books, published in twenty-one languages, include *The Minds of Boys: Saving Our Sons from Falling Behind in School and Life* (2005), *Nurture the Nature: Understanding and Supporting Your Child's Unique Core Personality* (2007), and *The Purpose of Boys: Helping Our Sons Find Meaning, Significance, and Direction in Their Lives* (2009). In the following essay for the *Washington Post,* Gurian alerts readers to the troubling way society treats boys in school.

AS YOU READ: How does Gurian characterize today's young men? What specific qualities do they have?

In the 1990s, I taught for six years at a small liberal arts college in Spokane, Wash. In my third year, I started noticing something that was happening right in front of me. There were more young women in my classes than young men, and on average, they were getting better grades than the guys. Many of the young men stared blankly at me as I lectured. They didn't take notes as well as the young women. They didn't seem to care as much about what I taught — literature, writing and psychology. They were bright kids, but many of their faces said, "Sitting here, listening, staring at these words — this is not really who I am."   1

That was a decade ago, but just last month, I spoke with an administrator at Howard University in the District. He told me that what I observed a decade ago has become one of the "biggest agenda items" at Howard. "We are   2 having trouble recruiting and retaining male students," he said. "We are at about a 2-to-1 ratio, women to men."

Howard is not alone. Colleges and universities across the country are grappling with the case of the mysteriously vanishing male. Where men once dominated, they now make up no more than 43 percent of students at American institutions of higher learning, according to 2003 statistics, and this downward trend shows every sign of continuing unabated.° If we don't reverse it soon, we will gradually diminish° the male identity, and thus the productivity and the mission, of the next generation of young men, and all the ones that follow.

The trend of females overtaking males in college was initially measured in 1978. Yet despite the well-documented disappearance of ever more young men from college campuses, we have yet to fully react to what has become a significant crisis. Largely, that is because of cultural perceptions about males and their societal role. Many times a week, a reporter or other media person will ask me: "Why should we care so much about boys when men still run everything?"

It's a fair and logical question, but what it really reflects is that our culture is still caught up in old industrial images. We still see thousands of men who succeed quite well in the professional world and in industry — men who get elected president, who own software companies, who make six figures selling cars. We see the Bill Gateses° and John Robertses° and George Bushes — and so we're not as concerned as we ought to be about the millions of young men who are floundering or lost.

But they're there: The young men who are working in the lowest-level (and most dangerous) jobs instead of going to college. Who are sitting in prison instead of going to college. Who are staying out of the long-term marriage pool because they have little to offer to young women. Who are remaining adolescents, wasting years of their lives playing video games for hours a day, until they're in their thirties, by which time the world has passed many of them by.

The old industrial promise — "That guy will get a decent job no matter what" — is just that, an old promise. So is the old promise that a man will be able to feed his family and find personal meaning by "following in his father's footsteps," which has vanished for millions of males who are not raised with fathers or substantial role models. The old promise that an old boys' network will always come through for "the guys" is likewise gone for many young men who have never seen and will never see such a network (though they may see a dangerous gang). Most frightening, the old promise that schools will take care of boys and educate them to succeed is also breaking down, as boys dominate the failure statistics in our schools, starting at the elementary level and continuing through high school.

---

unabated: Without losing force.   **diminish:** Lessen, make smaller.   **Bill Gates:** Founder of the Microsoft corporation.   **John Roberts:** Chief Justice of the United States Supreme Court.

Of course, not every male has to go to college to succeed, to be a good   8
husband, to be a good and productive man. But a dismal future lies ahead
for large numbers of boys in this generation who will not go to college. Statistics show that a young man who doesn't finish school or go to college in
2005 will likely earn less than half what a college graduate earns. He'll be
three times more likely to be unemployed and more likely to be homeless.
He'll be more likely to get divorced, more likely to engage in violence against
women and more likely to engage in crime. He'll be more likely to develop
substance abuse problems and to be a greater burden on the economy, statistically, since men who don't attend college pay less in Social Security and
other taxes, depend more on government welfare, are more likely to father
children out of wedlock and are more likely not to pay child support.

When I worked as a counselor at a federal prison, I saw these statistics up   9
close. The young men and adult males I worked with were mainly uneducated, had been raised in families that didn't promote education, and had
found little of relevance in the schools they had attended. They were passionate people, capable of great love and even possible future success. Many of
them told me how much they wanted to get an education. At an intuitive
level, they knew how important it was.

Whether in the prison system, in my university classes or in the schools   10
where I help train teachers, I have noticed a systemic problem with how we
teach and mentor boys that I call "industrial schooling," and that I believe is
a primary root of our sons' falling behind in school, and quite often in life.

Two hundred years ago, realizing the necessity of schooling millions of   11
kids, we took them off the farms and out of the marketplace and put them in
large industrial-size classrooms (one teacher, 25 to 30 kids). For many kids,
this system worked—and still works. But from the beginning, there were
some for whom it wasn't working very well. Initially, it was girls. It took more
than 150 years to get parity° for them.

Now we're seeing what's wrong with the system for millions of boys. Be-   12
ginning in very early grades, the sit-still, read-your-book, raise-your-hand-
quietly, don't-learn-by-doing-but-by-taking-notes classroom is a worse fit for
more boys than it is for most girls. This was always the case, but we couldn't
see it 100 years ago. We didn't have the comparative element of girls at par in
classrooms. We taught a lot of our boys and girls separately. We educated
children with greater emphasis on certain basic educational principles that
kept a lot of boys "in line"—competitive learning was one. And our families
were deeply involved in a child's education.

Now, however, the boys who don't fit the classrooms are glaringly clear.   13
Many families are barely involved in their children's education. Girls outperform boys in nearly every academic area. Many of the old principles of education are diminished. In a classroom of 30 kids, about five boys will begin to
fail in the first few years of pre-school and elementary school. By fifth grade,

parity: Equality.

they will be diagnosed as learning disabled, ADD°/ADHD,° behaviorally disordered or "unmotivated." They will no longer do their homework (though they may say they are doing it), they will disrupt class or withdraw from it, they will find a few islands of competence (like video games or computers) and overemphasize those.

Boys have a lot of Huck Finn° in them — they don't, on average, learn as 14 well as girls by sitting still, concentrating, multitasking, listening to words. For 20 years, I have been taking brain research into homes and classrooms to show teachers, parents and others how differently boys and girls learn. Once a person sees a PET or SPECT scan of a boy's brain and a girl's brain, showing the different ways these brains learn, they understand. As one teacher put it to me, "Wow, no wonder we're having so many problems with boys."

Yet every decade the industrial classroom becomes more and more pro- 15 tective of the female learning style and harsher on the male, yielding statistics such as these:

The majority of academic scholarships go to girls and young women.   16

Boys and young men comprise the majority of high school dropouts, as 17 high as 80 percent in many cities.

Boys and young men are 1 1/2 years behind girls and young women in 18 reading ability (this gap does not even out in high school, as some have argued, a male reading/writing gap continues into college and the workplace).

The industrial classroom is one that some boys do fine in, many boys just 19 "hang on" in, many boys fall behind in, many boys fail in, and many boys drop out of. The boys who do fine would probably do fine in any environment, and the boys who are hanging on and getting by will probably reemerge later with some modicum° of success, but the millions who fall behind and fail will generally become the statistics we saw earlier.

Grasping the mismatch between the minds of boys and the industrial 20 classroom is only the first step in understanding the needs of our sons. Lack of fathering and male role models take a heavy toll on boys, as does lack of attachment to many family members (whether grandparents, extended families, moms or dads). Our sons are becoming very lonely. And even more politically difficult to deal with. The boys-are-privileged-but-the-girls-are-shortchanged emphasis of the last 20 years (an emphasis that I, as a father of two daughters and an advocate of girls, have seen firsthand), has muddied the water for child development in general, pitting funding for girls against funding for boys.

We still barely see the burdens our sons are carrying as we change from an 21 industrial culture to a post-industrial one. We want them to shut up, calm down and become perfect intimate partners. It doesn't matter too much who boys and men are — what matters is who we think they should be. When I think back to the kind of classroom I created for my college students, I feel

---

ADD: Attention Deficit Disorder.   **ADHD:** Attention Deficit Hyperactivity Disorder.
Huck Finn: Footloose title character of Mark Twain's novel *The Adventures of Huckleberry Finn*.   **modicum:** Small amount.

regret for the males who dropped out. When I think back to my time working in the prison system, I feel a deep sadness for the present and future generations of boys whom we still have time to save.

And I do think we can save them. I get hundreds of e-mails and letters 22 every week, from parents, teachers and others who are beginning to realize that we must do for our sons what we did for our daughters in the industrialized schooling system—realize that boys are struggling and need help. These teachers and parents are part of a social movement—a boys' movement that started, I think, about 10 years ago. It's a movement that gets noticed for brief moments by the media (when Columbine° happened, when Laura Bush talked about boys) and then goes underground again. It's a movement very much powered by individual women—mainly mothers of sons—who say things to me like the e-mailers who wrote, "I don't know anyone who doesn't have a son struggling in school," or, "I thought having a boy would be like having a girl, but when my son was born, I had to rethink things."

We all need to rethink things. We need to stop blaming, suspecting and 23 overly medicating our boys, as if we can change this guy into the learner we want. When we decide—as we did with our daughters—that there isn't anything inherently wrong with our sons, when we look closely at the system that boys learn in, we will discover these boys again, for all that they are. And maybe we'll see more of them in college again.

Questions to Start You Thinking

1. **Considering Meaning:**   What problems face men who do not finish high school or go to college, according to Gurian? Does he suggest that every male should go to college?

2. **Identifying Writing Strategies:**   In paragraph 6, Gurian uses a series of sentence fragments. Why do you think he does this? What effect do they have?

3. **Reading Critically:**   Why is this disparity between males and females occurring now, according to Gurian, rather than earlier? How does he explain the origins of the problem?

4. **Expanding Vocabulary:**   Gurian writes that as a counselor in a federal prison, he worked with young men and adult males. Most were uneducated yet, "at an intuitive level," well aware of the importance of education (paragraph 9). What does *intuitive* mean in this context? Why is it significant to Gurian's larger point?

5. **Making Connections:**   In "The High Cost of Manliness" (pp. 532–35), Robert Jensen also addresses problems men face with the very concept of masculinity. How are his views of men similar to Gurian's? How are they different?

Columbine: A Colorado high school where two seniors shot and killed twelve students in 1999.

Link to the Paired Essay

Linda Babcock and Sara Laschever ("Low Goals and Safe Targets," pp. 548–51) analyze how differences in negotiating styles lead to gender gaps in income, property ownership, and leisure time. How would Gurian respond to their evidence and their overall argument? How does Gurian's tone differ from that of Babcock and Laschever? To what extent does that difference in tone reflect a difference in purpose?

Journal Prompts

1. Gurian worries about the lack of role models and mentors for young men. Who are your role models? How have they affected your life? Can a role model be someone of a gender other than your own?

2. Gurian describes disengaged and bored students, especially boys who do not fit into the "sit-still, read-your-book, raise-your-hand-quietly, don't-learn-by-doing" method of instruction (paragraph 12). In what respects do his observations match your own? Do you see — or identify with — students like this?

Suggestions for Writing

1. According to Gurian, our society pits resources for girls against resources for boys to the detriment of young males. Do you agree with Gurian? Write a personal essay explaining why or why not.

2. Gurian claims that "the industrial classroom becomes more and more protective of the female learning style and harsher on the male" (paragraph 15). After further reading and research, write an essay that examines learning styles in relation to gender.

Responding to an Image

Read this comic strip frame by frame, and summarize its basic story. What is the significance of its title? Overall, what is the comic strip's purpose? How does it combine text and visual images to comment on our ability to counter the effects of advertising? Why do you think the writer/artist chose to convey her message through a comic strip?

Web Search

Visit adflip <www.adflip.com>, a site that archives both classic and modern print advertisements. Click on "Current Ads," and choose one that interests you. Then search one of the site's classic-ad collections, looking for a similar product from a different decade. Compare and contrast the two ads. How do their visual and written components differ? What techniques or appeals do the advertisers use to sell the products? What does each ad reveal about the culture of its decade or about its intended audience? Write an essay using specific details from the ads to support your thesis or main idea about the pair.

For reading activities linked to this chapter, visit **<bedfordstmartins .com/bedguide>**.

Stephen King
Why We Crave Horror Movies

Stephen King was born in 1947 in Portland, Maine, and attended the University of Maine at Orono. He now lives in Bangor, Maine, where he writes his best-selling horror novels, many of which have been made into popular movies. The prolific King is also the author of screenplays, teleplays, short fiction, essays, e-books, and (under the pseudonym Richard Bachman) novels. His well known horror novels include *Carrie* (1974), *Firestarter* (1980), *Pet Sematary* (1983), *Misery* (1987), *The Green Mile* (1996), *Wizard and Glass* (1997), and *Hearts in Atlantis* (1999). His recent books include *On Writing: A Memoir of the Craft* (2000), the novels *Cell* (2006) and *Lisey's Story* (2006), and the final installments of his epic fantasy series *The Dark Tower,* which he is currently adapting into a comic-book series for Marvel. Since 2003, King has also written a regular column on pop culture for *Entertainment Weekly.* In the following essay, first published in *Playboy* in December 1981, King draws on his extensive experience with horror to explain the human craving to be frightened.

For more about Stephen King, visit **<bedfordstmartins .com/bedguide>**.

AS YOU READ: Identify the needs that King says horror movies fulfill for viewers.

I think that we're all mentally ill; those of us outside the asylums only hide it 1 a little better—and maybe not all that much better, after all. We've all known people who talk to themselves, people who sometimes squinch their faces into horrible grimaces when they believe no one is watching, people who have some hysterical fear—of snakes, the dark, the tight place, the long drop . . . and, of course, those final worms and grubs that are waiting so patiently underground.

When we pay our four or five bucks and seat ourselves at tenth-row center 2 in a theater showing a horror movie, we are daring the nightmare.

Why? Some of the reasons are simple and obvious. To show that we can, 3 that we are not afraid, that we can ride this roller coaster. Which is not to say that a really good horror movie may not surprise a scream out of us at some point, the way we may scream when the roller coaster twists through a complete 360 or plows through a lake at the bottom of the drop. And horror movies, like roller coasters, have always been the special province° of the young; by the time one turns forty or fifty, one's appetite for double twists or 360-degree loops may be considerably depleted.

We also go to reestablish our feelings of essential normality; the horror 4 movie is innately conservative, even reactionary. Freda Jackson as the horrible melting woman in *Die, Monster, Die!* confirms for us that no matter how far we may be removed from the beauty of a Robert Redford or a Diana Ross, we are still light-years from true ugliness.

And we go to have fun. 5

Ah, but this is where the ground starts to slope away, isn't it? Because this 6 is a very peculiar sort of fun indeed. The fun comes from seeing others menaced — sometimes killed. One critic suggested that if pro football has become the voyeur's° version of combat, then the horror film has become the modern version of the public lynching.

It is true that the mythic, "fairy-tale" horror film intends to take away the 7 shades of gray. . . . It urges us to put away our more civilized and adult penchant° for analysis and to become children again, seeing things in pure blacks and whites. It may be that horror movies provide psychic relief on this level because this invitation to lapse into simplicity, irrationality, and even outright madness is extended so rarely. We are told we may allow our emotions a free rein . . . or no rein at all.

If we are all insane, then sanity becomes a matter of degree. If your in- 8 sanity leads you to carve up women like Jack the Ripper or the Cleveland Torso Murderer, we clap you away in the funny farm (but neither of those two amateur-night surgeons was ever caught, heh-heh-heh); if, on the other hand, your insanity leads you only to talk to yourself when you're under stress or to pick your nose on your morning bus, then you are left alone to go about your business . . . though it is doubtful that you will ever be invited to the best parties.

The potential lyncher is in almost all of us (excluding saints, past and 9 present; but then, most saints have been crazy in their own ways), and every now and then, he has to be let loose to scream and roll around in the grass. Our emotions and our fears form their own body, and we recognize that it demands its own exercise to maintain proper muscle tone. Certain of these emotional muscles are accepted — even exalted — in civilized society; they are, of course, the emotions that tend to maintain the status quo° of civilization itself. Love, friendship, loyalty, kindness — these are all the emotions that we applaud, emotions that have been immortalized in the couplets of Hallmark cards and in the verses (I don't dare call it poetry) of Leonard Nimoy.

When we exhibit these emotions, society showers us with positive rein- 10 forcement; we learn this even before we get out of diapers. When, as children, we hug our rotten little puke of a sister and give her a kiss, all the aunts and uncles smile and twit and cry, "Isn't he the sweetest little thing?" Such cov-

---

province: Area.   **voyeur:** One who takes inordinate pleasure in the act of watching.
penchant: Strong inclination.   **status quo:** Existing state of affairs.

eted treats as chocolate-covered graham crackers often follow. But if we deliberately slam the rotten little puke of a sister's fingers in the door, sanctions
follow — angry remonstrance° from parents, aunts, and uncles; instead of a
chocolate-covered graham cracker, a spanking.

But anticivilization emotions don't go away, and they demand periodic   11
exercise. We have such "sick" jokes as "What's the difference between a truckload of bowling balls and a truckload of dead babies?" (You can't unload the
truckload of bowling balls with a pitchfork . . . a joke, by the way, that I heard
originally from a ten-year-old.) Such a joke may surprise a laugh or a grin out
of us even as we recoil, a possibility that confirms the thesis: if we share a
brotherhood of man, then we also share an insanity of man. None of which is
intended as a defense of either the sick joke or insanity but merely as an explanation of [how] the best horror films, like the best fairy tales, manage to be
reactionary, anarchistic, and revolutionary all at the same time.

The mythic horror movie, like the sick joke, has a dirty job to do. It deliber-   12
ately appeals to all that is worst in us. It is morbidity unchained, our most base
instincts let free, our nastiest fantasies realized . . . and it all happens, fittingly
enough, in the dark. For those reasons, good liberals often shy away from horror films. For myself, I like to see the most aggressive of them — *Dawn of the
Dead,* for instance — as lifting a trapdoor in the civilized forebrain and throwing a basket of raw meat to the hungry alligators swimming around in that
subterranean river beneath.

Why bother? Because it keeps them from getting out, man, it keeps them   13
down there and me up here. It was Lennon and McCartney who said that all
you need is love, and I would agree with that.

As long as you keep the gators fed.   14

Questions to Start You Thinking

1. **Considering Meaning:** What does King mean when he says that
   "we're all mentally ill" (paragraph 1)? Is this a serious statement? Why,
   or why not?

2. **Identifying Writing Strategies:** How does King use analysis, breaking a complex topic into parts, to support his argument?

3. **Reading Critically:** Why do you think King uses the inclusive pronoun *we* so frequently throughout his essay? What effect does the use
   of this pronoun have on your response to his argument?

4. **Expanding Vocabulary:** Define *innately* (paragraph 4). What does
   King mean when he says horror movies are "innately conservative"?
   Does he contradict himself when he says they are also "reactionary,
   anarchistic, and revolutionary" (paragraph 11)? Why, or why not?

5. **Making Connections:** In "Black Men and Public Space" (pp. 536–38),
   Brent Staples writes about the reflexive fear and anxiety he arouses in

remonstrance: Objection.

people when walking at night. How might King's view of human nature help explain the reactions to Staples?

Journal Prompts

1. What is your response to "sick" jokes? Why?
2. Recall a movie that exercised your "anticivilization emotions" (paragraph 11). Describe your state of mind before, during, and after the movie.

Suggestions for Writing

1. What genre of movie do you prefer to watch, and why? What cravings does this type of movie satisfy?
2. Do you agree that "the horror film has become the modern version of the public lynching" (paragraph 6)? Write an argument in which you defend or refute this suggestion, citing examples from King's essay and from your own moviegoing experience to support your position.

For more about Sarah Seltzer, visit <**bedfordstmartins.com/bedguide**>.

Sarah Seltzer
The (Girl) Geek Stands Alone

Sarah Seltzer is a freelance journalist and book critic from New York City. After her graduation from Harvard, Seltzer taught English for a year in the Bronx. Her feminist writing has appeared in the *Los Angeles Times, Publishers Weekly, Alternet, The Daily Beast, The Huffington Post, BITCH, Venus Zine,* and on NPR. Her other work can be found at RHRealityCheck.org and forward.com as well as *The Christian Science Monitor, The Nation,* and *Mother Jones.* She is working on her first novel. In this essay, Seltzer uses a feminist lens to examine a seemingly trivial matter of popular culture: how "geeks" are portrayed on the screen.

AS YOU READ: Why does Seltzer's title highlight the solitude of the girl "geek" above her other qualities?

Imagine this scene from a comedy: A group of female friends sit around smoking a bowl° and working on the Wikipedia page for *Lord of the Rings.* Their fashion sense is decidedly iconoclastic° and several sport thick-rimmed glasses. Without a trace of self-consciousness, they have a hilariously ribald° discussion on the relative sexual merits of elves and orcs.

Awesome as it is, you'll never see this scene onscreen. No mainstream movie or TV series would dare group so many female nerds together—or celebrate them so unabashedly.°

1

2

bowl: Pipe used to smoke marijuana. **iconoclastic:** Attacking cherished or accepted beliefs, traditions, or ideas. **ribald:** Indecent, gross, obscenely funny. **unabashedly:** Without embarrassment.

The story is not the same for dorks with Y chromosomes, who have re-   3
cently ascended to It-Boy status thanks to the success of a clutch of slacker-
themed movies and the TV series *Beauty and the Geek.* Two new TV shows,
Chuck and *The Big Bang Theory,* also feature geek-boy main characters paired
(platonically,° for the time being) with hot women. More than ever before, a
man with a mind for useless trivia and a socially inept posse can charm nu-
bile° women and audiences alike.

A pop culture that rewards guy geeks and leaves their female counter-   4
parts isolated—and often asexual—reflects a wider culture where men are
still judged on their cerebral achievements and women on their looks. Hollywood's expansive embrace of the geek is just an extension of a classic sexist
fantasy.

Take *Beauty and the Geek.* Dubbed a "social experiment" by producer Ash-   5
ton Kutcher, the show pairs awkward, blinking male twentysomethings with
spray-tanned women who are identified as "cigar model" and "ultimate
Hooters girl," pitting them against their fellow mismatched pairs in contests
of rocket science (for the beauties) and romance (for the geeks). They're competing for a cash prize, of course, but the show's real goal is that both the
ditzy and the dorky contestants will end up gushing about how much they've
learned from each other.

Still, the show's premise that beauty and brains are mutually exclusive is   6
inherently distasteful. Rubik's Cube° proficiency, lightsaber collections, and
mad quantum physics skills catapult men onto the show; *BATG*'s legion of
geeks may be laughable when they wax lyrical about Captain Kirk,° but
they're also enthusiastic and intelligent. Their putative° partners, however,
seem to have been chosen expressly for their low IQs: "Beauty," in this show's
parlance, by necessity equates with "painful stupidity." Several of this season's contestants couldn't answer the question, "Who wrote Beethoven's
Fifth?" On the other hand, one noted that her boobs cost 8,000 bucks—and
were worth it. Based on the dropped jaws and schoolboy giggles that greeted
her appearance, the geeks seemed to agree. (Then again, it's worth questioning how much the one-sidedness displayed by both the beauties and the
geeks is embellished for the cameras. Potential contestants must be aware
that, to get on the show, they have to play up their lack of either social savvy
or smarts—the more cringe-worthy the contestants, after all, the more likely
the audience is to tune in.)

For the 2007 season, *Beauty and the Geek* added a lone female geek and   7
male beauty to their usual lineup. Sam, the handsome guy, immediately
started getting busy with one of the distaff° hotties, leaving the bespectacled
Nicole without the attention of her partner. Her presence underscored the
stereotype of the anomalous female dork: While the male geeks underwent
normalcy training together, bonding along the way, Nicole's transformation

---

platonically: Without physical or sexual desire.   **nubile:** Sexually mature and attractive.
Rubik's Cube: Mechanical puzzle popular in the 1970s and 1980s.   **Captain Kirk:** Character on the 1960s science-fiction television show *Star Trek.*   **putative:** Supposed.   **dis-
taff:** Female.

out of geekdom was solo. (Though her makeover did wow beauties and geeks alike.)

BATG hinges on the expectation that the competition will help beauties 8 learn to appreciate their own competence—even if it's just in the ancient art of hot-oil massage—and the geeks will gain social pluck. But after four seasons of socially retarded guys and pneumatic° blondes, the show's take-home isn't, "Hey, don't be so judgy." Rather, the message is that modelesque babes should look for the inner worth of all the men around them—not just the beefcake—and value them appropriately. The geek guys, however, aren't encouraged to see the beauty in one of their own. Apparently, some real-life geeks have taken that message to heart: A computer club at Washington State University recently auctioned off dates with nerds—with makeovers by sorority girls—as a step toward boosting female enrollment. (This plan was apparently more popular than the simple "reach out to girls who like computers" option.)

For the most part, it's still true that even outside the boundaries of reality 9 TV, men are judged on their merits first and their looks second, while for women, unattractiveness is a dealbreaker. There's an underlying assumption that men have something to bring to the dating pool despite their looks, while women without good looks are essentially removed from the dating pool altogether. This unfair standard is magnified onscreen, so for *BATG*'s producers to reverse genders is commercially risky—and completely necessary. Nicole herself is aware of the hurdle gals like her face, telling the *Boston Herald* that in real life "a woman would be attracted to a guy geek more so than a guy to a girl geek. . . . That is kind of a raw deal."

If the show's producers let Nicole lead the way for a new season of female 10 geeks and male beauties, or even a slightly better gender balance of geeky contestants, the show might end up being truly subversive while retaining its sweet message. As it is, the original setup has outlived any novelty it may have had: Gorgeous women selflessly nurturing awkward-but-brilliant men is a trope° that these days is all too common.

The nerdy doofus and his comely girlfriend are hardly a new pairing, but 11 filmmaker Judd Apatow has been reinvigorating this strain of male-director wish fulfillment with a vengeance. His movies epitomize what *New Yorker* critic David Denby calls the "slacker-striver" dynamic, which pairs under-achieving, sloppy heroes with ultrasuccessful women. *The 40-Year-Old Virgin* and *Knocked Up* (which Apatow directed) and *Superbad* (which he produced) all center on immature guys. The women in the films are outgoing, attractive, and have matured to the point of rejecting the college-dude sensibility that the movies themselves embrace. The female leads in both *The 40-Year-Old Virgin* and *Knocked Up* are likable, but they're at the mercy of a narrative that, as critic David Denby points out, "reduces the role of women to vehicles. Their only real function is to make the men grow up."

pneumatic: Filled with compressed air.   **trope:** Commonly used or clichéd theme or plot device.

Within the universe of Apatow's films, male geeks are occupied by mining   12
cultural annals for comedic material—they're "joke jocks," writes *Time*'s film
critic Richard Corliss, constantly trying to top each other with witty references to Cat Stevens and *Star Wars*.

Apatow's women are too bland, too non-nerdy to confront his men at a   13
level beyond exasperated chastisement.° We chuckle when they sound off,
but they're not trying to make us laugh. So while they're technically successful, they're failures within the reclaimed male confines of comedy. (Presumably, they're not smart or funny enough to compete in the joke-jock arena.)

"The Apatow dictum° . . . is that women can't aspire to equality in crack-   14
ing jokes, but guys will indulge them and let them be the receptive audience,"
writes Corliss. And these nerds do meet with a receptive audience: On chicks-
and-media blog Jezebel's thread about *Knocked Up,* for instance, commenter
after commenter gushes about how lead doofus Ben's sense of humor over-
rides his less-than-conventionally-attractive looks. Perhaps what Ben's enthusiastic fans are saying is simply that not all heroes need to look like Brad Pitt
or Denzel Washington. But there has to be a way to acknowledge that geeky
qualities can be attractive in both sexes without fetishizing° uneven—and
somewhat improbable—male-female pairings.

While current films may be a wasteland for the female nerd, a spate of   15
'90s teen movies (*Ten Things I Hate About You, She's All That, Never Been Kissed*)
featured girl geeks as protagonists. Each of these heroines was a misunderstood eccentric on a journey toward happiness—and the prom. But unlike
today's merry male *Star Wars* fanboys and hackers, these quirky girls were
angry. Julia Stiles in *10 Things* and Rachel Leigh Cook in *She's All That* both
built their characters around don't-touch-me snarls. Both teen girls wrote
and made art, but they didn't have the same enthusiasm for pencils and
brushes that male geeks might feel toward their calculator or robotics kit. Instead, their pastimes were an outlet for pain.

In the geeky girls' lives, the subsiding of that pain begins when they real-   16
ize they are romantically desirable. Stiles begins to melt as she is serenaded
by Heath Ledger from the school bleachers, and Cook blooms when she tries
on a girly dress and takes off her glasses, turning wispy and feminine. They
literally stop being nerds when conventional femininity comes to the forefront.

"There's a myth that geeky girls have to be sexually unappealing," says   17
Annalee Newitz, editor of *She's Such a Geek! Women Write About Science, Technology, and Other Nerdy Stuff.* Unlike Apatow's dudes, who are attractive because of
their geekiness, these nerd girls must overcome it to become attractive—after
which, we're meant to understand they can never go back. What's proposed as
so bizarre about a girl who willingly chooses sci-fi over stilettos is that she
knowingly rejects her prescribed social role. If being an unabashed dork is a
uniquely male province, then so are all its perks: being judged for intelligence

---

chastisement: Severe criticism.   **dictum:** Principle.   **fetishizing:** Giving something excessive, unreasonable attention or reverence.

and wit rather than looks, for one. The female dork chooses her own narrative over the narrative of a conformist society and demands to be accepted for who she is. And as punishment, pop culture robs her of her sex appeal.

The same social fear that desexualizes female dorks also robs them of [18] friends. Newitz notes that for pop-culture consumers to find actual depictions of women bonding, we have to look for cheerleading or shoe-shopping scenes. And nerd girls in movies like *Never Been Kissed* and *Mean Girls,* or TV series like *Freaks and Geeks* are invariably asked to make a Faustian° bargain wherein they trade in their nerd-girl pal for a shot at a makeover and the ascent to popularity and dates. "It's very rare that you get a posse of girl geeks," Newitz says. There's a fear, apparently, that if smart, rational girls get together, they will discover that they don't need men. Of course, as Newitz points out, when real-life dorky women gather, they're far more likely to discuss iPhones and television than to plan separatist communes. But the cultural taboo persists, keeping images of female dorks from being celebratory or even benign; they remain moody Cinderellas waiting for that invitation to the ball that will spring them from geek ignominy.°

Would the real world look different if the pop-cultural one allowed fic- [19] tional femme-nerds to embrace their dorkitude, rather than pout about it? After all, Apatow's dudes and the *BATG* geeks love the things that make them nerdy: They choose to spend all their time comparing action figures, building websites, and running around with swords in live-action role play. *Knocked Up* contains a pivotal scene in which a man sneaks out at night — not to cheat with another woman, as his wife fears, but to play fantasy sports with his buddies. *Superbad,* meanwhile, closes a raucous° night of partying with its two goofball leads cuddled side by side in sleeping bags, remnants of pizza bagels scattered around them. In real life, female geeks have those sleeping-bag parties and groups of friends who engage in obsessive pastimes, too. Those pot-smoking, Wiki-editing, *Lord of the Rings*-loving girls undoubtedly exist in more than one dorm or suburban bedroom. But girl geeks are still waiting for the day when pop culture no longer demands that their nerdiness be redeemed, transformed, or made over — but can, like the dudes', be what makes them desired.

Questions to Start You Thinking

1. **Considering Meaning:** According to Seltzer, what is the lesson of the show *Beauty and the Geek*? In what ways do you think of television shows as imparting lessons or values?

2. **Identifying Writing Strategies:** Seltzer combines different types of writing in this essay. Where does she compare and contrast?

Faustian: Sacrificing spiritual or other higher values for power or material gain.   **ignominy:** Disgrace.   **raucous:** Rowdy or disorderly.

3. **Reading Critically:**   How would you characterize the tone and style of this essay? What do they suggest about Seltzer's overall purpose, as well as her audience?

4. **Expanding Vocabulary:**   According to Seltzer, if *Beauty and the Geek* featured female geeks and male beauties or better balanced male and female geeks, the show could "end up being truly subversive while retaining its sweet message" (paragraph 10). What does *subversive* mean? How could this show become subversive?

5. **Making Connections:**   In "The High Cost of Manliness" (pp. 532–35), Robert Jensen writes that men and women behave differently—and are perceived differently—not so much because they are "fundamentally different," but because "a political system has been creating differences between men and women" (paragraph 12). Do you think Seltzer would agree with this statement? Does her essay support Jensen's argument?

Journal Prompts

1. Discussing a "reality" television show, Seltzer writes that "the more cringe-worthy the contestants, after all, the more likely the audience is to tune in" (paragraph 6). Why would the spectacle of people behaving badly or embarrassing themselves appeal to audiences?

2. In her title and throughout her essay, Seltzer uses the slang terms *geek, nerd, dork, goofball,* and *doofus,* among others. Does she mean them to be insulting? Are they offensive? Do you use them? What do they mean, exactly, and do they have other synonyms?

Suggestions for Writing

1. Seltzer suggests that the girl geek creates her own story but is punished for doing so (paragraph 17). Write a personal essay to consider whether you have chosen your own story. How does society force a "narrative" on you or suggest a "storyline" that people like you are supposed to follow?

2. "For the most part," Seltzer writes, "it's still true that even outside the boundaries of reality TV, men are judged on their merits first and their looks second, while for women, unattractiveness is a dealbreaker" (paragraph 9). Do you agree with this assertion? Write an argumentative essay that takes a stand on this issue. Support your position with your personal experience, if you wish, but also consider evidence from popular culture (as Seltzer does), business, education, or politics, using magazines, journals, or other sources.

Ruth La Ferla

Latino Style Is Cool. Oh, All Right: It's Hot

Ruth La Ferla was born in 1936, in Munich, Germany, and moved to Chicago, Illinois, with her family in 1939. She earned a bachelor's degree from Knox College and a master's degree in German literature from the University of Illinois. In 2000, she took a position at the *New York Times* as a fashion writer, publishing articles in the Thursday Styles pages and in the Sunday Lifestyle section. She has also worked as a fashion editor for *Women's Wear Daily* and *Avenue*. "Latino Style Is Cool. Oh, All Right: It's Hot" first appeared in the *New York Times* on April 15, 2001, around the time that Jennifer Lopez introduced her new clothing line, JLo. La Ferla wanted to explore the rise of Latino stars in the media and how their visibility might affect the fashion industry. During her investigation, she discovered Latino culture's proud expression of heritage through fashion.

AS YOU READ: Identify the primary characteristics of the Latino style that La Ferla describes.

For more about Ruth La Ferla, visit <bedfordstmartins .com/bedguide>.

O   n a recent Friday afternoon, Lisa Forero, her dark, shoulder-length   1
hair parted in the center, stalked the corridors of La Guardia High School of Performing Arts in Manhattan, perched on four-inch platform boots. Ms. Forero, a drama major, played up her curves in a form-fitting gray spandex dress and wore outsize gold hoops on her ears. Her fingertips were airbrushed in tints of pink and cream.

Did she fret that her image — that of a saucy bombshell — bordered on   2
self-parody? Not a bit. Dressing up as a familiar stereotype is Ms. Forero's pointedly aggressive way of claiming her Latino heritage, she says. Ms. Forero, seventeen, acknowledged that she had not always been so bold. "Two or three years ago, I didn't usually wear gold," she said, "and I usually wouldn't get my nails done. But as I've gotten older, I've needed to identify more with my cultural background."

Her sandy-haired classmate Kenneth Lamadrid, seventeen, is just as   3
brash. "Because of the way I look and because my parents called me Ken, a lot of people don't know that I'm Cuban," he said. But Mr. Lamadrid takes pains to set them straight. That afternoon, he was wearing a souvenir from a recent family reunion, a snug T-shirt emblazoned with the names of all of his relatives who have emigrated to the United States from Cuba. "I'm wearing my family history," he said. "You have to be proud of who you are."

Ms. Forero and Mr. Lamadrid are members of a population that, accord-   4
ing to the 2000 census, seems on the verge of becoming America's largest minority group. Wildly heterogeneous,° its members come from more than twenty countries and represent a mixture of races, backgrounds, and even religions. What Latinos share, as Ms. Forero well knows, is a common language — Spanish — and rapidly expanding cultural clout.°

heterogeneous: From diverse sources.   **clout:** Power.

"Hispanic is hip," she observed dryly. "Right now, it's the thing to be." In- 5
deed, in the last couple of years Latinos have been surprised and flattered to
find themselves courted as voters, consumers, workers, and entertainers. And
now many are bemused to discover that, like hip-hop–influenced African
Americans before them, they are admired as avatars° of urban chic.

"There is an emerging Latino style, and I think it appeals to more than 6
just Latinos," said Clara Rodriguez, a professor of sociology at Fordham University in Manhattan and the author of *Latin Looks: Images of Latinas and
Latinos in the U.S. Media* (Westview Press, 1997). Dr. Rodriguez made a point of
distinguishing between pervasive archetypes—the smoldering vamp, the bril-
liantined° Lothario°—and the fashion personas adopted by young urban
Hispanics, which allude to those types without aping them. These Latin Gen
X-ers are rediscovering their roots and flaunting them, she said, while communicating solidarity by the way they dress.

Rodrigo Salazar, the editor of *Urban Latino,* a general-interest magazine for 7
young Hispanics, expressed a similar view. "As we stake our claim in the culture, we are starting to take control of our own images," Mr. Salazar said.
Young, trend-conscious Latinos do that in part, he said, by experimenting with
fashion and cultivating a street-smart style that is more overtly sensual than
hip-hop and is at the same time heavily steeped in Hispanic iconography.°

Flounces, ruffles, and ear hoops are among the generic, ostentatiously° His- 8
panic symbols being tossed into a pan-Latino° blender these days. Even crosses
are part of the mix, not as a symbol of faith but as a hip accessory. Mr. Salazar
conceded that such items lend themselves to ethnic stereotyping but argued
that perhaps that is all the more reason to flaunt them. For many young Hispanics, he said, they are a visual shorthand that signals their identity.

Latino style also incorporates the provocative cropped T-shirts, low-slung 9
chinos, stacked heels, and chains that are the fashion insignia of cholos,
members of Latin street gangs. And it incorporates components of a style
adopted by young Puerto Rican New Yorkers in the late 1970s: fitted shirts in
phantasmagorical° patterns, hip-riding denims, cropped halters, blouses tied
at the midriff, navel-baring T-shirts, and platform shoes. Similar regalia sur-
vives as the style uniform of pop icons like Ricky Martin and Jennifer Lopez.

But the look is also indebted to the traditional garb favored by an earlier 10
generation of Latino immigrants. On some days, for example, Mr. Lamadrid,
the drama student, wears a guayabera, a loose multipocket shirt like the ones
his Cuban grandfather used to wear. Nowadays, the shirts, worn by many
young Hispanics as a badge of their heritage, have been appropriated by non-
Hispanics as well.

"We take our lead from the things we've seen our parents wear and the 11
things we've seen in movies," Mr. Salazar said, "but our style is evolving as

---

avatars: Perfect representations.   **brilliantined:** Hair slicked back with a shiny pomade.
Lothario: A man known for seducing women.   **iconography:** Symbolism.   **ostenta-
tiously:** Marked by showiness.   **pan-Latino:** Across Latino culture.   **phantasmagorical:**
Fantastic, as related to what is not real.

our influence is growing. We're seeing ourselves in the street, and we're following the cues of our friends and celebrities who are Latino."

Mr. Salazar was describing a cultural pastiche° that has become increasingly identifiable — and some maintain, consummately marketable. Its potential mass appeal is surely not lost on Ms. Lopez, the singer and actress, who is negotiating with Andy Hilfiger, Tommy's younger brother, to market her own brand of Latina glam in a fashion line. 12

At the same time, Latina chic is being packaged for mass consumption by some leading apparel makers. In the last several months, Ralph Lauren, Nike, Tommy Hilfiger, and the Gap have played to the current fascination with Latina exoticism in advertisements featuring variations on the full-lipped, south-of-the-border sexpot. Ralph Lauren's campaign showcases the Spanish film star Penélope Cruz in a snug top and a swirling skirt, performing what looks like flamenco. Both Guess and Sergio Valente display ads in which halter tops and rump-clutching denims encase Brazilian brunettes. And Vertigo, a midprice sportswear company, is showing its scarlet trouser suit on a raven-haired vamp, a ringer — it can't be coincidence — for a young Bianca Jagger. 13

"Our industry has become enamored with the dark, mysterious confidence that these women portray," said Steven Miska, the president of Sergio Valente. 14

Magazine editors, too, find the Latin look compelling. The March issue of Italian *Vogue,* the fashionista's bible, has a feature in which young Latino-Americans model the season's key looks. 15

Is the industry trying to market Latinness as a commodity? "Definitely," said Sam Shahid, the president and creative director of Shahid, a New York advertising agency with fashion clients. Mr. Shahid employed Hispanic models for the latest Abercrombie & Fitch catalog. "No one moves as freely," he said, then added: "Selling a Latin look doesn't mean it has to be a Carmen Miranda,° cha-cha type thing. 'Latin' can simply be a sultry sex appeal." 16

Should Mr. Hilfiger and Ms. Lopez reach an agreement, industry insiders speculate that the collection will draw heavily on Ms. Lopez's Puerto Rican heritage. "Her flash look, the stacked heels, the low-rise jeans — these things are already being emulated by people well outside the Hispanic community," said Tom Julian, a trend analyst for Fallon Worldwide, a Minneapolis branding company. 17

Deliberately packaging an urban Hispanic look for mass consumption makes sense to Mr. Julian. "Ethnicity is good in today's marketplace," he said. "All of a sudden you are talking about hair, makeup, clothing, and accessories that are part of a lifestyle that is distinctive, that has a point of view." Noting that so-called urban apparel — the streetwise casual wear favored by young blacks and Hispanics — is a $5 billion-a-year business, he ventured that a Latino subgenre could generate at least half that amount. 18

pastiche: Mixture.   **Carmen Miranda:** Brazilian singer, actress, and star of 1940s American movie musicals, noted for her outrageous costumes (including headdresses made from fruit) and thick, comic accent.

Some Hispanics bristle at the reduction of their identity to a handful of   19
styling cues, which might then be peddled as Latin chic. They are uneasy
about being lumped by outsiders into an undifferentiated cultural mass. "I
think the world would often like to describe us as a bunch of hot tamales,"
said Betty Cortina, the editorial director of *Latina,* a lifestyle magazine for
young women. "That happens to be the way many Latinas see themselves,"
she conceded, "but if our cultural identity is all wrapped up in a sexy sense of
style, then we have a lot of work to do."

Others maintain that a degree of cultural stereotyping is inevitable and   20
may not be all bad. "It's important for people to understand that within the
Latin community there is range," said Elisa Jimenez, a New York fashion designer and performance artist of part-Mexican descent. At the same time, an
attraction to certain cultural stereotypes can be positive, she asserted, if "it
inspires us to be happier, more expressive—any or all of those things that we
want to be more of."

Latino-influenced apparel and grooming are seductive to many non-   21
Latins intent on borrowing elements of a culture that they perceive as more
authentic, spontaneous, and alluring than their own. "Latin equals sexy,"
said Kim Hastreiter, the editor of *Paper,* a magazine that features a generous
sampling of Latino artists, models, fashion, film, and pop stars in its April
issue. "It's heat and a certain aliveness."

Ms. Hastreiter might have been describing Cindy Green, a New York per-   22
formance artist and the graphic design director of the DKNY fashion house.
Ms. Green flaunts acrylic-tipped nails airbrushed in hot pink and silver, a hy-
perfeminine look copied from the young Latina women she sees on her way
to work. "I'm completely obsessed with my nails," she said, adding that she is
just as much taken with the tight ponytails, dark lip liner, and extreme
makeup worn by many young Hispanic women. "I come from Ohio," she
said, "and all this is very exotic to me."

Danielle Levitt, a New York City fashion photographer, is equally besot-   23
ted. "I can't explain my attraction to things that are Latin," she said. "I think
it's the glamour." Ms. Levitt likes to pile on Latina-style gold bangles and
heart-shaped pendants. At her throat she wears an elaborate gold nameplate,
similar to those worn on the air by the stars of *Sex and the City,* a show that is
arguably influenced by Latina style.

Ms. Jimenez had never designed clothes that were identifiably Latin until   24
Kbond, a vanguard Los Angeles clothing store, asked her recently for a look
that was patently Hispanic. She responded by lopping the sleeves off a series
of ruffled men's tuxedo shirts—"tricking them out," as she put it, into "sexy
little halters" for women.

At the moment she is selling a line of sportswear steeped in Latin   25
kitsch—"La Vida Loca" T-shirts, for example, printed with the characteristi-
cally Mexican images of a rose, a pair of dice, and a skull. "It's time to get our
heritage out there," Ms. Jimenez declared with mingled defiance and mirth.
She envisions her designs teamed with uptight little handbags and immacu-
late white jeans.

Who's going to wear them?   26

"Are you kidding?" she said. "They're going to be the height of Upper   27
East Side° chic."

Questions to Start You Thinking

1. **Considering Meaning:** What are some of the reasons La Ferla gives
   for young Latino women and men adopting exotic styles associated
   with traditional Hispanic culture?

2. **Identifying Writing Strategies:** How does La Ferla use cause and
   effect in this essay? Why is this strategy particularly appropriate to her
   purpose?

3. **Reading Critically:** Skim through the essay again, paying particular
   attention to the quotations La Ferla includes—from teenage Latinos and
   Latinas, a sociology professor, fashion editors and designers, and advertising and marketing experts. Why do you think she chose to interview
   this wide variety of people? What is the effect of the many quotations?

4. **Expanding Vocabulary:** Define *allude, aping, flaunting,* and *solidarity*
   (paragraph 6). How do these words help readers understand the sources
   of contemporary Latino style?

5. **Making Connections:** According to La Ferla, as Latinos return to their
   roots (paragraph 6), the fashion industry is converting those roots to a
   commodity (paragraph 16). What are the differences or similarities
   between those who embrace "Latino chic" fashion as a source of ethnic
   pride, and Harold Taw ("Finding Prosperity by Feeding Monkeys,"
   pp. 628–29), who honors his native country's traditions and rituals by
   feeding monkeys?

Journal Prompts

1. What do you identify as your cultural or ethnic heritage? How does this
   identification contribute to your personal style? (Keep in mind that
   your personal style may be a reaction against your family heritage.)

2. How fashion conscious are you? Do you follow the latest trends, intentionally buck them, or just ignore them altogether? Why do you feel
   about fashion as you do?

Suggestions for Writing

1. Take some time to observe the different fashion choices (clothing, hairstyles, accessories, and so forth) that characterize various groups in your
   community. You might, for example, observe people on your campus, at
   a shopping center or supermarket, or, if you live in a city, simply on the

Upper East Side: An upper-class neighborhood in New York City.

street. Make notes on your observations, and then write an essay in which you classify the various styles you observed.

2. In paragraph 4, La Ferla refers to the fact that 2000 census data suggest that Hispanic residents are "on the verge of becoming America's largest minority group." Do some research about the causes of this boom in the Hispanic population and the responses it has generated among both non-Hispanics and Hispanics. Then write an essay explaining these causes and effects.

Frank Deford

NFL: Dodging the Concussion Discussion?

Benjamin "Frank" Deford III was born in 1938 in Baltimore, Maryland. After graduating from Princeton University, he began working at *Sports Illustrated*. He has written fifteen books, including one on *Sports Illustrated*'s list of Top 25 Sports Books of All Time, *Everybody's All-American* (1981), which was made into a movie. *Alex: The Life of a Child* (1983), his memoir about his daughter's struggle with cystic fibrosis, was also made into a movie in 1986 and led him to chair the Cystic Fibrosis Foundation for seventeen years. Along with his work as a journalist at *Sports Illustrated,* he has worked with National Public Radio, *Vanity Fair,* and *Newsweek,* and he was the editor in chief of *The National.* He is in the National Sportscasters and Sportswriters Hall of Fame, has been selected U.S. Sportswriter of the Year six times, and earned an Emmy for his coverage of the Seoul Olympics in 1988. In this essay, originally a broadcast for his regular NPR show *Sweetness and Light,* Deford takes the National Football League to task for turning a blind eye to players in danger.

For more about Frank Deford, visit **< bedfordstmartins .com/bedguide>**.

AS YOU READ: Do the problems Deford considers here transcend football? Is this solely a "sports" story?

Unlike baseball, basketball and ice hockey, football is strictly an all-American game. Oh, there are a few Samoans in the NFL, the odd Canadian, but unlike most popular American cultural components, football has never succeeded as an export. Either it's just our thing, like bullfighting in Spain, or other people are too smart to risk playing it.   1

Luckily for the NFL, there's no dearth° of homegrown candidates. As students head back to high school, some 1.2 million will suit up in helmets and shoulder pads.   2

But an old NFL star who suffered a few concussions asks me: "How many mothers would let their boys play football if we knew what concussions could mean when these boys get older?"   3

The fact is, we don't know for sure how dangerous our American game is to the brains of the people who play it. We do know that high school players will experience more than 40,000 concussions this season, and that boys experience greater acceleration to the head than do older players. We know that in   4

dearth: Shortage, lack.

a full season of games and practice, players endure more than 3,000 hits, and frequently these collisions are at 100 g of force, the equivalent of a car crash.

Because so many former players have been found to suffer from dementia or depression, the NFL can no longer ignore the issue, but still, the league sounds more like the tobacco companies of a few decades ago. It dismissed a study by the University of North Carolina that used essentially the same methodology as smoking-and-cancer studies. In the study, 20 percent of retired players who had had three or more concussions said they suffered from depression. 5

Basically, the NFL wants to be its own research institute, even though, bit by bit, the evidence grows that football simply is not good for the brain. 6

"Anyone who doesn't recognize the severity of the problem is in tremendous denial," says Dr. Ann McKee of Boston University's School of Medicine. McKee conducted a study on players suffering from repetitive head trauma. 7

The NYU Medical School has proposed a definitive study on early-onset dementia. It wants to sample the brainwaves of 100 NFL rookies and 100 retired players. I asked Robert Batterman, the league's labor counsel, for help obtaining the rookie subjects needed. Batterman replied with a curt e-mail, saying only that NYU was talking to the wrong former players. 8

In other words: Hey, what's the problem? Not everybody who plays football gets brain damage. Not everybody who smokes gets cancer. Alas, if NYU can't get the young players to study, it can't do the study. 9

The old player I talked to says his wife stiffens every time he forgets something or can't remember a word. And, he says: "Frank, I never stop thinking that my mind's the next one to go." 10

Questions to Start You Thinking

1. **Considering Meaning:** What is the NFL's attitude toward the possibility that head injuries are causing high rates of depression and dementia in football players?

2. **Identifying Writing Strategies:** Deford's point is that football is dangerous, but he confesses that the danger of playing football is uncertain in paragraph 4. How does the paragraph as a whole support his argument?

3. **Reading Critically:** Deford compares the NFL with pre-settlement tobacco firms (paragraph 5). What does the comparison suggest? Is this analogy accurate and effective?

4. **Expanding Vocabulary:** According to a physician in Deford's article, "Anyone who doesn't recognize the severity of the problem is in tremendous denial" (paragraph 7). What does it mean to be in denial? How is it different from merely disagreeing with a point of view or denying the validity of a claim?

5. **Making Connections:** In his essay "In Defense of Consumerism" (pp. 638–41), Llewellyn H. Rockwell Jr. argues that the free market

serves everyone. How might he respond to Deford's essay, especially now that congressional hearings could lead to government intervention in an enormously popular and profitable sports industry?

Journal Prompts

1. Do you engage in any high-risk sports or activities? How do you assess the risks? Would new information highlighting dangers change your behavior? Why, or why not?

2. How is football uniquely American, in comparison to other sports? Why has it remained at home?

Suggestions for Writing

1. After reading this essay, would you allow your child to play football? Why or why not? If continuing research concludes that football injuries significantly affect mental health and cognitive functioning, could you see banning the sport outright? Write a personal essay about your views.

2. In his short essay, Deford focuses more on the NFL's response to the "concussion controversy" than the growing evidence that football is "not good for the brain" (paragraph 6). Investigate the current research on — and discussion about — the issue; then make your own evaluation of the dangers involved. Does Deford overstate the case, or is the NFL "in denial"?

Kate Dailey and Abby Ellin

America's War on the Overweight

Kate Dailey graduated from Pennsylvania State University and Columbia University's Graduate School of Journalism. She is currently the health and lifestyle editor for *Newsweek* and also runs *Newsweek*'s blog "The Human Condition." **Abby Ellin** has a graduate degree in creative writing from Emerson College. Her work has appeared in publications such as the *New York Times, Time, Village Voice, Marie Claire, Glamour, The Daily Beast,* and the *Boston Phoenix.* She is also the author of *Teenage Waistland: A Former Fat Kid Weighs In on Living Large, Losing Weight and How Parents Can (and Can't) Help.* In this *Newsweek* essay, Dailey and Ellin grapple with the complicated issues surrounding weight and health in modern America.

AS YOU READ: According to the authors, why do so many people have a fat bias?

P ractically the minute President Obama announced Regina M. Benjamin, a zaftig° doctor who also has an M.B.A. and is the recipient of a MacArthur "genius grant," as a nominee for the post of Surgeon General, the criticism started.

For more about Kate Dailey and Abby Ellin, visit **<bedfordstmartins .com/bedguide>**.

1

zaftig: Full-bodied.

The attacks were vicious—Michael Karolchyk, owner of a Denver "anti- 2
gym," told Fox News' Neil Cavuto, "Obesity is the No. 1 issue facing our
country in terms of health and wellness, and she has shown not that she was
born this way, not that she woke up one day and was obese. She has shown
through being lazy, and making poor food choices, that she's obese."

"This is totally disgusting to have someone so big to be advocating 3
health," wrote one YouTube commenter.

The anger about Benjamin wasn't the only example of vitriol° hurled at 4
the overweight. Cintra Wilson, style columnist for *The New York Times*, recently
wrote a column so disdainful of JCPenney's plus-size mannequins that the
Times' ombudsman° later wrote that he could read "a virtual sneer" coming
through her prose. A *Newsweek* post about *Glamour's* recent plus-size model
(in fact, a normal-sized woman with a bit of a belly roll) had several com-
menters lashing out at the positive reaction the model was receiving. "This
model issue is being used as a smoke screen to justify [a] self-destructive lifestyle that cost[s] me more money in health care costs," one wrote. Health guru
MeMe Roth has made a career out of bashing fat—she called size 12 *American
Idol* Jordin Sparks a "bad role model" on national television, and derided
size 2 Jennifer Love Hewitt for having cellulite. (That Roth is considered
something of an extremist doesn't stop the media attention.) Virtually any
news article about weight that is posted online garners a slew of comments
from readers expressing disgust that people let their weight get so out of control. The specific target may change, but the words stay the same: Self-destructive. Disgusting. Disgraceful. Shameful. While the debate rages on about obesity and the best ways to deal with it, the attitudes Americans have toward
those with extra pounds are only getting nastier. Just why do Americans hate
fat people so much?

Fat bias is nothing new. "Public outrage at other people's obesity has a lot 5
to do with America from the turn of the 20th century to about World War I,"
says Deborah Levine, assistant professor of health policy and management at
Providence College. The rise of fat hatred is often seen as connected to the
changing American workplace; in the early 20th century, companies began to
offer snacks to employees, white-collar jobs became more prominent, and
fewer people exercised. As thinness became rarer, says Peter N. Stearns, author of *Fat History: Bodies and Beauty in the Modern West* and professor of history at George Mason University, it was more prized, and conversely, fatness
was more maligned.

At the same time, people also paid a lot of attention to President Taft's 6
girth; while Taft was large, he wasn't all that much heavier than earlier presidents. Newspapers questioned how his weight would affect diplomacy and
solicited the funniest "fat Taft" joke. "This [period] is also when you get
ready-to-wear clothing," says Levine. "For the first time, [people were] buying

vitriol: Abusive and bitter thought or expression.   **ombudsman:** A person who investigates problems or complaints and attempts to resolve them.

clothes in a certain size, and that encourages a comparison amongst other people." Actuarial tables° began to connect weight and shorter lifespan, and cookbooks published around World War I targeted the overweight. "There was that idea that people who were overweight were hoarding resources needed for the war effort," Levine says. She adds that early concerns were that overweight American men would not be able to compete globally, participate in international business, or win wars.

Fatness has always been seen as a slight on the American character. Ours   7
is a nation that values hard work and discipline, and it's hard for us to accept that weight could be not just a struggle of will, even when the bulk of the research—and often our own personal experience—shows that the factors leading to weight gain are much more than just simple gluttony. "There's this general perception that weight can be controlled if you have enough will-power, that it's just about calories in and calories out," says Dr. Glen Gaesser, professor of exercise and wellness at Arizona State University and author of *Big Fat Lies: The Truth About Your Weight and Your Health,* and that perception leads the nonfat to believe that the overweight are not just unhealthy, but weak and lazy. Even though research suggests that there is a genetic propensity for obesity, and even though some obese people are technically healthier than their skinnier counterparts, the perception remains "[that] it's a failure to control ourselves. It violates everything we have learned about self-control from a very young age," says Gaesser.

In a country that still prides itself on its Puritanical ideals, the fat self is   8
the "bad self," the epitome° of greed, gluttony, and sloth. "There's a wide-spread belief that fat is controllable," says Linda Bacon, author of *Health at Every Size: The Surprising Truth About Your Weight.* "So then it's unlike a disability where you can have compassion; now you can blame the individual and attribute all kinds of mean qualities to them. Then consider the thinner people that are always watching what they eat carefully—fat people are symbols of what they can become if they weren't so virtuous."

But considering that the U.S. has already become a size XL nation—   9
66 percent of adults over 20 are considered overweight or obese, according to the Centers for Disease Control—why does the stigma,° and the anger, remain?

Call it a case of self-loathing. "A lot of people struggle themselves with   10
their weight, and the same people that tend to get very angry at themselves for not being able to manage their weight are more likely to be biased against the obese," says Marlene Schwartz, director of the Rudd Center for Food Policy and Obesity at Yale University. "I think that some of this is that anger is confusion between the anger that we have at ourselves and projecting that out onto other people." Her research indicates that younger women, who are

---

actuarial tables: Calculations and statistics used by insurance companies to determine life expectancy of their policyholders.   **epitome:** Perfect example.   **stigma:** A mark of infamy or disgrace.

under the most pressure to be thin and who are also the most likely to be self-critical, are the most likely to feel negatively toward fat people.

As many women's magazines' cover lines note, losing the last five pounds can be a challenge. So why don't we have more compassion for people struggling to lose the first 50, 60, or 100? Some of it has to do with the psychological phenomenon known as the fundamental attribution error, a basic belief that whatever problems befall us personally are the result of difficult circumstances, while the same problems in other people are the result of their bad choices. Miss a goal at work? It's because the vendor was unreliable, and because your manager isn't giving you enough support, and because the power outage last week cut into premium sales time. That jerk next to you? He blew his quota because he's a bad planner, and because he spent too much time taking personal calls.

The same can be true of weight: "From working with so many people struggling with their weight, I've seen it many times," says Andrew Geier, a postdoctoral fellow in the psychology department at Yale University. "They believe they're overweight due to a myriad of circumstances: as soon as my son goes to college, I'll have time to cook healthier meals; when my husband's shifts change at work, I can get to the gym sooner. . . ." But other people? They're overweight because they don't have the discipline to do the hard work and take off the weight, and that lack of discipline is an affront to our own hard work. (Never mind that weight loss is incredibly difficult to attain: Geier notes that even the most rigorous behavioral programs result in at most about a 12.5 percent decrease in weight, which would take a 350-pound man to a slimmer, but not svelte,° 306 pounds.)

But why do the rest of us care so much? What is it about fat people that makes us so mad? As it turns out, we kind of like it. "People actually enjoy feeling angry," says Ryan Martin, associate professor of psychology at the University of Wisconsin, Green Bay, who cites studies done on people's emotions. "It makes them feel powerful, it makes them feel greater control, and they appreciate it for that reason." And with fat people designated as acceptable targets of rage—and with the prevalence of fat people in our lives, both in the malls and on the news—it's easy to find a target for some soul-clearing, ego-boosting ranting.

And it may be that, like those World War I–era cookbook writers, we feel that obese people are robbing us of resources, whether it's space in a row of airline seats or our hard-earned tax dollars. Think of health care: when President Obama made reforming health care a priority, it led to an increased focus on obesity as a contributor to health-care costs. A recent article in *Health Affairs,* a public-policy journal, reported that obesity costs $147 billion a year, mainly in insurance premiums and taxes. At the same time, obesity-related diseases such as type 2 diabetes have spiked, and, while diabetes can be treated, treatment is expensive. So the overweight, some people argue, are

svelte: Gracefully slender.

costing all of us money while refusing to alter the behavior that has put them in their predicament in the first place (i.e., overeating and not exercising).

The reality is much more complicated. It's a fallacy to conflate the un- 15 healthy action—overeating and not exercising—with the unhealthy appearance, says Schwartz: some overweight people run marathons; eat only organic, vegetarian fare; and have clean bills of health. Even so, yelling at the overweight to put down the doughnut is far from productive. "People are less likely to seek out healthy behaviors when they're criticized by friends, family, doctors, and others," says Schwartz. "If people tell you that you're disgusting or a slob enough times, you soon start to believe it." In fact, fat outrage might actually make health-care costs higher. In a study published in the 2005 issue of the *Journal of Health Politics, Policy and Law,* Abigail Saguy and Brian Riley found that many overweight people decide not to get help for medical conditions that are more treatable and more risky than obesity because they don't want to deal with their doctor's harassment about their weight. (For instance, a study from the University of North Carolina found that obese women are less likely to receive cervical exams than their thinner counterparts, in part because they worry about being embarrassed or belittled by the doctor because of their weight.)

The bubbling rage against fat people in America has put researchers like 16 Levine in a difficult position. On the one hand, she says, she wants to ensure that obesity is taken seriously as a medical problem, and pointing out the costs associated with obesity-related illnesses helps illustrate the severity of the situation. On the other hand, she says, doing so could increase the animosity people have toward the overweight, many of whom may already live healthy lives or may be working hard to make healthier choices.

"The idea is to fight obesity and not obese people," she says, and then 17 pauses. "But it's very hard for many people to disentangle the two."

Questions to Start You Thinking

1. **Considering Meaning:**   What is "the fundamental attribution error" (paragraph 11)? Why is it significant for understanding negative attitudes toward overweight people?

2. **Identifying Writing Strategies:**   The first four paragraphs of the article provide specific examples of "fat bias." How do they fit into the overall structure of the essay? Why do you think Dailey and Ellin chose these examples?

3. **Reading Critically:**   The authors claim that "fat bias is nothing new" (paragraph 5). How effectively do they support this claim? How well do they connect contemporary "fat bias" with a longer historical tradition?

4. **Expanding Vocabulary:**   According to one expert, "It's a fallacy to conflate the unhealthy action—overeating and not exercising—with the unhealthy appearance" (paragraph 15). What is a *fallacy*?

5. **Making Connections:** Dailey and Ellin acknowledge that the United States "has already become a size XL nation — 66 percent of adults over 20 are considered overweight or obese" (paragraph 9). They agree with health experts about the "severity of the situation" (paragraph 16). How might Juliet Schor ("The Creation of Discontent," pp. 634–36) interpret this weight problem?

Link to the Paired Essay

Dailey and Ellin highlight a culture-wide anger at fat people in America. Does Michael Pollan ("The Cooking Animal," pp. 581–84) appear to have any "fat bias"? Does he view obesity through the lens of character flaws or poor self-discipline? Support your answer with evidence showing how he addresses the issue.

Journal Prompts

1. Do you agree that Americans believe in hard work, self-discipline, and willpower (paragraph 7) and expect such efforts to prevent weight gain? Explore why you agree, do not agree, or want to qualify this assertion.

2. According to the article, younger women are most pressured about weight, but that pressure seems to cross many demographic lines. Have you ever felt pressure to lose weight? Was it difficult or easy to do so? Did your experience give you any insight about weight, weight loss, or fat bias?

Suggestions for Writing

1. According to one source in the article, people like being angry because that emotion boosts their sense of power (paragraph 13). Do you agree with this? Write a personal essay exploring why or how people experience anger.

2. Dailey and Ellin describe American hostility toward overweight people as a "bubbling rage" (paragraph 16), examining examples of "fat bias," its history in America, and its psychological origins. Investigate American culture through magazines, movies, music, books, television shows, or politics for evidence to support your own thesis in an essay about attitudes toward fatness and thinness.

Michael Pollan
The Cooking Animal

Michael Pollan was born in 1955 on Long Island. He attended Bennington College and Oxford University before earning his master's in English at Columbia University. He is the Knight Professor of Science and Environmental Journalism at the University of California at Berkeley. Besides writing for the *New York Times Magazine* since 1987, Pollan has contributed articles to *Harper's, Mother Jones, Gourmet, Vogue, Travel + Leisure,* and *House and Garden.* Among his numerous awards are the James Beard Award for best magazine series in 2003 and the 2000 Reuters–I.U.C.N. Global Award for Environmental Journalism. Pollan has written many books, including *The Botany of Desire: A Plant's-Eye View of the World* (2001), *The Omnivore's Dilemma: A Natural History of Four Meals* (2006), *In Defense of Food: An Eater's Manifesto* (2008), and *Food Rules: An Eater's Manual* (2010). In this selection, Pollan ponders the intersection between modern eating habits and popular culture — especially television.

For more about Michael Pollan, visit **<bedfordstmartins .com/bedguide>**.

AS YOU READ: What picture of the "American food system" does Pollan present?

In 1773, the Scottish writer James Boswell, noting that "no beast is a cook," called *Homo sapiens* "the cooking animal," though he might have reconsidered that definition had he been able to gaze upon the frozen-food cases at Wal-Mart. Fifty years later, in *The Physiology of Taste,* the French gastronome Jean-Anthelme Brillat-Savarin claimed that cooking made us who we are; by teaching men to use fire, it had "done the most to advance the cause of civilization." More recently, the anthropologist° Claude Lévi-Strauss, writing in 1964 in *The Raw and the Cooked,* found that many cultures entertained a similar view, regarding cooking as a symbolic way of distinguishing ourselves from the animals.   1

For Lévi-Strauss, cooking is a metaphor for the human transformation of nature into culture, but in the years since *The Raw and the Cooked,* other anthropologists have begun to take quite literally the idea that cooking is the key to our humanity. Earlier this year, Richard Wrangham, a Harvard anthropologist, published a fascinating book called *Catching Fire,* in which he argues that it was the discovery of cooking by our early ancestors — not tool-making or language or meat-eating — that made us human. By providing our primate forebears with a more energy-dense and easy-to-digest diet, cooked food altered the course of human evolution, allowing our brains to grow bigger (brains are notorious energy guzzlers) and our guts to shrink. It seems that raw food takes much more time and energy to chew and digest, which is why other primates of our size carry around substantially larger digestive tracts and spend many more of their waking hours chewing: up to six hours a day. (That's nearly as much time as Guy Fieri° devotes to the activity.) Also, since   2

anthropologist: One who deals with the origins, physical and cultural development, biological characteristics, social customs, and beliefs of human beings.   **Guy Fieri:** Food Network television personality.

cooking detoxifies many foods, it cracked open a treasure trove of nutritious calories unavailable to other animals. Freed from the need to spend our days gathering large quantities of raw food and then chewing (and chewing) it, humans could now devote their time, and their metabolic resources, to other purposes, like creating a culture.

Cooking gave us not just the meal but also the occasion: the practice of eating together at an appointed time and place. This was something new under the sun, for the forager of raw food would likely have fed himself on the go and alone, like the animals. (Or, come to think of it, like the industrial eaters we've become, grazing at gas stations and skipping meals.) But sitting down to common meals, making eye contact, sharing food, all served to civilize us; "around that fire," Wrangham says, "we became tamer." 3

If cooking is as central to human identity and culture as Wrangham believes, it stands to reason that the decline of cooking in our time would have a profound effect on modern life. At the very least, you would expect that its rapid disappearance from everyday life might leave us feeling nostalgic for the sights and smells and the sociality of the cook-fire. Bobby Flay and Rachael Ray° may be pushing precisely that emotional button. Interestingly, the one kind of home cooking that is actually on the rise today (according to Harry Balzer°) is outdoor grilling. Chunks of animal flesh seared over an open fire: grilling is cooking at its most fundamental and explicit, the transformation of the raw into the cooked right before our eyes. It makes a certain sense that the grill would be gaining adherents° at the very moment when cooking meals and eating them together is fading from the culture. (While men have hardly become equal partners in the kitchen, they are cooking more today than ever before: about 13 percent of all meals, many of them on the grill.) 4

Yet we don't crank up the barbecue every day; grilling for most people is more ceremony than routine. We seem to be well on our way to turning cooking into a form of weekend recreation, a backyard sport for which we outfit ourselves at Williams-Sonoma,° or a televised spectator sport we watch from the couch. Cooking's fate may be to join some of our other weekend exercises in recreational atavism:° camping and gardening and hunting and riding on horseback. Something in us apparently likes to be reminded of our distant origins every now and then and to celebrate whatever rough skills for contending with the natural world might survive in us, beneath the thin crust of 21st-century civilization. 5

To play at farming or foraging for food strikes us as harmless enough, perhaps because the delegating of those activities to other people in real life is something most of us are generally O.K. with. But to relegate the activity of cooking to a form of play, something that happens just on weekends or mostly on television, seems much more consequential. The fact is that not 6

Bobby Flay and Rachael Ray: Hosts of cooking shows on television.   **Harry Balzer:** Consumer expert on American eating habits and trends.   **adherents:** Supporters or followers. **Williams-Sonoma:** American company that sells high-end kitchenware and home furnishings.   **atavism:** A throwback, a type from the past that reappears after an absence.

cooking may well be deleterious° to our health, and there is reason to believe that the outsourcing° of food preparation to corporations and 16-year-olds has already taken a toll on our physical and psychological well-being.

Consider some recent research on the links between cooking and dietary   7
health. A 2003 study by a group of Harvard economists led by David Cutler found that the rise of food preparation outside the home could explain most of the increase in obesity in America. Mass production has driven down the cost of many foods, not only in terms of price but also in the amount of time required to obtain them. The French fry did not become the most popular "vegetable" in America until industry relieved us of the considerable effort needed to prepare French fries ourselves. Similarly, the mass production of cream-filled cakes, fried chicken wings and taquitos, exotically flavored chips or cheesy puffs of refined flour, has transformed all these hard-to-make-at-home foods into the sort of everyday fare you can pick up at the gas station on a whim and for less than a dollar. The fact that we no longer have to plan or even wait to enjoy these items, as we would if we were making them ourselves, makes us that much more likely to indulge impulsively.

Cutler and his colleagues demonstrate that as the "time cost" of food   8
preparation has fallen, calorie consumption has gone up, particularly consumption of the sort of snack and convenience foods that are typically cooked outside the home. They found that when we don't have to cook meals, we eat more of them: as the amount of time Americans spend cooking has dropped by about half, the number of meals Americans eat in a day has climbed; since 1977, we've added approximately half a meal to our daily intake.

Cutler and his colleagues also surveyed cooking patterns across several   9
cultures and found that obesity rates are inversely correlated with the amount of time spent on food preparation. The more time a nation devotes to food preparation at home, the lower its rate of obesity. In fact, the amount of time spent cooking predicts obesity rates more reliably than female participation in the labor force or income. Other research supports the idea that cooking is a better predictor of a healthful diet than social class: a 1992 study in *The Journal of the American Dietetic Association* found that poor women who routinely cooked were more likely to eat a more healthful diet than well-to-do women who did not.

So cooking matters—a lot. Which when you think about it, should come   10
as no surprise. When we let corporations do the cooking, they're bound to go heavy on sugar, fat and salt; these are three tastes we're hard-wired to like, which happen to be dirt cheap to add and do a good job masking the shortcomings of processed food. And if you make special-occasion foods cheap and easy enough to eat every day, we will eat them every day. The time and work involved in cooking, as well as the delay in gratification built into the process, served as an important check on our appetite. Now that check is gone, and we're struggling to deal with the consequences.

---

deleterious: Harmful.   **outsourcing:** Purchasing or obtaining goods or services from an outside supplier.

The question is, Can we ever put the genie back into the bottle? Once it 11 has been destroyed, can a culture of everyday cooking be rebuilt? One in which men share equally in the work? One in which the cooking shows on television once again teach people how to cook from scratch and, as Julia Child° once did, actually empower them to do it?

Let us hope so. Because it's hard to imagine ever reforming the American 12 way of eating or, for that matter, the American food system unless millions of Americans—women and men—are willing to make cooking a part of daily life. The path to a diet of fresher, unprocessed food, not to mention to a revitalized local-food economy, passes straight through the home kitchen.

But if this is a dream you find appealing, you might not want to call 13 Harry Balzer right away to discuss it.

"Not going to happen," he told me. "Why? Because we're basically cheap 14 and lazy. And besides, the skills are already lost. Who is going to teach the next generation to cook? I don't see it.

"We're all looking for someone else to cook for us. The next American 15 cook is going to be the supermarket. Takeout from the supermarket, that's the future. All we need now is the drive-through supermarket."

Crusty as a fresh baguette, Harry Balzer insists on dealing with the world, 16 and human nature, as it really is, or at least as he finds it in the survey data he has spent the past three decades poring over. But for a brief moment, I was able to engage him in the project of imagining a slightly different reality. This took a little doing. Many of his clients—which include many of the big chain restaurants and food manufacturers—profit handsomely from the decline and fall of cooking in America; indeed, their marketing has contributed to it. Yet Balzer himself made it clear that he recognizes all that the decline of everyday cooking has cost us. So I asked him how, in an ideal world, Americans might begin to undo the damage that the modern diet of industrially prepared food has done to our health.

"Easy. You want Americans to eat less? I have the diet for you. It's short, 17 and it's simple. Here's my diet plan: Cook it yourself. That's it. Eat anything you want—just as long as you're willing to cook it yourself."

Questions to Start You Thinking

1. **Considering Meaning:** Why does Pollan consider the "outsourcing of food preparation" (paragraph 6) harmful? Why is it also harmful to turn cooking into recreation?

2. **Identifying Writing Strategies:** Pollan begins by citing three sources: James Boswell, Jean-Anthelme Brillat-Savarin, and Claude Lévi-Strauss. Why does he do this? What point do these writers make? How is it related to the overall purpose of Pollan's essay?

Julia Child: American chef, author, and television personality from the 1960s and 1970s.

3. **Reading Critically:**   What distinction does Pollan make between current cooking shows and ones from the past, such as Julia Child's? Why is this difference significant? Is the distinction valid?

4. **Expanding Vocabulary:**   Pollan writes that the disappearance of cooking from daily life could produce nostalgia "for the sights and smells and the sociality of the cook-fire" (paragraph 4). What does the word *sociality* mean? Why do you think Pollan chose to use the term in this context?

5. **Making Connections:**   Pollan is critical of fast food and processed food from corporations, which are "heavy on sugar, fat and salt," tastes that we are "hard wired to like" (paragraph 10). How might Llewellyn H. Rockwell Jr. ("In Defense of Consumerism," pp. 638–41) or Juliet Schor ("The Creation of Discontent," pp. 634–36) respond to Pollan's view of the "American food system" (paragraph 12)?

Link to the Paired Essay

Both Pollan and Dailey and Ellin ("America's War on the Overweight," pp. 575–79) discuss the issue of obesity in the United States. How are their explanations different? How are they similar?

Journal Prompts

1. How would you judge your diet and attitude toward food as compared to the "industrial eaters" (paragraph 3) Pollan describes in his essay?

2. Pollan looks at both food and the social event it can generate (paragraph 3). Examine your own eating habits, now and in the past. Do you generally eat regular meals? Do you eat alone or with others? Are these habits significant?

Suggestions for Writing

1. Pollan hopes that Americans can return to cooking at home and reform the country's way of eating. In contrast, consumer expert Harry Balzer claims that the project is impossible (paragraph 14). Do you agree with Pollan or Balzer? Do you think the way Americans eat needs to change? Write a personal essay that takes a stand on this issue.

2. Pollan examines the roles of chain restaurants, food manufacturers, and others in shaping our relationship with food. Drawing on a few sources, write an essay that identifies and analyzes a specific factor that influences American attitudes and behaviors about food.

28 E-Technology

Responding to an Image

At first glance, how would you describe the overall feeling conveyed by this image? What is significant about the perspective from which the photograph was taken? What is the mood of the picture? What point does the image seem to be making about the impact of communication technology? Translate that point into a caption for the illustration or into a thesis for an essay. (You also might want to compare and contrast this image with the one on the cover of this book.)

Web Search

Think of a topic of great personal interest to you—a hobby, a political or social issue, a subject of study, something you know a lot about. Then look for varied Web sites devoted to this topic, especially social-networking pages, chat rooms, blogs, and other interactive sites where individuals come together to share their thoughts on and experiences with the topic. As you browse through such sites, think about the kinds of communities the Web creates. How do people relate to one another online? What do they learn from one another, and where do they fail to connect? Ultimately, do you think of the Internet as a unifying force—bringing together people who would not normally come into contact? Or do you view the Internet as an isolating force—allowing people to remain anonymous and to avoid direct human contact?

For reading activities linked to this chapter, visit **<bedfordstmartins .com/bedguide>**.

Clive Thompson
The New Literacy

Clive Thompson is a science and technology writer for the *New York Times Magazine, Wired,* and *New York Magazine,* the video-game columnist for *Slate,* and a finance columnist for *Details.* He has received the National Magazine Award in Canada twice, and in 2002–2003 was the Knight Science Journalism fellow at MIT. His commentary can be heard on NPR, CNN, and the Canadian Broadcasting Corporation. He also keeps a blog, "Collision Detection," which "collects bits of offbeat research…and musings thereon." Here, Thompson discusses some counterintuitive research by Professor Andrea Lunsford on literacy in the digital age.

For more about Clive Thompson, visit **<bedfordstmartins .com/bedguide>**.

AS YOU READ: What did the Stanford Study of Writing discover about student writing?

As the school year begins, be ready to hear pundits° fretting once again about how kids today can't write—and technology is to blame. Facebook encourages narcissistic° blabbering, video and PowerPoint have replaced carefully crafted essays, and texting has dehydrated language into "bleak, bald, sad shorthand" (as University College of London English professor John Sutherland has moaned). An age of illiteracy is at hand, right?   1

Andrea Lunsford isn't so sure. Lunsford is a professor of writing and rhetoric at Stanford University, where she has organized a mammoth project called the Stanford Study of Writing to scrutinize° college students' prose. From 2001 to 2006, she collected 14,672 student writing samples—everything from in-class assignments, formal essays, and journal entries to emails, blog posts, and chat sessions. Her conclusions are stirring.   2

"I think we're in the midst of a literacy revolution the likes of which we haven't seen since Greek civilization," she says. For Lunsford, technology   3

pundits: Critics and commentators.   **narcissistic:** Self-centered.   **scrutinize:** Examine carefully.

isn't killing our ability to write. It's reviving it—and pushing our literacy in bold new directions.

The first thing she found is that young people today write far more than any generation before them. That's because so much socializing takes place online, and it almost always involves text. Of all the writing that the Stanford students did, a stunning 38 percent of it took place out of the classroom— life writing, as Lunsford calls it. Those Twitter updates and lists of 25 things about yourself add up.

It's almost hard to remember how big a paradigm shift this is. Before the Internet came along, most Americans never wrote anything, ever, that wasn't a school assignment. Unless they got a job that required producing text (like in law, advertising, or media), they'd leave school and virtually never construct a paragraph again.

But is this explosion of prose good, on a technical level? Yes. Lunsford's team found that the students were remarkably adept at what rhetoricians call *kairos*—assessing their audience and adapting their tone and technique to best get their point across. The modern world of online writing, particularly in chat and on discussion threads, is conversational and public, which makes it closer to the Greek tradition of argument than the asynchronous° letter and essay writing of 50 years ago.

The fact that students today almost always write for an audience (something virtually no one in my generation did) gives them a different sense of what constitutes good writing. In interviews, they defined good prose as something that had an effect on the world. For them, writing is about persuading and organizing and debating, even if it's over something as quotidian° as what movie to go see. The Stanford students were almost always less enthusiastic about their in-class writing because it had no audience but the professor: It didn't serve any purpose other than to get them a grade. As for those texting short-forms and smileys defiling° *serious* academic writing? Another myth. When Lunsford examined the work of first-year students, she didn't find a single example of texting speak in an academic paper.

Of course, good teaching is always going to be crucial, as is the mastering of formal academic prose. But it's also becoming clear that online media are pushing literacy into cool directions. The brevity of texting and status updating teaches young people to deploy haiku°-like concision.° At the same time, the proliferation° of new forms of online pop-cultural exegesis°—from sprawling TV-show recaps to 15,000-word videogame walkthroughs—has given them a chance to write enormously long and complex pieces of prose, often while working collaboratively with others.

asynchronous: Not occurring at the same time.   **quotidian:** Ordinary, commonplace. **defiling:** Making dirty; corrupting.   **haiku:** Japanese form of poetry having three unrhymed lines of five, seven, and five syllables.   **concision:** The quality of being brief; brevity.   **proliferation:** Rapid increase.   **exegesis:** Explanation or analysis.

We think of writing as either good or bad. What today's young people   9
know is that knowing who you're writing for and why you're writing might
be the most crucial factor of all.

Questions to Start You Thinking

1. **Considering Meaning:**   According to the author, what is the effect of
   the Internet on writing?

2. **Identifying Writing Strategies:**   Where does Thompson use comparison and contrast? How does it support his argument?

3. **Reading Critically:**   Who seems to be the intended audience for this
   essay? What is the writer's purpose? How well do you think he achieves it?

4. **Expanding Vocabulary:**   In paragraph 5, Thompson writes, "It's
   almost hard to remember how big a paradigm shift this is." What is a *paradigm shift*? Why is this concept important to Thompson's larger purpose?

5. **Making Connections:**   According to Thompson, the Internet and other
   new media forms are stimulating literacy. How might Sherry Turkle
   ("How Computers Change the Way We Think," pp. 602–7) respond to
   Thompson's article? What would she make of this "paradigm shift"?

Journal Prompts

1. Thompson claims that people are writing more than ever as they socialize online (paragraph 4). Consider your own time spent writing online,
   texting, or tweeting. Has this time and involvement made you a better
   writer? Why, or why not?

2. According to Thompson, students surveyed in the Stanford Study of
   Writing "defined good prose as something that had an effect on the
   world" (paragraph 7). Do you agree with this definition? Can you think
   of a better one? What examples come to mind?

Suggestions for Writing

1. Drawing on your own experience and observations, write an essay in
   which you explore the cause-and-effect relationship, positive or negative, between the use of the Internet (or another new media form) and
   its consequences for writing.

2. In his opening sentence, Thompson anticipates commentary blaming
   technology for educational gaps or failures, just as video games, television, radio, and even early novels have been criticized over the years as
   negative influences. Investigate one or several historical examples of
   people worrying about the bad effects of a new technology. Then, write
   an essay that examines those concerns and their validity, in retrospect.

David Gelernter

Computers Cannot Teach Children Basic Skills

David Gelernter was born in 1955. Although his undergraduate degree from Yale University is in classical Hebrew literature, he went on to earn a PhD in computer science from the State University of New York at Stony Brook. Gelernter has been a professor of computer science at Yale since 1983, and his books, articles, and theories on technology have been highly influential. He is also a painter and an art critic who serves on the National Council for the Arts. In 1993, he lost part of his right hand and the sight in one eye after opening a mail bomb sent by Theodore Kaczynski, the "Unabomber" terrorist opposed to the advancement of technology, who targeted prominent professors and business executives. Gelernter chronicled his recovery in the memoir *Drawing Life: Surviving the Unabomber* (1997). His many other books include *1939: The Lost World of the Fair* (1995), *Machine Beauty* (1998), and *Americanism: The Fourth Great Western Religion* (2007). In "Computers Cannot Teach Children Basic Skills," first published in *New Republic* in 1994, Gelernter challenges the widely held view that computers are always a "godsend" in the classroom.

For more about David Gelernter, visit **<bedfordstmartins .com/bedguide>**.

AS YOU READ: Identify the solution Gelernter proposes for making effective use of computers in the classroom.

Over the last decade an estimated $2 billion has been spent on more than 2 million computers for America's classrooms. That's not surprising. We constantly hear from Washington that the schools are in trouble and that computers are a godsend. Within the education establishment, in poor as well as rich schools, the machines are awaited with nearly religious awe. An inner-city principal bragged to a teacher friend of mine recently that his school "has a computer in every classroom . . . despite being in a bad neighborhood!"

Computers Teach Some Things Well

Computers should be in the schools. They have the potential to accomplish great things. With the right software, they could help make science tangible or teach neglected topics like art and music. They could help students form a concrete idea of society by displaying on-screen a version of the city in which they live — a picture that tracks real life moment by moment.

In practice, however, computers make our worst educational nightmares come true. While we bemoan the decline of literacy, computers discount words in favor of pictures and pictures in favor of video. While we fret about the decreasing cogency° of public debate, computers dismiss linear argument and promote fast, shallow romps across the information landscape. While we worry about basic skills, we allow into the classroom software that will do a student's arithmetic or correct his spelling.

cogency: Logic, persuasiveness.

Computers Lower Reading Skills

Take multimedia. The idea of multimedia is to combine text, sound, and pictures in a single package that you browse on-screen. You don't just *read* Shakespeare; you watch actors performing, listen to songs, view Elizabethan buildings. What's wrong with that? By offering children candy-coated books, multimedia is guaranteed to sour them on unsweetened reading. It makes the printed page look even more boring than it used to look. Sure, books will be available in the classroom, too—but they'll have all the appeal of a dusty piano to a teen who has a Walkman handy.   4

So what if the little nippers don't read? If they're watching Olivier° instead, what do they lose? The text, the written word along with all of its attendant pleasures. Besides, a book is more portable than a computer, has a higher-resolution display, can be written on and dog-eared, and is comparatively dirt cheap.   5

Hypermedia, multimedia's comrade in the struggle for a brave new classroom,° is just as troubling. It's a way of presenting documents on-screen without imposing a linear start-to-finish order. Disembodied paragraphs are linked by theme; after reading one about the First World War, for example, you might be able to choose another about the technology of battleships, or the life of Woodrow Wilson, or hemlines in the '20s. This is another cute idea that is good in minor ways and terrible in major ones. Teaching children to understand the orderly unfolding of a plot or a logical argument is a crucial part of education. Authors don't merely agglomerate° paragraphs; they work hard to make the narrative read a certain way, prove a particular point. To turn a book or a document into hypertext is to invite readers to ignore exactly what counts—the story.   6

The real problem, again, is the accentuation° of already bad habits. Dynamiting documents into disjointed paragraphs is one more expression of the sorry fact that sustained argument is not our style. If you're a newspaper or magazine editor and your readership is dwindling, what's the solution? Shorter pieces. If you're a politician and you want to get elected, what do you need? Tasty sound bites. Logical presentation be damned.   7

Another software species, "allow me" programs, is not much better. These programs correct spelling and, by applying canned grammatical and stylistic rules, fix prose. In terms of promoting basic skills, though, they have all the virtues of a pocket calculator.   8

In Kentucky, as the *Wall Street Journal* reported, students in grades K–3 are mixed together regardless of age in a relaxed environment. It works great, the *Journal* says. Yes, scores on computation tests have dropped 10 percent at one   9

Olivier: Laurence Olivier, a British actor noted for his Shakespearean performances. **brave new classroom:** Reference to the Aldous Huxley novel *Brave New World,* in which technology makes life happy but empty.   **agglomerate:** Jumble together.   **accentuation:** Making more intense.

school, but not to worry: "Drilling addition and subtraction in an age of calculators is a waste of time," the principal reassures us. Meanwhile, a Japanese educator informs University of Wisconsin mathematician Richard Akey that in his country, "calculators are not used in elementary or junior high school because the primary emphasis is on helping students develop their mental abilities." No wonder Japanese kids blow the pants off American kids in math. Do we really think "drilling addition and subtraction in an age of calculators is a waste of time"? If we do, then "drilling reading in an age of multimedia is a waste of time" can't be far behind.

Prose-correcting programs are also a little ghoulish, like asking a computer for tips on improving your personality. On the other hand, I ran this viewpoint through a spell checker, so how can I ban the use of such programs in schools? Because to misspell is human; to have no idea of correct spelling is to be semiliterate. 10

Conditions on the Use of Computers

There's no denying that computers have the potential to perform inspiring feats in the classroom. If we are ever to see that potential realized, however, we ought to agree on three conditions. First, there should be a completely new crop of children's software. Most of today's offerings show no imagination. There are hundreds of similar reading and geography and arithmetic programs, but almost nothing on electricity or physics or architecture. Also, they abuse the technical capacities of new media to glitz up old forms instead of creating new ones. Why not build a time-travel program that gives kids a feel for how history is structured by zooming you backward? A spectrum program that lets users twirl a frequency knob to see what happens? 11

Second, computers should be used only during recess or relaxation periods. Treat them as fillips,° not as surrogate teachers. When I was in school in the '60s, we all loved educational films. When we saw a movie in class, everybody won: teachers didn't have to teach, and pupils didn't have to learn. I suspect that classroom computers are popular today for the same reasons. 12

Most important, educators should learn what parents and most teachers already know: you cannot teach a child anything unless you look him in the face. We should not forget what computers are. Like books—better in some ways, worse in others—they are devices that help children mobilize their own resources and learn for themselves. The computer's potential to do good is modestly greater than a book's in some areas. Its potential to do harm is vastly greater, across the board. 13

fillips: Things that are added for excitement but are not essential.

Questions to Start You Thinking

1. **Considering Meaning:** What are the primary shortcomings Gelernter believes computers have as educational tools?

2. **Identifying Writing Strategies:** Where in the essay does Gelernter propose his solution as to how computers should be used in the classroom? Do you find this placement effective? Why, or why not?

3. **Reading Critically:** In several places in the essay, Gelernter compares computers with books. Review what he has to say about computers and books. Do you think he makes an effective argument here? Why, or why not?

4. **Expanding Vocabulary:** Define *bemoan, literacy, fret, linear,* and *romps* (paragraph 3). Then, in your own words, summarize Gelernter's point in paragraph 3. What does his word choice suggest about his intended audience?

5. **Making Connections:** What might Gelernter say about Clive Thompson's "The New Literacy" (pp. 587–89)? Which writer is more persuasive, and why?

Journal Prompts

1. What kind of learning have you done on computers? How effective do you find such learning?

2. In his final paragraph, Gelernter claims "you cannot teach a child anything unless you look him in the face." What does he mean? Do you agree?

Suggestions for Writing

1. To what extent do you agree or disagree with Gelernter? Write an essay in which you take a stand about the value of computers in the classroom. Focus on the basic skills of reading, writing, and mathematics, but feel free to consider computers as teaching tools in other areas, too.

2. Gelernter wrote this essay in 1994. Do some research on how the classroom use of computers has changed since then. For example, what kinds of educational software have been developed? How much time does the average student spend on a classroom computer? Are computers used to teach basic skills? Write an essay, using your findings to support your position about how Gelernter would feel about the use of classroom computers today.

Joseph Turow

Have They Got a Deal for You

Joseph Turow is the Robert Lewis Shayon Professor of Communication at the University of Pennsylvania's Annenberg School of Communication. He specializes in mass media industries. Some of his books include *Breaking Up America: Advertisers and the New Media World* (1997), *Niche Envy: Marketing Discrimination in the Digital Age* (2006), and *The Hyperlinked Society: Questioning Connections in the Digital Age* (2008). Turow's articles have appeared in *American Demographics* magazine, the *Boston Globe,* and the *Los Angeles Times.* His essay, originally published in the *Washington Post,* explores privacy and advertising in today's cyber-market.

AS YOU READ: What is the culture of suspicion that Turow investigates?

For more about Joseph Turow, visit **<bedfordstmartins .com/bedguide>**.

A couple of years ago, in an undergraduate seminar I taught called "Spam° and Society," discussion veered a bit off topic. One of the students asserted confidently that airline Web sites give first-time users lower prices than returning customers. Most of the others immediately agreed. They said the motive was to suck in potential buyers; then, when they returned, the airline could quietly raise prices.

I hear this kind of claim fairly often among heavy computer users. It seems to have become an article of faith that the unseen moguls behind all sorts of Web sites are cherry-picking consumers, customizing ads, manipulating prices, and changing product offers based on what they've learned about individual users without the users' knowledge.

In my research on Internet marketing, I talk to lots of Web workers and consultants and read the trade press, and it's pretty clear that this is going on. But it's extraordinarily hard to verify when it occurs, why any particular offer is made, or how a vendor is evaluating any given customer. Online merchants don't have to tell anyone how they operate, so generally they don't. University of Utah professor Rob Mayer, an adviser to Consumers Union's WebWatch project, told me he once asked an online travel industry executive whether travel sites offer certain customers different prices depending on their online history. The reply was cryptic,° yet telling: "I won't say it doesn't happen."

Lighten up, you might say. Nobody's forcing anyone to buy airline tickets or anything else. But I'm disturbed by what this reflects about our general retail environment—the evolution of what I would call a culture of suspicion. From airlines to supermarkets, from banks to Web sites, American consumers increasingly believe they are being spied on and manipulated. But they continue to trade in the marketplace because they feel powerless to do anything about it.

---

spam: Intrusive advertisements posted on a computer network or sent as e-mail.   **cryptic:** Short and mysterious.

This is a profound change. Broadly speaking, the past 150 years saw what   5
you might call the democratization of shopping in the United States. Beginning around the mid-1800s, department stores such as Stewart's in New York
City and Wanamaker's in Philadelphia moved away from the haggling° mode
of selling and began to display goods and uniform prices for all to see. Part of
the motive was self-interest: Given the wide variety of merchandise and the
large number of employees, the store owners didn't trust their clerks to bargain well with customers. But the result was a more or less egalitarian,° transparent marketplace—one that Americans have come to take for granted.
When they have to negotiate—most notably in car dealerships— they see it as
an unusual, nerve-racking experience.

This reliance on evenhanded, fair dealing lies at the heart of American   6
capitalism or at least the way we'd like to think of it. It's not always practiced,
by any means, as antitrust° suits and many consumer complaints attest. But
it's a worthy goal, and such institutions as the Securities and Exchange Commission and the Federal Trade Commission were established, in part, to aim
for it.

The scaffolding of this system is shaken if a retailer changes its offerings   7
to individual consumers based on information about the consumers that the
consumers don't know or that they suspect but can't verify. Take airline tickets. The Consumers Union's WebWatch investigators visited airline sites
many hundreds of times, finding a bewildering array of prices that seemed
weirdly random and virtually unpredictable (some prices changed between
log-on and checkout). The airlines say it's the result of a necessarily complex
pricing structure, but how can we tell that's all that's going on?

In September 2000, Amazon.com got headlines when customers found   8
that the same DVDs were being offered to different buyers at discounts of 30,
35, or 40 percent. Amazon insisted the discounts were part of a random
"price test," but critics suggested they were based on customer profiling.
After weeks of bad press, the firm offered to refund the difference to buyers
who had paid the higher prices. The company vowed it wouldn't happen
again.

Frequent computer users I've talked to—like my fairly hip students—   9
don't really believe such assurances. Frankly, it's hard for any dispassionate
observer to believe there's no "price customization" when associates from the
influential McKinsey consulting firm write in a 2004 *Harvard Business Review*
article that online companies are missing out on a "big opportunity" if they
are not tracking customers and adjusting prices accordingly—either to attract new buyers or get more of their money.

Meanwhile, this sort of thing goes on quite openly in brick-and-mortar   10
retail stores. In a hypercompetitive environment, where trying to beat

---

haggling: Bargaining.   **egalitarian:** Affirming, promoting, or characterized by equality.
antitrust: Opposed to monopolies or large combined businesses in order to maintain competition.

Wal-Mart and Costco on price is all but impossible, department stores and supermarkets compete with them by trying to hook the right customers. Operating on the financial industry's premise that about 20 percent of the customers bring in 80 percent of profits, they try to identify who belongs in that 20 percent—who will spend money and come back to spend more. And they're happy to get rid of those who hold out for bargains or return too many purchases.

Note that this is subtly different from the 20th-century model, in which 11 storekeepers stocked certain brands of soap or pasta or disposable diapers because they sold well, thus pleasing customers and making money at the same time. While that certainly continues, the new goal is to make money by identifying individuals who fit "best customer" profiles and then reinforce their purchases for reasons and in ways that are hidden from them.

It happens everywhere. Many banks give customers scores based on their 12 deposits and financial backgrounds; their phone representatives use friendlier scripts for high scorers. Supermarket cash registers spit out customized coupons at checkouts, tailored to the previous purchases recorded on "preferred customer" cards. If you buy Coke, you might get a coupon for Pepsi—or perhaps one for Coke, to make sure you return; if you buy coffee, they'll offer you a discount latte. Some grocery chains are already testing "shopping buddies," small computers that you actually carry around the store, getting personally tailored recommendations and discounts from the moment you enter.

The idea used to be that you, the consumer, could shop around, compare 13 goods and prices, and make a smart choice. But now the reverse is also true: The vendor looks at its consumer base, gathers information, and decides whether you are worth pleasing or whether it can profit from your loyalty and habits. You may try to jump from site to site to hunt for the best buy, but that's time consuming. And there are comparative shopping sites such as Bizrate or Nextag, but these can be tough to navigate and companies are learning quickly how to game the system.

This all might make sense for retailers. But for the rest of us, it can feel 14 like our simple corner store is turning into a Marrakech bazaar—except that the merchant has been reading our diary while we're negotiating blindfolded, behind a curtain, through a translator.

Considering the manic nature of retail and media competition and tech- 15 nological developments, this kind of marketing is likely to grow and become more sophisticated. I've spoken to telemarketing executives who claim they can target TV commercials to specific households. It is even possible, they say, to digitally place different products or dialogue into the scene of a show. Sure, there are financial and technical roadblocks to implementing these customized commercials—not to mention some charmingly old-fashioned concerns about privacy—but I'll bet they're coming.

Certainly, being targeted by marketers has its benefits. I like getting cou- 16 pons for my favorite breakfast cereal. I like Amazon.com suggesting films I might enjoy. And I like being treated well on the phone by a company that thinks I'm valuable. But I also like feeling that I'm in control of buying the product, not that the seller is choosing me.

In the early 20th century, "keeping up with the Joneses" was a real ideal,   17
and it spurred consumption. But the mysteries surrounding database marketing will increasingly make us not so much competitive as wary: Are our neighbors getting a better deal not because they shopped harder or bargained smarter but because of some database demographic we don't know about and can't fight?

Lack of knowledge breeds suspicion. A survey I directed this year for the   18
Annenberg Public Policy Center found a startling degree of high-tech ignorance among Americans who use the Internet. Eighty percent of those interviewed knew that companies can track their activities across the Web. Yet a substantial majority believe, too, that it is illegal for merchants and charities to sell information about them, even though it's legal and goes on all the time. Sixty-four percent believe incorrectly that "a site such as Expedia or Orbitz that compares prices on different airlines must include the lowest airline prices." And only 25 percent knew that the following statement was false: "When a website has a privacy policy, it means the site will not share my information with other websites and companies." Our report calls for changing the Orwellian label "Privacy policy" to the more honest "Using your information."

We also call for merchants to be more open about their database activi-   19
ties. A friend of mine phoned Citibank about his credit card and got a representative from India who wasn't able to understand his problem. My friend had never before gotten an "outsourced" operator and, knowing something about databases, concluded that Citibank had pushed him down a notch in status, reserving the U.S.-based service people for better customers. The reality is, he knows nothing about how Citibank operates and has no idea what it thinks about his status. My point is, precisely because he's Internet savvy, he's automatically suspicious that information may be used against him without his knowing it.

We used to say, "My money's as good as anyone else's." But in the 21st   20
century, that may no longer be true. My students can hardly remember a time before Internet cookies° and frequent flying and preferred shopping. They and their kids will try to beat the system to get the best deals, all the while assuming that they don't know all the rules of the marketplace. They'll be automatically mistrustful. It's a new world out there.

Questions to Start You Thinking

1. **Considering Meaning:**   What is the main problem that Turow identifies in this essay? What solutions does he offer?

---

cookies: Small pieces of information stored by Internet users' browsers.

2. **Identifying Writing Strategies:**   Where in the essay does Turow compare and contrast? How does comparison further his overall purpose?

3. **Reading Critically:**   Where does Turow anticipate objections or counterarguments in this essay? How effectively does he do so?

4. **Expanding Vocabulary:**   In paragraph 18, Turow says, "Our report calls for changing the Orwellian label 'Privacy policy' to the more honest 'Using your information.'" Who was Orwell? What is an *Orwellian label*? How do Orwellian terms work?

5. **Making Connections:**   How would Sherry Turkle ("How Computers Change the Way We Think," pp. 602–7) view the "culture of suspicion" that Turow discusses? On what grounds might she agree or disagree with Turow?

Journal Prompts

1. How much do you shop online? Are you generally mistrustful of the Internet marketplace, or have you found it reputable and easy to navigate?

2. Turow writes about commercial targeting based on a consumer's demographics. What demographic groups do you belong to? Have you been targeted by marketers and advertisers? What are the benefits and drawbacks of such targeting?

Suggestions for Writing

1. What does "keeping up with the Joneses" (paragraph 17) mean? How does the idea of "keeping up with the Joneses" influence people's buying habits and aspirations? Write a brief personal essay that defines the phrase and explores its significance.

2. Choose a commercial Web site that you frequent or have used in the past. Investigate its "privacy policy," the quality of its services, and its use of Web tracking, targeted marketing, targeted advertising, variable pricing, cookies, or similar services. Then, write an evaluation of the site, including your criteria for commercial sites.

Emily Yoffe
Seeking

Emily Yoffe was born in 1955 in Newton, Massachusetts. She regularly contributes to NPR as well as the *New York Times,* the *Washington Post,* and *O Magazine.* For her regular column in *Slate* magazine, "Human Guinea Pig," she has tried undergoing hypnosis, being a telephone psychic, and even entering the Mrs. America pageant, as well as other activities suggested by her readers. Her book *What the Dog Did: Tales from a Formerly Reluctant Dog Owner* (2005) was named Book of the Year by Dogwise.com. Here Yoffe discusses how and why we can become so addicted to new media technologies.

AS YOU READ: How does Yoffe characterize users of the Internet and other electronic devices?

For more about Emily Yoffe, visit **<bedfordstmartins .com/bedguide>**.

Seeking. You can't stop doing it. Sometimes it feels as if the basic drives for food, sex, and sleep have been overridden by a new need for endless nuggets of electronic information. We are so insatiably° curious that we gather data even if it gets us in trouble. Google searches are becoming a cause of mistrials as jurors, after hearing testimony, ignore judges' instructions and go look up facts for themselves. We search for information we don't even care about. [My colleague] Nina Shen Rastogi confessed... "My boyfriend has threatened to break up with me if I keep whipping out my iPhone to look up random facts about celebrities when we're out to dinner." We reach the point that we wonder about our sanity. Virginia Heffernan in the *New York Times* said she became so obsessed with Twitter posts about the Henry Louis Gates Jr. arrest that she spent days "refreshing my search like a drugged monkey." . . .

It is an emotional state that [Washington State University neuroscientist Jaak] Panksepp tried many names for: *curiosity, interest, foraging,° anticipation, craving, expectancy.* He finally settled on *seeking.* Panksepp has spent decades mapping the emotional systems of the brain he believes are shared by all mammals, and he says, "Seeking is the granddaddy of the systems." It is the mammalian motivational engine that each day gets us out of the bed, or den, or hole to venture forth into the world. It's why, as animal scientist Temple Grandin writes in *Animals Make Us Human,* experiments show that animals in captivity would prefer to have to search for their food than to have it delivered to them.

For humans, this desire to search is not just about fulfilling our *physical* needs. Panksepp says that humans can get just as excited about abstract rewards as tangible ones. He says that when we get thrilled about the world of ideas, about making intellectual connections, about divining meaning, it is the seeking circuits that are firing.

The juice that fuels the seeking system is the neurotransmitter dopamine. The dopamine circuits "promote states of eagerness and directed purpose," Panksepp writes. It's a state humans love to be in. So good does it feel that we seek out activities, or substances, that keep this system aroused. . . .

insatiably: Without being capable of satisfaction.   **foraging:** Searching.

University of Michigan professor of psychology Kent Berridge has spent   5
more than two decades figuring out how the brain experiences pleasure. . . .
In a series of experiments, he and other researchers have been able to tease
apart that the mammalian brain has separate systems for what Berridge calls
wanting and *liking*. . . . Wanting and liking are complementary. The former
catalyzes° us to action; the latter brings us to a satisfied pause. Seeking needs
to be turned off, if even for a little while, so that the system does not run in
an endless loop. . . .

But our brains are designed to more easily be stimulated than satisfied.   6
"The brain seems to be more stingy with mechanisms for pleasure than for
desire," Berridge has said. This makes evolutionary sense. Creatures that lack
motivation, that find it easy to slip into oblivious rapture, are likely to lead
short (if happy) lives. So nature imbued° us with an unquenchable° drive to
discover, to explore. Stanford University neuroscientist Brian Knutson has
been putting people in MRI scanners and looking inside their brains as they
play an investing game. He has consistently found that the pictures inside
our skulls show that the possibility of a payoff is much more stimulating
than actually getting one. . . . So we find ourselves letting one Google search
lead to another, while often feeling the information is not vital and knowing
we should stop. "As long as you sit there, the consumption renews the appetite," he explains.

Actually all our electronic communication devices — e-mail, Facebook   7
feeds, texts, Twitter — are feeding the same drive as our searches. Since we're
restless, easily bored creatures, our gadgets give us in abundance qualities the
seeking/wanting system finds particularly exciting. Novelty is one. Panksepp
says the dopamine system is activated by finding something unexpected or
by the anticipation of something new. If the rewards come unpredictably — as
e-mail, texts, updates do — we get even more carried away. No wonder we call
it a "CrackBerry."

The system is also activated by particular types of cues that a reward is   8
coming. In order to have the maximum effect, the cues should be small, dis-
crete, specific — like the bell Pavlov° rang for his dogs. Panksepp says a way to
drive animals into a frenzy is to give them only tiny bits of food: This simultaneously stimulating and unsatisfying tease sends the seeking system into
hyperactivity.

Berridge says the "ding" announcing a new e-mail or the vibration that   9
signals the arrival of a text message serves as a reward cue for us. And when
we respond, we get a little piece of news (Twitter, anyone?), making us want
more. These information nuggets may be as uniquely potent for humans as a
Froot Loop to a rat. When you give a rat a minuscule dose of sugar, it engen-
ders "a panting appetite," Berridge says — a powerful and not necessarily
pleasant state.

catalyzes: Makes happen.   **imbued:** Filled.   **unquenchable:** Unable to be satisfied or
suppressed.   **Pavlov:** Scientist who performed experiments on conditioning, training dogs
to salivate when a bell was rung.

If humans are seeking machines, we've now created the perfect machines 10 to allow us to seek endlessly. This perhaps should make us cautious. In *Animals in Translation*, Temple Grandin writes of driving two indoor cats crazy by flicking a laser pointer around the room. They wouldn't stop stalking and pouncing on this ungraspable dot of light—their dopamine system pumping. She writes that no wild cat would indulge in such useless behavior: "A cat wants to *catch* the mouse, not chase it in circles forever." She says "mindless chasing" makes an animal less likely to meet its real needs "because it short-circuits intelligent stalking behavior." As we chase after flickering bits of information, it's a salutary° warning.

Questions to Start You Thinking

1. **Considering Meaning:** Why does Yoffe maintain that we should be "cautious" (paragraph 10) about technologies like the Internet?

2. **Identifying Writing Strategies:** Where in the essay does Yoffe use comparison and contrast? How does this method of development support her thesis?

3. **Reading Critically:** Who is Yoffe's audience? How can you tell? How might that audience affect the style and content of the essay?

4. **Expanding Vocabulary:** Yoffe presents Panksepp's claim that "humans can get just as excited about abstract rewards as tangible ones" (paragraph 3). What do the words *abstract* and *tangible* mean in this context? How does this distinction further the writer's point?

5. **Making Connections:** In "The Creation of Discontent" (pp. 634–36), Juliet Schor argues that consumer desire ends up creating permanent discontent among consumers. What insight does "Seeking" provide about Schor's claim?

Journal Prompts

1. Do you agree with Yoffe that we need to be "cautious" (paragraph 10) about technologies like the Internet? Are you generally wary of new technology? Why, or why not?

2. Write about seeking in your own life, giving specific instances of the process or its effects.

Suggestions for Writing

1. In paragraphs 5 and 6, Yoffe cites brain research suggesting that we like desiring things more than we enjoy obtaining or achieving them. Using personal experience and observation, write an essay that agrees or disagrees with this assertion.

salutary: Healthy.

2. Read further about research on seeking, or analyze popular Web sites, advertisements, magazines, or other materials that seem to rely on seeking. Write an essay using these sources to support your own thesis about the nature or implications of seeking.

For more about
Sherry Turkle, visit
**<bedfordstmartins
.com/bedguide>**.

Sherry Turkle

How Computers Change the Way We Think

Sherry Turkle was born in 1948 in New York City. A graduate of Radcliffe College, the University of Chicago, and Harvard University, she is a clinical psychologist and a professor of sociology at the Massachusetts Institute of Technology. She also founded and directs the MIT Initiative on Technology and Self, a research center devoted to "the social and psychological dimensions of technological change." Turkle's teaching and writing, which focus on people's relationship with technology, have earned her the nickname *cybershrink*. Her books include *The Second Self: Computers and the Human Spirit* (1984, revised 2005), *Life on the Screen: Identity in the Age of the Internet* (1995), and *Simulation and Its Discontents* (2009). In the following essay, first published in the *Chronicle of Higher Education* in 2004, Turkle explores how technologies such as online chat, PowerPoint, word processors, and simulation games are radically affecting our "habits of mind."

AS YOU READ: Identify the areas in which Turkle sees computers changing the way people think. Does she present her opinions on whether these changes are good or bad?

The tools we use to think change the ways in which we think. The invention of written language brought about a radical shift in how we process, organize, store, and transmit representations of the world. Although writing remains our primary information technology, today when we think about the impact of technology on our habits of mind, we think primarily of the computer.

My first encounters with how computers change the way we think came soon after I joined the faculty at the Massachusetts Institute of Technology in the late 1970s, at the end of the era of the slide rule and the beginning of the era of the personal computer. At a lunch for new faculty members, several senior professors in engineering complained that the transition from slide rules to calculators had affected their students' ability to deal with issues of scale. When students used slide rules, they had to insert decimal points themselves. The professors insisted that that required students to maintain a mental sense of scale, whereas those who relied on calculators made frequent errors in orders of magnitude. Additionally, the students with calculators had lost their ability to do "back of the envelope" calculations, and with that, an intuitive feel for the material.

That same semester, I taught a course in the history of psychology. There, I experienced the impact of computational objects on students' ideas about their emotional lives. My class had read Freud's essay on slips of the tongue, with its famous first example: the chairman of a parliamentary session opens a meeting by declaring it closed. The students discussed how Freud interpreted such errors as revealing a person's mixed emotions. A computer-science major disagreed with Freud's approach. The mind, she argued, is a computer. And in a computational dictionary—like we have in the human mind—"closed" and "open" are designated by the same symbol, separated by a sign for opposition. "Closed" equals "minus open." To substitute "closed" for "open" does not require the notion of ambivalence or conflict.

"When the chairman made that substitution," she declared, "a bit was dropped; a minus sign was lost. There was a power surge. No problem."   4

The young woman turned a Freudian slip into an information-processing error. An explanation in terms of meaning had become an explanation in terms of mechanism.   5

Such encounters turned me to the study of both the instrumental and the subjective sides of the nascent° computer culture. As an ethnographer and psychologist, I began to study not only what the computer was doing *for* us, but what it was doing *to* us, including how it was changing the way we see ourselves, our sense of human identity.   6

In the 1980s, I surveyed the psychological effects of computational objects in everyday life—largely the unintended side effects of people's tendency to project thoughts and feelings onto their machines. In the twenty years since, computational objects have become more explicitly designed to have emotional and cognitive effects. And those "effects by design" will become even stronger in the decade to come. Machines are being designed to serve explicitly as companions, pets, and tutors. And they are introduced in school settings for the youngest children.   7

Today, starting in elementary school, students use e-mail, word processing, computer simulations, virtual communities, and PowerPoint software. In the process, they are absorbing more than the content of what appears on their screens. They are learning new ways to think about what it means to know and understand.   8

What follows is a short and certainly not comprehensive list of areas where I see information technology encouraging changes in thinking. There can be no simple way of cataloging whether any particular change is good or bad. That is contested terrain. At every step we have to ask, as educators and citizens, whether current technology is leading us in directions that serve our human purposes. Such questions are not technical; they are social, moral, and political. For me, addressing that subjective side of computation is one of the more significant challenges for the next decade of information technology in higher education. Technology does not determine change, but it encourages us to take certain directions. If we make those directions clear, we can more easily exert human choice.   9

nascent: Just being born.

Thinking about Privacy

Today's college students are habituated to a world of online blogging, instant messaging, and Web browsing that leaves electronic traces. Yet they have had little experience with the right to privacy. Unlike past generations of Americans, who grew up with the notion that the privacy of their mail was sacrosanct,° our children are accustomed to electronic surveillance as part of their daily lives.

I have colleagues who feel that the increased incursions on privacy have put the topic more in the news, and that this is a positive change. But middle-school and high-school students tend to be willing to provide personal information online with no safeguards, and college students seem uninterested in violations of privacy and in increased governmental and commercial surveillance. Professors find that students do not understand that in a democracy, privacy is a right, not merely a privilege. In ten years, ideas about the relationship of privacy and government will require even more active pedagogy.° (One might also hope that increased education about the kinds of silent surveillance that technology makes possible may inspire more active political engagement with the issue.)

Avatars° or a Self?

Chat rooms, role-playing games, and other technological venues offer us many different contexts for presenting ourselves online. Those possibilities are particularly important for adolescents because they offer what Erik Erikson described as a moratorium, a time out or safe space for the personal experimentation that is so crucial for adolescent development. Our dangerous world—with crime, terrorism, drugs, and AIDS—offers little in the way of safe spaces. Online worlds can provide valuable spaces for identity play.

But some people who gain fluency in expressing multiple aspects of self may find it harder to develop authentic selves. Some children who write narratives for their screen avatars may grow up with too little experience of how to share their real feelings with other people. For those who are lonely yet afraid of intimacy, information technology has made it possible to have the illusion of companionship without the demands of friendship.

From Powerful Ideas to PowerPoint

In the 1970s and early 1980s, some educators wanted to make programming part of the regular curriculum for K–12 education. They argued that because information technology carries ideas, it might as well carry the most powerful ideas that computer science has to offer. It is ironic that in most elementary schools today, the ideas being carried by information technology are not ideas from computer science like procedural thinking, but more likely to be those embedded in productivity tools like PowerPoint presentation software.

sacrosanct: Most sacred or holy.   **pedagogy:** Teaching.   **avatars:** Graphic representations of people in a virtual reality environment such as the Internet.

PowerPoint does more than provide a way of transmitting content. It carries its own way of thinking, its own aesthetic° —which not surprisingly shows up in the aesthetic of college freshmen. In that aesthetic, presentation becomes its own powerful idea. 15

To be sure, the software cannot be blamed for lower intellectual standards. Misuse of the former is as much a symptom as a cause of the latter. Indeed, the culture in which our children are raised is increasingly a culture of presentation, a corporate culture in which appearance is often more important than reality. In contemporary political discourse, the bar has also been lowered. Use of rhetorical devices at the expense of cogent° argument regularly goes without notice. But it is precisely because standards of intellectual rigor outside the educational sphere have fallen that educators must attend to how we use, and when we introduce, software that has been designed to simplify the organization and processing of information. 16

In *The Cognitive Style of PowerPoint* (Graphics Press, 2003), Edward R. Tufte suggests that PowerPoint equates bulleting with clear thinking. It does not teach students to begin a discussion or construct a narrative. It encourages presentation, not conversation. Of course, in the hands of a master teacher, a PowerPoint presentation with few words and powerful images can serve as the jumping-off point for a brilliant lecture. But in the hands of elementary-school students, often introduced to PowerPoint in the third grade, and often infatuated with its swooshing sounds, animated icons, and flashing text, a slide show is more likely to close down debate than open it up. 17

Developed to serve the needs of the corporate boardroom, the software is designed to convey absolute authority. Teachers used to tell students that clear exposition depended on clear outlining, but presentation software has fetishized° the outline at the expense of the content. 18

Narrative, the exposition of content, takes time. PowerPoint, like so much in the computer culture, speeds up the pace. 19

Word Processing versus Thinking

The catalog for the Vermont Country Store advertises a manual typewriter, which the advertising copy says "moves at a pace that allows time to compose your thoughts." As many of us know, it is possible to manipulate text on a computer screen and see how it looks faster than we can think about what the words mean. 20

Word processing has its own complex psychology. From a pedagogical point of view, it can make dedicated students into better writers because it allows them to revise text, rearrange paragraphs, and experiment with the tone and shape of an essay. Few professional writers would part with their computers; some claim that they simply cannot think without their hands on the keyboard. Yet the ability to quickly fill the page, to see it before you can think it, can make bad writers even worse. 21

---

aesthetic: Conception of beauty.   **cogent:** Logical.   **fetishized:** Turned into an object of irrational devotion.

A seventh grader once told me that the typewriter she found in her   22
mother's attic is "cool because you have to type each letter by itself. You have
to know what you are doing in advance or it comes out a mess." The idea of
thinking ahead has become exotic.

Taking Things at Interface Value

We expect software to be easy to use, and we assume that we don't have to   23
know how a computer works. In the early 1980s, most computer users who
spoke of transparency meant that, as with any other machine, you could
"open the hood" and poke around. But only a few years later, Macintosh
users began to use the term when they talked about seeing their documents
and programs represented by attractive and easy-to-interpret icons. They
were referring to an ability to make things work without needing to go below
the screen surface. Paradoxically, it was the screen's opacity that permitted
that kind of transparency. Today, when people say that something is transparent, they mean that they can see how to make it work, not that they know
how it works. In other words, transparency means epistemic opacity.

The people who built or bought the first generation of personal com-   24
puters understood them down to the bits and bytes. The next generation of
operating systems were more complex, but they still invited that old-time re-
ductive understanding. Contemporary information technology encourages
different habits of mind. Today's college students are already used to taking
things at (inter)face value; their successors in . . . [a decade] will be even less
accustomed to probing below the surface.

Simulation and Its Discontents

Some thinkers argue that the new opacity is empowering, enabling anyone to   25
use the most sophisticated technological tools and to experiment with simulation in complex and creative ways. But it is also true that our tools carry the
message that they are beyond our understanding. It is possible that in daily
life, epistemic opacity can lead to passivity.

I first became aware of that possibility in the early 1990s, when the first   26
generation of complex simulation games were introduced and immediately
became popular for home as well as school use. SimLife teaches the principles of evolution by getting children involved in the development of complex ecosystems; in that sense it is an extraordinary learning tool. During one
session in which I played SimLife with Tim, a thirteen-year-old, the screen before us flashed a message: "Your orgot is being eaten up." "What's an orgot?"
I asked. Tim didn't know. "I just ignore that," he said confidently. "You don't
need to know that kind of stuff to play."

For me, that story serves as a cautionary tale. Computer simulations en-   27
able their users to think about complex phenomena as dynamic, evolving systems. But they also accustom us to manipulating systems whose core assumptions we may not understand and that may not be true.

We live in a culture of simulation. Our games, our economic and political   28
systems, and the ways architects design buildings, chemists envisage mole-
cules, and surgeons perform operations all use simulation technology. In ten
years the degree to which simulations are embedded in every area of life will
have increased exponentially. We need to develop a new form of media literacy: readership skills for the culture of simulation.

We come to written text with habits of readership based on centuries of civ-   29
ilization. At the very least, we have learned to begin with the journalist's traditional questions: who, what, when, where, why, and how. Who wrote these
words, what is their message, why were they written, and how are they situated
in time and place, politically and socially? A central project for higher education during the next ten years should be creating programs in information-
technology literacy, with the goal of teaching students to interrogate simulations in much the same spirit, challenging their built-in assumptions.

Despite the ever-increasing complexity of software, most computer envi-   30
ronments put users in worlds based on constrained choices. In other words,
immersion in programmed worlds puts us in reassuring environments where
the rules are clear. For example, when you play a video game, you often go
through a series of frightening situations that you escape by mastering the
rules—you experience life as a reassuring dichotomy° of scary and safe. Children grow up in a culture of video games, action films, fantasy epics, and
computer programs that all rely on that familiar scenario of almost losing
but then regaining total mastery: there is danger. It is mastered. A still-more-
powerful monster appears. It is subdued. Scary. Safe.

Yet in the real world, we have never had a greater need to work our way out   31
of binary° assumptions. In the decade ahead, we need to rebuild the culture
around information technology. In that new sociotechnical culture, assumptions about the nature of mastery would be less absolute. The new culture
would make it easier, not more difficult, to consider life in shades of gray, to
see moral dilemmas in terms other than a battle between Good and Evil. For
never has our world been more complex, hybridized, and global. Never have we
so needed to have many contradictory thoughts and feelings at the same time.
Our tools must help us accomplish that, not fight against us.

Information technology is identity technology. Embedding it in a culture   32
that supports democracy, freedom of expression, tolerance, diversity, and
complexity of opinion is one of the next decade's greatest challenges. We cannot afford to fail.

When I first began studying the computer culture, a small breed of   33
highly trained technologists thought of themselves as "computer people."
That is no longer the case. If we take the computer as a carrier of a way of
knowing, a way of seeing the world and our place in it, we are all computer
people now.

---

dichotomy: Division into two opposite groups.   **binary:** Marked by two parts.

Questions to Start You Thinking

1. **Considering Meaning:** In your own words, explain the six major ways in which Turkle says that computers are changing the way people think. Why does she think it is important that we pay attention to these changes?

2. **Identifying Writing Strategies:** Why do you think Turkle presents the six areas of change in the order that she does? Does there seem to be a logic behind this order?

3. **Reading Critically:** How clearly does Turkle establish causes and effects in this selection? Do you find her arguments convincing? Why, or why not?

4. **Expanding Vocabulary:** Reread paragraph 23, in which Turkle writes about the fact that most computer users have little understanding of how computers work. Define *transparency, epistemic,* and *opacity,* and explain what Turkle means at the end of this paragraph when she says that "transparency means epistemic opacity."

5. **Making Connections:** How might Turkle respond to David Gelernter's arguments in "Computers Cannot Teach Children Basic Skills" (pp. 590–92)? How might Gelernter respond to Turkle? Explain whether the two are basically in agreement or disagreement.

Link to the Paired Essay

Although Turkle's essay and Michael Agger's "Lazy Eyes" (pp. 609–12) discuss a similar subject, they are written in dramatically different styles. Compare and contrast the two writers' styles, paying close attention to their purposes and audiences. Be sure to point to specific passages in each essay to support your thesis about their styles.

Journal Prompts

1. Choose one of the changes Turkle writes about here, and explore your own thoughts about it. Do you essentially agree with Turkle? Why, or why not?

2. To what extent do you rely on computers in your daily life? How would your life be different without computers?

For more on supporting a position with sources, see Ch. 12. For more on finding and documenting sources, see the Quick Research Guide beginning on p. A-18.

Suggestions for Writing

1. What are some possible negative effects of people's reliance on computers? Drawing on your own observations, write an essay in which you

explore a cause-and-effect relationship between computer use and some particular human behavior or way of thinking.

2. In paragraph 31, Turkle writes, "Never has our world been more complex, hybridized, and global. Never have we so needed to have many contradictory thoughts and feelings at the same time." Write an essay in which you identify several important challenges the world faces over, say, the next fifty years. Discuss the extent to which computer technology might contribute to solving them or to making them worse. Consult outside sources to support your position.

Michael Agger
Lazy Eyes

Michael Agger grew up in Bethlehem, Pennsylvania, and earned a BA from Yale University. He currently lives in Brooklyn, New York, where he works as a writer and editor for the online magazine *Slate.* His work has also appeared in *The New Yorker* and *New York Magazine.* In this essay, Agger takes a playful approach to "usability expert" Jakob Nielsen's advice about writing online. To experience this text online, go to < http:// www.slate.com/id/2193552>.

AS YOU READ: What point does "Lazy Eyes" make about online texts? How does its style contribute to its point? Note: Words and phrases that appear in blue indicate live links in the original.

For more about Michael Agger, visit **< bedfordstmartins .com/bedguide>**.

You're probably going to read this.   1

It's a short paragraph at the top of the page. It's surrounded by white   2
space. It's in small type.

To really **get your attention**, I should write like this: 3

- Bulleted list
- Occasional use of **bold** to prevent skimming
- Short sentence fragments
- Explanatory subheads
- No puns
- Did I mention lists?

What Is This Article About?

For the past month, I've been away from the **computer screen**. Now I'm   4
back **reading** on it many hours a day. Which got me thinking: How do we
read online?

It's a Jungle Out There

That's <u>Jakob Nielsen</u>'s theory. He's a **usability expert**° who writes an influential <u>biweekly column</u> on such topics as <u>eye-tracking research</u>, <u>Web design errors</u>, and <u>banner blindness</u>. (**Links**, btw, give a text **more authority**, making you more likely to stick around.) 5

Nielsen champions the idea of <u>information foraging</u>. Humans are **informavores**.° On the Internet, we hunt for facts. In earlier days, when switching between sites was time-consuming, we tended to stay in one place and dig. Now we assess a site quickly, looking for an "**information scent**." We move on if there doesn't seem to be any food around. 6

Sorry about the long paragraph. (<u>Eye-tracking studies show</u> that online readers tend to **skip** large blocks of text.) 7

Also, I'm probably forcing you to scroll at this point. Losing some **incredible percentage** of readers. Bye. Have fun on **Facebook**. 8

Screens vs. Paper

What about the **physical process** of reading on a screen? How does that compare to paper? 9

When you look at <u>early research</u>, it's fascinating to see that even in the days of green phosphorus monitors, studies found that there wasn't a huge difference in speed and comprehension between reading on-screen and reading on paper. Paper was the clear winner only when test subjects were asked to skim the text. 10

The studies are not definitive, however, given all the factors that can affect online reading, such as scrolling, font size, user expertise, etc. Nielsen holds that on-screen reading is <u>25 percent slower than reading on paper</u>. Even so, experts agree on what you can do to make screen reading more comfortable: 11

- Choose a **default font** designed for screen reading; e.g., Verdana, Trebuchet, Georgia.
- **Rest** your eyes for 10 minutes every 30 minutes.
- Get a **good monitor**. Don't make it too bright or have it too close to your eyes.
- Minimize reflections.
- Skip long lines of text, which promote fatigue.
- Avoid **MySpace**.

Back to the Jungle

Nielsen's apt description of the online reader: **"[U]sers are selfish, lazy, and ruthless."** You, my dear user, pluck the low-hanging fruit. When you arrive 12

---

usability expert: One who studies the effectiveness, efficiency, and user-friendliness of computer applications.   **informavores:** Consumers of information.

on a page, you don't actually deign to read it. You scan. If you don't see what you need, you're gone.

And it's not you who has to **change**. It's me, the writer: 13

- **One idea** per paragraph
- Half the **word count** of "conventional writing"! (Ouch!)
- Other stuff along these lines

Nielsen often sounds like a cross between **E. B. White**° and the **Terminator**. Here's his advice in a column titled "Long vs. Short Articles as Content Strategy": "A good editor should be able to cut 40 percent of the word count while removing only 30 percent of an article's value. After all, the cuts should target the least valuable information."   14

[*Ed. Note:* **Fascinating asides** about the writer's voice, idiosyncrasies, and **fragile ego** were cut here.]   15

He's Right

I kid about Nielsen, but he's very sensible. We're **active participants** on the Web, looking for **information** and **diversion**. It's natural that people prefer short articles. As Nielsen states, motivated readers who want to know everything about a subject (i.e., parents trying to get their kid into a New York **preschool**) will read long treatises with semicolons, but the rest of us are snacking. His advice: **Embrace hypertext**. Keep things short for the masses, but offer links for the Type A's.°   16

No Blogs, Though

Nielsen may be **ruthless** about brevity, but he doesn't advocate blogging. Here's his logic: "Such postings are good for generating controversy and short-term traffic, and they're definitely easier to write. But they don't build sustainable value."   17

That's a **debatable point**. My experience has been that a thoughtful blogger who tags his posts can cover a subject well. But Nielsen's idea is that people will read (and maybe even pay) for **expertise** that they can't find anywhere else. If you want to **beat the Internet**, you're not going to do it by blogging (since even OK thinkers occasionally write a great blog post) but by offering a **comprehensive take** on a subject (thus saving the reader time from searching many sites) and supplying **original thinking** (offering trusted insight that cannot be easily duplicated by the nonexpert).   18

Like a lot of what Nielsen says, this is both obvious and thoughtful.   19

E. B. White: Essayist, writer, and coauthor, with William Strunk, of a famous writing guide, *The Elements of Style.*   **Type A:** Stereotype of a personality that is impatient, ambitious, aggressive, and competitive.

Ludic Reading

Nielsen focuses on how to hold people's attention to convey information. 20
He's not overly concerned with **pleasure reading**.

Pleasure reading is also known as **"ludic reading."** Victor Nell has stud- 21
ied pleasure reading (PDF). Two fascinating notions:

- When we like a text, we read more slowly.
- When we're really engaged in a text, it's like being in an effortless trance.

Ludic reading can be achieved on the Web, but the environment works 22
against you. Read a nice sentence, get dinged by IM, never return to the story
again.

I suppose ludic readers would be the little sloths hiding in the jungle 23
while everyone else is out rampaging around for fresh meat.

Final Unnecessary Thought

We'll do more and more reading on screens, but they won't replace paper — 24
never mind what your friend with a Kindle tells you. Rather, paper seems to
be the new Prozac.° A balm° for the distracted mind. It's contained, offline,
tactile.° William Powers writes about this elegantly in his essay "Hamlet's
BlackBerry: Why Paper Is Eternal." He describes the white stuff as "a still
point, an anchor for the consciousness."

Moby Dick has become a spa.   25

Slate is Grand Central Station.   26

OK, you may leave now.   27

Questions to Start You Thinking

1. **Considering Meaning:** How does Agger see the value of blogs and bloggers?

2. **Identifying Writing Strategies:** What is the relationship between the form and style of Agger's essay and his subject matter? Do you find this essay effective? What are its benefits and drawbacks?

3. **Reading Critically:** How does Agger view his readers? How does he shape the form and substance of his essay for his audience?

4. **Expanding Vocabulary:** In paragraphs 20 and 21, Agger refers to "ludic reading." What does the word *ludic* mean? How does ludic reading contrast with other kinds of reading?

5. **Making Connections:** Agger approvingly cites a description of online readers as "selfish, lazy, and ruthless" (paragraph 12). Do you think Emily Yoffe ("Seeking," pp. 599–601) would agree or disagree? How might she characterize such readers?

Prozac: Brand name of a common antidepressant medication.   **balm:** Anything that heals, soothes, or lessens pain.   **tactile:** Touchable.

Link to the Paired Essay

In "How Computers Change the Way We Think" (pp. 602–7), Sherry Turkle writes, "The tools we use to think change the ways in which we think" (paragraph 1). For her, computer software and computer applications not only convey information and materials but also carry their "own way of thinking" and their "own aesthetic" (paragraph 15). How does Agger's essay illustrate and support Turkle's main argument? How might Turkle react to the style of "Lazy Eyes"?

Journal Prompts

1. Agger considers the value of blogs in his essay, especially ones that save time and enlighten readers (paragraph 18). What blogs do you read regularly? Why? Do you consider blogs "ludic reading"?

2. According to Agger, the Internet requires a particular style of writing that is significantly different from that of "conventional writing" (paragraph 13). Do you like this online style? What are its advantages and disadvantages?

Suggestions for Writing

1. Agger makes a distinction between reading for information and reading for pleasure. How would you categorize your reading—online, offline, assigned for courses, self-selected, and so on? Write an essay classifying the different kinds of reading you do, using specific examples.

2. "Lazy Eyes" is based largely on the research and insight of one "usability expert," Jakob Nielsen. Do your own Web research, perhaps examining sites and reading other views. Then create your own style guide or set of principles for online writing.

29 Explorations on Living Well

Responding to an Image

Look carefully at one of these four photographs. What time of day do you imagine the photograph was taken? Where are the people, and what are they doing? What relationships and emotions does the image suggest? Write about what the photograph seems to be saying about one or more possible elements of a happy life or a life well lived. If the photograph reminds you of your own experiences, either similar or dissimilar, bring those recollections into your written response to the photograph.

Web Search

American and global economic and social changes during recent years have challenged many people to examine their assumptions about what it means to live well. For example, two of the readings in this chapter originated as radio essays in the *This I Believe* series on National Public Radio. These personal statements—and their 1950s predecessors—are archived at http://www.npr.org and http://thisibelieve.org. From another angle, the surveys and polls conducted by the Pew Research Center for the People and the Press report on public opinions and beliefs at http://people-press.org. Likewise, the United States Census Bureau site, http://www.census.gov, supplies local, regional, and national data about American values and preferences, as suggested by employment, education, and other life factors. Explore these or other sites that investigate possible definitions of a life well lived. What method of addressing this question do you find most compelling? Why? Use the Internet to find at least one other reliable source of information on this matter. Be able to explain how you found your source and which criteria you used to evaluate its reliability and usefulness.

Sarah Adams

Be Cool to the Pizza Dude

Sarah Adams grew up in Wisconsin. She is a professor of English at Olympic Community College in Seattle, Washington. Adams's essay, "Be Cool to the Pizza Dude," was one of the first listener-submitted pieces read on National Public Radio's *This I Believe* series. In this piece, Adams discusses her personal philosophy of life, through the lens of pizza delivery.

AS YOU READ: What are Adams's four principles?

For more about Sarah Adams, visit **<bedfordstmartins .com/bedguide>**.

1 If I have one operating philosophy about life, it is this: "Be cool to the pizza delivery dude; it's good luck." Four principles guide the pizza dude philosophy.

2 Principle 1: Coolness to the pizza delivery dude is a practice in humility and forgiveness. I let him cut me off in traffic, let him safely hit the exit ramp from the left lane, let him forget to use his blinker without extending any of my digits° out the window or toward my horn because there should be one moment in my harried° life when a car may encroach or cut off or pass and I let it go. Sometimes when I have become so certain of my ownership of my lane, daring anyone to challenge me, the pizza dude speeds by in his rusted Chevette. His pizza light atop his car glowing like a beacon reminds me to check myself as I flow through the world. After all, the dude is delivering pizza to young and old, families and singletons, gays and straights, blacks,

---

digits: Fingers.   **harried:** Bothered or distracted by nuisances.

whites, and browns, rich and poor, and vegetarians and meat lovers alike. As he journeys, I give safe passage, practice restraint, show courtesy, and contain my anger.

Principle 2: Coolness to the pizza delivery dude is a practice in empathy. 3 Let's face it: We've all taken jobs just to have a job because some money is better than none. I've held an assortment of these jobs and was grateful for the paycheck that meant I didn't have to share my Cheerios with my cats. In the big pizza wheel of life, sometimes you're the hot bubbly cheese and sometimes you're the burnt crust. It's good to remember the fickle spinning of that wheel.

Principle 3: Coolness to the pizza delivery dude is a practice in honor, and 4 it reminds me to honor honest work. Let me tell you something about these dudes: They never took over a company and, as CEO,° artificially inflated the value of the stock and cashed out their own shares, bringing the company to the brink of bankruptcy, resulting in twenty thousand people losing their jobs while the CEO builds a home the size of a luxury hotel. Rather, the dudes sleep the sleep of the just.

Principle 4: Coolness to the pizza delivery dude is a practice in equality. 5 My measurement as a human being, my worth, is the pride I take in performing my job—any job—and the respect with which I treat others. I am the equal of the world not because of the car I drive, the size of the TV I own, the weight I can bench-press, or the calculus equations I can solve. I am the equal to all I meet because of the kindness in my heart. And it all starts here—with the pizza delivery dude.

Tip him well, friends and brethren, for that which you bestow freely and 6 willingly will bring you all the happy luck that a grateful universe knows how to return.

Questions to Start You Thinking

1. **Considering Meaning:** In your own words, briefly explain the four principles of Adams's philosophy—and how the "pizza dude" helps reveal each of them.

2. **Identifying Writing Strategies:** Why do you think Adams chooses to focus on the "pizza dude," specifically? How would her essay work if her guidelines were more general? How would you describe her writing voice and style—for example, her use of the term *dude*?

3. **Reading Critically:** Adams claims that her philosophy is "good luck" (paragraph 1). In her conclusion, she says that following her advice "will bring you all the happy luck that a grateful universe knows how to return" (paragraph 6). What assumptions on the writer's part do these statements reveal? Do you share them?

CEO: Chief executive officer, the highest-ranking executive at a company.

4. **Expanding Vocabulary:**   Why do you think Adams uses the word *cool* in the way she does here? Is it merely synonymous with *kind* or *nice,* or does it have other important connotations? What are they? What is the history of the term *cool* in slang usage?

5. **Making Connections:**   How might William F. Buckley Jr., author of "Why Don't We Complain?" (pp. 618–22), respond to Adams's guidelines? Which of these writers' views—and experiences—seem more realistic or valid? Why?

Journal Prompts

1. Adams writes that the pizza dude reminds her to show restraint, even when her impulses and instincts would have her do otherwise. Write about a time when you have checked yourself in the way Adams describes. What values does such behavior promote?

2. The writer makes a distinction between unscrupulous CEOs and those like the pizza dude, who do "honest work" (paragraph 4). What does the term *honest work* mean to you? Do you think Adams's generalizations are fair? Why, or why not?

Suggestions for Writing

1. Come up with your own four-point "operating philosophy," based on your experiences or observations, and present it in a personal essay. Create guidelines, as Adams does, that can be summarized in one memorable sentence.

2. Read further about various workers and their jobs, or observe and interview someone whose work seems to embody certain values. Write your own essay, based on your reading or your field work, about one job and the value it carries.

William F. Buckley Jr.

Why Don't We Complain?

William F. Buckley Jr. was born in 1925 and died in 2008. Buckley entered Yale in 1946 and chaired the *Yale Daily News*. His first book, *God and Man at Yale: The Superstitions of "Academic Freedom"* (1951), was an attack on Yale and members of its faculty that brought Buckley to prominence as a conservative commentator. In 1955, after a stint in the CIA in Mexico City, Buckley founded the magazine *National Review* and was its editor for thirty-five years. His twice-weekly syndicated newspaper column "On the Right" began in 1962 and, at its peak, appeared in three hundred newspapers across the country. His television debate show, *Firing Line,* began in 1966 and ran until 1999. During his lifetime, he wrote over forty books and edited at least five more. In this essay, originally published in *Esquire* in 1961, Buckley argues against what he sees as his own and his fellow Americans' growing passivity.

AS YOU READ: How does Buckley observe people reacting to problems? How does he believe people should react?

For more about William F. Buckley Jr., visit **<bedfordstmartins .com/bedguide>**.

It was the very last coach and the only empty seat on the entire train, so there was no turning back. The problem was to breathe. Outside, the temperature was below freezing. Inside the railroad car the temperature must have been about 85 degrees. I took off my overcoat, and a few minutes later my jacket, and noticed that the car was flecked with the white shirts of the passengers. I soon found my hand moving to loosen my tie. From one end of the car to the other, as we rattled through Westchester County, we sweated; but we did not moan. 1

I watched the train conductor appear at the head of the car. "Tickets, all tickets, please!" In a more virile age, I thought, the passengers would seize the conductor and strap him down on a seat over the radiator to share the fate of his patrons. He shuffled down the aisle, picking up tickets, punching commutation cards. *No one addressed a word to him.* He approached my seat, and I drew a deep breath of resolution. "Conductor," I began with a considerable edge to my voice. Instantly the doleful° eyes of my seatmate turned tiredly from his newspaper to fix me with a resentful stare: What question could be so important as to justify my sibilant° intrusion into his stupor°? I was shaken by those eyes. I am incapable of making a discreet fuss, so I mumbled a question about what time we were due in Stamford° (I didn't even ask whether it would be before or after dehydration could be expected to set in), got my reply, and went back to my newspaper and to wiping my brow. 2

The conductor had nonchalantly° walked down the gauntlet° of eighty sweating American freemen, and not one of them had asked him to explain why the passengers in that car had been consigned° to suffer. There is noth- 3

---

doleful: Sad.   **sibilant:** Hissing.   **stupor:** Mental numbness.   **Stamford:** City in Connecticut.   **nonchalantly:** Indifferently, coolly, without concern.   **gauntlet:** A double row of attackers, ready to hit anyone passing between them.   **consigned:** Given into the care of another.

ing to be done when the temperature *outdoors* is 85 degrees, and indoors the air conditioner has broken down; obviously when that happens there is nothing to do, except perhaps curse the day that one was born. But when the temperature outdoors is below freezing, it takes a positive act of will on somebody's part to set the temperature *indoors* at 85. Somewhere a valve was turned too far, a furnace overstocked, a thermostat maladjusted: something that could easily be remedied by turning off the heat and allowing the great outdoors to come indoors. All this is so obvious. What is not obvious is what has happened to the American people.

It isn't just the commuters, whom we have come to visualize as a supine° breed who have got on to the trick of suspending their sensory faculties twice a day while they submit to the creeping dissolution of the railroad industry. It isn't just they who have given up trying to rectify irrational vexations.° It is the American people everywhere.   4

A few weeks ago at a large movie theater I turned to my wife and said, "The picture is out of focus." "Be quiet," she answered. I obeyed. But a few minutes later I raised the point again, with mounting impatience. "It will be all right in a minute," she said apprehensively. (She would rather lose her eyesight than be around when I make one of my infrequent scenes.) I waited. It was *just* out of focus—not glaringly out, but out. My vision is 20-20, and I assume that is the vision, adjusted, for most people in the movie house. So, after hectoring° my wife throughout the first reel, I finally prevailed upon her to admit that it *was* off, and very annoying. We then settled down, coming to rest on the presumption that: a) someone connected with the management of the theater must soon notice the blur and make the correction; or b) that someone seated near the rear of the house would make the complaint in behalf of those of us up front; or c) that—any minute now—the entire house would explode into catcalls and foot stamping, calling dramatic attention to the irksome° distortion.   5

What happened was nothing. The movie ended, as it had begun, *just* out of focus, and as we trooped out, we stretched our faces in a variety of contortions to accustom the eye to the shock of normal focus.   6

I think it is safe to say that everybody suffered on that occasion. And I think it is safe to assume that everyone was expecting someone else to take the initiative in going back to speak to the manager. And it is probably true even that if we had supposed the movie would run right through the blurred image, someone surely would have summoned up the purposive° indignation to get up out of his seat and file his complaint.   7

But notice that no one did. And the reason no one did is because we are all increasingly anxious in America to be unobtrusive;° we are reluctant to make our voices heard, hesitant about claiming our rights; we are afraid that our cause is unjust, or that if it is not unjust, that it is ambiguous; or if not   8

supine: Lying on one's back; passive.   **vexations:** Annoyances or irritations.   **hectoring:** Harassing.   **irksome:** Annoying.   **purposive:** Serving a purpose.   **unobtrusive:** Not noticeable.

even that, that it is too trivial to justify the horrors of a confrontation with Authority; we will sit in an oven or endure a racking headache before undertaking a head-on, I'm-here-to-tell-you complaint. That tendency to passive compliance, to a heedless endurance, is someting to keep one's eyes on — in sharp focus.

I myself can occasionally summon the courage to complain, but I cannot, as I have intimated, complain softly. My own instinct is so strong to let the thing ride, to forget about it — to expect that someone will take the matter up, when the grievance is collective, in my behalf — that it is only when the provocation is at a very special key, whose vibrations touch simultaneously a complexus of nerves, allergies, and passions, that I catch fire and find the reserves of courage and assertiveness to speak up. When that happens, I get quite carried away. My blood gets hot, my brow wet, I become unbearably and unconscionably sarcastic and bellicose;° I am girded° for a total showdown. 9

Why should that be? Why could not I (or anyone else) on that railroad coach have said simply to the conductor, "Sir" — I take that back: that sounds sarcastic — "Conductor, would you be good enough to turn down the heat? I am extremely hot. In fact, I tend to get hot every time the temperature reaches 85 degr — ." Strike that last sentence. Just end it with the simple statement that you are extremely hot, and let the conductor infer the cause. 10

Every New Year's Eve I resolve to do something about the Milquetoast° in me and vow to speak up, calmly, for my rights, and for the betterment of our society, on every appropriate occasion. Entering last New Year's Eve I was fortified in my resolve because that morning at breakfast I had had to ask the waitress three times for a glass of milk. She finally brought it — after I had finished my eggs, which is when I don't want it anymore. I did not have the manliness to order her to take the milk back, but settled instead for a cowardly sulk, and ostentatiously refused to drink the milk — though I later paid for it — rather than state plainly to the hostess, as I should have, why I had not drunk it, and would not pay for it. 11

So by the time the New Year ushered out the Old, riding in on my morning's indignation and stimulated by the gastric juices of resolution that flow so faithfully on New Year's Eve, I rendered my vow. Henceforward I would conquer my shyness, my despicable disposition to supineness. I would speak out like a man against the unnecessary annoyances of our time. 12

Forty-eight hours later, I was standing in line at the ski repair store in Pico Peak, Vermont. All I needed, to get on with my skiing, was the loan, for one minute, of a small screwdriver, to tighten a loose binding. Behind the counter in the workshop were two men. One was industriously engaged in servicing the complicated requirements of a young lady at the head of the line, and obviously he would be tied up for quite a while. The other — "Jiggs," 13

---

bellicose: Eager to fight.   **girded:** Prepared.   **Milquetoast:** A timid, spineless person; named after Casper Milquetoast, a cartoon character created by Harold Webster in the 1920s.

his workmate called him—was a middle-aged man, who sat in a chair puffing a pipe, exchanging small talk with his working partner. My pulse began its telltale acceleration. The minutes ticked on. I stared at the idle shopkeeper, hoping to shame him into action, but he was impervious to my telepathic reproof and continued his small talk with his friend, brazenly° insensitive to the nervous demands of six good men who were raring to ski.

Suddenly my New Year's Eve resolution struck me. It was now or never. I 14 broke from my place in line and marched to the counter. I was going to control myself. I dug my nails into my palms. My effort was only partially successful.

"If you are not too busy," I said icily, "would you mind handing me a 15 screwdriver?"

Work stopped and everyone turned his eyes on me, and I experienced that 16 mortification° I always feel when I am the center of centripetal shafts of curiosity, resentment, perplexity.

But the worst was yet to come. "I am sorry, sir," said Jiggs deferentially, 17 moving the pipe from his mouth. "I am not supposed to move. I have just had a heart attack." That was the signal for a great whirring noise that descended from heaven. We looked, stricken, out the window, and it appeared as though a cyclone had suddenly focused on the snowy courtyard between the shop and the ski lift. Suddenly a gigantic army helicopter materialized, and hovered down to a landing. Two men jumped out of the plane carrying a stretcher, tore into the ski shop, and lifted the shopkeeper onto the stretcher. Jiggs bade his companion good-bye and was whisked out the door, into the plane, up to the heavens, down—we learned—to a nearby army hospital. I looked up manfully—into a score of man-eating eyes. I put the experience down as a reversal.

As I write this, on an airplane, I have run out of paper and need to reach 18 into my briefcase under my legs for more. I cannot do this until my empty lunch tray is removed from my lap. I arrested the stewardess as she passed empty-handed down the aisle on the way to the kitchen to fetch the lunch trays for the passengers up forward who haven't been served yet. "Would you please take my tray?" "Just a *moment,* sir!" she said, and marched on sternly. Shall I tell her that since she is headed for the kitchen *anyway,* it could not delay the feeding of the other passengers by more than two seconds necessary to stash away my empty tray? Or remind her that not fifteen minutes ago she spoke unctuously into the loudspeaker the words undoubtedly devised by the airline's highly paid public relations counselor: "If there is anything I or Miss French can do for you to make your trip more enjoyable, *please* let us—" I have run out of paper.

I think the observable reluctance of the majority of Americans to assert 19 themselves in minor matters is related to our increased sense of helplessness in an age of technology and centralized political and economic power. For

---

brazenly: Boldly.   **mortification:** Embarrassment.

generations, Americans who were too hot, or too cold, got up and did something about it. Now we call the plumber, or the electrician, or the furnace man. The habit of looking after our own needs obviously had something to do with the assertiveness that characterized the American family familiar to readers of American literature. With the technification of life goes our direct responsibility for our material environment, and we are conditioned to adopt a position of helplessness not only as regards the broken air conditioner, but as regards the overheated train. It takes an expert to fix the former, but not the latter; yet these distinctions, as we withdraw into helplessness, tend to fade away.

Our notorious political apathy is a related phenomenon. Every year, 20 whether the Republican or the Democratic Party is in office, more and more power drains away from the individual to feed vast reservoirs in far-off places; and we have less and less say about the shape of events which shape our future. From this alienation of personal power comes the sense of resignation with which we accept the political dispensations of a powerful government whose hold upon us continues to increase.

An editor of a national weekly news magazine told me a few years ago 21 that as few as a dozen letters of protest against an editorial stance of his magazine was enough to convene a plenipotentiary° meeting of the board of editors to review policy. "So few people complain, or make their voices heard," he explained to me, "that we assume a dozen letters represent the inarticulated views of thousands of readers." In the past ten years, he said, the volume of mail has noticeably decreased, even though the circulation of his magazine has risen.

When our voices are finally mute, when we have finally suppressed the 22 natural instinct to complain, whether the vexation is trivial or grave, we shall have become automatons,° incapable of feeling. When Premier Khrushchev° first came to this country late in 1959 he was primed, we are informed, to experience the bitter resentment of the American people against his tyranny, against his persecutions, against the movement which is responsible for the great number of American deaths in Korea, for billions in taxes every year, and for life everlasting on the brink of disaster; but Khrushchev was pleasantly surprised, and reported back to the Russian people that he had been met with overwhelming cordiality (read: apathy), except, to be sure, for "a few fascists who followed me around with their wretched posters, and should be horsewhipped."

I may be crazy, but I say there would have been lots more posters in a soci- 23 ety where train temperatures in the dead of winter are not allowed to climb to 85 degrees without complaint.

plenipotentiary: Having full power or authority.   **automatons:** Robots.   **Nikita Khrushchev** (1894–1971): Premier of the former Soviet Union from 1958 to 1964.

Questions to Start You Thinking

1. **Considering Meaning:** The writer focuses mostly on our tolerance for minor inconveniences, such as overheated commuter trains and inattentive waiters. But what larger implications and consequences follow from our inability to assert ourselves, according to Buckley?

2. **Identifying Writing Strategies:** Buckley's goal is to point out a general tendency among Americans and highlight its negative consequences. How does he implicate himself in this trend? Why do you think he does this?

3. **Reading Critically:** Who is Buckley's audience? What aspects of his essay indicate his likely readership?

4. **Expanding Vocabulary:** In his second paragraph, Buckley refers to a "more virile age." What do you think he is referring to? How does it contribute to his argument?

5. **Making Connections:** In "The Creation of Discontent" (pp. 634–36), Juliet Schor acknowledges that the growth in consumption has improved our lives in some ways but claims that it has not made us "happy" over the last forty years. In what ways do Schor's observations of modern life connect with Buckley's?

Journal Prompts

1. Do you have an inner Milquetoast, or do you tend to be more assertive? Recall an incident when you wanted to speak up for yourself. Did you? What were the consequences?

2. In this 1961 essay, Buckley writes about our "notorious political apathy" (paragraph 20). Do you think his generalization is or is not still true? What instances come to mind?

Suggestions for Writing

1. Write your own letter of complaint, directed to a person or institution that has affected you negatively in the present or the past.

2. According to Buckley, Americans were traditionally assertive and looked after their own needs (paragraph 19). Write an essay that reflects on the idea of American assertiveness and self-reliance. Choose examples from literature, history, or any aspect of American popular culture to support your view—or to respond to Buckley's.

William Zinsser

The Right to Fail

William Zinsser was born in New York City in 1922. After receiving his BA from Princeton University in 1944, he worked as a feature writer for the *New York Herald Tribune* and later became the newspaper's drama and film critic. Although he has covered subjects ranging from American landmarks to jazz in his many books and magazine articles, he is probably best known for his classic guides to writing: *On Writing Well* (1976), *Inventing the Truth* (1987), *Writing to Learn* (1988), and *Writing about Your Life* (2004). Zinsser has taught humor and nonfiction writing at Yale University, and he currently teaches at the New School University and the Columbia University Graduate School of Journalism in New York City. In "The Right to Fail," an excerpt from *The Lunacy Boom* (1970), Zinsser makes the case that failure is an important aspect of human experience.

For more about William Zinsser, visit <bedfordstmartins.com/bedguide>.

AS YOU READ: Identify the benefits of failure that Zinsser presents.

1 I like "dropout" as an addition to the American language because it's brief and it's clear. What I don't like is that we use it almost entirely as a dirty word.

2 We only apply it to people under twenty-one. Yet an adult who spends his days and nights watching mindless TV programs is more of a dropout than an eighteen-year-old who quits college, with its frequently mindless courses, to become, say, a VISTA volunteer. For the young, dropping out is often a way of dropping in.

3 To hold this opinion, however, is little short of treason in America. A boy or girl who leaves college is branded a failure—and the right to fail is one of the few freedoms that this country does not grant its citizens. The American dream is a dream of "getting ahead," painted in strokes of gold wherever we look. Our advertisements and TV commercials are a hymn to material success, our magazine articles a toast to people who made it to the top. Smoke the right cigarette or drive the right car—so the ads imply—and girls will be swooning into your deodorized arms or caressing your expensive lapels. Happiness goes to the man who has the sweet smell of achievement. He is our national idol, and everybody else is our national fink.°

4 I want to put in a word for the fink, especially the teen-age fink, because if we give him time to get through his finkdom—if we release him from the pressure of attaining certain goals by a certain age—he has a good chance of becoming our national idol, a Jefferson° or a Thoreau,° a Buckminster Fuller° or an Adlai Stevenson,° a man with a mind of his own. We need

---

fink: Tattletale or other contemptible person.   **Jefferson:** Thomas Jefferson (1743–1826), the third president of the United States and the main author of the Declaration of Independence.   **Thoreau:** Henry David Thoreau (1817–1862), an American writer and naturalist. **Buckminster Fuller:** American inventor, architect, and engineer (1895–1983) who dropped out of Harvard to work on solving global resource and environmental problems.   **Adlai Stevenson:** American politician (1900–1965) who was greatly admired for championing liberal causes but badly lost two presidential elections.

mavericks° and dissenters and dreamers far more than we need junior vice presidents, but we paralyze them by insisting that every step be a step up to the next rung of the ladder. Yet in the fluid years of youth, the only way for boys and girls to find their proper road is often to take a hundred side trips, poking out in different directions, faltering, drawing back, and starting again.

"But what if we fail?" they ask, whispering the dreadful word across the   5 Generation Gap to their parents, who are back home at the Establishment, nursing their "middle-class values" and cultivating their "goal-oriented society." The parents whisper back: "Don't!"

What they should say is "Don't be afraid to fail!" Failure isn't fatal.   6 Countless people have had a bout with it and come out stronger as a result. Many have even come out famous. History is strewn with eminent dropouts, "loners" who followed their own trail, not worrying about its odd twists and turns because they had faith in their own sense of direction. To read their biographies is always exhilarating, not only because they beat the system, but because their system was better than the one that they beat.

Luckily, such rebels still turn up often enough to prove that individual-   7 ism, though badly threatened, is not extinct. Much has been written, for instance, about the fitful scholastic career of Thomas P. F. Hoving, New York's former Parks Commissioner and now director of the Metropolitan Museum of Art. Hoving was a dropout's dropout, entering and leaving schools as if they were motels, often at the request of the management. Still, he must have learned something during those unorthodox years, for he dropped in again at the top of his profession.

His case reminds me of another boyhood—that of Holden Caulfield in   8 J. D. Salinger's *The Catcher in the Rye,* the most popular literary hero of the postwar period. There is nothing accidental about the grip that this dropout continues to hold on the affections of an entire American generation. Nobody else, real or invented, has made such an engaging shambles of our "goal-oriented society," so gratified our secret belief that the "phonies" are in power and the good guys up the creek. Whether Holden has also reached the top of his chosen field today is one of those speculations that delight fanciers of good fiction. I speculate that he has. Holden Caulfield, incidentally, is now thirty-six.

I'm not urging everyone to go out and fail just for the sheer therapy of it,   9 or to quit college just to coddle° some vague discontent. Obviously it's better to succeed than to flop, and in general a long education is more helpful than a short one. (Thanks to my own education, for example, I can tell George Eliot from T. S. Eliot. I can handle the pluperfect tense in French, and I know that Caesar beat the Helvetii because he had enough frumentum.°) I only mean that failure isn't bad in itself, or success automatically good.

---

mavericks: Nonconformists.   **coddle:** Indulge; satisfy.   **frumentum:** Latin word for corn or grain.

Fred Zinnemann, who has directed some of Hollywood's most honored   10
movies, was asked by a reporter, when *A Man for All Seasons* won every prize,
about his previous film *Behold a Pale Horse*, which was a box-office disaster. "I
don't feel any obligation to be successful," Zinnemann replied. "Success can
be dangerous—you feel you know it all. I've learned a great deal from my failures." A similar point was made by Richard Brooks about his ambitious
money loser, *Lord Jim*. Recalling the three years of his life that went into it,
talking almost with elation about the troubles that befell his unit in Cambo-
dia, Brooks told me that he learned more about his craft from this considerable failure than from his many earlier hits.

It's a point, of course, that applies throughout the arts. Writers, play-   11
wrights, painters, and composers work in the expectation of periodic defeat,
but they wouldn't keep going back into the arena if they thought it was the
end of the world. It isn't the end of the world. For an artist—and perhaps for
anybody—it is the only way to grow.

Today's younger generation seems to know that this is true, seems willing   12
to take the risks in life that artists take in art. "Society," needless to say, still
has the upper hand—it sets the goals and condemns as a failure everybody
who won't play. But the dropouts and the hippies are not as afraid of failure
as their parents and grandparents. This could mean, as their elders might
say, that they are just plumb lazy, secure in the comforts of an affluent state.
It could also mean, however, that they just don't buy the old standards of
success and are rapidly writing new ones.

Recently it was announced, for instance, that more than two hundred   13
thousand Americans have inquired about service in VISTA (the domestic
Peace Corps) and that, according to a Gallup survey, "more than three million American college students would serve VISTA in some capacity if given
the opportunity." This is hardly the road to riches or to an executive suite.
Yet I have met many of these young volunteers, and they are not pining
for traditional success. On the contrary, they appear more fulfilled than the
average vice president with a swimming pool.

Who is to say, then, if there is any right path to the top, or even to say   14
what the top consists of? Obviously the colleges don't have more than a
partial answer—otherwise the young would not be so disaffected with an
education that they consider vapid.° Obviously business does not have the
answer—otherwise the young would not be so scornful of its call to be an
organization man.

The fact is, nobody has the answer, and the dawning awareness of this   15
fact seems to me one of the best things happening in America today. Success
and failure are again becoming individual visions, as they were when the
country was younger, not rigid categories. Maybe we are learning again to
cherish this right of every person to succeed on his own terms and to fail as
often as necessary along the way.

vapid: Dull.

Questions to Start You Thinking

1. **Considering Meaning:**   What does Zinsser mean when he says that "dropping out is often a way of dropping in" (paragraph 2)? Why is this especially true for young adults?

2. **Identifying Writing Strategies:**   Identify some of the concrete examples that Zinsser uses to illustrate his points. Are his examples extensive and varied enough to be convincing? Why, or why not?

3. **Reading Critically:**   Zinsser is savvy enough to admit that his position is "little short of treason in America" (paragraph 3). Where else does he acknowledge that his advice might seem outlandish? How does he counter the opposition?

4. **Expanding Vocabulary:**   In paragraph 3, Zinsser writes, "Our advertisements and TV commercials are a hymn to material success." Define *hymn*. What does the word suggest about the American attitude toward material success? How does Zinsser feel about the American dream?

5. **Making Connections:**   Writing in 1970, Zinsser claims that "dropping out is often a way of dropping in" (paragraph 2) and seems cynical about our "goal-oriented society" (paragraph 8). Compare his essay with Michael Gurian's "Disappearing Act: Where Have All the Men Gone? No Place Good" (pp. 552–56). How does Gurian's argument affect your view of Zinsser's?

Journal Prompts

1. What is your definition of the "American dream" (paragraph 3)?

2. Who would you like to share Zinsser's essay with in order to open up that person's mind about failure? Why?

Suggestions for Writing

1. In paragraph 10, Zinsser offers the following quote from a movie director: "Success can be dangerous — you feel you know it all. I've learned a great deal from my failures." Write an essay in which you recall a personal experience that illustrates this statement.

2. Originally written in 1970, Zinsser's essay includes some examples that may not be familiar to you. Write an essay that supports and updates Zinsser's position by drawing on more current examples from history, literature, sports, current events, or popular culture. Imagine a specific audience for your essay (perhaps a sibling, a friend, or a high school class), and be sure that your examples will have an impact on those readers.

Harold Taw

Finding Prosperity by Feeding Monkeys

Harold Taw is a novelist, screenwriter, and attorney. After graduating Phi Beta Kappa from the University of California at Berkeley with a degree in anthropology, Taw was a Fulbright scholar studying the spread of AIDS in rural Thailand. He graduated from Yale Law School, where he was an articles editor for the *Yale Law Journal.* His first novel was *Adventures of the Karaoke King,* and his first screenplay was *Dog Park,* a top-ten finalist in the November 2009 Red Inkworks Screenwriter's Competition and a semifinalist in the 2009 Screenplay Festival Competition. His essay originally appeared as a radio broadcast on National Public Radio's series *This I Believe.*

For more about Harold Taw, visit <bedfordstmartins.com/bedguide>.

AS YOU READ: How does Taw explain causes and effects in this essay?

1   I could say that I believe in America because it rewarded my family's hard work to overcome poverty. I could say that I believe in holding on to rituals and traditions because they helped us flourish in a new country. But these concepts are more concretely expressed this way: I believe in feeding monkeys on my birthday—something I've done without fail for thirty-five years.

2   When I was born, a blind, Buddhist° monk, living alone in the Burmese° jungle, predicted that my birth would bring great prosperity to the family. To ensure this prosperity, I was to feed monkeys on my birthday.

3   While this sounds superstitious, the practice makes karmic sense. On a day normally given over to narcissism, I must consider my family and give nourishment to another living creature. The monk never meant for the ritual to be a burden. In the Burmese jungle, monkeys are as common as pigeons. He probably had to shoo them away from his sticky rice and mangoes. It was only in America that feeding monkeys meant violating the rules.

4   As a kid, I thought that was cool. I learned English through watching bad television shows, and I felt like Caine from *Kung Fu,°* except I was the chosen warrior sent to defend my family. Dad and I would go to the zoo early in the morning, just the two of us. When the coast was clear, I would throw my contraband peanuts to the monkeys.

5   I never had to explain myself until my eighteenth birthday. It was the first year I didn't go with my father. I went with my friends and arrived ten minutes after the zoo gates closed.

6   "*Please,*" I beseeched the zookeeper. "I feed monkeys for my family, not for me. Can't you make an exception?"

7   "Go find a pet store," she said.

8   If only it were so easy. That time, I got lucky. I found out that a high school classmate had trained the monkeys for the movie *Out of Africa,°* so he allowed me to feed his monkey. I've had other close calls. Once, a man with a

Buddhist: Follower of a religion that originated in India, but is common in China, Myanmar, Japan, Tibet, and other parts of Southeast Asia.   **Burmese:** Native to Burma, a country in southeast Asia, now Myanmar.   *Kung Fu:* American television show from the 1970s. *Out of Africa:* 1985 film based on a book by Isak Dinesen.

pet monkey suspected that my story was a ploy, and that I was an animal-rights activist out to liberate his monkey. Another time, a zoo told me that outsiders could not feed their monkeys without violating the zookeepers' collective bargaining agreement. In a pet store once, I managed to feed a marmoset° being kept in a birdcage. Another time, I was asked to wear a bio-hazard suit to feed a laboratory monkey.

It's rarely easy and, yet, somehow I've found a way to feed a monkey every year since I was born. 9

Our family has prospered in America. I believe that I have ensured this prosperity by observing our family ritual and feeding monkeys on my birthday. Do I believe that literally? Maybe. But I have faith in our family, and I believe in honoring that faith in any way I can. 10

Questions to Start You Thinking

1. **Considering Meaning:**   What is the meaning of Taw's birthday ritual? In what ways is it literal? How is it symbolic?

2. **Identifying Writing Strategies:**   How does Taw use repetition in his opening paragraph? How is it related to his overall meaning?

3. **Reading Critically:**   In what ways has Taw's attitude about the ritual changed over the years? Did its meaning change?

4. **Expanding Vocabulary:**   According to Taw, birthdays are "normally given over to narcissism" (paragraph 3). What does *narcissism* mean? How does feeding the monkeys counteract narcissism?

5. **Making Connections:**   Taw writes, "I could say that I believe in holding on to rituals and traditions because they helped us flourish in a new country" (paragraph 1). How might Richard Rodriguez ("Public and Private Language," pp. 524–29) respond to that statement?

Journal Prompts

1. Do you specifically honor your family in any way? How do you express your faith in family?

2. Taw writes that he had to "explain" himself and his annual custom after he turned eighteen (paragraph 5). Have you ever had to explain or justify a practice — religious, ethnic, personal, or otherwise — to someone unfamiliar with it? How did you do it? Was it difficult? Recount the experience.

Suggestions for Writing

1. "Finding Prosperity by Feeding Monkeys" was presented as part of *This I Believe,* a radio series in which people share brief essays about core

marmoset: Small monkey found in South and Central America.

values that shape their lives. (For another essay from this series, see Sarah Adams, "Be Cool to the Pizza Dude," pp. 615–16.) Write your own *This I Believe* essay that relates a personal philosophy or value system.

2. Taw acknowledges that his belief "sounds superstitious" (paragraph 3). What are superstitions? What purposes do they serve? Investigate a particular superstition. Then write an essay explaining its function, origins, variations, significance, or other aspects to support your thesis about it.

Eric Weiner

from *The Geography of Bliss*

Eric Weiner has been a correspondent with National Public Radio since 1993. In that time, he has traveled to over 30 countries as well as around the United States. He has written for the *New York Times* and the *Los Angeles Times*, and he was a Knight Journalism Fellow at Stanford University. His *New York Times* best-seller *The Geography of Bliss: One Grump's Search for the Happiest Places in the World* (2008) tells of his search through at least ten countries for the happiest place on earth. The excerpt from *The Geography of Bliss* reprinted here begins with Weiner's visit to Dutch professor Ruut Veenhoven, who runs "The World Database of Happiness."

AS YOU READ: What does Weiner learn about what makes people happy?

For more about Eric Weiner, visit **\<bedfordstmartins .com/bedguide\>**.

I pause to take in the moment. On these computers, right in front of me, is humanity's accumulated knowledge of happiness. After virtually ignoring the subject for decades, social scientists are now making up for lost time, churning out research papers at a prodigious° rate. Happy, you might say, is the new sad. 1

The research findings are alternatively obvious and counterintuitive,° expected and surprising. In many cases, the findings validate the great thinkers of centuries past—as if the ancient Greeks need validation. Here are a few of the findings, in no particular order. 2

Extroverts are happier than introverts; optimists are happier than pessimists; married people are happier than singles, though people with children are no happier than childless couples; Republicans are happier than Democrats; people who attend religious services are happier than those who do not; people with college degrees are happier than those without, though people with advanced degrees are less happy than those with just a BA; people with an active sex life are happier than those without; women and men are equally happy, though women have a wider emotional range; having an affair will make you happy but will not compensate for the massive loss of happiness that you will incur when your spouse finds out and leaves you; people are least happy when they're commuting to work; busy people are happier than those 3

prodigious: Enormous and amazing.   **counterintuitive:** Contrary to what common sense would indicate.

with too little to do; wealthy people are happier than poor ones, but only slightly.

So what should we do with these findings? Get married but don't have kids? Start going to church regularly? Drop out of that PhD program? Not so fast. Social scientists have a hard time unraveling what they call "reverse causality" and what the rest of us call the chicken-and-egg problem. For instance, healthy people are happier than unhealthy ones; or is it that happy people tend to be healthier? Married people are happy; or maybe happy people are more likely to get married? It's tough to say. Reverse causality is the hobgoblin that makes mischief in many a research project.

What I really want to know, though, is not who is happy but where they are happy—and why.... Believe it or not, most people in the world say they are happy. Virtually every country in the world scores somewhere between five and eight on a ten-point scale. There are a few exceptions: The sullen Moldovans consistently score about 4.5, and for a brief period in 1962 the citizens of the Dominican Republic could muster only a 1.6, the lowest level of happiness ever recorded on the planet. But, as I said, these are rare exceptions. Most of the world is happy....

America's place on the happiness spectrum° is not as high as you might think, given our superpower status. We are not, by any measure, the happiest nation on earth. One study, by Adrian White at the University of Leicester in Britain, ranked the United States as the world's twenty-third happiest nation, behind countries such as Costa Rica, Malta, and Malaysia. True, most Americans—84 percent, according to one study—describe themselves as either "very" or "pretty" happy, but it's safe to say that the United States is not as happy as it is wealthy.

Indeed, there is plenty of evidence that we are less happy today than ever before, as psychologist David Myers has shown in his book *The American Paradox: Spiritual Hunger in an Age of Plenty*. Since 1960, the divorce rate has doubled, the teen-suicide rate tripled, the violent-crime rate quadrupled, and the prison population quintupled. Then there are the increased rates of depression, anxiety, and other mental-health problems. (There is robust evidence that what we're witnessing is a genuine increase in these disorders and not merely a greater willingness to diagnose them.)...

The self-help industrial complex hasn't helped. By telling us that happiness lives inside us, it's turned us inward just when we should be looking outward. Not to money but to other people, to community and to the kind of human bonds that so clearly are the sources of our happiness.

Americans work longer hours and commute greater distances than virtually any other people in the world. Commuting, in particular, has been found to be detrimental to our happiness, as well as our physical health. Every minute spent on the road is one less minute that we can spend with family and friends—the kind of activities, in other words, that make us happy.

spectrum: Range.

Political scientist Robert Putnam makes a convincing case in his book 10
Bowling Alone that our sense of connection is fraying. We spend less time visiting family and friends; we belong to fewer community groups. Increasingly,
we lead fragmented lives. The Internet and other technologies may salve° our
loneliness, but they have not, I believe, eliminated it. . . .

One way Americans pursue happiness is by physically moving. Indeed, 11
ours is a nation founded on restlessness. What were the pilgrims if not he-
donic° refugees, searching for happiness someplace else? And what is our
much-heralded "frontier spirit" if not a yearning for a happier place? "In
America, getting on in the world means getting out of the world we have
known before," wrote the editor and teacher Ellery Sedgwick in his autobiography, *The Happy Profession.*

Sedgwick wrote those words in 1946. Since then, we've become even more 12
mobile. Every year, nearly forty million Americans move. Some, no doubt,
pick up stakes for job opportunities or to be near a sick relative. But many
move simply because they believe they'll be happier somewhere else. . . .

Where is the happiest place in the United States? Here the science of hap- 13
piness fails me. I could not find one definitive report that answers that question. Christopher Peterson of the University of Michigan told me that people
get happier the farther west they move. His theory, though, contradicts the
findings of David Schkade of the University of California at San Diego. He
and his colleagues surveyed people in California and Michigan and found
that they were equally happy (or unhappy, depending on your perspective).
The people in Michigan *thought* they would be happier if they moved to California, a belief that Schkade calls a "focusing illusion." Sitting in cold, bleak
Michigan, these people imagined a happier life in California, but they failed
to take into account the negative side to life there: traffic jams, high real-
estate prices, and wildfires, to name a few. "Nothing you focus on will make
as much difference as you think," he concludes. . . .

A slippery seal, happiness is. On the road, I encountered bushels of incon- 14
sistencies. The Swiss are uptight and happy. The Thais are laid-back and
happy. Icelanders find joy in their binge drinking, Moldovans only misery.
Maybe an Indian mind can digest these contradictions, but mine can't. Exasperated, I call one of the leading happiness researchers, John Helliwell. Perhaps he has some answers.

"It's simple," he says. "There's more than one path to happiness." 15

Questions to Start You Thinking

1. **Considering Meaning:** Explain the idea of a "focusing illusion"
   (paragraph 13) in your own words. Why is it significant to happiness
   research?

salve: Soothe or heal.   **hedonic:** Relating to pleasure.

2. **Identifying Writing Strategies:**   How does Weiner use main clauses that could stand alone as complete sentences and semicolons in paragraph 3? How does this stylistic choice support the overall meaning of his essay?

3. **Reading Critically:**   Weiner writes that the "self-help industrial complex" has not made us happier, as "it's turned us inward just when we should be looking outward" (paragraph 8). What do you think the "self-help industrial complex" is? What do people find when they look "inward" or "outward"?

4. **Expanding Vocabulary:**   Although Weiner emphasizes happiness in this essay, his book (from which this is an excerpt) is called *The Geography of Bliss.* What does *bliss* mean, and how is it different from *happiness?* How are these terms related to words like *contentment* and *pleasure?*

5. **Making Connections:**   What geography of bliss is implied by Cheryl Mendelson in "My Secret Life" (pp. 545–47)? What is her version of happiness? Do you think Weiner would agree with her views?

Journal Prompts

1. In paragraph 3, Weiner lists findings from happiness researchers. He then asks, "So what should we do with these findings?" (paragraph 4). Do any of these categories apply to you? Do the findings seem obvious or surprising? Would you change your life based on such research?

2. Weiner discusses the problem of a "focusing illusion" (paragraph 13) as it affects our perceptions of happiness. Write about a place, achievement, or ambition (personal or professional) that you expect to make you happy. Then, examine your own "focusing illusion" by taking into account any negative aspects of your goal or desire.

Suggestions for Writing

1. Write a personal essay about your own "geography of bliss." What places do you associate with your own happiness? How has geography contributed to—or detracted from—your happiness? Is there a location that you aspire to or that you see as essential to your future happiness?

2. Conduct your own happiness research experiment. (Be sure to check and follow your campus regulations about research involving human subjects.) Your study could be as basic as asking a range of people—students, friends, instructors, family members—to define happiness in a sentence or two. You could also pick a specific factor—gender, major, career ambition, employment—and look for patterns of happiness based on those factors. If possible, begin with a tentative hypothesis (for example, returning students are happier than new students), and then

test the hypothesis. Write a report to summarize your study and report your findings.

Juliet Schor
The Creation of Discontent

Juliet Schor is a professor of sociology at Boston College. Her undergraduate degree is from Wesleyan University and her PhD from the University of Massachusetts. Currently, Schor is studying trends in work and leisure, consumerism, and the relationship between work and family. Her awards have included the Maurer-Stump Award from the Reading-Berks Chapter of the Democratic Socialists of America and the George Orwell Award for Distinguished Contributions to Honesty and Clarity in Public Language from the National Council of Teachers of English. Her books include *The Overspent American: Why We Want What We Don't Need* (1998), *Do Americans Shop Too Much?* (2000), *Born to Buy: The Commercialized Child and the New Consumer Culture* (2004), and *The Overworked American: The Unexpected Decline of Leisure* (1992), from which this reading is taken. Here, Schor examines Americans' increasing material wealth and questions the assumption that it leads to greater fulfillment.

AS YOU READ: How does Schor connect material prosperity and unhappiness?

For more about Juliet Schor, visit **<bedfordstmartins.com/bedguide>**.

I never knew how poor I was until I had a little money.
— a banker

There is no doubt that the growth of consumption has yielded major improvements in the quality of life. Running water, washing machines, and electrical appliances eliminated arduous, often backbreaking labor. Especially for the poor women who not only did their own housework, but often someone else's as well, the transformation of the home has been profoundly liberating. Other products have also enhanced the quality of life. The compact disc raises the enjoyment of the music lover; the high-performance engine makes the car buff happy; and the fashion plate loves to wear a designer suit.

But when we add up all the items we consume, and consider the overall impact, rather than each in isolation, the picture gets murkier. The farther we get from the onerous° physical conditions of the past, the more ambiguous° are the effects of additional commodities. The less "necessary" and more "luxurious" the item, the more difficult it is automatically to assume that consumer purchases yield intrinsic value.

In an era when the connections between perpetual growth and environmental deterioration are becoming more apparent, with the quality of public life declining in many areas (public safety, decline of community, failing education system), shouldn't we at least step back and re-examine our commitment to ever-greater quantities of consumer goods? Do Americans need

onerous: Heavy, oppressive.   **ambiguous:** Lacking in clearness; having several possible meanings.

high-definition television, increasingly exotic vacations, and climate control in their autos? How about hundred-dollar inflatable sneakers, fifty-dollar wrinkle cream, or the ever-present (but rarely used) stationary bicycle? A growing fraction of homes are now equipped with jacuzzis (or steam showers) and satellite receivers. Once we take the broader view, can we still be so sure that all these things are really making us better off?

We do know that the increasing consumption of the last forty years has not made us happier. The percentage of the population who reported being "very happy" peaked in 1957, according to two national polls. By the last years these polls were taken (1970 and 1978), the level of "very happy" had not recovered, in spite of the rapid growth in consumption during the 1960s and 1970s. Similar polls taken since then indicate no revival of happiness.[1]

Despite the fact that possessions are not creating happiness, we are still riding the consumer merry-go-round. In fact, for some Americans the quest for material goods became more intense in the last decade: according to the pollster Louis Harris, "by the mid-1980s, the American people were far more oriented toward economic growth and materialism than before. Most significant, young people were leading the charge back to material values" (148).

Materialism has not only failed to make us happy. It has also bred its own form of discontent—even among the affluent.° Newspaper and magazine articles chronicle the dissatisfaction. One couple earning $115,000 tallied up their necessary expenses of $100,000 a year and complained that "something's gone terribly wrong with being 'rich'" (Hewitt). An unmarried Hollywood executive earning $72,000 worried about bouncing checks: "I have so much paid for by the studio—my car, my insurance, and virtually all food and entertainment—and I'm *still* broke." Urbanites° have it especially hard. As one New York City inhabitant explained, "It's incredible, but you just can't live in this city on a hundred thousand dollars a year" (Tobias 24). According to the *New York Times,* the fast lane is not all it's cracked up to be, and Wall Streeters are "Feeling Poor on $600,000 a Year." "When the Joneses they are keeping up with are the Basses . . . $10 million in liquid capital° is not rich" (Kroeger).

Whatever we think of these malcontents°—whether we find them funny, pathetic, or reprehensible°—we must acknowledge that these feelings are not confined to those in the income stratosphere. Many who make far less have similar laments. Douglas and Maureen Obey earn $56,000 a year—an income that exceeds that of roughly 70 percent of the population (Mishel 25). Yet

---

affluent: Wealthy.   **urbanites:** People who live in cities.   **liquid capital:** Cash, or assets that can be easily converted into cash.   **malcontents:** People who are never satisfied. **reprehensible:** Deserving of criticism or blame.

1. A number of polls ask identical questions, yet give different levels of happiness. For example, the General Social Survey polls yield consistently higher results than the Survey Research Center or the National Opinion Research Corporation. SRC and NORC polls end in the 1970s; the GSS poll continues through the 1980s. The conclusion that "very happy" has not recovered is based on the GSS poll, which begins in 1972 and is the only poll still being taken during the 1980s. The GSS peaks in 1973 and does not recover throughout the 1980s. See Niemi, 290.

they complain that they are stretched to the breaking point. Douglas works two jobs "to try to keep it all together. . . . I feel I make a fairly good income that should afford a comfortable life style, but somehow it doesn't. . . . [I'm] in hock° up to my eyeballs." The Obeys own their home, two cars, a second rental property, and a backyard pool (Coakley 1).

Complaints about life style have been particularly loud among the baby-boom generation. One writer explained a state of mind shared by many in her generation: she was convinced she would not achieve the comfortable middle-class life style enjoyed by her parents (four-bedroom house, two-car garage, private schools for the children, and cashmere blankets at the bottom of the beds): "I thought bitterly of my downward mobility . . . and [had] constant conversations with myself about wanting . . . a new couch, a weekend cottage, a bigger house on a quieter street" (Butler 34). Eventually she realized that more money was not the answer. Her needs were satisfied. As she acknowledged: "Discontent was cheating me of the life I *had*" (37). 8

Works Cited

The sources for Schor's study are presented in MLA style.

Butler, Katy. "The Great Boomer Bust." *Mother Jones* June 1989: 32–38. Print.

Coakley, Tom. "One Couple's Lament Captures Anti-tax Mood." *Boston Globe* 2 Feb. 1990: 1. Print.

Harris, Louis. *Inside America.* New York: Vintage, 1987. Print.

Hewitt, Paul S. "Something's Gone Terribly Wrong with Being 'Rich.'" *Los Angeles Herald Tribune* 7 Jan. 1989. Print.

Kroeger, Brooke. "Feeling Poor on $600,000 a Year." *New York Times* 26 Apr. 1987. Print.

Mishel, Lawrence, and David Frankel. *The State of Working America.* 1990–1991 ed. Armonk: Sharpe, 1991. Print.

Niemi, Richard G., John Mueller, and Tom W. Smith. *Trends in Public Opinion: A Compendium of Survey Data.* New York: Greenwood Press, 1989. Print.

Tobias, Andrew. "Getting by on $100,000 a Year." *Esquire* 23 May 1978: 24. Print.

Questions to Start You Thinking

1. **Considering Meaning:**   How does increasing consumption and materialism also increase discontent, according to Schor?

2. **Identifying Writing Strategies:**   Schor begins this essay with a quotation from an anonymous banker. How does this quotation function as an introduction to her essay?

3. **Reading Critically:**   What is the purpose of Schor's first paragraph? What point is she making? Why is it necessary?

4. **Expanding Vocabulary:**   Schor notes that it is increasingly unclear whether the items people buy have any "intrinsic value" (paragraph 2).

hock: Debt.

What does it mean for something to have intrinsic value? Why is "intrinsic value" important to Schor's argument about consumption and happiness?

5. **Making Connections:** Both Schor and Eric Weiner ("The Geography of Bliss," pp. 630–32) make the point that Americans have not become happier over the last forty to fifty years. How do their explanations differ? Do you think that the two explanations are compatible or mutually exclusive?

Link to the Paired Essay

In paragraph 3, Schor asks a series of rhetorical questions such as, "Do Americans need high-definition television, increasingly exotic vacations, and climate control in their autos? How about hundred-dollar inflatable sneakers, fifty-dollar wrinkle cream, or the ever-present (but rarely used) stationary bicycle?" How might Llewellyn H. Rockwell Jr. ("In Defense of Consumerism," pp. 638–41) react to these questions? How do you think he would respond to other aspects of Schor's essay? Which writer do you find more persuasive, and why?

Journal Prompts

1. Schor argues that the differences between "necessary" and "luxurious" consumer purchases have become blurred (paragraph 2). Have you ever bought something that you felt was a necessity, but that others might view as a luxury, or vice versa? What made you decide that the item was a luxury or a necessity?

2. In 1986, a newspaper writer coined the term "retail therapy," which is the practice of buying things in order to change your mood or state of mind, not because you need a particular product. Have you ever engaged in "retail therapy"? Did you find it helpful or harmful?

Suggestions for Writing

1. Schor writes about a woman who worries that she will never have as comfortable a lifestyle as her parents had when she was growing up (paragraph 8). Do you expect to lead a better or worse lifestyle than your parents? What elements of their lifestyle would you like to experience? What elements would you prefer not to include in your own life?

2. Schor cites a pollster who asserts that by the mid-1980s, increased materialism was primarily being driven by young people (paragraph 5). Is that still the case today? Based on your own experiences and observations of today's culture and on some research about current economics, write an essay discussing what segment of society drives consumer spending.

For more about Llewellyn H. Rockwell Jr., visit **<bedfordstmartins .com/bedguide>**.

Llewellyn H. Rockwell Jr.

In Defense of Consumerism

Llewellyn H. Rockwell Jr. was born in 1944 in Boston, Massachusetts. He received his degree in English from Tufts University. He is an American political commentator and chairman of the libertarian Ludwig von Mises Institute. From 1978 to 1982, he was Ron Paul's congressional chief of staff. His work includes *Speaking of Liberty,* an anthology of editorials and speeches, and the *Journal of Libertarian Studies,* which he publishes with the Ludwig von Mises Institute. His work also appears in *Conservative Digest.* He maintains a Web site, LewRockwell.com, where he blogs, records podcasts, and reprints articles with a libertarian perspective. In this essay, written for the Ludwig von Mises Institute, Rockwell offers a spirited defense of consumption and free-market capitalism.

AS YOU READ: How does Rockwell defend consumerism?

'm beginning to think that the epithet° "consumerism" is just another word for freedom in the marketplace.   1

It's true that the market is delivering goods, services, and technological advances by leaps, day after day. People claim that they are so inundated° with techno advances that they don't want anymore. Say no to the latest gizmo!   2

But we really don't mean it. No one wants to be denied web access, and we want it faster and better with more variety. We want to download songs, movies, and treatises on every subject. No amount of information is too much when it is something specific we seek.   3

And that's not all.   4

We want better heating and cooling in our homes and businesses. We want more varieties of food, wine, cleaning products, toothpaste, and razors. We want access to a full range of styles in our home furnishing. If something is broken, we want the materials made available to repair it. We want fresh flowers, fresh fish, fresh bread, and new cars with more features. We want overnight delivery, good tech support, and the newest fashions from all over the world.   5

The libraries are going online, as is the world's art. Commerce has made the shift. New worlds are opening to us by the day. We find that phone calls are free. We can link with anyone in the world through instant messaging, and email has become the medium that makes all communication possible. We are abandoning our tube-televisions and landline telephones—staples of 20th-century life—for far superior modes of information technology.   6

We want speed. We want wireless. We want access. And improvements. Clean and filtered water must flow from our refrigerators. We want energy drinks, sports drinks, bubbly drinks, juicy drinks, and underground spring water from Fiji. We want homes. We want safety and security. We want service. We want choice.   7

We are getting all these things. And how? Through that incredible production and distribution machine called the market economy, which is really   8

epithet: Insult.   **inundated:** Flooded.

nothing but billions of people cooperating and innovating to make better lives for themselves. There's no dog-eat-dog. Competition is really nothing but entrepreneurs and capitalists falling over themselves in a quest to win the hearts and minds of the consuming public.

Sure, it's easy to look at all this and shout: ghastly consumerism! But if 9 by "consume" we mean to purchase products and services with our own money in order to improve the human condition, who can't help but plead guilty?

The whole history of ideas about society has been spent trying to come 10 up with some system that serves the common man rather than just the elites, the rulers, and the powerful. When the market economy, and its capitalistic structure, came into being, that institution was finally discovered. With the advent of economic science, we came to understand how this could be. We began to see how it is that billions of unplanned economic choices could conspire to create a beautiful global system of production and distribution that served everyone. And how do the intellectuals respond to this? By denouncing it as providing too much to too many.

But are people buying superfluous° things that they can do without? Cer- 11 tainly. But who is to say for sure what is a need as versus a mere want? A dictator who knows all? How can we know that his desires will accord with my needs and yours? In any case, in a market economy, wants and needs are linked, so that one person's necessities are met precisely because other people's wants are met.

Here is an example.   12

If my grandchild is desperately sick, I want to get her to a doctor. The 13 urgent-care clinic is open late, as is the drug store next door, and thank goodness. I'm in and out, and I have the medicine and materials necessary to restore her to health. No one would say that this is a superficial demand.

But it can only stay open late because its offices are nestled in a strip mall 14 where the rents are low and the access is high. The real estate is shared by candy stores, sports shops selling scuba gear, a billiard hall, and a store that specializes in party favors—all stores selling "superficial" things. All pay rent. The developer who made the mall wouldn't have built the place were it not for these less urgent needs.

The same is true for the furniture and equipment and labor used in the 15 urgent-care clinic. They are less expensive and more accessible than they otherwise would be due to the persistence of non-essential consumer demands. The computers they use are up-to-date and fast precisely because technicians and entrepreneurs have innovated to meet the demands of gamers, gamblers, and people who use the web to do things they shouldn't.

The same point can be made about "luxury goods" and bleeding-edge 16 technologies. The rich acquire them and use them until the bugs are gone, the imitators are aroused, capitalists seek out cheaper suppliers, and eventually prices tumble and the same technology hits the mass market. Moreover,

superfluous: Unnecessary.

it is the rich who donate to charity, the arts, and to religion. They provide the capital necessary for investment. If you think through any service or good that is widely considered to be a need, you will find that it employs products, technologies, and services that were first created to meet superficial demands.

Maybe you think quality of life is no big deal. Does it really matter whether people have access to vast grocery stores, drug stores, subdivisions, and technology? Part of the answer has to do with natural rights: people should be free to choose and buy as they see fit. But another argument is buried in data we don't often think about. 17

Consider life expectancy in the age of consumerism. Women in 1900 typically died at 48 years old, and men at 46. Today? Women live to 80, and men to 77. This is due to better diet, less dangerous jobs, improved sanitation and hygiene, improved access to health care, and the entire range of factors that contribute to what we call our standard of living. Just since 1950, the infant mortality rate has fallen by 77 percent. Population is rising exponentially as a result. 18

It's easy to look at these figures that suggest that we could have achieved the same thing with a central plan for health, while avoiding all this disgusting consumerism that goes along with it. But such a central plan was tried in socialist countries, and their results showed precisely the opposite in mortality statistics. While the Soviets decried our persistent poverty amidst rampant consumerism, our poverty was being beaten back and our longevity was increasing, in large part because of the consumerism for which we were being reviled.° 19

Nowadays we are being told that consumption is aesthetically displeasing, and that we should strive to get back to nature, stop driving here and there, make a compost pile, raise our own vegetables, unplug our computers, and eat nuts off trees. This longing for the primitive is nothing but an attempt to cast a pleasing gloss on the inevitable effects of socialist policies. They are telling us to love poverty and hate plenty. 20

But the beauty of the market economy is that it gives everyone a choice. For those people who prefer outhouses to indoor plumbing, pulling their teeth to dentistry, and eating nuts from trees rather than buying a can of Planters at Wal-Mart, they too have the right to choose that way of life. But don't let them say that they are against "consumerism." To live at all requires that we buy and sell. To be against commerce is to attack life itself. 21

Questions to Start You Thinking

1. **Considering Meaning:** According to Rockwell, why is superfluous spending (paragraph 11) and "rampant consumerism" (paragraph 19) a good thing?

reviled: Verbally attacked.

2. **Identifying Writing Strategies:**   Why does Rockwell write much of the essay in the first person plural (using *we*). What effect does it have?

3. **Reading Critically:**   Other than including statistics on life expectancy in paragraph 18, Rockwell cites no sources, no supporting evidence, and no one who opposes his point of view. How does this choice affect the effectiveness of his essay? What does it suggest about his audience? What sources might he have included to support his argument?

4. **Expanding Vocabulary:**   Rockwell writes, "Nowadays we are being told that consumption is aesthetically displeasing . . ." (paragraph 20). What does *aesthetically displeasing* mean? Why would people describe consumption in this way?

5. **Making Connections:**   According to Rockwell, consumerism increases connections with others (paragraph 6). Would Eric Weiner ("The Geography of Bliss," pp. 630–32) agree with this assessment? What effect does such technology have on our sense of connection?

Link to the Paired Essay

Rockwell states that "to be against commerce is to attack life itself" (paragraph 21). How might Juliet Schor ("The Creation of Discontent," pp. 634–36) respond to Rockwell's conception of "life," as stated here?

Journal Prompts

1. Rockwell argues that we may say that we do not want more goods or technological advancements, but "we don't really mean it" (paragraph 3). Do you have any hesitations or mixed emotions about consumption or new technologies in the marketplace?

2. According to Rockwell, freedom of individual consumption "has to do with natural rights" (paragraph 17). What is a "natural right"? Do you consider freedom of choice as a consumer a "natural right"? How do your rights as a consumer and your rights as a citizen differ?

Suggestions for Writing

1. Write an essay that articulates your own view of consumption and consumer culture. Do you see it as an unqualified good, as Rockwell does? Do you take a more skeptical view, along the lines of Juliet Schor?

2. Rockwell disparages those who believe that people should live closer to nature — making compost, growing vegetables, reducing driving, and so forth — because he sees their more primitive lifestyle as a result of socialism (paragraph 21). Write an essay agreeing or disagreeing with him, using evidence from popular culture, contemporary politics, or recent history to support or refute his claim.

A
WRITER'S
RESEARCH
MANUAL

A Writer's Research Manual Contents

Introduction: The Nature of Research

Does cell phone use cause brain tumors?

What steps can law enforcement take to help prevent domestic violence?

How do prison sentences affect crime rates?

Is it true that about a million children in the United States are homeless?

Why is baseball exempt from antitrust laws?

You may have asked questions like these. Perhaps you discussed the issues with friends or read articles about them. If so, you were conducting informal research to satisfy your curiosity.

In your day-to-day life, you also conduct practical research as you solve problems and make decisions. You may want to buy a digital camera, consider an innovative medical procedure, or plan a vacation. To become better informed, you may talk with friends, search the Internet, request product information, compare prices, read articles, and check advertising. You pull together and weigh as much information as you can, preparing yourself to make a well-informed decision. At work you may do the same — conduct research by gathering information, pulling it together, and using it to make decisions about feasibility, marketing, or best practices.

When one of your college professors assigns a research paper due in a month or two, you won't be expected to discover the secrets of the human brain or to solve the problem of world hunger. On the other hand, research isn't merely pasting together information and opinions from others. Instead, the excitement lies in using research to draw conclusions and arrive at your own fresh view. The key is to start your investigation as professional researchers do — with a research question that you truly want to learn more about. Like a detective, you will need to plan your work but remain flexible, backtracking or jumping ahead or going sideways if you meet an obstacle.

Whenever you use research to come to a conclusion based on facts and expert opinions — whether in your personal life, for a college class, or on the job — this research manual will provide you with effective, efficient strategies and procedures.

30 Planning and Managing Your Research Project

Conducting research is a lifelong skill, valuable in college, at work, and in your personal life. Yet this skill is increasingly complex. Years ago, students would have figured that a term paper required finding a few articles and books on the library shelf, reading them, taking notes, and pulling things together in a paper. Today, you must still find, read, record, and write. But now you can't simply look on the shelf. Instead, you must actively inquire, search, access, evaluate, integrate, and synthesize information from moving, not fixed, targets. Electronic databases are fluid, the content of sources may change, and details may shift with the medium or date of presentation.

As a result, a research project requires information literacy — the capacity to handle information — as well as critical reading and thinking as you join the academic exchange. The graphic on page 647 identifies major stages in a typical research process, moving from the exploration of a topic to the evaluation, analysis, and synthesis that eventually evolve into a final paper with well-integrated sources.

Beginning Your Inquiry

A research paper is often the most engaging and complex assignment in a course. This chapter will help you plan and manage your project by creating a research schedule and building a research archive. Armed with these skills and tools, you will be ready to accomplish even the most formidable research task.

The Assignment: Writing from Sources

Find a topic that intrigues you, and develop a focused research question about it. After conducting whatever research is necessary, synthesize the information you assemble to develop your own reasonable answer to the research question. Then write a paper, persuasively using a variety of source material to convey your conclusions.

Because your final paper answers your research question, you are writing for a reason, not just stacking up facts. Reading and digesting the ideas of others is just the first step. You'll also analyze, evaluate, and synthesize,

The Research Process

Engage: Explore a topic that intrigues you, following your assignment (see pp. 646, 648).

⬇

Inquire: State your research question (see pp. 648–52).

⬇

Organize: Manage your project (see pp. 653–57).

- Create a schedule and plan a method of recording information.
- Organize a research archive.

⬇

Investigate: Work with your sources (see Ch. 31).

- Start a working bibliography, and draw the details from sources.
- Quote, paraphrase, and summarize to capture information in your notes (see pp. 669–75).

⬇

Search: Seek and evaluate reliable sources that might help to answer your question (see Chs. 32 and 33).

- Use the library catalog, databases, and reference materials.
- Search carefully on the Internet.
- Interview, observe, or conduct other field research.
- Analyze and evaluate the reliability and relevance of each source.

⬇

Synthesize: Integrate reliable information and evidence to support your answer to your research question.

- Use sources ethically to avoid plagiarism (see Chs. 31 and 34).
- Quote, paraphrase, summarize, and synthesize to capture and integrate source materials in your paper (see Chs. 31 and 34).
- Clarify the thesis that answers your question, and support it as you write your paper (see Ch. 35).
- Cite and list your sources (see pp. 660–67 and Ch. 36 or 37).

For advice on
scheduling your
research project, see
pp. 653–54.

thinking critically to achieve your purpose. Answering your question will probably require you to return to writing situations and purposes you addressed in Part Two—comparing, explaining causes, taking a stand, proposing a solution, evaluating, or supporting a position. You also may turn to field methods such as observing or interviewing.

Aim to persuade your audience to consider, respect, accept, or act on the answer to your question. If possible, use this project to benefit your college, employer, local community, or campus cause. Having a real audience will help you select what to include or exclude as you write your paper.

Generating Ideas and Asking a Research Question

> What assistance most effectively helps members of the military return to civilian life after a stressful tour of duty?
>
> How accurately do standardized tests measure learning?
>
> What can be done to aid hungry children in your community?

To define a narrow research question, start with your interests and research goals. Choose a territory—a research topic that stimulates your curiosity. If you need ideas, listen to the academic exchanges around you. Perhaps the reading, writing, or discussion in your geography course alerts you to the global threats to forests. To target your research, narrow "global threats to forests," maybe to "farming practices that threaten rain forests." As you learn more, continue to narrow your topic and your question about it.

DISCOVERY CHECKLIST

☐ What experience can you recall that raises intriguing questions or creates unusual associations in your mind?

☐ What have you observed recently—at school or work, online, or on television today—that you could more thoroughly investigate?

☐ What new perspectives on issues or events have friends, classmates, instructors, commentators, bloggers, or others offered?

☐ What problem would you like to solve?

☐ What have you read about lately that you would like to pursue further?

Exploring Your Territory

Like explorers in little-known territory, research writers first get a broad overview to see what viewpoints, changes, and trends look promising. Then they zero in on one small area.

Begin in the Library. Say you are looking for preliminary information on families. Your college library probably subscribes to many specialized databases (like *Sociological Abstracts, PsycINFO, Medline, ERIC,* and the *MLA Bibliography*). Start here to familiarize yourself with your topic and the available sources.

Go Online. You can browse on the Internet, visiting Web sites and reading blogs or messages posted to discussion forums. Search engines, such as Google, can lead to a range of Web pages or help you locate groups and lists (<http://groups.google.com>) related to your topic, such as exchanges on family law or parenting.

For more on electronic searches, see Ch. 32.

Talk with Experts. If you're curious about America's fascination with cars, meet with a professor, such as a sociologist or a journalist, who specializes in the area. Talk with friends who are passionate about their cars. Or go to an auto show, observing and talking with people who attend.

For more on interviewing, see pp. 692–93 and Ch. 6.

Revisit Your Purpose and Audience. Refine the purpose of your research and your analysis of your audience in light of what you have discovered thus far. Consider what goal you'd like your research to accomplish—whether in your personal life, for a college class, or on the job.

For more on purpose and audience, see pp. 11–16 and 400–01.

Satisfy curiosity	Analyze a situation
Take a new perspective	Substantiate a conclusion
Make a decision	Support a position
Solve a problem	Advocate for change

Suppose your survey of campus programs leads you to a proposal by the International Students Office for matching first-year students with host families during holidays. You wonder what such programs cost, how they work, what they offer foreign students and host families. At first, you think that your purpose is to persuade the community to participate. As you learn more, you see that the real challenge is to persuade the director of activities to support the project.

Turning a Topic into a Question

As you explore, move from broad to specific by asking more precise questions. Ask exactly what you want to find out, and your task will leap into focus.

BROAD OVERVIEW	Family structures
TOPIC	Blended families
SPECIFIC QUESTION	How do blended families today differ from those a century ago?
BROAD OVERVIEW	Contemporary architecture

TOPIC	Landscape architecture
SPECIFIC QUESTION	In what ways have the principles of landscape architecture shaped the downtown redevelopment?

For more on generating ideas, see Ch. 19.

Generate Ideas. Freewrite, map, or brainstorm whatever questions come to mind. Then, select one that appears promising. Your instructor also may have suggestions, but you will probably be more motivated investigating a question you choose.

Size Up Your Question. Focus to find a workable research question:

- Is your question debatable? Does it allow for a range of opinions? Will you be able to support your own view rather than explain something that's generally known and accepted?
- Is it interesting to you? Will your discoveries interest your readers?
- Is it narrow enough to allow for a productive investigation in the few weeks you have? Does it stick to a single focus?

BROAD QUESTION	How is the climate of the earth changing?
NARROWER QUESTION	How will El Niño affect climate changes in California during the next decade?
BROAD QUESTION	Who are the world's best living storytellers?
NARROWER QUESTION	How is Irish step dancing a form of storytelling?
BROAD QUESTION	Why are people homeless?
NARROWER QUESTION	What housing programs succeed in our region?

Although you should restrict your topic, a question can be too narrow or too insignificant. If so, it may be impossible to find relevant sources.

TOO NARROW	How did John F. Kennedy's maternal grandfather influence the decisions JFK made during his first month as president?

A question may also be so narrow that it's uninteresting. Avoid questions that can be answered with a simple yes or no or with a few statistics.

TOO NARROW	Are there more black students or white students in the entering class this year?
BETTER	How does the racial or ethnic diversity of students affect campus relations at our school?

Shape a question that will lead you into the heart of a lively controversy. The best research questions ask about issues that others take seriously and debate, issues likely to be of real interest to you and your readers.

Hone Your Question. Make your question specific and simple: identify one thing to find out, not several. The very phrasing of a well-crafted question can suggest keywords for searches.

QUESTION What has caused a shortage of affordable housing in northeastern cities?

POSSIBLE SEARCH TERMS Housing shortage, affordable urban housing

Refine Your Question. Until you start your research, you can't know how fruitful your first question will be. At least, it can establish a starting point. If it doesn't lead you to definite facts or reliable opinions, if it doesn't start you thinking critically, reword it or throw it out and ask a new question.

RESEARCH CHECKLIST
Questioning Your Question

☐ Does your question probe an issue that engages you personally?

☐ Is the scope of your question appropriate—not too immense and not too narrow? Will you be able to answer it given the time you have and the length limits for your paper?

☐ Can you find both current and background information about it?

☐ Have you worded your question concretely and specifically, so that it states exactly what you are looking for?

Predict an Answer in a Working Thesis. Some writers find a project easier to tackle if they have in mind not only a question but also an answer, perhaps a working thesis. However, you need to be flexible, ready to change your answer or even your question as your research progresses.

For more on stating and using a thesis, see pp. 401–10.

RESEARCH QUESTION How does a nutritious lunch benefit students?

WORKING THESIS Nutritious school lunches can improve students' classroom performance.

Use Your Working Thesis to Guide Your Research. Even though you probably will revise or replace your working thesis before you finish your paper, you can let your thesis guide you now.

- Identify terms to define or subtopics to explore.
- List or informally outline points you might develop.
- Note alternative or opposing views likely to emerge.

This early exploration will help you pursue the sources and information you need but avoid chasing after any wild hares that dart out to distract you.

On the other hand, if all you find is support for what you already think, your working thesis may be too dominant. You may no longer be conducting true research. To avoid this possibility, some writers delay stating a thesis until they've done substantial research or even begun drafting.

Surveying Your Resources

You can quickly test whether your question is likely to lead to an ample research paper with a fast search at the library site. You'll need enough ideas, opinions, facts, statistics, and expert testimony to address your question. If your survey turns up a skimpy list or, more likely, hundreds of sources, refine your question. Try to pick a question that is the focus of a dozen or twenty available sources. If you need help, ask a librarian for advice.

In addition, decide which types of sources to target. Some research questions require a wide range of sources. Others are better suited to a narrower range, perhaps restricted by date or discipline.

To review the types of evidence, see pp. 43–44.

- Opinions on controversies? Turn to newspaper editorials, opinion columns, issue-oriented sites, and partisan groups for diverse views.
- News and analysis? Look for stories from newsmagazines, newspapers, news services, and public broadcasting.
- Statistics and facts? Try census or other government data, library databases, annual fact books, and almanacs.
- Professional or workforce information? Turn to reports, surveys, and studies with academic, government, and corporate sponsors to reduce possible bias.
- Research-based analysis? Try scholarly or well-researched nonfiction, government reports, specialized references, and academic databases.
- Original records or images? Check archives, online historical records, and materials held by institutions such as the Library of Congress.

Using Keywords and Links

To practice using keywords, visit the Bedford Research Room Web site at **<bedfordstmartins/ researchroom .com>**.

Keywords are terms or phrases that identify the topics discussed in a research source. When you enter keywords into an electronic search engine (whether in a library catalog, in a database, or on the Web), the engine will return to you a list of all the sources it can find with those words. Finding the best keywords for a topic and search engine is essential. Start with the main terms in your research question. Write down or print out the keywords you try, noting whether they produce too few or too many results.

For search strategies, see p. 689. For more on search engines and advanced searches, see p. 688.

For advice on creating a working bibliography, see pp. 658–68.

As keywords lead to Web sites compiled by specialists or people who share an interest, browse through the irrelevant information, resources, and *links* — lists of related sites. These links, in turn, often contain their own lists of related Web pages. By following these connections systematically, you can rapidly expand your knowledge. However, avoid looking only for information to support a preconceived notion.

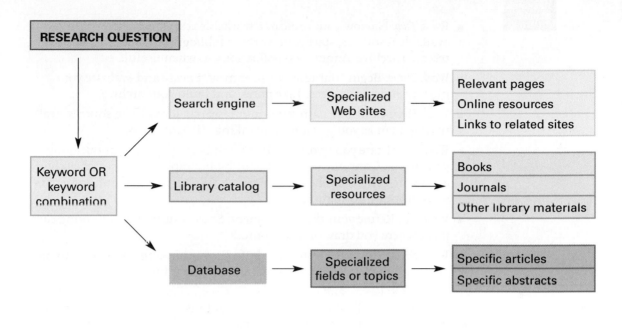

Learning by Doing Proposing Your Project

Assemble your research materials — topic ideas, research question, any working thesis, notes on resources and keywords, and anything else you've planned or gathered. Review your materials, and then write a short informal proposal that sums up what you want to discover and how you plan to proceed. In a small group, present your proposals, and exchange ideas about how to continue your inquiry.

Managing Your Project

No matter what your question or where you plan to look for material, you will want to keep track of where you've been and where you need to go.

Creating a Schedule

If your instructor doesn't assign a series of deadlines, set some for yourself. You can count on a research paper taking longer than you expect. If you procrastinate and try to toss it together in a desperate all-night siege, you will not be satisfied with the result. Instead, start with a clear-cut schedule that breaks your project into a series of small tasks.

For downloadable sample schedules (and research checklists), visit **<bedfordstmartins .com/bedguide>**.

SAMPLE SCHEDULE

- *Week One:* If you are not assigned a topic, start thinking about your interests. Explore by searching through your library or on the Internet.

- *Week Two:* Narrow your topic to a workable research question. Survey available resources, start your working bibliography, and organize your research archive. Annotate possible sources when useful.

- *Week Three:* Begin your research in earnest. Locate and evaluate your most promising sources. Take notes, and build your archive.

- *Week Four:* Continue narrowing your research, identifying sources, evaluating them as you go along, and taking efficient notes.

- *Week Five:* State your working thesis, and begin planning or outlining your paper. Continue to update your bibliography and research archive, arranging sources in the order in which you might use them. Target any gaps in your information.

- *Week Six:* Refine your thesis statement. Start your first draft, noting each place where you draw on your sources.

- *Week Seven:* Complete your first draft. Begin thinking about ways to revise and improve it. Seek feedback from a peer editor.

- *Week Eight:* Revise and edit your draft. Check that you have correctly presented and credited all quotations, paraphrases, and summaries from your sources. Proofread the entire paper, checking for any errors.

Each week you can make up a more detailed schedule, identifying tasks by the day or by the type to increase your efficiency.

DAILY SCHEDULE	ACTIVITY SCHEDULE
Monday — finish library catalog search	library search — *EBSCOhost* and *InfoTrac*
Tuesday — start article indexes	Web search — government sites
Thursday — read e-mails and printouts from databases	reading — new printouts and e-mails from databases
Sunday night — organize files and add notes	writing — revised research question — thesis?

Planning Collaborative Research

Research groups, in class or at work, require cooperative effort but can produce deeper and more creative outcomes than one individual could achieve. If your research project is collaborative, you will need to make agreements with others and meet your commitments. Your team might consolidate all its work or share the research but produce separate papers or presentations. With your instructor's approval, divide up the tasks so that all members are responsible for their own portions. Then agree on your due dates and group meetings.

SAMPLE SCHEDULE FOR A GROUP PROJECT

- *Week One:* Meet to get acquainted and to select someone to act as an organizer, e-mailing or calling to make sure things progress as planned. Individually investigate options for a project topic.

- *Week Two:* Meet again to select a topic, narrow it, and develop a research question that your instructor approves.
- *Week Three:* Individually survey resources and contribute entries and annotations to a collaborative working bibliography. Meet to assign tasks; individually gather material for the group's research archive.
- *Weeks Four and Five:* Continue to find, read, evaluate, and record notes on sources.
- *Week Six:* Meet to evaluate the sources and information gathered; decide what is missing or weak. Draft a working thesis and outline for presenting what everyone has learned.
- *Week Seven:* Individually draft assigned sections. Swap drafts, read them over, and respond with suggestions.
- *Week Eight:* Work together to consolidate the revised draft and agree on final changes. Appoint one member to prepare a polished copy and one or two others to act as final editors and proofreaders.

Recording Information

Plan ahead so your system produces what you need: relevant evidence from reliable sources to develop and support your answer to your research question. Avoid two extremes — collecting everything or counting only on memory.

Use Time-Honored Methods for Depth. Try this trusty advice: copy judiciously and take notes. Selective copying (photocopying or saving to a file) will help you accumulate material, but copying whatever you find wastes time. Instead, take notes, annotate, highlight, quote, paraphrase, and summarize — all time-honored methods for absorbing, evaluating, and selecting information from a source. Using such methods helps you identify potentially useful materials and, later, integrate them smoothly into your paper.

For advice on working with sources, see Ch. 31; for advice on integrating sources, see Ch. 34.

Innovate for Efficiency. Develop efficient techniques such as these:

- Write a summary on the first page of a printout or photocopy.
- Add a paraphrase in the margin next to a key section of a printout.
- Identify a lively or concrete quotation with a highlighter.
- E-mail information from a library database to yourself so that it is easy to move into an electronic folder or file.
- Record key quotations (noting sources and page numbers) in a computer file so that you can easily reorganize them.
- Summarize sources on sticky notes or cards so that you can quickly rearrange them in various orders.
- Use a graphics program or a sheet of poster board to sketch a "storyboard" for the main "events" that you want to cover in your paper.

Many researchers use note cards (with one note on each) or word-processing files (with clearly separated entries). Both are more flexible than notebook pages. When the time comes to organize, it's easy to reshuffle cards or move electronic notes into a logical order.

For more on critical reading, see Ch. 2.

Read as a Skeptical Critic. Distinguish what's significant for answering your research question and what's only slightly related. If you wish, add your own ratings (*, +, !! or – , ??) at the top or in the margin.

Take Accurate and Thorough Notes. Read the entire article or section of a book before beginning to take notes. Then decide what—and how much—to record so you dig out the useful nuggets without distorting the meaning. Double-check all statistics and lists. Record full enough notes and citations so that, once they're written, you are totally independent of the source.

Starting a Research Archive

Organize your information from library, Internet, and field sources by creating a research archive. An *archive* is a place where information is systematically stored for later use. Clearly distinguish the sources you save from your own notes about sources. Use highlighting and other markers to make key passages easy to find in any format.

File Paper Copies. If you prefer a paper format, photocopy book passages and articles, print out electronic sources (with your date of access), and keep field material. File these pages in a separate folder for each source, labeled with title or subject and author. Attach sticky notes to mark key passages, or highlight them. Make sure the author (or short title) and page number are identified on each page so you can credit your source.

Save Computer Files. Save Web pages, e-mails, posts to newsgroups and lists, transcripts of chats, and database records to a drive or other storage device. Note URLs or search paths, dates of access, and similar details. Give each file a descriptive name so that you can find the information quickly later on. You can also organize the files in different electronic folders or directories, clearly named. Back up all electronic records.

Save Favorites and Bookmarks. Save the locations of Web sites in your browser so that you can easily return to these *favorites* (Microsoft Internet Explorer) or *bookmarks* (Mozilla Firefox and Netscape Navigator). Annotate and organize them into folders.

Save Search Results. If a database or Internet search is productive, note where you searched and what keywords you used. Then, to pursue each relevant source, you can easily repeat the search at a later date, print out the search results, or save them to a computer file.

RESEARCH CHECKLIST
Getting Organized

☐ Have you identified and stated an intriguing research question?

☐ What has your quick survey of library and online sources revealed? Can you find enough information—but not too much—to answer your question?

☐ Which types of sources might be best for beginning your research?

☐ Have you created a realistic schedule based on your deadlines? Have you allowed plenty of time for research while meeting other commitments?

☐ Have you decided how you want to record research information? Have you tested whether your method will be easy to keep up and will help you compile useful and accurate information?

☐ Have you begun organizing your research archive—opening files, setting up electronic folders, or buying file folders for paper copies?

31 Working with Sources

A s you turn to sources, you will gather different kinds of information.

- First, in a source entry, record the details that identify each source so you can find it and eventually credit it correctly in your paper. Gather these entries in a working bibliography.

- Second, in source notes, capture information of value to your inquiry as quotations, paraphrases, or summaries ready for use in your paper.

- Finally, if useful or required, combine a source entry with a summary to build an annotated bibliography.

Drawing the Details from Your Sources

For more examples, see Ch. 36 on MLA style and Ch. 37 on APA style.

The Source Navigators on pages 660–67 show how to find the details needed to identify several types of sources you are likely to use. Each source is keyed to a menu to show where you might look for the details you need to record in a source entry, ready to be copied from a working bibliography to the list of sources ending the paper. Each entry also is accompanied by sample source notes.

The sample source entries show two common academic styles: MLA (Modern Language Association) and APA (American Psychological Association). Because MLA and APA entries differ, you should stick to the style your instructor expects. However, both require much the same information. The chart on page 668 summarizes what you'll need to record, both the basics — details nearly always required to identify each type of source — and the common additions or complications likely to crop up. When in doubt, record more than you're likely to need so you won't have to return to a source later on.

Starting a Working Bibliography

Your working bibliography is a detailed and evolving list of the articles, books, Web sites, and other resources that you plan to consult. It guides your research by recording the sources you have and intend to examine.

Each entry in your working bibliography eventually needs to follow the format your instructor expects, generally either MLA or APA style.

Choose a Method. Pick the method that you can use most easily and efficiently.

- Note cards, recording one source per card
- Small notebook, writing on one side of the page
- Word-processing program
- Computer database

Keep Careful Records. The more carefully you record possible sources, the more time you'll save later when you list the works you actually used and cited. At that point, you'll be grateful to find all the necessary titles, authors, dates, page numbers, and other details at your fingertips—and you'll avoid a frantic, last-minute database search or library trip.

When you start a bibliographic entry for a source, your information may be incomplete: "Find bionic ears article—probably in 2010 science magazine." For field research, you might simply start with the name of a possible contact: "Dr. Edward Denu—cardiologist—interview about drug treatments." Start with whatever clues you can gather—key words, partial titles, authors, relevant publications, rough dates. Once you locate or contact the source, you can add more detail and correct any early information. Eventually each entry should include everything necessary to find the source as well as to prepare the list of sources at the end of your paper. As your working bibliography develops, you may find that your research circumstances require different methods of recording information. For example, when you find that science magazine with the article on bionic ears, you may read a printed copy or print the full text from a database. Either way, you can easily take notes using your usual method: on cards, in a notebook, or in an electronic file. However, should you interview Dr. Denu or someone from his staff about medication for heart patients, you might make an audio recording of the conversation (with that person's permission) or jot notes in a handheld electronic storage tool as you talk. Then, right after the interview, you can transfer the significant information to your usual method so that you keep all your notes in the same format and in the same place.

Learning by Doing 🔲 Building a Working Bibliography

Present your initial source material to classmates. Share ideas about how to improve the accuracy of entries and the usefulness of notes.

Article in a Magazine

Record this information in your notes about each source:

1 The complete name of the author
2 The title and any subtitle of the article
3 The title and any subtitle of the magazine
4 The full date of the issue

5 The article's page numbers
6 The periodical's volume and issue numbers if available (for APA)
7 The medium of publication (for MLA)

Regaining BALANCE with Bionic Ears

Electronic implants in the inner ear may one day restore clear vision and equilibrium in some patients who experience disabling unsteadiness

By Charles C. Della Santina

KEY CONCEPTS

- Disorders of the vestibular system of the inner ear can cause vertigo and shaky, blurred vision.

- Three semicircular structures in the inner ear are responsible for measuring head rotation.

- Prostheses that would replace the function of the semicircular canals and thus restore balance are under development.
  —*The Editors*

Ask friends to list the body's senses, and they will usually stop after five: taste, touch, sight, smell and hearing. Most do not even notice their sixth sense—the sensation of how one's head is oriented and moving. But losing this capacity can cause dramatic, disabling vertigo, followed by chronic unsteadiness and blurred vision when the head is in motion. Fortunately, good progress is being made toward the development of bionic ear implants to restore balance in people who suffer from damage to the vestibular labyrinth of the inner ear—the part that provides us with our sixth sense.

The availability of these prostheses cannot come too soon for Richard Gannon, a 57-year-old retired steamfitter, who has homes in Pennsylvania and Florida. Gannon lost much of his sensation of balance seven years ago after suffering an apparent viral illness. "Let me be the first to get a vestibular implant," he says. "I've been waiting for a call for five years. As soon as they can do it, I'll walk to the hospital if I have to."

"I moved to a house near the beach when I retired because I love the water. But since I lost my balance, I can't walk straight, especially on sand," reports Gannon, a formerly avid swimmer. "Now mothers pull their kids away from me, thinking I'm drunk. Standing in two inches of surf makes me feel like I'm going to fall. I barely drive now, and never at night, because for every headlight, I see 20."

Although he feels fairly comfortable during daytime driving, he remarks that the cometlike trails left by road lights as they streak across his eyes at night are "like a laser show. I'd give up my hearing if it would mean getting my balance back." The recent advances toward bionic ear implants offer hope for Gannon and tens of thousands like him who have sustained damage to the inner ear from certain antibiotics (such as gentamicin) or chemotherapy or from meningitis, Ménière's disease or other illnesses.

Staying Upright and Steady

Much like cochlear implants, which restore hearing by electrically stimulating parts of the auditory nerve, this new type of bionic ear will provide stability by electrically stimulating the vestibular nerve, which normally conveys signals from the vestibular labyrinth to the brain. The device's electrical connection to the nerve will bypass the defective vestibular system.

The healthy labyrinth performs two important jobs. One is measuring which way is up and which way you are heading. You need this information to stand and walk normally. The second is sensing how your head is turning. You need this information to keep your eyes on target. Whenever your head turns up, for instance, the

GERARD SLOTA

Create a source entry out of the information you collect:

MLA

Source entry in MLA style

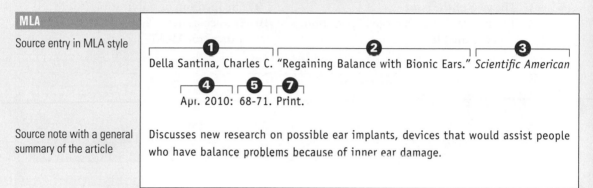

Della Santina, Charles C. "Regaining Balance with Bionic Ears." *Scientific American*
Apr. 2010: 68-71. Print.

Source note with a general summary of the article

Discusses new research on possible ear implants, devices that would assist people who have balance problems because of inner ear damage.

APA

Source entry in APA style

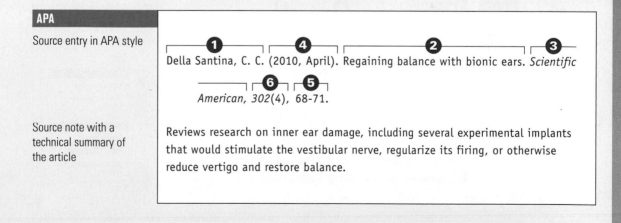

Della Santina, C. C. (2010, April). Regaining balance with bionic ears. *Scientific American, 302*(4), 68-71.

Source note with a technical summary of the article

Reviews research on inner ear damage, including several experimental implants that would stimulate the vestibular nerve, regularize its firing, or otherwise reduce vertigo and restore balance.

Article in a Scholarly Journal from a Database

Record this information in your notes about each source:

1 The complete name of the author
2 The title and any subtitle of the article
3 The title and any subtitle of the journal
4 The journal volume and issue numbers
5 The year of the issue
6 The printed article's original page numbers if available

7 The name of the database, subscriber service, or library service (for MLA)
8 DOI (digital object identifier) if available or URL for journal's home page (for APA)
9 The medium of publication (for MLA)
10 The access date when you used the source (for MLA)

---

(7)

http://www.jstor.org/stable/30250069 · Go

Trusted archives for scholarship

Login · Help · Contact Us

JSTOR

SEARCH BROWSE ABOUT PARTICIPATE RESOURCES MyJSTOR

Latest Issue of JSTORNEWS Now Available

Your access to JSTOR provided by JSTOR

> List of all Volumes > Volumes/Issues List > Issue Table of Contents > Item View

(2) "I'm Not Stupid": How Assessment Drives (In)Appropriate Reading Instruction
Danielle V. Dennis **(1)**

(3) *Journal of Adolescent & Adult Literacy*, Vol. 53, No. 4 (Dec., 2009 - Jan., 2010), pp. 283-290
Published by: International Reading Association

Save citation (Requires login)
Export this Citation
Item Information
PDF

(6) **(4)** **(5)**

< Previous Item | Next Item >

Page 283 of 283-290 | Select a page

JSTOR
References
Items by Danielle V. Dennis

(8)

Journal of Adolescent & Adult Literacy 53(4)
Dec 2009 / Jan 2010
doi:10.1598/JAAL.53.4.2
© 2009 International Reading Association
(pp. 283-290)

Google Scholar
Related Items
Items Citing this Item
Items by Danielle V. Dennis

"I'm Not Stupid": How Assessment Drives (In)Appropriate Reading Instruction

Create a source entry out of the information you collect:

MLA

Source entry in MLA style, e-mailed from database and recorded in a computer file

Dennis, Danielle V. **(1)** "'I'm Not Stupid': How Assessment Drives (In)Appropriate **(2)** Reading Instruction." *Journal of Adolescent & Adult Literacy* **(3)** 53.4 **(4)** (2009/2010): **(5)** 283-290. **(6)** *JSTOR*. **(7)** Web. **(9)** 23 Mar. 2010. **(10)**

Source note with a paraphrase of one paragraph in the article

Pressured to improve scores, school districts may just buy general reading programs for middle school students like the writer's. Although districts use those scores to put students in special classes, they do not find out exactly what students can do (p. 287).

APA

Source entry in APA style, e-mailed from database and recorded in a computer file

Dennis, D. V. **(1)** (2009/2010). **(5)** "I'm not stupid": How assessment drives **(2)** (in)appropriate reading instruction. *Journal of Adolescent & Adult Literacy,* **(3)** *53*(4), **(4)** 283-290. **(6)** doi:10.1598/JAAL.53.4.2 **(8)**

[If no digital object identifier (DOI) is specified, use the Internet address of the periodical's home page.]

Source note with a summary of the article's recommendations

Dennis recommends five steps for a middle-school reading program: screening with state scores, adding frequent individual assessments, grouping for instruction and self-assessment strategies, engaging students in setting goals, and drawing all teachers into the program (pp. 288-89).

Source Navigator

Book

Record this information in your notes about each source:

1 The complete name of the author
2 The title and any subtitle of the book
3 The place of publication, using the first city listed
4 The name of the publisher
5 The date of publication (from the front or back of the title page)

6 The medium of publication (for MLA)
7 The call number or library location (for your future use)
8 Keyword or author (for your filing system)

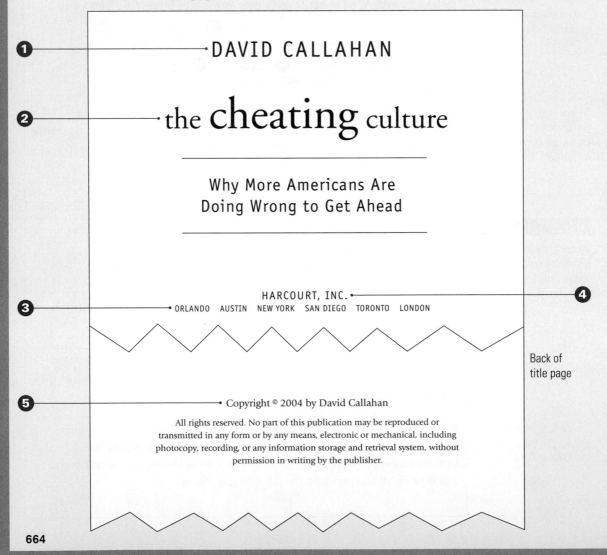

1 ·DAVID CALLAHAN

2 the **cheating** culture

Why More Americans Are
Doing Wrong to Get Ahead

HARCOURT, INC.· **4**

3 ORLANDO   AUSTIN   NEW YORK   SAN DIEGO   TORONTO   LONDON

Back of
title page

5 Copyright © 2004 by David Callahan

All rights reserved. No part of this publication may be reproduced or
transmitted in any form or by any means, electronic or mechanical, including
photocopy, recording, or any information storage and retrieval system, without
permission in writing by the publisher.

Create a source entry out of the information you collect:

Source entry in MLA style, recorded on a card

(7)
HF5387

C334

2004

(8)
Callahan

(1) **(2)**
Callahan, David. *The Cheating Culture: Why More Americans Are Doing Wrong to Get*

(3) **(4)** **(5)** **(6)**
Ahead. Orlando: Harcourt, 2004. Print.

Source note with a summary and quotation from the source

Looks at how the competitiveness of American culture has led to an epidemic of cheating in business, school, and sports. Page 116 says, "As making money moved front and center, young people stopped caring about other things."

Source entry in APA style, recorded on a card

(8)
Medical ethics

(1) **(5)** **(2)**
Callahan, D. (2004). *The cheating culture: Why more Americans are doing wrong*

(3) **(4)**
to get ahead. Orlando, FL: Harcourt.

Source note with a summary and a lead to another source

A comprehensive study of the extent of, and factors behind, cheating in business, academia, and other arenas. Cites book called *Branded* by Alissa Quart on teen consumerism (p. 117).

Page from a Web Site

Record this information in your notes about each source:

1 The complete name of the author, if available, often from the beginning or end of the page
2 The title of the page
3 The name of the site
4 The name of any sponsoring organization

5 The date of the last update
6 The medium of publication (for MLA)
7 The access date when you used the source
8 The Internet address (URL) (for APA)

Trends in College Pricing - Mozilla Firefox

File Edit View History Delicious Bookmarks Tools Help

http://www.trends-collegeboard.com/college_pricing/2_3_regional_variation_charges.html — **8**

Trends in College Pricing

CollegeBoard
inspiring minds™

Trends in College Pricing — **3**
2009

T R E N D S   I N   H I G H E R   E D U C A T I O N   S E R I E S

OVERVIEW   PUBLISHED PRICES   VARIATION IN PRICES   NET PRICE   INSTITUTIONAL FINANCES   ENROLLMENT & INCOME

Variation in Prices > By Region > Table 6   Back to Trends Main Page

2 — ## Regional Variation in Charges

▼ REGIONAL VARIATION
  Figure 6
  Table 6
  Table 6a
  Table 6b

Published prices and the rates of change in those prices vary considerably across regions of the country. In 2009-10, average published tuition and fees for public four-year colleges range from $5,802 in the South to $9,391 in New England.

Table 6: Average Student Expenses by College Board Region, 2009-10 (Enrollment-Weighted)

Key Points

- In 2009-10, average published tuition and fees for public two-year colleges range from $1,475 in the West to $3,992 in the New England region.
- Over the decade from 1999-2000 to 2009-10, dollar increases in average public four-year tuition and fees ranged from $2,180 (in 2009 dollars) in the Middle States to $3,349 in New England. Percentage increases ranged from 37% in the Middle States to 93% in the Southwest.
- In 2009-10, the highest average public four-year tuition and fees were in New England, which also had the highest average total

Region	Sector	Tuition & Fees	Add'l Chrgs*	Books & Supplies	Resident Room & Board	Resident Transp.	Resident Other Costs	Commuter Room & Board **	Commuter Transp.	Commuter Other Costs
National	Public Two-Year	$2,544	$4,772	$1,098	—	—	—	$7,202	$1,445	$1,996
	Public Four-Year	$7,020	$11,528	$1,122	$8,193	$1,079	$1,974	$7,969	$1,483	$2,318
	Private Four-Year	$26,273		$1,116	$9,363	$849	$1,427	$8,163	$1,332	$1,788
New England	Public Two-Year	$3,992	$6,501	$967	—	—	—	$6,959	$1,339	$1,906
	Public Four-Year	$9,391	$13,357	$1,001	$9,003	$672	$1,379	$7,923	$1,122	$1,581
	Private Four-Year	$32,857		$1,028	$11,027	$617	$1,215	$10,122	$965	$1,410

Trends in College Pricing - Mozilla Firefox

File Edit View History Delicious Bookmarks Tools Help

http://www.trends-collegeboard.com/college_pricing/2_3_regional_variation_charges.html

Trends in College Pricing

4 — site map | contact us | about us | press | careers | link to us | compliance | terms of use | privacy policy
© 2009 The College Board   Updated: 12/1/09

5

Create a source entry out of the information you collect:

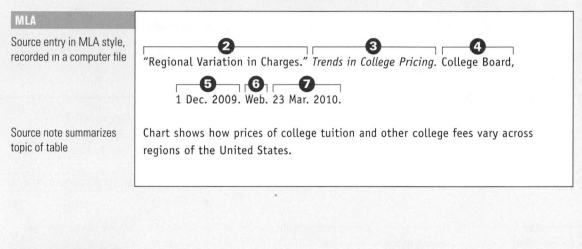

MLA

Source entry in MLA style, recorded in a computer file

"Regional Variation in Charges." *Trends in College Pricing*. College Board, 1 Dec. 2009. Web. 23 Mar. 2010.

Source note summarizes topic of table

Chart shows how prices of college tuition and other college fees vary across regions of the United States.

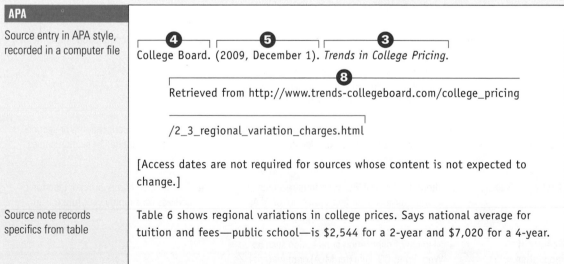

APA

Source entry in APA style, recorded in a computer file

College Board. (2009, December 1). *Trends in College Pricing*.

Retrieved from http://www.trends-collegeboard.com/college_pricing /2_3_regional_variation_charges.html

[Access dates are not required for sources whose content is not expected to change.]

Source note records specifics from table

Table 6 shows regional variations in college prices. Says national average for tuition and fees—public school—is $2,544 for a 2-year and $7,020 for a 4-year.

Type of Information to Record

	The Basics	Common Additions
Names	▪ Complete name of the author, as supplied in the source, unless not identified	▪ Names of coauthors, in the order listed in the source ▪ Names of any editor, compiler, translator, or contributor
Titles	▪ Title and any subtitle of an article, Web page, or posting (in quotation marks for MLA) ▪ Title and any subtitle of a journal, magazine, newspaper, book, or Web site (italicized)	▪ Title of a journal special issue ▪ Title of a series of books or pamphlets and any item number
Publication Details for Periodicals	▪ Volume and issue numbers for a journal (and a magazine for APA) ▪ DOI (digital object identifier) article number (for APA) ▪ Section number or letter for a newspaper	▪ Any edition of a newspaper (for MLA)
Publication Details for Books	▪ City of publication, using the first city listed (for MLA) with state or country (for APA) ▪ Name of the publisher	▪ Edition number (4th) or description (revised) ▪ Volume number and total volumes, if more than one ▪ Names and locations of copublishers ▪ Publisher's imprint
Publication Details for Electronic Sources	▪ Name (italicized) of the database, subscriber service, or library service (for MLA) ▪ Name of any site sponsor or publisher	▪ Details of any original or alternate print publication ▪ Document numbers
Dates	▪ Year of publication, full date (periodical), or date of creation or last update (electronic source) ▪ Your access date for an electronic source as printed or written on your hard copy (for MLA) or only for documents that change (for APA)	▪ Original date of publication for a literary work or classic
Location of Information	▪ Article's opening and concluding page numbers and any page for citing exact location of material in source	▪ Paragraph, screen, chapter, or section numbers if supplied or section names
Location of Source	▪ Internet address (URL, or uniform resource locator) for a hard-to-find source or, for APA, publication or publisher home page if no DOI	▪ Call number, library area, or electronic address (to simplify your future use)
Medium of Publication	▪ Medium of publication or reception such as Web, Print, CD, Film (for MLA) or of material reviewed (Motion picture, Book) or type of source (Computer software) (for APA)	

Capturing Information in Your Source Notes by Quoting, Paraphrasing, and Summarizing

Read critically to decide what each source offers. If you cannot grasp a source that requires specialized background, don't take notes or use it in your paper. On the other hand, if a source seems accurate, logical, and relevant, consider exactly how you want to record it in your notes.

Identify What's from Where. Clearly identify the author of the source, a brief title if needed, and the page number (or other location) where a reader could find the information. These details connect each source note to your corresponding bibliography entry. Adding a keyword at the top of each note will help you cluster related material in your paper.

Also identify which ideas are yours and which are your source's. For example, you might mark your source notes with these labels:

"...": quotation marks to set off all the exact words of the source

para: your paraphrase, restatement, or translation of a passage from the source into your own words and sentences

sum: your overall summary of the source's main point

paste: your cut-and-paste, quoting a passage moved electronically

JN (your initials) or [ ]: your own ideas, connections, or reactions

A system like this helps you develop your ideas, distinguish them from your paraphrase or cut-and-paste, and avoid accidental plagiarism, using another writer's words or ideas without appropriate credit.

Decide What You Need. When it comes time to draft your paper, you will incorporate your source material in three basic ways:

- Quoting: transcribing the author's exact words directly from the source
- Paraphrasing: fully rewording the author's ideas in your own words
- Summarizing: reducing the author's main point to essentials

Your notes, too, should use these three forms. Weighing each source carefully and guessing how you might use it—even as you are reading—is part of the dynamic process of research. Always think critically about how you will use your sources—otherwise, they'll end up using you.

Quoting

If you intend to use a direct quotation, capture it carefully, copying by hand or pasting electronically. Reproduce the words, spelling, order, and punctuation exactly, even if they're unusual. Put quotation marks around the material in your notes so you'll remember that it's a direct quotation.

For more examples of capturing information from sources, see pp. 234–42, pp. 707–13, and D in the Quick Research Guide, pp. A-26–A-31.

To practice quoting, paraphrasing, and summarizing, visit **<bedfordstmartins.com/bedguide>**.

Sample Quotations, Paraphrase, and Summary (MLA Style)

Passage from Original Source

Obesity is a major issue because (1) vast numbers of people are affected; (2) the prevalence is growing; (3) rates are increasing in children; (4) the medical, psychological, and social effects are severe; (5) the behaviors that cause it (poor diet and inactivity) are themselves major contributors to ill health; and (6) treatment is expensive, rarely effective, and impractical to use on a large scale.

Biology and environment conspire to promote obesity. Biology is an enabling factor, but the obesity epidemic, and the consequent human tragedy, is a function of the worsening food and physical activity environment. Governments and societies have come to this conclusion very late. There is much catching up to do.

Sample Quotations from Second Paragraph

Although human biology has contributed to the pudgy American society, everyone now faces the powerful challenge of a "worsening food and physical activity environment" (Brownell and Horgen 51). As Brownell and Horgen conclude, "There is much catching up to do" (51).

Sample Paraphrase of First Paragraph

The current concern with increasing American weight has developed for half a dozen reasons, according to Brownell and Horgen. They attribute the shift in awareness to the number of obese people and the increase in this number, especially among youngsters. In addition, excess weight carries harsh consequences for individual physical and mental health and for society's welfare. Lack of exercise and unhealthy food choices worsen the health consequences, especially because there's no cheap and easy cure for the effects of eating too much and exercising too little (51).

Sample Summary

After outlining six reasons why obesity is a critical issue, Brownell and Horgen urge Americans to eat less and become more active (51).

Works Cited Entry (MLA Style)

Brownell, Kelly D., and Katherine Battle Horgen. *Food Fight: The Inside Story of the Food Industry, America's Obesity Crisis, and What We Can Do about It.* Chicago: Contemporary-McGraw, 2004. Print.

RECORDING A GOOD QUOTATION

1. Quote sparingly, selecting only strong passages that might add support and authority to your assertions.

2. Mark the beginning and the ending with quotation marks.

3. Carefully write out or copy and paste each quotation. Check your copy — word by word — for accuracy.

4. Record the exact number of the page where the quotation appears in the source. If it falls on two pages, note both, marking where the page turns.

Sometimes it doesn't pay to copy a long quotation word for word. If you take out one or more irrelevant words, indicate the omission with an ellipsis mark (...). If you need to add wording, especially so that a selection makes sense, enclose your addition in brackets [like this].

Paraphrasing

When paraphrasing, restate an author's ideas in your own words and sentences. Express them fairly and accurately. Avoid judging, interpreting, or merely echoing the original. A good paraphrase may retain the organization, emphasis, and details of the original, so it may not be much shorter. Even so, paraphrasing is useful when you want to walk your readers through the points made in the original source.

For more on quotations and ellipsis marks, see C3 in the Quick Editing Guide, beginning on p. A-52, or book sections 25 and 27e–f.

ORIGINAL	"In staging an ancient Greek tragedy today, most directors do not mask the actors."
TOO CLOSE TO THE ORIGINAL	Most directors, in staging an ancient Greek play today, do not mask the actors.
A GOOD PARAPHRASE	Few contemporary directors of Greek tragedy insist that their actors wear masks.

WRITING A GOOD PARAPHRASE

1. Read the entire passage through several times.
2. Divide the passage into its most important ideas or points, either in your mind or by highlighting or annotating the passage.
3. Look away from the original, and restate the first idea in your own words. Sum up the support for this idea. Review the section if necessary.
4. Go on to the next idea, and do the same. Continue in this way.
5. Go back and reread the original passage one more time, making sure you've conveyed its ideas faithfully without repeating its words or sentence structure. Revise your paraphrase if necessary.

Summarizing

Sometimes a paraphrase uses up too much space or disrupts the flow of your own ideas. Instead, all you need is a summary to capture the main ideas of a source "in a nutshell" by restating them in your own words. This strategy can save space, distilling detailed text into one or two succinct sentences. Be careful as you reduce a long passage that you do not distort the original meaning or emphasis.

WRITING A GOOD SUMMARY

1. Read the original passage several times.

2. Without looking back, recall and state its central point.

3. Reread the original passage one more time, making sure you've conveyed its ideas faithfully. Revise your summary if necessary.

To practice quoting, paraphrasing, and summarizing, visit **<bedfordstmartins .com/bedguide>**.

RESEARCH CHECKLIST
Taking Notes with Quotations, Paraphrases, and Summaries

☐ For each source note, have you identified the source (by the author's last name or a keyword from the title) and the exact page? Have you added a keyword heading to each note to help you group ideas?

☐ Have you made a companion source entry in your working bibliography for each new source discovered during your research?

☐ Have you remained true to the meaning of the original source?

☐ Have you quoted sparingly—selecting striking, short passages?

☐ Have you quoted exactly? Do you use quotation marks around significant words, phrases, and passages from the original sources? Do you use ellipsis marks or brackets to show where any words are omitted or added?

☐ Are most notes in your own words—paraphrasing or summarizing?

☐ Have you avoided paraphrasing too close to the source?

For more exercises on incorporating sources, visit **<bedfordstmartins .com/bedguide>**.

Learning by Doing 🎥 Capturing Information from Sources

Select one of the following passages, and study it until you understand it thoroughly. Use this passage as you respond to the activities that follow.

PASSAGE 1

Within the next decades education will change more than it has changed since the modern school was created by the printed book over three hundred years ago. An economy in which knowledge is becoming the true capital and the premier wealth-producing resource makes new and stringent demands on the schools for educational performance and educational responsibility. A society dominated by knowledge workers makes even newer—and even more stringent—demands for social performance and social responsibility. Once again we will have to think through what an educated person is. At the same time, how we learn and how we teach are changing drastically and fast—the result, in part, of new theoretical understanding of the learning process, in part of new technology. Finally, many of the traditional disciplines of the schools are becoming sterile, if not obsolescent.

We thus also face changes in what we learn and teach and, indeed, in what we mean by knowledge.

—Peter F. Drucker, *The New Realities*

PASSAGE 2

When I look to the future of humanity beyond the twenty-first century, I see on my list of things to come the extension of our inquisitiveness from the objective domain of science to the subjective domain of feeling and memory. Homo sapiens, the exploring animal, will not be content with merely physical exploration. Our curiosity will drive us to explore the dimensions of the mind as vigorously as we explore the dimensions of space and time. For every pioneer who explores a new asteroid or a new planet, there will be another pioneer who explores from the inside the minds of our fellow passengers on planet Earth. It is our nature to strive to explore everything, alive and dead, present and past and future. When once the technology exists to read and write memories from one mind into another, the age of mental exploration will begin in earnest. Instead of admiring the beauties of nature from the outside, we will look at nature directly through the eyes of the elephant, the eagle, and the whale. We will be able, through the magic of science, to feel in our own minds the pride of the peacock and the wrath of the lion. That magic is no greater than the magic that enables me to see the rocking horse through the eyes of the child who rode it sixty years ago.

—Freeman Dyson, *Infinite in All Directions*

1. Quoting
   Identify one notable quotation from the passage you selected. Write a brief paragraph justifying your selection, explaining why you find it notable and why you might want to use it in a paper. Share your paragraph with classmates who have worked with the same passage. Did any of you select the same quotation? In what ways were your reasons similar or different? If you selected different quotations, what were your reasons?

2. Paraphrasing
   Write a paraphrase of your passage. Use your own language to capture what it says without parroting its words or sentence patterns. Compare and contrast your version with those of classmates who selected the same passage. What are its strengths and weaknesses? Where might you want to freshen the language?

3. Summarizing
   In one or two sentences, summarize the passage you selected. Capture its essence in your own words. Compare and contrast your summary with those of classmates who have worked on the same passage. What are its strengths and weaknesses? Where might you want to simplify or clarify?

4. Reflecting and Exchanging
   After completing 1, 2, and 3 above, decide which method of working with a passage proved most challenging. Write out specific tips for yourself about how to make that task easier, faster, and more successful. Compare your tips with those of your classmates so that you all gain fresh ideas about how to quote, paraphrase, and summarize.

Developing an Annotated Bibliography

An annotated bibliography is a list of your sources—those read to date or those credited in your final paper—that includes a short summary or an annotation for each source entry. This common assignment quickly informs a reader about the direction and depth of your research. It also demonstrates your mastery of two major college research skills: identifying a source and writing a summary.

For more on the MLA and APA formats, see Chs. 36 and 37.

When you develop an annotated bibliography, clarify two points from the beginning. First, find out which format you are expected to use as you identify your sources. Next, determine what your annotation should do—summarize only, add evaluation, or meet a special requirement (such as interpretation). A summary is a brief, neutral explanation in your own words of the thesis or main points covered in a source. In contrast, an evaluation is a judgment of the source, generally assessing its accuracy, reliability, or relevance to your research question.

For selections from an annotated bibliography, see p. 490.

Summary with Evaluation. As Stephanie Hawkins worked on the annotated bibliography for her APA-style paper "Japanese: Linguistic Diversity," she wanted to show her critical thinking. Besides briefly summarizing her sources, she also evaluated their contributions, relationships, or usefulness to her study.

> Abe, H. N. (1995). From stereotype to context: The study of Japanese women's speech. *Feminist Studies, 21*(3), 647-671.
>
> Abe discusses the roots of Japanese women's language, beginning in ancient Japan and continuing into modern times. I was able to use this peer-reviewed source to expand on the format of women's language and the consequences of its use.

> Kristof, N. (1995, September 24). On language: Too polite for words. *New York Times Magazine,* pp. SM22-SM23.
>
> Kristof, a regular columnist for the *New York Times Magazine,* briefly describes the use of honorifics as an outlet for sarcasm and insults. Although the article discusses cultures other than Japanese, it provides insight into the polite vulgarity of the Japanese language.

Summary with Interpretation. Often an annotated bibliography includes unfamiliar materials, and your readers can benefit from extra explanation, background, or context. Examples include primary (original, not secondhand) sources, music, images, artistic works, texts from other times or cultures, or translations. In such cases, you may want to summarize the source and also interpret it for your readers, as this annotation illustrates.

Virginia Slims Lights. Advertisement. *Family Circle*. 26 Dec. 1985: 34–35. Print.

This advertisement for cigarettes, one of five in this issue of a popular women's magazine, illustrates how advertisers appealed to women smokers during this era. The ad's heading, "Introducing the LONGEST Slims of all," runs across two pages with a long-legged woman smoker lying on her side also stretched across both pages. She is dressed not in alluring evening wear but in a blue-flowered sweater and woolly gold slacks. Both her attire and her wholesome look suit the issue's date and holiday features which include read-aloud stories, cookie recipes, and holiday decorating. Her head is thrown back and she smiles, holding her cigarette, which apparently promises enjoyment and relaxation at a busy time of the year for the magazine's readers.

32 Finding Sources in the Library, on the Internet, and in the Field

What would you pay for access to a 24/7 Web site designed to make the most of your research time? What if it also screened and organized reliable sources for you—and tossed in free advice from information specialists? Whatever your budget, you've probably already paid—through your tuition—for these services. To get your money's worth, simply use your student ID to access your college library, online or on campus.

Visit the library home page for an overview of resources such as these:

- the online catalog for finding the library's own books, journals, newspapers, and materials you can read or check out on campus
- databases (with subscription fees paid) for electronic access to scholarly or specialized citations, abstracts, articles, and other resources
- a consortium catalog for access to the resources of the state, region, or nation through interlibrary loan or a trip to a nearby library
- links for finding specialized campus libraries, archives, or collections
- pages, tutorials, and tours for advice on using the library productively

To introduce you to the campus library, your instructor may arrange a class orientation or tour. If not, visit both the library Web site and the on-campus facility yourself.

RESEARCH CHECKLIST
Investigating Your Campus Library

☐ What services, materials, and information does the home page present?

☐ How do you gain online access to the library from your own computer? What should you do if you have trouble logging in?

☐ How can you get advice from library staff: by drop-in visit, appointment, phone, e-mail, text message, chat, or other technology?

☐ What resources—such as the library catalog and databases—can you search in the library, from campus terminals, or from your computer?

☐ How can you identify databases that might be useful for your project? What tutorials from the library or vendor show how to use them efficiently?

☐ How are print books, journals, magazines, or newspapers organized?

☐ How do you find resources such as government documents, maps, legal records, statistics, videos, images, recordings, or local historical archives?

☐ Where can you study individually or meet with a group in the library?

☐ What links or no-fee access to reliable Web sites, search engines such as Google Scholar, or academic style guides does the library provide?

For links to free reliable research resources, visit **<bedfordstmartins .com/bedguide>.**

Searching the Library Online

Your campus library may surprise you with its sophisticated technology and easy access to an overwhelming array of resources. However, if it lacks what you need, try a regional public library, often your link to a statewide library association.

Target Your Search. Identify and hunt for what you want to find.

- Do you need a mixture of sources? Use the catalog to find specialized books or journals, databases to identify individual articles, reference books to look up definitions or overviews, or government sites or indexes to find reports.

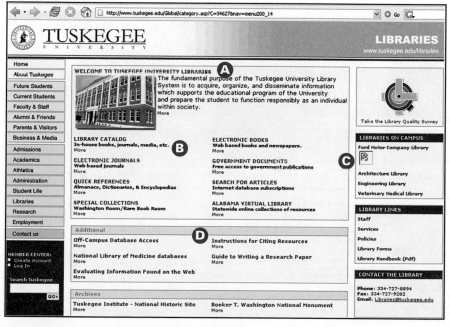

Figure 32.1 Sample home page from the Tuskegee University Libraries

A. Overview of libraries and their purpose
B. Access to library holdings and resources
C. Information on specific campus libraries
D. Other research resources

■ Do you need immediate or vintage information? Look for articles in periodicals (regularly published newspapers, magazines, and journals) for news of the day, week, or year—now or in the past. Turn to scholarly books for well-seasoned discussions.

■ Does your instructor require articles from peer-reviewed journals? Use databases to identify articles on your topic and to screen for refereed journals that rely on expert reviewers to assess articles considered for publication.

■ Do you need opinions about current issues? Search databases for newspapers or magazines that carry opinion pieces, issue-oriented or investigative articles, or contrasting regional, national, or international views.

■ Do you need the facts? Check state or federal agencies or nonprofit groups for statistics about people such as those in your zip code, including education, employment, or health.

To practice using keywords, visit the Bedford Research Room Web site at **<bedfordstmartins .com/researchroom>.**

Search the Library Catalog Creatively. Electronic catalogs may allow many search options, as the following chart illustrates. Consult a librarian or follow the prompts to find out which searches your catalog allows.

Sort Your Search Results. When your search produces a list of possible sources, click on the most promising items to learn more about them. See Figure 32.2 for a sample keyword search and Figure 32.3 for the sample

Figure 32.2 General results of a keyword search on "disabled children" using an online library catalog

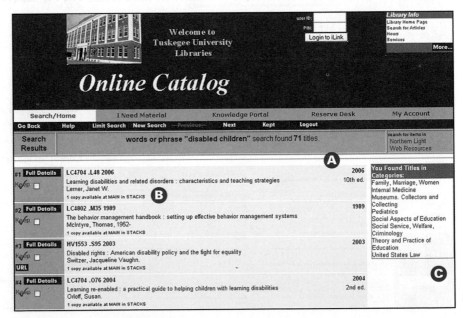

A. Number of search results
B. Results screen (linked to full entries) with call numbers, titles, authors, and availability
C. Topic areas where results found

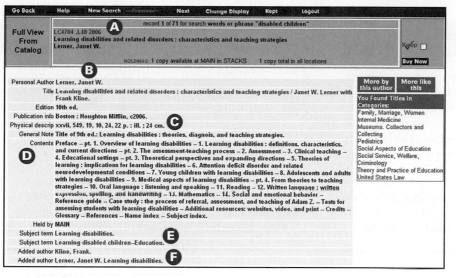

Figure 32.3 Specific record selected from keyword search results

A. Call number, title, and author
B. Availability and location
C. Number of pages, illustrations, and height of book
D. Contents by part and chapter
E. Alternate subject heading (often hyperlinked)
F. Additional author

Type of Search	Explanation	Examples	Search Tips
Keyword	Terms that identify topics discussed in the source, including works by or about an author, but may generate long lists of relevant and irrelevant sources	■ workplace mental health ■ geriatric home health care ■ Creole cookbook ■ Jane Austen novels	Use a cluster of keywords to avoid broad terms (whale, nursing) or to reduce irrelevant topics using the same terms (people of color, color graphics)
Subject	Terms assigned by library catalogers, often following the *Library of Congress Subject Headings* (*LCSH*)	■ motion pictures (not films) ■ developing countries (not third world) ■ cookery (not cookbooks)	Consult the *LCSH,* a set of large red books often shelved near the catalog terminals, to find the exact phrasing used
Author	Name of individual, organization, or group, leading to list of print (and possibly online) works by author	■ Hawthorne, Nathaniel ■ Colorado School of Mines ■ North Atlantic Treaty Organization	Begin as directed with an individual's last name or first; for a group, first use a keyword search to identify its exact name

(continued)

Type of Search	Explanation	Examples	Search Tips
Title	Name of book, pamphlet, journal, magazine, newspaper, video, CD, or other material	■ *Peace and Conflict Studies* ■ *Los Angeles Times* ■ *Nursing Outlook*	Look for a separate search option for titles of periodicals (journals, newspapers, magazines)
Identification Numbers	Library or consortium call numbers, publisher or government publication numbers	■ MJ BASI, local call number for recordings by Count Basie	Use the call number of a useful source to find related items shelved nearby
Dates	Publication or other dates used to search (or limit searches) for current or historical materials	■ Elizabeth 1558 (when she became queen of England) ■ science teaching 2011	Add dates to keyword or other searches to limit the topics or time of publication

online record for one source. Besides the call number or shelf location, the record will identify the author, title, place of publication, date, and often the book's contents, length, scope, and search terms that may help focus your search. Use these clues to help you select options wisely.

Sample the Field. Many libraries supply electronic lists of well-regarded starting points for research within a field. These valuable shortcuts help you quickly find a cluster of useful resources. The chart on page 681 supplies only a small sampling of the specialized indexes, dictionaries, encyclopedias, handbooks, yearbooks, and other resources available.

Browse the Shelves. A call number, like a building's address, tells where a book "resides." College libraries generally use the Library of Congress system with letters and numbers rather than the numerical Dewey Decimal system, but both systems group items by subject. With a call number from an online record, follow the library map and section signs to the shelf with a promising book. Once there, browse through its intriguing neighbors, which will treat the same subject.

Searching Library Databases

To practice using databases, visit the Bedford Research Room Web site at **<bedfordstmartins .com/researchroom>.**

Databases gather information. Your library may subscribe to dozens or hundreds to give you easy access to current, screened resources, including hard-to-find fee-based Web sources. Check your library's site for database descriptions and lists by topic or discipline. Match your research question to the databases likely to provide what you need.

■ General databases with citations, abstracts, or full-text articles from many fields: Academic Search Premier, One File, LexisNexis, Wilson OmniFile

Field

Field	Specialized Indexes	Reference Works	Government Resources	Internet Resources
Humanities	Essay and General Literature Index	The Humanities: A Selective Guide to Information Sources	EDSITEment at <edsitement.neh.gov>	Voice of the Shuttle at <vos.ucsb.edu>
Film and Theater	Film Literature Index	McGraw-Hill Encyclopedia of World Drama	Smithsonian Archives Center: Film, Video, and Audio Collections at <http://americanhistory.si.edu/archives/d-4.htm>	Performing Arts Links at <www.theatrelibrary.org/links/ActorsHistory.html>
History	Historical Abstracts	Dictionary of Concepts in History	The Library of Congress: American Memory at <memory.loc.gov/ammem/index.html>	WWW Virtual Library: History Central Catalogue at <www.vlib.iue.it/history/index.html>
Literature	MLA International Bibliography	Encyclopedia of the Novel	National Endowment for the Humanities at <www.neh.gov>	American Studies Crossroads at <www.crossroads.georgetown.edu/>
Social Sciences	Social Sciences Citation Index	International Encyclopedia of the Social and Behavioral Sciences	Fedstats at <www.fedstats.gov>	Intute: Social Sciences at <www.intute.ac.uk/socialsciences/>
Education	Education Index	International Encyclopedia of Education	National Center for Education Statistics at <nces.ed.gov>	ERIC: Education Resources Information Center at <www.eric.ed.gov>
Political Science	ABC Pol Sci: Bibliography of Current Contents: Political Science and Government	State Legislative Sourcebook: A Resource Guide to Legislative Information in the 50 States	Fedworld at <www.fedworld.gov/>	Political Resources on the Net at <www.politicalresources.net> National Security Archive at <www.gwu.edu/~nsarchiv>
Women's Studies	Women's Studies Abstracts	Women in World History: A Biographical Encyclopedia	U.S. Department of Labor Women's Bureau at <www.dol.gov/wb/>	Institute for Women's Policy Research at <www.iwpr.org/index.cfm>
Science and Technology	General Science Index	McGraw-Hill Encyclopedia of Science and Technology	National Science Foundation at <www.nsf.gov>	EurekAlert! at <www.eurekalert.org>
Earth Sciences	Bibliography and Index of Geology	Facts on File Dictionary of Earth Science	USGS (U.S. Geological Survey): Science for a Changing World at <www.usgs.gov>	Center for International Earth Science Information Network at <www.ciesin.org>
Environmental Studies	Environmental Abstracts	Encyclopedia of Environmental Science	EPA: U.S. Environmental Protection Agency at <www.epa.gov>	EnviroLink at <www.envirolink.org>
Life Sciences	Biological Abstracts	Encyclopedia of Human Biology	National Agricultural Library at <www.nal.usda.gov>	CAPHIS Top 100 List at <caphis.mlanet.org/consumer/index.html>

- General-interest databases with the news and culture of the time: Reader's Guide Full-Text or Retrospective (popular periodicals); New York Times Historical, America's Newspapers (news stories)
- Specialized databases focused by type of material: JSTOR, Project Muse, Sage (scholarly journals); Biological Abstracts (summaries of sources); WorldCat (books), American Periodical Series Online (digitized magazines from 1741 to 1900)
- Specialized databases focused by discipline or field: MEDLINEplus, ScienceDirect, GreenFILE (biology, medicine, health); Business Index ASAP (business)
- Issue-oriented databases: PAIS International (on public affairs), CQ Researcher (on featured issues), Opposing Viewpoints Resource Center (on debatable topics)
- Reference databases: Gale Virtual Reference Library, Britannica Online

For specific information, select a database that covers the exact field, scholarly level, type of source, or time period that you need. Databases do not identify sources in publications they do not analyze or for dates that they do not cover. Take tricky problems to a librarian who may suggest a different database or older print or CD-ROM indexes for historical research.

Keywords. Start your search with the keywords in your research question:

college costs   campus budgets   wetlands

If your first search produces too many sources, narrow your terms:

college tuition increases	state campus budget cuts	Illinois wetlands

Or add specifics, such as an author, title, or date.

Advanced Searches. Fill in the database's advanced search screen, or try common search options. For example, a database might allow wildcard or truncation symbols to find all forms of a term, often * for multiple or ? for individual characters:

child*   children, childcare, childhood
Colorad*   Colorado, Coloradan, Coloradans

A database also might allow Boolean searches that combine or rule out terms:

AND (narrows: all terms must appear in a result)   Colorado and River
OR (expands: any one of the terms must appear)   Colorado or River
NOT (rules out: one term must not appear)   Colorado not River

Search Returns. Your search calls up a list of records or entries that include your search terms. Click on one of these for specifics about the item

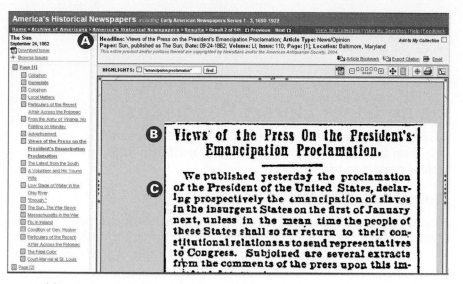

Figure 32.4 Search result from *America's Historical Newspapers*

A. Publication name, date, volume number, page number

B. Article title (and author, if available)

C. Text of article

(title, author, publication information, date, and other details) and possibly a description or summary (often called an abstract) or a link to the full text of the item. When you find a useful item, read, take notes, print, e-mail the citation or article to yourself, or save it, as your system allows. If the database supplies only an abstract, read it to decide whether you need to track down the full article elsewhere.

RESEARCH CHECKLIST
Selecting Periodical Articles from a Database

☐ What does the title of the periodical suggest about its audience, interest area, and popular or scholarly orientation? How likely are the articles in that periodical to supply what you need to find?

☐ Have the periodical articles been peer-reviewed (evaluated by other scholars prior to acceptance for publication), edited and fact-checked by journalists, or accepted for publication based on popular appeal?

☐ Does the title or description of the article suggest that it will answer your research question? Or does the entry sound intriguing but irrelevant?

☐ Does the date of the article fit your need for current, contemporary, eyewitness, or classic material?

☐ Does the length of the article suggest that it is a short review, a concise overview, or an exhaustive discussion? How much detail will you need?

☐ Does the database offer the full text of the article? If not, is the periodical containing the article likely to be available from another database, the publication's Web site, your library's shelves, or its microform files?

Using Other Library Resources

Many other library resources are available to you beyond what you can access from your library's home page. If you need help locating or using materials, consult a librarian.

Consulting Reference Materials

The library and all of its resources — whether electronic or print — are designed to help researchers like you to find information quickly and efficiently. Here you can familiarize yourself with a topic or fine-tune your research by filling in detailed definitions, dates, statistics, or facts.

General Encyclopedias. Multivolume references, such as the *New Encyclopaedia Britannica* and *Encyclopedia Americana,* can help you survey a topic, serving you best by preparing you to move to specialized resources.

Specialized Encyclopedias. These references cover a field in much greater depth than general encyclopedias do, as these sample titles suggest:

Dictionary of American History   *Encyclopedia of Psychology*

Encyclopedia of Human Biology   *Encyclopedia of Sociology*

The Gale Encyclopedia of Science   *Encyclopedia of World Cultures*

New Grove Dictionary of Music and Musicians

Dictionaries. Large and specialized dictionaries cover foreign languages, abbreviations, and slang as well as the terminology of a particular field, as in *Black's Law Dictionary, Stedman's Medical Dictionary,* or the *Oxford Dictionary of Natural History.* Unabridged dictionaries, often available on dictionary stands, define even the most obscure words.

Handbooks and Companions. Concise surveys of terms and topics on a specific subject feature articles longer than dictionary entries but more concise than those in encyclopedias.

Blackwell Encyclopaedia of Political Thought

Bloomsbury Guide to Women's Literature

Dictionary of the Vietnam War

Oxford Companion to English Literature

Statistical Sources. If numbers are a key type of evidence for your research, you can find sources for statistics in the library and online.

- The *Statistical Abstract of the United States*. Perhaps the most useful single compilation of statistics, this resource contains hundreds of tables relating to population, social issues, economics, and so on.
- *Gallup Poll*. The surveys conducted by the Gallup Organization are good resources for public-opinion statistics.
- *<www.census.gov>*. The federal government collects an extraordinary amount of statistical data and releases much of it on the Web. Check also <www.fedworld.gov> and <www.fedstats.gov>.

Atlases. For a geographical angle, use maps and atlases of countries, regions, and the world as well as history, natural resources, ethnic groups, and other topics.

Biographical Sources. Directories list basic information — degrees, work history, honors, addresses — for prominent people. Tools such as *Biography Index* and the *Biography and Genealogy Master Index* locate resources like these: *American Men and Women of Science, The Dictionary of American Biography, The Dictionary of National Biography, Who's Who in Politics, Who's Who in the United States.*

Bibliographies. When you use a bibliography — a list of sources on a specific subject — you take advantage of the research others have already done. Every time you find a good book or article, look at the sources the author draws on; some of these may be useful to you, too. Sometimes you may locate a book-length bibliography on your subject, compiled by a researcher and published so that others (including you) won't have to duplicate the work. Bibliographies cite a wide variety of materials and can lead to sources that you wouldn't otherwise find.

For example, *The Essential Shakespeare: An Annotated Bibliography of Major Modern Studies* lists the best books and articles published on each of Shakespeare's works, a wonderful shortcut when you look for worthwhile criticism. If you're lucky, adding the word *bibliography* to a subject or keyword search on your topic will turn up a similarly helpful list of sources with annotations.

For more on keyword searches, see pp. 678–80.

RESEARCH CHECKLIST
Managing Your Project

☐ Are you on schedule? Do you need to adjust your timetable to give yourself more or less time for any of the stages?

☐ Are you using your research question to stay on track and avoid digressions?

For downloadable sample schedules (and research checklists), visit **<bedfordstmartins .com/bedguide>**.

☐ Are you keeping your materials up-to-date — listing new sources in your working bibliography and storing new material in your archives?

☐ Do you have a clear idea of where you are in the research process?

Locating Special Materials

Your library is likely to have other collections of materials, especially on regional or specialized topics, but you may need to ask what's available.

Periodicals on Microform. This technology puts a large amount of printed material — for example, two weeks of the *New York Times* — on a durable roll of film (microfilm) that fits into a small box or on a set of plastic sheets the size of index cards (microfiche). The machines used to read microforms often print out full-sized copies of pages.

Primary Materials on Microform. Many libraries have primary, or first-hand, material in microform. For example, the *American Culture Series* reproduces books and pamphlets (1493 to 1875) with a good subject index, making it possible to view colonial religious tracts or nineteenth-century abolitionist pamphlets without traveling to a special collection. *American Women's Diaries* provides firsthand glimpses of the past through the words of westbound women.

Primary Materials in Digitized Format. Firsthand diaries, letters, speeches, and interviews are increasingly available in searchable databases. Examples include *Black Thought and Culture, Oral History Online,* and *North American Immigrant Letters, Diaries, and Oral Histories* (1840 on).

Resources from Organizations. Your library may collect pamphlets and reports distributed by companies, trade groups, and professional organizations. The *Encyclopedia of Associations,* organized by subject or group name, and the *United States Government Manual,* listing government agencies, can lead to useful materials and contacts, especially for field research.

Government Documents. The U.S. government, the most prolific publisher in the world, makes an increasing number of documents available for all citizens on the Web, along with indexes like these:

- *Monthly Catalog of United States Government Publications,* which is the most complete index to federal documents available
- *CIS Index,* which specializes in congressional documents with a handy legislative history index
- *Congressional Record Index,* which indexes daily reports on Congress

Besides congressional hearings, presidential papers, and reports from federal agencies, the government has published on practically any topic you can think of. If you plan to use government documents, often hard to locate, ask a librarian for help.

Using the Internet for Research

The Internet contains an ever-growing number of resources that vary greatly in quality and purpose. For example, a quick search for information about Yellowstone National Park turns up nearly anything you might want to find: official park information, contacts for cabin reservations, photographs of family trips, scientific studies of the wolf population, the Old Faithful Webcam, and technical reports such as the official Yellowstone Wildland Fire Management Plan. The sheer bulk of this information makes searching for relevant materials both too easy and too difficult, but a few basic principles can help.

Finding Recommended Internet Resources

Go first to online resources recommended by your instructor, department, or library. Their recommendations save the time required to search and screen randomly chosen sites. More important, their suggestions can take you directly to respected resources prepared by experts (scholars or librarians) and directed to academic researchers (like you). Browse to find resources such as these on your library or other campus Web site:

For a checklist for finding recommended sources, see B1 in the Quick Research Guide on p. A-23.

For more on evaluating sources, see Ch. 33.

- Self-help guides or Internet databases organized by area (social sciences or business), topic (literary analysis), or type of information, such as the extensive Auraria Library *Statistics and Facts* guide at <http://guides.auraria.edu/statistics>.
- Research Web sites sponsored by another library, academic institution, or consortium such as ipl2, the Internet Public Library at <www.ipl.org>, the Michigan eLibrary at <http://mel.org>, InfoMine <http://infomine.ucr.edu>, or the authoritative World Wide Web Virtual Library <http://vlib.org>.
- Other research centers or major libraries with their own collections of links, such as the Library of Congress page "Newspaper & Current Periodical Reading Room" at <http://www.loc.gov/rr/news/lists.html>.
- Specialty search engines for government materials— <www.fedworld.gov>, <www.usa.gov>, or <www.google.com/unclesam>—along with advice about using them such as that on the California State University Northridge Web site at <http://library.csun.edu/Find_Resources/Government_Publications/finddocs.html>.
- Specialty search engines for specific materials such as images at Google Images at <http://images.google.com>, including the *Life* magazine photo archive, or AltaVista Image Search at <http://www.altavista.com/image/>.

- Collections of online sources such as those for the humanities created by the EText Center, now available at <http://lib.virginia.edu/digital/collections/finding_digital.html>.

- Collections of e-books, including reference books and literary texts now out of copyright, such as *Bartleby.com* at <www.bartleby.com/> and *Project Gutenberg* at <www.gutenberg.org/>.

- Web databases with "unrestricted access" (not online subscription services restricted to campus users) as varied as the country-by-country data of *InfoNation* at <http://cyberschoolbus.un.org/infonation/index.asp> and the extensive health resources of *MedlinePlus* at <http://www.nlm.nih.gov/medlineplus/>.

- Community resources or organizations, often useful for local research and service learning reports.

Selecting Search Engines

Unlike a library, the Internet has no handy, systematic catalog, and search engines are not unbiased, objective searchers. Each has its own system of locating material, categorizing it, and establishing the sequence for reporting results. One search site, patterned on a library catalog or index, might be selective, designed to advance academic investigations. Another might carry extensive advertising but separate it from search results, while a third pops up sites that pay advertising fees ("sponsors") first in the list, even though sites listed later might be better matches.

The best search engine is one you select and learn to use well. If you have a favorite, check its search practices under About, Search Tips, or Help. As you work out a combination of search terms relevant to your research question, think of your wording as a zoom lens. Tinker with it to search as narrowly as possible, finding relevant sites but avoiding endless options. Then try the identical search with another search engine to compare the results.

RESEARCH CHECKLIST
Comparing Search Engine Results

☐ What does the search engine's home page suggest its typical users want—academic information, business news, sports, shopping, or music?

☐ What does the search engine gather or index—information from and about a Web page (Google), each word on a Web page (AltaVista), academic sources (Google Scholar), a collection of other search engines (Metacrawler, Dogpile, SurfWax, or other metasearch engines), or returns compared for several engines (RearWindow, TurboScout)?

☐ What can you learn from a search engine's About, Search Tips, or Help?

☐ How does the advanced search work? Does it improve your results?

☐ Does the search engine respond to questions (Ask, Wolframalpha), categorize by source type (text, images, news, blogs), or group information into directories by topic (About, Google Directory)?

☐ How well does the search engine target your "query" — the words that define your specific search?

☐ Can you easily distinguish results (responses to your query), sponsors (advertisers who pay for priority placement), and other ads by placement, color, or other markers?

Learning by Doing 🎥 Comparing Web Searches

Working with some classmates, agree on the topic and terms for a test search. (Or agree to test terms each of you selects.) Have everyone conduct the same search using different search engines, and then compare the results. Use the checklist above to suggest features for comparison. If possible, sit together, using your laptops or campus computers so that you can easily see, compare, and evaluate the search engine results. Sum up your conclusions, and report them to the class.

Conducting Advanced Electronic Searches

Search engines contain millions of records on Web sites, much as a database or library catalog contains records on books, periodicals, or other materials found in a library. Generally, search engines can be searched by broad categories such as *education* or *health* or by more specific keywords.

Limit the Search. When you limit your search to keywords and broad categories, you may be overwhelmed with information. For example, Figure 32.5 illustrates a keyword search for sources on *foster care* on Google that produced more than 20 million entries. A keyword search may be ideal if you search for a highly specialized term or topic, such as training for distance runners. For a more general topic — such as *foster care* — you may turn up seemingly endless results. Instead, try to limit your search in order to find more relevant results. As Figure 32.6 shows, an advanced search produced fewer sources on one aspect of foster care — placing teenagers.

For more on keywords, see p. 652 and pp. 679–80.

Select Limitations for Advanced Searches. Google and Metacrawler, for example, allow you to limit searches to all, exactly, any, or none of the words you enter. Look for directions for limitations such as these:

- A phrase such as *elementary school safety*, requested as a unit (exactly these words) or enclosed in quotation marks to mark it as a unit
- A specific language (human or computer) such as English or Spanish

Figure 32.5 Results of a keyword search for *foster care* using Google, reporting more than 20 million entries

A. Search terms
B. Total number of entries located
C. Highlighted search terms found in entries

- A specific format or type of software such as a PDF file
- A date range (before, after, or between creation, revision, or indexing)
- A domain such as .edu (educational institution), .gov (government), .org (organization), or .com (commercial site or company), which indicates the type of group sponsoring the site
- A part of the world, such as North America or Africa
- The location (such as the title, the URL, or the text) of the search term
- The audio or visual media enhancements
- The file size

Finding Specialized Online Materials

You can locate a variety of material online, ranging from e-zines (electronic magazines) to conversations among people interested in your topic.

Look for Electronic Publications. Wide public access to the Internet has given individuals and small interest groups an economical publication option. Evaluate and use such texts cautiously.

Figure 32.6
Advanced search results on *foster care + "placing teenagers"* using Google, reporting 163 entries

A. Search terms
B. Total number of entries located
C. Highlighted search terms found in entries

Browse the Blogs. Globe of Blogs at <www.globeofblogs.com> indexes many blogs (short for "Web logs"), providing access to the personal, political, and topical commentaries of individuals around the globe. Google features blog searches by topic at <blogsearch.google.com>. Given the rapid growth of blogs, you may want to use RSS (often expanded as "Real Simple Syndication") software to alert you to breaking news or to sample wide-ranging commentary on a current topic.

Keep Up with the News. Try sites such as <http://news.google.com> for easy access to current national or international coverage of major stories by thousands of newspapers or news services. Personalize the page to rearrange it to suit your interests, track a topic during the preceding month, or focus on a specific country or news source. RSS feeds and mailing lists are available for news as well as specialized topics, such as daily quotes, biographies, and historical events on the current date from *Britannica Online* at <http://newsletters.britannica.com/toolbox/> or "Blogs, Opinion and Analysis" at <http://abcnews.go.com/technology/blogs>.

Search Newsgroups and Mailing Lists. Newsgroups and mailing lists generate an enormous amount of text each day. Both support the discussion of topics such as adult education or immigration among people with a shared interest. The archives of such groups require cautious reading but may supply detailed analyses by interested members of the public or acknowledged experts. Google (at <groups.google.com>) allows you to search for mailing lists and newsgroups.

Finding Sources in the Field

The goal of field research is the same as that of library and Internet research — to gather the information you need to answer your research question and then to marshal persuasive evidence to support your conclusions. When you interview, observe, or ask questions of people, you generate your own first-hand (or primary) evidence. Almost any paper will be enriched by authentic and persuasive field sources, and you'll almost certainly learn more about your topic by going into the field. Before you begin, be sure to find out from your instructor whether you need institutional approval for research involving other people ("human subjects approval").

Interviewing

For more on interviewing, see Ch. 6.

Interviews — conversations with a purpose — may prove to be your main source of field material. Whenever possible, interview an expert in the field or, if you are researching a group of people, someone representative or typical. Either way, prepare carefully.

TIPS FOR INTERVIEWING

- Be sure your prospect is willing to be quoted in writing.
- Make an appointment for a day when the person will have enough time — an hour if possible — to have a thorough talk with you.
- Arrive promptly, with carefully thought-out questions to ask.
- Come ready to take notes, including key points, quotations, and descriptive detail. If you also want to record, ask permission.
- Really listen. Let the person open up.
- Be flexible, and allow the interview to move in unanticipated directions.
- If a question draws no response, don't persist; go on to the next one.
- At the end of the interview, thank your interviewee, and arrange for an opportunity to clarify comments and confirm direct quotations.
- Make additional notes right after the interview to preserve anything you didn't have time to record during the interview.

If you can't talk to an expert in person, try a telephone interview. Make an appointment for a convenient time, write out questions before you dial, and take notes. Federal regulations, by the way, forbid recording a phone interview without notifying the person talking that you are doing so.

Observing

An observation may provide essential information about a setting such as a business or a school. If so, make an appointment and, on arrival, identify yourself and your purpose. Some receptionists will insist on identification; ask your instructor for a statement on college letterhead declaring that you are a student doing field research.

For more on observing, see Ch. 5.

TIPS FOR OBSERVING

- Establish a clear purpose — exactly what you want to observe and why.

- Take notes so that you don't skip important details in your paper.

- Record facts, telling details, and sensory impressions. Notice the features of the place, the actions or relationships of the people who are there, or whatever relates to the purpose of your observation.

- Consider using a still or video camera if you have the equipment and can operate it without being distracted from the scene. Photographs can illustrate your paper and help you recall and interpret details while you write. If you are in a private place, get written permission from the owner (or other authority) and any people you film or photograph.

- Pause, look around, fill in missing details, and check the accuracy of your notes before you leave the observation site.

- Thank the person who arranged your observation so you will be welcome again if you need to return to fill gaps or test new ideas.

Using Questionnaires

Questionnaires are widely used to gather the responses of a number of people to a fixed set of questions. Professional researchers carefully design their questions and randomly select representative people to respond in order to reach reliable answers. Because your survey will not be that extensive, avoid generalizing about your findings as if they were unimpeachable facts. It's one thing to say that "many of the students" who filled out a questionnaire hadn't read a newspaper in the past month; it's another to claim that this is true of 72 percent of the students at your school — especially when your questionnaires went only to those at the gym on Friday, and most of them just threw out the forms.

A more reliable way to treat questionnaires is as group interviews: assume that you collect typical views, use them to build your overall knowledge, and cull the responses for compelling details or quotations. Use a questionnaire to concentrate on what a group thinks as a whole or when an interview to cover all your questions is impractical. (See Figure 32.7 for a sample questionnaire.)

QUESTIONNAIRE

Thank you for completing this questionnaire. All information you supply will be kept strictly confidential.

1. What is your age? _____
2. What is your gender? _____
3. What is your class? _____

   _____ Freshman   _____ Sophomore   _____ Junior   _____ Senior

4. How old were you when you first began using the Internet? _____
5. How do you currently access the Internet? Indicate which of the following statements is true for you.

   _____ With my own computer   _____ With computers at the library or campus lab

   _____ With my laptop   _____ Someone I live with has a computer

   _____ Other (please specify): _____

6. Approximately how many hours a week do you use the Internet? _____
7. What is your primary reason for using the Internet?

   _____ Personal   _____ School-related   _____ Work-related

8. Check all of the ways in which you use the Internet.

   _____ E-mailing

   _____ Visiting social networking sites or chatting

   _____ Recreational Web surfing

   _____ Recreational media use (listening to music, watching videos, playing games)

   _____ Taking an online course

   _____ Conducting optional research for a class

   _____ Conducting mandatory research for a class

   _____ Conducting personal research (such as planning travel, evaluating products)

   _____ Searching for a job or an internship

   _____ Posting résumés or job applications

   _____ Managing financial accounts

   _____ Maintaining a Web site or blog

   Other: _____

9. For which activities above do you use the Internet most? _____
10. On a scale of 1 to 5, rate how comfortable you are using the Internet.

    (not very comfortable) 1 2 3 4 5 (very comfortable)

11. Do you feel that you could benefit from further instruction in using the Internet?

    _____ Yes   _____ No   _____ Maybe

Figure 32.7 Questionnaire asking college students about Internet use

TIPS FOR USING A QUESTIONNAIRE

- Ask yourself what you want to discover with your questionnaire. Then thoughtfully invent questions to fulfill that purpose.

- State your questions clearly, and supply simple directions for easy responses. Test your questionnaire on classmates or friends before you distribute it to the group you want to study.

- Ask questions that call for checking options, marking yes or no, circling a number on a five-point scale, or writing a few words so responses are easy to tally. Try to ask for one piece of information per question.

- If you wish to consider differences based on age, gender, or other variables, include some demographic questions.

- Write unbiased questions that solicit factual responses. Do not ask, "How religious are you?" Instead ask, "What is your religious affiliation?" and "How often do you attend religious services?" Then you could report actual numbers and draw logical inferences about respondents.

- When appropriate, ask open-ended questions that call for short written responses. Although qualitative responses are more difficult to tally than quantitative, the answers may supply worthwhile quotations or suggest important issues or factors.

- Try to distribute questionnaires at a set location or event, and collect them as they are completed. If necessary, have them returned to your campus mailbox or another secure location. The more immediate and convenient the return, the higher your return rate is likely to be.

- Use a blank questionnaire or make an answer grid to mark and add up the answers for each question. Total the responses to say that a certain percentage selected a specific answer.

- For fill-in or short answers, type each answer into a computer file. (Code each questionnaire with a number, and note it if you might want to return to the individual questionnaire.) You can rearrange the answers in the file, looking for logical groups, categories, or patterns that accurately reflect the responses and enrich your analysis.

Corresponding

Does a person with views you need live too far away to interview? Do you need information from a group such as the American Red Cross or from an elected official? Check your library or the Internet for directories of professional organizations, businesses, government agencies, or special-interest groups that might supply expert information. Visit a group's Web site for an e-mail option for your request, a correspondence address, a FAQ page (that answers frequently asked questions), or files of brochures.

For advice on writing e-mail messages and business letters, see pp. 361–62.

TIPS FOR CORRESPONDING

- Plan ahead, and allow plenty of time for responses to your requests.

- Make your message short and polite. Identify yourself, and explain your request. List any questions. Thank your correspondent.

- Enclose a stamped, self-addressed envelope with a letter. Include your e-mail address in your message.

Attending Public and Online Events

College organizations bring interesting speakers to campus. Check the campus schedule of events and the newspaper. In addition, professionals and special-interest groups convene for regional or national conferences. A lecture or conference can be a source of fresh ideas and an excellent introduction to the language of a discipline.

TIPS FOR ATTENDING EVENTS

- Take notes on the lectures, usually given by experts in the field who supply firsthand opinions or research findings.
- Ask questions from the audience or talk informally with a speaker later.
- Record who attended the event, how the audience reacted, or other background details that could prove useful in writing your paper.
- Depending on the gathering, a speaker might distribute the paper presented or be willing to send you a copy. Conferences often publish their proceedings—usually a set of the lectures delivered—but publication takes months. Try the library for past proceedings.

If you join an online discussion, you can observe, ask a question, or save or print the transcript for your records.

fter you locate and collect information, you need to think critically and evaluate — in other words, judge — your sources.

For more on critical reading and thinking, see Chs. 2–3.

- Which of your sources are reliable?
- Which of these sources are relevant to your topic?
- What evidence from these sources is most useful for your paper?

Evaluating Library and Internet Sources

Not every source you locate will be equally reliable or equally useful. Sites recommended by your library have been screened by professionals, but each has its own point of view or approach, often a necessary bias to restrict its focus. Sources from the Web require special care. Like other firsthand materials, postings, blogs, and sites reflect the biases, interests, or information gaps of their writers or sponsors. Commercial and organizational sites may supply useful material, but they provide only what supports their goals — selling their products, serving their clients, enlisting new members, or persuading others to accept their activities or views. See Figure 33.1 for a sample evaluation of a Web site that provides both informative and persuasive materials.

For exercises on evaluating Web sources, visit **<bedfordstmartins .com/bedguide>**.

How can you simplify evaluation? Begin with your selection of sources. When you draw information from an article in a print or online peer-reviewed journal, the evaluation of that article actually began when the editors of the journal first read the article and then asked expert reviewers to evaluate whether it merited publication. Similarly, a serious book from a major publishing company or university press probably has been submitted to knowledgeable reviewers. Such reviewers may be asked to assess whether the article or book is well reasoned, logically presented, and competently researched. However, such reviewers can't decide if the work is pertinent to your research question or contains evidence useful for your paper.

How do you know what evidence is best? Do what experienced researchers do — ask key questions. Use the time-tested journalist's questions — who, what, when, where, why, and how — to evaluate each source you consider using.

Figure 33.1
Evaluating the purpose, audience, and bias of a Web site offering informative and persuasive materials

A. Identifies group as organization (.org), not school (.edu) or company (.com)
B. Uses engaging animal graphics
C. Appeals for support
D. Explains purpose of group and provides toolbar link to contact information
E. Links to information and recommends action about issues that concern animal lovers

RESEARCH CHECKLIST
Evaluating Sources

Who?

☐ Who is the author of the source? What are the author's credentials and profession? What might be the author's point of view?

☐ Who is the intended audience of the source? Experts in the field? Professionals? General readers? People with a special interest? In what ways does the source's tone or evidence appeal to this audience?

For advice on evaluating field sources, see pp. 703–04.

☐ Who is the publisher of the source or the sponsor of the site? Is it a corporation, a scholarly organization, a professional association, a government agency, or an issue-oriented group? Have you heard of this publisher or sponsor before? Is it well regarded? Does it seem reputable and responsible? Is it considered academic or popular?

☐ Who has reviewed the source prior to publication? Only the author? Peer reviewers who are experts in the area? An editorial staff?

What?

☐ What is the purpose of the publication or Web site? Is it to sell a product or service? To entertain? To supply information? To publish new research? To shape opinion about an issue or a cause?

☐ What bias or point of view might affect the reliability of the source?

☐ What kind of information does the source supply? Is it a primary source (a firsthand account) or a secondary source (an analysis of primary material)? If it is a secondary source, does it rely on sound evidence from primary sources?

☐ What evidence does the source present? Does it seem trustworthy, sufficient, and relevant given what you know about the subject? Does its argument or analysis seem logical and complete, or does it leave questions unanswered? Does it identify and list its sources or supply active links?

When?

☐ When was the source published or created? Is its information current?

☐ When was it last revised or updated? Is its information up-to-date?

Where?

☐ Where did you find the source? Is it prescreened, available through your campus library? Is it a Web site that popped up in a general search?

☐ Where has the source been recommended? On an instructor's syllabus or Web page? On a library list? In another reliable source? During a conference with an instructor or a librarian?

Why?

☐ Why should you use this source rather than others?

☐ Why is its information directly relevant to your research question?

How?

☐ How does the selection of evidence in the source reflect the interests and expertise of its author, publisher or sponsor, and intended audience? How might you need to qualify its use in your paper?

☐ How would its information add to your paper? How would it help answer your research question and provide evidence to persuade your readers?

Who Is the Author?

Learn about each author's credentials, affiliations, and reputation so that any author who shapes or supports your ideas is reliable and trustworthy.

Print Credentials. Check for the author's background in any preface, introduction, or concluding note in an article or a book. National newsmagazines (for example, *Newsweek, Time,* and *U.S. News & World Report*) usually identify any experts before or next to their contributions. However, most of their articles are written by reporters who try to substantiate facts and cover multiple views, perhaps compiling regional contributions. In contrast, some other magazines select facts to mirror editorial opinions.

Internet Credentials. For a Web site, look for a link to author information and an e-mail address so you could contact the author about his or her background. If your source is a posting to a newsgroup or a mailing list, deduce what you can from the writer's e-mail address and any signature file. Try a Web search for the person's name, looking for associated sites or links to or from the author's site. If you can't find out about the author, treat the information as background for you, not as evidence in your paper.

Field Credentials. For field research, you may be able to select your sources. To investigate safety standards for infant car seats, a personal interview with a local pediatrician will probably produce different information than an interview with a sales representative. Distributing a questionnaire to a certain group of people or observing a particular setting also may affect your research results. Delve deeply, widely, and fairly.

Reputation. The best measure of someone's expertise is the regard of other experts. Do others cite the work of your source's author? Does your instructor or someone else on campus who knows the field recognize or recommend the author? Is the author listed in a biographical database?

Material with No Author Identified. If no author is given, try to identify the sponsor or publisher. On a Web site, check the home page or search for a disclaimer, contact information, or an "About This Site" page. If a print source doesn't list an author, consider the publication: Is the article in a respected newspaper like the *Wall Street Journal* or a supermarket tabloid? Is the brochure published by a leader in its field?

Who Else Is Involved?

Intended Audience. A source written for authorities in a field is likely to assume that readers already have plenty of background knowledge. Such sources typically skip overviews and tailor their details for experts. In contrast, sources written for general audiences usually define terms and supply background. Instead of beginning your paper on HIV treatments with an article in a well-known medical journal for physicians that discusses the most favorable chemical composition for a protease inhibitor drug, turn first to a source that defines *protease inhibitor* and discusses how it helps HIV patients.

Publisher or Sponsor. The person, organization, government agency, or corporation that prints or sponsors a source also may shape its content. Like authors, publishers often hold a point of view. Businesses are likely to present their products more favorably than those of competitors. Political parties or special-issue groups, such as the American Civil Liberties Union or the National Rifle Association, are likely to publish materials supporting policies they favor. To learn about a Web site sponsor, look for a mission statement or an "About" page (see Figure 33.1).

Ask critical questions about what might motivate a publisher. Is a Web site created for commercial (.com) purposes, such as selling a product or service? Is it sponsored by an organization devoted to a cause (.org, as in Figure 33.1) or a government agency (.gov)? Is it the work of an individual with strong opinions but little expertise? Is a newsgroup or mailing list limited to a particular interest? Is a publisher noted for its works in a specific field or with a specific political agenda? Does a periodical have a predictable point of view? For example, a faith-based publication will take a different view than a newsmagazine, just as a conservative publication will differ from a liberal one. Because these questions can be difficult, consult a librarian if you need help.

For an example showing how a URL identifies a publisher, see A on p. 698.

Reviewers before Publication. Consider whether a publisher has an editorial staff, an expert editor, or an advisory board of experts. Does it rely on peer reviewers to critique articles or books under consideration? Does it expect research to meet professional standards? Does it outline such standards in its advice for prospective authors or its description of its mission? Does a sponsor have a solid reputation as a professional organization?

What Is the Purpose?

A reference book in a library serves a different purpose from a newspaper editorial, a magazine advertisement, or a Web site that promotes a service. To understand the purpose or intention of a source, ask critical questions: Is the purpose of this source to explain or inform? To report new research? To persuade? To offer another viewpoint? To sell a product? Does the source acknowledge its purpose in its preface, mission statement, or "About Us" or FAQ (Frequently Asked Questions) page?

Bias. A *bias* is a preference for a particular side of an issue. Because most authors and most publishers have opinions on their topics, there's little point in asking whether they are biased. Instead, ask how that viewpoint affects the presentation of information and opinion. What are the author's or sponsor's allegiances? Does the source treat one side of an issue more favorably than another? Is that bias hidden or stated? Having a strong bias does not invalidate a source. However, if you recognize such bias early on, you may want to look for other viewpoints to avoid lopsided analyses.

Primary or Secondary Information. A *primary source* is a firsthand account written by an eyewitness or a participant. It contains raw data and immediate impressions. A *secondary source* is an analysis of information in one or more primary sources. Primary sources for investigating the Korean War might include diaries or letters written by military personnel, accounts of civilian witnesses, articles by journalists on the scene, and official military reports. If a historian used those accounts as evidence in a study of military strategy or if a peace activist used them in a book on consequences of warfare for civilians, these resulting works would be secondary sources.

Most research papers benefit from both primary and secondary sources. If you repeatedly cite a fact or an authority quoted in someone else's analysis, try to go to the primary source. After all, a bombing raid that spared 70 percent of a village also leveled 30 percent of it. The original research (published as a primary source) can help you learn where facts end and interpretation begins.

When Was the Source Published?

Try to rely on current sources. In most fields, new information and discoveries appear every year, so a source needs to be up-to-date or at least still timely. New information may appear first in Web postings, media broadcasts, newspapers, and eventually magazines, though such sources may not allow time to consider information thoughtfully. Later, as material is more fully examined, it may appear in scholarly articles and books. For this reason, older materials can supply a valuable historical, theoretical, or analytical focus.

Where Did You Find the Source?

Is it recommended by your instructor? Is it in the library's collection? When instructors or academic units direct you to sources, you benefit from both their subject-matter and teaching expertise. On the other hand, when you find a Web source while randomly browsing or pick up a magazine at the dentist's office, you'll need to do all the source evaluation yourself.

Why Would You Use This Source?

Why use one source rather than another? Is its information useful for your purposes? Would its strong quotations or hard facts be effective? Does it tackle the topic in a relevant way? For one paper, you might appropriately rely on a popular magazine; for another, you might need the findings in the scholarly article on which the magazine relied. Look for the best sources for your purpose, asking not only "Will this do?" but also "Would something else be better?"

For more on selecting sources, see section B in the Quick Research Guide, pp. A-22–A-23.

For more on testing evidence, see pp. 42–43.

How Would This Source Contribute to Your Paper?

The evidence in a source—its ideas, facts, and expert or other opinions—can tell you about its reliability and usefulness for your project. Is its evidence complete, up-to-date, and carefully assembled? Is there enough convincing evidence to support its claims? Does visual material enhance the source rather than distract from its argument or information? Does the source identify its own sources in citations and a bibliography? Even a highly reliable source needs to be relevant to your research question and your ideas about how to answer that question. An interesting fact or opinion could be just that—interesting. Instead, you need facts, expert opinions, information, and quotations that relate directly to your purpose and audience.

Learning by Doing 🎧 Evaluating Your Sources

Select a source that you expect to be useful for your paper. Using the checklist on pages 699–700, jot down notes as you closely examine the source for reliability and relevance. Working with a classmate or group, present your evaluations to each other. Then discuss strategies for dealing with the strengths and limitations of the sources you have evaluated.

Evaluating Field Sources

Each type of field research can raise particular questions. For example, when you observe an event or a setting, are people aware of being observed? If so, have they changed their behavior? Is your random sampling of people truly representative? Have you questioned everyone in a group thoroughly enough? Besides the general criteria for evaluating sources, you might want to ask these questions as well.

RESEARCH CHECKLIST
Evaluating Field Sources

☐ Does your source seem biased or prejudiced? If so, is this viewpoint so strong that you have to discount some of the source's information?

☐ Does your source provide evidence to support or corroborate claims? Have you compared different people's opinions, accounts, or evidence?

☐ Is any evidence hearsay—one person telling you the thoughts of another or recounting actions that he or she hasn't witnessed? If so, can you check the information with another source or a different type of evidence?

☐ Does your source seem to respond consistently, seriously, and honestly? Has time possibly distorted memories of past events?

Reconsidering Your Purpose and Your Thesis

Once you have gathered and evaluated a reasonable collection of sources, it's time to step back and consider them as a group.

- Have you found enough relevant and credible sources to satisfy the requirements of your assignment? Have you found enough to suggest sound answers to your research question?

- Are your sources thought provoking? Can you tell what is generally accepted, controversial, or possibly unreliable? Have your sources enlightened you while substantiating, refining, or changing your ideas?

- Are your sources varied? Have they helped you achieve a reasonably complete view of your topic, including other perspectives, approaches, alternatives, or interpretations? Have they deepened your understanding and helped you reach well-reasoned, balanced conclusions?

- Are your sources appropriate? Do they answer your question with evidence your readers will find persuasive? Do they have the range and depth necessary to achieve your purpose and satisfy your readers?

Use these questions to check in with yourself. Make sure that you have a clear direction for your research—whether it's the same direction you started with or a completely new one. Perhaps you are ready to answer your research question, refine your thesis, and begin a draft that pulls together your ideas and those of your sources. On the other hand, you may want to find other sources to support or challenge your assumptions, to counter strong evidence against your position, or to pursue a tantalizing new direction.

Integrating Sources 34

Your paper should project your own voice and showcase your ideas — your thesis and main points about your research question. It also should marshal compelling support, using the evidence that you have quoted, paraphrased, and summarized from sources. Add this support responsibly, identifying both the sources and the ideas or exact words captured from them.

For more on using sources in your writing, see Ch. 12 and D1–D6 in the Quick Research Guide, pp. A-26–A-27.

Using Sources Ethically

Research can be a complex, lively process, enriched by the exchange of ideas. However, discussions of research ethics sometimes reduce that topic to one issue: plagiarism. Plagiarism is viewed especially seriously in college because it shows a deep disrespect for the work of the academic world — investigating, evaluating, analyzing, interpreting, and synthesizing ideas. And it may have serious consequences — failing a paper, failing a course, or being dismissed from the institution.

Plagiarists intentionally present someone else's work as their own whether they dishonestly submit as their own a paper purchased from the Web, pretend that passages copied from an article are their own writing, appropriate the ideas of others without identifying their sources, or paste in someone else's graphics without acknowledgment or permission.

Although college writers may not intend to plagiarize, most campus policies look at the outcome, not the intent. Working carefully with sources and treating the ideas and expressions of others respectfully can help build the skills necessary to avoid mistakes. Educating yourself about the standards of your institution, instructor, and profession also can protect you from ethical errors that may carry heavy consequences. The following chart illustrates how to avoid or remedy common situations that can generate problems.

Plagiarism Problem	Remedy
You have dawdled. Someone tells you about a site that sells papers, but you know this is wrong. Plus their topics don't sound like your assignment, and you need to hand in drafts and an annotated bibliography, too.	Don't buy the paper. Ask your instructor for more time, even with a penalty. Cancel your social life for the week, and hunt for recommended sources. Be proud that you showed integrity and didn't risk your college career.
You've fully investigated a serious research question about a problem affecting your family, but now you're mixing up what you've quoted, summed up, and thought up yourself. You're afraid your disorganization will look like plagiarism.	Stop and get organized. Link every note or file to its source with the author's last name (or brief title) and page number. Treat unidentified leftover notes as background. Don't add what you can't credit.
You found a great book in the library but had only a minute to record the basics. Later you found these notes: InDfCult, HUP, Cambridge, Carol Padden, Tom Humphries, 5 122 For Df voice/technol = issue Relates to cult def	Go back to the library. Spell out clear information about *Inside Deaf Culture* by Carol Padden and Tom Humphries, published in Cambridge, MA, by Harvard University Press in 2005. Turn back to p. 122. Decide what to do: quote (exact words with quotation marks) or paraphrase (your own words, not "parroting").
You've never read a book with hard words like *transmogrify* and *heuristic*. You can't restate them because you don't understand them. You're afraid your instructor will think you're a cheater who just copied, not an embarrassed student who can't read well enough.	Don't use a source you can't understand. Look for others shelved nearby or listed under the same keywords. If the source is required, reread and sum up each passage in turn to master it. Spend time improving your reading using campus or community resources.
You're struggling to start writing. Finally you're creating sentences, then pasting in notes. You suddenly wonder how you'll figure out where to add your source citations. What if you didn't identify a few sources or add the page numbers for quotations?	Backtrack fast. Add notes (color, brackets, or comments) to mark exactly where you need to add a source citation later. For yourself, note the basics — author and page. Add quotation marks for words directly from the source.
In your home country, you and your friends worked together to state the answer the teacher expected. Everyone handed it in, so nobody was left out. Here your teacher wants different papers, and you are afraid yours will be wrong.	Different cultures have different expectations. Research papers here often are explorations, not right answers. Think about ideas of classmates or sources, but write down your own well-reasoned thoughts. Get advice from the ESL or writing center.

Careful researchers acknowledge intellectual obligations and responsibilities, showing respect for all engaged in the academic exchange:

- researchers whose studies provide a sturdy foundation
- readers curious about discoveries, reasons, and evidence
- themselves as they gain experience with credible research practices

RESEARCH CHECKLIST
Learning How to Conduct Research Ethically

☐ Have you accepted the responsibility of reviewing your campus standards for ethical academic conduct? Have you checked your syllabus for any explanation about how those standards apply in your course?

☐ Are you regularly recording source entries in your working bibliography?

☐ Are you carefully distinguishing your own ideas from those of your sources when you record notes or gather material for your research archive?

☐ Are you sticking to your research schedule to avoid a deadline crisis?

☐ Have you analyzed your paper-writing habits to identify any, such as procrastination, that might create ethical problems for you? How do you plan to change such habits to avoid problems?

☐ Have you used this book to practice and improve research skills (such as quoting, paraphrasing, or summarizing)?

☐ Have you found the chapter in this book that explains the documentation style you'll use in your paper?

☐ Have you identified and followed campus procedures for conducting field research involving other people?

☐ Have you recorded contact information so that you can request permission to include any visual materials from sources in your paper?

☐ If your research is part of a group project, have you honored your agreements, meeting your obligations in a timely manner?

☐ If you feel ill prepared for doing research, have you sought help from your instructor or staff at the library, writing center, or computer lab?

☐ Have you asked your instructor's advice about any other ethical issues that have arisen during your research project?

Capturing, Launching, and Citing Evidence from Sources

Sources alone do not make for an effective research paper. Instead, the ideas, explanations, and details from your sources need to be integrated—combined and mixed—with your own thoughts and conclusions about the question you have investigated. Together they eventually form a unified whole that conveys your perspective and the evidence that logically supports it. To make sure that your voice isn't drowned out by your sources, keep your research question and working thesis—maybe still evolving—in front of you as you integrate

For more on stating a thesis, see pp. 404–07.

information. On the other hand, identify and credit your sources appropriately, treating them with the respect they deserve.

To practice quoting, paraphrasing, and summarizing, visit **<bedfordstmartins.com/bedguide>.**

For more about how to quote, paraphrase, and summarize, see pp. 236–41, 763–71, and 669–75.

Once you have recorded a source note, you may be tempted to include it in your paper at all costs. Resist. Include only material that answers your research question and supports your thesis. A note dragged in by force always sticks out like a pig in the belly of a boa constrictor.

When material does fit, consider how to incorporate it effectively and ethically. Quoting reproduces an author's exact words. Paraphrasing restates an author's ideas in your own words and sentences. Summarizing extracts the essence of an author's meaning. You also need to launch captured material by introducing it to readers and to cite it by crediting its source.

Quoting and Paraphrasing Accurately

To illustrate the art of capturing source material, let's first look at a passage from historian Barbara W. Tuchman. In *A Distant Mirror: The Calamitous Fourteenth Century* (New York: Knopf, 1978), Tuchman sets forth the effects of the famous plague known as the Black Death. In her foreword, she admits that any historian dealing with the Middle Ages faces difficulties. For one, large gaps exist in the recorded information. Here is her original wording:

ORIGINAL

> A greater hazard, built into the very nature of recorded history, is overload of the negative: the disproportionate survival of the bad side – of evil, misery, contention, and harm. In history this is exactly the same as in the daily newspaper. The normal does not make news. History is made by the documents that survive, and these lean heavily on crisis and calamity, crime and misbehavior, because such things are the subject matter of the documentary process – of lawsuits, treaties, moralists' denunciations, literary satire, papal Bulls. No Pope ever issued a Bull to approve of something. Negative overload can be seen at work in the religious reformer Nicolas de Clamanges, who, in denouncing unfit and worldly prelates in 1401, said that in his anxiety for reform he would not discuss the good clerics because "they do not count beside the perverse men."

Capture	Launch	Cite
▪ Quote ▪ Paraphrase ▪ Summarize ▪ Synthesize	▪ Identify authority ▪ Provide credentials for credibility ▪ Usher in the source ▪ Connect support to your points	▪ Credit the source ▪ Link the citation to your final list of sources ▪ Specify the location of the material used

Disaster is rarely as pervasive as it seems from recorded accounts.
The fact of being on the record makes it appear continuous and   15
ubiquitous whereas it is more likely to have been sporadic both in time
and place. Besides, persistence of the normal is usually greater than the
effect of disturbance, as we know from our own times. After absorbing
the news of today, one expects to face a world consisting entirely of
strikes, crimes, power failures, broken water mains, stalled trains, school   20
shutdowns, muggers, drug addicts, neo-Nazis, and rapists. The fact is
that one can come home in the evening—on a lucky day—without
having encountered more than one or two of these phenomena.

Although you might copy or highlight this entire passage when you
read it, it is too long to include in your paper. Quoting it directly would let
your source overshadow your own voice. Instead, you might want to quote
a striking line or so and paraphrase the rest by restating the details in your
own words. In the following paraphrase, the writer puts Tuchman's ideas
into other words but retains her major points and credits her ideas.

PARAPHRASE WITH QUOTATION

Tuchman points out that historians find some distortion of the truth hard to
avoid, for more documentation exists for crimes, suffering, and calamities than
for the events of ordinary life. As a result, history may overemphasize the
negative. The author reminds us that we are familiar with this process from
our contemporary news coverage, which treats bad news as more interesting
than good news. If we believed that news stories told all the truth, we would
feel threatened at all times by technical failures, strikes, crime, and violence—
but we are threatened only some of the time, and normal life goes on. The
good, dull, ordinary parts of our lives do not make the front page, and the
praiseworthy tend to be ignored. "No Pope," says Tuchman, "ever issued a
Bull to approve of something." But in truth, social upheaval did not prevail
as widely as we might think from the surviving documents of medieval life.
Nor, the author observes, can we agree with a critic of the church, Nicolas de
Clamanges, in whose view evildoers in the clergy mattered more than men of
goodwill (xviii).

In this reasonably complete and accurate paraphrase, about three-fourths
as long as the original, most of Tuchman's points have been spelled out.
The writer doesn't interpret or evaluate Tuchman's ideas—she only passes
them on. Paraphrasing enables her to emphasize ideas important to her research. It also makes readers more aware of them as support for her thesis
than if the whole passage had been quoted directly. The writer has directly
quoted Tuchman's remark about papal Bulls because it would be hard to
improve on that short and memorable statement.

Often you paraphrase to emphasize one point. This passage comes from Evelyn Underhill's classic study *Mysticism* (New York: Doubleday, 1990):

ORIGINAL

In the evidence given during the process for St. Teresa's beatification, Maria de San Francisco of Medina, one of her early nuns, stated that on entering the saint's cell whilst she was writing this same "Interior Castle" she found her [St. Teresa] so absorbed in contemplation as to be unaware of the external world. "If we made a noise close to her," said another, Maria del Nacimiento, "she neither ceased to write nor complained of being disturbed." Both these nuns, and also Ana de la Encarnacion, prioress of Granada, affirmed that she wrote with immense speed, never stopping to erase or to correct, being anxious, as she said, to write what the Lord had given her before she forgot it.

Suppose that the names of the witnesses do not matter to a researcher who wishes to emphasize, in fewer words, the renowned mystic's writing habits. That writer might paraphrase the passage (and quote it in part) like this:

PARAPHRASE WITH QUOTATION

Underhill has recalled the testimony of those who saw St. Teresa at work on *The Interior Castle*. Oblivious to noise, the celebrated mystic appeared to write in a state of complete absorption, driving her pen "with immense speed, never stopping to erase or to correct, being anxious, as she said, to write what the Lord had given her before she forgot it" (242).

Summarizing Concisely

To illustrate how summarizing can serve you, this example sums up the passage from Tuchman:

For Tuchman's original passage, see pp. 708–09.

SUMMARY

Tuchman reminds us that history lays stress on misery and misdeeds because these negative events attracted notice in their time and so were reported in writing; just as in news stories today, bad news predominates. But we should remember that suffering and social upheaval didn't prevail everywhere all the time (xviii).

As you can see, this summary merely abstracts from the original. Not everything has been preserved — not Tuchman's thought about papal Bulls, not examples such as Nicolas de Clamanges or the modern neo-Nazis. But the gist — the summary of the main idea — echoes Tuchman faithfully.

Before you write a summary, an effective way to sense the gist of a passage is to pare away examples, details, modifiers, and nonessentials. Here is the quotation from Tuchman as one student marked it up on a photocopy, crossing out elements she decided to omit from her summary.

~~A greater hazard,~~ built into the ~~very~~ nature of recorded history, is ~~overload of the negative:~~ the disproportionate survival of the bad side ~~— of evil, misery, contention, and harm. In history~~ this is exactly the same as in the daily newspaper. ~~The normal does not make news. History is made by the~~ documents that survive, ~~and these~~ lean heavily on crisis and calamity, crime and misbehavior, because such things are the subject matter of the documentary process ~~— of lawsuits, treaties, moralists' denunciations, literary satire, papal Bulls. No Pope ever issued a Bull to approve of something. Negative overload can be seen at work in the religious reformer Nicolas de Clamanges, who, in denouncing unfit and worldly prelates in 1401, said that in his anxiety for reform he would not discuss the good clerics because "they do not count beside the perverse men."~~

Disaster is rarely as pervasive as it seems from recorded accounts. ~~The fact of being on the record makes it appear continuous and ubiquitous whereas~~ it is more likely to have been sporadic both in time and place. Besides, persistence of the normal is usually greater than the effect of disturbance, as we know from our own times. ~~After absorbing the news of today, one expects to face a~~ world consisting entirely of ~~strikes, crimes, power failures, broken water~~ mains, stalled ~~trains, school shutdowns, muggers, drug addicts, neo Nazis, and rapists. The fact is that one can come home in the evening — on a lucky day — without having encountered more than one or two of these phenomena.~~

Rewording what was left, she wrote the following condensed version:

SUMMARY

History, like a morning newspaper, reports more bad than good. Why? Because the documents that have come down to us tend to deal with upheavals and disturbances, which are seldom as extensive and long-lasting as history books might lead us to believe (Tuchman xviii).

In writing her summary, the student could not simply omit the words she had deleted. The result would have been less readable and still long. She knew she couldn't use Tuchman's very words: that would be plagiarism. To make a compact, honest summary that would fit smoothly into her paper, she had to condense the passage into her own words.

Avoiding Plagiarism

Never lift another writer's words or ideas without giving that writer due credit and transforming them into words of your own. If you do use words or ideas without giving credit, you are plagiarizing. When you introduce

For more on avoiding plagiarism and using accepted methods of adding source material, see Ch. 12 and D1 in the Quick Research Guide, pp. A-26–A-27.

honest summarizing and paraphrasing, clearly indicate that the ideas belong to the originator, here Barbara Tuchman or Evelyn Underhill. In contrast, the next examples are unacceptable paraphrases of Tuchman's passage that lift, without thanks, her ideas and even her very words. Finding such gross borrowings in a paper, an instructor might hear the ringing of a burglar alarm. The first example lifts both thoughts and words, highlighted here with their lines in the original noted in the margin.

For Tuchman's original passage, see pp. 708–09.

PLAGIARIZED THOUGHTS AND WORDS

Sometimes it's difficult for historians to learn the truth about the everyday lives of people from past societies because of the disproportionate survival of the bad side of things. Historical documents, like today's newspapers, tend to lean rather heavily on crisis, crime, and misbehavior. Reading the newspaper could lead one to expect a world consisting entirely of strikes, crimes, power failures, muggers, drug addicts, and rapists. In fact, though, disaster is rarely so pervasive as recorded accounts can make it seem.

Quoted from line 2

Close to lines 5–6

Close to line 19

Lists from lines 19–21

Close to ¶ 2 opening

For more on managing a research project, see Ch. 30.

The writer of this paraphrase did not understand the passage well enough to put Tuchman's ideas in his or her own words. Those who allow enough time to read, to think, and to write are likely to handle sources more effectively than those who procrastinate or rush through their research.

This next example is a more subtle theft, lifting thoughts but not words.

PLAGIARIZED THOUGHTS

It's not always easy to determine the truth about the everyday lives of people from past societies because bad news gets recorded a lot more frequently than good news does. Historical documents, like today's news channels, tend to pick up on malice and disaster and ignore flat normality. If I were to base my opinion of the world on what is on the news, I would expect death and destruction around me all the time. Actually, I rarely come up against true disaster.

By using the first-person pronoun *I*, this student suggests that Tuchman's ideas are his own. That is just as dishonest as quoting without using quotation marks, as reprehensible as not citing the source of ideas.

The next example fails to make clear which ideas belong to the writer and which to Tuchman.

For a tutorial on avoiding plagiarism, visit <bedfordstmartins .com/rewriting>.

PLAGIARIZED WITH FAULTY CREDIT

Barbara Tuchman explains that it can be difficult for historians to learn about the everyday lives of people who lived long ago because historical documents tend to record only bad news. Today's news is like that, too: disaster, malice, and confusion take up a lot more room than happiness and serenity. Just as the ins and outs of our everyday lives go unreported, we can suspect that upheavals do not play as important a part in the making of history as they seem to.

After rightly attributing ideas in the first sentence to Tuchman, the writer makes a comparison to today's world in sentence 2. In sentence 3, she returns to Tuchman's ideas without giving Tuchman credit. The placement of sentence 3 suggests that this last idea is the student's, not Tuchman's.

As you write, use ideas and words from your sources carefully, and credit those sources. Supply introductory and transitional comments to launch and attribute quotations, paraphrases, and summaries to the original source ("As Tuchman observes . . ."). Rely on quotation marks and other punctuation to show exactly which words come from your sources.

For more on working with sources, see Chs. 12 and 31 as well as the Quick Research Guide, beginning on p. A-51. For more on quotation marks, ellipses, and brackets, see C3 in the Quick Editing Guide, p. A-52.

RESEARCH CHECKLIST
Avoiding Plagiarism

☐ Have you identified the author of material you quote, paraphrase, or summarize? Have you credited the originator of facts and ideas you use?

☐ Have you clearly shown where another writer's ideas stop and yours begin?

☐ Have you checked each paraphrase or summary against the original for accuracy? Do you use your own words? Do you avoid words and sentences close to those in the original? Do you avoid distorting the original meaning?

☐ Have you checked each quotation against the original for accuracy? Have you used quotation marks for both passages and significant words taken directly from your source?

☐ Have you used an ellipsis mark (. . .) to show your omissions from the original? Have you used brackets ([ ]) to indicate your changes or additions in a quotation? Have you avoided distorting the original meaning?

Launching Source Material

You need to write a launch statement to identify the source of each detail and each idea—whether a quotation, summary, or paraphrase—drawn from reading or field research. Whenever possible, help readers understand why you have selected particular sources, why you find their evidence pertinent, or how they support your conclusions. Use your launch statements to show not only that you have read your sources but also that you have absorbed and applied what they say about your research question. The following strategies suggest ways to strengthen your launch statements.

- Name the author in the sentence that introduces the source:

    As Wood explains, the goal of American education continues to fluctuate between gaining knowledge and applying it (58).

- Add the author's name in the middle of the source material:

    In *Romeo and Juliet,* "That which we call a rose," Shakespeare claims, "By any other word would smell as sweet" (2.2.43–44).

- Note the professional title or affiliation of someone you've interviewed to add authority and increase the credibility of your source:

    According to Jan Lewis, a tax attorney at Sands and Gonzales, . . .

    Briefly noting relevant background or experience can do the same:

    Recalling her tour of duty in Iraq, Sergeant Nelson noted . . .

- Identify information from your own field research:

    When interviewed about the campus disaster plan, Natalie Chan, Director of Campus Services, confirmed . . .

- Name the author only in the source citation in parentheses if you want to keep your focus on the topic:

    A second march on Washington followed the first (Whitlock 83).

- Explain for the reader why you have selected and included the material:

    As Serrano's three-year investigation of tragic border incidents shows, the current policies carry high financial and human costs.

- Interpret what you see as the point or relevance of the material:

    Stein focuses on stem-cell research, but his discussion of potential ethical implications (18) also applies to other medical research.

- Relate the source clearly to the thesis or point it supports:

    Although Robinson analyzes workplace interactions, her conclusions (289–92) suggest the need to look at the issues in schools as well.

- Compare or contrast the point of view or evidence of two sources:

    While Desmond emphasizes the European economic disputes, Lewis turns to the social stresses that also set the stage for World War II.

For more on connections and transitions, see pp. 433–37.

Adding transitional expressions to guide readers can strengthen your launch statements by relating one source to another (*in addition, in contrast, more recently, in a more favorable view*) or particular evidence to your line of reasoning (*next, furthermore, in addition, despite, on the other hand*).

Regardless of how you launch sources, you need to figure out how to integrate and synthesize them effectively. Use the Take Action chart (p. 715) for this purpose. Skim across the top to identify questions you might ask about your draft. When you answer a question with "Yes" or "Maybe," move straight down the column to Locate Specifics under that question. Use the activities there to identify gaps or weaknesses. Then move straight down to Take Action. Use the advice that suits your problem as you revise.

Citing Each Source Clearly

For examples of citations, see Ch. 36 for MLA or Ch. 37 for APA.

Often your launch statement does double duty: naming a source as well as introducing the quotation, paraphrase, or summary from it. Naming, or citing, each source both credits it and helps locate it in the list of sources at the end of your paper. There you provide full publication information so that readers could find your original sources if they wished.

Take Action Integrating and Synthesizing Sources

Ask each question at the top of the chart to consider whether your draft might need work on that issue. If so, follow the ASK—LOCATE SPECIFICS—TAKE ACTION sequence to revise.

	Weak Group of Sources?	**Unclear Connections?**	**No New Ideas?**
1 **ASK**	Do I need to reexamine the group of sources that I plan to synthesize?	Do I need to relate my sources more deeply and clearly to each other?	Do I need to deepen my synthesis so it goes beyond my sources to my own ideas?
2 **LOCATE SPECIFICS**	■ List the sources you're synthesizing. ■ Write out principles you have used (or could use) to select and group them—chronology to show change over time, theme to show aspects of a topic, comparison to show similarities, or another system. ■ Eliminate any fudging about your sources: pin down your guesses; summarize or paraphrase quotes; specify rather than generalize.	■ For each source, review your notes and draft discussion of it so you can sum up its focus. ■ Highlight connective statements or transitions already used in your draft to link the sources. ■ Mark any jumps from source to source without transitions. ■ Read your draft out loud to yourself, marking any weak or incomplete synthesis of sources.	■ Schedule several blocks of time so that you can concentrate on your intellectual task. ■ Mark a check by any part of your synthesis that reads like a grocery list (bread, eggs, milk or Smith, Jones, Chu). ■ Star each spot where you repeat the source's point without relating it to your point or adding your interpretation.
3 **TAKE ACTION**	■ Write down how each source develops your principles. ■ Redefine your principles or your ideas about what each source shows, as needed. ■ Revise your group: drop or add sources; move some if they don't fit well. If a source fits at several places, pick the best spot or fill a gap.	■ If a connection is missing, review the focus for the source; add a statement to connect it to the source before or after it. ■ Brainstorm or jot notes to refine, restate, or expand connections. ■ Use your notes to deepen connections as you refine your synthesis.	■ Generate ideas to build a cache of notes about how you want to relate your sources to your ideas and what they collectively suggest. Be creative; let your original ideas emerge. ■ For each check or star, use your own voice and ideas to fill gaps, deepen connections, or state relationships.

To make this connection clear, identify each source by mentioning the author (or the title if no author is identified) as you add information from the source to your paper. (In APA style, also add the date.) You can emphasize this identification by including it in your launch statement, or you can tuck it into parentheses after the information. Then, supply the specific location of any quotation or paraphrase (usually the page number in the original) so that a reader could easily turn to the exact material you have used. Check your text citations against your concluding list of sources to be sure that the two correspond.

Synthesizing Ideas and Sources

For more on synthesizing, see p. 245. To Take Action on synthesizing, see p. 715.

Integrating source notes into your paper generally requires positioning materials in a sequence, fitting them in place, and then reworking and interpreting them to convert them into effective evidence that advances your case. Synthesizing sources and evidence weaves them into a unified whole. Build your synthesis on critical reading and thinking: pulling together what you read and think, relating ideas and information, and drawing conclusions that go beyond those of your separate sources. If you have a sure sense of your paper's direction, you may find this synthesis fairly easy. On the other hand, if your research question or working thesis has changed or you have unearthed persuasive information at odds with your original direction, consider these questions:

- Taken as a whole, what does all this information mean?
- What does it actually tell you about the answer to your research question?
- What's the most important thing you've learned?
- What's the most important thing you can tell your readers?

Learning by Doing 🎥 Integrating and Synthesizing Your Sources

What do your sources need most? Your effort on working ethically? Capturing material (quoting, paraphrasing, summarizing)? Launching and citing sources? Synthesizing several sources? Start with your source notes or a draft passage, and tackle that priority. Exchange before and after versions with a classmate. Then focus on your next priority.

Y ou may have your own tried-and-true system of moving from research notes to a rough draft. If so, feel free to stick to your own system. On the other hand, you may be worried about how to pull together your paper — perhaps the longest and most complex you've ever written. If so, try some suggestions here as you plan, draft, revise, and edit.

Planning and Drafting

You began gathering material from library, Internet, and field sources with a question in mind. By now, if your research has been thorough and fruitful, you know your answer. The moment has come to weave together the material you have gathered. We can vouch for two time-proven methods.

The Thesis Method. Decide what your research has led you to believe. Sum up what it all means in a sentence. That sentence is your thesis, the one main idea your paper will demonstrate. Then plan and draft, including only what supports your thesis and makes it clear.

For advice on stating and using a thesis, see pp. 401–10.

The Answer Method. You may prefer to plunge in and start writing without stating any thesis at all. If so, recall your original research question. Start writing with the purpose of answering it, lining up evidence as you go and discovering what you want to say as you write. (With this method, allow more time for revising than with the thesis method.)

For more on research questions, see pp. 648–52.

Using Your Sources to Support Your Ideas

Moving from nuggets of information to a smooth, persuasive analysis or argument is the most challenging part of the research process. Though every writer's habits of mind are different, you'll probably cycle through four basic activities: interpreting your sources, refining your thesis, organizing your ideas, and forming a draft.

Interpret Your Sources. On their own, your source notes are only pieces of information. They need your interpretation to transform them into effective evidence. What does each mean in the context of your paper? Is it

For more on evidence, see pp. 42–43, 163–71, and section A in the Quick Research Guide, pp. A-19–A-22.

strong enough to bear the weight of your claim? Do you need more evidence to shore up an interesting but ambiguous fact? Keep your sources in their supporting role and your voice in the lead. Alternate statements and support to sustain this balance.

Refine Your Thesis.   Your thesis clearly, precisely states the point you want to make. It helps you decide what to say and how to say it. When it is clear to your readers, it prepares them for your scope and general message.

If you've used a working thesis to guide your research, sharpen and refine it before drafting, even if you change it again later. Explicitly stating your thesis in your opening paragraph is only one option. Sometimes you can craft your opening so that readers know exactly what your thesis is even though you only imply it. (Check this option with your instructor if you're unsure about it.) Make your thesis precise and concrete; don't claim more than you can show. If your paper is argumentative—you take a stand, propose a solution, or evaluate something—make your stand, solution, or appraisal clear.

TOPIC	Americans' attitudes toward sports
RESEARCH QUESTION	Is America obsessed with sports?
THESIS	The national obsession with sports must end.

Organize Your Ideas.   It isn't enough for your paper to describe your research steps or to string data together in chronological order. Instead, you need to report the significance of what you found out. If you began with a clear research question, select and organize your evidence to answer it. But don't be afraid to reorganize around a new question. If your material resists taking shape, arrange your source notes or archive in an order that makes sense. Then this sequence becomes a plan to follow as you write. Or write out an informal or formal outline on paper or on the computer, using the outline tool. If you lack source notes for a certain section, reconsider your plan, or seek other sources to fill the gap.

For more on organizing, drafting, and developing ideas, see Chs. 20–22.

Begin to Draft.   An outline is only a skeleton until you flesh it out with details. Use yours as a working plan, but change the subdivisions or sequence if you discover a better way as you draft. Even if everything hasn't fallen into perfect order, get something down on paper. Start at the beginning or wherever you feel most comfortable. Try also to connect the parts of your paper. For example, summarizing the previous section will refresh readers' memories, especially in a long paper.

For more on outlining, see pp. 410–21.

Launching and Citing Your Sources as You Draft

Citing your sources as you draft saves fuss when you put your paper into final form. And it prevents unintentional plagiarism. Right after every idea, fact, quotation, paraphrase, or summary captured from your reading or field research, refer your readers to the exact source of your material. In

MLA style, note the name of the author and the page of the source. (In APA style, add the date.) If you quote a field source, name the person speaking, if possible.

When you add a quotation to your draft, you can just copy and paste the passage from your note file, setting it off with quotation marks. Or you can just tape a note card into a handwritten or printed draft. If your draft looks sloppy, who cares? Then, you can shape the words to launch or introduce the source to show why you have quoted it or what authority its author lends to your paper.

If no transition occurs to you as you place a quotation or borrowed idea in your draft, don't sit around waiting for one. A series of slapped-in summaries and quotations makes rough reading, but you can write yourself a reminder and add connective tissue later.

Beginning and Ending

Perhaps you will think of a good beginning and conclusion only after you have written the body of your paper. The head and tail of your paper might simply make clear your answer to your initial question. But that is not the only way to begin and end a research paper.

Build to Your Finish. You might start out slowly with a clear account of an event to draw your readers into the paper. You could then build up to a strong finish, saving your strongest argument until the end—after you have presented all the evidence to support your thesis. Suppose your paper argues that American children are being harmed by the national obsession with sports:

- Begin with a real event, putting you and your reader on the same footing.
- Explore that event's implications to prepare your reader for your view.
- State your thesis: "The national obsession with sports must end."
- Support your thesis with evidence captured from well-chosen sources, moving to your strongest argument.
- Then end with a rousing call to action, stopping the sports mania.

Sum Up the Findings of Others. Another way to begin a research paper is to summarize the work of other scholars. One research biologist, Edgar F. Warner, has reduced this time-tested opening to a formula.

> First, in one or two paragraphs, you review everything that has been said about your topic, naming the most prominent earlier commentators. Next you declare why all of them are wrong. Then you set forth your own claim, and you spend the rest of your paper supporting it.

That pattern may seem cut and dried, but it is useful because it places your research and ideas into a historical and conceptual framework. If you

For more on launching source material, see pp. 713–14 and D6 in the Quick Research Guide, pp. A-29–A-30.

For exercises on opening and concluding writing, visit <bedfordstmartins.com/bedguide>.

For more strategies for opening and concluding, see pp. 428–32.

For more on transitions, see pp. 433–37.

browse in specialized journals, you may be surprised to see how many articles begin this way. Of course, one or two other writers may be enough to argue with. For example, a student writing on the American poet Charles Olson starts her research paper by disputing two views of him.

To Cid Corman, Charles Olson of Gloucester, Massachusetts, is "the one dynamic and original epic poet twentieth-century America has produced" (116). To Allen Tate, Olson is "a loquacious charlatan" (McFinnery 92). The truth lies between these two extremes, nearer to Corman's view.

Whether or not you fully stated your view at the beginning, you will certainly need to make it clear in your closing paragraph. A suggestion: before writing the last lines of your paper, read over what you have written. Then, without referring to your paper, try to put your view into writing.

Revising and Editing

For advice on integrating sources and avoiding plagiarism, see Ch. 34.

For more revising and editing strategies, see Ch. 23.

Looking over your draft, you may find your essay changing. Don't be afraid to develop a whole new interpretation, shift the organization, strengthen your evidence, drop a section, or add a new one.

REVISION CHECKLIST

For more on using your own voice, see pp. 245–46.

☐ Have you said something original, not just heaped up statements by others? Does your voice interpret and unify so your ideas dominate, not your sources?

☐ Is your thesis (main idea) clear? Do all your points support your main idea? Does all your evidence support your points?

☐ Does each new idea follow from the one before it? Can you see any stronger arrangement? Have you used transitions to connect the parts?

☐ Do you need more — or better — evidence to back up any point? If so, where might you find it?

☐ Are the words that you quote truly memorable? Are your paraphrases and summaries accurate and clear? Have you launched everything?

☐ Is the source of every quotation, fact, or idea unmistakably clear?

After you have revised your research paper, edit and proofread it. Carefully check the grammar, word choice, punctuation, and mechanics — and then correct any problems. Check your documentation, too — how you identify sources and how you list the works you have cited.

Peer Response   Writing Your Research Paper

Have a classmate or friend read your draft and suggest how you might make your paper more informative, tightly reasoned, and interesting. Ask your peer editor to answer questions such as these about writing from sources:

For general questions for a peer editor, see p. 465.

- What is your overall reaction to this paper?
- What is the research question? Does the writer answer that question?
- How effective is the opening? Does it draw you into the paper?
- How effective is the conclusion? Does it merely restate the introduction? Is it too abrupt or too hurried?
- Is the organization logical and easy to follow? Are there any places where the essay is hard to follow?
- Do you know which ideas are from the writer and which from sources?
- Does the writer need all the quotations he or she has used?
- Do you have any questions about the writer's evidence or the conclusions drawn from the evidence? Point out any areas where the writer has not fully backed up his or her conclusions.
- If this paper were yours, what is the one thing you would be sure to work on before handing it in?

EDITING CHECKLIST

☐ Have you used commas correctly, especially in complicated sentences that quote or refer to sources?   **C1**

☐ Have you punctuated quotations correctly?   **C3**

☐ Have you used capital letters correctly, especially in titles of sources?   **D1**

☐ Have you used correct manuscript form?   **D3**

☐ Have you used correct documentation style?

For more help, find the relevant checklist sections in the Quick Editing Guide on p. A-36. Turn also to the Quick Format Guide, beginning on p. A-1.

For more on documentation, see Ch. 36 (MLA) or Ch. 37 (APA).

Documenting Sources

A research paper calls on you to follow special rules in documenting your sources — in citing them as you write and in listing them at the end of your paper. In humanities courses and the social sciences, most writers of research papers follow the style of the Modern Language Association (MLA) or the American Psychological Association (APA). Your instructor will probably suggest which style to follow; if you are not told, use MLA. The first time you prepare a research paper in either style, you'll need extra time to look up exactly what to do in each situation. (See Ch. 36 or 37.)

For exercises on citing and listing sources, visit **<bedfordstmartins .com/bedguide>.**

Additional Writing Assignments

Using library, Internet, and field sources, write a research paper on one of the following topics or another that your instructor approves. Proceed as if you had chosen to work on the main assignment described on pages 646–47.

1. Investigate career opportunities, workplace changes, or trends for work that interests you. Include data from interviews with people in the field.

2. Compare student achievement in schools with different characteristics — for example, those with limited or extensive technology access or those with low and high numbers of students who move.

3. Study the growth of telecommuting or another technological advance that has changed the relationship between work and home.

4. Write a portrait of life in your town or neighborhood as it was in the past, using sources such as local library archives, photographs or other visual evidence, articles in the local newspaper, and interviews with longtime residents or a local historian.

5. Write a short history of your immediate family, drawing on interviews, photographs, scrapbooks, old letters, and any other available sources.

6. Study the reasons students today give for going to college. Gather information from interviews or surveys of a variety of students at your college.

7. Investigate a current trend you have noticed on television or online, collecting evidence by observing programs, commercials, sites, or pages.

8. Write a survey of recent films of a certain kind (such as horror movies, martial arts films, comedies, or love stories), supporting your generalizations with evidence from your film watching.

MLA Style for Documenting Sources **36**

The *MLA Handbook for Writers of Research Papers,* Seventh Edition (New York: MLA, 2009), supplies extensive recommendations for crediting sources. If you want more detailed advice than that given here, you can purchase a copy of the *MLA Handbook* or consult a copy in the reference room of your college library. Additional advice from MLA is available at <mla.org/style_faq>.

MLA style is frequently used in the humanities, including composition, literature, and foreign languages. Other disciplines follow other style guides, so it's useful to practice at least one style to become accustomed to scholarly practice. MLA style uses a two-part system to credit sources. First, you briefly cite or identify the source in your text, either by mentioning it directly in your discussion or by noting it in parentheses right after you use the information drawn from it. In most cases, the page number in the original source follows this identification. Second, you lead from this brief identification, usually the author's last name, to a full description of the source in your concluding alphabetical list, called "Works Cited." Prepare each entry there by looking up a sample for that type of source. Follow its pattern, noting sequence of details, format, punctuation, and spacing. If you have several similar entries — perhaps newspaper articles or journal articles from databases — check them all for consistency at one time.

Use the Take Action chart (p. 726) to figure out how to improve the MLA style in your draft. Skim across the top to identify questions you might ask about your draft. When you answer a question with "Yes" or "Maybe," move straight down the column to Locate Specifics under that question. Use the activities there to identify problems. Then move straight down to Take Action. Use the advice that suits your draft as you revise.

For a brief overview of MLA style, see E1–E2 in the Quick Research Guide, pp. A-30–A-35. Turn also to the Quick Format Guide beginning on p. A-1.

To review how to find details about sources, turn to the Source Navigators on pp. 660–67.

Citing and Listing Sources in MLA Style

Skim the following directory to find sample entries to guide you as you cite and list your sources. Notice that the examples are organized according to questions you might ask and that comparable print and electronic sources are grouped together. Also see pages 743–51 for a sample paper that illustrates MLA style.

Citing and Listing Sources in MLA Style (*continued*)

Citing Sources in MLA Style

The core of an MLA citation is the author of the source. That person's last name links your use of the source in your paper with its full description in your list of works cited. The most common addition to this name is a specific location, usually a page number, identifying where the material appears in the original source: (Valero 231). This basic form applies whatever the type of source — article, book, or Web page.

As you check your MLA style, keep in mind these three questions:

- Who wrote it?
- What type of source is it?
- How are you capturing the source material?

Take Action Citing and Listing Sources in MLA Style

Ask each question at the top of the chart to consider whether your draft might need work on that issue. If so, follow the ASK—LOCATE SPECIFICS—TAKE ACTION sequence to revise.

	Different Citations in Your Text and Your List?	**Incorrect Author Formats?**	**Incorrect Source Title Formats?**
1 **ASK**	Do any of my text citations differ from my Works Cited entries—or vice versa?	Have I inconsistently or incorrectly presented any of the authors in my list of works cited?	Have I inconsistently or incorrectly presented any source titles in my list of works cited?
2 **LOCATE SPECIFICS**	■ Circle any material from a source that is not identified. ■ Add a ✓ by each text citation that matches a works cited entry. ■ Add a ✓ by each works cited entry that matches a text citation. ■ Circle any source not checked in both places.	■ Read only the author part of each entry. ■ Circle any spot where you need to check the arrangement of first and last names. ■ Circle any spot where you need to check spelling or punctuation. ■ Mark any entries out of alphabetical order. ■ Circle any repeated problems.	■ Read only the title part of each entry, checking the format of each article, journal, book, Web site, or other title. ■ Circle any entry that you need to correct or look up by type, especially complications (such as an anthology) or tricky details (such as a newspaper section). ■ Circle any repeated problems.
3 **TAKE ACTION**	■ Correct circled items by adding what's missing. ■ Drop from your works cited any source not cited in your draft. (Or add it to your draft if it belongs there.) ■ Confirm that names of authors are spelled the same in both places so that the citation and list entry match.	■ Look up and correct all circled items. ■ Correct spelling or punctuation errors, such as a missing comma after the first name of the first of several authors. ■ Conclude each author section with a period. ■ Rearrange entries alphabetically as needed. ■ If you find patterns—repetition of an error—check all entries only for that problem and correct it.	■ Look up and correct all circled items. ■ Use quotation marks for an article or posting title; italicize a book, journal, or site title. ■ Correct the capitalization, spelling, or punctuation. ■ End each title with a period before the final quotation mark or after italics. ■ If you find patterns—repetition of an error—check all entries only for that problem and correct it.

Citing Sources in MLA Style   **727**

Who Wrote It?

Individual Author Not Named in Sentence

Place the author's last name in parentheses, right after the source information, to keep readers focused on the sequence and content of your sentences.

One approach to the complex politics of Puerto Rican statehood is to return to the island's colonial history (Negrón-Muntaner 3).

Individual Author Named in Sentence

Name the author in your sentence, perhaps with credentials or experience, to capitalize on the persuasive value of the author's "expert" status.

The analysis of filmmaker and scholar Frances Negrón-Muntaner connects Puerto Rican history and politics with cultural influences (xvii).

Two or Three Authors

Include each author's last name either in your sentence or in parentheses.

As magazines and newspapers multiplied in eighteenth-century Europe, they supplied new knowledge while popularizing old folk traditions (Davies and de Blécourt 6).

Four Authors or More

Name all the authors, or follow the name of the first author with the abbreviation "et al." (Latin for "and others"). Identify the source the same way in your list of works cited.

See the listing on p. 732.

Between 1870 and 1900, the nation's cities grew at an astonishing rate (Roark et al. 671).

Organization Author

If a source is sponsored by a corporation, a professional society, or another group, name the sponsor as the author if no one else is specified.

Each year, the Kids Count program (Annie E. Casey Foundation) alerts children's advocates about the status of children in their state.

Author of an Essay from a Reader or Collection

Cite the author of the essay, not the editor of the collection where it appears. Suppose you consulted Amy Tan's essay "Mother Tongue" in a collection edited by Wendy Martin. You'd cite Tan as the author, not Martin, and begin your works cited entry with her name (see p. 737).

Amy Tan explains the "Englishes" of her childhood and family (32).

Unidentified Author

For a source with an unknown author, supply the complete title in your sentence or the first main word or two of the title in parentheses.

According to a recent study, drivers are 42% more likely to get into an accident if they are using a wireless phone while driving ("Driving Dangerously" 32).

Same Author with Multiple Works

If you are citing several of an author's works, the author's name alone won't identify which one you mean. Add the title, or identify it with a few key words. For example, you would cite two books by Ann Charters, *Major Writers of Short Fiction* and *The Story and Its Writer*, as follows.

One observer notes the flood of magazine fiction, including "stories of real distinction" (Charters, *Major Writers* 1408). In fact, Charters believes that "the range and quality of the writer's mind are the only limitations on a story's shape" (*Story* 3).

Use italics, not underlining, in MLA style for titles of books, periodicals, and Web sites. For more style conventions, see p. 732.

Different Authors of Multiple Works

Separate more than one source in parentheses with a semicolon. For easy reading, favor shorter, separate references, not long strings of sources.

Ray Charles and Quincy Jones worked together for many years and maintained a strong friendship throughout Charles's life (Jones 58-59; Lydon 386).

What Type of Source Is It?

Because naming the author is the core of a citation, the basic form applies to any type of source. Even so, a few types of sources may present complications.

Multivolume Work

Add both volume and page numbers, with a colon between.

Malthus has long been credited with this conservative shift in population theory (Durant and Durant 11: 400-03).

Indirect Source

If possible, find the original source. If you can't access it, add "qtd. in" to show that the material was "quoted in" the source you cite.

Zill says that, psychologically, children in stepfamilies, even those living in a two-parent household, most resemble children in single-parent families (qtd. in Derber 119).

Visual Material

When you include a visual, help your reader connect it to your text. In your discussion, identify the artist or the artwork, and refer to its figure number.

For advice about permission to use visuals, see B1 in the Quick Format Guide, pp. A-8–A-9.

Johnson's 1870 painting *Life in the South* is a sentimental depiction of African Americans after the Civil War (see fig. 1).

Below the visual, supply a figure number and title, including the source.

Fig. 1. Eastman Johnson, *Life in the South,* High Museum of Art, Atlanta.

How Are You Capturing the Source Material?

How you capture source material—in your own words or in a short or long quotation—affects how you credit it. Always set off words directly from a source using quotation marks or the indented form for a long "block" quotation.

For more on capturing and integrating source materials, see pp. 234–41, pp. 669–72, and Ch. 34.

If material, quoted or not, comes from a specific place in a source, add a page number or other location, such as the paragraph or screen number supplied in an electronic source or the chapter or line in a literary work. No page number is needed for general material (an overall theme or concept), a one-page source, or a source without page numbers (a Web site, film, recording, performance).

For a sample block quotation, see p. 730.

For sample quotations from literature, see pp. 730–31.

Overall Summary or Important Idea

Terrill's *Malcolm X: Inventing Radical Judgment* takes a fresh look at the rhetorical power and strategies of Malcolm X's speeches.

Specific Summary or Paraphrase

One analysis of Malcolm X's 1964 speech "The Ballot or the Bullet" concludes that it exhorts listeners to the radical action of changing vantage point (Terrill 129-31).

If you paraphrase or summarize a one-page article, no page number is needed because it will appear in your list of works cited.

Vacuum-tube audio equipment is making a comeback, with aficionados praising the warmth and glow from the tubes, as well as the sound (Patton).

Blended Paraphrase and Quotation

When your words are blended with those of your source, clearly distinguish the two. Use quotation marks to set apart the words of your source.

Some less-than-perfect means have been used to measure television viewing habits, including a sensor that scans rooms for "hot bodies" (Larson 69).

Brief Quotation with Formal Launch Statement

Frank opens with a powerful claim: "Suffering has always animated life writing" (174).

Brief Quotation Integrated in Sentence

Pain, illness, and disability all contribute to the heartache that "has always animated life writing" (Frank 174).

"Suffering," according to Arthur Frank, "has always animated life writing" (174).

In "Moral Non-fiction: Life Writing and Children's Disability," Frank observes, "Suffering has always animated life writing" (174).

Long Quotation

When a quotation is longer than four typed lines, double-space and indent the entire quotation one inch instead of placing quotation marks around it. If the quotation is one paragraph or less, begin its first line without any extra paragraph indentation. Use ellipsis marks (. . .) to show where you omit anything from the middle of the quotation.

Cynthia Griffin Wolff comments on Emily Dickinson's incisive use of language:

> Language, of course, was a far subtler weapon than a hammer. Dickinson's verbal maneuvers would increasingly reveal immense skill in avoiding a frontal attack; she preferred the silent knife of irony to the strident battering of loud complaint. . . . Scarcely submissive, she had acquired the cool calculation of an assassin. (170-71)

Quotation from the Bible

Instead of the page, note the version, book, chapter, and verse numbers.

Once again, the author alludes to the same passage: "What He has seen and heard, of that He testifies" (*New American Bible,* John 3.32).

Quotation from a Novel or Short Story

First note the page number in your own copy. If possible, add the section or chapter where the passage could be found in any edition.

In *A Tale of Two Cities,* Dickens describes the aptly named Stryver as "shouldering himself (morally and physically) into companies and conversations" (110; bk. 2, ch. 4).

Quotation from a Play

For a verse play, list the act, scene, and line numbers, divided by periods.

Love, Iago says, "is merely a lust of the blood and a permission of the will" (*Oth.* 1.3.326).

Quotation from a Poem

Add a slash to show where a new line begins. Use "line" or "lines" in the first reference but only numbers in subsequent references, as in these examples from William Wordsworth's "The World Is Too Much with Us." The first reference:

"The world is too much with us; late and soon, / Getting and spending, we lay waste our powers" (lines 1-2).

The subsequent reference:

"Or hear old Triton blow his wreathed horn" (14).

If a poem has multiple parts, include the part and line numbers, separated by a period, without the word "line."

In "Ode: Intimations of Immortality," Wordsworth ponders the truths of human existence, "Which we are toiling all our lives to find, / In darkness lost, the darkness of the grave" (8.116-17).

RESEARCH CHECKLIST
Citing Sources in MLA Style

☐ Have you double-checked to be sure that you have acknowledged all material from a source?

☐ Have you placed your citation right after your quotation, paraphrase, summary, or other reference to the source?

☐ Have you identified the author of each source in your text or in parentheses?

☐ Have you used the first few words of the title to cite a work without an identified author?

☐ Have you noted a page number or other location when needed and available?

☐ Have you added necessary extras, whether volume numbers or poetry lines?

☐ Have you checked your final draft to be sure that every source cited in your text also appears in your list of works cited?

For a sample works cited page, see pp. 751–52 and section A in the Quick Format Guide, pp. A-1–A-7.

Listing Sources in MLA Style

At the end of your paper, list the sources from which you have actually cited material. Center the title "Works Cited" at the top of a new, double-spaced page. Alphabetize entries by authors' last names or, for works with no author, by title. When an entry exceeds one line, indent the following lines one-half inch. (Use your software menu—Format-Paragraph-Indentation—to set this special "hanging" indentation.)

Listing sources correctly depends on following patterns and paying attention to details such as capitalization and punctuation. The basic MLA pattern places a period after each of an entry's main parts such as author, title, publication details, and medium. MLA style simplifies many details:

- Abbreviate months and scholarly terms.
- List only the first city, and no state, to locate a publisher.
- List only the first name (without initials) of a publishing company.
- Drop "Inc.," "Co.," and "Press" from the company name, and abbreviate "University Press" as "UP."
- Use the most recent copyright date for a book.
- Add the medium of publication, reception, or delivery such as Print, Web, Television, Radio, CD, DVD, Film, Performance, Lecture.
- Omit the URL (uniform resource locator), or Internet address, unless the source would otherwise be hard to find or your assignment requests it.

As you prepare your own entries, begin with the author: first things first. The various author formats apply no matter what your source. Then, from the following examples, select the format for the rest of the entry depending on the type of work you have used—article, book, Web page, or other material. Match your entry to the example, supplying the same information in the same order with the same punctuation and other features. As you work on your list, keep in mind these two key questions, which are used to organize the sample entries that follow:

Who wrote it?

What type of source is it?

Who Wrote It?

Individual Author

Hazzard, Shirley. *The Great Fire*. New York: Farrar, 2003. Print.

Two or Three Authors

Name the authors in the order in which they are listed on the title page.

Steil, Benn, and Manuel Hinds. *Money, Markets, and Sovereignty*. New Haven: Yale UP, 2009. Print.

Four Authors or More

Name all the authors, or follow the name of the first author with the abbreviation "et al." (Latin for "and others"). Identify the source in the same way you cite it in the text.

Roark, James L., et al. *The American Promise*. Boston: Bedford, 1998. Print.

See the citation on p. 727.

Same Author with Multiple Works

Arrange the author's works alphabetically by title. Use the author's name for the first entry only; for the rest, replace the name with three hyphens.

Gould, Stephen Jay. *The Mismeasure of Man*. Rev. ed. New York: Norton, 1996. Print.

---. *Triumph and Tragedy in Mudville: A Lifelong Passion for Baseball*. New York: Norton, 2003. Print.

Organization Author

Name the organization as author without its opening "the," "a," or "an." (The name may reappear as the publisher.)

Canadian Standards Association. *Manufactured Homes*. Mississauga: Canadian Standards Assn., 2009. Print.

Author and Editor

If your paper focuses on the work or its author, cite the author first.

Marx, Karl, and Frederick Engels. *The Communist Manifesto*. 1848. Ed. John E. Toews. Boston: Bedford, 1999. Print.

If your paper focuses on the editor or the edition used, cite the editor first.

Toews, John E., ed. *The Communist Manifesto*. By Karl Marx and Frederick Engels. 1848. Boston: Bedford, 1999. Print.

Author and Translator

Hoeg, Peter. *Tales of the Night*. Trans. Barbara Haveland. New York: Farrar, 1998. Print.

If your paper focuses on the translation, cite the translator first.

Haveland, Barbara, trans. *Tales of the Night*. By Peter Hoeg. New York: Farrar, 1998. Print.

Unidentified Author

"2010 Cars: Safety." *Consumer Reports* Apr. 2010: 70–74. Print.

What Type of Source Is It?

Once you have found the format that fits the author, look for the type of source and the specific entry that best matches yours. Mix and match the patterns illustrated as needed. For example, a two-volume printed book in its second edition might send you to several examples until you have covered all of its elements.

Article in a Printed or an Electronic Periodical

Article from a Printed Journal

Provide the volume number, issue number, year, page numbers, and medium for all journals.

McHaney, Pearl Amelia. "Eudora Welty (1909-2001)." *South Atlantic Review* 66.4
(2001): 134-36. Print.

Article from an Online Journal

Supply the information that you would for a print article, using "n. pag." if the article does not have page numbers; end with the medium and your access date.

Purdy, James P., and Joyce R. Walker. "Digital Breadcrumbs: Case Studies of Online
Research." *Kairos* 11.2 (2007): n. pag. Web. 29 May 2010.

Article Accessed Online through a Library or Subscription Database

To see how to create the listing for a journal article from a database, turn to pp. 662–63.

If you find a source through a library database or a subscription service, include the name of the service, the medium, and your access date.

Vanacore, Andrew. "Free TV Could Get Its Curtain Call." *Boston Globe* 30 Dec. 2009:
B1. *Newsbank: America's Newspapers*. Web. 1 Mar. 2010.

Article from a Printed Magazine

To see how to create the listing for a magazine article, turn to pp. 660–61.

Give the month and year of the issue, or its specific date.

Jenkins, Lee. "He's Gotta Play Hurt." *Sports Illustrated* 26 Oct. 2009: 42-3. Print.

If the article's pages are not consecutive, add a + after its initial page.

"A User's Guide to the Brain." *Time* 29 Jan. 2007: 55+. Print.

Article from an Online Magazine

Bowden, Mark. "Jihadists in Paradise." *TheAtlantic.com*. Atlantic Monthly Group,
Mar. 2007. Web. 8 Mar. 2007.

Article from a Printed Newspaper

If the newspaper has different editions, indicate after the date the one where the article can be found: natl. ed. If the pages for the article are not consecutive, add a + after its initial page.

Associated Press. "Quake Slams Chile." *Denver Post* 28 Feb. 2010: A1+. Print.

Article from an Online Newspaper

Richmond, Riva. "Five Ways to Keep Online Criminals at Bay." *New York Times.* New
  York Times, 19 May 2010. Web. 29 May 2010.

Editorial from a Printed Periodical

McGrath, Neal. "Concussion Care for Student-Athletes." Editorial. *Boston Globe*
  30 Dec. 2009, Opinion sec.: 17. Print.

"Media Reform's Moment." Editorial. *Nation* 29 Jan. 2007: 4. Print.

Editorial from an Online Periodical

Duncan, Arne. "Investing in Students, Not the Banks." Editorial. *Washington Post.*
  26 Feb. 2010. Web. 1 Mar. 2010.

Letter to the Editor

Hoogendyk, Chris. Letter. *Discover* Dec. 2009: 6. Print.

Review

Include the words "Rev. of" before the title of the work reviewed.

Coukell, Allan. "The Cell That Wouldn't Die." Rev. of *Culturing Life: How Cells Became
  Technologies,* by Hannah Landecker. *Discover* Feb. 2007: 68. Print.

Printed or Electronic Book

Printed Book

Wrangham, Richard W. *Catching Fire: How Cooking Made Us Human.* New York: Basic,
  2009. Print.

To see how to create
the listing for a book,
turn to pp. 664–65.

Online Book

For an online book, supply what you would for a printed book. Then add the name of the site, the medium, and your access date.

Wharton, Edith. *The Age of Innocence.* New York: Appleton, 1920. N. pag.
  Bartleby.com: Great Books Online. Web. 8 Mar. 2010.

Multivolume Work

To cite the full work, include the number of volumes ("vols.") after the title.

Who Built America? Working People and the Nation's Economy, Politics, Culture,
    and Society. 2 vols. New York: Worth, 2000. Print.

To cite only one volume, give its number after the title. If you wish, you then can add the total number of volumes after the date.

Who Built America? Working People and the Nation's Economy, Politics, Culture, and
    Society. Vol. 1. New York: Worth, 2000. Print. 2 vols.

Revised Edition

Volti, Rudi. *Society and Technological Change.* 6th ed. New York: Worth, 2010. Print.

Book Published in a Series

After the title, add the series name as it appears on the title page, followed by any series number.

Smith, Philip E., II, ed. *Approaches to Teaching the Works of Oscar Wilde.* New York:
    MLA, 2008. Print. Approaches to Teaching World Lit. 103.

Book with Copublishers

If a book has more than one publisher, list them in the order on the title page, separated by a semicolon. (If the publisher uses an imprint name for a line of books, identify both with the imprint first: AltaMira-Rowman.)

Hiatt, Alfred. *The Making of Medieval Forgeries: False Documents in Fifteenth-Century*
    England. London: British Library; Toronto: U of Toronto P, 2004. Print.

Book without Publisher, Date, or Page Numbers

Provide what's available. Bracket information gained outside the source. Use "c." (meaning "around," from the Latin *circa*) to indicate an inexact date: c. 1995. Show doubt with a question mark: [1972?].

    If the date is unknown, use "n.d." (no date). Use "n.p." for no publisher or no place, or simply leave out the publisher's name if the work is pre-1900: New York, 1882. If pages are not numbered, use "n. pag." (no pagination), which will clarify why you have not given page references.

Rosholt, Malcolm. *Days of the Ching Pao: A Photographic Record of the Flying*
    Tigers-14th Air Force in China in World War II. N.p.: n.p., 1978. Print.

Part of a Printed or an Electronic Book

Give the author of the part first. Add the editor of the book after its title and the page numbers of the selection after the publication information. For an online book, add the site and your access date.

Selection from a Printed Book

Burke, Kenneth. "A Grammar of Motives." *The Rhetorical Tradition: Readings from Classical Times to the Present*. Ed. Patricia Bizzell and Bruce Herzberg. Boston: Bedford, 2001. 1298-324. Print.

Selection from an Online Book

Webster, Augusta. "Not Love." *A Book of Rhyme*. London, 1881. *Victorian Women Writers Project*. Web. 8 Mar. 2007.

Preface, Introduction, Foreword, or Afterword

Harjo, Joy. Introduction. *The Secret Powers of Naming*. By Sara Littlecrow-Russell. Tucson: U of Arizona P, 2006. ix-xi. Print.

Essay, Short Story, or Poem from an Edited Collection

Rothman, Rodney. "My Fake Job." *The Best American Nonrequired Reading*. Ed. Dave Eggers. Boston: Houghton, 2002. 117-32. Print.

Two or More Works from the Same Edited Collection

If you list more than one selection from an anthology, you can prepare an entry for the collection (instead of repeating it for each selection) and refer to it from the entries for the readings.

Cisneros, Sandra. "Only Daughter." Martin 10-13.

Martin, Wendy, ed. *The Beacon Book of Essays by Contemporary American Women*. Boston: Beacon, 1996. Print.

Tan, Amy. "Mother Tongue." Martin 32-37.

Article from a Printed Reference Work

No editor, publisher, or place of publication is needed for well-known references such as *Webster's, World Book Encyclopedia,* or *Encyclopaedia Britannica.* No volume and page numbers are needed when a reference book is organized alphabetically. If an article's author is identified by initials, check the book's list of contributors, which should supply the full name.

Raymer, John D., and Margarita Nieto. "Octavio Paz." *Notable Latino Writers*. Pasadena: Salem, 2006. Print.

Article from an Online Reference Work

"'Hansel and Gretel' by the Brothers Grimm." *Encyclopedia Mythica*. 2004. Web.
     1 Mar. 2010.

Other Printed or Electronic Document

Printed Government Document

Generally, the "author" will be the name of the government and the agency, separated by periods. If the document names an author or editor, that name may be provided either before the title or after it, if you identify the agency as author.

United States. Census Bureau. *Statistical Abstract of the United States, 2007:*
     The National Data Book. 126th ed. Washington: GPO, 2007. Print.

Online Government Document

United States. National Institutes of Health. "Improving Student Fitness." *NIH News*
     in Health. NIH, Dec. 2009. Web. 8 Mar. 2010.

Online Document

First identify the document; then supply the details about its electronic location.

Carter, Jimmy. "Inaugural Address of Jimmy Carter." 20 Jan. 1977. *The Avalon*
     Project. Yale Law School, 2008. Web. 29 May 2010.

Pamphlet

Campus Recreation at Auraria. *Drop-in Schedule: Spring 2010*. Denver: Campus
     Recreation at Auraria, 2010. Print.

Doctoral Dissertation or Master's Thesis

If the study is unpublished, place the title in quotation marks; if published, italicize the title. Follow the title with "Diss." (for a dissertation) or with an apt master's abbreviation (such as "MA thesis").

Beilke, Debra J. "Cracking Up the South: Humor and Identity in Southern Renaissance
     Fiction." Diss. U of Wisconsin, Madison, 1997. Print.

Internet or Electronic Source

Helping a reader find the material you cited and listed can be difficult with Internet materials. Sources such as Web sites exist only electronically and may change. When new forms (such as blogs) rapidly develop, adapt the formats as needed.

Personal Web Page

If no title is available, include an identification such as "Home page."

Tannen, Deborah. Home page. Georgetown U and Deborah Tannen, 2009. Web.
    26 Feb. 2010.

See the directory on pp. 724–25 for entries for other electronic sources, including books and articles.

Organization Web Page

"Library Statistics." *American Library Association*. Amer. Lib. Assn., 2010. Web.
    26 Feb. 2010.

Home Page for a Campus Department or Course

CSUN Department of Communication Studies. CSUN, n.d. Web. 26 Feb. 2010.

Blog or Blog Entry

To cite a blog entry, give the title of the entry in quotation marks. If it lacks a title, use a label such as "Blog comment." If there is no apparent sponsor, use "N.p." for no publisher.

To see how to create the listing for a Web page, turn to pp. 666–67.

Knight, Christopher. "The Watts Towers' Perpetual State of Crisis." *Culture Monster*.
    Los Angeles Times, 28 May 2010. Web. 29 May 2010.

Wray, William. Blog comment. *Culture Monster*. Los Angeles Times, 28 May 2010. Web.
    29 May 2010.

Publication on CD-ROM

Sheehy, Donald, ed. *Robert Frost: Poems, Life, Legacy*. New York: Holt, 1997. CD-ROM.

Visual or Audio Source

Advertisement

Feeding America. Advertisement. *Time* 21 Dec. 2009: 59. Print.

Comic or Cartoon

Supply the cartoonist's name and identification as a comic strip or cartoon.

Adams, Scott. "Dilbert." Comic strip. *Denver Post* 1 Mar. 2010: 8C. Print.

Photograph

Supply the place (museum or gallery and city) where the photograph is housed. If you are citing it from a publication, identify that source.

Stieglitz, Alfred. *Self Portrait*. J. Paul Getty Museum, Los Angeles. *Stieglitz: A
    Beginning Light*. By Katherine Hoffman. New Haven: Yale UP, 2004. 251. Print.

Strand, Paul. *Fifth Avenue, New York*. 1915. Photograph. Museum of Modern Art, New York.

For a family or personal photograph, identify who took it and when.

Bay Street Food Pantry. Personal photograph by author. 6 Nov. 2010.

Work of Art

Botticelli, Sandro. *The Birth of Venus*. 1482-86. Tempera on canvas. Uffizi Gallery, Florence.

Audiotape or Recording

Begin with the name of the artist, composer, speaker, writer, or other contributor, based on your interest in the recording. Include the medium, such as "Audiocassette," "CD," or "LP."

Byrne, Gabriel. *The James Joyce Collection*. Dove Audio, 1996. Audiocassette.

Program on Television or Radio

"The Wounded Platoon." *Frontline*. PBS. WGBH, Boston, 18 May 2010. Television.

"'How Sweet It Was': The Cultural Impact of Gospel." *Morning Edition*. Natl. Public Radio. KCFR, Denver, 30 May 2010. Radio.

Film

Start with the title, unless you wish to emphasize the work of a person connected with the film.

Lord of the Rings: The Return of the King. Dir. Peter Jackson. New Line Cinema, 2003. Film.

Jackson, Peter, dir. *Lord of the Rings: The Return of the King*. New Line Cinema, 2003. Film.

Live Performance

Rock 'n' Roll. By Tom Stoppard. Dir. Trevor Nunn. Perf. Nicole Ansari, Louise Bangay, Anthony Calf, and Martin Chamberlain. Royal Court Theatre, London. 5 June 2006. Performance.

Conversation or Field Artifact

Personal, Telephone, or E-mail Interview

Indicate how you conducted the interview: in person, by telephone, or by e-mail.

Boyd, Dierdre. Personal interview. 5 Feb. 2010.

Broadcast Interview

Begin with the person interviewed; if you wish, you may also add the interviewer (Interview by X).

Schatz, Amy. "Net Neutrality: Who's in Charge of the Internet?" Interview by Terry Gross. *Fresh Air*. Natl. Public Radio. KCFR, Denver. 25 May 2010. Radio.

Published Interview

Marshall, Chan. Interview. *Spin*. Dec. 2006: 72-75. Print.

Speech or Lecture

Wexel, Beth. Fall Convocation. Craig Hall, Wilton College. 29 Aug. 2010. Address.

Personal Letter

Use "MS" for handwritten manuscript or "TS" for typescript or printout.

Finch, Katherine. Letter to the author. 1 Nov. 2010. TS.

E-mail

Moore, Jack. Message to the author. 11 Oct. 2010. E-mail.

Online Posting

Use the subject line as the title; label as "Online posting" if it has no title.

Robinson, Meena. "Mansfield Park." *PBS Discussions*. PBS, 28 Jan. 2008. Web. 18 May 2008.

Cite a posting to a discussion group as you would an e-mail message.

Walsh, Karen. "Responsible Use of Technology." Message to the education technology discussion list. 28 May 2009. E-mail.

RESEARCH CHECKLIST
Listing Sources in MLA Style

☐ Have you begun each entry with the right pattern for the author's name?

☐ Have you figured out what type of source you have used? Have you followed the sample pattern for that type as exactly as possible?

☐ Have you used quotation marks and italics correctly for titles?

☐ Have you used the conventional punctuation — periods, commas, colons, parentheses — in your entry?

☐ Have you accurately recorded the name of the author, title, and publisher?

☐ Have you checked the accuracy of numbers for pages, volumes, and dates?

☐ Have you identified the medium of publication, reception, or delivery?

☐ Have you arranged your entries in alphabetical order?

☐ Have you checked your final list against your text citations so that every source appears in both places?

☐ Have you double-spaced your list, just like the rest of your paper? Have you allowed an inch margin on all sides?

☐ Have you begun the first line of each entry at the left margin? Have you indented each additional line one-half inch?

For a list of labels, see p. 732.

A Sample MLA Research Paper

In her paper "Meet Me in the Middle: The Student, the State, and the School," Candace Rardon investigates the rising costs of a college education and how schools have responded to the problem. Besides incorporating many features of effective research papers, this paper also illustrates the conventions for citing and listing sources in MLA style. Because an outline also was required, it precedes the paper.

1"

½"

Outline

Meet Me in the Middle:

The Student, the State, and the School

Thesis: By taking steps such as practicing cost containment, using new technological advancements and classroom alternatives, and exploring new revenue streams, many schools have been able to keep prices down and keep their doors open.

I. Among the various factors to consider when choosing a college, cost is increasingly becoming the most important and, to many, a barrier.

A. In the challenge to fund a university education, there are three players in the game: the student, the state, and the school.

B. By taking steps such as practicing cost containment, using new technological advancements and classroom alternatives, and exploring new revenue streams, many schools have been able to keep prices down and keep their doors open.

II. Prices for undergraduate tuition at both public and private institutions have steadily increased over the past decades.

A. The National Center for Education Statistics reports on cost increases.

B. The cost of college tuition and fees has risen each year.

III. Students have increasingly taken on more debt in paying for college.

A. Financial aid in the form of loans and grants is significant.

B. Most students graduate from a public four-year institution with education debt.

IV. State governments have been forced to decrease their funding to public colleges and universities.

A. In the current economic situation, states have been forced to cut budgets and reduce their levels of funding.

B. In 2008 and 2009, 39 states cut the amount they allotted in their budgets to higher education.

Rardon ii

    V. With students undertaking a record amount of debt
and states forced to cut their budgets, public colleges
and universities have a unique opportunity—even
responsibility—to change.

      A. Cost containment is the first step in decreasing a
school's budget and reliance on state funds.

      B. Operational changes can result in even more savings,
such as the use of online elements and technological
resources.

      C. Schools have explored new, alternative revenue streams
including grants, patents, and real estate opportunities.

   VI. By cutting past costs, thinking differently about present
operations, and looking to new future revenues, schools are
ensuring their own vitality and that of their students'
success.

½"

Candace Rardon

Professor Snyder

English Composition I

10 May 2010

Meet Me in the Middle:

The Student, the State, and the School

½" indent In December 2009, hundreds of students gathered on the campus of UCLA to protest the school's decision to raise tuition prices by 32%. Images of the protestors lying on the ground, representing the "Death of Public Education," are a sober picture of the current state of college tuition costs in the country. For students, among the various factors to consider when choosing a college—academics, athletics, student life, location, and so on—cost is increasingly becoming the most important and, for many, a barrier. In the challenge to pay for a public university education, there are three players in the game: the student, the state, and the school. With tuition prices and student loans at an all-time high, and state funding threatened by economic recession, universities themselves are now in a unique position to meet students and states in the middle of the crisis. The schools have an opportunity to bridge the funding gap and reevaluate their spending habits. By taking steps such as practicing cost containment, using new technological advancements and classroom alternatives, and exploring new revenue streams, many schools have been able to keep prices down and their doors open.

Prices for undergraduate tuition at both public and private institutions have progressively increased over the past decades and now "exceed inflation every year" (Hayden). The National Center for Education Statistics reports that "Between 1997-98 and 2007-08, prices for undergraduate tuition, room, and board at public institutions rose by 30 percent" and "at private institutions rose by 23 percent" (United States). In fact, as CreditUnions.com recently reported in a graph, the increase in higher education prices has steadily outpaced that of both

---

Margin annotations:

1"

½"

Writer's last name and page number ½" from top of page

Writer's name

Instructor's name

Course

Date

Title, centered

For more on beginning a research paper, see pp. 719–20.

Opening with current event to spark interest

Double-spacing throughout

1" 1"

Comments on current situation

Thesis previews development and central argument

For more on a thesis for a research paper, see p. 118.

Paragraph establishes background for the paper's general topic

No page number available in online source

1"

Figure cited in text

Rardon 2

medical costs and house prices (see fig. 1). This chart compares how much the cost of a college education has risen in recent years with how much health care costs and house prices have risen over the same period. While the cost of all three has risen, the expense of college has increased the most.

As the graph shows, the prices of tuition, medical care, and houses are plotted against both time and the Consumer Price Index. Computed by the Department of Labor's Bureau of Labor Statistics, the Consumer Price Index is a calculation generally used to measure inflation over a period of time, based on how the prices of common goods and services change. From 1989 to 2008, the price of higher education has consistently risen more than the prices of medical care and houses, a burden that often falls on the student.

Key term is defined

Trends in student borrowing point to a crisis in the amount of debt that students and families have to shoulder to afford an education. *Trends in Student Aid 2009,* a College Board report, states that in 2008-09, only 38% of students who graduated with a bachelor's degree from a public four-year institution did

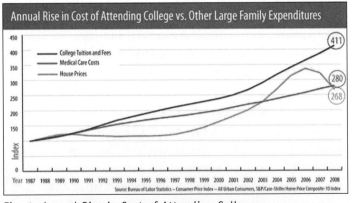

Fig. 1. Annual Rise in Cost of Attending College.

Source presents and credits findings of another study

Figure labeled in caption; source information provided

Source: Bureau of Labor Statistics, Consumer Price Index, and All Urban Consumers, Standard & Poor/Case-Schiller Home Price Composite-10 Index (Hoffman).

Rardon 3

so without education debt (Baum, Payea, and Steele). In 2007-08, college students graduated with a median debt of $11,000, and two-thirds had a median debt of $20,000. These numbers demonstrate the rising financial burden placed on college students, a situation that cannot be ignored, especially for the many students who are "making decisions and trade-offs among schools, living arrangements, work, and finances" (Bozick 278). Economist Richard Vedder has summed up the situation: "What we have now is an unsustainable trend" (qtd. in Sandler 199).

In the current economic recession, states have been forced to cut their budgets and reduce their funding to higher education. The Center on Budget and Policy Priorities reports that in 2009 and 2010, 39 states decreased the amount allotted to higher education in their budgets, leading to "reductions in faculty and staff in addition to tuition increases" (Johnson, Oliff, and Williams 6). Just as the University of California announced its huge increase, the state of Florida was also forced to raise tuition by 15% in 2009-10. The tuition increases that result from a lack of state funds are quickly becoming a nationwide threat.

With students accepting a record debt and states forced to cut their budgets, public colleges and universities have a unique opportunity—even responsibility—to change. Rather than raising tuition costs to make up for the loss of state funds, many schools across the country have begun to cut costs and diminish their need for future funds. A first step is cost containment so that schools can decrease their operating budgets and their reliance on state funds. In an article for *Time,* Sophia Yan outlines reductions on more than twenty campuses. For instance, Harvard University saved $900,000 by cutting hot breakfasts during the week in the dining halls. Western Washington University saved $485,000 by cutting its football team, and Whittier College saved $50,000 by cutting first-year orientation by a day. On the theory that "every little bit helps," schools are already looking for and finding ways to save money.

Only one citation needed for material in sequence in a paragraph and clearly from the same source

Facts and statistics support main point

For an explanation of statistics as evidence, see p. 41.

Page numbers provided for quotations

Paper continues to lay out background of argument

Transition from background to central argument

Specific examples provide evidence for point

For more on integrating sources, see Ch. 34.

Rardon 4

Point from last paragraph used for transition to new point

Going beyond cutbacks in services, schools have also considered operational changes that will result in even more savings. The Delta Project on Postsecondary Education Costs, Productivity, and Accountability is a nonprofit group that analyzes college costs and spending trends. In a recent policy advisory, the Delta Project recommends that schools use emergency funds from the 2009 American Recovery and Reinvestment Act to increase productivity:

Launch statement names organization as author

Direct quotation of longer than four lines set off from text without quotation marks, followed by page number in parentheses

Make investments in course redesign and other curricula changes that will make for a more cost-effective curriculum. . . . This includes redesigning large undergraduate courses, creating cost-effective developmental education modules that can be delivered statewide; and redesigning the general education curriculum to enhance community college transfer. (4)

Other suggestions include making current buildings more energy efficient and creating work opportunities for jobless students, either as interns or research assistants (4). Such changes can lead to substantial savings and help the budgets of schools across the country.

Transition leads to another way to avoid raising tuition costs

Another alternative to raising tuition is for schools to embrace technological advances and to explore alternatives to the ways universities are traditionally run. As Kamenetz observes, "Whether hybrid classes, social networks, tutoring programs, games, or open content, technology provides speed skates for students and teachers, not crutches." Specific models have come from the National Center for Academic Transformation, a nonprofit organization that uses information technology to raise student performance and lower costs. Its six course redesign models vary in how much in-class instruction is replaced by technology from the supplementary model, which creates "technology-based, out-of-class activities" (Natl. Center, "Six Models" 1), to the emporium model, which replaces lectures with an online learning resource center (3). When the University

Quotation and source clearly identified but pages are not numbered in source

Short title added to distinguish two sources by the same author

Basic models are explained before giving a specific example

of Alabama adopted the emporium model for Intermediate Algebra, the redesign increased student success, met individual needs, and saved 30% of costs (Natl. Center, "Program"). Of course, such course redesign cannot always be applied across the curriculum, but schools giving serious thought to current technology can transform the classroom, saving money and helping students.

    Finally, schools can supplement income from student tuition by considering additional sources of revenue. *Business Week* writer Francesca Di Meglio reports that many schools are already looking to grants, patents, real estate, and popular graduate courses to "protect [their] bottom line from fiscal and demographic trends that are making the college business more challenging." As early as the 1950s, three Indiana University researchers patented Crest toothpaste, and its returns went on to fund an on-campus dental research institute. As recently as 2004, Emmanuel College allowed Merck, a large pharmaceuticals company, to build a research facility on an acre of land the Boston school owns with a 75-year lease for $50 million. Di Meglio's examples show how schools can tap into these alternative income streams and reduce some of the pressure on tuition.

    Rising tuition costs, growing student borrowing, and shrinking government funding have endangered widespread access to a college education. As President Obama himself said in the 2010 State of the Union Address, "in the United States of America, no one should go broke because they chose to go to college. . . . it's time for colleges and universities to get serious about cutting their own costs—because they, too, have a responsibility to help solve this problem." In an era of economic strain, schools can embrace this chance to think creatively about the way they operate. By cutting costs where they spent money in the past, thinking differently about how they operate in the present, and looking to new ways of bringing in revenue in the future, schools can ensure their own vitality and that of

---

Margin annotations:

Direct quotation selected to make critical point

Statistics support claims

Third point of the argument is introduced

Launch statement names publication and author

Brackets identify words added to original text

Paraphrase of original source

Final sentence in paragraph connects examples from source with overall argument

For more on concluding a research paper, see pp. 719–20.

Ellipses show where words are omitted

Conclusion emphasizes critical points in argument

Rardon 6

their students' success. When public colleges and universities take such steps to ensure that a college education is available to everyone, meeting students and states in the middle with innovative ideas, then it is possible to reverse the decisions that led to protests such as the one on the UCLA campus. Instead of

Conclusion returns to event in opening

lying down, students can stand and welcome in an era of continued and increased college access and attendance.

Rardon 7

Works Cited

Baum, Sandy, Kathleen Payea, and Patricia Steele. *Trends in Student Aid 2009*. Washington: College Board, 2009. *Trends in Higher Education Series*. Web. 20 Apr. 2010.

Bozick, Robert. "Making It through the First Year of College: The Role of Students' Economic Resources, Employment, and Living Arrangements." *Sociology of Education* 80.3 (2007): 216-84. *JSTOR*. Web. 23 Apr. 2010.

Delta Project on Postsecondary Education Costs, Productivity, and Accountability. "Postsecondary Education Spending Priorities for the American Recovery and Reinvestment Act of 2009." Washington: Delta Project, Feb. 2009. Web. 20 Apr. 2010.

Di Meglio, Francesca. "Colleges Explore Alternative Revenue Streams." *BusinessWeek.com,* 7 Aug. 2008. Web. 2 May 2010.

Hayden, Tom. "Rising Cost of College? We Can't Afford to Be Quiet." *Chronicle of Higher Education* 28 Mar. 2010: n. pag. *Academic OneFile*. Web. 20 Apr. 2010.

Hoffman, Teri. "Graph of the Week: Annual Rise in Cost of Attending College vs. Other Large Family Expenditures." *CreditUnions.com*. Callahan & Associates, 27 July 2009. Web. 2 May 2010.

Johnson, Nicholas, Phil Oliff, and Erica Williams. "An Update on State Budget Cuts." *Center on Budget and Policy Priorities*. Washington: CBPP, 19 Apr. 2010. Web. 26 Apr. 2010.

Kamenetz, Anya. "The Virtual University." *American Prospect* 21.4 (2010): 22+. *LexisNexis Academic*. Web. 23 May 2010.

National Center for Academic Transformation. "Program in Course Redesign: The University of Alabama." *The National Center for Academic Transformation*. NCAT, 2005. Web. 2 May 2010.

---. "Six Models for Course Redesign." *The National Center for Academic Transformation*. NCAT, 2008. Web. 2 May 2010.

Obama, Barack. "Remarks by the President in State of the Union Address." United States Capitol, Washington, DC. 27 Jan. 2010. Address.

List of works cited on a separate page

List alphabetized by names of authors or by titles (when no author is named)

First line of entry at left margin, additional lines indented ½"

Use appropriate abbreviations if no information is given for publisher or date

No URLs for accessible Internet sources unless required by instructor

1"

½"

Sandler, Corey. *Cut College Costs Now! Surefire Ways to Save Thousands of Dollars.* Avon: Adams Media, 2006. Print.

United States. Dept. of Education. National Center for Education Statistics. "Fast Facts: Average Undergraduate Tuition and Fees and Room and Board Rates." 2009. *Digest of Education Statistics,* 2008. Web. 26 Apr. 2010.

Yan, Sophia. "Colleges Find Creative Ways to Cut Back." *Time* 21 Sept. 2009: 81. Print.

The American Psychological Association (APA) details the style most commonly used in the social sciences in its *Publication Manual,* Sixth Edition (Washington, D.C.: APA, 2010). For advice and updates, visit <apastyle.apa.org>, purchase the manual, or use a library copy.

APA style uses a two-part system to credit sources. First, you briefly cite or identify the author and date of the source in your text, either by mentioning them in your discussion or by noting them in parentheses right after you refer to the information drawn from the source. In many cases, you also supply the page number or other location in the original source. Second, you lead from this brief identification, through the author's name, to a full description of the source in your concluding list, called "References."

For a brief overview of APA style, see E1–E2 in the Quick Research Guide, pp. A-30–A-35.

Citing Sources in APA Style

The core of an APA citation is the author of the source. That person's last name links your use of the source in your paper with its full description in your list of references. Next comes the date of the source, which often establishes its current or classic status for readers. (Within a paragraph, you don't need to repeat this date if you refer to the source again unless a reader might mix up the sources under discussion.)

A common addition is a specific location, such as a page number (using "p." for "page" or "pp." for "pages"), that tells where the material appears in the original source. Unless the source lacks page numbers or other locators, this information is required for quotations and recommended for paraphrases and key concepts. When you supply these elements in parentheses, separate them with commas: (Westin, 2005, p. 48). This basic form applies whatever the type of source — article, book, or Web page.

As you check your APA style, keep in mind these three questions:

- Who wrote it?
- What type of source is it?
- How are you capturing the source material?

753

Citing and Listing Sources in APA Style

Skim the following directory to find sample entries to guide you as you cite and list your sources. Notice that the examples are organized according to questions you might ask and that comparable print and electronic sources are grouped together. Also see pages 769–75 for a sample paper that illustrates APA style.

Citing and Listing Sources in APA Style (*continued*)

Who Wrote It?

Individual Author Not Named in Sentence

Some experts feel that adolescent boys who bully are depressed and acting out in an aggressive manner (Pollack, 2000).

Individual Author Named in Sentence

Pollack (2000) contends that boys tend to contain their pain for fear of appearing vulnerable and inviting ridicule.

Two Authors

List the last names of coauthors in the order in which they appear in the source. Join the names with "and" if you mention them in your text and with an ampersand (&) if the citation is in parentheses.

A group's cultural development enhances its chance for survival, providing both physical and psychological protection (Anderson & Ross, 1998).

Anderson and Ross (1998) maintain that the development of a group's culture provides both physical and psychological protection.

Three Authors or More

For three to five authors, include all the last names in your first reference. In any later references, identify only the first author and add "et al." (for "and others"), whether in the text or in parentheses. For six authors or more, simply use the name of the first author with "et al." for all citations.

Conservation biology has developed in response to the accelerating rate at which species are being lost (Purves, Orians, & Heller, 1999). Purves et al. explore the consequences of human activities in relation to this acceleration.

Organization Author

Important as nutrition is for healthy people, it is even more critical for cancer patients who may have specific dietary needs (American Cancer Society, 2003, p. 7).

Author of an Essay from a Reader or Collection

Cite the author of the essay; identify the editor of the collection later in your reference list.

See the listing on p. 765.

Although rapes occur each year in campus fraternity houses, research studies have yet to investigate why these locations are more likely venues for rape than other college gathering places (Martin & Hummer, 2003).

Unidentified Author

Identify the source with the full title in your text or with the first few words in parentheses so that it is easy to locate in your alphabetical list of references.

Parents need to monitor their child's online activities ("Social Networking," 2006).

Same Author with Multiple Works

Three significant trends in parent-school relations evolved (Grimley, 2007) after the original multistate study (Grimley, 1987).

Different Authors with Multiple Works

Within a single citation, list the authors of multiple works in alphabetical order (as in your reference list). Separate the works with semicolons.

Several studies have examined minority educational attainment (Bowen & Bok, 1998; Charles, Dinwiddie, & Massey, 2004; Glazer, 1997).

What Type of Source Is It?

Naming the author is the core of a citation, regardless of the type of source used. Even so, a few types may present complications.

Indirect Source

If possible, locate and cite the original source. Otherwise, begin your citation with "as cited in" and name your source.

According to Claude Fischer, the belief in individualism favors "the individual over the group or institution" (as cited in Hansen, 2005, p. 5).

Government or Organization Document

If no specific author is identified, treat the sponsor as the author. Give its full name in your first citation. If the name is complicated or commonly shortened, you may add an abbreviation in brackets.

The *2005 National Gang Threat Assessment* (National Alliance of Gang Investigators Associations [NAGIA], 2005, pp. vii-viii) identified regional trends that have helped to account for the city's recent gang violence.

In later citations, use just the abbreviation and the date:

(NAGIA, 2005)

Source without a Date

When the date is unknown, use "n.d." ("no date").

Interval training encourages rotation between high-intensity spurts and "active recovery, which is typically a less-intense form of the original activity" (*Interval training,* n.d., para. 2).

A Classic

If the date is unknown, use "n.d." ("no date"). If the original date is known, show it along with your edition's date: (Burton, 1621/1977). For ancient texts, use the year of the translation: (Homer, trans. 1990). For a quotation from a classic, identify lines, sections, or other standard divisions so that a passage could be located in any edition. For biblical references, specify the version in your initial citation. Classics—ancient or religious—need not be added to your reference list.

Many cultures affirm the importance of religious covenant in accounts as varied as the biblical "Behold, I make a covenant" in Exodus 34:10 (King James Version) and

The Iliad (Homer, trans. 1990), which opens with the cause of the Trojan War, "all because Agamemnon spurned Apollo's priest" (Book 1, line 12).

Visual Material

To refer to your own figure or table, mention its number in your sentence: "As Figure 2 shows, . . ." Clearly identify a visual cited from a source.

Teenagers who play video games with a high degree of violence are more likely to show aggressive behavior (Anderson & Bushman, 2001, Table 1).

To include or adapt a table or a visual from a source, you may need to request permission from the author or copyright holder. Many sources—from scholarly journals to Web sites—state their permissions policy in the issue or on the site. (Ask your instructor for advice if you are uncertain about how to proceed.) Credit such material in a "From" or "Adapted from" note below it.

Personal Communication

Personal communications—such as face-to-face or telephone interviews, letters, memos, and e-mail—are not included in the reference list because your readers would not be able to find and use such sources. Simply name your source and the date of the communication in your paper.

J. T. Moore (personal communication, October 10, 2010) has made specific suggestions for stimulating the local economy.

How Are You Capturing the Source Material?

For more on capturing and integrating source material, see pp. 234–41, 669–72, and Ch. 34.

The way that you have captured source material—whether in your own words or in a quotation—affects how you present and credit it. Always identify words taken directly from a source by using quotation marks or the indented form for a long "block" quotation. Specify the location of quoted words. If you present in your own words material from a specific place in your source, APA also recommends that you add the location. A citation, but no location, is needed for general information, such as your summary of an overall finding.

To identify the location of material in a source, supply the page number. For an unpaginated source, especially online, give the paragraph number it supplies ("para. 3"). If it does not use either system, give the section name (or a short version), and identify the paragraph within the section (Methods section, para. 2). If appropriate, identify other parts: Chapter 5, Figure 2, Table 3.

The next four examples illustrate how Ross Rocketto varied his presentation of sources in his paper "Robin Hood: Prince of Thieves? An Analysis of Current School Finance Legislation in Texas."

Overall Summary or Important Idea

The resulting educational inequities have become particularly problematic because of technological changes that require higher levels of education for higher paying jobs (Wilson, 1996).

Blended Paraphrase and Quotation

According to William Julius Wilson (1996), the economic restructuring of the 1970s created what he refers to as "new urban poverty"—"segregated neighborhoods in which a substantial majority of individual adults are either unemployed or have dropped out of the labor force altogether" (p. 19).

Brief Quotation Integrated in Sentence

According to Castells, the city is the "most efficient and convenient form of collective consumption" (as cited in Savage, 2003, p. 162), that is, the best means of providing public housing, transport, education, and so on.

Long Quotation

If you quote forty words or more, indent the quotation one-half inch and double-space it instead of using quotation marks. After it, add your citation with no additional period, including whatever information you have not already mentioned in your launch statement.

This phenomenon is explained further by Hoxby (1998):

> First, districts that are good, efficient providers of schooling tend to be rewarded with larger budgets. This fiscal reward process works because a district's budget nearly always depends on property taxes, which in turn depend on home prices within the district, which in turn depend on how the marginal home buyers value the local schools. (p. 48)

RESEARCH CHECKLIST
Citing Sources in APA Style

☐ Have you double-checked to be sure that you have acknowledged all material from a source?

☐ Does your citation fall right after a quotation or reference to a source?

☐ Have you identified the author of each source in your text or in parentheses?

☐ Have you used the first few words of the title to cite a work without an identified author?

☐ Have you noted the date (or added "n.d." for "no date") for each source?

☐ Have you added a page number or other location whenever needed?

☐ Have you checked your final draft to be sure that every source cited in your text also appears in your list of references?

Listing Sources in APA Style

For a sample reference page, see p. 775 or p. A-6.

List your sources at the end of your paper. Title a new page with "References" centered. Double-space your list, and organize it alphabetically by authors' last names (or by titles for works without an identified author). Arrange several works by the same author by date, moving from earliest to most recent. If an author has two works published in the same year, arrange these alphabetically, and add a letter after each date (2009a, 2009b) so the date in your text citation leads to the correct entry.

Format each entry with a "hanging indent" so that subsequent lines are indented one-half inch (about five to seven spaces), just as a paragraph is. (Use the menu in your software—Format-Paragraph-Indentation—to set up this hanging or special indentation.) Include only sources that you actually cite in your paper unless your instructor requests otherwise.

APA style simplifies the following details:

- Supply only initials (with a space between them) for an author's first and middle names.

- Use an ampersand (&), not "and," before the name of the last of a series of authors (as you would in a citation in parentheses even though you would write "and" in your paper).

- Spell out names of months, but abbreviate terms common in academic writing (such as "p.m.," "Vol." for "Volume," or "No." for "Number").

- Capitalize only the first word, proper names, and the first word after a colon in the title of a book, article, or Web site. Capitalize all main words in the title of a journal or other periodical.

- Do not use quotation marks or italics for an article title in your reference list (even though you would use quotation marks if you mentioned it in your paper).

- Italicize a Web site, book, or periodical title (and its volume number).

- List only the first of several cities where a publisher has offices, and add the abbreviated state (unless a university's name identifies it). For locations abroad, spell both city and country.

- Shorten the name of a publisher, but include "Press."

- Use "Author" instead of the publisher's name if the two are the same.

- For articles, give volume, issue (if each begins with page 1), and any digital object identifier (DOI) numbers. If no DOI is available for an online article, supply the URL for the journal or publisher home page, even if you used a database.

- Include an access date only for online sources that might change.
- Omit a final period after the URL.

As you prepare your own entries, begin with the author. The various author formats apply whatever your source — article, book, Web page, or other material. Then, from the following examples, select the format for the rest of the entry, depending on the type of source you have used. Follow its pattern in your entry, supplying the same information in the same order with the same punctuation and other features. Keep in mind these two key questions, which are used to organize the sample entries that follow:

Who wrote it?

What type of source is it?

Who Wrote It?

Individual Author

O'Reilly, B. (2006). *Culture warrior*. New York, NY: Broadway Books.

Two Authors

Boggs, C., & Pollard, T. (2007). *The Hollywood war machine: U.S. militarism and popular culture*. Boulder, CO: Paradigm.

Three Authors or More

Provide names for three to six authors; for more than six, simply use "et al." ("and others") instead of adding more names.

Evans, B., Joas, M., Sundback, S., & Theobald, K. (2005). *Governing sustainable cities*. London, England: Earthscan.

Same Author with Multiple Works

Arrange the titles by date, the earliest first. If some share the same date, arrange them alphabetically, and letter them after the date.

Gould, S. J. (1996). *Full house: The spread of excellence from Plato to Darwin*. New York, NY: Harmony.

Gould, S. J. (2003a). *The hedgehog, the fox, and the magister's pox: Mending the gap between science and the humanities*. New York, NY: Harmony.

Gould, S. J. (2003b). *Triumph and tragedy in Mudville: A lifelong passion for baseball*. New York, NY: Norton.

Organization Author

American Red Cross. (2004). *CPR/AED for the professional rescuer*. Washington, DC:
Author.

Author of Edited Work

Bolles, E. B. (Ed.). (1999). *Galileo's commandment: 2,500 years of great science
writing*. New York, NY: Freeman.

Author and Translator

Ishinomori, S. (1988). *Japan Inc.: Introduction to Japanese economics* (B. Scheiner,
Trans.). Berkeley: University of California Press. (Original work published 1986)

Unidentified Author

Environment awareness: No child left inside. (2007, February 10). *The Economist,
382*, 32-33.

What Type of Source Is It?

Once you have found the appropriate author format, look for the type of
source and the specific entry that best matches yours. Mix and match the
patterns illustrated as needed. For example, the revised edition of an edited
collection of articles might send you to several examples until you have
identified all of its elements.

Article in a Printed or an Electronic Periodical

Article from a Journal Paginated by Volume

If the pages for the year's volume are numbered consecutively, no issue
number is needed. Italicize the volume number as well as the journal title.

Barker, T. (2009). Hong Kong film, Hollywood and the new global cinema: No film is
an island. *Asian Journal of Social Science, 37*, 970-971. doi:10.1163/1568484
09X12526657425668

Article from a Journal Paginated by Issue

If each issue begins with page 1, add the issue number in parentheses, without italics, leaving no space after the volume number.

Kissam, E. (2005). The fulcrum for immigrant civic engagement. *Journal of
Latino-Latin American Studies, 1*(4), 191-205.

If you want to list a special issue about a topic, rather than singling out an
article, begin with the issue editor or, if none, with the issue title.

Latinos in rural America [Special issue]. (2005). *Journal of Latino-Latin American Studies, 1*(4).

Article from a Journal with a DOI

Give volume, issue (if needed), and digital object identifier (DOI) numbers.

Het, S., & Wolf, O. T. (2007). Mood changes in response to psychosocial stress in healthy young women: Effects of pretreatment with cortisol. *Behavioral Neuroscience, 121*(1), 11-20. doi:10.1037/0735-7044.121.1.11

Article from a Journal without a DOI

If an article you found online has no DOI, add the journal's home page URL.

Doherty, S. D., & Rosen, T. (2006). Shark skin laceration. *Dermatology Online Journal, 12*(6), 6. Retrieved from http://dermatology.cdlib.org

Article Accessed through a Library or Subscription Database

Supply any DOI, or search for and identify the home page for the journal. Name the database only for a source otherwise hard to find.

Allison, S. (2004). On-screen smoking influences young viewers. *Youth Studies Australia, 23*(3), 6. Retrieved from http://acys.info/home

To see how to create the listing for a journal article from a database, turn to pp. 662–63.

Abstract for an Article

If you use only the abstract, cite it, not the full article. Add "Abstract" in brackets after the title, or use it to begin the retrieval line.

Powrie, P. (2003). Thirty years of doctoral theses on French cinema. *Studies in French Cinema 3*(3), 199-203. Abstract retrieved from Academic Search Premier Database.

Article from a Printed Magazine

Ricks, D. (2009, December). Flu wars. *Discover, 30,* 40-45, 74.

To see how to create the listing for a magazine article, turn to pp. 760–61.

Article from an Online Magazine

Chandler, K. (2005, June 18). Anger management. *Salon.com*. Retrieved from http://www.salon.com

Article from a Newsletter

Anti-evolution teachings gain in U.S. schools. (2005, January). *Newsletter on Intellectual Freedom, 54*(3), 27-28.

Article from a Printed Newspaper

Stein, R. (2004, March 11). Breast-cancer drug changes suggested. *The Boston Globe,* p. A4.

Article from an Online Newspaper

Martin, A. (2007, March 7). Makers of sodas try a new pitch: They're healthy. *The New York Times.* Retrieved from http://www.nytimes.com

Editorial

Rushed primaries. [Editorial]. (2007, March 19). *The Nation, 284,* 3.

Letter to the Editor

Lardner, G. (2007, March 19). Impeach, impeach, impeach [Letter to the editor]. *The Nation, 284,* 24.

Review

Rose, T. (1998, February 24). Blues sisters [Review of the book *Blues legacies and black feminism: Gertrude "Ma" Rainey, Bessie Smith, and Billie Holliday*]. *The Village Voice,* pp. 139-141.

Printed or Electronic Book

Printed Book

To see how to create a listing for a book, turn to pp. 664–65.

Zelden, C. L. (2009). *The Supreme Court and elections.* Washington, DC: CQ Press.

Online Book

Oblinger, D. G., & Oblinger, J. L. (Eds.). (2005). *Educating the Net generation.* Retrieved from http://www.educause.edu/educatingthenetgen/

Multivolume Work

Friedman, H. S. (Ed.). (1998). *Encyclopedia of mental health* (Vols. 1-3). San Diego, CA: Academic Press.

Revised Edition

Coleman, J. W. (2006). *The criminal elite: Understanding white-collar crime* (6th ed.). New York, NY: Worth.

Book without a Date

Reade, T. (n.d.). *American Originals.* Wichita, KS: Midtown Press.

Part of a Printed or an Electronic Book

Selection from a Printed Book

Martin, P. Y., & Hummer, R. A. (2003). Fraternities and rape on campus. In
  M. Silberman (Ed.), *Violence and society: A reader* (pp. 215-222). Upper Saddle
  River, NJ: Prentice Hall.

See the citation on p. 756.

Selection from an Online Book

Brown, M. (2005). Learning spaces. In D. G. Oblinger & J. L. Oblinger
  (Eds.), *Educating the Net generation* (chap. 12). Retrieved from
  http://www.educause.edu/educatingthenetgen/

Preface, Introduction, Foreword, or Afterword

Godwin, M. (1996). Foreword. In P. Ludlow (Ed.), *High noon on the electronic frontier*
  (pp. xiii-xvi). Cambridge, MA: MIT Press.

Article from a Reference Work

Norman, C. E. (2003). Religion and food. In *Encyclopedia of food and culture*
  (Vol. 3, pp. 171-176). New York, NY: Charles Scribner's Sons.

Printed or Electronic Report or Other Document

Many research reports and similar documents are collaborative products,
prepared under the auspices of government, academic, or other organizational sponsors. Start with the agency name if no specific author is identified.
In parentheses, add any report number assigned by the agency right after the
title. Add the publisher (unless it is also the author) before the URL.

Printed Government Document

U.S. Bureau of the Census. (2009). *Statistical abstract of the United States: The
  national data book: 2010.* (129th ed.) (NTIS Order Number: PB2010-965801).
  Washington, DC: U.S. Government Printing Office.

Online Government Document

U.S. Federal Trade Commission. (2010). *Medical Identity Theft.* Retrieved from
  http://www.ftc.gov/bcp/edu/pubs/consumer/idtheft/idt10.pdf

Research Report

Liu, J., Allspach, J. R., Feigenbaum, M., Oh, H.-J., & Burton, N. (2004). *A study of
  fatigue effects from the new SAT* (RR-04-46). Princeton, NJ: Educational Testing
  Service.

Online Research Report

National Institute on Drug Abuse. (2009). *Inhalant abuse* (NIH Publication
No. 09-3818). Retrieved from http://www.drugabuse.gov/PDF/RRInhalants.pdf

Online Research Report from a Database

Ross, D. B., & Driscoll, R. (2006). *Test anxiety: Age appropriate interventions.*
Retrieved from ERIC database. (ED493897)

Report from an Academic Institution

Bunn, M., Wier, A., & Holdren, J. P. (2003). *Controlling nuclear warheads and
materials: A report card and action plan.* Cambridge, MA: Harvard University,
Belfer Center for Science and International Affairs.

Pamphlet

Label the source in brackets as a brochure.

U.S. Department of the Interior. (2002). *Lewis and Clark Trail: National historic trail,
Illinois to Oregon* [Brochure]. Washington, DC: Author.

Doctoral Dissertation

Richter, P. (2004). *Improving nursing in the age of managed care* (Unpublished
doctoral dissertation). University of Wisconsin, Madison.

Internet or Electronic Source

To help a reader find the same material you used, identify a specific document and give its URL.

Section or Page from an Online Document

Detweiler, L. (1993). What is the future of privacy on the Internet? In *Identity,
privacy, and anonymity on the Internet* (sec. 2.12). Retrieved from
http://eserver.org/internet/Identity-Privacy-Anonymity.txt

Document from a Campus Web Site

Identify the university and sponsoring program or department (if applicable) before giving the URL for the specific page or document.

Allin, C. (2010). *Common sense for college students: How to do better than you
thought possible.* Retrieved from Cornell College, Department of Politics Web
site: http://www.cornellcollege.edu/politics/gb-resources-students/policies
/common-sense-cwa.shtml

See the directory on pp. 754–55 for entries for other electronic sources, including books and articles.

For any updates on online formats, visit the APA Web site at <apastyle.apa.org>.

To see how to create the listing for a Web page, turn to pp. 666–67.

Computer Software

Microsoft Office 2010 [Computer software]. Redmond, WA: Microsoft.

Visual or Audio Source

Audiotape or Recording

Ellis, A. (Writer/Producer). (1995). *Helping students develop their IEPs* [Audiotape]. Washington, DC: National Dissemination Center for Children with Disabilities.

Program on Television or Radio

Clark, L. (Writer/Director/Producer). (2004). Descent into the ice [Television series episode]. In P. Aspell (Executive producer), *Nova*. Boston, MA: WGBH.

Film

Lustig, B., Molen, G., & Spielberg, S. (Producers). (1993). *Schindler's list* [Motion picture]. United States: Universal.

Conversation or Field Artifact

Personal Interview

Omit a personal interview from your reference list because it is not accessible to readers. Instead, mention it in your paper as a personal communication.

See the citation on p. 758.

E-mail or Electronic Posting

Cite inaccessible messages as personal communications. Otherwise, supply author, date, title, a description such as [Web log post], and a "Retrieved from" line with the URL.

See the citation on p. 758.

RESEARCH CHECKLIST
Listing Sources in APA Style

☐ Have you started each entry with the appropriate pattern for the author's name? Have you left spaces between the initials for each name?

☐ Have you used "&" (not "and") to add the last coauthor's name?

☐ Have you included the date in each entry?

☐ Have you followed the sample pattern for the type of source used?

☐ Have you used capitals and italics correctly for the titles in your entries?

☐ Have you included the conventional punctuation—periods, commas, colons, parentheses—in your entry?

☐ Have you accurately recorded names of the author, title, and publisher?

☐ Have you checked the accuracy of dates, pages, and other numbers?

☐ Have you correctly typed or pasted in the DOI or URL of an electronic source? Have you split a long URL before a punctuation mark? Have you ended without adding a final period after a DOI or URL?

☐ Have you arranged your entries in alphabetical order?

☐ Have you checked your final list of references against your text citations so that every source appears in both places?

☐ Have you double-spaced your reference list, like the rest of your paper? Have you allowed an inch margin on all sides?

☐ Have you begun the first line of each entry at the left margin? Have you used your software to indent each additional line one-half inch (or five to seven spaces)?

A Sample APA Research Paper

In "Crucial Choices: Who Will Save the Wetlands If Everyone Is at the Mall?" Linn Bourgeau explores the loss of the Illinois wetlands, including both consequences and possible remedies. Her paper illustrates APA paper format and the APA conventions for citing and listing sources.

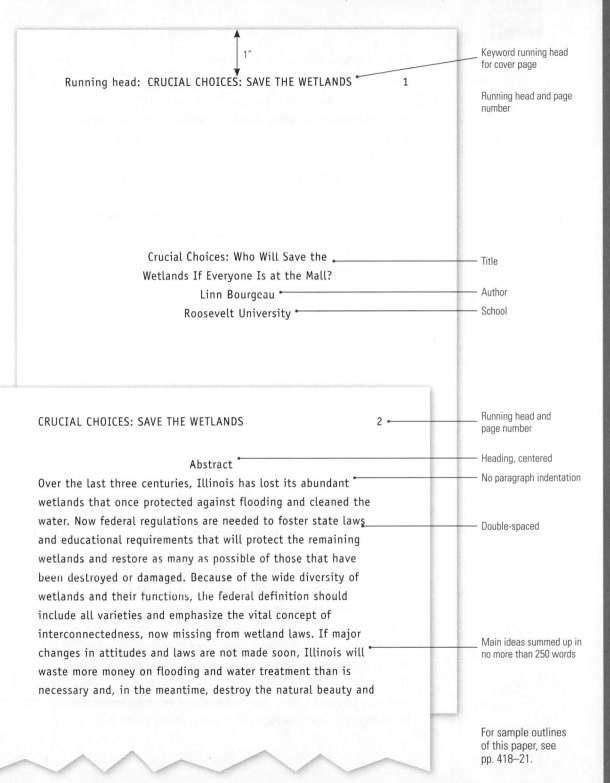

Running head: CRUCIAL CHOICES: SAVE THE WETLANDS

Keyword running head for cover page

Running head and page number

1

Crucial Choices: Who Will Save the
Wetlands If Everyone Is at the Mall?

Linn Bourgeau

Roosevelt University

Title

Author

School

CRUCIAL CHOICES: SAVE THE WETLANDS

2

Running head and page number

Abstract

Heading, centered

Over the last three centuries, Illinois has lost its abundant
wetlands that once protected against flooding and cleaned the
water. Now federal regulations are needed to foster state laws
and educational requirements that will protect the remaining
wetlands and restore as many as possible of those that have
been destroyed or damaged. Because of the wide diversity of
wetlands and their functions, the federal definition should
include all varieties and emphasize the vital concept of
interconnectedness, now missing from wetland laws. If major
changes in attitudes and laws are not made soon, Illinois will
waste more money on flooding and water treatment than is
necessary and, in the meantime, destroy the natural beauty and

No paragraph indentation

Double-spaced

Main ideas summed up in no more than 250 words

For sample outlines
of this paper, see
pp. 418–21.

½"

CRUCIAL CHOICES: SAVE THE WETLANDS   1"   3

Title centered ——————————• Crucial Choices: Who Will Save the

½" indent
(or 5 spaces)
Wetlands If Everyone Is at the Mall?

←→Each person, as part of nature's ecosystem, has the choice

Double-spaced
throughout
to interact with nature as that individual chooses. Because that

interaction includes valuable resources such as the wetlands,

poor choices carry huge consequences. It is crucial that federal

regulations foster state laws and educational requirements to

help protect the few wetlands that are left, restore as many as

possible of those that have been destroyed, and take measures

to improve the damage from over-development.

According to the Illinois Chapter of the Sierra Club (2003),

our ntation has lost over half its wetlands since Columbus

arrived, and Illinois has lost even more:

Long quotation (40 words
or longer) indented ½"
without quotation marks
The situation is even more grim in Illinois. In 1818 there

were over 8 million acres, or 23% of the total land area, of

wetlands in the state. Today, only 1,251,240 acres (2.5% of

the State) remains as wetlands. A staggering 90% of Illinois'

wetlands have been destroyed. (p. 2)

If the current trend of destroying wetlands continues, Illinois

will have more flooding and poorer water quality. The complex

1"   1"
←→ability of wetlands to stave off floods, to clean the water supply,←→

and to add to the aquifers that store water is not understood or

protected to the same degree that the wetlands protect and

serve humankind.

First-level heading,
bold and centered
—————————————• **Flood Protection**

Floods are dramatic and visible consequences of not

protecting wetlands, but wetlands are rarely mentioned in the

same newspaper headline with flooding. The cost of flooding

can be tallied, not only in dollars spent on post-flood

reconstruction but in lives. Thirteen people died in floods in

the decade between 1988 and 1998. Since that time, flooding

has consistently cost Illinois approximately $39 million annually

(Illinois Chapter of the Sierra Club, 2003, p. 5). Moreover,

Gaddie and Regens (2000) reported that the Great Midwestern

Flood of 1993, which damaged land and property along the

1"

Mississippi and Missouri rivers, could have been avoided along with billions of dollars spent in reconstruction (p. 24). At that time Illinois was not only one of the states with the most devastation, but also one of six states with the largest loss of wetlands (p. 25). Construction of roads, buildings, and other infrastructure along these rivers had changed the natural floodplain channels, preventing wetlands from doing their work of diverting and absorbing excess water. Understandably, then, the areas historically known as wetlands were also the areas with the worst destruction.

Specific pages noted

Preventing floods is one of the most valuable roles of wetlands. Their plant and soil composition is designed to hold and slowly release excess water. It has been estimated by Mitsch and Gosselink (2000) that, prior to the human interventions of levees and drainage, the storage capacity of the Mississippi River floodplain was 60 days' worth of overflow as opposed to the current 12 days (p. 586). This difference in holding capacity contributes to the increased occurrence of floods along the Mississippi (Belt, 1975, as cited by Mitsch & Gosselink, 2000, p. 586). Despite this fact, the drainage of wetlands has accelerated since 1950 (Mitsch & Gosselink, 2000, p. 587).

Names of two authors joined by "and" in text but "&" in parentheses

Legal Mitigation and Misconceptions

The laws regarding wetlands largely misinterpret or ignore the basic understanding of wetlands. Some laws established to address wetland issues, called wetland mitigation, have attempted to remedy the lack of wetlands but do little to protect existing wetlands. These laws are continually truncated by litigation brought to the Supreme Court. One such decision in favor of an Illinois developer in January 2001 limited the protection of "isolated wetlands" and, according to a 2003 report from the Illinois Chapter of the Sierra Club, led to a run on dredging and filling wetlands.

If legislators understood how wetlands bridge dry and aquatic soil as part of a large and complex ecosystem, they

CRUCIAL CHOICES: SAVE THE WETLANDS   5

would know that an "isolated wetland" simply does not exist.
The distance that water travels within a given area is called a
watershed, a crucial concept misunderstood by regulatory
organizations. Some created wetlands have road runoff as a
water source, not tides or streams, resulting in wrong water
levels. (Mitsch & Wilson, 1996, p. 78). In actuality, nature's
system cannot filter the low-quality runoff water if it does not
soak into the soil quickly. According to the Citizens for
Conservation restoration chairperson, water needs to be filtered
as it travels some distance through the soil, possibly through
numerous wetlands before being fed into a water source

Personal communication noted in text but not in References because it is not available to readers

(Vanderpoel, personal communication, 2006) such as a lake,
an aquifer, or a water treatment plant.

The law does not consider the interconnections within
natural water systems or protect areas that are dry, isolated, and
far from "navigable water," such as prairie potholes. These

Additional source cited in source where it was mentioned

seemingly dry areas, identified in a study by Weller (as cited in
Mitsch & Gosselink, 2000) as the type of wetlands that most
directly contributes to replenishing our underground water supply
(2000), are being dredged and filled on a regular basis, limiting
the potential for cleaner water. Citizens for Conservation (2006)

Brackets used to identify addition to quotation

states the undeniable fact that "everyone lives [within] a
watershed," noting that studies have shown that pollution from
Illinois is carried all the way to the Gulf. Healthy wetlands
within a watershed have proven benefits for water quality: the
removal of contaminants by aquatic wetland plants has been
replicated in laboratory studies (Weiss, Hondzo, & Semmens,
1983, pp. 1040-41). Middleton (1999) points out that while
wetlands are often conceptualized as standing water, such a
situation is actually detrimental to the naturally filtering and
flowing properties within watersheds.

As people destroy more wetlands, chances for naturally
purified water decrease while chances for lower-quality water are
multiplied exponentially by miles of pavement covering our land.
In a three-year study, Chicago Wilderness (n.d.) cites a high

CRUCIAL CHOICES: SAVE THE WETLANDS   6

correlation between "impervious cover" and "water sources such as lakes, reservoirs and aquifers" (p. 82). Though our conventional lawns may be considered benign or even beneficial as a type of vegetation, their root systems are not porous or deep enough to allow water to be absorbed into the local watershed. They are just as impervious as our streets and sidewalks and carry polluted water over, instead of into, the soil (Applied Ecological Services, 2004, p. 5), which has fewer filtering properties as the wetlands disappear.

Implementation of What We Know

New federal laws should require implementation of what we know, based on the many well-researched proposals already in place. One such plan, "Biodiversity: Business Guide," was compiled by Applied Ecological Services (2006) for the city of Schaumburg. This plan and many others have suggestions for everyone from the average homeowner to the hotel developer. One suggestion for commercial developers is to "retrofit" man-made ponds with vegetation that would prevent shoreline erosion. With such ponds in Schaumburg, aquatic vegetation would also filter the water headed for aquifers and roadside flooding (p. 7). By implementing well-researched alternatives such as these, the federal government could take the lead in curbing a potential water quality crisis and minimize the flooding crisis that already depletes funds and natural resources.

Education for Interconnectedness

Because of the wide diversity of wetlands and their functions, the federal definition of wetlands should include all the varieties of wetlands, including the concept of watersheds, a vital concept of interconnectedness now missing from wetland laws. These connections extend not only from marsh to lake but from state to state. The National Wildlife Federation (n.d.) stresses the need for federal protection by pointing to the many lakes and rivers that are shared by states.

This idea of interconnectedness, not in the forefront of our individualistic nation, means reeducating everyone from

Definition supplied

legislators to fourth-graders. Presently the social and political consciousness is a consumer-oriented, throw-away mentality, even regarding natural resources. Incorporating ecology into the curriculum at every grade level by 2030, as proposed by Chicago Wilderness advocate Packard (2006), is not only feasible, but imperative. How to educate politicians, developers, and legislators is a larger, more difficult endeavor clouded by the complexity of economic and political issues.

Who Will Save the Wetlands If Everyone Is at the Mall?

For certain, the value of wetlands is not an isolated issue any more than wetlands are isolated from one another. But, as ominous as that sounds, if people don't even know exactly how the basic necessity of water is being purified, it is difficult to guess what lies ahead for water supplies and flood control. What is known is that healthy wetlands protect against flooding and clean the water people need. Both Illinois and the country have made many poor choices by not heeding this evidence and protecting shared lakes and rivers (National Wildlife Federation, n.d.).

The current course must change so that both laws and civic conduct reflect the realities of wetlands' complexity and importance. Once a person understands the drawbacks of destroying wetlands, he or she should not only be motivated but also find it imperative to stop wetland destruction. If major changes in attitudes and laws are not made soon, Illinois will waste more money on flooding and water treatment than is necessary and, in the meantime, destroy the natural beauty and benefits of wetlands. The choices people make in their schools, legislative systems, and daily lives will impact the future of water quality and flooding.

CRUCIAL CHOICES: SAVE THE WETLANDS   8

References

Applied Ecological Services. (2006). *Biodiversity: Business guide for commercial, industrial and municipal development in the village of Schaumburg*. Retrieved from http://www.schaumburg.il.us

Chicago Wilderness. (n.d.). *Biodiversity recovery plan*. Retrieved from http://www.chicagowilderness.org/pubprod/brp/index.cfm

Citizens for Conservation. (2006). *Flint Creek Watershed Partnership* [Brochure]. Barrington, IL: Author.

Gaddie, R. K., & Regens, J. L. (2000). *Regulating wetlands protection*. Albany: State University of New York Press.

Illinois Chapter of the Sierra Club. (2003). *Isolated: Illinois wetlands at risk*. Retrieved from http://www.illinois.sierraclub.org

Middleton, B. A. (1999). *Wetland restoration, flood pulsing, and disturbance dynamics*. New York, NY: Wiley.

Mitsch, W. J., & Gosselink, J. G. (2000). *Wetlands*. New York, NY: Wiley.

Mitsch, W. J., & Wilson, R. F. (1996). Improving the success of wetland creation and restoration with know-how, time, and self-design. *Ecological Applications, 6*(1), 77-83. doi:10.2307/2269554

National Wildlife Federation. (n.d.). *Weakening the Clean Water Act: What it means for Illinois*. Retrieved from http://www.nwf.org/wildlife/pdfs/CleanWaterAct

Packard, S. (2006, Spring). Chicago wilderness, 2030: Visions for the future. *Chicago Wilderness Magazine*. Retrieved from http://www.chicagowildernessmag.org

Weiss, J. D., Hondzo, M., & Semmens, M. (1983). Storm water detention ponds: Modeling heavy metal removal by plant species and sediments. *Journal of Environmental Engineering, 132*(9), 1034-1042. doi:10.1061/(ASCE)0733-9372(2006)132:9(1034)

Page numbering continues

Heading, centered

First line of entry at left margin, additional lines indented ½"

List alphabetized by names of authors

All author names begin with last name

No period after URL

First word in title and after colon and all proper nouns capitalized

For more sample student research papers, visit **<bedfordstmartins.com/bedguide>**.

A
WRITER'S
HANDBOOK

A Writer's Handbook Contents

Introduction:
Grammar, or The Way Words Work

Every speaker of English, even a child, commands a grammatical system of tremendous complexity. Take the sentence "A bear is occupying a telephone booth while a tourist impatiently waits in line." In theory, there are nineteen billion different ways to state the idea in that sentence.[1] (Another is "A tourist fumes while he waits for a bear to finish yakking on a pay phone.") How do we understand a unique sentence like that one? For we do understand it, even though we have never heard it before—not in those very same words, not in the very same order.

To begin with, we recognize familiar words and we know their meanings. Just as significantly, we recognize grammatical structures. As we read or hear the sentence, we know that it contains a familiar pattern of **syntax,** or word order, that helps the sentence make sense to us. Ordinarily we aren't even conscious of such an order, but to notice it, all we need to do is rearrange the words of our sentence:

> Telephone a impatiently line in waits tourist bear a occupying is a booth while.

The result is nonsense: it defies English grammar. The would-be sentence doesn't follow familiar patterns or meet our expectations of order.

Hundreds of times a day, with wonderful efficiency, we perform tasks of understanding and constructing complex sentences. Why, then, think about grammar in college? Isn't it entirely possible to write well without contemplating grammar at all? Yes. If your innate sense of grammar is reliable, you can write clearly and logically and forcefully without knowing a predicate nominative from a handsaw. Most successful writers, though, have practiced for many years to gain this sense. When you doubt a word or a construction, a glance in a handbook often can clear up your confusion and restore your confidence—just as referring to a dictionary can help your spelling.

The grammatical conventions you'll find in this handbook are not mechanical specification but accepted ways in which skilled writers and speakers put words together to convey meaning clearly. The amateur writer can learn by following their example, just as an amateur athlete, artist, or even auto mechanic can learn by watching the professionals.

[1] Richard Ohmann, "Grammar and Meaning," *American Heritage Dictionary* (Boston: Houghton, 1979), pp. xxxi–xxxii.

38 Grammatical Sentences

1 | Sentence Fragments

Unlike a complete sentence, a **fragment** is partial or incomplete. It may lack a subject (naming someone or something), a predicate (making an assertion about the subject), or both. A fragment also may otherwise fail to express a complete thought. Unless you add what's missing or reword what's incomplete, a fragment cannot stand alone as a sentence. Even so, we all use fragments in everyday speech, where their context and delivery make them understandable and therefore acceptable.

> That bicycle over there.
>
> Good job.
>
> Not if I can help it.

In writing, fragments like these fail to communicate complete, coherent ideas. Notice how much more effective they are as complete sentences.

> I'd like to buy that bicycle over there.
>
> You did a good job sanding the floor.
>
> Nobody will steal my seat if I can help it.

Some writers use fragments on purpose. Advertisers are fond of short, emphatic fragments that command attention, like quick jabs to the head.

> For seafood lovers. Every Tuesday night. All you can eat.

sentence: A word group that includes both a subject and a predicate and can stand alone

Those who text-message or tweet compress what they write because time and character space are limited. They rely on the recipient of the message to fill in the gaps.

> Thru with lab. CU @ 8. Pizza?

In college writing, though, it is good practice to express your ideas in complete sentences. Besides, complete sentences usually convey more information than fragments — a big advantage in essay writing.

If you sometimes write fragments without recognizing them, learn to edit your work. Luckily, fragments are fairly easy to correct. Often you can attach a fragment to a neighboring sentence with a comma, a dash, or a colon. Sometimes you can combine two thoughts without adding any punctuation at all.

1a If a fragment is a phrase, link it to a nearby sentence, or make it a complete sentence.

You have two choices for revising a fragment if it is a phrase: (1) link it to an adjoining sentence, using punctuation such as a comma or a colon, or (2) add a missing subject or verb to make it a complete sentence.

FRAGMENT	Malcolm has two goals in life. *Wealth and power.*
SENTENCE	Malcolm has two goals in life: wealth and power. [The phrase *Wealth and power* has no verb; a colon links it to *goals.*]
FRAGMENT	Al ends his stories as he mixes his martinis. *With a twist.*
SENTENCE	Al ends his stories as he mixes his martinis, with a twist. [The prepositional phrase *With a twist* has no subject or verb; a comma links it to the main clause.]
FRAGMENT	*To stamp out the union.* That was the bosses' plan.
SENTENCE	To stamp out the union was the bosses' plan. [The infinitive phrase *To stamp out the union* has no main verb or subject; it becomes the sentence subject.]
FRAGMENT	The students taking the final exam in the auditorium.
SENTENCE	The students were taking the final exam in the auditorium. [The helping verb *were* completes the verb and makes a sentence.]

1b If a fragment is a subordinate clause, link it to a nearby sentence, or drop the subordinating conjunction.

Some fragments are missing neither subject nor verb. Instead, they are subordinate clauses, unable to express complete thoughts unless linked with main clauses. When you find a subordinating conjunction at the start or in

For more on editing for fragments, see A1 in the Quick Editing Guide, p. A-38.

phrase: Two or more related words that work together but may lack a subject (*will walk*), a verb (*my uncle*), or both (*to the attic*)

subject: The part of a sentence that names something — a person, an object, an idea, a situation — about which the verb in the predicate makes an assertion: The *king* lives.

verb: A word that shows action (The cow *jumped* over the moon) or a state of being (The cow *is* brown) the middle of a word group, that word group may be a subordinate clause. If you have treated it as a complete sentence, you can correct the problem in two ways: (1) combine the fragment with a main clause (a complete sentence) nearby, or (2) make the subordinate clause into a complete sentence by dropping the subordinating conjunction.

subordinating conjunction: A word (such as *because, although, if, when*) used to make one clause dependent on, or subordinate to, another: *Unless* you have a key, we are locked out. (See 14d–14f.)

FRAGMENT	The new law will help create jobs. *If it passes.*
SENTENCE	The new law will help create jobs, if it passes.
FRAGMENT	*Because Jay is an avid skier.* He loves winter in the mountains.
SENTENCE	Because Jay is an avid skier, he loves winter in the mountains.
SENTENCE	Jay is an avid skier. He loves winter in the mountains.

1c If a fragment has a participle but no other verb, change the participle to a main verb, or link the fragment to a nearby sentence.

A present participle (the *-ing* form of the verb) can serve as the main verb in a sentence only when it is accompanied by a form of *be* ("Sally *is working* harder than usual"). When a writer mistakenly uses a participle alone as a main verb, the result is a fragment.

FRAGMENT	Jon was used to the pressure of deadlines. *Having worked the night shift at the daily newspaper.*

One solution is to combine the fragment with an adjoining sentence.

SENTENCE	Jon was used to the pressure of deadlines, having worked the night shift at the daily newspaper.

A second solution is to choose another form of the verb.

SENTENCE	Jon was used to the pressure of deadlines. He *had worked* the night shift at the daily newspaper.

1d If a fragment is part of a compound predicate, link it with the complete sentence containing the subject and the rest of the predicate.

compound predicate: A predicate consisting of two or more verbs linked by a conjunction: My sister *stopped and stared.*

For punctuation advice, see 14a.

FRAGMENT	In spite of a pulled muscle, Jeremy ran the race. *And won.*

A fragment such as *And won* sounds satisfyingly punchy, but it lacks a subject. Create a sentence by linking the two verbs in the compound predicate.

SENTENCE	In spite of a pulled muscle, Jeremy *ran* the race *and won.*

To emphasize the second verb, add punctuation and another subject.

SENTENCE	In spite of a pulled muscle, Jeremy ran the race—and *he* won.

ESL Guidelines 🌐 Using Participles, Gerunds, and Infinitives

A **verbal** is a form of a verb that cannot function as the main verb in a sentence but can function as an adjective, an adverb, or a noun.

Using participles

When used as an adjective, the present (*-ing*) form expresses cause, and the past (*-ed* and *-d*) forms express effect or result.

> The movie was *terrifying to the children*. [The movie caused terror.]

> The children were *terrified by the movie*.
> [The movie resulted in terrified children.]

Using verbs with gerunds and infinitives

Some verbs are followed by gerunds (verb + *-ing*, functioning as a noun), others by infinitives (*to* + base verb), and still others by either.

- Verbs that are followed by gerunds

  appreciate, avoid, consider, deny, discuss, enjoy, finish, imagine, keep, miss, practice, recall, and *suggest,* among others

  > My family enjoys *going* to the beach.

- Verbs that are followed by infinitives

  agree, decide, expect, pretend, refuse, and *want,* among others

  > My mother decided *to eat* dinner at the Salad Shop.

- Verbs that can be followed by either a gerund or an infinitive

  continue, like, love, hate, remember, forget, start, and *stop,* among others

  > I like going to the museum, but Nadine likes *to go* to the movies.

NOTE: Some verbs, such as *stop, remember,* and *forget,* have significantly different meanings when followed by a gerund or by an infinitive.

> I stopped *smoking*. [I do not smoke anymore.]

> I stopped *to smoke*. [I stopped so that I could smoke.]

- *Used to* (meaning "did in the past") is followed by the basic form of the verb. *Be used to* or *get used to* (meaning "be or become accustomed to") is followed by a gerund.

  > I *used to live* in Rio, but now I live in Ohio. [I lived in Rio in the past.]

  > I *am used to living* in Ohio. [I am accustomed to living in Ohio.]

  > I *got used to living* in Ohio. [I became accustomed to living in Ohio.]

For practice, visit
**<bedfordstmartins
.com/bedguide>**.

For more practice, visit **<bedfordstmartins .com/bedguide>**.

Exercise 1-1 ▪ Eliminating Fragments

Eliminate any fragments in the following examples. Some sentences may be correct. Possible revisions for the lettered sentences appear in the back of the book. Example:

> Bryan hates parsnips. And loathes squash.
>
> Bryan hates parsnips *and* loathes squash.

a. Michael had a beautiful Southern accent. Having lived many years in Georgia.

b. Pat and Chris are determined to marry each other. Even if their families do not approve.

c. Jack seemed well qualified for a career in the air force. Except for his tendency to get airsick.

d. Lisa advocated sleeping no more than four hours a night. Until she started nodding off through her classes.

e. They met. They talked. They fought. They reached agreement.

1. Being the first person in his family ever to attend college. Alex is determined to succeed.

2. Does our society rob children of their childhood? By making them aware too soon of adult ills?

3. Richard III supposedly had the young princes murdered. No one has ever found out what really happened to them.

4. For democracy to function, two elements are crucial. An educated populace and a collective belief in people's ability to chart their own course.

5. You must take his stories as others do. With a grain of salt.

Exercise 1-2 ▪ Eliminating Fragments

Rewrite the following paragraph, eliminating all fragments. Explain why you made each change. Example:

> Many people exercise to change their body image. And may become obsessed with their looks.
> [The second word group is a fragment because it has no subject.]
>
> Many people exercise to change their body image *and* may become obsessed with their looks.
> [This revised sentence links the fragment to the rest of the sentence.]

Some people assume that only women are overly concerned with body image. However, men often share this concern. While women tend to exercise vigorously to stay slender, men usually lift weights to "bulk up." Because of their desire to look masculine. Both are trying to achieve the "ideal" body form. The muscular male and the slim female. Sometimes working out begins to interfere with other aspects of life. Such as sleeping, eating regularly, or going to school or work. These are warning signs. Of too much emphasis on physical appearance. Preoccupation with body image may turn a healthy lifestyle into an unhealthy obsession. Many people believe that looking attractive will bring them happiness. Unfortunately, when they become compulsive. Beautiful people are not always happy.

2 | Comma Splices and Fused Sentences

Splice two ropes, or two strips of movie film, and you join them into one. Splice two main clauses by putting only a comma between them, however, and you get a faulty construction called a **comma splice.** Here, for instance, are two perfectly good main clauses, each separate, each able to stand on its own as a sentence:

> The detective wriggled on his belly toward the campfire. The drunken smugglers didn't notice him.

Now let's splice those sentences with a comma.

COMMA SPLICE The detective wriggled on his belly toward the campfire, the drunken smugglers didn't notice him.

The resulting comma splice makes for difficult reading.

Even more confusing than a comma splice is a **fused sentence:** two main clauses joined without any punctuation.

FUSED SENTENCE The detective wriggled on his belly toward the campfire the drunken smugglers didn't notice him.

Lacking clues from the writer, a reader cannot tell where to pause. To understand the sentence, he or she must halt and reread.

main clause: A group of words that has both a subject and a verb and can stand alone as a complete sentence: *My friends play softball.*

For more on editing for comma splices and fused sentences, see A2 in the Quick Editing Guide, pp. A-38–A-40.

Sentence Parts at a Glance

The **subject (S)** identifies some person, place, thing, situation, or idea.

The **predicate (P)** includes a verb (expressing action or state of being) and makes an assertion about the subject.

An **object (O)** is the target or recipient of the action described by the verb.

A **complement (C)** renames or describes a subject or object.

       S   P   C   S   P   O

The *campus center is beautiful.* The new *sculpture draws crowds.*

The next two pages show five easy ways to eliminate both comma splices and fused sentences, also called **run-ons.** Your choice depends on the length and complexity of your main clauses and the effect you desire.

2a Write separate complete sentences to correct a comma splice or a fused sentence.

COMMA SPLICE	Sigmund Freud has been called an enemy of sexual repression, the truth is that he is not a friend of free love.
FUSED SENTENCE	Sigmund Freud has been called an enemy of sexual repression the truth is that he is not a friend of free love.

sentence: A word group that includes both a subject and a predicate and can stand alone

Neither sentence yields its meaning without a struggle. To point readers in the right direction, separate the clauses.

SENTENCE	Sigmund Freud has been called an enemy of sexual repression. The truth is that he is not a friend of free love.

2b Use a comma and a coordinating conjunction to correct a comma splice or a fused sentence.

If both clauses are of roughly equal weight, you can use a comma to link them — as long as you add a coordinating conjunction after the comma.

coordinating conjunction: A one-syllable linking word (*and, but, for, or, nor, so, yet*) that joins elements with equal or near-equal importance: Jack *and* Jill, sink *or* swim

For advice on coordination, see 14a–14c.

COMMA SPLICE	Hurricane winds hit ninety miles an hour, they tore the roof from every house on Paradise Drive.
SENTENCE	Hurricane winds hit ninety miles an hour, *and* they tore the roof from every house on Paradise Drive.

2c Use a semicolon or a colon to correct a comma splice or a fused sentence.

A semicolon can connect two closely related thoughts, emphasizing each one.

COMMA SPLICE	Hurricane winds hit ninety miles an hour, they tore the roof from every house on Paradise Drive.
SENTENCE	Hurricane winds hit ninety miles an hour; they tore the roof from every house on Paradise Drive.

If the second thought illustrates or explains the first, add it with a colon.

SENTENCE	The hurricane caused extensive damage: it tore the roof from every house on Paradise Drive.

The only punctuation powerful enough to link two main clauses single-handedly is a semicolon, a colon, or a period. A lone comma won't do the job except in the case of joining certain very short, similar main clauses.

> Jill runs by day, Tom walks by night.

> I came, I saw, I conquered.

Commas are not obligatory with short, similar clauses. If this issue is confusing, you can stick with semicolons to join all main clauses, short or long.

> Jill runs by day; Tom walks by night.

> I came; I saw; I conquered.

2d Use subordination to correct a comma splice or a fused sentence.

If one main clause is more important than the other or you want to give it more importance, make the less important one subordinate, which throws weight on the main clause. In effect, you show your reader how one idea relates to another: you decide which matters more.

FUSED SENTENCE	Hurricane winds hit ninety miles an hour they tore the roof from every house on Paradise Drive.
SENTENCE	*When hurricane winds hit ninety miles an hour,* they tore the roof from every house on Paradise Drive.
SENTENCE	Hurricane winds, *which tore the roof from every house on Paradise Drive,* hit ninety miles an hour.

main clause: A group of words that has both a subject and a verb and can stand alone as a complete sentence: *My friends play softball.*

For advice on subordination, see 14d–14f. For a list of subordinating words, see p. 842.

2e Use a conjunctive adverb with a semicolon and a comma to correct a comma splice or a fused sentence.

If you want to cram more than one clause into a sentence, you may join two clauses with a **conjunctive adverb.** Conjunctive adverbs show relationships such as addition (*also, besides*), comparison (*likewise, similarly*), contrast (*instead, however*), emphasis (*namely, certainly*), cause and effect (*thus, therefore*), or time (*finally, subsequently*). These transitional words and phrases can be a useful way of linking clauses — but only with the right punctuation.

COMMA SPLICE	Freud has been called an enemy of sexual repression, however the truth is that he is not a friend of free love.

A writer might consider a comma plus the conjunctive adverb *however* enough to combine the two main clauses, but that glue won't hold. Stronger binding — the semicolon along with a comma — is required.

For a list of conjunctive adverbs, see p. 842.

SENTENCE	Freud has been called an enemy of sexual repression; however, the truth is that he is not a friend of free love.

Exercise 2-1 ■ Revising Comma Splices and Fused Sentences

For more
practice, visit
**<bedfordstmartins
.com/bedguide>**.

In the following examples, correct each comma splice or fused sentence in two ways, and decide which way works better. Be creative: don't correct every one in the same way. Some sentences may be correct as written. Possible revisions for the lettered sentences appear in the back of the book. Example:

> The castle looked eerie from a distance, it filled us with nameless fear.
>
> The castle looked eerie from a *distance;* it filled us with nameless fear.
>
> *Or*
>
> The castle, *which looked eerie from a distance,* filled us with nameless fear.

a. We followed the scientist down a flight of wet stone steps at last he stopped before a huge oak door.

b. Dr. Frankenstein selected a heavy key, he twisted it in the lock.

c. The huge door gave a groan it swung open on a dimly lighted laboratory.

d. Before us on a dissecting table lay a form with closed eyes to behold it sent a quick chill down my spine.

e. The scientist strode to the table, he lifted a white-gloved hand.

1. Dr. Frankenstein flung a switch, blue streamers of static electricity crackled about the table, the creature gave a grunt and opened smoldering eyes.

2. "I've won!" exclaimed the scientist in triumph he circled the room doing a demented Irish reel.

3. The creature's right hand strained, the heavy steel manacle imprisoning his wrist began to creak.

4. Like a staple wrenched from a document, the manacle yielded.

5. The creature sat upright and tugged at the shackles binding his ankles, Frankenstein uttered a piercing scream.

Exercise 2-2 ■ Revising Comma Splices and Fused Sentences

Revise the following passage, using subordination, a conjunctive adverb, a semicolon, or a colon to correct each comma splice or fused sentence. You may also write separate complete sentences. Some sentences may be correct. Example:

> English can be difficult to learn, it is full of expressions that don't mean what they literally say.

English can be difficult to learn *because* it is full of expressions that don't mean what they literally say.

Have you ever wondered why you drive on parkways and park on driveways, that's about as logical as your nose running while your feet smell! When you stop to think about it, these phrases don't make sense yet we tend to accept them without thinking about what they literally mean we simply take their intended meanings for granted. Think, however, how confusing they are for a person who is just learning the language. If, for example, you have just learned the verb *park*, you would logically assume that a parkway is where you should park your car, of course when most people see a parkway or a driveway they realize that braking on a parkway would be hazardous, while speeding through a driveway will not take them very far. However, our language is full of many idiomatic expressions that may be difficult for a person from another language background to understand. Fortunately, there are plenty of questions to keep us *all* confused, such as why Americans commonly refer to going to work as "punching the clock."

3 | Verbs

Most verbs are called **action verbs** because they show action (*swim, eat, sleep, win*). Some verbs are called **linking verbs** (*is, become, seem, feel*) because they show a state of being by linking the subject of a sentence with a word that renames or describes it. A few verbs accompany a main verb to give more information about its action; they are called **helping** or **auxiliary verbs** (*have, must, can*).

For help editing verbs, see A3 in the Quick Editing Guide, pp. A-40–A-42.

Verb Forms

3a Use a linking verb to connect the subject of a sentence with a subject complement.

A linking verb (LV) shows what the subject of a sentence *is* or is *like*. The verb creates a sort of equation, either positive or negative, between the subject and its complement (SC)—a noun, a pronoun, or an adjective.

LV SC
Julia will *make* a good *doctor*. [Noun]

LV SC
Jorge *is* not the *one*. [Pronoun]

LV SC
London weather *seems foggy*. [Adjective]

A verb may be a linking verb in some sentences and not in others. If you focus on what the verb means, you can usually tell how it is functioning.

subject complement: A noun, an adjective, or a group of words that follows a linking verb and renames or describes the subject: This plum tastes *ripe*.

I often *grow* sleepy after lunch.
[Linking verb + subject complement *sleepy*]

I often *grow* tomatoes in my garden.
[Transitive verb + direct object *tomatoes*]

transitive verb: An
action verb that
must have an object to
complete its meaning:
Alan *hit* the ball.

Common Linking Verbs at a Glance

Some linking verbs tell what a noun is, was, or will be.

  be, become, remain: I *remain* optimistic.

  grow: The sky is *growing* dark.

  make: One plus two *makes* three.

  prove: His warning *proved* accurate.

  turn: The weather *turned* cold.

Some linking verbs tell what a noun might be.

  appear, seem, look: The child *looks* cold.

Most verbs of the senses can operate as linking verbs.

  feel, smell, sound, taste: The smoothie *tastes* sweet.

3b Use helping verbs to add information about the main verb.

Adding a **helping** or **auxiliary verb** to a simple verb (*go, shoot, be*) allows you to express a wide variety of tenses and moods (*am going, did shoot, would have been*). (See 3g–3l and 3n–3p.) The parts of this combination, called a **verb phrase,** need not appear together but may be separated by other words.

  I probably *am going* to France this summer.

  You *should* not *have shot* that pigeon.

  This change *may* well *have been contemplated* before the election.

Helping Verbs at a Glance

Of the twenty-three helping verbs, fourteen can also act as main verbs that identify the central action.

  be, is, am, are, was, were, being, been

  do, does, did

  have, has, had

The other nine act only as helping verbs, never as main verbs. As **modals,** they show actions that are possible, doubtful, necessary, required, and so on.

  can, could, should, would, may, might, must, shall, will

3c Use the correct principal parts of the verb.

The **principal parts** are the forms the verb can take—alone or with helping verbs—to indicate the full range of times when an action or a state of being does, did, or will occur. Verbs have three principal parts: the base form or infinitive, the past tense, and the past participle.

For the principal parts of many irregular verbs, see **<bedfordstmartins .com/bedguide>**.

- The **infinitive** is the simple, base, or dictionary form of the verb (*go, sing, laugh*), often preceded by *to* (*to go, to sing, to laugh*).
- The **past tense** signals completed action (*went, sang, laughed*).
- The **past participle** is combined with helping verbs to indicate action at various past or future times (*have gone, had sung, will have laughed*). With forms of *be*, it makes the passive voice. (See 3m.)

All verbs also have a present participle, the *-ing* form of the verb (*going, singing, laughing*). This form is used to make the progressive tenses. (See 3k and 3l.) It also can modify nouns and pronouns ("the *leaking* bottle") or, as a gerund, function as a noun ("*Sleeping all day* pleases me").

3d Use *-d* or *-ed* to form the past tense and past participle of regular verbs.

Most verbs in English are **regular verbs:** they form the past tense and past participle in a standard, predictable way. Regular verbs that end in *-e* add *-d* to the infinitive; those that do not end in *-e* add *-ed*.

INFINITIVE	PAST TENSE	PAST PARTICIPLE
(to) smile	smiled	smiled
(to) act	acted	acted

3e Use the correct forms for the past tense and past participle of irregular verbs.

At least two hundred **irregular verbs** form the past tense and past participle in some way other than adding *-d* or *-ed*: *go, went, gone*. Most irregular verbs, familiar to native English speakers, pose no problem.

For the forms of *be* and *have*, see A4 in the Quick Editing Guide, pp. A-42–A-43.

3f Use the correct forms of *lie* and *lay* and *sit* and *set*.

Try taking two easy steps to eliminate confusion between *lie* and *lay*.

- Learn the principal parts and present participles of both (see p. 792).
- Remember that *lie,* in all its forms, is intransitive and never takes a direct object: "The island *lies* due east." *Lay* is transitive, so its forms always require an object to answer "Lay what?": "*Lay* that pistol down."

The same distinction exists between *sit* and *set*. Usually, *sit* is intransitive: "He *sits* on the stairs." *Set,* on the other hand, almost always takes an

intransitive verb: A verb that is complete in itself and needs no object: The surgeon *paused.*
transitive verb: An action verb that must have an object to complete its meaning: Alan *hit* the ball.

Forms of *Lie* and *Lay, Sit* and *Set*

lie, lay, lain, lying: recline

PRESENT TENSE		PAST TENSE	
I lie	we lie	I lay	we lay
you lie	you lie	you lay	you lay
he/she/it lies	they lie	he/she/it lay	they lay

PAST PARTICIPLE
lain (We have *lain* in the sun long enough.)

PRESENT PARTICIPLE
lying (At ten o'clock he was still *lying* in bed.)

lay, laid, laid, laying: put in place, deposit

PRESENT TENSE		PAST TENSE	
I lay	we lay	I laid	we laid
you lay	you lay	you laid	you laid
he/she/it lays	they lay	he/she/it laid	they laid

PAST PARTICIPLE
laid (Having *laid* his clothes on the bed, Mark jumped in the shower.)

PRESENT PARTICIPLE
laying (*Laying* her cards on the table, Lola cried, "Gin!")

sit, sat, sat, sitting: be seated

PRESENT TENSE		PAST TENSE	
I sit	we sit	I sat	we sat
you sit	you sit	you sat	you sat
he/she/it sits	they sit	he/she/it sat	they sat

PAST PARTICIPLE
sat (I have *sat* here long enough.)

PRESENT PARTICIPLE
sitting (Why are you *sitting* on that rickety bench?)

set, set, set, setting: place

PRESENT TENSE		PAST TENSE	
I set	we set	I set	we set
you set	you set	you set	you set
he/she/it sets	they set	he/she/it set	they set

PAST PARTICIPLE
set (Paul has *set* the table for eight.)

PRESENT PARTICIPLE
setting (Chanh-Duy has been *setting* traps for the mice.)

object: "He *sets* the bottle on the counter." There are, however, a few easily memorized exceptions. The sun *sets*. A hen *sets*. Gelatin *sets*. You *sit* the canter in a horse show.

Exercise 3-1 ▪ Using Irregular Verb Forms

Underline each incorrectly used irregular verb in the following sentences, and substitute the verb's correct form. Some sentences may be correct. Answers for the lettered sentences appear in the back of the book. Example:

For more
practice, visit
**<bedfordstmartins
.com/bedguide>**.

> We have already <u>drove</u> eight hundred miles from campus.
>
> We have already *driven* eight hundred miles from campus.

a. Benjamin wrote all the music, and his sister sung all the songs.

b. After she had eaten her bagel, she drank a cup of coffee with milk.

c. When the bell rung, darkness had already fell.

d. Voters have chose some new senators, who won't take office until January.

e. Carol threw the ball into the water, and the dog swum after it.

1. He brought along two of the fish they had caught the day before.

2. By the time the sun set, the birds had all went away.

3. Teachers had spoke to his parents long before he stole the bicycle.

4. While the cat laid on the bed, the mouse ran beneath the door.

5. For the past three days the wind has blew hard from the south, but now the clouds have began to drift in.

Tenses

The **simple tenses** indicate whether the verb's action took place in the past, takes place in the present, or will take place in the future. The **perfect tenses** narrow the timing further, specifying that the action was or will be completed by the time of some other action. The **progressive tenses** add precision, indicating that the action did, does, or will continue.

For advice on
consistent verb
tense, see 9a.

3g Use the simple present tense for actions that take place once, repeatedly, or continuously in the present.

The simple present tense is the infinitive form of a regular verb plus *-s* or *-es* for the third-person singular (used with *a singular noun* or *he, she,* or *it*).

I like, I watch	we like, we watch
you like, you watch	you like, you watch
he/she/it likes, he/she/it watches	they like, they watch

ESL Guidelines 🌐 Selection of Verbs to Show the Past, Present, and Future

TIME OF ACTION OR STATE + ITS DURATION OR TIME RELATIONSHIP	PAST TIME Yesterday, some time ago, long ago	PRESENT TIME Right now, today, or at this moment	FUTURE TIME Tomorrow, soon, or at some expected or possible moment
Action or state occurs once	The team *lost* the game last week. (past tense)	Everyone *is* now on the field. (present tense)	The bus *will leave* at noon on Friday. (future tense) The bus *leaves* after lunch. (present tense)
Action or state occurs repeatedly	The team *won* every home game. (past tense)	The team *wins* when everyone *concentrates* on the game. (present tense)	The bus *will leave* at noon on Fridays. (future tense) The bus *leaves* at noon on Fridays. (present tense)
Action or state occurs continuously	The players *followed* the coach's directions. (past tense)	The coach always *encourages* the players. (present tense)	The bus *will leave* at noon from now on. (future tense) The bus always *leaves* at noon. (present tense)
Action or state is a general or timeless fact		Coaching *is* a challenging job. (present tense)	
Action or state completed before the time of another action	The players *had practiced* for only two weeks in August before their games began. (past perfect tense)	The team *has played* every week this fall. (present perfect tense)	The team *will have played* at six other campuses before the season ends. (future perfect tense)
Action or state begun in the past but still going on		The players *have practiced* every day. (present perfect tense)	

Verb Tenses at a Glance

NOTE: The examples show first person only.

SIMPLE TENSES

Present	*Past*	*Future*
I cook	I cooked	I will cook
I see	I saw	I will see

PERFECT TENSES

Present perfect	*Past perfect*	*Future perfect*
I have cooked	I had cooked	I will have cooked
I have seen	I had seen	I will have seen

PROGRESSIVE TENSES

Present progressive	*Past progressive*	*Future progressive*
I am cooking	I was cooking	I will be cooking
I am seeing	I was seeing	I will be seeing

Present perfect progressive	*Past perfect progressive*	*Future perfect progressive*
I have been cooking	I had been cooking	I will have been cooking
I have been seeing	I had been seeing	I will have been seeing

Some irregular verbs, such as *go,* form their simple present tense following the same rules as regular verbs (*go/goes*). Other irregular verbs, such as *be* and *have,* are special cases for which you should learn the correct forms.

I am, I have	we are, we have
you are, you have	you are, you have
he/she/it is, he/she/it has	they are, they have

You can use the simple present tense for an action happening right now ("I *welcome* this news"), happening repeatedly in the present ("Judy *goes* to church every Sunday"), or ongoing in the present ("Wesley *likes* ice cream"). In some cases, if you want to ask a question, intensify the action, or form a negative, use the helping verb *do* or *does* before the main verb.

I *do think* you should take the job. I *don't think* it will be difficult.

Does Christos *want* it? *Do* you *want* it? *Doesn't* anyone *want* it?

You can use the simple present for future action: "Football *starts* Wednesday." With *before, after,* or *when,* use it to express a future meaning: "When the team bus *arrives,* the players will board." Use it also for a general or timeless truth, even if the rest of the sentence is in a different tense:

Columbus proved in 1492 that the world *is* round.

Mr. Hammond will argue that people *are* basically good.

3h Use the simple past tense for actions already completed.

Regular verbs form the past tense by adding *-d* or *-ed* to the infinitive; the past tense of irregular verbs must be memorized. Use the past tense for an action at a specific past time, stated or implied.

> Jack *enjoyed* the party. [Regular verb]

> Akira *went* home early. [Irregular verb]

Though speakers may not pronounce the *-d* or *-ed* ending, standard written English requires that you add it to regular past tense verbs.

> NONSTANDARD   I *use* to wear weird clothes when I was a child.

> STANDARD   I *used* to wear weird clothes when I was a child.

In the past tense, you can use the helping verb *did* (past tense of *do*) to ask a question or intensify the action. Use *did* (or *didn't*) with the infinitive form of the main verb for both regular and irregular verbs.

I went.	I did go.	Why did I go?
You saw.	You did see.	What did you see?
She ran.	She did run.	Where did she run?

3i Use the simple future tense for actions that are expected to happen but have not happened yet.

Although the present tense can indicate future action ("We *go* on vacation next Monday"), most actions that have not yet taken place are expressed in the simple future tense, including promises and predictions.

> George *will arrive* in time for dinner.

> *Will* you please *show* him where to park?

To form the simple future tense, add *will* to the infinitive form of the verb.

I will go	we will go
you will go	you will go
he/she/it will go	they will go

You can also use *shall* to inject a tone of determination ("We *shall* overcome!") or in polite questions ("*Shall* we dance?").

3j Use the perfect tenses for actions completed at the time of another action.

The present perfect, past perfect, and future perfect tenses consist of a form of the helping verb *have* plus the past participle (*-ed* or *-en* form). The tense of *have* indicates the tense of the whole verb phrase.

For practice, visit
**<bedfordstmartins
.com/bedguide>**.

ESL Guidelines 🌐 Negatives

You can make a sentence negative by using **not** or another negative adverb such as *seldom, rarely, never, hardly, hardly ever,* or *almost never.*

- With **not:** subject + helping verb + **not** + main verb

  Gina did *not* go to the concert.

  They will *not* call again.

- For questions: helping verb + *n't* (contraction for *not*) + subject + main verb

  Didn't [for *Did not*] Gina go to the concert?

  Won't [for *Will not*] they call again?

- With a negative adverb: subject + negative adverb + main verb *or* subject + helping verb + negative adverb + main verb

  My son *seldom* watches TV.

  Danh may *never* see them again.

- With a negative adverb at the beginning of a clause: negative adverb + helping verb + subject + verb

  Not only does Emma struggle with tennis, but she also struggles with golf.

  Never before have I been so happy.

NOTE: Do not pile up several negatives for intensity or emphasis in a sentence. Readers may consider double negatives (*not never, not hardly, wouldn't not*) sloppy repetition or assume that two negatives cancel each other out.

FAULTY	The students did *not never* arrive late.
CORRECT	The students did *not* ever arrive late.
CORRECT	The students *never* arrived late.

The action of a **present perfect** verb was completed before the sentence is uttered. Its helping verb is in the present tense: *have* or *has.*

I *have* never *been* to Spain, but I *have been* to Mexico.

Have you *seen* Mr. Grimaldi? Mr. Grimaldi *has gone* home.

You can use the present perfect tense for an action completed before some other action: "I *have washed* my hands of the whole affair, but I am watching from a distance." With *for* or *since,* it shows an action begun in the past and still going on: "Max *has worked* in this office for years."

The action of a **past perfect** verb was completed before some other action in the past. Its helping verb is in the past tense: *had*.

The concert *had ended* by the time we found a parking space.

Until I met her, I *had* not *pictured* Jenna as a redhead.

Had you *wanted* to clean the house before your parents arrived?

In informal writing, the simple past may be used when the relationship between actions is made clear by *when, before, after,* or *until*.

Observers *saw* the plane catch fire before it landed.

The action of a **future perfect** verb will be completed by some point (specified or implied) in the future. Its helping verb is in the future tense: *will have*.

The builders *will have finished* the house by June.

When you get the new dime, *will* you *have collected* every coin you want?

The store *will* not *have closed* by the time we get there.

3k Use the simple progressive tenses for actions in progress.

The present progressive, past progressive, and future progressive tenses consist of a form of the helping verb *be* plus the present participle (the *-ing* form). The tense of *be* determines the tense of the whole verb phrase.

The **present progressive** expresses an action that began in the past and is taking place now. Its helping verb is in the present tense: *am, is,* or *are*.

I *am thinking* of a word that starts with *R*.

Is Stefan *babysitting* while Marie *is visiting* her sister?

You can express future action with the present progressive of *go* plus an infinitive phrase or with other words that make the time clear.

Are you *going to sign up* for the CPR class? Jeff *is taking* it Monday.

Use the present tense, not the present progressive, when verbs express being or emotion (*seem, be, belong, need*) rather than action.

I *guess* that the library is open. I *like* to study there.

The **past progressive** expresses an action that took place continuously at some time in the past, whether or not that action is still going on. Its helping verb is in the past tense: *was* or *were*.

The old men *were sitting* on the porch when we passed.

Lucy *was planning* to take the weekend off.

The **future progressive** expresses an action that will take place continuously at some time in the future. Its helping verb is in the future tense: *will be*. It also can use a form of *be* with *going to be*.

They *will be answering* the phones while she is gone.

She *is going to be flying* to Rome.

Will we *be dining* out every night on our vacation?

31 Use the perfect progressive tenses for continuing actions that began earlier.

Use the present perfect, the past perfect, or the future perfect progressive tense for an action that began earlier and did, does, or will continue.

The **present perfect progressive** indicates an action that started in the past and is continuing in the present. Form it by adding the present perfect of *be* (*has been, have been*) to the present participle (*-ing* form) of the main verb. Often *for* or *since* are used with this tense.

Fred *has been complaining* about his neighbor since the wild parties began.

Have you *been reading* Uma's postcards from England?

The **past perfect progressive** expresses a continuing action that was completed before another past action. Form it by adding the past perfect of *be* (*had been*) to the present participle of the main verb.

By the time Khalid finally arrived, I *had been waiting* for half an hour.

The **future perfect progressive** expresses an action that is expected to continue into the future for a specific time and then end before or continue beyond another future action. Form it by adding *will have been* to the present participle of the main verb.

They *will have been driving* for three days by the time they get to Oregon.

By fall Joanne *will have been attending* school longer than anyone else I know.

Exercise 3–2 ▪ Identifying Verb Tenses

For more practice, visit **<bedfordstmartins .com/bedguide>**.

Underline each verb or verb phrase and identify its tense in the following sentences. Answers for the lettered sentences appear in the back of the book. Example:

John is living in Hinsdale, but he prefers Joliet.

John is living [present progressive] in Hinsdale, but he prefers [simple present] Joliet.

a. He has been living like a hunted animal ever since he hacked into the university computer lab in order to change all of his grades.

b. I have never appeared on a reality television show, and I will never appear on one unless my family gets selected.

c. James had been at the party for only fifteen minutes when his host suddenly pitched the caterer into the swimming pool.

d. As of next month, I will have been studying karate for six years, and I will be taking the test for my orange belt in July.

e. The dachshund was running at its fastest speed, but the squirrel strolled toward the tree without fear.

1. As of May 1, Ira and Sandy will have been going together for a year.
2. She will be working in her study if you need her.
3. Have you been hoping that Carlos will come to your party?
4. I know that he will not yet have returned from Chicago.
5. His parents had been expecting him home any day until they heard that he was still waiting for the bus.

Voice

> Intelligent students read challenging books.

> Challenging books are read by intelligent students.

These two statements convey similar information, but their emphasis is different. In the first sentence, the subject (*students*) performs the verb's action (*read*); in the second sentence, the subject (*books*) receives the verb's action (*are read*). One sentence states its idea directly, the other indirectly. We say that the first sentence is in the **active voice** and the second is in the **passive voice.**

3m Use the active voice rather than the passive voice.

Verbs in the **active voice** consist of principal parts and helping verbs. Verbs in the **passive voice** consist of the past participle (*-ed* or *-en* form) preceded by a form of *be* ("you *are given*," "I *was given*," "she *will be given*"). Most writers prefer the active to the passive voice because it is clearer and simpler, requires fewer words, and identifies the actor and the action more explicitly.

ACTIVE VOICE   *Sergeants give* orders. *Privates obey* them.

Normally the subject of a sentence is the focus of readers' attention. If that subject does not perform the verb's action but instead receives the action, readers may wonder: What did the writer mean to emphasize?

PASSIVE VOICE   *Orders are given* by sergeants. *They are obeyed* by privates.

Other writers misuse the passive voice to try to lend pomp to a humble truth (or would-be truth). For example, "Slight technical difficulties are being experienced" may replace "The airplane needs repairs." Some even use the passive voice deliberately to obscure the truth.

You do not need to drop the passive voice entirely from your writing. Sometimes the performer of a verb's action is irrelevant, as in a lab report, which emphasizes the research, not the researcher. Sometimes the performer is understood: "Automobiles are built in Detroit." (It is understood that they are built *by people*.) Other times the performer is unknown and simply omitted: "Many fortunes were lost in the stock market crash of 1929." It's a good idea, though, to substitute the active voice for the passive unless you have a good reason for using the passive.

Exercise 3–3 ▪ Using Active and Passive Voice Verbs

For more practice, visit **<bedfordstmartins .com/bedguide>**.

Revise the following passage, changing the passive voice to the active voice in each sentence, unless you can justify keeping the passive. Example:

> The Galápagos Islands were reached by many species of animals in ancient times.

> Many species of animals *reached* the Galápagos Islands in ancient times.

The unique creatures of the Galápagos Islands have been studied by many scientists. The islands were explored by Charles Darwin in 1835. His observations led to the theory of evolution, which he explained in *On the Origin of Species*. Thirteen species of finches on the islands were discovered by Darwin, all descended from a common stock; even today this variety of species can be seen by visitors to the islands. Each island species has evolved by adapting to local conditions. A twig is used by the woodpecker finch to probe trees for grubs. Algae on the ocean floor are fed on by the marine iguana. Salt water can be drunk by the Galápagos cormorant, thanks to a salt-extracting gland. Because of the tameness of these animals, they can be studied by visitors at close range.

Mood

Still another characteristic of every verb is its **mood: indicative, imperative,** or **subjunctive.** The indicative mood is the most common. The imperative and subjunctive moods add valuable versatility.

3n **Use the indicative mood to state a fact, to ask a question, or to express an opinion.**

Most verbs in English are in the indicative mood.

FACT	Danika *left* home two months ago.
QUESTION	*Will* she *find* happiness as a belly dancer?
OPINION	I *think* not.

3o   Use the imperative mood to make a request or to give a command or direction.

The understood but usually unstated subject of a verb in the imperative mood is *you*. The verb's form is the base form or infinitive.

REQUEST	Please *be* there before noon. [*You* please be there. . . .]
COMMAND	*Hurry!* [*You* hurry!]
DIRECTION	*Drive* east on State Street. [*You* drive east. . . .]

3p   Use the subjunctive mood to express a wish, requirement, suggestion, or condition contrary to fact.

The subjunctive mood is used in a subordinate clause to suggest uncertainty: the action expressed by the verb may or may not actually take place as specified. In any clause opening with *that* and expressing a requirement, the verb is in the subjunctive mood and takes the base or infinitive form.

For practice, visit
**<bedfordstmartins
.com/bedguide>**.

ESL Guidelines 🌐 Conditionals

Conditional sentences usually contain an *if* clause, which states the condition, and a result clause.

- When the condition is true or possibly true in the present or future, use the present tense in the *if* clause and the present or future tense in the result clause. The future tense is not used in the *if* clause.

    If Jane *prepares* her essay early, she usually *writes* very well.

    If Maria *saves* enough money, she *will buy* a car.

- When the condition is not true in the present, for most verbs use the past tense in the *if* clause; for the verb **be,** use **were.** Use **would, could,** or **might** + infinitive form in the result clause.

    If Carlos *had* a computer, he *would need* a monitor, too.

    If Claudia *were* here, she *could do* it herself.

- When the condition was not true in the past, use the past perfect tense in the *if* clause. If the possible result was in the past, use **would have, could have,** or **might have** + past participle (*-ed* or *-en* form) in the result clause. If the possible result is in the present, use **would, could,** or **might** + infinitive form in the result clause.

    If Claudia *had saved* enough money, she *could have bought* a car. [Result in the past]

    If Annie *had finished* law school, she *might* be a successful lawyer now. [Result in the present]

Professor Vogt requires that every student *complete* the essay promptly.

She asked that we *be* on time for all meetings.

When you use the subjunctive mood to describe a condition that is contrary to fact, use *were* if the verb is *be*; for other verbs, use the simple past tense. Wishes, whether present or past, follow the same rules.

If I *were* rich, I would be happy.

If I *had* a million dollars, I would be happy.

Elissa wishes that Ted *were* more goal oriented.

Elissa wished that Ted *knew* what he wanted to do.

For a condition that was contrary to fact at some point in the past, use the past perfect tense.

If I *had been* awake, I would have seen the meteor showers.

If Jessie *had known* you were coming, she would have cleaned her room.

Although use of the subjunctive has grown scarcer over the years, it still sounds crude to write "If I *was* you. . . ." If you ever feel that the subjunctive makes a sentence sound stilted, rewrite it with an infinitive phrase.

Professor Vogt requires every student *to complete* the essay promptly.

infinitive: The base form of a verb, often preceded by *to* (*to go*, *to play*)

Exercise 3–4 ■ Using the Correct Mood of Verbs

Find and correct any errors in mood in the following sentences. Identify the mood of the incorrect verb as well as its correct replacement. Some sentences may be correct. Answers for the lettered sentences appear in the back of the book. Example:

For more practice, visit <bedfordstmartins .com/bedguide>.

The law requires that each person files a tax return by April 15.

The law requires that each person *file* a tax return by April 15.
[Incorrect: *files*, indicative; correct: *file*, subjunctive]

a. Dr. Belanger recommended that Juan flosses his teeth every day.

b. If I was you, I would have done the same thing.

c. Tradition demands that Daegun shows respect for his elders.

d. Please attends the training lesson if you plan to skydive later today.

1. If she was slightly older, she could stay home by herself.

2. If they have waited a little longer, they would have seen some amazing things.

3. Emilia's contract stipulates that she works on Saturdays.

4. If James invested in the company ten years ago, he would have made a lot of money.

For more on editing for subject-verb agreement, see A4 in the Quick Editing Guide, pp. A-42–A-43.

4 | Subject-Verb Agreement

What does it mean for a subject and a verb to agree? Practically speaking, it means that their forms match: plural subjects take plural verbs, third-person subjects take third-person verbs, and so forth. When your subjects and verbs agree, you prevent a mismatch that could distract readers from your message.

subject: The part of a sentence that names something—a person, an object, an idea, a situation—about which the predicate makes an assertion: The *king* lives.

verb: A word that shows action (The cow *jumped* over the moon) or a state of being (The cow *is* brown)

4a A verb agrees with its subject in person and number.

Subject and verb agree in person (first, second, or third):

> *I write* my research papers on my laptop. [Subject and verb in first person]

> *Eamon writes* his papers in the lab. [Subject and verb in third person]

Subject and verb agree in number (singular or plural):

> *Grace has enjoyed* college. [Subject and verb singular]

> *She and Jim have enjoyed* their vacation. [Subject and verb plural]

The present tense of most verbs is the infinitive form, with no added ending except in the third-person singular. (See 3g–3l.)

I enjoy	we enjoy
you enjoy	you enjoy
he/she/it enjoys	they enjoy

Forms of the verb *be* vary.

I am	we are
you are	you are
he/she/it is	they are

4b A verb agrees with its subject, not with any words that intervene.

> My *favorite* of O. Henry's short stories *is* "The Gift of the Magi."

> *Home sales,* once driving the local economy, *have fallen* during recent years.

A singular subject linked to another noun or pronoun by a preposi-
tional phrase beginning with wording such as *along with, as well as,* or *in addition to* remains a singular subject and takes a singular verb.

prepositional phrase: The preposition and its object (a noun or pronoun), plus any modifiers: *in the bar, under a rickety table*

> My cousin *James* as well as his wife and son *plans* to vote for Levine.

4c   Subjects joined by *and* usually take a plural verb.

In most cases, a compound subject takes a plural verb.

> *"Howl" and "Gerontion" are* Barry's favorite poems.
>
> *Sugar, salt, and fat* adversely *affect* people's health.

However, phrases like *each boy and girl* or *every dog and cat* consider subjects individually, as "each one" or "every one," and use a singular verb.

> *Each man and woman* in the room *has* a different story to tell.

Use a singular verb for two singular subjects that form or are one thing.

> *Lime juice and soda quenches* your thirst.

compound subject: A subject consisting of two or more nouns or pronouns linked by *and: Scott and Liz drove home.*

4d   With subjects joined by *or* or *nor,* the verb agrees with the part of the subject nearest to it.

> Either they or *Max is* guilty.

Subjects containing *not . . . but* follow this rule also.

> Not we but *George knows* the whole story.

You can remedy awkward constructions by rephrasing.

> Either they are guilty or Max is.
>
> We do not know the whole story, but George does.

4e   Most collective nouns take singular verbs.

When a collective noun refers to a group of people acting as one, use a singular verb.

> The *jury finds* the defendant guilty.

When the members of the group act individually, use a plural verb.

> The *jury do* not yet *agree* on a verdict.

If you feel that using a plural verb results in an awkward sentence, re-word the subject so that it refers to members of the group individually.

> The *jurors do* not yet *agree* on a verdict.

collective noun: A singular noun that represents a group of people or items, such as *committee, family, jury, trio*

For more on agreement with collective nouns, see 7e.

4f   Most indefinite pronouns take a third-person singular verb.

The indefinite pronouns *each, one, either, neither, anyone, anybody, anything, everyone, everybody, everything, no one, nobody, nothing, someone, somebody,* and *something* are considered singular and take a third-person singular verb.

> *Someone is bothering* me.

For a list of indefinite pronouns, see A6 in the Quick Editing Guide, pp. A-44–A-46.

Even when one of these subjects is followed by a phrase containing a noun or pronoun of a different person or number, use a singular verb.

Each of you *is* here to stay.

One of the pandas *seems* dangerously ill.

4g The indefinite pronouns *all, any,* and *some* use a singular or plural verb, depending on their meaning.

I have no explanation. *Is any* needed?

Any of the changes considered critical *have* been made already.

All is lost.

All of the bananas *are gone.*

Some of the blame *is* mine.

Some of us *are* Democrats.

For more on agreement with indefinite pronouns, see 7d.

None—like *all, any,* and *some*—takes a singular or a plural verb, depending on the sense in which the pronoun is used.

None of you *is* exempt.

None of his wives *were* blond.

4h In a subordinate clause with a relative pronoun as the subject, the verb agrees with the antecedent.

For more information on subordination, see 14d–14f.

To determine the person and number of the verb in a subordinate clause whose subject is *who, which,* or *that,* look back at the word to which the pronoun refers. This word, known as an antecedent, is usually (but not always) the noun closest to the relative pronoun.

relative pronoun: A pronoun (*who, which, that, what, whom, whomever, whose*) that opens a subordinate clause, modifying a noun or pronoun in another clause: The gift *that* I received is very practical.

I have a roommate *who studies* day and night.
[The antecedent of *who* is the third-person singular noun *roommate.* Therefore, the verb in the subordinate clause is third-person singular, *studies.*]

I bought one of the new cars *that have* defective brakes.
[The antecedent of *that* is *cars,* so the verb is third-person plural, *have.*]

This is the only one of the mayor's new ideas *that has* any worth.
[Here *one,* not *ideas,* is the antecedent of *that.* Thus, the verb in the subordinate clause is third-person singular, *has,* not *have.*]

4i A verb agrees with its subject even when the subject follows the verb.

Introductory expressions such as *there* or *here* change the ordinary order so that the subject follows the verb. Remember that verbs agree with subjects and that *here* and *there* are never subjects.

Here *is* a *riddle* for you.

There *are* forty *people* in my law class.

Under the bridge *were* a broken-down *boat and* a worn *tire*.

4j A linking verb agrees with its subject, not its subject complement.

When a form of the verb *be* links two or more nouns, the subject is the noun before the linking verb. Nouns that follow the linking verb are subject complements. Make the verb agree with the subject of the sentence, not the subject complement.

> *Jim is* a gentleman and a scholar.
>
> Amy's *parents are* her most enthusiastic audience.

4k When the subject is a title, use a singular verb.

> When I was younger, *Harry Potter and the Sorcerer's Stone was* my favorite book.
>
> *"People"* sung by Barbra Streisand *is* my aunt's favorite song.

4l Singular nouns that end in *-s* take singular verbs.

Some nouns look plural even though they refer to a singular subject: *measles, logistics, mathematics, electronics.* Such nouns take singular verbs.

> The *news is* that *economics has become* one of the most popular majors.

linking verb: A verb (*is, become, seem, feel*) that shows a state of being by linking the sentence subject with a word that renames or describes the subject: The sky *is* blue. (See 3a.)

subject complement: A noun, an adjective, or a group of words that follows a linking verb and renames or describes the subject: This plum tastes *ripe*. (See 3a.)

For more practice, visit **<bedfordstmartins .com/bedguide>**.

Exercise 4–1 ▪ Making Subjects and Verbs Agree

Find and correct any subject-verb agreement errors in the following sentences. Some sentences may be correct. Answers for the lettered sentences appear in the back of the book. Example:

> Addressing the audience tonight is the nominees for club president.
>
> Addressing the audience tonight *are* the nominees for club president.

a. For many college graduates, the process of looking for jobs are often long and stressful.

b. Not too long ago, searching the classifieds and inquiring in person was the primary methods of job hunting.

c. Today, however, everyone also seem to use the Internet to search for openings or to e-mail their résumés.

d. My classmates and my cousin sends most résumés over the Internet because it costs less than mailing them.

e. All of the résumés arrives quickly when they are sent electronically.

1. There are many people who thinks that interviewing is the most stressful part of the job search.

2. Sometimes only one person conducts an interview, while other times a whole committee conduct it.

3. Either the interviewer or the committee usually begin by asking simple questions about your background.

4. Making eye contact, dressing professionally, and appearing confident is some of the qualities an interviewer may consider important.

5. After an interview, most people sends a thank-you letter to the person who conducted it.

For advice on editing pronoun case, see A5 in the Quick Editing Guide, pp. A-43–A-44.

5 | Pronoun Case

As you know, pronouns come in distinctive forms. The first-person pronoun can be *I*, or it can be *me, my, mine, we, us, our,* or *ours.* Which form do you pick? It depends on what job you want the pronoun to do.

Depending on a pronoun's function in a sentence, we say that it is in the **subjective case,** the **objective case,** or the **possessive case.** Some pronouns change form when they change case, and some do not. The personal pronouns *I, he, she, we,* and *they* and the relative pronoun *who* have different forms in the subjective, objective, and possessive cases. Other pronouns, such as *you* and *it* have only two forms: the plain case (which serves as both subjective and objective) and the possessive case.

We can pin the labels *subjective, objective,* and *possessive* on nouns as well as on pronouns. Like the pronouns *you* and *it,* nouns shift from plain form only in the possessive (*teacher's* pet, *Jonas's* poodle, her *parents'* home).

When you are not sure which case to choose, beware of falling back on a reflexive pronoun (*myself, himself*). Instead of writing, "Return the form to John or *myself*" or "John and *myself* are in charge," replace the reflexive pronoun: "Return the form to John or *me*"; "John and *I* are in charge."

5a Use the subjective case for the subject of a sentence or clause.

Jed and *I* ate the granola.

Who cares?

Maya recalled that *she* played baseball.

Election officials are the people *who* count.

A pronoun serving as the subject for a verb is subjective even when the verb isn't written but is only implied:

Jed is hungrier than *I* [am].

subject: The part of a sentence that names something—a person, an object, an idea, a situation—about which the predicate makes an assertion: The *king* lives.

Don't be fooled by a pronoun that appears immediately after a verb, looking as if it were a direct object but functioning as the subject of a clause. The pronoun's case is determined by its role, not by its position.

The judge didn't believe *I* hadn't been the driver.

We were happy to interview *whoever* was running. [Subject of *was running*]

5b Use the subjective case for a subject complement.

When a pronoun functions as a subject complement, it plays essentially the same role as the subject and its case is subjective.

The phantom graffiti artist couldn't have been *he*. It was *I*.

5c Use the subjective case for an appositive to a subject or subject complement.

A pronoun in apposition to a subject or subject complement is like an identical twin to the noun it stands beside. It has the same meaning and case.

The class *officers*—Ravi and *she*—announced a senior breakfast.

5d Use the objective case for a direct object, an indirect object, the object of a preposition, or a subject of an infinitive.

The custard pies hit *him* and *me*. [Direct object]

Mona threw *us* towels. [Indirect object]

Mona threw towels to *him* and *us*. [Object of a preposition]

We always expect *him* to win. [Subject of an infinitive]

5e Use the objective case for an appositive to a direct or indirect object or the object of a preposition.

Mona helped us *all*—Mrs. Van Dumont, *him*, and *me*.
[*Him* and *me* are in apposition to the direct object *us*.]

Bob gave his favorite *students*, Tom and *her*, an approving nod.
[*Her* is in apposition to the indirect object *students*.]

Yelling, the team ran after *us*—Mona, *him*, and *me*.
[*Him* and *me* are in apposition to *us*, the object of the preposition *after*.]

5f Use the possessive case to show ownership.

Possessive pronouns can function as adjectives or as nouns. *My, your, his, her, its, our,* and *their* function as adjectives by modifying nouns or pronouns.

My new bike is having *its* first road test today.

subject complement: A noun, an adjective, or a group of words that follows a linking verb (*is, become, feel, seem,* or another verb that shows a state of being) and that renames or describes the subject: This plum tastes *ripe*. (See 3a.)

appositive: A word or group of words that adds information by identifying a subject or object in a different way: my dog *Rover,* Hal's brother *Fred*

direct object: The target of a verb that completes the action performed by the subject or asserted about the subject: I met *the sheriff*.

indirect object: A person or thing affected by the subject's action, usually the recipient of the direct object, through the action indicated by a verb such as *bring, get, offer, promise, sell, show, tell,* and *write*: Charlene asked *you* a question.

object of a preposition: The noun or pronoun that follows the preposition (such as *in, on, at, of, from*) that connects it to the rest of the sentence: She opened the door to the *garage*.

infinitive: The base form of a verb, often preceded by *to*: *to go, to play*

The possessive pronoun *its* does not contain an apostrophe. *It's* with an apostrophe is a contraction for *it is*, as in "*It's* a beautiful day for bike riding."

The possessive pronouns *mine, yours, his, hers, ours,* and *theirs* can discharge the whole range of noun duties, serving as subjects, subject complements, direct objects, indirect objects, or objects of prepositions.

> *Yours* is the last vote we need. [Subject]
>
> This day is *ours*. [Subject complement]
>
> Don't take your car; take *mine*. [Direct object]
>
> If we're honoring requests, give *hers* top priority. [Indirect object]
>
> Give her request priority over *theirs*. [Object of a preposition]

5g Use the possessive case to modify a gerund.

A possessive pronoun (or possessive noun) is the appropriate escort for a gerund. As a noun, a gerund requires an adjective for a modifier.

> Mary is tired of *his griping*. [The possessive pronoun *his* modifies the gerund *griping*.]
>
> I can stand *their being* late every day but not *his drinking* on the job. [The possessive pronoun *their* modifies the gerund *being*; the possessive pronoun *his* modifies the gerund *drinking*.]

However, editing possessives can be confusing because two different verb forms both end in *-ing*: gerunds that act as nouns and present participles that act as adjectives. If you are not sure whether to use a possessive for a gerund or an objective pronoun with a word ending in *-ing*, look closely at your sentence. Which word—the pronoun or the *-ing* word—is the object of your main verb? That word functions as a noun; the other word modifies it.

> Mr. Phipps remembered *them* smoking in the boys' room. [Mr. Phipps remembers *them*, those naughty students. *Them* is the object of the verb, so *smoking* is a participle modifying *them*.]
>
> Mr. Phipps remembered *their* smoking in the boys' room. [Mr. Phipps remembers *smoking*, that nasty habit. The gerund *smoking* is the object of the verb, and the possessive pronoun *their* modifies it.]

In everyday speech, the rules about pronoun case apply less rigidly. Someone who correctly says, "To whom are you referring?" is likely to sound pretentious. Say, if you like, "It's *me*," but in formal situations write "It is *I*." Say, if you wish, "*Who* did he ask to the party?" but write "*Whom* did he ask?"

Exercise 5–1 ▪ Using Pronouns Correctly

Replace any pronouns used incorrectly in the following sentences. Explain why each pronoun was incorrect. (Consider all these examples as written—not spoken—English, so apply the rules strictly.) Some sentences may be

---

Sidebar notes (left margin):

For a chart of possessive personal pronouns, see C2 in the Quick Editing Guide, p. A-51.

gerund: A form of a verb, ending in *-ing*, that functions as a noun: Lacey likes *playing* in the steel band.

present participle: A form of a verb ending in *-ing* that cannot function alone as a main verb but can act as an adjective: *Leading* the pack, Michael crossed the finish line.

For more practice, visit <bedfordstmartins .com/bedguide>.

correct. Answers for the lettered sentences appear in the back of the book. Example:

> That is her, the new university president, at the podium.
>
> That is *she*, the new university president, at the podium. [*She* is a subject complement.]

a. I didn't appreciate you laughing at her and I.

b. Lee and me would be delighted to serenade whomever will listen.

c. The managers and us servers are highly trustworthy.

d. The neighbors were driven berserk by him singing.

e. Jerry and myself regard you and she as the very people who we wish to meet.

1. Have you guessed the identity of the person of who I am speaking?

2. It was him asking about the clock that started me suspecting him.

3. They—Jerry and her—are the troublemakers.

4. Mrs. Van Dumont awarded the prize to Mona and I.

5. The counterattack was launched by Dusty and myself.

6 | Pronoun Reference

The main use of pronouns is to refer in a brief, convenient form to some **antecedent** that has already been named. A pronoun usually has a noun or another pronoun as its antecedent. Often the antecedent is the subject or object of the same clause in which the pronoun appears.

> Josie hit the *ball* after *its* first bounce.
>
> Smashing into *Greg*, the ball knocked off *his* glasses.

The antecedent also can appear in a different clause or even a different sentence from the pronoun.

> *Josie* hit the *ball* when *it* bounced back to *her*.
>
> The *ball* smashed into *Greg*. *It* knocked off *his* glasses.

A pronoun as well as a noun can be an antecedent.

> My *dog* hid in the closet when *she* had *her* puppies. [*Dog* is the antecedent of *she*; *she* is the antecedent of *her*.]

6a Name the pronoun's antecedent: don't just imply it.

When editing, be sure you have identified clearly the antecedent of each pronoun. A writer who leaves a key idea unsaid is likely to confuse readers.

> VAGUE   Ted wanted a Norwegian canoe because he'd heard that *they* produce the lightest canoes afloat.

antecedent: The word to which a pronoun refers: *Lyn* plays golf, and *she* putts well.

For more on choosing *that* or *which,* see 21e.

For practice, visit
<bedfordstmartins .com/bedguide>.

ESL Guidelines 🌐 Adjective Clauses and Relative Pronouns

Be sure to use relative pronouns (*who, whose, which, that*) correctly in sentences with adjective clauses. Use *who,* not *which,* for a person. Select *that* to introduce necessary information that defines or specifies; reserve *which* for additional, but not defining, information.

- Do not omit the relative pronoun when it is the subject within the adjective clause.

  INCORRECT   The woman *gave us directions to the museum* told us not to miss the Picasso exhibit.

  CORRECT   The woman *who gave us directions to the museum* told us not to miss the Picasso exhibit.
  [*Who* is the subject of the adjective clause.]

- In speech and informal writing, you can imply (not state) a relative pronoun when it is the object of a verb or preposition within the adjective clause. In formal writing, you should use the relative pronoun.

  FORMAL   Jamal forgot to return the book *that I gave him.*
  [*That* is the object of *gave.*]

  INFORMAL   Jamal forgot to return the book *I gave him.*
  [The relative pronoun *that* is implied.]

  FORMAL   This is the box *in which we found the jewelry.*
  [*Which* is the object of the preposition *in.*]

  INFORMAL   This is the box *we found the jewelry in.*
  [The relative pronoun *which* is implied.]

NOTE: When the relative pronoun is omitted, the preposition moves to the end of the sentence but must not be left out.

- *Whose* is the only possessive form of a relative pronoun. It is used with persons, animals, and things.

  INCORRECT   I bought a chair *that its* legs were wobbly.

  CORRECT   I bought a chair *whose* legs were wobbly.

NOTE: When in doubt about a pronoun, you can rephrase the sentence: I bought a chair *with wobbly legs.*

What noun or pronoun does *they* refer to? Not to *Norwegian,* which is an adjective. We may guess that this writer has in mind Norwegian canoe builders, but no such noun has been mentioned. To make the sentence work, the writer must supply an antecedent for *they.*

CLEAR   Ted wanted a Norwegian canoe because he'd heard that Norway produces [*or* Norwegians produce] the lightest canoes afloat.

Watch out for possessive nouns. They won't work as antecedents.

VAGUE   On William's canoe, *he* painted a skull and bones.

CLEAR   On his canoe, William painted a skull and bones.

VAGUE   In Hemingway's story, he describes the powerful sea.

CLEAR   In the story, Hemingway describes the powerful sea.

6b Give the pronoun *it, this, that,* or *which* a clear antecedent.

Vagueness arises, thick as fog, whenever *it, this, that,* or *which* points to some-thing a writer assumes is said but indeed isn't. Often the best way out of the fog is to substitute a specific noun or expression for the pronoun.

VAGUE   I was an only child, and *it* was hard.

CLEAR   I was an only child, and my solitary life was hard.

VAGUE   Judy could not get along with her younger brother. *This* is the reason she wanted to get her own apartment.

CLEAR   Because Judy could not get along with her younger brother, she wanted to get her own apartment.

antecedent: The word to which a pronoun refers: *Lyn* plays golf, and *she* putts well.

6c Make the pronoun's antecedent clear.

Confusion strikes if a pronoun points in two or more directions. When more than one antecedent is possible, the reader wonders which the writer means.

CONFUSING   Hanwei shouted to Kenny to take off his burning sweater.

Whose sweater does *his* mean—Kenny's or Hanwei's? Simply changing a pronoun won't clear up the confusion. The writer needs to revise enough to move the two possible antecedents out of each other's way.

CLEAR   "Kenny!" shouted Hanwei. "Your sweater's on fire! Take it off!"

CLEAR   Flames were shooting from Kenny's sweater. Hanwei shouted to Kenny to take it off.

CLEAR   Hanwei realized that his sweater was on fire and shouted to Kenny for help.

6d Place the pronoun close to its antecedent to keep the relationship clear.

Watch out for distractions that slip in between noun and pronoun. If your sentence contains two or more nouns that look like antecedents to a pro-noun, your readers may become bewildered.

CONFUSING   Harper steered his dinghy alongside the cabin cruiser that the drug smugglers had left anchored under an overhanging willow in the tiny harbor and eased it to a stop.

What did Harper ease to a stop? By the time readers reach the end of the sentence, they are likely to have forgotten. To avoid confusion, keep the pronoun and its antecedent reasonably close together.

CLEAR   Harper steered his dinghy into the tiny harbor and eased it to a stop alongside the cabin cruiser that the drug smugglers had left anchored under an overhanging willow.

Never force your readers to stop and think, "What does that pronoun stand for?" You, the writer, have to do this thinking for them.

antecedent: The word to which a pronoun refers: *Lyn* plays golf, and *she* putts well.

Exercise 6–1 ▪ Making Pronoun Reference Clear

For more practice, visit **<bedfordstmartins .com/bedguide>**.

Revise each sentence or group of sentences so that any pronoun needing an antecedent clearly points to one. Possible revisions for the lettered sentences appear in the back of the book. Example:

> I took the money out of the wallet and threw it in the trash.
>
> I took the money out of the wallet and threw *the wallet* in the trash.

a. I could see the moon and the faint shadow of the tree as it began to rise.

b. Katrina spent the summer in Paris and traveled throughout Europe, which broadened her awareness of cultural differences.

c. Most managers want employees to work as many hours as possible. They never consider the work they need to do at home.

d. I worked twelve hours a day and never got enough sleep, but it was worth it.

e. Kevin asked Mike to meet him for lunch but forgot that he had class at that time.

1. Bill's prank frightened Josh and made him wonder why he had done it.

2. Korean students study up to twenty subjects a year, including algebra, calculus, and engineering. Because they are required, they must study them year after year.

3. Pedro Martinez signed a baseball for Chad that he had used in a game.

4. When the bottle hit the windshield, it shattered.

5. My friends believe they are more mature than many of their peers because of the discipline enforced at their school. However, it can also lead to problems.

---

7 | Pronoun-Antecedent Agreement

A pronoun's job is to fill in for a noun, much as an actor's double fills in for the actor. Pronouns are a short, convenient way to avoid repeating the noun.

> The sheriff drew a six-shooter; he fired twice.

In this action-packed sentence, first comes a noun (*sheriff*) and then a pronoun (*he*) that refers back to it. *Sheriff* is the antecedent of *he*. Just as verbs need to agree with their subjects, pronouns need to agree with the nouns they stand for without shifting number, person, or gender in midsentence.

7a Pronouns agree with their antecedents in person and number.

A pronoun matches its antecedent in person (first, second, or third) and in number (singular or plural), even when intervening words separate the pronoun and its antecedent.

For more on editing for pronoun-antecedent agreement, see A6 in the Quick Editing Guide, pp. A-44–A-46.

> FAULTY   All *campers* should bring *your* knapsacks

Here, noun and pronoun disagree in person: third person *campers*; second person *your*.

> FAULTY   Every *camper* should bring *their* knapsack.

Here, noun and pronoun disagree in number: singular *camper*; plural *their*.

> REVISED   All *campers* should bring *their* knapsacks.

> REVISED   Every *camper* should bring *his or her* knapsack. (See also 7f.)

7b Most antecedents joined by *and* require a plural pronoun.

A **compound subject** is plural; use a plural pronoun to refer to it.

> *George,* who has been here before, *and Jenn,* who hasn't, will need *their* maps.

If the nouns in a compound subject refer to the same person or thing, they make up a singular antecedent. Use a singular pronoun too.

> The *owner and founder* of this company carries *his* laptop everywhere.

compound subject: A subject consisting of two or more nouns or pronouns linked by *and*: *Scott and Liz drove home.*

7c A pronoun agrees with the closest part of an antecedent joined by *or* or *nor.*

If your subject is two or more nouns (or a combination of nouns and pronouns) connected by *or* or *nor,* look closely at the subject's parts. Are they all singular? If so, your pronoun should be singular.

> Neither *Joy nor Jean* remembered *her* book last week.

> If *Sam, Arthur, or Dieter* shows up, tell *him* I'm looking for *him.*

If the part of the subject closest to the pronoun is plural, the pronoun should be plural.

> Neither *Joy nor her sisters* rode *their* bikes today.

> If you see *Sam, Arthur, or their friends,* tell *them* I'm looking for *them.*

7d An antecedent that is a singular indefinite pronoun takes a singular pronoun.

For a list of indefinite pronouns, see A6 in the Quick Editing Guide, pp. A-44–A-46. For more on agreement with indefinite pronouns, see 4f and 7f.

Most indefinite pronouns (such as *everyone* and *anybody*) are singular in meaning, so the pronouns that refer to them are also singular.

> *Either* of the boys can do it, as long as *he's* on time.
>
> Warn *anybody* who's still in *her* swimsuit that a shirt is required for dinner.

An indefinite pronoun that is plural (such as *both, many*) takes a plural pronoun.

> Tell *both* the guests I will see *them* soon.

7e Most collective nouns used as antecedents require singular pronouns.

When the members of a group (such as a committee, family, jury, or trio) act as a unit, use a singular pronoun to refer to them.

> The *cast* for the play will be posted as soon as the director chooses *it*.

For more on agreement with collective nouns, see 4e.

When the group members act individually, use a plural pronoun.

> The *cast* will go *their* separate ways when summer ends.

7f A pronoun agrees with its antecedent in gender.

> If *one of your parents* brings you to camp, invite *him* for lunch.

For more on bias-free language, see 18.

While technically correct (the singular *he* refers to the singular *one*), this sentence overlooks the fact that some parents are male, some female.

> If *one of your parents* brings you to camp, invite *him or her* for lunch.
>
> If your *parents* bring you to camp, invite *them* for lunch.

Exercise 7-1 ■ Making Pronouns and Antecedents Agree

For more practice, visit **<bedfordstmartins .com/bedguide>**.

If any nouns and pronouns disagree in number, person, or gender in the following sentences, substitute pronouns that agree with the nouns. If you prefer, strengthen any sentence by rewriting it. Some sentences may be correct. Possible revisions for the lettered sentences appear in the back of the book. Example:

> A cat expects people to feed them often.
>
> A *cat* expects people to feed *it* often. *Or*
>
> *Cats* expect people to feed *them* often.

a. Many architects find work their greatest pleasure.

b. Neither Melissa nor James has received their application form yet.

c. He is the kind of man who gets their fun out of just sipping one's beer and watching his Saturday games on TV.

d. Many a mother has mourned the loss of their child.

e. When one enjoys one's work, it's easy to spend all your spare time thinking about it.

1. All students are urged to complete your registration on time.

2. When a baby doesn't know their own mother, they may have been born with some kind of vision deficiency.

3. Each member of the sorority has to make her own bed.

4. If you don't like the songs the choir sings, don't join them.

5. Young people should know how to protect oneself against AIDS.

8 | Adjectives and Adverbs

An adjective's job is to provide information about the person, place, object, or idea named by the noun or pronoun.

For advice on nouns and articles, see pp. 820–21.

> Karen bought a *small red* car.

> The radios *on sale* are an *excellent* value.

An adverb describes a verb, adjective, or other adverb.

> Karen bought her car *quickly*.

> The phones arrived *yesterday*; we put them *in the electronics department*.

For more on editing adjectives and adverbs, see A7 in the Quick Editing Guide, pp. A-46–A-47.

8a Use an adverb, not an adjective, to modify a verb, adjective, or another adverb.

FAULTY   Karen bought her car *quick*.

FAULTY   It's *awful* hot today.

Adjectives and Adverbs at a Glance

ADJECTIVES
1. Typically answer the question Which? or What kind?
2. Modify nouns or pronouns

ADVERBS
3. Answer the question How? When? Where? or sometimes Why?
4. Modify verbs, adjectives, and other adverbs

Though an informal speaker might get away with these sentences, a writer cannot. *Quick* and *awful* are adjectives, so they can modify only nouns or pronouns. Adverbs are needed to modify the verb *bought* and the adjective *hot*.

> EDITED　　Karen bought her car *quickly*.
>
> EDITED　　It's *awfully* hot today.

8b Use an adjective, not an adverb, as a subject complement or an object complement.

subject complement: A noun, an adjective, or a group of words that follows a linking verb (*is, become, feel, seem*, or another verb that shows a state of being) and renames or describes the subject: This plum tastes *ripe*. (See 3a.)

object complement: A noun, an adjective, or a group of words that renames or describes a direct object: The judges rated Hugo *the best skater*.

If we write, "Her old car looked awful," the adjective *awful* is a **subject complement**: it follows a linking verb and modifies the subject, *car*. An **object complement** completes the description of a direct object and can be an adjective or a noun, but never an adverb.

> Early to bed and early to rise makes a man *healthy, wealthy,* and *wise*.
> [Adjectives modifying the direct object *man*]

When you are not sure whether you're dealing with an object complement or an adverb, look closely at the word's role in the sentence. If it modifies a noun, it is an object complement and should be an adjective.

> The coach called the referee *stupid* and *blind*.
> [*Stupid* and *blind* are adjectives modifying the direct object *referee*.]

If it modifies a verb, you want an adverb instead.

> In fact, the ref had called the play *correctly*.
> [*Correctly* is an adverb modifying the verb *called*.]

8c Use *good* as an adjective and *well* as an adverb.

linking verb: A verb (*is, become, seem, feel*) that shows a state of being by linking the sentence subject with a word that renames or describes the subject: The sky *is* blue. (See 3a.)

> This sandwich tastes *good*. [The adjective *good* is a subject complement following the linking verb *tastes* and modifying the noun *sandwich*.]
>
> Al's skin healed *well* after surgery.
> [The adverb *well* modifies the verb *healed*.]

Only if the verb is a linking verb can you safely follow it with *good*. Other kinds of verbs need adverbs, not subject complements.

> FAULTY　　After a bad start, the game ended *good*.
>
> EDITED　　After a bad start, the game ended *well*.

Complications arise when we write or speak about health. It is perfectly correct to say *I feel good*, using the adjective *good* as a subject complement after the linking verb *feel*. However, generations of confusion have nudged the adverb *well* into the adjective category, too. A nurse may speak of "a well baby"; greeting cards urge patients to "get well"—meaning, "become healthy." Just as *healthy* is an adjective here, so is *well*.

ESL Guidelines 🌐 Cumulative Adjectives

Cumulative adjectives are two or more adjectives used directly before a noun and not separated by commas or the word *and*.

She is an *attractive older French* woman.

His *expressive large brown* eyes moved me.

Cumulative adjectives usually follow a specific order of placement before a noun. Use this list as a guide, but keep in mind that the order can vary.

1. Articles or determiners
   a, an, the, some, this, these, his, my, two, several
2. Evaluative adjectives
   beautiful, wonderful, hardworking, distasteful
3. Size or dimension
   big, small, huge, obese, petite, six-foot
4. Length or shape
   long, short, round, square, oblong, oval
5. Age
   old, young, new, fresh, ancient
6. Color
   red, pink, aquamarine, orange
7. Nation or place of origin
   American, Japanese, European, Bostonian, Floridian
8. Religion
   Protestant, Muslim, Hindu, Buddhist, Catholic, Jewish
9. Matter or substance
   wood, gold, cotton, plastic, pine, metal
10. Noun used as an adjective
    car (as in *car mechanic*), *computer* (as in *computer software*)

For advice on using commas with adjectives, see 21d.

For practice, visit <**bedfordstmartins.com/bedguide**>.

When someone asks, "How do you feel?" you can duck the issue with "Fine!" Otherwise, in speech *good* or *well* is acceptable; in writing, use *good*.

8d Form comparatives and superlatives of most adjectives and adverbs with *-er* and *-est* or *more* and *most*.

Comparatives and superlatives are forms that describe one thing in relation to another. Put most adjectives into comparative form (for two things) by adding *-er* and into superlative form (for three or more) by adding *-est*.

For practice, visit
<**bedfordstmartins
.com/bedguide**>.

ESL Guidelines 🌐 Count and Noncount Nouns and Articles

Count Nouns and Articles

Nouns referring to items that can be counted are called **count** (or **countable**) nouns. Count nouns can be made plural.

table, chair, egg   two *tables,* several *chairs,* a dozen *eggs*

Singular count nouns must be preceded by a **determiner.** The class of words called determiners includes **articles** (*a, an, the*), **possessives** (*John's, your, his, my,* and so on), **demonstratives** (*this, that, these, those*), **numbers** (*three, the third,* and so on), and **indefinite quantity words** (*no, some, many,* and so on).

a dog, *the* football, *one* reason, *the* first page, *no* chance

Noncount Nouns and Articles

Nouns referring to items that cannot be counted are called **noncount** (or **uncountable**) nouns. Noncount nouns cannot be made plural.

INCORRECT   I need to learn more *grammars.*

CORRECT   I need to learn more *grammar.*

- Common categories of noncount nouns include types of **food** (*cheese, meat, bread*), **solids** (*dirt, salt, chalk*), **liquids** (*milk, juice, gasoline*), **gases** (*methane, hydrogen, air*), and **abstract ideas,** including emotions (*democracy, gravity, love*).

- Another category of noncount nouns is **mass** nouns, which usually represent a large group of countable nouns (*furniture, mail, clothing*).

- The only way to count noncountable nouns is to use a countable noun with them, usually to indicate a quantity or a container.

  one *piece* of furniture, two *quarts* of water, an *example* of jealousy

- Noncount nouns, such as *advice,* are never preceded by an indefinite article; they are often preceded by *some.*

  INCORRECT   She gave us *a* good advice.

  CORRECT   She gave us good advice.

  CORRECT   She gave us *some* good advice.

- When noncount nouns are *general* in meaning, no article is required, but when the context makes them specific (usually in a phrase or a clause after the noun), the definite article is used.

  GENERAL   Good continues to fight *evil.*

  SPECIFIC   The *evil* that humans do lives after them.

indefinite article: An article (*a* or *an*) that indicates any one of many possible items: I will make *a* cake or *an* apple pie.

definite article: An article (*the*) that indicates one particular item: I ordered *the* spaghetti, not *the* lasagna.

ESL Guidelines 🌐 Definite and Indefinite Articles

The Definite Article (*the*)

- Use *the* with a specific count or noncount noun mentioned before or familiar to both the writer and the reader.

  She got a huge box in the mail. *The* box contained oranges from Florida. [*The* is used the second time the noun (*box*) is mentioned.]

  Did you feed *the* baby? [Both reader and writer know which baby.]

- Use *the* before specific count or noncount nouns when the reader is given enough information to identify what is being referred to.

  The furniture in my apartment is old and faded. [Specific furniture]

- Use *the* before a singular count noun to state a generality.

  The dog has been a companion for centuries. [*The dog* refers to all dogs.]

- Use *the* before some geographical names.

  Collective Nations: the United States, the United Kingdom

  Groups of Islands: the Bahamas, the Canary Islands

  Large Bodies of Water (except lakes): the Atlantic Ocean, the Dead Sea, the Monongahela River, the Gulf of Mexico

  Mountain Ranges: the Rockies, the Himalayas

- Use *the* or another determiner when plural count nouns name a definite or specific group; use no article when they name a general group.

  Hal is feeding *the horses* in the barn, and he has already fed *his cows*.

  Horses don't eat meat, and neither do *cows*.

The Indefinite Article (*a, an*)

- Use *a* or *an* with a nonspecific, singular count noun when it is not known to the reader or to the writer.

  Jay has *an* antique car.
  [The car's identity is unknown to the reader.]

  I saw *a* dog in my backyard this morning.
  [The dog's identity is unknown to the writer.]

- Use *a* or *an* when the noun is first used; use *the* when it is repeated.

  I saw *a* car that I would love to buy. *The* car was red with tan seats.

- Use *some* or no article with general noncount or plural nouns.

INCORRECT	I am going to buy *a* furniture for my apartment.
CORRECT	I am going to buy *some* furniture for my apartment.
CORRECT	I am going to buy furniture for my apartment.

count noun: A noun with both singular and plural forms that refers to an item that can be counted: *apple, apples*

noncount noun: A noun that cannot be made plural because it refers to an item that cannot be counted: *cheese, salt, air*

The budget deficit is *larger* than the trade deficit.

This year's trade deficit is the *largest* ever.

We usually form the comparative and superlative of potentially cumbersome long adjectives with *more* and *most* rather than with *-er* and *-est.*

The lake is *more beautiful* than I'd imagined.

The shoreline is the *most beautiful* in the region.

For short adverbs that do not end in *-ly,* usually add *-er* and *-est.* With all others, use *more* and *most.* (Also see 8f.)

The trade deficit grows *fastest* and *most uncontrollably* when exports are down.

For negative comparisons, use *less* and *least* for adjectives and adverbs.

Michael's speech was *less dramatic* than Louie's.

Paulette spoke *less dramatically* than Michael.

Use irregular adjectives and adverbs (such as *bad* and *badly*) with care.

Tom's golf game is *bad,* but no *worse* than George's.

Tom plays golf *badly,* but no *worse* than George does.

For a chart of comparative forms of irregular adjectives and adverbs, see A7 in the Quick Editing Guide, p. A-46.

8e Omit *more* and *most* with an adjective or adverb that is already comparative or superlative.

Some words become comparative or superlative when we tack on *-er* or *-est.* Others, such as *top, favorite,* and *unique,* mark whatever they modify as one of a kind. Neither category requires further assistance to make its point. To say "a *more worse* fate" or "my *most favorite* movie" is redundant.

FAULTY	Lisa is *more uniquely* qualified for the job than any other candidate.
EDITED	Lisa is *better* qualified for the job than any other candidate.
EDITED	Lisa is *uniquely* qualified for the job.

8f Use the comparative form of an adjective or adverb to compare two people or things, the superlative form to compare more than two.

No matter how wonderful something is, we can call it the *best* only when we compare it with more than one other thing. Any comparison between two things uses the comparative form (*better*), not the superlative (*best*).

FAULTY	Chocolate and vanilla are both good, but I like chocolate *best.*
EDITED	Chocolate and vanilla are both good, but I like chocolate *better.*

Exercise 8-1 ■ Using Adjectives and Adverbs Correctly

For more practice, visit <**bedfordstmartins .com/bedguide**>.

Find and correct any incorrect adjectives and adverbs in the following sentences. Some sentences may be correct. Answers for the lettered sentences appear in the back of the book. Example:

> The deal worked out good for both of us.
> The deal worked out *well* for both of us.

a. Credit-card debt is becoming increasing common among students.

b. Students often lack the necessary experience to use their credit cards wisely.

c. Some students charge many items on different cards and make only the lower payments possible each month.

d. Unfortunately, when juggling multiple credit cards, many students lose sight of how rapid the debt is accumulating.

e. It is a well idea to charge only as much as you can pay in full each month.

1. A popular trend in television today is voyeurism, or the act of secret watching people as they go about their daily lives.

2. In the late 1990s, the popularity of MTV's *The Real World* sparked increasingly interest in this concept.

3. Music videos and commercials also began to incorporate voyeuristic elements, although, of the two, videos used the technique most frequently.

4. With the millennium came a flood of new "reality" programs, all trying to capitalize more distinctively on the current trend.

5. On the program *Survivor,* contestants are filmed living in challenging settings with limited supplies, while viewers at home watch breathless to see how the contestants will behave.

---

9 | Shifts

Just as you can change position to view a scene from different vantage points, in your writing you can change the time or perspective. However, shifting tense or point of view unconsciously or unnecessarily within a passage creates ambiguity and confusion for readers.

9a Maintain consistency in verb tense.

In a passage or an essay, use the same verb tense unless the time changes.

INCONSISTENT	The driver *yelled* at us to get off the bus, so I *ask* him why, and he *tells* me it *is* none of my business.

tense: The time when the action of a verb did, does, or will occur

CONSISTENT PRESENT

The driver *yells* at us to get off the bus, so I *ask* him why, and he *tells* me it *is* none of my business.

CONSISTENT PAST

The driver *yelled* at us to get off the bus, so I *asked* him why, and he *told* me it *was* none of my business.

9b If the time changes, change the verb tense.

To write about events in the past, use past tense verbs. To write about events in the present, use present tense verbs. If the time shifts, change tense.

> I *do* not *like* the new television programs this year. The comedies *are* too realistic to be amusing, the adventure shows *don't have* much action, and the law enforcement dramas *drag* on and on. Last year the programs *were* different. The sitcoms *were* hilarious, the adventure shows *were* action packed, and the dramas *were* fast paced. I *prefer* last year's reruns to this year's shows.

The time and the verb tense change appropriately from present (*do like, are, don't have, drag*) to past (*were, were, were, were*) back to present (*prefer*), contrasting this year's *present* with last year's *past* programming.

NOTE: When writing about literature, the accepted practice is to use present tense verbs to summarize what happens in a story, poem, or play. When discussing other aspects of a work, use present tense for present time, past tense for past, and future tense for future.

> Steinbeck *wrote* "The Chrysanthemums" in 1937.
> [Past tense for past time]

> In "The Chrysanthemums," Steinbeck *describes* the Salinas Valley as "a closed pot" cut off from the world by fog.
> [Present tense for story summary]

9c Maintain consistency in the voice of verbs.

For more on using active and passive voice, see 3m.

Shifting unnecessarily from active to passive voice may confuse readers.

INCONSISTENT

My roommates and I *sit* up late many nights talking about our problems. Grades, teachers, jobs, money, and dates *are discussed* at length.

CONSISTENT

My roommates and I *sit* up late many nights talking about our problems. We *discuss* grades, teachers, jobs, money, and dates at length.

9d Maintain consistency in person.

For more on pronoun forms, see 5 and also A5 in the Quick Editing Guide, pp. A-43–A-44.

Person indicates your perspective as a writer. First person (*I, we*) establishes a personal, informal relationship with readers as does second person (*you*), which brings readers into the writing. Third person (*he, she, it, they*) is more formal and objective. In a formal scientific report, second person is seldom appropriate, and first, if used, might be reserved for reporting procedures. In a personal essay, using *he, she,* or *one* to refer to yourself would sound stilted. Choose the person appropriate for your purpose, and stick to it.

INCONSISTENT   College *students* need transportation, but *you* need a job to pay for the insurance and the gasoline.

CONSISTENT   College *students* need transportation, but *they* need jobs to pay for the insurance and the gasoline.

INCONSISTENT   *Anyone* can go skydiving if *you* have the guts.

CONSISTENT   *Anyone* can go skydiving if *he or she* has the guts.

CONSISTENT   *You* can go skydiving if *you* have the guts.

9e Maintain consistency in the mood of verbs.

Avoid shifts in mood, usually from indicative to imperative.

For examples of the three moods of verbs, see 3n–3p.

INCONSISTENT   Counselors *advised* students to register early. Also *pay* tuition on time. [Shift from indicative to imperative]

CONSISTENT   Counselors *advised* students to register early. They also *advised* them to pay their tuition on time. [Both indicative]

9f Maintain consistency in level of language.

Attempting to impress readers, writers sometimes inflate their language or slip into slang or informal wording. The level of language should be appropriate to your purpose and your audience throughout an essay.

If you are writing a personal essay, use informal language.

INCONSISTENT   I felt like a typical tourist. I carried an expensive digital camera with lots of icons I didn't quite know how to decode. But I was in a quandary because there was such a plethora of picturesque tableaus to record for posterity.

Instead of suddenly shifting to formal language, the writer could end simply: *But with so much beautiful scenery all around, I couldn't decide where to start.*

If you are writing an academic essay, use formal language.

INCONSISTENT   Puccini's *Turandot* is set in a China of legends, riddles, and fantasy. Brimming with beautiful melodies, this opera is music drama at its most spectacular. It rules!

Cutting the last sentence avoids an unnecessary shift in formality.

Exercise 9-1 ▪ Maintaining Grammatical Consistency

For more practice, visit <bedfordstmartins .com/bedguide>.

Revise the following sentences to eliminate shifts in verb tense, voice, mood, person, and level of language. Possible revisions for the lettered sentences appear in the back of the book. Example:

> I needed the job at the restaurant, so I tried to tolerate the insults of my boss, but a person can take only so much.

> I needed the job at the restaurant, so I tried to tolerate the insults of my boss, but *I could* take only so much.

a. Dr. Jamison is an erudite professor who cracks jokes in class.

b. The audience listened intently to the lecture, but the message was not understood.

c. Scientists can no longer evade the social, political, and ethical consequences of what they did in the laboratory.

d. To have good government, citizens must become informed on the issues. Also, be sure to vote.

e. Good writing is essential to success in many professions, especially in business, where ideas must be communicated in down-to-earth lingo.

1. Our legal system made it extremely difficult to prove a bribe. If the charges are not proven to the satisfaction of a jury or a judge, then we jump to the conclusion that the absence of a conviction demonstrates the innocence of the subject.

2. Before Morris K. Udall, Democrat from Arizona, resigns his seat in the U.S. House of Representatives, he helped preserve hundreds of acres of wilderness.

3. Anyone can learn another language if you have the time and the patience.

4. The immigration officer asked how long we planned to stay, so I show him my letter of acceptance from Tulane.

5. Archaeologists spent many months studying the site of the African city of Zimbabwe, and many artifacts were uncovered.

10 | Misplaced and Dangling Modifiers

The purpose of a **modifier,** such as an adjective or adverb, is to give readers more information. To do so, the modifier must be linked clearly to whatever it is meant to modify or describe. If you wrote, "We saw a stone wall around a house on a grassy hill, beautiful and distant," your readers would have to guess what was *beautiful* and *distant:* the wall, the house, or the hill. Edit your modifiers—especially prepositional phrases and subordinate clauses—to make sure each is in the right place.

For more on editing for misplaced or dangling modifiers, see B1 in the Quick Editing Guide, p. A-47.

10a Keep modifiers close to what they modify.

Misplaced modifiers—phrases and clauses that wander away from what they modify—produce results more likely to amuse readers than to inform them. Place your modifiers as close as possible to whatever they modify.

MISPLACED	She offered toys to all the children in colorful packages. [Does the phrase *in colorful packages* modify *toys* or *children*?]
CLEAR	She offered toys in colorful packages to all the children.
MISPLACED	We need to remove the dishes from the crates that got chipped. [Does the clause *that got chipped* modify *dishes* or *crates*?]
CLEAR	We need to remove from the crates the dishes that got chipped.

10b Place each modifier so that it clearly modifies only one thing.

A **squinting modifier** is one that looks two ways, leaving the reader uncertain whether it modifies the word before or after it. To avoid ambiguity, place your modifier close to the word it modifies and away from another that might cause confusion.

SQUINTING The book that appealed to Amy *tremendously* bored Marcus.

CLEAR The book that *tremendously* appealed to Amy bored Marcus.

CLEAR The book that appealed to Amy bored Marcus *tremendously*.

Exercise 10-1 ▪ Placing Modifiers

For more practice, visit **<bedfordstmartins.com/bedguide>**.

Revise the following sentences, which contain modifiers that are misplaced or squinting. Possible revisions for the lettered sentences appear in the back of the book. Example:

Patti found the cat using a flashlight in the dark.

Using a flashlight in the dark, Patti found the cat.

a. The bus got stuck in a ditch full of passengers.
b. He was daydreaming about fishing for trout in the middle of a meeting.
c. The boy threw the paper airplane through an open window with a smirk.
d. I reached for my sunglasses when the glare appeared from the glove compartment.
e. High above them, Sally and Glen watched the kites drift back and forth.

1. In her soup she found a fly at one of the best restaurants in town.
2. Andy learned how to build kites from the pages of an old book.
3. Alex vowed to return to the island sometime soon on the day he left it.
4. The fish was carried in a suitcase wrapped in newspaper.
5. The reporters were informed of the crimes committed by a press release.

10c State something in the sentence for each modifier to modify.

main clause: A group of words that has both a subject and a verb and can stand alone as a complete sentence: *My friends play softball.*

Generally readers assume that a modifying phrase at the start of a sentence refers to the subject of the main clause to follow. If readers encounter a modifying phrase midway through a sentence, they assume that it modifies something just before or (less often) after it.

Feeling tired after the long hike, Jason went to bed.

Alicia, while sympathetic, was not inclined to help.

Sometimes a writer slips up, allowing a modifying phrase to dangle. A **dangling modifier** is one that doesn't modify anything in its sentence.

DANGLING   *Noticing a pain behind his eyes,* an aspirin seemed a good idea. [The opening doesn't modify *aspirin* or, in fact, anything.]

To correct a dangling modifier, first figure out what noun, pronoun, or noun phrase the modifier is meant to modify. Then make that word or phrase the subject of the main clause.

CLEAR   *Noticing a pain behind his eyes,* he decided to take an aspirin.

Another way to correct a dangling modifier is to turn the dangler into a clause that includes the missing noun or pronoun.

DANGLING   Her progress, *although talented,* has been slowed by poor work habits.

CLEAR   *Although she is talented,* her progress has been slowed by poor work habits.

Sometimes rewriting will clarify what the modifier modifies.

CLEAR   *Although talented,* she has been hampered by poor work habits.

Exercise 10-2 ▪ Revising Dangling Modifiers

Revise any sentences that contain dangling modifiers. Some sentences may be correct. Possible revisions for the lettered sentences appear in the back of the book. Example:

For more practice, visit <bedfordstmartins.com/bedguide>.

Angry at her poor showing, geology would never be Joan's favorite class.
Angry at her poor showing, Joan knew that geology would never be her favorite class.

a. Unpacking the suitcase, a horrible idea occurred to me.
b. After fixing breakfast that morning, the oven might be left on at home.
c. Trying to reach my neighbor, her phone was busy.
d. Desperate to get information, my solution was to ask my mother to drive over to check the oven.
e. With enormous relief, my mother's call confirmed everything was fine.

1. After working six hours, the job was done.
2. Further information can be obtained by calling the specified number.
3. To compete in the Olympics, talent, training, and dedication are needed.

4. Pressing hard on the brakes, the car spun into a hedge.
5. Showing a lack of design experience, the architect advised the student to take her model back to the drawing board.

11 | Incomplete Sentences

For advice on editing fragments, see 1 and also A1 in the Quick Editing Guide, p. A-38.

A fragment fails to qualify as a sentence because it lacks a subject or a predicate (or both) or it fails to express a complete thought. However, a sentence with the essentials can still miss the mark. If it lacks a crucial word or phrase, the sentence may be *incomplete*. When you make comparisons and use elliptical constructions, be certain that you complete the thought you want to express.

Comparisons

11a Make your comparisons clear by stating fully what you are comparing with what.

INCOMPLETE   Roscoe loves spending time online more than Diane.

Does Roscoe prefer the company of a keyboard to the company of his friend? Or, of these two people, is Roscoe (and not Diane) the online addict? Adding a word would complete the comparison.

CLEAR   Roscoe loves spending time online more than Diane *does.*

CLEAR   Roscoe loves spending time online more than *with* Diane.

11b When you start to draw a comparison, finish it.

The unfinished comparison is a favorite trick of advertisers — "Our product is better!" — because it dodges the question "Better than what?" A sharp writer (or shopper) knows that any item must be compared *with* something else.

INCOMPLETE   Scottish tweeds are warmer.

COMPLETE   Scottish tweeds are warmer *than any other fabric you can buy.*

11c Be sure the things you compare are of the same kind.

A sentence that compares should reassure readers on two counts: the items are similar enough to compare, and the terms of comparison are clear.

INCOMPLETE   The engine of a Ford truck is heavier than a Piper Cub airplane.

What is being compared? Truck engine and airplane? Or engine and engine? Because a truck engine is unlikely to outweigh a plane, we can guess the writer meant to compare engines. Readers, however, should not have to make the effort to complete a writer's thought.

CLEAR   The engine of a Ford truck is heavier than *that of* a Piper Cub airplane.

CLEAR   A Ford truck's engine is heavier than a *Piper Cub's*.

In this last example, parallel structure (*Ford truck's* and *Piper Cub's*) helps to make the comparison concise as well as clear.

For more on parallel structure, see 13.

11d To compare an item with others of its kind, use *any other.*

A comparison using *any* shows how something relates to a group without belonging to the group.

Alaska is larger than *any* country in Central America.

A comparison using *any other* shows how one member of a group relates to other members of the same group.

Death Valley is drier than *any other* place in the United States.

Exercise 11-1 ▪ Completing Comparisons

Revise the following sentences by adding needed words to any comparisons that are incomplete. (There may be more than one way to complete some comparisons.) Some sentences may be correct. Possible revisions for the lettered sentences appear in the back of the book. Example:

For more practice, visit **<bedfordstmartins .com/bedguide>**.

I hate hot weather more than you.

I hate hot weather more than you *do. Or*

I hate hot weather more than *I hate* you.

a. The movie version of *The Brady Bunch* was much more ironic.
b. Taking care of a dog is often more demanding than a cat.
c. I received more free calendars in the mail for 2011 than any year.
d. The crime rate in the United States is higher than Canada.
e. Liver contains more iron than any meat.

1. Driving a sports car means more to Jake than his professors.
2. People who go to college aren't necessarily smarter, but they will always have an advantage at job interviews.
3. I don't have as much trouble getting along with Michelle as Karen.
4. A hen lays fewer eggs than a turtle.
5. Singing is closer to prayer than a meal of Chicken McNuggets.

Elliptical Constructions

Robert Frost begins his well-known poem "Fire and Ice" with these lines:

Some say the world will end in fire, / Some say in ice.

When Frost wrote that opening, he avoided needless repetition by implying certain words rather than stating them. The result is more concise and more effective than a complete version of the same sentence would be:

Some say the world will end in fire, some say the world will end in ice.

This common tactic produces an **elliptical construction** — one that leaves out (for conciseness) words that are unnecessary but clearly understood by readers. Elliptical constructions can be confusing, however, if a writer gives readers too little information to fill in those missing words.

11e When you eliminate repetition, keep all the words essential for clarity.

An elliptical construction avoids repeating what a reader already knows, but it should omit only words that are stated elsewhere in the sentence, including prepositions. Otherwise, your reader may fill the gap incorrectly.

> INCOMPLETE   The train neither goes nor returns from Middletown.

Readers are likely to fill in an extra *from* after *goes*. Write instead:

> COMPLETE   The train neither goes *to* nor returns from Middletown.

11f In a compound predicate, leave out only verb forms that have already been stated.

compound predicate: A predicate consisting of two or more verbs linked by a conjunction: My sister *stopped and stared.*

Compound predicates are prone to incomplete constructions, especially if the verbs are in different tenses. Be sure no necessary part is missing.

> INCOMPLETE   The mayor never has and never will vote to raise taxes.
>
> COMPLETE   The mayor never has *voted* and never will vote to raise taxes.

11g If you mix comparisons using *as* and *than,* include both words.

For more on comparative forms, see 8d–8f.

To contrast two things, use the comparative form of an adjective followed by *than: better than, more than, fewer than.* To show a similarity between two things, sandwich the simple form of an adjective between *as* and *as: as good as, as many as, as few as.* Often you can combine two *than* or two *as* comparisons into an elliptical construction.

The White House is smaller [than] and newer than Buckingham Palace.

Some elegant homes are as large [as] and as grand as the White House.

However, merging a *than* comparison with an *as* comparison won't work.

> INCOMPLETE   The White House is smaller but just as beautiful as Buckingham Palace.
>
> COMPLETE   The White House is smaller *than* but just *as* beautiful *as* Buckingham Palace.

Exercise 11-2 ▪ Completing Sentences

Revise the following sentences by adding needed words to any constructions that are incomplete. (There may be more than one way to complete some constructions.) Some sentences may be correct. Possible revisions for the lettered sentences appear in the back of the book. Example:

For more practice, visit **<bedfordstmartins .com/bedguide>**.

> The general should have but didn't see the perils of invasion.
>
> The general should have *seen* but didn't see the perils of invasion.

a. Eighteenth-century China was as civilized and in many respects more sophisticated than the Western world.

b. Pembroke was never contacted, much less involved with, the election committee.

c. I haven't yet but soon will finish my research paper.

d. Ron likes his popcorn with butter, Linda with parmesan cheese.

e. George Washington always has been and will be regarded as the father of this country.

1. You have traveled to exotic Tahiti; Maureen to Asbury Park, New Jersey.

2. The mayor refuses to negotiate or even talk to the civic association.

3. Building a new sewage treatment plant would be no more costly and just as effective as modifying the existing one.

4. You'll be able to tell Jon from the rest of the team: Jon wears white Reeboks, the others black high-tops.

5. Erosion has and always will reshape the shoreline.

---

12 | Mixed Constructions and Faulty Predication

Sometimes a sentence contains all the necessary ingredients but still doesn't make sense. The problem may be a discord between two or more of its parts: phrases or clauses that don't fit together (a *mixed construction*) or a verb and its subject, object, or modifier (*faulty predication*) that don't match.

phrase: Two or more related words that work together but may lack a subject (as in *will walk*), a verb (*my uncle*), or both (*to the attic*)

clause: A group of related words that includes both a subject and a verb: *The sailboats raced* (independent clause) *until the sun set* (subordinate clause).

12a Link phrases and clauses logically.

A **mixed construction** results when a writer connects phrases or clauses (or both) that don't work together as a sentence.

> MIXED   In her efforts to solve the tax problem only caused the mayor additional difficulties.

The prepositional phrase *In her efforts to solve the tax problem* is a modifier; it can't act as the subject of a sentence. The writer, however, has used this phrase as a noun—the subject of the verb *caused*. To untangle this mixed con-

preposition: A transitional word (such as *in, on, at, of, from*) that leads into a phrase such as *in the bar, under a rickety table*

For more on coordination and subordination, see 14a–14f.

coordinating conjunction: A one-syllable linking word (*and, but, for, or, nor, so, yet*) that joins elements with equal or near-equal importance: Jack *and* Jill, sink *or* swim

subordinating conjunction:
A word (such as *because, although, if, when*) used to make one clause dependent on, or subordinate to, another: *Unless* you have a key, we are locked out.

ESL Guidelines 🌐 Mixed Constructions, Faulty Predication, and Subject Errors

Mixed constructions result when phrases or clauses are joined even though they do not logically go together. Combine clauses with either a coordinating conjunction or a subordinating conjunction, never both.

> INCORRECT   *Although* baseball is called "the national pastime" of the United States, *but* football is probably more popular.
>
> CORRECT   *Although* baseball is called "the national pastime" of the United States, football is probably more popular.
>
> CORRECT   Baseball is called "the national pastime" of the United States, *but* football is probably more popular.

Faulty predication results when a verb and its subject, object, or modifier do not match. Do not use a noun as both the subject of the sentence and the object of a preposition.

> INCORRECT   *In my neighborhood has* several good restaurants.
>
> CORRECT   *My neighborhood has* several good restaurants.
>
> CORRECT   *In my neighborhood, there are* several good restaurants.

Common **subject errors** include leaving out and repeating subjects of clauses.

- Do not omit *it* used as a subject. A subject is required in all English sentences except commands (imperatives).

> INCORRECT   *Is* interesting to visit museums.
>
> CORRECT   *It is* interesting to visit museums.

- Do not repeat the subject of a sentence with a pronoun.

> INCORRECT   *My brother-in-law, he* is a successful investor.
>
> CORRECT   *My brother-in-law* is a successful investor.

struction, the writer has two choices: (1) rewrite the phrase so that it works as a noun, or (2) use the phrase as a modifier, not a subject.

REVISED   Her efforts to solve the tax problem only caused the mayor additional difficulties.
[With *in* gone, *efforts* becomes the subject.]

REVISED   In her efforts to solve the tax problem, the mayor created additional difficulties.
[The phrase now modifies the verb *created*.]

To avoid mixed constructions, check your links—especially prepositions and conjunctions.

MIXED   Jack, although he was picked up by the police, but was not charged.

Using both *although* and *but* gives this sentence one link too many.

REVISED   Jack was picked up by the police but was not charged.

REVISED   Although he was picked up by the police, Jack was not charged.

12b Relate the parts of a sentence logically.

Faulty predication refers to a skewed relationship between a verb and some other part of a sentence.

FAULTY   *The temperature of water freezes* at 32 degrees Fahrenheit.

At first glance, that sentence looks all right. It contains both subject° and predicate. It expresses a complete thought. What is wrong with it? The writer has slipped into faulty predication by mismatching the subject and verb. The sentence tells us that *temperature freezes,* when science and common sense tell us it is *water* that freezes. To correct this error, the writer must select a subject and verb that fit each other.

REVISED   *Water freezes* at 32 degrees Fahrenheit.

Faulty predication also results from a mismatched verb and direct object.

FAULTY   Rising costs *diminish college* for many students.

Costs don't *diminish college.* To correct this error, the writer must change the sentence so that its direct object follows logically from its verb.

REVISED   Rising costs *diminish the number of students who can attend college.*

Subtler predication errors result when a writer uses a linking verb to forge a false connection between the subject and a subject complement.

FAULTY   *Industrial waste* has become *an important modern priority.*

subject: The part of a sentence that names something—a person, an object, an idea, a situation—about which the predicate makes an assertion: The *king* lives.
predicate: The part of a sentence that makes an assertion about the subject involving an action (Birds *fly*), a relationship (Birds *have feathers*), or a state of being (Birds *are warm-blooded*)
direct object: The target of a verb that completes the action performed by or asserted about the subject: I met *the sheriff.*
linking verb: A verb (*is, become, seem, feel*) that shows a state of being by linking the sentence subject with a subject complement that renames or describes the subject: The sky *is* blue. (See 3a.)

Is it *waste* that has become a *priority*? Or is it *solving problems caused by careless disposal of industrial waste*? A writer who says all that, though, risks wordiness. Why not just replace *priority* with a closer match for *waste*?

For more on using active and passive voice, see 3m.

REVISED   *Industrial waste* has become a *modern menace.*

Mismatches between a verb and another part of the sentence are easier to avoid when the verb is active rather than passive.

FAULTY   The idea of giving thanks for a good harvest *was not done* first by the Pilgrims.

REVISED   The idea of giving thanks for a good harvest *did not originate* with the Pilgrims.

12c Avoid starting a definition with *when* or *where.*

A definition needs to fit grammatically with the rest of the sentence.

FAULTY   Dyslexia is when you have a reading disorder.

REVISED   Dyslexia is a reading disorder.

FAULTY   A lay-up is where a player dribbles close to the basket and then makes a one-handed, banked shot.

REVISED   To shoot a lay-up, a player dribbles in close to the basket and then makes a one-handed, banked shot.

12d Avoid using *the reason is because* . . .

Anytime you start an explanation with *the reason is,* what follows *is* should be a subject complement: an adjective, a noun, or a noun clause. *Because* is a conjunction; it cannot function as a noun or adjective.

FAULTY   *The reason* Al hesitates *is because* no one supported him last year.

REVISED   *The reason* Al hesitates *is that* no one supported him last year.

REVISED   Al hesitates *because* no one supported him last year.

REVISED   *The reason* Al hesitates *is simple:* no one supported him last year.

Exercise 12-1 ■ Correcting Mixed Constructions and Faulty Predication

For more practice, visit **<bedfordstmartins .com/bedguide>**.

Correct any mixed constructions and faulty predication you find in the following sentences. Possible revisions for the lettered sentences appear in the back of the book. Example:

The storm damaged the beach erosion.

The storm worsened the beach erosion. *Or*

The storm damaged the beach.

a. The cost of health insurance protects people from big medical bills.

b. In his determination to prevail helped him finish the race.

c. The AIDS epidemic destroys the body's immune system.

d. The temperatures are too cold for the orange trees.

e. A recession is when economic growth is small or nonexistent and unemployment increases.

1. The opening of the new shopping mall should draw out-of-town shoppers for years to come.

2. The reason the referendum was defeated was because voters are tired of paying so much in taxes.

3. In the glacier's retreat created the valley.

4. A drop in prices could put farmers out of business.

5. The researchers' main goal is cancer.

13 | Parallel Structure

You use **parallel structure,** or parallelism, when you create a series of words, phrases, clauses, or sentences with the same grammatical form. The pattern created by the series—its parallel structure—emphasizes the similarities or differences among the items, whether things, qualities, actions, or ideas.

> My favorite foods are roast beef, apple pie, and linguine with clam sauce.
>
> Louise is charming, witty, intelligent, and talented.
>
> Manuel likes to swim, ride, and run.
>
> Dave likes movies that scare him and books that make him laugh.

Each series is a perfect parallel construction, composed of equivalent words: nouns in the first example, then adjectives, verbs, and adjective clauses.

For more on editing for parallel structure, see B2 in the Quick Editing Guide, p. A-48.

13a In a series linked by a coordinating conjunction, keep all elements in the same grammatical form.

A coordinating conjunction (*and, but, for, or, nor, so, yet*) cues your readers to expect a parallel structure. Whether your series consists of single words, phrases, or clauses, its parts should balance one another.

AWKWARD   The puppies are *tiny, clumsily bumping* into each other, *and cute.*

Two elements in this series are parallel one-word adjectives (*tiny, cute*), but the third, the verb phrase *clumsily bumping,* is inconsistent.

For more on coordination, see 14a–14c.

PARALLEL   The puppies are *tiny, clumsy, and cute.*

Don't mix verb forms, such as gerunds and infinitives, in a series.

AWKWARD	Plan a winter vacation if you like *skiing and to skate*.
PARALLEL	Plan a winter vacation if you like *skiing and skating*.
PARALLEL	Plan a winter vacation if you like *to ski and to skate*.

In a series of phrases or clauses, be sure that all elements in the series are similar in form, even if they are not similar in length.

AWKWARD	The fight in the bar takes place *after the two lovers have their scene together* but *before the car chase*. [The clause starting with *after* is not parallel to the phrase starting with *before*.]
PARALLEL	The fight in the bar takes place *after the love scene* but *before the car chase*.
AWKWARD	You can take the key, or don't forget to leave it under the mat. [The declarative clause starting with *You can* is not parallel to the imperative clause starting with *don't forget*.]
PARALLEL	You can *take the key*, or you can *leave it* under the mat.

13b In a series linked by correlative conjunctions, keep all elements in the same grammatical form.

When you use a correlative conjunction, follow each part with a similarly structured word, phrase, or clause.

AWKWARD	I'm looking forward *to either attending* Saturday's wrestling match *or to seeing* it on closed-circuit TV. [*To* precedes the first part (*to either*) but follows the second part (*or to*).]
PARALLEL	I'm looking forward *either to attending* Saturday's wrestling match *or to seeing* it on closed-circuit TV.
AWKWARD	Take my advice: try *neither to be first nor last* in the lunch line. [*To be* follows the first part but not the second part.]
PARALLEL	Take my advice: try to be *neither first nor last* in the lunch line.

13c Make the elements in a comparison parallel in form.

A comparative word such as *than* or *as* cues the reader to expect a parallel structure. This makes logical sense: to be compared, two things must resemble each other, and parallel structure emphasizes this resemblance.

AWKWARD	Philip likes *fishing* better than *to sail*.
PARALLEL	Philip likes *fishing* better than *sailing*.
PARALLEL	Philip likes *to fish* better than *to sail*.

gerund: A form of a verb, ending in *-ing*, that functions as a noun: Lacey likes *playing* in the steel band.

infinitive: The base form of a verb, often preceded by *to* (*to go*, *to play*)

correlative conjunction: A pair of linking words (such as *either/or*, *not only/but also*) that appear separately but work together to join elements of a sentence: *Neither* his friends *nor* hers like pizza.

For more on comparisons, see 11a–11d and 11g.

AWKWARD	*Maintaining* railway lines is as important to the public transportation system as *to buy* new trains.
PARALLEL	*Maintaining* railway lines is as important to the public transportation system as *buying* new trains.

13d Reinforce parallel structure by repeating rather than mixing lead-in words.

Parallel structures are especially useful when a sentence contains a series of clauses or phrases. For example, try to precede potentially confusing clauses with *that, who, when, where,* or some other connective, repeating the same connective every time to help readers follow them with ease.

> No one in this country needs a government *that* aids big business at the expense of farmers and workers, *that* ravages the environment in the name of progress, or *that* slashes budgets for health and education.

If the same lead-in word won't work for all elements in a series, try changing the order of the elements to minimize variation.

AWKWARD	The new school building is large but not very comfortable, and expensive but unattractive.
PARALLEL	The new school building is large and expensive, but uncomfortable and unattractive.

Exercise 13–1 ▪ Making Sentences Parallel

For more practice, visit **<bedfordstmartins .com/bedguide>**.

Revise the following sentences by substituting parallel structures for awkward ones. Possible revisions for the lettered sentences appear in the back of the book. Example:

> In the Rio Grande Valley, the interests of conservationists, government officials, and those trying to immigrate collide.
>
> In the Rio Grande Valley, the interests of conservationists, government officials, and immigrants collide.

a. The border separating Texas and Mexico marks not only the political boundary of two countries, but it also is the last frontier for some endangered wildlife.

b. In the Rio Grande Valley, both local residents and the people who happen to be tourists enjoy visiting the national wildlife refuges.

c. The tall grasses in this valley are the home of many insects, birds, and there are abundant small mammals.

d. Two endangered wildcats, the ocelot and another called the jaguarundi, also make the Rio Grande Valley their home.

e. Many people from Central America are desperate to immigrate to the United States by either legal or by illegal means.

1. Because the land along the Rio Grande has few human inhabitants and the fact that the river is often shallow, many illegal immigrants attempt to cross the border there.

2. To capture illegal immigrants more easily, the U.S. government has cut down tall grasses, put up fences, and the number of immigration patrols has been increased.

3. For illegal immigrants, crossing the border at night makes more sense than to enter the United States in broad daylight, so the U.S. government has recently installed bright lights along the border.

4. The ocelot and the jaguarundi need darkness, hiding places, and to have some solitude if they are to survive.

5. Neither the immigration officials nor have wildlife conservationists been able to find a solution that will protect both the U.S. border and these endangered wildcats.

---

14 | Coordination and Subordination

Coordination and subordination can use conjunctions to specify relationships between ideas. Coordination connects thoughts of equal importance; subordination shows how one thought affects another.

14a Coordinate clauses or sentences that are related in theme and equal in importance.

> The car skidded for a hundred yards. It crashed into a brick wall.

These two clauses make equally significant statements about the same subject, a car accident. Because the writer has not linked the sentences, we can only guess that the crash followed from the skid.

> The car skidded for a hundred yards, and it crashed into a brick wall.

Now the sequence is clear: first the car skidded; then it crashed. That's coordination. To tighten it, reduce the clauses to a compound predicate.

> The car skidded for a hundred yards and crashed into a brick wall.

Now the connection is so clear we can almost hear screeching brakes. Once you decide to coordinate two clauses, try these three ways to do it.

1. Join two main clauses with a coordinating conjunction.

UNCOORDINATED   Ari does not want to be placed on your mailing list. He does not want a salesperson to call him.

---

conjunction: A linking word that connects words or groups of words through coordination (*and, but*) or subordination (*because, although, unless*)

clause: A group of related words that includes both a subject and a verb: *The sailboats raced* (independent clause) *until the sun set* (subordinate clause).

compound predicate: A predicate consisting of two or more verbs linked by a conjunction: My sister *stopped and stared.*

coordinating conjunction: A one-syllable linking word (*and, but, for, or, nor, so, yet*) that joins elements with equal or near-equal importance: Jack *and* Jill, sink *or* swim

COORDINATED	Ari does not want to be placed on your mailing list, nor does he want a salesperson to call him.
COORDINATED	Ari does not want to be placed on your mailing list or called by a salesperson.

2. Join two main clauses with a semicolon and a conjunctive adverb. Conjunctive adverbs show relationships such as addition, comparison, contrast, emphasis, cause and effect, or time (see p. 842).

UNCOORDINATED	The guerrillas did not observe the truce. They never intended to.
COORDINATED	The guerrillas did not observe the truce; furthermore, they never intended to.

3. Join two main clauses with a semicolon or a colon.

UNCOORDINATED	The army wants to negotiate. The guerrillas prefer to fight.
COORDINATED	The army wants to negotiate; the guerrillas prefer to fight.
UNCOORDINATED	The guerrillas have two advantages. They know the terrain, and the people support them.
COORDINATED	The guerrillas have two advantages: they know the terrain, and the people support them.

> **conjunctive adverb:** A linking word that can connect independent clauses and show a relationship between two ideas: Jen studied hard; *finally,* she passed the exam.
>
> For more on semicolons and colons, see 22 and 23.

14b Coordinate clauses only if they are clearly and logically related.

Whenever you hitch together two sentences, make sure they get along. Will the relationship between them be evident to your readers?

FAULTY	The sportscasters were surprised by Easy Goer's failure to win the Kentucky Derby, but it rained on derby day.

Readers need enough information to see why two clauses are connected.

COORDINATED	The sportscasters were surprised by Easy Goer's failure to win the Kentucky Derby; *however, he runs poorly on a muddy track,* and it rained on derby day.

Choose a coordinating conjunction, conjunctive adverb, or punctuation mark that accurately reflects this relationship.

FAULTY	The sportscasters all expected Easy Goer to win the Kentucky Derby, and Sunday Silence beat him.
COORDINATED	The sportscasters all expected Easy Goer to win the Kentucky Derby, *but* Sunday Silence beat him.

For common types of sentences using coordination and subordination, see p. 847.

Coordinating and Subordinating Words at a Glance

Coordinating Conjunctions

and, but, for, nor, or, so, yet

Correlative Conjunctions

as . . . as	just as . . . so	not only . . . but also
both . . . and	neither . . . nor	whether . . . or
either . . . or	not . . . but	

Common Conjunctive Adverbs

accordingly	finally	likewise	otherwise
also	furthermore	meanwhile	similarly
anyway	hence	moreover	still
as	however	nevertheless	then
besides	incidentally	next	therefore
certainly	indeed	nonetheless	thus
consequently	instead	now	undoubtedly

Common Subordinating Conjunctions

after	before	since	until
although	even though	so	when
as	how	so that	whenever
as if	if	than	where
as soon as	in order that	that	wherever
as though	once	though	while
because	rather than	unless	why

Relative Pronouns

that, which	what	who	whom
whose	whatever	whoever	whomever

14c Coordinate clauses only if they work together to make a coherent point.

When a writer strings together several clauses in a row, often the result is excessive coordination. Packing too much information into a single sentence can make readers dizzy, unable to pick out which points really matter. Each key idea deserves its own sentence so readers see its importance.

EXCESSIVE   Easy Goer was the Kentucky Derby favorite, and all the sportscasters expected him to win, but he runs poorly on a muddy track, and it rained on derby day, so Sunday Silence beat him.

REVISED	Easy Goer was the Kentucky Derby favorite, and all the sportscasters expected him to win. However, he runs poorly on a muddy track, and it rained on derby day. Therefore, Sunday Silence beat him.

Excessive coordination may result from repeating the same conjunction.

EXCESSIVE	Phil was out of the house all day, so he didn't know about the rain, so he went ahead and bet on Easy Goer, so he lost twenty bucks, so now he wants to borrow money from me.
REVISED	Phil was out of the house all day, so he didn't know about the rain. He went ahead and bet on Easy Goer, and he lost twenty bucks. Now he wants to borrow money from me.

One solution to excessive coordination is subordination: making one clause dependent on another instead of giving both clauses equal weight.

For advice on subordination, see 14d.

Exercise 14–1 ▪ Using Coordination

For more practice, visit **<bedfordstmartins.com/bedguide>**.

Revise the following sentences, adding coordination where appropriate and removing faulty or excessive coordination. Possible revisions for the lettered sentences appear in the back of the book. Example:

> The wind was rising, and leaves tossed on the trees, and the air seemed to crackle with electricity, and we knew that a thunderstorm was on the way.

> The wind was rising, leaves tossed on the trees, and the air seemed to crackle with electricity. We knew that a thunderstorm was on the way.

a. Professional poker players try to win money and prizes in high-stakes tournaments. They may lose thousands of dollars.

b. Poker is not an easy way to make a living. Playing professional poker is not a good way to relax.

c. A good "poker face" reveals no emotions. Communicating too much information puts a player at a disadvantage.

d. Hidden feelings may come out in unconscious movements. An expert poker player watches other players carefully.

e. Poker is different from most other casino gambling games, for it requires skill and it forces players to compete against each other, and other casino gambling pits players against the house, so they may win out of sheer luck, but skill has little to do with winning those games.

1. The rebels may take the capital in a week. They may not be able to hold it.

2. If you want to take Spanish this semester, you have only one choice. You must sign up for the 8 a.m. course.

3. Peterson's Market has raised its prices. Last week tuna fish cost $1.29 a can. Now it's up to $1.59.

4. Joe starts the morning with a cup of coffee, which wakes him up, and then at lunch he eats a chocolate bar, so that the sugar and caffeine will bring up his energy level.

5. The *Hindenburg* drifted peacefully over New York City. It exploded just before landing.

14d Subordinate less important ideas to more important ideas.

For a list of subordinating words, see p. 842.

Subordination is extremely useful because it shows your readers the relative importance of ideas, how one follows from another or affects another. You stress what counts, thereby encouraging your readers to share your viewpoint. You can subordinate one sentence to another in any of these three ways.

1. Turn the less important idea into a subordinate clause by introducing it with a subordinating conjunction such as *because, if,* or *when.*

Jason has a keen sense of humor. He has an obnoxious, braying laugh.

From those sentences, readers don't know what to feel about Jason. Is he likable or repellent? The writer needs to show which trait matters more.

Although Jason has a keen sense of humor, he has an obnoxious, braying laugh.

This revision makes Jason's sense of humor less important than his annoying hee-haw. The less important idea is stated as a subordinate clause opening with *Although*; the more important idea is stated as the main clause.

The writer could reverse the meaning by combining the other way:

Although Jason has an obnoxious, braying laugh, he has a keen sense of humor.

That version makes Jason sound fun to be with, despite his mannerism.

Which of Jason's traits to emphasize is up to the writer. What matters is that, in both combined versions, the writer takes a clear stand by making one sentence a main clause and the other a subordinate clause.

2. Turn the less important idea into a subordinate clause by introducing it with a relative pronoun such as *who, which,* or *that.*

Jason, *who has an obnoxious, braying laugh,* has a keen sense of humor.

Jason, *whose sense of humor is keen,* has an obnoxious, braying laugh.

3. Turn the less important idea into a phrase.

Jason, *a keen humorist,* has an obnoxious, braying laugh.

Despite his obnoxious, braying laugh, Jason has a keen sense of humor.

main clause: A group of words that has both a subject and a verb and can stand alone as a complete sentence: *My friends play softball.*

relative pronoun: A pronoun (*who, which, that, what, whom, whomever, whose*) that opens a subordinate clause, modifying a noun or pronoun in another clause: The gift *that* I received is very practical.

phrase: Two or more related words that work together but may lack a subject (as in *will walk*), a verb (*my uncle*), or both (*to the attic*)

14e Express the more important idea in the main clause.

Sometimes a writer accidentally subordinates a more important idea to a less important one and turns the sentence's meaning upside down.

> FAULTY
> SUBORDINATION
>
> Although the heroism of the Allied troops on D-Day lives on in spirit, many of the World War II soldiers who invaded Normandy are dead now.

This sentence is accurate. Does the writer, however, want to stress death over life? This is the effect of putting *are dead now* in the main clause and *lives on* in the subordinate clause. Instead, the writer can reverse the two.

> REVISED
>
> Although many of the World War II soldiers who invaded Normandy are dead now, the heroism of the Allied troops on D-Day lives on in spirit.

14f Limit the number of subordinate clauses in a sentence.

Excessive subordination strings too many ideas together without helping readers pick out what matters.

> EXCESSIVE
> SUBORDINATION
>
> Debate over the Strategic Defense Initiative (SDI), which was originally proposed as a space-based defensive shield that would protect America from enemy attack, but which critics have suggested amounts to creating a first-strike capability in space, has to some extent focused on the wrong question.

> REVISED
>
> Debate over the Strategic Defense Initiative (SDI) has to some extent focused on the wrong question. The plan was originally proposed as a space-based defensive shield that would protect America from enemy attack. Critics have suggested, however, that it amounts to creating a first-strike capability in space.

subordinate clause: A group of words that contains a subject and a verb but cannot stand alone because it depends on a main clause to help it make sense: *When it snows, a truck plows our road.*

Exercise 14–2 ▪ Using Subordination

Revise the following sentences, adding subordination where appropriate and removing faulty or excessive subordination. Possible revisions for the lettered sentences appear in the back of the book. Example:

> Some playwrights like to work with performing theater companies. It is helpful to hear a script read aloud by actors.
>
> Some playwrights like to work with performing theater companies *because* it is helpful to hear a script read aloud by actors.

For more practice, visit **<bedfordstmartins .com/bedguide>**.

a. Cape Cod is a peninsula in Massachusetts. It juts into the Atlantic Ocean south of Boston. The Cape marks the northern turning point of the Gulf Stream.

b. The developer had hoped the condominiums would sell quickly. Sales were sluggish.

c. Tourists love Italy. Italy has a wonderful climate, beautiful towns and cities, and a rich history.

d. At the end of Verdi's opera *La Traviata,* Alfredo has to see his beloved Violetta again. He knows she is dying and all he can say is good-bye.

e. I usually have more fun at a concert with Rico than with Morey. Rico loves music. Morey merely tolerates it.

1. Although we occasionally hear horror stories about fruits and vegetables being unsafe to eat because they were sprayed with toxic chemicals or were grown in contaminated soil, the fact remains that, given their high nutritional value, these fresh foods are generally much better for us than processed foods.

2. English has become an international language. Its grammar is filled with exceptions to the rules.

3. Some television cartoon shows have become cult classics. This has happened years after they went off the air. Examples include *Rocky and Bullwinkle* and *Speed Racer*.

4. Although investors have not fully regained confidence in the stock market, stock prices have gone up.

5. Violetta gives away her money. She bids adieu to her faithful servant. After that she dies in her lover's arms.

15 | Sentence Variety

Most writers rely on some patterns more than others to express ideas directly and efficiently, but sometimes they combine sentence elements in unexpected ways to emphasize ideas and to surprise readers.

15a Normal Sentences

In a **normal sentence,** a writer puts the subject before the verb at the beginning of the main clause. This pattern is the most common in English because it expresses ideas in the most straightforward manner.

Most college *students* today *want* interesting classes.

Types of Sentences at a Glance

A **simple sentence** contains only one main clause, even with modifiers, objects, complements, and phrases in addition to its subject and verb.

```
┌────────────────── MAIN CLAUSE ──────────────────┐
```
Even amateur stargazers can easily locate the Big Dipper in the night sky.

It may have a compound subject (*Fred and Sandy*) or a compound verb (*laughed and cried*). Sometimes its subject is unstated but clearly understood: "Run!"

A **compound sentence** consists of two or more main clauses joined by a coordinating conjunction such as *and* or *but,* by a semicolon, or by a semicolon followed by a conjunctive adverb such as *however* or *nevertheless.*

```
                                      MAIN CLAUSE
┌────── MAIN CLAUSE ──────┐         ┌──────┐
```
I would like to accompany you, but I can't.

```
┌── MAIN CLAUSE ──┐          ┌────── MAIN CLAUSE ──────┐
```
My car broke down; therefore, I missed the first day of class.

A **complex sentence** has one main clause and one or more subordinate clauses.

```
      MAIN              SUBORDINATE
┌──── CLAUSE ────┐   ┌── CLAUSE ──┐
```
I will be at the airport when you arrive.

The relative pronoun linking the clauses may be implied.

```
   MAIN
 CLAUSE    SUBORDINATE
┌──┐   ┌── CLAUSE ──┐
```
I know [that] you saw us.

A **compound-complex sentence** combines a compound sentence (two or more main clauses) and a complex sentence (at least one subordinate clause).

```
   MAIN         SUBORDINATE     SUBORDINATE      MAIN
┌─ CLAUSE ─┐ ┌── CLAUSE ──┐ ┌─ CLAUSE ─┐ ┌─ CLAUSE ─┐
```
I'd gladly wait until you're ready; but if I do, I'll miss the boat.

For lists of coordinating and subordinating words, see p. 842.

15b Inverted Sentences

In an **inverted sentence,** a writer inverts or reverses the subject-verb order to emphasize an idea in the predicate.

NORMAL   *My peers are uninterested* in reading.

INVERTED   How *uninterested* in reading *are my peers*!

15c Cumulative Sentences

In a **cumulative sentence,** a writer piles details at the end of a sentence to help readers visualize a scene or understand an idea.

> They came walking out in heavily brocaded yellow and black costumes, the familiar "toreador" suit, heavy with gold embroidery, cape, jacket, shirt and collar, knee breeches, pink stockings, and low pumps.
> — Ernest Hemingway, "Bull Fighting a Tragedy"

15d Periodic Sentences

The positions of emphasis in a sentence are the beginning and the end. In a **periodic sentence,** a writer suspends the main clause for a climactic ending, emphasizing an idea by withholding it until the end.

> Leaning back in his chair, shaking his head slowly back and forth, frustrated over his inability to solve the quadratic equation, Franklin scowled.

Exercise 15-1 ▪ Increasing Sentence Variety

For more practice, visit **<bedfordstmartins .com/bedguide>**.

Revise the following passage, adding sentence variety to create interest, emphasize important ideas, and strengthen coherence.

> We are terrified of death. We do not think of it, and we don't speak of death. We don't mourn in public. We don't know how to console a grieving friend. In fact, we have eliminated or suppressed all the traditional rituals surrounding death.
>
> The Victorians coped with death differently. Their funerals were elaborate. The yards of black crepe around the hearse, hired professional mourners, and solemn procession leading to an ornate tomb are now only a distant memory. They wore mourning jewelry. They had a complicated dress code for the grieving process. It governed what mourners wore, and it governed how long they wore it. Many of these rituals may seem excessive or even morbid to us today. The rituals served a psychological purpose in helping the living deal with loss.

16 | Appropriateness

When you talk to people face-to-face, you can gauge their reactions to what you say. Often their responses guide your tone and your choice of words. When you write, you cannot gauge your readers' reactions as easily because you cannot see them. Instead, you must imagine yourself in their place, focusing especially closely on their responses when you revise.

Besides affecting how well you accomplish your purpose as a writer, your language can also affect how well you are regarded by others. When you accurately assess the tone, formality, and word choice expected in a situation, you use the power of language to enhance your own position. When you misjudge, you may find that others judge you harshly in response. Your prospective employer, your teacher, your supervisor, or others in positions of authority may or may not be aware of their power to set language expectations or of their own responses to your use of language. However, when they see your efforts to write and speak as they feel a situation requires, they will appreciate your effort to become one who can use language powerfully, adjusting it to your audience and situation.

16a Choose a tone appropriate for your topic and audience.

Like a speaker, a writer may come across as friendly or aloof, furious or merely annoyed, playful or grimly serious. This attitude is the writer's **tone** and, like a speaker's tone, it strongly influences the audience's response. A tone that seems right to a reader conveys your concern for the reader's reaction. For instance, taking a humorous approach to a disease such as cancer or AIDS might create an inappropriate tone that ignores a reader's feelings and thus meets with rejection. To convey your tone, use sentence length, level of language, and vocabulary. Choose formal or informal language, coolly objective words, or words loaded with emotional connotations. The key is to be aware of your readers and their expectations.

16b Choose a level of formality appropriate for your tone.

Considering the tone you want to convey to your audience helps you choose words that are neither too formal nor too informal. By **formal** language, we mean the impersonal language of educated persons who consider topics seriously. Usually written, formal language is marked by relatively complex sentences and a large vocabulary. It doesn't use contractions (such as *doesn't*). In contrast, **informal** language more closely resembles ordinary conversation. It uses relatively short sentences and common words. It may include contractions, slang, and references to everyday objects and activities (cheeseburgers, T-shirts, CDs). The writer may use *I* and address the reader as *you*.

The right language for most college essays lies somewhere between formal and informal. If your topic and tone are serious (say, for a research paper on terrorism), then your language may lean toward formality. If your topic is not weighty and your tone is light (say, for a humorous essay about giving your dog a bath), then your language may be informal.

For more practice, visit <**bedfordstmartins .com/bedguide**>.

Exercise 16–1 ▪ Choosing an Appropriate Tone and Level of Formality

Revise the following passages to ensure that both the tone and the level of formality are appropriate for the topic and audience. Example:

> I'm sending you this letter because I want you to meet with me and give me some info about the job you do.
>
> I'm writing to inquire about the possibility of an informational interview about your profession.

1. Dear Senator Crowley:
   I think you've got to vote for the new environmental law, so I'm writing this letter. We're messing up forests and wetlands — maybe for good. Let's do something now for everybody who's born after us.
   Thanks,
   Glenn Turner

2. The United States Holocaust Memorial Museum in Washington, D.C., is a great museum dedicated to a real bad time in history. It's hard not

to get bummed out by the stuff on show. Take it from me, it's an experience you won't forget.

3. Dear Elaine,

I am so pleased that you plan on attending the homecoming dance with me on Friday. It promises to be a gala event, and I am confident that we will enjoy ourselves immensely. I understand a local group by the name of Electric Bunny will provide musical entertainment. Please call me at your earliest convenience to inform me when to pick you up.

Sincerely, Bill

16c Choose common words instead of jargon.

Jargon is the term for the specialized vocabulary used by people in a certain field, such as music, carpentry, law, or sports. Nearly every academic, professional, and recreational field has its own jargon. To a specialist addressing other specialists, jargon is convenient and necessary. Without technical terms, after all, two surgeons could hardly discuss a patient's anatomy. To an outsider, though, such terms may be incomprehensible. To communicate information to readers without making them feel excluded or confused, avoid unnecessary jargon.

Jargon also can include ways of using words. Some politicians and bureaucrats like to make nouns into verbs by tacking on suffixes like *-ize*.

JARGON   The government intends to *privatize* federal land.

CLEAR   The government intends to *sell* federal land to *private buyers*.

Although *privatize* implies merely "convert to private ownership," usually its real meaning is "sell off"—as might occur were a national park to be auctioned to developers. *Privatize* thus also can be called a *euphemism*, a pleasant term that masks an underlying different meaning (see 16d).

Similarly, technology terms such as *access, format, interface, database,* and *parameters* are useful to explain technical processes. When thoughtlessly applied to nontechnical ideas, they can obscure meaning.

JARGON   A democracy needs the electorate's *input*.

CLEAR   A democracy needs the electorate *to vote and to express its views to elected officials*.

Avoid needless jargon by favoring a perfectly good old word over a trendy one. Also avoid the jargon of a special discipline—say, psychology or fly-fishing—unless you are writing for readers familiar with the field's details and terms. If you're writing for general readers, define any specialized terms. When you use plain words, you'll rarely go wrong.

For more practice, visit <**bedfordstmartins .com/bedguide**>.

Exercise 16–2 ▪ Avoiding Jargon

Revise the following sentences to eliminate the jargon. If necessary, revise extensively. If you can't tell what a sentence means, decide what it might mean, and rewrite it so that its meaning is clear. Possible revisions for the lettered sentences appear in the back of the book. Example:

> The proximity of Mr. Fitton's knife to Mr. Schering's arm produced a violation of the integrity of the skin.
>
> Mr. Fitton's knife cut Mr. Schering's arm.

a. Everyone at Boondoggle and Gall puts in face time at the holiday gatherings to maximize networking opportunities.

b. This year, in excess of fifty nonessential employees were negatively impacted by Boondoggle and Gall's decision to downsize effective September 1.

c. The layoffs made Jensen the sole point of responsibility for telephone interface in the customer-service department.

d. The numerical quotient of Jensen's telephonic exchanges increased by a factor of three post-downsizing, yet Jensen received no additional fiscal remuneration.

e. Jensen was not on the same page with management re her compensation, so she exercised the option to terminate her relationship with Boondoggle and Gall.

1. The driver-education course prepares the student for the skills of handling a vehicle on the highway transportation system.

2. In the heart area, Mr. Pitt is a prime candidate-elect for intervention of a multiple bypass nature.

3. The deer hunter's activity of quietizing a predetermined amount of the deer populace balances the ecological infrastructure.

16d Use euphemisms sparingly.

Euphemisms are plain truths dressed attractively, sometimes hard facts stated gently. To say that someone *passed away* instead of *died* is a common euphemism—humane, perhaps, in breaking terrible news to an anxious family. In such language, an army that *retreats* makes *a strategic withdrawal,* a person who is *underweight* turns *slim,* and an acne cream treats not *pimples* but *blemishes.* Even if you aren't prone to using euphemisms, note them when you read evidence from partisan sources and spokespersons.

16e Avoid slang in formal writing.

Slang, especially when new, can be colorful ("She's not playing with a full deck"), playful ("He's wicked cute!"), and apt (*ice* for diamonds, a *stiff* for a corpse). Most slang, however, quickly comes to seem as old and wrinkled as the Jazz Age's gleeful *twenty-three skidoo!* Your best bet is to stick to Standard English, seeking words that are usual but exact.

Exercise 16-3 ▪ Avoiding Euphemisms and Slang

Revise the following sentences to replace euphemisms with plainer words and slang with Standard English. Possible revisions for the lettered sentences appear in the back of the book. Example:

> Some dude ripped off my wallet, so I am currently experiencing a negative cash flow.
>
> *Someone stole* my wallet, so I am now *in debt.*

a. At three hundred bucks a month, the apartment is a steal.

b. The soldiers were victims of friendly fire during a strategic withdrawal.

c. Churchill was a wicked good politician.

1. Saturday's weather forecast calls for extended periods of shower activity.

2. The caller to the talk-radio program sounded totally wigged out.

3. We anticipate a downturn in economic vitality.

For more practice, visit **<bedfordstmartins .com/bedguide>**.

17 | Exact Words

What if you read that a leading citizen is a *pillow of the community*? Good writing depends on knowing what words mean and how to use them precisely.

17a Choose words for their connotations as well as their denotations.

The **denotation** of a word is its basic meaning—its dictionary definition. *Excited, agitated,* and *exhilarated* all denote a similar state of physical and emotional arousal. The **connotations** of a word are the shades of meaning that set it apart from its synonyms. You might be *agitated* by the prospect of final exams next week, but *exhilarated* by your plans for the vacation afterward. When you choose one of several options, you base your choice on connotation.

IMPRECISE	Advertisers have given light beer a macho image by showing football players *sipping* the product with *enthusiasm.*
REVISED	Advertisers have given light beer a macho image by showing football players *guzzling* the product with *gusto.*

preposition: A transitional word (such as *in, on, at, of, from*) that leads into a phrase such as *in the bar, under a rickety table*

For practice, visit **<bedfordstmartins .com/bedguide>**.

ESL Guidelines 🌐 *In, On, At:* Prepositions of Location and Time

Location Expressions

Elaine lives *in* Manhattan *at* a swanky address *on* Fifth Avenue.

- *In* means "within" or "inside of" a place, including geographical areas, such as cities, states, countries, and continents.

  I packed my books *in* my backpack and left to visit my cousins *in* Canada.

- Where *in* emphasizes *location* only, *at* is often used to refer to a place when a specific *activity* is implied: *at the store* (to shop), *at the office* (to work), *at the theater* (to see a play), and so on.

  Angelo left his bicycle *in* the bike rack while he was *at* school.

- *On* means "on the surface of" or "on top of" something and is used with floors of buildings and planets. It is also used to indicate a location *beside* a lake, river, ocean, or other body of water.

  The service department is *on* the fourth floor.

  We have a cabin *on* Lake Michigan.

- *In, on,* and *at* can all be used in addresses. *In* is used to identify a general location, such as a city or neighborhood. *On* is used to identify a specific street. *At* is used to give an exact address.

  We live *in* Boston *on* Medway Street.

  We live *at* 20 Medway Street.

- *In* and *at* can both be used with the verb *arrive. In* indicates a large place, such as a city, state, country, or continent. *At* indicates a smaller place, such as a specific building or address. (*To* is never used with *arrive.*)

  Alanya arrived *in* Alaska yesterday; Sanjei will arrive *at* the airport soon.

Time Expressions

- *In* indicates the span of time during which something occurs or a time in the future; it is also used in the expressions *in a minute* (meaning "shortly") and *in time* (meaning "soon enough" or "without a moment to spare"). *In* is also used with seasons, months, and periods of the day.

  He needs to read this book *in* the next three days.
  [During the next three days]

  I'll meet you *in* the morning *in* two weeks. [Two weeks from now]

- *On* is used with the days of the week, with the word *weekend,* and in the expression *on time* (meaning "punctually").

  Let's have lunch *on* Friday.

- *At* is used in reference to a specific time on the clock as well as a specific time of the day (*at night, at dawn, at twilight*).

  We'll meet again next Monday *at* 2:15 p.m.

ESL Guidelines 🌐 *To, For:* Indirect Objects and Prepositions

These sentences mean the same thing:

I sent the president a letter.

I sent a letter to the president.

In the first sentence, *the president* is the **indirect object:** he or she receives the direct object (*a letter*), which was acted on (*sent*) by the subject of the sentence (*I*). In the second sentence, the same idea is expressed using a **prepositional phrase** beginning with *to.*

- Some verbs can use either an indirect object or the preposition *to: give, send, lend, offer, owe, pay, sell, show, teach, tell.* Some verbs can use an indirect object or the preposition *for: bake, build, buy, cook, find, get, make.*

  I paid *the travel agent* one hundred dollars.

  I paid one hundred dollars *to the travel agent.*

  Margarita cooked *her family* some chicken.

  Margarita cooked some chicken *for her family.*

- Some verbs cannot have an indirect object; they must use a preposition. The following verbs must use the preposition *to: describe, demonstrate, explain, introduce,* and *suggest.*

  INCORRECT   Please explain me indirect objects.

  CORRECT   Please explain indirect objects *to me.*

- The following verbs must use the preposition *for: answer* and *prepare.*

  INCORRECT   He prepared me the punch.

  CORRECT   He prepared the punch *for me.*

- Some verbs must have an indirect object; they cannot use a preposition. The following verbs must have an indirect object: *ask* and *cost.*

  INCORRECT   Sasha asked a question to her.

  CORRECT   Sasha asked *her* a question.

Two-Word Verbs: Particles, Not Prepositions

Many two-word verbs end with a **particle,** a word that can be used as a preposition on its own but becomes part of a **phrasal verb.** Once the particle is added, the verb takes on a new idiomatic meaning that must be learned.

break up: to separate; to end a romantic relationship; to laugh

decide on: to select or to judge a person or thing

eat at: to worry or disturb a person

feel for [a person]: to sympathize with another's unhappiness

see to: to take care of a person or situation

take in [a person]: to house a person; to trick by gaining a person's trust

indirect object: A person or thing affected by the subject's action, usually the recipient of the direct object, through the action indicated by a verb such as *bring, get, offer, promise, sell, show, tell,* and *write:* Charlene asked *you* a question.

17b Avoid clichés.

A **cliché** is a trite expression, once vivid or figurative but now worn out from too much use. When a story begins, "It was a dark and stormy night," then its author is obviously using dull, predictable words. Many a strike is settled after a *marathon bargaining session* that *narrowly averts a walkout.* Fires customarily *race* and *gut.* And when everything is *terrific,* a reader will suspect that it isn't. Clichés abound when writers and speakers try hard to sound lively but don't bother to invent anything vigorous, colorful, and new. When editing your writing, you can often recognize an annoying cliché if you feel a sudden guilty desire to surround it with quotation marks. You might also show your papers to friends, asking them to look for anything trite.

COMMON CLICHÉS

a sneaking suspicion	last but not least
above and beyond the call of duty	little did I dream
add insult to injury	make a long story short
beyond a shadow of a doubt	piece of cake
come hell or high water	stab me in the back
cool as a cucumber	that's the way the ball bounces
few and far between	through thick and thin
greased lightning	tip of the iceberg
hard as a rock	tried and true

17c Use idioms in their correct form.

Every language contains **idioms,** or **idiomatic expressions:** phrases that, through long use, have become standard even though their construction may defy logic or grammar. For example, although *fender bender* may suggest the outcome of a minor collision between two cars, someone unfamiliar with that expression might struggle to connect the literal words with the idiomatic meaning. In addition, many idiomatic expressions require us to choose the right preposition. We work *up* a sweat while working *out* in the gym. We argue *with* someone but *about* something, *for* or *against* it. And someone who decides to *set up* a meeting doesn't expect to be *upset.* Sometimes we must know which article to use before a noun—if any. We can be *in motion,* but we have to be *in the swim.* We're occasionally in *a tight spot* but never in *a trouble.* Idioms also can involve choosing the right verb: we *seize* an opportunity, but we *catch* a plane.

The dictionary can help you choose the appropriate idiom for your sentence. Look up *agree* for instance, and you will probably find examples showing when to use *agree to, agree with,* or *agree that.*

For more practice, visit **<bedfordstmartins .com/bedguide>**.

Exercise 17–1 ▪ Selecting Words

Revise the following passage to replace inappropriate connotations, clichés, and faulty idioms. Example:

> The Mayan city of Uxmal is a common tourist attraction. The ruins have stood alone in the jungle since time immemorial.

> The Mayan city of Uxmal is a *popular* tourist attraction. The ruins have stood alone in the jungle since *ancient times.*

We spent the first day of our holiday in Mexico arguing around what we wanted to see on our second day. We finally agreed to a day trip out to some Mayan ruins. The next day we arrived on the Mayan city of Uxmal, which is as old as the hills. It really is a sight for sore eyes, smack-dab in a jungle stretching as far as the eye can see, with many buildings still covered in plants and iguanas moving quickly over the decayed buildings. The view from the top of the Soothsayer's Temple was good, although we noticed storm clouds gathering in the distance. The rain held up until we got off of the pyramid, but we drove back to the hotel in a lot of rain. After a day of sightseeing, we were so hungry that we could have eaten a horse, so we had a good meal before we turned in.

18 | Bias-Free Language

Thoughtful writers try to avoid harmful bias in language. They respect their readers and don't want to insult them, anger them, or impede communication. You may not be able to eliminate discrimination from society, but you can eliminate discriminatory language in your writing. Be on the lookout for words that insult or stereotype individuals or groups by gender, age, race, ethnic origin, sexual preference, or religion.

18a To eliminate sexist language, use alternatives that make no reference to gender.

Among the prime targets of American feminists in the 1960s and 1970s was the male bias built into the English language. Why, they asked, do we talk about *prehistoric man, manpower,* and *the brotherhood of man,* when by *man* we mean the entire human race? Why do we focus attention on the gender of an accomplished woman by calling her a *poetess* or a *lady doctor*? Why does a letter to a corporation have to begin "Gentlemen:"? On the other hand, to substitute "Everyone prefers their own customs" for "Everyone prefers *his* own customs" replaces sexism with bad grammar. Although there are no perfect solutions, sensitive writers try to minimize the sexist constraints of the English language.

18b Avoid terms that include or imply *man.*

One way to expand the meaning of *man* or a word starting with *man* is to substitute *human.* The result, however, is often clumsy.

SEXIST	Mankind studies man's inhumanity to man.
NONSEXIST	*Humankind* studies *humans'* inhumanity to *other humans.*

Adding *hu-* to *man* alleviates sexism but weighs down the sentence. Usually you can find a more graceful solution.

REVISED	*Human beings* study *people's* cruelty to one another.

Similarly, you need not simply replace the ending *-man* with *-person.* Instead, think about meaning and find a truly neutral synonym.

SEXIST	Did you leave a note for the mailman?
REVISED	Did you leave a note for the *letter carrier*?
SEXIST	Ask your steward [or stewardess] for a pillow.
REVISED	Ask your *flight attendant* for a pillow.

18c Use plural instead of singular forms.

Replace the singular with the plural (*they* and *their* for *he* and *his*).

SEXIST	Today's student values his education.
REVISED	Today's students value *their* education.

18d Where possible, omit words that denote gender.

You can make your language more bias-free by omitting pronouns and other words that needlessly indicate gender.

SEXIST	There must be rapport between a stockbroker and his client, a teacher and her student, a doctor and his patient.
REVISED	There must be rapport between stockbroker and *client,* teacher and *student,* doctor and *patient.*

Also treat men and women equally in terms of description or title.

SEXIST	I now pronounce you man and wife.
REVISED	I now pronounce you *husband* and wife.
SEXIST	Please page Mr. Pease, Mr. Mankodi, and Susan Brillantes.
REVISED	Please page Mr. Pease, Mr. Mankodi, and *Ms.* Brillantes.

18e Avoid condescending labels.

A responsible writer does not call women *chicks, babes, woman drivers,* or any other names that imply that they are not to be taken seriously. Nor should an employee ever be called a *girl* or *boy.* Avoid terms that put down individuals or groups because of age (*old goat, the grannies*), race or ethnicity (*Indian giver, Chinaman's chance*), or disability (*gimpy, handicapped*).

CONDESCENDING	The girls in the office bought Mr. Baart a birthday cake.
REVISED	The *administrative assistants* bought Mr. Baart a birthday cake.
CONDESCENDING	My neighbor is just an old fogy.
REVISED	My neighbor *has old-fashioned ideas.*

When describing a group, try to use the label or term that its members prefer, even if it is difficult to determine.

| POSSIBLY OFFENSIVE | Alice wants to study Oriental culture. |
| REVISED | Alice wants to study *Asian* culture. |

18f Avoid implied stereotypes.

Sometimes a stereotype is linked to a title. Aside from obvious exceptions, never assume that all the members of a group are of the same gender.

| STEREOTYPE | Pilots have little time to spend with their wives and children. |
| REVISED | Pilots have little time to spend with their *families.* |

Avoid stereotyping individuals or groups, negatively or positively.

STEREOTYPE	Roberto isn't very good at paying his rent on time, which doesn't surprise me because he is from Mexico.
REVISED	Roberto isn't very good at paying his rent on time.
STEREOTYPE	I assume Ben will do very well in medical school because his parents are Jewish.
REVISED	I assume Ben will do very well in medical school.

18g Use *Ms.* for a woman with no other known title.

Ms. is the preferred title of polite address for women because, like *Mr.* for men, it does not indicate marital status. Use *Miss* or *Mrs.* only if you know that the woman prefers this form. If a woman holds a doctorate, professional office, or position with a title, use that title rather than *Ms.*

Ms. Jane Doe, Editor | Dear Ms. Doe:
Professor Jane Doe, Department of English | Dear Professor Doe:
Senator Jane Doe, Washington, D.C. | Dear Senator Doe:

For more practice, visit **<bedfordstmartins .com/bedguide>**.

Exercise 18-1 ▪ Avoiding Bias

Revise the following sentences to eliminate bias. Possible revisions for the lettered sentences appear in the back of the book. Example:

A fireman needs to check his equipment regularly.

Firefighters need to check *their* equipment regularly.

a. Our school's athletic program will be of interest to black applicants.

b. The new physicians include Dr. Scalia, Anna Baniski, and Dr. Morton.

c. The diligent researcher will always find the sources he seeks.

1. Simon drinks like an Irishman.

2. Like most Asian Americans, Soon Li excels at music and mathematics.

3. Dick drives a Porsche because he likes the way she handles on the road, despite the little old ladies who slow down traffic.

For strategies for cutting extra words, see Ch. 23.

19 | Wordiness

Conciseness takes more effort than wordiness, but it pays off in clarity. Some expressions can be omitted (*area of, field of, kind of, sort of, type of, very*); others can be simplified.

SAMPLE WINDY WORDS AND PHRASES

WORDY	CONCISE
a period of a week	a week
arrive at an agreement, conclude an agreement	agree
at an earlier point in time	before, earlier
a large number of	many
lend assistance to	assist, aid, help
past experience, past history	experience, history
persons of the Methodist faith	Methodists
plan ahead for the future	plan
resemble in appearance	look like
sufficient number (or amount) of	enough
true facts	facts, truth
utilize, make use of	use

For more
practice, visit
**<bedfordstmartins
.com/bedguide>**.

Exercise 19–1 ▪ Eliminating Wordiness

Revise the following passage to eliminate wordiness. Example:

> At this point in time, a debate pertaining to freedom of speech is raging across our campuses.

> A debate *about* freedom of speech is raging across our campuses.

The media in recent times have become obsessed with the conflict on campuses across the nation between freedom of speech and the attempt to protect minorities from verbal abuse. Very innocent remarks or remarks of a humorous nature, sometimes taken out of context, have got a large number of students into trouble for the violation of college speech codes. Numerous students have become very vocal in attacking these "politically correct" speech codes and defending the right to free speech. But is the campaign against the politically correct really pertaining to freedom of speech, or is it itself a way in which to silence debate? Due to the fact that the phrase "politically correct" has become associated with liberal social causes and sensitivity to minority feelings, it now carries a very extraordinary stigma in the eyes of conservatives. To accuse someone of being politically correct is to refute their ideas before hearing their argument. The attempt to silence the opposition is a dangerous sign of our times and suggests that we are indeed in a cultural war.

41 Punctuation

20 | End Punctuation

Three marks can signal the end of a sentence: the period, the exclamation point, and the question mark.

20a Use a period to end a declarative sentence, a directive, or an indirect question.

Most sentences are **declarative,** meaning that they make a statement.

> Most people on earth are malnourished.

A period, not a question mark, ends an **indirect question,** which states that a question was asked or is being asked.

> The counselor asked Marcia why she rarely gets to class on time.

> I wonder why Roland didn't show up.

Written as **direct questions,** those sentences require a question mark.

> The counselor asked, "Marcia, why do you rarely get to class on time?"

> Why, I wonder, didn't Roland show up?

20b Use a period after some abbreviations.

A period within a sentence shows that what precedes it has been shortened.

> Dr. Robert A. Hooke's speech will be broadcast at 8:00 p.m.

The names of most organizations (YMCA, PTA), countries (USA, UK), and people (JFK, FDR) are abbreviated using all capitals without periods. Other abbreviations, such as those for designations of time, use periods. When an abbreviation ends a sentence, follow it with one period, not two.

For more on abbreviating names, see 28e.

20c Use a question mark to end a direct question.

> How many angels can dance on the head of a pin?

The question mark comes at the end of the question even if the question is part of a longer declarative sentence.

> "What'll I do now?" Marjorie wailed.

It can indicate doubt about the accuracy of a number or date.

> Aristophanes, born in 450(?) BC, became the master comic playwright of Greece's Golden Age.

Often the same purpose can be accomplished more gracefully in words:

> Aristophanes, born around 450 BC, became the master comic playwright of Greece's Golden Age.

In formal writing, avoid using a question mark to express irony or sarcasm: *her generous (?) gift*. If your doubts are worth including, state them directly: *her meager but highly publicized gift*.

For advice on punctuating indirect quotations and questions, see 25a. For examples of indirect questions, see 20a.

20d Use an exclamation point to end an interjection or an urgent command.

Rarely used in college writing, an exclamation point signals strong emotion or emphasis.

> We've struck an iceberg! We're sinking! I can't believe it!

It may mark an **interjection** or an urgent directive.

> Oh, no! Fire! Hurry up! Help me!

Exercise 20–1 ▪ Using End Punctuation

Where appropriate, correct the end punctuation in the following sentences. Give reasons for any changes you make. Some sentences may be

interjection: A word or expression (*oh, alas*) that inserts an outburst of feeling at the beginning, middle, or end of a sentence

A Writer's Handbook

For more practice, visit <**bedfordstmartins .com/bedguide**>.

correct. Answers for the lettered sentences appear in the back of the book. Example:

> Tom asked Cindy if she would be willing to coach him in tennis?
>
> Tom asked Cindy if she would be willing to coach him in tennis. [Not a direct question]

a. The question that still troubles the community after all these years is why federal agents did not act sooner?

b. I wonder what he was thinking at the time?

c. If the suspect is convicted, will lawyers appeal the case?

1. What will Brad and Emilia do if they can't take vacations at the same time.

2. When a tree falls in a forest, but no one hears it, does it make a sound.

3. What will happen next is anyone's guess.

21 | Commas

For more on comma usage, see C1 in the Quick Editing Guide, pp. A-50–A-51.

Like a split-second pause in conversation, a well-placed comma helps your readers to catch your train of thought. It keeps them from stumbling over a solid block of words or drawing an inaccurate conclusion.

> Lyman paints fences and bowls.

From this statement, we can deduce that Lyman is a painter who works with both a large and a small brush. But add commas and the portrait changes:

> Lyman paints, fences, and bowls.

Now Lyman wields a paintbrush, a sword, and a bowling ball. What we learn about his activities depends on how the writer punctuates the sentence.

21a Use a comma with a coordinating conjunction to join two main clauses.

main clause: A group of words that has both a subject and a verb and can stand alone as a complete sentence: *My friends play softball.*

When you join main clauses with a coordinating conjunction (*and, but, for, or, nor, so, yet*), add a comma after the first clause, right before the conjunction.

> The pie whooshed through the air, but the agile Hal ducked.

If your clauses are short and parallel in form, you may omit the comma.

> Spring passed and summer came.
>
> They urged but I refused.

Or you may keep the comma to throw emphasis on your second clause.

> Spring passed, and summer came.
>
> They urged, but I refused.

CAUTION: Don't use a comma with a coordinating conjunction that links two phrases or that links a phrase and a clause.

FAULTY   The mustangs galloped, and cavorted across the plain.

EDITED   The mustangs galloped and cavorted across the plain.

21b Use a comma after an introductory clause, phrase, or word.

Weeping, Lydia stumbled down the stairs.

Before that, Arthur saw her reading an old love letter.

If he knew who the writer was, he didn't tell.

Placed after any such opening word, phrase, or subordinate clause, a comma tells your reader, "Enough preliminaries: now the main clause starts."

EXCEPTION: You need not use a comma after a single introductory word or a short phrase or clause if there is no danger of misreading.

Sooner or later Lydia will tell us the whole story.

Exercise 21-1 ▪ Using Commas

Add any necessary commas to the following sentences, and remove any commas that do not belong. Some sentences may be correct. Answers for the lettered sentences appear in the back of the book. Example:

Your dog may have sharp teeth but my lawyer can bite harder.

Your dog may have sharp teeth, but my lawyer can bite harder.

a. Farmers around the world tend to rely on just a few breeds of livestock so some breeds are disappearing.

b. Older breeds of livestock are often less profitable, for they have not been genetically engineered to grow quickly.

c. For instance modern breeds of cattle usually grow larger, and produce more meat and milk than older breeds.

d. In both wild and domestic animals genetic diversity can make the animals resistant to disease, and parasites so older breeds can give scientists important information.

e. Until recently, small organic farmers were often the only ones interested in raising old-fashioned breeds but animal scientists now support this practice as well.

1. During the summer of the great soybean failure Larry paid little attention.

2. Unaware of the world he worked two jobs to earn his tuition.

phrase: Two or more related words that work together but may lack a subject (as in *will walk*), a verb (*my uncle*), or both (*to the attic*)

clause: A group of related words that includes both a subject and a verb: *The sailboats raced* (indirect clause) *until the sun set* (subordinate clause).

For more practice, visit **<bedfordstmartins .com/bedguide>**.

3. While across the nation farmers were begging for mortgages he fed the livestock every morning.

4. Neither the mounting agricultural crisis, nor any other current events, disturbed his dinner shift at the restaurant.

5. In fact you might have called him oblivious.

21c Use a comma between items in a series.

When you list three or more items, whether they are nouns, verbs, adjectives, adverbs, or entire phrases or clauses, separate them with commas.

> Country ham, sweet corn, and potatoes weighted Grandma's table.

> Joel prefers music that shakes, rattles, and rolls.

> In one afternoon, we climbed the Matterhorn, voyaged beneath the sea, and flew on a rocket through space.

Notice that no comma *follows* the final item in the series.

NOTE: Some writers omit the comma *before* the final item in the series. This custom may throw off the rhythm of a sentence and, in some cases, obscure the writer's meaning. Using the comma in such a case is never wrong and is preferred in academic style; omitting it can create confusion.

> I was met at the station by my cousins, brother and sister.

Are these people a brother-and-sister pair who are the writer's cousins? Or are they a group consisting of the writer's cousins, her brother, and her sister? If they are more than two people, a comma would clear up the confusion.

> I was met at the station by my cousins, brother, and sister.

21d Use a comma between coordinate adjectives but not between cumulative adjectives.

Adjectives that function independently of each other, though they modify the same noun, are called **coordinate adjectives.** Set them off with commas.

> Ruth was a clear, vibrant, persuasive speaker.

> Life is nasty, brutish, and short.

CAUTION: Don't use a comma after the final adjective before a noun.

> FAULTY   My professor was a brilliant, caring, teacher.

> EDITED   My professor was a brilliant, caring teacher.

To check whether adjectives are coordinate, apply two tests. Can you rearrange the adjectives without distorting the meaning of the sentence? (*Ruth was a persuasive, vibrant, clear speaker.*) Can you insert *and* between them? (*Life is nasty and brutish and short.*)

If the answer to both questions is yes, the adjectives are coordinate. Removing any one of them would not greatly affect the others. Use commas between them to show that they are separate and equal.

NOTE: If you link coordinate adjectives with *and* or another conjunction, omit the commas except in a series (see 21c).

> New York City is huge and dirty and beautiful.

Cumulative adjectives work together to create a single unified picture of the noun they modify. Remove any one of them and you change the picture. No commas separate cumulative adjectives.

> Ruth has two small white poodles.

> Who's afraid of the big bad wolf?

If you rearrange cumulative adjectives or insert *and* between them, the effect is distorted (*two white small poodles; the big and bad wolf*).

conjunction: A linking word that connects words or groups of words through coordination (*and, but*) or subordination (*because, although, unless*)

For more on cumulative adjectives, see p. 819.

Exercise 21–2 ▪ Using Commas

Add any necessary commas to the following sentences, remove any commas that do not belong, and change any punctuation that is incorrect. Some sentences may be correct. Answers for the lettered sentences appear in the back of the book. Example:

> Mel has been a faithful hardworking consistent band manager.

> Mel has been a faithful, hardworking, consistent band manager.

For more practice, visit **<bedfordstmartins .com/bedguide>**.

a. Mrs. Carver looks like a sweet, little, old lady, but she plays a wicked electric guitar.

b. Her bass player, her drummer and her keyboard player all live in the same retirement community.

c. They practice individually in the afternoon, rehearse together at night and play at the community's Saturday night dances.

d. The Rest Home Rebels have to rehearse quietly, and cautiously, to keep from disturbing the other residents.

e. Mrs. Carver has organized the group, scheduled their rehearsals, and acquired backup instruments.

1. When she breaks a string, she doesn't want her elderly crew to have to grab the guitar change the string and hand it back to her, before the song ends.

2. The Rest Home Rebels' favorite bands are U2, Arcade Fire and Lester Lanin and his orchestra.

3. They watch a lot of MTV because it is fast-paced colorful exciting and informative and it has more variety than soap operas.

4. Just once, Mrs. Carver wants to play in a really, huge, sold-out, arena.

5. She hopes to borrow the community's big, white, van to take herself her band and their equipment to a major, professional, recording studio.

21e Use commas to set off a nonrestrictive phrase or clause.

modifier: A word (such as an adjective or adverb), phrase, or clause that provides more information about other parts of a sentence: Plays *staged by the drama class* are *always successful.*

A **nonrestrictive modifier** adds a fact that, while perhaps interesting and valuable, isn't essential. You could leave it out of the sentence and still make sense. Set off the modifier with commas before and after it.

> Potts Alley, *which runs north from Chestnut Street,* is too narrow for cars.

> At the end of the alley, *where the fair was held last May,* a getaway car waited.

A **restrictive modifier** is essential. Omit it and you significantly change the meaning of the modified word and the sentence. Such a modifier is called *restrictive* because it limits what it modifies: it specifies this place, person, or action and no other. Because a restrictive modifier is part of the identity of whatever it modifies, no commas set it off from the rest of the sentence.

> They picked the alley *that runs north from Chestnut Street* because it is close to the highway.

> Anyone *who robs my house* will be disappointed.

Leaving out the modifier in that last sentence changes the meaning from potential robbers to humankind.

NOTE: Use *that* to introduce (or to recognize) a restrictive phrase or clause. Use *which* to introduce (or to recognize) a nonrestrictive phrase or clause.

> The food *that I love best* is chocolate.

> Chocolate, *which I love,* is not on my diet.

21f Use commas to set off nonrestrictive appositives.

appositive: A word or group of words that adds information by identifying a subject or object in a different way: my dog *Rover*, Hal's brother *Fred*

Like the modifiers discussed in 21e, an **appositive** can be either restrictive or nonrestrictive. If it is nonrestrictive—if the sentence still makes sense when it is omitted or changed—then set it off with commas before and after.

> My third ex-husband, *Hugo,* will be glad to meet you.

> We are bringing dessert, *a blueberry pie,* to follow dinner.

If the appositive is restrictive—if you can't take it out or change it without changing your meaning—then include it without commas.

> Of all the men I've been married to, my ex-husband *Hugo* is the best cook.

Exercise 21-3 ▪ Using Commas

For more practice, visit <**bedfordstmartins .com/bedguide**>.

Add any necessary commas to the following sentences, and remove any commas that do not belong. You may have to draw your own conclusions about what the writer meant to say. Some sentences may be correct. Possible revisions for the lettered sentences appear in the back of the book. Example:

> Jay and his wife the former Laura McCready were college sweethearts.
>
> Jay and his wife, the former Laura McCready, were college sweethearts.

a. We are bringing a dish vegetable lasagna, to the potluck supper.

b. I like to go to Central Bank, on this side of town, because this branch tends to have short lines.

c. The colony, that the English established at Roanoke disappeared mysteriously.

d. If the base commanders had checked their gun room where powder is stored, they would have found that several hundred pounds of gunpowder were missing.

e. Brazil's tropical rain forests which help produce the air we breathe all over the world, are being cut down at an alarming rate.

1. The aye-aye which is a member of the lemur family is threatened with extinction.

2. The party, a dismal occasion ended earlier than we had expected.

3. The general warned that the concessions, that the military was prepared to make, would be withdrawn if not matched by the rebels.

4. Although both of Don's children are blond, his daughter Sharon has darker hair than his son Jake.

5. Herbal tea which has no caffeine makes a better after-dinner drink than coffee.

21g Use commas to set off conjunctive adverbs.

When you drop a conjunctive adverb into the middle of a clause, set it off with commas before and after it.

> Using lead paint in homes has been illegal, *however,* since 1973.
>
> Builders, *indeed,* gave it up some twenty years earlier.

21h Use commas to set off parenthetical expressions.

Use a pair of commas around any parenthetical expression or any aside from you to your readers.

conjunctive adverb: A linking word that can connect independent clauses and show a relationship between two ideas: Jen studied hard; *finally,* she passed the exam. (See 14a-14c.)

parenthetical expression: An aside to readers or a transitional expression such as *for example* or *in contrast*

Home inspectors, *for this reason,* sometimes test for lead paint.

Cosmic Construction never used lead paint, *or so their spokesperson says,* even when it was legal.

21i Use commas to set off a phrase or clause expressing contrast.

It was Rudolph, *not Dasher,* who had a red nose.

EXCEPTION: Short contrasting phrases beginning with *but* need no commas.

It was not Dasher but Rudolph who had a red nose.

21j Use commas to set off an absolute phrase.

> **absolute phrase:** An expression, usually a noun followed by a participle, that modifies an entire clause or sentence and can appear anywhere in the sentence: The stallion pawed the ground, *chestnut mane and tail swirling in the wind.*

The link between an absolute phrase and the rest of the sentence is a comma or two commas if the phrase falls in midsentence.

Our worst fears drawing us together, we huddled over the letter.

Luke, *his knife being the sharpest,* slit the envelope.

Exercise 21–4 ▪ Using Commas

> For more practice, visit **<bedfordstmartins .com/bedguide>**.

Add any necessary commas to the following sentences, and change any punctuation that is incorrect. Answers for the lettered sentences appear in the back of the book. Example:

> The officer a radar gun in his hand gauged the speed of the passing cars.
>
> The officer, a radar gun in his hand, gauged the speed of the passing cars.

a. The university insisted however that the students were not accepted merely because of their parents' generous contributions.

b. This dispute in any case is an old one.

c. It was the young man's striking good looks not his acting ability that first attracted the Hollywood agents.

d. Gretchen learned moreover not always to accept as true what she had read in celebrity magazines.

e. The hikers most of them wearing ponchos or rain jackets headed out into the steady drizzle.

1. The lawsuit demanded furthermore that construction already under way be halted immediately.

2. It is the Supreme Court not Congress or the president that ultimately determines the legality of a law.

3. The judge complained that the case was being tried not by the court but by the media.

4. The actor kneeling recited the lines with great emotion.

5. Both sides' patience running thin workers and management carried the strike into its sixth week.

21k Use commas to set off a direct quotation from your own words.

When you briefly quote someone, distinguish the source's words from yours with commas (and, of course, quotation marks). When you insert an explanation into a quotation (such as *he said*), set that off with commas.

For advice on using punctuation marks with quotations, see 25g–25i; for advice on using quotation marks, see 25a–25d and C3 in the Quick Editing Guide, pp. A-52–A-53.

> Shakespeare wrote, "Some are born great, some achieve greatness, and some have greatness thrust upon them."

> "The best thing that can come with success," commented the actress Liv Ullmann, "is the knowledge that it is nothing to long for."

The comma always comes *before* the quotation marks.

EXCEPTION: Do not use a comma with a very short quotation or one introduced by *that*.

> Don't tell me "yes" if you mean "maybe."

> Jules said that "Nothing ventured, nothing gained" is his motto.

Don't use a comma with any quotation run into your own sentence and read as part of it. Often such quotations are introduced by linking verbs.

linking verb: A verb (*is, become, seem, feel*) that shows a state of being by linking the sentence subject with a word that renames or describes the subject: The sky *is* blue. (See 3a.)

> Her favorite statement at age three was "I can do it myself."

> Shakespeare originated the expression "my salad days, when I was green in judgment."

21l Use commas around *yes* and *no,* mild interjections, tag questions, and the name or title of someone directly addressed.

YES AND NO	*Yes,* I'd like a Rolls-Royce, but, *no,* I didn't order one.
INTERJECTION	*Well,* don't blame it on me.
TAG QUESTION	It would be fun to ride in a Silver Cloud, *wouldn't it?*
DIRECT ADDRESS	Drive us home, *James.*

interjection: A word or expression (*oh, alas*) that inserts an outburst of feeling at the beginning, middle, or end of a sentence

21m Use commas to set off dates, states, countries, and addresses.

On June 6, 1990, Ned Shaw was born.

East Rutherford, New Jersey, seemed like Paris, France, to him.

His family moved to 11 Maple Street, Middletown, Ohio.

Do not add a comma between state and zip code: *Bedford, MA 01730.*

For more practice, visit <**bedfordstmartins .com/bedguide**>.

Exercise 21–5 ▪ Using Commas

Add any necessary commas to the following sentences, remove any commas that do not belong, and change any punctuation that is incorrect. Some sentences may be correct. Answers for the lettered sentences appear in the back of the book. Example:

> When Alexander Graham Bell said "Mr. Watson come here, I want you" the telephone entered history.

> When Alexander Graham Bell said, "Mr. Watson, come here, I want you," the telephone entered history.

a. César Chávez was born on March 31 1927, on a farm in Yuma, Arizona.

b. Chávez, who spent years as a migrant farmworker, told other farm laborers "If you're outraged at conditions, then you can't possibly be free or happy until you devote all your time to changing them."

c. Chávez founded the United Farm Workers union and did indeed, devote all his time to changing conditions for farmworkers.

d. Robert F. Kennedy called Chávez, "one of the heroic figures of our time."

e. Chávez, who died on April 23, 1993, became the second Mexican American to receive the highest civilian honor in the United States, the Presidential Medal of Freedom.

1. Yes I was born on April 14 1988 in Bombay India.

2. Move downstage Gary, for Pete's sake or you'll run into Mrs. Clackett.

3. Vicki my precious, when you say, "great" or "terrific," look as though you mean it.

4. Perhaps you have forgotten darling that sometimes you make mistakes, too.

5. Well Dotty, it only makes sense that when you say, "Sardines!," you should go off to get the sardines.

21n Do not use a comma to separate a subject from its verb or a verb from its object.

FAULTY   The athlete driving the purple Jaguar, was Jim Fuld.
[Subject separated from verb]

EDITED   The athlete driving the purple Jaguar was Jim Fuld.

FAULTY   The governor should not have given his campaign manager, such a prestigious appointment.
[Verb separated from direct object]

EDITED   The governor should not have given his campaign manager such a prestigious appointment.

21o Do not use a comma between words or phrases joined by correlative or coordinating conjunctions.

For lists of coordinating words, see p. 842.

Do not divide a compound subject or predicate unnecessarily with a comma.

FAULTY   Neither Peter Pan, nor the fairy Tinkerbell, saw the pirates sneaking toward their hideout. [Compound subject]

EDITED   Neither Peter Pan nor the fairy Tinkerbell saw the pirates sneaking toward their hideout.

FAULTY   The chickens clucked, and pecked, and flapped their wings. [Compound predicate]

EDITED   The chickens clucked and pecked and flapped their wings.

21p Do not use a comma before the first or after the last item in a series.

FAULTY   We had to see, my mother's doctor, my father's lawyer, and my dog's veterinarian, in one afternoon.

EDITED   We had to see my mother's doctor, my father's lawyer, and my dog's veterinarian in one afternoon.

21q Do not use a comma to set off a restrictive word, phrase, or clause.

A restrictive modifier is essential to the definition or identification of whatever it modifies; a nonrestrictive modifier is not.

For an explanation of restrictive modifiers, see 21e.

FAULTY   The fireworks, that I saw on Sunday, were the best I've ever seen.

EDITED   The fireworks that I saw on Sunday were the best I've ever seen.

21r Do not use commas to set off indirect quotations.

When *that* introduces a quotation, the quotation is indirect and requires neither a comma nor quotation marks.

For more on quoting someone's exact words, see 25a–25c.

FAULTY   He told us that, we shouldn't have done it.

EDITED   He told us that we shouldn't have done it.

This sentence also could be recast as a direct quotation.

EDITED   He told us, "You shouldn't have done it."

22 | Semicolons

A semicolon is a sort of compromise between a comma and a period: it creates a stop without ending a sentence.

22a Use a semicolon to join two main clauses not joined by a coordinating conjunction.

Suppose, having written one statement, you want to add another that is closely related in sense. You decide to keep them both in a single sentence.

> Shooting baskets was my brother's favorite sport; he would dunk them for hours at a time.

A semicolon is a good substitute for a period when you don't want to bring your readers to a complete stop.

> By the yard life is hard; by the inch it's a cinch.

coordinating conjunction: A one-syllable linking word (*and, but, for, or, nor, so, yet*) that joins elements with equal or near-equal importance: Jack *and* Jill, sink *or* swim

NOTE: When you join a subordinate clause to a main one or join two statements with a coordinating conjunction, you can generally use just a comma. Reserve the semicolon to emphasize a close connection or to avoid confusion when long, complex clauses include internal punctuation.

22b Use a semicolon to join two main clauses that are linked by a conjunctive adverb.

You can use a conjunctive adverb to show a relationship between clauses such as addition (*also, besides*), comparison (*likewise, similarly*), contrast (*instead, however*), emphasis (*namely, certainly*), cause and effect (*thus, therefore*), or time (*finally, subsequently*). When a second statement begins with (or includes) a conjunctive adverb, you can join it to the first with a semicolon. No matter where the conjunctive adverb appears, the semicolon is placed between the two clauses.

For punctuation with conjunctive adverbs within clauses, see 21g.

> Bert is a stand-out player; *indeed,* he's the one hope of our team.

> We yearned to attend the concert; tickets, *however,* were hard to come by.

22c Use a semicolon to separate items in a series that contain internal punctuation or that are long and complex.

The semicolon is especially useful for setting off one group of items from another. More powerful than a comma, it divides a series of series.

> The auctioneer sold clocks, watches, and cameras; freezers of steaks and tons of bean sprouts; motorcycles, cars, speedboats, canoes, and cabin cruisers; and rare coins, curious stamps, and precious stones.

Exercise 22–1 ▪ Using Semicolons

For more practice, visit <bedfordstmartins .com/bedguide>.

Add any necessary semicolons to the following sentences, and change any that are incorrectly used. Some sentences may be correct. Answers for the lettered sentences appear in the back of the book. Example:

They spent all their money, they barely had enough to get home.

They spent all their money; they barely had enough to get home.

a. By the beginning of 2010, Shirley was eager to retire, nevertheless, she agreed to stay on for two more years.

b. The committee was asked to determine the extent of violent crime among teenagers, especially those between the ages of fourteen and sixteen, to act as a liaison between the city and schools and between churches and volunteer organizations, and to draw up a plan to reduce violence, both public and private, by the end of the century.

c. The leaves on the oak trees near the lake were tinged with red, swimmers no longer ventured into the water.

d. The football team has yet to win a game, however, the season is still young.

1. Although taking the subway is slow, it is still faster than driving to work.

2. The Mariners lost all three games to Milwaukee, worse yet, two star players were injured.

3. There was nothing the firefighters could do; the building already had been consumed by flames.

4. Chess is difficult to master; but even a child can learn the basic rules.

23 | Colons

A colon introduces a further thought, one added to throw light on a first. In using it, a writer declares: "What follows will clarify what I've just said." Some writers use a capital letter to start any complete sentence that follows a colon; others prefer a lowercase letter. Whichever you choose, be consistent. A phrase that follows a colon always begins with a lowercase letter.

23a Use a colon between two main clauses if the second exemplifies, explains, or summarizes the first.

Like a semicolon, a colon can join two sentences into one. The chief difference is this: a semicolon says merely that two main clauses are related; a colon, like an abbreviation for *that is* or *for example*, says that the second clause gives an example or explanation of the point in the first clause.

> She tried everything: she scoured the Internet, made dozens of phone calls, wrote e-mails, even consulted a lawyer.

main clause: A group of words that has both a subject and a verb and can stand alone as a complete sentence: *My friends play softball.*

23b Use a colon to introduce a list or a series.

A colon can introduce a word, a phrase, a series, or a second main clause, sometimes strengthened by *as follows* or *the following*.

> The dance steps are as follows: forward, back, turn, and glide.

When a colon introduces a series of words or phrases, it often means *such as* or *for instance*. A list of examples after a colon need not include *and* before the last item unless all possible examples have been stated.

> On a Saturday night many kinds of people crowd our downtown area: drifters, bored senior citizens, college students out for a good time.

23c Use a colon to introduce an appositive.

A colon preceded by a main clause can introduce an **appositive.**

> I have discovered the key to the future: robots.

appositive: A word or group of words that adds information by identifying a subject or object in a different way: my dog *Rover*, Hal's brother *Fred*

23d Use a colon to introduce a long or comma-filled quotation.

Sometimes you can't conveniently introduce a quoted passage with a comma. Perhaps the quotation is too long or heavily punctuated, or your prefatory remarks demand a longer pause. In either case, use a colon.

> God told Adam and Eve: "Be fruitful, and multiply, and replenish the earth, and subdue it."

23e Use a colon when convention calls for it.

AFTER A SALUTATION	Dear Professor James:
BIBLICAL CITATIONS	Genesis 4:7 [The book, chapter, verse]
TITLES: SUBTITLES	*Convergences: Essays on Art and Literature*
SOURCE REFERENCES	Welty, Eudora. *The Eye of the Story*. New York: Random, 1978.
TIME OF DAY	2:02 p.m.

23f Use a colon only at the end of a main clause.

In a sentence, a colon always follows a complete sentence, never a phrase. Avoid using a colon between a verb and its object, between a preposition and its object, and before a list introduced by *such as*.

main clause: A group of words that has both a subject and a verb and can stand alone as a complete sentence: *My friends play softball.*

FAULTY	My mother and father are: Bella and Benjamin.
REVISED	My mother and father are Bella and Benjamin.
FAULTY	Many great inventors have changed our lives, such as: Edison, Marconi, and Glutz.
REVISED	Many great inventors have changed our lives, such as Edison, Marconi, and Glutz.
REVISED	Many great inventors have changed our lives: Edison, Marconi, Glutz.

Exercise 23–1 ▪ Using Colons

For more practice, visit <**bedfordstmartins .com/bedguide**>.

Add, remove, or replace colons wherever appropriate in the following sentences. Where necessary, revise the sentences further to support your changes in punctuation. Some sentences may be correct. Possible revisions for the lettered sentences appear in the back of the book. Example:

> Yum-Yum Burger has franchises in the following cities; New York, Chicago, Miami, San Francisco, and Seattle.

> Yum-Yum Burger has franchises in the following cities: New York, Chicago, Miami, San Francisco, and Seattle.

a. The Continuing Education Program offers courses in: building and construction management, engineering, and design.

b. The interview ended with a test of skills, taking messages, operating the computer, typing a sample letter, and proofreading documents.

c. The sample letter began, "Dear Mr. Rasheed, Please accept our apologies for the late shipment."

1. In the case of *Bowers v. Hardwick,* the Supreme Court decided that: citizens had no right to sexual privacy.

2. He ended his speech with a quotation from Homer's *Iliad,* "Whoever obeys the gods, to him they particularly listen."

3. Professor Bligh's book is called *Management, A Networking Approach.*

24 | Apostrophes

Use apostrophes for three purposes: to show possession, to indicate an omission, and to add an ending to a number, a letter, or an abbreviation.

For advice on editing for apostrophes, see C2 in the Quick Editing Guide, pp. A-51–A-52.

24a To make a singular noun possessive, add -'s.

The *plumber's* wrench left grease stains on *Harry's* shirt.

Add -'s even when your singular noun ends with the sound of *s*.

Felix's roommate enjoys reading *Henry James's* novels.

Some writers find it awkward to add -'s to nouns that already end in an -s, especially those of two syllables or more. You may, if you wish, form such a possessive by adding only an apostrophe.

The Egyptian king *Cheops'* death occurred hundreds of years before *Socrates'.*

> ### Possessive Nouns and Plural Nouns at a Glance
>
> Both plural nouns and possessive nouns often end with -s.
>
> - *Plural* means more than one (two *dogs,* six *friends*), but *possessive* means ownership (the *dogs'* biscuits, my *friends'* cars).
> - If you can substitute the word *of* for the -s' (the biscuits *of* the dogs, the cars *of* my friends), you need the plural possessive with an apostrophe after the -s.
> - If you cannot substitute *of,* you need the simple plural with no apostrophe (the *dogs* are well fed, my *friends* have no money for gas).

24b To make a plural noun ending in *-s* possessive, add an apostrophe.

A *stockbrokers'* meeting combines *foxes'* cunning with the noisy chaos of a *boys'* locker room.

24c To make a plural noun not ending in *-s* possessive, add *-'s.*

Nouns such as *men, mice, geese,* and *alumni* form the possessive case the same way as singular nouns: with *-'s.*

What effect has the *women's* movement had on *children's* literature?

24d To show joint possession by two people or groups, add an apostrophe or *-'s* to the second noun of the pair.

I left my *mother and father's* home with *friends and neighbors'* good wishes.

If the two members of a noun pair possess a set of things individually, add an apostrophe or *-'s* to each noun.

Men's and *women's* marathon records are improving steadily.

24e To make a compound noun possessive, add an apostrophe or *-'s* to the last word in the compound.

A compound noun consists of more than one word (*commander in chief, sons-in-law*); it may be either singular or plural.

The *commander in chief's* duties will end on July 1.

Esther does not approve of her *sons-in-law's* professions.

24f To make an indefinite pronoun possessive, add -'s.

Indefinite pronouns such as *anyone, nobody,* and *another* are usually singular; they form the possessive case with -'s. (See 24a.)

> What caused the accident is *anybody's* guess, but it appears to be *no one's* fault.

24g To indicate the possessive of a personal pronoun, use its possessive case.

The personal pronouns° are irregular; each has its own possessive form, none with an apostrophe. Resist the temptation to add an apostrophe or -'s.

NOTE: *Its* (no apostrophe) is always a possessive pronoun.

> I retreated when the Murphys' German shepherd bared *its* fangs.

It's (with an apostrophe) is always a contraction of *it is.*

> *It's* [It is] not our fault.

personal pronoun: A pronoun (*I, me, you, it, he, we, them*) that stands for a noun that names a person or thing: Mark awoke slowly, but suddenly *he* bolted from the bed.

24h Use an apostrophe to indicate an omission in a contraction.

> *They're* [They are] too sophisticated for me.
>
> Pat *didn't* [did not] finish her assignment.
>
> Americans grow up admiring the Spirit of *'76* [1776].
>
> *It's* [It is] nearly eight *o'clock* [of the clock].

For a chart of possessive personal pronouns, see C2 in the Quick Editing Guide, p. A-51.

24i Use an apostrophe to form the plural of a letter or word mentioned as a word.

LETTER	How many *n*'s are there in *Cincinnati*?
WORD	Try replacing all the *should*'s in that list with *could*'s.

No apostrophes are needed for plural numbers and most abbreviations.

DECADE	The 1990s differed greatly from the 1980s.
NUMBER	Cut out two 3s to sew on Larry's shirt.
ABBREVIATION	Do we need IDs at YMCAs in other towns?

For advice on italicizing a letter, word, or number named as a word, see p. 899.

Exercise 24–1 ▪ Using Apostrophes

Correct any errors in the use of the apostrophe in the following sentences. Some sentences may be correct. Answers for the lettered sentences appear in the back of the book. Example:

> Youd better put on you're new shoes.
>
> *You'd* better put on *your* new shoes.

For more practice, visit <**bedfordstmartins .com/bedguide**>.

a. Joe and Chucks' fathers were both in the class of 90.

b. They're going to finish their term papers as soon as the party ends.

c. It was a strange coincidence that all three womens' cars broke down after they had picked up their mother's-in-law.

d. Don't forget to dot you're *i*s and cross you're *t*s.

e. Mario and Shelley's son is marrying the editor's in chief's daughter.

1. The Hendersons' never change: their always whining about Mr. Scobee farming land thats rightfully their's.

2. Its hard to join a womens' basketball team because so few of them exist.

3. I had'nt expected to hear Janice' voice again.

4. Don't give the Murphy's dog it's biscuit until it's sitting up.

5. Isnt' it the mother and fathers' job to tell kid's to mind their *p*s and *q*s?

25 | Quotation Marks

Quotation marks always come in pairs: one at the start and one at the finish of a quoted passage. In the United States, the double quotation mark (") is preferred over the single one (') for most uses. Use quotation marks to set off quoted or highlighted words from the rest of your text.

> "Injustice anywhere is a threat to justice everywhere," wrote Martin Luther King Jr.

25a Use quotation marks around direct quotations from another writer or speaker.

Enclose someone's exact words in quotation marks.

> Anwar al-Sadat reflected the Arab concept of community when he said, "A man's village is his peace of mind."

Use an indirect quotation to credit and report someone else's idea accurately. Do not use his or her exact words or quotation marks.

> Anwar al-Sadat asserted that a community provides a sense of well-being.

25b Use single quotation marks around a quotation inside another quotation.

Sometimes you may quote a source that quotes someone else or puts words in quotation marks. When that happens, use single quotation marks around the internal quotation (even if your source used double ones); put double quotation marks around the larger passage you are quoting.

> "My favorite advice from Socrates, 'Know thyself and fear all women,'" said Dr. Blatz, "has been getting me into trouble lately."

For more on editing quotation marks, see C3 in the Quick Editing Guide, pp. A-52–A-53.

For more on quoting, paraphrasing, and summarizing, see Ch. 12, D3–D5 in the Quick Research Guide (pp. A-27–A-28), or Chs. 31 and 34 in *A Writer's Research Manual.*

For capitalization with quotation marks, see 29j.

For punctuation of direct and indirect quotations, see 21r.

ESL Guidelines 🌐 Direct and Indirect Quotations

When you quote directly, use the exact words of the original writer or
speaker; set them off with double quotation marks. When you change a
direct quotation into an indirect quotation (someone else's idea reported
without using his or her exact words), be sure to reword the quotation.
Do not repeat the original wording from a source.

- Be sure to change the punctuation and capitalization. You also may
  need to change the verb tense.

  DIRECT QUOTATION   Pascal said, "The assignment is on Chinua
                             Achebe, the Nigerian writer."

  INDIRECT QUOTATION   Pascal said that the assignment was on Chinua
                             Achebe, the Nigerian writer.

- If the direct quotation is a question, you must change the word order
  in the indirect quotation.

  DIRECT QUOTATION   Jean asked, "How far is it to Boston?"

  INDIRECT QUOTATION   Jean asked how far it was to Boston.

  NOTE: Use a period, not a question mark, with questions in indirect
  quotations.

- Very often, you must change pronouns when using an indirect
  quotation.

  DIRECT QUOTATION   Antonio said, "I think you are mistaken."

  INDIRECT QUOTATION   Antonio said that he thought I was mistaken.

For practice, visit
**<bedfordstmartins
.com/bedguide>**.

According to the Organic Farming Research Foundation Web site at
<http://ofrf.org/resources/organicfaqs.html>, "All products sold as
'organic' must be certified."

25c Instead of using quotation marks, indent longer quotations.

Suppose you are writing an essay about the value of a college education.
You might include a paragraph like this:

In his 2004 commencement address at the College of William & Mary, comedian Jon
Stewart advised students to look beyond academic definitions of success:

> College is something you complete. Life is something you experience. So
> don't worry about your grade, or the results or success. Success is defined
> in myriad ways, and you will find it, and people will no longer be grading
> you, but it will come from your own internal sense of decency, which I
> imagine, after going through the program here, is quite strong . . .

although I'm sure downloading illegal files . . . but, nah, that's a different story.

For more on the MLA and APA styles, see section E in the Quick Research Guide (pp. A-30–A-35) and Chs. 36–37.

Indenting the passage shows that it is a direct quotation. You need not frame it with quotation marks. In MLA style, indent quotations of five lines or more by one inch. In APA style, indent quotations of forty words or more by about one-half inch. In both styles, double-space the quoted lines, and cite the source.

Follow the same practice if you quote four or more lines of a poem.

Phillis Wheatley, the outstanding black poet of colonial America, often made emotional pleas in her poems:

> Attend me, Virtue, thro' my youthful years
> O leave me not to the false joys of time!
> But guide my steps to endless life and bliss.
> Greatness, or Goodness, say what I shall call thee,
> To give me an higher appellation still,
> Teach me a better strain, a nobler lay,
> Oh thou, enthron'd with Cherubs in the realms of day (15-21).

For advice on capitalization and quotations, see 29j.

Notice that not only the source's words but her punctuation, capitalization, and line breaks are quoted exactly.

25d In dialogue, use quotation marks around a speaker's words, and mark each change of speaker with a new paragraph.

Randolph gazed at Ellen and sighed. "What extraordinary beauty."

"They are lovely," she replied, staring at the roses, "aren't they?"

25e Use quotation marks around the titles of a speech, an article in a newspaper or magazine, a short story, a poem shorter than book length, a chapter in a book, a song, and an episode of a television or radio program.

The article "An Updike Retrospective" praises "Solitaire" as the best story in John Updike's collection *Museums and Women*.

For advice on italicizing or underlining titles, see 31a and the chart on p. 899.

In Chapter 5, "Expatriates," Schwartz discusses Eliot's famous poem "The Love Song of J. Alfred Prufrock."

25f Avoid using quotation marks to indicate slang or to be witty or ironic.

INADVISABLE   By the time I finished my "chores," my "day off" was over.

REVISED   By the time I finished my chores, my day off was over.

No quotation marks are needed after *so-called* or similar words.

FAULTY   The meet included many so-called "champions."

REVISED   The meet included many so-called champions.

25g Put commas and periods inside quotation marks.

A comma or a period is always placed before quotation marks, even if it is not part of the quotation.

> We pleaded, "Keep off the grass," in hope of preserving the lawn.

> The sign warned pedestrians: "Keep off the grass."

For more on commas with quotations, see 21k.

25h Put semicolons and colons outside quotation marks.

> We said, "Keep off the grass"; they still tromped onward.

25i Put other punctuation inside or outside quotation marks depending on its function in the sentence.

Parentheses that are part of the quotation go inside the quotation marks. Parentheses that are your own, not part of the quotation, go outside.

> We said, "Keep off the grass (unless it's artificial turf)."

> They tromped onward (although we had said, "Keep off the grass").

If a question mark, exclamation point, or dash is part of the quotation, place it inside the quotation marks. Otherwise, place it after them.

> Who hollered "Fire"? She hollered, "Fire!"

Don't close a sentence with two end punctuation marks, one inside and one outside the quotation marks. If the quoted passage ends with a dash, exclamation point, question mark, or period, you need not add any further end punctuation. If the quoted passage falls within a question asked by you, however, the sentence should finish with a question mark, even if that means dropping other end punctuation (*Who hollered "Fire"?*).

Exercise 25-1 ▪ Using Quotation Marks

Add quotation marks wherever they are needed in the following sentences, and correct any other errors. Answers for the lettered sentences appear in the back of the book. Example:

> Annie asked him, Do you believe in free will?

> Annie asked him, "Do you believe in free will?"

For more practice, visit **<bedfordstmartins .com/bedguide>**.

a. What we still need to figure out, the police chief said, is whether the victim was acquainted with his assailant.

b. A skillful orator, Patrick Henry is credited with the comment Give me liberty or give me death.

c. I could hear the crowd chanting my name—Jones! Jones!—and that spurred me on, said Bruce Jones, the winner of the 5,000-meter race.

d. The video for the rock group Guns and Roses' epic song November Rain is based on a short story by Del James.

e. In response to a possible asteroid strike on Earth, former astronaut Rusty Schweickart says, Every country is at risk.

1. That day at school, the kids were as "high as kites."

2. Notice, the professor told the class, Cassius's choice of imagery when he asks, Upon what meat doth this our Caesar feed, / That he is grown so great?

3. "As I was rounding the bend," Peter explained, "I failed to see the sign that said Caution: Ice.

4. John Cheever's story The Swimmer begins with the line It was one of those midsummer Sundays when everyone sits around saying, I drank too much last night.

5. Who coined the saying Love is blind?

26 | Dashes

A **dash** is a horizontal line used to separate parts of a sentence—a dramatic substitute for a comma, semicolon, or colon. Your software may turn a typed dash, made by hitting your hyphen key twice without adding any spaces, to an unbroken line.

26a Use a dash to indicate a sudden break in thought or shift in tone.

The dash signals that a surprise is in store: a shift in viewpoint, perhaps, or an unfinished statement.

> Ivan doesn't care which team wins—he bet on both.

> I didn't notice my parents' accented speech—at least not at home.

26b Use a dash to introduce an explanation, an illustration, or a series.

appositive: A word or group of words that adds information by identifying a subject or object in a different way: my dog *Rover,* Hal's brother *Fred*

Use a dash to add an informal preparatory pause or to introduce an appositive that needs drama or contains commas.

> My advice to you is simple—stop complaining.

> Longfellow wrote about three young sisters—grave Alice, laughing Allegra, and Edith with golden hair—in "The Children's Hour."

26c Use dashes to set off an emphatic aside or parenthetical expression from the rest of a sentence.

It was as hot—and I mean *hot*—as the Fourth of July in Death Valley.

parenthetical expression: An aside to readers or a transitional expression such as *for example* or *in contrast*

26d Avoid overusing dashes.

The dash becomes meaningless if used too often. Use it only when a comma, a colon, or parentheses don't seem strong enough.

To compare dashes with commas, see 21, and with parentheses, see 27a–27b.

EXCESSIVE   Algy's grandmother—a sweet old lady—asked him to pick up some things at the store—milk, eggs, and cheese.

EDITED   Algy's grandmother, a sweet old lady, asked him to pick up some things at the store: milk, eggs, and cheese.

Exercise 26-1 ▪ Using Dashes

Add, remove, or replace dashes wherever appropriate in the following sentences. Some sentences may be correct. Possible answers for the lettered sentences appear in the back of the book. Example:

Stanton had all the identifying marks, boating shoes, yellow slicker, sunblock, and an anchor, of a sailor.

Stanton had all the identifying marks—boating shoes, yellow slicker, sunblock, and an anchor—of a sailor.

a. I enjoy going hiking with my friend John—whom I've known for fifteen years.

b. Pedro's new boat is spectacular: a regular seagoing Ferrari.

c. The Thompsons devote their weekends to their favorite pastime, eating bags of potato chips and cookies beside the warm glow of the television.

1. The sport of fishing—or at least some people call it a sport—is boring, dirty—and tiring.

2. At that time, three states in the Sunbelt, Florida, California, and Arizona, were the fastest growing in the nation.

3. LuLu was ecstatic when she saw her grades, all A's!

For more practice, visit **<bedfordstmartins .com/bedguide>**.

27 | Parentheses, Brackets, and Ellipses

Parentheses (singular, *parenthesis*) work in pairs. So do brackets. Both surround bits of information to make a statement perfectly clear. An ellipsis mark is a trio of periods inserted to show that something has been cut.

Parentheses

27a **Use parentheses to set off interruptions that are useful but not essential.**

FDR (as people called Franklin D. Roosevelt) won four presidential elections.

In fact, he occupied the White House for so many years (1933 to mid-1945) that babies became teenagers without having known any other president.

The material within the parentheses may be helpful, but it isn't essential. Without it, the sentences would still make good sense. Use parentheses to add a qualification, a helpful date, or a brief explanation — words that, in conversation, you might introduce in a changed tone of voice.

27b **Use parentheses around letters or numbers indicating items in a series.**

Archimedes asserted that, given (1) a lever long enough, (2) a fulcrum, and (3) a place to stand, he could move the earth.

No parentheses are needed for numbers or letters in an indented list.

For more practice, visit **<bedfordstmartins .com/bedguide>**.

Exercise 27-1 ▪ Using Parentheses

Add, remove, or replace parentheses wherever appropriate in the following sentences. Some sentences may be correct. Possible answers for the lettered sentences appear in the back of the book. Example:

The Islamic fundamentalist Ayatollah Khomeini — 1900–1989 — was a cleric and leader of Iran in the late twentieth century.

The Islamic fundamentalist Ayatollah Khomeini (1900–1989) was a cleric and leader of Iran in the late twentieth century.

a. Our cafeteria serves the four basic food groups: white — milk, bread, and mashed potatoes — brown — mystery meat and gravy — green — overcooked vegetables and underwashed lettuce — and orange — squash, carrots, and tomato sauce.

b. The hijackers will release the hostages only if the government, 1, frees all political prisoners and, 2, allows the hijackers to leave the country.

c. When Phil said he works with whales (as well as other marine mammals) for the Whale Stranding Network, Lisa thought he meant that his group lures whales onto beaches.

1. The new pear-shaped bottles will hold 200 milliliters, 6.8 fluid ounces, of lotion.
2. World War I, or "The Great War," as it was once called, destroyed the old European order forever.
3. The Internet is a mine of fascinating, and sometimes useless, information.

Brackets

Brackets, those open-ended typographical boxes, work in pairs like parentheses. Their special purpose is to mark changes in quoted material.

27c Use brackets to add information or to make changes within a direct quotation.

A quotation must be quoted exactly. If you add or alter a word or a phrase in a quotation from another writer, place brackets around your changes.

Suppose you are writing about James McGuire's being named chairman of the board of directors of General Motors. In your source, the actual words are these: "A radio bulletin first brought the humble professor of philosophy the astounding news." But in your paper, you want readers to know the professor's identity. So you add that information, in brackets.

> "A radio bulletin first brought the humble professor of philosophy [James McGuire] the astounding news."

Never alter a quoted statement any more than you have to. Ask yourself: Do I really need this quotation, or should I paraphrase?

For advice on quoting, paraphrasing, and summarizing, see Ch. 12, D3–D5 in the Quick Research Guide (pp. A-27–A-28), or Chs. 31 and 34 in *A Writer's Research Manual.*

27d Use brackets around *sic* to indicate an error in a direct quotation.

When you faithfully quote a statement that contains an error, follow the error with a bracketed *sic* (Latin for "so" or "so the writer says"). Usually you're better off paraphrasing an error-riddled passage.

> The book *Cake Wrecks* includes a photo of a cake with this message written on top in icing: Happy Thanksgiven [sic].

Ellipses

27e Use ellipses to signal that you have omitted part of a quotation.

Occasionally you will want to quote just the parts of a passage that relate to your topic. Acknowledge your cuts with **ellipses:** three periods with a space between each one (. . .). If ellipses conclude a sentence, precede them with a period placed after the end of the sentence.

Suppose you want to quote from Marie Winn's book *Children without Childhood* (New York: Penguin, 1984), but omit some of its detail. Use ellipses to show each cut:

> According to Winn, children's innocence can be easily lost: "Today's nine- and ten-year-olds . . . not infrequently find themselves involved in their own parents' complicated sex lives, . . . at least as advisers, friendly commentators, and intermediaries."

27f Avoid using ellipses at the beginning or end of a quotation.

For more on quoting, paraphrasing, and summarizing, see Ch. 12, D3–D5 in the Quick Research Guide (pp. A-27–A-28), or Chs. 31 and 34 in *A Writer's Research Manual*.

Even though a source continues after a quoted passage, you don't need ellipses at the end of your quotation. Nor do you need to begin a quotation with three dots. Save the ellipses for words or sentences you omit *inside* whatever you quote. If you plan to cut more than a section or two, think about paraphrasing instead.

For more practice, visit **<bedfordstmartins .com/bedguide>**.

Exercise 27-2 ▪ Using Brackets and Ellipses

The following are two hypothetical passages from original essays. Each one is followed by a set of quotations. Paraphrase or adapt each quotation, using brackets and ellipses, and splice it into the essay passage.

1. ESSAY PASSAGE

Most people are willing to work hard for a better life. Too often, however, Americans do not realize that the desire for more possessions leads them away from the happiness they hope to find. Many people work longer and longer hours to earn more money and as a result have less time to devote to family, friends, and activities that are truly important. When larger houses, sport-utility vehicles, and wide-screen TVs fail to bring them joy, they find even more things to buy and work even harder to pay for them. This cycle can grind down the most optimistic American. The only solution is to realize how few material possessions people absolutely need to have.

QUOTATIONS

a. Only when he has ceased to need things can a man truly be his own master and so really exist. —Anwar al-Sadat

b. I like to walk amidst the beautiful things that adorn the world; but private wealth I should decline, or any sort of personal possessions, because they would take away my liberty. —George Santayana

c. To live content with small means; to seek elegance rather than luxury, and refinement rather than fashion; to be worthy, not respectable and wealthy, not rich; to study hard, think quietly, talk gently, act frankly; to listen to stars and birds, to babes and sages, with open heart; to bear all

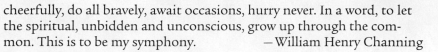

cheerfully, do all bravely, await occasions, hurry never. In a word, to let
the spiritual, unbidden and unconscious, grow up through the common. This is to be my symphony.   —William Henry Channing

2. ESSAY PASSAGE

Every human life is touched by the natural world. Before the modern
industrial era, most people recognized the earth as the giver and supporter
of existence. Nowadays, with the power of technology, we can (if we choose)
destroy many of the complex balances of nature. With such power comes
responsibility. We are no longer merely nature's children, but nature's
parents as well.

QUOTATIONS

a. The overwhelming importance of the atmosphere means that there are
   no longer any frontiers to defend against pollution, attack, or propa-
   ganda. It means, further, that only by a deep patriotic devotion to
   one's country can there be a hope of the kind of protection of the
   whole planet, which is necessary for the survival of the people of other
   countries.   —Anthropologist Margaret Mead

b. The survival of our wildlife is a matter of grave concern to all of us in
   Africa. These wild creatures amid the wild places they inhabit are not
   only important as a source of wonder and inspiration but are an inte-
   gral part of our natural resources and of our future livelihood and
   well-being.   —Former president of Tanzania Julius Nyerere

42 Mechanics

28 | Abbreviations

Abbreviations enable a writer to include necessary information in capsule form. Limit abbreviations to those common enough for readers to recognize, or add an explanation so that a reader does not wonder, "What does this mean?" Remember: when in doubt, spell it out.

28a Use abbreviations for some titles with proper names.

Abbreviate the following titles:

For advice on punctuating abbreviations, see 20b.

Mr. and Mrs. Hubert Collins	Dr. Martin Luther King Jr.
Ms. Martha Reading	St. Matthew

Write out other titles in full, including titles that are unfamiliar to readers of English, such as *M.* (for the French *Monsieur*) or *Sr.* (for the Spanish *Señor*).

General Douglas MacArthur	Senator Dianne Feinstein
President Barack Obama	Professor Shirley Fixler

Spell out most titles that appear without proper names.

FAULTY   Tomás is studying to be a dr.

REVISED   Tomás is studying to be a doctor.

When an abbreviated title (such as an academic degree) follows a proper name, set it off with commas. Don't add commas otherwise.

> Alice Martin, CPA, is the accountant for Charlotte Cordera, PhD.

> My brother has a BA in economics.

Avoid repeating forms of the same title before and after a proper name. Use either *Dr. Jane Doe* or *Jane Doe, DDS*, but not *Dr. Jane Doe, DDS*.

28b Use *a.m., p.m., BC, AD,* and *$* with numbers.

> 9:05 a.m.   3:45 p.m.   2000 BC   AD 1066

In case you are curious about abbreviations pinpointing years and times, *a.m.* means *ante meridiem*, Latin for "before noon"; *p.m.* means *post meridiem*, "after noon." AD is *anno domini*, Latin for "in the year of the Lord"—that is, since the official year of Jesus' birth. BC stands for "before Christ" and BCE for "before the common era."

For exact prices that include cents and for amounts in the millions, use a dollar sign with figures (*$17.95, $10.52, $3.5 billion*). Avoid combining an abbreviation with wording that means the same: *$1 million,* not *$1 million dollars; 9:05 a.m.* or *9:05 in the morning,* not *9:05 a.m. in the morning.*

28c Avoid abbreviating names of months, days of the week, units of measurement, or parts of literary works.

Many abbreviations in citations should be spelled out in MLA essay style.

NAMES OF MONTHS AND DAYS OF THE WEEK

After their session on September 3 [*or* the third of September], they did not meet until Friday, December 12.

UNITS OF MEASUREMENT

It would take 10,000 pounds of concrete to build a causeway 25 feet by 58 inches.

PARTS OF LITERARY WORKS

Von Bargen's reply appears in volume 2, chapter 12, page 187.

Leona first speaks in act 1, scene 2 [*or* the second scene of act 1].

28d Use the full English version of most Latin abbreviations.

Follow the conventions of your citation style when you use Latin abbreviations in source citations, parentheses, and brackets. However, unless you are writing for an audience of ancient Romans, translate most Latin abbreviations into English in your text.

For the use of *sic* to identify an error, see 27d.

COMMON LATIN ABBREVIATIONS

ABBREVIATION	LATIN	ENGLISH
et al.	*et alia*	and others, and the others (people)
etc.	*et cetera*	and so forth, and others, and the rest
i.e.	*id est*	that is
e.g.	*exempli gratia*	for example, such as

28e Use abbreviations for familiar organizations, corporations, and people.

Most sets of initials that are capitalized and read as letters do not require periods between the letters (CIA, JFK, UCLA). A set of initials that is pronounced as a word is called an **acronym** (NATO, AIDS, UNICEF) and never has periods between letters.

To avoid misunderstanding, write out an organization's full name the first time you mention it, followed by its initials in parentheses. Then, in later references, you can rely on initials alone. (For very familiar initials, such as FBI or CBS, you need not give the full name.)

28f Avoid abbreviations for countries.

When you mention the United States or another country in your text, give its full name unless the repetition would weigh down your paragraph.

> The president will return to the United States [*not* US] on Tuesday from a trip to the United Kingdom [*not* UK].

EXCEPTION: Unlike *US* as a noun, the abbreviation, used consistently with traditional periods or without, is acceptable as an adjective: *US Senate, U.S. foreign policy.* For other countries, find an alternative: *British ambassador.* Follow the conventions of your citation style when you cite or list government documents.

For more
practice, visit
**<bedfordstmartins
.com/bedguide>**.

Exercise 28-1 ▪ Using Abbreviations

Substitute abbreviations for words and vice versa wherever appropriate in the following sentences. Correct any incorrectly used abbreviations. Answers for the lettered sentences appear in the back of the book. Example:

> Please return this form no later than noon on Wed., Apr. 7.
>
> Please return this form no later than noon on *Wednesday, April 7.*

a. Prof. James has office hours on Mon. and Tues., beginning at 10:00 a.m.

b. Emotional issues, e.g., abortion and capital punishment, cannot be settled easily by compromise.

c. The red peppers are selling for three dollars and twenty-five cents a lb.

1. Hamlet's famous soliloquy comes in act three, sc. one.

2. A.I.D.S. has affected people throughout U.S. society, not just gay men and IV-drug users.

3. The end of the cold war between the U.S. and the Soviet Union complicated the role of the U.N. and drastically altered the purpose of N.A.T.O.

29 | Capital Letters

Use capital letters only with good reason. If you think a word will work in lowercase letters, you're probably right.

For advice and a useful chart on capitalization, see D1 in the Quick Editing Guide, p. A-53.

29a Capitalize proper names and adjectives made from proper names.
Proper names designate individuals, places, organizations, institutions, brand names, and certain other distinctive things. Any proper noun can have an adjective form, also capitalized.

For capitalization following a colon, see 23.

Miles Standish	University of Iowa	Australian beer
Belgium	a Volkswagen	a Renaissance man
United Nations	a Xerox copier	Shakespearean comedy

29b Capitalize a title or rank before a proper name.

During her second term, Senator Wilimczyk proposed several bills.

In his lecture, Professor Jones analyzed fossil evidence.

Titles that do not come before proper names usually are not capitalized.

Ten senators voted against the research appropriation.

Jones is the department's only full professor.

EXCEPTION: The abbreviation of an academic or professional degree is always capitalized. The informal name of a degree is not capitalized.

Dora E. McLean, MD, also holds a BA in music.

Dora holds a bachelor's degree in music.

29c Capitalize a family relationship only when it is part of a proper name or when it substitutes for a proper name.

Do you know the song about Mother Machree?

I have invited Mother to visit next weekend.

I would like you to meet my aunt, Emily Smith.

29d Capitalize the names of religions, their deities, and their followers.

Christianity	Muslims	Jehovah	Krishna
Islam	Methodists	Allah	the Holy Spirit

29e Capitalize proper names of places, regions, and geographic features.

Los Angeles	the Black Hills	the Atlantic Ocean
Death Valley	Big Sur	the Philippines

Do not capitalize *north, south, east,* or *west* unless it is part of a proper name (*West Virginia, South Orange*) or refers to formal geographic locations.

Drive south to Chicago and then east to Cleveland.

Jim, who has always lived in the South, likes to read about the Northeast.

A common noun such as *street, avenue, boulevard, park, lake,* or *hill* is capitalized when part of a proper name.

Meinecke Avenue	Hamilton Park	Lake Michigan

29f Capitalize days of the week, months, and holidays, but not seasons or academic terms.

During spring term, by the Monday after Passover, I have to choose between the January study plan and junior year abroad.

29g Capitalize historical events, periods, and documents.

Black Monday	the Roaring Twenties
the Civil War [*but* a civil war]	Magna Carta
the Holocaust [*but* a holocaust]	Declaration of Independence
the Bronze Age	Atomic Energy Act

29h Capitalize the names of schools, colleges, departments, and courses.

West End School, Central High School [*but* elementary school, high school]

Reed College, Arizona State University [*but* the college, a university]

Department of History [*but* history department, department office]

Feminist Perspectives in Nineteenth-Century Literature [*but* literature course]

29i Capitalize the first, last, and main words in titles.

When you write the title of a paper, book, article, work of art, television show, poem, or performance, capitalize the first and last words and all main words in between. Do not capitalize articles (*a, an, the*), coordinating conjunctions (*and, but, for, or, nor, so, yet*), or prepositions (such as *in, on, at, of, from*) unless they come first or last in the title or follow a colon.

ESSAY	"Once More to the Lake"
NOVEL	*Of Mice and Men*
VOLUME OF POETRY	*Poems after Martial*
POEM	"A Valediction: Of Weeping"

For advice on using quotation marks and italics for titles, see 25e and 31a.

29j Capitalize the first letter of a quoted sentence.

Oscar Wilde wrote, "The only way to get rid of a temptation is to yield to it."

Only the first word of a quoted sentence is capitalized, even when you break the sentence with words of your own.

"The only way to get rid of a temptation," wrote Oscar Wilde, "is to yield to it."

If you quote more than one sentence, start each one with a capital letter.

"Art should never try to be popular," said Wilde. "The public should try to make itself artistic."

Select a quoted passage carefully so that you can present its details accurately as it blends in with your sentence.

For advice on punctuating quotations, see 25g–25i.

For advice on using brackets to show changes in quotations, see 27c.

Exercise 29-1 ▪ Using Capitalization

Correct any capitalization errors you find in the following sentences. Some sentences may be correct. Answers for the lettered sentences appear in the back of the book. Example:

"The quality of mercy," says Portia in Shakespeare's *The Merchant Of Venice*, "Is not strained."

"The quality of mercy," says Portia in Shakespeare's *The Merchant of Venice*, "is not strained."

For more practice, visit **<bedfordstmartins .com/bedguide>**.

a. At our Family Reunion, I met my Cousin Sam for the first time, as well as my father's brother George.

b. I already knew from dad that his brother had moved to Australia years ago to explore the great barrier reef.

c. When my Uncle announced that he was moving to a Continent thousands of miles Southwest of the United States, his Mother gave him a bible to take along.

1. My Aunt, Linda McCallum, lived in the San Fernando valley and received her Doctorate from one of the State Universities in California.

2. She has pursued her interest in Hispanic Studies by traveling to South America from her home in Northeastern Australia.

3. She uses her maiden name — Linda McCallum, PhD — for her nonprofit business, Hands across the Sea.

30 | Numbers

Unless you are writing in a scientific field or your essay relies on statistics, you'll generally want to use words (*twenty-seven*). Figures (*27*) are most appropriate in contexts where readers are used to seeing them, such as times and dates (*11:05 p.m. on March 15*).

30a In general, write out a number that consists of one or two words, and use figures for longer numbers.

Short names of numbers are easily read (*ten, six hundred*); longer ones take more thought (*two thousand four hundred eighty-seven*). For numbers of more than a word or two, use figures.

Two hundred fans paid twenty-five dollars apiece for that shirt.

A frog's tongue has 970,580 taste buds; a human's has six times as many.

EXCEPTION: For multiples of a million or more, use a figure plus a word.

The earth is 93 million miles from the sun.

30b Use figures for most addresses, dates, decimals, fractions, parts of literary works, percentages, exact prices, scores, statistics, and times.

For examples, see Figures at a Glance on p. 897.

Using figures is mainly a matter of convenience. If you think words will be easier for your readers to follow, you can always write out a number.

Figures at a Glance

ADDRESSES	4 East 74th Street; also, One Copley Place, 5 Fifth Avenue
DATES	May 20, 2007; 450 BC; also, Fourth of July
DECIMALS	98.6° Fahrenheit; .57 acre
FRACTIONS	3½ years; 1¾ miles; half a loaf, three-fourths of voters
PARTS OF LITERARY WORKS	volume 2, chapter 5, page 37 act 1, scene 2 (*or* act I, scene ii)
PERCENTAGES	25 percent; 99.9 percent; also, 25%, 99.9%
EXACT PRICES	$1.99; $200,000; also, $5 million, ten cents, a dollar
SCORES	a 114–111 victory; a final score of 5 to 3
STATISTICS	men in the 25–30 age group; odds of 5 to 1 (*or* 5–1 odds); height 5'7"; also, three out of four doctors
TIMES	2:29 p.m.; 10:15 tomorrow morning; also, half past four, three o'clock (always with a number in words)

30c Use words or figures consistently for numbers in the same category throughout a passage.

Switching back and forth between words and figures for numbers can be distracting to readers. Choose whichever form suits like numbers in your passage, and use that form consistently for all numbers in the same category.

For more on the plurals of figures (*6s, 1960s*), see 24i.

> Of the 276 representatives who voted, 97 supported a 25 percent raise, while 179 supported a 30 percent raise over five years.

30d Write out a number that begins a sentence.

When a number starts a sentence, either write it out, move it deeper into the sentence, or reword the opening.

> Five percent of the frogs in our aquarium ate sixty-two percent of the flies.

> Ten thousand people packed an arena built for 8,550.

Exercise 30-1 ▪ Using Numbers

Correct any inappropriate uses of numbers in the following sentences. Some sentences may be correct. Answers for the lettered sentences appear in the back of the book. Example:

For more practice, visit **<bedfordstmartins .com/bedguide>**.

As Feinberg notes on page 197, a delay of 3 minutes cost the researchers 5 years' worth of work.

As Feinberg notes on page 197, a delay of *three* minutes cost the researchers *five* years' worth of work.

a. A program to help save the sea otter transferred more than eighty animals to a new colony over the course of 2 years; however, all but 34 otters swam back home again.

b. 12 percent or so of the estimated fifteen billion plastic water bottles purchased annually in the United States are recycled.

c. In act two, scene nine, of Shakespeare's *The Merchant of Venice*, Portia's 2nd suitor fails to guess which of 3 caskets contains her portrait.

1. *Fourscore* means 4 times 20; a *fortnight* means 2 weeks; and a *brace* is two of anything.

2. 50 years ago, traveling from New York City to San Francisco took approximately 15 hours by plane, 50 hours by train, and almost 100 hours by car.

3. At 7 o'clock this morning the temperature was already ninety-seven degrees Fahrenheit.

31 | Italics

Italic type—as in this line—slants to the right. In handwriting, indicate italics by underlining. Slightly harder to read than perpendicular type, it is usually saved for emphasis or other special uses.

31a Italicize certain titles, names, and words. Use italics for the types of titles, names, and words shown on page 899.

We read the story "Araby" in James Joyce's book *Dubliners*.

The Broadway musical *My Fair Lady* was based on Shaw's play *Pygmalion*.

31b Use italics sparingly for emphasis.

When you absolutely *must* stress a term, use italics. In most cases, the structure of your sentence should give emphasis where emphasis is due.

He put the package *under* the mailbox, not *into* the mailbox.

People living in affluent countries may not be aware that nearly *sixteen thousand children per day* die of starvation or malnutrition.

For titles that need to be placed in quotation marks, see 25e.

Italics at a Glance

Titles

MAGAZINES, NEWSPAPERS, AND SCHOLARLY JOURNALS

Newsweek   the *London Times*   *Film & History*

LONG LITERARY WORKS

The Bluest Eye (a novel)   *The Less Deceived* (a collection of poems)

FILMS

Psycho   *Casablanca*   *Avatar*

PAINTINGS AND OTHER WORKS OF ART

Four Dancers (a painting)   *The Thinker* (a sculpture)

LONG MUSICAL WORKS

Aïda   Handel's *Messiah*

CDS AND RECORD ALBUMS

Crash   *The Chronic*

TELEVISION AND RADIO PROGRAMS

Heroes   *All Things Considered*

Other Words and Phrases

NAMES OF AIRCRAFT, SPACECRAFT, SHIPS, AND TRAINS

the *Orient Express*   the *Challenger*

A WORD OR PHRASE FROM A FOREIGN LANGUAGE IF IT IS NOT IN EVERYDAY USE

Gandhi taught the principles of *satya* and *ahimsa:* truth and nonviolence.

EVERYDAY USE

I prefer provolone to mozzarella.

A LETTER, NUMBER, WORD, OR PHRASE WHEN YOU DEFINE IT OR REFER TO IT AS A WORD

The neon *5* on the door identified the club's address.

The rhythmic motion of the alimentary canal is called *peristalsis.*

What do you think *fiery* suggests in the second line?

When you give a synonym or translation — a definition of just a word or so — italicize the word and put its definition in quotation marks.

　The word *orthodoxy* means "conformity."

　Trois, drei, and *tres* are all words for "three."

EXCEPTION: The names of the Bible (King James Version, Revised Standard Version), the books of the Bible (Genesis, Matthew), and other sacred books (the Koran, the Rig-Veda) are not italicized.

For more
practice, visit
**<bedfordstmartins
.com/bedguide>**.

Exercise 31–1 ▪ Using Italics

Add or remove italics as needed in the following sentences. Some sentences may be correct. Answers for the lettered sentences appear in the back of the book. Example:

> Hiram could not *believe* that his parents had seen *the Beatles'* legendary performance at Shea Stadium.

> Hiram could not believe that his parents had seen the Beatles' legendary performance at Shea Stadium.

a. Does "avocado" mean "lawyer" in Spanish?

b. During this year's *First Night* celebrations, we heard Verdi's Requiem and Monteverdi's Orfeo.

c. It was fun watching the passengers on the Europa trying to dance to *Blue Moon* in the midst of a storm.

1. Jan can never remember whether Cincinnati has three n's and one t or two n's and two t's.

2. My favorite comic bit in "The Pirates of Penzance" is Major General Stanley's confusion between "orphan" and "often."

3. In Tom Stoppard's play "The Real Thing," the character Henry accuses Bach of copying a *cantata* from a popular song by *Procol Harum*.

32 | Hyphens

The hyphen, the transparent tape of punctuation, is used to join words and to connect parts of words.

32a Use hyphens in compound words that require them.

Compound words in the English language take three forms:

1. Two or more words combined into one (*crossroads, salesperson*)

2. Two or more words that remain separate but function as one (*gas station, high school*)

3. Two or more words linked by hyphens (*sister-in-law, window-shop*)

Compounds fall into these categories more by custom than by rule. When you're not sure which way to write a compound, refer to a current collegiate dictionary. If the compound is not listed, write it as two words.

Use a hyphen in a compound word containing one or more elements beginning with a capital letter.

Bill says that, as a *neo-Marxist* living in an *A-frame* house, it would be politically incorrect for him to wear a Mickey Mouse *T-shirt.*

Exceptions to this rule include *unchristian,* for one.

32b Use a hyphen in a compound adjective preceding, but not following, a noun.

Jerome, a devotee of *twentieth-century* music, has no interest in the classic symphonies of the *eighteenth century.*

I'd like living in an *out-of-the-way* place better if it weren't so far *out of the way.*

In a series of hyphenated adjectives with the same second word, you can omit that word (but not the hyphen) in all but the last adjective of the series.

Julia is a lover of eighteenth-, nineteenth-, and twentieth-century music.

The adverb *well,* when coupled with an adjective, follows the same hyphenation rules as if it were an adjective.

It is *well known* that Tony has a *well-equipped* kitchen, although his is not as *well equipped* as the hotel's.

Do *not* use a hyphen to link an adverb ending in *-ly* with an adjective.

The sun hung like a newly minted penny in a freshly washed sky.

32c Use a hyphen after the prefixes *all-, ex-,* and *self-* and before the suffix *-elect.*

Lucille's *ex-husband* is studying *self-hypnosis.*

This *all-important* debate pits Senator Browning against the *president-elect.*

32d Use a hyphen in most cases if an added prefix or suffix creates a double vowel, a triple consonant, or an ambiguous pronunciation.

It is also acceptable to omit the hyphen in the case of a double *e: reeducate.*

The contractor's *pre-estimate* did not cover any *pre-existing* flaws in the house.

The recreation department favors the *re-creation* of a summer program.

32e Use a hyphen in spelled-out fractions and compound whole numbers from twenty-one to ninety-nine.

When her sister gave Leslie's age as six and *three-quarters,* Leslie corrected her: "I'm six and *five-sixths!*"

The fifth graders learned that *forty-four* rounds down to forty while *forty-five* rounds up to fifty.

32f Use a hyphen to indicate inclusive numbers.

The section covering the years 1975-1980 is found on pages 20-27.

32g Use a hyphen to break a word between syllables at the end of a line.

Academic style guides (such as MLA and APA) prefer that you turn off your word processor's automatic hyphenation function. If you are designing a text that requires breaking a word, check your dictionary for its syllable divisions.

Exercise 32-1 ▪ Using Hyphens

For more practice, visit <bedfordstmartins.com/bedguide>.

Add necessary hyphens and remove incorrectly used hyphens in the following sentences. Some sentences may be correct. Answers for the lettered sentences appear in the back of the book. Example:

Her exhusband works part-time as a short order cook.

Her *ex-husband* works part-time as a *short-order* cook.

a. Jimmy is a lively four year old boy, and his sister is two years old.
b. The badly damaged ship was in no condition to enter the wide-open waters beyond the bay.
c. Tracy's brother in law lives with his family in a six room apartment.

1. Heat-seeking missiles are often employed in modern air-to-air combat.
2. *The Piano* is a beautifully-crafted film with first-rate performances by Holly Hunter and Harvey Keitel.
3. Nearly three fourths of the money in the repair and maintenance account already has been spent.

33 | Spelling

For a list of commonly confused homonyms, see D2 in the Quick Editing Guide, pp. A-53–A-56. See also A Glossary of Troublemakers, p. A-57.

English spelling so often defies the rules that many writers wonder if, indeed, there *are* rules. How, then, are you to cope? You can proofread carefully and use your spell checker. You can refer to lists of commonly misspelled words and of **homonyms,** words that sound the same, or almost the same, but are spelled differently.

For more spelling information and practice, visit <**bedfordstmartins .com/bedguide**>.

You can also use several tactics to teach yourself to be a better speller.

1. *Use mnemonic devices.* To make unusual spellings stick in your memory, invent associations. Using such mnemonic devices (tricks to aid memory) may help you with whatever troublesome spelling you are determined to remember. *Weird* behaves *weirdly.* Rise ag*ain*, Brit*ain*! One *d* in *dish,* one in *radish.* Why isn't *math*ematics like *athl*etics? You write a *letter* on station*ery.* Any silly phrase or sentence will do, as long as it brings tricky spellings to mind.

2. *Keep a record of words you misspell.* Buy yourself a little notebook in which to enter words that invariably trip you up. Each time you proofread a paper you have written and each time you receive one back from your instructor, write down any words you have misspelled. Then practice pronouncing, writing, and spelling them out loud until you have mastered them.

3. *Check any questionable spelling by referring to your dictionary,* your good-as-gold best friend. Use it to check words as you come up with them and to double-check them as you proofread and edit. If you are multilingual and originally learned British English, a good dictionary will distinguish American and British spellings (*color, colour; terrorize, terrorise*).

4. *Learn commonly misspelled words.* If you know that you are likely to confuse different words that sound alike, turn to the list of Commonly Confused Homonyms in the "Quick Editing Guide" (see p. A-55) and the Glossary of Troublemakers following that guide. Checkmark the words that you consider the trickiest—but don't stop there. Spend a few minutes each day going over them. Spell every troublesome word out loud; write it ten times. Do the same with any common problem words that your spell checker routinely catches, such as *nucular* for *nuclear* or *exercize* for *exercise.* Your spelling will improve rapidly.

Quick Format Guide

When you think about a newspaper, a specific type of publication comes to mind because the newspaper is a familiar *genre,* or form. Almost all newspapers share a set of defined features: a masthead, headlines, pictures with captions, graphics, and articles arranged in columns of text. Even if the details vary, you can still recognize a newspaper as a newspaper. Popular magazines, academic journals, letters of recommendation, corporate annual reports, and many other types of writing can be identified and distinguished by such features.

Readers also have expectations about how a college paper should be written and how it should look. They also may have expectations about the presentation of visual material such as graphs, tables, photographs, or other illustrations, depending on the field and the assignment. How can you find out what's expected? Check your course materials. Look for directions about format, advice about common problems, requirements for a specific academic style — or all three.

A | Following the Format for an Academic Paper

You can easily spot the appealing features of a magazine, newspaper, or Web site with bold headlines, colorful images, and creative graphics. Such lively materials serve their purpose, attracting your attention and promoting the interests of the publication's owners, contributors, or sponsors. In contrast, academic papers may look plain, even downright dull. However, their aim is not to entertain you with neon colors or dancing cats. Instead,

(continued on p. A-7)

MLA FIRST PAGE

Running head with writer's last name, one space, and the page number on every page

Writer's name

Instructor's name

Course

Date

Title, centered but not in quotes or italics

Double-spaced throughout

Uneven right margin with no automatic hyphenation

Thesis previewing paper's development

Launch statement names publication and author

Long quotation (5 prose or 4 poetry lines or more) indented without quotation marks

Ellipses show omissions and brackets show additions within a quotation

Page number locates information in source

Electronic sources without page numbers cited only by author or by title with organization as author

---

1″

½″

Williams 1

Christopher Williams

Professor Smith

Composition I

12 May 2010

Watercoolers of the Future

½″ indent or 5 spaces

1″   The traditional office environment includes many challenges such as commuting in rush-hour traffic, spending long hours in a cubicle, and missing family events due to strict work hours. These challenges are all changing, however, now that technology is altering how and where people work. With more and more freelance and home-based possibilities, a trend known as co-working has led to the development of shared workspaces. As technology changes the traditional office workspace, new co-working cooperatives are creating the watercoolers of the future, positive gathering spots where working people can meet and share ideas.   1″

New technology is leading the shift away from corporate offices. In *The Future of Work,* Malone explains this move away from the physical office with four walls:

1″

Dispersed physically but connected by technology, workers are now able . . . to make their own decisions using information gathered from many other people and places. . . . [They] gain the economic benefits of large organizations, like economies of scale and knowledge, without giving up the human benefits of small ones, like freedom, creativity, motivation, and flexibility. (4)

Working at a distance or from home can take a toll on workers, however. Loneliness and lack of social opportunities are some of the largest problems for people who do not work in a traditional office (Miller). This is where co-working comes in. Independent workers such as freelancers, people starting their own businesses, and telecommuters share office space. They often pay a monthly fee in exchange for use of the rented area and whatever it provides, such as desk space, meeting rooms,

1″

MLA WORKS CITED

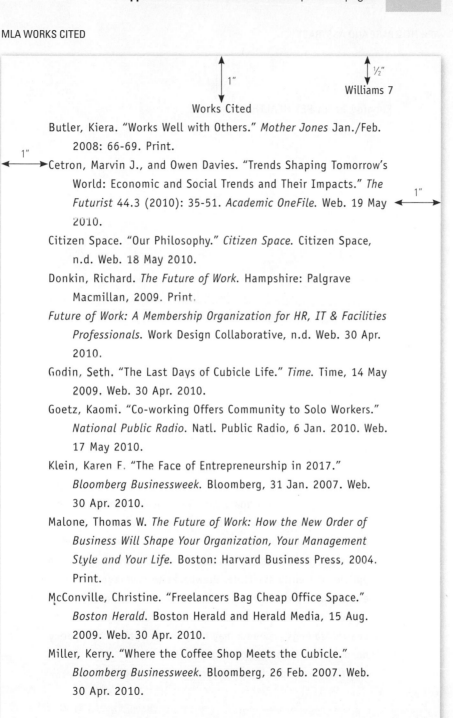

Works Cited

Butler, Kiera. "Works Well with Others." *Mother Jones* Jan./Feb.
2008: 66-69. Print.

Cetron, Marvin J., and Owen Davies. "Trends Shaping Tomorrow's
World: Economic and Social Trends and Their Impacts." *The
Futurist* 44.3 (2010): 35-51. *Academic OneFile*. Web. 19 May
2010.

Citizen Space. "Our Philosophy." *Citizen Space*. Citizen Space,
n.d. Web. 18 May 2010.

Donkin, Richard. *The Future of Work*. Hampshire: Palgrave
Macmillan, 2009. Print.

*Future of Work: A Membership Organization for HR, IT & Facilities
Professionals*. Work Design Collaborative, n.d. Web. 30 Apr.
2010.

Godin, Seth. "The Last Days of Cubicle Life." *Time*. Time, 14 May
2009. Web. 30 Apr. 2010.

Goetz, Kaomi. "Co-working Offers Community to Solo Workers."
National Public Radio. Natl. Public Radio, 6 Jan. 2010. Web.
17 May 2010.

Klein, Karen F. "The Face of Entrepreneurship in 2017."
Bloomberg Businessweek. Bloomberg, 31 Jan. 2007. Web.
30 Apr. 2010.

Malone, Thomas W. *The Future of Work: How the New Order of
Business Will Shape Your Organization, Your Management
Style and Your Life*. Boston: Harvard Business Press, 2004.
Print.

McConville, Christine. "Freelancers Bag Cheap Office Space."
Boston Herald. Boston Herald and Herald Media, 15 Aug.
2009. Web. 30 Apr. 2010.

Miller, Kerry. "Where the Coffee Shop Meets the Cubicle."
Bloomberg Businessweek. Bloomberg, 26 Feb. 2007. Web.
30 Apr. 2010.

List of Works Cited on a
separate page

Running head continues

List alphabetized by last
names of authors or by
titles (when no author is
named)

First line of entry at
left margin

Additional lines
indented ½"

Double-spaced
throughout

APA TITLE PAGE AND ABSTRACT

Running head with
short title in capital
letters on left and page
number on right

Double-spaced 12-point
Times New Roman font
recommended

Title, centered

Author

School

↕ 1"

Running head: PET HEALTH INSURANCE   1

Limitations of Pet Health Insurance
Jennifer Miller
Springfield Community College

Running head continues

Heading, centered

No paragraph
indentation

Double-spaced

Main ideas summed up in
no more than 250 words

Key words, common for
journal articles, also may
be expected by your
instructor

PET HEALTH INSURANCE   2

Abstract

In recent years, the amount of money spent annually in the
United States on veterinary care for household pets has risen
into the billions of dollars. One option for owners is to buy a pet
health insurance policy. Using the findings of several studies,
this report examines the advantages and disadvantages of the
policies currently available. Drawbacks to coverage include the
exclusion of pre-existing conditions and hidden fees. In the end,
this examination of pet health insurance concludes that interest-
bearing savings accounts may be a better option than policy
premiums for most pet owners.

Key words: pet health insurance, pet ownership

APA FIRST PAGE OF TEXT

PET HEALTH INSURANCE   3

½" (or 5–7   Limitations of Pet Health Insurance
spaces)
←→The Humane Society of the United States (2009) reports in

U.S. Pet Ownership Statistics that over 77 million dogs and

93 million cats are owned as household pets. However, only

3% of household pets are insured. Furthermore, in 2007, "only

850,000 pet insurance policies [were] in effect . . . according to

the National Commission on Veterinary Economic Issues"

(Weston, 2009). Recent studies suggest that, despite the

growing availability of insurance plans for pet health-care, these

policies may not be the cheapest way to care for a household

pet. Pet owners need to consider a number of factors before

buying a policy, including the pet's age, any pre-existing

diseases that an insurance carrier might decide not to cover, and

a policy's possible hidden fees.

Types of Pet Health Insurance Currently Available

Pet ownership is important to many people, and pets can do

a great deal to improve the mental health and quality of life for

their owners (McNicholas et al., 2005, p. 1252). However, paying

for a pet's own health care can be stressful and expensive.

Mathews (2009) reported on the costs in the *Wall Street Journal:*

½" This year, pet owners are expected to spend around $12.2

←→billion for veterinary care, up from $11.1 billion last year

and $8.2 billion five years ago, according to the American

Pet Products Association. Complex procedures widely used

for people, including chemotherapy and dialysis, are now

available for pets, and the potential cost of treating certain

illnesses has spiked as a result. (Introduction section,

para. 4)

Many providers currently offer plans to insure household

pets. The largest of the providers is the long-standing Veterinary

Pet Insurance (VPI), holding over two-thirds of the country's

market (Weston, 2009). Other companies include ASPCA Pet

Health Insurance, Petshealth Care Plan, and AKC Pet Healthcare

Plan. All offer plans for dogs and cats, yet VPI is one of only a

Running head continues

Title centered

Launch statement names organization as author with date added in parentheses

Double-spaced throughout

Uneven right margin with no automatic hyphenation

Brackets show additions and ellipses show omissions within a quotation

Electronic source without page cited only by author and date

Thesis previewing paper's development

First-level heading in bold type and centered

Citation identifies authors, date, and location in the source (required for quotation and preferred for paraphrase)

Long quotation (40 words or more) indented without quotation marks

Section name and paragraph number locate quotation in electronic source without page numbers

APA REFERENCES

Running head with page
numbering continues

Heading, centered

List alphabetized by
last names of authors
or by titles (when no
author is named)

First line of entry at
left margin

Additional lines
indented ½"

Double-spaced
throughout

No period after URL

No period after DOI
(digital object identifier)
for article

URL before period

PET HEALTH INSURANCE   12

References

Barlyn, S. (2008, March 13). Is pet health insurance worth the price?
The Wall Street Journal, p. D2.

Busby, J. (2005). *How to afford veterinary care without mortgaging
the kids.* Bemidji, MN: Busby International.

Calhoun, A. (2008, February 8). What I wouldn't do for my cat.
Salon. Retrieved from http://www.salon.com

Darlin, D. (2006, May 13). Vet bills and the priceless pet: What's a
practical owner to do? *The New York Times.* Retrieved from
http://www.nytimes.com

Humane Society of the United States (2009). U.S. pet ownership
statistics. Retrieved from http://www.humanesociety.org/issues
/pet_overpopulation/facts/pet_ownership_statistics.html

Kenney, D. (2009). *Your guide to understanding pet health insurance.*
Memphis, TN: PhiloSophia.

Mathews, A. W. (2009, December 9). Polly want an insurance policy?
Wall Street Journal. Retrieved from http://online.wsj.com

McNicholas, J., Gilbey, A., Rennie, A., Ahmedzai, S., Dono, J., &
Ormerod, E. (2005). Pet ownership and human health: A brief
review of evidence and issues. *British Medical Journal, 331,*
1252-1254. doi:10.1136/bmj.331.7527.1252

Price, J. (2010, April 9). Should you buy pet health insurance?
Christian Science Monitor. Retrieved from http://www.csmonitor
.com

Weston, L. P. (2009, December 21). Should you buy pet insurance?
MSN Money. Retrieved from http://articles.moneycentral.msn
.com

(continued from p. A-1)
they want to engage your mind. As a result, the conventions—the accepted expectations—for college papers vary by field but typically are designed to support core academic values: to present ideas, reduce distractions, and integrate sources. A conventional format reassures readers that you respect the values behind the guidelines.

Common Academic Values	Common Paper Expectations and Format
Clear presentation of ideas, information, and research findings	■ Word-processed text on one side of a white sheet of paper, double-spaced with one-inch margins ■ Paper printed in crisp, black, 12-point Times New Roman type with numbered pages
Investigation of an intriguing issue, unanswered question, unsolved puzzle, or unexplored relationship	■ Title and running head to clarify focus for reader ■ Abstract in social sciences or sciences to sum up paper ■ Opening paragraph or section to express thesis, research question, or conclusions ■ Closing paragraph or section to reinforce conclusions
Academic exchange of ideas and information, including evidence from reliable authorities and investigations	■ Quotations from sources identified by quotation marks or block format ■ Paraphrase, summary, and synthesis of sources ■ Citation of each source in the text when mentioned ■ Well-organized text with transitions and cues to help readers make connections ■ Possibly headings to identify sections
Identification of evidence to allow a reader to evaluate its contribution and join the exchange	■ Full information about each source in a concluding list ■ Specific format used for predictable, consistent arrangement of detail

MLA (Modern Language Association) style, explained in the *MLA Handbook for Writers of Research Papers,* Seventh Edition (New York-MLA, 2009), is commonly used in the humanities. APA (American Psychological Association) style, explained in the *Publication Manual of the American Psychological Association,* Sixth Edition (Washington, D.C.: Amer. Psychological Assn., 2010), is commonly used in the social and behavioral sciences. Both MLA and APA, like other academic styles, specify how a page should look and how sources should be credited. (See pp. A-2–A-6.)

For examples showing how to cite and list sources in MLA and APA styles, see E in the Quick Research Guide, pp. A-30–A-35.

B | Integrating and Crediting Visuals

Adding visuals to your text can engage readers, convey information, and re-inforce your words. The MLA and APA academic style guides divide visuals into two groups:

- **Tables** are grids that report numerical data or other information clearly and efficiently in columns (running up and down) and rows (running across).
- **Figures** include charts, graphs, diagrams, drawings, maps, photographs, or other images.

Much of the time you can create pie charts, bar charts, or tables in your text file using your software, spreadsheet, or presentation options. Try a drawing program for making diagrams, maps, or sketches or an image editor for scanning print photographs or adding your own digital shots.

When you add visuals from other sources, your simplest method may be to add an extra page break in your text where you want to place the material, print your file, and use the numbered blank page to photocopy or present the material. Alternatives include scanning printed material, picking up existing online graphics, or turning to the computer lab for sophisticated software or equipment. For a complex project, get help well ahead of your deadline, and allow plenty of time to learn new techniques.

Select or design visuals that are clear, easy to read, and informative. Use them to:

- Present statistical information, use graphs, charts, or tables.
- Discuss a conflict in a certain geographical area, supply a map.
- Illustrate a reflective essay, scan an image of yourself as a child or at an important moment.
- Clarify stages or steps in a process, procedure, or set of directions, add a diagram.

B1 Position visuals and credit any sources.

Introduce each visual by providing a context for it, identifying and explaining it in your text, and helping a reader see how it supports your point. Following your style guide, identify and number it as a table or figure and if needed, clarify its location within your paper.

Place the visual near the related text discussion so readers can easily connect the two. Solve any layout problems in your final draft as you arrange text and visual on the page. For instance, align an image with the left margin so that it continues the text's forward movement. Use it to balance and support, not overshadow, text. Let the visual draw a reader's eye with an appropriate — not excessive — share of the page. If you wish to present a long table or large photograph on its own page, simply add page breaks before and after it. If you need to include tables or figures for reference, such as your survey forms, consider placing them in an appendix or collecting them in an electronic supplement, as APA suggests.

Acknowledge visual sources as carefully as textual sources. When your material comes from a source, printed or electronic, credit it as you present the visual. Ask permission, if required, to use an image from a copyrighted source, including most printed books, articles, and other materials, and credit the owner of the copyright. If you download an image from the Web, follow the site guidelines for the use of images. If you are uncertain about whether you can use an image from a source, ask your teacher's advice.

B2 Prepare tables using MLA or APA format.

If you conduct a small survey, use the insert or table menu to create a simple table to summarize responses. Supply a label and a title or caption before the table. (Italicize its name if you are using APA style.) Double-space, add lines to separate sections, and use letters to identify any notes.

TABLE FORMAT FOR PRESENTING YOUR SURVEY FINDINGS

Table 1

Sources of Financial Support Reported by Survey Participants[a]

Type of Support	First-Year Students (n = 20)	Other Undergraduates (n = 30)
Scholarship or Campus Grant	25%	20%
Student Loans	40%	57%
Work Study	20%	7%
Family Support	50%	40%
Part-Time or Full-Time Job	25%	57%
Employer or Military Contribution	10%	17%
Other	5%	7%

a. Percentages based on the total number of respondents (n) were calculated and rounded to the nearest whole number.

(Margin labels: Label with number · Title or caption · Letter keyed to note · Column headings · Pair of rules or lines to enclose heading · Rule or line to mark end · Note of explanation if needed)

If your results came from only a few students at one campus, you might want to compare them with a table showing state or national findings, as in the next sample table. When you include a table or an image from a source, credit it, and identify it as a source (MLA) or as adapted (APA) if you have modified it.

TABLE FORMAT FOR MLA AND APA SOURCE CREDITS

Label with number

Table 2

Title or caption

Percentages of Undergraduates Receiving Selected Types of Financial Aid, by Type of Institution, Attendance Pattern, Dependency Status, and Income Level: 2007-08

Column headings

Institution Characteristics	Any Grants	Any Student Loans	Work-Study	Veterans Benefits
		Public		
2-year	39.6	13.2	0	2.0
4-year (non-doctorate)	52.5	43.4	7.3	2.4
4-year (doctorate)	53.1	47.8	8.0	2.0

Spanner heading (for all rows) centered

MLA source credit

Source: United States, Dept. of Educ., Inst. of Educ. Statistics, Natl. Center for Educ. Statistics; *2007-08 National Postsecondary Student Aid Study;* US Dept. of Educ., Apr. 2009; Web; 1 Feb. 2010; table 1.

The credit above follows MLA style; the credit below follows APA style. At the end of the entry, add the date and name of any copyright holder as requested.

APA source credit

Note. Adapted from U.S. Department of Education, Institute of Education Sciences, National Center for Education Statistics. 2009. *2007-08 National Postsecondary Student Aid Study* (NCES Publication No. NPSAS:08), Table 1.

B3 Add diagrams, graphs, charts, and other figures.

Select or design figures to convey information to readers. Consider your purpose and your readers' needs as you decide which types might be effective. A diagram to help readers see the sequence of steps in a process. A graph can show how different groups of people behave over time. A sketch of an old building can illustrate the style of its era. Add a clear caption or title to identify what you are illustrating as well as labels for readers to note key elements, add numerical or textual detail, and use visual elements — size, shape, direction, color — to emphasize, connect, or contrast.

- A process diagram can provide an overview that simplifies a complex process and clarifies its stages. Figure A.1 shows the stages in waste-water treatment.

- A comparative line graph can show how trends change over time. Figure A.2 compares trends in food allergies over a decade, marking percentages on the vertical line and years on the horizontal line.

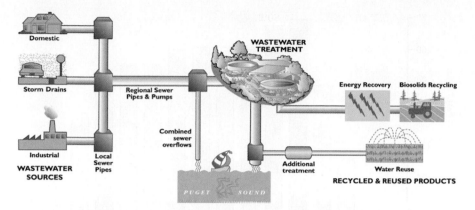

Figure A.1 A Diagram Showing the Process of Wastewater Treatment in King County, Washington. Source: King County, Washington, Department of Natural Resources Wastewater Treatment Division

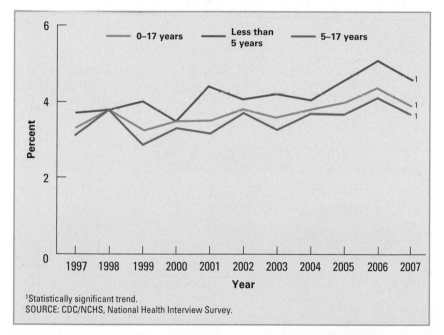

Figure A.2 A Comparative Line Graph Showing the Percentage of Children with a Reported Food or Digestive Allergy from 1997 through 2007 by Age Group. Source: The Centers for Disease Control and Prevention

- A column or bar graph can compare relative values. Figure A.3 illustrates the relative levels of alcohol usage among different age groups.
- A pie chart can compare components with each other and the whole. Figure A.4 shows how the total energy bill (100%) for a single family home is spent on various uses.

For a tutorial on preparing effective graphs and charts, see **<bedfordstmartins .com/bedguide>**.

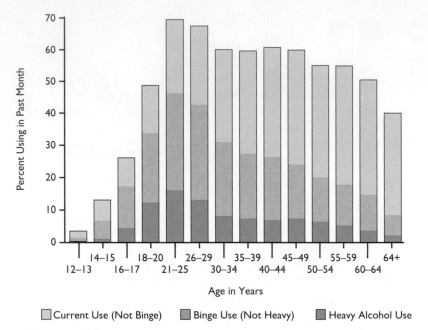

Figure A.3 A Bar Chart Presenting Numerical Comparisons. Source: U.S. Department of Health and Human Services, Substance Abuse and Mental Health Services Administration, Office of Applied Studies.

Where Does My Money Go?

Annual Energy Bill for a typical Single Family Home is approximately $2,200.

■ **Heating**

■ **Cooling**

■ **Water Heating**

■ **Appliances**
(includes refrigerator, dishwasher, clothes washer and dryer)

■ **Lighting**

  Electronics
(includes computer and monitor and TV and DVD player)

■ **Other***
(Includes external power adapters, telephony, set-top boxes, ceiling fans, vent fans and home audio)

Figure A.4 Pie Chart Showing Energy Consumption for a Typical Single Family Home in 2009. Source: ENERGYSTAR, The U.S. Environmental Protection Agency, The U.S. Department of Energy

C | Preparing a Document Template

Unless your teacher encourages creative formatting, avoid experimenting with a college paper. Follow the assigned format and style; check your finished paper against your instructor's directions and against examples (such as the MLA and APA samples in this format guide). Use your software's Help function to learn how to set font, page, format, or template features such as these:

- Placement of information on the first page
- Margin widths for the top, bottom, and sides of the page (such as 1″)
- Name of font (Times New Roman), style (regular roman, italics, or bold), and size of type (12 point)
- Running head with automatic page numbering
- Double spacing (without extra space between paragraphs)
- Text alignment, even on the left but not on the right (left alignment, not centered text, with automatic hyphenation of words turned off)
- Width of the paragraph indentation and special "hanging" indentation for your final list of sources
- Any other features of the required format

A template simplifies using expected features every time you write a paper with the same specifications. If you have trouble setting features or saving the template, ask for help from your instructor, from a classmate, at the writing center, or at the computer lab. Follow these steps to create your template:

1. Format your paper the way you want it to look.
2. Create a duplicate copy of your formatted file.
3. Delete all of the text discussion in the duplicate document.
4. Use the Save As feature to save the file as a document template.
5. Give the template a clear name ("Comp paper" or "MLA form").
6. To open a new file, select this template from your template folder.

D | Solving Common Format Problems

Because software programs differ, as do different versions of the same software, watch for default settings or format shifts that do not match an academic format.

- When you find unconventional features, such as extra lines between paragraphs or automatic hyphenation, reset these features.

- Use your software's Help function to look up the feature by naming it (paragraph), identifying the issue (paragraph spacing), or specifying what you want to do (troubleshoot paragraph spacing).
- Print the Help screens if the path seems complicated or the directions confusing.

Other problems might arise because academic style guides make their own assumptions about the texts their users are likely to write. For example, MLA style assumes that you will write an essay, simply separate items in a list with commas, and probably limit additions to tables and illustrations. On the other hand, APA style assumes that you might need section headings, lists (numbered, bulleted, or lettered within a sentence), and appendices, especially for research materials such as sample questionnaires. In addition, your instructor might require an outline or links for online sources. Follow your instructor's advice if your paper requires formatting that the style you are using (MLA or APA) does not recognize.

Readers appreciate your consideration of their practical problems, too. For example, your instructor might ask you to reprint a paper if your toner cartridge is nearly empty. Clear papers in a standard format are easier on the eyes than those with faint print or unusual features. In addition, such papers have margin space for comments so that they are easy to grade. Other readers may read your electronic file on a screen so they value your particular attention to online formatting conventions. Just as you want to address your readers' information needs, you also want to present a clear, neat, usable, readable document — one that readers can readily absorb.

E | **Designing Other Documents for Your Audience**

Four key principles of document design can help you prepare effective documents in and out of the classroom: know your audience, satisfy them with the features and format they expect, consider their circumstances, and remember your purpose.

DISCOVERY CHECKLIST

☐ Who are your readers? What matters to them? How might the format of your document acknowledge their values, goals, and concerns?

☐ What form or genre do readers expect? What features and details do they see as typical of that form? What visual evidence would they expect or accept as appropriate?

☐ What problems or constraints will your readers face as they read your document? How can your design help to reduce these problems?

☐ What is the purpose of your document? How can its format help achieve this purpose? How might it enhance your credibility as a writer?

☐ What is the usual format of your document? Find and analyze a sample.

E1   Select type font, size, and face.

Typography refers to the appearance of letters on a page. You can change typeface or font, style from roman to bold or italics, or type size for a passage by highlighting it and clicking on the appropriate toolbar icon. Selecting Font in the Format menu usually leads to options such as superscript, shadows, or small capitals.

Most college papers and many other documents use Times New Roman in a 12-point size. Signs, posters, and visuals such as slides for presentations might require larger type (with a larger number for the point size). Test such materials for readability by printing samples in various type sizes and standing back from them at the distance of your intended audience. Size also varies with different typefaces because they occupy different amounts of horizontal space on the page. Figure A.5 shows the space required for the same sentence written in four different 12-point fonts.

Times New Roman	An estimated 40 percent of young children have an imaginary friend.
Courier New	An estimated 40 percent of young children have an imaginary friend.
Arial	An estimated 40 percent of young children have an imaginary friend.
Comic Sans MS	An estimated 40 percent of young children have an imaginary friend.

Figure A.5 Space Occupied by Different Typefaces

Fonts also vary in design. Times New Roman and Courier New are called *serif* fonts because they have small tails, or serifs, at the ends of the letters. Arial and the more casual Comic Sans MS are *sans serif*—without serifs—and thus have solid, straight lines without tails at the tips of the letters.

Times New Roman (serif) K k P p

Arial (sans serif) K k P p

Sans serif fonts have a clean look, desirable for headlines, ads, "pull quotes" (in larger type to catch the reader's eye), and text within APA-style figures.

More readable serif fonts are used for article (or "body") text. In fact, Times New Roman, the common word-processor default font preferred for MLA and APA styles, was developed for the *Times* newspaper in London for its own use. As needed, use light, slanted *italics* (for certain titles) or dark **bold** (for APA headings).

E2   Organize effective lists.

The placement of material on a page — its layout — can make information more accessible for readers. MLA style recognizes common ways of integrating a list within a sentence: introduce the list with a colon or dash (or set it off with two dashes); separate its items with commas, or use semicolons if the items include commas. APA style adds options, preceding each item in a sentence with a letter enclosed by parentheses: (a), (b), and (c) or using display lists — set off from text — for visibility and easy reading.

APA recommends one type of displayed list, the numbered list, to emphasize priorities, conclusions, or processes such as steps in research procedures, how-to advice, or instructions, as in this simple sequence for making clothes:

NUMBERED LIST

1. Select your pattern and fabric.
2. Lay out the pattern and pin it to the fabric, noting the arrows and grain lines.
3. Cut out the fabric pieces, following the outline of the pattern.
4. Sew the garment together using the pattern's step-by-step instructions.

Another type of displayed list sets off a bit of information with a bullet, most commonly a small round mark (•) but sometimes a square (■), from the Toolbar or Symbol menu. Bulleted lists are common in résumés and other business documents but not necessarily in academic papers, though APA style now recognizes them. Use them to enumerate steps, reasons, or items when you do not wish to suggest any order of priority.

BULLETED LIST

- Let your hair dry without running a hair dryer.
- Commute by public transportation.
- Turn down the thermostat by one or two degrees.
- Unplug your phone charger and TV during the day.

E3   Consider adding headings.

In a complex research report, business proposal, or Web document, headings can provide a useful pathway, showing readers how the document is structured, which sections are most important, and how parts are related.

Headings also name sections so readers know where they are and where they are going. Headings at the same level should be consistent and look the same; headings at different levels should differ from each other and from the main text in placement and style, making the text easy to scan for key points.

For academic papers, MLA encourages writers to organize by outlining their essays but does not recommend or discuss text headings to help readers follow the organization. In contrast, APA illustrates five levels of headings beginning with these two:

First-Level Heading Centered in Bold

Second-Level Heading on the Left in Bold

Besides looking the same, headings at the same level in your document should be brief, clear, and informative, using consistent parallel phrasing. If you write a level-one heading as an *-ing* phrase, do the same for all the level-one headings that follow. Here are some examples of four common patterns for phrasing headings.

-ING PHRASES	QUESTIONS
Using the College Catalog	What Is Hepatitis C?
Choosing Courses	Who Is at Risk?
Declaring a Major	How Is Hepatitis C Treated?

NOUN PHRASES	IMPERATIVE SENTENCES
The Benefits of Electronic Commerce	Initiate Your IRA Rollover
The Challenges of Electronic Commerce	Learn Your Distribution Options
The Characteristics of the Online Shopper	Select New Investments

For more on parallel structure, see section B2 in the Quick Editing Guide, pp. A-48–A-49.

Web pages—especially home pages and site guides—generally have more headings than other documents because they are designed to help readers find information quickly, within a small viewing frame. If you design a Web page or post your course portfolio, consider what different readers might want to find. Then clearly connect your headings and content to users' needs.

When you begin college, you may feel uncertain about what to say and how to speak up. As you gain experience, you will join the intellectual exchange around you by reading, thinking, and writing with sources. You will be expected to turn to articles, books, and Web sites for evidence to support your thesis and develop your ideas. This expectation reflects the academic view that knowledge advances through exchange: each writer reads and responds to the writing of others, building and expanding the conversation.

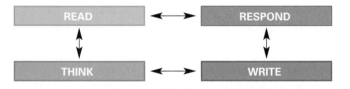

Conducting any research requires time to explore, to think, and to respond. However, efficient and purposeful research can produce greater success in less time than optimistic browsing. Perhaps you are writing about your experience, but you want to add a dash of supporting evidence from a source or two. Maybe you need a warm-up to build your confidence before a major research project. Possibly you need good advice fast: you've procrastinated, you're overwhelmed, or you're uncertain about how to succeed. To help you in such cases, this Quick Research Guide concentrates on five key steps.

TURNING TO SOURCES FOR SUPPORTING EVIDENCE

A | Defining Your Quest

Especially when your research goals are limited, you're more likely to succeed if you try to define the hunt in advance.

PURPOSE CHECKLIST

☐ What is the thesis that you want to support, the point that you want to demonstrate, or the question you want to answer?

For more about stating and using a thesis, see pp. 401–10.

☐ Does the assignment require or suggest any specific research focus — certain types of supporting evidence, sources, or presentations of material?

☐ Which ideas do you want to support with good evidence?

☐ Which ideas might you want to check, clarify, or change?

☐ Which ideas or opinions of others do you want to verify or counter?

☐ Do you want to analyze material yourself (for example, comparing different articles or Web sites) or to find someone else's analysis?

☐ What kinds of evidence do you want to use — facts, statistics, or expert testimony? Do you also want to add your own firsthand observation?

For more about types of evidence, see pp. 40–43.

TWO VIEWS OF SUPPORTING EVIDENCE

COLLEGE WRITER	COLLEGE READER
• Does it answer my question and support my thesis?	• Is it relevant to the purpose and assignment?
• Does it seem accurate?	• Is it reliable, given academic standards?
• Is it recent enough?	• Is it current, given the standards of the field?
• Does it add enough depth?	• Is it of sufficient quantity, variety, and strength?
• Is it balanced enough?	• Is it typical, fair, and complex?
• Will it persuade my audience?	• Does the writer make a credible case?

For evidence checklists, see p. 42 and p. A-22.

A1   Decide what supporting evidence you need.

When you want to add muscle to your college papers, you need reliable resources to supply facts, statistics, and expert testimony to back up your claims. Sometimes you won't need comprehensive information, but you will want to hunt—quickly and efficiently—for exactly what you do need. That evidence should satisfy you as a writer and also meet the criteria of your college readers—your instructors and possibly your classmates. Suppose, for example, that you are proposing solutions to your community's employment problem.

> WORKING THESIS
>
> Many residents of Aurora need more—and more innovative—postsecondary education to improve their job skills and career alternatives.

Because you already have ideas based on your firsthand observations and the experiences of people you know, your research goals are limited. First, you want to add accurate facts and figures that will show why you believe a compelling problem exists. Next, you want to visit the Web sites of local educational institutions and possibly locate someone to interview about existing career development programs.

A2   Decide where you need supporting evidence.

Sometimes, as you plan or draft, you may tuck in notes to yourself—find this, look that up, add some numbers here. Other times, you may not know exactly what or where to add. One way to determine where you need supporting evidence is to examine your draft, sentence by sentence.

- What does each sentence claim or promise to a reader?
- Where do you provide supporting evidence to demonstrate the claim or fulfill the promise?

The answers to these questions—your statements and your supporting evidence—often fall into a common alternating pattern:

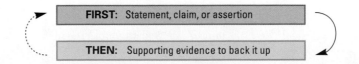

FIRST: Statement, claim, or assertion

THEN: Supporting evidence to back it up

For more about arguments based on claims of substantiation, evaluation, or policy, see pp. 168–70.

When you spot a string of assertions without much support, you have found a place where you might need more evidence. Select your evidence so that it substantiates the exact statement, claim, or assertion that precedes it. Likewise, if you spot a string of examples, details, facts, quotations, or other evidence, introduce or conclude it with an interpretive statement that explains the point the evidence supports. Make sure your general statement connects and pulls together all of the particular evidence.

When Carrie Williamson introduced her cause-and-effect paper, "Rain Forest Destruction," she made a general statement and then supported it by quoting facts from a source. Then she repeated this statement-support pattern, backing up her next statement in turn. By using this pattern from the very beginning, Carrie reassured her readers that she was a trustworthy writer who would try to supply convincing evidence throughout her paper.

For more on inductive and deductive reasoning, see pp. 46–48.

For the source entries from Carrie Williamson's MLA list of works cited, see pp. A-32–A-34.

The tropical rain forests are among the most biologically diverse communities in the world. According to the Rainforest Alliance, "The forests of the Neotropics are the habitat for tens of thousands of plant and wildlife species," as is the case for only one "square mile of tropical forest in Rondonia, Brazil," which is home to "1,200 species of butterflies—twice the total number found in the United States and Canada" ("Neotropical Rainforests"). These amazing communities depend on each part being intact in order to function properly but are being destroyed at an alarming rate. Each year "an area larger than Italy" (Soltani) is destroyed. Many rain forest conservationists debate the leading cause of deforestation. Regardless of which one is the major cause, the fact remains that both logging and slash-and-burn farming are destroying more and more acres of rain forests each year.

Statement

Supporting evidence: Information and statistics about species

Statement

Supporting evidence: Facts about destruction

Statement identifying cause-and-effect debate

Statement previewing points to come

The table below shows some of the many ways this common statement-support pattern can be used to clarify and substantiate your ideas.

First: Statement, Claim, or Assertion	Then: Supporting Evidence
Introduces a topic	Facts or statistics to justify the importance or significance of the topic
Describes a situation	Factual examples or illustrations to convey reality or urgency
Introduces an event	Accurate firsthand observations to describe an event that you have witnessed
Presents a problem	Expert testimony or firsthand observation to establish the necessity or urgency of a solution
Explains an issue	Facts and details to clarify or justify the significance of the issue
States your point	Facts, statistics, or examples to support your viewpoint or position
Interprets and prepares readers for evidence that follows	Facts, examples, observations, or research findings to develop your case
Concludes with your recommendation or evaluation	Facts, examples, or expert testimony to persuade readers to accept your conclusion

Use the following checklist to help you decide whether—and where—you might need supporting evidence from sources.

EVIDENCE CHECKLIST

☐ What does your thesis promise that you'll deliver? What additional evidence would ensure that you effectively demonstrate your thesis?

☐ Are your statements, claims, and assertions backed up with supporting evidence? If not, what evidence might you add?

☐ What evidence would most effectively persuade your readers?

☐ What criteria for useful evidence are most important to your readers? What evidence would best meet these criteria?

☐ Which parts of your paper sound weak or incomplete to you?

☐ What facts or statistics would clarify your topic?

☐ What examples or illustrations would make the background or the current circumstances clearer and more compelling for readers?

☐ What does a reliable expert say about the situation your topic involves?

☐ What firsthand observation would add authenticity?

☐ Where have peers or your instructor suggested more or stronger evidence?

B | Searching for Recommended Sources

When you need evidence, you may think first of the Internet. However, random Web sites require you to do extra work—checking what's presented as fact, looking for biases or financial motives, and searching for what's not stated rather than accepting what is. Such caution is required because anyone—expert or not—can build a Web site, write a blog, post a message, or send an e-mail. Repetition does not ensure accuracy, reliability, or integrity because the Internet has no quality controls.

On the other hand, when your college library buys books, subscribes to scholarly journals, and acquires references, print or electronic, these publications are expected to follow accepted editorial practices. Well-regarded publishers and professional groups turn to peer reviewers—experts in the field—to assess articles or books before they are selected for publication. These quality controls bring readers material that meets academic or professional standards. When you need to search efficiently, begin with reliable sources, already screened by professionals.

B1   Seek advice about reliable sources.

Although popular search engines can turn up sources on nearly any topic, will those sources meet your criteria and those of your readers? After all, your challenge is not simply to find any sources but to find solid sources with reliable evidence. The following shortcuts can help you find solid sources fast — ideally already screened, selected, and organized for you.

RESOURCE CHECKLIST

☐ Has your instructor suggested to the class where you might begin? Have you talked with your instructor after class, during office hours, or by e-mail to ask for advice about resources for your topic? Have you checked the assignment, syllabus, handouts, or class Web site?

☐ Have your classmates recommended useful academic databases, disciplinary Web sites, or similar resources?

☐ Does the department offering the course have a Web site with lists of resources available at the library or links to sites well regarded in that field?

☐ Does your textbook Web site provide links to additional resources?

☐ Which library databases does the librarian at the reference desk recommend for your course level and your topic?

☐ Which databases or links on your library's Web site lead to government (federal, state, or local) resources or articles in journals and newspapers?

☐ Which resources are available on library terminals or in the new periodicals or reference area of your campus library?

B2   Select reliable sources that meet readers' criteria.

If you planned to investigate common Internet hoaxes for a paper about online practices, you might deliberately turn to sources that are, by definition, unreliable. However, in most cases, you want to turn right away to reliable sources. For certain assignments, you might be expected to use sources as varied as reports from journalists, advice from practitioners in the field, accounts of historical eyewitnesses, or opposing opinions on civic policy. For other assignments, your instructor might expect you to turn not to popular but to scholarly sources—also identified as peer-reviewed or refereed sources—with characteristics such as these:

- in-depth investigation or interpretation of an academic topic or problem
- discussion of previous studies, which are cited in the text and listed at the end for easy reference by readers
- use of research methods accepted in a discipline or several fields

- publication by a reputable company or sponsoring organization
- acceptance for publication based on reviews by experts (peer reviewers) who assess the quality of the study
- preparation for publication supervised by academic or expert editors or by authors and professional staff

Your instructors may favor the quality controls of such publications, whether in print or online. Your campus librarian can help you limit your searches to peer-reviewed journals or check the scholarly reputation of sources that you find.

C | Evaluating Possible Sources

For exercises on evaluating Web sources in particular, visit **<bedfordstmartins .com/bedguide>**.

You may dream that your research will instantly turn up the perfect source. Like the perfect wave or the perfect day, such a source is hard to come by. Instead of looking for perfect sources, evaluate sources on the basis of practical needs, standards, and solid evidence.

C1 Evaluate sources as a practical researcher.

Your situation as a writer may determine how long or how widely you can search or how deeply you can delve into the sources you find. For example, if you are worried about finishing your paper on time or about juggling several assignments at once, you will need to search efficiently, evaluating sources first in terms of your own practical criteria.

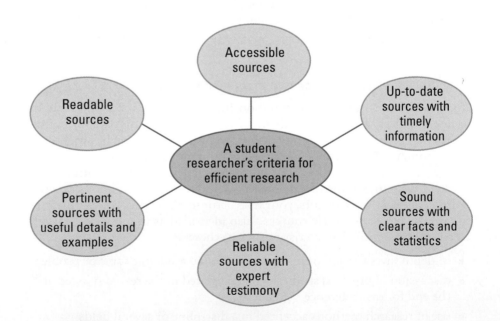

C2 Evaluate sources as your readers would.

Consider what your readers expect of the sources you select. If you are uncertain about college requirements, start with recommended sources that are easily accessible, readable, and up-to-date. Look for sources that are chock-full of reliable facts, statistics, research findings, case studies, observations, examples, and expert testimony that will persuade your readers.

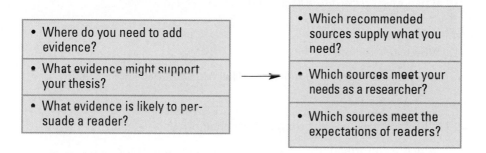

- Where do you need to add evidence?
- What evidence might support your thesis?
- What evidence is likely to persuade a reader?

→

- Which recommended sources supply what you need?
- Which sources meet your needs as a researcher?
- Which sources meet the expectations of readers?

C3 Evaluate sources for reliable and appropriate evidence.

When you use evidence from sources to support your points, both you and your readers are likely to hold two simple expectations:

- that your sources are reliable so you can trust their information
- that the information you select from them is appropriate for your paper

After all, how could an unreliable source successfully support your ideas? And what could unsuitable or mismatched information contribute? The difficulty, of course, is learning how to judge what is reliable and appropriate. The following checklist suggests how you can use the time-tested journalist's questions to evaluate each print or electronic source that you consider.

EVALUATION CHECKLIST

Who?

☐ Who is the author? What are the author's credentials and experience?

☐ Who is the intended audience? Is it general or academic?

☐ Who publishes or sponsors the source? Is this publisher well regarded?

☐ Who has reviewed the source before publication? Only the author? Expert peer reviewers? An editorial staff?

What?

☐ What is the purpose of the publication or Web site? Is it trying to sell, inform, report, or shape opinion?

☐ What bias or point of view might affect the reliability of the source?

☐ What evidence does the source present? Does the source seem trustworthy and logical? Does it identify its sources or supply active links?

When?

☐ When was the source published or created?

☐ When was it revised to stay up-to-date?

Where?

☐ Where did you find the source?

☐ Where is the source recommended? Has your library prescreened it?

Why?

☐ Why would you use this source rather than others?

☐ Why is its information relevant to your research question?

How?

☐ How does the source reflect its author, publisher or sponsor, and audience? How might you need to qualify its use in your paper?

☐ How would it support your thesis and provide persuasive evidence?

D │ Capturing, Launching, and Citing Evidence Added from Sources

For exercises on supporting a thesis statement, visit **<bedfordstmartins .com/bedguide>**.

For examples in both MLA and APA style, see E1–E2.

For exercises on incorporating source material and avoiding plagiarism, visit **<bedfordstmartins .com/bedguide>**.

Sometimes researchers concentrate so hard on hunting for reliable sources that they forget what comes next. The value of every source remains potential until you successfully capture its facts, statistics, expert testimony, examples, or other information in a form that you can incorporate into your paper. In addition, you need to launch — or introduce — the information in order to identify its source or its contribution to your paper. Finally, you must accurately cite, or credit, both in the text of your paper and in a final list of sources, each source whose words or ideas you use.

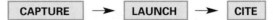

D1 Avoid plagiarism.

Allow enough time to add information from sources skillfully and correctly. Find out exactly how your instructor expects you to credit sources. Even if you do not intend to plagiarize — to use another writer's words or ideas without appropriately crediting them—a paper full of sloppy or careless shortcuts can look just like a paper deliberately copied from unacknowledged sources. Instead, borrow carefully and honestly.

Identify the source of information, an idea, a summary, a paraphrase, or a quotation right away, as soon as you write it in your notes. Carry that acknowledgment into your first draft and all that follow. You generally do not need to identify a source if you use what is called "common knowledge"—quotations, expressions, or information widely known and widely accepted. If you are uncertain about whether you need to cite a source, ask your instructor, or simply provide the citation.

D2 Read your source critically.

Before you pop any outside material into your paper, read critically to evaluate the reliability and suitability of the source. If you cannot understand a complicated source that requires specialized background, don't use it in your paper. If its ideas, facts, claims, or viewpoint seem unusual, incorporate only what you can substantiate in other, unrelated sources. On the other hand, if its evidence seems accurate, logical, and relevant, consider exactly how you might want to add it to your paper. Carefully distinguish it from your own ideas, whether you quote, paraphrase, or summarize.

For more on critical reading, see Ch. 2. For more on evaluating evidence, see pp. 42–43. For more on logical fallacies, see pp. 50–54, and 178–79.

D3 Quote accurately.

As you take notes, record as many quotations as you want if that process helps you master the material. When you add quotations to your paper, be selective. A quotation in itself is not necessarily effective evidence, and too many quotations will suggest that your writing is padded or lacks original thought. Quote exactly, and credit your source using the format expected.

For more on punctuating quotations and using ellipsis marks, see C3 in the Quick Editing Guide, pp. A-52–A-53.

QUOTATION CHECKLIST

☐ Have you quoted only a notable passage that adds support and authority?

☐ Have you checked your quotation word by word, for accuracy?

☐ Have you marked the beginning and the ending with quotation marks?

☐ Have you used ellipses (. . .) to mark any spot where you have left out words in the original?

☐ Have you identified the source of the quotation in a launch statement (see p. A-29) or in parentheses?

☐ Have you specified in parentheses the page number where the quotation appears in the source?

D4 Paraphrase carefully.

For more about how to
quote, paraphrase, and
summarize, see
pp. 234–53.

A paraphrase presents a passage from a source in your own words and sentences. It may include the same level of detail as the original, but it should not slip into the original wording (unless you identify those snippets with quotation marks). Credit the original source, just as you do when you quote.

PARAPHRASE CHECKLIST

☐ Have you read the passage critically to be sure you understand it?

☐ Have you paraphrased accurately, reflecting both the main points and the supporting details in the original?

☐ Does your paraphrase use your own words without repeating or echoing the words or the sentence structure of the original?

☐ Does your paraphrase stick to the ideas of the original?

☐ Have you revised your paraphrase so it reads smoothly and clearly?

☐ Have you identified the source of the paraphrase in a launch statement (see D6) or in parentheses?

☐ Have you specified in parentheses the page number where the passage appears in the source?

D5 Summarize fairly.

A summary clearly identifies the source and reduces its ideas to their essence. Using your own words, your summary may boil a book, a chapter, an article, or a section down to a few sentences that accurately and clearly sum up the sense of the original.

SUMMARY CHECKLIST

☐ Have you read critically to be sure you understand the source?

☐ Have you fairly stated the author's thesis, or main point, in your own words?

☐ Have you briefly stated any supporting ideas that you wish to summarize?

☐ Have you stuck to the overall point without bogging down in details?

☐ Has your summary remained respectful of the ideas and opinions of others, even if you disagree with them?

☐ Have you revised your summary so it reads smoothly and clearly?

☐ Have you identified the source of the summary in a launch statement (see D6) or in parentheses?

☐ Have you specified in parentheses the page number where any specific passage appears in the source?

D6 Launch and cite each quotation, paraphrase, summary, and synthesis.

Weave ideas from sources into your paper so that they effectively support the point you want to make. As you integrate each idea, take three steps.

1. Capture. Begin with the evidence you have captured from your source. Refine this material so that it will fit smoothly into your paper. Reduce your quotation to its most memorable words, freshen the wording of your paraphrase, or increase the precision of your summary. Synthesize by pulling together your own ideas and those of your sources so that you reach new insights. Position the evidence where it is needed to support your statements, claims, or assertions.

2. Launch. Launch, or introduce, the material captured from each source. Avoid tossing stand-alone quotations into your paper or stacking up a series of paraphrases and summaries. Instead, use your launch statement to lead smoothly into your source information. Try to draw on the authority of the source, mention the author's credentials, or connect the material to other sources or to your points. Let readers know why you have selected this evidence and what you think it contributes to your paper.

Dalton, long an advocate of "green" construction, recommends . . . (18).

As a specialist in elder law, attorney Tamara Diaz suggests . . . .

Like Westin, regional director Neil urges that ". . ." (308). Brown, however, takes an innovative approach to local conservation practices and recommends . . . (108).

Another policy analyst, arguing from principles expressed in the Bill of Rights, maintains . . . (Frank 96).

While Congress pits secure borders against individual liberties, immigration analyst Smith proposes a third possibility that might . . . (42).

3. Cite. Identify each source briefly yet accurately. Follow MLA, APA, or another academic format.

- Name the author in parentheses (unless named in your launch statement).
- In APA style, add the date of the source.

For more on launch statements, see pp. 244–45.

For more on punctuating quotations, see C3 in the Quick Editing Guide, pp. A-52–A-53.

For examples showing how to cite and list sources in your paper, see section E.

- Add an exact page number to locate the original passage.
- If a source has no author, begin the citation with the first words of the title.
- Add a full entry for each source to a list at the end of your paper.

E | Citing and Listing Sources in MLA or APA Style

For exercises on citing and listing sources in MLA style, visit **<bedfordstmartins .com/bedguide>**.

MLA style is the format for crediting sources that is recommended by the Modern Language Association and often required in English classes. APA style is the format recommended by the American Psychological Association, often used in the social sciences, business, and some composition classes. These two styles are widely used in college papers, but your specialized courses may require other academic styles, depending on the field. Because instructors expect you to credit sources carefully, follow any directions or examples supplied, or refer to the style manual required. Although academic styles all credit sources, they have many detailed differences. Stick to the one expected.

In both the MLA and APA styles, your sources need to be identified twice in your paper: first, briefly, at the very moment you draw upon the source material and later, in full, at the end of your paper. The short reference includes the name of the author of the source (or a short form of the title if the source does not name an author), so it's easy for a reader to connect that short entry in your text with the related full entry in the final alphabetical list.

E1   Cite and list sources in MLA style.

Cite in the text. At the moment you add a quotation, paraphrase, or summary, identify the source. Citations generally follow a simple pattern: name the author, and note the page in the original where the material is located.

(Last Name of Author ##)   (Talia 35)   (Smitt and Gilbert 152–53)

Place this citation immediately after a direct quotation or paraphrase.

> When "The Lottery" begins, the reader thinks of the "great pile of stones" (Jackson 191) as children's entertainment.

If you name the author in your launch, the citation is even simpler.

> As Hunt notes, the city faced "deficits and drought" (54) for a decade.

For quotations from poems, plays, or novels, supply line, act and scene, or chapter numbers rather than page numbers.

> The speaker in Robinson's poem describes Richard Cory as "richer than a king" (line 9), an attractive man who "fluttered pulses when he said,/ 'Good-morning'" (7–8).

If you use only one source, identify it at the beginning of your essay. Then just give page or line numbers in parentheses after each quotation or paraphrase.

CITATION CHECKLIST

☐ Have you placed your citation right after your quotation, paraphrase, or summary?

☐ Have you enclosed your citation with a pair of parenthesis marks?

☐ Have you provided the last name of the author either in your launch statement or in your citation?

☐ Have you used a short title for a work without an identified author?

☐ Have you added the exact page or other location number (such as a Web paragraph, poetry line, novel chapter, or play act and scene), as numbered in the source, to identify where the material appears?

List at the end. For each source mentioned in the text, supply a corresponding full entry in a list called Works Cited at the end of your paper.

WORKS CITED CHECKLIST

☐ Have you figured out what type of source you have used? Have you followed the sample pattern for that type as exactly as possible?

☐ Have you used quotation marks and italics correctly for titles?

☐ Have you used correct punctuation—periods, commas, colons, parentheses?

☐ Have you checked the accuracy of numbers: pages, volumes, dates?

☐ Have you accurately recorded names: authors, titles, publishers?

☐ Have you correctly typed the address of an electronic source that a reader could not otherwise find or that your instructor requires?

☐ Have you correctly arranged your entries in alphabetical order?

☐ Have you checked your final list against your text citations so that every source appears in both places?

☐ Have you double-spaced your list just like your paper, without any extra space between entries?

☐ Have you begun the first line of each entry at the left margin and indented each additional line as you would indent a paragraph?

For format examples, see the Quick Format Guide, pp. A-2–A-6.

Follow MLA patterns. Use the following examples as patterns for your entries. For each type of source, supply the same information in the same order, using the same punctuation or other features.

Book

If you need to find formats for other types of sources, consult the current *MLA Handbook for Writers of Research Papers,* often available in the library, or check your research manual or research guide for more information.

TEXT CITATION

(Rosenzweig 7)

WORKS CITED ENTRY

Author's name   Period   Title of book, in italics

Rosenzweig, Michael L. *Win-Win Ecology: How the Earth's Species Can Survive in the*

   Midst of Human Enterprise. New York: Oxford UP, 2003. Print.——————— Period

                     Period   City of   Publisher   Year of   Period   Medium
                              publication   publication   of publication

Essay, Story, or Poem from a Book

See the title page of this book and the reading on pp. 542–45 to find the details needed for this entry.

TEXT CITATION

(Brady 542)

WORKS CITED ENTRY

Author of   Title of selection,   Original date   Title of book or
selection   in quotation marks   (optional)   anthology, in italics

Brady, Judy. "I Want a Wife." 1971. *The Bedford Guide for College Writers.* 9th ed.

   Ed. X. J. Kennedy, Dorothy M. Kennedy, and Marcia F. Muth.—— Authors or editors
                                                                      of book
   Boston: Bedford, 2011. 542-44. Print.——————— Period

   City of   Publisher   Year of   Page numbers   Medium
   publication   of book   publication   of the selection   of publication

Popular Magazine Article

The author's name and the title generally appear at the beginning of an article. Typically, the magazine name, the date, and page numbers appear at the bottom of pages. Arrange the date in this order: 4 Oct. 2010.

TEXT CITATION

(Lobel 45)

WORKS CITED ENTRY

                   Title of article,   Title of magazine,   Medium of
Author's name   in quotation marks   in italics   publication

Lobel, Hannah. "Infinity or Bust." *Utne Reader* Nov.-Dec. 2006: 44-46. Print.

                                       Date of publication   Page numbers of the article

If the author is not identified, simply begin with the title of the article.

"How We Celebrate July 4th." *Parenting* June-July 2003: 22-23. Print.

Scholarly Journal Article

TEXT CITATION

(Goodin and Rice 903)

WORKS CITED ENTRY

Authors' names   Title of article, in quotation marks

Goodin, Robert E., and James Mahmud Rice. "Waking Up in the Poll Booth."

    Perspectives on Politics 7.4 (2009): 901-910. Print.

Title of journal,   Volume   Year   Page   Medium of
in italics   and issue   Colon   numbers   publication
                    numbers   of the article

Article from a Library Database

In databases, the publication information for the print source often appears at the top of the online entry. A printout usually records this information as well as your date of access. Follow the first page number of the print source by a hyphen if the full page range is not known.

TEXT CITATION

Omit the page number when it is not available in the online version.

(Soltani)

See p. A-21 for the text reference from Carrie Williamson's paper.

WORKS CITED ENTRY

Author's   Title of article,   Title of magazine,
name   in quotation marks   in italics

Soltani, Atossa. "Every Tree Killed Equals Another Life Lost." *Wood and Wood*

    Products 100.3 (1995): 86-. *Academic OneFile*. Web. 24 Feb. 2010.

Volume and   Date   Name of   Medium of   Date of
issue numbers   Colon   database,   publication access
                            in italics

First page of
print version

Page from a Web Site

The page title and site title often appear at the top of a given page. The date when a site was posted or last updated often appears at the bottom, as does the name of the sponsor (which also may appear as a link). A printout of the page will record this information as well as the date of access.

See p. A-21 for the text reference from Carrie Williamson's paper.

TEXT CITATION

The site is identified by title because it does not name an author. No page or paragraph numbers are available for the Web page.

According to the Rainforest Alliance, . . .

WORKS CITED ENTRY

No author   Title of page,   Title of site,   Sponsor   Date posted
identified   in quotation marks   in italics   name   or updated

"Neotropical Rainforests." *Rainforest-alliance.org.* Rainforest Alliance, 2010. Web.

    25 Feb. 2010.
                                      Medium of
      Date of visit   publication

E2 Cite and list sources in APA style.

Cite in the text. After the author's last name, add the date. Use p. (for "page") or pp. (for "pages") before the page numbers.

(Last Name of Author, Date, p. ##)   (Talia, 2010, p. 35)
(Smith & Gilbert, 2008, pp. 152–153)

List at the end. Call your list of sources References. Include all the sources cited in your text except for personal communications and classics.

Follow APA patterns. Use the following examples as patterns for your entries. For each type of source, supply the same information in the same order using the same punctuation or other features.

Book

TEXT CITATION

(Rosenzweig, 2003, p. 7)

REFERENCES ENTRY

Rosenzweig, M. L. (2003). *Win-win ecology: How the earth's species can survive in the midst of human enterprise.* Oxford, England: Oxford University Press.

Work or Section in a Book

Turn to the title page of this book and the reading selection on pp. 542–45 to find the details needed for this entry.

TEXT CITATION

(Brady, 1971/2011, p. 542)

REFERENCES ENTRY

Brady, J. (2011). I want a wife. In X. J. Kennedy, D. M. Kennedy, & M. F. Muth (Eds.), *The Bedford guide for college writers* (9th ed., pp. 542-44). Boston, MA: Bedford/St. Martin's. (Original work published 1971)

Popular Magazine Article

TEXT CITATION

("How We Celebrate," 2003, p. 22)

REFERENCES ENTRY

How we celebrate July 4th. (2003, June/July). *Parenting,* 22-23.

Scholarly Journal Article

For a magazine or journal article, add any volume number in italics and any issue number in parentheses, without a space or italics.

TEXT CITATION

(Goodin & Rice, 2009, p. 903)

REFERENCES ENTRY

Goodin, R. E., & Rice, J. M. (2009). Waking up in the poll booth. *Perspectives on Politics, 7,* 901-910. doi:10.1017/S1537592709991873

Article from a Library Database

IN-TEXT CITATION

No exact page or paragraph number may be available for an online article.

(Soltani, 1995)

REFERENCES ENTRY

The database does not need to be named unless a reader would have trouble finding the item without the archive's URL.

Soltani, A. (1995). Every tree killed equals another life lost. *Wood and Wood Products, 100*(3), 86-.

Page from a Web Site

TEXT CITATION

The site is identified by the sponsor because it does not identify an author.

According to the Rainforest Alliance, . . .

REFERENCES ENTRY

Your access date is not needed unless the material is likely to change.

Rainforest Alliance. (2010). Neotropical rainforests. Retrieved from Rainforest Alliance website: http://www.rainforest-alliance.org/aar.cfm?id=conservation

Quick Editing Guide

Editing and proofreading are needed at the end of the writing process because writers—*all* writers—find it difficult to write error-free sentences the first time they try. Sometimes as a writer you pay more attention to what you want to say than to how you say it. Sometimes you inaccurately remember spelling or grammar or punctuation. At other times you are distracted or simply make keyboarding errors. Once you are satisfied that you have expressed your ideas, you should make sure that each sentence and word is concise, clear, and correct.

Your grammar checker can help you catch some errors, but not others. For this reason, you always need to consider the grammar checker's suggestions carefully before accepting them, and you still need to edit on your own.

- A grammar checker cannot always correctly identify the subject or verb in a sentence; it may question whether a sentence is complete or whether its subject and verb agree, even when the sentence is correct.

- Grammar checkers are likely to miss certain problems such as misplaced modifiers, faulty parallelism, possessives without apostrophes, or incorrectly positioned commas.

- Most grammar checkers do a good job of spotting problems with adjectives and adverbs, such as confusing *good* and *well*.

You can also conduct searches for some of your problems.

- Keep track of your mistakes so that you develop an "error hit list."

- Use your software's Find and Replace capacity (try the Edit menu) to check quickly for searchable problems such as instances of *each* (always singular) or *few* (always plural) to see if all the verbs agree.

The computer can also help you read your draft more closely. For example, you can automatically isolate each sentence so that you are less likely to skip over sentence errors. First make a copy of your draft. Then use Replace in the Edit menu to convert every period in the file to a period and two returns. This change will create a version with each sentence separated by several spaces so that you can easily edit every one for fragments, comma splices, or other problems.

To help you edit, this Quick Editing Guide provides an overview of grammar, style, punctuation, and mechanics problems typical of college writing. Certain common errors in Standard Written English are like red flags to careful readers: they signal that the writer is either ignorant or careless. Use the editing checklist below to check your paper for these problems; then use the editing checklists in each section to help you correct specific errors. Concentrate on any problems likely to reappear in your writing.

For editing and proofreading strategies, see pp. 473–77.

EDITING CHECKLIST
Common and Serious Problems in College Writing

Grammar Problems

☐ Have you avoided writing sentence fragments?   A1

☐ Have you avoided writing comma splices or fused sentences?   A2

☐ Have you used the correct form for all verbs in the past tense?   A3

☐ Do all verbs agree with their subjects?   A4

☐ Have you used the correct case for all pronouns?   A5

☐ Do all pronouns agree with their antecedents?   A6

☐ Have you used adjectives and adverbs correctly?   A7

Sentence Problems

☐ Does each modifier clearly modify the appropriate sentence element?   B1

☐ Have you used parallel structure where needed?   B2

Punctuation Problems

☐ Have you used commas correctly?   C1

☐ Have you used apostrophes correctly?   C2

☐ Have you punctuated quotations correctly?   C3

Mechanics Problems

☐ Have you used capital letters correctly?   D1

☐ Have you spelled all words correctly?   D2

A | Editing for Common Grammar Problems

A1 Check for any sentence fragments.

A complete sentence is one that has a subject, has a predicate, and can stand on its own. A **sentence fragment** lacks a subject, a predicate, or both, or for some other reason fails to convey a complete thought. It cannot stand on its own as a sentence.

Though common in advertising and fiction, fragments are usually ineffective in college writing because they do not communicate coherent thoughts. To edit for fragments, check that each sentence has a subject and a verb and expresses a complete thought. To correct a fragment, complete it by adding a missing part, dropping an unnecessary subordinating conjunction, or joining it to a nearby sentence, if that would make more sense.

FRAGMENT	Roberto has two sisters. Maya and Leeza.
CORRECT	Roberto has two sisters, Maya and Leeza.
FRAGMENT	The children going to the zoo.
CORRECT	The children were going to the zoo.
CORRECT	The children going to the zoo were caught in a traffic jam.
FRAGMENT	Last night when we saw Cameron Diaz's most recent movie.
CORRECT	Last night we saw Cameron Diaz's most recent movie.

EDITING CHECKLIST
Fragments

☐ Does the sentence have both a subject and a complete verb?

☐ If the sentence contains a subordinate clause, does it contain a clause that is a complete sentence too?

☐ If you find a fragment, can you link it to an adjoining sentence, eliminate its subordinating conjunction, or add any missing element?

A2 Check for any comma splices or fused sentences.

A complete sentence has a subject and a predicate and can stand on its own. When two sentences are combined as one sentence, each sentence within the larger one is called a *main clause*. However, writers who fail to follow the rules for joining main clauses may create serious sentence errors. A

---

subject: The part of a sentence that names something—a person, an object, an idea, a situation—about which the predicate makes an assertion: The *king* lives.
predicate: The part of a sentence that makes an assertion about the subject involving an action (Birds *fly*), a relationship (Birds *have feathers*), or a state of being (Birds *are warm-blooded*)
subordinating conjunction: A word (such as *because, although, if, when*) used to make one clause dependent on, or subordinate to, another: *Unless* you have a key, we are locked out.

For exercises on fragments, visit **<bedfordstmartins .com/bedguide>**.

Take Action Improving Sentence Clarity

Ask each question at the top of the chart to consider whether your draft might need work on that issue. If so, follow the
ASK—LOCATE SPECIFICS—TAKE ACTION sequence to revise.

	Disconnected or Scattered Ideas?	Wordy Sentences?	Any Other Improvements in Sentence Style?
1 ASK	Have I tossed out my ideas without weighting or relating them?	Have I used more words than needed to say what I mean?	After a final look at the sentences in my draft, should I do anything else to improve them?
2 LOCATE SPECIFICS	■ Highlight the transitional words (*first, second, for example, however*). ■ Star all the sentences or sentence parts in a passage that seem to be of equal weight.	■ Read your draft out loud. Put a check by anything that sounds long-winded, repetitive, chatty, or clichéd. ■ Use past papers to help you list your favorite wordy expressions (such as *a large number of* for *many*) or extra words (such as *very* or *really*).	■ Read your draft out loud. Mark any sentences that sound incomplete, awkward, confusing, boring, or lifeless. ■ Ask your peer editors how you might make your sentences stronger and more stylish.
3 TAKE ACTION	■ Review passages with little highlighting; add more transitions to relate ideas. ■ In your starred sentences, strengthen the structure. Introduce less significant parts with subordinating words (*because, although*). Use *and* or *but* to coordinate equal parts.	■ At each check, rephrase with simpler or more exact words. ■ Search with your software for wordy expressions; replace or trim them. ■ Highlight a passage; use the Tools menu to count its words. See how many extra words you can drop.	■ Return to each mark to make weak sentences clear, emphatic, interesting, and lively. ■ Consider the useful suggestions of your peers. ■ Review sections A and B of this guide, and edit until your sentences express your ideas as you wish.

main clause: A group of words that has both a subject and a verb and can stand alone as a complete sentence: *My friends like baseball.*

coordinating conjunction: A one-syllable linking word (*and, but, for, or, nor, so, yet*) that joins elements with equal or near-equal importance: Jack *and* Jill, sink *or* swim

subordinating conjunction: A word (such as *because, although, if, when*) used to make one clause dependent on, or subordinate to, another: *Unless* you have a key, we are locked out.

For exercises on comma splices and fused sentences, visit **<bedfordstmartins .com/bedguide>**.

comma splice is two main clauses joined with only a comma. A **fused sentence** is two main clauses joined with no punctuation at all.

COMMA SPLICE	I went to the shop, I bought a new coat.
FUSED SENTENCE	I went to the shop I bought a new coat.

To find comma splices and fused sentences (also called run-ons), examine the main clauses in each sentence to make sure they are joined correctly. If you find a comma splice or fused sentence, correct it in one of these four ways, depending on which makes the best sense:

ADD A PERIOD	I went to the shop. I bought a new coat.
ADD A COMMA AND A COORDINATING CONJUNCTION	I went to the shop, and I bought a new coat.
ADD A SEMICOLON	I went to the shop; I bought a new coat.
ADD A SUBORDINATING CONJUNCTION	I went to the shop, where I bought a new coat.

EDITING CHECKLIST
Comma Splices and Fused Sentences

☐ Can you make each main clause a separate sentence?

☐ Can you link the two main clauses with a comma and a coordinating conjunction?

☐ Can you link the two main clauses with a semicolon or, if appropriate, a colon?

☐ Can you subordinate one clause to the other?

---

verb: A word that shows action (The cow *jumped* over the moon) or a state of being (The cow *is* brown)

A3 **Check for correct past tense verb forms.**

The **form** of a verb, the way it is spelled and pronounced, can change to show its **tense**—the time when its action did, does, or will occur (in the past, present, or future). A verb about something in the present will often have a different form than a verb about something in the past.

PRESENT	Right now, I *watch* only a few minutes of television each day.
PAST	Last month, I *watched* television shows every evening.

Many writers fail to use the correct form for past tense verbs for two different reasons, depending on whether the verb is regular or irregular.

Regular verbs are verbs whose forms follow standard rules; they form the past tense by adding -*ed* or -*d* to the present tense form:

watch/watched   look/looked   hope/hoped

Check all regular verbs in the past tense for one of these endings.

FAULTY	I *ask* my brother for a loan yesterday.
CORRECT	I *asked* my brother for a loan yesterday.

FAULTY	Nicole *race* in the track meet last week.
CORRECT	Nicole *raced* in the track meet last week.

TIP: If you say the final -*d* sound when you talk, you may find it easier to add the final -*d* or -*ed* when you write past tense regular verbs.

Because **irregular verbs** do not follow standard rules for their forms, their past tense forms are unpredictable and must be memorized. In addition, the past tense may differ from the past participle. Consult a dictionary for these forms.

participle: A form of a verb that cannot function alone as a main verb, including present participles ending in -*ing* (*dancing*) and past participles often ending in -*ed* or -*d* (*danced*)

FAULTY	My cat *laid* on the tile floor to take her nap.
CORRECT	My cat *lay* on the tile floor to take her nap.

FAULTY	I *have swam* twenty laps every day this month.
CORRECT	I *have swum* twenty laps every day this month.

TIP: In college papers, follow convention by using the present tense, not the past, to describe the work of an author or the events in a literary work.

FAULTY	In "The Lottery," Shirley Jackson *revealed* the power of tradition. As the story *opened,* the villagers *gathered* in the square.
CORRECT	In "The Lottery," Shirley Jackson *reveals* the power of tradition. As the story *opens,* the villagers *gather* in the square.

Irregular Verbs at a Glance

INFINITIVE (BASE)	PAST TENSE	PAST PARTICIPLE
begin	began	begun
burst	burst	burst
choose	chose	chosen
do	did	done
eat	ate	eaten
go	went	gone
lay	laid	laid
lie	lay	lain
speak	spoke	spoken

For a list of the principal parts of common irregular verbs (infinitive, past tense, and past participle forms), visit **<bedfordstmartins .com/bedguide>**.

For exercises on verbs, visit <bedfordstmartins.com/bedguide>.

EDITING CHECKLIST
Past Tense Verb Forms

☐ Have you identified the main verb in the sentence?

☐ Is the sentence about the past, present, or future? Does the verb reflect this time?

☐ Is the verb regular or irregular? Have you used its correct form?

A4   Check for correct subject-verb agreement.

The **form** of a verb, the way it is spelled and pronounced, can change to show **number**—whether the subject is singular (one) or plural (more than one). It can also show **person**—whether the subject is *you* or *she,* for example.

SINGULAR	Our instructor *grades* every paper carefully.
PLURAL	Most instructors *grade* tests using a standard scale.
SECOND PERSON	You *write* well-documented research papers.
THIRD PERSON	She *writes* good research papers, too.

A verb must match (or *agree with*) its subject in terms of number and person. Regular verbs (those whose forms follow a standard rule) are problems only in the present tense. There they have two forms: one that ends in *-s* or *-es* and one that does not. Only the subjects *he, she, it,* and singular nouns use the verb form that ends in *-s* or *-es.*

I like	we like
you like	you like
he/she/it/Dan/the child likes	they like

The verbs *be* and *have* are irregular, so their present tense forms must be memorized. The verb *be* is also irregular in the past tense.

> ### Forms of *Be* and *Have* at a Glance
>
> **THE PRESENT TENSE OF *BE***
>
> | I am | we are |
> |---|---|
> | you are | you are |
> | he/she/it is | they are |
>
> **THE PAST TENSE OF *BE***
>
> | I was | we were |
> |---|---|
> | you were | you were |
> | he/she/it was | they were |
>
> **THE PRESENT TENSE OF *HAVE***
>
> | I have | we have |
> |---|---|
> | you have | you have |
> | he/she/it has | they have |
>
> **THE PAST TENSE OF *HAVE***
>
> | I had | we had |
> |---|---|
> | you had | you had |
> | he/she/it had | they had |

verb: A word that shows action (The cow *jumped* over the moon) or a state of being (The cow *is* brown)

subject: The part of a sentence that names something—a person, an object, an idea, a situation—about which the predicate makes an assertion: The *king* lives.

Problems in agreement often occur when the subject is hard to find, is an indefinite pronoun, or is confusing. Make sure that you include any -s or -es endings and use the correct form for irregular verbs.

FAULTY	Jim *write* at least fifty e-mails a day.
CORRECT	Jim *writes* at least fifty e-mails a day.
FAULTY	The students *has* difficulty with the assignment.
CORRECT	The students *have* difficulty with the assignment.
FAULTY	Every one of the cakes *were* sold at the fundraiser.
CORRECT	Every one of the cakes *was* sold at the fundraiser.

EDITING CHECKLIST
Subject-Verb Agreement

☐ Have you correctly identified the subject and the verb in the sentence?

☐ Is the subject singular or plural? Does the verb match?

☐ Have you used the correct form of the verb?

A5 Check for correct pronoun case.

Depending on the role a pronoun plays in a sentence, it is said to be in the **subjective case, objective case,** or **possessive case.** Use the subjective case if the pronoun is the subject of a sentence, the subject of a subordinate clause, or a subject complement (after a linking verb). Use the objective case if the pronoun is a direct or indirect object of a verb or the object of a preposition. Use the possessive case to show possession.

SUBJECTIVE	*I* will argue that our campus needs more parking.
OBJECTIVE	This issue is important to *me*.
POSSESSIVE	*My* argument will be quite persuasive.

Writers often use the subjective case when they should use the objective case—sometimes trying to sound formal and correct. Instead, choose the correct form based on a pronoun's function in the sentence. If the sentence pairs a noun and a pronoun, try the sentence with the pronoun alone.

FAULTY	My company gave my husband and *I* a trip to Hawaii.
PRONOUN ONLY	My company gave *I* a trip?
CORRECT	My company gave my husband and *me* a trip to Hawaii.
FAULTY	My uncle and *me* had different expectations.
PRONOUN ONLY	*Me* had different expectations?
CORRECT	My uncle and *I* had different expectations.

---

indefinite pronoun: A pronoun standing for an unspecified person or thing, including singular forms (*each, everyone, no one*) and plural forms (*both, few*). *Everyone* is soaking wet.

For exercises on subject-verb agreement, visit **<bedfordstmartins .com/bedguide>**.

pronoun: A word that stands in place of a noun (*he, him,* or *his* for *Nate*)

subject: The part of a sentence that names something—a person, an object, an idea, a situation—about which the predicate makes an assertion: The *king* lives.

subject complement: A noun, an adjective, or a group of words that follows a linking verb (*is, become, feel, seem,* or another verb that shows a state of being) and that renames or describes the subject: This plum tastes *ripe*.

object: The target or recipient of the action of a verb: Some geese bite *people*.

Personal Pronoun Cases at a Glance

SUBJECTIVE	OBJECTIVE	POSSESSIVE
I	me	my, mine
you	you	your, yours
he	him	his
she	her	hers
it	it	its
we	us	our, ours
they	them	their, theirs
who	whom	whose

FAULTY	Jack ran faster than my brother and *me*.
PRONOUN ONLY	Jack ran faster than *me* ran?
CORRECT	Jack ran faster than my brother and *I*.

A second common error with pronoun case involves gerunds. Whenever you need a pronoun to modify a gerund, use the possessive case.

FAULTY	Our supervisor disapproves of *us* talking in the hallway.
CORRECT	Our supervisor disapproves of *our* talking in the hallway.

EDITING CHECKLIST
Pronoun Case

☐ Have you identified all the pronouns in the sentence?

☐ Does each one function as a subject, an object, or a possessive?

☐ Given the function of each, have you used the correct form?

---

gerund: A form of a verb, ending in *-ing*, that functions as a noun: Lacey likes *playing* in the steel band.

For exercises on pronoun case, visit **<bedfordstmartins .com/bedguide>**.

pronoun: A word that stands in place of a noun (*he, him,* or *his* for *Nate*)

A6 **Check for correct pronoun-antecedent agreement.**

The **form** of a pronoun, the way it is spelled and pronounced, can change to show **number**—whether the subject is singular (one) or plural (more than one). It also can change to show **gender**—masculine or feminine, for example—or **person:** first (*I, we*), second (*you*), or third (*he, she, it, they*).

SINGULAR	My brother took *his* coat and left.
PLURAL	My brothers took *their* coats and left.
MASCULINE	I talked to Steven before *he* had a chance to leave.
FEMININE	I talked to Stephanie before *she* had a chance to leave.

In most cases, a pronoun refers to a specific noun or pronoun nearby, called the pronoun's **antecedent.** The connection between the two must be clear so that readers know what the pronoun means in the sentence. The two need to match (or *agree*) in number and gender.

A common error is using a plural pronoun to refer to a singular antecedent. This error often crops up when the antecedent is difficult to find, is an indefinite pronoun, or is confusing for another reason. Look carefully to find the antecedent, and make sure you know whether it is singular or plural. Then make the pronoun match its antecedent.

FAULTY	Neither Luz nor Pam received approval of *their* financial aid.
CORRECT	Neither Luz nor Pam received approval of *her* financial aid.
	[*Neither Luz nor Pam* is a compound subject joined by *nor*. Any pronoun referring to it must agree with only the nearer part of the compound: *her* agrees with *Pam,* which is singular.]

Indefinite pronouns as antecedents are troublesome when they are grammatically singular but create a plural image in the writer's mind. Fortunately, most indefinite pronouns are always singular or always plural.

FAULTY	Each of the boys in the club has *their* own custom laptop.
CORRECT	Each of the boys in the club has *his* own custom laptop.
	[The word *each,* not *boys,* is the antecedent. *Each* is an indefinite pronoun and is always singular, so any pronoun referring to it must be singular as well.]
FAULTY	Everyone in the meeting had *their* own cell phone.
CORRECT	Everyone in the meeting had *his or her* own cell phone.
	[*Everyone* is an indefinite pronoun that is always singular, so any pronoun referring to it must be singular as well.]

indefinite pronoun: A pronoun standing for an unspecified person or thing, including singular forms (*each, everyone, no one*) and plural forms (*both, few*). *Everyone* is soaking wet.

Indefinite Pronouns at a Glance

ALWAYS SINGULAR			ALWAYS PLURAL
anybody	everyone	nothing	both
anyone	everything	one (of)	few
anything	much	somebody	many
each (of)	neither (of)	someone	several
either (of)	nobody	something	
everybody	no one		

For exercises on pronoun-antecedent agreement, visit **<bedfordstmartins.com/bedguide>**.

EDITING CHECKLIST
Pronoun-Antecedent Agreement

☐ Have you identified the antecedent for each pronoun?

☐ Is the antecedent singular or plural? Does the pronoun match?

☐ Is the antecedent masculine, feminine, or neuter? Does the pronoun match?

☐ Is the antecedent first, second, or third person? Does the pronoun match?

A7 Check for correct adjectives and adverbs.

Adjectives and **adverbs** describe or give information about (*modify*) other words. Many adverbs are formed by adding *-ly* to adjectives: *simple, simply; quiet, quietly.* Because adjectives and adverbs resemble one another, writers sometimes mistakenly use one instead of the other. To edit, find the word that the adjective or adverb modifies. If that word is a noun or pronoun, use an adjective (to describe which or what kind). If that word is a verb, adjective, or another adverb, use an adverb (to describe how, when, where, or why).

FAULTY	Kelly ran into the house *quick*.
CORRECT	Kelly ran into the house *quickly*.
FAULTY	Gabriela looked *terribly* after her bout with the flu.
CORRECT	Gabriela looked *terrible* after her bout with the flu.

Adjectives and adverbs with similar comparative and superlative forms can also cause trouble. Always ask whether you need an adjective or an adverb in the sentence, and then use the correct word.

FAULTY	His scar healed so *good* that it was barely visible.
CORRECT	His scar healed so *well* that it was barely visible.

Good is an adjective; it describes a noun or pronoun. *Well* is an adverb; it modifies or adds to a verb (*heal*, in this case) or an adjective.

modifier: A word (such as an adjective or adverb), phrase, or clause that provides more information about other parts of a sentence: Plays *staged by the drama class* are *always successful*.

Irregular Adjectives and Adverbs at a Glance

POSITIVE ADJECTIVES	COMPARATIVE ADJECTIVES	SUPERLATIVE ADJECTIVES
good	better	best
bad	worse	worst
little	less, littler	least, littlest
many, some, much	more	most

POSITIVE ADVERBS	COMPARATIVE ADVERBS	SUPERLATIVE ADVERBS
well	better	best
badly	worse	worst
little	less	least

EDITING CHECKLIST
Adjectives and Adverbs

☐ Have you identified which word the adjective or adverb modifies?

☐ If the word modified is a noun or pronoun, have you used an adjective?

☐ If the word modified is a verb, adjective, or adverb, have you used an adverb?

☐ Have you used the correct comparative or superlative form?

For exercises on adjectives and adverbs, visit **<bedfordstmartins .com/bedguide>**.

B | Editing to Ensure Effective Sentences

B1 Check for any misplaced or dangling modifiers.

For a sentence to be clear, the connection between a modifier and the thing it modifies must be obvious. Usually, a modifier should be placed just before or just after what it modifies. If the modifier is too close to some other sentence element, it is a **misplaced modifier.** If the modifier cannot logically modify anything in the sentence, it is a **dangling modifier.** Both errors can confuse readers — and sometimes create unintentionally humorous images. As you edit, place a modifier directly before or after the word modified and clearly connect the two.

modifier: A word (such as an adjective or adverb), phrase, or clause that provides more information about other parts of a sentence: Plays *staged by the drama class* are *always successful.*

MISPLACED	Dan found the leftovers when he visited in the refrigerator.
CORRECT	Dan found the leftovers in the refrigerator when he visited.
	[In the faulty sentence, *in the refrigerator* seems to modify Dan's visit. Obviously the leftovers, not Dan, are in the refrigerator.]
DANGLING	Looking out the window, the clouds were beautiful.
CORRECT	Looking out the window, I saw that the clouds were beautiful.
CORRECT	When I looked out the window, the clouds were beautiful.
	[In the faulty sentence, *looking out the window* should modify *I,* but *I* is not in the sentence. The modifier dangles without anything logical to modify until *I* is in the sentence.]

EDITING CHECKLIST
Misplaced and Dangling Modifiers

☐ What is each modifier meant to modify? Is the modifier as close as possible to that sentence element? Is any misreading possible?

☐ If a modifier is misplaced, can you move it to clarify the meaning?

☐ What noun or pronoun is a dangling modifier meant to modify? Can you make that word or phrase the subject of the main clause? Or can you turn the dangling modifier into a clause that includes the missing noun or pronoun?

For exercises on misplaced and dangling modifiers, visit **<bedfordstmartins .com/bedguide>**.

B2 Check for parallel structure.

correlative
conjunction: A pair
of linking words (such
as *either/or, not only/
but also*) that appear
separately but work
together to join
elements of a
sentence: *Neither*
his friends *nor* hers
like pizza.

A series of words, phrases, clauses, or sentences with the same grammatical form is said to be **parallel.** Using parallel form for elements that are parallel in meaning or function helps readers grasp the meaning of a sentence more easily. A lack of parallelism can distract, annoy, or even confuse readers.

To use parallelism, put nouns with nouns, verbs with verbs, and phrases with phrases. Parallelism is particularly important in a series, with correlative conjunctions, and in comparisons using *than* or *as.*

FAULTY	I like to go to Estes Park for skiing, ice skating, and to meet interesting people.
CORRECT	I like to go to Estes Park to ski, to ice skate, and to meet interesting people.
FAULTY	The proposal is neither practical, nor is it innovative.
CORRECT	The proposal is neither practical nor innovative.
FAULTY	Teens need a few firm rules rather than having many flimsy ones.
CORRECT	Teens need a few firm rules rather than many flimsy ones.

Edit to reinforce parallel structures by repeating articles, conjunctions, prepositions, or lead-in words as needed.

AWKWARD	His dream was that he would never have to give up his routine but he would still find time to explore new frontiers.
PARALLEL	His dream was that he would never have to give up his routine but *that* he would still find time to explore new frontiers.

EDITING CHECKLIST
Parallel Structure

For exercises
on parallel
structure, visit
**<bedfordstmartins
.com/bedguide>**.

☐ Are all the elements in a series in the same grammatical form?

☐ Are the elements in a comparison parallel in form?

☐ Are the articles, conjunctions, prepositions, or lead-in words for elements repeated as needed rather than mixed or omitted?

Use the Take Action chart (pp. A-39 and A-49) to help you figure out how to improve your draft. Skim across the top to identify questions you might ask about the sentences in your draft. When you answer a question with "Yes" or "Maybe," move straight down the column to Locate Specifics under that question. Use the activities there to pinpoint gaps, problems, or weaknesses. Then move straight down the column to Take Action. Use the advice that suits your problem as you revise.

Take Action Improving Sentence Style

Ask each question at the top of the chart to consider whether your draft might need work on that issue. If so, follow the
ASK—LOCATE SPECIFICS—TAKE ACTION sequence to revise.

	Passive Voice?	Faulty Parallelism?	Repetitive Sentence Patterns?
1 ASK	Have I relied on sentences in the passive voice instead of the active voice?	Have I missed opportunities to emphasize comparable ideas by stating them in comparable ways?	Do my sentences sound alike because they repeat the same opening, pattern, or length?
2 LOCATE SPECIFICS	■ Reread your sentence. If its subject also performs the action, it is in the active voice. (Underline the performer; double underline the action.) ■ If the sentence subject does not perform the action, your sentence is in the passive voice. You have tucked the performer into a *by* phrase or have not identified the performer.	■ Read your sentences, looking for lists or comparable items. ■ Underline items in a series to compare the ways you present them. **Draft:** Observing primates can reveal <u>how they cooperate</u>, <u>their tool use</u>, and <u>building</u> secure nests.	■ Add a line break at the end of every sentence in a passage so you can easily compare sentence openings, patterns, or lengths. ■ Use your software (or yourself) to count the words in each sentence. ■ Search for variations such as colons (:) and semicolons (;) to see how often you use them.
3 TAKE ACTION	■ Consider changing passive voice to active. Make the performer of the action the sentence subject (which reduces extra words by dropping the *by* phrase). **Passive:** The primate play area <u>was arranged</u> by the <u>zookeeper</u>. (9 words; emphasizes object of the action) **Active:** <u>The zookeeper arranged</u> the primate play area. (7 words; emphasizes zookeeper who performed the action)	■ Rework so that items in a series all follow the same grammatical pattern. ■ Select the common pattern based on the clarity and emphasis it adds to your sentence. **Parallel:** Observing primates can reveal how they <u>cooperate</u>, <u>use</u> tools, and <u>build</u> secure nests.	■ Rewrite for variety if you repeat openings (*During, After, Then, And, Because*). ■ Rewrite for directness if you repeat indirect openings (*There are, There is, It is*). ■ Rewrite to vary sentence lengths. Tuck in a few short sentences. Combine choppy sentences. Add a complicated sentence to build up to your point. ■ Try some colons or semicolons for variety.

C | Editing for Common Punctuation Problems

C1 Check for correct use of commas.

The **comma** is a punctuation mark indicating a pause. By setting some words apart from others, commas help clarify relationships. They prevent the words on a page and the ideas they represent from becoming a jumble.

1. Use a comma before a coordinating conjunction (*and, but, for, or, so, yet, nor*) joining two main clauses in a compound sentence.

   The discussion was brief, *so* the meeting was adjourned early.

2. Use a comma after an introductory word or word group unless it is short and cannot be misread.

   After the war, the North's economy developed rapidly.

3. Use commas to separate the items in a series of three or more items.

   The chief advantages will be *speed, durability,* and *longevity.*

4. Use commas to set off a modifying clause or phrase if it is nonrestrictive— that is, if it can be taken out of the sentence without significantly changing the essential meaning of the sentence.

   Good childcare, *which is difficult to find,* should be provided by the employer.

   Good childcare *that is reliable and inexpensive* is the right of every employee.

5. Use commas to set off a nonrestrictive appositive, an expression that comes directly after a noun or pronoun and renames it.

   Sheri, my sister, has a new job as an events coordinator.

6. Use commas to set off parenthetical expressions, conjunctive adverbs, and other interrupters.

   The proposal from the mayor's commission, however, is not feasible.

appositive: A word or group of words that adds information about a subject or object by identifying it in a different way: Terry, *the drummer,* manages the band.

parenthetical expression: An aside to readers or a transitional expression such as *for example* or *in contrast*

conjunctive adverb: A linking word that can connect independent clauses and show a relationship between two ideas: Jen studied hard; *consequently,* she passed the exam.

For exercises on commas, visit **<bedfordstmartins .com/bedguide>**.

EDITING CHECKLIST
Commas

☐ Have you added a comma between two main clauses joined by a coordinating conjunction?

☐ Have you added commas needed after introductory words or word groups?

☐ Have you separated items in a series with commas?

☐ Have you avoided commas before the first item in a series or after the last?

☐ Have you used commas before and after each nonrestrictive word, phrase, or clause?

☐ Have you avoided using commas around a restrictive word, phrase, or clause that is essential to the meaning of the sentence?

☐ Have you used commas to set off appositives, parenthetical expressions, conjunctive adverbs, and other interrupters?

C2 Check for correct use of apostrophes.

An **apostrophe** is a punctuation mark that either shows possession (*Sylvia's*) or indicates that one or more letters have intentionally been left out to form a contraction (*didn't*). An apostrophe is never used to create the possessive form of a pronoun; use the possessive pronoun form instead.

FAULTY　　　*Mikes* car was totaled in the accident.

CORRECT　　*Mike's* car was totaled in the accident.

FAULTY　　　*Womens'* pay is often less than *mens'*.

CORRECT　　*Women's* pay is often less than *men's*.

FAULTY　　　Che *did'nt* want to stay at home and study.

CORRECT　　Che *didn't* want to stay at home and study.

FAULTY　　　The dog wagged *it's* tail happily. [it's = it is? No.]

CORRECT　　The dog wagged *its* tail happily.

FAULTY　　　*Its* raining.

CORRECT　　*It's* raining. [it's = it is]

Possessive Personal Pronouns at a Glance

PERSONAL PRONOUN	POSSESSIVE CASE
I	my, mine
you	your, yours (*not* your's)
he	his
she	her, hers (*not* her's)
it	its (*not* it's)
we	our, ours (*not* our's)
they	their, theirs (*not* their's)
who	whose (*not* who's)

For exercises on apostrophes, visit <**bedfordstmartins .com/bedguide**>.

EDITING CHECKLIST
Apostrophes

☐ Have you used an apostrophe when letters are left out in a contraction?

☐ Have you used an apostrophe to create the possessive form of a noun?

☐ Have you used the possessive case—not an apostrophe—to show that a pronoun is possessive?

☐ Have you used *it's* correctly (to mean *it is*)?

C3 **Check for correct punctuation of quotations.**

When you quote the exact words of a person you have interviewed or a source you have read, enclose those words in quotation marks. Notice how student Betsy Buffo presents the words of her subject in this passage from her essay "Interview with an Artist":

> Derek is straightforward when asked about how his work is received in the local community: "My work is outside the mainstream. Because it's controversial, it's not easy for me to get exposure."

She might have expressed and punctuated this passage in other ways:

> Derek says that "it's not easy" for him to find an audience.

> Derek struggles for recognition because his art falls "outside the mainstream."

If your source is quoting someone else (a quotation within a quotation), put your subject's words in quotation marks and the words he or she is quoting in single quotation marks. Always put commas and periods inside the quotation marks; put semicolons and colons outside. Include all necessary marks in the correct place or sequence.

> As Betsy Buffo explains, "Derek struggles for recognition because his art falls 'outside the mainstream.'"

Substitute an ellipsis mark (. . .)—three spaced dots—for any words you have omitted from the middle of a direct quotation. If you are following MLA style, you may place the ellipses inside brackets ([. . .]) when necessary to avoid confusing your ellipsis marks with those of the original writer. If the ellipses come at the end of a sentence, add another period to conclude the sentence. You don't need an ellipsis mark to show the beginning or ending of a quotation that is clearly incomplete.

In this selection from "Playing Games with Women's Sports," student Kelly Grecian identifies quotations (from "Why Men Fear Women's Teams," *Ms.*, Jan.–Feb. 1991) and an omission:

For more about quotations from sources, see D3 in the Quick Research Guide, p. A-27.

> "The importance of what women athletes wear can't be underestimated," Rounds claims. "Beach volleyball, which is played . . . by bikini-clad women, rates network coverage" (44).

EDITING CHECKLIST
Punctuation with Quotations

☐ Are the exact words quoted from your source enclosed in quotation marks?

☐ Are commas and periods placed inside closing quotation marks?

☐ Are colons and semicolons placed outside closing quotation marks?

☐ Have you used ellipses to show where any words are omitted from the middle of a quotation?

For exercises on using and punctuating quotation marks, visit **<bedfordstmartins.com/bedguide>**.

D | Editing for Common Mechanics Problems

D1 Check for correct use of capital letters.

Capital letters are used in three general situations: to begin a new sentence; to begin names of specific people, nationalities, places, dates, and things (proper nouns); and to begin main words in titles.

FAULTY   During my Sophomore year in College, I took World Literature, Biology, American History, Psychology, and French—courses required for a Humanities Major.

CORRECT   During my sophomore year in college, I took world literature, biology, American history, psychology, and French—courses required for a humanities major.

EDITING CHECKLIST
Capitalization

☐ Have you used a capital letter at the beginning of each complete sentence, including sentences that are quoted?

☐ Have you used capital letters for proper nouns and pronouns?

☐ Have you avoided using capital letters for emphasis?

☐ Have you used a capital letter for the first, last, and main words in a title? (Main words exclude prepositions, coordinating conjunctions, and articles.)

For exercises on using capital letters, visit **<bedfordstmartins.com/bedguide>**.

preposition: A transitional word (such as *in, on, at, of, from*) that leads into a phrase
coordinating conjunction: A one-syllable linking word (*and, but, for, or, nor, so, yet*) that joins elements with equal or near-equal importance
article: The word *a, an,* or *the*

D2 Check spelling.

Misspelled words are difficult to spot in your own writing. You usually see what you think you wrote, and often pronunciation or faulty memory may interfere with correct spelling. If you know the words you habitually misspell, use your software's Search or Find functions to locate all instances

---

Capitalization at a Glance

THE FIRST LETTER OF A SENTENCE, INCLUDING A QUOTED SENTENCE
She called out, "Come in! The water's warm."

PROPER NAMES AND ADJECTIVES MADE FROM THEM

Smithsonian Institution	a Freudian reading	Marie Curie

RANK OR TITLE BEFORE A PROPER NAME

Ms. Olson	Professor Santocolon	Dr. Frost

FAMILY RELATIONSHIP ONLY WHEN IT SUBSTITUTES FOR OR IS PART OF A PROPER NAME

Grandma Jones	Father Time

RELIGIONS, THEIR FOLLOWERS, AND DEITIES

Islam	Orthodox Jew	Buddha

PLACES, REGIONS, GEOGRAPHIC FEATURES, AND NATIONALITIES

Palo Alto	the Berkshire Mountains	Egyptians

DAYS OF THE WEEK, MONTHS, AND HOLIDAYS

Wednesday	July	Labor Day

HISTORICAL EVENTS, PERIODS, AND DOCUMENTS

the Boston Tea Party	the Middle Ages	the Constitution

SCHOOLS, COLLEGES, UNIVERSITIES, AND SPECIFIC COURSES

Temple University	Introduction to Clinical Psychology

FIRST, LAST, AND MAIN WORDS IN TITLES OF PAPERS, BOOKS, ARTICLES, WORKS OF ART, TELEVISION SHOWS, POEMS, AND PERFORMANCES

The Decline and Fall of the Roman Empire	"The Lottery"

For a list of commonly confused words, see p. A-55.

and check the spelling. Consider keeping track of misspelled words in your papers for a few weeks so you can use this feature.

Spell checkers offer a handy alternative to the dictionary, but you need to know their limitations. A spell checker compares the words in your text with the words in its dictionary, and it highlights words that do not appear there, including most proper nouns. Spell checkers ignore one-letter words and will not flag an error such as *s truck* for *a truck*. Nor will they highlight words that are misspelled as different words, such as *except* for *accept, to* for *too*, or *own* for *won*. Always check the spelling in your text by eye *after* you've used your spell checker.

For a list of commonly misspelled words and spelling exercises, visit **<bedfordstmartins .com/bedguide>**.

EDITING CHECKLIST
Spelling

☐ Have you checked for the words you habitually misspell?

☐ Have you checked for commonly confused or misspelled words?

☐ Have you checked a dictionary for any words you are unsure about?

☐ Have you run your spell checker? Have you read your paper carefully for errors that it would miss?

COMMONLY CONFUSED HOMONYMS

accept (v., receive willingly); **except** (prep., other than)

     Mimi could *accept* all of Lefty's gifts *except* his ring.

affect (v., influence); **effect** (n., result)

     If the new rules *affect* us, what will be their *effect*?

capital (adj., uppercase; n., seat of government); **capitol** (n., government building)

     The *Capitol* building in our nation's *capital* is spelled with a *capital* C.

cite (v., refer to); **sight** (n., vision or tourist attraction); **site** (n., place)

     Did you *cite* Aunt Peg as your authority on which *sites* feature the most interesting *sights*?

complement (v., complete; n., counterpart); **compliment** (v. or n., praise)

     For Lee to say that Sheila's beauty *complements* her intelligence may or may not be a *compliment*.

desert (v., abandon; n., hot, dry region); **dessert** (n., end-of-meal sweet)

     Don't *desert* us by leaving for the *desert* before *dessert*.

elicit (v., bring out); **illicit** (adj., illegal)

     By going undercover, Sonny should *elicit* some offers of *illicit* drugs.

led (v., past tense of *lead*); **lead** (n., a metal)

     Gil's heart was heavy as *lead* when he *led* the mourners to the grave.

principal (n. or adj., chief); **principle** (n., rule or standard)

     The *principal* problem is convincing the media that the high school *principal* is a person of high *principles*.

stationary (adj., motionless); **stationery** (n., writing paper)

     Hubert's *stationery* shop stood *stationary* until a flood swept it away.

their (pron., belonging to them); **there** (adv., in that place); **they're** (contraction of *they are*)

     Sue said *they're* going over *there* to visit *their* aunt.

to (prep., toward); **too** (adv., also or excessively); **two** (n. or adj., numeral: one more than one)

     Let's not take *two* cars *to* town — that's *too* many unless Hal comes *too*.

who's (contraction of *who is*); **whose** (pron., belonging to whom)

     Who's going to tell me *whose* dog this is?

your (pron., belonging to you); **you're** (contraction of *you are*)

     You're not getting *your* own way this time!

A Glossary of Troublemakers

Usage refers to the way in which writers customarily use certain words and phrases, including matters of accepted practice or convention. This glossary lists words and phrases whose usage may trouble writers. Not every possible problem is listed—only some that frequently puzzle students. Refer to this brief list when needed, and follow its cross-references to *A Writer's Handbook*.

a, an   Use *an* only before a word beginning with a vowel sound. "*An* asp can eat *an* egg *an* hour." (Some words, such as *hour* and *honest*, open with a vowel sound even though spelled with an *h*.)

above   Using *above* or *below* to refer back or forward in an essay is awkward and may not be accurate. Instead, try "the *preceding* argument," "in the *following* discussion," "on the *next* page."

accept, except   *Accept* is a verb meaning "to receive willingly"; *except* is usually a preposition meaning "not including." "This childcare center *accepts* all children *except* those under two." Sometimes *except* is a verb, meaning "to exempt." "The entry fee *excepts* children under twelve."

advice, advise   *Advice* is a noun, *advise* a verb. When someone *advises* you, you receive *advice*.

affect, effect   Most of the time, the verb *affect* means "to act on" or "to influence." "Too much beer can *affect* your speech." *Affect* can also mean "to put on airs." "He *affected* a British accent." *Effect*, a noun, means "a result": "Too much beer has a numbing *effect*." But *effect* is also a verb, meaning "to bring about." "Pride *effected* his downfall."

agree to, agree with, agree on   *Agree to* means "to consent to"; *agree with*, "to be in accord." "I *agreed to* attend the lecture, but I didn't *agree with* the speaker's views." *Agree on* means "to come to or have an understanding about." "Chuck and I finally *agreed on* a compromise: the children would go to camp but not overnight."

ain't   Don't use *ain't* in writing; it is nonstandard English for *am not, is not* (*isn't*), and *are not* (*aren't*).

a lot   Many people mistakenly write the colloquial expression *a lot* as one word: *alot*. Use *a lot* if you must, but in writing *much* or *a large amount* is preferable. See also *lots, lots of, a lot of.*

already, all ready   *Already* means "by now"; *all ready* means "set to go." "At last our picnic was *all ready,* but *already* it was night."

altogether, all together   *Altogether* means "entirely." "He is *altogether* mistaken." *All together* means "in unison" or "assembled." "Now *all together*—heave!" "Inspector Trent gathered the suspects *all together* in the drawing room."

among, between   *Between* refers to two persons or things; *among,* to more than two. "Some disagreement *between* the two countries was inevitable. Still, there was general harmony *among* the five nations represented at the conference."

amount, number   Use *amount* to refer to quantities that cannot be counted or to bulk; use *number* to refer to countable, separate items. "The *number* of people you want to serve determines the *amount* of ice cream you'll need."

an, a   See *a, an.*

and/or   Usually use either *and* or *or* alone. "Tim *and* Elaine will come to the party." "Tim *or* Elaine will come to the party." For three options, write, "Tim *or* Elaine, *or both,* will come to the party, depending on whether they can find a babysitter."

ante-, anti-   The prefix *ante-* means "preceding." *Antebellum* means "before the Civil War." *Anti-* most often means "opposing": *antidepressant.* It needs a hyphen in front of *i* (*anti-inflationary*) or in front of a capital letter (*anti-Marxist*).

anybody, any body   When *anybody* is used as an indefinite pronoun, write it as one word: "*Anybody* in his or her right mind abhors murder." Because *anybody* is singular, do not write "Anybody in *their* right mind." (See 7d.) *Any body,* written as two words, is the adjective *any* modifying the noun *body*. "Name *any body* of water in Australia."

anyone, any one   *Anyone* is an indefinite pronoun written as one word. "Does *anyone* want dessert?" The phrase *any one* consists of the pronoun *one* modified by the adjective *any* and is used to single out something in a group: "Pick *any one* of the pies—they're all good."

anyplace   *Anyplace* is colloquial for *anywhere* and should not be used in formal writing.

anyways, anywheres   These nonstandard forms of *anyway* and *anywhere* should not be used in writing.

as   Sometimes using the subordinating conjunction *as* can make a sentence ambiguous. "*As* we were climbing the mountain, we put on heavy sweaters." Does *as* here mean "because" or "while"? Whenever using *as* would be confusing, use a more specific term instead, such as *because* or *while*.

as, like   Use *as, as if,* or *as though* rather than *like* to introduce clauses of comparison. "Dan's compositions are tuneful, *as* [not *like*] music ought to be." "Jeffrey behaves *as if* [not *like*] he were ill." *Like,* because it is a preposition, can introduce a phrase but not a clause. "My brother looks *like* me." "Henrietta runs *like* a duck."

as to   Usually this expression sounds stilted. Use *about* instead. "He complained *about* [not *as to*] the cockroaches."

at   See *where at, where to.*

bad, badly   *Bad* is an adjective; *badly* is an adverb. Following linking verbs (*be, appear, become, grow, seem, prove*) and verbs of the senses (*feel, look, smell, sound, taste*), use the adjective form. "I feel *bad* that we missed the plane." "The egg smells *bad.*" (See 8a, 8b.) The adverb form is used to modify a verb or an adjective. "The Tartans played so *badly* they lost to the last-place team, whose *badly* needed victory saved them from elimination."

being as, being that   Instead of "*Being as* I was ignorant of the facts, I kept still," write "*Because* I was ignorant" or "*Not knowing* the facts."

beside, besides   *Beside* is a preposition meaning "next to." "Sheldon enjoyed sitting *beside* the guest of honor." *Besides* is an adverb meaning "in addition." "*Besides,* he has a sense of humor." *Besides* is also a preposition meaning "other than." "Something *besides* shyness caused his embarrassment."

between, among   See *among, between.*

between you and I   The preposition *between* always takes the objective case. "Between *you* and *me* [not *I*], Joe's story sounds suspicious." "Between *us* [not *we*], what's going on between Bob and *her* [not *she*] is unfathomable." (See 5a–5f.)

but that, but what   "I don't know *but what* [or *but that*] you're right" is a wordy, imprecise way of saying "Maybe you're right" or "I believe you're right."

can, may   Use *can* to show ability. "Jake *can* bench-press 650 pounds." *May* involves permission. "*May* I bench-press today?" "You *may,* if you *can.*"

capital, capitol   A *capital* is a city that is the center of government for a state or country. *Capital* can also mean "wealth." A *capitol* is a building in which legislators meet. "Who knows what the *capital* of Finland is?" "The renovated *capitol* is a popular attraction."

center around   Say "Class discussion *centered on* [or *revolved around*] her paper." In this sense, the verb *center* means "to have one main concern"—the way a circle has a central point. (To say a discussion centers *around* anything is a murky metaphor.)

cite, sight, site   *Cite,* a verb, means "to quote from or refer to." *Sight* as a verb means "to see or glimpse"; as a noun it means "a view, a spectacle." "When the police officer *sighted* my terrier running across the playground, she *cited* the leash laws." *Site,* a noun, means "location." "Standing and weeping at the *site* of his childhood home, he was a pitiful *sight.*"

climatic, climactic   *Climatic,* from *climate,* refers to meteorological conditions. Saying "climatic conditions," however, is wordy—you can usually substitute "the climate": "*Climatic* conditions are [or "The *climate* is"] changing because of the hole in the ozone layer." *Climactic,* from *climax,* refers to the culmination of a progression of events. "In the *climactic* scene, the hero drives his car off the pier."

compare, contrast *Compare* has two main meanings. The first, "to liken or represent as similar," is followed by *to*. "She *compared* her room *to* a jail cell." The second, "to analyze for similarities and differences," is generally followed by *with*. "The speaker *compared* the American educational system *with* the Japanese system."

    Contrast also has two main meanings. As a transitive verb, taking an object, it means "to analyze to emphasize differences" and is generally followed by *with*. "The speaker *contrasted* the social emphasis of the Japanese primary grades *with* the academic emphasis of ours." As an intransitive verb, *contrast* means "to exhibit differences when compared." "The sour taste of the milk *contrasted* sharply *with* its usual fresh flavor."

complement, compliment *Compliment* is a verb meaning "to praise" or a noun meaning "praise." "The professor *complimented* Sarah on her perceptiveness." *Complement* is a verb meaning "to complete or reinforce." "Jenn's experiences as an intern *complemented* what she learned in class."

could care less This is nonstandard English for *couldn't care less* and should not be used in writing. "The cat *couldn't* [not *could*] *care less* about which brand of cat food you buy."

could of *Could of* is colloquial for *could have* and should not be used in writing.

couple of Write "a *couple of* drinks" when you mean two. For more than two, say "a *few* [or *several*] drinks."

criteria, criterion *Criteria* is the plural of *criterion,* which means "a standard or requirement on which a judgment or decision is based." "The main *criteria* for this job are attention to detail and good computer skills."

data *Data* is a plural noun. Write "The data *are*" and "*these* data." The singular form of *data* is *datum*—rarely used because it sounds musty. Instead, use *fact, figure,* or *statistic.*

different from, different than *Different from* is usually the correct form to use. "How is good poetry *different from* prose?" Use *different than* when a whole clause follows. "Violin lessons with Mr. James were *different than* I had imagined."

don't, doesn't *Don't* is the contraction of *do not,* and *doesn't* is the contraction of *does not.* "They *don't* want to get dressed up for the ceremony." "The cat *doesn't* [not *don't*] like to be combed."

due to *Due* is an adjective and must modify a noun or pronoun; it can't modify a verb or an adjective. Begin a sentence with *due to* and you invite trouble: "*Due to* rain, the game was postponed." Write instead, "*Because of* rain." *Due to* works after the verb *be.* "His fall was *due to* a banana peel." There, *due* modifies the noun *fall.*

due to the fact that A windy expression for *because.*

effect, affect See *affect, effect.*

either Use *either* when referring to one of two things. "Both internships sound great; I'd be happy with *either.*" When referring to one of three or more things, use *any one* or *any.* "*Any one* of our four counselors will be able to help you."

et cetera, etc. Sharpen your writing by replacing *et cetera* (or its abbreviation, *etc.*) with exact words. Even translating the Latin expression into English ("and other things") is an improvement, as in "high-jumping, shot-putting, and other field events."

everybody, every body When used as an indefinite pronoun, *everybody* is one word. "Why is *everybody* on the boys' team waving his arms?" Because *everybody* is singular, it is a mistake to write, "Why is *everybody* waving *their* arms?" (See 7d.) *Every body* written as two words refers to separate, individual bodies. "After the massacre, they buried *every body* in *its* [not *their*] own grave."

everyone, every one Used as an indefinite pronoun, *everyone* is one word. "*Everyone* has *his or her* own ideas." Because *everyone* is singular, it is incorrect to write, "*Everyone* has *their* own ideas." (See 7d.) *Every one* written as two words refers to individual, distinct items. "I studied *every one* of the chapters."

except, accept See *accept, except.*

expect In writing, avoid the informal use of *expect* to mean "suppose, assume, or think." "I *suppose* [not *expect*] you're going on the geology field trip."

fact that This is a wordy expression that, nearly always, you can do without. Instead of "*The fact that* he was puny went unnoticed," write, "That he was puny went unnoticed." "Because [not *Because of the fact that*] it snowed, the game was canceled."

farther, further In your writing, use *farther* to refer to literal distance. "Chicago is *farther* from Nome than from New York." When you mean additional degree, time, or quantity, use *further:* "Sally's idea requires *further* discussion."

fewer, less *Less* refers to general quantity or bulk; *fewer* refers to separate, countable items. "Eat *less* pizza." "Salad has *fewer* calories."

field of In a statement such as "He took courses in *the field of* economics," omit *the field of* to save words.

firstly The recommended usage is *first* (and *second,* not *secondly; third,* not *thirdly;* and so on).

former, latter *Former* means "first of two"; *latter,* "second of two." They are an acceptable but heavy-handed pair, often obliging your reader to backtrack. Your writing generally will be clearer if you simply name again the persons or things you mean. Instead of "The *former* great artist is the master of the flowing line, while the *latter* is the master of color," write, "Picasso is the master of the flowing line, while Matisse is the master of color."

further, farther See *farther, further.*

get, got *Get* has many meanings, especially in slang and colloquial use. Some, such as the following, are not appropriate in formal writing:

To start, begin: "Let's start [not *get*] painting."

To stir the emotions: "His frequent interruptions finally started annoying [not *getting to*] me."

To harm, punish, or take revenge on: "She's going to take revenge on [not *get*] him." Or better, be even more specific: "She's going to spread rumors about him to ruin his reputation."

good, well To modify a verb, use the adverb *well,* not the adjective *good.* "Jan dives *well* [not *good*]." Linking verbs (*be, appear, become, grow, seem, prove*) and verbs of the senses (such as *feel, look, smell, sound, taste*) call for the adjective *good.* "The paint job looks *good." Well* is an adjective used only to refer to health. "She looks *well*" means that she seems to be in good health. "She looks *good*" means her appearance is attractive. (See 8b, 8c.)

hanged, hung Both words are the past tense of the verb *hang. Hanged* refers to an execution. "The murderer was *hanged* at dawn." For all other situ-

ations, use *hung.* "Jim *hung* his wash on the line to dry."

have got to In formal writing, avoid using the phrase *have got to* to mean "have to" or "must." "I *must* [not *have got to*] phone them right away."

he, she, he or she Using *he* to refer to an indefinite person is considered sexist; so is using *she* with traditionally female occupations or pastimes. However, the phrase *he or she* can seem wordy and awkward. For alternatives, see 18.

herself See *-self, -selves.*

himself See *-self, -selves.*

hopefully *Hopefully* means "with hope." "The children turned *hopefully* toward the door, expecting Santa Claus." In writing, avoid *hopefully* when you mean "it is to be hoped" or "let us hope." "*I hope* [not *Hopefully*] the posse will arrive soon."

if, whether Use *whether,* not *if,* in indirect questions and to introduce alternatives. "Father asked me *whether* [not *if*] I was planning to sleep all morning." "I'm so confused I don't know *whether* [not *if*] it's day or night."

imply, infer *Imply* means "to suggest"; *infer* means "to draw a conclusion." "Maria *implied* that she was too busy to see Tom, but Tom *inferred* that Maria had lost interest in him."

in, into *In* refers to a location or condition; *into* refers to the direction of movement or change. "The hero burst *into* the room and found the heroine *in* another man's arms."

infer, imply See *imply, infer.*

in regards to Write *in regard to, regarding,* or *about.*

inside of, outside of As prepositions, *inside* and *outside* do not require *of.* "The students were more interested in events *outside* [not *outside of*] the building than those *inside* [not *inside of*] the classroom." In formal writing, do not use *inside of* to refer to time or *outside of* to mean "except." "I'll finish the assignment *within* [not *inside of*] two hours." "He told no one *except* [not *outside of*] a few friends."

irregardless *Irregardless* is a double negative. Use *regardless.*

is because See *reason is because, reason . . . is.*

is when, is where Using these expressions results in errors in predication. "Obesity *is when* a person is greatly overweight." "Biology *is where* students dissect frogs." *When* refers to a point in time, but *obesity* is not a point in time; *where* refers to a place, but *biology* is not a place. Write instead, "Obesity is the condition of extreme overweight." "Biology is a laboratory course in which students dissect frogs." (See 12c.)

its, it's   *Its* is a possessive pronoun, never in need of an apostrophe. *It's* is a contraction of *it is.* "Every new experience has *its* bad moments. Still, *it's* exciting to explore the unknown." (See 24g.)

it's me, it is I   Although *it's me* is widely used in speech, don't use it in formal writing. Write "It is I," which is grammatically correct. The same applies to other personal pronouns. "It was *he* [not *him*] who started the mutiny." (See 5.)

kind of, sort of, type of   When you use *kind, sort,* or *type*—singular words—make sure that the sentence construction is singular. "That *type* of show *offends* me." "Those *types* of shows *offend* me." In speech, *kind of* and *sort of* are used as qualifiers. "He is *sort of* fat." Avoid them in writing. "He is *rather* [or *somewhat* or *slightly*] fat."

latter, former   See *former, latter.*

lay, lie   The verb *lay,* meaning "to put or place," takes an object. "*Lay* that pistol down." *Lie,* meaning "to rest or recline," does not. "*Lie* on the bed until your headache goes away." Their principal parts are *lay, laid, laid* and *lie, lay, lain.* (See 3f.)

less, fewer   See *fewer, less.*

liable, likely   Use *likely* to mean "plausible" or "having the potential." "Jake is *likely* [not *liable*] to win." Save *liable* for "legally obligated" or "susceptible." "A stunt man is *liable* to injury."

lie, lay   See *lay, lie.*

like, as   See *as, like.*

likely, liable   See *liable, likely.*

literally   Don't sling *literally* around for emphasis. Because it means "strictly according to the meaning of a word (or words)," it will wreck your credibility if you are speaking figuratively. "Professor Gray *literally* flew down the hall" means that Gray traveled on wings. Save *literally* to mean that you're reporting a fact. "Chemical wastes travel on the winds, and the skies *literally* rain poison."

loose, lose   *Loose,* an adjective, most commonly means "not fastened" or "poorly fastened." *Lose,* a

verb, means "to misplace" or "to not win." "I have to be careful not to *lose* this button—it's so *loose.*"

lots, lots of, a lot of   Use these expressions only in informal speech. In formal writing, use *many* or *much.* See also *a lot.*

mankind   This term is considered sexist by many people. Use *humanity, humankind, the human race,* or *people* instead.

may, can   See *can, may.*

media, medium   *Media* is the plural of *medium* and most commonly refers to the various forms of public communication. "Some argue that, of all the *media,* television is the worst for children."

might of   *Might of* is colloquial for *might have* and should not be used in writing.

most   Do not use *most* when you mean "almost" or "nearly." "*Almost* [not *Most*] all of the students felt that Professor Crey should receive tenure."

must of   *Must of* is colloquial for *must have* and should not be used in writing.

myself   See *-self, -selves.*

not all that   *Not all that* is colloquial for *not very;* do not use it in formal writing. "The movie was *not very* [not *not all that*] exciting."

number, amount   See *amount, number.*

of   See *could of, might of, must of, should of.*

O.K., o.k., okay   In formal writing, do not use any of these expressions. *All right* and *I agree* are possible substitutes.

one   Like a balloon, *one,* meaning "a person," tends to inflate. One *one* can lead to another. "When *one* is in college, *one* learns to make up *one's* mind for *oneself.*" Avoid this pompous usage. Whenever possible, substitute *people* or a more specific plural noun. "When *students* are in college, *they* learn to make up their minds for *themselves.*"

ourselves   See *-self, -selves.*

outside of, inside of   See *inside of, outside of.*

percent, per cent, percentage   When you specify a number, write *percent* (also written *per cent*). "Nearly 40 *percent* of the listeners responded to the offer." The only time to use *percentage,* meaning "part," is with an adjective, when you mention no number. "A high *percentage* [or *a large percentage*] of listeners responded." *A large number* or *a large proportion* sounds better yet.

phenomenon, phenomena *Phenomena* is the plural of *phenomenon,* which means "an observable fact or occurrence." "Of the many mysterious supernatural *phenomena,* clairvoyance is the strangest *phenomenon* of all."

precede, proceed *Precede* means "to go before or ahead of"; *proceed* means "to go forward." "The fire drill *proceeded* smoothly; the children *preceded* the teachers onto the playground."

principal, principle *Principal* means "chief," whether used as an adjective or as a noun. "According to the *principal,* the school's *principal* goal will be teaching reading." Referring to money, *principal* means "capital." "Investors in high-risk companies may lose their *principal.*" *Principle,* a noun, means *rule* or *standard.* "Let's apply the *principle* of equality in hiring."

proved, proven Although both forms can be used as past participles, *proved* is recommended. Use *proven* as an adjective. "They had *proved* their skill in match after match." "Try this *proven* cough remedy."

quote, quotation *Quote* is a verb meaning "to cite, to use the words of." *Quotation* is a noun meaning "something that is quoted." "The *quotation* [not *quote*] next to her photograph fits her perfectly."

raise, rise *Raise,* meaning "to cause to move upward," is a transitive verb and takes an object. *Rise,* meaning "to move up (on its own)" is intransitive and does not take an object: "I *rose* from my seat and *raised* my arm."

rarely ever *Rarely* by itself is strong enough. "George *rarely* [not *rarely ever*] eats dinner with his family."

real, really *Real* is an adjective, *really* an adverb. Do not use *real* to modify a verb or another adjective, and avoid overusing either word. "*The Ambassadors* is a *really* [not *real*] fine novel." Even better: "*The Ambassadors* is a fine novel."

reason is because, reason...is *Reason...is* requires a clause beginning with *that.* Using *because* is nonstandard. "The *reason* I can't come *is that* [not *is because*] I have the flu." It is simpler and more direct to write, "I can't come because I have the flu." (See 12d.)

rise See *raise, rise.*

-self, -selves Don't use a pronoun ending in *-self* or *-selves* in place of *her, him, me, them, us,* or *you.* "Nobody volunteered but Jim and *me* [not *myself*]." Use the *-self* pronouns to refer back to a noun or another pronoun and to lend emphasis. "*We* did it *ourselves.*" "Sarah *herself* is a noted musician."

set, sit *Set,* meaning "to put or place," is a transitive verb and takes an object. *Sit,* meaning "to be seated," is intransitive and does not take an object. "We were asked to *set* our jewelry and metal objects on the counter and *sit* down." (See 3f.)

shall, will; should, would The helping verb *shall* formerly was used with first-person pronouns. It is still used to express determination ("We *shall* overcome") or to ask consent ("*Shall* we march?"). Otherwise, *will* is commonly used with all three persons. "I *will* enter medical school in the fall." *Should* is a helping verb that expresses obligation; *would,* a helping verb that expresses a hypothetical condition. "I *should* wash the dishes before I watch TV." "He *would* learn to speak English if you *would* give him a chance."

she, he or she See *he, she, he or she.*

should of *Should of* is colloquial for *should have* and should not be used in writing.

sight See *cite, sight, site.*

since Sometimes using *since* can make a sentence ambiguous. "*Since* the babysitter left, the children have been watching television." Does *since* here mean "because" or "from the time that"? If using *since* might be confusing, use an unambiguous term (*because, ever since*).

sit See *set, sit.*

site See *cite, sight, site.*

sort of See *kind of, sort of, type of.*

stationary, stationery *Stationary,* an adjective, means "fixed, unmoving." "The fireplace remained *stationary* though the wind blew down the house." *Stationery* is paper for letter writing. To spell it right, remember that *letter* also contains *-er.*

suppose to Write *supposed to.* "He was *supposed to* read a novel."

sure *Sure* is an adjective, *surely* an adverb. Do not use *sure* to modify a verb or another adjective. If you mean "certainly," write *certainly* or *surely* instead. "He *surely* [not *sure*] makes the Civil War come alive."

than, then *Than* is a conjunction used in comparisons; *then* is an adverb indicating time. "Marlene is brainier *than* her sister." "First crack six eggs; *then* beat them."

that, where See *where, that.*

that, which Which pronoun should open a clause—*that* or *which*? If the clause adds to its sentence an idea that, however interesting, could be left out, then the clause is nonrestrictive. It should begin with *which* and be separated from the rest of the sentence with commas. "The vampire, *which* hovered nearby, leaped for Sarah's throat."

If the clause is essential to your meaning, it is restrictive. It should begin with *that* and should not have commas around it. "The vampire *that* Mel brought from Transylvania leaped for Sarah's throat." The clause indicates not just any old vampire but one in particular. (See 21e.)

Don't use *which* to refer vaguely to an entire clause. Instead of "Jack was an expert drummer in high school, *which* won him a scholarship," write "Jack's skill as a drummer won him . . ." (See 6b.)

that, who, which, whose See *who, which, that, whose.*

themselves See *-self, -selves.*

then, than See *than, then.*

there, their, they're *There* is an adverb indicating place. *Their* is a possessive pronoun. *They're* is a contraction of *they are.* "After playing tennis *there* for three hours, Lamont and Laura went to change *their* clothes because *they're* going out to dinner."

to, too, two *To* is a preposition. *Too* is an adverb meaning "also" or "in excess." *Two* is a number. "Janet wanted to go *too,* but she was *too* sick to travel for *two* days. Instead, she went *to* bed."

toward, towards *Toward* is preferred in the United States, *towards* in Britain.

try and Use *try to.* "I'll *try to* [not *try and*] attend the opening performance of your play."

type of See *kind of, sort of, type of.*

unique Nothing can be *more, less,* or *very unique. Unique* means "one of a kind." (See 8e.)

use to Write *used to.* "Jeffrey *used to* have a beard, but now he is clean-shaven."

wait for, wait on *Wait for* means "await"; *wait on* means "to serve." "While *waiting for* his friends, George decided to *wait on* one more customer."

well, good See *good, well.*

where, that Although speakers sometimes use *where* instead of *that,* you should not do so in writing. "I heard on the news *that* [not *where*] it got hot enough to fry eggs on car hoods."

where . . . at, where . . . to The colloquial use of *at* or *to* after *where* is redundant. Write "*Where* were you?" not "*Where* were you *at*?" "I know *where* she was rushing [not *rushing to*]."

whether See *if, whether.*

which, that See *that, which.*

who, which, that, whose *Who* refers to people, *which* to things and ideas. "Was it Pogo *who* said, 'We have met the enemy and he is us'?" "The blouse, *which* was green, accented her dark skin." *That* refers to things but can also be used for a class of people. "The team *that* increases sales the most will get a bonus." Because *of which* can be cumbersome, use *whose* even with things. "The mountain, *whose* snowy peaks were famous the world over, was covered by fog." See also *that, which.*

who, whom *Who* is used as a subject, *whom* as an object. In "*Whom* do I see?" *Whom* is the object of *see.* In "*Who* goes there?" *Who* is the subject of "goes." (See also 5a.)

who's, whose *Who's* is a contraction of *who is* or *who has.* "*Who's* going with Phil?" *Whose* is a possessive pronoun. "Bill is a conservative politician *whose* ideas are unlikely to change."

whose, who, which, that See *who, which, that, whose.*

will, shall See *shall, will; should, would.*

would, should See *shall, will; should, would.*

would of *Would of* is colloquial for *would have* and should not be used in writing.

you *You,* meaning "a person," occurs often in conversation. "When *you* go to college, *you* have to work hard." In writing, use *one* or a specific, preferably plural noun. "When *students* go to college, *they* have to work hard." See *one* and 18c.

your, you're *Your* is a possessive pronoun; *you're* is the contraction of *you are.* "*You're* lying! It was *your* handwriting on the envelope."

yourself, yourselves See *-self, -selves.*

Answers for Lettered Exercises

EXERCISE 1–1 ▪ Eliminating Fragments, p. 784

Suggested revisions:

a. Michael had a beautiful Southern accent, having lived many years in Georgia.
b. Pat and Chris are determined to marry each other, even if their families do not approve.
c. Jack seemed well qualified for a career in the air force, except for his tendency to get airsick.
d. Lisa advocated sleeping no more than four hours a night until she started nodding through her classes.
e. Complete sentences

EXERCISE 2–1 ▪ Revising Comma Splices and Fused Sentences, p. 788

Suggested revisions:

a. We followed the scientist down a flight of wet stone steps. At last he stopped before a huge oak door.
We followed the scientist down a flight of wet stone steps until at last he stopped before a huge oak door.
b. Dr. Frankenstein selected a heavy key; he twisted it in the lock.
Dr. Frankenstein selected a heavy key, which he twisted in the lock.
c. The huge door gave a groan; it swung open on a dimly lighted laboratory.
The huge door gave a groan and swung open on a dimly lighted laboratory.
d. Before us on a dissecting table lay a form with closed eyes. To behold it sent a quick chill down my spine.
Before us on a dissecting table lay a form with closed eyes; beholding it sent a quick chill down my spine.
e. The scientist strode to the table and lifted a white-gloved hand.
The scientist strode to the table; he lifted a white-gloved hand.

EXERCISE 3–1 ▪ Using Irregular Verb Forms, p. 793

a. Benjamin wrote all the music, and his sister *sang* all the songs.
b. Correct
c. When the bell *rang*, darkness had already *fallen*.
d. Voters have *chosen* some new senators, who won't take office until January.

e. Carol threw the ball into the water, and the dog *swam* after it.

EXERCISE 3–2 ▪ Identifying Verb Tenses, p. 799

a. has been living: present perfect progressive; hacked: simple past; change: simple present **b.** have never appeared: present perfect; will never appear: simple future; gets selected: simple present **c.** had been: past perfect; pitched: simple past **d.** will have been studying: future perfect progressive; will be taking: future progressive
e. was running: past progressive; strolled: simple past

EXERCISE 3–4 ▪ Using the Correct Mood of Verbs, p. 803

a. Dr. Belanger recommended that Juan *floss* his teeth every day. (Incorrect *flosses,* indicative; correct *floss,* subjunctive)
b. If I *were* you, I would have done the same thing. (Incorrect *was,* indicative; correct *were,* subjunctive)
c. Tradition demands that Daegun *show* respect for his elders. (Incorrect *shows,* indicative; correct *show,* subjunctive)
d. Please *attend* the training lesson if you plan to skydive later today. (Incorrect *attends,* indicative; correct *attend,* imperative)

EXERCISE 4–1 ▪ Making Subjects and Verbs Agree, p. 807

a. For many college graduates, the process of looking for jobs *is* often long and stressful.
b. Not too long ago, searching the classifieds and inquiring in person *were* the primary methods of job hunting.
c. Today, however, everyone also *seems* to use the Internet to search for openings or to e-mail *his or her* résumés.
d. My classmates and my cousin *send* most résumés over the Internet because it costs less than mailing them.
e. All of the résumés *arrive* quickly when they are sent electronically.

EXERCISE 5–1 ▪ Using Pronouns Correctly, p. 810

a. I didn't appreciate *your* laughing at her and *me.* (*Your* modifies the gerund *laughing; me* is an object of the preposition *at.*)
b. Lee and *I* would be delighted to serenade *whoever* will listen. (*I* is a subject of the verb phrase *would be delighted; whoever* is the subject of the clause *whoever will listen.*)

c. The managers and *we* servers are highly trustworthy. (*We* is a subject complement.)
d. The neighbors were driven berserk by *his* singing. (The gerund *singing* is the object of the verb *driven;* the possessive pronoun *his* modifies *singing.*) *Or*
Correct as is. (*Him* is the object of the verb *driven; singing* is a participle modifying *him.*)
e. Jerry and *I* regard you and *her* as the very people *whom* we wish to meet. (*I* is a subject of the verb *regard; her* is a direct object of the verb *regard; whom* is the object of the infinitive *to meet.*)

EXERCISE 6-1 ■ Making Pronoun Reference Clear, p. 814

Suggested revisions:

a. As the moon began to rise, I could see the faint shadow of the tree.
b. While she spent the summer in Paris, Katrina broadened her awareness of cultural differences by traveling throughout Europe.
c. Most managers want employees to work as many hours as possible. They never consider the work their employees need to do at home.
d. Working twelve hours a day and never getting enough sleep was worth it.
e. Kevin asked Mike to meet him for lunch but forgot that Mike had class at that time. *Or*
Kevin forgot that he had class at the time he asked Mike to meet him for lunch.

EXERCISE 7-1 ■ Making Pronouns and Antecedents Agree, p. 816

Suggested revisions:

a. Correct
b. Neither Melissa nor James has received an application form yet. *Or*
Melissa and James have not received their application forms yet.
c. He is the kind of man who gets his fun out of just sipping his beer and watching his Saturday games on TV.
d. Many a mother has mourned the loss of her child. *Or*
Many mothers have mourned the loss of their children.
e. When you enjoy your work, it's easy to spend all your spare time thinking about it. *Or*
When one enjoys one's work, it's easy to spend all one's spare time thinking about it.

EXERCISE 8-1 ■ Using Adjectives and Adverbs Correctly, p. 823

a. Change *increasing* to *increasingly.* b. Correct. c. Change *lower* to *lowest.* d. Change *rapid* to *rapidly.* e. Change *well* to *good.*

EXERCISE 9-1 ■ Maintaining Grammatical Consistency, p. 826

Suggested revisions:

a. Dr. Jamison is an erudite professor who tells amusing anecdotes in class. (Formal) *Or* Dr. Jamison is a funny teacher who cracks jokes in class. (Informal)
b. The audience listened intently to the lecture but did not understand the message.
c. Scientists can no longer evade the social, political, and ethical consequences of what they do in the laboratory.
d. To have good government, citizens must become informed on the issues. Also, they must vote.
e. Good writing is essential to success in many professions, especially in business, where ideas must be communicated clearly.

EXERCISE 10-1 ■ Placing Modifiers, p. 828

Suggested revisions:

a. The bus full of passengers got stuck in a ditch.
b. In the middle of a meeting, he was daydreaming about fishing for trout.
c. With a smirk, the boy threw the paper airplane through an open window.
d. When the glare appeared, I reached for my sunglasses from the glove compartment.
e. Sally and Glen watched the kites high above them drift back and forth.

EXERCISE 10-2 ■ Revising Dangling Modifiers, p. 829

Suggested revisions:

a. As I was unpacking the suitcase, a horrible idea occurred to me.
b. After fixing breakfast that morning, I might have left the oven on at home.
c. Although I tried to reach my neighbor, her phone was busy.
d. Desperate to get information, I asked my mother to drive over to check the oven.
e. I felt enormous relief when my mother's call confirmed everything was fine.

EXERCISE 11-1 ■ Completing Comparisons, p. 831

Suggested revisions:

a. The movie version of *The Brady Bunch* was much more ironic *than the television show.*
b. Taking care of a dog is often more demanding than *taking care of* a cat.
c. I received more free calendars in the mail for the year 2011 than *I have for* any other year.
d. The crime rate in the United States is higher than *it is in* Canada.
e. Liver contains more iron than any *other* meat.

EXERCISE 11-2 ▪ Completing Sentences, p. 833

Suggested revisions:

a. Eighteenth-century China was as civilized *as* and in many respects more sophisticated than the Western world.
b. Pembroke was never contacted *by,* much less involved with, the election committee.
c. I haven't yet *finished* but soon will finish my research paper.
d. Ron likes his popcorn with butter; Linda *likes hers* with parmesan cheese.
e. Correct

EXERCISE 12-1 ▪ Correcting Mixed Constructions and Faulty Predication, p. 836

Suggested revisions:

a. Health insurance protects people from big medical bills.
b. His determination to prevail helped him finish the race.
c. AIDS destroys the body's immune system.
d. The temperatures are too low for the orange trees.
e. In a recession, economic growth is small or nonexistent, and unemployment increases.

EXERCISE 13-1 ▪ Making Sentences Parallel, p. 839

Suggested revisions:

a. The border separating Texas and Mexico marks not only the political boundary of two countries but also the last frontier for some endangered wildlife.
b. In the Rio Grande Valley, both local residents and tourists enjoy visiting the national wildlife refuges.
c. The tall grasses in this valley are the home of many insects, birds, and small mammals.
d. Two endangered wildcats, the ocelot and the jaguarundi, also make the Rio Grande Valley their home.
e. Many people from Central America are desperate to immigrate to the United States by either legal or illegal means.

EXERCISE 14-1 ▪ Using Coordination, p. 843

Suggested revisions:

a. Professional poker players try to win money and prizes in high-stakes tournaments; however, they may lose thousands of dollars.
b. Poker is not an easy way to make a living, and playing professional poker is not a good way to relax.
c. A good "poker face" reveals no emotions, for communicating too much information puts a player at a disadvantage.
d. Hidden feelings may come out in unconscious movements, so an expert poker player watches other players carefully.
e. Poker is different from most other casino gambling games, for it requires skill and it forces players to compete against each other. Other casino gambling pits players against the house, so they may win out of sheer luck, but skill has little to do with winning those games.

EXERCISE 14-2 ▪ Using Subordination, p. 845

Suggested revisions:

a. Cape Cod is a peninsula in Massachusetts that juts into the Atlantic Ocean south of Boston, marking the northern turning point of the Gulf Stream.
b. Although the developer had hoped the condominiums would sell quickly, sales were sluggish.
c. Tourists love Italy because it has a wonderful climate, beautiful towns and cities, and a rich history.
d. At the end of Verdi's opera *La Traviata,* Alfredo has to see his beloved Violetta again, even though he knows she is dying and all he can say is good-bye.
e. I usually have more fun at a concert with Rico than with Morey because Rico loves music while Morey merely tolerates it.

EXERCISE 16-2 ▪ Avoiding Jargon, p. 852

Suggested revisions:

a. Everyone at Boondoggle and Gall attends holiday gatherings in order to meet and socialize with potential business partners.
b. This year, more than fifty employees lost their jobs after Boondoggle and Gall's decision to reduce the number of employees by September 1.
c. The layoffs left Jensen in charge of all telephone calls in the customer-service department.
d. Jensen was responsible for handling three times as many telephone calls after the layoffs, yet she did not receive any extra pay.
e. Jensen and her managers could not agree on a fair compensation, so she decided to quit her job at Boondoggle and Gall.

EXERCISE 16-3 ▪ Avoiding Euphemisms and Slang, p. 853

Suggested revisions:

a. At three hundred dollars a month, the apartment is a bargain.
b. The soldiers were accidentally shot by members of their own troops while they were retreating.
c. Churchill was an excellent politician.

EXERCISE 18-1 ▪ Avoiding Bias, p. 860

Suggested revisions:

a. Our school's athletic program will be of interest to *many* applicants.
b. The new physicians include Dr. Scalia, *Dr.* Baniski, and Dr. Morton.
c. *Diligent researchers* will always find the sources *they* seek.

EXERCISE 20-1 ▪ Using End Punctuation, p. 863

a. The question that still troubles the community after all these years is why federal agents did not act sooner. [Not a direct question]

b. I wonder what he was thinking at the time. [Not a direct question]

c. Correct

EXERCISE 21-1 ▪ Using Commas, p. 865

a. Farmers around the world tend to rely on just a few breeds of livestock, so some breeds are disappearing.

b. Correct

c. For instance, modern breeds of cattle usually grow larger and produce more meat and milk than older breeds.

d. In both wild and domestic animals, genetic diversity can make the animals resistant to disease and parasites, so older breeds can give scientists important information.

e. Until recently, small organic farmers were often the only ones interested in raising old-fashioned breeds, but animal scientists now support this practice as well.

EXERCISE 21-2 ▪ Using Commas, p. 867

a. Mrs. Carver looks like a sweet little old lady, but she plays a wicked electric guitar.

b. Her bass player, her drummer, and her keyboard player all live in the same retirement community.

c. They practice individually in the afternoon, rehearse together at night, and play at the community's Saturday night dances.

d. The Rest Home Rebels have to rehearse quietly and cautiously to keep from disturbing the other residents.

e. Correct

EXERCISE 21-3 ▪ Using Commas, p. 869

Suggested revisions:

a. We are bringing a dish, vegetable lasagna, to the potluck supper.

b. I like to go to Central Bank on this side of town because this branch tends to have short lines.

c. The colony that the English established at Roanoke disappeared mysteriously.

d. If the base commanders had checked their gun room, where powder is stored, they would have found that several hundred pounds of gunpowder were missing.

e. Brazil's tropical rain forests, which help produce the air we breathe all over the world, are being cut down at an alarming rate.

EXERCISE 21-4 ▪ Using Commas, p. 870

a. The university insisted, however, that the students were not accepted merely because of their parents' generous contributions.

b. This dispute, in any case, is an old one.

c. It was the young man's striking good looks, not his acting ability, that first attracted the Hollywood agents.

d. Gretchen learned, moreover, not always to accept as true what she had read in celebrity magazines.

e. The hikers, most of them wearing ponchos or rain jackets, headed out into the steady drizzle.

EXERCISE 21-5 ▪ Using Commas, p. 872

a. César Chávez was born on March 31, 1927, on a farm in Yuma, Arizona.

b. Chávez, who spent years as a migrant farmworker, told other farm laborers, "If you're outraged at conditions, then you can't possibly be free or happy until you devote all your time to changing them."

c. Chávez founded the United Farm Workers union and did, indeed, devote all his time to changing conditions for farmworkers.

d. Robert F. Kennedy called Chávez "one of the heroic figures of our time."

e. Correct

EXERCISE 22-1 ▪ Using Semicolons, p. 874

a. By the beginning of 2010, Shirley was eager to retire; nevertheless, she agreed to stay on for two more years.

b. The committee was asked to determine the extent of violent crime among teenagers, especially those between the ages of fourteen and sixteen; to act as a liaison between the city and schools and between churches and volunteer organizations; and to draw up a plan to reduce violence, both public and private, by the end of the century.

c. The leaves on the oak trees near the lake were tinged with red; swimmers no longer ventured into the water.

d. The football team has yet to win a game; however, the season is still young.

EXERCISE 23-1 ▪ Using Colons, p. 877

Suggested revisions:

a. The Continuing Education Program offers courses in building and construction management, engineering, and design.

b. The interview ended with a test of skills: taking messages, operating the computer, typing a sample letter, and proofreading documents.

c. The sample letter began, "Dear Mr. Rasheed: Please accept our apologies for the late shipment."

EXERCISE 24-1 ▪ Using Apostrophes, p. 879

a. Joe's and Chuck's fathers were both in the class of '90.

b. Correct

c. It was a strange coincidence that all three women's cars broke down after they had picked up their mothers-in-law.

d. Don't forget to dot your *i*'s and cross your *t*'s.

e. Mario and Shelley's son is marrying the editor in chief's daughter.

EXERCISE 25–1 ▪ Using Quotation Marks, p. 883

a. "What we still need to figure out," the police chief said, "is whether the victim was acquainted with his assailant."

b. A skillful orator, Patrick Henry is credited with the phrase "Give me liberty or give me death."

c. "I could hear the crowd chanting my name—'Jones! Jones!'—and that spurred me on," said Bruce Jones, the winner of the 5,000-meter race.

d. The video for the rock group Guns and Roses' epic song "November Rain" is based on a short story by Del James.

e. In response to a possible asteroid strike on Earth, former astronaut Rusty Schweickart says, "Every country is at risk."

EXERCISE 26–1 ▪ Using Dashes, p. 885

Suggested revisions:

a. I enjoy going hiking with my friend John, whom I've known for fifteen years.

b. Pedro's new boat is spectacular—a regular seagoing Ferrari.

c. The Thompsons devote their weekends to their favorite pastime—eating bags of potato chips and cookies beside the warm glow of the television.

EXERCISE 27–1 ▪ Using Parentheses, p. 886

Suggested revisions:

a. Our cafeteria serves the four basic food groups: white (milk, bread, and mashed potatoes), brown (mystery meat and gravy), green (overcooked vegetables and under-washed lettuce), and orange (squash, carrots, and tomato sauce).

b. The hijackers will release the hostages only if the government (1) frees all political prisoners and (2) allows the hijackers to leave the country.

c. Correct

EXERCISE 28–1 ▪ Using Abbreviations, p. 892

a. *Professor* James has office hours on Monday and Tuesday, beginning at 10:00 a.m.

b. Emotional issues, *for example,* abortion and capital punishment, cannot be settled easily by compromise.

c. The red peppers are selling for *$3.25 a pound.*

EXERCISE 29–1 ▪ Using Capitalization, p. 895

a. At our family reunion, I met my cousin Sam for the first time, as well as my father's brother George.

b. I already knew from Dad that his brother had moved to Australia years ago to explore the Great Barrier Reef.

c. When my uncle announced that he was moving to a continent thousands of miles southwest of the United States, his mother gave him a Bible to take along.

EXERCISE 30–1 ▪ Using Numbers, p. 897

a. A program to help save the sea otter transferred more than eighty animals to a new colony over the course of *two* years; however, all but *thirty-four* otters swam back home again.

b. *Twelve percent* or so of the estimated *15 billion* plastic water bottles purchased annually in the United States is recycled.

c. In act II, scene ix, of Shakespeare's *The Merchant of Venice,* Portia's *second* suitor fails to guess which of *three* caskets contains her portrait.

EXERCISE 31–1 ▪ Using Italics, p. 900

a. Does *avocado* mean "lawyer" in Spanish?

b. During this year's First Night celebrations, we heard Verdi's *Requiem* and Monteverdi's *Orfeo.*

c. It was fun watching the passengers on the *Europa* trying to dance to "Blue Moon" in the midst of a storm.

EXERCISE 32–1 ▪ Using Hyphens, p. 902

a. Jimmy is a lively four-year-old boy, and his sister is two years old.

b. Correct

c. Tracy's brother-in-law lives with his family in a six-room apartment.

Acknowledgments *(continued from p. iv)*

Adams, Sarah, "Be Cool to the Pizza Dude" by Sarah Adams. Copyright 2005 by Sarah Adams. *This I Believe* edited by Jay Allison and Dan Gediman. Copyright © 2006 by This I Believe, Inc. Reprinted by arrangement with Henry Holt and Company, LLC.

Agger, Michael, "Lazy Eyes." Copyright © 2008 by Michael Agger. Reprinted with the permission of the author.

Babcock, Linda, and Sara Laschever, "Low Goals and Safe Targets" from *Women Don't Ask*. Copyright © 2003 Linda Babcock and Sara Laschever. Published by Princeton University Press. Reprinted by permission of Princeton University Press.

Baker, Russell, "The Art of Eating Spaghetti." Reprinted by permission of Don Congdon Associates, Inc. © 1982 by Russell Baker.

Barry, Dave, "From Now On, Let Women Kill Their Own Spiders." First published in the *Miami Herald*, February 12, 1999. Copyright © 1999 by Dave Barry. Reprinted with the permission of the author.

Brady, Judy, "I Want a Wife." Copyright © 1971 by Judy Brady. Reprinted with the permission of the author.

Britt, Suzanne, "Neat People vs. Sloppy People" from *Show and Tell* (Raleigh, North Carolina: Morning Own Press, 1982). Copyright © 1982 by Suzanne Britt. Reprinted with the permission of the author.

Brooks, Joe, excerpts from "How to Catch More Trout." First published in *Outdoor Life*, May 2006. Copyright © 2006 by Time4 Media, Inc. Reprinted with the permission of the publishers. All rights reserved. Reproduction in any medium is strictly prohibited without permission from Time4 Media, Inc. Such permission may be requested from *Outdoor Life* magazine.

Buckley Jr., William F., "Why Don't We Complain?" Copyright © 1960 by William F. Buckley Jr. First published in *Esquire* magazine. Used by permission of The Wallace Literary Agency, Inc.

Dailey, Kate, and Abby Ellin, "America's War on the Overweight" from *Newsweek*, August 26, 2009. © 2009 Newsweek, Inc. All rights reserved. Used by permission and protected by the Copyright Laws of the United States. The printing, copying, redistribution, or retransmission of the Material without express written permission is prohibited.

Deford, Frank, "NFL: Dodging the Concussion Discussion?" Copyright © 2009. Reprinted with the permission of the author.

Edmonds, David, pages 1-4 from *Rousseau's Dog: Two Great Thinkers at War in the Age of Enlightenment* by David Edmonds and John Eidinow. Reprinted by permission of HarperCollins Publishers and David Higham Associates.

Frost, Robert, "Putting in the Seed" and "The Road Not Taken" from *The Poetry of Robert Frost*, edited by Edward Connery Lathem. Copyright 1916, 1969 by Henry Holt and Company. Reprinted with the permission of Henry Holt and Company, LLC.

Garretson, Marjorie Lee, "More Pros than Cons." Copyright © 2010. Reprinted by permission of the author, Marjorie Lee Garretson.

Gelernter, David, "Computers Cannot Teach Children Basic Skills" from *The New Republic*. Copyright © 1994. Reprinted with the permission of the publisher.

Gurian, Michael, "Disappearing Act: Where Have the Men Gone? No Place Good." Copyright © 2005 by Michael Gurian. Michael Gurian, founder of the Gurian Institute, is the author of *The Minds of Boys* (with Kathy Stevens) and *Boys and Girls Learn Differently*. Reprinted by permission of the author.

Halpern, Jake, excerpt from *Fame Junkies: The Hidden Truth behind America's Favorite Addiction* by Jake Halpern. Copyright © 2007 by Jake Halpern. Reprinted by permission of Houghton Mifflin Harcourt Publishing Company. All rights reserved.

Harjo, Suzan Shown, "Last Rites for Indian Dead." First published in the *Los Angeles Times*, September 16, 1989. Copyright © 1989 by Suzan Shown Harjo. Reprinted with the permission of the author.

Jackson, Shirley, "The Lottery" from *The Lottery* by Shirley Jackson. Copyright © 1948, 1949 by Shirley Jackson. Copyright renewed 1976, 1977 by Laurence Hyman, Barry Hyman, Mrs. Sarah Webster and Mrs. Joanne Schnurer. Reprinted by permission of Farrar, Straus and Giroux, LLC.

Jensen, Robert, "The High Cost of Manliness." Originally posted on <www.AlterNet.org>, September 8, 2006. Copyright © 2006 Independent Media Institute. Reprinted with permission. All rights reserved.

King, Stephen, "Why We Crave Horror Movies." Reprinted with permission. Copyright © Stephen King. All rights reserved. Originally appeared in *Playboy* (1982).

Kluger, Jeffrey, excerpt from "The New Science of Siblings" from *Time*, July 10, 2006: 47-48. Copyright © 2006 by Time, Inc. Reprinted with permission.

Knight, Al, "Perhaps We Should Move to Save Dogs from Their Owners" from the *Denver Post*, November 21, 2006. Reprinted with the permission of the author.

Kohn, Alfie, "When a Parent's 'I Love You' Means 'Do as I Say'" from *The New York Times*. Copyright © September 15, 2009, *The New York Times*. All rights reserved. Used by permission and protected by the Copyright Laws of the United States. The printing, copying, redistribution, or retransmission of the material without express written permission.

La Ferla, Ruth, "Latino Style Is Cool. Oh, All Right: It's Hot" from *The New York Times*. Copyright © April 15, 2001, *The New York Times*. All rights reserved. Used by permission and protected by the Copyright Laws of the United States. The printing, copying, redistribution, or retransmission of the material without written permission is prohibited.

Liu, Eric, "The Chinatown Idea," from *The Accidental Asian: Notes of a Native Speaker* by Eric Liu. Copyright © 1998 by Eric Liu. Used by permission of Random House, Inc.

Leving, Jeffrey M., and Glenn Sacks, "Women Don't Want Men? Ha!" from the *Chicago Tribune*, January 21, 2007. Reprinted with the permission of the authors.

Mann, Charles C., and Mark L. Plummer, "The Butterfly Problem." First published in the *Atlantic Monthly* 269, No. 1, January 1992. Copyright © 1992 by Charles C. Mann and Mark L. Plummer. Reprinted with the permission of the authors.

McCain, John, excerpt from "The Virtues of the Quiet Hero." Copyright © 2005 by John McCain. From the book *This I Believe: The Personal Philosophies of Remarkable Men and Women*, edited by Jay Allison and Dan Gediman. Copyright © 2006 by This I Believe, Inc. Reprinted by arrangement with Henry Holt and Company, LLC.

Mendelson, Cheryl, "Home Comforts" from *Home Comforts: The Art and Science of Keeping House*. Copyright © 1999. Reprinted with the permission of Cheryl Mendelson.

Miller, Christy De'on, "Timeless" from *Operation Homecoming*, edited by Andrew Carroll. Copyright © 2006 by Random House, Inc. Used by permission of Random House, Inc.

Nash, Madeleine J., excerpt from "The Case for Cloning" in *Time*, February 9, 1998. Copyright © 1998 by Time, Inc. Reprinted by permission.

Pfeffer, Jeffrey, "Lay Off the Layoffs" from *Newsweek,* February 5, 2010, Newsweek, Inc. All rights reserved. Used by permission and protected by the Copyright Laws of the United States.

Pollan, Michael, excerpt from *Out of the Kitchen, Onto the Couch.* Reprinted by permission of International Creative Management, Inc. Copyright © 2009 by Michael Pollan for *The New York Times.*

Razdan, Anjula, "What's Love Got to Do with It?" Reprinted from *Utne Reader* (May–June 2003). Copyright © 2003 by Ogden Publications. www.utne.com

Rideau, Wilbert, "Why Prisons Don't Work." First published in *Time,* March 21, 1994. Reprinted with the permission of the author.

Rockwell, Llewellyn H., "In Defense of Consumerism" from *Mises Daily,* May 18, 2006. Copyright © by Llewellyn Rockwell. Reprinted with the permission of the author.

Rodriguez, Richard, "Public and Private Language" from *Hunger of Memory* by Richard Rodriguez Copyright © 1982 by Richard Rodriguez. Reprinted by permission of George Borchardt, Inc., on behalf of the author.

Saletan, William, excerpt from "Please Do Not Feed the Humans" from *Slate,* © September 2, 2006, The Slate Group. All rights reserved. Used by permission and protected by the Copyright Laws of the United States.

Schor, Juliet, "The Creation of Discontent" from *The Overworked American.* Copyright © 1993, Perseus Books Group.

Seltzer, Sarah, "The (Girl) Geek Stands Alone." Copyright © 2007 by Sarah Seltzer. Reprinted with the permission of the author.

Senna, Danzy, "The Color of Love." Originally published in *O, The Oprah Magazine.* Copyright © 2000 by Danzy Senna. Reprinted with permission of The Wylie Agency LLC.

Solotaroff, Paul, "The Surfing Savant" from *Rolling Stone,* April 15, 2010. © 2010 Rolling Stone LLC. All rights reserved. Reprinted by permission.

Staples, Brent, "Black Men and Public Space." First published in *Ms.* Magazine, September 1986. Copyright © 1986 by Brent Staples. Reprinted with the permission of the author.

Stevenson, Seth, "Soft Sell: Why Quiet, Understated TV Ads Are So Effective" from *Slate,* © February 1, 2010, The Slate Group. All rights reserved. Used by permission and protected by the Copyright Laws of the United States. The printing, copying, redistribution, or retransmission of the Material without express written permission is prohibited.

Tan, Amy, "Mother Tongue." Copyright © 1990 by Amy Tan. First appeared in *The Threepenny Review.* Reprinted by permission of the author and the Sandra Dijkstra Literary Agency.

Taw, Harold, "Finding Prosperity by Feeding Monkeys." Copyright © 2005 by Harold Taw. *This I Believe,* edited by Jay Allison and Dan Gediman. Copyright © 2006 by This I Believe, Inc. Reprinted by arrangement with Henry Holt and Company, LLC.

Thompson, Clive, "New Literacy." Copyright © 2009 by Clive Thompson. Reprinted with the permission of the author.

Tsu, Lillian, excerpt from "A Woman in the White House." First published in *Cornell Political Forum,* 1997. Copyright © 1997 by Lillian Tsu. Reprinted with the permission of the author.

Turkle, Sherry, "How Computers Change the Way We Think." First published in the *Chronicle of Higher Education,* 2004. Copyright © 2004 by Sherry Turkle. Reprinted with the permission of the author.

Turow, Joseph, "Have They Got a Deal for You." Copyright © 2005 by Joseph Turow. Reprinted with the permission of the author.

Underwood, Anne, "The Good Heart" from *Newsweek,* October 3, 2005, Newsweek, Inc. All rights reserved. Used by permission and protected by the Copyright Laws of the United States.

Warner, Judith, "Helicopter Parenting Turns Deadly" from *The New York Times.* Copyright © November 29, 2007, *The New York Times.* All rights reserved. Used by permission and protected by the Copyright Laws of the United States. The printing, copying, redistribution, or retransmission of the Material without express written permission is prohibited.

Weiner, Eric, excerpt from *The Geography of Bliss.* Copyright © 2008 by Eric Weiner. By permission of Grand Central Publishing.

White, E. B., excerpt from "Once More to the Lake" from *One Man's Meat.* Copyright © 1941 by E. B. White. Copyright renewed. Reprinted by permission of Tilbury House, Publisher, Gardiner, Maine.

Yoffe, Emily, "Seeking" from *Slate,* © August 12, 2009, The Slate Group. All rights reserved. Used by permission and protected by the Copyright Laws of the United States. The printing, copying, redistribution, or retransmission of the Material without express written permission is prohibited.

Zinsser, William, "The Right to Fail." Copyright © 1969, 1970 by William K. Zinsser. Reprinted by permission of the author.

Art Credits (in order of appearance):

Page 4: "Government Center Steps." Pelle Cass.

Page 15: *Atlantic Monthly* subscription advertisement. Copyright © The Atlantic Monthly Group/Tribune Media Services. Reprinted by permission. All rights reserved.

Page 31: Jeffrey Leving. Courtesy of Jeffrey Leving.

Page 31: Glenn Sacks. Courtesy of Glenn Sacks.

Page 33: Heat maps of Web pages from eye-tracking studies. Copyright © by Jakob Nielsen. All rights reserved.

Page 41: Candy bar. istockphoto.

Page 52: Al Knight. Courtesy of Al Knight.

Page 53: Dog riding in truck. Tristan Davison and Jeff McNeill/Getty Images.

Page 56: "Boston Public Garden (Red)." Pelle Cass.

Page 58: Photo collage of recalled experiences. Michael Schwarz/The Image Works; Mario Tama/Getty Images; D. Miller/CLASSICSTOCK/Robertstock/Aurora Photos; Lawrence Migdale/Photo Researchers, Inc.

Page 60: Russell Baker. Yvonne Hemsey/Getty Images.

Page 61: Lady Macbeth. © Tristram Kenton/Lebrecht/The Image Works.

Page 68: Soccer player scoring goal. Robert Llewellyn/Aurora Photos.

Page 76: People dancing on the roof. © Josef Lindau/Corbis.

Page 76: Rock-climber in ocean cave. Carlos Hernandez/Aurora Photos.

Page 75: Group of women at table. Veer/Corbis Photography.

Page 77: Artist performing "levitation" act. Uwe Meinhold/AFP/Getty Images.

Page 79: Eric Liu. Photo by Alan Alabastro.

Page 81: Market in New York City's Chinatown. Dorling Kindersley/Getty Images.

Page 85: Emergency room. David Joel/Getty Images.

Page 87: Elvis impersonators. Chris Jackson/Getty Images.

Page 94: Girl sitting under table. Veer/Cultural Photography.

Page 94: Server at party. Doug Mills/*The New York Times*/Redux Pictures.

Page 95: Climbers on Mt. Rushmore. Kevin Steele/Aurora Photos.

Page 96: Photo collage of famous people. Photo by Stacey Ilyse Photography/The White House via Getty Images; AP Photo; NBAE/Getty Images; Shaun Heasley/Getty Images.

Page 98: Paul Solotaroff. Photo by Jim Herrington.

Page 99: Clay Marzo surfing. CBS/Landov.

Page 106: Frost/Nixon interview. AP Photo/Ray Stubblebine.

Page 114: Census interview in desert landscape. REUTERS/STR/Landov.

Page 115: Job interviews. AP Photo/The State, Gerry Melendez.

Page 115: FEMA worker interviewing flood victim. Getty Images.

Page 116: Couple at Woodstock, 1969 and 2009. © Burk Uzzle/Courtesy Laurence Miller Gallery, New York; Richard Harbus/Daily News Pix.

Page 118: Suzanne Britt. Courtesy of Suzanne Britt.

Page 119: Einstein's desk. Photo by Ralph Morse/Time Life Pictures/Getty Images.

Page 129: Baseball fans watching game on television, sitting on hill overlooking stadium. Charles Steele/Zuma Press.

Page 129: Basketball players. John Biever/Sports Illustrated/Getty Images.

Page 134: Families with a week's worth of food. © Peter Menzel.

Page 136: Forests showing damage from clearcutting. Daniel Dancer/Peter Arnold, Inc.

Page 138: Jeffrey Pfeffer. Courtesy of Jeffrey Pfeffer.

Page 146: Series showing car and crane falling into water. © Nicholas Griffin.

Page 154: Chart showing declining music industry sales. Courtesy of Enders Analysis.

Page 154: Elderly shopper in record store. Michael Nagle/The New York Times/Redux Pictures.

Page 154: Photo of student listening to music. © Andrew Dillon Bustin.

Page 155: Photo of student protest against sweatshops. Jeff Greenberg/The Image Works.

Page 157: Suzan Shown Harjo. AP Photo/Manuel Balce Ceneta.

Page 158: Funeral procession for re-burial of Native American remains. AP Photo/The Albuquerque Journal, Eddie Moore.

Page 163: Joan of Arc. Getty Images.

Page 181: Girl overlooking Jimmy Fund race. Suzanne Kreiter/Boston Globe/Landov.

Page 182: Cell phone tower disguised as tree. © Robert Voit, courtesy of Amador Gallery, New York.

Page 181: Family reading. Nicole Bengiveno/The New York Times/Redux Pictures.

Page 185: Surfrider Foundation's "Plastic Surprise." Photo by Matt Cobleigh.

Page 185: Wilbert Rideau. Courtesy of Wilbert Rideau.

Page 191: Living wall. © Gil Snyder, AIA.

Page 195: "Don't Mess With Texas" anti-littering sign. AP Photo/Donna McWilliam.

Page 197: Agriculture student. Jack Dykinga/ARS/USDA.

Page 201: Traffic congestion. Timothy Fadek/Bloomberg via Getty Images.

Page 200: Graffiti on train car. Martha Cooper/Peter Arnold Inc.

Page 201: Student with heavy backpack. Heather Stone/Chicago Tribune/Newscom.

Page 202: Judges at pumpkin competition. Norm Eggert Photography.

Page 204: Seth Stevenson. Courtesy Seth Stevenson.

Page 205: DeBeers shadow advertisement. Image courtesy of The Advertising Archives.

Page 210: George Gershwin. Getty Images.

Page 211: Still from The Cabinet of Dr. Caligari. Goldwyn/Photofest.

Page 219: Swatch advertisement with shark. Image courtesy of The Advertising Archives.

Page 219: Omega advertisement with Daniel Craig (James Bond). Image courtesy of The Advertising Archives.

Page 218: Photo of church at Auvers. Pierre-Franck Colombier/AFP/Getty Images.

Page 218: The Church at Auvers by Vincent Van Gogh. Getty Images.

Page 220: Photo collage of source usage. Scott Bauer/ARS/USDA; Sam Javanrouh; Jeff Greenberg/The Image Works.

Page 222: Jake Halpern. © Neil Giordano, courtesy of Jake Halpern.

Page 235: Mojave desert. © Kate Leigh/iStockphoto.

Page 253: Pedestrian on cell phone. Richard Perry/The New York Times/Redux Pictures.

Page 253: Gamblers in Las Vegas. Mike Mergen/Bloomberg/Getty Images.

Page 251: Contestant in child beauty pageant. Konstantin Zavrazhin/Getty Images.

Page 254: "Photographers." Pelle Cass.

Page 257: Shirley Jackson. AP Photo.

Page 280: Kate Chopin. The Granger Collection.

Figure 14.1: Public-service announcement with one prominent element. Copyright © 2005 by the American Psychological Association. <http://actagainstviolence.apa.org/materials/psa/ADCA04B0113-Driver.pdf>.

Figures 14.2–14.5: Photo of four children (Kodak Picture of the Day). © Merrilee A. Giegerich.

Figure 14.6: Volkswagen advertisement. Courtesy Volkswagen of America, Inc.

Figure 14.7: Oldsmobile advertisement. Courtesy of Leo Burnett.

Figure 14.8: "Stairway" type design. © Hyunmee Kum, Samsung Art and Design Institute.

Figure 14.9: "Type as cultural cliché" from Roy Paul Nelson, Publication Design © 1990. Reprinted with permission of the McGraw-Hill Companies.

Figure 14.10: Photograph conveying a mood. Jonathan Nourok/PhotoEdit.

Figure 14.11: Photograph with missing element. Courtesy of the National Park Service.

Figure 14.12: Public-service advertisement showing wordplay. D. Reed Monroe.

Figure 14.13: Billboard showing wordplay. Bill Aron/PhotoEdit.

Figure 14.14: Poster conveying a theme. The Advertising Council, Inc. Reprinted with permission.

Page 306: Photo essay on wheelchair basketball team. © Josh Birnbaum/www.joshbirnbaum.com.

Page 348: Apartment buildings. © Jeff Greenberg/The Image Works.

Page 348: City from above. Creatas/Jupiter Images.

Page 348: Map of New York City, 1807. The Granger Collection.

Page 366: Brochure design showing prominent elements. Studio InFlux/The Art Institute of Boston at Lesley University: Jenny Barrett, ManChing Cheng, Lisa Goode, and Yehudit Massouda-Winiarz.

Page 370: "Football, Cypress Field, Brookline MA." Pelle Cass.

Page 372: Erin Schmitt. Courtesy of Erin Schmitt.

Page 381: Peter Hertli. Courtesy of Alice Hertli.

Page 496: Photo of family gathered for a meal. Tom McCarthy/PhotoEdit.

Page 513: Danzy Senna. Ulf Andersen/Getty Images.

Page 506: Judith Warner. Jean-Louis Atlan.

Page 509: Alfie Kohn. Courtesy of Alfie Kohn.

Page 518: Amy Tan. Will Ragozzino/Getty Images.

Page 524: Richard Rodriguez. Photo © Christine Alicino, courtesy of Richard Rodriguez.

Page 531: Father holding baby. © Bill Varie/Alamy. Page 531: Firefighter seated on truck. Marc Asnin/Redux.

Page 532: Robert Jensen. Photo by Christina Murrey, courtesy of Robert Jensen.

Page 536: Brent Staples. Courtesy of *The New York Times*.

Page 539: Dave Barry. © Daniel Portnoy Photography, courtesy of Dave Barry.

Page 542: Judy Brady. Photo by Ron Ngata, courtesy of Judy Brady.

Page 545: Cheryl Mendelson. Courtesy of Cheryl Mendelson.

Page 548: Linda Babcock. Photo by Cynthia Byrd, courtesy of Linda Babcock.

Page 548: Sara Laschever. Courtesy of Sara Laschever.

Page 552: Michael Gurian. Photo by Colin Mulvaney, courtesy of Michael Gurian.

Page 558: "Sign Language" cartoon. © Lee Lorenz/The New Yorker Collection/www.cartoonbank.com.

Page 559: Stephen King. AFP/Getty Images.

Page 562: Sarah Seltzer. Courtesy of Sarah Seltzer.

Page 573: Frank Deford. Newscom.

Page 575: Kate Dailey. Photo by Susanna Schrobsdorff, courtesy of Kate Dailey.

Page 575: Abby Ellin. Courtesy *The Daily Beast*.

Page 581: Michael Pollan. Newscom.

Page 586: People on laptops in a café. Dominik Eckelt/Getty Images.

Page 587: Clive Thompson. Courtesy of Clive Thompson.

Page 590: David Gelernter. Courtesy of David Gelernter.

Page 594: Joseph Turow. Photo by Kyle Cassidy, courtesy of Joseph Turow.

Page 599: Emily Yoffe. © Chris Leaman.

Page 602: Sherry Turkle. Pat Greenhouse/*Boston Globe*/Landov.

Page 609: Michael Agger. Courtesy of Michael Agger.

Page 614: Photo collage of ways to live well. © Finbarr O'Reilly/Reuters/Corbis; Blend Images/John Lund/Marc Romanelli/Getty Images; Floresco Productions/Getty Images; Blend Images/Jon Feingersh.

Page 615: Sarah Adams. Nubar Alexanian.

Page 618: William F. Buckley Jr. Time & Life Pictures/Getty Images.

Page 624: William Zinsser. Photo by Thomas Victor, courtesy of William Zinsser.

Page 628: Harold Taw. Nubar Alexanian.

Page 630: Eric Weiner. Photo by Chuck Berman, courtesy of Twelve Books.

Page 634: Juliet Schor. © Gary Gilbert, courtesy of Juliet Schor.

Page 638: Llewellyn H. Rockwell Jr. Courtesy of the Ludwig von Mises Institute.

Page 660: Facsimile for Source Navigator: From "Regaining Balance with Bionic Ears" by Charles C. Della Santina in *Scientific American*. Reprinted with permission. Copyright © 2010 Scientific American, a division of Nature America, Inc. All rights reserved.

Page 662: Facsimile for Source Navigator: From JSTOR Web site. Reprinted courtesy of JSTOR and International Reading Association. JSTOR © 2010. All rights reserved.

Page 664: Facsimile for Source Navigator: From *The Cheating Culture: Why More Americans Are Doing Wrong to Get Ahead*, copyright © 2004 by David Callahan, reproduced by permission of Houghton Mifflin Harcourt Publishing Company. This material may not be reproduced in any form or by any means without prior written permission of the publisher.

Page 666: Facsimile for Source Navigator: SOURCE: *Trends in College Pricing, 2009*. Copyright © 2009. The College Board. www.collegeboard.com. Reproduced with permission.

Figure 32.1: Library home page courtesy of the Ford Motor Company Library, Tuskegee University, Tuskegee, Alabama. Courtesy of the Tuskegee University Libraries. Reprinted with permission.

Figure 32.2: Multiple entries from an online catalog courtesy of the Ford Motor Company Library, Tuskegee University, Tuskegee, Alabama. Courtesy of the Tuskegee University Libraries. Reprinted with permission.

Figure 32.3: Single entry from an online catalog courtesy of the Ford Motor Company Library, Tuskegee University, Tuskegee, Alabama. Courtesy of the Tuskegee University Libraries. Reprinted with permission.

Figure 32.4: Search result from America's Historical Newspapers Web site. Newsbank–Readex. Archive of Americana.

Figure 33.1: Screenshots from the American Society for the Prevention of Cruelty to Animals (ASPCA) Web site. Copyright © 2010. The American Society for the Prevention of Cruelty to Animals (ASPCA). All rights reserved.

Page 736: Line graph comparing rise in higher education costs with medical and housing costs. Source: CreditUnions.com: http://www.CreditUnions.com © 2008 Callahan & Associates, Inc.

Page A-11: Diagram of wastewater treatment. Courtesy of King County Wastewater Treatment Division.

About the Photographs that Open Parts 1–4

Selected People (2009)
A Series of Photographs by Pelle Cass

Reflecting on the process he used to create the series *Selected People*, artist Pelle Cass noted, "Most photographs record a single instant in time. My photographs record many moments at once." To create each composite photograph in the series, he set up his tripod and took dozens of candid images from a single spot, over a span of time ranging from several minutes to many hours. He studied the images, selected the ones he wanted to use, and then found the image of the scene with the fewest people to use as a "blank canvas." In Photoshop, he cut and pasted each figure (up to 200 layers in Photoshop) into the blank canvas, in the precise position it occupied in the original scene. In this way, he included only the figures he selected. Nothing is changed, only selected.

"This series of photos reminds me of the name of a poem by X. J. Kennedy: 'The Purpose of Time Is to Prevent Everything from Happening at Once.'"
—Pelle Cass

Part 1: "Government Center Steps" (pages 4–5)

"I organize the figures in my scenes by the color of their clothing, by mood, age, attractiveness, gesture, position, race, or even just by oddness."

How is the artist organizing the figures here? What overall effect does the photograph create? What, if anything, is it saying to you, the viewer?

Part 2: "Boston Public Garden—Red, with Blossoms" (pages 56–57)

"Untold number of people must have walked on every square of pavement, and innumerable small gestures and glances must have occurred over and over, for as long as there were people. It struck me as almost supernatural."

What mood or effect does this photo create? What would you describe as the photograph's theme or symbolic content? What elements in it contribute to its effect? What is the difference between this photograph and one that records a single moment?

Part 3: "Boston Public Garden—Photographers" (pages 254–55)

"All these pictures are partly about attention, about the way your mind filters things and sorts data according to your interests."

What are people in the park photographing, and why? What, if anything, does this photograph say about our shared public life?

Part 4: "Football, Cypress Field, Brookline" (pages 370–71)

"No matter how I try to trick photography into doing things it's not quite meant to do, it stays linked to the real world somehow, and it's the link to reality that I value the most."

What do you see as the meaning of this photograph? What effect does it create? How does it compare with a short movie? How is it linked or not linked to the real world?

INDEX

PROOFREADING SYMBOLS

Use these standard proofreading marks when making minor corrections in your final draft. If extensive revision is necessary, type or print out a clean copy.

Symbol	Meaning
∽	Transpose (reverse order)
≡	Capitalize
/	Lowercase
#	Add space
⌒	Close up space
℘	Delete
⌣⋯	Stet (undo deletion)
∧	Insert
⊙	Insert period
⋀	Insert comma
;/	Insert semicolon
:/	Insert colon
⌄	Insert apostrophe
⌄⌄ ⌄⌄	Insert quotation marks
|=|	Insert hyphen
¶	New paragraph
no ¶	No new paragraph

CORRECTION SYMBOLS

Many instructors use these abbreviations and symbols to mark errors in student papers. Refer to this chart to find out what they mean.

Abbreviation or Symbol	Meaning	For more information in Handbook	For more information in Quick Editing Guide
abbr	abbreviation	28 (p. 890)	
adj	misuse of adjective	8 (p. 817)	A7 (p. A-46)
adv	misuse of adverb	8 (p. 817)	A7 (p. A-46)
agr	faulty agreement	4 (p. 804), 7 (p. 814)	A4 (p. A-42), A6 (p. A-44)
awk	awkward		
cap	capital letter	29 (p. 893)	
case	error in case	5 (p. 808)	A5 (p. A-43)
coord	faulty coordination	14a–c (p. 840)	
cs	comma splice	2 (p. 785)	A2 (p. A-38)
dm	dangling modifier	10c (p. 828)	B1 (p. A-41)
f	format (see Quick Format Guide)		
frag	fragment	1 (p. 780)	A1 (p. A-38)
fs	fused sentence	2 (p. 785)	A2 (p. A-38)
gl or gloss	see Glossary of Troublemakers		A (p. A-56)
hyph	error in use of hyphen	32 (p. 900)	
inc	incomplete construction	11 (p. 830)	
irreg	error in irregular verb	3e–f (p. 791)	A3 (p. A-40)
ital	italics	31 (p. 898)	
lc	use lowercase letter	29 (p. 893)	D1 (p. A-53)
mixed	mixed construction	12 (p. 833)	
mm	misplaced modifier	10a–b (p. 827)	B1 (p. A-41)
mood	error in mood	3n–p, 9e (pp. 801, 825)	
num	error in the use of numbers	30 (p. 896)	
p	error in punctuation	20–27 (p. 862)	C (p. A-50)
pass	ineffective passive voice	3m (p. 800)	
ref	error in pronoun reference	6 (p. 811)	A6 (p. A-44)
rep	careless repetition	19 (p. 860)	
rev	revise		
run-on	comma splice or fused sentence	2 (p. 785)	A2 (p. A-38)
sp	misspelled word	33 (p. 902)	D2 (p. A-53)
sub	faulty subordination	14d–f (p. 844)	
t or tense	error in verb tense	3g–l, 9a–b (pp. 793, 823)	A3 (p. A-40)
v	voice	3m, 9c (pp. 800, 824)	
vb	error in verb form	3a–f (p. 789)	A3 (p. A-40)
wc	word choice		
w	wordy	19 (p. 860)	
—( )[ ]…	dash, parentheses, brackets, ellipses	26–27 (pp. 884, 885)	
//	faulty parallelism	13 (p. 837)	B2 (p. A-48)
x	obvious error		

Add your instructor's own abbreviations below:

A GUIDE TO THE HANDBOOK

Learning by Doing

A Selected List of Activities

Checklists

A Selected List of Guidelines